Encyclopedia of Adult Development

Edited by Robert Kastenbaum

Oryx Press
1993

The rare Arabian Oryx is believed to have inspired the myth of the unicorn. This desert antelope became virtually extinct in the early 1960s. At that time several groups of international conservationists arranged to have 9 animals sent to the Phoenix Zoo to be the nucleus of a captive breeding herd. Today the Oryx population is nearly 800 and over 400 have been returned to reserves in the Middle East.

Copyright © 1993 by The Oryx Press
4041 North Central at Indian School Road
Phoenix, Arizona 85012-3397

Published simultaneously in Canada

Printed and Bound in the United States of America

∞ The paper used in this publication meets the minimum requirements of American National Standard for Information Science—Permanence of Paper for Printed Library Materials, ANSI Z39.48, 1984

Library of Congress Cataloging-in-Publication Data

Encyclopedia of adult development / edited by Robert Kastenbaum.
    p.   cm.
  Includes bibliographical references and index.
  ISBN 0-89774-669-4
  1. Adulthood—Psychological aspects—Encyclopedias.
2. Developmental psychology—Encyclopedias. I. Kastenbaum, Robert.
  BF724.5.E53   1993
  155.6—dc20   92-46666
                                                    CIP

noted earlier, however, it is also possible to theorize about change throughout the total life course without giving so much emphasis to developmental processes as such. One such alternative is offered by information-processing theory (e. g., Klahr & Wallace, 1976; Salthouse, 1985). Social learning theory (e. g. Bandura, 1977) offers another major alternative in which adult behavior patterns are thought to be acquired through social interactions and influences rather than emerging from a "developmental process." Skinner's (1953) behaviorism stands in even more striking contrast to the mainstream developmental theories in its attempt to explain complex patterns of behavior and interaction as the outcome of multiple and repeated episodes of conditioning in which particular "responses" have been "reinforced."

The continuing competition between developmental and nondevelopmental models of the adult life course may prove valuable in "developing" or "reinforcing" the greatest strengths of each approach.

▼ ROBERT KASTENBAUM

See also: Contextualism; Development and Aging; Disengagement Theory; Habituation: A Key to Lifespan Development and Aging?; Mid-Life Crisis; Spiritual Development and Wisdom: A Vedantic Perspective.

References

Allport, G. (1955). *Becoming.* New Haven, CT: Yale University Press.

Bandura, A. (1977). *A Social Learning Theory.* Englewood Cliffs, NJ: Prentice-Hall.

Buhler, C. (1953). The curve of life as studies in biographies. *Journal of Applied Psychology, 19:* 405-09.

———. (1962). *Psychologie im Leben unserer Zeit.* Munich: Droemer-Knaur.

Buhler, C., & Massarik, F. (Eds.). (1968). *The Course of Human Life.* New York: Springer.

Buss, A. R. (1979). Toward a unified framework for psychometric concepts in the multivariate developmental situation: Intraindividual change and inter- and intraindividual differences. In J. R. Nesselroade & P. B. Baltes (Eds.), *Longitudinal Research in the Study of Behavior and Development.* New York: Academic Press, pp. 41-60.

Coles, R. (1970). *Erik H. Erikson: The Growth of His Work.* Boston: Little, Brown.

Connidis, I. A. (1988). *Family Ties and Aging.* Toronto; Vancouver: Butterworth.

Cumming, R. B., & Henry, W. E. (1961). *Growing Old.* New York: Basic Books.

Erikson, E. H. (1950). *Childhood and Society.* New York: W. W. Norton.

———. (1959). *Identity and the Life Cycle: Selected Papers.* New York: International Universities Press.

———. (1969). *Gandhi's Truth: On the Origins of Militant Nonviolence.* New York: Norton.

———. (1979). Reflections on Dr. Borg's Life Cycle. In D. D. Van Tassel (Ed.), *Aging, Death, and the Completion of Being.* Philadelphia: University of Pennsylvania Press, pp. 29-68.

Freud, S. (1900/1968). *The Interpretation of Dreams.* London: Hogarth Press.

———. (1933/1966). *Introductory Lectures on Psychoanalysis.* New York: Norton.

Gould, R. L. (1978). *Transformations: Growth and Change in Adult Life.* New York: Simon & Schuster.

Jung, C. G. (1933). *Modern Man in Search of a Soul.* New York: Harvest.

Klahr, D., & Wallace, J. G. (1976). *Cognitive Development: An Information-Processing Approach.* Hillsdale, NJ: Erlbaum.

Levenson, D. J. (1978). *The Seasons of a Man's Life.* New York: Alfred E. Knopf.

Maslow, A. H. (1968). *Toward a Psychology of Being.* New York: Van Nostrand Reinhold.

———. (1970). *Motivation and Personality.* New York: Harper & Row.

Miller, P. H. (1983). *Theories of Developmental Psychology.* San Francisco: W. H. Freeman.

Mullen, P. B. (1992). *Listening to Old Voices.* Chicago; Urbana: University of Illinois Press.

Murry, H. A. (1981). *Endeavors in Psychology.* New York: Harper.

Piaget, J. (1926). *The Language and Thought of the Child.* New York: Basic Books.

———. (1954). *The Construction of Reality in the Child.* New York: Basic Books.

Rogers, C. R. (1951). *Client-centered Therapy: Its Current Practice, Implications, and Theory.* Boston: Houghton Mifflin.

———. (1961). *On Becoming a Person: A Therapist's View of Psychotherapy.* Boston: Houghton Mifflin.

Rose, A. M. (1965). The subculture of the aging: A framework in social gerontology. In A. M. Rose & W. A. Peterson (Eds.), *Older People and Their Social World.* Philadelphia: F. A. Davis, pp. 3-16.

Salthouse, T. A. (1985). *A Theory of Cognitive Aging.* Amsterdam: North-Holland.

Sheehy, G. (1976). *Passages: Predictable Crises of Adult Life.* New York: Dalton.

Skinner, B. F. (1953). *Science and Human Behavior.* New York: Macmillan.

Wyatt-Brown, A. M. (1992). Literary gerontology comes of age. In T. R. Cole, D. D. Van Tassel, & R. Kastenbaum (Eds.), *Handbook of the Humanities and Aging.* New York: Springer, p. 331-51.

Ya, L. H. (1988). A Confucian theory of human development. In R. M. Thomas (Ed.), *Oriental Theories of Human Development.* New York: Peter Lang.

AFRICAN-AMERICAN EXPERIENCES THROUGH THE ADULT YEARS

African Americans are often portrayed in the scientific literature in a simplistic and undifferentiated manner. An underlying assumption of the literature is a large degree of homogeneity in values, motives, social and psychological statuses, and behaviors among African Americans (Jackson, 1991; Jaynes & Williams, 1989). It is true that categorical treatment based on race produces extensive group uniformity in attitudes and behaviors. It is equally true, however, that a rich heterogeneity exists among blacks in these same status, attitudinal, and behavioral dimensions.

Research demonstrates that African Americans span the same spectrum of structural circumstances, psychological statuses, and social beliefs as Americans of other ethnic and cultural backgrounds (Jackson, 1991; Stanford, 1990). But the unique history and nature of their individual and group developmental experiences place vast numbers of African-Americans at disproportionate risk for physical, social, and psychological harm. Population statistics reflect this harm in an alarming and increasing gap between blacks and other ethnic groups in mortality, unemployment, disintegrating neighborhoods, and growing numbers of women and children living in poverty.

In the face of these harsh realities of life, recent research findings show African Americans to possess a wide array of group and personal resources at every point in the lifespan (Jackson, 1991; Stanford, 1990). The changing age structure, however, will influence the health and effective functioning of older blacks (Gibson, 1986; Richardson, 1991). Since the older black American of the year 2046 has already been born, the continuing imbalanced sex ratio, segregated geographic distribution, and proportion in poverty, among other black structural factors, will have profound influences upon family structure, health status, and the well-being of older blacks over the next 50 to 60 years.

A lifespan framework is needed to explore how environmental stressors influence and interact with group and personal resources both to impede and to enhance the quality of life for successive cohorts of African Americans over their life course. It is the premise of a lifespan perspective that already born and aging cohorts of blacks are and have been exposed to health status risks as they reach older ages in the years and decades to come (Baltes, 1987; Barresi, 1987).

Notable improvements, particularly in health, have occurred over the last 40 years in the life situations of blacks (Farley, 1987; Jackson, 1981). Recent literature, however, points to the continuation of negative life events and structural barriers, especially for poor blacks (Gibson, 1986; Jaynes & Williams, 1989). These problems include high infant morbidity and mortality, childhood diseases, lack of preventive health care, deteriorating neighborhoods, poverty, adolescent violence, unemployment and underemployment, teen pregnancy, drug and alcohol abuse, broken marriages, and all the difficulties associated with single-parent households. Although the causal relationships are not known (Williams, 1990), these are clearly all predisposing factors for high morbidity and mortality across the entire lifespan of blacks (Dressler, 1991; Haan & Kaplan, 1985; Hamburg, Elliott, & Parron, 1982).

The Role of Race and Ethnic Categorization

More work is needed to understand the conceptual status of race (Wilkinson & King, 1987), and how, and under what conditions, race, ethnicity, and sociocultural and socioeconomic factors may serve as resources for the coping processes and adaptation of racially different groups to their environmentally disadvantaged circumstances (Dressler, 1985, 1991; Wilkinson & King, 1987).

Cooper (1984, 1991) suggests that the biologic concept of race has no scientific meaning. According to Cooper's position, the social definitions of race and ethnicity should be viewed solely as clues for searching out environmental causes of observed differences between groups. Studies on illness behavior also point to the independent role of cultural and life-style differences among racial groups in accounting for behavioral and health outcomes (Cooper, 1984; 1991; Dressler, 1985, 1991; Driedger & Chappell, 1988; Richardson, 1991).

Most researchers and writers tend to treat race or ethnicity as just one of many sociocultural factors. A sounder approach is to treat race as a distinct predisposing cultural and social environment indicator (Jackson, Antonucci, & Gibson, 1990a). This more focused approach encourages the study of the role of sociocultural factors in health behaviors within racial and ethnic groups. James (1984, 1985), Myers (1984), and Jackson (1988) have even questioned the appropriateness and validity of socioeconomic status and other sociocultural measures (such as occupation) when making comparisons across race and ethnic groups (Markides, Liang, & Jackson, 1990).

Aging and the lifecourse are the central concerns in an approach to understanding ostensible race effects. In our overall framework we assume that the various ethnic and racial groups have divergent life experiences because of socioeconomic and cultural reasons (Driedger & Chappell, 1988). These divergent experiences have profound influences, both positive and negative, on individual, family, and group well-being at all stages of the lifecourse. Ultimately these experiences will also influence the adjustment to major transitions in the later years of life (e.g., retirement, disability, loss of spouse). Conceptually, we use race as first and foremost a summary construct that "stands in" for a host of other psychological and possibly biological variables (Wilkinson & King, 1987). We try to study and understand how these variables provide coping and adaptive mechanisms that alleviate the distinct socioeconomic and psychological disadvantages of categorical racial membership (Stanford, 1990).

Race-Relevant Coping Mechanisms

In our own work we have been primarily concerned with how blacks do as well as they do in the face of severe structural, social, and technological constraints. We have conducted numerous studies that address the coping skills and adaptability of Americans of African descent at different points in the life course (Jackson, 1991). We have also argued that the type of data needed to assess this approach has been lacking. Large national data sets with adequate numbers of black and white respondents to significant questions remain to be developed (Jackson, Antonucci, & Gibson, 1990a; Markides, Living, & Jackson, 1990).

Previous work and speculation lead us to believe that the most important race effects are probably interactions with other ethnic, structural, or cultural factors, such as religion, socioeconomic status, and worldviews. We also expect these effects to be related more to differences between blacks and whites in underlying mediating processes than in differences in the level of particular variables of interest. For example, our findings indicate that blacks and whites do not differ significantly (for the most part) on the level of various measures of individual aging. Blacks and whites do differ, however, in their coping processes (Jackson, Antonucci, & Gibson, 1990b). This finding is consistent with our general model of coping and adaptation (Jackson, Antonucci, & Gibson, 1990b; Jackson, 1991), which suggests that throughout the entire lifespan blacks and whites may utilize different mechanisms to maintain comparable levels of productivity, mental and physical health, well-being, and effective functioning.

One adaptive mechanism that may be race-relevant is the use of a *fatalistic orientation*. In the face of severe structural barriers, a view of life that emphasizes the existence of these barriers may be very important among blacks for explaining why hard work does not lead to positive outcomes. This may become even more important as both blacks and whites move through their life course and come to grips with the failures and missed opportunities of their own lives. A coping orientation that has a reasonable and accurate *external referent* can lead to external attributions of success and failure. This strategy protects blacks from some of the life disappointments that result from *internal attributions* (self-blaming), which are normal for all of us as we age, and from those abnormal barriers that are due to racism and discrimination.

Another possible protective mechanism may be the *sense of collectivity* or *group identity and consciousness* that places the good of the group alongside or above the good of the individual. Thus, even though individual mobility and achievement may not be great, concerns about the group as a whole may serve as a significant way of interpreting one's own contributions. *Religious orientations* seem to serve a similar role for blacks, perhaps as part of a group worldview that provides a guiding set of charitable and spiritual values for life.

Period and Cohort Influences in the Aging of Blacks

We have attempted to develop a coherent lifecourse framework within which the economic, social, and psychological lives of black Americans can be comprehended and explained in the context of historical and current structural disadvantage and blocked mobility opportunities (Jackson, 1991; Jackson, Antonucci, & Gibson, 1990a, 1990b). Our data collections explore the nature of African-American reactions to their unequal status in the United States. Specifically, this research has addressed the question of how structural disadvantages in the environment are translated at different points in the individual and group life course into physical, social, and psychological aspects of group and self. Self-esteem, personal efficacy, close personal and social relationships, neighborhood and family integration, physical and mental health, group solidarity, and political participation have been among the major variables studied.

The age cohort into which blacks are born; the social, political, and economic events that occur to blacks born at a particular time, and the individual aging process at different points in a person's life course all influence the adaptation and quality of life. For example, blacks born before the 1940s faced very different environmental constraints and have experienced a very different set of life tasks than those born in the 1970s (Baker, 1987). Significant health care advances, changes in the legal structure and in family patterns, urban migration, and macro-economic influences have given each succeeding cohort a different set of experiences (Richardson, 1991).

For example, blacks born since the Civil Rights Movement have a different set of expectations of what life should offer than those who came to age before the movement. Although there is clearly a sharing of knowledge and attitudes over the generations within families as well as across birth cohorts, the movement and its corollary events changed irrevocably the level of aspirations and expectations of African Americans.

In many ways this post-Civil Rights Movement group may be considered the "disappointment generation." Not only have their legitimate aspirations remained unfulfilled, but the nature of racial oppression has changed dramatically from the pre-Civil Rights Movement period. The struggle for equal opportunity has proven to be both different and more difficult than the struggle for equal rights under the law.

How this discovery will affect the "disappointment generation" as they age is a matter of pure speculation. It may be that the adaptive mechanisms of fatalism, worldview, or religious orientation may not be as effective for a still deprived but more cynical group of aging African Americans. On the other hand, greater access to health care (through Medicare, Medicaid, etc.) may offset somewhat the negative consequences of little structural change in mobility and real achievement. In a more pessimistic vein, it may be that African Americans who were middle-aged at the time of the Civil Rights Movement benefited most from the "radical" changes of the 1960s and 1970s. By contrast, new cohorts of middle-aged and elderly blacks may face an environment with fewer tangible goods and services as well as a more pessimistic and worsening psychological and social atmosphere.

The overall context of our research is how these different birth cohorts, historical and current environmental events, and individual differences in aging processes interact with one another.

Adult Health Status. The examination of black health status, especially with regard to aging adults, has been conducted in something of a vacuum. Several authors have indicated the necessity of considering lifespan models and history, cohort, and period effects (e.g., Barresi, 1987; Manton & Soldo, 1985). However, few have actually collected the type of data or conducted the types of analyses that would shed any light on this process. The lack of good conceptual models of older black adult health status has contributed to this lack of quality data on large and representative samples of black Americans as they move through their adult years.

Many blacks bring a history of poor health into their later years. The available cohort data for cause-specific mortality and morbidity across the lifecourse for the recent decades indicates that there are accumulated deficits that place older black people at greater risk than whites of the same age (Jackson, 1991). Similarly, the fact that blacks actually outlive their white counterparts in the most advanced age groups suggests that selection factors may be at work that result in hardier survivors among the "oldest old" blacks (Gibson & Jackson, 1987, 1991).

Cohort experiences of blacks undoubtedly play a major role in their health experiences over the lifecourse. This influence operates through the quality of health care available from birth onward, and the continuing exposure to risk factors throughout the years. Furthermore, the stressful nature of prejudice and discrimination is pervasive across the lifespan, but differs in form as a function of birth cohort, period, and age (Baker, 1987; Cooper, Steinhauer, Schatzkin, & Miller, 1981; Dressler, 1991).

Socioeconomic Status and the Life Course of African Americans

Socioeconomic status (SES) has also been recognized as a major risk factor (Haan & Kaplan, 1985). Impressive evidence points to SES as a major factor in a wide variety of diseases; higher levels of SES are associated with better health and lower morbidity. This relationship has been shown both at the individual and the ecological level with respect to general mortality, blood pressure, cancer, cardiovascular heart diseases, cerebrovascular disease, diabetes, and obesity.

What has not been shown is *how* SES affects these health outcomes from birth (James, 1985). If the proper statistical controls and interactions were examined, one would probably find that advantaged blacks would be similar to their white counterparts over the lifespan. Blacks who are currently at middle or high SES would be at an intermediate position, and blacks who had been disadvantaged across their entire life course would continue to show worse health care status than comparable low SES whites. This nonsymmetrical effect of SES has been reported by some researchers (e.g., Haan & Kaplan, 1985), and James (1985) believes that this holds true specifically for cardiovascular disease.

An emerging pattern of findings, then, indicates that similarities in education and income equate upper-income race groups on health outcomes but have less effect on lower-income groups (Kessler & Neighbors, 1986). The causes of these observed effects are not know. Perhaps income and other socioeconomic control variables under-equate different race groups at lower income levels and over-equate at upper income levels. Blacks at the upper socioeconomic positions may, in general, have more of "whatever it is" that is correlated with education, income, or occupation levels than comparable whites, thus countering the effects of discrimination, and may also show equal or superior health outcomes. It may take a hardier or more gifted person to reach the top in the struggle for success when one must cope all the way with the discrimination and perils of a racially divided society (Jaynes & Williams, 1989).

On the other hand, blacks with lower education, income, or occupational levels are not as well off as comparable whites because of discrimination and lack of resources. It is probable that whites at these levels would still maintain a decided advantage over blacks, who would show decidedly poorer health outcomes.

Attention should also be given to the fact that older blacks—at all SESs--have suffered the stresses associated with racial group membership longer. We might expect, then, that older black groups at upper socioeconomic levels would be less superior to their white counterparts, and show continued health deficits. Older blacks in lower SES positions might be expected to show continued poorer health outcomes.

These differences should be much less prominent among younger adults, who may show no appreciable differences at either the upper- or lower-status levels when the appropriate statistical controls are used. An examination of National Center for Health Statistics data for the most part confirms this speculation. It may be important to distinguish clearly between younger and older adult cohorts in examining the relationship between SES and health status.

A New Generation at Risk

Blacks being born today will be at considerable risk despite some health care advances and other positive developments in recent years. They are most likely to spend their childhood in low-income, single-parent households. They will have inadequate diets and inadequate educational opportunities. Their job prospects will be poor in young adulthood, and a large proportion will die or suffer chronic disease before reaching middle adulthood.

Only a comparative few will inherit anything from their parents. Even for those born into contemporary middle-class homes, few will receive a legacy or financial support for college. Dental visits, preventive health maintenance, well-baby checkups, sensory adjustments for poor hearing and vision, and similar services will be lacking. Survival itself will be paramount. Other "luxuries" of life will remain as difficult for this new cohort of African Americans to afford as they have been for previous cohorts.

None of these issues strikes at the individual and social psychological phenomena of life among black Americans: discouragement, lack of perceived control, and other ravages of racism and discrimination that sap energy and the aspirations and expectations of a successful life. When combined with real structural barriers to educational and occupational mobility and the high probability of exposure to environmental risk factors, the early morbidity, disability, and excess mortality of black Americans become easy to understand (Jaynes & Williams, 1989).

Aging: Some Positives

Older age among blacks, however, is not a time of inevitable decline (Rowe, 1985). The evidence suggests that changes in lifestyle, environmental risk reduction, and medication interventions can have positive influences on both the length and quality of life among older black adults. Survey data show that many older blacks are free from functional disability and limitations of activity related to chronic illness (e.g., Gibson & Jackson, 1987, 1991). In fact, after the age of 65, blacks and whites (within sex groups) differ very little in life expectancy.

Health care has improved significantly for older black adults, and consecutive cohorts are better educated and better able to take advantage of available opportunities. On the other hand, without extensive environmental intervention, a significant proportion of older black adults of the year 2047 (born in 1992) will likely be at severe risk for impoverished conditions and poor social, physical, and psychological health in old age. This poor prognosis is not predicated on biological dimensions of racial differences but on the physical, social, psychological, and environmental risk factors that are correlated with racial and ethnic group membership in this society.

Cradle-to-Grave Pathways of African Americans

From cradle to grave, African Americans are at greater risk for debilitating social, psychological, and physical harm. These relentless negative influences contribute to higher rates of fetal death and adolescent and adult homicide, along with greater levels of morbidity and mortality in the later years of life.

On the other hand, not all blacks are born into such circumstances. There exists a sizable black middle-class, though its precise numbers are disputed. Many blacks in this country can look forward to relatively comfortable styles of living throughout the adult years.

The Pathway of Poverty. The first pathway is one of poverty and deprivation. The "typical" American of African descent who travels this pathway is most likely to have been conceived by a single woman, to have received no prenatal care, and to have been born at a low birth weight in a public health setting. There will be little if any postnatal or day care. He or she will likely live with a poor, unmarried mother and several siblings in a decaying apartment in the inner urban area of a rust belt city, or in a poor rural area of the South. Preschool will not be available, nor will there be much inclination or wherewithal to provide educational materials and toys in the home.

The poor resources and decaying surroundings will continue to shadow his or her childhood. (Estimates are that by 2000 nearly 80 percent of all black children will spend a sizable proportion of childhood in poverty.) School will be chaotic, with many teachers poorly trained or unmotivated. His or her academic performance will fall over the years of schooling because of progressively poorer teaching and resources, while the dangers of drugs and violence increase.

Many children will fall prey to gang membership or illegal drug use and the drug business. Teen prostitution will become a distinct possibility. College will not be an option for most, even if high school is completed. In some urban areas only 45 percent of entering freshmen in high school leave with a diploma. Available opportunities and the cost of higher education are major barriers to even thinking seriously about college for many black children.

Jobs, if any are to be had, will be at minimum wage or otherwise inadequate for individual and family support. A disproportionate number of young black people will wind up on welfare because of the lack of both educational opportunities and jobs. A sizable proportion of women will not marry, or, if they do, will nevertheless spend most their lives in single status. If work is found in young and middle adulthood, it will either be in a dead-end job or in the lower end of the service industry. Because of poor wages and benefits, health insurance will be minimal and preventive health care will be unavailable or provided only at a bare minimum. Growing old, he or she is not likely to have a private pension plan and will have to manage somehow with only Social Security or Supplemental Security Income.

The Middle-Class Pathway. There are more black families that include both individuals in extreme poverty and in working- and middle-class situations. Given the presence of two parents in the household, the chances of receiving good pre- and postnatal care increase to approximately half the births. For the most part, these are families with both parents employed by the government. They have steady if not lucrative positions and adequate health benefits and pensions. Because of racial discrimination and housing barriers, however, many do not live in areas that provide the best schooling opportunities. Furthermore, since both salaries are needed for day-to-day survival, little can be saved for the future or for college education. Cutbacks in college loan programs hurt them much more than whites of comparable incomes since the latter group has greater personal and family assets.

Because of racially exclusive housing patterns, black children in these circumstances are most likely to rub shoulders with children whose life situations are much different from their own. As children of middle-class parents, they can at best hope to achieve the same economic and occupational level themselves, with the higher strata obstructed by race-related blockages. As they enter the later years of life, they will have a more favorable situation than blacks born into meaner economic conditions, but they will have have to manage their budgets carefully with little extra available for amenities or sharing with others.

The life course is a struggle, both psychologically and physically, for African Americans at every income level and at every stage. Even with economic and social resources, the pernicious nature of discrimination and blocked opportunities can have a strong negative influence on the aspirations and expectations of young adults—aspirations and expectations that the majority assumes to be a given right of citizenship. We need to keep in mind that the often portrayed success stories of African-Americans in sports, the arts, and entertainment are exceptions to the working-class, near-poverty, or poverty existence of most blacks.

The older black American of half a century from now has already started his or her life. Unfortunately, we can accurately predict what the most probable life experiences will be for a majority of these African Americans. Fortunately, it is in our power as a nation to comprehend, intervene, and ameliorate these conditions, using time and foreknowledge to change the life pathways of future African-American elders.   ▼ JAMES S. JACKSON

See also: Cardiac Health; Cohort and Generational Effects; Contextualism; Drug Use and Abuse; Grandparent Communication Skills; Grandparent Education to Enhance Family Strength; Happiness, Cohort Measures of; Housing as a Factor in Adult Life; Interethnic Relationships; Longevity; Place and Personality in Adult Development; Religion and Coping with Crisis; Risk to Life through the Adult Years; Rural Living: What Influence on Adult Development?; Social Class and Adult Development; Stress; Subcultural Influences on Lifelong Development; Suffering; Suicide.

References

Anderson, N.B., & Shumaker, S.A. (1989). Race, reactivity, and blood pressure regulation. *Health Psychology, 8:* 483-86.

Baker, F.M. (1987). The Afro-American life cycle: Success, failure, and mental health. *Journal of the National Medical Association, 7:* 625-33.

Baltes, P.B. (1987). Theoretical propositions of life-span developmental psychology: On the dynamics between growth and decline. *Developmental Psychology, 23:* 610-26.

Barresi, C.M. (1987). Ethnic aging and the life course. In D. E. Gelfand & C. M. Barresi (Eds.), *Ethnic Dimensions of Aging*. New York: Springer, pp. 18-34.

Cooper, R. (1984). A note on the biological concept of race and its application in epidemiological research. *American Heart Journal, 108:* 715-23.

———. (1991). Celebrate diversity—or should we? *Ethnicity and Disease, 1:* 3-7.

Cooper, R., Steinhauer, M., Schatzkin, A., & Miller, A. (1981). Improved mortality among U. S. blacks, 1968-1978: The role of antiracist struggle. *International Journal of Health Services, 11:* 511-22.

Dressler, W. (1985). Extended family relationships, social support, and mental health in a Southern black community. *Journal of Health and Social Behavior, 26:* 39-48.

———. (1991). Social class, skin color, and arterial blood pressure in two societies. *Ethnicity and Disease, 1:* 60-77.

Driedger, L., & Chappell, N. (1988). *Aging and Ethnicity: Toward an Interface.* Toronto: Butterworth.

Farley, R. (1987). Who are black Americans?: The quality of life for black Americans twenty years after the civil rights revolution. *The Milbank Quarterly, 65* (Supplement 1): 9-34.

Gibson, R.C. (1986). Blacks in an aging society. *Daedalus, 115*: 349-72.

Gibson, R.C., & Jackson, J.S. (1987). Health, physical functioning, and informal supports of the black elderly. *Milbank Quarterly, 65* (Supplement 1): 1-34.

———. (1991). The black oldest old: Health, functioning, and informal support. In R.M. Suzman, D.P. Willis, & K.G. Manton (Eds.), *The Oldest Old.* New York: Oxford University Press, pp. 506-15.

Haan, M.N., & Kaplan, G.A. (1985). The contribution of socioeconomic position to minority health. In *Crosscutting Issues in Minority Health, Volume II. Report of the Secretary's Task Force on Black and Minority Health.* Washington, DC: U.S. Department of Health and Human Services.

Hamburg, D.A., Elliott, G.R., & Parron, D.L. (1982). *Health and Behavior: Frontiers of Research in the Biobehavioral Sciences.* Washington, DC: National Academy Press.

Jackson, J.J. (1981). Urban black Americans. In A. Harwood (Ed.), *Ethnicity and Medical Care.* Cambridge, MA: Harvard University Press, pp. 16-28.

———. (1985). Race, national origin, ethnicity, and aging. In R. B. Binstock & E. Shanas (Eds.), *Handbook of Aging and the Social Sciences.* New York: Van Nostrand Reinhold, pp. 264-303.

———. (1988). Social determinants of the health of aging black populations in the United States. In J. S. Jackson (Ed.), *The Black American Elderly: Research on Physical and Psychosocial Health.* New York: Springer, pp. 107-35.

Jackson, J.S. (Ed.). (1988). *The Black American Elderly: Research on Physical and Psychosocial Health.* New York: Springer.

———. (1991). *Life in Black America.* Newbury Park, CA: Sage.

Jackson, J.S., Antonucci, T.C., & Gibson, R.C. (1990a). Cultural, racial, and ethnic minority influences on aging. In J. E. Birren & K. W. Schaie (Eds.), *Handbook of the Psychology of Aging.* Third Edition. New York: Academic Press, pp. 103-23.

———. (1990b). Social relations, productive activities, and coping with stress in late life. In M.A.P. Stephens, J.H. Crowther, S.E. Hobfoll, & D.L. Tennenbaum (Eds.), *Stress and Coping in Later Life Families.* Washington, DC: Hemisphere, pp. 80-97.

James, S.A. (1984). Coronary heart disease in black Americans: Suggestions for research on psychosocial factors. *American Heart Journal, 108*: 833-38.

———. (1985). Coronary heart disease in black Americans: Suggestions for future research on psychosocial factors. In A. M. Ostfield (Ed.), *Measuring Psychological Variables in Epidemiologic Studies of Cardiovascular Disease.* Washington, DC: NIH Publication No. 85-2270, Public Health Service, U.S. Department of Health and Human Services.

Jaynes, G.D., & Williams, R.M., Jr., (Eds.). (1989). *A Common Destiny: Blacks and American Society.* Washington, DC: National Academy Press.

Kessler, R., & Neighbors, H. (1986). A new perspective on the relationships among race, social class, and psychological distress. *Journal of Health and Social Behavior, 27*: 107-15.

Manton, K.G., & Soldo, B.J. (1985). Dynamics of health changes in the oldest old: New perspectives and evidence. *Milbank Quarterly, 63*: 206-85.

Markides, K.S., Liang, J., & Jackson, J.S. (1990). Race, ethnicity, and aging: Conceptual and methodological issues. In L. K. George & R. H. Binstock (Eds.), *Handbook of Aging and the Social Sciences.* Third Edition. New York: Academic Press, pp. 112-29.

Myers, H.F. (1984). Summary of workshop III: Working group on socioeconomic and sociocultural influences. *American Heart Journal, 108*: 706-10.

Richardson, J. (1991). *Aging and Health: Black Elders.* Stanford Geriatric Education Center Working Paper Series, No. 4. Stanford: Stanford University Division of Family & Community Medicine.

Rowe, J.W. (1985). Health care of the elderly. *New England Journal of Medicine, 312*: 827-35.

Stanford, E.P. (1990). Diverse black aged. In Z. Harel, E. A. McKinney, & M. Williams (Eds.), *Black Aged: Understanding Diversity and Service Needs.* Newbury Park, CA: Sage.

Wilkinson, D.T., & King, G. (1987). Conceptual and methodological issues in the use of race as a variable: Policy implications. *The Milbank Quarterly, 65* (Supplement 1): 56-71.

Williams, D.R. (1990). Socioeconomic differentials in health: A review and redirection. *Social Psychology Quarterly, 53*: 81-99.

AGE AND MATE CHOICE

Recent lifespan evidence suggests a biological origin for the differences between men's and women's preferences in the age of their mates, and contradicts longstanding theories in the social sciences. Among social scientists who have studied human relationships, it was considered "common knowledge" that American women choose to date and marry men older than themselves, while American men choose to date and marry relatively younger women. Many social scientists who commented on this phenomenon assumed that these patterns are rooted in a norm of Western culture that specifies that it is inappropriate for women to show interest in younger men and for men to show interest in older women (Cameron et al., 1977; Presser, 1975).

Recent data from diverse societies and time periods suggest that this assumption of cultural relativity was incorrect; the phenomenon appears to be universal across human cultures (Buss, 1989; Harpending, 1992; Kenrick & Keefe, 1992). Further, when the data on mating preferences are examined within the context of lifespan development, it is found that only men beyond their twenties show a strong preference for relatively younger women. On the other hand men in their twenties show interest in both relatively younger and relatively older women. Men in their teens show preferences that are incompatible directly with the supposed social norms, expressing a stronger attraction toward women a few years older than they are. This finding challenges the assumptions of social scientists, since young men are usually more likely to comply with sex-role norms (Deutsch, Zalenski, & Clark, 1986).

If age preferences in mates are not the products of social norms, how can they be explained? In combination, the cross-cultural and lifespan data on age preferences suggest that those preferences are the products of biological evolution; when it came to reproduction, our male and female ancestors needed to play a slightly different game. The nature of those evolved differences is described below.

Age Preferences Across the Lifespan

When Henry VIII married his first wife, Catherine of Aragon, he was in his late teens and she was in her early twenties. He married his second wife, Anne Boleyn, when he was 42 and she was about 24. He married his sixth and final wife, Catherine Parr, when he was 52 and she was 31. The age differences between the infamously fickle monarch and his mates are similar to those found among modern Americans (Kenrick & Keefe, 1992; Kenrick, Engstrom, Cornelius, & Keefe, 1992).

We analyzed data from "singles" advertisements placed by middle-class men and women in the western United States, as well as similar advertisements placed by wealthy men and women in the eastern United States. We also examined marriage records from different cities and administered questionnaires to teenagers (who usually have not yet had a chance to leave records of their preferences via advertisements or marriage licenses). Regardless of the data source, men in their forties and fifties are interested in women several years younger than themselves, whereas younger men show an interest in women around their own age or even older than themselves.

Usually, however, women in their twenties do not reciprocate the sexual interest of men in their teens. Women at all ages show a preference for men ranging from their own age up to five or ten years older. However, Catherine of Aragon probably made an exception in Henry's case because he possessed an abundance of other characteristics that women find attractive. He was powerful, wealthy, and high in social status. Researchers have found that women around the world place more value on these characteristics than do men (e.g., Buss, 1989; Hill, 1984; Mealey, 1985; Sadalla, Kenrick, & Vershure, 1987). Usually, teenage men have not had much chance to acquire substantial resources or social status.

Compared with women, men around the world place relatively less emphasis on the material resources of their partners, and relatively more emphasis on the partner's physical condition. From an evolutionary perspective, this discrepency is rooted in the most obvious and basic difference between the sexes—only women bear children (Daly & Wilson, 1983; Kenrick & Trost, 1989). Since females carry their offspring within their bodies, and nurse them for some time afterwards, their youthfulness and physical health are of the utmost importance to the offspring's survival. The contribution of her own physical resources to her own offspring is quite costly to a female mammal, and older females and their offspring living under natural conditions are increasingly less likely to survive (Trivers, 1985).

In humans, the evolution of menopause has resulted in complete infertility in older women. Therefore, men who selected older women as mates would have been less likely to pass their genes on to future generations. That would explain why only older men show a strong preference for women younger than themselves. If a 45-year-old man has a choice between marrying a woman a few years younger than he is and one who is a few years older, choosing the younger woman offers the greater likelihood of children. On the other hand, if a 17-year-old man faces the same choice, it will make less difference to his reproductive success if he chooses the older woman. In fact, women in their twenties are more fertile than women in their teens.

When a woman selects a man, on the other hand, his youthfulness is less important. Men do not go through menopause, and grandfathers are physiologically capable of reproducing (Nieschlag & Michel, 1986). Since older males are able to accumulate wealth and social status, and to form increasing social alliances, our female ancestors would probably have benefited from mating with

males who were older than they were (Leonard, 1989). The older male's resources and social connections would have indirectly helped the offspring survive.

Age Preferences in Different Cultures and Time Periods

If the evolutionary perspective is correct, and if the lifespan changes in age preferences are due to features of human evolution, then one would expect that the pattern found in the United States would also show up in other cultures. Although other cultures do not share our social norms, they do share the same biological differences between men and women, which would have worked to make the two sexes show different patterns of mate preference.

An examination of "singles" advertisements from Holland and Germany revealed that men and women in those countries show preferences just like those found in the United States. The Dutch data are depicted in Figure 1.

Of course, Holland and Germany are both European cultures, and might be expected to share a number of social norms with American society. Marital advertisements from India, on the other hand, indicate a very different set of cultural norms. Those advertisements request information about caste, subcaste, and horoscope, for instance. Nevertheless, they show a pattern very similar to the one demonstrated in American and European societies (see Figure 1). In India, women at all ages indicate a preference for older men, whereas men, as they age, express more and more interest in relatively younger women.

One could argue that even Indian advertisements might reflect the influence of Euro-American culture. That argument is weakened by an examination of marriage data from the island of Poro, a remote fishing community in the Philippines. The residents of this island had had little contact with Western culture. Yet the same pattern of preferences found today in the U.S., Europe, and India was found in marriages recorded on Poro between 1913 and 1939 (Kenrick &

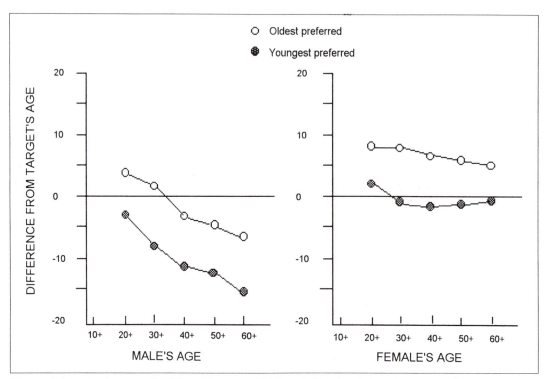

Figure 1. Age Preferences for Mates Expressed in Dutch Singles Advertisements. The same pattern was found in American and German advertisements, in American marriages, and in marital advertisements from India and marriages recorded early in this century on the island of Poro. (Figure from D.T. Kenrick & R.C. Keefe, "Age Preferences in Mates Reflect Sex Differences in Human Reproductive Strategies." *Behavioral and Brain Sciences 15* (1992): 75-133.)

Keefe, 1992). More recently, anthropologists have uncovered the same pattern in traditional African cultures (Broude, 1992; Harpending, 1992). Thus, the sex difference in mate preference across the lifespan appears to be a universal feature of human societies.

Implications of These Findings

The findings on sex differences in age preferences are part of a larger body of evidence suggesting that some features of "human nature" are the result of biological influences rooted in the evolutionary past. Researchers have uncovered cross-cultural universals in subtle flirtation gestures (Eibl-Eibesfeldt, 1975), in emotional expressions (Ekman & Friesen, 1971), in homicide patterns (Daly & Wilson, 1988), and in various aspects of human mating arrangements (Daly

& Wilson, 1983). It is important to keep in mind, however, that biological and cultural factors always interact with one another (Lumsden & Wilson, 1981). Although men commit more murders than women in all societies, for instance, and that seems to reflect a biological influence, some societies have very low frequencies of homicides in both men and women, and that seems to reflect cultural factors. To say that biological factors influence human behavior is therefore not to say that humans are controlled, like robots, by their hormones and primitive brain structures.

It is also important to keep in mind that to say that some phenomenon is "natural" does not mean that it is somehow morally correct or socially desirable. Heart attacks, ulcers, and viral infections are all "natural" biological phenomena, but very few people would advocate social programs to increase their prevalence. Some consequences of the "natural" influences on age preferences would probably not be regarded as socially desirable. For instance, they lead to a great discrepancy in remarriage rates between older men and women. Compared with women over 50, more than twice as many men over 50 got married in Seattle during January 1986, for example. The same discrepancy occurs all over the world. In Mauritius in 1975, for instance, 559 men over 50 got married, compared to 180 women. In Fiji during the same year, 123 men over 50 but only 46 women over 50 got married (Kenrick & Keefe, 1992). The discrepancy results from the universal patterns of mate preference described above. Older men prefer to marry younger women, whereas women, even older women, are seeking older men. This leaves older men with more options than older women, and since there are also many more women who survive into the decades over 50 there are many more unmarried older women than older men.

Meanwhile, teenage men are from 4 to 25 times less likely to get married than are teenage women (Kenrick & Keefe, 1992). In some societies the "surplus" of younger males and older females leads to an interesting social arrangement—young men are introduced to heterosexual relations by unattached older women (Marshall, 1971). This phenomenon is a good example of the interaction between biological realities and cultural norms.

▼ Douglas T. Kenrick, Richard C. Keefe, and Guus Van Heck

See also: Gender as a Shaping Force in Adult Development and Aging; Loving and Losing; Marital Development; Menopause; Sex in the Later Adult Years; Sexuality.

References

Broude, G.J. (1992). The May-September algorithm meets the 20th century actuarial table. *Behavioral and Brain Sciences, 15:* 94-95.

Buss, D.M. (1989). Sex differences in human mate preference: Evolutionary hypothesis tested in 37 cultures. *Behavioral and Brain Sciences, 12:* 1-49.

Cameron, C., et al. (1977). Courtship American style—newspaper ads. *Family Coordinator, 26:* 27-30.

Daly, M., & Wilson, M. (1983). *Sex, Evolution, and Behavior.* Second Edition. Belmont, CA: Wadsworth.

———. (1988). *Homicide.* New York: Aldine deGruyter.

Deutsch, F.M., Zalenski, C.M., & Clark, M.E. (1986). Is there a double standard of aging? *Journal of Applied Social Psychology, 16:* 771-75.

Eibl-Eibesfeldt, I. (1975). *Ethology: The biology of behavior.* Second Edition. New York: Holt, Rinehart & Winston.

Ekman, P., & Friesen, W. V. (1971). Constants across cultures in the face and emotion. *Journal of Personality and Social Psychology, 17:* 124-29.

Harpending, H. (1992). Age differences between mates in southern African pastoralists. *Behavioral and Brain Sciences, 15:* 102-03.

Hill, J. (1984). Prestige and reproductive success in man. *Ethology and Sociobiology, 5:* 77-95.

Kenrick, D.T., Engstrom, C., Cornelius, C., & Keefe, R.C. (1992). Age preferences for dating partners among teenagers: Support for an evolutionary model. Unpublished manuscript, Arizona State University.

Kenrick, D.T., & Keefe, R.C. (1992). Age preferences in mates reflect sex differences in human reproductive strategies. *Behavioral and Brain Sciences, 15:* 75-133.

Kenrick, D.T., & Trost, M.R. (1989). A reproductive exchange model of heterosexual relationships: Putting proximate economics in ultimate perspective. In C. Hendrick (Ed.), *Review of Personality & Social Psychology.* Newbury Park, CA: Sage.

Leonard, J.L. (1989). Homo sapiens: A good fit to theory, but posing some enigmas. *Behavioral & Brain Sciences, 12:* 26-27.

Lumsden, C.J., & Wilson, E.O. (1981). *Genes, Mind, and Culture: The Coevolutionary Process.* Cambridge, MA: Harvard University Press.

Marshall, D.S. (1971). Sexual behavior on Mangaia. In D.S. Marshall & R.G. Suggs (Eds.), *Human Sexual Behavior: Variations in the Ethnographic Spectrum.* New York: Basic Books.

Mealey, L. (1985). The relationship between social status and biological success: A case study of the Mormon religious hierarchy. *Ethology and Sociobiology, 6:* 249-57.

Nieschlag, E., & Michel, E. (1986). Reproductive functions in grandfathers. In L. Mastroianni, Jr. & C.A. Paulsen (Eds.), *Aging, Reproduc-*

tion, and the Climacteric. New York: Plenum Press, pp. 59-71.

Presser, H.B. (1975). Age differences between spouses: Trends, patterns, and social implications. *American Behavioral Scientist, 19:* 190-205.

Sadalla, E.K., Kenrick, D. T., & Vershure, B. (1987). Dominance and heterosexual attraction. *Journal of Personality and Social Psychology, 52:* 730-38.

Trivers, R.L. (1985). *Social Evolution.* Menlo Park, CA: Benjamin/Cumming.

AGE 21

The age of 21 has long been a legal watershed, particularly in the United States and Great Britain, and throughout the British Commonwealth. There are no doubt many who, upon reaching their twenty-first birthday, celebrate by going to a bar with friends to proudly display an identity card and (this time legally) order a pitcher of beer.

No evidence exists to support the notion that significant emotional or physiological changes occur at 21. According to prevalent theories of developmental psychology, 21-year-olds do not necessarily, or even usually, enter a new stage of the life course. Nonetheless, the U.S. legal system, at least until recently, has operated as if human development does proceed in that fashion. For centuries throughout the Anglo-Saxon world, 21 was considered "the age of majority," that is, the age at which a person was considered competent to enter into a binding contract without the use of an adult intermediary. Consider, for example, the situation in Great Britain until at least the 1970s: At 21, individuals would become eligible to make wills, marry without parental consent, apply for naturalization, hold legal estate in land, obtain liquor licenses, serve on juries, and secure a passport without the signature of an adult (Committee on the Age of Majority, 1967).

As early as the thirteenth century, age 21 was an important marker in Britain, at least for men. This was the age, for example,

when they could begin to serve as knights. It was believed that the physical requirements of combat—to wear a heavy suit of armor and simultaneously lift a sword or lance—could be met only by men who had attained age 21. In the same historical era, peasants and other workers were considered adults after they had learned their trade, or by age 15. By the seventeenth century, the age of 21 as a life course marker filtered down from the elite to become the age of majority for all English men and women (Committee on the Age of Majority, 1967, p. 20)

It is likely that whatever legal status the age of 21 has in the United States derives from its English heritage. The Fourteenth Amendment to the Constitution, enacted in 1968, stipulates 21 as the voting age. This threshold was altered in 1971 with enactment of the Twenty-Sixth Amendment, lowering the voting age to 18. Many states stipulate 21 as the minimum legal drinking age, which is nowadays what many people would consider the prime significance of 21, although there are still a number of states in which an individual must be 21 in order to consent to medical treatment (Institute of Law Research and Reform, 1975). Until the 1970s, Canadians under 21 needed the permission of a parent or guardian to receive an operation or anesthetic, but the tendency nowadays is for physicians to accept the consent of those over 16 (Institute of Law Research and Reform, 1975, p. 4). The words of one wise observer are pertinent here: "What history does show is that there is nothing particularly god-given about the age of 21 as such, and that things do change in the light of changing circumstances" (Committee on the Age of Majority, 1967, p. 23).

What is curious is that age 21, rather than 20, should have become a significant legal marker. Our counting system, is, after all, governed by the decimal system. This makes the ages of 30, 40, and 50 a lot more salient to most people than the numbers in between. One possibility is that 21 is the multiple of 3 and 7, both of which are formulaic numbers having high citation frequencies in the Bible and bearing diverse folklore meanings. Roman law divided youth into several categories, including *infantia* for those under 7, and *tutela impuberes*, which, for boys at least, lasted between 7 and 14. For girls, puberty was said to end at 12, yet another formulaic number having significant biblical and folklorist overtones. While the ancient Romans defined full maturity (*plena maturitas*) as beginning at 25, in Britain the law evolved such that maturity was defined as 21 and over. In fact, for centuries, the Latin word *infantia* was used in English law for everyone under 21 (Committee on the Age of Majority, 1967). Members of the British Commonwealth and former British colonies, the United States included, are heirs to this tradition of deeming 21 as a significant marker of personal growth and responsibility.

▼ STANLEY H. BRANDES

See also: Age 40; Age 65; Centenarians; Development and Aging in Historical Perspective.

References

Committee on the Age of Majority. (1967). *Report*. London: Parliament of Great Britain.

Institute of Law Research and Reform. (1975). *The Consent of Minors to Medical Treatment*. Edmonton, Alberta, Canada: University of Alberta Press.

AGE 40

In the United States, as in much of the Western world, the age of 40 is perceived to be a major turning point in adult development. Critical life changes do not necessarily occur at age 40 nor do a majority of individuals necessarily experience age 40 as pivotal. Change at 40 is certainly not genetically programmed. Nonetheless, age 40 is a salient feature of what Robert LeVine (1980) calls our "life plan," or "organized system of...shared expectancies about how lives are lived" (p. 82). It is part of a culturally determined configuration of ideas about normal, predictable progression through childhood and adulthood. In other words, when Americans tell a story about how they mature and grow old, 40 is likely to be part of the plot.

Age 40 is commonly associated with three main types of personal transformation. The most frequently cited change is the onset of a diffuse sense of restlessness and unhappiness. In a whimsical moment, Jules Henry (1973) dubbed this syndrome the "forty year old jitters." He and others (e.g., Davitz & Davitz, 1976; Mayer, 1978) describe age 40 as a time of emotional upheaval, when individuals lose the firm control over their lives that they had developed over the course of several preceding decades.

Most of what we hear about emotional trauma at 40 is based on impressionistic evidence. However, scholars and clinicians reinforce these ideas. For example, Daniel Levinson and associates (1978) report that, for the vast majority of their research sample, the age 40 is "a time of moderate or severe crisis. Every aspect of [the informants'] lives comes into question and they are horrified by much of what is revealed. They are full of recriminations against themselves and others" (p. 199). Levinson's report is consonant with Carl Jung's claim, first articulated in 1931, that there occurs a "rise in the frequency of depressions in men around forty."

A second, more concrete symptom refers to the physiological aspects of aging, including declining bodily strength, deteriorating appearance, and reduced sexual energy. This idea is as old as Shakespeare's second sonnet, which begins:

> When forty winters shall besiege thy brow,
> And dig deep trenches in thy beauty's field,
> Thy youth's proud livery, so gaz'd on now,
> Will be a tatter'd weed, of small worth held.

A contemporary expression of the same theme is represented in pop psychologist Barbara Fried's (1967) contention that "Forty tends to be morbidly convinced that he is actually very sick...and to grieve over the degeneration, both real and imagined, of his physical and mental capacities" (pp. 11-12).

A third symptom at 40 is the presumed occurrence of an occupational crisis. The popular media repeatedly remind us that suddenly, at age 40, people begin to reassess their careers and strike out in new directions. This is the age when they begin to feel trapped by jobs they no longer find satisfying, and yet are limited in their options by the vastly reduced opportunities that confront their generation. In fact, there is little doubt that men and women over 40 have long suffered from discriminatory employment practices.

Resentment against age discrimination in the United States reached a fevered pitch with the publication in 1948 of Conrad Miller Gilbert's *We Over Forty: America's Human Scrap Pile*. A response to adverse employment conditions gave rise in 1967 to the Age Discrimination in Employment Act, which specifically aimed to protect people between ages 40 and 65. Although a 1979 modification of the law raised the upper limit to 70, the lower figure—40 years old—has remained constant.

The various changes attributed to 40-year-olds—the descent into psychological crisis, as well as physiological and occupational transitions—are part of a centuries-old notion that age 40 is a critical divide between two major life periods. This notion explains why all America laughed when comedian Jack Benny refused to admit that he was older than 39. Like most successful humorists, Benny had hit upon a sensitive issue in the personal lives of his public. By openly expressing his anxiety about reaching 40, as well as the fantasy of never having to do so, his joke became ingrained in American folklore. For similar reasons, the title of Walter Pitkin's phenomenal bestseller, *Life Begins at Forty* (1932), became proverbial. The title gained popularity not so much because it reflected reality, but rather because it represented—and continues to represent—a denial of the aging process, which our culture defines as beginning at 40. In the end, the fear of turning 40 amounts to a fear of death. Age 40 is when people commonly begin to think about how many years they have left to live rather than how long they have already been alive.

Why 40?

At this point it is reasonable to ask why 40 has come to represent the developmental turning point of adulthood. Demographic patterns are certainly not responsible. According to no accepted definition of the lifespan—whether referring to actual or anticipated years of life—can 40 be considered the midpoint of human existence. Nor can career patterns provide a sufficient explanation. Age discrimination after 40 is more an effect than a cause of our life plan; it is a by-product of the implicit story that we tell ourselves and one another about how human beings grow old.

Possibly the importance of 40 derives from the fact that this age coincides with critical changes in the developmental cycle of family and household. The empty-nest syndrome, which produces temporary parental depression when children leave home (Glick & Parke, 1965; Rogers, 1982), often coincides with age 40. Age 40 also frequently occurs during the stage of life that has been termed "midolescence" (McMorrow, 1974), a middle-aged period in which parents begin to imitate the erratic behavior and emotional ups and down of their adolescent children. And yet, both the empty-nest syndrome and midolescence encompass time spans long enough that the cultural focus on the specific age of 40 as a turning point still remains a mystery.

Of course, if we compare ourselves with other, vastly different cultures, certain basic explanations come to mind. The mere fact that our language, unlike others, permits us to count to 40 (Gay & Cole, 1967; Tylor, 1958) and our reliance on the decimal system are cultural elements that could make 40 a salient number. Equally significant is the fact that we live in a society in which counting and quantification are highly valued endeavors. Our economic regime has made it necessary for us to measure our world with assiduousness and exactitude. No doubt our obsessive measurement of time, money, and other valuables has influenced us to count ages with equivalent concern and precision. Yet all of these basic cultural underpinnings—language, the decimal system, quantitative biases—merely facilitate our views of the age of 40. They are not truly explanatory.

Number Symbolism

Number symbolism offers the best explanation. Specifically, the importance we attribute to the *age* of 40 derives in good measure from the significance of the *number* 40. The United States shares with the rest of the Western world an implicit emphasis on certain numerals—including 3, 7, 10, 12, and 40—that have become formulaic. We organize our lives with reference to these numbers and think of the world in terms of them with only the barest, if any, awareness that we are doing so. With specific regard to the number 40, there exist at least four different symbolic meanings, which are, in the main, ancient in origin. Each of these meanings corresponds to different ways in which age 40 has been perceived within the context of the lifespan.

First, there is 40 as meaning "many, a lot." Consider what the *Oxford English Dictionary* says about 40: "Used indefinitely to express a large number." This denotation has produced a number of colloquial expressions. A deceitful person can be called "40-faced," as in "40-faced liar" or "40-faced flirt." An angry or alarmed person is said to have "40 fits." In some English dialects, extreme distaste or contempt may be indicated by saying, "I wouldn't touch it with a 40-foot pole." The symbolic meaning of 40 as *many* is consonant with the popular notion that people who are 40 are old; that is, that they have accrued a large number of years.

If 40 has been used as a symbolic equivalent of many, it has also been employed at least as commonly to indicate the specific quantitative measure 4 times 10. There is abundant indication of this usage in the Judeo-Christian tradition. Hence, according to the Bible, the Flood lasted "forty days and forty night" (Genesis 7:4). Moses was on the Mount "forty days and forty nights" (Exodus 16:35). The Israelites were made to "wander in the wilderness forty years" (Numbers 14:13). Elijah went "forty days and forty nights into Horeb the mount of God" (1 Kings 19:8).

The story of Moses is filled with references to 40. Haggada, for example, "divides the life of Moses into three equal periods. He is said to have lived forty years in Egypt, forty in Midian, and forty in the wilderness" (Ginzberg, 1938, p. 404). He prophesied for 40 years, and after he received the Ten Commandments in the wilderness, "Israel feasted for forty days" (p. 250). The meaning of 40 as the specific quantity 4 times 10 is consonant with stage theories of human development that view the years up to age 40 as representing a single developmental entity, the first or second half of life.

There is yet a third symbolic meaning of 40: its association with birth, whether spiritual or natural. For example, The Prophet Mohammed's conversion occurred when he was 40 years old. In Jewish tradition, religious and historical personages typically begin new stages of life at 40. And natural birth, from ancient times to the present, is often accompanied by the new mother's 40-day period of seclusion, abstinence, or purification. Even in the United States until the 1960s, physicians routinely recommended abstention from coitus for six weeks before and after parturition. The association of 40 with *birth or rebirth* corresponds to cultural ideas of self-actualization. It is at 40, we are told, that men start new families, people enter new careers, and opportunities present themselves for personal growth.

This brings us to the fourth and final facet of 40: its symbolic meaning as a period of *sacrifice and transition* from one state of being to another. In the Bible, for example, "forty days or years is the common duration of punishment, fasting, repentence, and vigil" (Buttrick et al., 1962, p. 565). Commonly, too, there exists an association between 40 and purification in Mediterranean mourning practices. From ancient times (Genesis 50:3) to the present (Hand, Casetta, & Thiederman, 1981), 40-day seclusions or quarantines have commonly followed upon a death. In fact, our own English term "quarantine" obviously derives from the Latin *quaraenta*, meaning "forty."

Overtones of repentence and punishment attached to the number 40 correspond to notions of a midlife crisis at age 40, a period of emotional agony, upheaval, and self-doubt. These feelings, according to popular ideas, are growing pains, necessary for rebirth as a new and better being, and required for restoring psychological equilibrium.

With such strikingly similar symbolic attributions to the number 40 and age 40 in ancient and contemporary tradition, it is likely that the meanings in one domain have carried over into the other. Our feelings about the number 40, as conveyed through folk speech, religion, and other aspects of culture, have no doubt exerted a strong unconscious influence on the way we react to the age of 40. Our ancient Mediterranean religious heritage particularly emphasizes the number 40—together with the American tendency to think in terms of age grading. This latter tendency is itself a by-product of our heavily age-graded educational and employment systems. Taken together, these historical and cultural influences have imparted special significance to the age of 40 in the U.S.

New Meanings

While age 40 has long been perceived as a developmental turning point in America, its symbolic meaning has undergone two specific changes in the post-World War II era. First, age 40 was transformed from mainly signifying the beginning of old age to principally representing middle age. This change in emphasis can be attributed to a number of factors, but most important is increasing longevity and the emergence of the category "senior citizens," marked by retirement age, as the quintessential category of elderly persons.

Second, age 40 is now perceived as more of a threshold for women than was the case formerly. It is above all the feminist movement, and especially the involvement of women in professional careers, that has produced this change in our collective perception. No longer is the female life course defined principally according to biological transitions (e.g., menarche, menopause, and the like) or family roles (e.g., wife, mother, widow). We now see women as subject to lifespan demarcators, like age 40, that are cultural. Correspondingly, American women now share with men feelings at turning 40, like emotional upset (Harris, 1975; Jacobs, 1979), that were more commonly reserved for periods of biological or family role transition.   ▼ STANLEY H. BRANDES

See also: Age 21; Age 65; Centenarians; Depression; Development and Aging in Historical Perspective; Gender as a Shaping Force in Adult Development and Aging; Humor; Mental Health in the Adult Years; Metaphors of the Life Course; Mid-Life Crisis; Parental Imperative; Stress; Work Capacity Across the Adult Years; Work Organization Membership and Behavior.

References

Brandes, S. (1985). *Forty*. Knoxville, TN: The University of Tennessee Press.

Buttrick, G.A., et al. (1962). *The Interpreter's Dictionary of the Bible*. Vol. 3. New York: Abingdon Press.

Davitz, J., & Davitz, L. (1976). *Making It from 40 to 50*. New York: Random House.

Fried, B. (1967). *The Middle-Age Crisis*. New York: Harper & Row.

Gay, J., & Cole, M. (1967). *The New Mathematics and an Old Culture: A Study of Learning among the Kpelle of Liberia*. New York: Holt, Rinehart & Winston.

Gilbert, C. (1967). When did a man in the Renaissance grow old? *Studies in the Renaissance*, 14: 7-32.

Ginzberg, L. (1938). *Legends of the Jews*. Seven volumes. Philadelphia: Jewish Publications Society of America.

Glick, P. C., & Parke, R., Jr. (1965). New approaches to studying the life cycle of the family. *Demography*, 2: 187-202.

Hand, W.D., Cassetta, A. & Theiderman, S.B., (Eds.). (1981). *Popular Beliefs and Superstitions: A Compendium of American Folklore from the Ohio Collection of Newhall Niles Puckett*. 3 vols. Boston: G.K. Hall.

Harris, J. (1975). *The Prime of Ms. America: The American Woman at Forty*. New York: Putnam.

Henry, J. (1973). *On Sham, Vulnerability, and Other Forms of Self-Destruction*. London: Penguin, pp. 128-44.

Jacobs, H. (1979). *Life After Youth: Female, Forty— What Next?* Boston: Beacon Press.

Jung, C. G. (1931/1969). *The Structure and Dynamics of the Psyche*. Princeton, NJ: Princeton University Press, pp. 387-403.

LeVine, R. (1980). Adulthood among the Gusii of Kenya. In N. J. Smelser & E. H. Erikson (Eds.), *Themes of Work and Love in Adulthood*. Cambridge, MA: Harvard University Press, pp. 77-104.

Levinson, D.J., et al. (1978). *The Seasons of a Man's Life*. New York: Ballantine.

Mayer, N. (1978). *The Male Mid-Life Crisis: Fresh Starts After Forty*. New York: Signet.

McMorrow, F. (1974). *Midolscence: The Dangerous Years*. New York: Quadrangle.

Pitkin, W. B. (1932). *Life Begins at Forty*. New York: McGraw-Hill.

Rogers, D. (1982). *The Adult Years: An Introduction to Aging*. Second Edition. Englewood Cliffs, NJ: Prentice-Hall.

Tylor, E. B. (1871/1958). *The Origins of Culture*. New York: Harper & Row.

AGE 65

Is there anything special about age 65? The answer depends on the frame of reference that has been selected. Statistically speaking, nothing much happens to health status between ages 64 and 65. The long-term trend toward increased morbidity and mortality throughout the later adult years shows up well before 65 and does not suddenly reach new peaks thereafter. Behavioral and cognitive competency likewise are not altered by approaching, crossing, and continuing past the age 65 threshold. If we examined a variety of performance measures across the adult years, we would not be able to put our finger on a particular place on the charts where learning, memory, vocabulary, and other functions deteriorate in a marked and predictable manner. Similarly, individuals do not suddenly lose their social and interpersonal skills at age 65.

In summary, from the standpoint of what can be reliably measured or observed, age 65 is but a phantom. Some aspects of human performance tend to decline systematically with age (e.g., response speed), some tend to remain stable or even improve a little (e.g., vocabulary), and still other aspects have to be evaluated in a more complex manner than decrement vs. increment (e.g., coping style).

From the historical perspective, age 65 reads more like a comedy of errors than a sequence of logically connected events. As Brandes (1985) reports there is a rich sociocultural tradition that has contributed to age 40 becoming especially salient to us, and, to a lesser degree, the same may be said of age 21. In contrast, 65 was introduced specifically as a marker of adult development with the intention of producing economic and political effects. A powerful German industry— the Krupp weapons and munitions factory system—established a pioneering program of employee benefits. Most Krupp workers engaged in very heavy physical labor, often under oppressive and hazardous conditions. The promise of a retirement pension and some other amenities was a move designed to ensure loyalty and productivity as well as to fulfill Krupp's self-image as a stern but loving father to his workers. Statisticians were ordered to determine the appropriate age for retirement and distribution of its newly available benefits. The shrewd industrialist made it clear that he did not want just any age selected. The most suitable age would be one that did not seem excessively advanced, but at the same time one that relatively few workers would achieve. And this was the entering wedge for 65 as a significant age in society's construction of adulthood and aging. In effect, the statisticians assured Krupp that most of his workers would die before becoming eligible for that tempting pension.

Kaiser Wilhelm (William II), the German ruler at the turn of the twentieth century, was a friend and admirer of Krupp. He saw to it that the Krupp plan became the model for his own pioneering civil service retirement program and carried over age 65 for this purpose. Industrialists and government leaders in the United States were impressed by the German retirement program initiatives and accepted age 65 with little if any critical scrutiny. Interestingly, the establishment of 65 as retirement age was followed by a significant increase in life expectancy in both Germany and the United States, as well as in other industrialized nations. The money-saving angle in selecting this age almost immediately started to become less efficient as more and more people actually lived long enough to claim their benefits.

Nothing in the history or current bureaucratic status of age 65 constitutes a rational argument on its behalf. This age was first selected and then disseminated and perpetuated as a significant marker for reasons of convenience to the reigning political and economic establishments. For example, when 65 was selected as the age of eligibility for Social Security in 1935, this decision had no data base in the biological, medical, or sociobehavioral sciences.

In recent years, age 65 has become a negotiable issue that is responsive to a number of political and economic trends. In the aftermath of World War II, "65 and out" came to be felt as an ever-increasing pressure. During this period, many workers felt threatened and frustrated by the rule that they must leave their long-term employment even if they felt as competent and productive as ever.

This narrow and rigid approach has been somewhat ameliorated as all parties involved—the working person, industry, and government—have had more experience and opportunity to adjust to population and technological change. Some workers now take advantage of options for early retirement and are therefore spared the once-dreaded encounter with "65 and out." In some occupations and some work settings, the retirement age has been moved back to 70. This is another change in policy that has moderated the power of age 65. Furthermore, mandatory retirement has been completely abolished in some settings, and the range of "uncapped" work situations will increase again in 1994 when new provisions of the amended Social Securities Act come into ef-

fect. It seems probable that age 65 will continue to diminish somewhat in its practical significance as industrialized nations continue to adjust to their changing populations and needs (Graebner, 1980; Robinson, Coberly, & Paul, 1985; Schulz, Borowski, & Crown, 1991).

From the bureaucratic and sociopolitical standpoint, age 65 has been a rather sad comedy because it has been taken so seriously and affected so many lives despite its lack of factual credibility. It has not been a success as a management tool either because many highly motivated and competent workers have been forced to leave their employment, to the detriment of the operation. Many a business and governmental agency could have benefited from the experience and judgment of the senior personnel who have been forced out by the arbitrary age criterion. Many people in managerial positions have mistakenly assumed that mandatory retirement at age 65 was working to their advantage. This assumption usually derives from the simplicity and convenience of relying upon chronological age as the sole criterion—and from the way it shields executives from making executive decisions. Instead of observing and assessing the contributions of each individual worker, executives could simply look at the calendar and push the "eject" button.

The one really convincing application of the "65 and out" rule was in all probability its first. A deeply pious man was so encumbered by administrative responsibilities that he could not find the time for meditation and personal spiritual development. The (not yet invented) light bulb flashed on over his head one day, and he drew up a new rule: At the age of 65, all church administrators in this district must resign their duties. I can imagine him smiling a little as he affixed his signature ("Raymond of Pennafort," later to be beatified St. Raymond) to this document on his own sixty-fifth birthday (in the year 1245). Raymond would live another 30 years after liberating himself from the yoke of mundane responsibilities.

Conclusion

Age 65 has become a part of the popular mind-set of our times and thus cannot be completely disregarded despite its unimpressive scientific and managerial credentials. Many people still regard 65 as a crucial threshold, with their adult life on one side and a dreaded "afterlife" on the other side. By now, however, millions have passed across this symbolic threshold only to discover that their lives are still very much their own and their powers undiminished. Unfortunately, "65 and out" has become a self-fulfilling prophecy for some people, especially when individuals intensely reinforce this view and social institutions fear the worst about aging and understand very little about it.

Neither 65 nor any other chronological age deserves to be taken seriously as a solid marker between "adulthood" and "old age." Even if our society is not ready to relinquish this simplistic marker, there are millions of independent and competent men and women whose vibrant lives thoroughly rebuff a stereotype that should no longer be tolerated by thinking people.   ▼ Robert Kastenbaum

See also: Age 21; Age 40; Career Age; Centenarians; Development and Aging in Historical Perspective; Japanese Perspectives on Adult Development; Retirement Preparation; Slowing of Behavior with Age; Suffering; Work Capacity Across the Adult Years.

References

Brandes, S. (1985). *Forty.* Knoxville, TN: The University of Tennessee Press.

Graebner, W. (1980). *A History of Retirement.* New Haven, CT: Yale University Press.

Robinson, P., Coberly, S., & Paul, C. (1985). Work and retirement. In R. Binstock & E. Shanas (Eds.), *Handbook of Aging and the Social Sciences.* Second Edition. New York: Van Nostrand Reinhold, pp. 503-27.

Schulz, J. H., Borowski, A., & Crown, W. H. (1991). *Economics of Population Aging.* Westport, CT: Auburn House.

ALCOHOL USE AND ABUSE

Alcohol is used by adults in almost every culture in the world and has been available for thousands of years. The Bible warns that kings and princes under the effect of alcohol cannot rule justly. But the Bible also recommends the use of alcohol as a remedy for those approaching death or consumed by bitterness. This dual vision of alcoholic beverages has continued to the present day. Controlled moderate use of alcohol is often appreciated and has been associated with positive effects. In contrast, alcohol abuse is associated with a litany of severe physical, social, and mental health problems.

The consumption of alcohol varies greatly from one culture to another. For example, the average consumption of alcohol per person per year is 15 liters in the United States and 17.5 liters in Canada. The average French person, however, consumes 25.9 liters. The average annual rates of alcohol consumption for a nation are related to the rates of alcoholism as well as to death rates from liver cirrhosis (deLint & Schmidt, 1971). As might be expected, populations with higher than average rates of consumption also have significantly more alcohol-related problems. Humans are the only species who will voluntarily drink enough to become intoxicated.

Drinking Patterns throughout the Adult Years

The pattern of drinking tends to change through the adult years. In looking at these differences it is important to distinguish between actual age-related changes and differences that exist between the generations, which are known as cohort effects. Persons who are now in their later adult years may drink relatively less than today's young people because they always had a pattern of relatively lower alcohol consumption. Other generations may drink more because they developed these behavior patterns earlier in life when societal attitudes were different. For example, the current generation of older persons includes many individuals who supported Prohibition, at least at the start. By contrast, today's young adults have been exposed to a high saturation of television beer advertising that could possibly influence their drinking habits in old age as well as at the present time.

Despite cohort differences in drinking patterns, both longitudinal and retrospective research suggests that people generally drink less as they grow older. Several studies show that although people drink just as frequently in their advancing years, they consume less alcohol than in earlier years (Vogel-Sprott, 1984). Significant changes occur in the proportion of fat and water in the body as people age. Even though the total body weight may remain unchanged, fat increases and water content decreases. This is a relevant difference because alcohol is primarily distributed in body water. A given amount of alcohol will therefore achieve a higher concentration in the bodies of older people.

The decline in alcohol consumption with age is possibly related to these changes in body composition. A person who enjoys alcoholic beverages may find that it takes less to obtain the same effect (McKim & Mishara, 1987). However, recent research has suggested that changes in body water may not account for the reduced use of alcohol. Evidence suggests that later in life many people reduce their alcohol intake because they are afraid of losing control or are concerned with the effect of drinking on their health (Mishara & Kastenbaum, 1980).

Men tend to drink more than women. This sex difference seems to be decreasing with recent generations, however. There is also a clear link between drinking and tobacco use: Smoking and drinking tend to go hand in hand.

Health Benefits and Risks

Alcoholism is considered a major health problem throughout the world. The World Health Organization (1952) has defined alcoholism as follows:

> Alcoholics are those excessive drinkers whose dependence upon alcohol has attained such a degree that it shows a notable mental disturbance or interference with their bodily and mental health, their interpersonal relations, and their smooth social and economic functioning; or those who show the prodromal effects of such developments.

In many recent studies the word "alcoholism" has been replaced by "problem drinking" in order to include a wide variety of consumption patterns in the definition. Alcoholics may drink large quantities daily or they may "binge" and drink tremendous amounts only on weekends or even just once a month. Research has shown that alcoholism and heavy drinking is six times more common in men than in women and is related to social and behavioral problems in the home. There is probably some genetic component in the determination of drinking. Identical twins, for example, have more similar drinking patterns than fraternal twins, who are less similar genetically. Even if genetic predispositions are conclusively established, however, this tendency does not provide a comprehensive explanation for why any given individual develops a drinking problem.

A high level of alcohol consumption significantly increases the risk of many disorders, including liver disease and cardiovascular problems (McKim, 1991). Moderate consumption, however, has been related to increased life expectancy in several studies (e.g., Colditz et al., 1985). In general, persons who consume in moderation—usually defined as one or two drinks per day— tend to live longer on the average than persons who abstain totally. It is not yet clear if the alcohol actually helps prolong life or if abstainers have special characteristics or engage in other health practices that result in increased risk of death. The area of greatest controversy continues to be the possible role of moderate alcohol consumption in protecting against cardiac problems. Every new study on this topic is scrutinized carefully by those who support and those who reject this proposition. While there is no clear evidence to suggest that moderate drinking has any negative effects for most individuals, there are suggestions that some may derive benefits.

Treatment

There is much debate regarding the etiology of alcoholism and how to effectively treat problem drinkers. Alcoholics Anonymous (AA), a nonprofit organization founded in 1935, has spread to 110 nations and has a world membership of more than one million. In the United States, AA is currently assisting as many alcoholics as all medical facilities combined, and it does so with apparent success. AA's goal is to help alcoholics stay sober. The organization takes the position that there is no cure for alcoholism itself, but that alcoholics can stop drinking. Members are expected to attend regular meetings for extended periods of time. New members may attend as many as five or six meetings a week to help them start to control their drinking. For many people, AA goes beyond being a treatment program to control or stop drinking and becomes a way of life. Alcoholics Anonymous has proven effective for many drinkers. However, AA has not participated in scientific evaluations of its treatment effects, so not all questions have been answered.

Other methods of treatment include traditional psychotherapy and counseling, behavior therapy (in which drinking behavior is punished or alternatives not compatible with drinking are reinforced), and the use of drugs such as disulfiram (Antabuse) that make people feel sick if they drink. Despite the panoply of treatment methods, there is no definitive evidence about which type is most effective. Alcoholics who are most likely to be helped in any treatment are those who have a high socioeconomic status, a stable social situation, are highly motivated to quit, and have spouses who participate in the effort (Baekeland, 1977). For still unknown reasons alcoholics between the ages of 40 and 45 seem to be the most responsive to treatment.

Alcohol Consumption and Effects in Old Age

Many studies have found positive effects when wine or beer is served in moderation to elderly people who reside either in their own homes or in an institution. It appears that drinking one or two glasses of either of these beverages per day can contribute to decreased depression, higher morale, more restful sleep, and greater participation in a variety of activities. In the most extensive experimental investigation of these effects, Mishara et al. (1975) compared experimental and control groups in two institutional settings for elderly adults. Recognizing that a favorable social setting makes its own contribution to well-being, the investigators worked with institutional officials to establish pleasant "social hour"-type environments in both facilities. Within each facility, those in the experimental group were given access to up to two drinks per day. Members of the control groups had identical opportunities for social interaction, but were offered nonalcoholic beverages. Medical and psychosocial evaluations of all participants were made prior to the study, after nine weeks, and after eighteen weeks. This study found that having alcoholic beverages available did not have any negative effect on the health and well-being of the elderly participants. In fact, members of the experimental group developed higher morale and slept better than did members of the comparable control groups. Improved social relations occurred with both experimental and control groups, confirming the need to differentiate between the effects of consuming alcohol and the effects of enjoying a social setting on a regular basis.

Research indicates that as people age there are fewer alcoholism problems, along with the general decrease in consumption. One explanation of this decrease may be the fact that alcoholism is a self-limiting disease: Alcoholics tend to die younger. Another explanation is that people tend to reduce drinking as they grow older. A third possibility is that older alcoholics may be more difficult to identify because they tend to drink alone and are less likely to get into trouble at work or with the police. Mishara (1985) underlined the importance of distinguishing between older persons whose alcoholic problems developed later in life and those who have had longstanding problems with alcohol but have managed to survive into old age. The "acute" group of alcoholics with their newly developed problems tend to respond well to interventions aimed at helping them stop drinking. However, "chronic" alcoholics may respond best to palliative measures that help them to survive, although not decisively terminating their drinking habits.

Although much remains to be learned about the use and abuse of alcohol across the adult years, it is evident that many alcoholics are able to stop or control their drinking after participating in appropriate treatment programs.

▼ BRIAN L. MISHARA AND WILLIAM A. MCKIM

See also: Cardiac Health; Cohort and Generational Effects; Driving: A Lifespan Challenge; Drug Use and Abuse; Gender as a Shaping Force in Adult Development and Aging; Longevity; Mental Health Resources for Adults; Mexican Americans: Life Course Transitions and Adjustment; Native American Perspectives on the Lifespan; Risk to Life through the Adult Years; Rural Living: What Influence on Adult Development?; Stress; Twins through the Lifespan.

References

Baekeland, F. (1977). Evaluation of treatment methods in chronic alcoholism. In B. Kissen & H. Begleiter (Eds.), *The Biology of Alcoholism.* Volume 5. New York: Plenum, pp. 383-440.

Colditz, G. A., et al. (1985). Moderate alcohol and decreased cardiovascular mortality in the elderly cohort. *American Heart Journal, 109*: 886-89.

deLint, J. S., & Schmidt, W. (1971). The epidemiology of alcoholism. In Y. Israel & J. Maidones (Eds.), *Biological Basis of Alcoholism.* New York: Wiley/Interscience, pp. 423-42.

McKim, W. A. (1991). *Drugs and Behavior.* Second Edition. Engelwood Cliffs, NJ: Prentice Hall.

McKim, W.A., & Mishara, B.L. (1987). *Drugs and Aging.* Toronto: Butterworth.

Mishara, B. L. (1985). What we know, don't know, and need to know about older alcoholics. In E. Gottheil, K. A. Druley, T. E. Skoloda, & H. M. Waxman (Eds.), *The Combined Problems of Alcoholism, Drug Addiction and Aging.* Springfield, IL: Charles C. Thomas, pp. 243-61.

Mishara, B. L., & Kastenbaum, R. (1980). *Alcohol and Old Age.* New York: Grune & Stratton.

Mishara, B.L., et al. (1975). Alcohol effects in old age: An experimental investigation. *Social Science and Medicine, 9*: 535-47.

Vogel-Sprott, M. (1984). Response measures of social drinking: Research implications and applications. *Journal of Studies on Alcohol, 44*: 817-36.

World Health Organization. (1952). *Expert Committee on Mental Health.* WHO Technical Report Series 42. Geneva: World Health Organization.

ATTACHMENT ACROSS THE LIFESPAN

Attachment is a term that developmental and clinical psychologists use when referring to the emotionally close and important social relationships that people have with each other. This concept of attachment was originally proposed by the late John Bowlby (1969), an innovative British psychiatrist who spent much of his career at the Tavistock Institute in London. Bowlby's Attachment Theory was an eclectic approach to social relationships that drew upon Freud's theory of psychoanalysis, Darwin's theory of evolution, and Lorenz's theory of ethology. The goal of Attachment Theory was to explain how relationships are formed and what role they play in the individual's development. Although Bowlby originally proposed Attachment Theory as a basis for understanding social relationships across the lifespan, much of the early work in this field concentrated on parent-child relationships, especially mother-infant dyads.

The focus of the early attachment literature and research was to understand how the young child came to view the world as a safe, stimulating, and challenging place to live. Attachment Theory suggests that significant social relationships provide the individual with a secure base from which to explore the world. With this secure base, the individual is motivated to seek out and investigate the challenges offered by the environment. In turn, this positive experience with the world helps the child to develop his or her confidence and abilities.

Ainsworth's Strange Situation

One research strategy had a particularly strong effect in guiding, and perhaps inadvertently limiting, the early studies of attachment. Ainsworth's Strange Situation (Ainsworth et al., 1978) offered a standardized approach for assessing the quality of infant relationships with adults. The eight-episode Strange Situation was designed for use with 12-month-old children and an "attachment figure," most often the mother.

Three broad categories of attachment relationships have been defined. The securely attached infant is successful at using the attachment figure as a secure base from which to explore the world. In the presence of the mother or other attachment figure, this child will freely explore the environment. If separated from the attachment figure, the child usually will express concern, may or may not accept comfort from a stranger, but will most obviously approach and greet the attachment figure on reunion.

A second group has been labeled the ambivalently attached-resistant group. These infants are not quite as able to use the attachment figure as a secure base. They show stress when separated from the attachment figure and are much less able to accept comfort from a stranger. Upon reunion, they greet the attachment figure with ambivalence, both approaching and pushing him or her away. This child may run to its mother but cry rather than smile or be calmed by her.

And, finally, the ambivalently attached-avoidant child seems much less able to use the attachment figure as a secure base from which to explore the world. This child cannot use the attachment figure for comfort when upset and is likely to avoid her or him during reunion episodes. Although these are infant behaviors and reactions to attachment relationships, these same relationship types may be continued and extended throughout adulthood (Antonucci, 1976).

Attachment in Adult Social Relationships

Just as with children, close and important social relationships with significant others may play a major role in the life experience of adults. Attachment as a lifespan concept was first explored in an American Psychological Association symposium that was later published as a special edition of *Human Development*. In this volume, infant researchers, clinicians, ethologists, and adult development psychologists offered their thoughts on how to extend the concept of attachment across the lifespan (Antonucci, 1976). Similarly, Lerner & Ryff (1978) noted that attachment was an ideal theoretical construct for extension over the life course because it can be applied so readily to different points along the age spectrum. More recently, infant attachment researchers have themselves become more interested in the adult implications of Bowlby's concept of representational models (Bretherton & Waters, 1985; Parkes & Stevenson-Hinde, 1982). This interest has often been stimulated by the continued development and aging of persons who first came to the researchers' attention as infants in their longitudinal studies. A retrospective Adult Attachment Interview has proven useful in noting the continuity of (recalled) attachment relationships and its transmission across generations (Main, Kaplan, & Cassidy, 1985). This approach has been found especially useful in studying relationships in maladaptive situations. Hazen & Shaver (1987, 1990) have also successfully applied the attachment concept to the study of adult romantic relationships.

The basic premise of attachment theory—that social relations with others provide a secure basis from which to explore the world—can readily be applied to adult social relationships. It is critical to maintain the perspective that social relationships are continuing, ongoing, and dynamic. Individuals grow and develop; their parents, siblings, friends, spouses, and children also grow and develop. Although relationships often build upon the past, we need to recognize that they naturally change as each individual matures, interacts with the larger world, and has new experiences as a result of experience with various life roles.

How Do Different Types of Attachment Relationships Develop?

Very little attention has been given to the systematic study of the underlying mechanisms that influence the development of different relationship types either in adults or children (see Belsky & Nezworski, 1988; Rutter, 1987). There have been some suggestions, however. Clinicians, for example, have observed that parents who provide their children with warm, supportive environments have children who themselves are warm, more competent, and better adjusted. These children, in turn, are likely to become warm and supportive parents. Furthermore, they seek adult relationships of the same type. On the other hand, children who were abused as children are themselves more likely to abuse their children. It has also been observed that people develop certain expectations based on their own experiences about what should be given and what should be received as part of the social relationships they have with others (Levitt, 1991). Nevertheless, despite the widespread acceptance of this idea, very little rigorous scientific investigation has addressed the question of the specific psychological mechanisms through which such continuity and discontinuity are achieved.

In seeking to understand how the relationship between infant and adult caregiver provides the infant a secure base from which to explore the world, researchers have learned that the physical characteristics of the environment do not lead to securely attached children. A clean and sanitary environment, for example, does not necessarily lead to positively attached children. The number of toys, furniture, or people available in the environment also has little relationship to the attachment outcome.

Close examination reveals that it is necessary to pinpoint specific characteristics of the environment, i.e., the people with whom the infant, the child, and the adult actually interact, and the nature of their interactions. Several theorists reached the same conclusion, although they used somewhat different terms in expressing their observations. The important elements in attachment formation have been described variously as quality rather than quantity, or loving care from important others or, more behavioristically, contingent responsivity. Despite such variations in terminology, the descriptive similarity across all these types is the notion that the child, and later the adult, interacts on a steady basis with an adult who is responsive to the child's specific behaviors or overture. The important point is not only that the infant's needs are met, but that the infant learns to communicate effectively what these needs are and experiences success in meeting these needs.

Although much of this research was conducted with infants, the fundamental message is directly applicable to adult attachment relationships. Few researchers have attempted to extend this theoretical perspective over the life course and to speculate on the mechanisms of this attachment relationship.

Antonucci and Jackson (1987) suggest that close social relationships such as attachment allow the transmission of self-efficacy through contingent feedback experiences that allow children to adjust their behavior by monitoring the responses of others. Under ideal conditions, individuals have close attachment relationships which provide them with the secure base from which to explore the world. In the case of adults, this secure base might take the form of feelings of self-efficacy or self-esteem that are developed as a result of success experiences supported or facilitated by significant others. As one moves from childhood to adolescence to young adulthood, one continues to be influenced by attachment figures. In the case of children, these attachment figures are usually parents. Later, the spouse and various significant others become attachment figures in adult life.

These are hypothesized to be additive experiences. The parent-child relationship, under ideal circumstances, enables the child to feel that there is a secure base from which to explore the world. At first, this feeling facilitates the child's learning experiences with the immediate environment—toys, people, objects in and around the house. The tasks of later childhood and adulthood are more complex. We already have research evidence suggesting that children who enjoy secure infant attachment relationships are more likely to be competent and resilient as personalities and more effective and social as students (Arend, Gove, & Sroufe, 1979). Antonucci and Jackson (1987) have proposed that this tendency may extend even further up the life cycle. Children who were made to feel secure as infants are likely to be better able to succeed at more adult tasks. They feel capable of striving for and achieving more adult goals. And the effects are cumulative in another sense as well. Individuals who move from childhood to adulthood with the "secure sense of attachment" are likely to choose for intimate companions the kind of people who will provide further support, efficacy, and esteem enhancement. As all these individuals continue to grow and mature, the nature of their relationships and interactions develops and changes along with them (Kahn & Antonucci, 1980).

Authentic Support and Continued Development

Attachment and other social relationships need not be universally or unrealistically positive. Although attachment relationships provide positive support in many areas of life, this support must also be authentic. The interpersonal feedback must be realistic.

Support figures reinforce the successes and support the failures of the individual. They acknowledge both the individual's strong and weak points. This type of realistic appraisal from supportive others allows securely attached children to become adults who are also less susceptible to abusive relationships, and more able to address problems in a genuine, informed, and confident manner. They will be the individuals who not only seek out supportive others to provide them with the same secure base as adults that their parents gave them in childhood, but also will be those who are best able to take on the challenges of life. They will recognize their own limitations while at the same time feeling empowered by supportive others to use every available asset to meet those challenges.

Nevertheless, the unique and extraordinary character of human beings allows them to be forever receptive to the changing nature of their social relations. One's relationships with parents can remain close and important throughout a lifetime, yet it is also a dynamic relationship that can continue to grow and develop. Attachments are close and important relationships that change over time. ▼ Toni C. Antonucci

See also: Adult Children and Their Parents; Contextualism; Friendships through the Adult Years; Grandparent Communication Skills; Grandparent Education to Enhance Family Strength; Loneliness; Marital Development; Narcissism; Native American Perspectives on the Lifespan; Parental Imperative; Sibling Relationships; Social Relationships, Convoys of; Spiritual Development and Wisdom: A Vedantic Perspective.

References

Ainsworth, M. D. S., et al. (1978). *Patterns of Attachment*. Hillsdale, NJ: Erlbaum.

Antonucci, T. C. (1976). Attachment: A lifespan concept. *Human Development, 19*: 135-42.

Antonucci, T. C., & Jackson, J. (1987). Social support, interpersonal efficacy and health. In L. L. Carstensen & B. A. Edelstein (Eds.), *Handbook of Clinical Gerontology*. New York: Pergamon, pp. 291-311.

Arend, R., Gove, F., & Sroufe, L. A. (1979). Continuity of individual adaptation from infancy to kindergarten: A predictive study of ego-resiliency and curiosity in preschoolers. *Child Development, 50*: 905-59.

Belsky, J., & Nezworski, T. (1988). *Clinical Implications of Attachment*. Hillsdale, NJ: Erlbaum.

Bowlby, J. (1969). *Attachment and Loss. Volume 1: Attachment*. New York: Basic Books.

Bretherton, I., & Waters, E., (Eds.). (1985). A move to the level of representation. *Monographs of the Society for Research in Child Development, 50*: 1-2.

Hazen, G., & Shaver, P. (1987). Romantic love conceptualized as an attachment process. *Journal of Personality and Social Psychology, 52*: 511-24.

———. (1990). Love and work: An attachment-theoretical perspective. *Journal of Personality and Social Psychology, 59*: 270-80.

Kahn, R. L., & Antonucci, T. C. (1980). Convoys over the life course: Attachment, roles, and social support. In P. B. Baltes & O. Brim (Eds.), *Life-Span Development and Behavior*. Volume 3. New York: Academic Press, pp. 234-86.

Lerner, R., & Ryff, C. (1978). Implementation of the life-span view of human development: The sample case of attachment. In P. B. Baltes (Ed.), *Life-Span Development and Behavior*. Volume 1. New York: Plenum Press, pp. 2-45.

Levitt, M. J. (1991). Attachment and close relationships: A life span perspective. In J. L. Gerwitz & W. F. Kurtines (Eds.), *Intersections with Attachment*. Hillsdale, NJ: Erlbaum, pp. 38-55.

Main, M., Kaplan, N., & Cassidy, J. (1985). Security in infancy, childhood, and adulthood: A move to the level of representation. In I. Bretherton & E. Waters (Eds.), *Growing Point in Attachment*. Monographs of The Society for Research in Child Development, 50: 66-106.

Parkes, C. M., & Stevenson-Hinde, J. (1982). *The Place of Attachment in Human Development*. New York: Basic Books.

Rutter, M. (1987). Continuities and discontinuities. In J. Osofsky (Ed.), *Handbook of Infant Development*. New York: Wiley, pp. 214-38.

B

BODY SENSES

When we look, listen, taste, or sniff we are extracting information from the external world. The sensory modalities involved in these operations generally receive more attention than the modalities that provide information on our own internal operations. Vision and hearing, the two most emphasized sensory modalities among humans, are directed toward the outer world and therefore are valuable for identifying threats and opportunities. Much of our overall conception of the world is based upon information extracted from visual and auditory scanning of the environment. The olfactory and gustatory senses are often of equal or even greater importance to other species, but usually play a secondary role to vision and audition for humans, especially in high-tech societies. Even the aroma and taste of food are replaced by their visual proxy in television commercials.

The inner—or body—senses receive little attention until something goes wrong. A person feels dizzy and has difficulty in maintaining balance, for example, or detects a loss in sensitivity to vibrations. Difficulties involving the body senses are more readily detected and understood if we have a baseline of knowledge regarding their normal development and functioning. Furthermore, the body senses are a vital component in our holistic functioning and cannot be disregarded if we hope to learn the full story of human development across the lifespan.

The distinction between externally oriented and body senses is of practical value, but does not represent the entire state of affairs. There are "inner" facets to the externally oriented senses, and "outer" facets to the body senses. For example, the images we derive through the visual system actually tell us quite a bit about the visual system and the signals it has received. A "color blind" person, for example, derives a different processed image than a person with unimpaired color vision. Fatigue, drugs, and age-associated changes in the visual and central nervous system all influence the "final product" of visual detection and processing (and the same may be said for audition, olfaction, and gustation). From a philosophical standpoint it can also be argued that we never do see, hear, taste, or smell the external world in the pure sense of these terms, but are always limited to an admixture of external signal and the operational characteristics of our perceptual system.

Similarly, the body senses carry out their self-monitoring functions through sensitivity to external as well as internal events. "I feel creepy," for example, is a body sense interpretation that may have been triggered by a curious spider landing on the back of the neck. The external and inner senses have different primary realms of responsibility, but both involve an integration of "messages from the beyond" with inner processes.

But the receptors do not tell the whole story, whether in the case of body senses or any other modality. Before a sensory impression becomes a functional element in our behavior it must be processed through higher structures in the nervous system. The status and special characteristics of our central control system must be taken into account, along with receptor organs themselves.

Introducing the Body Senses

The body senses can be divided into two broad realms. The *somesthetic* senses provide information about touch, pressure, pain and other sensations, and temperature. These sensory functions might be regarded as monitoring devices that provide "status reports" on the condition of our bodies and thereby help us to detect problems, make adjustments, and orient ourselves effectively within our environment.

The *vestibular* sense plays a critical role in our ability to maintain balance. It provides us with a continuing pattern of information concerning the position and movements of our body. It is the physical-sense counterpart of a motion picture. For example, in walking across an icy street, we rely upon our vestibular sense to judge when we are in danger of losing our balance in time to make adjustments. The vestibular system is versatile enough not only to help us remain upright when circumstances threaten our balance, but also to reward athletes by enabling them to execute marvels of athletic movement in gymnastics or other sporting events. The vestibular system is particularly well suited to offering information on the position of the head.

Each of the modalities involved in the body senses will now be briefly described.

Touch. The *cutaneous* system makes possible the sensation of touch. Pressure-sensitive receptors of various types are located in the skin. These structures respond to physical contact such as brushing against a wall, receiving a friendly pat, or becoming the landing site for a thirsty mosquito. Although not as complex as the visual or auditory systems, the cutaneous receptor system has its own specialists.

- Bunched receptors known as Merkel's discs specialize in conveying information about continuous pressure at the surface of the skin.
- Ruffini end-organs provide information about pressure that can be detected at their deeper level within the skin structure.
- Hair-cell receptors tremble at light touches.
- Meissner's corpuscles detect light contacts on areas of the skin that lack hair-cell receptors.
- Pacinian corpuscles are expert in picking up quick changes in touch or pressure by firing off rapid bursts of signals at first contact and then decreasing the signal rate.

All touch receptors have thresholds of sensitivity, i.e., a minimal level of contact that is required to reliably detect the presence or location of touch.

Pain. Receptors for pain are located throughout the body. These take the form of free nerve endings. Some share the skin with touch-pressure receptors; others are found in joints, arterial walls, the skull, and in various body organs. More than one kind of stimulus can evoke the pain response through the same free nerve endings. For example, excessive mechanical pressure, muscle spasms, stretching of ligaments and joints, and swelling of internal organs are all likely to register as "pain." Additionally, thermal sensitivity can be converted into pain perception, e.g., "painfully cold," or "a burning sensation."

Research into pain and its control has proven frustrating because it is difficult to establish a standard and dependable measure of this phenomenon. What appears to be the same intensity of the same stimulus might be experienced as "stimulating" by one person, "a little annoying" by another, and "very painful" by still another. Pain is real, but it is also a complex and idiosyncratic experience. Individuals differ in their pain thresholds and in how they interpret and cope with the experience. Pain tolerance is the highest intensity of undesirable sensation that a person can withstand, and cultural and personality characteristics clearly influence this level. For example, open and gregarious people are more likely to talk about their painful experiences, but also more likely to tolerate high levels of pain, while anxious people tend to have lower levels of pain tolerance (Whitbourne, 1985). People who have learned to "suffer in silence" as part of ethnic or cultural values will also respond differently from those who have been encouraged to seek assistance and relief whenever anything goes wrong.

There are also marked individual differences in response to placebos (nonactive substances that are given to patients who believe they are receiving actual medication). The fact that one person may experience substantial relief from use of a "fake" pill, while another remains in pain even after receiving real medication should alert us to the pervasive role of personality, expectation, and individual differences in general when trying to understand pain sensitivity and tolerance.

Thermal Sensitivity. Temperature recognition makes an important contribution to homeostasis. Tissue damage can result from prolonged exposure to extreme temperatures, whether these have external or internal sources. For example, heat stroke can be a risk for heavily padded football players who exert themselves on a hot day. But there is also risk of dehydration, heart failure, and other negative outcomes for the person who is running a very high fever and not receiving adequate care.

The receptor system involved in thermal sensitivity has not been firmly established. Whitbourne (1985) suggests that there are separate receptors for warmth and cold, each probably taking the form of free nerve endings. On the basis of the limited available data, she also suggests that the cold receptors are more numerous. Whitbourne also makes an interesting point about the rate of change in temperature:

> Within a narrow range, the individual cannot sense changes in temperature if they occur gradually. This range corresponds to temperatures slightly above and slightly below physiological zero, which is the skin temperature at which neither warmth nor cold is felt. The temperature at which physi-ological zero is achieved varies according to area of the body, having an average value of about 7 degrees below the normal body temperature. The zone above and below physiological zero serves several important functions. Because of the relative insensitivity of thermal receptors to skin temperature in the range of physiological zero, discomfort from warmth and cold is experienced only when the temperature of the skin reflects outside conditions that can potentially threaten to lower or raise the body's core temperature below or above safe levels. The protective nature of this zone is apparent from the fact that temperature changes away from it are sensed as more intense than changes toward it. As a result, there is a greater likelihood of behavioral changes oriented toward achieving homeostasis when the possibility of risk is greater from escalating or descending temperatures relative to the risk of harm to the body's tissues. (p. 194)

There are significant differences in thermal sensitivity at various bodily locations. The area most sensitive to warming and cooling is the forehead, which thereby provides the best index of what is taking place temperature-wise in the environment. The abdominal area has the least sensitivity to thermal changes. Along with differential bodily sensitivity to thermal change, one must also take into account the disconcerting fact that different approaches to measurement also yield different results. Although much remains to be learned, it is already clear that thermal sensitivity involves a set of complex processes concerned with protecting the body from the effects of extreme temperatures.

Position and Balance. We tend to take for granted our ability to maintain and adjust our positions in space and to achieve and regain balance while in motion. Unfortunately, this set of abilities may become less reliable with advancing age, as will be described below. For young and for old, position and balance are mediated by kinesthetic feedback processes and the vestibular system (Kornhuber, 1974; Van der Laan & Oostervald, 1974; Wilson & Peterson, 1981).

Kinesthesia is the term given to the receptive side of the positioning and balancing process. When we have adequate kinesthetic acuity we are able to monitor the position and status of our body in space; we "have a feeling for where we are." For example, even with our eyes closed or in the dark we know the relative displacement and orientation of our arms, legs, and torso, and can locate the tip of our nose with an index finger should this seem like a trick worth doing. Receptors are located in the skin, so arranged that each Golgi ending reports on a small angle of movement while the larger grouping encompasses the entire range of movement. In executing a successful movement one is taking advantage of a series of feedback messages between kinesthetic receptors and those divisions of the central nervous system that are most concerned with the direction of skilled motor actions.

The vestibular system accomplishes its function of maintaining our desired orientation in space in a rather interesting way: In effect, it computes gravitational and accelerative force signals as these register on our heads. More specifically, the device that bears the primary responsibility for this operation is a structure located within the inner ear. The vestibular system consists of two spherical compartments and three looping semicircular canals. Within the two compartments (known respectively as the *utricle* and the *saccule*) are sensitive little hair cells that are surrounded by a sort of jelly with crystals on top. These tiny crystals of calcium carbonate are known as *otoconia*. When we move our heads, the otoconia also shift position and this ruffles the hair cells which, in turn, induce the vestibular nerve to flash a neural signal. This "alarm" keeps ringing until we shift our head position again. If we shake our head in dismay at the complexity of this process, then we are merely inciting the vestibular system into action! Actually the continuous feedback process is a good deal more involved than what has been sketched here, but enough has been described to help us appreciate how much our control over our total body orientation depends on events that take place within the inner ear.

Body Sense Changes through the Adult Years

Although less is known about lifespan development and change in the body senses, this area of inquiry has started to attract a growing cadre of researchers. The quest for general understanding has been intensified by concern about problems in later adulthood that seem to be related to breakdowns in the ability to maintain balance and carry out intended actions. It should also be acknowledged at the outset that the study of body sense through the adult years poses methodological and analytic challenges parallel to those encountered in other topic areas. Of particular relevance is the difficulty in differentiating between changes that should be attributed to intrinsic processes ("aging") and those that are secondary to disease, disability, or life-style factors.

What has been learned?

The Pathology-Deficit Connection. A review of the research literature has led Kenshalo (1979) to a conclusion that might not have been anticipated on the basis of the reigning assumptions regarding age-related deficit. Kenshalo first noted that "Current clinical descriptions of somesthetic acuity report a uniform decline with advancing years." This was not at all surprising. Kenshalo also noticed that some investigators report that "losses in certain measures of somesthetic sensitivity are by no means general in the aged population...This raises a question concerning the etiology of somesthetic deficits. Is the aging of this system a physiological or pathological state? Stated another way, is aging physiological involution or the result of disease? (p. 189).

Kenshalo tentatively concludes that decline in somesthetic acuity through the adult years is more closely related to pathological processes than to "aging" per se. Many people do experience such declines, but some are spared or recover function after loss. He presents a challenging view that is still viable today, although in need of more definitive research.

In those systems where regeneration of the sensory processes is slow or nonexistent, such as vision or audition, aging appears more physiological than pathological. In systems such as the cutaneous or chemical senses where regeneration of neurological structures and functions is considerable, pathology seems to account better for sensory deficits than physiological involution. (Kenshalo, pp. 189-90)

All that declines over time is not necessarily aging, then, and the capacity for regeneration and recovery of function may be greater than is usually supposed, at least within the relatively "primitive" body sense systems.

Persistence and Change: A Mixed Picture. Some components of the body sense systems show clear patterns of change with age, but some do not. This mixed picture exists even within the same sphere of functioning. For example, the dermal nerve net, the most numerous set of sensory receptors in the skin, remain fairly constant in number, density, and form throughout the adult years. By contrast, the previously mentioned Meissner corpuscles "undergo remarkable changes during the lifetime of the individual. At birth and in infants they are almost spherical and they elongate with age. In young individuals they are cylindrical, and each corpuscle is attached firmly to the epidermis above and the general elastic framework of the dermis below. With age the corpuscle loosens from the epidermis and may become detached" (Kenshalo, p. 193). The number of Meissner corpuscles decreases steadily from the first decade of life through all the adult years, with some areas losing more of the receptor cells than others. To make matters even more complicated, the pacinian corpuscles behave differently in different individuals! These somesthetic receptor organs actively remodel and regenerate themselves in some people and not in others. Examples such as these suggest that it would be premature to generalize about age-related changes in somesthetic sensitivity; rather, we should be as specific as we can in examining particular modes of body sense and their underlying structures.

Still as Sensitive to Touch? Yes and No. The mixed picture of structural changes over the adult years also shows up at the level of personal experience. This is especially clear in the case of touch. With advancing adult age, one tends to become less sensitive to touch on the surface of the hand, ordinarily a region that is quite sensitive. However, there is little or no decline in touch sensitivity on those body areas that are normally covered with hair. Furthermore, vibratory signals are still as well detected in the upper part of the body, but less well detected in the lower part after about age 50 (Whitbourne, 1985).

We know little about the practical implications of this heterogeneous pattern. Do people tend to develop increased "touch cravings" around midlife because of reduced sensitivity to touch in certain regions of the body? Are there corresponding modifications in erotic feeling that are associated with the mixed picture of persistence and change in touch sensitivity? There is obviously a need for research that would combine measures of touch and vibration sensitivity with exploration of the individual's total world of personal and interpersonal experience.

No Changes in Thermal Sensitivity? Here we have chosen to raise a question rather than offer a firm conclusion. The very limited research on thermal sensitivity throughout the adult years was examined by Kenshalo (1979) and Whitbourne (1985), both of whom were properly cautious about drawing inferences from the meager data available. Not much has changed in this area in recent years. We are left, then, with results based on so few individuals that it might be best to say nothing at all until help arrives.

However, the scant available data are too provocative to pass up completely. It appears that adults of varying ages (from about 18 through the mid 60s) do not show differences in response to thermal stimulation. Differences in sensitivity were noted among individuals, but not among age-grouped individuals. Another way of putting this is that people seem to retain their baseline abilities to detect warmth and coldness through at least a large sector of the adult years. Whitbourne (1985) tried to account for these findings by speculating that elderly people studied in their homes had adapted to lower temperatures caused by the need to control heating bills.

> Small increments in temperature would therefore be perceived as warm, even though the skin temperature was actually quite low. Alternatively, it is plausible that the older persons had a lower skin temperature primarily because of defective homeostatic defense mechanisms, and that this intrinsic age effect makes them likely to feel warm at a lower temperature. (Whitbourne, 1985, p. 197)

And yet, as a resident of Arizona and a former director of a geriatric facility, I have found that heat-seeking behavior is one of the most pervasive characteristics of elderly adults. Adults at midlife and beyond often report decreased tolerance for the wintry blasts of their native environs and become heliotropic visitors or immigrants to Sun Belt locations. Furthermore, in a roomful of people of different ages, it is generally the elders who ask to have the heat turned up or start to look around for a sweater. Perhaps we need to distinguish more consistently between the ability to detect thermal levels and changes and the zone of comfort.

Increasing Vulnerability to Pathological Conditions. It has already been noted that pathology rather than intrinsic age-related changes may play a significant role in body sense declines over the adult years. With increasing adult age, people also become more susceptible to pathological conditions that can interfere with somesthetic and vestibular functioning and thereby destabilize a broad range of activities that are part of everyday life.

Peripheral vestibular disorders constitute an entire class of pathological conditions that make it difficult to walk, step, adjust to environmental barriers, etc. Although these are not the only types of pathology that we might encounter in the later adult years, they will do as our major example here. Peripheral vestibular disorders take three basic forms: vestibular distortion, vestibular loss, and fluc-

tuating function. Each of these forms can manifest itself in a variety of clinical syndromes. We will focus only on vestibular distortion.

Damage to the vestibular system increases the "noise" or error factor in the flow of information moving from receptors in the inner ear to the central nervous system. For example, the afflicted individual may suffer vertigo and other distressing symptoms simply by tilting his or her head, and thereby inciting the semicircular canals to file misleading reports that make the central nervous system believe a full rotation of the head has occurred (Horak, Mirka, & Schupert, 1989). Several other types of misinformation can also be generated by the vestibular apparatus when it has been damaged by external or internal trauma (e.g., a ruptured membrane through which fluid leaks into the middle ear).

Complaints of dizziness, vertigo, unsteadiness, and similar problems should be taken seriously and receive thorough medical assessment. The common tendency to dismiss such complaints as "only what you have to expect with getting old" or "just looking for attention" neglect a real problem that can often be alleviated.

Falls Are a Major Risk Factor. Geriatricians and gerontologists know that falls constitute one of the major risk factors for elderly adults; this is now a very active area for environmental design, rehabilitation techniques, and research. It is estimated that between 20 percent and 40 percent of people over age 65 who live at home experience a fall during the course of a year, with perhaps twice as many suffering a fall within an institutional setting (Horak, Mirka, & Schupert, 1989).

Every adult who exhibits unsteadiness, frailty, and difficulties in gaining and maintaining balance should be evaluated for susceptibility to falls. Exercise programs and dietary regimes may help to prevent falls, and safety precautions in the home and in the institutional and public sectors can also help reduce these incidents. Improved lighting deserves particular consideration. (Some falls are secondary to stroke or other conditions not directly related to posture and balance.)

One might well advocate educational programs for all adults as the middle years of life approach. Detecting, correcting, or compensating for possible difficulties with body senses and the preservation of postural and motion control might prevent many a fall and its complications. ▼ ROBERT KASTENBAUM

See also: Chronic Pain as a Lifespan Problem; Exercise; Individuality; Information Processing; Listening; Risk to Life through the Adult Years; Taste and Smell; Vision.

References

Horak, F. B., Mirka, A., & Schupert, C. L. (1989). The role of peripheral vestibular disorders in postural dyscontrol in the elderly. In M. H. Woolacott & A. Shumway-Cook (Eds.), *Development of Posture and Gait Across the Life Span.* Columbia, SC: University of South Carolina Press.

Kenshalo, D. R., Sr. (1979). Aging effects on cutaneous and kinesthetic sensibilities. In S. S. Han & D. H. Coons (Eds.), *Special Senses in Aging.* Ann Arbor, MI: University of Michigan Institute of Gerontology, pp. 189-218.

Kornhuber, H. H. (Ed.). (1974). *Vestibular System: Handbook of Sensory Physiology.* Berlin: Springer-Verlag.

Van der Laan, F. L., & Oostervald, W. S. (1974). Age and vestibular function. *Aerospace Medicine, 45:* 540-47.

Whitbourne, S. K. (1985). *The Aging Body.* New York: Springer-Verlag.

Wilson, V. J., & Peterson, B. (1981). Vestibulospinal and reticulo-spinal systems. In V. B. Brooks (Ed.), *Handbook of Physiology. Volume 2: Motor Control.* Bethesda, MD: American Physiological Society, pp. 667-702.

C

CARDIAC HEALTH

Cardiac health has become increasingly synonymous with overall health in the later adult years. Heart disease is the most common cause of death for senior adults, as well as a major cause of disability and loss of time from work. Furthermore, cardiac health is as important for women as for men, although heart disease generally strikes men earlier than women.

Treatment for heart disease is advancing at a rapid pace. Revascularization techniques such as coronary artery bypass surgery and percutaneous transluminal coronary angioplasty may be modifying the actual disease process by restoring the arteries to a more normal state. In addition, new drugs may be able to stop a heart attack in progress. Often survival is dependent on the early reporting of symptoms, prompt treatment, and enhanced emergency response systems.

Although heart disease remains the nation's number one health problem, its prevalence has diminished considerably during the past two decades and continued improvement is likely to occur (Gorlin, 1990).

One reason for the decline in heart disease is that people have taken seriously the data on risk factors for heart disease and hypertension. Many people are modifying their behavior to live healthier lives. The risk factors that have been identified for heart disease are:

1. Age
2. Sex
3. Family history of heart disease
4. Hypertension
5. Diabetes
6. Smoking
7. Lipid parameters (various types of cholesterol)
8. Diet (especially fat intake)
9. Sedentary lifestyle
10. Obesity
11. Stress
12. Hostility and Type A behavior pattern
13. Caffeine intake
14. Alcohol

Some of these risk factors (6-14) are modifiable, i.e., one could stop smoking, or adopt a more active life-style. Some risk factors (4-5) can be controlled although not eliminated, and some are not amenable to intervention (1-3). Understanding how and why these factors are related to heart disease is the object of current research. What should be an individual's attitude toward developing a risk factor profile and how can the data be interpreted? Until all facts are in, the recommendation from sources such as the American Heart Association (1989) is to modify as many of the behaviors as possible. Smoking is often singled out as a major risk factor in heart disease and there is little disagreement about the negative effects of smoking on cardiac health (as well as on the respiratory system). The data on the other risk factors and their interactions continue to evolve. Before making decisions about a personal program of risk factor modification it would be wise to read both the popular and the scientific literature and to discuss one's own unique situation with experts.

A useful brief introduction to the understanding of heart disease is provided by

Sullivan (1987). He notes that major problems can include circulation in the coronary arteries that supply blood directly to the heart, the heart muscle itself, the heart valves, or maintenance of the rhythm of the heart beat. Thus, heart disease is one of the disorders of the cardiovascular system, which includes the heart and the blood vessels. Other diseases of the cardiovascular system also become increasingly common with advancing age. Prominent among these are hypertension (or high blood pressure) and cerebrovascular accidents (stroke).

Correcting the Myths

Four myths about heart disease must be dispelled:

1. "Women don't get heart disease."
2. "If you don't have symptoms, don't worry."
3. "If you don't have a heart attack before age 60, you are safe and won't have one."
4. "It doesn't matter what you do, if you're going to get heart disease, you will get it."

These common statements do not stand up to the facts and should therefore not lead us to form premature conclusions.

Coronary Disease in Women. By age 60, one man out of five has suffered a heart attack. The comparable rate for women is one in seventeen. These numbers have promoted the tendency to think of heart disease as a problem for men only. However, heart disease is the major cause of death for women by age 67, and the chances of survival after a heart attack are less favorable for women (Altman, 1991; American Heart Association, 1989; Healy, 1991).

Silent Heart Disease. Not all heart disease is symptomatic. The absence of chest pains does not necessarily mean that a person is free from disease and risk. It is important for people with characteristics that put them at higher risk to make use of screening procedures. The same risk factors already noted apply also to silent heart disease (Cohn, 1988).

Age of Onset and Risk of Disease. The Framingham Study is a major, long-term epidemiologic investigation of a sample of persons who were aged 30-59 in 1949 and lived in this community 18 miles west of Boston. All participants were free of coronary heart disease at the time the study started. These 2,845 women and 2,282 men are the prime source of much of our information about the relationship of risk factors to the development of heart disease. Dawber (1990) provides an extremely readable account of the design and purposes of this study.

The Framingham Study has found that the prevalence (number of cases at any one time) of heart disease increases with age. The annual rate for men and women differs appreciably throughout the adult years. (This rate is calculated as number of cases per 1,000 persons.)

		Men	*Women*
Ages	35-44	5	1
	45-54	11	4
	55-64	18	10
	65-74	23	14
	75-84	30	22
	85+	Insufficient data	41

Heart disease is a source for concern not only at midlife but also into very old age.

Risk Factor Modification. A main reason that rates of heart disease have declined is because people have changed their habits, notably smoking and diet (American Heart Association, 1989). Data also suggest that modifying risky behavior such as smoking at any age can have a positive impact on risk of disease. Recent research has shown that in persons with coronary heart disease, blockages in the coronary arteries can be reversed with an extremely low-fat diet and rigorous exercise (Ornish et al., 1990).

Recent studies show risk factor modification to be a reasonable approach. How this approach should best be tailored to each individual, however, has not been fully worked out. Furthermore, both social and economic resources have also been identified as contributing to enhanced survival. After accounting for differences in the severity of the disease, it has been found that coronary patients with a supportive spouse or confidant and with adequate economic resources were likely to make stronger recoveries (Williams et al., in press). These findings may begin to point the way to other types of intervention that could reduce the morbidity and mortality associated with heart disease.

Two other issues are of particular importance: management of cardiac disease to reduce disability and enhance the quality of life, and understanding the impact that this disease can have on psychological functioning. As many as four million Americans have coronary artery disease, chronic angina (chest pain), or a history of myocardial infarctions (heart attacks). In its various forms, cardiac disease accounts for approximately 30 percent of the total cost of Social Security Disability and 13 percent of the total claims (Guilette et al., 1988). Learning to live with cardiac disease is obviously an important consideration for many people.

Understanding the contribution of cardiac health or disease to psychological functioning is important because we cannot fully understand adult development and aging unless we are able to distinguish between processes of normal aging and the effects of a particular disease process (Siegler, 1989). Cognitive decline is one significant area that invites serious consideration in this regard. Is cardiac disease responsible for such cognitive changes as difficulties in memory and information processing in the later years of life? If so, then prevention or treatment of the disease might be expected to result in improved cognitive functioning. If, however, cognitive decline is an aspect of "normal aging," then the researcher's task may be directed to understanding the basic processes involved in aging, while caregivers attempt to develop more effective ways to help people cope with cognitive change. Whatever might be learned through future research, it is already clear that cardiac health is an important factor in overall physical and psychological well-being throughout the lifespan.

▼ ILENE C. SIEGLER

See also: Alcohol Use and Abuse; Gender as a Shaping Force in Adult Development and Aging; Health Education and Adult Development; Information Processing; Learning and Memory in Everyday Life; Longevity; Memory; Religion in Adult Life; Risk to Life through the Adult Years; Slowing of Behavior with Age; Social Support for the Chronically Ill; Stress.

References

Altman, L. K. (1991). Men, women and heart disease: More than a question of sexism. *The New York Times*, 6 August, pp. B5, B8.

American Heart Association. (1989). *Silent Epidemic: The Truth About Women and Heart Disease*. Dallas: American Heart Association.

Cohn, P.F. (1988). *Silent Myocardial Ischemia & Infarction*. New York: Marcus Decker.

Dawber, T. R. (1990). *The Framingham Study: The Epidemiology of Atherosclerotic Disease*. Cambridge, MA: Harvard University Press.

Gorlin, R. (Ed.). (1990). Evolving concepts in ischemic heart disease. *Circulation, 82:* II1-II160.

Guilette, W., et al. (1988). Committee report on economic administrative and legal factors influencing the insurability and employability of patients with ischemic heart disease. *Journal of the American College of Cardiology, 14:* 1010-15.

Healy, B. (1991). The Yentl Syndrome. *New England Journal of Medicine, 325:* 274-76.

Ornish, D., et al. (1990). Can lifestyle changes reverse coronary heart disease? *Lancet, 336:* 129-33.

Siegler, I. C. (1989). Developmental health psychology. In M. Storandt & G. R. Vanden Bos (Eds.), *The Adult Years: Continuity and Change*. Washington, DC: American Psychological Association, pp. 115-42.

Sullivan, R. J. (1987). Cardiovascular system. In G. L. Maddox, R. C. Atchley, L. W. Poon, R. S. Roth, I. C. Siegler, & R. M. Steinberg (Eds.), *The Encyclopedia of Aging*. New York: Springer Publishing Company, pp. 84-89.

Williams, R. B. (1989). *The Trusting Heart*. New York: Times Books.

Williams, R. B., et al. (In press). Survival in patients with angiographically documented coronary artery disease: Prognostic importance of social and economic resources in medically treated patients. *Journal of the American Medical Association*.

CAREER AGE

Aging has been defined in chronological, biological, social, and functional terms. But career age, one of the newer conceptions of aging, is virtually age-neutral—in fact, almost an anti-aging definition of age. Career age measures the length of time one has spent in his or her chosen occupation; the relative distance one has traveled since entering the field. The starting point for career age can be set at any of several logical points of reference: (a) the date of graduation from one's highest earned degree, (b) the first day of permanent employment in one's chosen field, or (c) the date that one stops holding mere "jobs" and begins a "career." The distinction between having jobs—usually unrelated and unsequential employments—and pursuing a career is central to the concept of career age. A career starts some place and has the potential to "get some place," to develop in progressively more responsible steps.

Career age assumes the elements of choice and of continuity within a single, more or less coherent field of endeavor. Progressive responsibility, promotions, and related salary increments may or may not occur. But regardless of rank, title, or chronological age, career age is calculated by measuring length of services provided and experiences gained in one's chosen field.

Career age accumulates so long as one remains in his or her chosen field; relocations within the same field do not affect it. By changing careers in midlife a chronologically older individual can nonetheless be a junior employee in the new career. Similarly, one can be senior in one career and junior in a second career. A 60-year-old accountant, for example, might have more than three decades of service and experience in the field and occupy a senior position in a major firm, but at the same time be an entry-level assistant for a local theater company in the hope of launching a satisfying second career.

Career Age in Higher Education

In the absence of research on career age in other professions, the concept is perhaps best understood as it is evidenced in higher education, where distinctions among chronological age, rank, and seniority are regularly observed. For example, most young faculty members are untenured, although a few will move quickly through the tenure and promotion system. Similarly, some older faculty may hold "temporary" appointments for decades. Others are tenured quickly under relatively lenient tenure policies or during periods of less competition for academic positions, but remain associate professors throught their careers. Still other faculty members earn early doctorates, pursue nonacademic careers, and then are hired into academia at full professor rank late in their careers. Others begin and complete their doctoral research in middle age and initiate their academic careers—usually as second careers—in their forties or fifties. While chronologically "older," they are "junior" in terms of career age. Thus, chronological age, years in service, and the rewards of tenure and promotion can interrelate in a variety of ways.

The advantage of career age over chronological age as the standard against which to compare job performances is that age-based variations such as those identified above are and should be minimized. Whether chronologically young or old, associate professors are expected to meet standards that are different from those applied to more junior assistant professors and to more senior full professors. Similarly, whether young or old, professors are expected to resign or retire when they no longer can perform the duties for which they were hired.

Regardless of career age-linked standards of scholarly performance, professors at all career ages are expected to demonstrate a measure of the generativity that dominates the life stage of middle adulthood (Erikson, Erikson, & Kivnick, 1986). Academic generativity can be expressed by nurturing students, guiding the institution, and contributing to the enlargement and refinement of a substantive body of knowledge. All these activities constitute career-appropriate expressions of generativity. Where other careers may accommodate the expression of generativity as middle-age professionals strive to balance this theme in their personal lives, higher education absolutely requires generative behavior in a variety of different domains.

Faculty Expectations

Perhaps the issues that most clearly reveal differential faculty expectations by career age are those regarding intellectual currency and academic "vitality." Five hundred faculty members from 37 research universities responded to a mail survey (Bader and McTavish, in preparation) with a wide range of responses. With respect to currentness, 36 percent of respondents under 44 years of age and 1 in 5 older respondents agreed with the statement "Once faculty are tenured, they lack incentive to keep current in their fields." One respondent maintained that faculty over 50 years of age invariably were suspect, no matter how recently or how long ago they had earned their degree. Another respondent wrote that senior faculty seem to be more up-to-date on current *issues* whereas junior faculty seem more up-to-date on *technologies*. Such assumptions deserve to be tested.

With respect to academic vitality, more than 90 percent of the respondents agreed with the statement that "young faculty bring essential new vitality to departments." It is undeniable that new vitality at times may be essential, but youthfulness alone does not guarantee such stimulation. Nor are young faculty members the only ones who are capable of shaking up stagnant departments. Newly hired or newly transferred faculty of any age may prove quite able and willing to do so. And senior faculty who are newly returned from sabbaticals or other professional development activities may also bring vitality to their departments.

Given the impending elimination of academic mandatory retirement (federally mandated to occur in 1994), further study of the interplay of chronological age, rank, and career age at various points in a career—(e.g., degree completion, hiring, promotion, resignation, and retirement)—is desirable. Any observed trends should be correlated with student demand and with scientific and creative productivity. Such resulting data will disclose the relative contributions of individual faculty at different ages and stages in their careers, and may counter the prevailing presumption of relative inadequacy and decline among older faculty. Rees and Smith (1991) have made an excellent contribution in this regard; their work should be compared with that of Bayer and Dutton (1977), who studied career age at a time when chronological and career age were virtually synonymous.

In Other Fields

Career age is also pertinent to fields other than higher education. For example, it operates in the same basic ways within U. S. public school systems, the military, commercial aviation, law enforcement, and fire fighting. In each of these examples, "experience" often is highly rated in evaluating an employee's day-to-day performance and relative worth, without respect to chronological age, rank, or seniority. However, conflicts can arise when only one of these variables is relied upon for decision making regarding promotion, retention, or retirement.

▼ JEANNE E. BADER AND HELEN Q. KIVNICK
See also: Age 65; Individuality; Military Service: Long-Term Effects on Adult Development; Work Organization Membership and Behavior.

References

Bader, J. & McTavish, D. (In preparation). Age and Seniority as Variables in Higher Education.

Bayer, A. E., & Dutton, J. E. (1977). Career-age and research-professional activities of academic scientists. *Journal of Higher Education, 48*: 259-73.

Erikson, E.H., Erikson, J.M., & Kivnick, H.Q. (1986). *Vital Involvement in Old Age.* New York: W.W. Norton.

Rees, A., & Smith, S. P. (1991). *Faculty Retirement in the Arts and Sciences.* Princeton, NJ: Princeton University Press.

CAREGIVING

John Kingery, an 84-year-old Alzheimer's patient, was abandoned at a dog racing track in Coeur d'Alene, Idaho. He could not communicate with those who found him. His identity was discovered after television news reports were seen by staff who had cared for him at a long-term care facility in Portland.

This widely publicized case in March 1992 illustrates a growing phenomenon that is often called "granny dumping." The American College of Emergency Physicians estimates that between 100,000 and 200,000 geriatric patients are abandoned nationwide in emergency rooms each year (Hastings Center Report, 1991). One of the underlying reasons for this trend is that caregiving can be overwhelming. Growing numbers of family members who care for aging parents are reaching their limits and feel unable or unwilling to care for them any longer.

Although the term *caregiving* can be used to describe a broad range of activities and circumstances, it is most commonly used to describe the informal or unpaid care that family members, relatives, or friends provide to someone who has a physical, mental, emotional, or economic impairment that limits his or her independence. To some extent, parents are caregivers to their children until the children establish independent life-styles. In the case of developmentally disadvantaged children, the parents are often lifelong caregivers.

Most of the national and international concern about caregiving, however, is not focused on what parents are expected to do for their young children, but rather on the caregiving required for the rapidly increasing numbers of older adults. The fastest growing age group in the United States is the oldest-old—persons age 85 and over. In 1900, the average life expectancy in the United States was 47 years. Today, woman can expect to live 78.8 years and men 71.9 years (U.S. Bureau of the Census, 1990). Population aging is a worldwide phenomenon; Canada, France, Germany, Japan, Sweden, and the United Kingdom all have rapidly increasing percentages of people reaching 80.

Many older people are healthy and active. This increased longevity, however, also results in increasing numbers of persons who are frail, dependent, and in need of care. According to the report *Aging America: Trends and Projections* (U.S. Department of Health & Human Services, 1991), most Americans age 65 and over have at least one chronic illness or impairment, but at any one point in time, only 5 percent of those in this age group live in nursing homes or other institutionalized settings. Between 20 and 25 percent of the over 65 population will enter a nursing home at some time in their lives (Kastenbaum & Candy, 1973). Older adults with chronic conditions such as arthritis, hypertension, heart disease, diabetes, hearing and visual impairments, and mental health disorders such as depression, stroke, and Alzheimer's disease often require assistance from others, usually family members, in order to manage tasks of daily living.

Alzheimer's disease has brought the issue of caregiving to the forefront of public attention because its effects are so devastating to the afflicted persons, their family members, and the health care system. Moreover, the disease is now considered to be highly prevalent among elderly adults. It has been estimated that about 47 percent of those age 85 and over have "probable" Alzheimer's disease (Evans et al., 1989). Persons in the advanced stages of this progressive deteriorative cognitive disease require almost constant attention because they become unable to bathe or feed themselves, frequently wander, have disrupted sleep patterns, and cannot remember who they are or where they are, or recognize family members. In some cases, the person can become violent, verbally and physically abusive, and dangerous to himself or herself and others.

Caregiving in these arduous situations has been referred to as the "36-hour day" (Mace & Rabins, 1981) because of the constant demands. Issues related to caregiving will become increasingly more salient and problematic in the future because the numbers and proportions of persons in need will continue to grow. Additionally, their impairments and frailties are becoming more severe, financial costs of long-term care are escalating, and the emotional, social, and physical demands on caregivers are becoming ever more stressful.

Who Are the Caregivers?

In the United States, the largest national studies of caregivers have been the 1982 National Long-Term Care Survey (LTC) with a sample of 6,393 Medicare enrollees, the Informal Caregivers Survey (ICS) of 1,924 caregivers who were identified from the LTC study (Stone, Cafferata, & Sangl, 1987), and the National Caregivers Survey of 754 caregivers (American Association of Retired Persons, 1988). Most of the information available from these and other studies deals with caregiving provided to older adults who are usually defined as persons aged 50 and over.

Family members are estimated to provide about 80 percent of all the informal care received by older adults. Approximately 8 percent of U.S. households include a caregiver (American Association of Retired Persons, 1988). It is also well documented that family members are highly stressed and burdened by care, but continue to do most of it, accept the responsibility willingly, and, in general, do an outstanding job (Brody, 1985).

The likelihood of being a primary caregiver—the person who provides most of the assistance—is dependent on gender, age, kin relationship, and geographic proximity to the care receiver. According to the previously mentioned studies, most of these caregivers (50-74 percent) live in the same house with the care receiver or at least within 20 minutes. Approximately 75 percent of

primary caregivers are women. Daughters (29 percent) and wives (23 percent) are more likely to be primary caregivers than are husbands (13 percent) or sons (8 percent). In fact, daughters-in-law are more likely than sons to become primary caregivers.

Our society's gender socialization process perpetuates a set of values and norms that suggest women are better than men at caregiving tasks; therefore, women are expected to be caregivers and should be more available. Most of the caregivers are between the ages of 45 and 57, but a substantial proportion (between 20 percent and 36 percent) are age 65 or over. Nearly half of the caregivers are employed either full- or part-time.

To appreciate the caregivers' experience, it is important to know that most of them have been providing care for about five years. About two-thirds are married, and about one-third have children living with them. Also, 55 percent of the primary caregivers are assisting the older persons in excess of 21 hours per week. Some caregivers (16 percent) report that their responsibilities are constant.

Caregivers assist with very basic tasks of daily living such as dressing, walking, bathing, toileting, and feeding, as well as grocery shopping, transportation, housework, preparing meals, managing finances, and administering medicine. Being a caregiver requires diverse skills, patience, dedication, sacrifice, perseverance, good physical and mental health, and, as many caregivers have said, "a good sense of humor" to cope with the many challenges.

Caregiving and Adult Development: Neglected Issues

One of the most neglected aspects of caregiving is how it might impact the lifelong developmental process of the caregiver. No studies have yet been done to examine the long-term consequences, both positive and negative. We have learned about the specific burdens that caregivers often experience, such as mental and physical fatigue, loss of social activities, frustration in coping with a complicated and fragmented system of care, and the pain and sorrow associated with watching a loved one become increasingly frail and dependent. In addition, we have learned that *burden levels are highest among caregivers who:*

- Work full-time
- Are raising young children
- Lack support and assistance from others
- Operate with very limited financial resources
- Provide care to aggressive or violent persons
- Do not feel much affection for or intimacy with the person they care for

More studies are needed to examine specific issues about caregiver burden as well as the extent to which specific services can help to alleviate some of the stress and burnout. However, an even higher priority should be given to obtaining more information concerning the impact of caregiving on the caregiver's life course, developmental processes, family life, and general well-being. Continued neglect of these issues increases the risk factor because federal, state, and local policy in the United States will be placing increasingly more pressure on family caregivers to assume even more responsibility in order to keep older adults out of nursing homes.

Saving money by delaying or preventing the use of nursing homes might sound like a logical, responsible, and humane policy. Unfortunately, it fails to consider the financial, social, psychological, and physical health costs that might result from expecting more and more from already heavily burdened family caregivers. Economists, politicians, and policymakers have access to a large set of data to document the enormous costs of providing long-term care, but they do not have a similar set of data to sum the costs when family members exceed their caregiving resources and capabilities.

Specific Developmental Issues

Nearly every aspect of a person's life can be impacted by being a primary caregiver to someone else. Simply for illustrative purposes, we might ask questions about the possible effects of caregiving on the caregiver's work life, marital and other family relationships, social and religious participation, attitudes about aging, recreation and leisure activities, spirituality, mental and physical health, emotions, and overall life satisfaction.

Researchers at the University of Utah Gerontology Center have completed one of the few longitudinal studies of caregivers in the United States by surveying nearly 900 caregivers on three separate occasions a year apart. Their findings reveal that not all caregivers experience the same levels of stress and difficulty because much depends on their age, life circumstances, relationship to the care receiver, and available resources (Harper & Lund, 1990). This team of investigators has raised questions about these neglected issues. For example, we need to know more specifically how caregiving responsibilities affect concentration at work, absenteeism, job turnover, and work satisfaction. As a developmental issue, caregiving could very well influence career choices and opportunities. For example, when women between the ages of 30 and 40 reduce their work hours or quit their jobs to become family caregivers, resuming their career path later can be made more difficult.

Disrupted and strained marital and family relationships can result from meeting caregiving responsibilities and neglecting relationships with others. Some divorced middle-aged women in the Utah study described how their family relationships had become strained because caregiving tasks had altered and restricted family activities such as vacations, mealtime discussions, and leisure time together. The quality of relationships with important persons such as parents, siblings, and children are central to many aspects of our lifespan development, and caregiving experiences are certainly capable of influencing these relationships because of the daily demands that may last for several years.

Outside of family relationships, caregivers often make sacrifices in their social activities because they do not have the time or energy to invest in them. Again, not being able to attend social gatherings, maintain friendships, or participate in community volunteer activities can restrict opportunities for personal growth and development of the heavily burdened caregiver. We know very little about the long-term consequences that result from giving up one's social life to be a caregiver. Self-esteem and feelings of connectedness with others can be seriously altered as one has fewer and fewer opportunities to interact with friends. The longer the disruption continues in the caregiver's social life, the more difficult it becomes to reestablish the strained or lost social relationships and activities.

Life transitions, traumatic experiences, and major losses often lead people to ask questions about meaning and purpose. As a difficult and demanding situation persists, some caregivers begin to ask themselves why this is happening to them. Some want to believe that there is a special purpose for them, such as being presented with a challenge that will ultimately help to develop skills and character. In the University of Utah study, a caregiving husband wrote, "through adversity comes a greater faith and strength." Not all caregivers, however, experience a sense of spiritual growth. Some report that their feelings of spirituality had changed because they believed that their caregiving experiences were unfair or unjust, or that it was inhumane of their god to allow such a moral person as their family member to deteriorate through the insidious effects of Alzheimer's disease. Caregiving experiences can lead to a broad range of consequences, many of which are influenced by how caregivers perceive the purpose or find personal meaning in their situation.

Personality, emotions, and overall life satisfaction can be impacted by long-term caregiving experiences. It is widely documented that at times many caregivers become depressed, anxious, irritable, frustrated, angry, guilty-ridden, emotionally overwhelmed, exhausted, and physically ill. When these feelings and conditions persist over time, the caregivers' assessments of their self-esteem and overall life satisfaction are likely to become increasingly more negative.

Also relevant to a caregiver's development are the attitudes that he or she forms about the care recipient, one's own aging, and whether or not one would like to be cared for in the future by younger family members. In the University of Utah study, 68 percent of the respondents reported that caregiving was the most stressful situation they had ever experienced. An even larger majority (80 percent) said that they had become more negative in their feelings toward their dependent family member, and 28 percent indicated that they get depressed about the thought of growing old.

One adult daughter in the study wrote that a person "having to work a full day, raise a family, and take care of an impaired relative would be susceptible to suicide, parent-abuse and possibly murder." All three of these options have obviously detrimental consequences for growth and development. Another adult daughter said, "I wouldn't want to put my kids through what I am going through." A daughter-in-law reported, "I hope I die before I have her kind of problems." These negative consequences of caregiving need to be acknowledged so that they might be prevented or minimized in the future. Personal sacrifices for the good of society and to meet family obligations can result in long-term difficulties for individual caregivers who exceed their resources and capabilities.

Positive Consequences of Caregiving

Up to this point, we have primarily emphasized negative impacts of caregiving on the development and well-being of the caregiver. This background was necessary to broaden our understanding of the topic of caregiving because many of these long-term developmental consequences have not received adequate national attention from researchers, counselors, service providers, public policymakers, and even caregivers themselves.

As mentioned earlier, stressful life transitions and events can create opportunities for personal growth if the person perceives the situation as a challenge; has personal, family, and community resources sufficient to assist in the process; and successfully manages the challenge. This is a possibility with caregiving.

Most caregivers are primary caregivers who end up performing most of the tasks themselves. Success means providing good care to the recipient; wanting to be a caregiver; protecting one's own physical, psychological, and social well-being; and developing new skills and abilities. Some assistance from others is often required to achieve and sustain this kind of success. The support can come from community services or adult siblings and children who actually share in performing tasks (rather than simply offering their best wishes).

Telephone directories can help lead caregivers to local voluntary and national organizations that provide valuable educational materials and other services. The National Alzheimer's Association has chapters in all 50 states and offers an array of helpful services. Emotional, social, and educational support are available in the form of mutual-help support groups run by many different organizations. Each state has an office or division on aging-related services that works in cooperation with local area agencies on aging. Caregivers who access these agencies often can benefit by receiving direct services or obtaining information that will make them better aware of what is available. Although the continuum of services has many gaps and the services are sometimes inconvenient and costly, they can include assistance with transportation, meals, home maintenance, home-care, companionship, and respite for caregivers. Respite—having some time away from providing care—has emerged as the number one service need identified by caregivers to dependent elders (Caserta et al., 1987).

When caregivers have these varied resources in place and are able to maintain a functioning personal and social life, they can experience growth from their caregiving situation. Caregivers in the University of Utah study have reported many different kinds of benefits. Some indicated that their sacrifices have helped them become less self-centered and more empathic, caring, understanding, and compassionate toward others. In some cases, caregivers said that they had become closer to and more loving of the care receiver because they believed that their services had been appreciated. Others reported that they felt better about themselves because they had met their responsibilities and obligations and now felt less guilty. Many caregivers learned to be more patient and appreciative of having good health. Some said that they learned to value life more and to take one day at a time. A few caregivers even reported that they had developed a sense of humor from their caregiving experiences because they needed to find enjoyment and, in some cases, laugh at situations and events.

The Time of Caregiving in the Life Course

People can become primary caregivers at almost any age. A twenty-year-old grandson might suddenly become a caregiver to his grandmother after a stroke has limited her speech and mobility. A 55-year-old daughter who spent the last 25 years raising her children and is now looking forward to pursuing new interests and activities might be confronted with a long-term caregiving career to both of her aging parents. It is not uncommon for a woman to spend 17 years caring for a child and 18 years helping an aging parent. With more people living beyond the age of 85, it will become more common to find 70-, 80-, and 90-year-old persons providing care to their aging spouses.

It is difficult to know how caregiving will impact the development of each specific caregiver, but it is important to recognize that the stress of caregiving can have both positive and negative consequences, depending on the individual's current life course circumstances. The 25-year-old grandson may have the physical energy to do caregiving work but be unprepared to make sacrifices that would restrict career choices, dating, and marriage plans. The 55-year-old daughter might expect caregiving demands at this time in her life, but she must assess how caregiving will influence her marriage, friendships, and social life. An 80-year-old spouse might be dedicated to doing everything possible for as long as possible, but might lack the physical requirements of caregiving. Women in the "sandwich generation"—those caring both for children at home and aging parents—are at risk of neglecting their own needs and development in order to be both the super-mom and the super-daughter.

An almost forgotten concern in most discussions of caregiving is an assessment of what happens to the children who have a parent (usually their mother) who devotes several years to being a caregiver. We cannot afford to neglect how caregiving influences the course of the child's development. Although children and adolescents can benefit from caregiving by learning how to share responsibilities and be compassionate, we need to be aware of some potential negative effects as well. Children of caregivers may sacrifice family vacations, privacy, and relationships with the caregiving parent.

In the University of Utah study, a teenager reported having suffered the embarrassing situation of having his friends watch his demented grandfather urinate on the living room carpet. This teenager stopped bringing his friends home after school. The teenage years are critical in a developmental life-course perspective because values, attitudes, norms, life goals, and self-concepts are being shaped. If caregiving experiences in the home are not managed well, they can adversely affect the child's academic performance, family life, and how self and others are viewed. The long-term consequences for these children might include negative attitudes about elders, caregiving, and their parents.

In forming our national public policy regarding who should be providing care and what caregivers should do, we would benefit from knowing more about these broader and long-term consequences. There are also potential monetary costs that have not yet been specified. Moreover, it is quite possible that a policy of expecting more and more from family caregivers could result in a future cohort of adult children who are fearful about aging and want nothing to do with caring for their aging parents.

A better understanding of how caregiving affects one's personal development would help caregivers in making decisions about their responsibilities and capabilities.   ▼ DALE A. LUND

See also: Adult Children and Their Parents; Depression; Gender as a Shaping Force in Adult Development and Aging; Gender Differences in the Workplace; Grandparent Communication Skills; Humor; Life Events; Marital Development; Mental Health Resources for Adults; Parental Imperative; Social Relationships, Convoys of; Social Support for the Chronically Ill; Stress; Suffering.

References

American Association of Retired Persons (1988). *A National Survey of Caregivers: Final Report.* Washington, DC: Opinion Research Corporation.

Brody, E. M. (1985). Parent care as a normative family stress. *The Gerontologist, 25:* 1-29.

Caserta, M., et al. (1987). Caregivers to dementia patients: The utilization of community services. *The Gerontologist, 27:* 209-14.

Evans, D., et al. (1989). Prevalence of Alzheimer's disease in a community population of older persons. *Journal of the American Medical Association, 262:* 2551-56.

Harper, S., & Lund, D. (1990). Wives, husbands, and daughters caring for institutionalized and noninstitutionalized dementia patients: Toward a model of caregiver burden. *International Journal of Aging and Human Development, 30:* 241-62.

Hastings Center Report (1991). *Throwing Granny Away.* Briar-Cliff Manor, NY: The Hastings Center.

Kastenbaum, R., & Candy, C. E. (1973). *International Journal of Aging and Human Development, 4:* 15-21.

Mace, N., & Rabins, P. (1981). *The 36-Hour Day.* Baltimore: The Johns Hopkins University Press.

Stone, R., Cafferata, G., & Sangl, J. (1987). Caregivers of the frail elderly: A national profile. *The Gerontologist, 27:* 616-26.

U.S. Bureau of the Census. (1990). Marital status and living arrangements: March, 1989. *Current Population Reports,* Series P-20, No. 445. Washington, DC: U. S. Government Printing Office.

U.S. Department of Health & Human Services. (1991). *Aging America: Trends and Projections.* Washington, DC.

CENTENARIANS

In a recently published book based on her 40 years of research on centenarians, Belle Boone Beard (1991) wrote, "Longevity is one of the oldest miracles, and 100 is the magic number. Ninety years is old, but 100 is news" (p. 3).

Beard cites a Peruvian with a reported age of 157 and a Russian with a reported age of 167. She personally interviewed six centenarians with an average verified age of 103 who gathered at a reunion of Union soldiers in 1949. That was said to be the first time ever that a gathering of six centenarians took place. The *Guinness Book of Records* cited Florence Knapp (born October 10, 1873) as the oldest living person in the United States when she reached the age of 114 in 1987. Ms. Knapp died two years later.

How Many Centenarians?

Centenarians are the fastest growing age group in the United States. The 1950 Census listed 4,475 centenarians in the United States. This total represented a ratio of three centenarians per 100,000 inhabitants. The 1980 Census listed more than 32,000 centenarians—a ratio of 14 per 100,000. The prediction for the yet to be released 1990 Census is that there will be 54,000 centenarians, a ratio of 22

per 100,000, and a sevenfold increase in the ratio since mid-century.

A Caucasian male born in 1980 in the United States has one chance in 250 to survive to the age of 100. If that person lives to 70 years, the probability improves to 6.5 chances per 1,000; at 80, 12 per 1,000; and at 90, 51 per 1,000. The 250 to 1 at-birth odds against becoming a centenarian will therefore have improved to 20 to 1 for those who attain their ninth decade.

The high odds against living to 100 years for most individuals explain the intrigue surrounding the magic age of 100. These long-lived individuals may possess special heredity characteristics; social, economic, and environmental support; exceptional personality or coping skills; intellectual abilities; care in their personal health and eating habits; or any combinations of the above. Some or all of these hypotheses concerning longevity could be supported in the examination of specific individuals. For example, Florence Knapp did enjoy a pedigree of long life. Three of her four grandparents lived to double the average life expectancy in the late eighteenth century. Her aunt, Mary Knapp, lived almost 108 years, and her parents to 78 and 86 years. The same pattern does not hold for all centenarians, however. Inspection of Beard's (1991) collection of centenarian data spanning more than 40 years (archived at the University of Georgia) reveals a wide diversity of patterns among centenarians, and systematic investigation is needed to analyze and clarify these patterns.

What Has Been Learned from Centenarian Research?

To date, research on centenarians has been primarily descriptive and limited generally to unidisciplinary and univariate studies. Clayton, Poon, and Martin (in press) provide a literature review of centenarian studies in the biomedical and psychosocial domains. Between 1970 and 1989, biomedical studies were far more numerous than psychological and sociological studies. Among the biomedical studies, half were autopsy investigations that attempted to isolate causes of death or describe change in body systems. These studies showed a variety of causes of death; no one cause was dominant. There was also tremendous variability in changes of body systems found among the centenarians.

A second cluster of biomedical studies examined physical decline among living centenarians and between centenarians and younger adults. These studies also found significant individual variation among centenarians in anthropomorphic measurements, age of death of parents and grandparents, blood pressure, angina, incontinence, depression, and loss of teeth. Diffused slowing of electroencephalographic (EEG) patterns was a common characteristic among centenarians; however, there were marked individual differences in the degree of slowing as well as in brain atrophy. Variability was found both in the immune system and in health-seeking behaviors. Recent psychological and sociological studies have also supported the general theme of heterogeneity among centenarians. Based upon the available data, then, it is difficult to speak of a "typical" centenarian.

Beard's cases studies, however, tend to demonstrate the existence of optimistic attitudes among centenarians. The studies of Beard and others found large individual variability, however, in personality traits, intellectual functioning, future ambitions, coping strategies, life-styles, and sensory functions.

Identification of the factors most responsible for the survival of centenarians remains a challenge. Delcros (1991) surveyed the current studies of centenarians worldwide and found increasing interest in their survival characteristics. Given the heterogeneity of individual characteristics among centenarians, studies are now relying more on multivariate designs to examine the independent and interactive contributions of biomedical and psychosocial factors. Among the current major research programs on this topic are the Georgia Centenarian Study (University of Georgia), Tokyo Metropolitan Institute of Gerontology (Japan), Ipsen Foundation (France), University of Lund (Sweden), and Semmelweiss University (Hungary). ▼ Leonard W. Poon

See also: Age 21; Age 40; Age 65; Individuality; Longevity; Risk to Life through the Adult Years.

References

Beard, B. B. (1991). *Centenarians, the New Generation.* New York: Greenwood Press.

Clayton, G. M., Poon, L. W., & Martin, P. (In press). Centenarian research: A literature update, 1970-89. *Journal of Applied Gerontology.*

Delcros, M. J. (1991). Centenarians: A survey of studies on psychology. Presented at the Fifth International Meeting of the International Psychogeriatric Association, Rome.

Poon, L. W. (Ed.). (1992). Special issue: The Georgia Centenarian Study. *International Journal of Aging & Human Development, 34* (1).

CHRONIC PAIN AS A LIFESPAN PROBLEM

Chronic pain may seem to be anachronistic in an era of massively advertised analgesics, but it is a daily reality to many persons, perhaps 25 to 30 percent of the U.S. population alone (Bonica, 1990). The unanswered questions that so often accompany chronic pain add to the burden and stress. Although there are signs of a growing interest in these questions, those who advocate attention to solving pain-related problems call for a sharp acceleration of progress.

Even the fundamental nature of pain itself is a question without a definitive answer. One view holds that four "domains" of human experience are involved:

• *Nociception,* or the detection of tissue damage by transducers in skin and deeper structures.

• *Pain,* or the recognition of nociceptive stimulation by the central nervous system.

• *Suffering,* or "the negative affective response to pain or other emotionally laden events."

- *Pain behavior,* or "what a person does or does not do or say that leads the observer to infer that the patient is suffering from a noxious stimulus." (Loeser & Egan, 1989)

When viewed within this frame of reference, pain is unmeasurable, as are nociception and suffering. All pain behaviors, however, are "real, and all are quantifiable." Even so, a frequent difficulty occurs. Many medical practitioners, unable to find a distinct cause-and-effect linkage between the chronic pain and a specific and identifiable cause, may regard the suffering and pain behavior as "psychosomatic," or, more precisely, psychogenic.

But pain specialists are likely to challenge the psychogenic label. They point out that diagnostic tests and treatment methods today are more advanced than they were even a decade ago and that they improve all the time. "What was considered psychogenic a few years ago may be recognized as an organic syndrome today, as researchers develop a better understanding of the mechanisms involved in chronic pain" (Hitchcock, 1991, p. 391).

Acute or Chronic Pain?

Acute pain is usually regarded as an essential signal that something is amiss in the human body. It is a temporary condition, subject to fairly specific actions for relief in most cases, although general practitioners are sometimes criticized for unfamiliarity with medications that would relieve temporary pain, particularly after surgery (Max, 1989, 1990; Neal, 1978; Schuchman & Wilkes, 1989).

Chronic pain is commonly defined as a condition that persists for at least six months (some authorities say three months is a better measure) despite efforts to stop it. A complete healing process is likely to be elusive, although pain may cease from time to time, often returning in either similar or new forms. Chronic pain has been called a "burglar alarm that nobody can shut off" (Budiansky, 1987).

The pioneering Multidisciplinary Pain Center at the University of Washington (Se-

attle) evaluates four kinds of problems: pain associated with cancer or cancer therapies; pain associated with injury to a nerve, the spinal cord, or brain; pain associated with illness, such as arthritis; and pain associated with an injury or operation (University of Washington Medical Center, Chronic Pain Service, 1991).

Subcategories are numerous. Low back pain is the most widespread. This condition is fairly common even in young adults, and becomes increasingly frequent through the middle years of life. Low back pain can develop as a consequence of a variety of job-related activities such as lifting objects repeatedly or sitting continuously for more than four hours a day. Low back pain is not only common, but also tends to be recurrent (Rucker et al., 1991).

Arthritis affects approximately 37 million Americans, its prevalence increasing markedly from about age 45. But younger persons suffer from this condition as well. In fact, more than 200,000 children in the United States have arthritis (Arthritis Foundation, 1991).

Children are affected in other ways as well. A haunting chapter in a landmark work describes leukemic youngsters who received little relief from the excruciating discomfort of weekly bone marrow withdrawals. The author describes communication failures between hospital staff and the children, along with misconceptions about medication dosages suitable for children. On the other hand, she also gives examples of responsive and sensitive procedures that help alleviate anxiety and pain. Overall, however, she cites a general tendency of the medical profession to refuse "to recognize the suffering of children, as if it were a distraction from the primary business of curing" (Neal, 1978).

Pain in the Later Years of Life

A dual challenge confronts researchers who focus on chronic pain and its effects on older persons. On the one hand, they point to laboratory findings that challenge the myth that "the older individual in some way feels pain differently than younger individuals because of age per se" (Harkins, 1988). They also question the underrepresentation of older persons in pain control clinics (Harkins, 1987; Melding, 1991).

In addition, researchers and advocates argue that pain problems must be overcome no matter what the age of the person who is experiencing them. This crusade against therapeutic nihilism still faces the resistance of a prevalent attitude among medical practitioners that pain and frailty are inevitable after a given age, therefore, geriatric pain is (erroneously) regarded as intractable (Butler & Gastel, 1980; Harkins, Kiwentus, & Price, 1990; Oriol, 1991). Fortunately, the alleviation of pain among terminally ill persons receiving hospice treatment through the use of narcotics and other techniques, once a matter of controversy (Butler, 1979), now appears to be more accepted and standardized (Kaiser, 1990).

Policy Questions

Chronic pain stirs criticism about research priorities at the National Institutes of Health and elsewhere. A typical complaint: "Since people rarely die from most of the illnesses that cause chronic pain, the medical field doesn't seem to take it seriously" (National Chronic Pain Outreach Association, 1991).

Another charge leveled at physicians and other medical practitioners is that there is a lag in the use of analgesics that have been proven to maintain comfort. This reluctance to provide adequate pain relief even when remedies are available may be particularly true in the treatment of acute, post-operative, and chronic cancer pain (Max, 1990).

The U.S. Social Security Administration faces a troublesome quandary in the assessment of pain in determining eligibility for disability payments. Members of Congress and other critics have questioned the SSA policy calling for objective medical evidence—i.e., medical signs or laboratory findings—that establish the existence of a physical or mental impairment that could reason-

ably be expected to produce the pain that is reported by the applicant. In recent years, SSA has awarded contracts to promote the design of pain assessment instruments related to the effect of pain on residual functional capacity and other matters (Oriol, 1991; Rucker et al., 1991).

Prospects

Breakthroughs in research and practice related to pain control appear to be increasing. One promising area of research at the National Institutes of Health is the track of potential genetic causes of pain (Oriol, 1991). Advances in understanding the mechanisms of pain control also appear to be on the increase (Budiansky, 1987; Rosenthal, 1990). Pain control centers now number more than a thousand nationwide, and many rely on a multidisciplinary approach to the understanding of, and coping with, pain. Indeed, the International Association for the Study of Pain has issued guidelines for "desirable characteristics for pain treatment facilities" (1990). Innovative treatment methods include devices to enable post-surgery patients to self-administer medications when they believe they are needed (subject to limits on total dosage).

Finally, there is increasing awareness that all pain—and chronic pain in particular—has far-reaching consequences for other family members, a situation that requires mutual accommodation and recognition of the many riddles that still cloud professional and lay understanding of pain's origins, processes, and consequences (Martel, 1991; Roy, 1989).   ▼ WILLIAM E. ORIOL

See also: Body Senses; Religion and Coping with Crisis; Social Support for the Chronically Ill; Stress; Suffering.

References

Arthritis Foundation. (1991). *The Arthritis Fact Book and the Media*. Atlanta: Arthritis Foundation.

Bonica, J. (Ed.). (1990). *The Management of Pain*. Second Edition. Philadelphia: Lea and Febiger.

Budiansky, S. (1987, June 29). Taking the pain out of pain. *U.S. News & World Report*: 50-57.

Butler, R. (1979). Compassion and relief from pain. *International Journal of Aging & Human Development 9*: 193-95.

Butler, R., & Gastel, B. (1980). Care of the aged: Perspectives on pain and discomfort. In L. K. Ng & J. J. Bonica (Eds.), *Pain, Discomfort, and Humanitarian Care*. Amsterdam: Elsevier, pp. 297-312.

Harkins, S. (1987). Pain. In G. Maddox (Ed.), *The Encyclopedia of Aging*. New York: Springer, pp. 509-11.

————. (1988). Pain in the elderly. In R. Dubner, G. F. Gebhart, & M. R. Bond (Eds.), *Proceedings of the Fifth World Congress on Pain*. Amsterdam: Elsevier, pp. 355-67.

Harkins, S., Kwentus, J., & Price, D. (1990). *Pain and suffering in the elderly*. In J. Bonica (Ed.), *The Management of Pain*. Second Edition. Philadelphia: Lea and Febiger, pp. 552-59.

Hitchcock, L. (1991). Myths and misconceptions about chronic pain. In R. Weiner (Ed.), *Innovations in Pain Management: A Practical Guide for Clinicians*. Volume 3. Orlando: Paul M. Deutsch Press, pp. 391-97.

International Association for the Study of Pain. (1990). *Desirable Characteristics for Pain Treatment Facilities and Standards for Physician Fellowship in Pain Management*. Seattle: IASP.

Kaiser, K. (1990). Removing barriers in hospice pain management. A family matter. *Caring Magazine, 9*: 42-49.

Loeser, J., & Egan, K. (Eds.). (1989). *Managing the Chronic Pain Patient*. New York: Raven Press.

Martel, L. (1991). Chronic pain and the family. *Lifeline*. Bethesda, MD: National Chronic Pain Outreach Association.

Max, M. (1989). Pain relief and the control of drug abuse: Conflicting or complementary goals? In C. S. Hill & W. S. Fields (Eds.), *Advances in Pain Research and Therapy*. Volume 11. New York: Raven Press, pp. 885-89.

————. (1990). Improving outcomes of analgesic treatment: Is education enough? *Annals of Internal Medicine, 113*: 885-89.

Melding, P. (1991). Is there such a thing as geriatric pain? (Editorial). *Pain, 46*: 119-21.

National Chronic Pain Outreach Association (1991). *Narrative Comments from 1991 NCPOA Member Survey*. Bethesda, MD: NCPOA, p. 3.

Neal, H. (1978). *The Politics of Pain*. New York: McGraw-Hill.

Oriol, W. (1991). Chronic pain: Its many impacts upon older Americans and their families. *Perspective on Aging, 20:* 6-13. Washington, DC: The National Council on the Aging.

Rosenthal, E. (1990, Feb. 14). Powerful new weapons change treatment of pain. *New York Times*, pp. C-1, C-12.

Roy, R. (1989). *Chronic Pain and the Family: A Problem-Centered Perspective*. New York: Human Sciences Press.

Rucker, K. S., et al. (1991). Musculoskeletal pain, disability, and pain assessment instruments development. *Journal of Back and Musculoskeletal Rehabilitation, 1:* 67-73.

Schuchman, M., & Wilkes, M. (1989, July 23). Suffering in silence. *New York Times Magazine*, pp. 36-37.

University of Washington Medical Center, Chronic Pain Service. (1991). *Information for Patients and Physicians*. (Brochure). Seattle: University of Washington Medical Center.

COHORT AND GENERATIONAL EFFECTS

The terms "cohort" and "cohort effects" are often used in discussing human development. There is good reason for their popularity: We have little hope of understanding developmental processes unless we also understand the relevance of cohort effects. "Generational effects" are less frequently mentioned, but also deserve attention.

What Is a Cohort?

A cohort is a group of persons sharing a certain statistical or demographic characteristic. One type of cohort is a set of individuals who begin life at the same time. We can select a cohort on the basis of highly specific criteria, for example: all females born in Manhattan, Kansas, on 29 February 1992. We might instead create a much broader cohort category: all babies born anywhere in the world in the year 1900. The size and specification of a particular cohort depends upon the purpose for which it is being identified. The number of people who qualify for the leap year birthday cohort in Manhattan, Kansas, might be zero; the very large number who qualify for the year 1900 can only be estimated. Nevertheless, both would qualify as cohorts: sets of people (real or hypothetical) who begin life at the same time. In practice, most cohorts are neither as radically delimited as the leap year girls of Manhattan, Kansas, or the worldwide births of 1900.

Here are several typical examples of established cohorts:

- All high school students who took a standard scholastic aptitude examination in 1950.
- All children who were vaccinated against polio in 1960.
- All adults who became eligible for Social Security benefits in 1980.

Why Is Cohort Analysis Useful?

These examples can also illustrate how cohort analysis is useful in understanding human development. By comparing two or more cohorts on the same timeline we can identify possible trends. Suppose, for example, that the scholastic aptitude scores earned by the 1960 cohort turn out to be lower than those of the 1950 cohort, and that the 1970 cohort has scores that are even lower, and a further decline is observed for the 1980 cohort. Should we conclude that "kids are getting dumber all the time?" Or would it be time to consider alternative explanations, such as: (a) Are we teaching as effectively as before? (b) Has the home environment become less supportive of classroom learning? (c) Is there something wrong with the way we are measuring scholastic aptitude? (to take just three possible hypotheses).

Comparing cohorts improves our ability to distinguish developmental processes in the individual from a variety of social and environmental influences. It does not guarantee that we will be successful because the interrelationships between individual and society are continuous, complex, and never fully available for documentation. Nevertheless, systematic attention to cohort effects helps us to avoid premature and simplistic conclusions.

Consider again the first cohort(s) of children who had the opportunity to be protected against polio. We might find that a higher percentage of these children were physically and socially active when they reached the age of 30, as compared with a 1950 cohort that had no such protection. Would it be more appropriate to conclude that there has been a burst of physical and social improvement in the later cohort, or that fewer had become disabled by polio?

And consider again the people who reached age 65 and became eligible for full Social Security retirement benefits in 1980. If we studied this cohort's attitude toward life, self-concept, and daily activities we might be tempted to conclude that "This is what 65-year-olds think, and what they do." But it would be wiser to add: "This is what 65-year-olds think, and what they do when they have this particular Social Security retirement package to draw upon; I wonder how much of their way of life is based upon turning 65, and how much upon the specific resources and challenges that this particular cohort confronted at that particular time?" Good questions—and similar in spirit to questions asked by many researchers regarding many aspects of adult development and experience.

The term "cohort" has roots in the best place: the soil. Agricultural experimentation was already well advanced while the behavioral and social sciences were still trying to find their way. In a typical experiment, we might have planted for broccoli. All the plantings might have been carried out in an identical manner during the same period of time. But one difference might have been introduced: let us say, the spacing between plants. The total set of plantings would be divided, then, into traditionally spaced, narrower spaced, and wider spaced sectors. These would be experimental co-horts for each other, the "hort" coming from horticulture. When the crops matured, we would have examined their quantity and quality, knowing that all came from similar seeds and grew during the same time period. Any differences discovered among the cohorts could probably be attributed to the differential spacing arrangements. Theoretically, there can be no co-horts without a "hort" being around some place, but one never reads about horts.

Generations

Cohorts should be distinguished from generations. A cohort can be any set of individuals with a common point of origin in time. Generations occur within lineages or descent lines. You, your parents, and your children comprise three distinct generations as well as three distinct cohorts. For a clear example of the cohort/generation difference, consider two instructors who have worked for many years in their respective schools. The first school is located in a highly stable neighborhood that has served many of the same families over the years. This instructor has had the experience of teaching successive generations of children. The second school is located in a neighborhood through which people of a number of different national origins, native languages, and ethnicities have passed over the past half century. The veteran instructor here has also taught wave after wave of youngster, but relatively few represent the same family lines.

When the cohort/generational difference is blurred, we may either overestimate the continuity between successive waves of individuals (treating independent people as though descendants of previous families) or underestimating the continuity (treating people with familial and genetic connections as though having only a random relationship with each other).

There is a link between cohorts and generations, however, since both concepts deal with waves of people who move forward through time. These concepts are mingled in an imaginative book that attempts to analyze "the history of America's future" from the year 1584 to the year 2069 (Strauss & Howe, 1991). The authors assert that several general types of cohorts or generations occur and reoccur in history in a cyclical manner, each bringing distinctive characteristics to society. Social scientists have barely absorbed,

let alone tested, this new theory, so it would be premature to offer an evaluation at this time. It will no doubt encounter some difficulty simply because it is a broad and bold theory that appears at a time when social scientists seem to be locked into a phase of tinkering with "models" of much more limited scope. Whether the Strauss & Howe theory eventually is supported or rejected, however, may be less important than the invitation it provides to think freshly about generational relationships and their possible effects on both individual lives and social processes.

What is the most significant point about cohort identification and analysis? Perhaps it is simply to remind us that none of us grows up and grows old in a vacuum. We are profoundly influenced by the social, symbolic, economic, and ecological characteristics of the times into which we are born. To understand who we are and why we are living our particular kind of lives we also need to understand something of the interplay between maturational development and social/symbolic forces.

▼ ROBERT KASTENBAUM

See also: Alcohol Use and Abuse; Contextualism; Divorce; Driving: A Lifespan Challenge; Drug Use and Abuse; Generational Equity; Grandparent Communication Skills; Grandparent Education to Enhance Family Strength; Happiness, Cohort Measures of; Intelligence—Crystallized and Fluid; Interethnic Relationships; Language Development; Longevity; Marital Development; Military Service: Long-Term Effects on Adult Development; Parental Imperative; Rural Living: What Influence on Adult Development?; Spiritual Development and Wisdom: A Vedantic Perspective; Travel: Stimulus to Adult Development.

References

Hayslip, B., & Panek, P. E. (1989). *Adult Development and Aging.* New York: Harper & Row, Publishers, pp. 96-97, 509-11.

Kastenbaum, R. (1987). Gerontology. In G. L. Maddox (Ed.), *The Encyclopedia of Aging.* New York: Springer, pp. 288-90.

Nydegger, C. N. (1987). Cohorts. In G. L. Maddox (Ed.), *The Encyclopedia of Aging.* New York: Springer, pp. 127-29.

Strauss, W., & Howe, N. (1991). *Generations*. New York: William Morrow.

COMMUNICATION

From the infant's cry to the aged person's last words, people are linked to each other through the process of communication. Effective communication is often a critical component in developing interpersonal relationships, establishing a positive self-image, and achieving desired results in the world. Furthermore, our guiding values and meanings are established, shaped, and challenged through communicational exchanges.

But what, precisely, *is* communication? DeVito (1986, p. 61) defines the communication act as "the total of all the elements and processes involved in the sending and receiving of messages." Often each participant is both sender and receiver, as in a conversation. Various *channels* may be used, such as visual, auditory, and touch. Communication may be restricted to one channel (e.g., the auditory during a telephone conversation), or may involve multiple channels (e.g., mother and baby smiling and vocalizing to each other while also in tactile contact).

Each act of communication is vulnerable to many possible sources of failure or distortion. Collectively, the various potential interferences are known as *noise*. This definition includes noise in the usual sense of sounds that interfere with hearing the intended message, but all channels can be affected. Having our sightlines blocked by people standing and moving about while watching a sports event would be an example of visual noise. Trying to discern what a political candidate actually means when he or she is emitting a smoke screen of ambiguous terms would be an example of semantic noise. The act of communication is also vulnerable to selective filtering and other forms of inattention, fatigue, limited channel capacity, difficulties in decoding messages, and numerous other problems.

The concept of *message* is not as simple as it might appear. For example, DeVito (1986, p. 201) defines message as "any signal or combination of signals that serves as a stimulus for a receiver." But what, then, is a *signal?* Is every stimulus—every sound we hear, every sight we see, every touch we feel—a signal? If everything is a message, then this term is of little use. It may be more useful to consider the act of communication as a symbolic exchange. If a sender-receiver interaction involves information and meanings, then we can speak of messages having been exchanged. If one sees merely movement and hears merely sounds without attaching meaning to them, then we have probably not had an act of communication.

A Developmental Approach to Communication

The mature adult communicates effectively in many ways to many other people, and perhaps to the dog or cat of the house as well. Developmentalists who focus on infancy and childhood devote a great deal of attention to the early growth of communication skills. Many of their observations are not only interesting for the information they provide, but also for helping us to understand the subsequent course of communicational behavior and experience throughout the adult life course.

The study of communication takes on new themes and challenges when we consider the teen and early adult years in which issues of identity, intimate relationships, and career decisions become more salient. In the middle adult years there are often new challenges to confront, e.g., communicating effectively with both one's maturing children and one's aging parents, reviewing and renewing a marital relationship that may have focused for many years on child rearing, and reconsidering one's balance of obligations and interests between work, family, and personal interests. In the later adult years communication skills may be called upon to ensure continued affection and support from younger generations, and to cope with such other challenges as hearing impairment, forgetfulness, and negative ageism on the part of society. Significant reductions in the ability to communicate effectively can imperil the elderly adult's health and financial status and increase the chances of being considered by others to require supervisory care.

We do not yet have a comprehensive lifespan developmental theory of communication, but many researchers and service providers—as well as a number of articulate people who speak for their own age echelon—are contributing useful information and ideas. It is likely that when such a theory does emerge it will give much attention to the socio-environmental context of communication as well as to the psychological and health characteristics of the individual.

What follows here is a selective overview of issues, findings, and implications in the study of communication across the lifespan, with particular emphasis on the adult years.

Early Development of Communication Skills

Communication skills start to develop very early and continue at a rapid pace through infancy and early childhood. Several major principles have emerged from observations of this early phase of development.

1. *Humans are active communicators from the very beginning.* Although they have literally everything to learn about socialized forms of communication, there is already an active self that does not need to be "turned on" like a mechanical toy or to passively await stimuli from the environment. "Infants begin to experience a sense of an emergent self from birth. They are predesigned to be aware of self-organizing processes. They never experience a period of total self/other undifferentiation. There is no confusion between self and other in the beginning or any point during infancy. They are also predesigned to be selectively responsive to external social events and

never experience an autistic-like phase" (Stern, 1985, p. 10). As Stern observes, even the youngest human is never locked into an isolated, autistic-like state (unless there is pathology involved), but possesses at least the rudiments of a self that seeks interaction and communication.

2. *This active orientation is supported by the rapidly developing ability to scan the socio-physical environment for information.* For example, newborns not only can discriminate among different sweet, sour, and bitter-tasting substances, but react to them with facial expressions that are similar, if longer lasting, to those of adults, (Steiner, 1979). Babies so young that they have yet to be nursed by their mothers displayed lingering "Mona Lisa-like" smiles at their first taste of sugar. Hearing begins in the womb, although the vibrations and sounds occasioned by the mother's voice come across quite differently than what will be perceived when the fetus has become a neonate. There is no basis for the proposition that the fetus "understands" what it hears, but there is evidence that communication and learning do occur via the auditory pathway even prior to birth (Maurer & Maurer, 1988). Newborns not only can see, but within a few days they show the ability to prefer some visual stimuli to others and to follow changes in the visual field. Interestingly, young babies have a fixed depth of focus at about 13 centimeters— the distance between the infant and the mother's face during nursing (Silverman, 1989). Babies soon find people and animals more interesting to watch than inanimate objects, and in numerous other ways demonstrate that they have their own guiding principles. The total configuration of rapid sensory development suggests that babies and young children are already primed for communicative interactions.

3. *Early communication flourishes within the mother-child relationship.* The broader principle is that human interaction in general fosters the development of communica-

tion from infancy onward. In practice, it has usually been the mother-infant relationship that has provided the most frequent and predictable framework for encouraging communication. It is more common to refer to this process as one of bonding or attachment. From a communication standpoint, the deepening relationship between mother and infant is achieved in part through their interactions and, in turn, stimulates further interactions.

One of the most important elements in this early attachment and communication pattern is the mother's response to the baby's expressions of its needs and desires. Stern (1985) and his colleagues have given particular attention to a response known as *affect attunement,* which leads to *interpersonal communion.* For the first few months of interaction, mother and baby establish a pattern of reciprocal behavior as she feeds, diapers, bathes, and cuddles the child. This pattern becomes transformed as the infant expands its range of action and expression. Some mothers excel at matching their own feeling-response to the mood of the infant:

> A nine-month-old girl becomes very excited about a toy and reaches for it. As she grabs it, she lets out an exuberant "aaaah!" and looks at her mother. Her mother looks back, scrunches up her shoulders, and performs a terrific shimmy with her upper body, like a go-go dancer. The shimmy lasts only about as long as her daughter's "aaaah!" but is equally excited, joyful, and intense (Stern, 1985, p. 140).

Attunement of mother (other adult) with the baby creates moments of interpersonal communion, which "means to share in another's experience with no attempt to change what that person is doing or believing" (Stern, p. 148). Such special interactions as affect attunement, along with a rich and repetitive pattern of positive communications through eye and ear contact and touch provide a context within which infants develop the confidence and practice the competence that can lead to the further growth of communication skills throughout the life course.

4. *Early disabilities can lead to long-term problems in communication, coping, and self-actualization.* Fortunately, increasing attention is being given to the recognition and management of disabilities by parents, teachers, health professionals, and researchers. Dyslexia (first known as "word blindness"), for example, was seldom diagnosed until recent years (Snowling, 1987). Many adults today have painful memories of difficulties in school and work that are related to undiagnosed and untreated dyslexia. Perhaps fewer children today will have to experience the stress and confusion that can be associated with this impairment when it is not recognized as such. Children who are hearing or sight impaired, as well as those with Down's syndrome and some other genetic conditions, face obstacles to communicational development that can also have a negative influence on their overall personality growth and sense of well-being (Lewis, 1987). Impairments and disabilities are usually much easier to cope with when recognized early. In this sense, one of the most effective ways to reduce the incidence of communicational impairment in the later adult years is to diagnose these conditions when they first show themselves in childhood and to provide educational and other services, along with encouragement and emotional support.

Communication in the Early and Middle Adult Years

How and how well adults communicate has a powerful bearing on the course of interpersonal relationships, occupational success, and integration with the larger community. Accounts of communication within specific contexts are offered in entries listed at the end of this article.

Attention should be given to the following additional facets of adult communication.

1. *Competent communication requires the ability to see the world as others see it, or at least to recognize that other people do have their own perceptions.* This ability is often known as perspective-taking. Infants and young children have an *egocentric* organization of the world (not to be confused with "egotistical"). They have not yet recognized that there are other perspectives than their own. In later childhood and the teen years, the individual starts to appreciate that his or her own point of view is only one of many. Ideally, one enters the adult years with the awareness that other people's viewpoints must be considered. Deeper relationships and fewer conflicts are among the rewards for those who make the effort to recognize others' viewpoints. Communicational interactions remain limited, brittle, and subject to misunderstandings when perspective-taking ability has not been well developed (Barnett, 1984). It is likely that those who have not mastered the ability—and the willingness—to consider the other person's point of view will be at greater risk for becoming cognitively rigid and socially isolated in their later adult years. Living a long life does not necessarily induce an attitude of communicational inflexibility and impermeability. But the failure to develop perspective-taking skills in the first place is probably a major influence on subsequent problems in understanding others and making oneself understood.

2. *Social communication skills may stabilize relatively early in adulthood or continue to develop throughout the lifespan.* By the third decade of life most people have established their own patterns of interpersonal relationships, occupational choice, leisure time interests, and so forth. They are competent in most routine and familiar situations, and able to cope somehow with the occasional emergency. At this point there is a temptation to settle into a secure pattern (or to make whatever pattern exists as secure as possible). It is not unusual for another three decades to pass without a marked advance in communication skills because the existing abilities seem to do the job well enough. There is likely to be an increasing dependence on a few communication strategies and "set speeches" that have served more or less adequately in the past. There may be some "smoothing of rough edges" over the years, e.g., one speaks tactfully instead of impulsively in a potential conflict situation. Nevertheless, the person at 60 may not differ appreciably in communicational practices from the person he or she was three decades previously.

Other individuals, however, continue to refine and extend—or even transform—their communicational skills. Realms within which communicational development can continue through the adult years if the individual is so disposed include:

a. Improved understanding of opposite-sex communicational needs and techniques. Recent contributions have confirmed and elaborated on the proposition that females and males tend to approach communicational interactions in different ways. Persons of either sex can experience a growth in personal understanding as well as greater effectiveness in their interactions with those of the opposite sex by building upon the insights of authors such as Tannen (1990).

b. Improved understanding of communicational techniques and modalities and development of new communication skills. These activities can range from developing the skills necessary to participate in a computer information network to taking courses in creative writing or public speaking, learning another language, or involving oneself in the lives of people who differ markedly from oneself in age, ethnicity, life-style, or religious or political persuasion. Travel often lends itself to the promotion of social communication skills if the individual is ready to open himself or herself to other viewpoints.

c. Improved ability to influence decisions and events in the public sphere. Relatively few Americans choose to participate in the political process—in either a narrow or broad sense of the term—in youth and early adulthood. By the time they have reached the middle adult years, there may be an entrenched habit of tending to personal affairs to the exclusion of involvement in the public sphere; furthermore, absorption in personal, family, and career issues may have preempted the cultivation of communication skills relevant to public influence and decision making. However, some people do reach beyond their accustomed routines to take an active interest in the political process at mid-life or later. This involvement may originate in a particular issue that touches on their own lives, or derive instead from an awakening of interest in the larger world and the motivation to make that world a better place. Once the motivation has arisen to influence events in the public sector, the mid-life adult may go on to refine existing communication skills and develop new abilities to meet this challenge.

In each of these realms, communication may either settle into a routine or become transformed into an increasingly enterprising and effective developmental asset. Erikson's (1963) well-known depiction of *generativity versus stagnation* as the primary mid-life challenge can find many applications in the realm of communication skills.

3. *In moving through the adult years one faces an increasing prospect of loss that challenges the ability to preserve meaning and communicate effectively.* Many of these losses are interpersonal. Some relationships end with the death of a family member or friend; other relationships may suffer atrophy and deterioration. There is a tendency for the balance to shift from starting important new relationships to coping with the decline or loss of existing relationships. Numerous communication challenges arise when relationships are ending or threatening to do so. For example, it is difficult to communicate well with a terminally ill friend if either or both of us are working hard at avoiding this central fact. Judgment, sensitivity, and confidence in the relationship are helpful in creating the opportunities to take leave of each other in our own way before we are separated by death. The strength of a relationship may be demonstrated through warm and honest communication even as that relationship comes to an unavoidable end. Providing—and accepting—emotional support after a death also calls upon mature and flexible communication skills.

A relationship may deteriorate for a variety of reasons, e.g., the middle-aged couple who decide that they had only stayed together for the children and would now rather go their own ways, or a rift between two adult children who disagree on who should do what to aid an aged parent. It can be helpful to recognize the communicational signs of relationship deterioration. Miller and Parks (1982) report that typical signs of relationship deterioration include: fewer interactions, shorter interactions, increased physical distance, reduced eye contact, shrinkage of conversation topics to small talk, decline or disappearance of self-disclosure statements, and more defensiveness and deception. The appearance of this pattern of communicational behaviors strongly suggests that the relationship is in trouble. Some individuals prefer not to notice this shift in the relationship because it is so distressing, but awareness of these negative communication signals can provide the opportunity to consider alternative responses, including reviewing and renewing the values of the relationship before it is too late.

Communication in the Later Adult Years

> In one's early years, one writes out of one's glands—really out of the juices of the libido—and everything seems absolutely marvelous and right and easy. But in one's early years you don't know enough, you're not wise enough, to say important things; you're merely reacting to experience. In late life you have wisdom to draw from. (Kunitz, 1992, p. 133)

Stanley Kunitz, the distinguished poet, still creative in his later adult years, exemplifies those who have continued to enrich their personalities and their communication abilities throughout a long life. Many creative artists are expressive and vital in old age, although subject to all the usual age-associated impairments and burdens. They are not only able to communicate adequately in everyday life, but also to contribute to culture's heritage of meaning. There is no fixed upper limit for communicational excellence in old age, nor is there a fixed age at which such excellence must cease.

The challenge of generativity versus stagnation continues from mid-life onward. One has the advantage of additional life experience to draw upon, but also the increased probability of physical impairment and the sorrow of interpersonal loss. Communication challenges in the later adult years include the following:

1. *Coping with losses in sensory acuity and mobility.* Changes in vision and hearing can lead to social withdrawal and a general reduction in one's range, frequency, and variety of communication. In turn, falling out of touch with others can lead to a decline in self-esteem, morale, and sense of control over one's life. Difficulties in getting around (e.g., loss of driving skills or license, problems in ambulation) can further contribute to reduced social interaction. Along with whatever ben-

efits a particular individual can derive from hearing aids, glasses, and such transportation assists as electric-powered carts, there is also the personal dimension to consider. Essentially, a person can give in to the limitations or develop ways to compensate for or circumvent them. A self-described "fiercely independent" woman, for example, may have to decide for herself that it is acceptable to have people help her get around. For all aging individuals there is likely to be a continuing process of adjustment to physical changes in order to preserve communication effectiveness and opportunity.

2. *Institutional residence often intensifies communication problems.* Elderly persons who are admitted for residential care to a nursing care or other specialized facility often bring communication problems with them. For example, a person may have suffered a stroke that has such residual effects as slurred speech and difficulties in finding the right word. Others may be in various phases of a progressive dementing condition such as Alzheimer's disease, or, perfectly alert, may simply have difficulties in operating a standard telephone or putting their thoughts in writing. It has become clear, however, that the institutional milieu often results in further social isolation (e.g., Gubrium, 1975). The residents have relatively little power and are subject to routines and procedures that are intended to serve the total institution more than the needs of individual men and women.

This situation poses a challenge not only to the elderly person, but to the institution and to society at large. Numerous efforts have been made to improve the quality of life for institutionalized elders, and there has been enough success to encourage improvements on a national and international level (e.g., Kastenbaum et al., 1981; Maguire, 1985; Weiler & Rathbone-McCuan, 1978). When family and friends show continued interest in the well-being of an institutionalized elderly person, that individual is likely to receive a higher level of care from the staff and to remain motivated to communicate.

3. *Careful evaluation—and reevaluation—is needed when there is a question of a dementing condition.* Communication problems in the later adult years can arise from a number of sources, including the reversible effects of illness or trauma, drug reactions, and anxiety or depression. Sometimes, however, communication disorders signify the existence of a dementing process. Today there is a new generation of service providers who are educated and motivated to diagnose problems such as these and recommend the most adequate treatment or management procedures available. Concerned family members would do well to seek out nurses, physicians, psychiatrists, psychologists, and social workers who have studied geriatric problems and are aware of the complexities and options involved. Both members of the general public and service providers can prepare themselves by reading informative books such as those by Bayles & Kaszniak (1987), Dreher (1987), and Hinrichsen (1990). The existence of an organically based cognitive/communicative disorder should never mean that the afflicted individual is to be abandoned, but, rather, that special consideration and support need to be provided to help this person remain an interactive participant in the human network.

Whether confronted with the challenge of carrying out effective communications on a very basic level or with writing the perfect poem, an elderly person is engaged in a universal quest for self-expression. As Kunitz adds:

> The beautiful thing about the poem before it is written is that it's perfect. We are mortal and fallible human beings, and we have our limitations. And the poem that is written is never as good as the poem I imagine I am going to write. (Kunitz, 1992, p. 133)

▼ ROBERT KASTENBAUM

See also: Adult Children and Their Parents; Attachment Across the Lifespan; Control and Vulnerability; Creativity; Divorce; Expressive Arts; Fictive Kin; Friendships through the Adult Years; Gender as a Shaping Force in Adult Development and Aging; Grandparent Communication Skills; Grandparent Education to Enhance Family Strength; Habituation: A Key to Lifespan Development and Aging?; Interethnic Relationships; Language Development; Listening; Loving and Losing; Marital Development; Maturity; Political Beliefs and Activities; Sibling Relationships; Social Relationships, Convoys of; Suicide; Travel: Stimulus to Adult Development; Trust as a Challenge in Adult Development; Twins through the Lifespan; Vision; The Voice; Widowhood: The Coping Response; Work Organization Membership and Behavior.

References

Barnett, M. A. (1984). Perspective taking and empathy in the child's prosocial behavior. In H. E. Sypher & J. L. Applegate (Eds.), *Communication by Children and Adults.* Beverly Hills, CA: Sage, pp. 43-62.

Bayles, K. A., & Kaszniak, A. W. (1987). *Communication and Cognition in Normal Aging and Dementia.* Boston: Little, Brown.

DeVito, J. A. (1986). *The Communication Handbook.* New York: Harper & Row.

Dreher, B. B. (1987). *Communication Skills for Working with Elders.* New York: Springer.

Erikson, E. H. (1963). *Insight and Responsibility.* New York: Norton.

Gubrium, J. F. (1975). *Living and Dying at Murray Manor.* New York: St. Martin's Press.

Hinrichsen, G. A. (1990). *Mental Health Problems and Older Adults.* Santa Barbara, CA: ABC-Clio.

Kastenbaum, R., et al. (1981). *Old, Sick, and Helpless: Where Therapy Begins.* Cambridge, MA: Ballinger.

Kunitz, S. (1992). In P. L. Berman & C. Goldman (Eds.), *The Ageless Spirit.* New York: Ballantine, pp. 131-37.

Lewis, V. (1987). *Development and Handicap.* New York: Basil Blackwell.

Maguire, G. H. (Ed.). (1985). *Care of the Elderly: A Health Team Approach.* Boston: Little, Brown.

Maurer, D., & Maurer, C. (1988). *The World of the Newborn.* New York: Basic Books.

Miller, G. R., & Parks, M. R. (1982). Communication in dissolving relationships. In S. Duck (Ed.), *Personal Relationships. 4: Dissolving*

Personal Relationships. New York: Academic Press, pp. 127-54.

Silverman, M. A. (1989). The first year after birth. In S. Greenspan & G. H. Pollock (Eds.), *The Course of Life. Volume 1. Infancy.* Madison, WI: International Universities Press, pp. 321-58.

Snowling, M. (1987). *Dyslexia. A Cognitive Developmental Perspective.* New York: Basil Blackwell.

Steiner, J. (1979). Human facial expressions in response to taste and smell stimulation. In H. Reese & L. P. Lipsitt (Eds.), *Advances in Child Development and Behavior.* New York: Academic Press, pp. 257-95.

Stern, D. N. (1985). *The Interpersonal World of the Infant.* New York: Basic Books.

Tannen, D. (1990). *You Just Don't Understand. Women and Men in Conversation.* New York: William Morrow.

Weiler, P. G., & Rathbone-McCuan, E. (1978). *Adult Day Care. Community Work with the Elderly.* New York: Springer.

CONFLICT AS A CHALLENGE IN ADULT DEVELOPMENT

Conflict stresses persons of all ages. Internally, conflict stresses the individual's link to his or her self-image. For example, when we cheat, lie, or steal, the guilt and shame that we feel is the product of internal conflict. Externally, conflict stresses the individual's linkages to important others. For example, when we quarrel over family plans, debate political issues, or compete with an associate for a promotion, the anger and frustration we feel is the product of external conflict. Whether the type of conflict being considered is an internal struggle of conscience or an external struggle for power and the allocation of scarce rewards, it produces stress and evokes activity to reduce that stress. Competent persons must be able to control both the initiation and the management of conflicts in order to protect and nurture both internal and external relationship links.

From a developmental perspective, conventional wisdom would suggest a tendency for young and old to experience more conflict episodes than middle-aged adults because they are either less skilled or less motivated in avoidance. Moreover, both young and old are assumed to permit each conflict episode to do more lasting damage to the relationship than is the case with middle-aged adults because they lack adequate skills or motivation to engage in problem-solving activity.

This U-shaped hypothesis about the developmental cycle of conflict management skills lends support to our culture's stereotypes of "hotheaded youth," "levelheaded adults," and "cantankerous old people." This kind of stereotyping is represented visually in Figure 1 below.

Thoughtful research and focused observation tend to discount these stereotypes. Nevertheless, the U-shaped hypothesis remains a useful starting place for the study of conflict across the lifespan.

Defining Conflict

Conflict will be defined here as a communication concept. From this standpoint, *conflict is a relationship crisis that is produced by failed predictions. The crisis is managed as the parties communicate to effect changes in the way the past is to be understood and the future is to be constructed.* For example, most parents do not expect their children to be thieves. If one's child is arrested for shoplifting, then an implicit prediction about that child has failed, and a conflict has been established.

Parent and child communicate about the past to discover errors of understanding that need to be changed so that the act of stealing is viewed as an unequivocally negative behavior. They communicate about the present to make sure that they are in agreement about the event and the tension it produced. They communicate about the future in order to understand changes that need to be made to repair damage done to the relationships that link the child to the parent, the damaged property owner, other family members, and social acquaintances.

Despite stylistic differences that indicate some persons enjoy a good fight, research basically indicates that persons of all

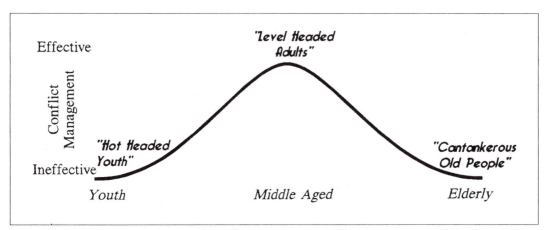

Figure 1. Stereotyped Perceptions of Conflict Management Effectiveness across the Lifespan

ages find conflict to be painful and therefore prefer to ignore or simply tolerate most situations in which behavioral predictions have failed. Consequently, it is not true that marriages end because two people prefer different ways of squeezing toothpaste from a tube. On the other hand, it is true that persons vary in terms of their tolerance for relationship tension. Some individuals seem to fight over trivialities while others allow even blatant acts of betrayal to go unmentioned. Many studies have explored these different predilections to conflict but have not reached a clear conclusion. Although intelligence, education, gender, social status, and cultural origin all influence the individual's ability to tolerate conflict, there is no pattern that predicts either a low or a high conflict threshold. Consequently, it is more fruitful to study the management of conflict than the origins of conflict.

Managing Conflict

From the management perspective, it has long been understood that conflict elicits a surge of adrenaline that leads to a "fight or flight" response (Pruitt & Rubin, 1986). These response tendencies—considered by some to be instincts—translate into three possible conflict outcomes: a win, a loss, or avoidance (Hocker & Wilmot, 1991). The possibility of a creative fourth option, the "win/win" potential found in effective problem solving, has

been addressed by recent work on conflict management. With this fourth alternative, it is reasoned that an individual's needs can be assessed and ways can be discovered to allocate the scarce resources available to the conflicting parties in such a way as to maximize rewards for everyone. Even in child custody disputes, for example, advocates of "win/win" conflict management believe that creative ways can be found to help both parents focus on giving the child a victory, and eventually give each other equally rewarding victories in the process.

Viewed through the eyes of the injured party, the management of conflict hinges on the ability to target a problem-solving future. Communication that simply explores the past is both pointless and counterproductive and leads to little more than a struggle to fix the blame for things that went wrong. In fact, although it is clearly a widespread communication tendency, the desire to ask the offending party "why" he or she has failed to behave in predicted ways seldom proves useful. Questions such as "Why did you lie?" simply produce denials, excuses, and appeals for mercy or forgiveness. The stage is then set for a relationship-destroying tirade wherein the parties struggle to fix the blame for the bruised feelings. Instead of simply looking back to the problem, the challenge is to look ahead to the solution.

In the example of the child who shoplifted, competent conflict management would begin when the parent targeted a problem-solving future. Perhaps the parent would decide that the child should be grounded, made to pay hard-earned money, participate in a counseling session, or even be shipped off to a special school. Whatever solution is chosen, effective conflict management is essentially a communication process in which future-oriented change is made necessary and reasonable.

Occasionally, of course, significant relationships encounter such destructive conflicts that no amount of change can solve the problems. The employee caught stealing, the spouse caught cheating, and the politician caught selling a vote are classic examples of betrayed trusts that can lead to the termination of relationships. Whenever persons feel that there can be no change in the future that makes up for damage done in the past, the relationship is terminated. All too frequently, however, relationships die needlessly.

One of the most useful insights from recent research into mediation, negotiation, and problem-solving practices indicates that creative alternatives can be devised for even the most dramatic conflicts, and relationships can be salvaged if all parties commit to the relationship. An especially popular treatment of this approach is found in the work of Fisher and Ury (1981), which summarizes insights from the Harvard Negotiation Project. Fisher and Ury point out that few conflicts need to be seen as a competition for position or power in which one party must win and the other lose, or in which one party makes all the adjustment and the other continues along his or her familiar path. Instead, they challenge persons in conflicts to commit to a "win/win" outcome in which a future is constructed that offers both parties an opportunity to nurture the relationship by maximizing rewards and minimizing punishments for one another.

Conflict Management Issues from Youth to Old Age

The very fact that this "win/win" approach is considered both new and relatively difficult helps to explain the U-shaped hypothesis about the developmental cycle for conflict management skill in our culture. Three key variables in effective conflict management change as we move from youth through middle age to old age—time, socialization, and power.

Time is a key variable for persons in conflict because the need to focus on productive future-oriented change requires the ability to image situations and events that may be months and even years distant. For the very young, the ability to image distant futures often is limited by impatience and inexperience. The impatience stems from the fact that "next year" often implies whole new realities that are bound up with changes of school or rites of passage. Even the notion of "next week" is distorted by a television-based world where media families discover and resolve conflicts in 30-minute time frames. Inexperience produces a similar distortion in youthful constructions of problem-solving futures. The ability to trust others to make enduring change comes through experience.

For the very old, the ability to image distant futures often is limited by impatience and experience. Impatience in this case derives from the awareness of a shrinking lifespan, while experience teaches that change is difficult both to accomplish and to maintain as accustomed habits attempt to reclaim their position. The work required for effective conflict management may seem excessive and the results uncertain for many elderly persons simply because they have had substantial experiences with promises that get broken and problems that recur. Only the stable adult has both the time frame and the experience to sense that the work invested in solving problems will prove both rewarding and enduring. This attitude exists in some young and some old adults, although it is more likely to be found among the middle-aged.

Socialization, viewed as the degree to which we need and value relationships with others, serves as the second major variable that influences our developmental experience with conflict. For the young, relationships often are overly important and excessively fragile. With no career to enrich their self-concepts, young people rely on the acceptance of peers and the rewards of stable interactions to define self-esteem. Failed predictions—perhaps a discovered lie or an overheard tease—become acts of betrayal that produce destructive and often permanent disruptions in youthful relationships. With respect to conflict management, this excessive socialization pressure produces a tendency for young people to sacrifice relationships that could have been repaired and nurtured by the more mature adult.

For elderly persons, relationships are equally important, but far less fragile than they are for young people or even middle-aged adults. Problems of self-concept and self-esteem are things of the past for many older persons. Consequently, criticism may not be perceived as a request for change or even a firm judgment of one's values. The disengagement from the world of work, for example, is also a partial disengagement from the need to accommodate the expectations of others.

The right to exhibit eccentric behavior and simply ignore mainstream social conventions is often an implicit privilege that accompanies old age. On the one hand, this decreased socialization suggests that many more conflicts are simply better tolerated among elderly persons than they are among the young and middle-aged. On the other hand, when conflict is enjoined, requests for change are often articulated more bluntly and more forcefully among elders than among either young or middle-aged persons.

Power, the last of the variables in our ability to manage conflict, has a more intuitive appeal than either time or socialization. Social power peaks during middle age. As a consequence, it is easier for the middle-aged adult to impose change on children, colleagues, friends, and even one's own self than it is for the very young and for retired elders. Parents of young children, for example, have both the moral authority and the financial resources to impose change on children who disappoint them. Working adults have the

capacity to threaten the destruction of a relationship and then carry through with such actions as resignations or terminations.

There is an exception to the U-shaped hypothesis. One aspect of social power tends to increase steadily across the lifespan. The legitimate power that comes from personal experience is limited only by our physical capacity to communicate effectively. So long as the individual is mentally sharp and capable of effective speech, it is likely that he or she can effect change in others simply by the power of reason. It is common, therefore, to find that our "elder statesmen" are, in fact, elderly even if they are not, in fact, men. Many persons garner ever increasing amounts of social power and thus become increasingly valued resources for conflict management right up to the moment of death.

Improving Conflict Management Skills

Conflict is never pleasant for men or women of any age, regardless of their social position. Because some conflict is inevitable, however, it must be studied and management practices must be developed to help young, middle aged, and elderly alike to protect their interpersonal relationships whenever conflicts are encountered. Toward this end, the key challenge facing persons of all ages has to do with the development of two skills: creative problem solving and future-oriented communication.

Creative problem solving produces many possible futures that can repair problems that have been produced by past behavior. Each potential change, moreover, is evaluated from a relationship perspective so that the action taken to resolve a conflict strengthens relationships as it solves problems. Divorces, terminations, angry lectures, and even most ultimatums draw attention to the past and help the injured party to inflict pain on the people who initiated conflict. By contrast, problem solving focuses on the future and views punishment as a bridge to strengthened relationships. Whatever the age, therefore, only the unskilled conflict manager would terminate the relationship when a valued friend betrays the relationship. The skilled conflict manager would invent options to repair the damage and would explore all possible conflict management tools, from heartfelt conversations to professional intervention by a trained therapist.

Future-oriented communication entails both the courage and the competence to take action to solve a problem. Courage is needed because most us are reluctant to initiate a conflict and assert our preference for what is to be said and done as the future unfolds. Competence is an element because most of us don't know how to manage the process of communication to keep it focused toward a positive future goal. We tend to let the other person escape the need to contemplate a specific change of some future-oriented behavior by allowing apologies, excuses, explanations, and topic-shifting questions to shift the discussion to the past. We end up, then, trying to fix the blame for the origin of the conflict rather than agreeing on a plan to solve the problem. We counter this drift to the past when we target the future, convince ourselves it is an appropriate future, and then communicate our vision clearly and enthusiastically.

Throughout the lifespan, both men and women can improve the way they manage conflicts. To the extent that it is a skill that can be mastered, there is nothing to suggest that our stereotypes should continue to favor the middle-aged adult. The more appropriate model would be a straight line indicating that we simply get better and better with each problem we solve, and each relationship we strengthen through the process of managing conflicts.   ▼ JOHN CRAWFORD

See also: Marital Development; Privacy Issues; Sibling Relationships; Social Class and Adult Development; Stress.

References

Fisher, R., & Ury, W. (1981). *Getting to Yes: Negotiating Agreement Without Giving In.* Boston: Houghton Mifflin.

Hocker, J. L., & Wilmot, W. W. (1991). *Interpersonal Conflict, 3rd Edition.* Dubuque, IA: William C. Brown.

Pruitt, D. G., & Rubin, J. Z. (1986). *Social Conflict: Escalation, Stalemate, and Settlement.* New York: Random House.

CONTEXTUALISM

How are things in the world related to one another? How does development occur? How does a person both change and remain the same during adulthood? Such basic questions address a person's fundamental assumptions, his or her way of seeing the world. Mechanism, organicism, contextualism, and formism are four worldviews that were identified by Stephen Pepper (1942) half a century ago, although all four have a much longer history. When one knows what worldview a particular individual holds, one is in a better position to understand not only the answers that person gives to questions like those above, but even the kind of questions he or she thinks it makes sense to ask.

Social and developmental psychologists have been especially interested in three of the worldviews described by Pepper: mechanism, organicism, and contextualism. The fourth view, formism, is less used today (Reese & Overton, 1970). Each view is formed around a central theme or metaphor, sometimes called a root metaphor. The metaphor of mechanism, not surprisingly, is the machine. Organicism takes the individual living organism as its root metaphor. Contextualism's metaphor is the network or relationship. All three metaphors and their worldviews have made important contributions to understanding adult development. Although the focus here is contextualism, the following description of mechanism and organicism will help in understanding what contextualism is by showing what it is not.

Mechanism and Organicism

A machine is entirely built and its structure, dimensions, power, and other characteristics are defined before it begins to operate. It then responds to inputs from the outside in a direct way. For example, turning the ignition key in a car begins a process that results in gasoline and air being burned in a combustion chamber. The energy produced is then used to drive a shaft that turns wheels, and so on. A specific input produces the same effect over and over. In this process of linear causality, a machine continues to do the same thing until it either wears out or is turned off.

In a mechanistic world view this model defines how people as well as machines operate. Development is a process of accumulation of exposure to stimuli and of responses to these stimuli. This model is called "incremental" because no sharp breaks occur in the sequence of stimuli and responses that is known as the lifespan. People develop the way they do because of the stimuli to which they are exposed over time. This relatively passive way of viewing development is exemplified by various learning theories (e.g., Bandura, 1977; Skinner, 1953) as well as by most information-processing theories (e.g., Fisher, 1978; Shannon & Weaver, 1949).

The organicist world view proceeds from a different starting point—the metaphor of a growing organism. A biological organism changes its structure during its lifetime—from a seed to a tree, a larva to a butterfly, or a human embryo to an elderly person. The genetic blueprint defines the scope of development, which is expressed as a process of unfolding, changing, and transformation. Development reacts to environmental events to the extent that these events "call forth" the structural changes that are an essential part of the nature of the organism. Unlike mechanism, organicism holds that stimuli do not determine development. Stimuli may have a role in allowing developmental changes to occur, but they do not themselves shape or cause developmental phenomena. Furthermore, stimuli that are not relevant to the inner developmental processes will have little or no effect.

Many developmental theories take an organicist model as their starting point. Piaget's (1954) theory is a good example of an organicist model for child development. Stage theories of adult development, such as Erikson's (1968), conceive of the adult life course as a set of changes that progressively build on one another. Erikson calls this process "epigenetic." The stages are thought to be ultimately rooted in biological and neural functioning.

Basic Concepts of Contextualism

Contextualism is an alternative to both mechanism and organicism (see Rosnow & Georgoudi, 1986, for a wide selection of applications; also Blank, 1989; McGuire, 1983). Rather than approaching behavior, thoughts, and actions as springing either from individual biological unfolding or from environmentally produced stimuli, contextualists view all of these as momentary products of ongoing transactions or relationships. These interconnected transactions include such varied components as physical environments, social structures, mental representations, historical events, and biology. None of these factors dominate in defining either the behavior that occurs at a particular moment or the development that occurs over an extended period of time. The interplay of all these elements is a creative process that makes each moment of development unique and constantly open to change.

Contextualism focuses on the concept of embeddedness. Current situations and events are embedded in or carried along with the ongoing flow that we call history. Correspondingly, individuals also are embedded in this changing array of contexts, and in their own distinctive histories of biological development, interpersonal relationships, and individual thoughts.

One particularly important type of thought is that which is concerned with meaning. People are constantly trying to relate what is going on both to their own goals and intentions and to the goals and intentions of those around them. The meanings they generate in turn create a new set of conditions for the individual and for those within his or her context.

For example, a parent may discipline a child "for his own good" because the parent believes the child will learn an important lesson. "Go to your room and don't come out until I say so" might be seen as a brief restriction that will help the child develop an enduring sense of responsibility. In this case the "meaning" to the parent is a necessary growth experience for the child. However, the parent may take the same action not to benefit the child but to compensate for having been browbeaten at work by an oppressive boss. The "same" action is in reality a very different one, depending on its relation to goals and intentions. In either case the child may invest exactly the same meaning in the action, such as "My mother hates me and wants my life to be boring and stupid." The mother reinterprets her relationship to her child partly on the basis of her analysis of her own behavior—its meaning—and partly in reaction to the behavior and expressed emotions of her child which, in turn, likely are based on a very different version of this particular action.

Contextualism does not offer the stability of mechanism or the ordered change of structural organicism. Development is not simply movement of a basically stable individual through the changing stimuli presented by an otherwise stable world, as in mechanism. Furthermore, development is not movement through a defined sequence of orderly changes within the organism, more or less regardless of the nature of the physical and social environment, as in organicism. Contextualism shares with dialectical thinking (Riegel, 1979) an emphasis on the often disorderly nature of change and the impossibility of ever totally capturing an inherently changing process in terms designed for stability and order.

Development is an evolutionary process. It is less clearly determined at its beginning than in worldviews in which development is completely necessitated by the form of that which is developing. It is also less defined by its results than in more "teleological" approaches that assert that the cause of development is the end product.

If one looks at development at a particular point in time—which is the way most research is done and also the way that most of us experience reality—then development is a reflection of the creative process that balances an array of forces, each producing its own level and type of tension or pressure. Making this kind of time-specific observation, one might describe what one sees as a person who "has such and such a personality" or shows a certain level of "maturity," or use some other label that seems to denote a stable aspect of the person. If one looks at development in a more contextual and historical sense, however, then development is in fact the process itself. Development is the creative balancing act. It is a dynamic patterning of the supposedly separate and independent forces. In other words, development now is recognized to be a set of relationships—not something that is caused by or that can be considered part of artificial boundaries such as "the person" or "the environment."

The crux of the contextualist question about development is "How does change occur in spite of the pressures and constraints to remain stable—and how does something remain stable in spite of the inexorable pressure to change, adapt, and react?"

The set of concepts and the research agenda involved in a contextualistic approach are in some ways very humble and in others very arrogant (Blank, 1989). Contextualists humbly insist that their own meanings—theories and interpretations of people's behaviors—are open to alteration in the process of describing them to others because meaning is intrinsically a relationship. It is the product of a negotiation process that can be renegotiated. Each interpretation, including contextualism, is necessarily incomplete and tentative. On the other hand, contextualists arrogantly insist that all prevailing theories are inadequate because they fail to account for the multidimensional nature of "reality" that is emphasized by the contextualist worldview.

Contextualism and Adult Development

A contextualist approach is in many ways suited to the concerns of adult developmentalists. It is apparent that many aspects of adult development are in large part defined by the historical flow of the individual through society. On the individual level this flow is called the life course (Sorensen, Weinert, & Sherrod, 1986). On the group level this same process is identified with age stratification (Riley, Johnson, & Foner, 1972), and an emphasis is placed on how cohorts move through the roles and transitions of society. Thus, history must be part of adult developmental theories and measures. For example, Erikson's theory of adult development clearly refers to each stage as being contained in all the others, dependent upon the past meanings assigned to personal experiences, and open to reinterpretation.

Many adult development theories are also concerned with what is often labeled the "dialectics" of personality growth and development—the back-and-forth interplay of the person and his or her range of contexts, including the physical world and the demands of society. Finally, many theories in adult development are tested primarily through qualitative methods, such as in-depth interviews, which emphasize the role of meaning and the construction of reality. These methods fit more easily into the contextual world view than any of its competitors.

Thus, many theories of adult development appear to be compatible with a contextualist approach. Nevertheless, few theorists and researchers have fully committed themselves to this model. Contextualism has seldom provided explicit guidance to the process of planning research and formulating theory.

How might a contextual worldview interact with the goals of those who are interested in adult development? Part of the answer is to consider how the balancing act of stability and change can be achieved. The answer lies in the importance of negotiation, of involvement in constructing a self, a society, and a life as time relentlessly proceeds, altering everything in its path and yet simultaneously requiring stability in order for change to make sense.

What is necessary for negotiation to proceed? Relationships. Negotiation cannot simply take the form of an individual thought process or act, although each person surely is a thinker, an actor, a negotiator. Similarly, society does not determine development independently of individuals. Instead, individuals compose a social setting which then "borrows" power from them to set roles, rules, right, and responsibilities before the individuals that form it. Chance, biological urges and constraints, social rules, and individual choice are all involved.

Once elements or actors are identified and acknowledged as co-creators of development, then adult developmentalists can begin in earnest to examine how negotiations of development occur. Researchers must always remember with humility that what they discover will itself have been restricted by the methods used, the historical moment or moments of investigation, and the particular set of actors.

Developing through Adulthood

As people move through adulthood, they also move through a variety of circumstances and contexts. These circumstances and contexts are often bound by the norms of society, by physical limitations or characteristics, by individual preferences, and so on. It is as though we are moving through a series of rooms, sometimes by choosing to open doors, but at other times by being pushed through them. Once we have moved through a door, we can be influenced by what we observed and learned in the previous rooms, but we can seldom go back. On the rare occasions when we do return to a previous context, the room will have been altered while we were gone. We also are never quite sure about what is beyond the next door, even though we are aware that at some point we will need to move through it.

In this process, some people have more power or control over their own lives and the lives of others, more "say" in who goes through what doors and when. For a concrete example, think of the negotiation of development as though it were a conversation. In some conversations, one person may dominate, never allowing others to contribute their ideas or help set the rules and scope of the discourse. Seldom is everyone's contribution completely equal to everybody else's. Instead, some people have a greater voice in the ongoing negotiation of development than do others.

These differences in "voice" are often related to age. Certainly this is the case early in life because adults have louder and more dominant voices than children. It is important to recognize, though, that children, even in infancy, do have voices and do partially determine not only their own development but also that of their parents and other adults. In fact, contextualism as a worldview has compelled theorists to recognize the grave limitations of any model that acts as though development is a one-way process at any time or in any circumstances. Most theories embedded in mechanism or organicism share these limitations (Lerner & Spanier, 1978). Still, the amount of influence or control is certainly weighted toward adults in most adult-child interactions.

In young adulthood and even more so in middle age, persons have a good chance of having their voices recognized as important to the conversation of development. They have the power and the social recognition necessary to be heard. The established adult has a number of different choices available, a number of doors to open.

In later life, however, events may occur that alter the trajectory of individual development in ways that either reduce one's voice to a whisper or allow others to ignore it even when it is loud and clear. Disability is one event that certainly produces a lessened capacity to be in control of one's destiny at any age, and becomes more and more likely to occur as a person ages. Well-documented reductions in activity level, especially in the broader communities of work, education, and commerce, give the person fewer opportunities to be involved in all the conversations necessary to continue the developmental negotiations. Loss through death of spouse,

friends, and others with whom one regularly negotiated and created one's life (the developmental convoy) leaves the person with fewer companions to whom one can turn and from whom one's voice is solicited.

A contextualist approach to adult development directs attention to the dynamic interplay of person and context. It attends to the continuing demands for change on the part of both person and context, if only to maintain a tension of forces to produce stability. Adults often work to maintain stability in relationships so that they can remain the "same" as they have been. At other times, however, they may need a conception of themselves as different, as changed, and it is then that they use the same raw materials—life events, role requirements, physical surroundings, self-concept, biological processes, relationships with others—to create the changes that are necessary for continued development. ▼ Thomas O. Blank

See also: Adult Development and Aging, Models of; Attachment Across the Lifespan; Cohort and Generational Effects; Disengagement Theory; Happiness, Cohort Measures of; Metaphors of the Life Course; Place and Personality in Adult Development.

References

Bandura, A. (1977). *Social Learning Theory.* Englewood Cliffs, NJ: Prentice-Hall.

Blank, T. O. (1989). Social psychology, contexts of aging, and a contextual world view. *International Journal of Aging & Human Development, 29:* 225-39.

Erikson, E. H. (1968). *Identity and the Life Cycle.* New York: W. W. Norton.

Fisher, B. A. (1978). *Perspectives on Human Communication.* New York: Macmillan.

Lerner, R. M., & Spanier, G. B. (1978). A dynamic interactional view of child and family development. In R. M. Lerner & G. B. Spanier (Eds.), *Child Influences on Marital and Family Interactions: A Lifespan Perspective.* New York: Academic Press.

McGuire, W. J. (1983). A contextualist theory of knowledge: Its implications for innovation and reform in psychological research. In L. Berkowitz (Ed.), *Advances in Experimental Social Psychology.* Volume 16. New York: Academic Press.

Overton, W. F. (1984). World views and their influence on psychological theory and research: Kuhn-Lakatos-Laudan. In H. W. Reese (Ed.), *Advances in Child Development and Behavior.* Volume 18. New York: Academic Press.

Pepper, S. C. (1942). *World Hypotheses: A Study in Evidence.* Berkeley, CA: University of California Press.

Piaget, J. (1954). *The Construction of Reality in the Child.* New York: Basic Books.

Reese, H. W., & Overton, W. F. (1970). Models of development and theories of development. In P. Baltes & L. Goulet (Eds.), *Lifespan Developmental Psychology: Research and Theory.* New York: Academic Press, pp. 116-49.

Riegel, K. F. (1979). *Foundations of a Dialectical Psychology.* New York: Academic Press.

Riley, M. W., Johnson, M., & Foner, A. (1972). *Aging and Society: A Sociology of Age Stratification.* New York: Russell Sage.

Rosnow, R. L., & Georgoudi, M. (1986). *Contextualism and Understanding in Behavioral Science: Implications for Research and Theory.* New York: Praeger.

Shannon, C., & Weaver, W. (1949). *The Mathematical Theory of Communication.* Urbana: University of Illinois Press.

Skinner, B. F. (1953). *Science and Human Behavior.* New York: Free Press.

Sorensen, A. B., Weinert, F. E., & Sherrod, L. R. (1986). *Human Development and the Life Course: Multidisciplinary Perspectives.* Hillsdale, NJ: Erlbaum.

CONTROL AND VULNERABILITY

Human development throughout the lifespan can be viewed from a variety of perspectives. One of the most useful perspectives may be derived from the observation and analysis of our quest for control. In its most basic forms, the quest for control represents the urgent need to reduce vulnerability. In its more elaborate forms, control may be placed in the service of additional motives and ambitions. The study of control and vulnerability is a relatively new area of theory and research. Before turning to the early results, however, an understanding of the main features of control as a key facet of development and aging is necessary.

Developing and Negotiating Control: A Brief Overview

Almost by definition, an adult is a person who is in control. It is the child who needs a significant degree of guidance and supervision because a child has not yet gained the ability to regulate his or her own behavior throughout a broad range of situations. In the later adult years the individual's behavior may come under increasing scrutiny from both self and others with the implicit question in mind: "*Still* in control?" This general pattern involves the interaction of individual and societal factors at every step. For example, it is the helplessness and vulnerability of the infant that call forth extensive caregiving efforts by the family. Because the baby cannot feed itself or extricate itself from hazardous situations, somebody else has to control the situation and see to the baby's survival and defense. This is a normative or "expectable" situation in the early phase of individual development.

During the teen years considerable testing of the individual's ability to control his or her own life takes place. Youths must somehow demonstrate to their elders (as well as themselves) that they are now able to exercise self-regulation. In today's industrialized societies, being given the keys to the car is often a milestone in a youth's acceptance as a member of adult society, i.e., a person who can be counted upon to exercise control in a responsible manner. It is generally accepted that this newly granted control has both an inner and an outer direction. The driver, for example, is expected to keep his or her temper under control (inner direction) and obey the laws and principles governing safe operation of a motor vehicle (outer direction).

When a society accepts a person as a fully enfranchised adult, a reversal in the flow of authority and responsibility usually occurs. In return for greater access to the resources and privileges of membership in society, the adult now is expected to provide guidance and control for those of junior standing. The chronological age at which full adult status is granted varies from society to society and may also be affected by circumstances; e.g., greater responsibilities may be thrust upon the young in times of war, or additional obstacles may be placed in the developmental paths of the young in times of high unemployment.

Having demonstrated to the satisfaction of self and society the ability to exercise adequate self-regulation, the adult is then in a position to use these control capabilities to pursue additional goals. Winning a mate, starting a family, and succeeding in a demanding and perhaps risky career are among the purposes that require substantial control-related abilities. Negotiating for even higher levels of control may also become a major issue, depending on one's ambitions and the sociocultural context. In past generations, adults who were coming into their own often had to negotiate for increased power with a tenacious but relatively small layer of elders at the same time that some advanced youths were starting to pressure them. Today, the "middle" in middle-aged adults deserves special emphasis because people in this situation have to cope with substantial power struggles from both below and above. Youth socialized into a fast-paced, high-expectation society want their satisfactions now, while a much larger and, generally, healthier cadre of elderly adults is not necessarily willing to step aside and yield power.

From the older adult's standpoint, the quest for control may have become part of a new and distinctive configuration. People in their seventies, for example, may have become quite proficient in exercising control over their own lives while also exercising substantial influence in their relationships, in the workplace, and perhaps in the community as well. It is natural for them to expect to continue in the effective exercise of control and influence. Sooner or later, however, this expectation may be challenged by illness or other physical impairment, reduced financial status, loss of significant relationships,

and encounters with age-discriminatory attitudes and practices. Depending on circumstances and personality, an individual may fear that "I'm slipping" or that "They're trying to take everything away from me."

What makes this situation even more complex is the frequent coexistence of an impulse toward what Jung (1961, 1966) has characterized as individuation, Maslow (1948, 1968) as self-actualization, and Van Tassel (1979) as completion of being. These views suggest that a long life provides the opportunity to "become who we really are" (Jung, 1966, p. 174). One can become more one's own self by shedding the outer layers of personality that are no longer needed and discovering and actualizing previously neglected potentialities. Some elderly adults may then find themselves in the disconcerting situation of reaching toward a new sense of liberation and actualization while at the same time feeling the need to struggle for continued control of their own lives and resources. At one extreme of the spectrum are aging men and women who are afflicted with progressive dementing conditions such as Alzheimer's disease and are gradually losing control over their most basic functions, while at the other extreme are those for whom age is bringing a new level of wisdom. Between these extremes, it is likely that many are struggling with the competing motivations for continued control over practical life circumstances and the inner quest for completion of being.

Finally, attention must be given to what might be called disorders or aberrations of control. The infant who does not know how to feed itself or buckle itself into a restraint seat in a car is showing neither a disorder nor an aberration. All of us must pass through a maturational process in order to develop basic self-regulatory and protective abilities. The obvious disorders of control that are related to impairments of the central nervous system vary widely in their patterns and consequences as well as their sources. Stroke victims may lose some degree of control over their ability to speak but remain alert and well oriented, whereas individuals at a particular stage of Alzheimer's disease may retain the ability to speak clearly but no longer recognize family members or recall their own life history.

Other aberrations of control are more closely related to personality and life history factors. Perhaps most consequential for experiences throughout the adult life course are the following two types of aberration.

- *Excessive dependence on self or others.* Some people cultivate a coping style in which they attempt to induce other people to take the risks and responsibilities for them. It is as though they have decided not to relinquish childhood techniques but to transform these temporary and normative methods into a permanent *modus operandi*. The opposite aberration on this bipolar dimension is known in psychoanalytic terminology as *counterdependency*. Although these individuals also have very strong needs for others to provide care and protection, they present to the world the persona of a fiercely independent person who is always in control of everything. Both of these styles, when taken to an extreme, significantly reduce the individual's ability to cope with a variety of challenges and circumstances. For example a counterdependent person might feel "I'd rather die than ask for help"—and proceed to do so.
- *Control as the primary end in itself.* It is often enjoyable to play with a new skill that one has just mastered. The pleasure derives not so much from what one can do with the new skill, but from success in having expanded or refined one's realm of control. Generally, control is valuable for the life-protecting and life-enhancing functions that it makes possible, but some people become addicted to control itself as their primary satisfaction. This character trait tends to have a negative effect on interpersonal relationships (e.g., When I say "Jump!" you say "How high?"), as well as on occupational success and personal safety. Ignoring any considerations other than the opportunity to exercise control and power, these individuals are catastrophes ready to happen.

With these background considerations in mind we will now draw upon the relatively new area of control/vulnerability research for further insights.

Sense of Control versus Helplessness

Much of the current interest in control, vulnerability, and related problems was inspired by the studies and ideas of Martin Seligman (e.g., 1975, 1991; see also Abramson, Metalsky, & Alloy, 1989; Meier & Seligman, 1976; Sweeney, Anderson, & Bailey, 1986). His theory of *learned helplessness* was first derived from laboratory experiments with animals. Subsequently, Seligman and other investigators designed studies more appropriate to observing human behavior in real-life situations.

Seligman's first recognition of the behavior he would call learned helplessness came about when a fellow graduate student complained that the dogs being studied in their laboratory experiments just were not being cooperative. "'It's the dogs,' said Bruce. 'The dogs won't do anything. Something's wrong with them. So nobody can do any experiments'" (Seligman, 1991, p. 19). As Seligman observed the dogs who had been accused of not being cooperative, he immediately grasped the principle that would soon guide much research into both human and animal control/vulnerability dynamics:

> The dogs first had to learn to jump over the barrier to escape the shock; once they'd learned that, they could then be tested to see if tones alone evoked the same reaction. It should have been a cinch for them. To escape the shock, all they'd have to do was jump over the low barrier that divided the shuttlebox. Dogs usually learn this easily. These dogs...had just lain down whimpering. They hadn't even tried to get away from the shocks. And that, of course, meant that nobody could proceed with what they really wanted to do—test the dogs with the tones.
>
> As I...looked at the whimpering dogs, I realized that something much more significant had already occurred than any result the transfer experiment might produce:

Accidentally, during the early part of the experiment, the dogs must have been taught to be helpless. That's why they had given up. The tones had nothing to do with it. During Pavlovian conditioning they felt the shocks go on and off regardless of whether they struggled or jumped or barked or did nothing at all. They had concluded...that nothing they did mattered. So why try? I was stunned by the implications. If dogs could learn something as complex as the futility of their actions, here was an analogy to human helplessness, one that could be studied in the laboratory. Helplessness was all around us—from the urban poor to the newborn child to the despondent patient with his face to the wall.... (Seligman, 1991, p. 20)

Now, many studies later, it has become clear that learned helplessness is a powerful concept that can help to guide preventive and interventive efforts with humans as well as animals. When the course of lifespan development goes well, children learn that they themselves can do things that make a difference. By behaving in certain ways they can win approval and admiration from others, solve some of their own problems, and achieve some of their own goals. They find it more effective and satisfying to do something themselves than to cry or rage until somebody else comes and does it for them. A general sense of being an effective person with control over his or her own life accompanies continued lifespan development if all continues to go well. This fortunate person enters adulthood with a firm sense of *learned optimism* (Seligman, 1991). "I can do it!," this person responds to an opportunity; "I can get out of this jam!" is the confident response to a challenge.

The scenario is not always this favorable, however. Like the depressed, do-nothing dogs observed by Seligman, people may encounter critical situations in their early development in which whatever they do seems to have no effect on the world—in practical terms, this usually occurs when young children are unable to win the love, approval, and protection of their parents. Crying doesn't do it, nor does screaming and

thrashing, nor silence and immobility. The earlier such situations arise and the longer they persist, the more likely it is that the individual will have (implicitly) decided that life is a futile enterprise. As adults these individuals lack confidence in their ability to make a mark on the world, and therefore they devote little energy to achieving what would normally be the emerging goals and needs of self-actualization. Furthermore, when a person has adopted a learned helplessness attitude, the likelihood of developing further skills and resources is significantly reduced, as is the ability to form and sustain meaningful interpersonal relationships.

The learned helplessness concept offers an alternative way of thinking about some of the behaviors that have often been ascribed to growing old: withdrawal from activities, depressive mood, even suicidal tendencies. This pattern of behavior is not "caused" by old age and does not need to occur in the later adult years. Instead, these behaviors could be regarded as the outcome of the individual's accumulated frustration in discovering that nothing he or she does seems to make any difference. Preventing or overcoming the learned helplessness attitude in the later adult years would therefore result in higher self-esteem, greater confidence, and a sense of control over one's own destiny.

Prior to the introduction of learned helplessness theory the author had designed a series of studies exploring the possibility of inducing "old behaviors" in young adults and "young behaviors" in old adults (Kastenbaum, 1971). One of these studies involved asking people to serve as advisers to a "city government" that was part of the simulation paradigm. The advisers eventually discovered that those representing the government were making their decisions without regard to the recommendations the advisers had prepared for them. Young adults who found themselves in the role of advisers-whose-advice-made-no-difference developed patterns of impotent rage, preoccupation with bodily discomfort, repetitious complaining, and increasingly aimless behavior. At the time, this response pattern was similar to the dark mood and ineffectual behavior observed among some men who had been forced to retire against their wishes. Seligman's subsequent description of learned helplessness provided a more general framework for understanding this kind of response. If older adults are excluded from situations in which their actions can have observable effects—e.g., through forced retirement and other forms of ageism—then a condition akin to learned helplessness may develop. Because placing a young adult in a structurally similar situation seems to induce the same kind of response, the situation rather than chronological age appears to be the important factor.

The therapeutic dimension was added by two studies in real-life settings that were designed soon after the appearance of the learned helplessness model. Schulz (1976) gave some elderly residents of a nursing home the opportunity to make their own decisions about when and if they would accept visits from students who were trying to improve their understanding of older adults. Other residents were also visited by students, but these residents were not given a choice about the scheduling. This seemingly very small difference—having or not having a choice regarding visitation—proved to make a significant difference in the residents' well-being. Those who had the opportunity to exercise choice, and therefore control, showed a pattern of improvement in morale, activity level, and self-esteem. The extent of this more optimistic outlook on life exceeded any changes that could be noted among those who received friendly visitations but who had no say in the matter.

The implications of this study were strengthened by another experimental intervention in the nursing home setting. Langner and Rodin (1976) saw to it that elderly residents were offered potted plants to keep and enjoy in their rooms. The experimental manipulation here also involved the individual's sense of control. Those who had been assigned to the control (actually "no control") condition were just told to enjoy the plants; the staff would water and look after them.

Those in the experimental condition were told that whether or not the plants survived and flourished was up to them. Again, the elderly men and women who had been encouraged to exercise their own control over the situation showed a marked improvement in self-esteem and well-being that surpassed the (slight if any) effects noted for those who had received plants but not the responsibility of caring for them.

Studies such as these have opened the way to a renewed appreciation for the importance of the individual's sense of control and responsibility. Furthermore, they have conveyed the message that learned helplessness sometimes can be reversed by providing opportunities to exercise effective control. This approach has been used by service providers and researchers who have tried a variety of techniques to empower institutionalized elderly adults. On a broader scale, such organizations as the American Association of Retired Persons may be helping a large number of older adults to retain or renew their confidence in being able to make their opinions known and count for something.

Other Issues

The adequate development and appropriate use of control throughout the lifespan requires attention to a great many issues, a few of which are discussed here.

• *Memory control.* It is difficult to feel confident and competent in everyday life if we are concerned about the reliability of our ability to recall information on demand. Whatever we do to strengthen and supplement our memory functioning as we move through the adult years is likely to bolster our general sense of control. And nowhere is it written that we must wait until the later adult years to give serious attention to our memory prowess.

• *Learning and information processing.* We can have little hope for control over our lives without cognitive control. This includes the entire process that encompasses attention, concentration, judgment, decision-making, and monitoring our own cognitive functioning. Techniques for developing and protecting cognitive control include the avoidance of alcohol and drug abuse, the willingness to explore new relationships and situations, and a devotion to lifelong learning.

- *Personal and spiritual development.* As Jung (1966) and others have suggested, we tend to carry into adulthood a burden of attitudes, assumptions, beliefs, and habits that interferes with discovering who we really are and who we might yet become. From the control perspective, this psychological debt to the past limits our freedom in the present and future. Whatever helps us to modify overcontrol from our past—e.g., life review or guided reminiscences, meditation, counseling, group discussions—can liberate us to explore new ways of being.

- *Age-related changes in control purpose and style.* Much remains to be learned about the dynamics of continuity and change in our personalities as we move through the lifespan. Building upon an idea offered by Jung (1966), Gutmann (1987) has presented cross-cultural research and theory that suggests men and women tend to alter their "mastery styles" in the later adult years. We still do not know much, however, about the variety of changes that might occur and their consequences for well-being and self-development. Emerging research approaches (e.g., Heil & Krampen, 1989; Lachman, 1986) may provide us with a whole new set of findings and ideas.

- *How much control do we need?* We do not have a dependable answer for this intriguing question. It seems to me that the appetite for overcontrol is whetted by deprivation. If we lose or think that we are losing control over some aspect of our lives, then we may intensify our control-seeking efforts. This orientation is more likely to lead to heightened power struggles than to ease the way for intergenerational transfers of control. It is also possible that outcroppings of bigotry in the later years

are part of the struggle to control perhaps more than what one actually can—or should—control (Kastenbaum, 1991, in press).

▼ ROBERT KASTENBAUM

See also: Alcohol Use and Abuse; Depression; Development and Aging; Disengagement Theory; Driving: A Lifespan Challenge; Drug Use and Abuse; Gender as a Shaping Force in Adult Development and Aging; Generational Equity; Grandparent Communication Skills; Grandparent Education to Enhance Family Strength; Habituation: A Key to Lifespan Development and Aging?; Individuality; Information Processing; Learning and Memory in Everyday Life; Maturity; Memory; Reminiscence and Life Review; Retirement Preparation; Spiritual Development and Wisdom: A Vedantic Approach; Suicide.

References

Abramson, L. Y., Metalsky, G. I., & Alloy, L. B. (1989). Hopelessness depression: A theory-based process-oriented sub-type of depression. *Psychological Review, 96:* 358-72.

Gutmann, D. (1987). *Reclaimed Powers.* New York: Basic Books.

Heil, F. E., & Krampen, G. (1989). Action-theoretical approaches to the development of control orientations in the aged. In P. S. Fry (Ed.), *Psychological Perspectives of Helplessness and Control in the Elderly.* New York: Elsevier Science.

Jung, C. G. (1961). *Memories, Dreams, and Reflections.* New York: Pantheon.

———. (1966). *Collected Works.* Volume 7: *Two Essays in Analytical Psychology.* London: Routledge & Kegan Paul.

Kastenbaum, R. (1971). Getting there ahead of time. *Psychology Today,* December, pp. 52-54; 82-84.

———. (1991). Racism and the older voter? Arizona's rejection of a paid holiday to honor Martin Luther King, Jr. *International Journal of Aging and Human Development, 32:* 199-209.

———. (1993). Encrusted elders: Arizona and the political spirit of postmodern aging. In T. Cole, A. Achenbaum, & R. Kastenbaum (Eds.), *Voices and Contexts: Toward a Critical Gerontology.* New York: Springer, pp. 160-83.

Lachman, M. E. (1986). Personal control in later life: Stability, change, and cognitive correlates. In M. M. Baltes & P. B. Baltes (Eds.),

The Psychology of Control and Aging. New York: Erlbaum, pp. 207-36.

Langner, E. J., & Rodin, J. (1976). The effects of choice and enhanced social responsibility: A field experiment in an institutional setting. *Journal of Personality and Social Psychology, 34:* 191-98.

Maslow, A. H. (1948). "Higher" and "Lower" needs. *Journal of Psychology, 25:* 433-36.

Maslow, A. H. (1968). *Toward a Psychology of Being.* Second edition. New York: Van Nostrand Reinhold.

Meier, S.F. & Seligman, M.E. (1976). Learned helplessness: Theory and evidence. *Journal of Experimental Psychology, 105:* 3-46.

Schulz, R. (1976). Effects of control and predictability on the physical and psychological well-being of the institutionalized aged. *Journal of Personality and Social Psychology, 33:* 563-73.

Seligman, M. E. P. (1975). *Helplessness: On Depression, Development, and Death.* San Francisco: Freeman.

———. (1991). *Learned Optimism.* New York: Knopf.

Sweeney, P., Anderson, K., & Bailey, S. (1986). Attributional style in depression: A meta-analytic review. *Journal of Personality and Social Psychology, 50:* 974-91.

Van Tassel, D. D. (1979). *Aging, Death, and the Completion of Being.* Philadelphia: University of Pennsylvania Press.

CREATIVITY

In his seventy-fifth year, an artist decided to change his name—for the fifth and final time. He now wanted to be known as "Manji, Old Man Mad about Painting" (Smith, 1988). The occasion was the publication (in 1834) of the first volume of his *One Hundred Views of Mt. Fuji.* Two additional volumes followed in what has become a unique artistic treasure appreciated not only by his fellow Japanese but by all the world. Manji—better known to history by one of his earlier names, Hokusai—prefaced the first volume with a personal declaration that can serve very well as our introduction to creativity through the adult years.

From the age of six I had a penchant for copying the form of things, and from about fifty, my pictures were frequently published; but until the age of seventy, nothing that I drew was worthy of notice. At seventy-three years, I was somewhat able to fathom the growth of plants and trees, and the structure of birds, animals, insects, and fish. Thus when I reach eighty years, I hope to have made increasing progress, and at ninety to see further into the underlying principles of things, so that at one hundred years I will have achieved a divine state in my art, and at one hundred and ten, every dot and every stroke will be as though alive. Those of you who live long enough, bear witness that these words of mine prove not false (quoted by Smith, 1988, p. 7).

Hokusai's personal philosophy and artistic achievement represent the high road in creativity, a level of awareness, engrossment, originality, industriousness, and talent that few attain in any sphere of human endeavor. We will return to Hokusai after surveying the broader area of creativity in adult development.

Fortunately, one does not have to be so prodigiously gifted as Hokusai to think and act creatively. Current theories, studies, and self-expressive techniques embrace the concept that creativity can be cultivated and enjoyed by most men and women and at all ages. Moreover, it is also recognized that creativity can be demonstrated in a great many ways. Although traditionally associated closely with the arts and sciences, creativity can be a facet of such activities as entertaining young children on a rainy day, playing games, inventing useful devices, and dealing with problems at work in new ways. Teachers at all educational levels can attest to the creativity often at work in concocting excuses for not completing assignments (e.g., "My boyfriend's dog swallowed the keys to my car, so I couldn't get to the library until he threw up—the dog, I mean—and he didn't").

Definitions of Creativity

There is more than one reasonable way to define *creativity.* The approach taken most often by researchers, which is also the approach that seems most closely to match the materialistic-productive spirit of industrialized societies, defines creativity as the ability to produce something. We know and judge creativity by its observable products, and some people produce more than others or produce things with a higher level of quality or value.

Despite its apparent clarity, this definition quickly runs into difficulties. An artist might turn out many paintings or a writer many stories that adhere to stereotyped formats. Is a product really creative if it is barely distinguishable from many others of the same genre? "Painting by the numbers" describes an approach that can apply to many fields of endeavor. Researchers are well aware of the problems involved in trying to specify how a creative product differs from something that has been produced in a mechanical and undistinguished way. Usually, one or more of the following criteria are used:

- Creative products are new, original, or unusual.
- Creative products are of higher merit or quality.
- Creative products are those that are recognized and honored by leading authorities over a period of time.

None of these criteria is fully adequate. In societies with long, past-dominated traditions, for example, originality may not be as valued as in fast-paced high-technology societies that constantly demand—and then quickly devour—the new, original, or unusual. Judgments of merit or quality are subject to many biases. The history of art, science, technology, and society is rich in examples of "worthless scribbles" that later are recognized as masterpieces, flying machines that "will never get off the ground" but that soon revolutionize transportation and global relationships, and "harebrained schemes" to give the vote to men who do not own property or even to women. Similarly, a consensus among "leading authorities" may reflect self-protective biases rather than the merits of a new theory, invention, or work of art. These prob-

lems do not entirely invalidate the study of creativity as a product, but they should be kept in mind as a limitation and a source of possible error.

One alternative way of defining creativity would emphasize the *process* rather than the product. The guiding assumption here is that there is something distinctive about the way we perceive, think, and behave when we are being creative as distinguished from simply responding to stimuli or obligations in a routine and predictable manner. A major advantage of this approach is its focus on the creative people themselves rather than on the products of their actions. For example, an interminable and frustrating meeting of public health administrators was given welcome comic relief when one participant summarized their miseries in a country-style song that he had constructed almost entirely from fragments of previous conversation. A moment later there was no "product"; the song had vanished with its one rendition. However, all the participants could hear for themselves how the themes and follies of their deliberations had been interwoven and put into perspective.

In this and in many other instances, the creative person has attended more carefully than others to passing words, events, and actions, selected those that showed some promise, and engaged in symbolic manipulations that brought these diverse elements together in a new way. Generally, the creative process involves an unusually fresh and keen awareness of what has been going on, along with a sense of freedom in manipulating these elements and giving them a new form and direction. A person who is behaving creatively is also more likely to try out several approaches to a situation rather than responding immediately with the first thought or action that comes to mind:

> Problem finders explore extensively before committing themselves to a direction, remain open to new directions, and resist viewing a work as finished. Problem finding promotes creativity specifically by downrating the weight of precedent and prior thought. (Perkins, 1988, p. 324)

Keen vision and hearing as such do not necessarily guarantee that the person will use these skills creatively. It has also been found repeatedly that neither normal nor superior intelligence automatically lends itself to creativity. Many adults are masters of the predictable and routine situation. They can also cope well with many problems and challenges by calling upon their own past experiences or the accumulated knowledge and opinion in their field. Nevertheless, even a mind that can deal with many facts in a highly competent manner may not come up with new ideas or insights. Whatever the creative process might be, it is not the relentless grinding of the mental mill, using the same stone to pound the same grain into the same flour.

Because intelligence alone does not guarantee creativity, some observers believe that personality is a critical factor. Carl C. Jung's (1933) theory of personal growth throughout the entire lifespan suggests that creativity is liberated when we become ready and willing to give our neglected inner potentials the opportunity for expression. The person who continues to shackle significant aspects of his or her personality in order to present a conformist face to the world will be neither a whole nor a creative person. In this view, the creative process must be nurtured by a personality that is free to explore and take risks.

The creative process/personality approach has become increasingly attractive to those who advocate lifelong learning, development, and self-actualization. It is somewhat more problematical, however, for behavioral scientists, who prefer to work with clear, nonambiguous, and quantifiable material. We cannot simply count the number of compositions, paintings, or scientific publications; instead we must deal with all the complexities and obscurities of what takes place within the individual's mind in the intricate process of moving from idea to "product."

Another alternative approach to creativity is even more difficult to define. Creativity could be considered to be the most distinctive human contribution, especially as it discovers, constructs, or affirms *meaning*. Humans have transformed the environment to suit themselves and have constructed symbolic systems that have been given such names as faith, belief, logic, and language. Long before they reach adulthood, people have already invested even the simplest of their actions with values and meanings. Certain foods may be considered taboo for religious reasons, for example, or certain parts of our own bodies may be considered "dangerous" or "naughty."

Many people spend much of their lives under the spell of whatever meanings have already been created by past generations. Sooner or later, however, individuals may find themselves in situations that raise questions about the prevailing values and meanings. These situations have arisen with increasing frequency in our own times with the interaction of people holding a variety of beliefs and the successive waves of technological change that challenge many traditional meanings.

"How could people do this to each other?" is an example of the crises in meaning that have arisen repeatedly during the remarkable violence that has characterized the twentieth century. "How could it come to this?" is another question posed by some people who have followed the established rules throughout their lives and now, in old age, find themselves excluded, abandoned, and characterized as "burdens" whose well-being is no longer "cost effective."

Individuals and groups, then, may be called upon to exercise their creativity in order to make sense of and reconstruct value in a world that can appear as disorderly, indifferent, and brutal. This is a far cry from creativity as a secondary leisure-time puttering around; it represents instead the urgent need to generate or regenerate meanings that one can live with, whether in youth, mid-life, or old age. This form or context of creativity has been the least adequately studied, but there is abundant material to work with in biographies and autobiographies, which is to say in the lives of people who have responded to the challenge of creative meaning-making (e.g., Berman, 1991; Berman & Goldman, 1992; Carlsen, 1991a, 1991b).

Major Research Findings

Most studies have focused on creativity as a product, although the variety of approaches is now increasing and includes efforts to explore the personal and contextual dimensions as well as the product. The following summary concentrates on findings that help us to understand the developmental course of creativity through the adult years.

1. *Creative productivity reaches its peak in the early adult years.* This finding, which many studies support (as reviewed, e.g., by Kastenbaum, 1992; Simonton, 1990), is most convincing with respect to the number of identifiable products. If we imagine artists, mathematicians, and scientists as laborers on an assembly line, their "output" will be highest before age 40 (in some domains, before 30).

2. *The peak for "product output" comes at different ages for different domains of activity.* Pure mathematics, theoretical physics, lyric poetry, and musical composition are fields in which accomplishment often comes early, with outstanding contributors often having made their mark in their twenties. Novelists, philosophers, historians, and others whose achievements seem to require more life experience and sense of perspective are among those who reach peaks later in their lives, usually around the late forties.

   Perhaps certain types of creative talent can be expressed early in life because they are relatively self-contained. Music and mathematics are examples. Other creative activities require the ability to integrate information from a variety of fields, appreciate the nuances and levels of human experience, and exercise judgment when no clear guideposts exist. These differences may explain why child prodigies are seldom encountered in historical scholarship.

3. *The quality ratio of creative products does not change with age.* Simonton (1990) has found that "Those periods in a creator's life that see the most masterpieces also witness the most easily forgotten productions, on the average" (p. 323). This finding implies that composers, for example, will have more "hits" in early adulthood because they are turning out more pieces. But in their later adult years the odds that their next symphony or opera will be a masterpiece are about the same as they were previously even though fewer works are produced.

4. *There are marked individual differences in the pattern of creativity across the lifespan.* What has already been described is the overall picture. Individual artists or scientists have distinctly different patterns. Perhaps the most obvious difference is attributable to longevity; the operas composed by Verdi in his old age cannot be compared with those of his friend Donizetti because the latter died young. Less obvious but fairly well demonstrated is the tendency for those who have been prolific when young to remain prolific when in their later adult years.

These first four findings come from studies in which creative products have been examined within a quantitative frame of reference (sometimes in quite a sophisticated manner; e.g., Simonton, 1980). Taken together, they indicate that both general and individual principles should be recognized. People tend to produce more creative products in youth, with the domain of creative endeavor having an important bearing on when the peak output occurs. There is little uniformity, however, regarding the age at which the most original, profound, or memorable products are created. In other words, we cannot dismiss the possibility of significant creativity in an aged person or assume that significant creativity will happen as a matter of course in a young person. Furthermore—and here we start to approach the biographical / qualitative area of research—it is often more useful to know just who the person is rather than to know his or her age.

The best predictor for continued creativity in the later adult years (given continued survival) seems to be that person's lifelong pattern of accomplishment.

Biographical and other qualitatively oriented studies offer observations that can stimulate and enrich our approach to creativity throughout the adult years, even though the findings seldom can be readily generalized and confirmed. The following statements are best regarded as viable hypotheses that are based on but not definitely proven by available observations.

5. *Cultures can encourage or discourage creativity at all age levels.* There is distressing evidence, for example, that deprivations and adverse experiences in primary education can stifle or distort creativity in childhood. In the past, this trend has often been attributed to inflexible and inappropriate attitudes that attempted to "beat education" into children rather than helping them explore themselves and the world in a natural and pleasurable manner. Today, however, the more daunting problem has to do with the overall quality of the educational experience, especially for racial and ethnic minorities (e.g., Kozol, 1991).

On the other end of the spectrum, cultural stereotypes known as "ageism" (Palmore, 1990) have portrayed elderly men and women as used up and useless. Vigorous creativity would be about the last thing that American society would expect from its elders. This negative expectation—or "nonexpectation"—can discourage older adults from creative activities, especially if they have not already established a lifelong pattern in this direction.

Fortunately, there are also well-documented examples of cultural traditions within which creativity is considered to be a core component of the aging experience. The late Renaldo Maduro (1974, 1980) reported a high level of creativity among elderly men in Northern India and explained how this activity is supported by the Hindu philosophical tradi-

tion. Becoming an ever more accomplished artist is intimately related to becoming an ever more spiritualized and developed human being. This does not mean that all people continue to develop personally and artistically with advancing age; it is easier to fail than to succeed in these challenges. However, the key point is that the creative and spiritual development of the aging person is regarded as an expression and culmination of basic cultural values—as distinct from the "worn-out machine" concept that is often still applied to the elders in the U.S.

6. *Creative and personal renewal is a possibility for many if not all individuals in the later adult years.* Freedom from obligations associated with the workplace or family can open the way to discovering or rediscovering potentials that had been laid aside years ago. Some people may have surrendered their deepest interests and liveliest enthusiasms to earn a steady salary or raise a growing family. Now, in their still vigorous sixties, seventies, or beyond they are often able to come back to these interests as a competent adult who has a better idea of how to do things effectively. Other people may have come to a period of stagnation in middle adulthood, perhaps associated with stress, depression, and disturbing life events. A new friendship, a turn of good fortune, or an inner process of healing and resolution may result in a rebirth of enthusiasm and creativity. The person who seemed "old and used up" at 60 may be vibrant and creative at 70.

7. *The construction or reconstruction of meanings can make it possible for the aging person to experience life fully to the very end and provide an invaluable model for others.* Two famous examples reveal a previously unsuspected "secret" of survival. In his old age, Tennyson had become the very image of the poet and of the British literary establishment; even people with no taste for poetry liked to wear a Tennysonian cape and try to capture his lofty and mysterious "look" (actually

nearsightedness). And in his old age, Picasso was admired for his "animal energy," passion for life, and unpredictability, even by those who were repelled by his later creations. People edging into their own later adult years could sense that Tennyson and Picasso each had a faith or meaning that gave his life direction. As it turns out, both Tennyson and Picasso went through very difficult and surprisingly comparable situations in their youth and had reason to doubt whether they could or should go on (Kastenbaum, 1989). Each turned to his respective art. Tennyson created a gallery of old men in his poetry, and Picasso did so in his Blue Period paintings. The troubled young men created their old men to serve as their own models and guides for the rest of their long journeys through the lifespan. When Old Tennyson and Old Picasso became models for others, they were themselves actualizing the life-saving future selves they had envisioned in their youth.

Investing or reinvesting life with meaning can occur in old age as well as in youth. The most perceptive and vital people often discover new depths in their lives and in the world as they achieve the perspective granted by age. They also tend to make a new creation of each day. Author May Sarton, for example, describes how she has several new days every day, e.g., a day in the garden with her animals, a writing day, a meditation day, and an involvement-with-the-world day (in Berman & Goldman, 1992, pp. 233-38). She also observes: "I suppose my whole life could be defined as an acute conflict between art and life, between what art asks and what life asks. The conflict is what keeps you alive" (p. 237).

There is no one way to live creatively throughout the adult years. Some focus on their own self-development, some on relationships with other people. And some, like Hokusai, feel that self and society are perhaps too confining and seek instead a communion with the universe at large. He created his own goal of *becoming his art* and

having his art become a part of the natural world ("and at one hundred and ten, every dot and every stroke will be as though alive"). Hokusai is perhaps for most of us an example too extreme to emulate, a person who almost defines and develops himself out of ordinary existence through his creative activity, becoming almost a fairy tale or mythic universal character.

If there is no one path for all to follow in creative development through the adult years, there may be a unique path for all individuals to discover for themselves.

▼ Robert Kastenbaum

See also: Conflict as a Challenge in Adult Development; Development and Aging in Historical Perspective; Expressive Arts; Fairy Tales as Commentary on Adult Development and Aging; Grandparent Communication Skills; Grandparent Education to Enhance Family Strength; Habituation: A Key to Lifespan Development and Aging?; Individuality; Information Processing; Interethnic Relationships; Japanese Perspectives on Adult Development; Life Events; Maturity; Spiritual Development and Wisdom: A Vendantic Perspective; Stress.

References

Berman, H. J. (1991). From the pages of my life. *Generations, 15:* 33-40.

Berman, P. L., & Goldman, C. (1992). *The Ageless Spirit.* New York: Ballantine.

Carlsen, M. B. (1991a). *Creative Meaning-Making.* New York: Norton.

———. (1991b). *Creative Aging: A Meaning-Making Perspective.* New York: Norton.

Jung, C. G. (1933). *Modern Man in Search of a Soul.* New York: Harcourt, Brace.

Kastenbaum, R. (1989). Old men created by young artists: Time-transcendence in Tennyson & Picasso. *International Journal of Aging & Human Development, 28:* 81-104.

———. (1992). The creative process: A lifespan approach. In T. Cole, D. D. Van Tassel, & R. Kastenbaum (Eds.), *Handbook of the Humanities and Aging.* New York: Springer, pp. 285-306.

Kozol, J. (1991). *Savage Inequalities.* New York: Crown.

Maduro, R. (1974). The old man as a creative artist in India. *International Journal of Aging & Human Development, 5:* 303-29.

———. (1980). Symbolic equations in creative process: Reflections on Hindu India. *Journal of Analytic Psychology, 25:* 59-90.

Palmore, E. (1990). *Ageism: Negative and Positive.* New York: Springer.

Perkins, D. N. (1988). Creativity and the quest for mechanism. In R. J. Sternberg & E. D. Smith (Eds.), *The Psychology of Human Thought.* Cambridge: Cambridge University Press, pp. 309-36.

Simonton, D. K. (1980). Thematic fame, melodic originality, and musical Zeitgeist: A biographical and transhistorical content analysis. *Journal of Personality & Social Psychology, 38:* 972-83.

———. (1990). Creativity and wisdom in aging. In J. E. Birren & K. W. Schaie (Eds.), *Handbook of the Psychology of Aging.* Third Edition. San Diego: Academic Press, pp. 320-29.

Smith, H. (Ed.). (1988). *Hokusai: One Hundred Views of Mt. Fuji.* New York: George Braziller.

CRIMINAL BEHAVIOR

Although the inverse (negative) correlation between age and crime is among the oldest and most robust findings in criminology, the study of criminal behavior across the life course has made very limited progress. Some of the difficulty is inherent in any study of a behavior as deviant as crime. Officially reported crime represents some unknown proportion of all crime. The number of crimes actually committed is significantly larger than indicated by the official statistics, although how much larger cannot be said with any certainty. Victimization surveys and self-report surveys of criminal activity do show age distributions similar to the officially reported aggregate crime statistics. Nevertheless, what is known as the "dark number" problem (Wiles, 1971) remains and may especially affect the study of crime across the lifespan. It is not known, for example, whether the convergent age distributions for official statistics, self-report surveys, and victimization surveys for young persons also hold true for older persons. Older persons most often commit crimes such as gambling, employee theft, embezzlement, and other "white collar" offenses, while teenagers and young adults tend toward such crimes as burglary, larceny, and robbery.

Crime has been little studied in a lifespan perspective, in part because of the very strength of the inverse relationship between age and crime (Cline, 1980). Most of what is known about the relation between age and crime is based on aggregate or group-level data investigated as a set of synchronic causes and interactions. Relatively little research has been designed to investigate criminal activity as a set of diachronic interactions: a complex process occurring across time and using the lifespan as a unit of analysis. Indeed, some researchers consider such designs to be of dubious value. In recent years, a very brisk debate has taken place over the Hirschi and Gottfredson (1983) thesis of an invariance in the age-crime relationship across offenses, time periods, and gender (Cohen & Land, 1987; Greenberg, 1985; Hirschi & Gottfredson, 1985; Shavit & Rattner, 1988; Steffensmeier & Streifel, 1991; Steffensmeier et al., 1989). Hirschi and Gottfredson (1983) have argued that cohort or other longitudinal designs are essentially irrelevant, contending that the identification of the causes of crime at *any* age will disclose those causes for *all* ages. Since much of what knowledge we do have about criminal activity across the lifespan has been gleaned from longitudinal studies, this debate has important implications for lifespan research.

Age and Crime in Industrial Society

If crime is partly a matter of opportunity, then youth has more than its share: the aged cannot very well snatch a gold chain and run off down the street. Another hypothesis is that the age-crime relationship owes something to the very characteristics of young people, particularly physical strength and agility. We find, however, that criminal activity is not as massively concentrated upon young people in less developed countries even though their youth are no less strong and agile.

Industrialization markedly concentrates the mass of common criminal activity among the young. Considered over the course of the twentieth century, the peak age of criminal participation, especially for low-return property crimes, has shifted to younger and younger persons (Christie, 1974; Greenberg, 1977).

Taken as a whole, criminal activity peaks in the teen years and declines rapidly thereafter. For example, in 1980, 18 was the peak age for all arrests across 20 offense categories (Steffensmeier et al., 1989; U.S. Federal Bureau of Investigation, 1985). The peak age was even younger for the most common property crimes: 16 for burglary, auto theft, and larceny, and 17 for robbery.

The fall-off is precipitous: 75 percent of all arrests for burglary in 1980 occurred among people under age 25 (Steffensmeier et al., 1989). The corresponding figures for auto theft, larceny, and robbery were 26, 32, and 28, respectively. Violent crime peaked several years later and fell off more slowly, but also showed a heavy concentration in the early stages of the lifespan.

Although some criminologists maintain that the age-crime relationship does not change over time (Hirschi & Gottfredson, 1983), the data do not seem to bear this out (Christie, 1974; Steffensmeier & Streifel, 1991; Steffensmeier et al., 1989). For most crimes, *the tendency in the United States is for younger and younger people to account for more and more of the transgressions, including violent crimes like homicide* (Cohen & Land, 1987). The peak age for all those arrested in 1980 was younger than in 1960, and the peak age in 1960 was younger than in 1940. The median age of all those arrested was 29 in 1940 and 30 in 1960. By 1980, it had fallen to 25 (Steffensmeier et al., 1989).

Major Theoretical Problems

Four major theoretical problems regarding crime emerge from the lifespan perspective. The first is why so many people are involved in delinquency in their early teens—or even before—and then, as far we can tell, largely cease criminal involvement as they grow older. When and why do so many people commit minor crimes in their early adolescence but do not do so later as well? Even for persons with marked antisocial propensities, middle adulthood usually brings an end to their public criminal careers. As part of its definition of those diagnosed as "anti-social personalities," the American Psychiatric Association *Diagnostic and Statistical Manual of Mental Disorders* (1980) concludes that even for them, criminal involvement tends to fall away in their thirties.

This pattern raises a second and distinct problem: when and why people who commit crimes as adolescents or young adults desist. Far more has been written about youthful entry into crime than about this later, staggered but massive exit from criminal participation.

Third, for those who continue some type of criminal involvement, what types of progressions occur? Here we need to distinguish so-called "career criminals," sometimes called habitual offenders, from "criminal careers" (Blumstein et al., 1986). *Career criminals* refers to those who identify with crime as a means of earning a living (Shover, 1985) and who, for major portions of their early and middle adulthood, pursue crime as a vocation. *Criminal careers* refers to the different shapes or trajectories that criminal participation may take throughout the lifespan. These can include intermittent, interrupted, or "retired" patterns of criminal activity, and they apply also to people for whom crime is a relatively unimportant part of their identity or vocational life. Within the variety of criminal careers we may ask what types of progression take place. Under what conditions do people begin with less serious property crime and move to more serious property or violent crime? Is there a progression from common street crime to more "mainstream" offenses (e.g., employee theft and tax cheating)? By contrast, do some careers move from high-risk to low-risk offenses?

Fourth and finally, who starts late? When and why do some people apparently commit crimes only later in life? To what extent do the early development histories of these criminal "late bloomers" mirror the histories of their contemporaries who become involved in crime in youth and desist in middle and later adulthood?

There is a good deal of research on the first problem and some on the second, but very little on the third and fourth. Viewed in a life course perspective, the most common pattern is never to have been arrested as a juvenile, young adult, or older adult (Cline, 1980). The most common "criminal career" is to have committed property crimes in one's youth and never to have been arrested again.

In this regard, criminal activity does not stand alone. As Robins (1980, p. 37) has written: "All common forms of deviance (drug use, theft, drinking, sexual promiscuity, fighting) seem to drop off with age, whether or not they have been labelled and whether or not their being labelled eventuated in intervention in the form of treatment or punishment." This is especially true of forms of deviance that bring risk or require physically demanding behavior (Gove, 1985). That much criminal behavior would taper off as we age makes sense. It stands to reason that the very young lack and the old have lost the strength and speed to commit most petty thefts or acts of vandalism. But what requires explanation is just how precipitous the drop is. Men in their late twenties can physically manage much of what they could in their mid-teens, however, their incidence of criminal participation is radically lower.

Some researchers have attributed this change to a process of psychological maturation in which age brings a greater need for social approval and a corresponding desire to behave in a socially reinforced manner (Gove, 1985; Jolin & Gibbons, 1987).

Traditional sociological explanations emphasize two other kinds of variables. The first set is composed of life course variables such as school, employment and career choice, marriage, and the formation of families. These tend to give young adults a greater stake in social conformity. Growing social status and economic self-sufficiency remove some of the reasons for youth crime. One's stake in the social order grows, and the risks entailed in challenging it—through crime, politics, or deviant subcultures—rise accordingly. In economic terms, the opportunity costs from continued criminal involvement go up, not least in terms of future earning power.

More Severe Penalties

The second set of variables concern the penalties associated with crime. These rise sharply with age. In English common law, children under age 7 are conclusively presumed to lack any criminal capacity and are therefore held blameless. Those between 7 and 14 are still presumed to lack that capacity, although this presumption can be refuted at trial (Moore, 1984). All other things being equal—such as social class, race, and the nature of the offense—there is a very sharp rise in the severity of penalties in the transition from adolescence to young adulthood. The sanctions against crime increase in harshness until we near the end of the life course.

In early adolescence, the possible consequences for anything but the most serious crimes of violence are rather insignificant. The typical acts of early adolescent delinquency (e.g., vandalism, minor thefts) present little social cost for each occurrence (although the cumulative social cost is, of course, quite great). Because of the sheer volume of such acts, society invests comparatively little in protecting against each individual occurrence or in apprehending the perpetrator. As a consequence, the chances of getting caught for any single delinquent act are slim. Social authorities—from parents to police to juvenile justices—tend to excuse some youthful delinquency as being part of normal adolescence. A far larger percentage of youth crime is therefore not reported in comparison with adult crime, and even when the youthful offender is caught, the admonishments and sanctions that follow often take place in informal ways that do not come to the attention of juvenile justice agencies.

As offenders enter and move through adulthood, neither the public nor the law and its agencies continue to take such a lenient view. Victims become more likely to report the crime, police to make an arrest, district attorneys to seek a criminal prosecution, and judges to punish. The protective shelter of adolescence is withdrawn, the offender is held responsible for his or her actions, and punitive sanctions are applied. As the costs of crime rise, aging offenders drop out of low-return criminal activity (Shover, 1985).

Aging Criminals

Both maturational and life course variables bear on another reason for abandoning criminal careers, namely, that it becomes increasingly difficult to deal with the stress of being punished—and aging criminals can get punished a lot. The risks and costs associated with crime extend to older career criminals (Cusson & Pinsonneault, 1986; Meisenhelder, 1977). Even among professional thieves—where the assumption might be that age carries with it greater expertise—age often brings with it inefficiency and fear, points made by Sutherland (1937) in his classic study, *The Professional Thief.* The Rand study of habitual offenders (Petersilia, Greenwood, & Lavin, 1978), conducted with a group of California prisoners, showed that the likelihood of arrest, conviction, and imprisonment increased with age.

The aging process that makes it more difficult to commit crimes requiring physical prowess also makes it more difficult to deal with the criminal subculture. It becomes increasingly difficult for older offenders to get by in prison. Studies of prisoner suicide, for example, suggest that the trauma of incarceration may worsen with age.

The convict world is increasingly a youth-oriented culture. Its normative values are those of youth, and it esteems the attributes of youth: slightly unpredictable and impulsive action, physical courage, ritual challenging, and, above all, physical strength (Sykes, 1958). Correctional institutions today are also far more violent than they were in earlier generations (Irwin, 1980). Older inmates are out of their depth in these youthful and menacing environments, and they fare increasingly poorly (Cardozo-Freeman, 1984; Shover, 1985).

Although overall arrest rates drop steeply for persons in their thirties and are very low for people over 40, this general pattern breaks down for particular offenses. If the aging process tends to close off some criminal opportunities, it can also bring others. For example, teenagers are seldom in a position to embezzle substantial sums, and one has to be old enough to form a family in order to start abusing them. Different types of criminal behavior peak at different ages. For example, those arrested in 1980 for embezzlement, fraud, and gambling had median ages of 28, 30, and 39, respectively, after which rates of participation leveled off or declined slowly with age (Steffensmeier et al., 1989). A few types of crime show peaks of participation in middle age (e.g., drunk driving), while involvement in certain other illegal activities continues largely unabated from the thirties to 50 and beyond (e.g., gambling and drunkenness).

Not only do we know little about "new criminals"—those who have not been arrested as juveniles or young adults—but we also know very little about the crimes of the affluent—the Leona Helmsleys, Ivan Boeskys, Pete Roses, and Charles Keatings, to take some representative criminals of the present time. We know that the looting of savings and loan associations was accomplished by middle-aged and older adults. Did their earlier delinquency go undetected? What contributes to later decisions to undertake criminal pursuits? Conversely, is "stock shrinkage" (the delightful insurance-driven euphemism for employee theft) disproportionately a function of delinquents who grew up or, indeed, do all employees steal and do so equally?

Women and Crime

Virtually every type of crime is committed most frequently by men. The exception is prostitution, an activity for which societal attitudes and age-old enforcement practices hold those selling their sexual services criminally responsible.

For a broad spectrum of crimes in 1980, men accounted for 84 percent of those arrested; in violent crimes, the ratio grew to 90 percent males to 10 percent females (Siegel, 1983). Among those arrested in 1985 for 19 index offenses collected in the Uniform Crime Reports, men outnumbered women decisively in all age groups reported (Table 1).

Even these ratios are misleading, since they include violations of sexual mores and other public order offenses. Among those arrested for prostitution in 1985, women outnumbered men by a ratio of three to one in the age groups in which most prostitution arrests are concentrated (those under 30). But the sex ratio was reversed for prostitution arrests of those 40 to 49, and stood at almost seven men to every woman for those 50 and older. This pattern reflects men's participation as procurers, pimps, and solicitors of sexual services throughout adulthood at ages when women tend to lose their marketability as sexual commodities (Chesney-Lind, 1986; Steffensmeier & Streifel, 1991).

By contrast, men outnumber women by ratios of at least 9 or 10 to 1 for the most common property crimes, such as auto theft, burglary, and robbery. Among common low-return property crimes, only in arrests for larceny do women represent more than 25 percent of criminal offenders. As for crimes against persons, the participation of women is either relatively small or negligible. Men

outnumber women at more than 5 to 1 in homicides (Dunn, 1977), and child molestation by women is still so rare that it tends to make sensational newspaper headlines (Barnard et al., 1989).

Recent decades have seen a significant increase in the rate of arrests for women that surpasses the rate increase for men's arrests. A number of researchers have concluded that, as women's rate of participation in the labor force rises, so will their rates of criminal participation (Adler, 1975; Simon, 1976, 1977). Like rising divorce rates, increased criminal activity by women has been dumped at the feet of the women's movement. Supposedly, the movement for equality has led women out of the kitchen and through other people's jimmied windows. For at least two decades it has been routinely hypothesized that the growing social equality of women with men brings with it striking shifts in the percentages of women involved in crime, and that with the women's movement a fast approaching parity in arrest rates looms (Deming, 1977; Weis, 1976).

The increase in the proportion of women arrested does appear real, rather than simply a function of changes in enforcement practices. Nevertheless, male supremacy remains substantially unchallenged in the domain of crime with the exception of sex-related public order offenses and possibly certain other crimes whose dimensions are still not very well known (shoplifting and employee theft). Although the rates of increase for arrests of women are greater than those for men, Steffensmeier (1980) has pointed out that the small numbers mean that even moderate absolute increases bring large percentage changes. The absolute numbers of men arrested have grown, and *the absolute gap between the numbers of men and women arrested has also grown* (Steffensmeier, 1980). Official arrest statistics and self-report surveys of criminal activity continue to indicate that the suggested relationship between the women's movement and crime is essentially a myth.

That women's criminal activity peaks later in the lifespan and declines more slowly than that of men was long a staple of classical

Table 1. Arrested Offenders by Sex and Age (1985)

Age Group	Ratio of Males to Females
10-19	4 to 1
20-29	5 to 1
30-39	5 to 1
40-49	6 to 1
50+	8 to 1

Based on data reported by D.J. Steffensmeier and C. Streifel, "Age, Gender and Crime across Three Historical Periods: 1935, 1960, and 1985." *Social Forces,* 69 (1991): 869-94.

criminology. The theory goes that, as people age, the gender roles of women become diffuse. The decline of certain nurturant, other-directed role behavior is thought to stimulate entry into male domains, including criminal activity (Farrington, 1986; Leonard, 1982; Sutherland & Cressey, 1978). In this view, women should therefore make up a growing percentage of criminal offenders in older age groups. The trouble with this theory is that it does not appear to be supported by contemporary empirical evidence, although some research in the first half of the century suggested a later entry into crime for women than for men. At the present time the peak ages and the median ages for criminal participation for most offenses, and the shape of the age distribution curve, are strikingly similar for men and women (Steffensmeier & Streifel, 1991).

Conclusion

A social policy crisis—and, increasingly, a fiscal one—drive the research agenda for criminal activity across the life course. We live in the age of the second "Great Confinement" (Cohen, 1979), a period that is characterized by an historically unprecedented rise not only in the numbers of federal, state, and county prisoners, but also in the rate of incarceration. The United States currently practices a higher rate of incarceration than any other advanced industrial nation, and it incarcerates people for longer periods of time (Currie, 1985). Prisoners 50 and older represent the fastest growing segment of the current prison population.

This extraordinary expansion in prisons, prisoners, and prison guards takes place at enormous social and financial cost. Among our announced national goals, there is no more obvious failure than the two decades-long pursuit of "law and order" through ever more draconian punishment.

The study of crime across the lifespan can tell us something about the "natural courses" of criminal careers, about the moments when deterrence of future crime, or incapacitation, counts and when it no longer

matters. There are diverse models of criminal careers, of the decisions that embark or sustain people on those careers at different stages of the life course, and, most especially, of the decisions that bring those careers to a close. One size cell and one size sentence do not fit all. Unless and until we consider the lives within the life of crime, too many of those lives will be wasted.   ▼ Joel Haycock

See also: Cohort and Generational Effects; Disengagement Theory; Driving: A Lifespan Challenge; Gender as a Shaping Force in Adult Development and Aging; Gender Differences in the Workplace; Stress; Subcultural Influences on Lifelong Development; Suicide.

References

Adler, F. (1975). *Sisters in Crime*. New York: McGraw-Hill.

American Psychiatric Association (1980). *Diagnostic and Statistical Manual of Mental Disorders*. Third Edition. Washington, DC: American Psychiatric Association.

Barnard, G. W., et al. (1989). *The Child Molester: An Integrated Approach to Evaluation and Treatment*. New York: Brunner/Mazel.

Blumstein, A., et al. (1986). *Criminal Careers and "Career Criminals."* 2 vols. Washington, DC: National Academy Press.

Cardozo-Freeman, I. (1984). *The Joint. Language and Culture in a Maximum Security Prison*. Springfield, IL: Charles C. Thomas.

Chesney-Lind, M. (1986). Women and crime: The female offender. *Signs: Journal of Women in Culture and Society, 12*: 78-96.

Christie, N. (1974). Criminological Data as Indicators on Contemporary Society. In *Crime of Industrialization*. Stockholm: Scandanavian Research Council for Criminology, pp. 144-88.

Clausen, J. (1986). *The Life Course: A Sociological Explanation*. Englewood Cliffs, NJ: Prentice-Hall.

Cline, H. F. (1980). Criminal behavior over the life span. In O. G. Brim, Jr. & J. Kagan (Eds.), *Consistency and Change in Human Development*. Cambridge, MA: Harvard University Press, pp. 642-74.

Cohen, L. E., & Land, K. C. (1987). Age structure and crime: Symmetry versus asymmetry and the projection of crime rates through the 1990s. *American Sociological Review, 52*: 170-83.

Cohen, S. (1979). The punitive city: Notes on the dispersal of social control. *Contemporary Crises, 3:* 333-63.

Cressey, D. (1971). *Other People's Money.* Belmont, CA: Wadsworth.

Currie, E. (1985). *Confronting Crime.* New York: Pantheon Books.

Cusson, M., & Pinsonneault, P. (1986). The decision to give up crime. In D. Cornish & R. Clarke (Eds.), *The Reasoning Criminal: Rational Choice Perspectives on Offending.* New York: Springer-Verlag, pp. 72-82.

Deming, R. (1977). *Women: The New Criminals.* Nashville: Thomas Nelson.

Dunn, C. (1977). *The Patterns and Distribution of Assault Incident Characteristics among Social Areas.* Washington, DC: U.S. Department of Justice, Law Enforcement Assistance Administration.

Farrington, D. (1986). Age and crime. In M. Tonry & N. Morris (Eds.), *Crime and Justice: An Annual Review of Research.* Chicago: University of Chicago Press, pp. 189-250.

Gove, W. R. (1985). The effects of age and gender on deviant behavior: A biopsychosocial perspective. In A. S. Rossi (Ed.), *Gender and the Life Course.* Chicago: Aldine, pp. 115-44.

Greenberg, D. F. (1977). Delinquency and the age structure of society. *Contemporary Crises, 1:* 189-223.

———. (1985). Age, crime, and social explanation. *American Journal of Sociology, 91:* 1-21.

Haycock, J. (1991). Crimes and misdemeanors: A review of recent research on suicides in prison. *Omega, 23:* 81-94.

Hirschi, T., & Gottfredson, M. (1983). Age and the explanation of crime. *American Journal of Sociology, 89:* 552-84.

———. (1985). Age and crime, logic and scholarship: Comment on Greenberg. *American Journal of Sociology, 91:* 22-27.

Irwin, J. (1980). *Prisons in Turmoil.* Boston: Little, Brown.

Jolin, A., & Gibbons, D. C. (1987). Age patterns in criminal involvement. *International Journal of Offender Therapy and Comparative Criminology, 31:* 237-60.

Leonard, E. (1982). *Women, Crime, and Society.* New York: Longman.

Matza, D. (1964). *Delinquency and Drift.* New York: Wiley.

McCarthy, B., & Langworthy, R. (Eds.). (1988). *Older Offenders: Perspectives in Criminology and Criminal Justice.* New York: Praeger.

Meisenhelder, T. (1977). An exploratory study of exiting from criminal careers. *Criminology,* 15: 319-34.

Moore, M. S. (1984). *Law and Psychiatry.* Cambridge: Cambridge University Press.

Petersilia, J. (1980). Criminal career research: A review of recent evidence. In N. Morris & M. Tonry (Eds.), *Crime and Justice: An Annual Review of Research.* Chicago: University of Chicago Press.

Petersilia, J., Greenwood, P. W., & Lavin, M. (1978). *Criminal Habits of Habitual Felons.* Washington, DC: U.S. Government Printing Office.

Robins, L. (1980). Alcoholism and labelling theory. In W. Gove (Ed.), *The Labelling of Deviance.* Beverly Hills, CA: Sage, pp. 35-47.

Rowe, A., & Tittle, C. (1977). Life cycle changes and criminal propensity. *The Sociological Quarterly, 18:* 223-36.

Runyan, W. M. (1982). *Life Histories and Psychobiography.* Oxford: Oxford University Press.

Shavit, Y., & Rattner, A. (1988). Age, crime and the early life course. *American Journal of Sociology, 93:* 1457-70.

Shover, N. (1985). *Aging Criminals.* Beverly Hills, CA: Sage.

Siegel, L. J. (1983). *Criminology.* St. Paul, MN: West Publishing Co.

Simon, R. J. (1976). American Women and Crime. *Annuals of the American Academy of Political and Social Science, 423:* 31-46.

———. (1977). *Women and Crime.* Lexington, MA: D. C. Heath.

Steffensmeier, D. J. (1980). Sex differences in patterns of adult crimes, 1965-1977: A review and assessment. *Social Forces, 58:* 1080-1108.

———. (1986). *The Fence: In the Shadow of Two Worlds.* Totowa, NJ: Rowman & Littlefield.

Steffensmeier, D. J., & Streifel, C. (1991). Age, gender and crime across three historical periods: 1935, 1960, and 1985. *Social Forces, 69:* 869-94.

Steffensmeier, D. J., et al. (1989). Age and the distribution of crime. *American Journal of Sociology, 94:* 803-31.

Sutherland, E. H. (1937). *The Professional Thief.* Chicago: University of Chicago Press.

Sutherland, E. H., & Cressey, D. R. (1978). *Criminology.* Tenth Edition. New York: Lippincott.

Sykes, G. M. (1958). *The Society of Captives: A Study of Maximum Security Prison.* Princeton, NJ: Princeton University Press.

U.S. Federal Bureau of Investigation. (1985). *Uniform Crime Reports.* Washington, DC: U.S. Government Printing Office.

Walters, G. D. (1990). *The Criminal Lifestyle*. Newbury Park, CA: Sage.

Weis, J. G. (1976). Liberation and crime: The invention of the new female criminal. *Crime and Social Justice, 3:* 17-27.

Wiles, P. (1971). Criminal statistics and sociological explanations of crime. In W. G. Carson & P. Wiles (Eds.), *Crime and Delinquency in Britain*. London: Martin Robertson, pp. 174-92.

Wolfgang, M. E., Figlio, R., & Sellin, T. (1972). *Delinquency in a Birth Cohort*. Chicago: University of Chicago Press.

D

DEPRESSION

For most people, the word *depression* is linked to personal experiences of feeling sad, unhappy, blue, down-in-the dumps, or the like. Indeed, occasional feelings of emotional depression are part and parcel of living. The capacity to feel depressed is part of a biological heritage that has endowed human beings with emotional reactivity to events in their lives and to those around them. People vary, however, in how often and how strongly they experience depression. For some, feelings of depression are not mild and occasional but are profound and disabling and continue for extended periods of time.

Many studies have been devoted to understanding what depression is, what causes it, how frequently people experience it, whether it is more common at particular points in adult development, and how it should be treated.

What Is Depression?

Depression is most commonly thought of as a state of feeling, but it can also refer to mental health problems that are so severe or long-lasting that they require professional attention. Such conditions are known as *clinical depression*. Clinically depressed individuals almost always experience depressed feelings, but may also undergo changes in the way they think, act, and view the world and themselves. It is as if depression has taken on a life of its own—perhaps comparable to weather's tropical depressions that develop into potentially devastating hurricanes.

A set of guidelines for distinguishing between the usual feelings of depression that most adults experience now and then and clinical depression is offered in the *Diagnostic and Statistical Manual of Mental Disorders* (referred to as *DSM-III-R* because it is a revision of the third edition of the manual; American Psychiatric Association, 1987). Two diagnostic categories represent the most serious kinds of depression: *major depressive episode* and *dysthymia*.

Major depressive episode (henceforth referred to as major depression) is the most severe type of depression. Changes may include feelings of depression and worthlessness, loss of interest in usual activities, problems in concentrating, and thoughts of death or suicide. Perhaps most characteristic of major depression, besides depressed mood, are physical or physiological changes in appetite, weight, sleep, energy, and activity level. Less commonly, persons who are severely depressed may experience delusions (believe things that are not true) or hallucinations (see or hear things that do not exist).

Major depression may come on suddenly or it may develop more gradually, emerging from milder feelings of depression. Once a major depression develops, it may last for weeks, months, or, in rare cases, years. Even without mental health treatment the "episode" of major depression will eventually end, but with treatment the episode usually ends earlier and the likelihood of another episode may be decreased.

Unfortunately, more than half of the people who have an episode of major depression will have later episodes as well. Some experience a single recurrence; others may experience many episodes throughout their lives. The first episode of major depression occurs on average around age 26, although people may experience major depression for the first time at any point throughout life—even in very advanced years.

Some individuals with major depression have times in their lives when they feel *especially* good, cheerful, happy, "high," "up," or irritable. This type of mental and emotional state, known as a *manic* episode, is different from the usual enthusiasm or happiness that people feel when things seem to be going well. The manic state is more extreme and is part of a condition formerly called manic depression but now called *bipolar disorder*, indicating two extremes of an emotional pole.

The other major type of depression is *dysthymia*, a condition that is less severe than major depression but tends to last longer, typically for two years or more. People with dysthymia experience the same difficulties as those with major depression—appetite and sleep changes, tiredness, poor self-esteem, problems concentrating, feelings of helplessness—but usually with a somewhat lesser degree of intensity. Another condition known as *cylothymia* is characterized by periods of feeling much better than usual interspersed with periods of feeling much worse. These feelings are less extreme and less disabling than in bipolar disorder.

The tenth leading cause of death in the U.S. is suicide, and many who attempt or actually complete a suicide are depressed (Blumenthal & Kupfer, 1990). For some people depression is so painful that they view the prospect of death as a relief. Several factors have been associated with relatively high risk for suicidal behavior: being male, having a family history of suicide, recent life stresses, medical illness, psychiatric illness, and a history of previous suicide attempts. Elderly white males have the highest rates of suicide within the general population (Kastenbaum,

1992). Canetto (1992) suggests that in American society white men stand to lose more power, status, and influence in later life than do women or nonwhite men. Becoming old may be a painful shock to men who have not developed adequate personal resources to adapt well to the challenges of later life.

Major depression and dysthmia are two ways of characterizing what are currently regarded as the most severe types of depression and depression-related problems. The depression that is frequently seen following the loss of an important other, such as a spouse or child—a state called bereavement—is considered an expectable response to the deep distress of being separated from a central person in one's life. The most intense feelings of grief and depression usually subside after a time, but for some people the distress intensifies and develops into a major depression.

Significant feelings of depression also may be experienced after a particularly stressful life event, for example, divorce or the loss of a job. Some individuals respond more intensely to loss and stress, a reaction that can make it difficult to meet day-to-day responsibilities. This condition is called an adjustment disorder.

The diagnostic classifications of depression described above offer mental health researchers and practitioners a useful way to characterize these emotional problems so they can be better understood and alleviated. But mental health professionals themselves debate about the best way to classify feeling states. Some argue that diagnostic classifications may promote a narrowing of focus on symptomatology with a concurrent failure to more fully appreciate the individual who is suffering from these symptoms. Obviously, the classification of depression encompasses only one band within the total spectrum of human emotional experience—but one that can be painful, disabling, and frightening.

What Causes Depression?

There are several causes of depression and these frequently interact with one another. Depression provides strong evidence that the body and mind are not separate. Genetics, biochemistry, personality, interpersonal relationships, life events, and even social and historical forces all may contribute to a depressive state.

The National Institute of Mental Health has declared the 1990s "The Decade of the Brain" (National Institute of Mental Health, 1988). This designation reflects the considerable growth in recent years in our understanding of the ways in which human behavior is affected by the structures and processes within the brain. Most people do not think of their emotional lives as influenced by brain chemistry, but scientific evidence has documented such a relationship. Information in the brain is communicated by electrical impulses between brain cells. This process involves a variety of substances known as *neurotransmitters*. Interference or disruption in this electrochemical process may have many behavioral effects, including poor regulation of mood and depression. The reason some people experience problems in the production and regulation of neurotransmitters is the subject of several theories and numerous studies.

It has long been observed that certain kinds of depression tend to run in families. Researchers have found that some persons with the most severe forms of mental illness have a genetic disposition to these conditions. For example, if an identical twin experiences serious depression or bipolar disorder, the other twin has a 70 percent chance of also having this condition. How the brain increases vulnerability to depression is only beginning to be understood. It may be that genetic heritage is linked to variations in brain structures or processes, or both.

Other possible causes of depression are medical problems and medications (Rodin, Craven, & Littlefield, 1991). Medical conditions associated with depression include several types of cancer as well as thyroid disease, heart problems, high blood pressure, and infections. Certain medications also trigger depression. People with serious depression may need to be evaluated for underlying medical problems that may need to be treated or medications that should be changed or discontinued.

Stressful life circumstances have also been tied to greater risk for depression. Health problems, interpersonal difficulties, financial pressures, and the death of loved ones are stressful life circumstances that may lead to depression (Brown & Harris, 1978). Further, ongoing life strains such as unhappy marriages, parenting pressures, chronic work problems, and similar difficulties also are associated with increased risk of depression (Mitchell, Cronkite, & Moos, 1983).

Psychological factors have been implicated in depression. Cognitive theories of depression suggest that some individuals are predisposed to think about themselves, the future, and the world in particularly negative ways (Beck, 1976), and this ongoing negative distortion contributes to depression. Behavioral approaches to depression operate on the premise that there is an important link between emotions and behavior (Lewinsohn, Biglan, & Zeiss, 1976). Changes in behavioral patterns that deprive an individual of satisfactions to which he or she is accustomed may result in feelings of depression which, in turn, make it less likely that the individual will engage in the very activities that are important to emotional well-being. Psychodynamic approaches emphasize the emotionally detrimental effect of conflicts within the individual of which he or she may not be aware (Bemporad, 1985). Feelings of depression are regarded as a signal that there are psychological or interpersonal problems with which the individual needs to more fully reckon.

How Common Is Depression?

Only recently has solid information become available to answer this question. In the 1980s, the National Institute of Mental Health sponsored a large research project— the Epidemiological Catchment Area Study (ECA)—that surveyed several thousand people living in the community and in certain institutional settings to determine how common various mental health problems were (Robins & Regier, 1991). The results challenged a number of common assumptions about depression, particularly the notion that elderly persons were more likely to suffer from it than younger persons.

First, the study found that almost one-third of the U.S. population had, at some point in their lives, experienced feelings of depression that lasted at least two weeks. Much smaller numbers had ever experienced major depression (4.9 percent) or dysthmia (2.7 percent). Many people with dysthymia had also experienced major depression at some point. In any one year, 2.7 percent of the sample were found to have experienced a major depression. The general factors associated with greater risk for major depressions were being a woman, being younger, being white or Hispanic (vs. black), being unemployed, living in an urban area, and having been divorced or separated.

Some of the most intriguing findings from the ECA study and from other research conducted throughout the world confirm that emotional well-being is linked to the social and historical circumstances in which people live. ECA data showed that, far from being especially vulnerable to depression, today's cohort of elderly persons is less likely than younger persons to have ever had diagnosable depression. Only 1.4 percent of the elderly population were found to have ever experienced major depression and only 1.7 percent had experienced dysthmia. Corresponding numbers for the entire population were 4.9 percent and 3.2 percent.

These findings are counterintuitive. By virtue of having lived longer, the elderly have had more years of being at risk for depression than have younger people. Further, given the many losses associated with the later years of life, the elderly would be expected to report greater rates of major depression. However, symptoms consistent with a major depression in the previous one-year period occurred in 2.7 percent of the general all-age sample and in only 0.9 percent of the elderly. In other words, it was three times more likely for nonelderly people to have experienced major depression symptoms.

ECA and other data further showed increasing rates of depression for successive age cohorts grouped by 10-year periods in which they were born: 1905-1914, 1915-1924, and so on through 1955-1964 (Klerman & Weissman, 1989). Social and behavioral scientists have long known that the outlook and behavior of people are influenced by the social and historical forces present during their formative years. People raised during the Great Depression of the 1930s look at the world differently than those who grew to maturity in the 25 years of prosperity following World War II (the so-called baby boomers). One explanation for the apparent relative immunity to depression in the current cohort of older adults is of particular interest. It suggests that people raised during the Great Depression had reduced expectations about what life would bring. When their lives turned out to be better than expected, the result was a state of emotional well-being. By contrast, baby boomers were weaned in an era of economic prosperity and taught to expect a great deal from life—materially, occupationally, and personally. As adults, they now live in a world of limited resources, heightened competition, and inevitable compromises, all of which produce a greater vulnerability to depression.

Other epidemiological data suggest that rates of depression rose for *all* age cohorts during the period 1965-1975. One explanation offered is that the social turbulence of that era was personally and interpersonally dislocating for all age groups, thereby increasing general vulnerability to depression. Some have argued, however, that these findings pertain only to very specific characterizations of depression. Even though the elderly have lower rates of diagnosable depression, they nonetheless appear to suffer from more symptoms of emotional distress than younger persons. Scientists continue to debate the implications of all the findings reported here; nonetheless, these data offer many clues to the complex interplay between self, society, and depression.

What Treatments Exist for Depression?

Estimates are that 70 to 80 percent of people with clinical depression improve with treatment. The treatments for depression fall into two general areas: somatic and nonsomatic. Somatic treatments primarily include antidepressant medications and electroconvulsive therapy (ECT). Nonsomatic treatments generally refer to psychotherapy.

Before receiving treatment for depression an individual should receive a thorough evaluation, including:

- A history of past and current mental health problems
- Inquiry about other problems that may not have been mentioned (e.g., thoughts of suicide or harming others, drug abuse, alcoholism)
- An inventory of medical conditions and medications
- An evaluation of life difficulties and stresses
- The status of significant relationships
- A sense of how cultural or ethnic issues influence the person's life.

Although individual states license those service providers who may assess and treat mental health problems, generally the core mental health providers are psychiatrists, psychologists, social workers, and nurses. Many people, particularly elders, bring emotional problems to the attention of their family physicians. Although some family physicians evaluate and treat depression in an appropriate manner, studies have found that they often overlook depression and sometimes fail to treat it with the most up-to-date methods (German, Shapiro, & Skinner, 1987). Conversely, some mental health professionals without medical training may make referrals for medical evaluation when it is necessary. In view of the varied and often interacting determinants of depression, a careful and thorough examination is important before developing a treatment plan.

A variety of antidepressant medications are given for the treatment of major depression. Studies indicate that one antidepressant is not necessarily better than another, but some *individuals* do respond better to certain antidepressants than to others. Antidepressant medications have different side effects such as dry mouth, blurry vision, and constipation, which may present special problems for persons with certain medical conditions. In general, those prescribing psychiatric medications must be especially careful with elderly adults because they usually require smaller doses and may be more sensitive to side effects than younger persons (Blazer, 1990).

The other major type of somatic treatment is ECT (Fink, 1979). ECT involves passing an electrical current through an individual's brain to induce a seizure while the individual is temporarily rendered unconscious. This procedure is usually done on several occasions over one or several weeks. Although the average person may consider such a procedure puzzling and even frightening, ECT has been found to be quite useful in the treatment of serious depression. However, ECT typically is given only to persons who do not respond to antidepressant medications, whose conditions are life-threatening and need immediate treatment, or who cannot receive antidepressants because of specific medical problems.

There are a variety of approaches to conducting psychotherapy in the treatment of depression, and many mental health professions make use of several approaches (Beckham & Leber, 1985). Cognitive and behavioral therapies emphasize changing habitual ways of thinking or behaving that may have a role in prompting or sustaining depression. Interpersonal therapy focuses on changing relationships with important others that may precipitate or maintain depression. Psychodynamic therapy emphasizes past or current life conflicts whose resolution will diminish depression. Research has demonstrated that psychotherapy is useful in the treatment of depression both alone and in combination with antidepressant somatic treatment. Psychotherapy is usually the treatment of choice for dysthmia although increasing efforts are being made to use antidepressant medications.

Not all mental health professionals agree about the most effective treatment for depression. Some argue that almost all persons with major depression should be given somatic treatments since these have been shown to reduce depressive symptomatology, usually within six weeks. Others argue that the evidence for the effectiveness of psychotherapy in the treatment of depression supports its use more often. Further, it has been suggested that there is an overemphasis on treating symptoms of depression to the neglect of the personal, interpersonal, and social factors that may be salient and that can be the focus of psychotherapy.

In summary, for most people depression is a brief period of feeling emotionally out-of-sorts. For some people, however, depression is a serious mental health problem. It is a complex phenomenon in which heredity, biology, personality, social relationships, and even historical factors may come to bear. Depression can occur at any point in adult life, and treatment can be effective at any point in shortening the duration of episodes and reducing the frequency of recurrence.

▼ GREGORY A. HINRICHSEN

See also: Age 40; Cohort and Generational Effects; Disengagement Theory; Happiness, Cohort Measures of; Life Events; Mental Health in the Adult Years; Mental Health Resources for Adults; Narcissism; Native American Perspectives on the Lifespan; Rural Living: What Influence on Adult Development?; Social Support for the Chronically Ill; Stress; Suffering; Taste and Smell; Widowhood: The Coping Response.

References

American Psychiatric Association (1987). *Diagnostic and Statistical Manual of Mental Disorders.* Third Edition, Revised. Washington, DC: American Psychiatric Association.

Beck, A. T. (1976). *Cognitive Theory and the Emotional Disorders.* New York: International Universities Press.

Beckham, E. E., & Leber, W. R. (Eds.). (1985). *Handbook of Depression: Treatment, Assessment, and Research.* Homewood: IL: Dorsey Press.

Bemporad, J. R. (1985). Long-term analytic treatment of depression. In E. E. Beckham & W. R. Leber (Eds.), *Handbook of Depression: Treatment, Assessment, and Research.* Homewood, IL: Dorsey Press, pp. 82-99.

Blazer, D. (1990). *Emotional Problems in Later Life: Intervention Strategies for Professional Caregivers.* New York: Springer.

Blumenthal, S. J., & Kupfer, D. J. (Eds.). (1990). *Suicide Over the Life Cycle: Risk Factors, Assessment, and Treatment of Suicidal Patients.* Washington, DC: American Psychiatric Press.

Brown, G. W., & Harris, T. O. (1978). *Social Origins of Depression: A Study of Psychiatric Disorder in Women.* New York: Free Press.

Canetto, S. (1992). Gender and suicide in the elderly. *Suicide and Life-Threatening Behavior, 22:* 80-97.

Fink, M. (1979). *Convulsive Therapy: Theory and Practice.* New York: Raven Press.

German, P. S., Shapiro, S., & Skinner, E. A. (1987). Detection and management of mental health problems of older patients by primary care providers. *Journal of the American Medical Association, 257:* 489-93.

Kastenbaum, R. (1992). Death, suicide, and the older adult. *Suicide and Life-Threatening Behavior, 22:* 1-14.

Klerman, G. L., & Weissman, M. M. (1989). Increasing rates of depression. *Journal of the American Medical Association, 261:* 2229-35.

Lewinsohn, P. M., Biglan, T., & Zeiss, A. (1976). Behavioral treatment of depression. In P. Davidson (Ed.), *Behavioral Management of Anxiety, Depression and Pain.* New York: Bruner/Mazel, pp. 91-146.

Mitchell, R. E., Cronkite, R. C., & Moos, R. H. (1983). Stress, coping and depression among married couples. *Journal of Abnormal Psychology, 92:* 443-48.

National Institute of Mental Health (1988). *Approaching the 21st Century: Opportunities for NIMH Neuroscience Research.* Rockville, MD: Department of Health and Human Services Publication No. (ADM) 89-1580.

Robins, L. N., & Regier, D. A. (Eds.). (1991). *Psychiatric Disorders in America: The Epidemiological Catchment Area Study.* New York: Free Press.

Rodin, G., Craven, J., & Littlefield, C. (1991). *Depression in the Medically Ill: An Integrated Approach.* New York: Bruner/Mazel.

DEVELOPMENT AND AGING

A traveler, tired, cold, and hungry, is given shelter one night in a farmer's humble dwelling. Soon after entering, the traveler blows vigorously on his hands. "Why are you doing that?" asks one of the children. "To warm my hands." When the meal is served, steam rises from the soup. The traveler blows across his bowl. "Why are you doing that?" asks another child. "To cool my soup." In extreme agitation, all the family unites in tossing the traveler back out into the night. "He must have been the Devil!" "Yes, who else can blow both hot and cold?"

Time is the "who else." It is time that at first seems to favor growth, but then alters its character and hobbles us with age. The newborn, whose very survival depends on adult caregiving, will be a parent with the competence to look after his or her own children— it is just a matter of what time brings forth. Time *continues* to bring forth, however, and the parents may reach a point in their lives when they need the help of others to protect their well-being.

The concepts of development and aging, then, are both linked and differentiated by time. This dynamic leads to a hypothetical moment in a person's life in which time seems to change from its life-enhancing to its life-threatening modality. Disengagement theory (Cumming & Henry, 1961) has seized upon this (remember: hypothetical) moment and asserted that this is precisely when we make the transition from adult to aging adult. According to this theory, we realize that all we have left is that disagreeable kind of time that erodes our abilities—and that even this time is starting to run out. (There is actually little evidence to support the proposition that most people actually experience this momentous moment: there are marked individual differences in our awareness and interpretation of time throughout the lifespan, e.g., Friedman, 1982; Kastenbaum, 1982).

In this respect, disengagement theory is also a sort of traveler's tale. It makes a provocative point but raises more questions than it answers. Perhaps the most fundamental question is why and how time seems to change its character at some point in our adult lives. "How does development become aging?" is another way of putting this question. Should aging be regarded as an independent process with its own sources and rules, or is it inherent in the same processes that generate growth and development? Is this two-part invention—development and aging— part of a master plan that cannot and should not be modified? Or is aging a disorder or aberration that could be corrected through ingenious research and genetic engineering?

Whether we are interested primarily in understanding the lifespan journey or intervening in it, it is useful to examine the concepts of development and aging with some care. These ideas go back a long way, and we are still influenced by theories that were first formulated more than 2,000 years ago.

Becoming: Aristotle's Theory of Development

Son of a physician to the king of Macedonia, student of Plato and the mentor of Alexander the Great, Aristotle (384-323 B.C.) set out to discover for himself what is "real." He faced the same problem that earlier philosophers had recognized: how to understand time or change. Some had argued that only that which does not change is real, and a few that change itself is the only reality. Aristotle proposed a way of integrating change with constancy and, in so doing, provided what might be regarded as the first lifespan developmental theory, or at least its prototype.

Growth, development, and life itself reveal a process of coming-to-be. Every living thing (and every element in the universe, for that matter) has its own distinctive form. Today we might think of each form as a set of rules that govern the actions and transformations that can take place, and think particularly of genes and DNA structures that control the rules or code. Aristotle's form is a higher-level abstraction but serves a similar purpose.

Development proceeds as a form moves from its potentiality to its actuality. An acorn and an oak are obviously very different from each other, yet also obviously intimately connected. For Aristotle, the oak is the actuality of the acorn and the acorn is the potentiality of the oak.

The transition of a form from potentiality to actuality requires change which, in turn, requires time. Operating within this framework, Aristotle could grant reality status to time and change while still speaking up for constancy and order. Development is change, but it is planned and orderly change. Furthermore, the same passage of time results in a variety of different actualizations because each has its own potentiality or distinctive form. In the same period of time, the kitten, the puppy, and the human infant will all show remarkable progress toward their respective actualizations, but each in its own way.

Most researchers and theoreticians today do not spend much time thinking about Aristotle; nevertheless, his influence lingers. Whenever we attempt to understand a person or predict his or her future actions by examining this individual's past experiences and behaviors, we are following in Aristotle's footsteps. The developmental (also known as genetic) approach has guided observers as different as Charles Darwin (1859), Sigmund Freud (1905), Arnold Gesell (1945), and B. F. Skinner (1938), who have made their distinctive contributions by attempting to discover the coming-to-be of actualized forms (such as adult behavior patterns). Few of Aristotle's specific observations have held up with time (e.g., his demonstration that the heart or its equivalent in "bloodless animals" is the "supreme organ of the sense faculties"; Aristotle, 1971, p. 714), but his zeal in the process of discovery has stimulated a great many others. When we search for what is particularly distinctive about a person or a group of people, we are also hewing to Aristotle's concept of distinctive forms. This is especially the case when we attempt to discern a basic meaning or goal—*teleos*, in Aristotle—for the life's journey of a particular person or of humankind in general.

Aristotle may have written a good deal more about the later adult years and aging than has come down to us. He regarded the middle adult years as the pinnacle of life, safely beyond the inexperience and impulsivity of youth and not yet burdened with age. Aristotle believed he had found a vital connection between youthful development on one hand and aging and death on the other:

> The source of life is lost to its possessors when the heat with which it is bound up is no longer tempered by cooling [and]...is consumed by itself. Hence, a small disturbance will speedily cause death in old age. ...It is just as though the heart contained a tiny feeble flame which the slightest movement puts out. Hence in old age death is painless, for no violent disturbance is required to cause death, and there is an entire absence of feeling when the soul's connexion is severed....Youth is the period of the growth of the primary organ of refrigeration, old age of its decay, while the intervening time is the prime of life. (p. 725)

Wrong again, of course! But Aristotle offers several themes here that remain attractive to some contemporary developmentalists and gerontologists:

- Development and aging can be understood in terms of the same principles. For Aristotle, this boiled down to "too cold, "too hot," and "just right" (middle age). Today, gerontologists tend to speak instead of deleterious changes in our genetic apparatus over time or of accumulated damage and errors that interfere with cell metabolism (Hayflick, 1987). Whatever the particular theory, it tends to obey Aristotle's premise that when we identify the process through which the form moves from potentiality to actuality we are also identifying the process through which the form decays.

- Death represents a relatively small step beyond aging. There is not much to dying and death for old people because they are already so feeble, dried up, and disengaged. Some of the most popular accounts of lifespan development, including

Erikson's (1950) epigenetic theory and Butler's (1963) life review concept, assert that preparing oneself to face death with equanimity is the major life task for old people. This view is consistent with Aristotle's belief that elderly men and women have but a frail hold on life and should find it easy to let go. The facts are not entirely in agreement with this premise, however. Many an elderly person is highly involved in life and eager to see what tomorrow brings. Aristotle does not provide us with a positive model for old age, instead tempting theoreticians to see preparing oneself for death as the most appropriate activity. Alternatively, one might assert that each phase of life has its own form to actualize, with neither youth nor age representing "undercooked" or "overcooked" versions of the middle-age ideal.

Competing Images of Development and Aging

From Aristotle to the present day there has been an increasingly intense competition among differing images of human development and aging. These rival versions have emerged within varied geopolitical, religious, and philosophical contexts and, in turn, have influenced such realities of daily life as the treatment of children, educational goals and methods, and the overall relationship between the state and the individual. As the following selected examples indicate, we are not dealing with bland academic discourse here, but with ideas that could—and did—spark revolution.

1. *Children are defective adults.* This idea would strike most people today as ludicrous. Nevertheless, this was the dominant view of children from medieval times to the dawn of the modern age and proved to be a stubborn opponent as more enlightened concepts appeared (Aries, 1962). Children basically were neither seen nor heard: diaries, histories, songs, and works of art seldom included boys and girls as significant characters.

When children were depicted by artists, they were presented as miniature adults. Their clothing and demeanor showed little or nothing of the characteristics associated with youth. Even in the innovative sixteenth century, children remained of little interest for themselves (Schorsch, 1978). In fact, children were classified as among the "lower animals" when they were not being ignored or criticized as unreliable and incompetent little adults.

So unimportant was the child that families of means quickly placed their children in the hands of servants and so-called nurses. Fathers who themselves had a place in society had very little to do with their young children, and many mothers did the same. During the "enlightened" eighteenth century, the children of lower-class families were still being neglected or placed in virtual slavery as apprentices, while the children of affluent families had little contact with their parents (Lorence, 1974).

This negative and dismissive attitude emerged from attitudes and social forces at work through much of Europe over many centuries. Modern advocates of "family values" would be appalled to learn how typical families actually functioned in these not-so-good and not-so-old days. The developmental viewpoint was seldom in evidence. Few people gave credence to the possibility that childhood might be a critical period for personal and social development, deserving loving and attentive care. Obedience might be beaten into the young, but otherwise they were on their own to sink and swim as they might.

2. *Old people would be admired if they gave themselves over to contemplation and other saintly qualities, but more often were mocked for their wrinkles, ailments, and follies* (Covey, 1991). When considered together with the weak and negative image of the child, it would appear that neither the beginnings nor the endings of life's journey (Cole, 1992) attracted the favorable

interest of society through much of Western history. (A different scenario, finding virtue in aging and the aged, developed in a number of Eastern cultures, as summarized by Kiefer, 1992.) Overall, few people seemed to hold a conception of the entire lifespan in which early development and the older adult years were seen as part of a coherent and positive whole.

3. *Children are empty vessels waiting to be filled by society.* John Locke, an English physician, took an interest in the education of children that was quite remarkable for the seventeenth century. He offered challenging new ideas about knowledge, society, and human development (Locke, 1689, 1690, 1693). Most important for our purposes, Locke was the first to make a strong case for the proposition that we do not come into this world with a set of wired-in or preexisting ideas. Instead, the mind of a newborn can be likened to a blank slate (*tabula rasa*) that will be written on by experience. Whether the child will turn out to be an adult who is informed or ignorant, thoughtful or reckless, law-abiding or criminal depends on the way society has "written on" this blank slate.

Locke's theory was controversial, of course, and in many quarters just what the establishment did *not* want to hear. His message was welcomed, however, by those who desired radical change. They quickly saw that, if Locke was right, any child might have the potential to be a resourceful adult and accomplish great things. The farmer or merchant's child could become a doctor, a bishop, a sea captain, or even a ruler. The politically volatile idea of equal opportunity now had a philosophical and psychological rationale.

Locke's ideas received a powerful political expression in the U.S. Constitution. Movements that led to educational opportunities for all children—and the controversies that still exist today—owe much to Locke's developmental thesis.

Children became much more important, as did teachers and the whole subject of education. Furthermore, Aristotle's theory of coming-to-be now had some serious competition. A person does not simply actualize his or her form over a period of time. Instead, who that person will become depends greatly on the kind of experiences made available to him or her. Each newborn has a variety of selves he or she could become instead of being limited to one fixed track that has already been laid down.

Locke's contributions had a very practical side. He offered detailed suggestions on how society could shape its young into valuable citizens. Behavior modification, schedules of reinforcement, and much of today's marketing and manipulating technology were clearly anticipated by Locke (although certainly he would not have approved of all the purposes to which these techniques have been applied). These techniques are important from the developmental standpoint for two almost opposite reasons:

a. The continuity of the individual from youth through adulthood is emphasized by the fact that the same principles can be applied to establishing, shaping, and strengthening desired patterns of behavior at all age levels.

b. The characteristics of the individual are less important than the nature of the educational and social experiences to which he or she is exposed. This implication has fueled a still active controversy between those who emphasize external or environmental factors and those who contend that the genetic endowment and overall status of the organism play an important role.

Interestingly, it would be quite a while before the Lockean emancipation found its way to the later adult years. There was no immediate realization of the implication that the newly envisioned possibilities of youth might also contribute to diverse and creative outcomes in old age as well. This concept has just started to attract widespread attention in recent years, and its derivation from Locke has yet to be appreciated.

4. *Children should develop in their own natural ways.* This idea is one that might well be the favorite of most children. It was introduced by Jean Jacques Rousseau (1712-1778), whose colorful life has been the subject of many biographies as well as his own autobiographical writings. Rousseau welcomed Locke's emphasis on child development, but he was skeptical about the intentions as well as the ability of society to provide effective learning opportunities. In fact, society was the menace. What his eighteenth-century contemporaries liked to praise as civilization and progress seemed like corruption and enslavement to Rousseau. It was he who penned the memorable phrase "Man is born free, but is everywhere in chains."

All that is wrong with human nature has resulted from society's distortion of our basic impulses and sensitivities. Left to their own intuitions, children will discover who they are and what the world is about. They will grow up to be truly free beings, unshackled by superstitions, fears, prohibitions, and all the foolish brutality of social custom. The "natural" child will grow into an independent-minded adult, not a mere replica of the docile and unthinking conformists one sees at every hand.

Clearly, any respectable upholder of the status quo who had not been outraged by Locke would now fly at Rousseau with fangs and claws exposed. Today, Rousseau's extremist message would be less shocking to a public that has become increasingly critical of many of its social institutions and is on better terms with its own impulses and fantasies than in the more oppressive times experienced by Rousseau.

There is reason to consider Rousseau to be the first thoroughgoing developmentalist. In one of his works (Rousseau, 1762) he urged that we pay attention to the child *as a child,* not as a future or incomplete adult. He then became the first of many stage theorists. Two centuries later we can read his account of four childhood stages and clearly envision the type of behavior he has in mind ("Yes, that sounds like a two year old all right!"). His description of the adolescent's mastery of abstract thinking abilities anticipated what Piaget (1936) and others would confirm many years later. Subsequent generations of developmental researchers often have been inspired by Rousseau's enthusiasm for the child as a child and his trust in the child's ability to profit from his or her own mistakes and to construct a worldview based on his or her own distinctive experiences.

If today we see children as active, creative, and basically well equipped for developmental challenges, then we are endorsing Rousseau's once-alarming contention. This will be further affirmed if we go easy on controlling, interfering, and punishing, but instead keep our faith in the child's own natural wisdom.

We know little about Rousseau's vision of the elderly person. Perhaps children who develop in an active and natural manner will avoid the routinization and hyperhabituation too often associated with adult life and will move into old age as strong individuals with the confidence to face their new challenges and opportunities. Nothing in Rousseau's view would insist upon a sudden or arbitrary cessation of personal growth. A "natural child" grown old might not be at all impressed by stereotyped expectations that he or she settle into a rocking chair and keep out of mischief.

Stages—and More Stages

Many current theories are organized around stages of development. Phenomena associated with aging are often compressed into the final stage, a sort of little red caboose bearing the black flag of death that brings up the rear. Detailed presentation of these theories would not be appropriate here because most focus primarily on the earlier years of life. We have already looked at some of the major guiding concepts, and Cole (1992) has also traced some of the connections (see also **Development and Aging in Historical Perspective**).

It is more useful to try to explore the general concept of developmental stages. The biological and medical sciences offer many examples of phenomena that can be said to occur in definite stages. These are well documented with physical specimens, photographs, and a variety of special instrumentation. Furthermore, in many instances one can observe the entire sequence as it takes place. The data base is so firm and so well replicated that one would be sincerely surprised to discover, for example, that a bullfrog had just reverted to being a tadpole. Similarly, the laboratory technician and the physician know that something momentous has happened when a Stage 3 tumor has regressed to Stage 1.

Stage theories have three apparent advantages. First, the concept of stages is attractive because it provides a way to bring some order to a mass of observations. Second, it is attractive because this order takes the form of a temporal sequence. People feel more comfortable when they know that a predictable course has been charted: This will be followed by that. Knowing what comes next tends to reduce anxiety and bolster one's sense of control. And, third, as we have just seen, the concept of stages has proven justifiable and useful in a number of biological and medical spheres.

Unfortunately, stages are seldom so clear, reliable, and well documented when we shift to the realm of individual behavior and social interaction. At their worst, "stages" of development are arbitrary terms that have been imposed on a collection of opportunistic and unrepresentative observations. These terms are then interpreted as the basis for rules of living. What begins as the assertion that Stage B follows Stage A becomes the moral prescription that Stage B *should* follow Stage A—and if it does not, then there must

be something amiss and the straggler should be pulled through from one stage to the next. And, just to round off our visit to this "little shop of theoretical horrors," we discover that the supposed scientific basis is little more than the reigning social values in disguise.

For some years now, the most popular type of developmental stage theories has interpreted the journey of life as a series of jobs or tasks that must be accomplished. One must complete this job in infancy, discharge that task in adolescence, and so on. The job-task-work approach to lifespan development has been accepted in a docile manner by many educators and consumers of theory because it has accorded so well with our society's emphasis on salvation through work and productivity. There are signs, however, that taking lifespan development to be just another form of work in an industrial society is an approach that is starting to falter, perhaps in response to an increased interest in discovering alternative ways of life. Although this has been a "worst case scenario" (with names withheld to protect the perhaps now regretful offenders), it is reasonable to suggest that developmental stages have enjoyed more popularity than they deserve.

On the positive side, several stage theories have stimulated valuable research—from both advocates and opponents—that otherwise might not have been carried out. A prime example is Jean Piaget's cognitive-developmental theory. In contrast to a number of other theories, the stages articulated by Piaget and his colleagues have been much more detailed and amenable to testing. Furthermore, the Piagetians have innovated methods for observing, manipulating, and analyzing their stages. Overall, the Piagetian cognitive-developmental theory has had its ups and downs with respect to confirmation and consensus, but there is no question that we have learned a great deal more not only about cognitive development but also about how to observe and think about cognitive development from this seminal approach. Among the valuable offshoots from Piaget's approach is the stage theory of moral development that has been formulated and tested by Lawrence Kohlberg (1973, 1981). At the very least, this theory has led to a renewed interest in moral development.

The careful thinker will glean whatever information and insights may be of value from stage theories, but not succumb too quickly to the assertion that all people everywhere go through all these "stages," and that the stages themselves represent a fixed sequence of qualitatively distinct levels or modes of functioning. The careful thinker will also be aware of the many ways in which the values held by society or the individual theoretician may have leaked into what has been packaged as pure science.

Alternative Concepts of Development and Aging

In recent years an avant-garde of lifespan developmental researchers and theoreticians has staked out new positions that require complex multivariate studies. The key difference here is that this new type of theoretician finds previous conceptualizations too simple and inflexible, not up to the challenge of integrating, predicting, and explaining the diverse phenomena that emerge from their studies (e.g., Nesselroade, 1977; Schaie, 1977; Schaie & Hertzog, 1985). "Development" and "aging" tend to disappear, at least temporarily, as researchers come up with tighter, narrower, and more mathematically oriented models of change. In fact, the general level of discourse has been altered. Instead of dealing with broad traditional concepts such as "development," "aging," and "stages," researchers are more inclined to work with computer generated or assisted models. We are likely to find them muttering over a set of superimposed curves that represent multiple measurements on multiple variables at several points in time. These models are highly relevant to what we more familiarly speak of as "development" and "aging," but are not as easily assembled into communication packages.

Most of the emerging models have in common the principle that both change and constancy can be found when we examine human behavior and experience across the lifespan. It is not useful to think of this pattern as having a single cause or as consisting of a series of isolated effects. Instead, we seem to be dealing with a dynamic field in which many action sequences from a variety of sources interact. It is easier to identify many of these influences than to discover how they operate and, particularly, what role is played by each individual in shaping his or her life.

A mechanistic or reductionistic interpretation would attempt to enter data from biological, psychological, and socioenvironmental sources and allow the computer to come up with the best descriptive model of what we have become accustomed to thinking of as development/aging. A more holistic model, and one that sees the individual as an active and creative force, would have to produce a methodological and theoretical approach that is equal to this contention— and the search is on. In other words, the increasing complexity of lifespan developmental data and data analysis does not necessarily replace choice and values. We can work with the emerging data and models in the service of alternative or competing conceptions of what it means to move through the lifespan journey.

And this brings us back to our mysterious traveler. Perhaps each individual has the option of blowing either hot or cold. Whatever terminology one prefers, it is clear enough that the physical capacities that once blossomed in time will, given enough time, wither to some extent. But it is also clear that a process of personal and spiritual growth can flourish even as time takes its toll. Some of the complexity apparent in the new multivariate models of development and aging may be attributable to the distinctive ways in which each person deals with the challenge of continuing to grow as a human being despite the onslaught of age-related impairments. A powerful and poignant image was created by the artist Francisco Goya in his old age. He depicted a man of great age, stooped over as he hobbled along supported by two walking sticks. Goya's caption: *"Aun aprendo"* ("Still learning").

▼ Robert Kastenbaum

See also: Adult Development and Aging, Models of; Contextualism; Creativity; Development and Aging in Historical Perspective; Disengagement Theory; Fairy Tales as Commentary on Adult Development and Aging; Habituation: A Key to Lifespan Development and Aging?; Individuality; Intelligence; Maturity; Metaphors of the Life Course; Mid-Life Crisis; Spiritual Development and Wisdom: A Vedantic Perspective.

References

Aries, P. (1962). *Centuries of Childhood.* New York: Vintage.

Aristotle. (1971). On youth and old age, on life and death, on breathing. In R. M. Hutchins (Ed.), *Great Books of the Western World.* Volume 8: *Aristotle I.* Chicago: Encyclopedia Britannica, pp. 714-26. (Original work, third century B.C.).

Butler, R. N. (1963). The life review: An interpretation of reminiscence in the aged. *Psychiatry, 26:* 65-76.

Cole, T. R. (1992). *The Journey of Life: A Cultural History of Aging in America.* Cambridge: Cambridge University Press.

Covey, H. C. (1991). *Images of Older People in Western Art and Society.* New York: Praeger.

Cumming, E., & Henry, W. E. (1961). *Growing Old: The Process of Disengagement.* New York: Basic Books.

Darwin, C. (1859). *The Origin of Species.* New York: Modern Library.

Erikson, E. H. (1950). *Childhood and Society.* New York: Norton.

Freud, S. (1905). Three contributions to the theory of sex. In A. A. Brill (Ed.), *The Basic Writings of Sigmund Freud.* New York: Modern Library, pp. 553-63.

Friedman, W. J. (Ed.). (1982). *The Developmental Psychology of Time.* New York: Academic Press.

Gesell, A. (1945). *The Embryology of Behavior.* New York: Harper & Row.

Hayflick, L. (1987). Biological aging theories. In G. L. Maddox (Ed.), *The Encyclopedia of Aging.* New York: Springer, pp. 64-68.

Kastenbaum, R. (1982). Time course and time perspective in later life. In C. Eisdorfer (Ed.), *Annual Review of Gerontology and Geriatrics.* Volume 3. New York: Springer, pp. 80-101.

Kiefer, C. W. (1992). Aging in Eastern cultures: A historical overview. In T. Cole, D. D. Van Tassel, & R. Kastenbaum (Eds.), *Handbook of the Humanities and Aging.* New York: Springer, pp. 96-124.

Kohlberg, L. (1973). Continuities in childhood and adult moral development revisited. In P. B. Baltes & K. W. Schaie (Eds.), *Life-span Developmental Psychology: Personality and Socialization.* New York: Academic Press, pp. 180-207.

———. (1981). *Essays on Moral Development.* New York: Harper & Row.

Locke, J. (1689/1960). *Two Treatises on Government.* Cambridge: Cambridge University Press.

———. (1690/1961). *Essay Concerning Human Understanding.* London: J. M. Dent & Sons.

———. (1693/1963). Some Thoughts Concerning Education. In P. Gay (Ed.), *John Locke on Education.* New York: Columbia University.

Lorence, B. W. (1974). Parents and children in Eighteenth-Century Europe. *History of Childhood Quarterly, 2:* 1-30.

Nesselroade, J. R. (1977). Issues in studying developmental change in adults from a multivariate perspective. In J. E. Birren & K. W. Schaie (Eds.), *Handbook of the Psychology of Aging.* New York: Van Nostrand Reinhold, pp. 59-69.

Piaget, J. (1936). *The Construction of Reality in the Child.* New York: Ballantine.

Rousseau, J. J. (1762/1948). *Emile, Or Education.* London: J. M. Dent & Sons.

Schaie, K. W. (1977). Quasi-experimental research designs in the psychology of aging. In J. E. Birren & K. W. Schaie (Eds.), *Handbook of the Psychology of Aging.* New York: Van Nostrand Reinhold, pp. 39-58.

Schaie, K. W., & Hertzog, C. (1985). Measurement in the psychology of adulthood and aging. In J. E. Birren & K. W. Schaie (Eds.), *Handbook of the Psychology of Aging.* Second Edition. New York: Van Nostrand Reinhold, pp. 61-94.

Schorsch, A. (1978). *Images of Childhood.* New York: Mayflower.

Skinner, B. F. (1938). *The Behavior of Organisms.* Englewood Cliffs, NJ: Prentice-Hall.

DEVELOPMENT AND AGING IN HISTORICAL PERSPECTIVE

Beginning in the nineteenth century, modern biology and medicine attempted to understand human development essentially without reference to religious beliefs or to social environment (Bernard, 1865; Charcot, 1881; Minot, 1908). By stripping away such "biases," modern science and experimental medicine sought "objective" descriptions and explanations of the phenomena under study. In recent years, however, it has become clear that the modern scientific search for detached, value-free knowledge of independently existing phenomena cannot be achieved. Aging and old age are certainly real, but they do not exist in some natural realm, independent of the ideals, images, and social practices that conceptualize, represent, and sustain them. In the late twentieth century, we are also witnessing renewed desire for a deeper understanding of the social and spiritual aspects of adult development and aging (Cole, 1992).

Ironically, our ancestors in the Greco-Roman and Christian West felt that they possessed such an understanding—rooted in their belief in the unity of knowledge and the interrelationship of "man" (to use the traditional language), nature, society, and the cosmos. This understanding was framed in two major concepts: the *ages (or stages) of life* and the *journey of life.* The archetypal power of these images derives from their capacity to help us approach the mystery of human temporality. Each offers a way of conceiving fragmented, sometimes chaotic, ever-changing "life time" as a unified whole.

The Ages of Life and the Journey of Life

The concept or images of the ages of life portray the processes of birth, growth, maturity, decay, and death as part of an inevitable cycle. As Cicero put it, "Life's race course is fixed. Nature has only a single path and that path is run but once, and to each stage of existence has been allotted its appropriate quality" (1923, p. 33). The journey of life refers to the individual experience of moving from stage to stage. The metaphor of the journey operates by narrating diverse experiences in time and space, bringing them under the control of a unified purpose. Tradition-

ally, it has emphasized the fluid and unique qualities of individual experience, the spiritual drama of the traveler's search.

Until the mid-sixteenth century, the English word "age" referred primarily to a stage or period of human life (Dove, 1986). Since numerical age had virtually no social significance, few people knew exactly how old they were. This historical meaning of the word "age" reflected a universal assumption that during the course of a life men passed through several distinct phases of existence. No one doubted that women also passed through the ages of life, but until the seventeenth century scholars, writers, physicians, and artists either subsumed women under the category of men or referred exclusively to men.

Ancient authors established three principal traditions of the ages of life: divisions into three, four, and seven. The fourfold division proved most congenial to the medieval world view, which assumed a divinely ordained correspondence between man, nature, and the cosmos. Greek medicine and physiology had created the four ages: childhood, youth, maturity, and old age. Each of these ages possessed its special physical, mental, and behavioral characteristics. These were explained by the particular age's relationship to the four humors (black bile, phlegm, yellow or red bile, and blood), the four qualities (hot, dry, cold, and moist,) the four elements (air, fire, earth, and water), and the four seasons.

Aristotle provided authority for the biological division of life into three ages: growth, stasis, and decline. In the *Rhetoric* (Book II, Chapters 12-14), Aristotle had also urged the moral superiority of middle age. Since men at the height of their powers are neither too trusting nor too cynical, he claimed that the ideal ruler is neither young nor old—an argument often repeated in medieval writings (Burrow, 1986). In general, the biological division of three ages, based on the rise and fall of physical power, was less hospitable to old age than was the fourfold scheme, which fell easily into medieval patterns of harmony between microcosm and macrocosm.

The third major scheme of the life course depicted seven ages, each explained according to the influence of a planet. In his astrological treatise *Tetrabiblos*, the second-century astronomer Ptolemy provided the authoritative version of this scheme, which did not become popular in the West until the late Middle Ages. Ptolemy's treatise provided the model for Jaques' monologue in Shakespeare's *As You Like It*:

> All the world's a stage
> And all the men and women merely players.
> They have their exits and their entrances;
> And one man in his time plays many parts,
> His acts being seven ages.

For Ptolemy, the last two ages were ruled by Jupiter and Saturn. The sixth age (from 56 to 68) brought thoughtfulness, dignity, and decorum, while the seventh age (68 until death) was considered old and cold, weak, easily offended, and hard to please.

Spiritual Ages: The Contributions of Christian Doctrine

"To everything there is a season, and a time to every purpose," medievals learned from Ecclesiastes. They believed that appreciating the harmonious relations between the course of life and all of God's creation opened one's soul to divine transcendence. Neither the number of (st)ages nor the exact chronology of each age was as important as the basic assumption that the natural divisions of a lifetime belong to the divine order of the universe.

Christian writers developed a doctrine of spiritual ages to complement the theory of bodily ages. As Thomas, Bishop of Brinton, preached in 1380: "Just as we speak of bodily age, whereby we proceed from infancy to boyhood...and so forth...so spiritual age is a progress from virtue to virtue, from grace to grace, from good to better, from perfection to greater perfection" (Burrow, 1986, p. 110). The concept of spiritual ages allowed for the paradoxical unity of physical decline and spiritual ascent. This unity played a central role in medieval thinking about aging and the life course. In *Il Covivio*, for example, Dante accepted Aristotle's theory of three ages. But he protested against the implication that "our life is no more than a mounting and descending." While he agreed that the physical and intellectual peak of life occurred in middle age, Dante believed that spiritual development continued—the "ennobled soul proceeds in due order (toward)...its ultimate fruit" (Dante, trans. Burrow, 1986, p. 6.).

Scientific Legacy of Antiquity

From antiquity, the Middle Ages received not only general ideas about the course of life, but also specific theories about the nature and causes of aging. Aristotle, Galen, Hippocrates, and Cicero were the principle authorities. In *On Youth and Old Age, on Life and Respiration*, Aristotle defined old age as that period of life when the body's innate heat diminishes. Heat was the essence of life according to Hippocratic medicine. The source of heat was the heart, conceived as a sort of furnace. From the heart, heat was sent to the whole body for the purpose of maintaining a healthful balance of humors. Both health and character depended on the regulation of the four humors.

Each individual possessed a finite amount of heat that steadily diminished in the natural course of life. Although it could be fortified or replenished temporarily, vital heat could never be wholly restored. In time, the fire of life eventually would be quenched.

The Roman physician Galen added another dimension to this classical theory of aging. Arguing that blood and semen, as sources of generation, required a drying element to produce tissue, he posited that vital heat began to dry these substances, producing an embryo. The drying process did not stop after formation of the embryo but continued throughout the individual's life. Thus Galen believed that an infant was mist and an old person quite dried out. In his theory, old age meant desiccation (Grant, 1963).

Ancient authors noted that behavioral changes accompanied physical signs. Aristotle considered old age a time when normal failings were magnified, when physical decline and the loss of inward heat depressed the spirit. Passions waned—a development that philosophers, equating passion with animal nature—considered one blessing in an otherwise baleful process.

Such was the scientific legacy that the Greco-Roman world bequeathed to scholars of the Middle Ages. Beginning at conception, the physiological process of drying out and growing cold continued inexorably until death. The stages of life were milestones marking diminution of natural heat and increased desiccation. Each change dictated its own behavioral patterns. This approach to aging and the ages of life arose in an intellectual milieu without boundaries between sciences, theology, and philosophy. Medieval writers combined the physical and the moral, interpreting behavioral signs in the light of physiology, individual character, and divine commandment.

Aging and the Fall of Humanity

Christianity added a new cause for sickness, aging, and death that went far beyond Hippocratic medicine's natural explanation. In medieval Christian theology, sickness, aging, and death were not the original condition of humanity. Rather, these were punishments that resulted from rebellion against God's commandment. In the Garden of Eden, Adam and Eve had lived in perfect health, their humors in balance—immune to the aging process. Once expelled from the Garden of Eden, however, they were no longer protected by the Tree of Life. They became subject to the processes of aging and illness that have been the fate of humankind ever since.

Christianity added a spiritual or moral cause to the physical causes of aging that had been emphasized by Greco-Roman writers. Aging and death result from original sin; they are necessitated by enforced separation from the primal source of youth and health. Medieval Christian writers, however, did not reject natural explanations. Rather, they took up Hippocratic remnants and stitched them into the fabric of scriptural and patristic teaching to create a world view in which physical processes were ordained and directed by God.

In the medieval synthesis, medicine and theology interact. Although it is natural to age and die, the ultimate cause lies in the fall of man. This religious belief conceived of aging as preparation for death and eternity. Ancient authors had understood aging as part of a journey from birth to death. In medieval Christian culture, the journey was transformed into a pilgrimage to God, the eternal source of life.

Medieval writers, in other words, subordinated the ages of life to the pilgrimage of life. Under the guiding hand of theology—known as the "Queen of the Sciences"—they wove theories of human development into a rich tapestry of astrology, humoral pathology, and natural philosophy. Until the end of the Middle Ages, these ideas remained the province of a courtly, ecclesiastical, or learned minority. But from the late fourteen century until the nineteenth century, new versions of the ages of life and the journey of life circulated more broadly. These included popular Protestant iconography of the life course and Bunyan's *Pilgrim's Progress*. These early modern concepts of human development provided Western society with cultural cognitive maps necessary for long-range thinking and planning about individual lifetime.

A seventeenth-century German portrayal (Figure 1) of both women and men moving together through the stages of life's journey is typical of the models of human development and aging that were becoming more common in society. There is reason to believe that such depictions of an orderly progression were intended to have a comforting effect, suggesting that everybody, young and old, female or male, has a place in the social and universal order.

Pilgrim's Progress (1678/1965) is one of the most popular pieces of prose fiction ever written. Its author, John Bunyan, was imprisoned for failing to conform to the Church of England. Part One of this folk epic describes the fictional journey of Christian, a kind of Everyman, whose passage through the stages of redemption takes the form of an exciting

Figure 1. The Ten Steps of Life (portrayed as ascending and descending a staircase) Germany, Seventeenth Century

adventure through unknown and dangerous territory. Filled with names of places and characters that have passed into world literature—e.g., Vanity Fair, the Iron Cage, the Slough of Despond—*Pilgrim's Progress* universalized the ideal of individual growth within the framework of Calvinist orthodoxy. In Part Two, Bunyan described the journey of Christiana (Christian's wife), thus emphasizing the spiritual quest of aging female believers (Cole, 1992).

A Competing Ideal: Scientific and Material Progress

Ironically, just as these two themes became more popular and socially important, scientists and scholars began to attack their ancient and medieval assumptions. By the middle of the eighteenth century, educated men and women generally espoused an ideal of scientific and material progress. The medieval Christian view of an imperfect earthly existence, whose only hope was divine intervention, seemed to rest on misguided fear and superstition. Galenic physiology was thoroughly discredited as a general theory of health and disease. Medicine and the life sciences turned their attention away from the essence of life and toward its phenomena. Within this context, the ages of life doctrine smacked of prescientific concern with astrology, myth, and religion.

After the decline of Galenic theory, medical thought turned increasingly to the nervous system to locate the regulatory powers traditionally ascribed to the four humors. Many Enlightenment physicians believed that an unknowable "vital force" activated all bodily processes. Aging consisted of the gradual deterioration of this force, resulting in a drying of the body, diminishing and souring of the humors, narrowing of the blood vessels, wearing out of the organs, and accumulation of earthy materials in the body (Grant, 1963).

During the first half of the nineteenth century, leading physicians of the Paris school of medicine rejected the traditional conception of illness as a general systematic condition. Instead, they devised nosologies based on specific disease entities whose existence could be confirmed by postmortem examination. Much of the empirical research of the Paris school was conducted on aged paupers at Salpetriere and Bicetre hospitals. French physicians wrote the first treatises in geriatric medicine, based on the idea of old age as a clinically distinct stage of life (Haber, 1983; Stearns, 1976).

While these French clinicians attempted to reduce the processes and diseases of aging to specific mechanisms and lesions, they often retained the principle of a life or "vital" force. However, with the growing knowledge of cellular biology in the 1830s and of bacteriology in the 1880s, the principle of an unobservable life force gradually fell out of favor. Degeneration of tissues and of cells replaced depletion of the life force as primary explanations of aging.

Although the life sciences discarded the ancient medical doctrine underlying the "ages of life," this image remained important in iconography and popular culture, particularly in rural areas, up to the eve of World War I. Even in medical and scientific thought, remnants of the old theory hung on. The notion of a "grand climacteric," for instance, appears in I. L. Nascher's pioneering *Geriatrics* (1914), as well as in G. Stanley Hall's *Senescence* (1922). Derived from the Greek word for step, staircase, or ladder, the "grand climacteric" referred to the last major transition in life—the "dangerous age" marking the difficult passage from middle age to old age.

By the end of the nineteenth century, Anglo-American academic writers began clamoring for specialized research on old age—often in the native view that laboratory science would "solve" the problems of aging

(Minot, 1908). The growing cultural dominance of a scientific worldview generally strengthened popular hostility to all forms of decline or decay—especially old age and death. Meanwhile, the steady erosion of religious authority weakened the vision of life as a sacred pilgrimage (Cole, 1992). New editions of John Bunyan's *Pilgrim's Progress*, which had been one of the most popular books in America in the nineteenth century, virtually disappeared around 1910.

Modern Scientific Faith and Its Limitations

The central tendency of modern gerontological thought has been to detach aging from any kind of religious or philosophical worldview. This tendency reflects the modern scientific faith that an accumulation of discrete, observable, quantifiable facts will someday add up to total knowledge of the natural and social worlds, allowing men and women to order their existence without conflict, suffering, or mystery.

As the twentieth century draws to a close, the limits as well as the benefits of this vision have become increasingly apparent. Scientific and technical progress have permitted spectacular gains in longevity, though the nature of biological aging and the future health status of an exploding aged population remain unclear. Contemporary Western culture is plagued by widespread cultural malaise and confusion over the meaning and purpose of human life—particularly in old age.

When Erik Erikson developed his theory of the "Eight Ages of Man" in 1950 (see Figure 2), he sought to recreate an integrated vision of the life cycle that was both descriptive and normative.

Erikson did not refer to his predecessors in the "ages of life" tradition, with their assumptions of the interrelationships between "man," "nature," "society," and the "cosmos." But in 1964 he did note that modern Western culture failed to provide coherent meaning for later life. "As we come to the last stage," he wrote, "we become aware...that

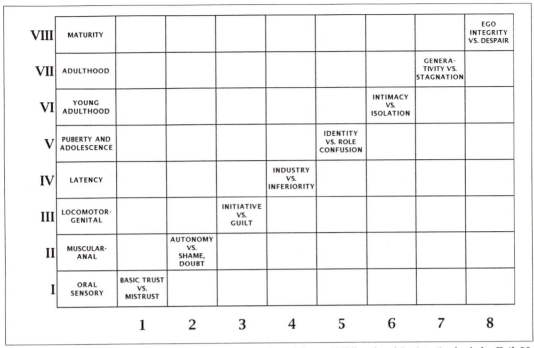

Figure 2. Erikson's "Eight Stages of Man." Reproduced from *Childhood and Society*, 2nd ed., by Erik H. Erikson, by permission of W.W. Norton & Company, Inc. Copyright 1950, © 1963 by W.W. Norton & Company, Inc. Copyright renewed 1978, 1991 by Erik H. Erikson.

our civilization really does not harbor a concept of the whole of life….As our world image is a one way street to never-ending progress…our lives are to be one way streets to success—and sudden oblivion" (Erikson, 1964, p. 132).

In the last decade of the twentieth century, we are witnessing renewed interest in metaphor, myth, symbolism, and other modes of conveying meaning. The positivist faith that all problems will yield to scientific explanation and control now appears not only inadequate, but destructive of a fundamental human need to envision life as a meaningful whole. As our postmodern culture searches for more adequate ways to understand and experience the second half of life, we would do well to remember the *ages of life* and the *journey of life*—two essential images in Western thinking about human development and aging (Cole, Van Tassel, & Kastenbaum, 1992).

▼ THOMAS R. COLE AND MARY G. WINKLER

See also: Age 65; Creativity; Development and Aging; Fairy Tales as Commentary on Adult Development and Aging; Gender Differences in the Workplace; Generational Equity; Individuality; Japanese Perspectives on Adult Development; Maturity; Metaphors of the Life Course; Mid-Life Crisis; Native American Perspectives on the Lifespan; Possessions; Suffering; Twins through the Lifespan.

References

Aristotle (1924). *Rhetoric*. (Chapters 12-14). Oxford: Oxford University Press.

Bernard, C. (1865). *An Introduction to the Study of Experimental Medicine*. Reprint. New York: Dover, 1957.

Bunyan, J. (1965). *Pilgrim's Progress*. Harmondsworth, England: Penguin.

Burrow, J.A. (1986). *The Ages of Man*. New York: Oxford University Press.

Charcot, J.M. (1881). *Clinical Lectures on the Diseases of Old Age*. New York: William Wood.

Cicero. *De Senectute* (1923). Cambridge: Cambridge University Press.

Cole, T.R. (1992). *The Journey of Life*. Cambridge: Cambridge University Press.

Cole, T.R., Van Tassel, D., & Kastenbaum, R. (Eds.) (1992). *Handbook of the Humanities and Aging*. New York: Springer.

Dove, M. (1986). *The Perfect Age of a Man's Life*. Cambridge: Cambridge University Press.

Erikson, E.H. (1950). *Childhood and Society*. New York: Norton.

———. (1964). *Insight and Responsibility*. New York: Norton.

Grant, R.L. (1963). Concepts of aging: An historical review. *Perspectives in Biology and Medicine*, 44: 10.

Haber, C. (1983). *Beyond Sixty-Five*. Cambridge: Cambridge University Press.

Hall, G.S. (1922). *Senescence: The Last Half of Life*. New York: D. Appleton.

Minot, C.S. (1908). *The Problem of Age, Growth, and Death*. New York: Putnam.

Nascher, I.L. (1914). *Geriatrics*. Reprint. New York: Arno Press, 1979.

Ptolemy (1940). *Tetrabiblos*. Cambridge: Cambridge University Press.

Stearns, P. (1976). *Old Age in European Society*. New York: Holmes and Meier.

DISENGAGEMENT THEORY

Almost all theories of human development focus upon infancy and childhood. This emphasis neither taxes our understanding nor requires apology. Clearly, it is useful to "begin from the beginning." Furthermore, the early phases of life are so rich in process and event that observers are afforded an exceptional opportunity to see growth and development in perhaps its most exuberant moments. For example, one day a baby still shy of her third month "decides" to invest her energies in attempting to turn herself over. For most of that day, turning is her top priority, and she accompanies her eventually successful efforts with screams and grunts, much like an athlete testing the limits of her ability. The next day she is tired and less active, but she now has turning over well incorporated into her behavioral repertoire. Turning still requires considerable effort, but it has already become a past accomplishment, so this activity no longer requires self-encouraging screams and grunts—only a day or so after developing this skill, it is merely something that Brianna does. The early life focus of typical developmental theories also serves a variety of practical purposes, e.g., improving our ability to identify and encour-

age superior child-rearing practices, detecting and alleviating problems that might otherwise interfere with continued physical, psychological, and social growth, and so on.

There is a cost to these theories, however, and it comes due in the middle and later adult years. The tendency to view the second half of the lifespan through the lens of early developmental theories has interfered with fresh and independent observations. The thoughts, feelings, actions, and relationships of mature adults often are regarded as the (frequently degraded) outcomes of earlier developmental processes. What might be new, different, and distinctive about the middle and later adult years can be obscured by reliance on concepts and methods that were established in youth-oriented research. Imagine what ideas we might now be favoring about infancy and childhood if we were laboring with assumptions derived from work with aged adults.

Disengagement theory has earned a place in history as the first influential modern approach to adult development that actually takes adult development as its starting point. The emergence of disengagement theory in the 1960s provided a jolt of new energy to the field of gerontology and kindled a number of interests that are still being pursued today. For both its historical significance and its inherent features, disengagement theory is well worth the attention of all who seek to understand the whole of human development.

Basic Concepts of Disengagement Theory

The gist of disengagement theory and its research origins have been succinctly characterized by its cofounder, Elaine Cumming:

> Disengagement theory was developed during a five-year study of a sample of aging people in an American city. These were 275 adults between the ages of 50 and 90 years; they were in good health and had the minimum of money for independence. Briefly, the theory proposes that under these conditions, normal aging is a mutual withdrawal

or "disengagement" between the aging person and others in the social system to which he belongs—a withdrawal initiated by the individual himself, or by others in the system. When disengagement is complete, the equilibrium that existed in middle life between the individual and society has given way to a new equilibrium characterized by greater distance and a changed basis for solidarity. (Cumming, 1964, p. 3)

The study itself (conducted in Kansas City) provided social gerontology with much needed information on elderly adults who were living independently in the community and introduced measures of social interaction and morale that were eagerly taken up by the field. Reported most fully in *Growing Old* (Cumming & Henry, 1961), the Kansas City study served as a foundation for many subsequent attempts to learn about the characteristics and coping techniques of senior adults. Even more stimulating at the time, however, was the theoretical approach that Cumming and her colleague, William E. Henry, generated from this study.

As the quoted passage indicates, disengagement theory proposed major hypotheses about the course of development in the second half of life. A synthesis of the most fundamental hypotheses can be drawn from the various writings of the coauthors (Cumming et al., 1960; Cumming & Henry, 1961; Cumming, 1964; Henry, 1965):

1. Disengagement is an inevitable and universal process: It will be experienced by all aging people, although its timing and quality will be influenced by personal and situational factors.

2. This process is normative (expectable) and therefore should not be regarded as pathological or abnormal. It is as much a part of nature for aging people and their societies to disengage from each other as it is for children to grow into adults who take up the burden of basic social obligations.

3. Disengagement is mutual. Under favorable conditions, the older person and society are both ready to alter their relationship. As in a ritualistic dance, each

partner bows to the other and takes several steps backward. From this point on, society will expect less from the disengaged person who, in turn, will be relieved of many of his or her former responsibilities and will enjoy the freedom afforded by less encumbered time and reduced obligations. Society may delay the disengagement of a relatively few elderly individuals who are considered indispensable; others may be forced out before they are ready to leave. Ready or not, however, the disengagement process eventually encompasses all people if they live long enough.

4. From the individual's standpoint, disengagement begins with the recognition that his or her remaining time is limited. Values tend to change with the perception that time is starting to run out. Instead of trying to keep doing everything, the individual reconsiders the values that are most meaningful and is likely to rearrange life's priorities. "The first stirrings of a willingness to disengage from the peak involvement of the middle years may be the feeling that there is not time to do everything we had meant to do" (Cumming & Henry, 1961, p. 22).

5. A significant corollary here is that the aging person is said to become more inward and reflective. Concepts such as "life review" and "heightened interiority" may be applied to this shift in the focus of thought.

6. The elderly person eventually *reengages* with society. This is a normal and essential part of the overall process. The new engagement is on a more optional and voluntary basis—instead of having to show up at work every day and perform to the boss's demands, for example, a person may decide to donate time and skill to a community project, or become a part-time student.

7. Gender differences are salient in adjustment to disengagement. Women may suffer a loss in status associated with their husband's retirement, but men are more vulnerable to anxiety and depres-

sion because they now have lost their primary function as breadwinners and are not as adept as women in the art of social relationships that becomes so important in the postoccupational years.

Biological, psychological, and sociocultural factors all play their roles in disengagement theory. Growing old involves physiological processes that bring about a progressive decrease in physical functioning and move the individual ever closer to death. Society responds to this basic fact—and to the need for renewing itself with vigorous youth—by easing or forcing aging people into less responsible positions. Caught between biological and sociocultural pressures, the individual engages in psychological processes that lead to recognition of the situation, reevaluation of priorities, and some form of reengagement.

Evaluating Disengagement Theory

The social gerontological establishment expressed particular interest in the implications of disengagement theory for individual coping and social policy. The most common reaction was to regard the disengagement hypothesis as a challenge to the assumption that people should continue to be active and involved in the later years of life. In the 1960s gerontology was a new field that combined interdisciplinary study and advocacy within a society that held prevailingly negative stereotypes about older people. Many gerontologists were attempting to promote a more enlightened perspective in which the experience and skills of elderly men and women would be appreciated and valued. To them, disengagement theory seemed to pose a threat. Is it really normal and proper for aging people to withdraw from society? If so, then perhaps there was little justification for a vigorous advocacy of active life-styles in old age.

Accordingly, a lively controversy centered over the rival claims of disengagement and activity theories. The latter theory was little more than a slogan at first, an insistence that one must and should be busy and involved, rather than passive and withdrawn. An actual theory was eventually offered (Lemon, Bengston, & Peterson, 1972), with emphasis on social roles and self-concept. As Hendricks and Hendricks (1981) note, however, this theory received little further elaboration or critical attention.

Although the disengagement vs. activity controversy generated many studies, the results were not as enlightening as one might have hoped. Many studies settled for simplistic measures of engagement or activity; significant variables such as physical and emotional health, socioeconomic class, and situational opportunities were often neglected. Perhaps most critically, there was a tendency to misinterpret the basic premises of disengagement theory. Never did Cumming and Henry insist that older people should not engage in pleasurable and meaningful activities, nor did they warn that it would be misguided or unnatural to provide rehabilitation services or other resources. The hypothesis that disengagement is inevitable and universal did suggest that one would have limited success in attempting to prevent or reverse the process. This is not the same thing, however, as insisting that we must enforce disengagement and refrain from any action that might foster continued activity among elderly people. On the contrary, the theory specifies that *reengagement* is a crucial part of the total process. After the detachment phase of the disengagement process, people may once again have a strong sense of involvement and participate in activities that are of particular importance to them.

Today, both of these positions seem a little naive. Thoughtful researchers realize that the number of activities in which a person engages may not be as important as their meaning to the individual. Furthermore, disengagement theory has given more attention to individual differences and has been willing to consider the possibility that the process might not be as immutable as first supposed. Research energies now are invested in a variety of more specific questions (e.g., how certain types of activity are related to particular health outcomes) that first became salient through the disengagement / activity controversy.

Other facets of disengagement theory remain of interest, although they have not received as much attention as the controversy already discussed. Cumming & Henry's (1961) exploration of gender-related experiences in later adulthood provides a useful historical baseline against which to compare subsequent socioeconomic developments. These developments include, for example, the changing pattern of female participation in the work force, both the progress and the frustrations encountered in the equal rights movement, and the continued growth of adult communities in Sun Belt states, all of which have provided a different context within which many people move into their later years. Attention to subcultural differences is also needed. The original sample for disengagement theory was middle-class, middle-America whites. Whether or not the same phenomena would be observed in other socioeconomic and ethnic groups remains to be determined.

Two of the most provocative disengagement theory hypotheses have received surprisingly little critical and empirical attention. Unlike all the controversy stirred up by the disengagement / activity issue, most gerontologists have been content to accept without question the proposition that people become more reflective and devoted to heightened interiority with advancing adult age. The work of David Guttmann (1987) is a significant exception. It remains unclear whether heightened interiority (and the life review) should be regarded as a general characteristic of the aging person or as a pathway of development that is taken by a relatively few inquiring minds. Research on time perspective in later life is not especially supportive of the notion that creative life reviewing and enhanced imagination occur frequently in later life (Kastenbaum, 1982).

The other dangling proposition concerns the aging adult's hypothetical encounter with mortality. Disengagement theory asserts that recognition of the shortage of time and the certainty of death are critical to the initiation of the entire detachment-reattachment process. Again, though, gerontology has given little systematic attention to this proposition, and the available observations fall short of demonstrating that such musings on mortality occur with all or even most people (Kastenbaum, 1992, Chapter 4). Some people are not much given to reflection in either youth or old age, and others prefer activity to troubling thoughts.

These unsettled issues do not detract from disengagement theory's contributions to our thinking about the second half of life. The stream of research and theory in adult development has moved past this seminal theory without answering all the questions that have been raised, but even those who have never opened *Growing Old* have benefited from its heritage of fact, method, and idea.   ▼ Robert Kastenbaum

See also: Adult Development and Aging, Models of; Contextualism; Depression; Gender as a Shaping Force in Adult Development and Aging; Gender Differences in the Workplace; Generational Equity; Individuality; Life Events; Mastery Types, Development, and Aging; Mid-Life Crisis; Retirement: An Emerging Challenge for Women; Social Class and Adult Development; Subcultural Influences on Lifelong Development; Work Organization Membership and Behavior.

References

Cumming, E. (1964). New thoughts on the theory of disengagement. In R. Kastenbaum (Ed.), *New Thoughts on Old Age*. New York: Springer, pp. 3-18.

———. (1975). Engagement with an old theory. *International Journal of Aging and Human Development, 6:* 187-91.

Cumming, E., & Henry, W. E. (1961). *Growing Old*. New York: Basic Books (reprint edition: New York: Arno Press, 1979).

Cumming, E., et al. (1960). Disengagement—a tentative theory of aging. *Sociometry, 23* (1).

Gutmann, D. (1987). *Reclaimed Powers*. New York: Basic Books.

Hendricks, J., & Hendricks, C. D. (1981). *Aging in Mass Society*. Second Edition. Cambridge, MA: Winthrop.

Henry, W. E. (1965). Engagement and disengagement: Toward a theory of adult development. In R. Kastenbaum (Ed.), *Contributions to the Psychobiology of Aging*. New York: Springer, pp. 19-36.

Kastenbaum, R. (1982). Time course and time perspective in later life. In C. Eisdorfer (Ed.), *Annual Review of Gerontology and Geriatrics*. Volume 3. New York: Springer, pp. 80-101.

———. (1992). *The Psychology of Death*. Second Edition. New York: Springer.

Lemon, W. B., Bengston, V. L., & Peterson, J. A. (1972). An exploration of the activity theory of aging: Activity types and life expectation among in-movers to a retirement community. *Journal of Gerontology*, 27: 511-23.

DIVORCE

Divorce is a complex legal, social, and personal process that affects people of all ages and has cross-generational implications. Marital separation and divorce, once associated with mental illness and other forms of social deviance, are now recognized to have elements of both crisis and challenge. How the process is resolved and whether the resolution leads to personal growth or stagnation depends not only on the divorcing individuals and their social supports but also on the economic and legal contexts.

Historical Background

Over a period of less than 40 years, the social institution of divorce has evolved from something unusual and suspect to a common and socially accepted phenomenon. After a temporary surge in divorces immediately following World War II when the soldiers returned home, divorce rates remained relatively stable until the mid-1950s. From 1957 to 1977, the incidence of divorce among persons aged 44 or younger more than doubled. Smaller increases occurred among middle-aged and elderly persons (Glick, 1984).

More recent figures reveal a changing demographic pattern. From 1983 through 1991, the divorce rate per 1,000 population dropped from approximately 5.1 to 4.7 (National Center for Health Statistics, 1991). Using 1985 data from the U.S. Bureau of the Census, Norton and Moorman (1987) projected that lifelong probabilities of divorce for women would reach their peak with the birth cohort that is currently in their thirties, and may have already begun to wane. Norton and Moorman also reported that approximately 56 percent of women in their thirties would divorce at some point in their lives. A slightly but encouragingly lower lifetime probability of divorce (54 percent) was estimated for women in their twenties. Rates were also lower for those in middle and later ages: 36 percent for women in their forties and 24 percent for women in their fifties.

Despite these fluctuations, however, the overall incidence of divorce remains high. It is estimated that well over two million persons divorce each year (e.g., National Center for Health Statistics, 1991). If one takes into consideration the children and the parents of divorcing persons, then it is reasonable to assume that more than six million people are affected by new divorces every year. Moreover, the ranks of those who have already divorced are steadily growing.

The increasing prevalence of divorced persons may lead to increases in the number of older adults who lack social supports and to greater numbers of people who find it hard to serve as caregivers to young and older generations. For example, there is evidence that divorce interferes with the amount of support that adult children provide to dependent parents (Cicirelli, 1983). Since the children of divorced parents themselves seem to have an increased risk of divorce, a vicious cycle of diminished intergenerational support may ensue (Chiriboga et al., 1991).

Age Differences in the Impact of Divorce

Although most researchers have focused their attention on young adults, increasing numbers of middle-aged and older adults are terminating their marriages. Furthermore, many of those who divorce in their twenties and thirties enter their middle and later years as divorced people. In a pioneering study, Goode (1956) reported that older women seemed more distressed by divorce. Although by "older" Goode was referring to women in their late thirties, the idea that advancing age might bring increased vulnerabilities with respect to divorce has been supported by more recent studies (e.g., Cooney et al., 1986). In a lifespan study of men and women who ranged in age from 20 to over 70, Chiriboga et al. (1991) found that the older the maritally separated adult, the lower the reported psychological well-being.

Gender Differences in the Impact of Divorce

Women traditionally have been viewed as the prime victims of divorce, women with children being particularly vulnerable. The reasons cited for the greater vulnerability of women include a more limited or interrupted work history, job discrimination, recent changes in divorce law that have reduced alimony payments, and the pressures and stresses experienced by single-parent mothers who must cope with the economic, emotional, and energy demands associated with child rearing (Weitzman, 1985).

More recent longitudinal and probability-based studies indicate that divorce takes its toll on men as well. Some evidence now suggests that women may experience a higher quality of life and more adequate psychological functioning than men in both short- and long-term adjustment to divorce (Chiriboga et al., 1991; Wallerstein, 1986). It is also apparent that the presence of young children may impede the recovery not only of women (e.g., Weiss, 1979), but of men as well (Chiriboga et al., 1991; Huntington, 1986).

There is some consensus that the problems faced by men and women during the process of divorce are quite different: While divorced mothers must contend with the challenge of combining work and child raising, men must contend with loneliness, finding a new home, the potential loss of their children's love, and filling in the "empty hours."

Stress and Negative Life Events

Divorce has become recognized in recent years as a devastatingly negative life event. Although stress methodologies and theories have been applied to divorce to only a limited degree, a linkage clearly exists between mental health and the multiple stressors that are encountered when marriages terminate (Caldwell, Bloom, & Hodges, 1983). In one of our studies of adult men and women, the author and his colleagues found that marital separation and divorce not only can be regarded as individual life events but also seem to act as triggers and catalysts for a host of subsequent events (Chiriboga et al., 1991). We considered both positive and negative events in 11 areas of stress, such as marital or dating relationship, family, work, finances, and home. The participants were 333 men and women aged 20 to 70+. Life events were reported both during the period of marital separation and at a follow-up some three and one-half years later. On both of these occasions, women reported having experienced more life events in such areas as home situation and finances. No age differences were found with respect to negative stressors during the period of marital separation. Fewer positive events, however, were reported by men and women aged 40 and over in such areas as work, marital or dating activities, and relationships outside the family.

When the participants were recontacted three and one-half years later, fewer negative life events were found for all age groups. Moreover, age differences also emerged at this point in exposure to negative events: Those aged 50 or over now reported fewer negative events than did the younger participants. Furthermore, the older men and women reported significant increases in the number of positive events they had experienced, while the younger participants reported somewhat fewer positive events. Evidently, the quality of life for divorced persons can differ appreciably from the time that the marital separation is occurring to a later point in time.

Social support can spell the difference between the individual's tendency to regard a situation as a crisis or a challenge. Kitson (1992) reports that people frequently lose friends when they divorce, a phenomenon that has also been reported in studies of bereavement. The social support system available to men may be more severely compromised by marital discord because, in general, men have fewer friends overall and are more likely to rely on their spouse as their prime confidant (Chiriboga et al., 1991).

A Ripple Across Time and Generation

Although divorce reaps its greatest harvest of distress during the months immediately following marital separation, some individuals are adversely affected for many years. For example, Wallerstein & Blakeslee (1989) report that at least half of the men they studied were still experiencing distress 10 years after the initial separation. An important point to keep in mind, however, is that the divorce is likely to have negative effects on many people besides the couple that is splitting up. As noted by Peck and Manocherian (1989) and by Johnson (1988), divorce often affects grandparents and children as well.

Grandparents may be distressed by the problems facing their divorcing child and also by the potential loss of their own visitation rights to grandchildren. Although several states have passed laws protecting the rights of grandparents, their views and concerns often are overlooked or not expressed. Potentially, the grandparents of today and tomorrow could play a valuable integrative role for both their divorcing children and their grandchildren. This positive view is based on the fact that each successive cohort of grandparents has been younger, healthier, and more financially secure than previous cohorts (Johnson, 1988). Whether or not many grandparents would choose to play a strong supportive role to the divorcing family is unknown at present.

Children of divorce can be affected at any age. Whether a young child or an adolescent, the individual may be adversely affected by the divorce, not only in the short run but over periods of 5 and 10 years (e.g., Wallerstein & Blakeslee, 1989). Younger children tend to blame themselves or feel it is up to them to get the parents together again. Older children are better able to understand the situation and to express their own anger at what is happening.

There is also evidence that adult children experience conflicts when their parents divorce (Ahrons & Rogers, 1987; Cooney et al., 1986). However, while they may experience anger and conflict over the breakup, adult children do not appear to develop the degree of intrapsychic damage that is experienced by young children.

Divorce and the Changing Structure of Families

Divorced men and women are likely to remarry. This is especially true of men and of both men and women under the age of 40. Many do not remarry, however, and some do so only to go through another divorce. More than half of the households in the United States are currently headed by women. It is estimated that approximately half the school-age children live in single-parent households or in households that include a stepparent (Brown, 1989).

The term *reconstituted family* is sometimes used to refer to families in which one or both partners were previously married and/or have children by a prior relationship. Such family structures are another side effect of divorce and are definitely on the increase (Ahrons & Rogers, 1987). The complexity of relationships in reconstituted families is reflected in the lack of familiar and appropriate kinship terms (Johnson, 1988). For example, what do children call their previous set of grandparents, as distinguished from the new set? Who is the "real" Daddy and Mommy when two or more people potentially occupy each status?

Of particular concern in the reconstituted family are the stepchildren. Not only may they have ambivalent feelings toward their stepparent, but the stepparent may encounter problems related to the lack of clear guidelines for his or her new parental role. White and Booth (1985) report that the risk of divorce among remarriages is approximately 50 percent greater when there is the presence of at least one stepchild.

Divorce as a Transitional Process

Divorce is increasingly viewed as a "normative transition," that is to say, a situation that can be expected to occur and that results in change of status and relationships (Ahrons & Rogers, 1987; Chiriboga et al., 1991; Peck & Manocherian, 1989). This attitude has been rapidly challenging the traditional assumption that marriages will endure "until death do us part." The concept of *transitions* is proving helpful in understanding the processes involved in divorce and providing a framework for counseling and other interventions when these are indicated (e.g., Schlossberg, 1984).

Anthropologists conceive of life transitions as taking place in three stages. Each of these stages of transition is associated with what might be called a developmental task. In the first stage, called Separation, the task is to detach oneself as completely as possible from the previous way of life. Those who fail to sever their social, emotional, or economic bonds with their former spouse may never resolve the multiple problems that accompany divorce. The Liminal stage comes next, and its task is to learn the new roles and role requirements that one faces after leaving the marital relationship. In the final stage, Aggregation, one reenters society with the readiness to take on new adult responsibilities. Divorce and some other types of transition may also have an earlier stage that occurs before Separation. During this period of Anticipation one considers the pros and cons of making such a significant role change (Chiriboga et al., 1991).

Perhaps the bottom line is that divorce confronts people with multiple demands for change. People move, change jobs or reenter the job market, and alter their relationships to family and friends. These changes are not always undesired. Men and women who are going through a divorce have been found to score higher on positive as well as negative life events (Chiriboga et al., 1991). Given the diversity of experiences that are made possible by divorce, it is not surprising that people vary widely in how they live through this transition. For some, it is an overwhelming crisis. For others, it is a challenge. For still others, it is essentially a relief. However they react, the lives of divorcing people will never be quite the same.   ▼ DAVID A. CHIRIBOGA

See also: Adult Children and Their Parents; Cohort and Generational Effects; Gender as a Shaping Force in Adult Development and Aging; Information Processing; Longevity; Risk to Life through the Adult Years; Sexuality; Slowing of Behavior with Age; Vision.

References

Ahrons, C. R., & Rogers, R. H. (1987). *Divorced Families: A Multi-Disciplinary Developmental View.* New York: Norton.

Brown, F. H. (1989). The postdivorce family. In B. Carter & M. McGoldrick (Eds.), *The Changing Family Life Cycle.* Second Edition. Boston: Allyn and Bacon, pp. 371-98.

Caldwell, R. A., Bloom, B. L., & Hodges, W. F. (1983). Sex differences in separation and divorce: A longitudinal perspective. *Issues in Mental Health Nursing, 5:* 103-20.

Chiriboga, D. A., et al. (1991). *Divorce: Crisis, Challenge, or Relief?* New York: New York University Press.

Cicirelli, V. (1983). A comparison of helping behavior to elderly parents of adult children with intact and disrupted marriages. *Gerontologist, 24:* 396-400.

Cooney, T. M., et al. (1986). Parental divorce in young adulthood: Some preliminary findings. *American Journal of Orthopsychiatry, 56:* 470-77.

Glick, P. (1984). Marriage, divorce, and living arrangements: Prospective changes. *Journal of Family Issues, 5:* 7-26.

Goode, W. J. (1956). *Women in Divorce.* New York: The Free Press.

Huntington, D. S. (1986). Fathers: The forgotten figures in divorce. In J. W. Jacobs (Ed.), *Divorce and Fatherhood: The Struggle for Parental Identity.* Washington, DC: American Psychiatric Association.

Johnson, C. L. (1988). *Ex Familia: Grandparents, Parents, and Children Adjust to Divorce.* New Brunswick, NJ: Rutgers University Press.

Kitson, G. C. (1992). *Portrait of Divorce.* New York: Guilford Press.

National Center for Health Statistics. (1991). Births, marriages, divorces, and deaths for May, 1991. *Monthly Vital Statistics Report, 40:* 1-24.

Norton, A. J., & Moorman, J. E. (1987). Current trends in marriage and divorce among American women. *Journal of Marriage and the Family, 49:* 3-14.

Peck, J. S., & Manocherian, J. R. (1989). Divorce in the changing family life cycle. In B. Carter & M. McGoldrick (Eds.), *The Changing Family Life Cycle.* Second Edition. Boston: Allyn and Bacon, pp. 335-69.

Schlossberg, N.K. (1984). *Counseling Adults in Transition: Linking Practice with Theory.* New York: Springer.

Wallerstein, J.S. (1986). Women after divorce: Preliminary report on a ten year follow-up. *American Journal of Orthopsychiatry, 56:* 65-77.

Wallerstein, J.S., & Blakeslee, S. (1989). *Second Chance: Men, Women and Children a Decade After Divorce.* New York: Ticknor & Fields.

Weiss, R.S. (1979). Growing up a little faster. *Journal of Social Issues, 35:* 97-111.

Weitzman, L.J. (1985). *The Divorce Revolution: The Unexpected Social and Economic Consequences for Women and Children in America.* New York: The Free Press.

White, L., & Booth, A. (1985). The quality and stability of remarriages: The role of stepchildren. *American Sociological Review, 50:* 689-98.

DRIVING: A LIFESPAN CHALLENGE

The introduction of the automobile was rather quickly followed by the introduction of the driver's license. Authorities could see that this alarming contrivance promised to be a source of nuisance and danger as well as a new way of getting from one place to another. American folklore has it that the operator of the first and only horseless carriage in town was such a reckless driver that he was re-quired to apply for the first license and operate the vehicle in a more responsible manner. The name of this gentleman was Henry Ford, as Paul Harvey has related in one of his popular "Now you know the rest of the story" broadcasts.

The automobile not only has changed the life-style of individuals and nations but has become virtually a member of the family and a symbol of adult identity and empowerment. Getting behind the wheel of a car and turning the ignition key has long been an act that symbolizes a youth's ability to seek his or her own place in the community. "This is my freedom. This is my entry into the world of power, status, opportunity, and independence," sings youth. "Slow down, keep your eyes on the road, and turn down that radio," warns the establishment.

From youth through advanced age, operating a motor vehicle involves the related themes of opportunity, responsibility, and identity. Achieving and maintaining a balance among these forces can be regarded as a measure of one's maturity and competence. The individual's pattern of driving behavior also represents the influence of sociocultural and environmental as well as developmental and personality factors. Particular attention will be given here to issues surrounding the continuation of driving behavior in the later adult years.

Opportunity, Responsibility, and Identity Issues

Motor vehicles serve many of the same opportunity functions throughout the adult age spectrum. Access to an automobile, truck, or motor bike enables many adults to meet a variety of needs and desires. They drive to work, to the supermarket, to visit their friends, or to the movies. In an emergency, they drive to the clinic or hospital. In one mood, they drive "to get away" from people, places, and situations; in another mood, they drive to "get back" to people, places, and situations that they long to see again, or they pack up their "significant others" and go off together. Just "driving to drive" has long been a favorite and relatively inexpensive pastime. Three generations may crowd into a car on an autumn ride to enjoy the changing colors of the leaves or to picnic in a favorite spot. Some of these activities could be carried out, if less conveniently, without a motor vehicle, but the total pattern of flexibility and freedom to come and go as they choose would be out of reach for many people without access to a car.

Theoretically, it is only access that one would need. As long as a qualified driver is available to operate the vehicle, perhaps it should not matter whether one is behind the wheel or rides as a passenger. The ability and license to drive, however, have both symbolic and functional implications. If grandmother never learned to drive, or has voluntarily surrendered her license, then she must be dependent upon others to take her places. This situation has the potential of being a source of discontent for both the nondriver and the driver because both must coordinate their schedules and make compromises. The desire to see one's self as independent and, in fact, to be in a position to decide and act as an independent person is strong among adults of all ages. For example, in a study of three-generational families, all reported themselves to be highly independent people on several measures (Kastenbaum & Cameron, 1969). Therefore, it can be as difficult for elderly as for young adults to be in situations in which they cannot exercise the valued sense of independence by turning the ignition key and heading off.

Nevertheless, there are some age and cohort differences despite the significance of perceived independence at all age levels as well as the functional purposes that are served by the automobile.

1. For youth, driving is particularly esteemed as a way of removing themselves, if temporarily, from family control. Once in the car, the live-at-home adolescent can more readily experience himself or herself as an independent and empowered person.

2. For elderly adults, driving is particularly valued as a way of demonstrating that they can *continue* to exercise their independence and competency. This ability also serves as a protection against the fear of losing their place in the world. "I'm not old, I can drive," as one respondent told researcher Susan Eisenhandler (1990).

3. Shopping, staying in contact with friends and family, and having the ability to respond to medical and other emergencies through the use of a car are among values especially associated with driving among older adults, while the need for transportation to paid employment and school has diminished.

4. Women in earlier-born cohorts are less likely to be experienced drivers—or to drive at all—compared with females born in more recent decades. Both men and women who are now in their later adult years are more likely to have developed "activist" orientations toward auto operation and maintenance, having had to deal with vehicles that were balkier (e.g., stalling, overheating) required more from the operator (e.g., pre-automatic transmissions), and had more maintenance and repair jobs that could be done by the average motorist without recourse to a mechanic. Younger drivers in today's more technologically advanced cars have a less active involvement in the routine operation of their vehicles. In this sense, drivers from earlier-born cohorts may, as a group, have a more highly developed sense of interaction with car and road.

Two other facets of driving are equally relevant among younger and older drivers: The cost of owning, operating, and insuring a motor vehicle is often a major concern for both teens and retired adults, and the perceived social status associated with possessing a desirable vehicle is valued by many adults at all ages.

The special meaning of maintaining one's license to drive in later adulthood emerged clearly in a recent study by Eisenhandler (1990). She characterizes the driver's license in old age as "the asphalt identikit." More specifically, by possessing a valid driver's license, the elderly adult has a tangible *disidentifier* to counter any possible allegations that he or she is "old" and therefore no longer an independent and empowered member of the adult community. "Elders maintain a continuing claim to identity and to membership in the larger community through this laminated piece of plastic that entitles them to drive anywhere in the country" (Eisenhandler, 1990, p. 3). This disidentifier is especially useful when elderly adults must deal with people and places that are outside the family circle. Faced with the prospect of being treated in a categorical manner rather than as a unique and worthy individual, they can use the driver's license as an indicator that they should be not lumped with "those other people" who really cannot take care of themselves any more.

Several other studies have also found that elderly adults who live independently in the community rely heavily on the automobile as the primary means of transportation (e.g., Krout, 1983; McGhee, 1983). In many areas, the alternatives to the private automobile are not very satisfactory, with public transportation being inconvenient, unreliable, or virtually nonexistent. To lose or surrender one's driver's license, then, would not only constitute a possibly damaging blow to self-esteem and sense of independence but would also contribute to social isolation and the inability to look after one's own needs.

Driver Competency and Safety Issues

The competency of the individual driver and the safety of his or her pattern of behavior within a particular sociophysical environment is an issue throughout the adult lifespan. Not all the variables are directly linked to age. For example, some young drivers take excellent care of their vehicles, thereby reducing the likelihood of accident, and some middle-aged and elderly drivers never think to replace defective brakes or check wheel alignments. People differ in their general affinity for and understanding of machines as well as in their attitudes toward automobile knowledge, care, and safety. There are also marked differences in role models and child-rearing patterns that give rise to differential lifespan relationships to competency and safety as a driver. The little girl of 1950 whose parents or older siblings welcomed her to the weekend ritual of puttering with the family car may be today's astute driver who makes sure her car is always in top shape and has never had an accident.

Symbolic and socioenvironmental influences also affect competency and safety. At various points in recent social history, automobiles have been advertised either as primarily an economical and reliable form of transportation or as a powerful, aggressive, and sexy extension of one's own imagined self. A particular cohort of people will have been influenced by various such images at different points in the lifespan. For example, today's middle-aged adults are hearing more about affordability, dependability, and safety features, but it was speed, size, and sex appeal that saturated advertisements when they were just starting to purchase their first cars. An adult driver's conception of what a car should be, what it should do, how it should be used, and what it should mean with respect to his or her life-style will be to some extent a product of the relentless sales messages that have come his or her way over many years. Similarly, the sociophysical environment in which one has developed a particular pattern of driving behavior will also be influential. For example, the complex of speed-aggression-independence-sexiness imagery may have different implications for safety in a resident of the wide open spaces and usually clear weather of New Mexico than in a resident of a congested urban area with frequent weather-related risks. Add differential attitudes toward the use of alcoholic beverages, and one can see that driving style and competency at any adult age depends on many factors other than age per se.

There is, however, good reason to associate age with safety issues. The available findings add up to a not altogether simple picture, a picture that itself must be completed by further research.

First, it has been well established that the highest frequency of automobile accidents occurs among drivers under the age of 20 (Hayslip & Panek, 1989).

Second, there is a gradual decrease in the rate of accidents in relationship to the number of miles driven after the early adult years, but the rate then increases significantly in the later decades. Both the youngest and the oldest drivers are overrepresented in the total motor vehicle accident rates. The young are responsible for a much greater number of accidents because their relatively high propensity for accidents is coupled with many hours behind the wheel. Older drivers are almost as accident-prone as the youngest drivers, but they drive less and therefore contribute a small number to the total (Huston & Janke, 1986).

Third, the types of accidents and, fourth, the likely causes of these accidents differ for young and old drivers. Younger drivers tend to have accidents caused by speeding, driving on the wrong side of the road, and using vehicles that are in poor repair and have various safety problems. Older drivers (65+) are more likely to have accidents involving inadequate control of the vehicle or inattentiveness, as shown through ignoring stop signs, failing to give way, and improperly turning (McFarland, Tune, & Welford, 1964). In general, older drivers involved in accidents tended to make more errors of omission, failing to take signals, signs, and other incoming information into account.

Older drivers are much less likely to experience an accident because of either excessive speed or equipment problems (Planek, 1973). They have relatively few single-car accidents, but considerably more two-vehicle accidents than do either young or middle-aged drivers (Campbell, 1966). Elderly drivers also have relatively few alcohol-related accidents. This is one of the major points of differentiation between the two most accident-prone age groups: Young drivers are overrepresented and elderly drivers are underrepresented with respect to accidents associated with alcohol consumption (Rothe, 1990).

One additional characteristic of accidents involving older drivers is of particular concern: The fatality rate is much higher among elderly drivers as well as elderly passengers (MacKay, 1988). It would appear that the capacity to recover from serious injury is less robust in elderly drivers and passengers.

Psychologists find that many accidents among both young and elderly drivers involve defects in information processing and decision making (Avolio & Panek, 1983; Panek & Rearden, 1987). These flawed decisions are more often made while traveling at a higher speed among young drivers, who also tend to have more impulsive personality characteristics. Middle-aged and older drivers are less likely to have impulsivity as a salient characteristic but are more likely to exercise "directiveness," defined as the attempt to exert one's will on others (Panek et al., 1978). It is not yet known whether this impulsivity/directiveness correlate of driving behavior is an abiding age-related characteristic or, rather, simply the characteristics of younger and older cohorts at the present time.

Vision, Competence, and Safety

Problems in visual functioning have so often been proposed or assumed as the cause of motor vehicle accidents involving older adults that this topic warrants special attention here. Visual acuity tests have become standard practice in assessing suitability for licensing and relicensing, with particular emphasis on the visual competency of older drivers. This practice is not without its detractors, who hold that (a) the tests routinely administered by state authorities do not sample the type of visual functioning that is actually significant when operating a motor vehicle under a variety of road and weather conditions and (b) other characteristics of the individual are often more decisive in competent and safe driving than visual acuity.

We have already seen that attentiveness, information processing, and decision-making tendencies are related to accidents, and that personality characteristics such as impulsivity and directiveness also seem to have a bearing. There is no doubt that it would be wise to assess a broader range of functions rather than depend so heavily on static (fixed position) visual acuity in assessing a person's ability to operate a motor vehicle in a safe manner.

Research on the vision/accident link in older drivers has not as comprehensively and definitively established this association as one might have supposed. Owsley et al. (1991) came to this conclusion in their recent review of the previous studies, some of which involved large numbers of motorists and accidents. Although a statistically significant correlation has been found for visual deficits and motor vehicle accidents, this correlation is so low that is useless for such practical purposes as trying to predict which elderly drivers would be at greatest risk for future accidents.

In their own study, Owsley et al. used a greater variety of visual measures and also studied a number of other characteristics of their elderly drivers. They learned that the best predictors of accident frequency were a combination of two variables: *early visual attention* and *mental status*. As these terms suggest, it was not visual acuity as such that differentiated between those who were most and those who were least likely to have experienced an accident while driving. Rather, it was the individual's general alertness and responsiveness as indexed by mental status and the ability or willingness to pay attention immediately when presented with visual stimuli. Findings of this type strengthen the case for considering more than static visual acuity in assessing driver competency and safety.

Another team of experienced researchers observes that "although there are well-recognized declines in visual functioning with age, their contribution to the problems of older persons on tasks in the natural environment, including driving, are largely unknown" (Kline et al., 1992, p. 27). This research group, who studied adults ranging in age from 22 to 92, found that "the visual problems of drivers increased with age along five different visual dimensions: unexpected vehicles, vehicle speed, dim displays, windshield problems, and sign reading." They also confirmed results of previous studies that showed age-related declines in visual processing speed, light sensitivity, dynamic vision, near vision, and visual search.

One important specific outcome of this study was a converging line of evidence indicating that many accidents occur when an older driver is "surprised" by other vehicles that come into his or her line of vision. Decreased visual functioning seems to combine with insufficient attentiveness to relevant events in the road environment so that the elderly driver faces more emergencies in what should have been anticipated and therefore routine situations.

Recommendations

It would be useful for motorists as well as motor vehicle authorities to give close attention to the type of research findings that have been summarized here. Not only would such attention hasten the development of more relevant and effective assessment procedures, but it could also lay the foundations for educational and training programs to help drivers remain competent and safe over a longer stretch of life's road.

Rothe (1990) emphasizes the importance of developing and implementing more effective educational programs for older drivers. On the basis of his own studies and a thorough review of the literature, he suggests that defensive driving, knowledge of traffic laws, and improved awareness of automobile features and technology be given particular attention. Furthermore, he challenges traffic safety educators to find ways of getting the message across to elderly drivers that they must operate more safely while making turns at intersections, when starting up after coming to a stop, and in right-of-way situations. He also recommends that the public transportation available to older people be improved to take their needs more fully into account and thus reduce their dependency on the automobile.

One must certainly agree that the safety issues involved are the responsibility of society as well as the individual: "The lack of convenient mass transit routes and schedules, increasing urban sprawl, shortage of rural medical health and other care facilities, and inattention to other viable transportation possibilities force the elderly to accept the automobile as a fundamental tool for retaining a desired life-style" (Rothe, 1990, p. 345).

▼ ROBERT KASTENBAUM

See also: Alcohol Use and Abuse; Cohort and Generational Effects; Gender as a Shaping Force in Adult Development and Aging; Information Processing; Longevity; Risk to Life through the Adult Years; Slowing of Behavior with Age; Vision.

References

Avolio, B.J., & Panek, P.E. (1983). Automobile accidents characteristic of young and old female drivers. Paper presented at the annual meetings of the American Psychological Association, Anaheim, CA, August 1983.

Campbell, B.J. (1966). Driver age and sex related to accident time and type. *Traffic Safety Research Review, 10*: 36-44.

Eisenhandler, S.A. (1990). The asphalt identity: Old age and the driver's license. *International Journal of Aging and Human Development, 30*: 1-14.

Hayslip, B. & Panek, P.E. (1989). *Adult Development and Aging.* New York: Harper & Row.

Huston, R., & Janke, M. (1986). *Senior Driver Facts* (Report CAL-DMV-RSS-86-82). Sacramento: California Department of Motor Vehicles.

Kastenbaum, R., & Cameron, P. (1969). Cognitive and emotional dependency in later life. In R.A. Kalish (Ed.), *The Dependencies of Old People.* Ann Arbor: Institute of Gerontology (University of Michigan), pp. 39-58.

Kline, D.W., et al. (1992). Vision, aging, and driving: The problems of older drivers. *Journal of Gerontology, 47*: 27-34.

Krout, J.A. (1983). Correlates of Service Utilization among the Rural Elderly. *Gerontologists.* 23: 500-04.

MacKay, M. (1988). Crash protection for older persons. In *Transportation in an Aging Society* (Special Report 218, Vol. 2). Washington, DC: Transportation Research Board, National Research Council, pp. 158-93.

McGhee, J.L. (1983) Transportation opportunities and the rural elderly. *Gerontologist, 23:* 505-11.

McFarland, R.A., Tune, C.S., & Welford, A.T. (1964). On the driving of automobiles by older people. *Journal of Gerontology, 19:* 190-97.

Owsley, C., et al. (1991). Visual / cognitive correlates of vehicular accidents in older drivers. *Psychology and Aging, 6:* 403-15.

Panek, P.E., & Rearden, J. (1987). Age and gender effects on accident types for rural drivers. *Journal of Gerontology, 6:* 332-46.

Panek, P.E., et al. (1977). A review of age changes in perceptual information processing ability with regard to driving. *Experimental Aging Research, 3:* 387-449.

———. (1978). Selected Hand Test personality variables related to accidents in female drivers. *Journal of Personality Assessment, 42:* 355-57.

Planek, T.W. (1973). The aging driver in today's traffic: A critical review. In *Aging and Highway Safety: The Elderly in a Mobile Society.* North Carolina Symposium on Highway Safety, Volume 7. Chapel Hill, NC: University of North Carolina, Safety Research Center.

Planek, T.W., & Fowler, R.C. (1971). Traffic accident problems and exposure characteristics of the aging driver. *Journal of Gerontology, 26:* 224-30.

Rothe, J.P. (1990). *The Safety of Elderly Drivers.* New Brunswick, NJ: Transaction Publishers.

DRUG USE AND ABUSE

Two distinct lifetime patterns of drug use can be identified. One pattern is characteristic of recreational drugs such as alcohol, caffeine, tobacco, and illegal substances; the other is associated with medicinal drugs such as pain relievers, psychotherapeutic medicines, prescriptions for hypertension, and so forth (McKim & Mishara, 1987).

The levels of use for six types of drugs throughout the adult lifespan are given in Figure 1. These include three recreational drugs (tobacco, marijuana, and cocaine) and three medicinal drugs (sleeping pills, tran-

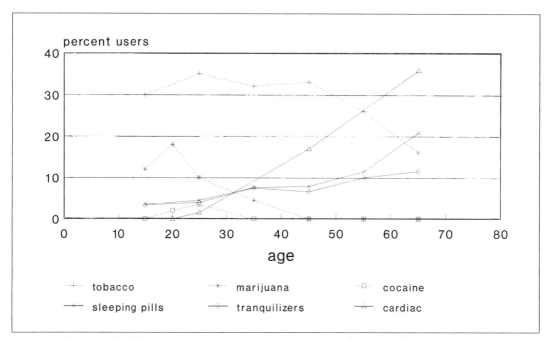

Figure 1. The Use of Different Drugs across the Adult Lifespan. This figure shows the percent of people in different age groups who report using each of six drugs: three recreational drugs (dotted lines), tobacco, marijuana, and cocaine; and three medicinal drugs (solid lines), sleeping pills, tranquilizers, and cardiac medications. The data are from three Canadian National Surveys: The Canada Health Survey (1981, p. 179); The Health Promotion Survey (Health and Welfare and Welfare Canada, 1988, p. 28 and p. 58); and the National Alcohol and Drug Survey (Health and Welfare Canada, 1990, Table 24).

quilizers, and cardiac and blood pressure medicines). The data were collated from several national surveys conducted in Canada but are typical of most Western industrialized nations.

As can be clearly seen, the use of recreational drugs tends to start during late adolescence, reach a peak in young adulthood, and then decline with age. (This pattern is also characteristic of alcohol use, a topic that is given separate treatment in this book.) The usage pattern for most medicines is exactly the opposite. Relatively few people use medicinal drugs during the early and middle adult years, but usage increases rather dramatically with advancing age.

In addition to these differences in patterns of drug use based on age, drug use also differs by gender. Recreational substances (with the exception of coffee) are used far more widely by men than by women at all stages of life, but medicinal drugs are used far more extensively by women than by men.

Smoking

In general, the smoking habit is acquired during the teen years and may persist throughout the lifespan. In the past, men were much more likely to take up smoking. As a consequence, current surveys show that men are disproportionately represented among older smokers. Current research, however, indicates that fewer and fewer young people are becoming smokers these days. Therefore, as the population ages, the percentage of smokers in all age groups will probably decline significantly. Because young men have shown a much larger decrease in smoking than young women, there have been signs of a crossover effect: the rate of young women smoking starting to exceed that of men (Health and Welfare Canada, 1988b). This trend suggests that in the years ahead the sex difference in smoking will disappear or perhaps even be reversed.

The decline in the number of smokers with increasing age could be a result of several factors. People in the older age categories may have been teenagers at a time when smoking was not so prevalent and, consequently, they never took up this habit. It has also been speculated, however, that the decline in the incidence of smokers in older age categories is a result of a higher death rate; i.e., smokers tend to die before they have the opportunity to grow old.

Caffeine

Caffeine causes no social problems and has not conclusively been linked to many specific health problems. It is a stimulant of the central nervous system, however, and it creates physical dependence and is habit forming. Significant amounts of caffeine are consumed in the form of tea and cola beverages, but coffee remains the primary form in which caffeine is consumed throughout the Western world.

The prevalence of coffee drinking is the same for both sexes. It increases until the middle adult years (35 to 65) and then remains stable. Tea shows a similar pattern, but there is a small decline in the number of tea drinkers in the 75+ age category. Caffeine-containing cola beverages are consumed primarily by people under the age of 30 (Barone & Roberts, 1984).

Illegal Drugs

As shown in Figure 1, the use of the most common illegal drugs is associated with the younger age categories and is exceedingly rare among people over age 35. It is not yet clear whether the decline in illicit drug use with age represents a cohort difference (i.e., the older people of today never used illicit drugs in their lifetime and never will) or whether it occurs because something about aging leads people to stop using illicit drugs in their later years.

It is likely that both explanations are important, although little direct evidence is available at present. For example, a phenom-enon called "maturing out" has been reported among heroin users. Maturing out usually occurs after 5 to 10 years of heroin use when users have reached their thirties or forties. It has been estimated that between one-fourth and two-thirds of heroin users spontaneously mature out. Those who do not spontaneously abandon the drug and who are not successfully treated continue to use heroin into old age and are seldom susceptible to treatment (McKim, 1991).

A similar phenomenon is thought to occur with other illicit substances such as marijuana, LSD, and cocaine. People who are not longtime heavy users may spontaneously discontinue the drugs as they mature, find other interests, and acquire different friends.

Use of Medicines

People use more prescription drugs as they age. Most surveys show that between 6 percent and 90 percent of people over age 65 consume at least one type of medicine regularly, while about 12 percent of men and 25 percent of women take more than three medicines simultaneously.

The figure reveals that the percentage of adults who use sleeping pills, tranquilizers, and antidepressants increases from almost no utilization by those under 25 to very high use by those over 65. In fact, the use of drugs from almost every therapeutic category shows a similar increase with increasing age. Notable exceptions are antibiotics; ear, nose, and throat preparations; antihistamines; and nonprescription medicines in general (also referred to as over-the-counter or OTC medications) (McKim & Mishara, 1987).

Reasons for Use

The reasons for these changes with age are not entirely clear. The most obvious explanation is that older people are sicker and need more medicines. Although it is true that older people tend to suffer from more chronic illness, we also know that more than ill health is involved in the use of medicine. Subjective assessment of health, increased stress in one's social roles, negative perceptions of one's capacities in relation to others, and dissatisfaction with past decisions are among the factors that have been shown to be related to the increased use of medicine in the later adult years (Crutchfield & Gove, 1984; Guttmann, 1978; McKim, Stones, & Kozma, 1990).

The use of medicines by older people is a complex phenomenon that involves not only illness but also one's response to a shifting mix of psychological and social variables. Attempts to understand medicine-taking behavior throughout the adult lifespan must draw extensively on the behavioral and social sciences, and cannot be usefully perceived as a "medical" issue exclusively.

Do Elderly People Take Too Many Medicines?

In a major study of the attitudes and practices of elderly people conducted by the American Association of Retired Persons (1984), 79 percent of the respondents agreed that most people their age took too many drugs—but only 6 percent agreed that they themselves used too many medicines. Older people seem to recognize that there is a problem but feel that it is only a problem for somebody else. Another survey has shown clearly that older people see medicines as important tools in managing their lives and count on this support to helping them remain active. More than a third of the elderly people surveyed report that they regularly depend on medicines for their normal functioning (Guttmann, 1978).

Medicine-Related Problems

Many studies have found that the number of unwanted side effects or adverse reactions from medicines increases as adults age. Among the reasons for this are changes in the way the body absorbs, distributes, and eliminates drugs. These changes frequently result in a heightened sensitivity to the effects of medicines, and physicians may have to prescribe lower dosages for older people to reduce the occurrence of side effects.

Often the adverse effects of medicines are symptoms such as memory loss, confusion, loss of balance, and drowsiness. Such symptoms would be noticed immediately in a younger person but may go unobserved in an older person—or be ascribed to aging and then treated with higher doses or additional drugs.

Even though age-related changes in sensitivity are responsible for many adverse side effects, the most frequent source of difficulty appears to be the large number of medicines that many elderly people use simultaneously. In general, taking three or more medicines increases the chance of making errors in taking the drugs and, therefore, the likelihood of adverse interactions among the drugs.

Compliance

Another problem associated with the use of many medications is a failure to use medicines in the manner intended by the physician. Such problems are often described as "noncompliance" or "nonadherence." Noncompliance has been found to increase with age, but it is generally conceded that this is not a direct result of being older. Instead, like increased adverse reactions, some noncompliance is probably a result of taking too many medicines at the same time.

In the American Association of Retired Persons (1984) survey 14 percent of those over age 65 reported that at some point in time they had failed to fill a prescription, and 33 percent reported discontinuing a prescription before it was finished. The most common reason given (42 percent) was fear of side effects, while others (31 percent) believed the drug was not doing them any good. In some circumstances, deliberate noncompliance can be viewed as a self-protective response to unnecessary medications and may be viewed as beneficial. However, deliberate noncompliance has been found to be responsible for 27 percent of drug-related admissions of older patients at a large Canadian hospital (Grymonpre et al., 1988). Older people may be justifiably suspicious of medicines, but they also resist using some that could be beneficial.

More often, when elderly people take medicines incorrectly it is by accident, as a result of confusion, memory loss, or the inability to open containers or read instructions. Much research is being directed toward developing methods that might improve compliance. Special containers and medicine dispensers have been developed, and a variety of calendars and other reminder devices have been introduced—so far with only limited success. The best method of preventing both deliberate and accidental noncompliance appears to be education. Patient education programs have been shown to improve the medicine-taking behavior of patients, just as education directed at physicians has also been shown to improve their prescribing practices (Raisch, 1990).

Conclusion

Drugs pose different threats at different stages of adult development. The period of adolescence and young adulthood is a time of heavy use of psychologically active drugs that are consumed for recreational purposes. Overindulgence at this stage carries the risk of addiction, damage to health, adoption of deviant life-styles, and missed opportunities. Such dangers are fairly well understood and appreciated.

The second high-risk period occurs later in life and involves drugs that are taken as medications. Even though these substances are legal, very often relieve distressing symptoms, and are used with the advice and encouragement of a physician, there is no guarantee that they will not do as much harm as the recreational drugs used by young people. The dangers to older adults posed by these respectable drugs are only now becoming understood, and attempts are being made to reduce the risks.

▼ WILLIAM A. McKIM AND BRIAN L. MISHARA
See also: Alcohol Use and Abuse; Chronic Pain as a Lifespan Problem; Cohort and Generational Effects; Gender as a Shaping Force in Adult Development and Aging; Health Education and Adult Development; Learning and Memory in Everyday Life.

References

American Association of Retired Persons. (1984). *Prescription Drugs: A Survey of Consumer Use, Attitudes, and Behavior.* Washington, DC: AARP.

Barone, J. J., & Roberts, H. (1984). Human consumption of caffeine. In P. B. Dews (Ed.), *Caffeine: Perspectives from Recent Research.* Berlin: Springer-Verlag, pp. 59-73.

Canada Health Survey. (1981). *The Health of Canadians: Report of the Canada Health Survey.* Ottawa: Minister of Supply and Services Canada.

Crutchfield, R. W., & Gove, W. R. (1984). Determinants of drug use: A test of the coping hypothesis. *Social Science and Medicine, 18:* 503-09.

Grymonpre, R. E., et al. (1988). Drug associated hospital admissions in older medical patients. *Journal of the American Geriatrics Society, 36:* 1092-98.

Guttmann, D. (1978). Patterns of legal drug use by older Americans. *Addictive Diseases: An International Journal, 3:* 337-56.

Health and Welfare Canada. (1988a). *Canada's Health Promotion Survey: Technical Report.* Ottawa: Minister of Supply and Services.

———. (1988b). *The Smoking Behavior of Canadians.* Ottawa: Minister of Supply and Services.

———. (1990). *The National Alcohol and Other Drug Survey: Technical Report.* Ottawa: Minister of Supply and Services.

McKim, W.A. (1991). *Drugs and Behavior: An Introduction to Behavioral Pharmacology.* Second Edition. Englewood Cliffs, NJ: Prentice-Hall.

McKim, W. A., & Mishara, B. L. (1987). *Drugs and Aging.* Toronto: Butterworth.

McKim, W. A., Stones, M. J., & Kozma, A. (1990). Factors predicting medicine use in institutionalized and noninstitutionalized elderly. *Canadian Journal on Aging, 9:* 23-34.

Raisch, D. (1990). A model of methods for influencing prescribing. Part II. A review of educational methods, theories of human inference, and delineation of the model. *Drug Intelligence and Clinical Pharmacy, 24:* 537-42.

E

EXERCISE

Much attention has focused on the importance of regular physical activity as a means of enhancing health and effective functioning. Although most early research focused on relatively young and healthy adults, in recent years a systematic effort has been made to extend our knowledge to a broader cross-section of the population. As our understanding of the physiological, psychological, and social significance of exercise has increased, so has the proportion of adults who voluntarily participate in some form of structured physical activity. Physicians and other health care professionals are beginning to recommend exercise as an adjunct to more traditional therapy for a wide variety of physical and behavioral disorders. For example, the American Medical Association recently acknowledged the prophylactic value of exercise when it enthusiastically endorsed participation in regular exercise programs for healthy adults of all ages (American Medical Council on Scientific Affairs, 1984).

In this brief overview of some of the physiological and psychological benefits of regular exercise, the principal focus is on the long-term effects of extended physical training. The short-term effects of a single bout of exercise are not addressed. The illustrative examples used are largely taken from the literature on exercise and aging. However, the principles underlying the physiological and psychological adaptations to exercise stress are not unique to any segment of the population, and in most cases these principles can be generalized to adults of all ages.

Physiological Adaptations to Exercise Stress

The physiological benefits of participation in regular physical activity are now well established. Physiological adaptations to exercise stress include improved cardiovascular and pulmonary performance, increased muscular strength and endurance, enhanced flexibility and range of motion, decreased adiposity, and improved lipid status (Lamb, 1984). Although most of these relations were first established in young adults, extensive efforts have been made in recent years to apply these findings to the elderly population. In a recent review, Goldberg and Hagberg (1990) suggested that the physiological responses of elderly adults to exercise training are essentially similar to those experienced by younger individuals.

A discussion of some of the more common physiological adaptations associated with regular exercise follows.

Cardiovascular Function. Maximal oxygen consumption (VO^2max) during an exercise stress test is generally accepted as the single best measure of overall cardiovascular performance (Lamb, 1984). At first it was thought that VO^2max declined linearly with age at the rate of about 10 percent per decade. This decline was considered to be relatively consistent across individuals and independent of physical activity status (Dehn & Bruce, 1972; Hodgson, 1971). However, recent research has shown that participation in regular exercise often can substantially reduce this rate of decline (Heath et al., 1981; Rogers et al., 1990). Indeed, several studies have found that exceptionally well-trained individuals who maintain high activity levels often experience little or no decline in VO²max over time periods of a decade or more (Kasch, Wallace, & Van Camp, 1985; Pollock et al., 1987).

The mechanism by which exercise influences cardiovascular performance in old age is complex. Nevertheless, several recent studies suggest that both central and peripheral factors are involved. Increased cardiac output has been identified as a contributing central mechanism, and increased oxidative capacity of the skeletal muscle is a contributing peripheral mechanism (Goldberg & Hagberg, 1990). It is unrealistic for most elderly adults to expect to escape totally the age-related declines in aerobic capacity, but increasingly strong evidence suggests that even modest levels of physical activity can result in significant increases in cardiovascular efficiency in old age.

Pulmonary Function. A number of well-documented structural changes have been shown to alter pulmonary efficiency with aging. Gross morphological changes which lead to decreases in elasticity and compliance have been found to reduce the elastic recoil capacity of the lungs (McKeown, 1965). Progressive degeneration of the vertebral discs often results in an alteration in the shape of the thoracic capacity with a resultant reduction in pulmonary volume (McKeown, 1965). Pulmonary efficiency is further compromised by age-related declines in the strength of the thoracic muscles (Dhar, Shastri, & Lenora, 1976), and also by calcification and ossification of the costovertebral and costochondral joints (Grant, 1972).

The extent to which regular exercise is able to influence the rate of these age-related declines is unclear. Aerobic exercise appears to have minimal effects on vital capacity, expiratory volume, and other measures of pulmonary performance in younger people who have not yet undergone significant age-related declines in pulmonary capacity (Shephard, 1978). In older individuals, however, regular exercise may be associated with a reduction in the rate of vertebral degeneration and also with an increase in thoracic muscle strength (Buskirk, 1985). These changes are likely to affect the rate of decline in pulmonary function and in the long run may result in fitness-related effects on pulmonary performance (Chodzko-Zajko & Ringel, 1987b). Further research is needed to clarify our understanding of the precise effects of exercise on pulmonary performance in elderly populations.

Blood Pressure. Hypertension is thought to afflict 20 million Americans over age 65 (Kannel & Vokonas, 1986). Although the precise mechanisms responsible for elevations in blood pressure are still poorly understood, there is little doubt that both systolic and diastolic blood pressure on average increase significantly with advancing age (Shephard, 1978).

Numerous studies have shown that regular exercise reduces systolic and diastolic blood pressure in young and middle-aged people with borderline hypertension (Goldberg & Hagberg, 1990). Until recently, relatively little was known about the effect of exercise on blood pressure in older adults. In a nine-month exercise training study, Hagberg et al. (1985) found that a six-month program of low-intensity walking significantly lowered both systolic and diastolic blood pressure in hypertensive adults who ranged in age from 60 to 65. These data suggest that exercise may have antihypertensive effects in older individuals similar to those previously reported in younger populations.

Blood Lipids. Age-related elevations in serum total cholesterol and serum triglycerides have been well established (Buskirk, 1985).

Hypercholesterolemia and hyperlipidemia are significant risk factors for the premature development of coronary artery disease (Castelli et al., 1977). Extensive research has focused on the effect of exercise training on coronary heart disease risk. A number of studies have shown that highly trained master athletes exhibit favorable biochemical profiles when compared with sedentary individuals of the same chronological age (Seals et al., 1984; Tamai et al., 1988). These studies included such measures as reduced low-density lipoprotein cholesterol and elevated high-density lipoprotein cholesterol. However, because almost all instances of improvement in biochemical profiles are associated with coincident decreases in body weight (Goldberg & Hagberg, 1990), dissociating the effects of exercise from the effects of weight loss is frequently difficult.

These problems notwithstanding, the evidence suggests that regular exercise is associated with a decrease in body fat which, in turn, is associated with a decrease in circulating lipids. It is worth noting that the effect of exercise on blood lipids is relatively transient and that blood lipids return to pre-exercise values within a few days of cessation of physical activity.

Flexibility, Muscle Strength, and Endurance. Flexibility, muscle strength, and endurance all decline significantly with advancing age (Shephard, 1978). Stretching exercises that emphasize range of motion and flexibility have been shown to increase ankle, knee joint, and lower back flexibility in older adults (Frekany & Leslie, 1975). The importance of pre-exercise stretching is reflected in the fact that almost all structured exercise programs recommend that aerobic exercises be preceded by calisthenic exercises (Stone, 1987).

Formerly, strength training was seldom emphasized as a component of exercise programs designed for elderly individuals. Lifting heavy weights requires maximal or near maximal muscular contractions, and this degree of effort has been shown to result in sharp increases in blood pressure. Because these acute elevations in blood pressure are potentially dangerous for hypertensive individuals, most exercise regimens have deemphasized strength training for older adults.

Recently, however, a number of studies have examined the effect of dynamic low-weight strength training in elderly adults. In one such study (Coggan et al., 1990), older

adults who trained with weights for 12 months showed appreciable increases in muscular strength and endurance. Since the maintenance of adequate levels of muscular strength is crucial for the successful performance of many of the activities of daily living, exercise scientists have started to reevaluate the importance of strength training as a component of exercise programs for elderly adults. The American College of Sports Medicine (1991) has recently recommended that low- to moderate-intensity strength exercises be included as part of the exercise training regimen for older adults.

The Psychological Benefits of Exercise

In addition to its physiological effects, increasingly strong evidence supports the hypothesis that regular exercise enhances psychological health and well-being. Regular exercisers reported significantly greater life satisfaction (Sidney & Shephard, 1976), increased self-esteem (Ingrebretsen, 1982), and fewer mood state disturbances (Chodzko-Zajko & Ismail, 1984; Chodzko-Zajko, 1990) than did sedentary adults who served as controls.

Of particular interest is the relation between exercise and affective disorders in old age. It is generally accepted that the incidence of depression increases significantly with age (LaRue, Dessonville, & Jarvik, 1985). However, several recent studies have suggested that the association between chronological age and depression may be confounded by the decreases in physical activity levels that usually accompany advancing age (Berkman et al., 1986; Parent & Whall, 1986). The author recently examined relationships between cardiovascular fitness, chronological age, and depression in a group of elderly men (Chodzko-Zajko, 1990). The findings revealed a small but significant increase in depressive tendencies with advancing age. However, when statistical tests were used to control for physiological fitness differences among the participants, the association between advancing age and depression proved to be no longer reliable. These data suggest a connection between age-related increases in depression and the tendency for physical activity levels to decline with age.

A number of authors have reported that participation in regular exercise programs reduces depression in patients with mild to moderate levels of clinical depression (Greist et al., 1979; Martinsen, Medhus, & Sandvik, 1985). Studies with nonclinical populations have also reported beneficial effects of exercise on mood state and anxiety (Morgan & O'Connor, 1987). Although most of these studies have not focused exclusively on older adults, the consensus is that elderly adults often experience a variety of psychological benefits as a result of participation in regular exercise programs (Berger & Hecht, 1989).

The possible effects of physical fitness on cognitive performance in old age have been the focus of a number of recent studies. In general, highly fit elderly adults respond to reaction time tasks significantly faster than their less fit contemporaries (Spirduso & MacRae, 1990). Whether the beneficial effects also extend to more complex cognitive tasks such as memory, problem solving, and geometric shape rotation is less clear (Chodzko-Zajko, 1991). One exercise training study demonstrated that four months of aerobic exercise significantly improved the performances of older adults on a wide variety of cognitive tasks, including memory, mental arithmetic, and problem solving (Dustman et al., 1984). A more recent study was unable to replicate these exercise effects, however (Blumenthal & Madden, 1988). It is evident that more research is needed to examine the nature of the relation between exercise and cognitive performance in elderly adults.

Exercise Prescription

Formulating a generic exercise prescription that can be applied across the board for all adults is difficult and probably inappropriate. Individual differences in health status, physical fitness, and previous exercise experience require that exercise prescription be tailored to meet the specific needs of each person. Older adults should be encouraged to seek advice from a health professional who can assist them in the preparation of an optimal program designed to meet their individual needs. Most professional health organizations recommend that individuals over age 35 obtain a thorough medical examination before embarking on an exercise program (American College of Sports Medicine, 1991).

In the past, a large percentage of the elderly population remained sedentary because of the mistaken belief that they were not candidates for participation in regular physical activity. The number of individuals for whom exercise is contraindicated on medical grounds is extremely small (Stone, 1987). The vast majority of elderly men and women can benefit from participation in some form of physical activity (American College of Sports Medicine, 1991). The emergence of specialized programs for specific clinical populations is a testament to the realization that the benefits of physical activity need not be restricted to "jocks" and exercise fanatics. These specialized programs include the Arthritis Foundation's PACE program and a variety of programs offered for diabetics and for people undergoing cardiac rehabilitation.

Although one must recognize the importance of individualized exercise prescriptions for elderly adults, some generalized comments about the frequency and intensity of exercise can be made.

Mode of Exercise. Low-intensity rhythmic activities that utilize large muscle groups are generally accepted as optimal for the enhancement of aerobic capacity. Common examples of such activities are walking, jogging, bicycling, and swimming. In most instances the particular activity selected by an individual is simply a matter of personal preference, although orthopedic and/or other medical factors may restrict the options available to some individuals. In recent years an increasing number of older adults have also enjoyed participation in activities such as aerobic dance and weight training. Although these activities may not be appropriate for all older individuals, many people can obtain significant physiological benefits as well as enjoyment from these modes of exercise (American College of Sports Medicine, 1991).

Frequency and Duration. Obtaining a reliable training effect from exercise is generally recognized to require a frequency of two to three times per week (Lamb, 1984). However, habitual exercisers often work out five or six days per week without adverse consequences (American College of Sports Medicine, 1991).

Duration. Most structured exercise programs are designed to last between 45 minutes and an hour. This time period usually is divided up into 15 or 20 minutes of warm-up activity, followed by 20-30 minutes of aerobic activity, and another 5-10 minutes of cooling-down activity. This format is flexible, but there is some evidence to suggest that the aerobic component of exercise programs should last at least 20 minutes to obtain optimal cardiovascular benefits (Lamb, 1984).

Intensity. Exercise intensity is generally determined by monitoring heart rate response during exercise. Target heart rates are calculated on the basis of age-adjusted values, and exercise heart rates are titrated according to the fitness level of each participant. In general, exercise intensities between 60 and 85 percent of the heart rate reserve are recommended for optimal aerobic benefits.

Exercising at these intensities need not lead to excessive fatigue, profound sweating, or shortness of breath. The popular misconception that high-intensity exercise is required for significant physiological gain, exemplified in the saying "no pain, no gain," is simply not true. Such misconceptions perpetuate inappropriate attitudes about exercise and result in large numbers of individuals avoiding potentially beneficial and highly enjoyable physical activities.

Conclusion

Advancing age is characterized by a progressive and insidious decline in the functional capacity of most physiological systems. Although this decline is largely inevitable and inescapable, there are often considerable differences among individuals with respect to its rate and extent. Several lines of research suggest that people who engage in healthful behaviors often can postpone or reduce the deleterious consequences of aging and thus deviate from expected patterns of linear senescence (Chodzko-Zajko & Ringel, 1987a).

In recent years a good deal of attention has focused on the importance of regular physical activity as a means of enhancing optimal health and effective functioning in old age. Although the prophylactic effects of exercise in old age sometimes are difficult to isolate, the evidence supports the contention that the vast majority of older adults would benefit substantially from participation in a regular program of physical activity. This evidence is leading a growing proportion of the population, regardless of age, to include regular exercise as an integral component of their everyday routine.

▼ Wotjek J. Chodzko-Zajko

See also: Body Senses; Depression; Health Education and Adult Development; Individuality; Learning and Memory in Everyday Life; Longevity; Risk to Life through the Adult Years; Slowing of Behavior with Age; Work Capacity Across the Adult Years.

References

American College of Sports Medicine. (1991). *Guidelines for Graded Exercise Testing and Exercise Prescription.* New York: Lea & Febiger.

American Medical Council on Scientific Affairs. (1984). Exercise programs for the elderly. *Journal of the American Medical Association,* 252: 544-46.

Berger, B. G., & Hecht, L. M. (1989). Exercise, aging, and psychological well-being: The mind body question. In A. C. Ostrow (Ed.), *Aging and Motor Behavior.* Indianapolis: Benchmark Press, pp. 307-23.

Berkman, L. F., et al. (1986). Depressive symptoms in relation to physical health and functioning in the elderly. *American Journal of Epidemiology,* 124: 372-88.

Blumenthal, J. A., & Madden, D. J. (1988). Effects of aerobic exercise training, age, and physical fitness on memory search performance. *Psychology and Aging, 3:* 280-85.

Buskirk, E. R. (1985). Health maintenance and longevity: Exercise. In C. E. Finch & E. L. Schneider (Eds.), *Handbook of the Biology of Aging*. New York: Van Nostrand Reinhold, pp. 894-931.

Castelli, W. P., et al. (1977). HDL cholesterol and other lipids in coronary heart disease: The Cooperative Lipoprotein Phenotyping study. *Circulation, 55:* 767-72.

Chodzko-Zajko, W. J. (1990). The influence of general health status on the relationship between chronological age and depressed mood state. *Journal of Geriatric Psychiatry, 23:* 13-22.

———. (1991). Physical fitness and cognitive performance. *Medicine and Science in Sports and Exercise, 23:* 868-72.

Chodzko-Zajko, W. J., & Ismail, A. H. (1984). MMPI interscale relationships in middle aged male subjects before and after an 8 months fitness program. *Journal of Clinical Psychology, 40:* 163-69.

Chodzko-Zajko, W. J., & Ringel, R. L. (1987a). Physical fitness measures and sensory and motor performance in aging. *Experimental Gerontology, 22:* 317-28.

———. (1987b). Physiological aspects of aging. *Journal of Voice, 1:* 18-26.

———. (1989). Evaluating the influence of physiological health on sensory and motor performance changes in the elderly. In A. C. Ostrow (Ed.), *Aging and Motor Behavior*. Indianapolis: Benchmark Press, pp. 307-23.

Coggan, A. R., et al. (1990). Histochemical and enzymatic characteristics of skeletal muscle in master athletes. *Journal of Applied Psychology, 68:* 1896-1901.

Dehn, M. M., & Bruce, R. A. (1972). Longitudinal variations in maximal oxygen intake with age and activity. *Journal of Applied Physiology, 33:* 805-07.

Dhar, S., Shastri, S.R., & Lenora, R. A. (1976). Aging and the respiratory system. *Medical Clinics of North America, 60:* 1121-39.

Dustman, R. E., et al. (1984). Aerobic exercise training and improved neuropsychological function of older individuals. *Neurobiology of Aging, 5:* 35-42.

Frekany, G. A., & Leslie, D. K. (1975). Effects of an exercise program on selected flexibility measures of senior citizens. *Gerontologist, 15:* 182-83.

Goldberg, A. P., & Hagberg, J. M. (1990). Physical exercise and the elderly. In E. L. Schneider & J. W. Rowe (Eds.), *Handbook of the Biology of Aging*. San Diego: Academic Press, pp. 407-23.

Grant, J. C. B. (1972). *Grant's Atlas of Anatomy*. Baltimore: Williams & Wilkins.

Greist, J. H., et al. (1979). Running as a treatment for depression. *Comprehensive Psychiatry, 20:* 41-54.

Hagberg, J. M., et al. (1985). A hemodynamic comparison of young and older endurance athletes during exercise. *Journal of Applied Physiology, 58:* 2041-46.

Heath, G. W., et al. (1981). A physiological comparison of young and older endurance athletes during exercise. *Journal of Applied Physiology, 58:* 2047-51.

Hodgson, J. L. (1971). *Age and Aerobic Capacity of Urban Midwestern Males*. Ph.D. dissertation. Minneapolis, MN: University of Minnesota.

Ingrebretsen, R. (1982). The relationship between physical activity and mental factors in the elderly. *Scandinavian Journal of Social Medicine, 29:* 153-59.

Kannel, W.B., & Vokonas, P. S. (1986). Primary risk factors for coronary heart disease in the elderly. The Framingham Study. In N. K. Wenger & C. D. Furburg (Eds.), *Current Heart Disease in the Elderly*. London: Elsevier, pp. 60-95.

Kasch, F. W., Wallace, J. P., & Van Camp, S. P. (1985). Effects of 18 years endurance exercise on the physical work capacity of older men. *Journal of Cardiopulmonary Rehabilitation, 5:*308-12.

Lamb, D. R. (1984). *Physiology of Exercise: Responses and Adaptations*. New York: Macmillan.

LaRue, A., Dessonville, C., & Jarvik, L. F. (1985). Aging and mental disorders. In J. E. Birren & K. W. Schaie (Eds.), *Handbook of the Psychology of Aging*. New York: Van Nostrand Reinhold.

Martinsen, E.W., Medhus, A., & Sandvik, L. (1985). Effects of aerobic exercise on depression: A controlled study. *British Medical Journal, 292:* 109-14.

McKeown, K. W. (1965). *Pathology of the Aged*. London: Butterworth.

Morgan, W. P., & O'Connor, P. J. (1987). Exercise and mental health. In R. K. Dishman (Ed.), *Exercise Adherence*. Champaign, IL: Human Kinetics.

Parent, C. J., & Whall, A. L. (1986). Are physical activity, self-esteem and depression related? *Journal of Geriatric Nursing, 20:* 8-11.

Pollock, M. L., et al. (1987). Effect of age and training on aerobic capacity and body composition of master athletes. *Journal of Applied Physiology, 62:* 725-31.

Rogers, M. A., et al. (1990). Decline in VO²max with aging in master athletes and sedentary men. *Journal of Applied Physiology, 68:* 2195-99.

Seals, D. R., et al. (1984). Elevated high density lipoprotein levels in older endurance athletes. *American Journal of Cardiology, 54:* 390-93.

Shephard, R. J. (1978). *Physical Activity and Aging.* Chicago: Croom Helm.

Sidney, K. H., & Shephard, R. J. (1976). Attitudes toward health and physical activity in the elderly: Effects of a physical training program. *Medicine and Science in Sports and Exercise, 8:* 246-52.

Spirduso, W. W., & MacRae, P. G. (1990). Motor performance and aging. In J. E. Birren & K. W. Schaie (Eds.), *The Handbook of the Psychology of Aging.* Third Edition. San Diego: Academic Press, pp. 184-97.

Stone, W. J. (1987). *Adult Fitness Programs.* Glenview, IL: Scott Foresman.

Tamai, T., et al. (1988). The effects of physical exercise on plasma lipoprotein and apoliprotein metabolism in elderly men. *Journal of Gerontology, 43:* M75-79.

EXPRESSIVE ARTS

Just as a plant needs rain, sun, and good earth to attain its maximum growth, so an individual needs to engage in self-expression, gain an understanding and acceptance of self, and become aware of the part played in directing his or her own life. In psychology, growth theories emphasize the realization of a person's full potential (Fleshman and Fryrear, 1981). The term *self-actualization* has been used frequently since it was introduced by Maslow (1968) and Rogers (1962) to describe the innate human tendency to develop whatever potential lies within the individual. Both of these observers equated self-actualization with the psychological growth dimension of creativity. In an influential book, Maslow (1959) described self-actualizing creativeness as a fundamental potentiality of all or most humans at birth, but, unfortunately, as a characteristic that was most often lost, buried, or inhibited as the person became enculturated.

This phenomenon can often be seen in early development. Children are experts in creative ways of learning and self-expression. They question, inquire, search, manipulate, experiment, create, explore, and play. However, as children enter school they find many restrictions placed on their curiosity and manipulativeness. Schools target the cognitive and intellectual areas for development. The areas of intuition, affect, and self-expression are often neglected and left to develop on their own, if at all. As a consequence, many children do not learn how to continue to develop their potential for self-expression (Dacey, 1976).

One of the most consistent findings of creativity research in children is that discontinuities in creative development often result in loss of interest in learning, increased behavioral problems, and increased emotional disturbances (Torrance, 1977). These periods can be so stressful that an individual's creativity is inhibited, reduced, or entirely lost as he or she ages (Torrance, Clements, & Goff, 1989). As a child moves into adulthood, further obstacles to the development of creativity and self-expressiveness are encountered. These obstacles include pressure to conform, ridicule of unusual ideas, a drive for success and rewards based on the demands and standards of others, and intolerance of a playful attitude (Dacey, 1976). All too often people lose touch with their creativity and inner potential as they grow up.

Although development is a continuous process, discontinuities or pauses do appear to occur in the developmental flow. These pauses can occur in childhood and persist throughout life. People frequently seek help as they become aware of areas in their lives that have been on pause. This help is available in many forms, one of which is creative-expressive therapy.

Creative-Expressive Therapy

Creative-expressive therapy is an interdisciplinary approach that uses elements of various art therapies but cannot be identified by one particular modality such as dance therapy, drama therapy, art therapy, or music therapy (Fleshman & Fryrear, 1981). This approach is oriented to meet an individual's changing and developing needs by encouraging self-expression and communication with both oneself and others (Weiss, 1984). Individuals are encouraged to realize their full potential by accepting themselves and creatively expressing their life experiences and/or dreams.

Two natural mediums for creative expression are art and play. Both are expressions created from the imagination, external representations of inner experiences and perspectives. Art and play involve the language of the imagination, the emotions, the senses, and the inner self (Rossman, 1987). Sensory expression is often the only way to reach people who are in severe states of emotional withdrawal, depression, or psychic confusion (McNiff, 1986). Art and play therapy allow for the ventilation and release of negative energy and encourage creative, growth-oriented self-expression and communication.

The arts are frequently used in therapeutic situations in which conventional modes of communication are not effective. The focus of art therapies is not on the tangible products, but rather on the process of communication involving all of the senses and the imagination. A basic belief in art therapies is that self-expression and creative expression have healing qualities. These include stress and anxiety reduction, increased self-esteem, feelings of accomplishment, improved communication skills, and self-discovery.

There has been an increase in creative-expressive educational interventions for adults of all ages in a variety of settings. The educational interventions have focused on the development of creative and expressive skills of adults outside of therapy. A basic belief of creative-expressive education is that personal development is a continuous cycle in which growth and change are the norm from conception through death. It is further believed that personal development requires a conscious effort to develop talents and unused potentials in order to become all that one is capable of becoming (self-actualization).

Educational Interventions at Three Adult Stages

Although development is a continuous process, there are particular phases/stages of life with particular needs. Adulthood has been characterized as consisting of three phases/stages: early, middle, and later adulthood (Strom, Bernard, & Strom, 1987). It has become increasingly popular among researchers to examine the transitions that mark adulthood in terms of what the individual is doing, rather than chronological age (Tavris, 1989).

Early adulthood begins with an individual assuming personal financial responsibility, defining career goals, developing and exercising the skills necessary for career satisfaction, forming a marriage, and starting a family (Levinson, 1978). According to Neugarten (1980), middle adulthood is a new prime of life because parental roles are less stressful, homemaking is less burdensome, and spouses have more time together. Later adulthood generally includes retirement and some degree of physical decline.

Educational interventions for early adulthood are primarily task specific—learning a new job or job skills; earning a college degree, certification, or licensure; learning about birth and child rearing; etc. During this period, lack of time is a frequently expressed reason for not engaging in creative-expressive activities and programs.

Task-specific educational interventions are common in middle adulthood as well. These include learning the skills necessary for a second or third career, earning advanced college degrees, or developing interests or hobbies into a second income. However, interventions for this segment of the population also may focus on noncredit courses on interpersonal and communication skills, new hobbies and interests, or other areas of personal development. The middle adult years often find individuals with somewhat more time available for leisure and learning pursuits.

Later adulthood had long been ignored by growth-oriented therapies and educational interventions. Most of society's efforts for this group have centered on basic maintenance needs such as housing, health care, income, and transportation. However, there is now a growing realization of the importance of self-expression and creative development for older adults (Strom, Bernard, & Strom, 1987).

A Quality of Life Educational Program

One creative-expressive program for older adults is being conducted by the University of Georgia in senior centers throughout northeast Georgia. The Quality of Life Program focuses on making service providers and caregivers more aware of the value of creative-expressive programming. On-site training is given to caregivers/service providers. Modules are offered in the areas of art, creativity, dance, drama, and fitness. The caregiver/service providers use these activities to teach their elderly clients both physical and expressive ways of improving their feelings of well-being. They also encourage the clients to pursue their own creativity and to communicate more freely with themselves and others.

Each module contains activities incorporating physical, social, emotional, and creative aspects of expression and learning (Torrance, Clements, & Goff, 1989). The activities are divided into monthly topics and emotional themes, utilizing the Torrance three-stage creative teaching model (Torrance & Safter, 1989). A centralized focus on play and fun contribute to the interdisciplinary and creative nature of the activities. Play is an important ingredient because it is a basic form of learning by doing and is also an active and natural form of stimulation (Goff & Torrance, in press). In adulthood, play offers a special freedom from work and the usually serious nature of life. Too often, the adult's sense of responsibility crushes the play spirit, leaving a sense of guilt about being playful. However, play is a necessary relief from the seriousness of life. The play process is refreshing and revitalizing even if it takes physically strenuous or mentally demanding forms (Fleshman & Fryrear, 1981).

Imaginative play and activity foster creativity and self-expression. Creative playing provides an opportunity to develop imagination and independent thinking, as well as an opportunity for cooperation and communication, a healthy release of emotions, freedom of choice, and health-engendering recreation (McCaslin, 1984). The fact that play is enjoyed is one of the main reasons it is conducive to health (Bowen & Mitchell, 1925). The ability to play is a recognized characteristic of mental health, and also has potential for maintaining mental health.

Imagination is another important element of mental health, self-expression, and creativity. Imagery in particular has been shown to be a powerful tool for recovering health, reducing pain and stress, and inducing relaxation. Through imagery one can also examine dilemmas from several angles and keep the mind working actively. A relatively new science—psychoneuroimmunology—is emerging as a result of investigations into the effect of imagery on health. There is already considerable evidence that various forms of imagery can alter psychophysiological functioning in the direction of increased health. Relief can be provided from states of hyperarousal and from the effects of prolonged stress. Some studies have found that imagery can help restore the body's natural ability to ward off disease through the immune system (e.g., Achterberg, 1985; Pelletier, 1977).

Mental images are also useful tools for self-discovery and for making changes in other areas of life in addition to health. Expressive arts speak the language of the imagination and inner self. The physical and tangible manifestations of expressive arts are external representations of the self-actualizing creative process.

Creative-expressive activities offer adults the opportunity to improve communication with each other and with themselves. Creative expression arouses the adventurous spirit within and generates a zest for living. The expressive arts can feed society's hunger for positive, life-affirming approaches to self-expression, self-discovery, and creativity. Furthermore, enhancing creativity and self-expressiveness may well contribute to improved levels of physical and mental wellness (Dunn, 1961; Torrance, 1978).

▼ E. PAUL TORRANCE AND KATHY GOFF

See also: Habituation: A Key to Lifespan Development and Aging?; Health Education and Adult Development; Learning and Memory in Everyday Life; Mental Health in the Adult Years; Stress.

References

Achterberg, J. (1985). *Imagery and healing.* Boston: New Science Library.

Bowen, W. P., & Mitchell, E. D. (1925). *The theory of organized play.* New York: A. S. Barnes & Co.

Dacey, J. S. (1976). *New ways to learn: The psychology of education.* Stamford, CT: Greylock Publishers.

Dunn, H. L. (1961). *High level wellness.* Arlington, VA: R. W. Beatty, Ltd.

Fleshman, B., & Fryrear, J. L. (1981). *The arts in therapy.* Chicago: Nelson-Hall.

Goff, K., & Torrance, E. P. (in press). The healing qualities of imagery and creativity. *Journal of Creative Behavior.*

Levinson, D. (1978). *The seasons of a man's life.* New York: Alfred A. Knopf.

Maslow, A. H. (1959). Creativity in self-actualizing people. In H. H. Anderson (Ed.), *Creativity and its cultivation.* New York: Harper & Brothers, pp. 83-95.

———. (1968). *Toward a psychology of being.* Second Edition. Princeton, NJ: Van Nostrand.

McCaslin, N. (1984). *Creative drama in the classroom.* New York: Longman.

McNiff, S. (1986). *Educating the creative arts therapist.* Springfield, IL: Charles C. Thomas.

Neugarten, B. L. (1980). Must everything be a midlife crisis? *Prime Time,* 2, February: 1-3.

Pelletier, K. R. (1977). *Mind as healer, mind as slayer.* New York: Delta.

Rogers, C. R. (1962). Toward a theory of creativity. In S. J. Parnes & H. F. Harding (Eds.), *A source book for creative thinking.* New York: Scribner's, pp. 66-72.

Rossman, M. L. (1987). *Healing yourself.* New York: Walker & Co.

Strom, R. D., Bernard, H. W., & Strom, S. K. (1987). *Human development and learning.* New York: Human Sciences Press.

Tavris, C. (1989). Old age is not what it used to be. In H. Cox (Ed.), *Aging.* Sixth Edition. Guilford, CT: Duskin Publishing Group, pp. 16-18.

Torrance, E. P. (1977). *Creativity in the classroom.* Washington, DC: National Education Association.

———. (1978). Healing qualities of creative behavior. *Creative Child and Adult Quarterly,* 3: 146-58.

Torrance, E. P., Clements, C. B., & Goff, K. (1989). Mind-body learning among the elderly: Arts, fitness and incubation. *Educational Forum,* 54: 123-33.

Torrance, E. P., & Safter, H. T. (1989). *The incubation model of teaching.* Buffalo, NY: Bearly Limited.

Weiss, J. C. (1984). *Expressive therapy with elders and the disabled: Touching the heart of life.* New York: Haworth Press.

F

FAIRY TALES AS COMMENTARY ON ADULT DEVELOPMENT AND AGING

Most adults cherish fairy tales from childhood. Whether Cinderella or Snow White, the drama is similar. A young man and woman fall in love, battle terrible enemies, win a great victory, and marry. Finally, the two live happily ever after. These fairy tales feature children or adolescents as their protagonists and reflect the psychology of youth (Bettelheim, 1976). A unique group of fairy tales, however, take grown-ups as their protagonists. Less familiar than "Sleeping Beauty" or "Rumpelstiltskin," these tales focus on the trials and tribulations of "old" people, not youth. Hence, I call them *elder tales*. Gathered from around the world, elder tales present strikingly similar themes that depict the developmental tasks of later life (Chinen, 1989). There is also another distinct group of fairy tales that center around middle-aged individuals (Chinen, 1992).

The idea that fairy tales can speak to adults may seem odd, since stories of this type usually are considered to be children's fare. Historically, however, fairy tales and folk stories were primarily for adults. Before the advent of printing and widespread literacy, fairy tales functioned as the chief medium of news and entertainment. Adults told the stories to each other, filling the tales with personal reflections on life. Only in the last few centuries were fairy tales banished to the nursery.

The stories still convey vital insights about adult life and human nature in general. The best way to illustrate this point is by recounting a prototypical elder tale, "The Shining Fish," from Italy.

An Elder Tale

Once upon a time, an old man and his wife lived in a house overlooking the sea. Through the years, all their sons died, leaving the old man and woman to poverty and loneliness. The old man barely earned a living by gathering firewood and selling it in the village. One day while working in the forest, the old man met a stranger with a long white beard. "I know all about your troubles," the stranger said, "and I want to help." He gave the old man a small leather bag and vanished. When the old man looked in the bag, he found it full of gold! The old man threw away his firewood and rushed home. But along the way, he began to think. "If I tell my wife about this money, she will waste it all." And so he said nothing to his wife. Instead, he hid the money under a pile of manure.

The next day, the old man awoke to find that his wife had cooked a wonderful breakfast, with sausages and bread. "Where did you find the money for this food?" he asked his wife.

"You did not bring any wood to sell yesterday," she said, "so I sold the manure to the farmer down the road." The old man ran out, shrieking with dismay. Sure enough, the manure was gone, and the gold, too. The old man went glumly back to work in the forest. Deep in the woods, he met the stranger again.

The stranger laughed. "I know what you did with the money, but I still want to help." So he gave the old man another purse filled with gold.

The old man rushed home, but along the way he started thinking again. "If I tell my wife, she will squander this fortune." And so he hid the money under the ashes in the fireplace. The next day he awoke to find his wife had cooked another hearty breakfast. "You did not bring back any firewood," she explained, "so I sold the ashes to the farmer down the road."

The old man ran to the fireplace and found it empty—no ashes and no gold. The old man sadly dragged himself back to work in the forest. There he met the stranger a third time. The stranger sighed. "It seems you are not destined to be rich," the stranger said, "but I still want to help." He offered the old man a large bag. "Take these frogs, and sell them in the village. Then use the money to buy the largest fish you can find—nothing else, just the largest fish!" With that, the stranger vanished.

The old man hurried to the village and sold his frogs. With the money in hand, he was tempted to buy cakes, beer, and sweetmeats. But the old man followed the stranger's instructions, and bought the largest fish. He returned home that night too late to clean the fish, so he hung it outside his house from the rafters. Then he and his wife went to bed.

That night, it stormed, and the old man and woman could hear the waves thundering on the rocks below their house. In the middle of the night, someone pounded on the door. The old man went to see who it might be, and found a group of young fishermen dancing and singing outside in the rain.

"Thank you for saving our lives!" they told the old man. "What do you mean?" he asked. The fishermen explained that they were caught at sea by the storm, and it was so dark, they did not know where land was. Then the old man put out his light for them. "A light?" the old man asked. The fishermen pointed, and the old man saw his fish hanging from the rafters, shining with such a great light it could be seen for miles around.

From that day on, the old man hung the shining fish each evening to guide the young fishermen safely home. For their part, they shared their catch with him. And so the old man and his wife lived in comfort and honor the rest of their days.

Commentary

The story opens with an old man and his wife living in poverty—a theme present in virtually every elder tale from around the world. The poverty makes a good symbol for the losses—real and feared—of old age. To emphasize the theme, the story notes that the old couple's children all died, so they have suffered perhaps the deepest loss an adult can experience. By beginning with such a dismal picture, the story warns us that it will not gloss over the problems of growing old.

In the middle of this dismal situation, the old man meets a stranger who gives him a bag of gold. This is the next theme found in elder tales around the world. These tales regularly depict magic erupting in the course of ordinary events. Several points are worth emphasizing here. First, notice that the old man does not seek his fortune in far-off lands, as do the *youthful* protagonists of more familiar fairy tales such as "Jack and the Beanstalk" or "Sinbad the Sailor" (Campbell, 1949). The stranger comes unbidden to the old man, and the old man's task is to *notice* and *accept* the magic. If the old man were suspicious or hostile, for instance, and fled the stranger, nothing further would have developed. Psychologically, the story depicts an important and difficult task for older individuals—to be open to new experiences, and to be psychologically flexible (Peck, 1968).

After receiving the gold from the stranger, the old man hides it without telling his wife. He acts out of suspicion and greed, and the story emphasizes the odious nature of his motivation in a humorous detail: The old man conceals the gold under manure! When the old man's wife inadvertently sells the dung the next day, he is effectively punished for his avarice. The old man does not learn the lesson, though. He receives a second bag of gold, hides this one also from his wife, and loses the treasure again.

Repeated misfortunes such as these are common in tales of youth. There, however, the youth suffers the loss because of a powerful and wicked adversary like a witch. Here, the old man's enemy is himself—his own greed and suspicion. Losing the gold forces the old man to face his faults. When the stranger gives the old man a third gift, and tells him to buy the largest fish available, the old man is tempted to do otherwise. Yet he does obey the stranger. Apparently the old man now realizes how poor his judgment can be, after hiding the gold in manure and ashes! He breaks out of his egocentric mode of thinking.

Such self-confrontation and reformation are major tasks for later life (Jung, 1930). This process is rare in youth tales, where young protagonists are virtuous and all misfortune is blamed on clear-cut villains. Fairy tales reflect real life here, because youth normally project their faults and troubles on other people. The challenge in old age is to reverse this "projection" (Mussen & Haan, 1981; Vaillant, 1977).

When the old man returns home with his fish, he hangs it from the rafters. This is an odd thing to do, even in an age without refrigerators, since the old man runs the risk of having his fish stolen by somebody or eaten by a stray cat. The old man's actions, in fact, are symbolic. They underscore just how much he has changed. He no longer tries to hoard his gift, the way he did with his bags of gold. Instead, he offers his gift to the whole world.

The story quickly elaborates on this theme. A terrible storm breaks out that night, threatening the lives of several young fishermen. They are saved by the old man's fish, which becomes a shining beacon, guiding the young men safely home. By hanging his fish in the open, the old man transforms a private boon into a public benefit. This is the final theme in elder tales, and another psychological challenge for older individuals—transmuting personal advantage into a helpful legacy for the next generations. And this is, of course, what Erikson (1983) meant by "generativity."

The old man and the young fishermen then come to an agreement. He hangs his fish to guide them each night, and they share their catch with him. Essentially, the old man mediates between a magical, supernatural realm and youth struggling in the secular, material world. This is a traditional role for elders in preindustrial societies. They instruct the young in the spiritual and philosophical traditions of their culture, symbolically connecting the sacred and the secular, for the benefit of society (Gutmann, 1987). Such a mediating role represents the real treasure that the old man receives from the stranger.

Other elder tales reinforce the theme. Gold and private wealth are not the goals of later life, but rather generative, spiritual activity (Bianchi, 1984; Biesele & Howell, 1981). Elder tales thus contrast sharply with stories about youth. The latter typically end with material rewards—the hero and heroine gain a great treasure, and become king or queen. But worldly reward *is* the goal of youth, who are taking their place in society and pursuing secular ambitions. Generativity and self-transcendence ideally replace those aims in later life (Brewi & Brennan, 1985; Brown, 1980; Katz, 1975).

Fairy tales of youth also reflect the traditional mediating role of the elder. A fairy godmother or wise old man rescues the young hero and heroine from a dreadful danger. "The Shining Fish" reveals how the elder gains that "magic" power and wisdom. It is through a long process of psychological maturation: grappling with the losses of old age, being psychologically flexible, confronting one's dark side, transcending egocentricity, and fostering a generative, spiritual connection with youth.   ▼ ALLAN B. CHINEN

See also: Development and Aging in Historical Perspective; Fictive Kin; Marital Development; Mastery Types, Development, and Aging; Suffering; Trust as a Challenge in Adult Development.

References

Bettelheim, B. (1976). *The Uses of Enchantment: The Meaning and Importance of Fairy Tales.* New York: Knopf.

Bianchi, E. C. (1984). *Aging as a Spiritual Journey.* New York: Crossroad.

Biesele, M., & Howell, N. (1981). The old people give you life: Aging among !Kung hunter-gatherers. In P. Amoss & S. Harrell (Eds.),

Other Ways of Growing Old. Stanford, CA: Stanford University Press, pp. 77-98.

Brewi, J., & Brennan, A. (1985). *Mid-life: Psychological and Spiritual Perspectives*. New York: Crossroads.

Brown, P. (1980). Religious needs of older persons. In J. Thorson & T. Cook (Eds.), *Spiritual Well-being of the Elderly*. Springfield, IL: Charles C. Thomas, pp. 76-82.

Campbell, J. (1949). *The Hero with a Thousand Faces*. Princeton, NJ: Princeton University Press.

Chinen, A. (1989). *In the Ever After: Fairy Tales and the Second Half of Life*. Wilmette, IL: Chiron.

———. (1992). *Once Upon a Noon Time: Fairy Tales and the Psychology of Men and Women at Mid-Life*. Los Angeles: Tarcher.

Erikson, E. H. (1983). *The Life Cycle Completed*. New York: Norton.

Gutmann, D. (1987). *Reclaimed Powers: Toward a New Psychology of Men and Women in Later Life*. New York: Basic Books.

Jung, C. G. (1930; reprinted 1967). The stages of life. In *Collected Works*, Volume 8. Princeton, NJ: Princeton University Press, pp. 387-403.

Katz, R. L. (1975). Jewish values and socio-psychological perspectives on aging. In S. Hiltner (Ed.), *Toward a Theology of Aging*. New York: Human Sciences Press, pp. 135-50.

Mussen, P., & Haan, N. (1981). A longitudinal study of patterns of personality and political ideologies. In D. Eichorn et al. (Eds.), *Present and Past in Middle Life*. New York: Academic Press, pp. 393-414.

Peck, R. (1968). Psychological developments in the second half of life. In B. Neugarten (Ed.), *Middle Age and Aging: A Reader in Social Psychology*. Chicago: University of Chicago Press.

Vaillant, G. (1977). *Adaptation to Life: How the Best and the Brightest Came of Age*. New York: Little, Brown.

Von Franz, M. L. (1977). *Individuation in Fairy Tales*. Dallas, TX: Spring.

FICTIVE KIN

Children often have imaginary playmates and courtesy relatives, ideal people who make few if any demands on them. As they grow older, they give up these playmates, and relationships with their courtesy relatives change. As people lose their innocence and give up these ought-to-be relationships, they seek to replace them through transforming the what-is into what-can-be. In other words, they create and then negotiate fictive kin relationships. These are also referred to by some observers as "constructed" ties or "kin-like nonkin relations" (Rubinstein et al., 1991). Fictive kin relationships may be substituted for and even preferred over one's kinship relations.

Despite their importance and meaning throughout the life course, however, we do not know much about how fictive kin relationships are established and maintained in adulthood. The lack of information may be a consequence of our traditional emphasis on the importance of family and friends in our lives. Fictive kin are neither and yet are simultaneously both friends and "family."

A fictive kin relationship is one in which two people have mutually transformed their friendship into a fictional family relationship which they publicly acknowledge. These are "chosen relatives." This is family as it ought to be, not necessarily as it is. The existence of fictive kinships contradicts the folk saying that we can choose our friends but not our relatives. Unlike "real" relatives, fictive kin are family without much friction. This is one of the reasons that fictive kin are important throughout life—they provide us with idealized relatives.

Many people carry throughout their lives a guiding wish, almost a myth, of what "family" ought to be, structurally, functionally, and relationally. When reality fails to meet these standards, they may create relatives. Through this process they can have siblings without rivalry, parents without power. As people age, fictive kin relationships may also develop when legal kin are either absent or prove unsatisfactory. As do all relationships, fictive kinships change throughout the life course in form (brother, sister, mother, father), function, emotional content, and social context.

Characteristics of Fictive Kin Relationships

The processes involved in adult fictive relationships can be viewed as acts of recreating, reconstituting, transforming, or transmuting a secondary relationship into a primary one. An "as though" tie is established.

We create and become fictive kin on an "as needed" basis. Because our feelings for people are defined by or expressed in the titles we give them—friend, enemy, confidant, colleague—when we move toward describing a person in family terminology, we are thereby emphasizing the importance of that relationship. We use family terminology because the family is the crucible in which our primary relationships are formed. Our fictive relationships thus become primary ones with reciprocal obligations, rights, and responsibilities. The emphasis is on the relationship and the mutuality through which it is created and defined.

The mutuality requirement of kinship relationships is not satisfied in all situations in which family terms are invoked. For example, nursing home staff may refer to residents as "granny," "auntie," or "uncle" in keeping with their own regional or social-class colloquialisms and, all too frequently, as a condescending or deprecating form of address. The use of kinship titles in such formal human services programs as Big Brothers, Big Sisters, or Adopt-a-Grandparent does not indicate that fictive kin relationships actually exist. Nevertheless, such relationships conceivably could develop between the formal service provider and the person to whom services are provided. Family terminology in and of itself does not necessarily indicate the existence, mutuality, or intensity of an interpersonal relationship.

The nature of a fictive kin relationship and the specific title used to designate it vary not only by age but also by the gender, social class, race, and ethnicity of the participants. However, for the relationship to be considered a fictive one, it must be defined in similar terms by both participants, acknowledged publicly, and undergirded by reciprocity.

Like other interpersonal relationships, fictive kinship has affective (emotional) content and is found in context. It has definition, function, duration, and fragility. From the viewpoint of definition, the two participants have defined their reciprocal relationship as being qualitatively different from friendship. Despite family terminology, however, such a relationship is neither legally nor traditionally a family relationship. It is voluntary rather than obligatory. Its affective content is more positive than negative; there is more clarity than ambiguity.

The specific kinship form (e.g., brother, sister, grandmother, grandfather) with which it is designated and the kinship role are a re-creation of the socioculturally familiar. From the viewpoint of the individuals involved, the definition depends upon each individual's life experiences with specific relationships or relatives—or on the idealized picture of what a relationship/relative should be. Thus, although two people may define themselves as "sisters" or "brothers," each has an experiential referent, real or imagined, of an ideal sister or brother. To this extent, fictive kin can be idealized versions of conventional kin. Quasi-mathematically, the new relationship reflects the difference between what-is and what-ought-to-be.

All interpersonal relationships wax and wane throughout the life course, and fictive kin relationships are no exception. If they vary by definition, function, and duration, so, too, do they vary by their degree of fragility (an aspect of waxing and waning). Because all interpersonal relationships have elements of fragility, all require some nurturing. Fictive relationships—neither friendship nor family, yet more than either—require ongoing reinforcement. They have no traditional kinship basis and therefore lack well-established norms either of friendship or kinship. The norms that are established have been co-created by the involved parties and are not societally defined. Thus, the role and nature of fictive kin relationships in adulthood and old age are negotiated on an ongoing basis. These negotiations are conducted within the context of the social and psychological characteristics of the involved participants. Although the functions of fictive kin may be similar to those of legal kin, there is an affective dimension in which obligation assumes a moral rather than legal tone.

The duration of a fictive relationship in adulthood varies. It may be of relatively short duration, as is true of "going for brothers" among men in a street corner society (Liebow, 1967). It may be lifelong, as is found among old women in Nova Scotia (McCrae, 1988). Some of these old women have had deeply emotional ties with the same fictive "sister" since childhood. Other types of fictive kin relationships may be based on the need to accomplish certain immediate tasks and therefore do not survive the short, situation-specific duration (Gubrium & Buckholdt, 1982).

From a developmental viewpoint, the specific title of the fictive relative reflects our age/stage of life. Siblings may be more important than parents in early adulthood. Aunts and uncles may be more important than "kissin' cousins" in childhood. For young mothers, older mothers may be more necessary than siblings.

A number of social and behavioral scientists have written about fictive kin relationships. Essentially, they describe such relationships as being "like" family. Unlike family relationships, however, these are voluntary and have no legal obligations. In some instances, having a number of fictive kin is a mark of prestige and a source of self-esteem (Liebow, 1967); in others, the emphasis is on the mutual aid aspects of the relationship. Some view physical proximity as an essential component in establishing and maintaining a relationship, arguing that geography is more important than genealogy (Stack, 1974). If need, function, and physical ability are seen as key elements in fictive relationships, then presumably there is also a cost-benefit element.

Social Factors and Fictive Kin

With rare exceptions (McCrae, 1988, for example), authors have not dealt with how the broad demographic changes occurring in our society might influence the creation of fictive kin in the future. Despite the fantasies and stereotypes entertained by many politicians and idealogues, family life in the United States is rapidly changing. Even our definition of what constitutes a family is changing.

The declining birthrate, increasing divorce rate, and increased out-of-wedlock births all contribute to new and different family structures. There are more four- and five-generation families than ever before. Life expectancies have been increasing so that marriages can last longer, far beyond the reproductive years, at least for women—and long after the children have "yo-yoed" out of the household. In some families the oldest two or three generations are all women because of the differences in the death rates between men and women. In some families there are few years between generations because of teenage pregnancies in each of the generations. Grandmothers in their thirties are different from those in their sixties.

There has been a large increase in "POSSSLQ" relationships. This recent neologism seemed to create itself from the ever-more common situation of "people of the opposite sex sharing the same living quarters." "UM" is another type of relationship that has been increasing rapidly. This term, coined by Mona Wasow of the University of Wisconsin, refers to the difficulties parents experience when they introduce one of their children along with his or her POSSSLQ partner: "This is Mary and her...um...um...." UM takes the place of a relationship for which we do not have a satisfactory consensual label.

Currently, there seems to be greater public acknowledgment and acceptance of gay and lesbian couplehood as well as a variety of other "created family" households. Given these demographic trends and changing definitions of what constitutes a family, the interesting question is whether there will be a major increase in the number of fictive kinships in the future to substitute for nonexistent legal kin. Will the low birthrate, for example, result in more older people establishing fictive parent-child relationships with younger people? If so, what will be the legal, financial, and moral obligations of the fictive kin for one another? It could well be that, in the absence of biological children, fictive ones will replace (f)actual ones and created relationships will replace legal/"blood" relatives. Along a broad front, there may be an increase in compensatory family relationships to fill in for nonexistent "real" kin.

Little systematic attention has been given to many of the issues that have been raised here. No studies have probed the processes by which a friend is transformed into a fictive kin. What are the means by which imaginary siblings are transformed into fictive siblings? How do we transform friendships into kinships, and is the basis for this transformation the same throughout the life course? What is the stimulus? Is it necessary for a specific function or need to be met? Does loneliness prompt the young mother, isolated from her own mother, to transform an older neighbor into a fictive mother in order to gain the reassurances and support she needs? What are the clues and signs the older neighbor gives to encourage or solicit this relationship? How do participants negotiate and mutually define their respective roles in the relationship?

If we need more information about how we transform friends into kin, we also need to learn the processes by which fictive kin are "de-kin-dled." What causes some fictive relationships to terminate? And how does the dissolution occur? And, as with all developmental research, we will need to know to what extent the presence or absence of fictive kinships in particular stages of life is a cohort or a developmental phenomenon.

▼ Mildred M. Seltzer

See also: Adult Children and Their Parents; Divorce; Fairy Tales as Commentary on Adult Development and Aging; Friendships through the Adult Years; Gender as a Shaping Force in Adult Development and Aging; Grandparent Education to Enhance Family Strength; Longevity; Sibling Relationships; Social Class and Adult Development; Social Relationships, Convoys of; Subcultural Influences on Lifelong Development.

References

Aoyagi, K. (1978). Kinship and friendship in Black Los Angeles: A study of migrants from Texas. In D. B. Shimkin, E. M. Shimkin, & D. A. Frate (Eds.), *The Extended Family in Black Societies.* The Hague: Mouton, pp. 271-353.

Goody, E. N. (1971). Forms of pro-parenthood: The sharing and substitution of parental roles. In J. Goody (Ed.), *Kinship.* Baltimore: Penguin, pp. 331-45.

Goody, J. (1971). Introduction to Part Eleven, "Fictive Kin." In J. Goody (Ed.), *Kinship.* Baltimore: Penguin, p. 323.

Gubrium, J. F., & Buckholdt, D. R. (1982). Fictive family: Everyday usage, analytic, and human service considerations. *American Anthropologist, 84*: 878-88.

Kemper, R. V. (1982). The compadrazgo in urban Mexico. *Anthropological Quarterly, 55*: 17-30.

Liebow, E. (1967). *Tally's Corner.* Boston: Little, Brown & Co.

McCrae, H. (1988). *Fictive kin: An unexplored yet important component of the social networks of elderly women.* Paper presented at the Canadian Association on Gerontology Scientific and Educational Meeting, Halifax, Nova Scotia.

Miller, S. J. (1986). Conceptualizing interpersonal relationships. *Generations, 10*: 6-9.

Mintz, S. W., & Wolf, E. R. (1971). Ritual co-parenthood (compadrazgo). In J. Goody (Ed.), *Kinship.* Baltimore: Penguin, pp. 346-61.

Rosman, A., & Rubel, P. G. (1985). *The Tapestry of Culture.* Second Edition. New York: Random House.

Rubinstein, R. L., et al. (1991). Key relationships of never-married, childless older women: A cultural analysis. *The Journal of Gerontology, 46*: 270-77.

Schneider, D. M., & Homans, G. C. (1975). Kinship terminology and the American kinship system. In J. P. Spradley & M. A. Rynkiewich (Eds.), *The Nacerima: Readings on American Culture.* Boston: Little, Brown, pp. 119-32.

Stack, C. B. (1974). *All Our Kin: Strategies for Survival in a Black Community.* New York: Harper & Row.

Sussman, M. B. (1976). The family life of old people. In R. Binstock & E. Shanas (Eds.), *Aging and the Social Sciences.* New York: Van Nostrand Reinhold, pp. 218-43.

FRIENDSHIPS THROUGH THE ADULT YEARS

Friendships are an important part of the informal social network of most adults. Friends provide companionship, assistance, and emotional support as they contribute to one's sense of well-being. The understanding of the concept "friend" appears to be universal, but the criteria used to determine what it is that makes a person a friend vary greatly among individuals. Definitions of friendship often focus either on the social or personal characteristics of the friend or on the relationship shared by two individuals (Roberto & Kimboko, 1989). This voluntary social bond is described by terms such as "acquaintances," "casual friends," "good friends," "close friends," "best friends," and "family friends." These various expressions suggest that not all friendships are alike and emphasize the personal and distinctive nature of each friendship relationship.

Despite the lack of consensus as to who constitutes a friend, the subject of friendship has become of increasing interest to researchers who study interpersonal relationships in adulthood. Over the past decade numerous journal articles and scholarly books have addressed this topic (e.g., Adams & Blieszner, 1989; Allan, 1989; Bell, 1981, Matthews, 1986). Age comparisons, gender differences, and exchanges between friends are the major focus of the research. These themes are taken up here to examine the structure and function of friends throughout the adult life cycle.

Age Comparisons

Most studies of adult friendships are cross-sectional in nature, providing a snapshot of the relationship at one point in time. These studies allow for an examination of potential age-related differences and similarities in the development and structure of friendships. Four basic descriptors of adult friendships emerge from these investigations: *residential proximity, age homogeneity, similarity,* and *complementarity.*

Residential proximity influences friendship development for younger and older adults but has only a modest effect on the friendships of middle-aged adults (Johnson, 1989). It is possible that this finding is related to the greater availability of age-segregated housing for people of college age and for older adults (e.g., dormitories, student apartments, retirement communities). Although a shared living environment does not guarantee the development of a friendship, it does provide the opportunity for individuals to meet. Young and middle-aged adults typically are more mobile than their elderly counterparts and can more easily venture beyond their immediate surroundings in search of friends. Physical and economic limitations can restrict older adults' opportunity for contact with friends who live outside their immediate residential environment. Elderly persons may need to rely more on phone and written correspondence as a means of associating with friends.

Age homogeneity is the norm among close friends. The common life-stage experiences shared by two individuals of similar ages bring a sense of mutual understanding to the relationship. These experiences include career decisions, mate selection, parenting challenges, and so forth.

As individuals move through their adult years, however, age-discrepant friendships become more frequent. Distinctive life circumstances centering around occupation, marital status, and organizational membership often create a context for the development of cross-age friendships (Matthews, 1986). The development and maintenance of friendships with individuals of different ages can be especially beneficial to older adults, who are more vulnerable to the loss of same-age friends.

In general, people prefer to be around others who are like themselves; therefore, most friendships are formed on the basis of high degrees of *similarity*. Shared interests, values, behaviors, and experiences are consistently related to the development and maintenance of friendships between adults. When underlying values are similar, then opposite or *complementary* personal characteristics also can contribute to the development and maintenance of adult friendships. Complementarity in friendships provides an opportunity for individualism, stimulation, and the balance of traits and behaviors that appear necessary for successful relationships.

Some researchers suggest that age influences the amount of time spent engaging in activities with friends as well as the importance of specific functions. For example, in their classic study of four generations, Weiss and Lowenthal (1975) observed an upsurge of friend activity in the pre-retirement years, following a long period of relatively less interaction with friends that lasted from high school through middle age. A steady decline in power as a function of women's friendship from adolescence through the later years has also been noted, while the role of intimacy-assistance remains constant (Candy, Troll, & Levy, 1981). Although the opportunity for interacting with friends seems to vary throughout life, the emotional rewards of friendships appear to be everlasting.

Matthews (1986) describes three distinct styles of interaction that govern patterns of friendship initiation, maintenance, and termination. Individuals categorized as *independent* live in the present, associating with friends who happen to be around. No continuity in friendships is ever expected. Those labeled *disconcerning* focus more on the past. The history they share with a few close friends is of primary importance in their lives. Close friendships are expected to continue, but lost friends are not likely to be replaced. The *acquisitive* type report both past and current friends. Although they expect current friendships to continue, they also look toward the development of new friends in the future. These findings highlight the need to recognize individual differences in the need for friends, the way people make friends, and individuals' willingness to start over again after losing friends.

Gender Differences

In general, women report having a greater number of friends than men. The responsibilities created (or curtailed) by the acquired roles of men and women as they progress through the life course engender different opportunities for the development and maintenance of friendships. For example, it has been noted that the friend network of women compared with that of men shrinks during the early years of marriage and parenthood, whereas the size of men's friend network relative to women's declines in the post-parental years (Fischer & Oliker, 1983).

Greater continuity has been found in the long-term close relationships of older women as compared with older men (Roberto & Kimboko, 1989). Women report contact with close friends from their childhood and adolescence, whereas men maintain relationships with close friends developed only since mid-life. These women also viewed friends as playing an even more significant role in their lives as they grew older. This increased importance may be a result of having more time to devote to the friendship as well as to the substitution of friends for family members who no longer live nearby or who are deceased.

The characterization of women's friendships as "face-to-face" and male friendships as "side-by-side" (Wright, 1982) reflects the interaction patterns between same-sex friends. In other words, women's friendship requires time purely for direct confrontation and shared conversation. Throughout the adult life course, women place greater emphasis on the personal, emotional, and affectual aspects of friendship; share more intimate information with friends; and are involved in more complex relationships with friends (Wright, 1989). By contrast, friendship between males tends to center around structured activities of mutual interest (Roberto & Scott, 1986; Weiss & Lowenthal, 1975; Wright, 1989). This is not to imply that men do not talk to one another, but rather that their conversations take place as part of a larger interaction.

Research on cross-sex friendships in adulthood is more limited. These relationships are more predominant among males than among females, among single compared with married individuals, and among younger versus older adults (Wright, 1989). The nature of cross-sex friendships seems to depend on structural and social norms. For example, men frequently name women as close friends and perceive their friendships with women as being more intimate than their relationships with male friends. The reverse, however, does not hold true. Women's friendships with men do not appear to be as self-disclosing as their friendships with other women. Cross-sex friends among married individuals are often "work friends" or individuals who become friends as a result of being part of a couple. In later life, friendships with members of the opposite sex are often restricted, particularly for women, as a result of the relative unavailability of older men and the view that such relationships must be romantic in nature (Adams, 1985).

Exchange Patterns

As individuals move through the life course, they continually surround themselves with a convoy or set of people with whom they relate through the giving and receiving of support (Kahn & Antonucci, 1980). Exchange, therefore, is one of the most crucial elements in a friendship.

Exchanges can be broadly defined as either instrumental or affective. Instrumental exchanges represent the nonpersonal provision of material assistance (e.g., help with a task, transportation, financial assistance). Affective exchanges are more intimate and provide for comfort, companionship, and the opportunity for self-disclosure. Affective exchanges predominate in the friendships of younger adults, while a combination of affective and instrumental exchanges are typical of friendships in later life (Roberto, 1989).

Reciprocity—the balance of giving and receiving—is an important aspect of adult friendships. Several factors influence the sig-

nificance that individuals place on reciprocity or the equity of exchanges within their friendships. For example, some individuals are non-exchange oriented and are less likely to be concerned with keeping track of the specific affective and instrumental transactions within their friendships (Roberto, 1989). Along with personality differences, there are also differences that are related to the intimacy or depth of the relationship. In friendships that involve limited intimacy, people tend to give to each other with the expectation of receiving something comparable in return; these have been called "exchange relationships." However, for people who are "best friends" or who maintain a "communal relationship," to receive does not necessarily create a specific debt that needs to be repaid (Clark, 1984). Reciprocity of exchanges is also more important when interacting with relatively new friends rather than with close or long-term friends. The immediate obligation to reciprocate becomes less salient as friendships continue to develop.

Conclusions

Friendships have been identified as a vital part of the social network of individuals throughout adulthood. As family and work demands require us to enter new personal and geographical arenas, we face the never-ending challenge of developing new friendships while maintaining old relationships. Lifelong friends provide us with a sense of identity and history, while new friendships bring opportunity for growth, fellowship, and the sharing of new experiences. The norms of friendship permit physical separation, however, ongoing contact through phone calls, letters, computers, or personal conversations is vital to the preservation of all types of friends.

Interactions with friends provide both men and women with the opportunity for the exchange of intimacy, support, and assistance. Reciprocity of these exchanges is an important element in differentiating levels of friendship. The most satisfying friendships appear to be those in which there is a balance of giving and receiving. Younger adults (perhaps because they perceive themselves as having more opportunities to develop new friendships) are more likely than older adults to terminate imbalanced relationships.

Although gender differences are apparent in the structure and function of friendships, the influence of age is less clear. The lack of longitudinal information limits our knowledge to cohort or group differences, rather than changes in friendships over time. Future research, using a lifespan developmental approach, is necessary in order to gain a clearer understanding of the structure and process of friendship across the adult life course. ▼ KAREN A. ROBERTO

See also: Attachment Across the Lifespan; Fictive Kin; Gender as a Shaping Force in Adult Development and Aging; Generational Equity; Housing as a Factor in Adult Life; Individuality; Military Service: Long-Term Effects on Adult Development; Place and Personality in Adult Development; Social Relationships, Convoys of; Work Organization Membership and Behavior.

References

Adams, R. (1985). Normative barriers to cross-sex friendships of elderly women. *The Gerontologist, 25:* 605-11.

Adams, R., & Blieszner, R. (Eds.). (1989). *Older Adult Friendships: Structure and Process.* Newbury Park, CA: Sage.

Allan, G. (1989). *Friendship: Developing a Sociological Perspective.* Boulder, CO: Westview.

Bell, R. (1981). *Worlds of Friendship.* Beverly Hills, CA: Sage.

Candy, S., Troll, L., & Levy, S. (1981). A developmental exploration of friendship functions in women. *Psychology of Women Quarterly, 44:* 373-81.

Clark, M. (1984). Record keeping in two types of relationships. *Journal of Personality and Social Psychology, 37:* 549-57.

Fischer, C., & Oliker, S. (1983). A research note on friendship, gender, and the life cycle. *Social Forces, 62:* 124-33.

Johnson, M. (1989). Variables associated with friendship in an adult population. *Journal of Social Psychology, 129:* 379-90.

Kahn, R., & Antonucci, T. (1980). Convoys over the life course: Attachment, roles, and social support. In P. Baltes & O. Brim (Eds.), *Life-span Development and Behavior.* Volume 3. New York: Academic Press, pp. 253-86.

Matthews, S. (1986). *Friendships Through the Life Course.* Beverly Hills, CA: Sage.

Roberto, K. (1989). Exchange and equity in friendships. In R. Adams & R. Blieszner (Eds.), *Older Adult Friendships: Structure and Process.* Newbury Park, CA: Sage, pp. 147-65.

Roberto, K., & Kimboko, P. (1989). Friendships in later life: Definitions and maintenance patterns. *International Journal of Aging and Human Development, 28:* 9-19.

Roberto, K., & Scott, J. P. (1986). Friendships of older men and women: Exchange patterns and satisfaction. *Psychology and Aging, 1:* 103-09.

Weiss, L., & Lowenthal, M. (1975). Life course perspectives on friendships. In M. Lowenthal, M. Thurher, & D. Chiriboga (Eds.), *Four Stages of Life.* San Francisco: Jossey-Bass, pp. 48-61.

Wright, P. (1982). Men's friendships, women's friendships and the alleged inferiority of the latter. *Sex Roles, 8:* 1-20.

———. (1989). Gender differences in adult's same- and cross-gender friendships. In R. Adams & R. Blieszner (Eds.), *Older Adult Friendships: Structure and Process.* Newbury Park, CA: Sage, pp. 197-221.

G

GENDER AS A SHAPING FORCE IN ADULT DEVELOPMENT AND AGING

Few can doubt that gender and sex are powerful influences in human development from youth through advanced age. Dolls and toy trucks are not randomly distributed among little girls and boys even in our more egalitarian times. Furthermore, the girl with her eye on the truck and the boy with his eye on the doll are apt to meet with differential patterns of social response. These differential patterns of influence begin even earlier in life. The couple expecting their firstborn to be a daughter may decorate the nursery in different colors and symbols than their neighbors who expect their newborn to be a son. Differential expectations, obligations, opportunities, and status are experienced throughout the entire lifespan—and perhaps beyond. My colleagues and I found that the death of males was more likely to be recognized through newspaper obituaries, long obituaries, and photographs than the death of females (Kastenbaum, Peyton, & Kastenbaum, 1977).

Several major aspects of the gender influence are examined here. It should be noted at the outset that the relationship between gender, development, and aging has been changing for many years and shows every sign of continuing to change. For example, the increasing number of women in the work force is both the result of socioeconomic change and the probable cause of additional changes.

Gender or Sex?

Both of these terms are often used in referring to male/female differences. Furthermore, gender has been divided into its role and identity aspects. In serious discussions it is helpful to make a clear distinction among these terms as does Huyck (1990): *"Sex* is used to indicate physiological differentiation between males and females. *Gender role* includes the social prescriptions or stereotypes associated with each sex, to which an individual may or may not conform, and *gender identity* includes the introspective part of gender role, such as the gender-linked qualities that one sees as part of the self" (p. 124).

These distinctions can be illustrated by referring again to the little girl and boy. Joanna and Jonathan have functionally significant differences in their anatomy and physiology, and these differences will exist no matter what gender roles might be prescribed for them. In other words, the sex differences will be there whether Joanna is expected to accommodate herself to the traditional roles of wife and mother or to pursue a demanding and highly competitive career. Similarly, even if Jonathan should have inner gender-identity yearnings to give birth, just like Mommy, his sexual biology will not cooperate in the matter.

To understand an individual's total sense of self and place in society, we would need to have the basic categorical information, "male or female," and then learn both what gender-related roles this person is expected to fill and how this person interprets his or own gender identity. A person may be quite content with the existing roles and identity or may be in serious conflict. Furthermore, this relationship with one's gender roles and identity is subject to change as one grows up, encounters a variety of life experiences, and grows old.

Conceptual Models of Gender Differences

The emphasis here is on gender rather than sex, to the extent that this theoretical distinction can actually be sustained in practice. In the health and longevity sphere in particular, it is often difficult to distinguish between sex-linked and societal/life-style influences. In fact, we turn now to the major theoretical positions that attempt to explain observed gender differences in development and aging.

Four such models are summarized by Huyck (1990). The *biogenetic* model is concise and powerful. Attention is focused tightly upon the genetic coding that is associated with the twenty-third pair of chromosomes. (The other 22 chromosome pairs are identical for both sexes.) Females have two X chromosomes; males have one X and one Y. The X chromosome is much larger than the Y and includes genes that are crucial for many basic functions that are not sex-related. Blood clotting, carbohydrate metabolism, and the production of protein for skeletal growth are among the functions that are guided by the X chromosome in both females and males (Smith & Warner, 1989). The Y chromosome carries the genetic coding for male sexual development.

Socioevolutionary models build upon the biogenetic. It is held that all societies assign certain types of functions differentially to males and females in order to take maximum advantage of the distinctive abilities of each sex. In this view, it would not be surprising to find that many if not all cultures have developed basically similar gender roles even though these cultures may differ markedly in many other ways. The female must have the opportunity to bring her young into the world

safely and care for them; the male must be a provider and protector. A sophisticated and challenging version of the socioevolutionary model has been offered by David Gutmann (1987; see also **Parental Imperative**).

Cognitive differentiation models focus on the information processing activities of the young child (e.g., Bem, 1985; Deaux & Kites, 1987; Money, 1987). Very early in life, the child recognizes that people are divided into males and females and that he or she is "one of those" or "one of them." Because the child arrives at this categorical conclusion so early, the male/female distinction becomes a continuing and cumulative way of organizing further information about self and others. The individual's way of thinking about gender-specific characteristics will change markedly as he or she reaches puberty, develops more advanced intellectual skills, and acquires additional experience with the world. Nevertheless, the very early and very basic distinction between the sexes remains as a powerful "filter" through which the individual perceives self and others and judges what kind of appearance and behavior is "right" for males and females.

Social learning models also emphasize the perceptions and thoughts of the young child. This approach, however, calls more attention to the variable nature of the social environment in which individual development takes place (e.g., Hess & Ferree, 1987). For example, a particular child may have few or many same-gender role models to use as the basis for his or her own behavior. There may also be either tolerance or punishment for exploratory behavior in the direction of opposite-sex gender roles, and the child may also be reinforced (socially rewarded) for some but not all of his or her same-sex gender-linked behaviors. A girl who expresses aggressive and competitive patterns of behavior might be reprimanded for engaging in "wrong gender" behavior, but a boy may also be discouraged from engaging in such behavior by parents or teachers who dislike this behavior even when it occurs as part of a traditional male role. In contrast to the cognitive differentiation model, then, the social learning approach suggests that a particular child's sense of what is appropriate gender-linked behavior is controlled more by society than by the individual's own cognitions.

Taken as a set, these models agree on the significance and universality of sex and gender influences in human development, and all the theories also see these influences as present right from the start. Biogenetic factors certainly must be considered by all theorists and also by all social institutions that are interested in exercising an influence on gender-related attitudes and behaviors. It is a long stretch, however, from the X and Y chromosomes to the realm of complex individual behavior and social dynamics. In trying to understand gender as a shaping force in adult development and aging, we must attend both to individual patterns of development from infancy onward, and to the needs, assumptions, obligations, and opportunities presented to the developing individual by society at large and by its own family.

Advantage: Female

As already mentioned, the clear theoretical distinction between sex and gender is not always so clear in practice. This "fuzziness" is particularly evident in one of the most significant areas of differential female/male experience—health and longevity. There is a clear pattern of advantage in being female as far as longevity and most specific causes of death are concerned. Gee (1989a) observes that "Mortality rates have declined substantially in this century for all ages and for both sexes....Women have experienced a larger mortality reduction than men, a trend that has been observed in all developed countries" (p. 185).

The reduced risk to health and survival in bearing children has been a major factor in the differential change. However, women have experienced their greatest increase in life expectancy at the upper age levels. Since 1900, the mortality rate for women aged 65+ has been cut in half. Over this same period of time, men aged 65+ have had a significant but lesser mortality rate decline of about a third.

Looking at today's leading cause of death in the United States, cardiovascular disease, one finds that the mortality rates throughout all adult age levels are lower for females, and that this pattern holds true among both whites and African Americans (Gee, 1989b). Females are also less frequently victims of fatal accidents.

Overall, women seem to experience more illnesses and physical problems that make it an effort to cope with the demands of everyday life, while men tend encounter severe and life-threatening conditions at a comparatively earlier age (Verbrugge, 1989). Some of this difference can be attributed to the higher frequency of heavy smoking and alcohol consumption among males as well as a more marked disposition toward risky and violent behavior. The gender gap in life expectancy is now 6.8 years among whites and 7.9 years among African Americans.

Why do females tend to live longer than males? Is the answer to be found in the biogenetic factors (therefore, *sex* differential) or in the divergent life-styles experienced by males and females from youth through old age (therefore, *gender* differential)? The debate is still with us. Most, if not all, researchers agree that both psychosocial and biogenetic factors are involved. For example, a "plus" for women throughout the twentieth century has been the notable improvements in caring for women before, during, and after childbirth. A "negative" was the increasing use of cigarettes among women as a result of advertising campaigns and the "fashionability" factor in the years following World War I (and, currently, the incidence of substance abuse). These are psychosocial rather than biogenetic factors.

Nevertheless, even after individual and social life-style factors have been taken into account, there is still reason to believe that sex (as distinguished from gender) factors are important in the differential mortality. In recent years particular attention has been given to the possibility that female sex hormones have a protective effect and/or male hormones may be implicated in some disease processes (e.g., Luria et al., 1982; Waldron, 1983).

The probabilities of an individual having the opportunity to grow old, as well as to enjoy good health along the way, are influenced to some extent by both sex- and gender-linked factors. It is well for us to remember that the current female advantage in life expectancy in most industrialized nations does not hold true throughout the world. Women remain at a substantially greater risk for illness, disability, and early death in nonindustrialized and impoverished nations, where continual childbearing and other hardships tend to age females prematurely (e.g., Weeks, 1988).

Gender-Related Differences in Personal and Social Resources

Regardless of gender, the person born with the proverbial silver spoon in his or her mouth is likely to experience a very different life course than the individual who seldom had enough food. Care must be taken to avoid comparing the resources available to people strictly on the basis of gender. Nevertheless, taking the population as a whole, some important trends can be noted.

In the later adult years, women are more likely than men to find themselves in difficult or downright impoverished financial circumstances. Elderly women who are members of an economically disadvantaged subpopulation may experience the cumulative effects of gender, age, and socioeconomic discrimination. Hess (1990) reports:

> In 1987, the poverty rate for older white females was 12.5 percent compared to 6.8 percent for white males. For African-Americans, the rates were 24.6 percent for men and 40.2 percent for women. For older women living alone as "unrelated individuals," 25 percent of whites and 63 percent of African-Americans fall below the poverty lines. Because many of these women are the survivors of poor men, their current status is a continuation of their earlier circumstances; others will be living on Social Security benefits earned many decades earlier when wages were lower. (p. 14)

Furthermore, Hess adds, it is probable that the actual extent of poverty among elderly women (and especially African Americans) is even greater than these figures suggest "because many will have moved to the residence of an adult child, while some others may have joined the uncounted legions of the homeless."

The female's general edge in survival, then, does not guarantee adequate financial resources to preserve health and enjoy life. A woman who in a sense owes her long life to a number of twentieth-century advances in disease control and other public health improvements may find herself now betrayed by a system that does not provide the opportunity for a safe and dignified standard of living. Although the overall income of elderly people has risen appreciably in recent years, many still live in impoverished and vulnerable circumstances. The salience of gender-related factors is again underscored by Hess: "When, as in the 1950's, the elderly poor were male unemployed workers and family heads, a vast extension of old-age benefits was a priority. Today, when the poor elderly are primarily women and people of color, such programs are in danger of further reduction" (1990, p. 15).

Throughout their adult years, women are more likely than men to be called upon as caregivers. It is most commonly a daughter or a wife, not a son or a husband, who provides direct personal care to an ill or disabled family member. Historically, it has also been primarily the woman's role to volunteer services to needy people of all kinds. Although men also feel a strong sense of obligation for the care of elderly and other needy individuals, the woman is the one usually expected to perform these services because she has been socialized into this role since she tended her "sick dolly" as a child. By contrast, men are usually socialized to delegate hands-on caregiving tasks (Matthews & Rosner, 1988). And, of course, men are more likely to be paid for what they do.

Often personal caregiving services are performed without pay. The cost of health, social, and educational services would long ago have soared beyond today's alarming levels if the care-for-pay establishment had not been supplemented by the voluntary efforts of many women of all adult ages and racial/ethnic backgrounds. Essentially, the woman has provided a "surplus" of caregiving and therefore been heavily relied on as a social resource, but she herself is less likely to receive such support on a sustained basis when the need is hers.

Adjustments and Transitions

All adults are faced with numerous challenges in moving from youth to age. Many of the same situations are encountered by both men and women. In youth, for example, both need to deal with the issue of leaving home and starting a more independent way of life. At mid-life, both may experience the death of people who have been significant in their lives. Adjusting to age-related physical changes is another challenge faced by both men and women.

Each individual brings a unique pattern of resources and experiences to bear upon such challenges, but each also has his or her own pattern of anxieties and concerns. These patterns have not been "caused" by gender-related influences as such, and it is obvious that there is considerable variation within both males and females in the way that they deal with adjustments and transitions. Gender-linked expectations and experiences do not determine how and how well adults cope, but they do provide frameworks within which individual plans of action are formulated.

For example, a comparison has been made between college students and community-dwelling elderly adults on their responses to Injustice and Personal Power scales (Degelman et al., 1991). Women at both age levels were more sensitive to possibilities of injustice than were men. Taken by itself, this finding suggests that gender is the more important predictor of adult attitudes. The picture changes, though, when we add that it was the older women—and *only* the older

women—who expressed a relatively low sense of personal power. Young women did not feel any less powerful than men. Should these findings be confirmed by further studies, it would then appear that sensitivity to injustice is a strongly linked gender characteristic, since both young and old cohorts share this type of response. However, the fact that personal powerlessness was reported only by elderly women raises at least two possibilities: (a) females lose power (or sense of empowerment) with age, or (b) the power status of women has been changing markedly in recent years. Should the latter alternative prove to be correct, then future cohorts of elderly women will feel more empowered than the present cohort and, therefore, approach their life challenges in a different and perhaps more assertive manner. The fact that elderly men felt no less empowered than did the young men could indicate a relative stability in the socially defined role for males—or, alternatively, that the fortunate and effective man is more likely to have survived and to have retained his independent-living status in the community.

There have long been cultural stereotypes to the effect that males and females differ markedly in their styles of coping and adjustment. Both sexes see males as being independent, logical, worldly, and adept in mathematics and business. Females are seen as having a superiority in being aware of others' feelings and behaving in a gentle and tactful manner (Broverman et al., 1972). Associated with these stereotypes is the view that women tend to be less mature and more "emotional" than men. A woman therefore runs the risk of seeming "immature" if she expresses the emotional side of her nature, and "unfeminine" if she does not. It should not go unnoticed that considering an active and responsive emotional expressivity to be "immature" is more of a value judgment than an objective finding. Cold logic and apparent disinterested objectivity do not always provide the most creative, compassionate, and positive way to face life's challenges.

Couples who are actively involved in raising children together tend to develop more "cross-gender" understanding and skills. In the later adult years there is also frequently a growing-together of male and female interests and values. With the extended lifespan now being experienced by many people, it is possible that a large number of adults will outgrow the gender roles and identities that had so much influence in their early socialization and years of primary social obligations. They may simultaneously discover more about how "the other half" really lives as well as about some of the relatively underdeveloped aspects of their own nature. ▼ ROBERT KASTENBAUM

See also: Adult Children and Their Parents; Age 40; Alcohol Use and Abuse; Cardiac Health; Contextualism; Disengagement Theory; Divorce; Driving: A Lifespan Challenge; Drug Use and Abuse; Fictive Kin; Friendships through the Adult Years; Gender Differences in the Workplace; Individuality; Longevity; Mastery Types, Development, and Aging; Menopause; Mexican Americans: Life Course Transitions and Adjustment; Parental Imperative; Privacy Issues; Retirement Preparation; Risk to Life through the Adult Years; Sexuality; Sibling Relationships; Social Relationships, Convoys of; Social Support for the Chronically Ill; Travel: Stimulus to Adult Development; The Voice.

References

Bem, S. L. (1985). Androgyny and gender schema theory: A conceptual and empirical integration. In T. B. Sonderegger (Ed.), *Nebraska Symposium on Motivation 1984: Psychology and Gender*. Lincoln, NE: University of Nebraska Press, pp. 170-95.

Broverman, I. K., et al. (1972). Sex-role stereotypes: A current appraisal. *Journal of Social Issues, 28*: 59-78.

Deaux, K., & Kites, M. E. (1987). Gender stereotypes: Some thoughts on the cognitive organization of gender-related information. *Academic Psychology Bulletin, 7*: 123-44.

Degelman, D., et al. (1991). Age and gender differences in beliefs about personal power and injustice. *International Journal of Aging and Human Development, 33:* 101-12.

Gee, E. (1989a). Mortality rate. In R. Kastenbaum & B. K. Kastenbaum (Eds.), *Encyclopedia of Death*. Phoenix: The Oryx Press, pp. 183-85.

———. (1989b). Causes of death. In R. Kastenbaum & B. K. Kastenbaum (Eds.), *Encyclopedia of Death*. Phoenix: The Oryx Press, pp. 38-41.

Gutmann, D. L. (1987). *Reclaimed Powers: Toward a New Psychology of Men and Women in Later Life*. New York: Basic Books.

Hess, B. B. (1990). The demographic parameters of gender and aging. *Generations, 14* (Summer): 12-16.

Hess, B. B., & Ferree, M. M. (1987). *Analyzing Gender: A Handbook of Social Science Research*. Newbury Park, CA: Sage.

Huyck, M. H. (1990). Gender differences in aging. In J. E. Birren & K. W. Schaie (Eds.), *Handbook of the Psychology of Aging*. Third Edition. New York: Academic Press, pp. 124-38.

Kastenbaum, R., Peyton, S., & Kastenbaum, B. K. (1977). Sex discrimination after death. *Omega, Journal of Death and Dying, 7:* 351-59.

Luria, M. H. (1982). Relationship between sex hormones, myocardial infarction, and occlusive coronary disease. *Archives of Internal Medicine, 142:* 42-44.

Matthews, S. H., & Rossner, T. T. (1988). Shared filial responsibility: The family as the primary caregiver. *Journal of Marriage and the Family, 50:* 185-95.

Money, J. (1987). Propaedeutics of diecious G-I/R: Theoretical foundations for understanding dimorphic gender identity roles. In J. M. Reinisch, L. A. Rosenblum, & S. A. Sanders (Eds.), *Masculinity/Femininity: Basic Perspectives*. New York: Oxford University Press, pp. 13-28.

Smith, D. W. E., & Warner, H. R. (1989). Does genotypic sex have a direct influence on longevity? *Experimental Gerontology, 24:* 277-88.

Verbrugge, L. M. (1989). Pathways of health and death. In R. D. Apple (Ed.), *The History of Women, Health, and Medicine in America*. New York: Garland, pp. 26-42.

Waldron, I. (1983). Sex differences in human mortality: The role of genetic factors. *Social Science and Medicine, 17*: 321-33.

Weeks, J.R. (1988). The demography of Islamic nations. *Population Bulletin 43* (4).

GENDER DIFFERENCES IN THE WORKPLACE

Discrimination against women in the work force is commonplace in the United States. Two of its major forms are economic inequality and gender segregation.

Wages and Salaries

Working women, who now make up approximately 60 percent of the labor force, are paid substantially lower wages and salaries than men with the same education, experience, and motivation who hold the same jobs (Christy, 1990). Pay in predominantly female occupations is lower by at least a fifth than the pay in predominantly male occupations after controlling for work characteristics and other factors (Sorenson, 1989).

Sex-based discrimination has been evident in the U.S. economy ever since records have been kept and is still pervasive. Contrary to what many believe, this situation has not changed substantially in recent decades. The ratio of female to male wages based on annual median incomes has been in the narrow range of 59 to 63 percent since 1967 (Christy, 1990). In other words, on the average, a woman is paid 63 cents for every dollar a man is paid on a comparable job.

A woman who has graduated from college does not make more money than a man who has only completed high school. A woman with a high school education receives the same wages as a male high school dropout. Women who become executives after graduating from business administration programs in prestigious colleges still earn only about half the salaries paid to men in similar positions (Bartlett & Miller, 1988).

The data showing that education and training do little to prevent economic discrimination against women in the workplace are widely acknowledged, but the practice continues—and it does so despite laws and policies that have been established to eliminate this form of injustice, such as the Equal Pay Act of 1964 and a number of more recent directives.

Gender Segregation

Another persistent form of discrimination is gender segregation in the workplace (Wharton, 1987). Women still compose between 70 and 97 percent of the employees in household work, food services, clerical positions, nursing, and elementary education, all of which are traditionally gender-stereotyped fields. Men still dominate (85 percent) as physicians and continue to occupy the large majority of professional positions in science, engineering, technology, private industry, commerce, banking, and all branches of government. Relatively few women receive doctorates in science and engineering—in fact, there has been a decline in these areas. Fewer women received bachelor degrees in science and engineering in 1990 than in 1984. In 1990 only 8.4 percent of the bachelor degrees in mathematics were awarded to women (Brush, 1991), and the percentages were even lower in physics and astronomy (4.7 percent) and engineering (3.1 percent).

Monetary compensation is considered a critical datum signifying the status and prestige that a particular occupation is accorded by society. Since the traditional male occupations consistently pay higher wages and salaries, it is not surprising that men remain in them. Even in professions in which women are underrepresented, there is further stereotyping and discrimination by gender into subspecialties with lower status and pay. For example, women lawyers tend to be in domestic law or trust specialties rather than corporate or criminal law. Women in medicine tend to be pediatricians, psychiatrists, or public health physicians (Christy, 1990).

Some recent reports hail so-called phenomenal advances that women have made in the labor force. On closer examination, however, the changes are far less impressive. For example, it has been reported that women-owned businesses increased more than 50 percent in the mid-1980s (O'Hare & Larson,

1991). But the size of the increase is largely an artifact brought about by changes in the Internal Revenue Service's taxing structure. Also, more than 80 percent of the women-owned businesses are concentrated in the social sciences (personal, health, and business), and half of them have no employees and receipts of less than $5,000 (U.S. Department of Commerce, 1990).

Real, But Limited, Progress

Still, considered from an historical perspective, women have made some progress in the workplace. The women's rights movement began with the industrial revolution in the nineteenth century in response to women's appalling working conditions, especially in the garment industry. It gained significant momentum, however, only after World War II. Moved by an appeal to their patriotism, both single and married women ventured forth to contribute to the war effort. They managed homes, farms, businesses, and production while the men were away fighting and winning the war. By 1944, for example, 63 percent of the professional and managerial and 70 percent of the semiskilled jobs were opened to women (Hartmann, 1982). Not surprisingly, when the men returned after the war, many women found it difficult to adjust to losing their jobs and the independence, status, and prestige they had enjoyed (Campbell, 1984).

Today, women have access to employment in virtually all fields, including those still considered by many to be the domain of men, such as the sciences, technology, truck driving, law enforcement, and the military. Although the ratios of women in these occupations are still small—in some cases, extremely small—an important barrier to economic equality is being removed nevertheless. Increased participation and success by women in male-dominated occupations will probably prove to be the single most important factor in eliminating gender stereotypes.

Male Exodus and Female Entry

The improved access of women to traditional male occupations is not necessarily the result of awakened consciences and goodwill of the male-dominated power structures. The pattern of occupational changes shows rather more pragmatic thinking. Specifically, women have entered jobs that men have vacated.

This trend can be seen in a number of occupations, from agriculture to psychology. A dramatic example is the changing composition of the U.S. military. At least one major reason for the recruitment of women—and minorities—into the military is the fact that young white males left the service or failed to enter. The public image of the military suffered following the Vietnam War, influencing President Nixon in 1972 to allow conscription to lapse and the armed forces to become an all-volunteer organization.

From that time forward, increasing numbers of women have enlisted in all branches of the military. In 1948 a 2 percent ceiling was established for enlisted women. At that time, about 1 percent of armed forces personnel were women. Between 1972 and 1975, the percentages quadrupled, reaching 12 percent in the mid-1980s (Segal, 1989). The influx of women into all branches of the military could be regarded as making this the most democratic organization in our total economy.

The last barrier for women in the armed forces—the combat exclusion laws—is currently under congressional debate and may disappear before long. It has been argued that the distinction between combat and noncombat positions has become of doubtful significance in today's high-technology military. Testimony given before a congressional committee indicates that the combat exclusion laws have the effect of keeping women from advancing in the military ranks to positions for which they are qualified (Ferber, 1988).

Much of the resistance to women in combat is based on the belief that women interfere with male bonding, thus detracting from a unit's cohesion and performance. A similar argument was also advanced against racial integration (Segal, 1989). Others fears the "feminization" of the armed forces. This hypothetical process is imagined as leading to the loss of strength and discipline, thereby threatening our national security (Mitchell, 1989). Such fears are hardly warranted. Although the number of women in the military has greatly increased, the armed forces are still composed largely of men (90 percent; National Guard, 89 percent), according to the Department of Defense (1989).

Although no studies are available on this issue, it is reasonable to suggest that women are eager to enter "male" occupations not primarily for the thrill of "invasion," but because of their own vocational interests and aptitudes and because these occupations offer better wages and salaries. In addition to increasing access to "male" occupations, a dramatic restructuring of the wage scales at all levels is needed to end gender-based inequities and discrimination. A recent survey of individuals graduated from a government-sponsored Job Training Partnership program showed that the average hourly wage of a typist was $4 compared with $16 for a truck driver (Hendren, 1991). Similar gender-based inequities can be found across the occupational board.

The Glass Ceiling

Although women's participation in male-dominated occupations has increased, women consistently have been prevented from advancing in these occupations. This phenomenon is called *the glass ceiling*. The term describes a barrier that is so subtle as to be transparent—and yet at the same time so strong that it prevents women from moving up the ladder in organizational hierarchies.

Evidence of this type of gender discrimination and inequality is pervasive. The glass ceiling exists at all levels, in the professions, in private industry, and in government (Hymowitz & Schellhardt, 1986; Morrison & Von Glinow, 1990). For example, although women occupy about a third of the manage-

ment positions in private industry (up from 16 percent in 1969), only 2 percent of the senior executives are women. Less than 5 percent of the members of boards of directors of the nation's 190 largest health care organizations are women.

The ratios are similar for management positions in government and educational institutions (Morrison & Von Glinow, 1990), where only 8 percent of the positions at senior levels are held by women. Only 5 percent of school superintendents are women, although women constitute nearly three-fourths of the work force (Kallestad, 1990). The percentages are even lower in higher education. Throughout the history of the U.S. Congress, only about 1 percent of the membership has been female. Today, only 2 percent of the U.S. Congress are women, and only 5 percent of state governors are women—yet women compose 51 percent of the population.

It is easy to see that progress toward economic gender equality is minimal when women are denied access to the top positions of the organizational hierarchies, thereby being kept from the highest levels of decision making, status, and prestige, as well as income. The glass ceiling actually reinforces the old gender stereotypes of female inferiority.

Explanations. Three explanations have been advanced for the glass ceiling phenomenon. These explanations can also be applied to other gender-specific forms of discrimination.

One explanation suggests actual deficiencies in women as the cause. In this view, women do not have the aptitude, ability, stamina, or personality characteristics that are required for responsible and demanding positions. This explanation is contradicted by psychological research that has provided strong evidence that gender-based differences do not exist in these characteristics. Women are not inferior to men with respect to abilities, motivation, and other personality factors that might influence their performance. Evidence shows that women actually perform their job responsibilities as adequately as men (Morrison & Von Glinow, 1990).

A second explanation is that gender discrimination and sexism are the major causes for the economic suppression of women. This explanation is accepted by most psychologists and by all feminists and humanistically inclined persons. In this view, discrimination takes on various forms, beginning in early childhood. Gender discrimination is experienced at home, in school, and throughout the community, and is disseminated and reinforced by the mass media. With respect to the sciences, for example, girls consistently receive messages that discourage their interest, undermine their self-confidence, and question their capabilities (Brush, 1991; Kantrowitz & Wingert, 1992).

The third explanation advanced for discrimination against women in the workplace—especially of the glass ceiling type—points to broader structural and systemic factors as the cause. Exclusion from informal social networks and the opportunity for mentoring are among the factors that have been suggested here (Morrison & Von Glinow, 1990). This explanation is also widely accepted and acknowledged.

For women to have equal access to the careers that suit their abilities and interests, it may be necessary for society to discard the restrictive attitudes and practices that begin early in childhood and remain as a burden and an obstacle to overcome as women prepare for fulfilling adult careers.

▼ HANNELORE L. WASS

See also: Development and Aging in Historical Perspective; Disengagement Theory; Gender as a Shaping Force in Adult Development and Aging; Military Service: Long-Term Effects on Adult Development; Retirement: An Emerging Challenge for Women; Sexuality; Work Capacity Across the Adult Years; Work Organization Membership and Behavior.

References

Bartlett, R. L., & Miller, T. I. (1988). Executive earnings by gender. *Social Science Quarterly, 69*: 892-907.

Brush, S. G. (1991). Women in science and engineering. *American Scientist, 79*: 404-19.

Campbell, D. A. (1984). *Women at War with America: Private Lives in a Patriotic Era*. Cambridge, MA: Harvard University.

Christy, S. (1990). Women, work and the workplace. In L. L. Lindsay (Ed.), *Gender Roles: A Sociological Perspective*. Englewood Cliffs, NJ: Prentice-Hall, pp. 179-92.

Department of Defense. (1989). *Military Women*. Volume 7. Washington, DC: The Pentagon.

Ferber, M. M. (1988). Combat exclusion laws for women in the military (Report No. GAO/T-NSIAD-88-8). Washington, DC: U.S. General Accounting Office.

Hartmann, S. (1982). *The Home Front and Beyond: American Women in the 1940's*. Boston: Twayne.

Hendren, J. (1991). Law may open new fields to women workers. *Gainesville Sun*, December 15.

Hymowitz, C., & Schellhardt, T. D. (1986). The glass ceiling. *The Wall Street Journal*, March 24.

Kallestad, B. (1990). Women's salaries still lag. *Gainesville Sun*, February 17.

Kantrowitz, B., & Wingert, P. (1992). Sexism in the schoolhouse. *Newsweek*, February 24, p. 62.

Mitchell, B. P. (1989). *Weak Link: The Feminization of the American Military*. Washington, DC: Regnery Gateway.

Morrison, A. M., & Von Glinow, M. A. (1990). Women and minorities in management. *American Psychologist*: 200-08.

O'Hare, W., & Larson, J. (1991). Women in business. *American Demographics*, July, pp. 34-38.

Segal, D. R. (1989). *Recruiting for Uncle Sam: Citizenship and Military Manpower*. Lawrence, KS: University Press of Kansas.

Sorenson, E. (1989). Measuring the pay disparity between typically female occupations and other jobs: A bivariate selectivity approach. *Industrial and Labor Relations Review, 42*: 624-38.

U.S. Department of Commerce. (1990). *1987 Economic Censuses: Women-Owned Businesses*. Washington, DC: Superintendent of Documents.

Wharton, A. S. (1987). Gender segregation in private-sector, public-sector and self-employed occupations 1950-1981. *Social Science Quarterly, 70*: 923-39.

GENERATIONAL EQUITY

Generational equity exists when there is a fair distribution of the available resources among all members of society according to their needs and regardless of their age. However, philosopher Norman Daniels (1983) urges that we go a step further and consider both justice between birth cohorts and justice between age groups. The issue of equity between *birth cohorts* (people born at the same time) can be illustrated by today's baby boomers, who will be tomorrow's elders. This cohort may not capitalize on the benefit ratios and replacement ratios that retirees currently enjoy under Social Security. The *age group* issue concerns the treatment of one particular segment of the population (e.g., children) in comparison with another segment (e.g., the elderly) in relation to their particular place in the lifespan. For example, loans for college students are subject to means tests for eligibility, but Social Security entitlements are not. The diverse entitlement programs existing today contain a number of significant examples in which one age group is treated more leniently or generously than another.

Although the population size and structure of the United States and other Western nations have changed appreciably, many of the questions about generational equity that are being raised today are not new. In 1882, Anthony Trollope published *The Fixed Period*, a futuristic novel in which older citizens seemed to have outlived their usefulness and were viewed as burdens to society. The action takes place nearly contemporaneously (1880) on Britannaula, a fictitious island. The younger citizens of the island had adopted a "fixed period" law under which all citizens age 67 or older were "deposited" in a special honorary college known as "necropolis." Here, members were expected to spend one year in deep thought and peaceful reflection before being chloroformed and cremated. This policy was intended to avoid the "imbecility and weakness of human life when pro-tracted beyond its fitting limits" and to dignify death with "circumstances of honor and glory" (Trollope, 1882).

Raising Questions in the 1980s

Slightly more than 100 years later, Governor Richard Lamm of Colorado echoed Trollope's message. Appearing on ABC's "Nightline" telecast (April 1984), Lamm stated that too much technology and money were being spent on the elderly during their last years of life in comparison with the young, who have their entire lives before them. Three years later, Daniel Callahan (1987) stated Lamm's case in more diplomatic terms. In *Setting Limits*, Callahan argued strenuously that medicine can keep some people alive far longer than is of any benefit to them. He concluded, therefore, that the United States should consider adopting age-based policies as a means of allocating health care resources across the lifespan. Great Britain, for example, prohibits public funding for kidney dialysis for those over age 55, and other nations have applied similar policies to various types of technologies. The United States, according to Callahan, should follow suit.

The comments of Lamm and the writings of Callahan eventually produced a much broader question that demands even greater attention: In an era of limited resources, are the aged receiving a disproportionately large share of the available resources in comparison with other groups? This became the generational equity issue, and it has quickly spawned a new debate in numerous participants.

Samuel Preston established the original parameters of the debate with his presidential address before the Population Association of America (Minneapolis, May 1984), and followed it up with his article in *Scientific American* later that year (Preston, 1984). He argued that we cannot simply wish away the possibility that there is direct competition between the young and the old for society's resources. Preston held that expenditures on elderly people can be thought of "mainly as consumption," while expenditures on behalf of the young are "a combination of consumption and investment."

Following in Preston's path, Richman and Stagner (1986) also framed the issues in terms of elderly people and children. They argued that an aging society poses two possible consequences for America's children: "They may become a treasured resource nurtured all the more for their scarcity and importance to the nation's future; or they may come to be regarded, amid the increasing clamor for resources and attention by other dependent groups, as only another needy minority." Others joined the debate as well. Philip Longman (1987), in *Born to Pay: The New Politics of Aging in America,* contends that an unfair burden has been placed on the baby boom generation to support a growing aged population through Social Security and Medicare. Longman argues that expenditures on the aged exceed the defense budget, and that the demand to expand these benefits will continue well into the next century. Similar points were raised in several editorials in *Newsweek.* Special articles in *The Nation* and the *New Republic* spoke in terms of a "health care generation war" and "the greedy geezers" problem.

The so-called middle generation is being challenged on two fronts. Longman contends that two-paycheck families with incomes over $20,000 will pay more in Social Security taxes than they will receive in benefits, a sharp contrast to returns enjoyed by current beneficiaries. For example, a person who retired in 1986 got the entirety of his or her contribution to Social Security back within 18 months. Simply put, today's beneficiary experienced much lower taxes and reaps much greater benefits than those 20 to 30 years younger. Furthermore, a *Business Week* article ("Those aging baby boomers," 1991) concluded that the age cohort born between 1929 and 1938 has an average household net worth twice that of the age cohort born between 1949 and 1958. This trend is expected to continue for other generations or cohorts well into the next century.

On a second front, today's family is being squeezed between two generations.

Not only is child care in great demand because of two-earner couples and single-parent households but so, too, is elder care. Almost 62 percent of women between the ages of 45 and 54 now are engaged in paid employment, as are 42 percent of those who fall into the 55 to 64 age bracket (U.S. Bureau of Labor Statistics, 1984). It is precisely these two groups of middle-aged females who are most likely to provide the necessary care to the disabled parent. Today, 1 of every 10 people aged 85 and older has a child who is at least 65 (Brody, 1986). As a result, for the first time in U.S. history the average couple has more parents than children (Preston, 1984). In short, today's middle-aged (40 to 59) are expected to provide care at both ends of the age scale, unlike previous middle-aged groups.

Organizations Enter the Debate

Several important organizations also took up the cause. For example, in April 1985, Democratic National Committee Chairman Paul Kirk suggested that the party consider a payment freeze and a means test for Social Security. Although eventually placed on hold, the proposal represented the Democrats' response to criticism of its history of expanded entitlement programs for elderly people. The generational equity question was rapidly becoming politicized.

Equally important, perhaps, was the formation of Americans for Generational Equity (AGE) in 1985. Founded by Senator David Durenburger and former Representative James Jones, AGE questioned the future of the $200 billion Social Security system and the assumption that the young should support the old. From fewer than 100 members and a budget of $88,000 in 1985, AGE grew to more than 1,000 members and $300,000 by 1990. A central theme in AGE's message is that elderly people are too expensive. Consequently, the young will be overburdened with the responsibility of covering these costs, and today's baby boomers are unlikely to receive the same level of old age benefits when they become elderly.

To counter groups such as AGE, more than 90 national organizations, including the National Council on Aging and the Child Welfare League of America, have banded together to form Generations United. Claiming to represent more than 30 million Americans of all ages, this coalition has focused on such intergenerational issues as health care, welfare reform, child and elder abuse, and day care both for children and dependent older adults.

Another significant event that played a major role in neutralizing AGE's influence was the Gerontological Society of America's publication of *Ties that Bind: The Interdependence of Generations* (Kingson, Hirshorn, & Cornman, 1986). A primary purpose of this work was to dispel the growing belief that the young and old are fighting over limited government resources. More specifically, the report attacked those popular myths that feed on intergenerational conflict. For example, the report emphasized that the voting behavior of older persons is guided more by party affiliation, social class, race, and political belief than by age. Further, opinion polls continued to show strong support by old and young alike for programs such as Social Security, Medicare, student loans, and food subsidies. And finally, the authors argued that concern over the elderly population depleting resources needed by the young does not take into account future economic growth, the potential for many to work beyond the age of 65, and the increase of women in the labor force.

The Major Themes

The debate over generational equity continues to encompass four major themes, regardless of whether the discussion is conducted in legislative chambers, university seminar rooms, or editorial board rooms at publishing houses. Furthermore, according to Kaye (1988) and Wisensale (1988), these themes are essentially flawed in structure and rooted in general misunderstanding about an aging society.

First, generational equity is commonly framed in terms of conflict between young and old and between the working and nonworking population. Yet the fact remains that the younger generation is more willing to support entitlements for elderly people in the present because it is aware that in the future it will have its own access to programs such as Social Security and Medicare. Although this is not to say that a war between generations will be avoided, the fact remains that whatever conflict exists between the two groups has yet to reach the level of intensity that has been forecast by groups such as AGE.

Second, another shortcoming of the generational equity argument is that it tends to pit spending for the aged against spending for children. Although generational equity advocates are accurate in pointing out that the poverty rate among elderly persons has declined dramatically while that for children has climbed significantly, they also play what can best be called a zero-sum game. In other words, it is assumed that the U.S. economic pie is finite in size and will not grow. Thus, spending priorities, particularly those affecting the Pentagon, must not be restricted. Under this simplistic "canes vs. kids" argument, elderly people are robbing children of their future. To counter such thinking, Binstock (1983) asks why the concern over how many workers are needed to support a retiree is not matched by an equal concern over the number of workers needed to support an aircraft carrier. (Recent global developments suggest that such concern may be rising to the surface.)

Third, Edward Wynne (1986) reminds us that elderly people practice reciprocity through the transfer of assets to their descendants by means of inheritance, as well as through substantial support for children through their childhood, adolescence, and young adulthood. Such contributions on the part of the aged often are overlooked in the assessment of intergenerational transfer. Generational equity advocates also tend to ignore the importance of Social Security, Medicare, and other established old age benefits in reducing the financial burdens that in past generations had been the responsibility of younger family members.

The fourth and perhaps strongest argument on behalf of generational equity is rooted in the assumption that Social Security is a poor investment for the young, and thus they will realize a poor rate of return when they retire. Although Social Security has indeed experienced a rocky history and has required major reform measures over the years to maintain its solvency, it remains strong and continues to accumulate impressive surpluses. It is not surprising, therefore, that conservative groups such as AGE continue their assaults against it. Likewise, other critics such as banks and insurance companies, including Metropolitan Life and the U.S. League of Savings Institutions, have consistently favored any cuts in Social Security benefits that would in turn boost the need for private pensions and individual savings plans.

Despite whatever arguments can be mustered to address the concerns of AGE and similar organizations, the generational equity issue continues to spill over into the political arena. Rightly or wrongly, it appears that, at least for now, an organized backlash aimed at the aged has begun and therefore must be addressed. As a result, the political landscape has shifted and we have witnessed important policy initiatives being put forth that are tied directly to the issue of generational equity. Two significant examples of these initiatives are the late Claude Pepper's family policy package, introduced two weeks before his death in 1989, and the final report of the Pepper Commission on Health Care, issued in 1990.

Claude Pepper's Family Policy Package

Long the leading advocate for the nation's elderly people, Senator Claude Pepper began to respond to the changing political winds in the 1980s by introducing a variety of intergenerational policy proposals. His Medical Long-Term Home Care Catastrophic Protection Act was designed to provide home care for technology-dependent children under 19, the disabled, and children and elderly people who are unable to perform two or more activities of daily living. Although endorsed by 110 diverse organizations, the bill failed to pass either house.

Just two weeks before his death in 1989, Pepper introduced what he referred to as his "package for keeping America's families together." Consisting of seven separate bills, the package included provisions for long-term home care for all chronically ill people regardless of age. It also created the nation's first "Young Americans Act" and proposed a "School Completion and Incentives Act." The package was rounded out by measures to reform Social Security and provisions to protect institutionalized older adults. Although appealing to some legislators, the support was not wide enough to achieve passage. However, the symbolism should not be overlooked. In the final weeks of his life, the older person's strongest advocate chose to move in the direction of intergenerational policies.

The Pepper Commission's Report

The Pepper Commission, a 15-member bipartisan panel, was established in 1989 to examine the status of health care in the U.S. The Commission's recommendations cut across the lifespan. In short, the recommendations were divided into two groups: those that concerned access to health insurance regardless of age, and those that focused on long-term health care for elderly people. On the former point, the Pepper Commission proposed the creation of a new public health plan to replace the current state-federal Medicaid program, recommended that employers with more than 100 workers be required to either provide employees and their nonworking dependents with private health insurance or contribute to the public plan on their behalf, and suggested that employers with fewer than 100 workers be encouraged to participate in the plan through a series of tax incentives and subsidies. The panel would also prevent private insurance companies from excluding coverage for preexisting conditions and from refusing coverage for an individual within a covered group.

Concerning long-term care of the aged, the Commission recommended federal payments for up to three months of care in a nursing home regardless of age or ability to pay, called for federal coverage of both home- and community-based care for the disabled of all ages, proposed an asset-protection policy for those entering nursing homes, and suggested the expansion of research on long-term disabilities and chronic illnesses. To finance both the universal access and long-term care programs, the Commission recommended that taxes be progressive, requiring higher contributions from those most able to pay.

Conclusion

The generational equity question has clearly made its way onto the political agenda. Whether or not the discussion is always anchored in accurate information is, of course, another question.

As we attempt to shape our social welfare policies for the future, we must address at least two fundamental questions. Is generational equity morally justified? Is generational equity something toward which our society should strive?

It can be argued that equity is always morally justified. The real question, however, is whether or not it can be achieved politically at a reasonable price. Obviously the fair allocation of resources between and among various birth cohorts and age groups is not an easy task. Nevertheless, theoretical models do exist and should be explored further. For example, Daniels (1983) has developed a framework from the work of John Rawls that could, in principle, justify age-based allocation or denial of resources according to an equitable distribution procedure over an entire lifespan. According to Daniels, instead of looking at birth cohorts or age cohorts as being in conflict over resources at any point in time, we should take each person's entire lifespan as the basic unit of consideration. Within this framework it would be reasonable to accept the proposition that the same person may gain differential access to differential resources over the course of his or her entire lifespan.

With respect to the second question, generational equity definitely is a goal toward which our society should strive. But equally important, the goal should also serve as our compass in this debate. To paraphrase H. R. Moody (1982) in his discourse on ethics and long-term care, generational equity should not be seen as a code word for "smart politics" or "sound public policy" or become the latest buzzword of "politically correct language." Instead, it should become a means to keep the debate going, to keep the dialogue responsible, and, whenever possible, to guide us toward a better understanding of our societal principles and toward wiser decisions in our personal lives.

▼ STEVEN K. WISENSALE

See also: Adult Children and Their Parents; Cohort and Generational Effects; Development and Aging in Historical Perspective; Disengagement Theory; Friendships through the Adult Years; Political Beliefs and Activities; Suffering.

References

Binstock, R. (1983). The aged as scapegoat. *The Gerontologist, 23*: 136-43.

Brody, E. (1986). Parent care as a normative family stress. In L. E. Troll (Ed.), *Family Issues in Current Gerontology*. New York: Springer.

Callahan, D. (1987). *Setting Limits: Medical Goals in an Aging Society*. New York: Simon and Schuster.

Daniels, N. (1983). Justice between age groups: Am I my parent's keeper? *Millbank Memorial Fund Quarterly*, Summer, pp. 489-522.

Kaye, L. (1988). Generational equity: Pitting young against old. *New England Journal of Human Services, 3*: 8-11.

Kingson, E., Hirshorn, B., & Cornman, J. (1986). *Ties that Bind: The Interdependence of Generations*. Cabin John, MD: Seven Locks Press.

Longman, P. (1987). *Born to Pay: The New Politics of Aging in America*. Boston: Houghton-Mifflin.

Moody, H. R. (1982). Ethical dilemmas in long-term care. *Journal of Gerontological Social Work, 5*: 97-111.

Preston, S. (1984). Children and the elderly in the U.S. *Scientific American, 250:* 44-49.

Richman, H., & Stagner, M. (1986). Children in an aging society: Treasured resource or forgotten minority? *Daedalus, 115:* 171-89.

Those aging baby boomers. (1991). *Business Week,* May 20, 106-12.

Trollope, A. (1882). *The Fixed Period.* Reprinted in N. J. Hall (Ed.), *Selected Works by Anthony Trollope.* 2 vols. Salem, NH: Ayer, 1981.

U.S. Bureau of Labor Statistics. (1984). Employment and Earnings. Washington, DC: U.S. Government Printing Office.

Wisensale, S. (1988). Generational equity and intergenerational policies. *The Gerontologist, 28:* 773-78.

Wynne, E. (1986). Will the young support the old? In A. Pifer & L. Bronte (Eds.), *Our Aging Society: Paradox and Promise.* New York: W. W. Norton.

GRANDPARENT COMMUNICATION SKILLS

When today's grandparents were growing up, there was less emphasis on learning from peers. In those days, teachers were seen as a sufficient source of instruction. Reading and listening to the teacher were considered the primary ways to learn. Student conversation during class was regarded as a waste of time, a practice to be discouraged and treated as misbehavior. Times have changed. Students are no longer obliged to just sit still, listen carefully, and write their responses to the teacher. They learn to express themselves orally, challenge the opinions of others, defend their points of view, and work together on group projects. This broader orientation is considered necessary for success in a society that encourages individuality, self-esteem, cooperation, and concern for others (Brilhart & Galenes, 1989; Brown, 1988; Duck & Silver, 1990; Schwartz, 1991; Toffler, 1991).

How do these differences in schooling affect family interaction? A "generation gap" is frequently identified as the reason for the decline in family conversation. Older people are thought to be rooted in the past while efforts of the younger generation are aimed at

the future. Because their schooling was focused on individual classroom activity, grandparents generally lack group learning skills. Commonly acquired by children today, these skills facilitate productive dialogue with peers and mutually respectful conversation within families. However, older adults can become effective participants in discussion groups, recognize peers as a potential source of learning, and demonstrate communication skills that support satisfying intergenerational relationships. What is needed to achieve this objective is guidance and an opportunity to practice in a low-risk setting. (Strom, Bernard, & Strom, 1989).

Age-Segregated Communication

Although churches and senior centers would seem to be good places for older adults to acquire and practice previously unlearned communication skills, this is seldom the case. These institutions are popular because they bring together people who have approximately the same sense of history and who share common experiences; communication among them is easier than with persons from other age groups. Since their dialogues begin with general agreement of definitions, assumptions, and interpretations, there is less ambiguity or likelihood of misinterpretation. Their conversations with age peers are relatively predictable, free of uncertainty, and usually judged to be pleasant.

But whatever our age it is unwise to make peers the only audience to hear our concerns just because talking to them is easier. When older people are limited to peers for extended conversations, they are less likely to acquire the up-to-date communication skills needed for successful interaction with people of other generations. Each of us must continue to interact with people whose experience differs from our own so that we can learn about them and make ourselves better known. Understanding how other age groups see things and feel about the world is necessary for a broad outlook and becoming responsive to the needs of others (Strom & Strom, 1990).

Some older persons contend that "We have always just done what comes naturally in carrying out our conversations. This has worked pretty well, so why should we change?" Even though everyone enjoys visiting, casual conversation does not offer the mental stimulation necessary for learning. In addition to the "natural" way of responding to others, it is also important for members of a group to engage in self-disclosure, remain focused, yield to other speakers, evaluate different points of view, call for clarification, and brainstorm. Older persons who learn to develop these abilities in a peer setting usually become effective discussants, and improve the quality of their communication with their own family members (Strom, Bernard, & Strom, 1989).

Guidelines for Discussion Groups

The authors' long-term project to develop education for older adults has included observations of grandparents' behavior in discussion groups. The purpose of grandparent education is to provide learning opportunities that contribute to mental health, family harmony, and intergenerational understanding. Based on anecdotal information, the authors formulated the following guidelines to promote more productive dialogue. These guidelines are given to the class members so they can monitor their own conduct as well as the behavior of peers. Some of these recommendations involve the logistics of group interaction, which can have a powerful effect on communication. Other suggestions are procedural and depend on accountability by the participants. In combination, these suggestions can enrich the outcomes of discussion groups for older adults (Strom & Strom, 1991a, 1991b, 1991c, 1992a, 1992b).

Provide Advance Agenda. The questions for discussion should be distributed in advance and should appear in large print for ease of reading. The participants are asked to read the agenda before coming to class. For older adults, the activities of everyday living are slower and less spontaneous. They feel more comfortable when they can take plenty of time and plan well ahead. This practice encourages reflection and reduces anxiety.

Limit the Scope of Discussion. People feel overwhelmed when there are too many questions for consideration. Elderly persons in particular feel rushed and disappointed if there is not enough time for them to express their views. It is best to limit the agenda to five questions and the duration of discussion to 20 or 30 minutes.

Consider Hearing Difficulties. Half of the older adult population suffer from some hearing impairment and many wear hearing aids. They often experience problems with listening, especially in a classroom setting. These difficulties can be partially overcome by proper seating. In the classroom, it helps to arrange individuals in small groups seated as far apart as possible. Everyone should know they are expected to look directly at other participants when they speak. After the end of the discussion period, reporters summarize group comments while they face the audience. Anybody who talks to the whole class should speak loudly enough to be heard. In a large room, this may require the use of a microphone. The hearing difficulties of older learners are seldom considered in the design of instructional facilities, so leaders should carefully select and prepare the best available meeting sites.

Form New Groups Regularly. The recommended size for a discussion group of older adults is four or five persons including a facilitator. More mental stimulation occurs when new groups are formed on a regular basis. Unless this is done, some members avoid meeting new people and seek comfort in the predictability of talking with the same persons each session. When a couple is participating in this learning experience, the spouses are urged to attend separate groups in all sessions so they will have more to share after class. The shifting membership composition of each group also helps to distribute and minimize the possible negative impact of a few individuals who may be difficult to get along with. It is possible, then, to minimize interpersonal conflicts and expose participants to a greater range of peer opinion by regularly changing the makeup of their discussion groups.

Select Relevant Group-Formation Criteria. Many criteria can be used to form groups. It is helpful to draw upon criteria that are appropriate to the nature and purpose of a particular session. For a lesson on single-parent and blended families, participants use the marital status of sons or daughters to assign themselves to a group. Thus, grandparents with a divorced son or daughter would be seated together. Those with blended families (second marriage for husband and/or wife where one/both parties bring children to the marriage) would compose another group, and those with husband-wife first-time marriages would constitute a third group. For establishing discussion groups during a lesson on child and adolescent thinking the age of a selected grandchild becomes the criterion. During a lesson concerned with individuality, the criterion shifts to the number of grandchildren. Gender of a grandchild is the criterion for the lesson on deciding about drugs and sex. For variation, discussion groups may be based on the favorite television programs of the participants (sports, sit coms, documentaries, movies, concerts, etc.), changes that people looking back would have made in their lives (gone to college, chosen a different career, traveled more, lived someplace else, etc.), or the ways in which members spend leisure time (playing cards, traveling, visiting friends and relatives, volunteering in the community, etc.).

Rely on Facilitators. The participants should be told that the group facilitator's purpose is to keep the conversation moving and focused on the topic under consideration. This requires making sure that each person talks to the whole group rather than speaking only to the facilitator and seeking only his or her reaction or advice. Facilitators can be chosen on a rotation basis by the group or appointed by the class leader. In either case, facilitators should avoid the expert role whenever someone invites their opinion in order to bring closure on a subject. Discussion is a time for sharing peer opinions rather than a time for instruction.

Record and Share Comments. Every group needs a recorder every session. This person can be chosen by rotation in the group or be appointed. The recorder's purpose is to write down views expressed by speakers regardless of whether or not the recorder agrees with these views. When the thrust of someone's views are unclear, the recorder should ask for clarification so that the person's points are understood and fairly represented. When a discussion ends, the recorder should be ready to orally summarize group comments if called upon and should also submit them to the group in writing. By listening to the recorders' oral summaries, the participants become more aware of the feelings of their peers.

Maximize the Participation. Group members are invited to choose at least one question that they are willing to talk about. Anyone who still has not spoken when the discussion is nearly over should be asked if he or she wants to offer a comment. Because the goal is participation by the full group, it may be necessary to ask a nonspeaker to react to points made by other members, for example, "Jim, how do you feel about Amy's comments?"

Respect Individual Opinion. Some older adults are accustomed to being ignored and have ceased to value their own opinion. They may suppose that their passive behavior is natural and explain, "I don't have anything important to say." This self-impression undermines the sense of worth that people should feel, and it prevents them from becoming known as individuals. One way to show people they are respected is by recognizing their views. All group members should continually reinforce the principle that everybody's opinions are valued.

During a visit to a city hospital, a group of Navajos allowed the authors to observe the group's procedure for solving problems and ensuring that everyone's views are considered. The leader held up an arrowhead and said, "Sometimes older people in our tribe have to come to the city for hospital care. During the time they are here they often feel bad because the spiritual support of their traditional medicine man is missing. What can we do when the Indian is disoriented like this at the hospital or nursing home? How can we help him in this time of difficulty?"

The leader then passed the arrowhead on to someone else in the circle and that person was expected to make a suggestion. In turn, each of the people had an opportunity to comment. The order of speakers was determined by their seating, and the speaker always held the arrowhead, passing it on whenever she or he was finished talking. Sometimes people expressed agreement with the views of others who had spoken before them; others took a new position or elaborated on a previous comment. In some cases a novel idea was presented. When everyone in the circle had spoken, the outcome was a greater range of possibilities. In this instance, the possibilities included visitation by the medicine man, ceremonies on the reservation in absentia, placement of religious artifacts blessed by the medicine man in the hospital room, and a videotape of the medicine man.

Limit Speaker Time. Some persons monopolize conversations. To make sure each person has an opportunity to talk, group members should be told to limit their remarks to three minutes. At the end of this time the facilitator should interrupt a speaker and invite another person to comment. Speaker dominance must be prevented if the group discussion is to successfully engage all members. Recognize that there are many motives for dominance. For example, after a spouse dies the survivor may have no one who will listen and share his or her feelings. When a person in this circumstance finds a ready audience, he or she may seem ready to talk indefinitely, even if others are bored.

Responses from peers are predictable. Most do not want to deal with a person who is perceived as talking too much. They feel it is the leader's task to confront an "offender." Some express a dislike for working in a group, while others prefer to move to another group. The facilitator should assume leadership in handling this situation, but everyone should develop a sense of personal responsibility for

ensuring the conditions that support group learning.

Wait for Responses. Older men and women may need or desire more time for reflection than younger people. This is certainly the case for persons who have suffered a stroke or other disabilities that affect their speech and cause them to respond slowly or resort to mazing, such as, "Well, ah, I think, ah, that the, ah...." Impatient group members are inclined to anticipate what the slow persons want to say and complete their sentences for them as if playing a game of charades. This second-guessing denies individuality of expression and contradicts the known benefits of awaiting the fruits of the other person's reflections. When you observe this kind of behavior, just say, "Please let him finish." This example will usually set the pattern for future group reaction to a slow respondent.

Encourage Brainstorming. During the group process known as brainstorming, the goal is to identify as many solutions as possible for a particular problem. When people share their ideas, a broader range of options emerges. Decision makers in business and industry credit brainstorming with the creation of better work procedures, improved products, and higher morale. To survive in the present international marketplace, companies need employees who are capable of group problem solving. Accordingly, children are being taught this procedure in elementary school. Older adults have much to gain from participation in brainstorming because it helps them to recover and sustain creative thinking abilities. Brainstorming experiences also encourage them to defer judgment until sufficient information is available instead of reaching premature conclusions.

Accept Spontaneity. The opportunity to react in a spontaneous way is preserved by facilitators who allow individuals to speak when they are ready. Accepting spontaneity requires approval of some interruption, balanced by a willingness to intervene when a pattern of dominance is apparent. Usually discussions are more stimulating when there is no established order for speaking. Otherwise, people tend to think about what they will say when their turn comes, and they fail to listen to what their peers are saying. The anxiety that goes with ordered speech can be overcome by letting individuals determine when they want to comment. Some topics may evoke strong emotions. This can be dealt with by allowing the option to say, "I pass," when a person prefers not to comment.

Challenge Statements. Many older people today are not accustomed to challenging the information sources that peers rely on. Perhaps it seems a courtesy to allow another person to say whatever she or he likes without monitoring the message, but this also has the unintended effect of reinforcing unwarranted generalizations and poor logic. When older adults display this kind of behavior outside the peer group, it lessens their chance to influence family members, and is particularly costly in terms of relationships with teenage grandchildren. Persons who consider a challenge to their viewpoint as an insult are depriving themselves of authentic conversations. One way to help is by urging speakers to substantiate or qualify statements that include exaggeration, for example, "You can't trust the government." One response might be to say, "I suppose that is true sometimes, but can you think of cases when it is necessary to trust the government?"

Candace, a middle-aged nurse, observed, "My mom, who lives at a long-term care facility, challenges statements by peers and she is rejected for it." Those who work with older adults in discussion groups should help them support this type of behavior rather than presume that someone who is trying to keep them on track is rude and out of bounds. Older people dislike being patronized, so they should discourage this behavior in peers as well.

Urge Conclusions. Some older people do not focus well in discussions of ideas and concepts. They prefer to talk about people and events that are often unknown to the other group members. Although this approach seems to qualify each speaker as an authority on whatever situation she or he is describing, it does not mean that the answer given is relevant to the discussion question before the group. When a speaker provides a personal observation but neglects to clarify the implication, the facilitator should try to draw the implication and then check for confirmation. For example, "Nancy, I think the point you are trying to make is...."

Sustain the Focus. When the discussion wanders from the topic, or the participants lose the topic altogether, the facilitator should present the focus again. By occasionally restating the question and briefly summarizing what has already been said about the issue, a facilitator can keep the group on track without embarrassment or reliance on memory.

Reinforce Insights. Wisdom often surfaces in discussions with older people. One way to augment the impact of insightful remarks is by reinforcing them, i. e., acknowledging them in some way and thereby rewarding the speaker for having made this valuable contribution. The facilitator can turn attentively to such speakers and emphasize their comments by requesting, "Would you say that again?" or "Tell us more." Alternately, the facilitator can contribute to a participant's self-esteem by saying, "What a perfect comment," or "Thanks for sharing that special insight."

Support Self-Disclosure. The willingness to take risks decreases with age, so older adults may need support to make their feelings and ideas known (Duck & Silver, 1990). Everyone can grow when they see the discussion group as a safe setting for giving personal opinions. For this to happen, a group response pattern must be established that accepts self-disclosure without criticism or unkind remarks. As people gain confidence in expressing their viewpoints to peers, they become more willing to do so with family members as well.

Monitor Behavior. Some people tell interesting stories during group discussion. But some older men and women unknowingly repeat stories to the class. By privately reminding the storyteller when she or he becomes repetitious, a facilitator helps identify the need to monitor more closely one's own conversations, for example, "John, that story about the flat tire was interesting but it is the third time we've heard it. How about sharing another experience that conveys the same message?"

Reminding another person about any aspect of their behavior that might be misinterpreted (e.g., "Zip up your pants") should be considered a courtesy rather than an insult. Instead, some observers say, "So what if you've already heard his story ten times? He likes to tell it, so just listen, and don't say anything to embarrass him." When older adults seek respect, it is important to realize that the behaviors young people most often associate with declining mental ability are repetitious storytelling and memory lapse. Group members should feel a sense of responsibility about helping their peers monitor their communicational behavior.

Maintain Optimism. Pessimism and optimism are explanatory styles that each of us learn and rely on to interpret troublesome situations. Whereas a pessimist might consider a defeat as permanent, overwhelming, and evidence of some personal weakness, an optimist could perceive the same misfortune as a temporary setback, an obstacle that can be overcome by approaching the problem in some other way. More is involved here than just a difference of opinion.

Optimists do better in the classroom, in athletics, and at work because they cheerfully persist in the face of setbacks while pessimists with equal ability decide to withdraw or give up. Negative thinkers have weaker immune systems, a higher incidence of infectious diseases, greater health problems from the middle of life onwards, and are far more likely to suffer depression (Seligman, 1991). They also are uncomfortable to be around. Together, these factors suggest that positive thinking should become more common among older people. When pessimism is expressed, try to acknowledge the individual's experience by stating that some people have gone through a lot; they have experienced a bad time. Then invite others in the group to share positive experiences that reflect their sense of optimism.

In summary, older adults want close and satisfying relationships with their sons, daughters, and grandchildren. The likelihood of achieving this goal improves considerably when men and women in peer group discussions help one another practice communication skills they were not taught earlier in life but need now to fulfill their important roles in the changing family.

▼ ROBERT D. STROM AND SHIRLEY K. STROM

See also: Adult Children and Their Parents; Attachment Across the Lifespan; Cohort and Generational Effects; Grandparent Education to Enhance Family Strength; Interethnic Relationships; Listening; Native American Perspectives on the Lifespan; Social Relationships, Convoys of.

References

Brilhart, J., & Galenes, G. (1989). *Effective Group Discussion.* Madison, WI: W. C. Brown.

Brown, R. (1988). *Group Processes: Dynamics Within and Between Groups.* New York: Basil Blackwell.

Duck, S., & Silver, R. (1990). *Personal Relationships and Social Support.* Newbury Park, CA: Sage Publications.

Schwartz, P. (1991). *The Art of the Long View.* New York: Doubleday.

Seligman, M. (1991). *Learned Optimism.* New York: Knopf.

Strom, R., and Strom, S. (1990). Raising expectations for grandparents: A three-generational study. *International Journal of Aging and Human Development, 31*(3): 161-67.

———. (1991a). *Becoming a Better Grandparent: A Guidebook for Strengthening the Family.* Newbury Park, CA: Sage Publications.

———. (1991b). *Becoming a Better Grandparent: Viewpoints on Strengthening the Family.* Newbury Park, CA: Sage Publications.

———. (1991c). *Grandparent Education: A Guide for Leaders.* Newbury Park, CA: Sage Publications.

———. (1992a). *Achieving Grandparent Potential: A Guidebook for Building Intergenerational Relationships.* Newbury Park, CA: Sage Publications.

———. (1992b). *Achieving Grandparent Potential: Viewpoints on Building Intergenerational Relationships.* Newbury Park, CA: Sage Publications.

Strom, R., Bernard, H. and Strom, S. (1989). *Human Development and Learning*. New York: Human Sciences Press.

Toffler, A. (1991). *Powershift*. New York: Bantam.

GRANDPARENT EDUCATION TO ENHANCE FAMILY STRENGTH

A strong family is one whose members enjoy mutually satisfying relationships and have the capacity to meet each other's needs (Stinnett & DeFrain, 1985). Efforts to strengthen families include classes that help parents acquire effective methods of guidance and set reasonable expectations for their children. A similar approach could benefit the 55 million grandparents in the United States. Observers agree that grandparents have the potential to make more significant contributions to their families (Bengston & Robertson, 1985; Elkind, 1990; Kornhaber, 1986). The status of grandparents can be enhanced by (a) better understanding of how family relationships are influenced by technological change, (b) widespread recognition of the need to establish educational expectations for grandparents, and (c) the development of a practical curriculum to help grandparents adjust to their emerging role.

Family Relationships and Technological Change

Learning in a Past-Oriented Society. When the older people of today were children, the world was changing less rapidly. With a relatively slower rate of progress, the past tended to dominate the present. Consequently, youngsters learned mostly from adults. In those days a father might reasonably say to his child: "Let me tell you about life and what to expect. I will give you the benefit of my experience. Now, when I was your age...." In this type of society the father's advice would be relevant because he had already confronted most of the situations

that his children would face. Given the slow pace of change, children could see their own future as they observed the day-to-day activities of their parents and grandparents.

Some past-oriented societies, where adults remain the only important source of a child's education, still exist. On the island of Bali in Indonesia, parents pass along their woodcarving and painting skills to sons and daughters who expect to earn a living in much the same way their parents have. Similarly, aboriginal tribes in Australia try to perpetuate their traditional community. Amish people in the United States maintain a pattern of living that closely resembles that of their ancestors. For children growing up in these static environments, the future seems essentially a repetition of the past. When life is so free of uncertainty, so predictable, it appears justified to teach boys and girls that they should adopt the life-style of their elders.

Thus, in slowly changing cultures, grandparents are viewed as experts, as authorities, as models for all age groups. Children are expected to be listeners and observers, precisely as the hoary cliche has it: "to be seen, but not heard" (Strom & Strom, 1987).

Learning in a Present-Oriented Society. When technology is introduced and accelerated in a society, the pace of social change increases correspondingly. Long-standing customs and traditions are permanently modified. Successive generations of grandparents, parents, and children come to have less in common.

Children today have many experiences that were not part of their parents' upbringing. This means that there are some things adults are too old to know, simply because they grew up a few years earlier. This situation is a reversal of the traditional comment to children: "You're too young to understand." Boys and girls now encounter conditions unique to history in their cohort. Access to drugs, life in a single-parent family, computer involvement, and global awareness are common among today's children. They are exposed to day care, racially integrated schools, and the fear of sexually transmitted diseases. Adults cannot remember most of these situations because they never experienced them in their childhood.

Drawing on childhood memories as a basis for offering advice ("When I was your age...") becomes less credible as the pace of social change quickens. Because of the gap between experiences of adults and children, individuals tend to seek advice mostly from their peers. An increasing number of people feel that the only persons who can understand them are those who are at the same stage of life as themselves or who share similar challenges. Unfortunately, when people are limited to their peers for extended conversations, they are less inclined to develop the communication skills needed for successful interaction with other generations.

A peer orientation undermines cultural continuity as it divides the population into special interest groups. Because a rapidly changing society assigns greater importance to the present than to the past, older people cease to be regarded as models for everyone. Each generation instead chooses to identify with famous people of their own or the next higher age group. Therefore, respect for elderly people declines. Older adults are no longer regarded as experts about much of anything except aging (Strom, Bernard, & Strom, 1989).

Learning in a Future-Oriented Society. The phase of civilization we are entering is sometimes referred to as the Information Age. Within this context, school for children begins earlier, continues longer, and includes a vast amount of knowledge that was unavailable to previous generations of students. Given these conditions, children are bound to view the world from a different vantage point and should be appreciated by adults as constituting an important source of learning.

Certainly, intergenerational dialogue is necessary to shape the future in a democratic society. Unless such contacts are sustained and mutually beneficial, the future could bring increasing conflict as low birth rates provide fewer working age taxpayers to meet the needs of a growing elderly population. Some social scientists expect relationships between the young and older populations to replace the relationship between races as the dominant domestic conflict in the next half century (Toffler, 1990).

Intergenerational relationships are valuable because they offer a broader orientation than can be gained from any peer group. Until recently, aging was assumed to be accompanied by a sense of perspective. This assumption still makes sense in slow-changing cultures. In technological societies, however, the attainment of perspective requires something more than simply getting older. Becoming aware of how age groups other than one's own see things and feel about the world is necessary for a broad perspective and being able to respond to the needs of others. Unless the viewpoints of younger generations are taken into account, perspective tends to diminish rather than grow as people age (Strom & Strom, 1985, 1991b).

Establishing Educational Expectations for Grandparents

The authors' efforts to help grandparents started with offering a free course for them at senior citizen centers and churches in the metropolitan Phoenix area. The 400 people who enrolled in these classes were told they would learn something of what it is like for children to be growing up in contemporary society and also how parents view their task of raising children at the present time. In return, the participants agreed to share their experiences as grandparents. This format was chosen because the literature on family relations revealed a patronizing attitude toward grandparents instead of educational programs to help them grow. Previous investigators had not made an effort to identify grandparent learning needs, so there were no educational solutions. The following assumptions emerged from the preliminary research and continue to guide the ongoing project (Strom & Strom, 1989).

Grandparent responsibilities can be more clearly defined. Mothers and fathers have access to parenting courses that help them maintain competence in their changing role, but similar opportunities are unavailable to grandparents. Instead, they are left alone to wonder: "What are my rights and my responsibilities as a grandparent? How can I continue to be a favorable influence as my grandchild gets older? How well am I doing as a grandparent?"

These kinds of questions are likely to persist until there are well-established guidelines for setting goals and for self-evaluation. Many grandparents have difficulty defining their roles and understanding how they could make a greater contribution. As a result, the responsibility for raising the young has become disproportionately distributed in many families, with grandparents assuming fewer obligations than is in everyone's best interest.

Grandparents can learn to improve their influence. Mothers and fathers who can count on grandparents to help provide caregiving and guidance seek support outside the family less often. Grandparents need to be aware of the parenting goals of sons and daughters and act as a partner in reinforcing these goals. However, even though research indicates that people remain capable of adopting new attitudes and skills during middle and later life, grandparent development has not received priority in adult education. This missing element lessens the possibility of a meaningful life for many grandmothers and grandfathers.

The concept of lifelong learning should include a concern for curriculum development. This means society has to reconsider its view that continuous learning is essential only for young people. The myth that aging is accompanied by wisdom has misled many older adults to underestimate their need for further education. When grandparents are mentally active, they remain a source of advice. Individuals at every age have a responsibility to keep growing in order to achieve their potential.

A practical grandparent program should be widely available. Older men and women have been led to believe that learning in later life should consist of whatever topics they find interesting, without any societal expectations such as exist for younger learners. But as

people continue to age, they should also continue to grow—and not just in terms of acquiring leisure-oriented skills. Some facets of education in later life should emphasize obligations and roles, just as the curriculum for younger age groups does. Senior citizens are the only population without any defined educational needs or cooperatively planned curricula. Since the size of this group is expected to increase faster than any other age segment, it seems reasonable to provide them educational opportunities that can help strengthen their families.

Society should set higher expectations for grandparents. By themselves, grandparents may be unable to generate the motivation necessary to stimulate educational commitment within their peer group. This is a difficult task because so many people think of retirement as a time when they can withdraw from active community responsibility. Peers reinforce the perception that being carefree and without obligation is an acceptable goal in later life. The problem is compounded by age segregation. When older adults are limited to one another for most of their interactions, they establish standards that may not be in accord with what the society as a whole believes is best.

It would be helpful if younger people raised their expectations for older adults and made these higher expectations known. The talent and potential contribution of seniors could enrich the lives of everyone. Accordingly, we should expect grandparents to demonstrate a commitment to personal growth, to concern themselves about others through volunteering, and to support the schools to ensure a better future for children. If educational expectations are not established for older adults, they will experience less influence and lower self-esteem.

The benefits of grandparent education can be assessed. Popular support can be expected for programs that help grandparents enlarge the scope of their influence, improve their ability to communicate with loved ones, become more self-confident, and experience greater respect within the family circle. These benefits would be even more credible if the sources confirming them included persons other than just the participating grandparents. By comparing the results from three-generational versions of the authors' Grandparent Strengths and Needs Inventory, the merits of various educational approaches to family development can be determined. This inventory also enables educators to adapt curricula in a way that honors group and individual differences (Strom & Strom, 1990; Strom, Strom, & Collinsworth, 1991).

Goals for Grandparent Development

Six fundamental aspects of the grandparent experience are addressed in the authors' program. Each of them has implications for child and adult development.

1. *Increase the satisfaction of being a grandparent.* Today's longer lifespan gives grandparents more years to influence their grandchildren, but the actual outcome depends on whether or not a particular relationship is mutually satisfying. The relationship is in jeopardy when family members avoid sharing their feelings or when they experience insufficient satisfaction with one another. Grandmothers and grandfathers who enjoy their role are better able to cope with difficulties.

2. *Improve grandparents' performance of their role.* The efforts of grandparents to guide grandchildren depend on how self-confident they feel in their family role. Those who seek to support the parenting goals of their sons and daughters will continue to teach grandchildren. These persons realize that it is unreasonable to expect parents to be exclusively responsible for the care and guidance of grandchildren. By being active contributors in the family, they are seen as a valuable and long-term source of influence.

3. *Enlarge the scope of guidance expected of grandparents.* There is abundant evidence that academic learning alone is an insufficient preparation for success in life. It follows that grandparents should help grandchildren acquire some of the out-of-school lessons they need. By defining the aspects of growth that should be obtained at home, it is possible to improve a child's total education and establish a helpful role for grandparents.

4. *Decrease the difficulties of being a grandparent.* Grandparents encounter some difficulty in getting along with sons, daughters, in-laws, and grandchildren. The manner in which these problems are handled is a sign of personal effectiveness. Every grandmother and grandfather should have access to education that focuses on their changing roles. When grandparents are aware of the child-rearing strategies of their sons and daughters, and they know the predictable difficulties to expect as grandchildren get older, they can prepare themselves by acquiring the skills necessary for continued success.

5. *Reduce the frustrations experienced by grandparents.* Some frustration is to be expected, but grandparents vary in the frequency with which they experience frustration. One way to reduce their discontent is by helping them to understand why certain types of child behavior occur and why some of these perhaps disconcerting or perplexing behaviors should be allowed to continue. When the expectations of grandparents are consistent with a child's needs, they will be more likely to offer support for the development of a favorable self-concept in the child.

6. *Reduce the family information needs of grandparents.* Grandparents need accurate perceptions about their grandchildren's abilities and social relationships. In addition to the information provided to them by teachers and parents, grandparents should listen to the grandchildren themselves to learn about their hopes, fears, goals, and concerns. If educational programs for grandparents can regularly include access to the views of people who are the same age as grandchildren, then it becomes easier for them to understand how family members resemble and differ from their peers.

Elements of Curriculum and Instruction

The learning activities that grandparents consider appealing deserve priority in planning educational programs for them. Just as young students need a variety of teaching methods, so older men and women can also benefit from a wide range of instructional techniques. The two courses the authors have developed on "Becoming a Better Grandparent" and "Achieving Grandparent Potential" follow the same format of focusing on all three generations. The lessons about grandparents concern keeping up with the times, giving and seeking advice, communicating from a distance, growing as a couple, and learning in later life.

Lessons about the middle generation call for recognizing indicators of parental success, helping single and blended families with stepparents, developing values and morals, building self-esteem in the child, and watching television together. The lessons on grandchildren emphasize getting along with others, sharing fears and worries, understanding children's thinking, deciding about sex and drugs, and encouraging the college student. All 24 lessons consist of the same instructional elements, each of which deserves a brief explanation.

Discussing and Brainstorming. Grandparents meet in small groups to consider agendas from their guidebook that encourage their expression of ideas, concerns, mistakes, goals, and solutions (Strom & Strom, 1991a, 1991c). During these discussions the participants inform, challenge, and reassure one another. They quickly discover that there is much to gain from sharing feelings and thoughts. Conversations with emotionally supportive peers reduce feelings of loneliness and help the participants organize their thinking and increase their awareness of the possibilities for becoming a better grandparent. Creative thinking is practiced during each session when the group shifts to consideration of a brainstorming task.

Problem Solving. The next activity invites grandparents to consider how they might handle a particular problem if they had to cope with it. A family incident is described that offers everyone the same information, including several possible solutions. Grandparents like to reflect and then discuss the pros and cons they see for each of the given choices. It is stimulating to think of additional options and to identify relevant information that may be missing. All participants have an opportunity to share their reasoning about the advice they consider to be the best. This scenario approach broadens the range of solutions individuals see and discourages premature judgment. Later, in the home, grandparents present the scenarios to relatives and discover their viewpoints.

Grandparent Principles. Several written principles accompany each unit. Grandparents rely on these practical guidelines for review, reflection, and personal application. Participants benefit from reading the companion volume of viewpoints that match each lesson in the guidebook (Strom & Strom, 1991b, 1991d). These essays, from which the principles are drawn, offer insights, observations, and suggestions for making the grandparent experience more satisfying. In addition, local resource persons can enrich the learning by acquainting grandparents with the ways problems are handled in their own community. Because each individual represents a unique family, grandparents must decide for themselves which principles are most appropriate in their present situation, which ones to apply immediately, and which ones can be deferred until a later time.

Self-Evaluation and Observation. Personal growth requires self-examination. Grandparents are encouraged to practice this important skill as part of their homework. Each homework assignment consists of several multiple-choice questions that give participants a chance to state their feelings about issues such as family relationships, communication problems, and expectations of children. The anonymous homework is submitted at the beginning of each class. After responses are tallied for each item, the previously unknown norms of perception and behavior are announced to the class. This helps individuals learn how their personal experiences as grandparents both resemble and differ from the experiences of their peers.

Intergenerational Conversations. Grandparents should strive to know each grandchild as an individual. The best way to achieve this goal is also the most direct: through interaction with the particular grandchild. However, most grandmothers and grandfathers admit that they sometimes have difficulty keeping a conversation going with youngsters. This is why they appreciate questions focusing on realms of experience that the generations commonly encounter, topics that transcend age. Every lesson includes a set of questions dealing with topics of mutual concern such as music, health, school, money, fears, friends, and careers. These questions help grandparents initiate a dialogue in face-to-face or telephone interactions. While most of the inquiries fit all grandchildren, some are more appropriate for teenagers. A portion of each class session is devoted to grandparents' comments about the insights they have acquired through intergenerational interviews.

Grandparents also need to know something about the norms of their grandchild's age group. It is unreasonable to suppose that all the information we need about the orientation of relatives will be provided by the relatives alone. In a society where peers have considerable influence, it is wise to find out how people in a grandchild's age group think and feel. This improves understanding of how loved ones resemble and differ from their peers. One useful approach is to videotape interviews with children and parents who express their views on topics such as peer pressure, school stress, and family conflict. This method reflects the authors' belief that the broad perspective of life each of us ought to acquire emerges only when the thoughts and feelings of other age groups are taken into account.

Evaluating Grandparent Success

The effectiveness of grandparent education has been confirmed by research. In one study 800 people representing three generations evaluated the attitudes of grandparents before and after their participation in the "Becoming a Better Grandparent" course. At the end of the program, grandparents reported that they had made significant improvements. This progress was corroborated by inventory scores of the parents and grandchildren (Strom & Strom, 1990). Specifically, grandparents benefit from the mentally stimulating experience by understanding how their role is changing, acquiring a broader perspective, learning new attitudes, gaining greater confidence and self-esteem, improving communication skills, and strengthening family relationships (Strom & Strom, 1985, 1989; Strom, Strom, & Collinsworth, 1990).

These representative feelings expressed by the grandparents show the importance of the program for them:

- "I realized that I must keep on growing in order to understand other family members and be seen by them as a positive influence."
- "Now I understand my privileges as a grandparent as well as the duties I owe my grandchildren."
- "I found that helping my son and daughter achieve their parenting goals has upgraded my status to that of a valued partner."
- "I feel so much better about myself as a grandmother and more optimistic about my grandchildren."

Sons and daughters also identified some important benefits of grandparent education:

- "My parents seem more willing to share their feelings with us and they are more supportive of the way we are bringing up the children."
- "Taking this class has really helped my mom think about her role in my child's life. She is working hard to get to know my children as individuals."
- "My dad has realized that listening and learning from his grandchildren is the key to being respected by them."

• "My mother has always been kind and loving to all of us, but now she is more interesting to be around. It's fun to hear what she is learning."

Grandmothers and Grandfathers

It would be pleasing to be able to report a balance in the proportion of men and women who seek to improve themselves through grandparent education. However, just as mothers significantly outnumber fathers in parenting classes, so grandmothers are overrepresented in classes for grandparent development (or, it could be said that grandfathers are underrepresented).

Usually, three out of four students in the courses are grandmothers. Does this ratio indicate that grandmothers need more guidance than grandfathers? On the contrary, it suggests that grandmothers are more motivated to keep growing in this aspect of life. This conclusion was reached after comparing the influence of 155 grandmothers and 55 grandfathers who had just completed the program. Assessments were made to determine how each gender was perceived by themselves and by their sons, daughters, and grandchildren. Although the grandmothers reported having less formal education than did the grandfathers, they were seen as more successful grandparents in the estimate of all three generations (Strom & Strom, 1989).

In this study, grandparents, parents, and grandchildren all portrayed grandmothers as being emotionally closer to grandchildren, better informed about family affairs, and more willing to commit themselves to helping others. They were better at seeing the positive side of situations, learning from other family members, and making their feelings known. Grandmothers were credited with knowing more than grandfathers about the fears and concerns of grandchildren as well as with spending more time with them. They were also regarded as more effective in teaching grandchildren how to show trust, get along with others, and handle arguments. Additionally, grandmothers were viewed as better at passing on family history and cul-

tural traditions, and more willing to accept help from grandchildren.

Strengths of grandfathers were recognized, too. They saw themselves as having less difficulty than grandmothers in giving advice to sons and daughters, and they were less frustrated by the televiewing and listening habits of grandchildren. Parents observed grandfathers as being more satisfied than grandmothers when grandchildren asked for advice. The grandchildren themselves felt that their outlook on life was appreciated more by grandfathers.

Perhaps it is unfair to compare grandfathers with grandmothers. Consider the more positive results that emerge when the emphasis is on identifying change in grandfather attitudes and behaviors after instruction. The grandfathers in this study felt that they made improvement in terms of satisfaction with their role, success in carrying out their obligations, effectiveness in teaching, overcoming difficulties, coping with frustrations, and becoming more informed. Parents and grandchildren confirmed that these gains had occurred. By joining grandmothers as participants in family-oriented education, grandfathers have proven that they can learn to build more successful relationships with their spouse, children, and grandchildren. Grandfathers have shown themselves able to grow along with their partner and become actively involved in strengthening the family (Strom & Strom, 1989).

Grandparenting Contributions in African-American Families

Educational programs designed to help grandparents fulfill their own developmental potential and contribute more effectively to overall family strength should take ethnic and socioeconomic factors into consideration. For example, children of African-American heritage in the United States continue to encounter greater risks to health and safety, such as inadequate medical care, improper nutrition, environmental hazards, exposure to violent behavior, and unwanted pregnancies (Besharov, 1990; Hewlett, 1991;

Zinsmeister, 1990). Although education would seem to offer the best possibility for escape from poverty, many African-American children experience school as a disappointing ordeal, and this leads to lower graduation rates at both the high school and college levels (Boyer, 1990; Louv, 1990).

Aging also brings additional burdens and difficulties for African-Americans, who are less likely to have the financial security of adequate retirement pensions and health insurance. They often leave the work force early, and live in poverty at twice the rate of Anglo older adults in the general population (McKinney & Harel, 1989). The current generations of elderly African-American men and women have more limited formal education and less income, reside in substandard housing, experience more health problems, and grew up during a time when racial prejudice had yet to be countered by civil rights legislation.

The positive side, however, offers strengths that can be built on through grandparent education. African-Americans have a tradition of shared commitment to support family members whenever help is needed and a willingness to honor and maintain intergenerational ties. More specifically, African-American grandparents have been found to engage in more reciprocal helping behaviors with their children and grandchildren, as compared with Anglos (Bureau of the Census, 1991; Jackson & Wood, 1976).

A recent study focused on 204 African-American grandparents and the same number of Anglo grandparents, along with 470 grandchildren (Strom et al., in press). Grandparents in both ethnic groups showed overall favorable self-perceptions, but the scores were significantly and consistently higher among the African-Americans. Both the grandparents and the grandchildren in this group placed particular emphasis on teaching, especially in the realm of caring about the feelings of others, acquiring good manners, developing a sense of right and wrong, and valuing the continued pursuit of learning throughout life. Furthermore, the African-American grandchildren reported that their grandparents were consistently willing to listen to them.

Nevertheless, the grandchildren also perceived their grandparents as needing improvement in such areas as coping with frustrations and understanding what it is like to be growing up today. There seemed to be a greater discrepancy among African-American than among Anglo generations in the older person's recognition of the world of challenge and experience that is encountered by the young.

This exploratory study suggests that there is great potential for grandparent education as a source of strength for African-American families, which already have a tradition of intergenerational teaching and an established interest in lifelong learning. Particular attention might be given to helping the grandparent generation to learn more about the attitudes, opinions, and behaviors that prevail in their grandchildren's peer groups and to become more adept in conversing on topics that are of interest to the grandchildren. The curriculum for African-American grandparents might usefully emphasize problem-solving techniques to help the grandchildren have more enjoyable and productive experiences in the classroom and to cope with the challenges and stresses of adolescence. Special attention might also be given to clarifying the concerns of single parents, identifying the risks these families commonly encounter, and illustrating the ways in which the grandparents can be supportive. Educators should make a concerted effort to recruit elderly grandmothers and grandfathers and emphasize their potential for continued influence, and to identify members of the African-American community who could serve as leaders of grandparent courses.

Conclusion

As we contemplate the future, it is important to bear in mind that the baby boomers, those persons born between 1946 and 1964, will become the largest group of older adults in history. This population of 77 million people will be better educated and healthier and will live longer than preceding generations. If the preparation they receive for retirement focuses only on financial and leisure readiness, then a life-style of strictly recreation could become the norm. On the other hand, if getting ready for leisure activities is augmented by an emphasis on continued responsibility as family members, then baby boomers can make an enormous contribution to society. This possibility is supported by the emerging concept of grandparent education (Strom & Strom, 1991e).

▼ ROBERT D. STROM AND SHIRLEY K. STROM

See also: Attachment Across the Lifespan; Cohort and Generational Effects; Divorce; Fictive Kin; Gender as a Shaping Force in Adult Development and Aging; Grandparent Communication Skills; Learning and Memory in Everyday Life; Reminiscence and Life Review.

References

Bengston, V., & Robertson, J. (1985). *Grandparenthood.* Beverly Hills, CA: Sage.

Besharov, D. (1990). *Recognizing Child Abuse: A Guide for the Concerned.* New York: Macmillan.

Boyer, E. (1990). A close look at college. In *America's Best Colleges.* Washington, DC: U.S. News & World Report, pp. 52-71.

Bureau of the Census (1991). *1990 Census of Population and Housing.* Washington, DC: Bureau of the Census, Data User Service Division.

Elkind, D. (1990). *Grandparenting.* Glenview, IL: Scott, Foresman.

Hewlett, S. (1991). *When the Bough Breaks: The Cost of Neglecting Our Children.* New York: Basic Books.

Jackson, M., & Wood, J. (1976). *Aging in America: Implications for the Black Aged.* Washington, DC: National Council on Aging.

Kornhaber, A. (1986). *Between Parents and Grandparents.* New York: St. Martin's Press.

Louv, R. (1990). *Childhood's Future.* Boston: Houghton Mifflin.

McKinney, E., & Harel, Z. (1989). *Black Aged.* Beverly Hills, CA: Sage.

Stinnett, N., & DeFrain, J. (1985). *Secrets of Strong Families.* Boston: Little, Brown.

Strom, R., & Strom, S. (1985). Becoming a better grandparent. In K. Struntz & S. Reville (Eds.) *Growing Together: An Intergenerational Sourcebook.* Washington, DC: American Association of Retired Persons and Elvirita Lewis Foundation, pp. 57-60.

———. (1987). Preparing grandparents for a new role. *The Journal of Applied Gerontology, 6:* 476-86.

———. (1989). *Grandparent Development.* Washington, DC: American Association of Retired Persons Andrus Foundation.

———. (1990). Raising expectations for grandparents: A three-generational study. *International Journal of Aging and Human Development, 31:* 161-67.

———. (1991a). *Achieving Grandparent Potential: A Guidebook for Building Intergenerational Relationships.* Newbury Park, CA: Sage.

———. (1991b). *Achieving Grandparent Potential: Viewpoints on Building Intergenerational Relationships.* Newbury Park, CA: Sage.

———. (1991c). *Becoming a Better Grandparent: A Guidebook for Strengthening the Family.* Newbury Park, CA: Sage.

———. (1991d). *Becoming a Better Grandparent: Viewpoints on Strengthening the Family.* Newbury Park, CA: Sage.

———. (1991e). *Grandparent Education: A Guide for Leaders.* Newbury Park, CA: Sage.

Strom, R., Bernard, H., & Strom, S. (1989). *Human Development and Learning.* New York: Human Sciences Press.

Strom, R., Strom, S., & Collinsworth, P. (1990). Improving grandparent success. *The Journal of Applied Gerontology, 9:* 480-92.

———. (1991). The Grandparent Strengths and Needs Inventory: Development and factorial validation. *Educational and Psychological Measurement, 51:* 135-42.

Strom, R., et al. (in press). Strengths and needs of black grandparents. *The International Journal of Aging and Human Development.*

Toffler, A. (1990). *Powershift.* New York: Bantam Books.

Zinsmeister, K. (1990). Growing up scared. *The Atlantic,* June, pp. 49-66.

H

HABITUATION: A KEY TO LIFESPAN DEVELOPMENT AND AGING?

When does aging begin? This question led to the articulation of habituation theory, which began with the proposal that the ideal way to understand aging would be to identify its earliest emergence and then proceed to track this process throughout the lifespan (Kastenbaum, 1980-1981; Kastenbaum, 1984). Habituation theory suggests that a process identifiable in very young children provides origins for both positive development and the progressively restricting phenomenon often known as aging. Habituation theory is unusual not only in its hypothesis that aging has its roots in infancy and early childhood but also in its intended role as an alternative model for theory construction, methodological innovations, and practice. In other words, whether or not the specific details of the theory prove valid, the general strategy introduced by habituation theory could be applied to the generation of useful approaches that select other sets of data and hypotheses as their substance.

A description of habituation in its traditional context will be followed by the elaboration and extension of this approach to lifespan development and aging and then a brief consideration of implications.

Habituation: Basic Concept and Findings

Habituation can be defined as the systematic decrement in the organism's state of attention with prolonged or repeated exposure to the same stimulus or signal. This dry and formal definition refers to a sequence of events that is actually very interesting to observe. Suppose that a particular study features Brianna, all of a month old. The challenge is to find a "researchable moment" when she is awake, alert, and not in urgent need of nourishment, cuddling, or cleanup. When Brianna appears unpressured by need states, the experimenter will introduce a stimulus that the baby has not previously encountered. A buzzer or some other sound is often used for this purpose.

"Wow!" responds Brianna. More specifically, her heart rate accelerates, her eyes dart toward the source of the sound, and she holds her breath for a moment, the better to take in the new attraction. She is doing all that a baby of her age can do to "pay attention." This pattern of behavior in itself is known as the *orienting reflex*. It is an unlearned response that seems to have adaptational value: "What's going on around here?" If the buzzer is sounded again a few moments later, she will again exhibit the "wow response." With further repetitions, however, Brianna will respond less actively to the stimulus and will eventually ignore it altogether. It is as though she has decided, "I've heard that one already! It's no longer very interesting." The same thing happens if the stimulus is continued for an extended period of time. After "too much" exposure, whether through repetition or endurance of the stimulus, Brianna and other healthy infants will become *habituated*. Offer her a new stimulus, however, and she will again become a "turned on" listener who is responding in a vigorous and holistic manner.

The significance of habituation has been well appreciated by many investigators of infant and child development. Thompson and Spencer (1966) were perhaps the first to realize that habituation represents a very early outcropping of mind. When Brianna ignores a repetition of the once-exciting buzz, she is exercising such cognitive abilities as memory, comparison, and judgment. For example, if she had no way of registering, preserving, and retrieving her previous exposures to the stimulus, then the next buzz would seem as new as the first and would call forth a similar response. Sokolov (1963) has suggested that the cerebral cortex generates a model for a repeated stimulus and that the reticular formation then compares subsequent stimuli against this model. If an incoming signal is perceived as different from the model, then the reticular system "turns on the juice," alerting us to the fact that we are confronted with something new that deserves our full attention.

Habituation not only discloses the operation of perceptual and cognitive processes but also serves important developmental functions. In particular, habituation makes it possible for the young organism to gain a little freedom from the tyranny of immediate stimuli. The child who is able to habituate effectively does not have to jump and twitch and stare at every incoming stimulus and therefore can concentrate his or her attention either on what is new and different or on his or her own plans (e.g., catching that cat's tail the next time it goes by). To reframe this phenomenon only slightly: Habituation allows the organism to filter out information that has already been processed and that does not require further attention at this time, thereby enhancing the ability to identify and process information that *is* new and potentially useful.

Further evidence for the positive contribution of habituation to normal development is found in studies that report correlations between an infant's or child's overall developmental level and his or her ability to habituate. For example, habituation is achieved more readily by full-term than by premature babies (Field et al., 1979) and becomes quicker and more effective with continued development through infancy and childhood (Clifton & Nelson, 1976).

We now leave the classical realm of habituation research—very early development—with the clear impression that habituation is a process that makes a vital and positive contribution to human development. So where does aging come in?

The Proposed Habituation-Aging Link

The General Case for a Habituation Theory. The approach to theory construction that motivates this theory first assembles a set of preliminary considerations (Kastenbaum, 1980-1981). Habituation is proposed as a candidate for a partial model of human aging for the following reasons.

- It is an observable *process*, not an abstraction from statistical analysis or a theory spinner's fancy.

- This process has been identified *very early* in life; therefore, we will not be entering the lifespan at too late a point to detect the origins of age-related phenomena.

- The process is *psychobiological*, i.e., it involves an overall pattern of response that includes basic physiological, behavioral, and cognitive functions—and we might well expect aging to involve all these components and functions as well.

- It is also a pattern that *generalizes* beyond one situation and one point in time; the developing person becomes ever more able to habituate across a broader span of signals and settings.

- It is a relatively *enduring* process; one tends to remain habituated unless special circumstances intervene or special efforts are made to bring about dyshabituation.

- It bears a striking *resemblance* to core features of "old behavior" (Kastenbaum, 1968)—especially the reduced intake of information.

- Habituation can be subjected to *experimental* investigation, i.e., one can attempt to produce and modify habituation by introducing carefully specified manipulations and variables, along with the appropriate controls.

This set of considerations is offered not as proof that habituation is, in fact, a key factor in development and aging, but rather as a way of presenting criteria that should be applied to any theoretical model of development/aging, using habituation as the present example.

The Specific Case. The specific case for habituation and aging centers on the proposition that reducing one's attention to the available information flow has both positive and negative implications. Habituation is a "sword that cuts both ways" because it both frees the organism from the obligation to respond to all signals all the time (positive) and establishes a strong precedent for ignoring signals that are vital for continued growth and adaptation (negative). In other words, maturation and aging diverge from the same process.

In this view, a person who "behaves oldly" shows a limited pattern of interaction with the environment. The routinization and overpredictability of behavior is closely associated with the failure to take new information into account. Unlike young Brianna, who responded so vigorously and holistically to a novel stimulus (the buzzer), the person who has established an "old" way of functioning tends to treat new signals as though they had been already encountered, evaluated, and dismissed. Consider the following possible responses to signals or stimuli shown in Table 1.

A person who has not achieved or who has lost the ability to habituate has difficulty in discriminating between signals and situations that should have become familiar and

Table 1. Signal Response Types

Signal Status	Phase 1	Phase 2	Process Type
Old	Attention	Respond	Unhabituated
New	Attention	Analyze	Habituated—Go
Old	Attention	Dismiss	Habituated—Stop
New	Attention	Dismiss	Hyperhabituated

those that are actually new to his or her experience. A very young or immature child or a person who has experienced brain trauma or some other form of severe stress may be unable to filter out redundant and extraneous information and will therefore feel overwhelmed by stimuli.

The person who has developed effective habituation is better able to differentiate useful from useless information. When a signal passes the first test ("This could be something new and interesting"), the habituation shield is lowered and active processing of the information begins. Often, however, there will be the energy-saving decision that "I have dealt with this before," and no additional perceptual and cognitive processing will be devoted to the signal. The well-habituated person has established a system of information recognition and processing that gives potentially new signals an opportunity for reception and appreciation, while screening out many other signals that can safely be ignored. By contrast, the *hyperhabituated* person has only a very limited "window of opportunity" for new signals to come through. There is a dominant tendency to classify all signals as though they were merely repetitions of previously received and disposed-of information.

Most people do continue to attend to most stimuli immediately (Phase 1). Vigilance is such a salient characteristic of our nervous systems/minds that we can hardly *not* observe. For observations to become part of our judgment, planning, and actions, however, requires further processing, and it is at Phase 2 (and beyond) that the differences arise among unhabituated, habituated, and hyperhabituated individuals.

Within this theoretical perspective, then, the pattern of "behaving oldly" is not intrinsically correlated with chronological age. An elderly person may be alert to external and internal signals and exhibit a spontaneity and responsiveness that the years have not diminished. Similarly, a 30-year-old may already be closed into a routinized mode of functioning and a very limited spectrum of response. One everyday situation in which this distinction often makes itself known is the individual's response to meeting somebody new. The hyperhabituated person is likely to assimilate the new person to his or her existing images of people previously known. "He reminds me a lot of...." "She's just another one of those...." The person with an effective habituation/discovery balance is more likely to notice and be fascinated by what is different about the new person. "She sure has a different way of looking at things...." "That fellow just seems full of surprises...."

According to habituation theory, then, "oldness" is not a necessary derivative of age but, rather, one pattern of functioning that a person might develop earlier or later in life and to a lesser or greater degree. To understand "oldness" in the general or the specific case, we would need to understand the conditions that affect the maturational vs. the aging potentials of habituation.

Habituation/Hyperhabituation: A Lifespan Overview

In summary, the theory suggests the following.

1. Habituation is a basic maturational process that begins in early infancy and serves as a marker for continued mental and socioemotional growth throughout childhood.

2. Social pressures, operating at first primarily through the family, relentlessly shape the youngster's total response potential into channels considered useful and proper by society; this influences the child's relationship to internal as well as external reality. The psychobiological process of habituation, then, is supplemented by a social selectivity process that also has the effect of reducing one's readiness to examine new signals without prejudice and form one's own judgments about them.

3. As the child develops language and symbolic skills, it becomes able either to command or to discard large realms of potential experience. For example, the boy may be pressured to regard "female" interests as irrelevant and unbecoming, while the girl is subjected to parallel pressures in the other direction. Instead of dismissing one signal at a time as redundant or irrelevant, the developing person gains the ability to treat entire realms of potential (inner-self or outer-world) information as not worth bothering with. This no-response set contributes significantly to what will later in life be recognized as "old behavior."

4. The early and relentless channeling of possible responsiveness and experiences has an accumulative effect, so that at a particular adult age some people have already reduced their new learning to a very limited band of situations (e.g., work-related), while others have continued to refine their information-seeking and information-processing skills.

5. Hyperhabituation becomes intensified throughout adult life, primarily because (a) it represents an apparent saving in energy, through eliminating many information-processing tasks; and (b) it offers the illusion of stability: One can increasingly live within a fixed personal model of self and universe rather than testing out one's beliefs every day against the hard edges of reality. This also becomes an increasing liability, isolating the individual from changes and limiting adaptational opportunities.

6. The negative effects of hyperhabituation may become synergic with fatigue, physical disorders, memory problems, and bereavement—all of which also tend to increase the distance between the individual and his or her sociophysical environment. He or she is left to defend a

shrinking realm with reduced resources and the nonadaptive habit of hyperhabituation. According to this theory, much of the observed decline in fluid intelligence with age is the result of the long-term practice of dismissing instead of welcoming new information and new kinds of interpersonal relationships.

In summary, "aging" or "oldness" is seen as an early emerging tendency to overadapt to one's own routines and expectations rather than coping flexibly and resourcefully with the world at large and exploring the heights and depths of one's inner potentials.

Norris-Baker and Scheidt (1989) have examined hyperhabituated behavior as it might be seen "in a relatively healthy, cognitively-intact...resident of a long-term care institution." They suggest that hyperhabituated functioning in this kind of setting can be inferred through "the routinized use of time; categorical judgments regarding the lack of novelty in several sectors of resident and personal life; generalized disinterest in maintaining and nurturing relations among residents, staff, and family members; constriction of social and physical environmental range or 'niche breadth'; passive (as against active) initiation of and participation in activities of the setting" (p. 252). These authors propose specific methodologies for investigating behaviors associated with the hyperhabituation pattern and call attention to its cross-situational aspects.

Reich and Zautra (1991) have since introduced a technique for assessing one major facet of hyperhabituation. Preliminary research enabled them to devise a simple true/false self-report scale concerned with the "trait of routinization" and to use this instrument as a basis for studying individual responses to socioexperimental interventions. Commenting on their findings, Reich and Zautra observe, "Reduced reactivity to the environment can reflect an avoidance of the anxiety generated by stimulation, or it can be a reflection of generalized habituation to entire classes of stimuli, or even 'mindlessness'" (pp. 177-78).

Those who are contributing to the elaboration, refinement, and testing of this new conceptual approach share the view that what is traditionally regarded as (negative) "oldness" is actually the result of an ineffective strategy for dealing with life that becomes the mainstay for some people during their early development and is relied on increasingly with advancing adult age. Prevention and intervention of hyperhabituation may well be within our means. It may be useful to realize that some people have the perspective and wisdom of age in their youth, and some elderly people retain the spontaneity and openness of youth: We do not have to doom ourselves to a self-constricted life on the too straight and narrow pathway of hyperhabituation.   ▼ Robert Kastenbaum

See also: Adult Development and Aging, Models of; Expressive Arts; Information Processing; Intelligence—Crystallized and Fluid; Language Development; Mid-Life Crisis; Parental Imperative; Social Class and Adult Development.

References

Clifton, R. K., & Nelson, M. N. (1976). Developmental study of habituation in infants: The importance of paradigm, response system, and state. In T. J. Tighe & R. H. Leaton (Eds.). *Habituation.* Hillsdale, NJ: Lawrence Erlbaum, pp. 159-206.

Field, T. M., et al. (1979). Cardiac and behavioral response to repeated tactile and auditory stimulation by preterm and term infants. *Developmental Psychology, 15:* 406-16.

Kastenbaum, R. (1968). Perspectives on the development and modification of behavior in the aged: A developmental perspective. *Gerontology,* 8: 280-84.

———. (1980-1981). Habituation as a model of human aging. *International Journal of Aging and Human Development,* 12: 159-70.

———. (1984). When aging begins: A lifespan developmental approach. *Research on Aging, 6:* 105-18.

Norris-Baker, C., & Scheidt, R. J. (1989). Habituation theory and environment-aging research: Ennui to joie de vivre? *International Journal of Aging and Human Development, 29:* 241-58.

Reich, J. W., & Zautra, A. J. (1991). Analyzing the trait of routinization in older adults. *International Journal of Aging and Human Development,* 32: 161-80.

Sokolov, E. N. (1963). *Perception and the Conditioned Reflex*. New York: Macmillan.

Thompson, R. G., & Spencer, W. A. (1966). Habituation: A model phenomenon for the study of neuronal substrates of behavior. *Psychological Review, 73*: 16-43.

HAPPINESS, COHORT MEASURES OF

Are older people happier than younger people? If results from a survey of contemporary adult Americans showed that older adults scored higher than younger adults on a scale measuring happiness, we might be tempted to conclude that increasing age is accompanied by increasing wisdom or the growth of some other perspective that enhances happiness across the adult lifespan. Alternatively, if the survey results showed that older people were less happy than younger people, we might assume that with increasing age comes illness, loss of physical vigor, and other misfortunes that diminish happiness.

Both examples encourage the assumption that the explanation for why people at different ages are more or less happy lies in some facet of the developmental or aging process. Wisdom increases, for example, or biological processes break down, and, therefore, changes occur in the level of happiness. There is another possibility to consider, however. When we see differences in happiness between people of different ages we might be observing cohort differences. In other words, degree of happiness may have more to do with people's experiences in the particular historical era in which they were raised and matured rather than with their chronological age. A cohort is a group of persons sharing a certain statistical or demographic characteristic, such as all Americans born in 1954 or all those who fought in Vietnam (see also **Cohort and Generational Effects**).

To the extent that cohort differences exist, we would not expect all adults to have the same patterns of aging because they have moved through different sectors of history.

For example, those who were adolescents during the Great Depression may have experienced ever-increasing levels of happiness throughout their adulthoods as difficult times gave way to greater financial security and personal opportunity. By contrast, later-born cohorts might experience more constant or even decreasing levels of happiness throughout their adult lives, e.g., as more competition is faced for fewer career opportunities.

Currently, social scientists believe that there are small but probably authentic differences in happiness levels between younger and older adult Americans. And they feel that at least some of these differences can be traced to the historical experiences of the various generations—experiences that have shaped the values and beliefs of various cohorts and thus altered the foundations on which people base their judgments of well-being. From the available information, it appears that both aging and cohort processes affect the reported well-being of adults in the United States.

A Growing Discontent?

The clues that we have about cohort-based changes in happiness levels come from national representative surveys of American adults that have been repeated year after year. Researchers find that before 1970 there had been a negative correlation between age and happiness. This observation supports the conventional assumption that wisdom declines with age.

This assumption no longer held true by the early 1970s. The relationship between age and well-being disappeared. An adult's reported level of happiness seemed to be independent of chronological age. The pattern has continued to change. More recent data indicate that older people are actually happier or more satisfied with life than are younger adults (Rodgers, 1982). Can it be that the experience of aging has changed so dramatically over the past decades that late life has now changed from a time of least happiness to a stage of life that is more enjoyable than young adulthood?

Most social scientists who have studied this situation are not persuaded that the circumstances of older and younger adults have changed as drastically as these shifting findings suggest. Instead, the consensus is that American society has been joined by increasingly discontented younger cohorts: More and more unhappy sets of younger adults have been entering the adult population pool and this has the effect of making older adults look comparatively happy (Glenn, 1980).

The question then becomes: Why over the past two decades have the cohorts of Americans reaching adulthood become more discontented than those who made the same transition in years past? One possibility is that there has been some genuine decrease in later-born cohorts' readiness for coping with the demands of the world. Changes in child-rearing, the family system, and educational patterns might all have led to inferior preparation for life's exigencies, leaving them less content with their circumstances.

There is a more likely explanation, however. Research over various historical periods in the United States suggests that cohorts differ not in their actual preparedness for facing life's demands, but in their styles of expressing their feelings (Glenn, 1980). For example, in one study it was learned that Americans had shifted in the way they evaluated their own happiness within a period of two decades (Veroff, Douvan, & Kulka, 1981). Between 1957 and 1976 there was a shift toward evaluating happiness on a more personal level and away from public role performances. Personal and psychological issues became more important factors as compared with meeting the expectations of society for achievement, status, and so forth. This "psychologizing" of our culture has made it easier for adults to embrace negative as well as positive emotions. The feeling of greater subjective distress, therefore, may not reflect a state of increased deprivation or frustration, but rather a greater willingness to admit to being unhappy.

The Role of Values in Well-Being

Styles of coping with personal problems have also changed from cohort to cohort. More recent adult cohorts are far more likely than older cohorts to seek support from others. Young adults are far less likely to say they intend to solve their problems themselves. This "cultural shift toward personal informality" (Veroff, Douvon, & Kulka, 1981, p. 539) has not affected members of earlier cohorts who are now in their later years of life. The older cohorts have proven to be relatively immune to the cultural trend toward reliance on psychological experts and the growing tendency to reveal problems to friends. This reticence may be part of the older generation's greater tendency both toward religiosity and the offering of socially acceptable answers (Herzog, Rodgers, & Woodworth, 1982).

In all, it appears that there are relatively important differences in the values that underlie people's evaluations of their happiness. Analyzing different cohorts' reports of happiness shows that adults born before 1903—a group with lower happiness overall than all other groups of American adults—have had their levels of happiness rise steadily over the years 1957 to 1978 (Rodgers, 1982). This pattern contrasts markedly with that experienced by adults who were born between 1923 and 1942. The latter show a dip in happiness levels that coincides with increased concern about justice and equality in the United States. Rodgers suggests that post-1920 cohorts base their experiences of happiness on "post-materialistic" values. Similarly, other studies have shown that the cohorts of adults born before 1903 had happiness levels that were more closely linked to survival needs and more firmly wedded to Protestant ethic values (Felton, 1987) than has been the case with subsequent cohorts.

Conclusion

We must pay attention to the prevailing values of the different historical eras in which adults have been brought up in order to understand how they arrive at judgments about their well-being. Older Americans today are likely to describe themselves as somewhat happier than younger people. The reasons for this difference have more to do with the values with which they grew up rather than with their current ages. Today's older adults judge their happiness in light of the Protestant ethic values that dictate their own individual responsibility for their own happiness (Moen, 1978). They are also likely to evaluate their happiness in light of how adequately they have performed important public social roles such as those of worker and parent (Bryant & Veroff, 1982).

By contrast, today's younger adults judge their happiness in light of their own personal or psychological standards. Less bound to the concept that they are responsible for their own happiness, they are freer to admit to discontentment and distress.

Aging processes will also influence the level of experienced well-being. A foreshortened sense of futurity, ill health, and the loss of friends and family to death are among the significant life changes that almost certainly influence the sense of well-being. Objective circumstances such as financial security and housing arrangements will also continue to vary across the lifespan and affect one's attitudes and self-appraisal. It is now clear, however, that cohort-based differences in adults' values also influence the individual's judgment of his or her happiness and well-being both in youth and old age. The values, events, and experiences that become part of a person's life while growing up during a particular moment in history are likely to continue exercising influences throughout the entire life course.   ▼ BARBARA J. FELTON

See also: Cohort and Generational Effects; Contextualism; Housing as a Factor in Adult Life; Longevity; Place and Personality in Adult Development; Religion and Coping with Crisis.

References

Bryant, F. B., & Veroff, J. (1982). The structure of psychological well-being: A sociohistoric analysis. *Journal of Personality and Social Psychology, 43:* 653-73.

Felton, B. J. (1987). Cohort variation in happiness: Some hypotheses and exploratory analyses. *International Journal of Aging and Human Development, 25:* 27-42.

Glenn, N. D. (1980). Values, attitudes, and beliefs. In O. G. Brim, Jr., & J. Kagan (Eds.), *Constancy and Change in Human Development.* Cambridge, MA: Harvard University Press, pp. 596-640.

Herzog, A. R., Rodgers, W. L., & Woodworth, J. (1982). *Subjective Well-Being among Different Age Groups.* Ann Arbor, MI: Institute for Social Research, University of Michigan.

Moen, E. (1978). The reluctance of the elderly to accept help. *Social Problems, 25:* 293-303.

Rodgers, W. L. (1982). Trends in reported happiness within demographically defined subgroups, 1957-1978. *Social Forces, 60:* 826-42.

Veroff, J., Douvan, E., & Kulka, R. A. (1981). *The Inner American: A Self-Portrait from 1957-1976.* New York: Basic Books.

HEALTH EDUCATION AND ADULT DEVELOPMENT

Most people wish to live long and well. Good health usually ranks high on the list of values for both women and men. Over the years, the health of the American people has improved in many ways. For example, average life expectancy has increased from 50 years at the beginning of the century to over 70 in the 1990s.

Health is determined by more than contact with bacteria or viruses. People now realize they can control many of the factors that affect health. These factors include public health measures (such as vaccination), life-style, income, nutrition and diet, and environmental hazards. Taken together, these factors have more influence on health, illness, and death than do health care services (Aaron, 1990; Fuchs, 1974).

Formal health education is one way of empowering adults to increase the probability of improving their health and thereby providing a solid basis for personal and social development. Today adults are enrolling in large numbers in general and specific-topic courses in universities and other educational settings. Nevertheless, there are no formal academic programs to develop adult health educators.

Maintaining or improving the health and well-being of adults is a national health priority for practical as well as humane reasons. Practical factors include the growth of the population aged 50 and over as a political force, the high cost of medical care with special reference to long-term care, and the health risks associated with aging.

Healthy People Year 2000 is a Public Health Service-led national program setting priority areas for improving the health of all Americans (U.S. Department of Health and Human Services, 1990). One priority is to increase the span of healthy life. Other priorities have to do with eliminating cancer; increasing activity and exercise; improving dental, mental, and nutritional health; preventing injury; and reducing the use of medications. Recently, *The Second Fifty Years: Promoting Health and Preventing Disability* (Berg & Cassells, 1990) focused on the health of adults aged 50 and older. It recommended that the nation give priority to 12 risk factors that are associated with disease and disability in aging adults: high blood pressure, medications, osteoporosis, sensory loss, infectious diseases, oral health, cancer, smoking, depression, physical activity, social isolation, and falls.

In 1991, guided by the priorities delineated in Healthy People Year 2000, the U.S. Administration on Aging embarked on its Eldercare programs to focus the nation's resources on improving the health, well-being, and care, and reducing the economic burden, of high-risk older adults. In similar fashion, The National Institute on Aging started developing and funding research initiatives.

Defining Health

The World Health Organization's definition of health reads: "Health is a state of complete physical, mental, and social well being and not merely the absence of disease and infirmity" (Steinfels, 1973, p. 4).

A modification is suggested that integrates the meaning given to time. Think of your death. Think of the world as you will leave it to your children and grandchildren. How does it affect your view of the future—especially what Lifton (1979) identifies as the themes of continuity, connection, and futurity? Think also of your roots, your history. What legacy were you left by your parents, grandparents, and others? What legacy do you wish to leave? The meaning that is given to time, especially present and future, can affect health-related behavior and priorities. For example, a person who feels that time is "running out" while young children are rapidly growing up may forsake faculty meetings or other low-priority tasks in order to have more opportunity to be with the children. Playing with one's children becomes a higher priority when it is realized that death may occur at any moment. One might forsake heavy tobacco consumption if one truly realized that death is a high probability.

The modified definition becomes: Health is not merely the absence of disease and infirmity but it is the perception of and progress toward acceptable physical, mental, and social well-being both here and now and as expected in the future.

What Is Health Education?

Health education is part of the public health model concerned with:

1. Prevention of disease and illness and enhancement of wellness
2. Rehabilitation (postvention)
3. Cure (intervention)

Intervention was the sole province of medicine until research indicated that psychosocial factors contribute both to the risk of contracting disease and illness as well as to their remediation. These factors include significant life events, adequacy of the social support system, and the meanings each individual gives to life.

Health education has been defined as any combination of learning experiences through which people voluntarily adapt behavior conducive to health (Feldman, 1989). Such a comprehensive definition encourages a variety of programs and courses, including exercise, stress reduction, and patient education. The programs vary in their goals, target population, site, and process.

Health Promotion and Wellness

Health promotion and the wellness movement are sometimes regarded as an integral part of health education and sometimes as a separate development. It all began with the publication of Halbert Dunn's (1961) influential book, *High-Level Wellness.* "Wellness" complemented the so-called medical model with its emphasis on disease prevention and cure. Courses and programs in nutrition, exercise, yoga, t'ai chi ch'uan, self-awareness, relaxation, and stress reduction proliferated. Programs of this type are still well attended by adults. Their common goal has been been to improve the health and well-being of the "total person."

A representative definition of health promotion is given by O'Donnell (1989):

> The science and art of helping people change their lifestyle to move toward a state of optimal health. Optimal health is defined as a balance of physical, emotional, social, spiritual and intellectual health. Lifestyle change can be facilitated through a combination of efforts to enhance awareness, change behavior, and create environments that support good health practices. Of the three, supportive environments will probably have the greatest impact in producing lasting changes. (p. 5)

Note the emphasis on "lifestyle," "lifestyle change," and "efforts." Efforts and change imply empowerment that enables a person to control his or her own health to a large degree. Still, health promotion needs to bear in mind that we cannot evade death, nor can we control our own destiny, as is often implied by health promotion advocates. A war here, a homicide or environmental catastrophe there—and poof—so much for "control." On the other hand, the goals of health education and health promotion seem well worth pursuing even though they are occasionally presented in an oversimplified and overly optimistic manner.

Combining the concepts of health education and health promotion, adult health education may be defined as any combination of learning experiences that is designed to improve knowledge, insights, and skills concerning health and well-being aspects of aging (including old age, dying, and death). Adult health education also facilitates the voluntary adaptation of behavior by adults that is conducive to health and well-being.

Theoretical Framework

Today, a variety of theories attempt to explain and/or predict health-related behavior. Nearly all these theories are derived from other disciplines, such as psychology, anthropology, and sociology (Feldman, 1989; Glanz, Lewis, & Rimer, 1990).

One of the first theories was the health belief model, introduced in the 1950s by Hochbaum and his colleagues in an effort to understand the failure of many public health programs (Rosenstock, 1990). This theory derived from cognitive psychology with its emphasis on the expectations and beliefs held by the individual. For example, it may be hypothesized that if prevention of a heart attack is one of an individual's values, and if this person expects that losing weight would be a useful way to reduce this risk, then the probability for maintaining a weight-reduction program will increase. In this instance, the effort to keep the weight down would be the action component that is associated with the value and expectation that have been described.

The health belief model has been modified so that it is now believed that individuals will take health-protective action:

- If they regard themselves as susceptible to the condition
- If they believe it to have potentially serious consequences
- If they believe that there is available a course of action that would be beneficial in

reducing either their susceptibility to or the severity of the condition

- If they believe that the anticipated barriers to (or costs of) taking the action are outweighed by its benefits (Rosenstock, 1990, pp. 42-43)

Communication and persuasion theory provided the framework for early health education research because verbal, visual, and written communications are the traditional tools of health education. Typical research investigated the effects of fear-arousal or threatening-to-health communications (Beck, 1991; Festinger, 1957; Glanz, Lewis, & Rimer, 1990; Hovland, Janis, & Kelley, 1953). Today, there are a wealth of additional concepts and theories that are valuable in understanding and predicting health behavior.

Symbolic Interaction Theory is one such theory, derived from sociology (see Glanz, Lewis, & Rimer, 1990, for a review of health-education related theories). Behavior is seen as a function of the way the person perceives and gives meaning to the world. Characteristic of this view is the Native American proverb that cautions people not to judge others until they have walked a mile in the other person's moccasins. Thus, Symbolic Interaction Theory emphasizes empathy as a path toward understanding another person's behavior. It also emphasizes understanding the meanings and symbols through which people construe themselves and the world. Symbolic interactionists often use the ISAS paradigm. Individual behavior is in response to Symbols relative to the Audience and the Situation (Leming & Dickinson, 1990). Each individual may give unique meanings to situations and objects; therefore, one should not make the mistake of overgeneralizing observations on the basis of group tendencies.

Health education theory is still being developed, tested, and modified. No single theory now predicts health behavior adequately in all situations. Perhaps that will be the status of health education theory for years to come, since development of a single comprehensive theory would be a difficult task. Factors to be considered include the quality of cognitive and physical functioning, perceptions of the environment, history and future expectations, social support, stress, and so forth. A second task would be to determine whether the theory was applicable to the individual, the group, or both.

Adult Health Education Courses and Programs

Programs of many types are in operation today. Some are comprehensive, others are more specialized in terms of content and target audience. An example of the latter is the Adult Health & Development Program at the University of Maryland. This intergenerational health education course is also a medical school elective. It attempts to bring both institutionalized and noninstitutionalized adults, aged 50 and over, into a "health and well-being groove." University and college students and volunteers ("staffers") are trained to work on a one-to-one basis with the assigned adult member. They serve as "friendly coaches." Play, physical activity, and formal health education are means to improving health as well as developing friendships between the staffer and his or her member and the group at large. Thus the staffer and member learn together, and often serve as teachers to each other (Leviton, 1989). Formal health education in the classroom includes topics such as coping with arthritis, developmental changes, taking control of one's health, intelligent use of medication, physical fitness, and memory, as well as specific areas of concern such as foot or dental problems. Evaluations by members over the years indicate significantly improved perception of overall health and well-being, social integration, physical fitness, health knowledge, and desire to return to the program (Leviton, 1989).

A conventional classroom approach has also been used at the University of Maryland since the early 1970s with both undergraduate and graduate courses offered to traditional university students and community adults.

One of the better evaluated adult health education programs was the Wallingford

Wellness Project (FallCreek & Mettler, 1984; FallCreek & Stam, 1982; Lalonde, Hooyman, & Blumhagen, 1988). The WWP was a three-year community-based health promotion program for the independent-living older adult. It offered 21 weeks of education in four areas: physical fitness, stress management, nutrition, and environmental awareness and action. Results indicate that the program was effective in promoting and sustaining healthy life-style changes up to six months after the course work ended (Lalonde, Hooyman, & Blumhagen, 1988).

Examples of specialized courses and programs include those in exercise; nutrition; weight control; smoking, alcohol, and drug cessation; yoga; t'ai chi ch'uan; and stress reduction. Some of these programs have stood the test of time very well. These include Richard Mance's exercise and physical activity programs at Prince George's Community College (Maryland), which attracts approximately 200 mobile adults each semester, and Margo Raynor's statewide program in North Carolina, which has included as many as 10,000 people in senior athletic games.

Patient education is another specialized form of adult health education. Usually the goal is to maintain or improve mobility, diet, or pulmonary, circulatory, or sexual functioning. Many such programs now exist under a variety of academic and community auspices.

Because the proportion of females to males increases with age, it is not surprising that women tend to predominate as participants in comprehensive adult health education programs. Little research is available on gender differences and motivation for becoming involved in comprehensive adult health education. Observation suggests that the motivations may be more similar than different. An exception may be in the area of physical fitness, where females tend to exclude strength building, perhaps because of cultural and historical stereotypes. On the other hand, as the public becomes more aware of research indicating the beneficial aspects of strength, women might be expected to participate as fully as men in weight-resistance training programs.

Sources of Information

Within the past decade, organizations concerned with adult health education have proliferated. Examples at the federal level are the National Institute on Aging, National Institute of Mental Health (Center on Aging), and the U.S. Office of Disease Prevention and Health Promotion. Nonprofit organizations include the National Council on Aging's Health Promotion Institute and the American Association of Retired Persons' National Resource Center on Health Promotion and Aging.

All of the foregoing organizations have a general mission with regard to adult health education. Organizations with a more specific focus include The National Council on Patient Information and Education (concerned with the proper use of medications), The Arthritis Foundation, and the Alzheimer's Disease and Related Disorders Association. Adult health education concerns are also addressed within large health-oriented organizations such as the American Public Health Association and the American Alliance for Health, Physical Education, Recreation, and Dance. The former has a gerontological health section, and the latter has a Council on Aging and Adult Development.

Resources such as Johns Hopkins University's *Over 50 Newsletter, Perspectives in Health Promotion and Aging,* bibliographies and other materials published by the National Resource Center for Health Promotion and Aging, publications by the National Institute on Aging, periodicals such as *The Journal of Aging and Health,* and an increasing number of research-based books and articles provide a growing data base for adult health education.

Conclusion and Recommendations

It is not only middle-aged and elderly adults who benefit from health education.

Younger people also benefit by increasing the probability of their aging well, along with learning how to become more helpful to older adults. Another gain is learning to understand and empathize with others as part of a mutual "civilizing" process.

Adult health education specialists in the future would be wise to include data and insights from thanatology, the study of death-related behavior and phenomena. Health education classes rarely address issues such as an "appropriate death" (Weisman, 1972) or the health consequences of grief. Adults have higher suicide, widowhood, and general mortality rates than younger age cohorts. Death-related behavior has economic effects as well. For example, about 30 percent of Medicare costs are expended for care in the last year of life (Berg & Cassells, 1990).

Grieving is associated with increased health risks. In a major study of the health consequences of bereavement, The Institute of Medicine concluded that loss of a loved one was associated with significant distress in practically everyone. "Some bereaved persons are at increased risk for illness and even death" (Osterweis, Solomon, & Green, 1984, p. 283). We know that the probability of widowhood increases with age, especially among females. Coping with the health challenges of widowhood in particular and bereavement in general might well be taken up as priorities by adult health education specialists.

One reason that adults are concerned with the future is their investment in children and grandchildren, who represent a form of "symbolic immortality" (Lifton, 1979). Thus, adult health education should include issues devoted to making the world a better place for the younger generations. This could be accomplished by eliminating those deaths that are attributable to human agency and that involve the motive to kill another person. Examples of "horrendous death" (Leviton, 1991a, 1991b) include war, homicide, terrorism, and death as a result of racism.

Another priority should be meeting the health education needs of adult minorities such as the foreign born, Native Americans, and African Americans.

Adult health education is an art, a profession, and a science with the potential of bringing together people of all generations and backgrounds to work toward the common goal of living long and well.

▼ DAN LEVITON AND MAUREEN EDWARDS

See also: African-American Experiences through the Adult Years; Alcohol Use and Abuse; Cardiac Health; Drug Use and Abuse; Exercise; Gender as a Shaping Force in Adult Development and Aging; Longevity; Risk to Life through the Adult Years; Sex in the Later Adult Years; Stress.

References

Aaron, H. (1990). A prescription for health care. In H. Aaron (Ed.), *Setting National Priorities: Policy for the Nineties*. Washington, DC: Brookings Institution, pp. 249-91.

Beck, K. (1991). Human response to threat. In D. Leviton (Ed.), *Horrendous death, health, and well-being*. Washington, DC: Hemisphere, pp. 31-47.

Berg, R., & Cassells, J. (Eds.). (1990). *The Second Fifty Years: Promoting Health and Preventing Disability*. Washington, DC: National Academy Press.

Dunn, H. (1961). *High-Level Wellness*. Arlington, VA: R. W. Beatty Co.

FallCreek, S., & Mettler, M. (1984). *A Healthy Old Age: A Sourcebook for Health Promotion with Older Adults*. New York: The Haworth Press.

FallCreek, S., & Stam, S. (Eds.). (1982). *The Wallingford Wellness Project: An Innovative Health Promotion Program with Older Adults*. Seattle: University of Washington, Center for Social Welfare Research.

Feldman, S. (1989). Gerontological health education research: Issues and recommendations. In J. Humphrey & R. Feldman (Eds.), *Advances in Health Education: Current Research*. New York: AMS Press, pp. 161-93.

Festinger, L. (1957). *A Theory of Cognitive Dissonance*. Evanston, IL: Row, Peterson.

Fuchs, V. (1974). *Who Shall Live?* New York: Basic Books.

German, P. (1978). The elderly: A target group highly accessible to health education. *International Journal of Health Education*, 21: 267-72.

Glanz, K., Lewis, F., & Rimer, B. (Eds.). (1990). *Health Behavior and Health Education: Theory, Research, and Practice*. San Francisco: Jossey-Bass.

Hovland, C., Janis, I., & Kelley, H. (1953). *Communication and Persuasion*. New Haven, CT: Yale University Press.

Lalonde, B., Hooyman, N., & Blumhagen, J. (1988). Long-term outcome effectiveness of a health promotion program for the elderly: The Wallingford Wellness Project. *Journal of Gerontological Social Work*, 13: 95-112.

Leming, M., & Dickinson, G. (1990). *Understanding Dying, Death, and Bereavement*. Fort Worth, TX: Holt, Rinehart & Winston.

Leviton, D. (1989). Intergenerational health education: The Adult Health and Development Programme. *Hygie: International Journal of Health Education*, 8: 26-29.

Leviton, D. (Ed.). (1991a). *Horrendous Death and Health: Toward Action*. Washington, DC: Hemisphere.

————. (1991b). *Horrendous Death, Health, and Well-Being*. Washington, DC: Hemisphere.

Lifton, R. (1979). *The Broken Connection*. New York: Simon & Schuster.

O'Donnell, M. (1989). Definition of health promotion. Part III: Expanding the definition. *American Journal of Health Promotion*, 3: 5.

Osterweis, M., Solomon, F., & Green, M. (Eds.). (1984). *Bereavement: Reactions, Consequences, and Care*. Washington, DC: National Academy Press.

Rosenstock, I. (1990). The health belief model: Explaining health behavior through expectancies. In K. Glanz, F. Lewis, & B. Rimer (Eds.), *Health Behavior and Health Education: Theory, Research, and Practice*. San Francisco: Jossey-Bass.

Steinfels, P. (1973). Introduction. *The Hastings Center Studies*, 1: 3-6.

U.S. Department of Health and Human Services. (1990). *Helping People 2000: Full Report*. Washington, DC: Superintendent of Public Documents.

Weisman, A. (1972). *On Death and Denying*. New York: Behavioral Publications.

HOMOSEXUALITY

Heterosexual white males are the only people who grow up and grow old. Theories and studies of lifespan development have often assumed a generic person who meets the foregoing description. Females, "nonwhites," and individuals from a variety of subcultures apart from the mainstream were seldom represented in scientific, educational, and programmatic endeavors. Times have changed—somewhat. The life course influences of gender, race, ethnicity, and socioeconomic status have been the subject of studies that are contributing to a more adequate understanding of both the commonalities and the diversities of human development.

One assumption, however, has been slow to change. Little attention has been given to homosexuality as an alternative set of pathways through the adult life course. This neglect is unfortunate for at least three reasons. First, of course, is the exclusion of a substantial percentage of the general population. The actual numbers have never been firmly determined. Some estimates are as low as 2 percent (Levine, 1988), others as high as 10 percent (Kimmel, 1978). One would also arrive at differing figures by asking for a statement of current sexual preference as distinguished from inquiring into any homosexual activity in which one may have engaged at any time in the past. All estimates are subject to dispute, but it has become clear that homosexuality is not uncommon.

Next, we cannot have much confidence in our understanding of the role of heterosexuality in lifespan development unless we become more knowledgeable about its similarities to and differences from homosexuality. Finally, it would be valuable to have a dependable data base when confronted with the divisive attitudes toward homosexuality within our society.

Same-Sex Attraction

The cause of homosexuality remains a mystery, although opinions abound. Some people believe that same-sex attraction is genetically determined, therefore biological. Others believe it is the result of cultural and social influences. Many take a stance in the middle, holding that being gay or lesbian is partly biological and partly social. This middle position is taken by Weinrich (1982), who, in exasperation, complains that "The *nature-nurture controversy* is dead. So why does it continue to occupy so much of our attention?" (p. 165, Weinrich's italics).

The answer lies not in any recent discoveries of biological or environmental causation but rather in the rhetorical importance of a root cause in determining social policy. Opponents of gay and lesbian rights tend to believe that sexual orientation is a choice; that is, individuals decide to engage or not engage in same-sex activities. In contrast, pro-gay and pro-lesbian rights activists assert that sexual orientation is not freely chosen (e.g., Brummett, 1979). In any case, same-sex attraction has been in existence from the beginning of recorded history. Although same-sex attraction is found in every era, culture, race, religion, and country, its meanings differ (Duberman, 1991; Foucault, 1988; Weinrich & Williams, 1991).

The discussion of same-sex attraction is complicated by the recognition that gays and lesbians do not typically define themselves either exclusively or primarily on the basis of their sexual activities. For example, some men who engage in same-sex activities do not define themselves as gay or homosexual (Doll et al., 1992). Participation in same-sex activities, then, is not necessarily the defining characteristic of homosexuals, at least from the individual's perspective. The social construction of sexual identity is much more complex (Weinberg, 1983), and more systematic research is needed on men who engage in same-sex activities but who do not define themselves as homosexual. Since we know so little about these men, it is impossible to place much confidence in statistical estimates of the overall homosexual population. Further complicating matters is the fact that some men and women do not engage exclusively in either homosexual or heterosexual activities throughout their adult lives.

From this confusing context the terms *homosexual, lesbian,* and *gay* emerge. As a term that was imposed by the scientific community in the nineteenth century, "homosexual" is frequently regarded as too stigmatizing and depersonalizing through its overemphasis on sexual activities (Downing, 1989). "Lesbian" and "gay," by contrast, are terms that have emerged from the lesbian and gay communities themselves. The term "lesbian" was used in a contemporary sense as early as the sixteenth century but did not gain currency until late in the nineteenth century, and the term "gay" did not make its appearance with a sexual denotation until the mid-twentieth century. It is probable that "lesbian" derives from a reference to the Agean island of Lesbos, home of the poet Sappho. The etymology of "gay" is obscure. Both terms, however, reflect the desire to move away from the mainstream social construction of "the homosexual" (Boswell, 1980).

In the United States, gay and lesbian culture has changed considerably over the past 50 years. What was once a taboo topic and shameful life-style is now becoming a recognized way of life, and communities have emerged with shared beliefs, values, attitudes, expectations, and perceptions. Although gays and lesbians share many political goals, gender differences pervade all aspects of their personal and social lives. The personal and social issues in gay and lesbian adult lives touched upon in the following discussion are not experienced in the same ways by gays and lesbians.

Personal Issues

Coming out is a process of self-identification and self-disclosure (Jandt & Darsey, 1981). It is often very difficult to redefine one's identity, whether as a gay or a lesbian (Gonsiorek & Rudolph, 1991). Although many people come out in their early adult years, there is no age limit. For example, some people come out after a heterosexual marriage and parenting children. Lesbians have been reported to recognize and act upon their same-sex attractions at a later age than gays (Nichols, 1990).

As a process of self-disclosure, many lesbians and gays find that they need to reveal their sexual orientation from time to time throughout their adult lives. *With the possible exception of public figures, coming out is not a single event, but an ongoing process of self-disclosure to selected individuals.* Fear of rejection by family, friends, and coworkers is one of the primary barriers to coming out. There can be negative consequences to this self-disclosure, but the desire to live openly, as opposed to *closeted*, is frequently an important motivation. "Coming out still means living at risk, but it is also the gesture that makes everything else possible: our development as individuals; our security as a community" (Goldstein, 1992, p. 42).

Romantic relationships and lifelong partnerships are of utmost importance for both gays and lesbians. One of the greatest myths held by the dominant culture is that gays and lesbians are interested first and foremost in the sex act. This is associated with the equally mistaken notion that gays and lesbians define themselves primarily through sexual activity. On the contrary, being gay or lesbian is an emotional activity. In lifelong relationships, the physical dimension of the partnership plays a role of lesser importance.

Finding romance and settling into a partnership is the challenge. In large cities, newspapers offer romance ads, or dating services are available. In many cases, however, gays and lesbians meet through friends or in nightclubs. The dating process and the development of relationships are not much different than the courtships experienced by heterosexuals. Potential couples meet, have dinner, compare interests, beliefs, and values, and arrange to meet again. If, over time, the relationship seems workable, then the couple makes a private and/or public commitment to each other.

Yet there are some differences between gay and lesbian relationships that have to do with gender rather than sexual orientation (Peplau, 1991). Legal marriages do not exist for same-sex couples, but some lesbians and gays conduct a public ceremony for their friends and/or family. Many make only a private commitment to each other and exchange rings on significant occasions such as an anniversary. Should the relationship not work out as expected, the separation involves many of the same problems that occur in heterosexual divorces: a division of property, sadness, loneliness, and, eventually, the

search for another relationship (Marcus, 1988; McWorther & Mattison, 1984; Wolf, 1979).

Gay and lesbian parenthood can become a complex issue when a man or woman is in a heterosexual marriage, has children, and then comes to terms with his or her sexuality and leaves the marriage. Often, the heterosexual parent assumes responsibility for the child, and the other parent starts a new life. The goal of both parents is to provide a healthy upbringing for the children, but frequently the stigma associated with homosexuality presents a dilemma. Some parents never mention the issue of sexuality, others discuss the situation openly and honestly, and still others wait until the children are adults to give them the facts.

In any case, parents usually do not know how to answer the forthright questions children often ask, such as, "Mommy, why aren't there any women at Daddy's house?" Recent books for children such as *Daddy's Roommate* (Willhoite, 1991) are intended to help parents answer these difficult questions. On the whole, however, more research is needed to help children learn to live with the truth (Wolf, 1979).

Childbirth is an issue that faces many lesbians, especially lesbian couples. Through sperm donors or artificial insemination, a woman can become pregnant and raise a child outside the context of heterosexual marriage. In most states, legal problems related to a lesbian couple having a child are easily resolved. The nonbiological mother is able to adopt the child so that if something happens to the birth mother, custody of the child remains within the family. Should the two women dissolve their partnership, custody is handled through the courts, in much the same way as in male-female divorces. Joint custody is not unusual.

The largest problem facing a lesbian couple's child is the stigma associated with lesbianism. The child is likely to face discrimination at school, in the neighborhood, and even in the extended family. Aunts, uncles, or cousins may disapprove of same-sex relationships and take this attitude out on the child. Ironically, those who discriminate against the child will often do so with the rationalization that the child cannot live a normal life with two women as parents—not realizing that they, not the parents, are the source of the problem.

Two fallacious assumptions regarding lesbian parenting are that (a) the child will be gay or lesbian and (b) one of the women will play the role of father. No empirical evidence exists to support either of these claims. In most instances, a child born into a lesbian family is provided with a safe, nurturing environment with two mothers. If all involved have the personal strength to overcome prejudice and discrimination, the child is then able to proceed through adolescence and into adulthood in a healthy manner (Wolf, 1979).

Gay communities are neighborhoods—typically in the major urban areas of the United States—where large numbers of gays and lesbians have chosen to congregate. While most of these neighborhoods seem to be oriented more toward gay men than lesbians, some have a decidedly lesbian focus. Businesses cater to both gay and lesbian consumers, but men tend to dominate the public domain. Some resort areas have now taken on a gay orientation. These include Provincetown, Massachusetts; Key West, Florida; Fire Island, New York; and the Russian River area of California. However, many gays and lesbians do not live in such communities. Gays and lesbians reside in all 50 states; in large cities, suburbs, and small towns, on farms and ranches; and in high-rise and single-family houses (Herdt, 1992; Miller, 1989).

Social activities for lesbians and gays are diverse. Nightclubs and bars are important in gay and lesbian culture. Some clubs are oriented more toward a gay clientele, others have a more lesbian orientation, and still others cater to both. For the many members of the community who live "in the closet," nightclubs become a place where sexual identity is open and conversation is not censored. Men can dance with men and women with women, and same-sex kissing is commonplace. A couple can hold hands and act like a couple, and potential dates can be identified without the nagging question, "Is he or she straight?" (Marcus, 1988).

Because excessive drinking can be a problem, some gays and lesbians turn to discussion groups, bridge clubs, softball leagues, and other such activities as an alternative to the bar scene. The intention is to find or create situations in which lesbians and gays can make friends, be open about their sexuality, and enjoy a nonhostile environment.

Social Issues

Religion plays a major role in gay and lesbian life, from both external and internal perspectives. Many religious leaders criticize homosexuality as sinful. Leaders of the Roman Catholic church and the fundamentalist Christian religions have been particularly vocal in their opposition to homosexuality. They see being gay or lesbian as a lifestyle preference rather than something not freely chosen.

Lesbians and gays who desire religious affiliation and experience have organized ways of meeting their needs in spite of the anti-homosexual rhetoric of church leaders. Dignity is an organization of gay and lesbian Roman Catholics. Affirmation is the organization for Mormons, and Integrity is for Episcopalians. Other groups such as the Brethren Mennonites Council, Jehovah's Witness Gay Support Group, Lutherans Concerned, Presbyterians for Lesbians and Gays, and various Jewish organizations exist to serve their respective memberships. Gays and lesbians who want to participate in organized religion but do not want to be a part of any of the traditional institutions have created their own churches and places of worship, the largest being the Metropolitan Community Church. Many religious options now are available for gays and lesbians (Preston, 1991). Currently, many traditional church bodies are struggling with the place of homosexuality within their denomination and are dealing with the issue of the ordination of gays and lesbians.

Many contemporary social issues are reflected in gay and lesbian communities. *Lookism,* closely related to *ageism,* has long been embedded in the gay male community. The tradition of celebrating male beauty has been an important part of the gay male sensibility that emphasizes youth and good looks. The high value placed on looks tends to have a negative effect on attitudes toward aging. Ageism is still pervasive in the United States (Palmore, 1990), and gay men have not resisted this cultural attitude. Lesbians have been much more successful at not playing into lookism. This resistance stems from the feminist rejection of patriarchal constructions of femininity and beauty by lesbian feminists.

Because "human development models have been seldom applied to gay men and lesbians in the scholarly or professional literatures" (D'Augelli, 1991, p. 218), there is little information on the *aging process.* Older gays and especially older lesbians have been largely invisible in the public arena: "The older female homosexual has remained hidden to an even greater extent than has her male counterpart; this is reflected in the newly emerging literature on the older homosexual, which focuses primarily on the male" (Berger, 1982, p. 13). Both gays and lesbians, however, "contribute as taxpayers throughout their working lives [and] are shortchanged when it comes to publicly funded social services" (Berger, 1982, p. 14). The pervasive assumption that elderly adults are heterosexual means that many social service providers are unprepared to deal adequately with all of their clientele.

Racial and ethnic differences are significant features of the gay and lesbian community. A number of organizations are directed toward serving the gays and lesbians of a particular racial or ethnic group (Preston, 1991). Each racial or ethnic group that has formed such organizations reflects its own distinctive concerns and issues. These include African-Americans (Beam, 1986; Hemphill, 1991; Lorde, 1985), Asian-Americans and Pacific Islanders (H., 1989), Jewish Americans (Beck, 1982), Latinos (Trujillo, 1991), and Native Americans (Roscoe, 1988).

Many of these groups are designed to promote pride and understanding of their racial or ethnic group as well as their sexuality. These groups also articulate their special interests within the larger gay and lesbian community.

The existence of these organizations underscores both the diversity of the gay and lesbian community and the vitality of its members. "We've [gays/lesbians] come to understand ourselves as the bearers of many cultures, each of which determines how we express our sexuality" (Goldstein, 1992, p. 40). Organizations such as Men of All Colors Together represent a desire to deal openly with racial and ethnic differences.

Internal struggles occur within the gay and lesbian community just as they do within other sectors of the population. At the present time, the lesbian community is attempting to cope with two markedly different orientations. Radical lesbian feminists have initiated the womyn's/wimmin's/women's movement—spelled various ways to "get the men out of wo-men." Those who take this approach resent being treated as sexual objects or symbols of mere physical beauty by the dominant, white male-centered culture (Davenport, 1983). They eschew makeup, miniskirts, the shaving of body hair, or anything else that promotes the image of womyn as social decorations for male pleasure. Radical lesbian feminists have spent some 30 years creating, advocating, and defending their movement.

They are at odds with a new generation of lesbians (who sometimes prefer being called gay women). These women enjoy their right to same-sex relationships but opt to appear "feminine" in the traditional sense. They choose to use cosmetics and wear designer clothes and jewelry, but they do not view themselves as objects of the patriarchy (Van Gelder, 1992). Lesbian scholars and social critics are in the process of exploring the complex issues related to women, especially gay women, in a male-dominated society. By and large, they prefer that these discussions occur in private circles rather than in the mass media (Allen, 1990).

Political Issues

Gay bashing—violence directed against gays and lesbians because of their sexual orientation—has become a more visible problem now that some police departments are keeping hate crime records on violence that is directed against gays and lesbians. (The Supreme Court overturned a St. Paul, Minnesota, ordinance against hate crimes on June 22, 1992, as a violation of free expression because it targeted the message of the offenders, not necessarily their words or deeds. What effect this ruling may have on the incidence and visibility of gay bashing and the response to it remains to be seen.)

Gays tend to be the victims of more anti-gay violence than lesbians. The cultural invisibility of lesbians may be a major reason for this difference. Another aspect may be the blame that gays receive for the AIDS epidemic (Herek, 1991).

It appears that gay bashing, like other hate crimes, is on the increase (Goldstein, 1992). Gay bashing can take a number of forms, ranging from verbal assault to murder, all motivated by *homophobia*—the irrational fear of gays and/or lesbians. Some have started to question the use of this term, however, as relevant data have not demonstrated that anti-gay and anti-lesbian hatred is an irrational fear response. Perhaps this attitude may be more accurately viewed as a social value rather than as individual pathology.

The advent of acquired immune deficiency syndrome (AIDS) has affected the gay community tremendously. When the virus first appeared in the U.S. in the early 1980s, it seemed to be restricted chiefly to the gay community and even thought of as a "gay disease." Research has since shown, however, that throughout the world, AIDS affects mostly heterosexuals. Straight women are the fastest-growing population affected. Nevertheless, AIDS and its agent, the human immunodeficiency virus (HIV), have had the most direct impact on gay men in the U.S., and the effects are felt in the political, social, cultural, and personal realms. AIDS Coalition to Unleash Power (ACT UP) is active in the effort to increase funding for AIDS research, and in most cities AIDS service organizations are operated by gay men or lesbians.

The AIDS crisis has brought the gay and lesbian communities together. Although some women resent being once again at the service of men, lesbians have rallied behind the efforts to educate and help their male counterparts. Perhaps the most discouraging dimension of the AIDS crisis is the isolation and stigma experienced by some gay men with HIV as they are abandoned by family, friends, and the health care system (Weitz, 1991).

Gay and lesbian rights legislation has become a political focal point. A number of states currently have nondiscrimination policies, as do more than 80 cities in the United States. Political goals are not limited to the establishment of nondiscrimination statements but reflect a larger social movement (Adam, 1987). Many gays and lesbians are concerned that their relationships are not legally recognized by the state, that they do not have clear survivorship rights, that crime statistics often do not include anti-gay and anti-lesbian hate crimes, that more monies need to be directed to AIDS research, and that it is difficult to adopt children.

Recent political focus has turned toward employment discrimination, "the one legal issue that presses on the daily existence of almost all gay citizens" (Rivera, 1991, p. 88). This situation affects both gays and lesbians, although not necessarily in the same ways (Levine & Leonard, 1985). When "hundreds of GIs serving in Operation Desert Storm came out, risking court-martial and dishonorable discharge" (Goldstein, 1992, p. 39), additional pressure was brought upon the Department of Defense to end the ban on gays and lesbians in the military. The focus on the military is not new, as some evidence suggests that World War II experiences played an important role in raising gay and lesbian consciousness (Bérubé, 1990).

Gays and lesbians have also pushed for domestic partner recognition by both cities and corporations. Domestic partner recognition confers the same benefits on the partners of gays and lesbians that are currently entitlements of heterosexual partners. As the political environment changes, the goals of the gay and lesbian rights movement will shift. In general, the goal of most gay and lesbian political involvement reflects a desire to be given the same legal and social opportunities available to heterosexuals as they pursue their own journeys through the adult life course.

▼ THOMAS K. NAKAYAMA AND FREDERICK C. COREY
   See also: Divorce; Fictive Kin; Friendships through the Adult Years; Gender as a Shaping Force in Adult Development and Aging; Gender Differences in the Workplace; Interethnic Relationships; Loving and Losing; Marital Development; Military Service: Long-Term Effects on Adult Development; Sex in the Later Adult Years; Sexuality.

References

Adam, B. D. (1987). *The Rise of a Gay and Lesbian Movement.* Boston: Twayne.

Allen, J. (Ed.). (1990). *Lesbian Philosophies and Cultures.* Albany, NY: State University of New York Press.

Barret, R. L., & Robinson, B. E. (1990). *Gay Fathers.* Lexington, MA: Lexington Books.

Beam, J. (Ed.). (1986). *In the Life: A Black Gay Anthology.* Boston: Alyson.

Beck, E. T. (Ed.). (1982). *Nice Jewish Girls: A Lesbian Anthology.* Watertown, MA: Persephone Press.

Berger, R. M. (1982). *Gay and Gray: The Older Homosexual Man.* Urbana, IL: University of Illinois Press.

Bérubé, A. (1990). *Coming Out Under Fire: The History of Gay Men and Women in World War Two.* New York: Penguin.

Boswell, J. (1980). *Christianity, Social Tolerance, and Homosexuality.* Chicago: University of Chicago Press.

Brummett, B. (1979). A pentadic analysis of ideologies in two gay rights controversies. *Central States Speech Journal, 30:* 250-61.

D'Augelli, A. R. (1991). Teaching lesbian/gay development: From oppression to exceptionality. *Journal of Homosexuality, 22:* 213-27.

Davenport, D. (1983). The pathology of racism: A conversation with third world wimmin. In C. Moraga & G. Anzaldua (Eds.), *This Bridge Called My Back: Writings by Radical Women of Color.* New York: Women of Color Press, pp. 85-90.

Doll, L. S., et al. (1992). Homosexually and nonhomosexually identified men who have sex with men: A behavioral comparison. *The Journal of Sex Research, 29:* 1-14.

Downing, C. (1989). *Myths and Mysteries of Same-Sex Love.* New York: Continuum.

Duberman, M. (1991). *About Time: Exploring the Gay Past.* New York: New American Library.

Duberman, M., Vicinus, M., & Chancey, G., Jr. (Eds.). (1989). *Hidden from History: Reclaiming the Gay and Lesbian Past.* New York: New American Library.

Foucault, M. (1978/1985). *The History of Sexuality.* Volumes 1 and 2. New York: Random House.

———. (1988). Sexual choice, sexual act: Foucault and homosexuality. In L. D. Kritzman (Ed.), *Politics, Philosophy, Culture: Interviews and Other Writings, 1977-1984.* New York: Routledge, pp. 286-303.

Goldstein, R. (1992). 1991, the Third Wave: Multiculti-queerism emerges. *The Advocate,* January 14, pp. 36-42.

Gonsiorek, J. C., & Rudolph, J. R. (1991). Homosexual identity: Coming out and other developmental events. In J. C. Gonsiorek & J. D. Weinrich (Eds.), *Homosexuality: Research Implications for Public Policy.* Newbury Park, CA: Sage, pp. 161-76.

Green, G. D., & Bozett, F. W. (1991). Lesbian mothers and gay fathers. In J. C. Gonsiorek & J. D. Weinrich (Eds.), *Homosexuality: Research Implications for Public Policy.* Newbury Park, CA: Sage, pp. 197-214.

H., P. (1989). Asian American lesbians: An emerging voice in the Asian American community. In Asian Women United of California (Ed.), *Making Waves: An Anthology of Writings by and about Asian American Women.* Boston: Beacon, pp. 282-90.

Hemphill, E. (1991). *Brother to Brother: New Writings by Black Gay Men.* Boston: Alyson.

Herdt, G. (Ed.). (1992). *Gay Culture in America: Essays from the Field.* Boston: Beacon Press.

Herdt, G., & Boxer, A. (1992). Introduction: Culture, history, and life course of gay men. In G. Herdt & A. Boxer (Eds.), *Gay Culture in America: Essays from the Field.* Boston: Beacon Press, pp. 1-28.

Herek, G. M. (1991). Stigma, prejudice, and violence against lesbians and gay men. In J. C. Soniorek & J. D. Weinrich (Eds.), *Homosexu-*

ality: Research Implications for Public Policy. Newbury Park, CA: Sage, pp. 60-80.

Jandt, F. E., & Darsey, J. (1981). Coming out as a communicative process. In J. W. Chesebro (Ed.), *Gayspeak: Gay Male and Lesbian Communication*. New York: Pilgrim Press, pp. 12-27.

Kimmel, D. C. (1978). Adult development and aging: A gay perspective. *Journal of Social Issues*, 34: 113-30.

Levine, M. P. (Ed.). (1988). *Gay Men: The Sociology of Male Homosexuality*. Revised Edition. New York: Harper & Row, 1988.

Levine, M. P., & Leonard, R. (1985). Discrimination against lesbians in the work force. In E. B. Freedman et al. (Eds.), *The Lesbian Issue: Essays from SIGNS*. Chicago: University of Chicago Press, pp. 187-97.

Lorde, A. (1985). *I Am Your Sister: Black Women Organizing Across Sexualities*. Latham, NY: Women of Color Press.

Marcus, E. (1988). *The Male Couple's Guide to Living Together*. New York: Harper & Row.

McWorther, D. P., & Mattison, A. M. (1984). *The Male Couple: How Relationships Develop*. Englewood Cliffs, NJ: Prentice-Hall.

Miller, N. (1989). *In Search of Gay America*. New York: Harper & Row.

Nichols, M. (1990). Lesbian relationships: Implications for the study of sexuality and gender. In D. P. McWhirter, S. A. Sanders, & J. M. Reinisch (Eds.), *Homosexuality/Heterosexuality: Concepts of Sexual Orientation*. New York: Oxford University Press, pp. 350-64.

Palmore, E. (1990). *Ageism: Negative and Positive*. New York: Springer.

Peplau, L. A. (1991). Lesbian and gay relationships. In J. C. Gonsiorek & J. D. Weinrich (Eds.), *Homosexuality: Research Implications for Public Policy*. Newbury Park, CA: Sage, pp. 177-96.

Preston, J. (1991). *The Big Gay Book*. New York: Plume/Penguin.

Rivera, R. R. (1991). Sexual orientation and the law. In J. C. Gonsiorek & J. D. Weinrich (Eds.), *Homosexuality: Research Implications for Public Policy*. Newbury Park, CA: Sage, pp. 81-100.

Roscoe, W. (Ed.). (1988). *Living the Spirit: A Gay American Indian Anthology*. New York: St. Martin's.

Trujillo, C. (Ed.). (1991). *Chicana Lesbians: The Girls Our Mothers Warned Us About*. Berkeley, CA: Third Woman Press.

Van Gelder, L. (1992). Lipstick liberation. *Los Angeles Times Magazine*, March 15, pp. 30-32, 34, 54.

Weinberg, T. S. (1983). *Gay Men, Gay Selves: The Social Construction of Homosexual Identities*. New York: Irvington Publishers.

Weinrich, J. D. (1982). Introduction, Part III: Biology. In W. Paul et al. (Eds.), *Homosexuality: Social, Psychological, and Biological Issues*. Newbury Park, CA: Sage, pp. 165-67.

Weinrich, J. D., & Williams, W. L. (1991). Strange customs, familiar lives: Homosexualities in other cultures. In J. C. Gonsiorek & J. D. Weinrich (Eds.), *Homosexuality: Research Implications for Public Policy*. Newbury Park, CA: Sage, pp. 44-59.

Weitz, R. (1991). *Life with AIDS*. New Brunswick, NJ: Rutgers University Press.

Willhoite, M. (1991). *Daddy's Roommate*. Boston: Alyson Wonderland.

Wolf, D. G. (1979). *The Lesbian Community*. Berkeley, CA: University of California Press.

HOUSING AS A FACTOR IN ADULT LIFE

"There is no place like home." "Home is where the heart is." These and other truisms suggest that adequate housing is a basic condition for an acceptable life for virtually everyone of every age. Housing provides an extension of the self and a sense of place that is so powerful that many persons experience grief upon moving from a long-term home. Housing is shelter, a barrier against the extremes of weather conditions and from the noises, pressures, and "invasions" of people one wishes to avoid.

Shelter, however, is only a foundation for the needs that are fulfilled by housing. The basic set of needs to be fulfilled and values to be satisfied applies to all age groups. One's home expresses the values that one holds about what is good and satisfying. Any particular place serves some needs and expresses some values well but is likely to be less effective in serving some other purposes (Blank, 1988). What some of those needs and values are and how they vary by age through adulthood, what kinds of housing adults of different ages inhabit and how well those housing types serve their needs, and how housing will change in the future will be explored briefly here.

What Needs Served? What Values Fulfilled?

Some needs and values relate to the housing unit itself: convenience, ease of usage, safety, security, beauty, and comfort. A convenient house is close to stores and services, friends and family, churches and community activities. Ease of use is concerned more with the interior arrangements of the house. For example, do the size and layout allow the person to clean the house efficiently and prepare meals with little wasted effort? One house may be placed in a convenient location but prove difficult to use by a family with a particular set of needs. Another house may be ideally organized for the family's purposes but lack reasonable access to schools, shopping, or public transportation.

Safety and security are twin needs. A secure house provides the family with a feeling of being safe from intrusion from the outside, such as criminal attack. A safe house minimizes concerns about the consequences of one's own activities, such as falling on slippery surfaces or on a poorly designed staircase. One's house should also reflect one's sense of beauty reasonably well. The totality of satisfying most of these needs and having familiar surroundings leads to a sense of comfort in one's home.

Beyond these basic needs, housing should also fulfill emotional needs and values such as privacy, community, independence, and control. Whether living alone or in a dormitory or institution, a person needs privacy on some occasions. Balancing this need for privacy is the need for companions and a sense of community. The neighborliness or friendliness of the adjacent community is often an important factor. A person's home should foster independence and a sense of being in control. Most adults want to feel that they can do what they want in their own homes, without being told what to do or constrained from living as they choose.

Of course, a house should also be spacious enough to meet all of one's demands but not so large as to be forbidding, and it should be within one's resources to afford. In fact, affordability has become an increasingly salient aspect of housing, especially for today's younger people who are trying to enter the housing market for the first time.

How Well Can Housing Fulfill All These Values?

No house perfectly fulfills all of one's values or needs. Some needs can be met fully only by reducing the ability of the home to fulfill other needs. For example, a person might feel totally safe only by eliminating all potential hazards and by establishing an ever-active monitoring system, but this might have the effect of making the residence appear sterile, unattractive, and low on satisfying privacy needs. Choice of housing is always a matter of trade-offs. In the best of cases, a person gives away high satisfaction of some values of lesser concern for the purpose of ensuring high satisfaction of the most critical values and needs. In many cases adult Americans succeed very well in negotiating these trade-offs; they are able to fulfill adequately their most important values and tolerate any shortcomings.

As people go through life, the basic needs and values associated with housing do not change. The importance attached to particular qualities and needs may shift, however. Young adults are likely to emphasize independence and privacy, but the most critical factor often is simply affordability. In the middle years of life many people give particular importance to beauty, security, and a community feeling as they raise their children and rise in their occupations. A spacious home at this point may not only meet the needs of a large and active family but also reflect the family's status. By comparison, many elderly people shift their priorities in the direction of convenience, ease of usage, safety, and security.

Where Do People Live?

Most adults of all ages live in "free market" housing. In other words, they do not live in a place that has been purposely set aside for only one age, nor do they live in housing that has been built or supported directly by the government. They are most likely to dwell in single-family homes; rental housing is the next most common arrangement (U.S. Bureau of the Census, 1990).

Age. A person's age has a significant influence on housing type and quality (see Table 1). Middle-aged and older persons are the most likely to own their homes, whereas young adults are more likely to rent. This difference is related both to affordability and mobility. Younger people have a difficult time entering the ownership market, and they are also less likely to make the attempt because of their tendency to move more often. Older persons often have lived in the same housing for more than 20 years, and their homes are more often older. Maintenance of these older homes often requires more effort or money, neither of which the older person may have available in abundance.

Older persons on the average spend a smaller percentage of income on housing because many own their homes free and clear. The situation is reversed for elderly persons who pay rent: Usually they pay a considerably higher percentage of their income than do younger adults who rent their premises. A much larger percentage of people live alone in old age than at any other time of life. On the average, the homes of older persons are smaller than those of other age groups. Middle-aged persons who require a larger than average home for raising families will eventually need to decide whether or not to move into smaller homes as they age.

For many decades elderly people were more likely to live in urban and rural areas while young and middle-aged adults chose the suburbs. Recently, however, the percentage of elderly people in the suburbs has been growing until this has now become their most common location. Young families tradi-

Table 1. Age-Related Differences in Housing
(Percentages by age of "householder" or primary resident)

A. Four Age Categories and Ownership

Age of Householder	% of Total Households	% Who Own
Under 30	16%	30%
30-44	33%	61%
45-64	29%	77%
65+	22%	75%

B. Elderly Compared to Total on Selected Variables

Number of Persons	% of All Households	% of Elderly Households
1	24%	44.5%
2	32%	45%
3-4	33%	9%
More than 4	11%	1/5%
Age of Structure Pre-1950	32%	42%
Owned Free & Clear	43%	83%
Median Value of Owned Home	$72,400	$62,300
Renters: % of Income to Rent	29%	36%

Adapted from information contained in Current Housing Reports, H-150-87, American Housing Survey for the United States in 1987.

tionally located in suburban areas for access to good schools and other amenities. However, the aging of persons who built suburban homes in the post-World War II housing boom and remained there has led to a "graying" of many of these areas. At the same time, the high cost of suburban housing has limited the influx of new younger families. This phenomenon is cause for some concern because suburban areas are much less likely to have either a wide range of services near residential areas or adequate transportation. Both of these factors are very important for older persons who may have limited mobility and are concerned about driving.

Race and Ethnicity. There are also important differences in housing type, quality, and cost by race and ethnicity. Unfortunately, the U.S. Census Bureau housing surveys do not at present provide refined data on this topic. Information is subdivided only into the categories of black and Hispanic, the latter grouping together all people who are Spanish-speaking and of Central or South American heritage. Nevertheless, the available information is important and helps to form at least a tentative picture of the housing problems faced by minority or ethnic groups as compared with the predominantly white and English-speaking population of the United States.

As shown in Table 2, both blacks and Hispanics are likely to encounter more problems with housing than the majority population. They are more likely to rent, to pay a larger percentage of their income for housing, and to live in housing that has serious deficiencies and in neighborhoods with a variety of serious problems. Blacks and Hispanics often are segregated into more or less clearly delineated center city or rural neighborhoods that provide a lower quality of services than surrounding areas. The larger percentage of income paid for rental housing by these people continues to exist despite the fact that relatively more members of minority populations live in public housing. Those who purchase housing on the open market are even worse off in this regard than the statistics reveal.

Housing Issues for Young and Middle-Aged Adults

A major goal of most younger persons is to establish their own home (whether dormitory, apartment, or house) as a means of fulfilling the need for independence from parental control. Unfortunately, housing is relatively expensive and consumes a large percentage of entry-level income. In response

Table 2. Selected Comparisons Between Total, Blacks, and Hispanics

	% of Total (or white)	% of Black	% of Hispanic
Owner occupant %	69%	43%	40%
Median Value	$72,400	$50,000	$73,500
Renters—% of Income	29%	32%	32%
Serious Problems	5%	18%	15%
Rats in evidence	5%	15%	13%
Holes in plaster	6%	13%	11%
Trash or litter in area	29%	49%	47%
Area			
Center City	33%	61%	54%
Suburban	45%	24%	36%
Rural	22%	14%	10%

Adapted from information contained in Current Housing Reports, H-150-87, American Housing Survey for the United States in 1987. Hispanics include both blacks and whites, depending on which race they choose on the census form. Other examples of problems that are classified as serious include lack of a toilet, exposed wiring, no heat for protracted time, water leaks, no light fixtures in hallways, etc.

to affordability problems in recent decades, lending institutions have developed a bewildering array of adjustable and balloon financing plans that begin the mortgage at an artificially low payment level with the expectation that in a few years the younger person will have become established and therefore be able to afford substantially higher mortgage payments.

Traditionally, middle-aged adults have "traded up" to larger homes, either to meet the space needs of their families or for the prestige value. The dangers of trading up lie in the possibility of financial overextension, especially if divorce makes it necessary to establish a second living arrangement.

Issues for Older Persons

Older persons often are forced by circumstance to change their hierarchical arrangement of values and needs. Their goals are likely to shift to maximizing control and independence (not unlike young adults, but for different reasons) and to emphasizing convenience and ease of usage. They may also desire to tap into the equity they have built up in a house to serve other purposes.

Elderly persons often have major needs for their housing environment to support them more extensively than was the case earlier in life. They are likely to move more slowly, experience vision and hearing problems, and have somewhat less strength and stamina. A variety of other physiological changes may also force them to rely more on their housing environment. This form of increasing dependence is sometimes called environmental docility. A well-known model of environmental relations connects a person's environmental competence (ability to influence the environment) to the demands made by the environment (Lawton & Nahemow, 1973). These demands may include the ability to climb steep stairs, reach up to high cabinets, or carry laundry and groceries for a long distance. The environmental competence model emphasizes the importance of having one's housing characteristics closely match one's ability to function within this environment.

Most people continue to be at least relatively well matched with the characteristics of their housing throughout the lifespan. However, many people experience some lowering of their competence level as they age, and they risk a mismatch unless their housing environment is modified appropriately or they move to a new and less taxing home. As the mismatch between an elderly person and the housing environment becomes greater, he or she may become increasingly vulnerable to danger because of insufficient security or safety. This consideration may lead elderly persons to sacrifice some measure of beauty, comfort, privacy, or independence in the interest of maximizing safety and security. Concurrently, they may require more money to pay for the maintenance of both the home and themselves. It is not unusual for an elderly person to become "house rich but cash poor."

Housing for Elderly and Disabled Persons

Although most Americans live in "regular" housing, there are several types of age-specialized (age-segregated) dwellings. A few types are for young persons, for example, dormitories or single apartment complexes. However, by far the greatest amount and variety of specialized housing is for elderly persons. Theoretically at least, elderly persons have more types of housing to choose from: all of the age-integrated types in addition to those intended only for older people. This variety is appropriate because a fairly significant portion of elderly persons (estimated at about 20 percent) have difficulty living in "regular" housing.

Types of age-segregated housing for older persons range on a continuum from apartment complexes that are very similar to ordinary community housing to environments that provide highly intensive nursing care. Blank (1988), Lawton (1986), and several resource books from the American Association of Retired Persons (1984, for example) provide detailed information about the full range of types, including emerging alternatives. Here three major types will be described.

Subsidized Rental Housing. About 3 percent (more than 1,400,000) of the elderly people in the U.S. live in housing units for people with disabilities that have been built through federal funding programs or subsidies. The tenants pay only 25 percent of their incomes for this housing (U.S. Department of Housing and Urban Development, 1972, 1984). Moderate- to low-income elderly persons who can still care for themselves and younger disabled persons are eligible to use this program.

This housing is often managed either by the housing authority of a local government or by a private sponsor, such as a church group. Some buildings provide virtually no services, making them similar to regular apartments except for the age or disability limitations and the low cost. Others include services such as meal programs, community rooms, transportation, and perhaps very limited personal care. Overall, this type of housing offers considerable security, safety, and convenience, but it is usually not very attractive. Privacy and independence are somewhat lower than in a regular apartment. Furthermore, recent changes in the regulations concerning disability have begun to increase the tensions between the elderly and disabled younger residents, especially those with mental disabilities. Another problem must also be noted: Since 1980 there has been a very sharp drop in additions to the stock of available disability housing, and many of the existing units are becoming old, worn, and difficult to maintain.

Congregate housing is a variation that is more "service rich." It offers supportive services such as homemaker services, most meals, and help with personal care and grooming (Chellis, Seagle, & Seagle, 1982; U.S. House of Representatives, 1986).

Nursing Homes. The most supportive housing is the type that first became known as nursing homes but in more recent years is described and regulated as care facilities (Harrington, Newcomer, & Estes, 1985; National Center for Health Statistics, 1987). Nursing homes are differentiated by level of care and by financial approach (nonprofit or proprietary). All provide at least some regular nursing care, meal services, and fairly extensive personal care. All also allow for only a minimum of privacy, sense of control, and independence, while maximizing security and safety. Many elderly people and others have developed a very negative stereotype of nursing homes; however, it is difficult to avoid sacrificing some values in order to maintain the level of monitoring and efficiency necessary to provide for persons who have a very low level of competency to care for themselves. Superior nursing homes recognize the need to give special attention to issues of privacy, independence, and resident control. At any given time, about 4 to 5 percent of the population over age 65 live in nursing homes; about 25 percent will spend some time in a nursing home during the course of their lives (Kastenbaum & Candy, 1973).

Life Care Communities. Adult-only communities include a variety of types of housing. Although often referred to as "retirement communities," many residents reject this designation and prefer to think of themselves as residents of active adult communities. By whatever name, age-segregated communities came into existence soon after the end of World War II (Morrison et al., 1986; Streib, LeGreca, & Folts, 1986). Most have been built specifically for their purpose, although some developed simply because many older persons gravitated to a particular area. Although more popular in the South and the West, adult-only communities exist in all parts of the country. Some provide virtually no services; these usually have a mix of housing that is similar to what is found in an age-integrated community.

Most planned retirement communities, however, include a package of services that range from activity programs to home and personal care. Establishments that call themselves "life care" or "continuing care" communities provide nursing home services when needed. To gain admittance to such communities, older persons typically pay an entrance fee that may range from $20,000 to well over $100,000, depending on the size of unit and type of community. Additionally, a maintenance fee is charged that is well in excess of what would be normal rental for their unit. This approach constitutes a long-term care insurance plan for the residents. Obviously, only those older persons who possess significant resources can afford to live in this type of housing: At present, this amounts to approximately 500,000 men and women.

The strengths and weaknesses of this approach to packaging housing, services, and long-term care have been discussed in various guides (e.g., American Association of Homes for the Aging, 1986; Raper, 1984) and in many articles in both professional journals and popular magazines (see Blank, 1988).

All told, these three major types as well as some less common age-segregated approaches provide useful options along the continuum of housing that is available for the approximately 15 percent of the over-65 population who need and desire arrangements of this type at any particular time.

What Will the Future Hold?

Demographic, social, economic, political, and technological trends will greatly affect the housing of the future for adults of all ages. The population will continue to age at least until the middle of the next century. This period will be characterized by longer lifespans and lower birthrates. Concurrently, family life patterns are becoming less stable, as indicated by higher rates of divorce and single parenting. These changes may lead to an emphasis on smaller houses and increase the importance of both specialized housing and improved ways to ensure proper maintenance.

In turn, these changes will require new types of financial arrangements to encourage home ownership among the young and the newly single middle-aged, and also to enable elderly persons to obtain additional resources to care adequately for themselves and their homes. Reverse annuity mortgages (RAMs) have already emerged as one new option. These financial devices enable long-term owners to use the equity in their home to provide for needed services without selling the home (Jacobs, 1986). RAMS are likely to become a normal component in a lifelong relationship between lending institutions and home owners that begins when people buy their first home.

The large cutbacks in the 1980s in almost every federal program for services and housing were accompanied by increasing home prices in otherwise recessionary times. This combination produced a large rise in the number of homeless persons, among whom elderly people and children are overrepresented. Lowering housing prices may improve this deplorable state of affairs, but the negative effects may continue to increase overall as existing public housing becomes less usable and is not replaced.

Technological advances will also influence housing, especially in the area of so-called "smart" houses (Blank, 1988; Geremia, 1987). Electronic controls will integrate telephones, all appliances from dishwashers to televisions, lighting, air quality control, security, computer files, and many other components of the house to maximize efficiency, comfort, monitoring, security, and maintenance. "Smart" houses may offer great benefits to elderly and disabled persons who have limited mobility or strength, although they also may have the potential danger of overcontrol.

The future of housing for developing individuals and a developing society will continue to build upon the foundation of the past and will continue to bring dramatic changes for society as a whole.

▼ THOMAS O. BLANK

See also: African-American Experiences through the Adult Years; Friendships through the Adult Years; Happiness, Cohort Measures of; Japanese Perspectives on Adult Development; Marital Development; Mexican Americans: Life Course Transitions and Adjustment; Place and Personality in Adult Development; Privacy Issues; Subcultural Influences on Lifelong Development; Vision.

References

American Association of Homes for the Aging. (1986). *The Continuing Care Retirement Community: A Guide for Consumers.* Washington, DC: American Association of Homes for the Aging.

American Association of Retired Persons. (1984). *Housing Options for Older Americans.* Washington, DC: American Association of Retired Persons.

Blank, T. O. (1988). *Older Persons and Their Housing—Today and Tomorrow.* Springfield, IL: Charles C. Thomas.

Chellis, R. D., Seagle, J. F., & Seagle, B. M. (1982). *Congregate Housing for Older People: A Solution for the 1980's.* Lexington, MA: Lexington Books.

Geremia, K. (1987). *Smart House.* Upper Marlboro, MD: Smart House Venture Development, Inc.

Harrington, C., Newcomer, R. J., & Estes, C. L. (1985). *Long-Term Care for the Elderly.* Beverly Hills, CA: Sage.

Jacobs, B. (1986). The national potential of home equity conversion. *The Gerontologist, 26:* 496-504.

Kastenbaum, R., & Candy, S. E. (1973). The 4% fallacy: Many die where few have lived. *International Journal of Aging and Human Development, 4:* 15-21.

Lawton, M. P. (1986). *Environment and Aging.* Albany, NY: Center for the Study of Aging.

Lawton, M. P., & Nahemow, L. (1973). Ecology and the aging process. In C. Eisdorfer & M. P. Lawton (Eds.), *Psychology of Adult Development and Aging.* Washington, DC: American Psychological Association, pp. 219-36.

Morrison, I. A., et al. (1986). *Continuing Care Retirement Communities: Political, Social, and Financial Issues.* New York: Haworth.

National Center for Health Statistics. (1987). *Use of Nursing Homes by the Elderly: Preliminary Data from the 1985 National Nursing Home Survey.* Hyattsville, MD: Public Health Service.

Raper, A. T. (1984). *National Continuing Care Directory.* Mt. Prospect, IL: AARP Books / Scott, Foresman.

Streib, G. F., LaGreca, A. J., & Folts, W. E. (1986). Retirement communities. In R. J. Newcomer, M. P. Lawton & T. O. Byerts (Eds.), *Housing and Aging Society.* New York: Van Nostrand Reinhold, pp. 142-62.

U.S. Bureau of the Census. (1990). *Statistical Abstracts of the United States, 1990.* Washington, DC: U.S. Government Printing Office.

U.S. Department of Housing and Urban Development. (1972). *Management of Housing for the Elderly: A HUD Guide.* Washington, DC: U.S. Government Printing Office.

———. (1984). *Section 202 Housing for the Elderly and Handicapped: A National Survey.* Washington, DC: U.S. Government Printing Office.

U.S. House of Representatives, Select Committee on Aging. (1986). *Maximizing Supportive Services for the Elderly in Assisted Housing: Experiences from the Congregate Housing Services Program.* Washington, DC: U.S. Government Printing Office.

HUMOR

Humor—a Neglected Sense?

A funny thing happened to me on my way through my developmental cycle. My sense of humor plateaued somewhere around pre-adolescence, maybe inching its way toward late adolescence and early adulthood. This happened because my cognitive stages stopped developing. All of my other sensory systems changed. Developmental psychologists and lifespan analysts have provided a plethora of information about these sensory system changes. We know in a fair amount of detail what happens to our visual and auditory systems. We learn about taste and tactile changes. Little attention, however, is given to our sense of humor. We are left with the belief that we possess a robust sense of humor but that the other person may not be similarly blessed.

Most authors agree that we know considerably more about humor and its development through childhood and early adolescence than we know about humor through the adult years, although there is a sprinkling of information on humor in and about old age. One reason for our limited knowledge about the lifespan developmental aspect of humor is that we tend to know more about early childhood and adolescence in general. The social and behavioral sciences have long been youth oriented. Research with a lifespan perspective is relatively recent. Another reason is that scientific research about humor is also a fairly recent endeavor. The study of humor was not considered a sufficiently "serious" topic for research, it was "too soft"— a scientific criticism that is almost worse than death.

Other reasons have to do with the difficulties in defining humor, in discriminating among and evaluating the many theories of humor, and in finding the most accurate and parsimonious theoretical approach. Additionally, there are problems in categorizing forms of humor—jokes, puns, spontaneous wit, comedy routines, and so forth.

We do not know the differences, if any, between the ability to *initiate* a humorous exchange and the ability to *appreciate* it. Do initiation and appreciation differ developmentally? Are initiation and appreciation of humor qualitatively different from each other? Also poorly understood are the relationships between laughter—the visible sign that a humorous event may have occurred— and humor itself. We know that there are age differences in the acoustic of laughter responses (LaPointe, Mower, & Case, 1990), but we do not know what these differences might tell us about the sense of humor as such.

Some Functions and Dangers of Humor

Theories about humor have been proposed over the centuries, from Aristotle (Janko, 1984) to Freud (1938, 1952), from Hobbes (1950) to Bergson (1980) to Grotjahn (1987). Much humor requires that we look at the world in a different way, recognizing its paradoxes and inconsistencies and its many levels of reality.

Humor can be used to express hostilities, both personal and social, to evidence anxieties, and to make fun of oneself and others. It can defuse touchy situations, expose pretension, and, according to some, enhance health (Cousins, 1976). Humor strengthens the bonds of group solidarity and distinguishes between "we," the in-group, and "they," the out-group. There seems to be agreement that a sense of humor is an important coping mechanism throughout life. We deal with our anxieties about death and medical care through jokes such as the following:

> A man dies and goes to heaven. St. Peter meets him at the gates and asks his name. The man tells him. St. Peter goes through all his books and can find no record of the man. "Are you sure I have the spelling right?" After numerous questions, St. Peter runs the man's name through the computer and returns to tell him, "You're not due here for eight more years. Tell me, who's your doctor?"

The dangers of humor are clearly defined in the novel (and motion picture) *The Name of the Rose* (Eco, 1983). Here murder is committed in a medieval monastery to prevent others from being exposed to the heresies implicit in humor. In the novel, Jorge of Burgos has hidden a rare manuscript of Aristotle's *Poetics II* in order to keep the evils and power of humor from infecting the world. To treat matters with humor is to question them—and questioning changes power relationships.

That Aristotle wrote about comedy is unquestioned. The existence of *Poetics II* is supported by Janko (1984), although this work is now thought to have been lost through the turmoil of the intervening centuries. Both *Poetics I* and *Poetics II* began life as lecture notes. Apparently we know Aristotle as we know George Herbert Mead: through the lecture notes of students. From his fragmentary surviving writings on this subject, we learn that Aristotle considered comedy a form of poetry. It involves the imitation of inferior persons and the ugly "of which the ludicrous is one part" (Aristotle, 1967, p. 23). Both the ugliness and the distortion are painless, however. Aristotle also recognized the role of incongruity in humor. Perhaps humor theory and studies would have developed quite differently had Aristotle's complete views on this subject come down to us across the years; in this sense, history itself may have played a sad joke on the great philosopher.

Current Interests in Humor

Today, there is a lively interest in humor among scholars. National and international conferences focus on humor, and an interdisciplinary publication (*Humor: International Journal of Humor Research*) has been serving this growing field since 1988. For information on current scholarly activities in this area, inquiries are invited by Alleen Nilsen, president of the International Society for Humor Studies (c/o Department of English, Arizona State University, Tempe, AZ 85287-2803). ISHS offers a great variety of bibliographies on such topics as "Medicine, Physiology," "Names," "19th Century America," "Puns, Ambiguity," and "Sex Roles," as well as on specific nations and peoples.

As a society we support a humor industry on stage, radio, and television. We value our comics and cartoonists. We enjoy "the life of the party." Nevertheless, some individuals continue to express fear of humor, and others believe that it is not just an appropriate topic for research. Still others feel strongly that nothing destroys humor more surely than the attempt to study it scientifically; certainly, there are not a lot of laughs in the typical research piece on this topic.

Given this background, what can be said about the developmental aspects of a sense of humor in adulthood? To play it safe, one would have to say very little. However, much of what follows is speculation stimulated by the limited research presently available on humor in the adult years.

Theories and Studies

The general study of adult development and aging has disclosed a number of age *differences* in thought and behavior, but information about age *changes* after adolescence remains limited. Several attempts have been made to establish a developmental approach to humor (e.g., Loeb & Wood, 1986; McGhee, 1983, 1986; McGhee, Ruch, & Hehl, 1990). The late Martin Loeb and Vivian Wood suggested an Eriksonian model of humor, while Paul McGhee and his colleagues drew on empirical findings to propose a developmental approach.

McGhee and his associates hold that a developmental theory of humor must take individual differences into account. Furthermore, one must consider the issue of stability vs. change. Do the content, initiation, appreciation, and other factors associated with humor change through the adult years and, if so, how? Are these changes seen in everyone, or do they vary markedly by individual dispositions? Other questions relate to the possible relationships between certain personality characteristics and preferences for particular forms of humor.

According to McGhee (1983), humor appreciation is related to the individual's cognitive stage of functioning and therefore should not be expected to change after adolescence unless there is some form of cognitive regression. In other words, once developed and barring dementia, the cognitive aspects of humor remain essentially unchanged, although its content may reflect different needs, concerns, and interests of different periods of life. The theme varies; the structure does not.

For example, while the structure of knock-knock jokes persists, their content varies. A child's knock-knock joke could go as follows:

"Knock, knock!"
"Who's there?"
"Dwayne."
"Dwayne who?"
"Dwayne the bathtub. I'm dwowning" (Mindess, 1987, p. 84).

An adult's variation, using the same structure, might go:

"Knock, knock!"
"Who's there?"
"Louisville."
"Louisville who?"
"Louise will, but Rosie won't!"

In a recent article, McGhee, Ruch, & Hehl (1990) emphasize the relationship between one's mastery of more advanced levels of cognitive functioning and humor. To consider something humorous, a person has to be at the right stage of development. For example, the following joke requires a grasp of Piagetian conservation (the concept that quantity or number remains the same regardless of changes in shape of position).

> A man goes to the pizza parlor and orders a pizza. He is asked whether it should be cut into six or eight slices. "Six. I'm not very hungry."

One has to master the skills at one's particular developmental level before one can play with them.

Drawing on a series of empirical studies, McGhee and his associates developed a developmental model of humor that extends to about age 60. They focused on two kinds of humor: nonsense and incongruity plus resolution. Consideration was also given to both positive and negative responses to various kinds of humor. Laughter is a positive response, for example, while the most obvious negative response is to view the humor as not humorous. People with different personality characteristics will also have varying kinds of responses to humor. Introverts and extroverts respond differently, as do those with either an internal or an external locus of control.

Loeb and Wood (1986) take a less quantitative approach. Using an Eriksonian model of development, they make the interesting suggestion that the more secure we are, the more we are able to use humor. If we are secure enough in the positive side of each of the eight Eriksonian normative bipolar crises, then we can use humor to help us deal with the negative aspects. For example, when we deal with the crisis of Intimacy vs. Isolation, we are more likely to trade jokes about marriage, bachelorhood, and "old maids" (a term that has dropped out of the social vocabulary except for the eponymous card game). Presumably, as we deal with the final Eriksonian crisis of Integrity vs. Despair, there are a series of death-related jokes. For example:

> A man dies and goes to heaven where he is met by the Virgin Mary. After processing his papers, she asks if he has any questions before entering heaven. "Yes, just one. I have always noticed how sad you look in all the pictures and statues of you. How come?" After a brief pause, the Virgin Mary responds, "Well, to tell you the truth, I always wanted a daughter."

Humor from Adolescence through Adulthood: Some Speculations

Although developmental psychology textbooks usually have little or nothing to say about humor, there is evidence that one's sense of humor undergoes developmental changes as one moves from adolescence through the adult years.

The ability to laugh at oneself or one's social category is adaptive. Furthermore, as Mindess (1987) observes, humor evidences one's hope and delight at being alive. With humor one can change the world, create or recreate one's realities. Humor involves, as Koestler (1964) pointed out, "an act of creation." Mindess (1987) emphasizes that "Creation, dissolution, and re-creation are embedded in human development" (p. 94). This suggests that our sense of humor can change and become more complex.

An equally optimistic approach stems from the work of Schaie (1977), who observed that most earlier models of intellectual development were limited to acquiring problem-solving skills. The pressures of adulthood require cognitive changes, according to Schaie. In adulthood we move through cognitive stages that emphasize the functions of being acquisitive, achieving, responsible, executive, and reintegrative. If cognitive development does not end in late adolescence or early adulthood, there is a strong possibility that there are also developmental changes in our sense of humor. One would expect increased complexity both in the humor we initiate and in the humor we appreciate. One would expect increased spontaneity in both initiation and appreciation, greater use of environmental stimuli, and greater discrimination in humor appreciation. We would be better able to understand what others laugh at even if we choose not to laugh at it ourselves. Increased tolerance for ambiguity brings with it greater opportunities for humor because one can entertain several frames of reference and enjoy the tensions and incongruities among them.

Personality is usually defined as an individual's enduring traits that differentiate her or him from other individuals. Given continuity in personality, then, one would expect the characteristics of humor initiation and appreciation to show some signs of stability over the lifespan. Continuity does not mean lack of change (Atchley, 1989). As we develop a greater repertoire of experiences, we have more possibilities upon which to draw in humor behavior. And if appreciation of complex humor is associated with intelligence, then we should expect both individual differences and a degree of within-individual stability. This would be accompanied by greater appreciation for more complex kinds of humor.

An individual's threshold for humor may remain stable, but the nature of the stimuli that reach this threshold may change. One's sense of timing may become more precise. One could also assume that with increased cognitive complexity there would be an increased humor reaction to paradoxical situations. An example is the famous Charles Addams cartoon that depicts a pair of ski tracks coming toward a tree, separating around the tree trunk, and then once again coming together.

The general hypothesis here is that developmental changes do occur in one's sense of humor throughout adulthood. This theory suggests that the complexity in the content of what one appreciates as humor increases, the sources of humor proliferate, appreciation widens, and creativity of the individual's humor shows an overall growth. Greater responsiveness to increasing sophistication in humor stimuli also develops.

This is not to deny individual differences in humor. With increasing adult age there are also increased individual differences in many aspects of thought and behavior. Furthermore, the existence of relatively humorless people cannot be denied. Nevertheless, the emphasis should be on the reality of growth and change in one's sense of humor through the adult years. Humor does not necessarily plateau any more than do other aspects of human development.

On Uses and Abuses of Humor

When Norman Cousins (1976) published his autobiographical *Anatomy of an Illness*, many learned from it that humor might be helpful in treating illness; others began to examine humor as a therapeutic technique. Renewed attention was given to the use of humor in the classroom to facilitate learning, by dentists to ease pain, and, possibly, in classrooms full of dentists to ease the pain of learning. Although this flurry of attention has been introducing some new concepts and techniques, the therapeutic use of humor is not unique to late twentieth-century thinking. Koller (1988) reminds us that centuries ago, people spoke of being in "good humors." This pleasant state could be achieved by having the right balance between the four (assumed) humors of bile, phlegm, choler, and blood.

As a society we seek practical applications of scientific findings. One result can be seen in the form of specialists who are advocating and implementing "applied humor" (Silberman, 1987). Professional organizations offer workshops to increase humor skills on the assumption that the humorless can become humorous. This attempt to put humor into utilitarian harness does not necessarily either add pleasure or heighten effectiveness. All too often, contrived humor replaces spontaneous humor, amid the insistence on *using* humor. ("Now it is your turn to say something funny, Mr. Hickenlooper!"). Forced, hence unfunny, humor can be more depressing than the lack of humor; consider, for example, annual meetings of nursing home associations!

The relentless humor approach has become sufficiently popular to have won media attention. For example, in the *Cincinnati Enquirer's* "Laughter, the Best Medicine," MacDonald (1991) describes humor seminars intended to help cancer patients. She writes about physicians and other health care workers who attend workshops and training sessions on "How to be Humorous." She also lists a source for a catalog of therapeutically humorous materials.

Contrived therapeutic humor, like the ersatz affection offered by some professional human service workers, threatens to become the false coin of significant interactions. When pursued in a narrow and unreflective manner, this approach leads us to seek the lowest common denominator in humor and, therefore, the lowest cognitive level. The power of humor is great, but, unlike penicillin, it is difficult to apply by prescription.

▼ MILDRED M. SELTZER

See also: Age 40; Body Senses; Individuality; Intelligence; Listening Across the Lifespan; Memory; Mental Health in the Adult Years; Taste and Smell; Vision.

References

Aristotle. (1967). *Poetics*. Ann Arbor, MI: University of Michigan Press. (original ca. 335 B.C.)

Atchley, R. C. (1989). A continuity theory of normal aging. *The Gerontologist, 29*: 183-89.

Berger, A. A. (1986). Humor, the psyche, and society. *American Behavioral Scientist, 30*: 6-15.

Bergson, H. (1980). Laughter. In W. Sypher (Ed.), *Comedy*. Baltimore: Johns Hopkins University Press, pp. 61-190.

Butcher, S. H. (1907). *Aristotle's Theory of Poetry and Fine Art with a Critical Text and Translation of the Poetics*. Fourth Edition. London: Macmillan.

Cousins, N. (1976). *Anatomy of an Illness*. New York: Norton.

Eco, U. (1983). *The Name of the Rose*. New York: Harcourt Brace Jovanovich.

Freud, S. (1938). *Wit and Its Relation to the Unconscious*. New York: Random House.

———. (1952). Humor. In J. Strachey (Ed.), *Sigmund Freud: Collected Papers*. Volume 5. London: The Hogarth Press, pp. 215-21.

Fry, W. F. (1987). Humor and paradox. *American Behavioral Scientist, 30*: 42-71.

Grotjahn, M. (1987). Dynamics of Jewish jokes. *American Behavioral Scientist, 30*: 96-99.

Haig, R. A. (1988). *The Anatomy of Humor: Biopsychological and Therapeutic Perspectives*. Springfield, IL: Charles C. Thomas.

Hobbes, T. (1950). *Leviathan*. Clinton, MA: The Colonial Press.

Janko, R. (1984). *Aristotle on Comedy: Towards a Reconstruction of Poetics II*. Berkeley, CA: University of California Press.

Koestler, A. (1964). *The Act of Creation*. New York: Dell.

Koller, M. R. H. (1988). *Humor and Society: Explorations in the Sociology of Humor*. Houston: Cap and Gown Press.

LaPointe, L. L., Mower, D. M., & Case. J. L. (1990). A comparative acoustic analysis of the laughter responses of 20- and 70-year-old males. *International Journal of Aging and Human Development, 31*: 1-9.

Loeb, M., & Wood, V. (1986). Epilogue: A nascent idea for an Eriksonian model of humor. In L. Nahemow, K. A. McCluskey-Fawcett, & P. E. McGhee (Eds.), *Humor and Aging*. New York: Academic Press, pp. 279-84.

MacDonald, S. (1991). Laughter: The best medicine. *The Cincinnati Enquirer*, December 11, pp. C1, C5.

McGhee, P. E. (1983). Humor development: Toward a life span approach. In P. E. McGhee & J. H. Goldstein (Eds.), *Handbook of Humor Research*. Volume 1, *Basic Issues*. New York: Springer-Verlag, pp. 109-34.

———. (1986). Humor across the lifespan: Sources of developmental change and individual differences. In L. Nahemow, K. A. McCluskey-Fawcett, & P. E. McGhee (Eds.), *Humor and Aging*. New York: Academic Press, pp. 27-51.

———. (1989). (Ed.). *Humor and Children's Development: A Guide to Practical Applications*. New York: The Haworth Press, pp. 1-12.

McGhee, P. E., Ruch, W., & Hehl, F. J. (1990). A personality-based model of humor development during adulthood. *International Journal of Humor, 3*: 121-46.

Mindess, H. (1987). The panarama of humor and the meaning of life. *American Behavioral Scientist, 30*: 82-95.

Nahemow, L. (1986). Humor as a data base for the study of aging. In L. Nahemow, K. A.

McCluskey-Fawcett, & P. E. McGhee (Eds.), *Humor and Aging*. New York: Academic Press, pp. 3-26.

Nahemow, L., McCluskey-Fawcett, K. A., & McGhee, P. E. (Eds.). (1986). *Humor and Aging*. New York: Academic Press.

Schaie, K. W. (1977). Toward a stage theory of adult cognitive development. *International Journal of Aging and Human Development, 8*: 129-37.

Seltzer, M. M. (1986). Timing: The significant common variable in both humor and aging. In L. Nahemow, K. A. McCluskey-Fawcett, & P. E. McGhee (Eds.), *Humor and Aging*. New York: Academic Press, pp. 121-37.

Silberman, I. N. (1987). Humor and Health. *American Behavioral Scientist, 30*: 100-12.

Simons, C. J. R., McCluskey-Fawcett, K. A., & Papini, D. R. (1986). Theoretical and functional perspectives on the development of humor during infancy, childhood, and adolescence. In L. Nahemow, K. A. McCluskey-Fawcett, & P. E. McGhee (Eds.), *Humor and Aging*. New York: Academic Press, pp. 53-80.

Veeser, H. A. (1988). Holmes goes to carnival: Embarrassing the signifier in Eco's anti-detective novel. In M. T. Inge (Ed.), *Naming the Rose: Essays on Eco's The Name of the Rose*. Jackson, MS: University Press of Mississippi, pp. 101-15.

The author is grateful to Lawrence W. Sherman of the Department of Educational Psychology, Miami University, for helpful comments.

INDIVIDUALITY

Our implicit understanding of the word *development* suggests a consistent process in which everyone changes in more or less the same way over time. Studies of adults' lives, however, indicate that people change in different ways, at different times, as a result of different experiences (Howe, 1982; Vaillant, 1977). This article is concerned with differences among adults in their characteristic patterns of development. It begins by considering the sources of continuity and change in adults' behavior and experiences. These observations provide a basis for understanding how adults create coherent patterns of differential behavior over time. The implications of these patterns for understanding adult development are then discussed.

Conceptual Background

Interactional Theory. Psychological theories of individual development are often based on an interactional approach (Kenrick & Furder, 1988; Lerner & Tubman, 1989; Magnusson, 1988). The interactional approach holds that (a) people decide to enter certain situations and (b) people's actions in these situations are influenced both by their own existing characteristics and by salient features of the situations or environmental events to which they are exposed. Just exposure to various situations induces changes in the individual through mechanisms such as learning and cognition, so the individual's actions

are held to induce changes in the situations to which they are exposed.

Studies of adults' lives have provided support for this interactional approach. In a longitudinal study of AT&T managers, Bray, Campbell, & Grant (1974) found that individuals whose characteristics indicated greater managerial potential were given more challenging assignments for their first jobs. Experience in these advanced positions, however, contributed to the more rapid development of managerial skills and more rapid career progression. In another longitudinal study, Caspi (1987) found that explosive individuals had problems in later life presumably because they could not adapt to the demands made by work and family situations in adulthood. In these and many other studies a pattern emerges in which the individual and the situation can be seen to influence each other.

Change. The situations to which individuals are exposed change in a systematic fashion throughout adulthood. At least five phenomena contribute to these ongoing changes in situational exposures:

1. Learning may lead individuals to change their perceptions and actions in a situation over time (Ackerman, 1986).
2. People may seek out new situations to promote their long-term well-being (Brandstadter, 1984).
3. Social and occupational role demands change over time as a result of other people's expectations (Havighurst, 1953).
4. Broad historic changes in society—such as war or the emergence of new tech-

nologies—may thrust people into new situations (Sternberg & Lubart, 1991).

5. Chance encounters may lead to exposure to new and unanticipated situations (Handal, 1987).

Because these forces lead to organized changes in the situations to which individuals are exposed, subsequent learning should lead to progressive change in the individual's differential characteristics. The literature on adult development provides ample support for this proposition. For example, Elder and Clipp (1989) found that exposure to combat experiences led to greater resilience after initial stress faded away. Schooler (1984) observed that exposure to cognitively demanding situations led to gains in intelligence throughout the lifespan. Similarly, Howard and Bray (1990) found that the cognitive demands of managerial jobs led to gains in cognitive abilities such as analytical reasoning as well as to personality attributes such as independence. These enhanced personal abilities in turn contributed to effective performance in the managerial positions. Finally, in an autobiographical study, Handal (1987) concluded that unanticipated events stand out in people's minds and seem to play an important role in shaping their lives.

Stability. The preceding observations concerning ongoing changes in situational exposure and their impact on the individual might lead one to suspect that people are in a constant state of flux even during the supposedly stable adult years. While few psychologists deny that people do change, it has become clear that change occurs in a highly systematic or structured manner. People are able to change, then, while still maintaining a substantial coherence in their lives.

Recent studies suggest that people seem to maintain their individual characteristics even as development leads to changes in the situations they encounter. Costa and McCrae (1980) and McCrae and Costa (1990) administered measures of neuroticism, openness, extraversion, agreeableness, and conscientiousness to adults between ages 25 and 90. Ten-year retest reliabilities in the .50 to .80 range were obtained: This consistency over time indicates substantially more stability in adult personality than might be expected on the basis of purely situational grounds. Other studies by Rokeach (1973), Campbell (1971), and Terman and Oden (1959) have provided evidence for the stability of values, interests, and cognitive abilities in adulthood. Howard and Bray's (1990) findings also indicate that change in adulthood often results in further growth in areas of strength. This is the individual developmental parallel to the proverb that "the rich get richer." Adults often improve themselves in areas that they perceive to be of special value to them. This directed and coherent growth, in turn, tends to maintain, extend, and stabilize existing characteristics rather than induce radical change.

Developmental Patterns

Ecology Model. At this point, a new question comes to the fore. How do individuals go about generating patterns of continuity and change during adulthood? The author and his colleagues have proposed a potential answer to this question by focusing on the origins of coherent developmental patterns vis-à-vis the ecology model (Mumford & Owens, 1984; Mumford, Stokes, & Owens, 1990; & Mumford, Uhlman, & Kilkullen, in press). The ecology model is intended to describe differential development in adulthood. This model holds that adults are active, goal-oriented entities who seek to maximize their long-term adaptation in a world that presents many changing environmental opportunities through their continued learning, cognition, and action.

However, adults are presented with a fundamental problem in their search for adaptation: the limitations on their time and energy. Adults must select situations and potential actions in these situations so as to maximize long-term adaptation. Individuals select situations based on their beliefs about the personal desirability of the situational outcomes (Baron & Boudreau, 1987). Once they have entered a situation, however, they become more knowledgeable about or sensitive to its implications (Wagner & Sternberg,

1984). At the same time, they are apt to develop personality characteristics or resources that will help them to achieve the desired outcomes (Hulin, Herry, & Noon, 1990). When outcomes are satisfying, the prior development of knowledge structures and those skills, abilities, and personality characteristics contributing to effective action should lead individuals to select similar situations in the future. Over time, this process of choice and development should lead to the emergence of a highly refined set of individual characteristics for the identification and exploitation of a certain class of situations.

Because no single class of situations is likely to satisfy all of an individual's needs, people must enter a number of different kinds of situations and engage in different actions within these situations. Furthermore, their differential characteristics will be developing in all these situations. Their choices must therefore be complementary and compensatory rather than competing. When the individual's choices are coupled with the explicit selective acts and the structured, self-reinforcing expectations that society has for individuals, then coherent patterns of differential behaviors and experiences should emerge (Abeles, Steel, & Wise, 1982; Caspi, Bem, & Elder, 1989). Thus, the unique but organized choices that adults make in their structured social environment enable them to create coherent patterns of continuity and change even when confronted with a shifting environment. Furthermore, change will often represent an extension of existing characteristics. This promotes stability and systematic transformations in behavior, based on situational demands. Difficulty in making choices similarly will lead to a continuing pattern that lacks coherency. For example, Pulkkinen (1982) found that adolescents who lacked self-control tended to do poorly in school and then encountered problems with social relationships, drugs, and employment as they entered young adulthood.

Patterns of Differential Development. People's unique experiences lead them to develop in unique ways. Nonetheless, situational exposures and people's differential characteristics are organized in a systematic fashion. To identify common patterns of differential development in adulthood, several investigators obtained descriptions of people's behavior and experiences at different points in their lives (Block, 1971; Mumford & Owens, 1984; Owens & Schoenfeldt, 1979). Subgroups of individuals who were similar with respect to their behavior and experiences at different points in their lives were identified through cluster analysis. The results indicated that most people's lives could be described by reference to a limited number of developmental patterns. One group, for example, could be described as the *Competent Nurturers*. This subgroup contained rather traditional women from warm, supportive families who did well in school and were interested in biology, medicine, and teaching. In the college years, they continued this pattern but became more involved in social activities. During their postcollege years, they were married, committed to their families, and involved in community service work.

Although this research identified a number of other patterns as well, virtually all of them display the same kind of coherence, reflecting systematic and predictable transformations in characteristic behavior and experiences as people use their existing characteristics to adapt to new situations. Further research investigating the characteristics of these patterns has provided support for other tenets of the ecology model. For instance, individuals expressing certain developmental patterns tended to enter and perform well in certain occupations and college majors (Schoenfeldt, 1974). Furthermore, patterns expressed in earlier years seem to condition the patterns of behavior and experience that are seen in the later adult years (Stokes, Mumford, & Owens, 1989). These patterns also seem to condition the implications of certain behaviors in a given developmental period such that individuals raised in a bad family environment were not adversely affected by adolescent rebellion. For individuals raised in a good family environment, however, adolescent rebellion presaged problems in adjustment and achievement in adulthood (Mumford, Stokes, & Owens, 1990). Finally, these subgroups have been found to be especially strong predictors of academic underachievement, responses to projective tests, and personal goals and values (Owens & Schoenfeldt, 1979).

Individuals might seek different outcomes and value fulfillments even when dealing with similar situations, and the resulting differences in their actions might lead to qualitative differences in their subsequent development. Mumford, Snell, and Hein (in press) examined this hypothesis in a recent study that was concerned with continuity and change in religious involvement. On the basis of the earlier work of William James (1902), they argued that adults' religious involvement might be conditioned either by the economic instrumental value of religious institutions or as a channel for emotional expression. Some subgroups were found to respond to religious institutions on the basis of their instrumental implications while others responded on the basis of their expressive implications. Subsequently, models of continuity and change were constructed for the two subgroups, instrumentals and expressives. Religious involvement was found to be somewhat more stable for instrumentals than for expressives between adolescence and young adulthood. Collegiate bohemianism and literary pursuits were associated with decreased religious involvement for expressives, while adolescent social effectiveness and family commitments in young adulthood contributed to religious involvement for instrumentals. It can be seen, then, that the variables influencing continuity and change depend on individuals' broader developmental pattern and the experiences that are implied by this pattern at a given point in their lives.

Pattern Emergence

We have already seen that developmental patterns are coherent and allow for both continuity and change. But how do these patterns begin in the first place? A recent study found that people tend to see their lives unfolding like a story (Howard, 1991). There is reason to believe that these stories might represent something more than retrospective construction. Mumford, Snell, and Reiter-Palmon (in press) draw upon the ecology model and the theory of self-maintained developmental patterns to suggest that people may make significant changes in a rapidly changing environment without resorting to extensive conscious analyses. One does not always have to stop and think through all the possible long-term implications of emerging situations and one's own action choices. Instead, people may compare the immediate situation to their guiding mental model or "opportunistic planning template" (Hayes-Roth & Hayes-Roth, 1979; Krietler & Krietler, 1987). This model represents an idealized image of how life should come out. It reflects a storylike integration of needs, values, beliefs about oneself, beliefs about the world, and role models provided by significant others. The fit of particular situations to this mental model or template is held to generate different kinds of affect (Higgins, 1987). This affect or feeling-state guides one's evaluation of the situation and choice of action. Fairly rapid comparison of the situation against one's preexisting mental model makes it possible to generate a coherent pattern of choices and differential development without the need for extensive conscious processing.

These mental models begin to form in late childhood or early adolescence, followed by a period of testing and refinement. At some point, however, developing individuals find a set of situations and social roles that enable them to express their personal story or mental model. This discovery or invention ends the period of exploration. It leads to the crystallization of developmental patterns as defined by a set of stable and coherent choices.

In the first test of this hypothesis, Mumford, Wesley, and Shaffer (1987) found that individuals differ in the time at which their developmental pattern crystallizes. The timing of crystallization depends on the ability of individuals to apply their models or stories effectively in the situations that confront them. As a result, individuals who could adapt to the traditional social roles that permeate the adolescent environment tended to crystallize relatively early, while individuals who were oriented toward more nontraditional intellectual approaches tended to crystallize in college.

In a later investigation, Wesley (1989) examined how crystallization influenced choices. He found that crystallized individuals were more likely to move into occupations that fit their broader developmental patterns. Furthermore, crystallized individuals tended to display more pronounced positive and negative emotional reactions to good and poor matches than individuals who had not yet crystallized and were still exploring their options. In accordance with this observation, Snell (1990) found that individuals were more sensitive to change influences in the period preceding crystallization. Thus, the degree of continuity and change observed in studies of individuality may depend on both the person and his or her prior developmental history.

Differential Capacities

Ability and Personality Characteristics. Not all choices can be made on the basis of affect or feeling-state alone. Furthermore, people must be capable of generating and implementing actions that will allow them to attain desired outcomes in a situation. Under conditions where the nature of situations is subject to change, one needs to apply intelligence, or the ability to reason with knowledge. The evidence compiled by Terman and Oden (1959) indicates that intelligence can have a marked impact on people's lives. More intelligent people are likely to have better jobs and happier marriages, and they are also likely to report more satisfaction with their lives.

Intelligence is not the only differential characteristic that influences behavior and experience. McCrae (1987), for instance, has shown that openness may have a significant

impact on the course of lives because it contributes to the willingness to try out new courses of action. The trait of openness enables some people to be more sensitive to change. Similarly, Bandura (1989) has illustrated how high self-esteem contributes to actions in various situations and to the capability for acquiring new knowledge or skills in these situations.

Psychologists have identified hundreds of cognitive abilities and personality characteristics. These characteristics can influence differential development in adulthood in a wide variety of ways. Personality characteristics typically lead individuals to prefer certain kinds of actions in their attempts to gain certain values or outcomes. Thus, an extroverted and rather social person might try to get a raise by working with others, while an introvert might try to get the same raise by writing a better report. The resulting differences in their actions may lead to the development of different skills that, in turn, will encourage them to enter different kinds of situations in the future and pursue different courses of development. Similarly, Ackerman (1986) and Fleishman (1972) have shown that broad cognitive abilities, such as intelligence and spatial visualization, promote the development of different kinds of skills and may therefore lead to differences in people's later experience—and thereby again influence differential development. Because the skills developing from personality and abilities will influence later decisions made by the individual, they will tend to contribute to the maintenance and growth of these characteristics.

Knowledge. Abilities and personality influence differential adult development in another way. By conditioning the person's experience in different areas, abilities and personality contribute to the development of knowledge. In turn, knowledge shapes our actions in a situation.

This observation has led Bandura (1989), Brandstadter (1984), and Sternberg and Lubart (1991) to suggest that knowledge may play an important role in guiding differential development. On a more subtle level, they suggest that the ability to acquire and apply certain kinds of knowledge can also influence differential development. For example, individuals differ with respect to their skills in problem finding, as well as their self-awareness and self-esteem, and each of these characteristics can either promote or restrict the acquisition and application of knowledge. One illustration of these principles can be found in studies of creativity (Sternberg & Lubart, 1991). The exposure to and the acquisition of different kinds of knowledge lead people to be creative in different ways at different points in their lives.

Conclusion

This consideration of a number of influences on differential development in adulthood supports the conclusion that adults are not static entities. They grow and change. The growth and change, however, are not random. They proceed from the past that conditions the individual's selection of actions in his or her changing life situations. Thus, adults display coherent patterns of development.

These coherent patterns of development, however, are not the same for all individuals because these individuals have not been exposed to the same situations. Furthermore, they seek different things in these situations. As a result, adults develop different realms and levels of knowledge, varying skills, abilities, and personality characteristics, enter different situations, and change in different ways at different times. To put the matter a little differently: The accumulation of experience with development does not eliminate differences—it accentuates them. Moreover, the developmental process itself reflects the unique characteristics of individuals as they choose the situations that make up their lives. Thus, one cannot understand either individuals or development as separate entities. One must seek to understand adult development from the perspective of the individual engaged in creating his or her life.

▼ Michael D. Mumford

See also: Body Senses; Career Age; Centenarians; Development and Aging in Historical Perspective; Disengagement Theory; Exercise; Friendships through the Adult Years; Gender as a Shaping Force in Adult Development and Aging; Information Processing; Intelligence; Learning and Memory in Everyday Life; Life Events; Mental Health in the Adult Years; Metaphors of the Life Course; Religion in Adult Life; Work Organization Membership and Behavior.

References

Abeles, R. P., Steel, L., & Wise, L. L. (1980). Patterns and implications of life-course organization: Studies from Project Talent. In P. B. Baltes & O. G. Brim (Eds.), *Life-span Development and Behavior*. New York: Academic Press, pp. 308-39.

Ackerman, P. C. (1986). Individual differences in information processing: An investigation of intellectual abilities and task performance during practice. *Intelligence, 10:* 100-39.

Bandura, A. (1989). Human agency and social cognitive theory. *American Psychologist, 44:* 1175-84.

Baron, R. M., & Boudreau, L. A. (1987). An ecological perspective on integrating personality and social psychology. *Journal of Personality and Social Psychology, 53:* 1222-28.

Block, J. (1971). *Lives Through Time*. Berkeley, CA: Bancroft.

Brandstadter, J. (1984). Personal self-regulation of development: Cross-sequential analyses of development-related control beliefs and emotions. *Developmental Psychology, 25:* 96-108.

Bray, D. W., Campbell, R. J., & Grant, P. L. (1974). *Formative Years in Business: A Long-Term AT&T Study of Managerial Lives*. New York: Wiley.

Campbell, D. P. (1971). *Manual for the Strong-Campbell Vocational Interest Invention*. Palo Alto, CA: Stanford University Press.

Caspi, A. (1987). Personality in the life course. *Journal of Personality and Social Psychology, 53:* 1203-13.

Caspi, A., Bem, D. J., & Elder, G. H. (1989). Continuities and consequences of interactional styles across the life course. *Journal of Personality, 57:* 375-405.

Costa, P. T., & McCrae, R. R. (1980). Still stable after all these years: Personality as a key to some issues in adulthood and old age. In P. B. Baltes & O. G. Brim (Eds.), *Life-span Development and Behavior*. Volume 3. New York: Academic Press, pp. 65-102.

Elder, G. H., & Clipp, E. C. (1989). Combat experience and emotional health. *Journal of Personality, 57:* 311-42.

Fleishman, E. A. (1972). On the relation between learning abilities and skill acquisition. *American Psychologist, 27:* 1017-32.

Handal, A. (1987). Personal theories about the lifespan development of one's self in autobiographical self-presentations of adults. *Human Development, 50:* 83-98.

Havighurst, R. (1953). *Human Development and Education.* New York: Longmans.

Hayes-Roth, B., & Hayes-Roth, F. (1979). A cognitive model of planning. *Cognitive Science, 3:* 275-310.

Higgins, T. E. (1987). Self Discrepancy: A theory relating self and affect. *Psychological Review, 94:* 319-40.

Howard, A., & Bray, D. W. (1990). *Managerial Lives in Transition: Advancing Age and Changing Times.* New York: Guilford Press.

Howard, G. S. (1991). Culture tales: A narrative approach to thinking, cross-cultural psychology, and psychotherapy. *American Psychologist, 46:* 186-97.

Howe, M. J. (1982). Biographical evidence and the development of outstanding individuals. *American Psychologist, 37:* 1071-81.

Hulin, C. L., Herry, R. A., & Noon, S. L. (1990). Adding a dimension: Time as a factor in the generalizability of predictive relationships. *Psychological Bulletin, 107:* 328-46.

James, W. (1902). *Varieties of Religious Experience.* Boston, MA: Houghton-Mifflin.

Kenrick, D. T., & Furder, D. C. (1988). Profiting from controversy: Lessons from the person-situation debate. *American Psychologist, 43:* 23-34.

Krietler, D., & Krietler, H. (1987). Plans and planning: Their motivational and cognitive antecedents. In S. C. Friedman, E. K. Scholnick, & R. R. Cocking (Eds.), *Blueprints for Thinking: The Role of Planning in Cognitive Development.* New York: Cambridge University Press, pp. 117-36.

Lerner, R. M., & Tubman, J. G. (1989). Conceptual issues in studying continuity and discontinuity in personality development across the lifespan. *Journal of Personality, 57:* 343-74.

Magnusson, D. (1988). Individual development from an interactional perspective. In D. Magnusson (Ed.), *Paths Through Life.* Hillsdale, NJ: Lawrence Erlbaum, pp. 1-21.

McCrae, R. R. (1987). Creativity, divergent thinking, and openness to experience. *Journal of Personality and Social Psychology, 52:* 1258-65.

McCrae, R. R., & Costa, P. T. (1990). *Personality in Adulthood.* New York: Guilford Press.

Mumford, M. D., & Owens, W. A. (1984). Individuality in a developmental context: Some empirical and theoretical considerations. *Human Development, 27:* 84-108.

Mumford, M. D., Snell, A. F., & Hein, M. B. (In press). Varieties of religious experience: Person influences on continuity and change. *Journal of Personality.*

Mumford, M. D., Snell, A. F., & Reiter-Palmon, R. (In press). Personality and background data: Life history and self-concepts in an ecological system. In G. S. Stokes, M. D. Mumford, & W. A. Owens (Eds.), *Handbook of Background Data Research: Theories, Measures, and Applications.* Palo Alto, CA: Consulting Psychologists Press.

Mumford, M. D., Stokes, G. S., & Owens, W. A. (1990). *Patterns of Life Adaptation: The Ecology of Human Individuality.* Hillsdale, NJ: Lawrence Erlbaum.

Mumford, M. D., Uhlman, E. E., & Kilkullen, R. J. (In press). The structure of life history: Implications for the construct validity of background data scales. *Human Performance.*

Mumford, M. D., Wesley, S. S., & Shaffer, G. S. (1987). Individuality in developmental context. II: The crystallization of developmental trajectories. *Human Performance, 30:* 292-321.

Owens, W. A., & Schoenfeldt, L. F. (1979). Toward a classification of persons. *Journal of Applied Psychology, 69:* 569-607.

Pulkkinen, C. (1982). Self control and continuity from childhood to adolescence. In P. B. Baltes & O. G. Brim (Eds.), *Life-span Development and Behavior.* Volume 4. New York: Academic Press, pp. 209-26.

Rokeach, M. (1973). *The Structure of Human Values.* New York: Free Press.

Schoenfeldt, L. F. (1974). Utilization of manpower: Development and evaluation of an assessment classification model for matching individuals with jobs. *Journal of Applied Psychology, 59:* 583-95.

Schooler, C. (1984). Psychological effects of couples environments during the life span: A review and theory. *Intelligence, 8:* 254-81.

Snell, A. F. (1990). *Crystallization as a Moderator of Continuity and Change in Religious Involvement.* Master's thesis, The Georgia Institute of Technology, Atlanta.

Sternberg, R. J., & Lubart, T. I. (1991). An investment theory of creativity and its development. *Human Development, 34:* 1-31.

Stokes, G. S., Mumford, M. D., & Owens, W. A. (1989). Life history prototypes in the study of human individuality. *Journal of Personality, 57:* 509-45.

Terman, L. M., & Oden, G. (1959). *The Gifted Group at Mid-Life.* Palo Alto, CA: Stanford University Press.

Vaillant, G. E. (1977). *Adaptation to Life.* Boston: Little, Brown.

Wagner, R. K., & Sternberg, R. J. (1984). Alternative conceptions of intelligence and their implications for education. *Review of Educational Research, 54:* 179-223.

Wesley, S.S. (1989). *Background Data Subgroups and Career Outcomes: Some Developmental Influences on Person-Job Matching.* Doctoral dissertation, The Georgia Institute of Technology, Atlanta.

INFORMATION PROCESSING

Human cognition is best understood through analysis of the mental representations and cognitive processes that intervene between the presentation of a stimulus and the occurrence of a response. This is the core principle within the information-processing framework. This framework is based on ideas that arose in the late 1950s with the weakening of the influence of behaviorism and the emergence of cognitive psychology.

A common activity such as driving an automobile can illustrate the breadth of the information processing perspective. The operator of a moving vehicle has to:

- Continuously perceive changing environmental stimulation
- Respond by selecting and making effective responses
- Monitor progress along the route
- Anticipate actions of other vehicles
- Converse with passengers, if present

Each of these activities involves a considerable amount of processing in the sense that numerous transformations occur between the stimuli and the responses. A primary goal of information-processing research is to understand the nature of these transformations and to discover the factors that limit the amount of processing that can be carried out at any given time.

Early research based on concepts derived from information theory was highly encouraging because it supported the proposition that humans could meaningfully be regarded as processors of information. For example, one discovery was that the time required to respond to a stimulus was a linear function of the amount of information in the stimulus. This finding held true when information was measured either in terms of the probability of the stimulus or in terms of the number of possible stimulus alternatives. Now known as the *Hick-Lyman Law* in honor of two of the first investigators of the phenomenon, this relationship has proven to be extremely robust and is still widely accepted as a fundamental characteristic of human performance. Another line of research inspired by information theory concepts focused on the *channel capacity* of the human information-processing system. These studies determined the maximum number of discrete values along a unidimensional continuum that could be accurately distinguished.

Much of the original information-processing research was based on quantitative measures of information defined in terms of *bits.* A bit corresponded to a 50 percent reduction in uncertainty. This formal interpretation of information was gradually abandoned, however. Most contemporary researchers consider information to be whatever is manipulated or transformed during the performance of a cognitive task. A goal shared by almost all proponents of the information-processing perspective is that of specifying the identity and sequence of the operations responsible for converting (stimulus) input into (response) output. Posner and McLeod (1982) described this orientation as follows:

> We take it as fundamental to all information processing models that they incorporate a certain number of elementary mental pro-

cesses or operations, a concatenation of which can produce complex behavior. (p. 478-79)

The information-processing perspective is clearly somewhat reductionistic. The primary aim is to determine the processes responsible for observed behavioral products. In other words, information-processing researchers attempt to focus on *what a person does* in a cognitive task, not simply on the number of successes achieved in a given number of opportunities. However, there are limits to the reductionism attempted, or even considered desirable, by information-processing researchers. A complete reductionism would express all explanations in terms of biochemical mechanisms. Many researchers judge that human cognitive phenomena are too complicated to allow tractable explanations at such a molecular level. More coherent interpretations are possible when concepts are invoked that are more similar in scope and level to the phenomena to be explained.

A basic assumption of the contemporary information-processing perspective, then, is that a useful and meaningful level of analysis exists that is intermediate between the overt behavior and the underlying neuropsychological processes. As implied in the Posner and McLeod (1982) quotation, the units in this intermediate level of analysis are mental processes and the representations on which they are presumed to operate.

Although early information-processing theorists had little interest in individual differences, other researchers soon realized the potential benefits of extending this perspective. The reasoning was quite simple: If cognitive behavior could be explained in terms of the processes or components intervening between stimulus and response, then it should also be possible to interpret individual differences in cognitive behavior in terms of strengths or weaknesses in one or more of these components.

Three examples of research within the information-processing tradition will be briefly described to indicate what is involved in this kind of analysis and to reveal how the procedures have been extended to the investigation of performance differences that are associated with age variation across the adult years.

Examples of Information-Processing Research in Adulthood

The first example is from the area of memory and is based on a relatively simple three-component model. According to this view, which has generated a considerable amount of research, memory involves processes that are concerned with *encoding, storage,* and *retrieval.* Effective memory is assumed to require accurate registration or encoding of the material, its accurate retention or storage until needed, and, finally, its successful recall or retrieval from storage.

Many studies in the field of adult development have attempted to determine which of these three hypothesized processes or components is primarily responsible for age-related memory impairments. One important early study focused on the retrieval component by comparing the performance of young and old adults on recall tests and on recognition or multiple-choice tests (Schonfield & Robertson, 1966). The guiding assumption was that the retrieval requirements of recognition tests would be minimal because the alternatives are present in the tests, but that the demands of traditional recall tests, where the individual has to generate the alternative, would be much more substantial. This assumption seems plausible because it is consistent with the common observation that it is easier to remember something, such as a person's name, when one merely has to select it from a set of alternatives rather than recall it without any other clues. Young adults in Schonfield and Robertson's (1966) experiment were found to be more accurate than older adults in recall tests but not in recognition tests, thus leading the investigators to infer that difficulties with the retrieval component are a major cause of age-associated memory problems.

This conclusion, however, has since been challenged by researchers investigating age-related influences on encoding and storage components. For example, the encoding component has been studied by requiring research participants to engage in various types of distracting activity, or to perform different kinds of operations on the stimulus material while it is being presented. A frequent finding in these studies has been that older adults are more affected by the manipulations than young adults. This has led to the inference that there are age differences in the memory component associated with encoding. Based on somewhat different manipulations, still other results have been interpreted as implicating an age difference in the storage component. With the benefit of hindsight, these inconsistencies in the results probably should not be considered too surprising because the close interdependence of the components suggests that even if quite localized at first, any deficiencies would probably come to affect the memory process in general.

Research on spatial abilities is another area in which information-processing models have been very influential. One model that has inspired a great deal of research was designed to account for performances in tasks requiring rapid decisions about stimuli in different angular orientations. A typical trial might involve the presentation of a geometric pattern or an alphanumeric character in one of several orientations. The research participant is asked to decide as rapidly as possible whether the test stimulus is a normal or a mirror-image version of the pattern or character. Tests of this type often are included in vocational aptitude batteries because they have been found to predict success in occupations such as architecture, engineering, and air transportation (e.g., pilots and air controllers).

The model proposed by Shepard and his colleagues postulates that this task is performed by a sequence of four processing components: *encode* the stimulus, *rotate* it to the upright orientation, *decide* whether the stimulus is normal or mirror image; and *respond*. Because only the second component would be expected to be sensitive to the angular orientation of the stimulus, an estimate of the duration of this component can be obtained from the slope of the line that relates decision time to angular orientation (Shepard & Metzler, 1971). The intercept of the line will then represent the total duration of the remaining components concerned with encoding, decision, and response.

About a dozen studies employing variants of the spatial rotation procedure have now found the slopes of the functions relating decision time to stimulus orientation to be larger for older than for young adults. As implied by Shepard's model, these results have been interpreted as indicating that older adults are less efficient than young adults at rotating, or otherwise transforming, mental representations. Although these results seem to be reliable, they are not sufficient to allow a conclusion that the age differences in spatial abilities have been traced to the processing component that is concerned with spatial transformation. The reason is that statistically significant age differences have also invariably been found in the intercept of the functions relating decision time to angular orientation. This suggests that older adults are also less efficient in one or more components associated with encoding, decision, or response. Adult developmental research guided by this particular information-processing model has led to more precise descriptions of the performance differences, but it has not yet resulted in the isolation of the age-related differences to a single processing component.

Information-processing analyses have also been applied to more complex cognitive tests, such as those designed to assess inductive reasoning ability. Most test batteries used to evaluate intellectual or cognitive abilities include one or more tests of this kind because they are assumed to measure higher-order thinking. An example is the series completion test in which the examinee is required to select the best continuation of a sequence of letters or numbers. Several different information-processing models have been proposed to explain performance on series completion tests, but most include components devoted to discovering the periodicity of the pattern and attempting to infer the relations among elements. In other words, determining the best continuation of a sequence is assumed to demand that one identify the relevant pattern ("which elements?") and then discover how these elements are connected ("which relation?").

One method of investigating possible age differences in components concerned with pattern periodicity and element relations involves manipulating a series completion test. For example, some problems might consist of a simple continuation such as 2-4-6-8-10-??. The successive elements here obviously are related by a rule of +2. Other problems might consist of two interleaved patterns such as 2-9-4-6-6-?? Here, the first, third, and fifth elements are linked by one relation (+2), and the second and fourth elements are linked by a different relation (-3). Finally, the abstractness of the relation can be manipulated by linking the elements with a second-order relation. An example would be 2-4-7-11-16-?? in which the increment from each element to the next is itself changed across elements. In this case the rule would be +2 as the initial value, with an increment of +1 for each successive element, so that $2 + (2) = 4$, $4 + (2 + 1) = 7$, $7 + (2 + 1 + 1) = 11$, etc.

Salthouse and Prill (1987) administered problems such as these to groups of young and old adults. A consistent finding in several independent experiments was that the accuracy difference between young and old adults was greater with the alternating patterns and with the second-order relational patterns than with problems based on a simple continuation. This suggests that both detection of the periodicity of the pattern and identification of the relations among elements were impaired by factors associated with increased age.

One of their experiments (Salthouse & Prill, 1987) extended the process analyses by presenting each element successively and monitoring the time devoted to examining the elements. Analyses of the durations that participants spent inspecting or processing each element revealed that the times were longer for the element in the sequence where the pattern first deviated from a simple continuation. The magnitude of these increases was greater for older than for young adults. These on-line measures obtained while the task was being performed provide valuable confirmation of the inferences that both processing components appear to be affected by age-related changes.

Limitations of the Information-Processing Perspective

Information-processing models have been widely used in guiding research involving adults of various ages. There is now a fairly substantial literature concerned with age differences in various information-processing components (see Salthouse, 1991, for a review). As noted in the preceding discussion, however, the research has tended to reveal age differences in nearly all components that have been investigated. This is apparent in measures that are presumed to reflect the efficiency or time of various components and in measures hypothesized to assess the effectiveness or accuracy of the components. An inference from this research is that *increased age seems to be associated with slower and less successful processing in nearly every processing component that has been investigated.*

The situation just described is clearly not a very desirable outcome if one is attempting to localize or isolate the source of age-related differences because localization or isolation is impossible if differences are evident in virtually every hypothesized component. At least three possible interpretations might account for the finding of age differences in nearly all components that have been investigated:

1. Perhaps the previous studies have been inconsistent because relevant variables were not carefully controlled. If so, more definitive localization of age differences would result from age-comparative studies relying on information-processing procedures after improvements in methodology help to identify, control, and manipulate other important variables.

2. Perhaps current information-processing models are themselves at fault. The existing models may be inadequate because relevant dimensions in which adults of different ages vary have been neglected. For example, many information-processing models have ignored the role of knowledge and experience as determinants of human performance. The implication of this position is that more consistent results will be obtained when more appropriate models have been formulated that include attention to a broader variety of adult development changes.

3. Perhaps neither the current methodology nor the existing models are deficient. Instead, it may be that age-related changes actually do affect many different aspects of processing. In other words, age-related changes may not be discrete and isolated to specific processing components, but instead may be relatively broad and general in nature. This last interpretation has led to an interest in factors that might be common to many facets of processing. The exact nature of these factors is still unknown, but they have come to be referred to as processing *resources* because they are assumed to enable or enhance many kinds of processing—but they are also "scarce," in that they exist in limited quantities. Research inspired by the notion of age-related decreases in some type of processing resources is still in its infancy, but promising results have begun to appear (Salthouse, 1991).

These three alternative interpretations for the lack of success in localizing adult age differences to a small number of critical processing components may appear somewhat abstract. However, the direction of future research concerned with adult age differences in information processing will depend largely on which view acquires the greatest acceptance among active researchers.

Compensation and Adaptation

Another topic that is beginning to receive more attention by researchers concerned with aging and cognition is how competency in many activities can be maintained at high levels. This question is especially important because information-processing research findings seem to suggest that the efficiency or effectiveness of relevant cognitive abilities declines with increased age.

No definitive conclusions are possible on the basis of the available research, but a number of intriguing possibilities have been identified. For example, *it is conceivable that at least some age-related declines are attributable to disuse*. Therefore, levels of performance might be maintained or even improved over the adult years if the individual continues to exercise these abilities. Another alternative is that although some components may be declining, other determinants of performance— perhaps related to knowledge acquired through experience—may be improving such that they *compensate for the declining aspects*. Still another possibility is that people might adapt to their decreased proficiency in certain aspects of cognitive functioning by shifting *the nature of their activities* to emphasize those dependent on components that either do not change with age or may even improve with age.

At present, all of these alternatives must be considered speculative because convincing empirical evidence is not yet available. The hypotheses are nevertheless interesting because they represent a potentially significant direction for future research concerned with information processing in adulthood.

The information-processing perspective emphasizes the analysis of cognitive behavior in terms of simpler processing components. This approach has been enthusiastically adopted by researchers interested in cognitive functioning across adulthood, although the goal of localizing age differences to specific processing components has not yet been achieved. Another important challenge for future information processing researchers is to explain the fact that people do maintain proficient performances in many activities despite age-related declines in relevant processing components.

▼ TIMOTHY A. SALTHOUSE

See also: Body Senses; Cardiac Health; Driving: A Lifespan Challenge; Habituation: A Key to Lifespan Development and Aging?; Individuality; Intelligence; Intelligence—Crystallized and Fluid; Learning and Memory in Everyday Life; Memory; Slowing of Behavior with Age.

References

Posner, M. I., & McLeod, P. (1982). Information processing models: In search of elementary operations. *Annual Review of Psychology, 33:* 477-514.

Salthouse, T. A. (1991). *Theoretical Perspectives in Cognitive Aging.* Hillsdale, NJ: Lawrence Erlbaum Associates.

Salthouse, T. A., & Prill, K. A. (1987). Inferences about age impairments in inferential reasoning. *Psychology and Aging, 2:* 43-51.

Schonfield, A. E. D., & Robertson, E. A. (1966). Memory storage and aging. *Canadian Journal of Psychology, 20:* 228-36.

Shepard, R. N., & Metzler, J. (1971). Mental rotation of three-dimensional objects. *Science, 171:* 701-03.

INTELLIGENCE

What Is Intelligence?

There are both theoretical and practical reasons for seeking an accurate and comprehensive picture of intelligence in adulthood. For example, our ideas about whether our intellectual skills decline as we age may influence such decisions as whether or not to return to school, seek a higher-paying position, or retire. From the societal standpoint, biases about the intellectual functioning of adults have an impact on the hiring, firing, and retraining of older workers in both the private and the public sectors. Mandatory retirement policies also are informed or misinformed by assumptions regarding the intellectual abilities of older workers. Careful and systematic attention is required if we are to understand intellectual change in adulthood. The picture is complex, a variety of theoretical outlooks exist, and methodological concerns in the

pursuit of dependable information cannot be ignored.

Many of the available approaches to intelligence are psychometric in origin, i.e., based on particular tests or measures. Some of these models hypothesize that intelligence consists of one basic or general primary ability, while other models hypothesize that a larger number of abilities and a more complex structure exist (Schaie, 1990). Among the most popular models of intelligence in the adult development literature is Thurstone and Thurstone's (1962) description of five primary mental abilities: verbal meaning, inductive reasoning, number skill, spatial orientation, and word fluency. Much attention has also been given in recent years to the distinction between crystallized and fluid intelligences (Cattell, 1987; Horn, 1985). Ideas about intelligence that are associated with the Wechsler Adult Intelligence Scale have also been quite influential. Piaget's analysis of formal vs. postformal reasoning represents quite a different approach and has stimulated much research and discussion (Rybash, Hoyer, & Roadin, 1986). Two other sets of distinctions are now starting to receive widespread attention: between exercised and unexercised intellectual abilities (Denny, 1982), and between the mechanics (information processing, problem solving) and the pragmatics (wisdom, life-planning skills) of intelligence (Baltes, Dittmann-Kohli, & Dixon, 1984). All of these approaches have contributions to make to our understanding of the nature of intelligence and its development throughout the lifespan.

The available data clearly indicate that intelligence is *multidimensional* or multifaceted. This conclusion leads to the further conclusion that the intelligence quotient (IQ) is *not* an adequate or accurate estimate of adult intelligence. Therefore, statements about the growth or decline of intelligence with age must recognize the complexity of intellectual functioning in adulthood. The evidence also overwhelmingly indicates that the concept of "general intelligence" is not adequate to explain performances on the myriad tests and scales that have been devised. Because intelligence is complex, it should not surprise us if, as we age, different aspects of intelligence change in different ways—and for different reasons in one person than in another.

The Complexity and Structure of Intelligence

The variety of ways in which investigators have attempted to define the particular form or structure that intelligence takes adds to the difficulty in examining the question of structural change with age. The question of structure has very definite implications for the assessment of intelligence across the lifespan. For example, a study of a group of children might require only one scale in which all items measure general ability. This single-scale, single-concept approach might be adequate in assessing intelligence for the purpose of predicting class performance. The situation is much different, however, when working with a sample of adults and attempting to predict their performance in complex job situations. This situation might well require measures of five different abilities. Comparing the scores obtained from each group of persons would not be appropriate because different abilities are being assessed.

How intelligence is organized deserves serious consideration here because of its implications for the assessment of intelligence in adulthood. *If intelligence is composed of more than one general ability, then it becomes questionable to compare persons of different ages in terms of IQ or any other overall index of intelligence.* An investigator might intentionally decide not to measure the same ability when trying to predict different types of intellectual performance. Howard Gardner (1983) has proposed a theory of multiple intelligence that is decidedly practical in that it specifies many domains of intelligence that seem to relate to the everyday world and to occupational success. For example, distinct sets of abilities may exist for linguistic, musical, logical-mathematical and bodily-kinesthetic intelligence. Essentially, we would need to change our way of thinking from "intelligence" to "intelligences." It remains to be seen whether or not this new view will come to be accepted as a viable approach to intelligence, particularly as it relates to our knowledge of adult development and aging.

There is an obvious practical implication of the multiple intelligences concept. One need not see oneself as more or less intelligent than others in an overall sense. Rather, it would be more accurate to say that some individuals are brighter than others with regard to certain classes of abilities. For example, the highly educated older person may have excellent verbal skills or command a wealth of information, yet do poorly in visualizing relationships between objects in space (a critical skill in assembling or dissembling an engine) or have difficulty in understanding and recalling directions.

The complexity of human intelligence supports the notion that people can develop their skills in some areas to compensate for deficiencies in other areas. Many middle-aged and older adults continue to improve their vocabulary skills and certain other areas of knowledge while shying away from tasks or situations in which they cannot use their past experience to their advantage. They often regard such situations as personally irrelevant, too difficult, or simply requiring too much effort (Hayslip, 1989). In effect, these adults devote themselves to maintaining and enhancing skills that are already intact, while neglecting skills that they do not see as critical or as demanded by their everyday life experience.

Intelligence in the Adults Years: Cross-Sectional Studies

Early studies by Miles and Miles (1932) and Jones and Conrad (1933) found noticeable declines in intellectual performance with increasing age. These were cross-sectional studies; i.e., the participants were people who differed in age at the time of measurement. This type of study is to be distinguished from longitudinal research in which the same people are tested and retested over a period of time. Cross-sectional studies such as those mentioned have contributed much to the belief that intellectual functions decline with age. For example, Doppelt and Wallace (1955) found that overall performance on the Wechsler Adult Intelligence Scale reached its peak between ages 00 and 34, then declined slowly until about age 60, and declined more severely after 60. Botwinick (1967) notes that this assumed decline with age is built in as an "age credit" correction to the definition of IQ: "the age corrected IQ scores do not reflect the actual differences between people of different ages" (p. 4). If the respondents' actual (uncorrected) test scores were compared, older adults would fare more poorly. Despite such findings, it is not wise to conclude immediately that intellectual performances necessarily decline with age: Longitudinal studies often show an increase in overall performance with age (Schaie & Labouvie-Vief, 1974).

A *classic aging pattern* of intelligence has been found through cross-sectional analysis of intelligence test data (Matarazo, 1972). Both sections of the Wechsler Adult Intelligence Scale show declines with age. However, the decrement for the Performance subtests is a great deal more severe than that for the Verbal subtests. This finding has been replicated in at least nine other major studies (Botwinick, 1984), and similar data have been found with another well-known test of intellectual abilities, the Stanford-Binet.

Botwinick (1984) observes that the patterns of uncorrected scores do reflect age trends, subject to the appropriateness of the testing content and the state of the person being tested. Nevertheless, individual differences in intelligence may outweigh age-related differences, especially for older persons. The relatively low correlations between age and intelligence seem to be based on the marked individual differences in intellectual level at all ages. Thus, predictions about intellectual functioning that are made on the basis of age alone are often not very useful.

Cross-Sectional Studies of Piagetian Intelligence

Jean Piaget and his colleagues identified "conservation" as one of the major intellectual abilities that develops through childhood. Conservation refers to the understanding that quantity or number remain the same regardless of changes in shape or position (e.g., the amount of water is still the same after being poured from a tall, thin vessel into a short, broad vessel). Conservation tasks can range from the simple to the complex. Several researchers have reported decrements in Piagetian conservation tasks in the later adult years (Hooper, Fitzgerald, & Papalia, 1971; Hornblum & Overton, 1976; Papalia, 1972; Papalia & Bielby, 1974). It has been suggested that this decline in conservation performance is parallel to the observed decrement in the ability to cope with new problems and situations that has been found by Horn and Cattell (1966, 1967). Both conservation ability and the fluid type of intelligence that is required in dealing with new situations seem to be relatively unaffected by formal schooling, culture, or specific life experiences.

There is another possible explanation, however. Perhaps older adults' thinking is of a different quality than that of younger adults. Elderly people might redefine the Piagetian tasks that are put to them, leading to different types of answers. Following this line of reasoning, one would not necessarily assume that there is an age-related decline in "formal operations," the Piagetian term for highly developed mental abilities. Instead, one might conceive of a new stage of intellectual development termed "postformal reasoning."

Advocates of this new stage suggest that postformal reasoning is relative, temporary, and highly dependent on the immediate context (Rybash, Hoyer, & Roadin, 1986). What is "right" in one situation may not "fit" another. In adult life we often encounter problems that do not have "right" or logical solutions attached to them. Instead, we must use our intellectual creativity as we apply ourselves to new situations in which previous solutions are no longer relevant.

Schaie (1977-1978), for example, suggests that young adults tend to use their skills to reach achievement-related goals and to solve real-life problems. Middle-aged persons, faced with heavy obligations and responsibilities, are more likely to apply their intellect to meeting the demands of an ever-changing world, such as making career choices, balancing both work and home, coping with technological change, and caring for both adolescent children and aging parents. As an older adult, intelligence is pressed into the service of reintegrating one's entire life, taking the past into account and considering a shift in values and priorities. To the extent that these changes do not take in the uses of intellectual ability throughout the adult years, it could be misleading to compare people who are in different life stages on any one type of cognitive performance.

Longitudinal Studies of Adult Intelligence

Most longitudinal studies (studies that follow the same individuals over a period of years) have not found age-related decrements in intellectual performance. Typically, longitudinal studies show that performances continue to improve for a number of years and then level off (e.g., Dearborn & Rothney, 1963). Owens (1966) found gains in Army Alpha total scores up to the 40-50 age range. Schaie's longitudinal data over the adult lifespan suggest that there is a gain in intellectual abilities through the forties. This is followed by relative stability for most intellectual skills through the fifties and early sixties. Significant declines for most abilities are not found until the sixties (Schaie, 1979, 1990).

These declines are greater for persons who are poorly educated, live in intellectually depriving environments, and have significant health difficulties (such as cardiovascular illness). The drop-off is also more apparent on tests that require people to work quickly against the clock (Schaie, 1979, 1990). Moreover, there are vast individual differences in the extent of decline after age 60. More than two-thirds of the participants did not show decrements in intellectual performances until age 74. Even by age 81, only 30 to 40 percent experienced significant declines (Schaie, 1990). The reduction becomes increasingly apparent in the eighties and nineties, although many individuals "selectively optimize" certain skills in familiar and supportive situations (Baltes, 1987). Other longitudinal investigations yield similarly positive data on adult developmental change in intelligence (e.g., Cunningham & Owens, 1983; Palmore et al., 1985; Shock et al., 1984).

What is perhaps most important to learn from Schaie's study of adult intelligences is that *the notion of irreversible, biologically based decline in abilities with age is clearly unfounded.* In most cases the age decrement in intelligence can be reduced or intensified, depending upon the interaction of the sociocultural environment (how stimulating? how supportive?) with the aging process. Thus, there is no such thing as universal, true age-related decline (Baltes & Schaie, 1976). Moreover, the nature of the interaction between aging and historical change seems to vary with cohort membership. Not only is the structure of intellect complex, but so is its interaction with the events and influences that are associated with a particular time period in history.

Methodological Concerns

Many researchers have highlighted the inadequacies of the traditional cross-sectional and longitudinal designs for assessing developmental changes in intellectual functioning. Cohort or generational differences, time of measurement effects, and regression effects are among the most notable sources of difficulty in drawing conclusions (see Baltes, 1968; Schaie, 1965, 1990). These factors, along with practice and attrition, can limit the confidence we place on available cross-sectional and longitudinal data, although the latter are clearly preferable in that they are more likely to reflect change due to age (Kaufman, 1990). Practice effects appear to be especially important when individuals are asked to give repeated performances on the Wechsler Adult Intelligence Scale (WAIS) (Kaufman, 1990).

Cohort Effects on Intelligence

One of the most important findings has been the recognition of cohort effects on intellectual functioning. Independent of the individual's age, certain characteristics of his or her intellectual performance can be shown to have a relationship to membership in a particular historical "wave" (Kaufman, 1990; Schaie, 1990). The most representative findings here are those of Schaie (1979, 1990), whose data clearly show that cohort effects are at least as important as maturation as an influence on intelligence in adulthood. Cohort effects influence the baseline reference point from which age-related changes in intelligence can be understood.

The direction of cohort differences can vary by type of ability. For example, younger cohorts perform better on primary mental ability measures of verbal meaning, spatial orientation, and inductive reasoning (1990). This pattern is thought to be related largely to the higher levels of education and better health that are characteristic of people who were born in more recent times. In contrast, younger cohorts perform less adequately on the primary mental abilities of number skill and word fluency. When controls are introduced for level of education, Verbal scores on the WAIS are affected more strongly than the Performance scores. This supports the conclusion that education is a major factor that influences adult intelligence—and educational experiences are cohort specific (Kaufman, 1990).

Schaie (1979) and Baltes, Reese, and Nesselroade (1986) believe that cross-sectional differences reflect the differing amounts of "information accumulation" that are gained by one generation compared with another. This difference reflects higher and lower baselines from which two generations started out. Age differences in crystallized intelligence or accumulated knowledge may reflect environmental opportunities and influ-

ences rather than actual change with age. Similarly, age differences in fluid intelligence (ability to deal with new situations or with existing situations in a new way) can be either overestimated or underestimated by cross-sectional studies (Schaie, 1970). Thus, the apparent difference between young and old adults may actually derive from the different baselines that existed for an earlier and a later cohort or generation. Generally, though, cohort differences have been found to be greater for crystallized than for fluid types of intelligence.

The available data suggest that cohort-specific patterns exist for a variety of intellectual abilities. This general finding leads to the caution that genuine maturational changes cannot be inferred when different cohorts are measured at different points in their lives. Likewise, longitudinal studies are cohort-specific and may not provide information that can be generalized to past or future cohorts. It is only when cross-sectional and longitudinal approaches yield similar trends that the results can be ascribed to the influence of maturational factors alone.

Intellectual Decline? A Summary of Major Findings

The following conclusions offered by Schaie (1979) remain viable today:

1. Reliable decrement cannot be found for all abilities for all persons.
2. Decrement is not likely at all until very late in life.
3. Decline is most evident when speed of response is important.
4. Decline is evident in most abilities for individuals of any age who have severe cardiovascular disease.
5. Decline is evident for individuals in their fifties and sixties who live in deprived environments.
6. Studies involving independent (cross-sectional) samples will overestimate the extent of age decrements in intellectual ability (when such losses exist at all).
7. Studies involving repeated-measure (longitudinal) samples will accurately esti-

mate age changes for adults who are in good health and live in stimulating environments but will underestimate loss for those in poor health and/or living in impoverished situations.

8. Cohort effects account for more of the variance in intelligence with age than do biologically based factors, with the latter assuming more importance only late in life.

9. Individual differences are substantial regarding both the type of skills that decline and the extent of the decline.

10. Many people sustain and even improve their intellectual skills, while others decline much earlier in life, depending on health, educational background, social interaction, and the level of skill maintenance they bring into the later years of life.

It is important to recognize that the conditions under which adult intelligence is tested will influence the findings and conclusions. Noncognitive factors may undermine the accurate assessment of intelligence in many adults (Hayslip & Kennelly, 1985). Examples of noncognitive influences might be fatigue, sensory loss, anxiety, speededness, attentional deficits, and depression (Kausler, 1990). Although a tired or anxious respondent might underperform on intellectual tests, a person who has already had successful practice with this procedure or who brings a high educational background to the task might optimize his or her performance. Selective attrition (the fact that some potential respondents have not remained in the sample because of ill health or have not survived) can also result in higher scores because those who do continue in the study tend to be people who enjoy superior physical and psychological health.

Everyday Intelligence

A recent development is the search for everyday intelligence (Kausler, 1991). Everyday intelligence is an idea that possesses what we might call ecological or functional validity (Schaie, 1978; Scheidt, 1981). In other words, it reflects the skills that adults actually call upon to function on an everyday basis in familiar situations. The everyday context in which persons exercise their abilities may provide a more accurate reflection of their intellectual prowess than what occurs when they are asked to deal with formal measures of intellectual functioning. Dealing with other persons in relationships, making decisions, weighing options in ambiguous life-planning situations, and evaluating one's standing in various life domains (e.g., disease and death, financial matters) may indeed provide reasonable estimates of intelligence as compared with items on intelligence tests such as the WAIS where a single "right" answer exists. Much work needs to be done in this relatively new sphere of intellectual-functioning research in adulthood.

Conclusion

A complex picture emerges from research on intellectual functioning in adulthood. The assumption that inevitable and irreversible declines in intelligence occur with age is clearly inaccurate. The conditions under which intelligence declines are highly dependent upon the individual. Stability or growth with age better represents the pattern of age changes for some dimensions of intelligence, while for other abilities, moderate (though not irreversible) declines can be noted.

That there are many types of intelligence, each changing in a different way, should encourage us to be flexible in evaluating both our own and others' intellectual skills. Both the use of a lifetime of experience and the ability to adapt to new situations are basic characteristics of adult intelligence.

▼ BERT HAYSLIP, JR.

See also: Cardiac Health; Humor; Individuality; Information Processing; Intelligence—Crystallized and Fluid; Language Development; Reminiscence and Life Review; Slowing of Behavior with Age; Work Organization Membership and Behavior.

References

Baltes, P. B. (1968). Longitudinal and cross-sectional sequences in the study of age and generation effects. *Human Development, 11:* 145-71.

———. (1987). Theoretical propositions of lifespan developmental psychology: On the dynamics between growth and decline. *Developmental Psychology, 23:* 611-26.

Baltes, P. B., Dittmann-Kohli, F., & Dixon, R. (1984). New perspectives on the development of intelligence in adulthood: Toward a dual process conception and model of selective optimization with compensation. In P. B. Baltes & O. Brim (Eds.), *Life-span Development and Behavior.* Volume 6. New York: Academic Press, pp. 33-76.

Baltes, P. B., Reese, H. W., & Nesselroade, J. R. (1986). *Life-span Developmental Psychology: Introduction to Research Methods.* Hillsdale, NJ: Lawrence Erlbaum.

Baltes, P.B., & Schaie, K.W. (1976). On the plasticity of intelligence in adulthood and old age: Where Horn and Donaldson fail. *American Psychologist, 31:* 720-25.

Botwinick, J. (1967). *Cognitive Processes in Maturity and Old Age.* New York: Springer.

———. (1984). *Aging and Behavior.* New York: Springer.

Cattell, R.B. (1987). *Intelligence: Its Structure, Growth and Action.* Amsterdam: Elsevier.

Cunningham, W., & Owens, W. (1983). The Iowa State Study of the adult development of intellectual abilities. In K. W. Schaie (Ed.), *Longitudinal Studies of Adult Psychological Development.* New York: Guilford, pp. 20-39.

Dearborn, W. F., & Rothney, J. W. (1963). *Predicting the Child's Development.* Cambridge, MA: Sci-Art.

Denny, N. W. (1982). *Aging and cognitive changes.* In B. B. Wolman (Ed.), Handbook of Developmental Psychology. Englewood Cliffs, NJ: Prentice-Hall, pp. 807-27.

Doppelt, J. E., & Wallace, W. L. (1955). Standardization of the Wechsler Adult Intelligence Scale for Older Persons. *Journal of Abnormal and Social Psychology, 51:* 312-30.

Gardner, H. (1983). *Frames of Mind: The Theory of Multiple Intelligences.* New York: Basic Books.

Hayslip, B. (1989). Alternative mechanisms for improvements in fluid ability performance among aged adults. *Psychology and Aging, 4:* 122-24.

Hayslip, B., & Kennelly, K. (1985). Cognitive and noncognitive factors affecting learning among older adults. In D. B. Lumsden (Ed.), *The Older Adult as Learner.* New York: Hemisphere, pp. 73-98.

Hooper, F., Fitzgerald, J., & Papalia, D. (1971). Piagetian theory and the aging process: Extensions and speculations. *International Journal of Aging and Human Development, 2:* 3-20.

Horn, J. L. (1978). Human ability systems. In P. B. Baltes (Ed.), *Lifespan Development and Behavior.* Volume 1. New York: Academic Press, pp. 211-56.

———. (1985). Remodeling old models of intelligence. In B. B. Wolman (Ed.), *Handbook of Intelligence: Theories, Methods, and Applications.* New York: Wiley Interscience, pp. 267-300.

Horn, J. L., & Cattell, R. B. (1966). Refinement and test of the theory of fluid and crystallized intelligence. *Journal of Educational Psychology, 57:* 253-70.

———. (1967). Age differences in fluid and crystallized intelligence. *Acta Psychologica, 26:* 107-29.

Hornblum, J. N., & Overton, W. F. (1976). Area and volume conservation among the elderly: Assessment and training. *Developmental Psychology, 12:* 68-74.

Jones, H. E., & Conrad, H. S. (1933). The growth and decline of intelligence: A study of a homogenous group between the ages of ten and sixty. *Genetic Psychology Monographs, 13:* 223-98.

Kaufman, A. S. (1990). Age and IQ across the adult lifespan. In A. S. Kaufman (Ed.), *Assessing Adolescent and Adult Intelligence.* Boston: Allyn and Bacon, pp. 181-232.

Kausler, D. H. (1991). *Experimental Psychology, Cognition, and Human Aging.* Second Edition. New York: Springer-Verlag.

Matarrazo, J. D. (1972). *Measurement and Appraisal of Adult Intelligence.* Baltimore: Williams & Wilkins.

Miles, C. C., & Miles, W. R. (1932). The correlation of intelligence scores and chronological age from early to later maturity. *American Journal of Psychology, 44:* 44-78.

Owens, W. A. (1966). Age and mental abilities: A second adult follow-up. *Journal of Educational Psychology, 57:* 311-25.

Palmore, E., et al. (1985). *Normal Aging III.* Durham, NC: Duke University Press.

Papalia, D. (1972). The status of several conservation abilities across the lifespan. *Human Development, 15:* 229-43.

Papalia, D., & Bielby, D. D. (1974). Cognitive functioning in middle aged and elderly adults: A review of research based on Piaget's theory. *Human Development, 17:* 424-43.

Rybash, J. M., Hoyer, W. J., & Roadin, P. A. (1986). *Adult Cognition and Aging.* New York: Pergamon Press.

Schaie, K. W. (1965). A general model for the study of developmental problems. *Psychological Bulletin, 64:* 92-107.

———. (1970). A reinterpretation of age-related changes in cognitive structure and functioning. In L. R. Goulet & P. B. Baltes (Eds.), *Life-span Developmental Psychology: Theory and Research.* New York: Academic Press, pp. 486-508.

———. (1977-1978). Toward a stage theory of adult intellectual development. *International Journal of Aging and Human Development, 8:* 120-38.

———. (1978). External validity in the assessment of intellectual development in adulthood. *Journal of Gerontology, 33:* 696-701.

———. (1979). The primary mental abilities in adulthood: An exploration in the development of psychometric intelligence. In B. Baltes & O. Brim (Eds.), *Life-span Development and Behavior.* Volume 2. New York: Academic Press, pp. 68-115.

———. (1990). Adult intellectual development. In J. E. Birren & K. W. Schaie (Eds.), *Handbook of the Psychology of Aging.* Third Edition. New York: Academic Press, pp. 292-309.

Schaie, K. W., & Labouvie-Vief, G. (1974). Generational versus ontogenetic components of change in adult cognitive behavior: A fourteen year cross-sequential study. *Developmental Psychology, 10:* 305-20.

Scheidt, R. (1981). Ecologically valid inquiry: Fait accompli? *Human Development, 23:* 225-28.

Shock, N., et al. (1984). *Normal Human Aging: The Baltimore Longitudinal Study of Aging.* Washington, DC: Government Printing Office.

Thurstone, L. L., & Thurstone, T. G. (1962). *SRA Primary Mental Abilities.* Chicago: Science Research Associates.

Wohlwill, J., (1970). The age variable in psychological research. *Psychological Review, 77:* 49-64.

INTELLIGENCE— CRYSTALLIZED AND FLUID

Any theory of intelligence must be evaluated in terms of its usefulness in organizing and explaining the available data on adult development. An approach to the understanding of intellectual functioning that goes a long way toward meeting this criterion is the theory of *fluid* and *crystallized* intelligence (Cattell, 1941, 1963; Horn & Cattell, 1966, 1967).

Raymond B. Cattell (1987) identifies several considerations that converged to suggest the existence of two general factors of intelligence rather than just one. Most important among these considerations are the following facts.

1. Age curves were obtained for "perceptual" or "content-free" tests, as distinguished from vocabulary and several other subscales of school intelligence tests.
2. Differing physiological correlates were found between measures of intellectual functioning that emphasize verbal knowledge and skills and measures that were intended to be more universal or "culture fair."
3. Each type of test showed its own distinctive pattern of age changes after early adulthood (about age 20).

Cattell points out that the fluid *(Gf)* versus crystallized *(Gc)* distinction should not be confused with the differences between performances on verbal and quantitative measures that have been found through the use of the Wechsler Adult Intelligence Scale, or with several other distinctions that had been made by other investigators.

What Are Crystallized and Fluid Forms of Intelligence?

Crystallized ability is called upon when we are asked to exercise cognitive (mental) skills that we have already established as the result of earlier learning and development.

By contrast, fluid ability shows up more in tests that require adaptation to new situations. When we cannot cope with a situation effectively on the basis of our previously established knowledge and skills, then it is time to make use of that general ability that Cattell describes as the fluid form of intelligence. Horn and Cattell (1966, p. 255) characterize fluid ability as "representing processes of reasoning in the immediate situation in tasks requiring abstracting, concept formation and attainment, and the perception and eduction of relations." Fluid factors are measured most purely in culture-fair tests whose elements are either extremely novel or are overlearned by everybody. The point is to eliminate or reduce the effects of differential educational opportunity.

Cultural influences are thought to affect the early development of fluid and crystallized abilities. A particular society might place greater emphasis on either one type of intellectual process or the other. During the adult years there is a general pattern of change in which crystallized abilities continue to increase with experience, while fluid intelligence tends to decay. The older the adult, then, the greater the likelihood of relatively high crystallized intelligence and relatively low fluid intelligence. According to Cattell (1963), fluid ability starts to decline in the early twenties and continues to diminish throughout the adult years. Crystallized skills increase until at least the late twenties and, according to some studies, may continue to increase well into the later adult years. The effects of brain damage are more evident on Gf. A person with brain damage is more likely to show a reduction in the ability to cope effectively with new situations than in the ability to utilize previous knowledge and skills, although particular types of injury can lead to particular deficits.

In childhood the two forms of general intelligence are closely interrelated, with crystallized ability often being the easiest to observe and measure. As individual development continues, the Gf-Gc correlation becomes less substantial. It becomes increasingly useful with increasing age to measure fluid intelligence with culture-fair tests. The rate of learning in any area will be a function of Gf, Gc, and the level of the specific ability factor in that area. When people are exploring areas of learning that are new to them, the influence of their fluid intelligence will be greater (Horn, 1985).

Horn and Cattell (1966) refined the theory with a sample of approximately 300 adults. They found that several other general factors also influenced performances on tests of intelligence: visualization, fluency, and speediness. To determine the importance of fluid and crystallized forms of intelligence in coping with a particular task, then, we should take into account the possible effects of these other characteristics as well.

Age Differences in Fluid and Crystallized Intelligence

Age differences in fluid and crystallized intelligence were evaluated and confirmed by Horn and Cattell (1967), who used a wide variety of cognitive tasks. For example, fluid intelligence was assessed by such tasks as the letter series, e.g., ABCD__, which provide a measure of inductive reasoning. Other tasks involved figural classification and matrices, e.g., ☐ is to ☐☐ as 0 is to __. Word analogies, nonsense equations, and associative memory were among the other measures used. Tasks assessing Gc included vocabulary, syllogistic reasoning and inferences, arithmetical reasoning, experiential evaluation of social situations, and ideational fluency. Gf was found to increase through childhood into young adulthood and to decline thereafter; in contrast, Gc increased throughout the adult years, well into the sixth decade of life (and possibly beyond). Several factors contribute to these differential age patterns.

The growth of Gf depends on the adequacy of physiological structures that reach their fullest growth and complexity during the late teens and early twenties. Injuries to the structures that support learning are irreversible. Early in life, the effects of such injuries can be masked by neural growth, learning, and other positive aspects of development. Later in adulthood, these masking effects become less effective and neural damage begins to take its toll, contributing to a decline of fluid intelligence throughout middle and later adulthood. Additionally, various types of new injury to the nervous system may be encountered as people age, e.g., through accidents, disease, or the cumulative effects of drug or alcohol use.

It has been suggested that the decrease in Gf with adult age may be the inevitable result of physiological decrements with aging (Cattell, 1987; Horn, 1982; Horn & Cattell, 1967). There are alternative possibilities, however. Declines in fluid intelligence may be linked to age-related deficits in effortful processing (Hayslip & Kennelly, 1982; Kennelly, Hayslip, & Richardson, 1985; Stankov, 1988). It has also been proposed that depression or fatigue might be responsible for the information processing deficits that older people experience (Hayslip, Kennelly, & Maloy, 1991).

Few have questioned the conclusion that Gf varies by age and Gc does not (see Figure 1). However, there have also been few attempts to collect longitudinal data on the growth and decline of both Gf and Gc in adulthood. Until further studies are completed, questions can be raised about the possible effects of cohort differences, selective sampling, selective attrition, or practice (Cunningham & Tomer, 1990). For example, the assumption that patterns of intellectual development and decline will be the same for people who are born at different points of time might not be substantiated if we had the opportunity to compare those who grew up in 1800, 1850, 1900, 1950, and so forth. Another question that has not yet received adequate attention is the basis for the apparent stability of Gc in adulthood. Schaie (1970, 1979) has argued that cohort or generation differences are greater for Gc than for Gf. Hayslip (1988) suggests, however, that older persons who are moderately anxious about their intellectual functioning may be more motivated to exercise their crystallized skills. This tendency could contribute to a decline in

their fluid abilities because of the lack of recent practice, or because of a culturally induced belief that their cognitive skills must inevitably decline with age. Many people seem able to make accurate estimates of their performances on tests of both Gc and Gf, and also express more confidence in their crystallized abilities (Lachman & Jelalian, 1984). Perhaps individuals' feelings about their intellectual strengths and weaknesses will emerge as a crucial factor in the growth of crystallized and the decline of fluid intellectual abilities over the adult years and into later adulthood.

Can Fluid Intelligence Be Improved by Training?

The most recent developments in Gf/Gc theory center on age shifts in the correlation between these two abilities and on the trainability of Gf skills.

Cunningham, Clayton, and Overton (1975) tested the Horn and Cattell (1966, 1967) hypothesis that there should be a less substantial relationship between fluid and crystallized abilities for elderly adults. This hypothesis was confirmed and supported again by Hayslip and Brookshire (1985) with the use of a different methodology, but still another study found that the correlation between fluid and crystallized abilities was weakest for middle-aged individuals (Hayslip & Stearns, 1979).

The decrement-oriented view of fluid intelligence in adulthood has been challenged by several investigators. Baltes (1987) and others have proposed that the degree of intellectual plasticity available to the aging adult is greater than has customarily been assumed. This approach has led to some convincing evidence that the performance of older adults on tasks requiring fluid ability can be improved through the use of problem-solving techniques. Providing elderly people with knowledge of the "solution rules" has been found effective in improving performances on Gf tasks (Baltes & Willis, 1982).

At present, disagreement centers on the methods that can most effectively be used to

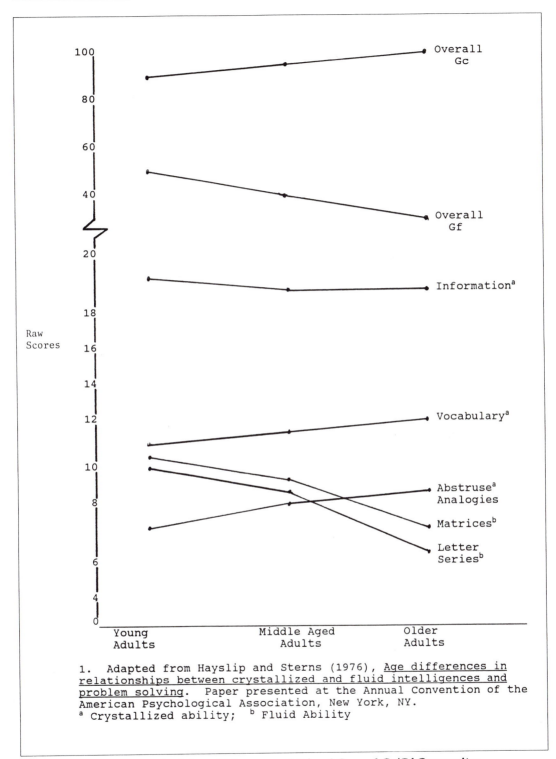

1. Adapted from Hayslip and Sterns (1976), <u>Age differences in relationships between crystallized and fluid intelligences and problem solving</u>. Paper presented at the Annual Convention of the American Psychological Association, New York, NY.
[a] Crystallized ability; [b] Fluid Ability

Figure 1. Age Differences in Selected Measures of Gf and Gc, and Gc/Gf Composites

enhance fluid intelligence training for older persons. Among the promising approaches that are being explored are rules-based training (Baltes & Willis, 1982) and anxiety reduction with performance enhancement (Hayslip, 1989a), practice alone (Hayslip, 1989b), and self-directed training (Baltes, Sowarka, & Kliegl, 1989; Blackburn & Papalia, 1988). There is reason for optimism that several strategies will prove effective and practical in overcoming the age-related decline in fluid intelligence.   ▼ Bert Hayslip, Jr.

See also: Cohort and Generational Effects; Habituation: A Key to Lifespan Development and Aging?; Information Processing; Intelligence; Learning and Memory in Everyday Life; Social Class and Adult Development; Subcultural Influences on Lifelong Development.

References

Baltes, P.B. (1987). Theoretical propositions of life-span developmental psychology: On the dynamics between growth and decline. *Developmental Psychology, 23:* 611-26.

Baltes, P.B., Sowarka, D., & Kliegl, R. (1989). Cognitive training research on fluid intelligence in old age: What can older adults achieve by themselves? *Psychology and Aging, 4:* 217-21.

Baltes, P.B., & Willis, S.L. (1982). Plasticity and enhancement of intellectual functioning in old age: Penn State's Adult Development and Enrichment Project (ADEPT). In F. I. M. Craik & S. E. Trehub (Eds.), *Aging and Cognitive Processes.* New York: Plenum, pp. 353-89.

Blackburn, J. L., & Papalia, D. (1988). Modifiability of fluid intelligence: A comparison of two training approaches. *Journal of Gerontology, 43:* 87-89.

Cattell, R. B. (1941). Some Theoretical Issues in Adult Intelligence Testing. *Psychological Bulletin, 38:* 592-610.

———. (1963). Theory of crystallized and fluid intelligence: A critical experiment. *Journal of Educational Psychology, 54:* 1-22.

———. (1987). *Intelligence: Its Structure, Growth and Action.* Amsterdam: Elsevier.

Cunningham, W. (1981). Ability factor structure differences in adulthood and old age. *Multivariate Behavioral Research, 16:* 3-22.

Cunningham, W., Clayton, V., & Overton, W. (1975). Fluid and crystallized intelligence in young adulthood and old age. *Journal of Gerontology, 30:* 54-55.

Cunningham, W., & Tomer, A. (1990). Intellectual abilities and age: Concepts, theories, and analyses. In E. A. Lovelace (Ed.), *Aging and Cognition: Mental processes, Self-awareness, and Interventions.* New York: Elsevier, pp. 379-406.

Hayslip, B. (1988). Personality-ability relationships in aged adults. *Journal of Gerontology, 43:* 79-84.

———. (1989a). Alternative mechanisms for improvements in fluid ability performance among aged adults. *Psychology and Aging, 4:* 122-24.

———. (1989b). Fluid ability training with aged people: A past with a future? *Educational Gerontology, 15:* 573-95.

Hayslip, B., & Brookshire, R. (1985). Relationships among abilities in elderly adults: A time lag analysis. *Journal of Gerontology, 40:* 748-50.

Hayslip, B., & Kennelly, K. J. (1982). Short-term memory and crystallized-fluid intelligence in adulthood. *Research in Aging, 4:* 314-32.

Hayslip, B., Kennelly, K. J., & Maloy, R. (1991). Fatigue, depression, and cognitive performance among aged persons. *Experimental Aging Research, 16:* 111-15.

Hayslip, B., & Sterns, H. L. (1979). Age differences in relationships between fluid and crystallized intelligences and problem solving. *Journal of Gerontology, 34:* 404-14.

Horn, J. L. (1970). Organization of data on life-span development of abilities. In L. R. Goulet & P. B. Baltes (Eds.), *Life-span Developmental Psychology: Theory and Research.* New York: Academic Press, pp. 424-66.

———. (1982). The aging of human abilities. In B. Wolman (Ed.), *Handbook of Developmental Psychology.* Englewood Cliffs, NJ: Prentice-Hall, pp. 847-70.

———. (1985). Remodeling old models of intelligence. In B. B. Wolman (Ed.), *Handbook of Intelligence: Theories, Measurements, and Applications.* New York: Wiley, pp. 267-300.

Horn, J. L., & Cattell, R. B. (1966). Refinement and test of the theory of fluid and crystallized intelligence. *Journal of Educational Psychology, 57:* 253-70.

———. (1967). Age differences in fluid and crystallized intelligence. *Acta Psychologica, 26:* 107-29.

Kennelly, K. J., Hayslip, B., & Richardson, S. (1985). Depression and helplessness-induced cognitive deficits in the aged. *Experimental Aging Research, 8:* 165-73.

Lachman, M., & Jelalian, E. (1984). Self-efficacy and attributions for intellectual performance in young and elderly adults. *Journal of Gerontology, 39:* 577-82.

Schaie, K. W. (1970). A reinterpretation of age-related changes in cognitive structure and functioning. In L. R. Goulet & P. B. Baltes (Eds.), *Life-span Developmental Psychology: Theory and Research.* New York: Academic Press, pp. 486-508.

———. (1979). The primary mental abilities in adulthood: An exploration in the development of psychometric intelligence. In P. Baltes & O. Brim (Eds.), *Life-span Development and Behavior.* Volume 3. New York: Academic Press, pp. 68-115.

Stankov, L. (1988). Aging, attention, and intelligence. *Psychology and Aging, 3:* 59-74.

Willis, S. L. (1990). Current issues in cognitive training research. In E. A. Lovelace (Ed.), *Aging and Cognition: Mental Processes, Self-awareness and Interventions.* New York: Elsevier, pp. 263-80.

INTERETHNIC RELATIONSHIPS

Interethnic relationships occur when persons who identify themselves with different ethnic groups (e.g., an African American and a Mexican American) interact. In a nation as culturally diverse as the United States, people of many different ethnic heritages come in contact with each other throughout their lives. The quality of life for individuals and the entire nation is affected by the quality of interethnic relationships.

The question of ethnic and cultural adaptation is complex. What makes one individual tolerant while another is not? Does adaptation require a behavior change or is it enough to have a tolerant attitude? These are among the issues considered here. A discussion of the general topic of racial attitudes and interethnic communication is followed by an examination of theories of adult development as they relate to these attitudes and behaviors and by some speculation on the shape of ethnic relations across the lifespan.

Beyond Tolerance

An attitude of tolerance certainly is one of the keys to effective interethnic relationships (Brislin, 1981). It is very difficult to get along with others if we are critical of all the ways in which they may differ or seem to differ from us. Tolerance, however, is not a simple attitude to acquire. It demands that a person be able to accept differences and the ambiguities they generate, have patience with the intricacies of other cultures, take a broad view when making judgments, and feel empathy for other points of view. Tolerance also requires that one become aware of stereotypes and be willing to modify them.

Even with all its advantages, a general feeling of tolerance may not be enough to encourage the development of positive interethnic relationships. People can remain prejudiced against another group without any specific feeling of personal animosity (Jackman & Crane, 1986). Indeed, one might still discriminate against a "friend" because she or he is not considered one's equal. For example, a Mexican-American told the authors about a white friend who, while expressing positive personal regard, labeled Mexican-Americans as incapable of anything other than manual labor. Perceptions of other groups and their members obviously are far from simple.

Some elements of intergroup relationships are less apparent than others. In previous eras it was common for prejudice to be expressed overtly and directly. Current forms of discrimination, especially that by whites against other ethnic groups, tend to be more subtle and indirect (Pettigrew, 1985) or symbolic (Giles & Evans, 1986; Harrison et al., 1990). In general, change in the behavior of whites toward other groups has lagged behind their increasing attitude of tolerance. For example, large numbers of whites oppose social programs such as affirmative action and minority scholarships despite their rejection of blatant discrimination. Underlying their opposition to some types of social programs may be a hostile attitude toward other ethnic groups. One can also expect more direct discrimination from older people than from younger adults because of changes in societal attitudes over recent decades.

Toward Positive Interactions

Recent surveys suggest that negative reactions to disempowered ethnic groups are decreasing (Gordon, 1986). Although respondents in the most recent surveys expressed a wide range of opinions and still held negative stereotypes, the overall pattern indicates that all groups are increasingly positive toward interethnic relationships.

Attitudes and relationships do not develop in a vacuum. We learn about other ethnic groups in a variety of ways: by direct interaction and observation, through the media, and so forth. Positive attitudes and behavior can be learned through direct contact between members of various groups. However, contact does not always help, and some forms of contact can even lead to more negative attitudes. The contact theory of prejudice (Jackman & Crane, 1986) attempts to explain the processes involved in positive and negative effects of direct interactions. The theory assumes that negative intergroup relationships are caused by irrational prejudices. Therefore, hostile relationships and attitudes can be improved by accurate information that is gained through sustained, one-to-one, informal contact. These contacts should occur in situations that are egalitarian, noncompetitive, and supported by authorities. Situations in which people of differing groups interact on an unequal footing, which emphasize competition for scarce resources or rewards, and which are fleeting or unsanctioned by authority are less likely to contribute to the growth of interethnic understanding and may even have negative effects.

In favorable interactive situations, positive information is shared and positive intergroup behaviors are modeled and reinforced. The effects of these processes can be seen among African-Americans who were raised in predominantly white suburbs. As children, many had positive interactions with both white and black peers in nonthreatening situations and thereby developed positive attitudes toward both ethnic groups (Banks, 1984).

Clearly, then, members of different groups can develop positive attitudes toward each other. However, cultural differences continue to exist, and even if the attitudes are positive, people must still discover ways of adapting to these differences (Coupland et al., 1988). Members of disempowered groups find numerous ways of adapting. Two of the most common techniques are biculturalism and code switching. Biculturalism is achieved by developing flexible social and ethnic roles that encompass aspects of both one's own cultural heritage and that of the larger society. Code switching refers to the ability to move to an alternative mode of interaction when one finds oneself in a different cultural context. Many individuals also benefit from traditional, ancestral worldviews that provide strength and loyalty to their own group along with appreciation of the dominant culture.

Members of the dominant culture also are called upon to adjust. This is particularly true in settings in which a disempowered culture dominates. Although less is known about these processes, one type of unsuccessful adjustment has been identified. In overaccommodation, members of one group try "too hard" to adjust to the other group. This attempt is interpreted as insincerity. In one research project, for example, a black woman reported being the only member of her ethnic group at a wedding. She complained that people continually brought up "black topics" such as Ray Charles and sports. This pattern of behavior was perceived by her as racist.

Successful adjustment entails a complicated process of adapting to the situation while at the same time maintaining group identity and loyalty. Families often are the most important source of help in achieving this delicate balance. Flexibility is encouraged when parents help their children create and maintain a positive self-image that is derived from their ethnicity. Successful adapters are usually taught to have pride in their ethnic identity, promote their own self-development, maintain an awareness of ethnic barriers, and act in an egalitarian fashion. Parents provide the models from which positive attitudes and behaviors are learned.

Changes Over Time

Once learned, does the capacity to adapt to other ethnic groups remain constant, or does it change as people age, develop different interethnic relationships, or experience historical events? Unfortunately, very little information is available to answer questions of this kind. We do know that the labels used to describe groups such as African Americans have changed over the years. In the 1950s "Negro" and "colored" were the most frequent labels. During the black power movement of the 1960s, "black" emerged as the label of choice. More recently, leaders such as Jesse Jackson have advocated the term "African American." Recent research suggests that these labels have differential meanings for African Americans and members of the mainstream culture (Hecht & Ribeau, 1987). Overall, "black" is the term that is regarded as most negative by whites and Mexican Americans, and there has been some shifting toward the term "African American" within this group. The popular use and meaning of ethnic labels has changed over time and may continue to do so. These changes, however, may not be embraced by all age cohorts. For example, some people in the generation that experienced the change in the standard terminology from "colored" to "black" might be less ready to accept the further change to "African American." Because people both within and outside a particular ethnic or racial group can find it difficult to adjust to new usages, these changes may place a further strain on intergroup relations.

Despite the scarcity of direct research, theories of human development suggest how ethnic relations are likely to develop across the lifespan. Attitudes and behaviors remain relatively stable across the lifespan (Barresi, 1990; Schaie & Geiwitz, 1982). Adult personality is very stable and resistant to change.

Individuals generally select environments that suit their existing personalities instead of adjusting their personalities to the environment.

Nevertheless, life experiences may influence personality. Significant events can alter the way a person thinks and behaves. The contact theory suggests that positive interethnic contact is one of these events. As a result, what might appear to be age difference might instead represent variations among generations (Kimmel, 1974). Different generations experience dissimilar child-rearing methods, education, historical events, media exposure, and so forth. Observed differences therefore may not be a function of chronological age but rather of the generation or age cohort within which the person develops.

The sociocultural and historical events experienced by a particular generation or age cohort may play an important role in their general development. The type of interethnic contact experienced by an age cohort can strongly influence its attitudes and behaviors. The influence of contacts experienced at an early age would be expected to be particularly significant.

Unfortunately, several factors tend to limit the number of positive interethnic relationships that develop during the course of adult development as a consequence of positive interactions. Elderly people seldom choose to develop new types of relationships (Kimmel, 1974). Elderly whites are more conservative about civil rights than are other groups (Crandall, 1980), while elderly blacks remain financially disadvantaged compared with their white peers. These attitudinal and economic differences tend to reinforce preexisting negative attitudes (Atchley, 1991). As a consequence, many elderly whites resist social contact with blacks, interpreting their differences as being the result of skin color and refusing to acknowledge the lifelong effects of racism.

These conclusions tend to hold true of other age groups as well. There continues to be a high degree of separation among members of various ethnic groups. Furthermore, whites in general do not view members of other groups as equals (Atchley, 1991; Crandall, 1980; Denton & Massey, 1988).

Overall, ethnic attitudes and relationships throughout the life course are influenced by *historical events* that affect both mainstream and empowered groups, by *individual contact*, and, secondarily, by one's *developmental stage* in life. If Americans growing up during the turbulent civil rights period of the 1960s experienced negative contact with members of other ethnic groups, this early shaping of racial attitudes would be likely to maintain itself throughout the lifespan of this cohort.

Conversely, today's college students have grown up in a society that either is dealing with civil rights issues in a more peaceful manner or has developed a relatively nonconfrontational way of ignoring them. This cohort may hold more positive attitudes toward different ethnic groups and may also have established more culturally diverse relationships than have preceding generations. It is possible that this cohort will continue to cultivate such relationships throughout their lives; if so, then longitudinal studies 50 years hence may demonstrate greater ethnic tolerance than is found among the elderly people of today.

The same promise does not hold true, however, for those who form negative attitudes early in life. Events associated with World War II may have had a negative effect on Americans growing up during that time period. The attitudes of Jewish Americans toward Germans and of the general American public toward the Japanese may have been shaped by this conflict. Intensely negative attitudes that were formed during recent threatening relations between Vietnamese immigrants and young residents of Texas fishing villages are unlikely to be altered by future events. Because older people are exposed to a highly selective body of information and their social groups tend to be less permeable or more difficult to enter, it is unlikely that contact in later life will foster improved relationships among these and other groups.

In this exploration of lifespan issues in interethnic relations, particular emphasis has been given to the importance of the nature of the contact that occurs between members of different groups and the prevailing social climate during key developmental periods. The more positive attitudes of current college students hold some promise for the future. Nevertheless, both the direct and the indirect stereotyping that is still prevalent in all age groups may continue to prevail throughout the lifespan of young and old and interfere with the development of meaningful interethnic relationships.

▼ Susan MacLaury and Michael L. Hecht

See also: African-American Experiences through the Adult Years; Cohort and Generational Effects; Humor; Information Processing; Language Development; Mexican Americans: Lifecourse Transitions and Adjustment; Native American Perspectives on the Lifespan; Reminiscence and Life Reviews; Slowing of Behavior with Age; Work Organization Membership and Behavior.

References

Atchley, R. C. (1991). *Social Forces and Aging.* Sixth Edition. Belmont, CA: Wadsworth.

Banks, J. A. (1984). Black youths in predominantly white suburbs: An exploratory study of their attitudes and self-concepts. *Journal of Negro Education, 53:* 3-17.

Barresi, C. M. (1990). Ethnogerontology: Social aging in national, racial, and cultural groups. In K. F. Ferrero (Ed.), *Gerontology: Perspectives and Issues.* New York: Springer, pp. 248-65.

Brislin, R. (1981). *Cross-Cultural Encounters: Face-to-Face Interactions.* Elmsford, NY: Pergamon.

Coupland, N., et al. (1988). Elderly self-disclosure: Interactional and intergroup issues. *Language and Communication, 8:* 109-33.

Crandall, R. C. (1980). *Gerontology: A Behavioral Science Approach.* New York: Random House.

Denton, M. A., & Massey, D. S. (1988). Residential segregation of Blacks, Hispanics, and Asians by socioeconomic status and generation. *Social Science Quarterly, 69:* 797-805.

Giles, H., & Evans, A. (1986). The power approach to intergroup hostility. *Journal of Conflict Resolution, 30:* 469-85.

Gordon, L. (1986). College student stereotypes of Blacks and Jews on two campuses: Four studies spanning 50 years. *Sociology and Social Research*, 70: 200-01.

Harrison, A. O., et al. (1990). Family ecologies of ethnic minority children. *Child Development*, 61: 347-62.

Hecht, M. L., & Ribeau, S. (1987). Afro-American identity labels and communicative effectiveness. *Journal of Language and Social Psychology*, 6: 319-26.

Jackman, M. R., & Crane, M. (1986). "Some of my best friends are black...": Interracial friendship and whites' racial attitudes. *Public Opinion Quarterly*, 50: 459-86.

Kimmel, D. C. (1974). *Adulthood and Aging.* Third Edition. New York: Wiley.

Pettigrew, T. F. (1985). New black-and-white patterns: How best to conceptualize them? *Annual Review of Sociology*, 11: 329-46.

Schaie, K. W., & Geiwitz, J. (1982). *Adult Development and Aging.* Boston: Little, Brown.

J

JAPANESE PERSPECTIVES ON ADULT DEVELOPMENT

The traditional Japanese perspective on adult development is diametrically opposed to the typical American perspective. The following two examples illustrate the contrasting views.

If you ask Americans to graph the ups and downs of the life course, they usually will draw a curve rising from birth to a peak somewhere in middle age and then declining to old age and death (Back & Bourque, 1970). In contrast, the traditional Japanese would draw a U-shaped curve starting with a high point in childhood, dropping to a low point in middle age, and then rising to old age (Benedict, 1946).

When you meet an older American, you do not usually ask, "How old are you?" This question is considered impolite or embarrassing. If you do happen to learn the person's age, you would probably hope to pay a compliment by saying, "My, you don't look that old!" This type of response, of course, encourages age denial. It is also what is sometimes called a "left-handed compliment" because it implies that "You don't look as decrepit and senile as most people your age!" In contrast, one of the polite things a traditional Japanese may ask an older person is, "How old are you, honorable elder?" The elder's age is usually given with pride, much as children in the United States brag about how old they are. Furthermore, the complimentary response on hearing the elder's age is: "Congratulations! You have achieved the venerable years."

In other words, old age is usually a source of shame and denial in our culture, while in traditional Japanese culture it is a source of honor and pride. Both of these perspectives are types of ageism, i.e., prejudice for or against people on the basis of their age (Palmore, 1990).

Sources of Respect

There are two main sources of respect for elders in Japan: the vertical society and filial piety. The vertical society establishes the right of all older persons to general respect from younger persons; filial piety specifies the obligations owed to one's own parents and grandparents (Palmore & Maida, 1985).

Japan has been called a vertical society because most Japanese relationships are determined by a graded hierarchy of vertical relationships (Nakane, 1972). These are the relationships between superior and inferior, such as parent and child, master and servant, teacher and student, senior and junior persons. These are in contrast to horizontal relationships, which are those between equals, such as between colleagues and friends. In Japan, even relationships between colleagues and friends become vertical, depending on age, sex, and other factors. Because age and seniority are among the most important criteria for these vertical rankings, the Japanese social structure tends to maintain high status for older persons.

Filial piety, the other source of respect for elders, goes back to both Confucian precepts and the even more ancient ancestor worship (Hearn, 1955). Integral to ancestor worship was the belief that the ancestral ghosts must be kept happy through reverence and nourishment because they have the power to control one's destiny for good or evil. It is but a small step from worship of one's dead ancestors to respect for one's living ancestors. Since reverence and devotion to dead ancestors are of supreme importance, respect and duty toward living ancestors became one of the most important duties in life.

Oyakoko, or obligation to parents, was one of two unconditional and absolute duties in traditional culture (the other was obligation to the Emperor and Japan). These duties were so absolute and unconditional that there was a special word for them, *gimu,* to distinguish them from all lesser duties. "It is hard for a Westerner to understand the unconditional nature of this filial piety: Filial piety became in Japan a duty one had to fulfill even if it meant condoning a parent's vice and injustice. It could be abrogated only if it came into conflict with one's obligation to the Emperor, but certainly not when one's parent was unworthy or when he was destroying one's happiness" (Benedict, 1946, p. 119).

Filial piety was also supported by Buddhism, which has a proverb: "Filial piety is the source of many good deeds and the beginning of all virtue."

Family Respect

One sign of family respect for elders is the fact that 70 percent of all Japanese over age 60 still live with their children, in contrast to only 13 percent of Americans (Palmore & Maida, 1985). Most of these arrangements appear to be motivated more by respect and by desire for companionship and mutual aid than by the housing shortage or financial necessity.

A traditional form of respect for elderly family members is the seating arrangement. The seat with the highest honor—nearest the *tokonoma,* an alcove in which scrolls or flowers are displayed—is occupied by the oldest male. His wife usually occupies the second highest seat, and all the other household members are arranged in descending order according to age and sex. The same order of prestige is followed in serving. The oldest male is served first; the youngest female is served last. Not only are the elders served first, they also get the choicest portions of whatever is served. In cooking, also, the tastes of the elders are usually given precedence. If the elders like the rice cooked soft for easier chewing, it will usually be cooked soft even if the young want it firm. If the elders like the food salty or sour, it will usually be prepared to this taste.

A similar order of precedence is usually followed in all household matters. The elders go through doors before younger persons and walk down the street in front of younger persons. The elders get to use the family bath first. The elders usually occupy the rooms with the best exposure and the finest silks, decorations, and bedding. When guests bring gifts, these will be chosen primarily to please the elders.

Adult children who have established their own families show respect and affection for their parents by returning to the family home to celebrate their parents' birthdays and special holidays. Throughout the year, dutiful sons and daughters keep in close contact with their parents through frequent visits, letters, and phone calls. Many adult children call their parents every day, even when they must use long distance.

Bowing to elders is learned at an early age: While the mother still carries the baby strapped to her back, she will push the infant's head down with her hand to bow. His first lessons as a toddler are to observe respectful behavior toward his parents and grandparents. When younger persons bow to their elders, the younger bow lower and stay down longer than the elders.

Public Respect

Perhaps the most pervasive form of respect for the elderly both in private and in public is the honorific language used in speaking to or about them. English has polite and impolite forms for some words, but Japanese is unusual in its extreme elaboration of different forms to show the proper degree of respect or deference. Differential respect is reflected not only in the different nouns, verbs, prefixes, suffixes, and other parts of speech, but also in the basic grammar and syntax of the language.

There are three basic forms of speech in Japanese. The honorific form is used in speaking to someone who is older or otherwise superior to oneself. The middle form is used in speaking to equals. The plain or blunt form is used in speaking to younger persons and other inferiors. Thus, respect for elders is one of the basic dimensions built into the Japanese language.

The importance given to public respect for elders in Japan can be illustrated by quoting from the 1963 National Law for the Welfare of the Elders: "The elders shall be loved and respected as those who have for many years contributed toward the development of society, and a wholesome and peaceful life shall be guaranteed to them." In contrast, the comparable law in the United States, the Older Americans' Act of 1965, does not make any mention of love and respect for elders, nor does it even attempt to "guarantee a wholesome and peaceful life."

To carry out its intention of guaranteeing a wholesome and peaceful life, the Japanese government has established a series of programs for elders, including free annual health examinations, homes for the aged, rest homes, old people's clubs, special employment opportunities, and counseling services.

The government has also designated September 15 as Respect for Elders Day. On this day various ceremonies are held in honor of elders. Children return to their family home to honor their elders, medals and gifts are given by the local and national government honoring those who became 75 during the year, and newspapers and magazines run special features on elders.

Another form of public respect for elders is linked to the fact that the legislature, corporations, universities, religious organizations, and most other such institutions are largely controlled by the elderly. This is a result of the seniority system in which prestige and power tend to increase with age. Japan does not have a true gerontocracy in which elders have all the power, but it is clear that they have a greater share of the power and prestige than other age groups.

Most Japanese believe this is as it should be, since they assume that maturity and wisdom tend to increase with age and that power should be given to those who are most mature and wise—the elders. Some younger people criticize this system. Perhaps not too surprisingly, however, they tend to join and defend the establishment as they grow older.

Because of this respect and because most Japanese believe that all able-bodied persons should remain useful regardless of age, the majority of workers continue in their occupations beyond age 65. They may "retire" to part-time or less demanding work, but they usually continue to be useful and productive in one way or another.

Obasute versus Respect

Ninety miles west of Tokyo is a mountain called *Obasute*, which means "discarding grandmother." There is no evidence that the Japanese have ever abandoned the aged as a matter of custom, but the *Obasute* theme can be traced through tales dating from the sixth century to the present (Plath, 1972).

The theme of resentment against the aged is also the main theme of some popular short stories and novels. These stories indicate that there is widespread resentment against the burdens of caring for those aged who are senile or incapacitated. On the other hand, there are also many stories that show respect for the elderly by portraying them as wise, skillful, and devoted.

Thus, there appears to be considerable ambivalence toward elders among many modern Japanese. They appear to respect elders and show deference to them in public, but in private may resent their power or the burden of caring for them.

Trends

Since World War II and the democratization of Japan, the power of the elderly and the respect accorded to them has diminished. An example of this declining power is the fact that the proportion of marriages arranged by parents or by an elderly matchmaker has declined from about two-thirds to less than one-third. Similarly, the proportion of elders living with their children has declined from about 90 percent to less than 70 percent, but it is still much higher than in the United States.

Despite some decline in status and respect, Japanese elders are still much more integrated into their society and are given much more respect and higher status than elders in the United States.

▼ Erdman B. Palmore

See also: Adult Children and Their Parents; Age 65; Development and Aging in Historical Perspective; Housing as a Factor in Adult Life; Religion in Adult Life; Social Class and Adult Development; Work Organization Membership and Behavior.

References

Back, K., & Bourque, L. (1970). Life graphs: Aging and cohort. *Journal of Gerontology, 25:* 249-55.

Benedict, R. (1946). *The Chrysanthemum and the Sword.* Boston: Houghton Mifflin.

Hearn, L. (1955). *Japan: An Interpretation.* Rutland, VT: Charles E. Tuttle.

Nakane, L. (1972). *Japanese Society.* Berkeley: University of California Press.

Palmore, E. (1990). *Ageism: Negative and Positive.* New York: Springer.

Palmore, E., & Maida, D. (1985). *The Honorable Elders Revisited.* Durham, NC: Duke University Press.

Plath, D. (1972). Japan: The after years. In D. Cowgill & L. Holmes (Eds.), *Aging and Modernization.* New York: Appleton-Century-Crofts.

L

LANGUAGE DEVELOPMENT

Language can be defined as the ability to communicate through the use of oral and written symbols (Benson, 1979). This ability, however, is dependent on a variety of other abilities: speech, comprehension of oral language, reading, writing, and pragmatics (knowing when a particular linguistic form is appropriate).

Childhood language acquisition has been the focus of most of the developmentally oriented research. Particular attention has been given to the years from birth to age 6. Less extensive attention has been given to the examination of language development in later childhood and adolescence. Generally, it has been assumed that language skills are preserved virtually intact into old age. This view assumes that language becomes "crystallized" fairly early in the individual's developmental career and remains stable thereafter. Perhaps because of this assumption, little scholarly attention has been given to either language development or language change across the adult years.

There is now reason to believe that language skills may not be as well preserved across the adult lifespan as has been traditionally assumed.

Second Language and Adult Register Development

Individuals are still able to acquire a variety of language skills well into late ado-

lescence and adulthood. These include foreign language fluency, more effective writing skills, and expanded vocabulary. It does appear, however, that most postchildhood language learning centers on the enrichment of existing skills.

One area in which adolescents and adults do continue to develop is in their use of different "registers." A register represents a particular style of speech. For example, people tend to have one style of speech that they use with their families, another style they use with their friends, and yet another for the workplace. Almost all social and professional groups, whether they are professors or surfers (or surfing professors, for that matter), have their own specialized language and idioms. The ability to learn different registers appears to continue through adulthood and into advanced old age.

It is often thought that second language acquisition is very difficult, if not impossible, for most adults. It is true that learning a *first* language with native proficiency requires that this process begin in childhood. There is more leeway, however, in the acquisition of a second (or third) language. Nonetheless, most individuals find it easier and achieve more success in learning a new language when this is accomplished before puberty. There are exceptions: Some people do acquire additional languages along with the native accent well into adulthood (Obler, 1989). At least one study also found that the ability to learn a language that is spoken in a related dialect (not one's own) increases from adolescence through young adulthood, and improves even further in those aged 30 to 40

(Sankoff, 1970). If, however, one does not continue to use a language, dialect, or register, both comprehension and production abilities may be lost.

Age-Related Changes in Spoken Language

Adult language development appears to be a lifelong process. Language undergoes a continual process of change in response to other changes that occur in adult cognition. Overall, verbal fluency shows a significant decrease with age. This decrease is not as great for persons with higher levels of education. Several aspects of oral language have been studied in connection with age-related processes. These aspects include phonology, lexicon (vocabulary), syntax (sentence structure), and comprehension. Phonology is the only aspect of oral language that appears to remain intact throughout the advanced adult years.

Older adults often complain of difficulty in finding the intended word or proper name. One study that required individuals to name objects and actions (Sandson, Obler, & Albert, 1987) found that correct answers decreased from ages 30 to 79. However, on tasks that require individuals to define target words—rather than retrieving words from memory—elderly adults are more likely to give superior explanations. Furthermore, there appears to be little or no age-related decrement in the passive access to one's lexicon. For example, older people perform just as well as young people when asked to recognize a label or name. Findings such as these suggest that lexical items are not being lost with advancing adult age, but rather, one tends to have more difficulty obtaining access to particular words on demand. In fact, vocabulary tends to grow throughout the adult years even though more difficulties are experienced in accessing words from memory. It is possible, however, that the ability to learn new words decreases somewhat in advanced old age, although new learning continues to take place.

The decreased ability to access words is probably related to decreased memory functioning as people age. Elderly people have been found to tend to engage in circumlocutions (roundabout explanations) and unnecessary comments when engaged in memory tasks. These appear to be strategies that are invoked when attempting to recall or describe a word. The explanations offered by older people tend to be longer, suggesting some difficulty in finding just the right words.

The speech of elderly people is often perceived by listeners as being tangential and circumlocutory. Studies of spoken discourse find that older groups use more paraphrasing and more indefinite terms, comments, and questions (Obler, 1989). The overall pattern of speech changes with age suggests that people tend to use more words to explain their ideas, tend to rephrase an idea several different ways in the same conversation, and tend to state their ideas less directly. These characteristics are not always perceived as negative: In cultures that place a high value on storytelling, the older storyteller is usually considered to be the most satisfying.

The increased elaborateness of language in the later adult years—the tendency to use more words and more and longer sentences to make the same point—is accompanied by another pattern of change. Despite the more elaborate production of speech, the overall structure of language becomes less complex and more errors are made by people as they age. The speech becomes more extended in terms of number of words spoken, but the sentence structure becomes simpler. One study found that the average number of clauses per sentence in spontaneous oral language decreased by 23 percent from ages 50 to 90 (Kemper et al., 1989). This finding suggests that as people age they use fewer sentences with embedded clauses. For example, elderly speakers are more likely to say: "I grew up in the nation's capitol. I have many happy memories of presidents, inaugurations, political feuds, and elections." A younger speaker is more likely to say, "I enjoyed growing up in Washington, D.C., with its active political life, such as elections, inaugurations, and political feuds." It is theorized that older adults' production of complex syntactic constructions is affected by decreases in their ability to retain and manipulate multiple language elements simultaneously.

Comprehension of oral language at the one-word level is unchanged in later adulthood. However, decreases with age appear at the level of the sentence, the paragraph, and other longer units. Furthermore, the more syntactically complex the language, the more difficult it is for elderly adults to retrieve it from memory. In tasks that require recalling information from a paragraph, older adults retrieve fewer items, concepts, and themes.

Overall, then, significant qualitative changes in language can be observed with normal aging. Although communication remains functional throughout the lifespan, elderly people tend to have a more elaborate discourse style, poorer retrieval of words from an intact lexicon, less complex syntax, and more difficulties on naming and comprehension tasks. Nevertheless, it is probable that most adults develop strategies for coping with memory and language change. Consequently, these underlying changes do not necessarily interfere with effective communication.

Age-Related Changes in Written Language

Studies of written language in adulthood show changes similar to those found in oral language. The written language of adults over age 70 is more likely to be marked by elaborateness of style, with more articles (the, a, an) and modifying words and phrases. Interestingly, 30-year-olds write more like 70-year-olds. At mid-life—about age 50—adults tend to use a more abbreviated or concise style. It is possible that younger people use an elaborated written style that gives way to a more economical style in mid-life but becomes elaborated again in later years. An alternative explanation could be cohort differences in writing style, but this possibility remains to be studied.

Examinations of adults' written texts indicate that an overall decrease in the complexity of sentences occurs in written as well as oral language use. In fact, the decline in the average number of clauses per utterance is even greater for written (44 percent) than for oral (23 percent) language. This shift in sentence complexity does not necessarily mean that the writing has become less effective. Judges of written discourse have rated the prose statements composed by elderly individuals as clearer and more interesting than those of young adults. Written communications tend to gain in interest and clarity across the entire adult age range. A comparison of written and spoken language suggests, however, that written language remains somewhat more complex than oral discourse for elderly people (Kemper et al., 1989).

The reduced complexity in writing that is produced by elderly adults has its parallel in the ability to read communications written by others. Elderly adults have difficulty in processing written material that contains complex sentences. Studies of text comprehension and recall disclose age-related decrements for the repetition and recall of complex syntactic constructions. Individuals with higher levels of verbal ability showed less decrement with age.

Limitations of Available Knowledge

Despite the research findings reported here, what must be kept in mind is the wide variation that exists across individuals of the same age. How much an individual's use of language actually changes over time to a large extent depends on his or her individual abilities and education. Some people have superior cognitive abilities that are expressed in early language development and continue to be operative throughout the entire lifespan. It is quite possible for a 70-year-old to have greater access to his or her vocabulary or to write more complex sentences than a less gifted 30-year-old.

Education level is also associated with language style and skill. Most of the research that has been conducted on language change across the adult years has focused on adults with relatively little advanced education. When adults with higher levels of education are included in the studies, they generally show considerably less decrement in their ability to process language. There are also some indications that older adults who continue to use their skills—through reading, writing, and learning activities—maintain their abilities longer and with fewer losses than those who do not.

Another caution to bear in mind is the possibility of cohort effects, as mentioned above. For example, more people attend college today than did so 50 years ago (this is particularly true for women). Therefore, what has been discovered to be true of 70-year-olds today may not be true of 70-year-olds as we near the middle of the twenty-first century. It is also possible that young people today read less and watch television more—this pattern could have many effects on the language skills that elderly people will possess half a century from now.

Finally, it is also possible that the way that most studies have been conducted may influence the findings. For example, asking elderly people to write an essay rather than using existing materials could influence the style and quality. If the participants were not motivated to perform well, they may not have produced examples of their best work (the same could possibly be true of the younger participants as well).

Despite these cautions, it does appear that the belief that language "crystallizes" after adolescence is in error. There are differences in both written and oral language across the adult lifespan. Precisely how these differences originate and what role they may play in the individual's overall cognitive and social functioning remain to be determined by future studies.   ▼ Jess Alberts

See also: Cohort and Generational Effects; Habituation: A Key to Lifespan Development and Aging?; Intelligence; Intelligence—Crystallized and Fluid; Learning and Memory in Everyday Life; Memory; The Voice.

References

Benson, D. F. (1979). *Aphasia, Alexia, and Agraphia.* New York: Churchill Livingston.

Kemper, S., & Rash, S. J. (1988). Speech and writing across the life-span. In M. M. Gruneberg, P. E. Morris, & P. E. Sykes (Eds.), *Practical Aspects of Memory: Current Research and Issues. II.* New York: John Wiley & Sons, pp. 107-12.

Kemper, S., et al. (1989). Life-span changes to adults' language: Effects of memory and genre. *Applied Psycholinguistics*, 10: 49-66.

Knoefel, J. E. (1990). Neurological aging. In E. Cherow (Ed.), Proceedings of the research symposium on communication sciences and disorders and aging. *American Speech-Language-Hearing Association Reports.*

Obler, L. K. (1989). Language beyond childhood. In J. B. Gleason (Ed.), *The Development of Language.* London: Merrill, pp. 275-302.

Sandson, J., Obler, L. K., & Albert, M. L. (1987). Language changes in healthy aging and dementia. In S. Rosenberg (Ed.), *Advances in Applied Psycholinguistics.* New York: Cambridge University Press.

Sankoff, G. (1970): *The Social Life of Language.* Philadelphia: University of Pennsylvania Press.

LEARNING AND MEMORY IN EVERYDAY LIFE

Maintaining their learning and memory skills is vitally important to many adults. Not being able to learn new procedures at work or to remember others' names can be both embarrassing and detrimental to personal and occupational well-being.

What is known about learning and memory in everyday adult life has grown from studies of these basic processes in the laboratory. The knowledge gained through research, however, does not fully serve its purpose until it is made available for use in our everyday world. This potentially valuable relationship between the laboratory and the everyday world emphasizes the need for "ecological" or "external" validity. Findings obtained under well-controlled experimental conditions and using somewhat contrived tasks may or may not generalize to the world outside the laboratory (Mook, 1983).

Concerns about external validity are also frequently expressed in the broad field of adult developmental research. Schaie (1978) and Scheidt (1981) have discussed the need for externally valid research in cognition. Investigators are urged to study learning, memory, problem solving, and other cognitive abilities in ways that have relevance to intellectual functioning in everyday life. Ecologically valid research should use stimuli that are truly representative of the larger world. In this way, the studies could be said to possess "functional validity" (Scheidt, 1981).

Familiar tasks or stimuli become unfamiliar, however, if they are extracted from the real-world context in which they usually occur (Hultsch & Hickey, 1978; Scheidt, 1981). For example, rather than presenting arbitrary lists of numbers or words to be recalled, studies of everyday learning and memory might more usefully evaluate the adult's ability to learn and recall real telephone numbers or actual grocery lists (e.g., West & Crook, 1990).

The fact that a study uses real world-type methods does not guarantee that the results will be applicable outside the laboratory (Banaji & Crowder, 1989), but there is a growing consensus that both specialized and naturalistic research approaches are necessary to help us understand learning and memory (Ceci & Bronfenbrenner, 1991; Conway, 1991; Tulving, 1991). In this connection it is useful to distinguish between *mechanistic* explanations of memory, in which underlying processes are identified, and *functional* explanations, which identify the everyday uses that are served by these processes (Bruce, 1991).

The adult learner can only be understood within the context of many interacting systems, such as the family and the culture (Sinnott, 1989a). Furthermore, an individual's learning and memory system is influenced by his or her sensory, perceptual, and motivational systems. The learning and memory

system cannot be separated from the other intrapersonal systems with which it must interact and the real-world systems in which the individual is embedded. Learning and memory in everyday life therefore must be understood in relative rather than absolute terms, especially if our focus is on the individual as acting upon the learning environment rather than being a passive recipient of stimuli and information. Instead of viewing a learner as competent or incompetent, this approach suggests that an individual's skills are simply more or less functional in solving everyday problems.

Performance is relative to (a) the nature of the information to be learned, (b) the needs, abilities, and motives of the individual, and (c) the requirements of the situation in which the individual uses his or her learning and memory skills. Moreover, those methods of intervention that might be used to help someone improve learning and memory skills must also be flexible.

Enhancing Adult Learning and Memory Skills

A number of factors are important in efforts to enhance the adult learner's performance.

1. *The learner's characteristics.* What is the level of the factual knowledge, existing skills, self-assessment of abilities, and susceptibility to factors that could interfere with the learning process (e.g., anxiety or fatigue)?

2. *Behaviors expected of the individual.* The individual can be helped to meet these expectations by being offered specific help in the areas of asking more effective questions, using mediational aids, conducting more effective rehearsals, or utilizing techniques to reduce anxiety.

3. *Nature of the training or intervention program.* This includes attention to the use of materials that are meaningful, concrete, and clearly understood, as well as to process (e.g., rewarding participants for responding to all items, reducing anxi-

ety, or providing feedback and practice with learning materials).

4. *Specific goals of the individual.* With each person's own goals and needs in mind, the program can be tightly focused on particular skills or, even if more broadly conceived, can be made personally meaningful to the learner (Willis, 1985).

A variety of noncognitive interventions interact with the learning situation and the learner's personality and skills (Hayslip & Kennelly, 1985). For example, fears about getting lost at night or about failing an important exam might actually make it more difficult for an adult learner to find his or her way or to do well on the exam. Other noncognitive factors include overarousal, fatigue, being unwilling to use learning or memory aids, not wanting to guess to avoid being wrong, sensory deficits, not understanding task instructions, and using tasks that are too rapidly paced.

It is especially important to ensure that older adults are "fresh" when they attempt new learning. Moreover, the registration of material that must be learned and recalled can be enhanced by minimizing the effect of sensory deficits. Visual presentation may be best for material that is personally meaningful and that can be reviewed (Arenberg, 1976; Dixon et al., 1982). On other hand, auditory augmentation may be more helpful when dealing with material that is less familiar and more complex. An example of auditory augmentation would be speaking as one is presenting slides—assuming that the auditory and visual inputs are well coordinated.

Personality also has a significant influence on learning and memory in adulthood (Kausler, 1990). An individual's personal beliefs, values, and perceptions can influence even the basic judgment as to whether he or she should attempt to maintain learning and memory skills (Hayslip & Panek, 1989). Believing that one has little control over events in one's life, not valuing one's intellectual skills, and excessive anxiety about possible failure are all personality factors that can set the stage for diminished cognitive functioning in adulthood. The assumption that one is "too old" to learn new things, or that memory naturally fails with increasing age, can undermine the development of new skills in adulthood, as well as lead to the decline of existing skills (Hayslip, 1989a). The individual's beliefs about the possibility of learning new things or about the inevitability of memory loss with age should be carefully explored before an attempt is made to develop new skills or enhance existing skills.

Learning and retention of new material are particularly difficult when the adult learner must divide his or her attention in complex situations, or when fatigue or depression is present (Kennelly, Hayslip, & Richardson, 1985). If depression is suspected, a separate evaluation is in order and, if necessary, treatment should be given before making any efforts at new learning.

Recent discussions of intervention programs reflect a sensitivity to the variety of influences on learning and memory performance (West, 1989). Enhancement techniques involve (a) assessing the learning and memory demands that a person faces, (b) identifying helpful strategies that individuals are able and willing to use in improving their skills (e.g., organizational techniques, mnemonic aids, overlearning, verbal elaboration), and (c) ensuring that such gains can be maintained and that they are generalizable over a variety of situations.

Learning versus Memory

Learning and memory are usually considered to be separate, yet highly interrelated, processes. Learning is often understood in terms of the acquisition of stimulus-response (S-R) associations (Kausler, 1991). From this standpoint, all learning is associative. Learning has also been defined as a systematic change in behavior "that occurs in some specified situation" (Estes, 1975, p. 9). The implication is that the learner has brought intention and effort into the situation, as distinguished from an entirely mechanistic S-R approach. Memory is usually defined as a more abstract process that is also dependent upon experience but not necessarily tied to a specific situation, as is the case with learning (Estes, 1975; Kausler, 1991).

The associative view of learning, based on the linking of stimuli and responses, has been challenged by several other approaches. Cognitive psychology sees the adult learner as an active processor of information (Schwartz & Reisberg, 1991). The main elements in learning here are the cognitive processes or operations that people actively perform on the information that is to be learned and remembered. For example, one might organize or categorize information to be stored for later retrieval or recall. This happens, for example, when trying to remember grocery items to be purchased or in learning and recalling people's names at a party. Still another approach to learning and memory relies on the integrity of brain cells (neurons). Depending on how the individual's neural network is organized, he or she is more or less efficient in learning and recalling information (Kausler, 1991). All these approaches have generated studies that are useful in improving our understanding of learning and memory in adulthood.

Although learning and memory are separate, they are also closely related to each other. In fact, learning must be inferred from memory and memory from learning because they cannot be observed directly and independently. For example, one's ability to learn new information often is assessed through measuring recall. Indeed, one cannot recall that which has not been learned. "If a man does not learn well, he has little to recall....If his memory is poor, there is no sign of his having learned much" (Botwinick, 1978, p. 261).

In practice, it is often difficult to make the distinction between learning and memory. For example, in studying for a test, one acquires information by reading, organizing, and reviewing. If the test will be given two days from now, the learner must be able to store or hold that information securely until it is time to retrieve the material for the test performance. The individual's learning and memory for the test material are inferred on the basis of the test score. In the context of everyday living, adequate learning and memory skills must be inferred on the basis of the adult's coping skills, decision making, or adaptation to stress and change.

Research on everyday learning and memory in adulthood has explored a variety of topics. Particular attention has been given to: (a) memory for text materials, (b) metamemory, (c) speech comprehension, (d) memory for spatial information, and (e) prospective memory.

Memory for Text Materials

Text comprehension is an active, constructive process in which the learner processes each sentence selectively, piecing it together with existing knowledge to generate a new interpretation about what a particular statement means (Hultsch & Dixon, 1984). Indeed, the processing of text materials reflects a variety of logical operations. The learner constructs the meaning of a text through a hierarchical organization of arguments or propositions that are linked together by verbs. In the learner's mind, arguments may or may not be connected in the text, depending on their relationships to each other.

A number of factors affect the ability to process and recall text in an efficient manner (Hultsch & Dixon, 1984). One important factor is the type of instruction and preparation that has been given to the learner. For example, the person may be asked to read a list of words for their meaning prior to reading the text materials. This exercise is found beneficial by young adults whose recall of text is enhanced after the preliminary reading, but the same procedure interferes with text learning among older persons. Furthermore, age differences in performance also can be affected by the modality through which the presentation of material is made (oral or visual) and whether the researchers are analyzing recall for details or main ideas. It can also make a difference whether the recall is tested immediately after learning or after a period of time has elapsed. The precise method of assessing the text learning can also influence the results. Generally, it is easier to recognize the correct item when given a choice among several possibilities than it is to come up with the right answer spontaneously (recall method).

Memory for text material depends on more than age. Breadth of prior knowledge, level of education, and verbal ability will all influence performance (Meyer & Rice, 1989). As might be expected, performance is poorest for those who have little prior knowledge of the topic, who are poorly educated, and who have the least verbal ability. Hartley (1986) found that the effectiveness of reading ability was a better predictor than age in determining memory for text. Age differences in memory for text may exist under certain circumstances, but these have yet to be fully determined.

A person's goals and strategies, reading habits, and personality also influence memory for text material. Although reading news articles, stories, and other materials in the "real world" could provide natural examples of text memory, adults are seldom required to absorb a passage with the goal of being able to recall it accurately and in detail (Hartley, 1989). For this reason, we still know little about what actual strategies might be used by adult readers as they pursue their own goals.

Metamemory

This term refers to "how much we know about what we know" (Lachman, Lachman, & Thronesberg, 1979). The study of metamemory is important because confidence in one's own abilities influences the amount of preparation and effort put into dealing with everyday tasks. For example, whether or not one makes a grocery list before leaving for the store depends on a personal estimate of memory skills. A common observation is that many adults underestimate their own learning or memory skills and therefore rely heavily on calendars, date books, or diaries to keep track of appointments.

The literature regarding age differences in metamemory is mixed. Many researchers

have found that older persons are as accurate in predicting what they can and cannot remember as are younger adults, regardless of whether old or new information is being dealt with (e.g., Lachman & Lachman, 1980; Rabinowitz et al., 1982). Others, however, have found that older persons are more likely than young adults to overestimate the extent of what they can remember (e.g., Bruce et al., 1982; Murphy et al., 1981). Just to confuse matters further, Zelinski, Gilewski, and Thompson (1980) found that older adults were *more* accurate than young adults in estimating their performances.

Again, there are mixed findings on the relationship between subjective estimates of memory skills and the older individual's actual objective performance. One study found little relationship between subjective estimates and objective performance (Zarit, Cole, & Guider, 1981), while another found a positive relationship (Poon & Schaffer, 1982). A key to resolving these inconsistent findings will be improvements in the measurement of metamemory (Poon, 1985).

Despite the mixed character of the available findings, this newly emerging area of research has promise for offering a firmer base for training programs that can enhance adult learning and memory performances. It may be that such programs can be more effective if they are targeted at the particular older learner whose metamemory skills are poor. Perhaps this person also has low self-esteem. Persons who are somewhat depressed and who have not used existing skills for some time may also have become isolated from social feedback and therefore may have lost touch with the state of their own learning and memory skills (Hayslip & Caraway, 1989). Reminding older learners to use memory strategies that have proven effective for them in the past, promoting an awareness of their metamemory skills, and clearly specifying goals are among the viable strategies that can enhance the memory performance of older persons both on laboratory tasks and in everyday situations (Poon, 1985).

People's estimates of their own abilities can be upgraded by reducing anxiety and by altering their general self-perceptions (Hayslip, 1989b). This again suggests that noncognitive factors might influence learning and memory, and should encourage continued exploration of how adults explain their learning and memory problems as well as their overall sense of intellectual efficacy (Bandura, 1977; Lachman & Jelalian, 1984; Lachman & McArthur, 1986). For example, when older persons experience memory difficulties, these problems are frequently attributed to a lack of competence. When such failures are experienced by younger persons, however, the explanation usually offered is lack of effort and attention (Erber, Szuchman, and Rothberg, 1990). This difference may reflect the lower expectations that both the young and the old have regarding the cognitive skills of older persons.

Speech Comprehension

Speech comprehension is relevant to adults of all ages if they are to interact with others effectively. How we process what is said to us in a conversation is "on-line" (Stine, Wingfield & Poon, 1989). Often we can go back and read something again or pick out a particular passage here and there. What we hear, though, is *sequential*: The listener must attend to every word as it is spoken to come away with an accurate understanding. Words must be recognized and a context for understanding must be constructed. For adults with uncorrected age-related hearing loss (presbycusis), there is a distortion in the basic sound information needed for processing and understanding. The faulty reception of auditory information makes it difficult to understand what has been said.

Fortunately, however, there is little decline in the ability to construct a linguistic context essential to comprehension and recall (Stine, Wingfield, & Poon, 1989). Noise and overly rapid speech can make it difficult for the older person to register the words clearly, but the basic ability to comprehend speech remains. Both younger and older adults are able to compensate to some extent for higher rates of speech by selecting longer sequences of words instead of concentrating on word-by-word attention. A deficit in processing individual words or word elements is more common among older adults, but often this can be compensated for by giving more attention to the larger pattern of discourse.

Memory for Spatial Information

Our knowledge of and memory for spatial activities and relationships comes into play when we search for an object that is usually left in a given place (e.g., our keys or glasses) or when trying to get our bearings when lost in an unfamiliar place. As with memory for prose and other ecological tasks, the learner's skills are important. The available findings clearly indicate age-related declines in memory for spatial locations (Kivasic, 1989). This is true in both small-scale (e.g., location of features on a map) and large scale situations (e.g., knowledge of one's residence or of landmarks in one's hometown). Moreover, a person's spatial abilities seem to predict knowledge of his or her own neighborhood (Krauss, Awad, & McCormick, 1981). In a study involving shopping in a familiar vs. an unfamiliar supermarket, younger adults' ability to execute an efficient shopping route in a new setting was not affected by their familiarity with an old setting (Kivasic, 1981). Older adults, however, did seem to be affected, suggesting that familiarity with one setting interfered somewhat with learning their way in the new setting. Interestingly, spatial skills had a different relationship to efficiency of shopping behavior in young and old adults. Spatial skills predicted shopping behavior in the novel setting for younger persons, while for older persons spatial skills predicted behavior in the familiar settings. As with other ecological tasks, much remains to be learned about the everyday spatial behavior of adults.

Prospective Memory

We use prospective memory skills when we intentionally memorize a list of things to be done in the future. Making decisions for future retirement, planning a vacation, or just getting through a hectic day are among the activities that involve carrying out plans and reaching previously set goals. Research in this newly emerging area is just starting to appear. Tasks that have been studied include remembering to mail a postcard or make a phone call at a particular time in the future. In almost every case, either no age differences or superior performances by older persons have been observed (Sinnott, 1989b).

A recent study (Einstein & McDaniel, 1990) found no age differences in prospective memory (as measured by remembering to press a key when the word "rake" appeared in a list of words to be recalled later). Additionally, the possession of a good short-term memory was not related to prospective memory skills. Both young and older adults showed improved prospective memory performances when they were permitted to use a memory aid, such as a note or a string tied to a finger. Moreover, as the distinctiveness of the stimulus to which they were to respond in the future increased, their performance improved. Unfamiliar or unique cues presumably create less interference, thereby leading to better prospective memory.

For effective prospective memory, it is important not only to remember that one must do something in the future but also to remember the particular cue or target that should elicit this behavior. For example, knowing right now that one must make an important phone call at noon three days from today does one little good if, when the time comes, one fails to remember that it is at noon that the call must be made. Prospective memory may prove to be a highly relevant process that enables adults to continue to function adaptively in everyday life.

The Adult Learner

Learning in adulthood can be thought of as self-directed (Hiemstra, 1985). It is learning that one decides to pursue because of one's own experiences and interests rather than what is required by school or other

external influences. Self-directed learning activities can have very positive effects on the adult's self-esteem and fulfillment. This predisposition to learn either for meaning or for achievement has been termed *learning style* (Schmeck, 1983). Older as well as younger adults are affected by their learning style. Davenport (1986) found that the personal and educational benefits of continued learning activities for older persons varied with sex and with various learning styles, but not with age.

Altering expectations about continued learning throughout adulthood can be an important influence on adults of all ages. Should they learn new skills? Can they continue to feel productive and worthwhile? Interventions and opportunities that are based on individual differences in abilities, interests, and personal goals are critical to enhancing learning skills.

Several possible goals for the adult learner have been suggested by Willis (1985):

1. Improving one's understanding of age-related changes and how the basic biological processes can affect everyday feelings and behaviors
2. Understanding and coping with technological and cultural change (e.g., becoming computer literate)
3. Developing new skills to help overcome the obsolescence generated by rapid cultural change so that one can maintain an independent life-style
4. Contributing to the development of second careers
5. Encouraging the formation of skills that are personally relevant, rather than occupationally relevant, after retirement

Education can serve many ends for different adult learners at different points in their lives. Individuals who begin such efforts early in adulthood are more likely to see their learning and memory skills in a positive light. Many adults do not see a reason to develop their cognitive skills or assume that such efforts would be doomed to failure. These attitudes are shaped by our society's youth-oriented "production mentality"

(Ansello & Hayslip, 1979). Unfortunately, many adults have come to subscribe to this negative view and therefore do not pursue formal or informal educational opportunities. Encouraging the adult learner to continue to "be alive" mentally requires changing our society's attitudes. Adults of all ages can build on their existing skills and develop new abilities in both instrumental (goal-oriented) and expressive (individually centered) areas. Equal attention should be given to the ends as well as the means for enhancing one's abilities throughout all the adult years.

▼ BERT HAYSLIP, JR.

See also: Cardiac Health; Drug Use and Abuse; Exercise; Expressive Arts; Grandparent Education to Enhance Family Strength; Individuality; Information Processing; Language Development; Listening; Memory; Subcultural Influences on Lifelong Development.

References

Ansello, E. F, & Hayslip, B. (1979). Older adult higher eduction: Academic stepchild and Cinderella. In H. Sterns et al. (Eds.), *Gerontology in Higher Education*. Belmont, CA: Wadsworth, pp. 262-73.

Arenberg, D. (1976). The effects of input condition on free recall in young and old adults. *Journal of Gerontology, 31:* 551-55.

Banaji, M., & Crowder, R. (1989). The bankruptcy of everyday memory. *American Psychologist, 44:* 1185-93.

Bandura, A. (1977). Self efficacy: Toward a unifying theory of behavioral change. *Psychological Review, 84:* 191-215.

Botwinick, J. (1967). *Cognitive Processes in Maturity and Old Age*. New York: Springer.

———. (1978). *Aging and Behavior*. Second Edition. New York: Springer.

———. (1981). *Aging and Behavior*. Third Edition. New York: Springer.

Bruce, D. (1991). Mechanistic and functional explanations of memory. *American Psychologist, 46:* 46-48.

Bruce, P., Coyne, A., & Botwinick, J. (1982). Adult age differences in metamemory. *Journal of Gerontology, 37:* 354-57.

Campbell, D. T., & Stanley, J. (1963). *Experimental and Quasi-experimental Designs for Research*. Chicago: Rand-McNally.

Ceci, S. J., & Bronfenbrenner, U. (1991). On the demise of everyday memory: "The rumors of my death are much exaggerated" (Mark Twain). *American Psychologist, 46:* 27-31.

Conway, M. (1991). In defense of everyday memory. *American Psychologist, 46:* 19-26.

Davenport, J. (1986). Learning style and its relationship to gender and age among Elderhostel participants. *Educational Gerontology, 12:* 205-17.

Dixon, R., et al. (1982). Text recall in adulthood as a function of level of information, input modality, and delay interval. *Journal of Gerontology, 37:* 358-64.

Einstein, G. O., & McDaniel, M. A. (1990). Normal aging and prospective memory. *Journal of Experimental Psychology, 16:* 717-26.

Erber, J. T., Szuchman, L. T., & Rothberg, S. T. (1990). Age, gender, and individual differences in memory failure appraisal. *Psychology and Aging, 5:* 600-03.

Estes, W. K. (1975). The state of the field: General problems and issues of theory and metatheory. In W. K. Estes (Ed.), *Handbook of Learning and Cognitive Processes*. Volume 1. Hillsdale, NJ: Lawrence Erlbaum, pp. 1-24.

Hartley, J. T. (1986). Reader and text variables as determinants of discourse memory in adulthood. *Psychology and Aging, 1:* 150-58.

———. (1989). Memory for prose: Perspectives on the reader. In L. W. Poon, D. C. Rubin, & B. A. Wilson (Eds.), *Everyday Cognition in Adulthood and Late Life*. Cambridge, MA: Cambridge University Press, pp. 135-56.

Hartley, J. T., Harker, J. O., & Walsh, D. (1980). Contemporary issues and new directions in adult development of learning and memory. In L. W. Poon (Ed.), *Aging in the 1980's: Contemporary Issues*. Washington, DC: American Psychological Association, pp. 239-52.

Hayslip, B. (1989a). Fluid ability training with aged people: A past with a future? *Educational Gerontology, 15:* 573-86.

———. (1989b). Alternative mechanisms for improvements in fluid ability performance in aged persons. *Psychology and Aging, 4:* 122-24.

Hayslip, B. & Caraway, M. (1989). Cognitive therapy with aged persons:Implications of research design for its implementation and evaluation. *Journal of Cognitive Psychotherapy, 3,* 255-71.

Hayslip, B., & Kennelly, K. J. (1985). Cognitive and noncognitive factors affecting learning among older adults. In D. B. Lumsden (Ed.),

The Older Adult as Learner. Washington, DC: Hemisphere, pp. 73-98.

Hayslip, B. & Panek, P. (1989). *Adult development and aging.* New York: HarperCollins.

Hiemstra, R. (1985). The older adult's learning projects. In D. B. Lumsden (Ed.), *The Older Adult as Learner.* Washington, DC: Hemisphere, pp. 165-96.

Horn, J. L. (1965). A rationale and test for the number of factors in factor analysis. *Psychometrika, 30,* 179-85.

Hultsch, D. F., & Dixon, R. (1984). Memory for text materials in adulthood. In P. Baltes & O. Brim (Eds.), *Lifespan Development and Behavior.* Volume 6. New York: Academic Press, pp. 77-108.

Hultsch, D.F., & Hickey, T. (1978). External validity in the study of human development: Theoretical and methodological issues. *Human Development, 21:* 76-91.

Kausler, D. F. (1990). Motivation, human aging, and cognitive performance. In J. E. Birren & K. W. Schaie (Eds.), *Handbook of the Psychology of Aging.* Third Edition. New York: Academic Press, pp. 171-81.

———. (1991). *Experimental Psychology, Cognition, and Human Aging.* New York: Springer-Verlag.

Kennelly, K. J., Hayslip, B., & Richardson, S. (1985). Depression and helplessness-induced cognitive deficits in the aged. *Experimental Aging Research, 8:* 165-73.

Kivasic, K. C. (1981). Studying the "hometown advantage" in elderly adult's spatial cognition and spatial behavior. Paper presented at the Annual Convention of the Society for Research in Child Development, Boston, MA, April 1981.

———. (1989). Acquisition and utilization of spatial information by elderly adults: Implications for day-to-day situations. In L. W. Poon, D. C. Rubin, & B. A. Wilson (Eds.), *Everyday Cognition in Adulthood and Late Life.* Cambridge, MA: Cambridge University Press, pp. 265-83.

Krauss, I., Awad, Z., & McCormick, D. (1981). Learning, remembering, and using spatial information as an older adult. Paper presented at the Annual Convention of the Society for Research in Child Development. Boston, MA, April 1981.

Lachman, J.L., & Lachman, R. (1980). Age and the actualization of world knowledge. In L. Poon, et al. (Eds.), *New Directions in Memory and Aging.* Hillsdale, NJ: Lawrence Erlbaum, pp. 285-311.

Lachman, J. L., Lachman, R., & Thronesberg, C. (1979). Metamemory throughout the adult lifespan. *Developmental Psychology, 15:* 543-51.

Lachman, M. E., & Jelalian, E. (1984). Self-efficacy and attributions for intellectual performance in young and elderly adults. *Journal of Gerontology, 39,* 577-82.

Lachman, M. E., & McArthur, J. (1986). Adult age differences in causal attributions for cognitive, physical, and social performance. *Psychology and Aging, 1,* 127-32.

Meyer, B. J., & Rice, G. E. (1989). Prose processing in adulthood: The text, the reader, and the task. In L. W. Poon, D. C. Rubin, & B. Wilson (Eds.), *Everyday Cognition in Adulthood and Late Life.* Cambridge, MA: Cambridge University Press, pp. 157-94.

Mook, D. G. (1983). In defense of external invalidity. *American Psychologist, 38:* 379-87.

Murphy, M., et al. (1981). Metamemory in the aged. *Journal of Gerontology, 36:* 185-93.

Poon, L. (1985). Differences in human memory with aging. In J. E. Birren & K. W. Schaie (Eds.), *Handbook of the Psychology of Aging.* Second Edition. New York: Van Nostrand Reinhold, pp. 427-62.

Poon, L., & Schaffer, G. (1982). Prospective memory in young and elderly adults. Paper presented at the Annual Convention of the American Psychological Association, Washington, DC, August, 1982.

Rabinowitz, J. C., et al. (1982). Aging and metamemory: The roles of relatedness and imagery. *Journal of Gerontology, 37:* 688-95.

Schaie, K. W. (1978). External validity in the assessment of intellectual development in adulthood. *Journal of Gerontology, 33:* 695-701.

Scheidt, R. J. (1981). Ecologically-valid inquiry: Fait accompli? *Human Development, 24:* 225-28.

Schmeck, R. R. (1983). Learning styles of college students. In R. F. Dillon & R. R. Schmeck (Eds.), *Individual Differences in Cognition.* Volume 1. New York: Academic Press, pp. 223-80.

Schwartz, B., & Reisberg, D. (1991). *Learning and Memory.* New York: Norton.

Sinnott, J. (1989a). General systems theory: A rationale for the study of everyday memory. In L. W. Poon, D. C. Rubin, & B. A. Wilson (Eds.), *Everyday Cognition in Adulthood and Late Life.* Cambridge, MA: Cambridge University Press, pp. 59-72.

———. (1989b). Prospective / intentional memory and aging. In L. W. Poon, D. C. Rubin, & B. A. Wilson (Eds.), *Everyday Cognition in Adulthood and Late Life*. Cambridge, MA: Cambridge University Press, pp. 352-72.

Stine, E. L., Wingfield, A., & Poon, L. W. (1989). Speech comprehension and memory through adulthood: The roles of time and strategy. In L. W. Poon, D. C. Rubin, & B. A. Wilson (Eds.), *Everyday Cognition in Adulthood and Late Life*. Cambridge, MA: Cambridge University Press, pp. 195-221.

Tulving, E. (1991). Memory research is not a zero-sum game. *American Psychologist, 46:* 41-42.

West, R.L. (1989). Planning practical memory training for the aged. In L. W. Poon, D. C. Rubin, & B. A. Wilson (Eds.), *Everyday Cognition in Adulthood and Late Life*. Cambridge, MA: Cambridge University Press, pp. 520-29.

West, R. L., & Crook, T. H. (1990). Age differences in everyday memory: Laboratory analogues of telephone number recall. *Psychology and Aging, 5:* 520-29.

Willis, S. L. (1985). Towards an educational psychology of the older adult learner: Intellectual and cognitive bases. In J. E. Birren & K. W. Schaie (Eds.), *Handbook of the Psychology of Aging*. Second Edition. New York: Van Nostrand Reinhold, pp. 818-47.

Zarit, S., Cole, K., & Guider, R. (1981). Memory training strategies and subjective complaints of memory in the aged. *The Gerontologist, 21:* 158-64.

Zelinski, E., Gilewski, M., & Thompson, L. (1980). Do laboratory tests relate to everyday remembering and forgetting? In L. Poon, et al. (Eds.), *New Directions in Memory and Aging*. Hillsdale, NJ: Lawrence Erlbaum, pp. 519-44.

LIFE EVENTS

Life events are identifiable, discrete changes in life patterns. Examples of life events that have received substantial research attention include starting and stopping work, marriage and parenthood, health problems, and loss of important relationships by death or estrangement. Most of the research literature emphasizes the facts that life events disrupt a person's usual behavior pattern and can threaten or challenge personal well-being.

Less commonly, it is noted that life events also can enhance well-being.

Because of their discrete character, the onset of life events can be clearly dated. The literature is vague about the duration of life events, probably because it is difficult to pinpoint when some types of life events can be considered to have ended. There is general consensus, however, that life events do have temporal boundaries and are most usefully regarded as episodes rather than ongoing patterns. A given life event may have long-term or even permanent consequences despite the fact that the event itself occurred within the relatively brief time framework.

How Life Events Are Studied

The occurrence of life events is usually identified and measured by self-reports. Two of the most widely used life event measures are the Schedule of Recent Events (Holmes & Rahe, 1967) and the Geriatric Social Readjustment Rating scale (Amster & Krauss, 1974). Most life event instruments inquire about events that have been experienced in the recent past (e.g., the past year). This approach is taken because (a) recent changes are expected to be those that are most strongly related to well-being and (b) memory problems can reduce the accuracy of reports regarding more remote events.

One of the major differences between life event measures is the presence or absence of weights. Many measures are scored simply by summing the number of life events that occurred over a defined period of time. This procedure reflects the assumption that larger numbers of events represent higher levels of change. Other measures are scored by summing the life events after they have been weighted to reflect the presumed amounts of change generated. For example, the Schedule of Recent Events gives widowhood a weight of 100 and assigns change in residence a weight of 20 (Holmes & Rahe, 1967). These weights suggest that widowhood generates five times greater change in usual behavior patterns than residential relocation. No definitive evidence supports the use of either weighted or unweighted life events. Most investigators, however, use unweighted scale scores as these do not require making assumptions about the relative importance of various life events to the individual.

During the past decade substantial attention has been given to what are broadly referred to as "life event qualities." This research has taken two basic forms. First, some investigators have questioned the appropriateness of simply summing up life events, whether weighted or unweighted. Of particular concern is whether information is lost by ignoring the specific kinds of events that individuals experience (Kessler & McLeod, 1985). Indeed, a number of researchers have suggested that life events should not be summed at all, that they should be studied individually. Reflecting the same concern, other investigators suggest that life events be aggregated into specific categories that are analyzed separately. Some researchers have proposed categories based on the life domain in which change is experienced, for example, work-related events, family-based events, and health-related events. Other investigators recommend categories based on other event characteristics, such as loss events (e.g., deaths of loved ones), exit events (e.g., retirement, divorce), and role gains (e.g., becoming a spouse or parent).

Second, many investigators now ask respondents not only to report the occurrence of life events but also to rate the characteristics of those events. Examples of event characteristics that are frequently examined include the perceived importance of the event, the degree to which the event was expected or unexpected, and, especially, whether the event was perceived as having a positive or negative effect on the respondent's life (e.g., Hughes, George, & Blazer, 1988). Perceptions of life event characteristics may be important because they indicate the meaning that the individual attaches to the event—and the impact of a life event may vary, depending on its meaning. For example, events that are perceived as important may have greater impact than those viewed as unimportant. Similarly, stress is more likely to be experienced if an event is viewed as negative than if it is perceived as positive.

Not only do the nature and degree of impact vary depending on the meaning of the event(s) for individuals, but it is also clear that few events are perceived in the same way by everybody (Hughes, George, & Blazer, 1988) For most events, respondents vary in the extent to which they view the event as positive versus negative, expected versus unexpected, and important versus unimportant. Even events such as health problems and death of a family member are occasionally reported to have positive effects.

In summary, the study of life events has evolved over time. Earlier studies were concerned primarily about the ability and willingness of study participants to report the occurrence of life events in an accurate manner. Current research is exploring the objective and subjective facets of life events that are related to differential impact or consequences.

Age Differences in Life Events

From the adult development perspective, it is important to know whether or not there are predictable age differences in the occurrence, qualities, and meanings of life events. There is strong consensual information about some of these issues; for others, information is scant and suggestive rather than definitive.

Strong and consistent evidence shows that older adults experience fewer life events than younger and middle-aged adults (e.g., Hughes, Blazer, & George, 1988; Lowenthal, Thurnher, & Chiriboga, 1975). Life event instruments developed for use with young and middle-aged adults have been criticized on the grounds that they may not be "age-fair"— that they neglect events that are unlikely to be experienced at younger ages but are common in later life. Although this criticism may have some merit, investigators who have enriched their life event measures to include events that are especially likely to occur in later adulthood also report that older adults experience fewer events than their younger peers.

Age groups also differ in predictable ways in the type of events they experience (Hughes, Blazer, & George, 1988). As expected, young adults are most likely to report marriage, parenthood, leaving education, gaining employment, and residential relocation. Middle-aged adults are most likely to experience departure of children from the parental home, promotions, illness of family members, and, for women, menopause and reentry into the labor force. Older adults are most likely to report the onset of health problems, retirement, widowhood, and the loss of friends and other family members. The relationships between age and the occurrence of specific events reflect complex, heterogeneous etiologies.

Biological factors clearly affect the distribution of fertility, menopause, and illness across age groups. Most age differences, however, appear to reflect the impact of social expectations or what has been called the "social clock." Given social institutions and norms, for example, it is not surprising that entry into the labor force usually occurs in young adulthood and retirement from the labor force occurs in later life. The predictability of these and other life events appears to rest upon social custom rather than the requirements of nature.

Age differences in the meaning of life events have received little attention. Only two studies include systematic examination of age differences in the subjective ratings assigned to specific life events. Chiriboga and Dean (1978) found that although older adults report fewer life events, they experience greater distress and more pervasive effects as a result of life events than do younger adults. More recently, Hughes, George, and Blazer (1988) examined age differences in ratings of the positive versus negative valence, expectedness, and importance of 19 life events, using data from a representative community sample (age range: 18 to 96). Only three significant age differences were observed. Compared with their younger peers, older adults were more likely to report that (a) family illness was expected, (b) personal hospitalization was negative, and (c) retirement was positive.

Life Events as Stressors

Scientific interest in life events was initiated by investigators who were interested in the relationships between stress and health. Early studies in this area now appear to have been overly simplistic. These pioneering studies focused on the extent to which life events, especially scales measuring total number of life events, predicted subsequent physical and mental illness. Small but significant relationships were found between life events and subsequent health problems. These studies assumed that stress was directly proportional to the amount of change generated by life events. Investigators explicitly hypothesized that the meaning of life events was inconsequential. For example, the effects on health of events perceived as positive were expected to be equally as strong as the effects of events perceived as negative.

As life events research has matured, it has become apparent that a more complex and multifaceted view of the relationships between life events and health outcomes is required. Two sources of complexity are especially important. First, the meanings that individuals attach to life events clearly influence their outcomes and consequences. The distinction between positive and negative events has proven to be especially critical. In general, negative outcomes are likely only if the life events are *perceived* as negative (e.g., Kessler & McLeod, 1985). Moreover, psychological distress (including but not limited to full-blown psychiatric disorder) is more responsive to negative life events than is physical distress, although decreased immune function, increased cardiac reactivity, and other negative physiological reactions also can result from negative life events (e.g., George, 1989).

Second, life events should not be studied in a vacuum. The individual's distinctive resources and deficits strongly influence the likelihood that negative life events will result in health problems (George, 1989). Life events are substantially more likely to have negative consequence for persons who lack personal and social resources than for those who are relatively advantaged. Indeed, the major focus of recent research is to delineate *the conditions under which* life events do and do not lead to negative outcomes. This is a more useful and sophisticated question than whether life events are risk factors for physical and mental illness.

Life Events as Markers of Adult Development

A developmental or life course perspective on life events has emerged to complement research based on life events as stressors. This perspective focuses on life events as transitional markers of adult development (e.g., Hultsch & Plemons, 1979). Unlike the stress perspective that views change per se as problematic and as increasing the risk of negative outcomes for the individual, the developmental life course perspective assumes that many kinds of change are predictable and normal, and may enhance well-being. And even when life events are perceived as negative, the adult development perspective reminds us that the negative consequences of undesirable events can be accompanied by psychosocial growth and enhanced mastery.

The adult development perspective on life events was launched in part by research on the *qualities* of life events. One characteristic that emerged as important was the extent to which life events were experienced as "on time" or "off time." A life event may be experienced as off time or "off schedule" if it occurs either earlier or later than expected. Substantial research indicated that negative outcomes were less likely to occur when events were experienced on time rather than off time (Hagestad, 1990). The distinction proved to be important even for events that are almost universally viewed as negative, such as widowhood. Death of one's spouse typically involves intense grief and pervasive behavioral and emotional adjustments. Nonetheless, adjustment to widowhood has been demonstrated to be more difficult for younger than older widows (e.g., Glick, Weiss, & Parkes, 1974). Recognition of the on-time/off-time distinction also suggests that in some

cases lack of change may be more problematic for well-being than is the experience of change. Research into the timing of life events now has moved beyond the question of whether a particular event occurs on time or off time. Issues such as age at marriage, age at the transition to parenthood, and age at retirement have been found to be associated not only with well-being but also with the resources available for making these events more or less difficult (Hagestad, 1990). For example, the likelihood of greater stress for a couple becoming parents "too early" might be significantly reduced by the availability of caring and competent family members to offer support and assistance.

In addition to its concern with the timing of life events, current research also focuses on sequences and consequences. For example, there is evidence that the individual's socioeconomic status and marital stability are influenced by the sequence in which he or she leaves school, enters an occupation, and marries (e.g., Hogan, 1978). Similarly, compression of multiple life events into a short time interval has different effects on well-being than experiencing the same events over a longer period.

Duration dependence also affects life course achievements and is a rich area of inquiry. "Duration dependence" refers to the fact that the length of time spent in one status or situation can either increase or decrease the likelihood that a life event will occur (Hagestad, 1990). For example, the longer the duration of schooling, the greater the likelihood of leaving school: Each year of education brings the individual closer to the end of his or her formal education. In contrast, the longer an individual remains in an occupation, the lower the likelihood that he or she will change occupations: The probability of major career changes decreases with job tenure. For some life events, the effect of duration changes over time. For example, between ages 18 and 35, the longer a person is unmarried, the more likely it is that marriage will occur in the future. After about age 35, however, the probability that a never-married person will wed decreases with age.

When performed appropriately, developmental studies of life events pay explicit attention to heterogeneity—to variability in the timing, sequencing, and duration dependence of life events and to the implications of those variations. Life events are rarely developmental in the sense of being universally observed at predictable ages (as compared, for example, with the emergence of the first tooth). Instead, life events are developmental in the sense that the past is prologue to the future, and the course of life event sequences has important implications for later behavior and well-being.

There is also a significant link between life events and clinical psychology (e.g., Danish, Smyer, & Nowak, 1980). Psychological distress, sometimes requiring professional help, can result from life events, especially those that are experienced as negative, involve loss, and occur off time (or fail to occur at all). Life events research is continuing to identify the kinds of problems that can arise when transitions go awry, and it is also providing information about the normative course of life events against which problematic transitions can be assessed.

▼ LINDA K. GEORGE

See also: Depression; Disengagement Theory; Individuality; Interethnic Relationships; Marital Development; Mental Health in the Adult Years; Mid-Life Crisis; Retirement: An Emerging Challenge for Women; Retirement Preparation; Social Support for the Chronically Ill; Stress; Widowhood: The Coping Response.

References

Amster, L. E., & Krauss, H. H. (1974). The relationship between life crises and mental deterioration in old age. *International Journal of Aging and Human Development, 5:* 51-55.

Chiriboga, D. A., & Dean, H. (1978). Dimensions of stress: Perspectives from a longitudinal study. *Journal of Psychosomatic Research, 22:* 47-55.

Danish, S. J., Smyer, M. A., & Nowak, C. (1980). Dimensions of stress: Perspectives from a longitudinal study. *Journal of Psychosomatic Research, 22:* 47-55.

George, L. K. (1989). Stress, social support, and depression over the life course. In K. S. Markides & C. L. Cooper (Eds)., *Aging, Stress, and Health*. Chichester, England: John Wiley.

Glick, I. O., Weiss, R. D., & Parkes, C. M. (1974). *The First Year of Bereavement*. New York: John Wiley.

Hagestad, G. O. (1990). Social perspectives on the life course. In R. H. Binstock & L. K. George (Eds.), *Handbook of Aging and the Social Sciences*. Third Edition. San Diego, CA: Academic Press.

Hogan, D. P. (1978). The variable order of events in the life course. *American Sociological Review, 40:* 553-69.

Holmes, T. H., & Rahe, R. H. (1967). The Social Readjustment Rating Scale. *Journal of Psychosomatic Research, 11:* 213-18.

Hughes, D. C., Blazer, D. G., & George, L. K. (1988). Age differences in life events: A multivariate controlled analysis. *International Journal of Aging and Human Development, 27:* 207-20.

Hughes, D. C., George, L. K., & Blazer, D. G. (1988). Age differences in life events qualities: Multivariate controlled analyses. *Journal of Community Psychology, 16:* 161-74.

Hultsch, D. R., & Plemons, J. K. (1979). Life events and life-span development. In P. B. Baltes & O. G. Brim, Jr. (Eds.), *Life-span Development and Behavior*. Volume 2. New York: Academic Press.

Kessler, R. C., & McLeod, J. D. (1985). Social support and mental health in community samples. In S. Cohen & S. L. Syme (Eds.), *Social Support and Health*. New York: Academic Press.

Lowenthal, M. F., Thurnher, M., & Chiriboga, D. (1975). *Four Stages of Life*. San Francisco: Jossey-Bass.

LISTENING

When one thinks of listening, one also thinks immediately of hearing. If one can hear, one can listen.

This perception is wrong for two reasons. First, listening involves more than the sense of hearing. One listens also through sight, touch, and smell. Second, sensing is only the first step of the listening process. One must analyze the sensory input, using his or her knowledge and experience to interpret or understand the input. In the psychological literature, this three-stage process is described as reception, attention, and perception. The literature on listening refers to it as receiving, attending, and assigning meaning to the stimulus (Wolvin & Coakley, 1988). All three stages must be completed before listening has occurred. If the message arrives in the auditory channel, hearing it would be only the first state. Likewise, seeing a stimulus would be the first stage of listening to a message in the visual channel.

As already noted, listening is more than an auditory process; it involves all of the senses. When another person is talking, one listens to the words and the way the words are stated (tone, pitch, rate, etc.), as well as the nonverbal messages of body posture, facial expressions, and eye contact. If the person is wearing a heavy cologne, the fragrance is also a message.

One additional distinction is important. In traditional models of communication, one finds what might be called listening referred to as feedback. Communication is described as a two-way process of message sending/receiving and feedback. Saying "I'm fine" to the stock question "How are you?" is a way of providing feedback to the communication. That response is also an indication that one had been listening to the communication in the first place. The listening response can be as simple as a smile, a nod of the head, or a minimal verbal reply, "OK." Just as communication messages are received through all the senses, listening responses are also likely to use those same senses.

When one provides a listening response nonverbally, one is engaging in what are called *nonverbal attending behaviors*. Positive attending behaviors include eye contact, leaning forward toward the speaker, nodding one's head, or smiling. One can listen to a verbal message without maintaining eye contact with the speaker. Clearly, some portion of the visual message would be lost without eye contact.

Verbal Listening Responses

Verbal listening responses can be categorized into four types. The following sample dialogue provides an example of each of these responses:

> *Speaker:* It sure is a wonderful day outside. It would be great to go for a picnic.
>
> *Listener A:* Yes, it's a great day and the picnic sounds nice.

The response of Listener A is on the same subject as the speaker's original statement. It is known as a *same* response.

> *Listener B:* Yeah.

This listener's response is labeled as *minimal*. It does not tell whether it is a nice day or a good day for a picnic or both. The listener's "Yeah" may simply mean that he or she heard the speaker's voice, not necessarily agreeing with or even attending to what was said.

> *Listener C:* Won't it be nice to go for a walk with this great weather.

This listener is using a *tangent* response. It is related to the nice day and the current conversation, but it is not a direct response to the speaker.

> *Listener D:* What time is it?

This listener has pretty much ignored the speaker altogether. This response, labeled *different*, has no reference to the speaker. In fact, the listener has started a new series of exchanges that themselves need a listener.

In their interactions, people usually provide both verbal and nonverbal listening responses, and, as just illustrated, these responses can have several types of relationship to the statements that elicited them.

A Model of Listening

The following model (Figure 1) offers a convenient way to encapsulate the critical elements that are involved in the listening process (Arnold, 1989).

This model presents the two dimensions on which the listener relies when re-

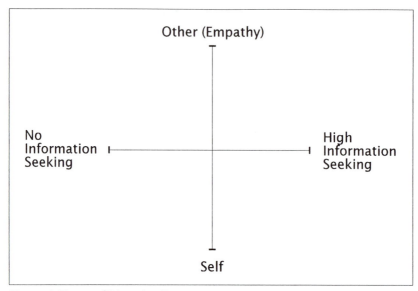

Figure 1. Types of Listening Responses

sponding to a communicator. The listener can respond in such a way as to seek information from the speaker. "Tell me more" and "Would you elaborate on that point?" are examples of information-seeking responses. Reporters and physicians who are seeking the cause of some set of events or symptoms are good examples of information-seeking listeners (Goss, 1982).

On the second continuum, a listener responds with the interest either of the speaker or of the self primarily in mind. "You are upset" or "Tell me more" reflects an interest in the other person. Responses such as "I just felt like that" or "Your point reminds me of a time when I..." reflect self-interest. A response that shows interest in the other person is called *empathic listening*. Counselors and best friends usually provide the most empathic listening. Since both of these dimensions are continual, one can respond anywhere within the model, not just at the extremes of other-self or high-low information seeking. For example, one can seek more information as a listener and still give an empathic response.

One obvious way to find out whether another person has listened to what one has said is to ask him or her. One could also try to assess the individual's listening comprehen-

sion by testing how much of the information has been remembered. Studies often present the reading of a passage of material and then test for memory of major themes and/or details. Another way to test a listener's effectiveness would be to employ the coding system described in Figure 1 on the four types of listening responses. This is a more complex approach that requires some knowledge of the listener's intent. For example, research has indicated that caregivers are judged by third parties as more comforting to Alzheimer's disease patients when they give same rather than different responses (Bohling & Arnold, 1990).

The issue of perspective is important because, from a speaker's perspective, one would prefer a listener who engages in all of the positive nonverbal attending behaviors and provides a majority of *same* verbal listening responses. From a listener's perspective, an orientation toward information seeking and self-interest may give a majority of *different* listening responses. To judge listening effectiveness, then, one must determine whether the interaction is being evaluated from the viewpoint of the speaker or the listener.

Listening Across the Lifespan

The early years of life are spent listening for information relative to self. Infants listen for cues that they are going to be fed or have their diapers changed. They listen for a soothing voice, a warm embrace, or a smile that they associate with having their needs met. Research shows that infants are able to respond to sounds and objects at a very early age. Hodgson (1978) describes the changes in auditory recognition from birth to three years. As they age, infants learn to complete the three-stage process of listening. It is one thing to possess the ability to hear and see. It takes more to ascribe meaning to the stimuli.

As people mature, they experience two major changes in their ability to listen. First, they are able to differentiate a greater range of sensory input, thereby enhancing their ability to listen effectively. Second, they are able to recognize that they can do more than respond as information seekers for self. They can listen empathically to another person. They can show caring for another person through their listening responses.

Unfortunately, with aging the acuity of hearing, vision (Bischof, 1976), and taste and smell sensitivity (Schiffman, Orlandi, & Erickson, 1979) diminish. These changes lessen one's ability to listen effectively. For example, studies have shown that individuals begin to notice hearing loss in the mid-forties, particularly in the range of high and low pitch sounds (Verbrugge, 1984). This type of hearing loss—called *presbycusis*—can make some sounds unintelligible. If all a person hears if "ffretr, e satg," a hearing aid will only increase the volume, so that what is heard is now, "FFRETR E SATG." Not all that helpful! Garbled sound becomes loud garbled sound.

The ravages of disease, strokes, and dementia also diminish the ability to listen. The loss caused by a lack of sensory input may be accompanied by an inability to provide a listening response. It has already been noted that both verbal and nonverbal responses are forms of listening. The ability to provide a listening response is lessened if one cannot make a connection between the input and meanings that are held in one's memory. One assigns meaning, the third step in listening, by turning to one's memory for prior experience. If, as people age, memory function diminishes, they may have limited abilities to respond and thus may not be able to let the speaker know that they are listening. These losses do not prevent people from listening, but they do make interaction more difficult. The likelihood of losing some of our sensory input ability and/or ability to provide a listening response increases with age, although, fortunately, few people suffer a total loss.

It is not always easy to determine when another person has a diminished capacity to listen or provide a listening response. A speaker cannot always tell whether another person can hear or see just by looking at the person. Instead, the speaker may become frustrated with or ignore the older person because he or she appears not to be listening. This can become a downward spiral because the older person may interpret this listening response or nonresponse as indicating "We don't care about you or what you are saying." The older person may then establish a pattern of avoiding circumstances that require speaking and listening, so as not to be embarrassed by deficiencies in this area.

The situation does not have to be as negative as described here. Some people who have become superior listeners throughout their development careers continue to exercise their skills effectively in the later years of life, despite some declines in sensory input. Furthermore, advances in research and innovations in re-education programs might well provide the knowledge base and the techniques for maintaining effective listening skills and, therefore, enhancing social interactions throughout the lifespan.

▼ William E. Arnold

See also: Body Senses; Grandparent Communication Skills; Grandparent Education to Enhance Family Strength; Humor; Information Processing; Learning and Memory in Everyday Life; Life Events; Memory; Taste and Smell; Vision; The Voice.

References

Arnold, W. E. (1989). Listening and information processing. Paper presented to the International Listening Association Convention, Atlanta, GA.

Bischof, L. (1976). *Adult Psychology*. Second Edition. New York: Harper & Row.

Bohling, H., & Arnold, W. (1990). Alzheimer's patients and selected listening response. Paper presented to the International Listening Association, Indianapolis, IN.

Carkhuff, R. (1969). *Helping and Human Relations.* New York: Holt, Rinehart and Winston.

Goss, B. (1982). Listening as information processing. *Communication Quarterly, 30:* 304-06.

Hodgson, W. R. (1978). Testing infants and young children. In J. Katz (Ed.), *Handbook of Clinical Audiology.* Baltimore: Williams & Wilkins, pp. 397-409.

Schiffman, S., Orlandi, M., & Erickson, R. P. (1979). Thresholds of food odors in the elderly. In J. H. Ordy & K. Brizzee (Eds.), *Sensory Systems and Communication in the Elderly.* Volume 10. New York: Raven Press, pp. 247-68.

Verbrugge, L. (1984). A health profile of older women with comparisons to older men. *Research on Aging, 6:* 291-322.

Wolvin, A., & Coakley, C. (1988). *Listening.* Third Edition. Dubuque, IA: W. C. Brown.

LONELINESS

Loneliness can be defined as the generalized lack of satisfying personal, social, or community relationships. The distinction between the objective manifestation of being alone and the subjective manifestation of experiencing loneliness is fundamental. A person who is alone (e.g., who lives alone) may or may not experience loneliness. A person *feeling* lonely may or may not be alone. It is not surprising, however, that feelings of loneliness are more common among those who do live alone.

If the proportion of adults in different age groups reporting loneliness were depicted as a curve, it would assume the character of a shallow U-shape. Loneliness is reported more frequently among people at both ends of the adult spectrum: young adults and those in the most advanced age groups, from approximately 75 on. However, loneliness is characterized by more than just its frequency: The nature or content of the loneliness feeling might also differ at various times of life. Furthermore, the feelings of loneliness might be more or less stable on the individual level. For example, it is possible that a person who feels lonely in his or her late 70s might have had these feelings for many years previously. The curve just described gives only one part of the total reality. Subdivisions also alter the picture. For example, the shape of the curve differs according to the proportion of married persons in each cohort. A division into marital status reveals that the largest proportion of feelings of loneliness can be found among unmarried people in young middle-age.

Many circumstances pertaining to loneliness have yet to be elucidated. One example of the elusiveness of the loneliness concept concerns the discrepancy between results from *cross-sectional* and *longitudinal* studies. In the higher age groups, cross-sectional studies show an increasing proportion of elderly people who feel lonely, while longitudinal studies show a decreasing proportion. Another example concerns the reaction following the loss of someone else. For those who experience such a loss, feelings of loneliness can be *less* common immediately following the loss than prior to the loss (loneliness should not be confused with grief).

In a thorough review of the literature, Perlman and Peplau (1982) conclude that loneliness has been looked at from several theoretical perspectives: psychodynamic, phenomenological, existential, sociological, interactionist, and cognitive. In comparing these approaches, the authors conclude that only the existentialists regard loneliness as being positive, and even this is seen as a potential rather than a given. According to the existential view, loneliness is universal—it comes with being human and persists throughout the lifespan.

Within the psychodynamic and phenomenological views, feelings of loneliness are regarded as pathological. The causes of loneliness are believed to be subjective and individual. The psychodynamic school focuses on the past, especially childhood experiences, while the phenomenologists emphasize the present situation. In contrast, the interactionist and cognitive positions hold that feelings of loneliness are normal. The reasons for them are to be found both in the individual and in the situation. In sociological analysis, the appropriate term to describe loneliness would be "normative." The cause is sought through both historical and contemporary perspectives.

Social Isolation versus Emotional Isolation

Early writers differed in their theorizing as to whether loneliness should be regarded as a unidimensional or a multidimensional construct. Today, loneliness most commonly is viewed as a multidimensional phenomenon. Particularly influential has been a typology emanating from Robert Weiss's (1973) distinction between social and emotional isolation. *Social isolation* is the individual's response to the absence of a place in an accepting community. *Emotional isolation* is the response to the absence of an attachment figure (also known as "significant other" by some writers). Although a plausible distinction, it has seldom been upheld in empirical research.

An overview on approaches to loneliness would not be complete without mentioning such related constructs as solitude, which refers to being alone in a positively valued manner. Negative constructs include meaninglessness, self-estrangement, and structural estrangement (Andersson, 1986). The last has been the most elaborated of these constructs. Loneliness that is caused by cultural or structural factors may arise because of the nature of the individual's bonds to established values and cultural norms.

It has been observed that avoiding social isolation requires *authentic community*. An individual's social role provides a public identity as well as reassurance of his or her worth. There is reason to assume that indi-

viduals in higher social strata are more bound by close ties to the societal life through the social norm system and formal social activities. There are also indications that the social isolation aspect of loneliness is particularly related to social position. The "cure" for emotional isolation takes a different form. Persons may experience loneliness as emotional isolation regardless of whether or not they are involved with others. Merely having companions is not sufficient. For example, individuals may experience emotional isolation resulting from major transitions. The problem may also be related to a deficit in the individual's capacity for socioemotional bonding. This suggests that one solution to the problem of emotional isolation would require a kind of psychological or emotional reworking of basic personality patterns that were developed in one's family during the early socialization process. Thus, it is assumed that early socialization can influence feelings of loneliness in later life stages—the source of the problem may be in the past, not the present.

From a developmental viewpoint, it seems reasonable that emotional isolation could have its origins in the earliest attachment-separation period, whereas social isolation would derive from the later socialization period in which external influences may be more prominent.

Situational versus Developmental Loneliness

The distinction between situational and developmental loneliness is fundamental. Causes of *situationally* bound loneliness are generally sought in factors related to the social network. Lack of friends and losses of companions and intimates are regarded as the main determinants of this experience. The underlying causes are factors such as moving, getting a new job, changing schools, divorce, death of close relatives and friends, and so forth. However, it has been claimed that the reaction to situational events is to some degree dependent on earlier socioemotional experiences. In this view, developmental loneliness determines situational loneliness. An alternative view holds that loneliness is like a recessive nondominant trait, which is fully experienced under the "right" conditions, such as dramatic changes in one's life.

Discussions about the *developmental* dimension of loneliness as originating from early childhood experiences are strongly influenced by *attachment theory*. Weiss (1973) suggests that emotional isolation can be regarded as an expression of an adult pattern of the attachment system that links infants to parent figures. He argues that the attachment system undergoes modification during adolescence, so that the individual integrates new objects as attachment figures, in addition to the parents. These new attachment figures become increasingly important as the influence of parents as attachment figures declines. Nevertheless, parents remain "on reserve," ready to be reinstated as primary attachment figures if necessary. Bowlby's work (1976, 1982, 1983, 1990) provides an important resource for the understanding of attachment and its possible relevance to loneliness.

Neglect versus Intrusion

Attachment theory holds that neglect—like childhood separation or loss—leads to relational problems in later years. For example, it has been suggested that parental divorce increases a child's feelings of loneliness by making the child feel powerless. This experience fosters persistent internal attributions for failure, which in turn may lead to persistent internal attributions for loneliness.

However, it is important to determine the associations between different types of attachment in childhood and loneliness in adulthood and old age. A multidimensional notion of the loneliness of emotional estrangement considers the possibility that different influences of one's family—too little or too much emotional fusion—result in similar deficits in the ability to form the requisite socioemotional bonds that would prevent emotional isolation. *Neglect* is one side of the

coin, signifying too little attention, while *intrusion* is the other side, indicating too much attention.

A distinction can be made between two types of neglectful upbringing: ambivalent or neglectful forms of interaction. Ambivalent interaction occurs with a parent who is characterized by narcissistic withdrawal. This type of parent is cold and rejecting but occasionally shows devotion and interest. In the neglectful mode of interaction the parent is prevailingly hostile and aggressive. It can be seen, then, that individuals can suffer from emotional isolation for opposite reasons. Both kinds of neglectful upbringing result in individuals who fear rejection because they have been rejected in the past. Furthermore, in their attempts to avoid the pain of rejection, they tend to act in ways that make further rejection likely. Either they are "clingy" in relationships, resulting in avoidance behavior from others, or they are distant and aloof, i.e., they make use of avoidance behavior themselves and ultimately are rejected by others.

Arguments pertaining to intrusive parental influence in childhood can be found in studies of narcissism. Intrusion is the situation in which the personality of the child is absorbed by the parent. It can be illustrated by Zilboorg's (1938) often-cited statement: "If the omnipotent baby learns the job of being admired and loved but learns nothing about the outside world, he may develop a conviction of his greatness and all importance which will lead to a narcissistic orientation to life—a conviction that life is nothing but being loved and admired. This narcissistic-megalomanic attitude will not be acceptable to the environment, which will respond with hostility and isolation of the narcissistic person."

According to Zilboorg, this is the basis for the development of loneliness. If the young child has an exaggerated sense of self that excludes emotional bonding with others, or fails to develop a self that is appropriately differentiated from others, there is a risk of loneliness. Note, however, that whether "being admired and loved" results in "learning nothing about the outside world" depends on the type of love. As indicated in developmental psychology, parental love is an important foundation for the psychological security that is necessary to make one's way effectively and affirmatively throughout the lifespan. On the other hand, parental love that is overly possessive may result in excessive efforts to control the child.

Thus, from a developmental viewpoint, loneliness originates in early experiences with attachment figures; it is caused by parental neglect or intrusion. However, Bowlby (1990) also emphasizes that it is important for parents to realize that their children also have the legitimate need to explore the world and to form other relationships both with peers and with other adults. Apart from the issue of a secure base, if a child is discouraged from exploring by an overprotective parent, there is the risk that he or she will be shy, fail to develop social skills, and become lonely. The loneliness experienced by an elderly person, then, may have its roots in early childhood relationships, but may be intensified by interpersonal and other losses that are associated with the hardships of later adulthood.

Developmental influences can also affect one's ability to cope with challenges, and weakness in this area could lead to loneliness of the situational type. The distinction between developmental and situational causes for loneliness also has clinical implications. The application of the accumulated knowledge is crucial, as research is impressive in documenting that loneliness represents a potential risk factor for both emotional and physical disorders among a range of populations and situations across the lifespan.

▼ Lars Andersson

See also: Attachment Across the Lifespan; Divorce; Life Events; Marital Development; Mental Health in the Adult Years; Narcissism; Parental Imperative; Social Relationships, Convoys of.

References

Andersson, L. (1986). A model of estrangement—including a theoretical understanding of loneliness. *Psychological Reports, 58*: 683-95.

———. (1990). Narcissism and loneliness. *International Journal of Aging and Human Development, 30*: 81-94.

Bowlby, J. (1976). *Separation.* New York: Basic Books.

———. (1982). *Loss.* New York: Basic Books.

———. (1983). *Attachment.* New York: Basic Books.

———. (1990). *A Secure Base.* New York: Basic Books.

Hojat, M., & Crandall, R. (Eds.). (1989). *Loneliness: Theory, Research, and Applications.* Newbury Park, CA: Sage.

Perlman, D., & Peplau, L. (Eds.). (1982). *Loneliness. A Sourcebook of Current Theory, Research, and Therapy.* New York: John Wiley & Sons.

Weiss, R. W. (Ed.). (1973). *Loneliness: The Experience of Emotional and Social Isolation.* Cambridge, MA: MIT Press.

Zilboorg, G. (1938). Loneliness. *Atlantic Magazine,* January, pp. 45-54.

LONGEVITY

Fascination with the "Ancient Ones"

The image of the "ancient ones" who survive into extreme old age has fascinated humankind over the centuries. The oriental heritage includes not only veneration for the wise elder but also a belief that it was once commonplace for people to live vigorously for 100 years and more. This idea was already more than 2,000 years old by the time that Kung Fu-tzu (fifth century B.C.) and Meng-tzu (fourth century B.C.) established the foundation for the influential ancestor-venerating tradition that has become known in the West as Confucianism (Kiefer, 1992; Ya, 1988).

Methuselah with his reported longevity of 969 years holds first rank among biblical personages, with Noah (950) and Adam (930) not far behind. At the dawn of the Christian era, several hermits who were said to have lived more than a century were among the earliest to be revered as saints. A study encompassing the entire Christian era finds that Roman Catholic saints (both men and women) had longer lives on the average than other people of their times. In fact, "a nation composed entirely of saints recruited from the first century onward would have a significantly higher percentage of aged adults than any current or projected population of modern times" (Kastenbaum, 1990, p. 104). Nevertheless, as we approach modern times, fewer saints attain great old age, thereby perhaps lessening the symbolic connection between piety and longevity.

A fictional conception of superlongevity captivated many readers and moviegoers when James Hilton (1936) drew upon both oriental and occidental thought for his novel *Lost Horizon*. An exceptionally long life was depicted as a blessing for the individual and a boon for the community, who would benefit from the wisdom of the aged. Extraordinary longevity, however, was depicted as highly dependent on contextual forces: Those who dared to leave Shangri-La were doomed to age very rapidly and crumble into dust.

Cultural history also affords examples of a more "morbid" type of fascination with superlongevity. Aurora, goddess of dawn, was in love with a mortal man. She begged Jupiter, her father, to bestow immortality on Tithon so they could live and love together through the ages. Jupiter finally acceded to her wishes, but—showing a nastily legalistic turn of mind—did not spare Tithon from the aging process. Tellings of this myth sometimes include the assertion that Tithon is still with us, now an aged cricket endlessly chirping his lament.

Captain Gulliver encounters another negative instance of superlongevity when his travels take him to the Land of the Luggnaggians (Swift, 1726). Here he learns that an occasional immortal is born in this kingdom, the total of "Struldbrugs" now having reached about 1,100. The Captain rhapsodizes:

> Happy nation, where every child hath at least a chance for being immortal! Happy people who enjoy so many living examples of ancient virtue, and have masters ready to instruct them in the wisdom of all former ages! But, happiest beyond all comparison are those excellent Struldbrugs, who being

born exempt from the universal calamity of human nature, have their minds free and disengaged, without the weight and depression of spirits caused by the continual apprehension of death. (p. 217)

Gulliver swiftly learns, however, that these immortals actually are opinionated, peevish, covetous, morose, vain, talkative, incapable of friendship, and "dead to all natural affection," as well as forgetful, aphasic, impotent, and envious. Far from being welcomed and honored, the Struldbrugs are roundly despised.

Overall, in both fact and fantasy society has expressed both strong fascination with and strong ambivalence toward those who attain great age. This attitudinal mix is still with us today. For example, the intensifying controversies associated with **Generational Equity** bespeak the fear that too many people may be living too long, while studies of **Suicide** suggest that self-destruction can be prompted by the aging person's perception that he or she is considered a burden rather than a treasure by others.

Longevity and Life Expectation: Basic Concepts

Although the long-lived person—in fact or fancy—is often the topic of popular discussion, there is a good deal more to the study of longevity. First, it will be useful to acquire an understanding of several terms that are encountered in this area. *Longevity* is given two somewhat different meanings. Often longevity refers to the upper limit of survival for a particular species. In this sense, longevity is identical with the concept of a maximum lifespan. Longevity is also used as the marker of the lifespan that is most commonly achieved. For example, a particular genetic line of the fruit fly *Drosophila melanogaster* has a maximum lifespan of about 70 days, but the average length of survival will depend much on temperature, food supply, population density, and other factors that have been manipulated in the laboratory (Lamb, 1986). Longevity in the sense of maximum lifespan will always be 70 days (unless and until proven otherwise), but observed average longevity will depend on particular circumstances.

The statistical tables and charts often seen in newspapers, magazines, and books usually provide information about average longevity of particular populations that have been monitored at a particular time, rather than on longevity in the sense of maximum lifespan. Indeed, the maximum lifespan for humans is still a matter of controversy, as reports of people living beyond the age of 120 or so generally have been discounted by experienced researchers. That some people can and do become centenarians is not in doubt, but there is doubt about claims for people said to have survived another 30 years or more.

Life expectancy indicates how much longer a person is likely to survive, given that individual's present age. This estimate can be refined by taking other factors into consideration, such as time of measurement (date), gender, and race. For example, in 1850 a newborn white female had a life expectancy of 40 years. The "same person" born in 1985 would have a life expectancy of about 79 years. The particular number generated for life expectancy will vary as we replace one cohort date with another, separate or combine the sexes, separate or combine different races, and so on.

It is useful, then, to have clearly in mind the framework within which a life expectancy estimate is generated. One should also remember that an averaged estimate assumes a broad range of variance. If the average life expectancy for a newborn white female in 1985 was 79, for example, then half of this cohort will survive past 79 and half will die before this age.

Mortality rate is often reported in association with longevity and life expectancy statistics. This concept gives us the other side of the coin: information on those who do not survive past a particular point in time. The mortality rate is calculated on the basis of number of deaths per 1,000 individuals within a one-year period (unless otherwise specified). Actually, there are two versions of the mortality rate that are in common usage, as well as a number of specialized versions that provide more refined information on well-defined topics (Gee, 1989). Perhaps the most frequently encountered version is the crude death rate (CDR). The CDR is calculated in two steps: first, by dividing all deaths that occur in a year by the average total population for that year, and then by expressing this proportion as a rate per 1,000 population. Using the standard of deaths per 1,000 population makes it possible to compare mortality rates between populations of different sizes. This comparison can involve either the general death rates or the mortality attributable to a particular cause.

A more complicated technique is used to calculate the ASMR, or age-standardized mortality rate. The ASMR attempts to adjust all populations to the same standard of age composition. Obviously, this can only be a statistical maneuver that does not actually affect the age composition of a given society during a given year. Nevertheless, this manipulation often provides a clearer picture of what the mortality rate signifies. The ASMR enables us to rule out the possibility that observed changes or differences in mortality are based on changes or differences in the age structure of populations. For example, as Gee (1989) notes, many Third World nations have higher mortality but lower CDRs than industrialized nations. This puzzling situation is explained by the fact that Third World nations tend to have a much higher proportion of younger people and therefore the general mortality rates do not reflect the high risk of dying that is found among the more substantial aged populations of industrialized nations.

A similar situation prevails when comparing mortality/longevity in the same nation over an extended period of time. Two related trends have been operating in opposite directions: the reduction of mortality/extension of life expectancy associated with public health improvements, and the increasing proportion of elderly people in the population with the heightened risk factors that accompany advanced age.

The informed consumer of information about health, longevity, and risks to life will want to examine sources to determine whether the mortality statistics adjust or fail to adjust for age. In reading more technical material, such as articles in scientific journals, one may also look for more refined mortality measures that take sex, race, and other variables into account.

Prolongevity, the newest of the longevity-related concepts, deals not so much with a statistical concept as with the attempt to extend longevity. Moderate prolongevity has the aim of enabling more people to survive up to the established limits of the human lifespan. The abundant attention given these days to diet, exercise, management of stress, and avoidance of harmful substances testifies to the present generation's interest in living long and healthy lives. Radical prolongevity is sympathetic to this goal but also has a more ambitious agenda: to break through the supposed outer limits of the lifespan. As one might expect, the radical prolongevity agenda is more controversial and seems to require further technological developments before it can be fully tested. In this realm we encounter such ideas as "protein engineering" and "genetic recombinant interventions."

Prolongevity has an ancient history that stretches back to the days of pre-Confucian Chinese alchemists and rambles through arcane writings, secret laboratories, and countless "mad scientists" right up to the present day (see Gruman, 1966, for an authoritative early history, and Mishara & McKim, 1989, for a concise survey of more recent developments; another recent contribution of interest is Drexler's 1987 *Engines of Creation*).

Current Issues and Prospects

There is general agreement on several major facets of human longevity (see **Risk to Life through the Adult Years**). These facets include a significant overall improvement in longevity and life expectation for populations in industrialized nations over the past century or so. By far the greatest contribution to this improvement occurred in the first half of the twentieth century, with slower progress in more recent years. That so many more people are surviving into the late adult years owes much to the sharp reduction of infant and child mortality. Another long-term trend has been the reversal of the once prevalent female longevity disadvantage. Although both sexes have experienced increases in average longevity, this change has been especially strong for females, who are now much less frequently victimized by maternal complications and infectious diseases. It is also thought by many researchers that females possess a sex-linked longevity advantage that has finally had a chance to express itself as the result of improved public health and quality of life.

There is also general agreement about many of the influences that determine length of life. Precisely how much influence each of these factors exerts and precisely how these influences operate remains a matter for continuing research to clarify. Nevertheless, almost everybody's list of longevity-influencing factors includes:

- Heredity
- Sex
- Race
- Intelligence
- Marital status
- Socioeconomic circumstances
- Dietary and substance use habits
- Exercise and stress management habits

If we go by the book, in Western industrialized societies the most advantaged person for longevity and life expectancy would be the daughter of long-lived white parents who proves to be bright, marries for keeps, and has a good income, and who further is a nonsmoker who eats a sensible diet, drinks in moderation and never during pregnancy, keeps herself physically active, and knows how to prevent stressful circumstances from getting out of hand. It is obvious that some of these influences are within the individual's potential control (e.g., smoking, learning effective stress management techniques), while others are not (e.g., choice of parents and genetic lineage).

Those well versed in longevity research also tend to agree that the influences are more dynamic and complex than any list can indicate. Here are two examples of what they mean. First, Palmore (1977) and his colleagues found that the correlation between the longevity of parents and offspring diminishes to the vanishing point as the child becomes an elderly man or woman. This series of studies (conducted by a multidisciplinary team at the Duke University Medical Center) suggests that genetic factors make a significant contribution to differential mortality in the earlier years of life. Once a person reaches mature adulthood, however, the genetic influence seems to become just one influence among many, and perhaps less important than life-style.

Second, recent studies have discovered that impaired functioning of the immune system has a major role in the morbidity and mortality rate of elderly people. To this recognition has been added the discovery that nutritional status seems to have a profound effect on immunocompetency in old age (Chandra, 1990). "Eating right," then, may be important throughout the lifespan but become an especially critical influence on survival in the later years. When one adds the fact that a particular elderly person may eat poorly because of such circumstantial factors as financial concerns, lack of transportation, or lack of companionship at mealtime, one can appreciate anew that each influence on longevity operates in conjunction with many others.

One other area of general agreement should be mentioned because it also provides the starting point for a number of divergent views. *The Gompertz curve* (also known as the Gompertz-Makeham law) is a graphic demonstration of changes in mortality rate over the lifespan. This pattern was first described quite some time ago (Gompertz, 1825) and has been found repeatedly in many other studies up to the present day. An example of the Gompertz curve is given in Figure 1. Age-adjusted death rates (ASMR) are shown on the vertical dimension and age in years is shown on the horizontal dimension. Notice also that ASMR are reported for six different populations for purposes of comparison. These populations include the United States at three points in time, as well as sampled years from India, Mexico, and Sweden (Finch, 1990).

The level of age-adjusted mortality differs among these sampled populations, but the basic curve or pattern is similar for all six. In fact, if it were practical or necessary to array 60 populations in the same figure, one would still observe the prevalence of the Gompertz curve. Any pattern that displays itself so consistently across a broad range of observations is certain to gain the interest and respect of researchers.

Essentially, the Gompertz curve demonstrates a relatively high survival rate during the earlier part of the lifespan, which then gives way to a systematic decline. The "force of mortality," as some have put it, becomes more intense in the later part of the lifespan. Figure 1 shows this in the steep rise of all the population mortality curves after midlife. The Gompertz curve, along with supplementary equations developed by other researchers, is well accepted as a description of longevity/mortality across the lifespan. There is little disagreement about the curve as such, especially when it is limited to the adult years (infant and early childhood mortality rates deserve independent attention). Furthermore, data from some nonhuman species also conform to the Gompertz curve (Finch, 1990).

If we knew for sure that processes are expressed by the Gompertz curve, we might know a great deal about "the force of mortality" and whether or not it is realistic to subscribe to a radical prolongevity view. Currently, there is lively and valuable controversy regarding the interpretation and implications of the Gompertz curve. This controversy is best followed by those who are willing and able to speak the language of biogenetic research. Nevertheless, the following concise sampling of assertions and counterassertions provides an introduction to this set of controversies.

Aging is detrimental vs. aging is adaptive. The most frequently expressed biological

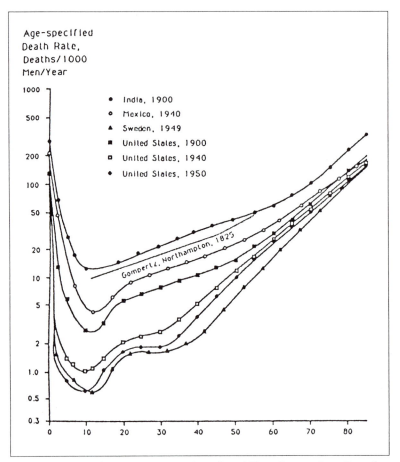

**Figure 1. Original Gompertz Data (1825) and Five Comparison Popula-
tions Demonstrate the "increasing force of mortality" with Advancing
Age.** Reprinted from E.C. Finch, *Longevity, Senescence & the Genome* (1990),
with permission of the publisher, The University of Chicago Press.

position holds that aging is a detrimental
phenomenon, i.e., "the overall process of
progressive, generalised impairment of the
functions of organs and tissues [that] results
in an increasing age-specific death rate"
(Kirkwood & Holliday, 1986). By implication, the basic mortality pattern is fixed and
inherent. Death is simply the end point of the
aging process, which is itself a kind of natural
law. However, not all researchers and theorists accept this proposition. An alternative
view comes from an evolutionary perspective which suggests that aging is a beneficial
characteristic or phenomenon—for the species, if not for the individual. Aging and
death clear the way for new generations to
emerge with their fresh energies. Kirkwood

& Holliday (1986, p. 4) find debilitating flaws
in this type of argument: "On the one hand
ageing is so rarely encountered in organisms
in the wild that the need and opportunity for
an adaptive ageing process to have evolved
would have been minimal...while on the other,
group selection for advantage to the species
is so much weaker than selection for advantage to the individual."

A variation of the evolutionary/adap-
tive argument, however, could recruit support from the sociocultural realm. Human
society, unlike "organisms in the wild," can
benefit from the experience, perspective, and
symbolic value of at least some of its aged
members. When conceived as a process of
acquiring experience, knowledge, wisdom,

and social-symbolic value, human aging may not be so easily dismissed as a process with adaptive value.

The rate of aging can/cannot be modified; therefore longevity can/cannot be extended. The prevalence of the same mortality pattern throughout numerous human and nonhuman populations suggests that we are dealing with a force of nature that will not easily be influenced by technological manipulations. Furthermore, several theories identify particular processes involved in aging that could be interpreted as being beyond significant human intervention (Hayflick, 1987). One can take a more optimistic position, however, noting the progress that has already been made both in genetic engineering and in the study of development and aging. In every realm of study one can make the argument that we are in a better position than ever to identify and intervene in processes that contribute to the overall pattern of age-related decline and mortality. For example, in exploring the biochemistry of Alzheimer's disease, researchers are already uncovering numerous points of possible intervention that could also have a bearing on aging and mortality within the general population (Morgan & May, 1990).

Moreover, what we call "aging" is not necessarily the same process in different species. Finch (1990) reviews the lifespan characteristics of many organisms, including microscopic entities, fungi, insects, plants, and both vertebrate and invertebrate animals. He observes that there are several markedly different patterns of fertility / reproduction and aging. For example, it would be difficult to apply the term "biological senescence" both to the short-lived hemaphroditic nematode and to humans and have this term convey anything like the same meaning. One might infer, then, that generalizations across species should be made only with great care and that the potentials for human (pro)longevity are not necessarily identical with those for other species.

The "biological limit" on the human lifespan is real/illusory. The prevailing view today is that the upper range of the human lifespan does not extend much beyond 100 years, and that the prospect of extending this limit is not within sight and may never be achievable. As already noted, this view is based on such considerations as the Gompertz curve and the rejection of many claims for examples of superlongevity. Gavrilov and Gavrilova (1991) further point out that mortality figures have more or less stabilized in recent years despite continuing medical advances, suggesting that industrialized nations may have already closely approached the feasible limits of longevity increase. However, they further observe that attitudinal and behavioral patterns have much to do with the deceleration of longevity enhancement. Improved health care too often is counterbalanced "by the negative consequences of modern life styles (stress, hypodynamia, obesity, smoking, etc.), the destruction of the ecological balance, and environmental pollution" (Gavrilov & Gavrilova, 1991, p. 107). Possibly, then, modifications of individual and sociocultural behavior could result in a new surge of average longevity increase, although not necessarily in breaking through the presumed outer limits of the lifespan.

A more optimistic or radical position has been taken, or at least acknowledged as worthy of respect, by some other major researchers. For example, familial trends in longevity have been found in many studies, most impressively in the case of monozygotic (identical) twins (e.g., Jarvik, Blum, & Varma, 1972). In more recent years there have been a number of discoveries that identify particular genes that seem to influence aging and longevity. Many of these genes appear to exercise their influence early in life; others have effects that seem to have a delayed expression in the later adult years. It might be premature to rule out the possibility of suppressing the expression of age-accelerating or life-foreshortening genes at this relatively early point in a promising and rapidly developing field of research.

In the meantime, each individual is free to reflect upon the alternative pathways that might be taken through the relatively long lifespans that many people do experience today. Are we to age as Tithons lamenting our lost youth, as Struldbrugs becoming more self-centered every day, as saints transcending everyday life, or as mature, caring, and involved participants in the give and take of human interaction? ▼ Robert Kastenbaum

See also: Alcohol Use and Abuse; Cardiac Health; Centenarians; Cohort and Generational Effects; Driving: A Lifespan Challenge; Drug Use and Abuse; Fictive Kin; Gender as a Shaping Force in Adult Development and Aging; Generational Equity; Happiness, Cohort Measures of; Health Education and Adult Development; Military Service: Long-Term Effects on Adult Development; Retirement: An Emerging Challenge for Women; Risk to Life through the Adult Years; Social Support for the Chronically Ill; Spiritual Development and Wisdom: A Vedantic Perspective; Suffering; Twins through the Lifespan.

References

Chandra, R. K. (1990). Nutrition is an important determinant of immunity in old age. In D. R. Prinsley & H. H. Sandstead (Eds.), *Nutrition and Aging.* New York: Alan R. Liss, pp. 321-34.

Drexler, K. E. (1987). *Engines of Creation.* New York: Doubleday.

Finch, C. E. (1990). *Longevity, Senescence, and the Genome.* Chicago: University of Chicago Press.

Gavrilov, L. A., & Gavrilova, N. S. (1991). *The Biology of Life Span.* London: Harwood.

Gee, E. (1989). Mortality rate. In R. Kastenbaum & B. Kastenbaum (Eds.), *Encyclopedia of Death.* Phoenix, AZ: The Oryx Press, pp. 183-85.

Gompertz, B. (1825). On the nature of the function expressive of the law of human mortality and on a new mode of determining life contingencies. *Philosophical Transactions of the Rural Society of London,* 115: 513-85.

Gruman, G. J. (1966). A history of ideas about the prolongation of life. The evolution of prolongevity hypotheses to 1800. *Transactions of the American Philosophical Society,* 56, Part 9.

Hayflick, L. (1987). Biological aging theories. In G. L. Maddox (Ed.), *The Encyclopedia of Aging.* New York: Springer, pp. 64-68.

Hilton, J. (1936). *Lost Horizon.* New York: William Morrow.

Jarvik, L. F., Blum, J. E., & Varma, A. D. (1972). Genetic components and intellectual functioning during senescence: A 20-year study of aging twins. *Behavior Genetics,* 2: 159-71.

Kastenbaum, R. (1990). The age of saints and the saintliness of age. *International Journal of Aging & Human Development,* 30: 95-118.

Kiefer, C. W. (1992). Aging in Eastern cultures: A historical overview. In T. R. Cole, D. D. Van Tassel, & R. Kastenbaum (Eds.), *Handbook of the Humanities and Aging.* New York: Springer, pp. 96-124.

Kirkwood, T. L. L., & Holliday, R. (1986). Ageing as a consequence of natural selection. In A. H. Bittles & K. J. Collins (Eds.), *The Biology of Human Aging.* Cambridge: Cambridge University Press, pp. 1-16.

Lamb, M. J. (1986). Insects as models for testing theories of ageing. In A. H. Bittles & K. J. Collins (Eds.), *The Biology of Human Aging.* Cambridge: Cambridge University Press, pp. 33-48.

Mishara, B. L., & McKim, W. A. (1989). Prolongation of life. In R. Kastenbaum & B. K. Kastenbaum (Eds.), *Encyclopedia of Death.* Phoenix, AZ: The Oryx Press, pp. 206-10.

Morgan, D. G., & May, P. C. (1990). Age-related changes in synaptic neurochemistry. In E. L. Schneider & J. W. Rowe (Eds.), *Handbook of the Biology of Aging.* Third Edition. New York: Academic Press, pp. 219-54.

Palmore, E. (1977). Predictors of longevity. In S. G. Haynes & M. Feinlieb (Eds.), *Epidemiology of Aging.* Bethesda, MD: National Institutes of Health, pp. 57-64.

Swift, J. (1726). *Gulliver's Travels.* Reference Edition. Boston: Beacon Press, 1963.

Ya, L. H. (1988). A Confucian theory of human development. In R. M. Thomas (Ed.), *Oriental Theories of Human Development.* New York: Peter Lang, pp. 117-33.

LOVING AND LOSING

The two powerful themes—loving and losing—have such an intimate and complex interrelationship that one can hardly be considered without the other. This connection has been explored for centuries in the poetry, songs, drama, prayers, and meditations of many lands. Love thwarted by family interference led to the suicides of a clerk and his wife in *Southeast the Peacock Flies,* a narrative poem written by an anonymous Chinese author in the second century (in Watson, 1984). *Love Song of the Dark Lord* (*Gitagovinda* in the original Sanskrit) is an extended religious/erotic lyric written in twelfth-century India by Jayadeva, since revered as a poet-saint. The Third Song depicts the anguish of the deserted lover, e.g.:

> Budding mango trees tremble from the embrace of rising vines.
> Brindaban forest is washed by meandering Jumna river waters.
> When spring's mood is rich, Hari roams here
> To dance with young women, friend—
> A cruel time for deserted lovers. (Miller, 1977, p. 75)

Happiness in love breeds anxiety about the inevitable separation and loss that time will bring. Shakespeare concludes his seventy-third sonnet with the couplet:

> This thou perceiv'st, which makes thy love more strong,
> To love that well, which thou must leave ere long.

In "To his coy mistress," Andrew Marvell whispers of "Time's winged chariot hurrying near" and ends with the often-quoted zinger:

> The grave's a fine and private place,
> But none, I think, do there embrace.

A British soldier mired in the killing trenches of World War I discovered a theme that is no less poignant for being much less common. In *Strange Meeting,* Wilfred Owen imagines having escaped from battle "down some profound dark tunnel...." There, one of the "encumbered sleepers" stares at him with piteous recognition. The poem concludes:

> I am the enemy you killed, my friend.
> I knew you in this dark, for so you frowned
> Yesterday through me as you jabbed and killed.
> I parried; but my hands were loath and cold.
> Let us sleep now.... (see Silkin, 1983, p. 198)

Owen, who was in fact to die near the end of the war, sensed a strong if unspoken bond between those who were being forced to destroy each other in a world gone mad with violence. A related message is expressed very differently in a poem by the contemporary Navajo author Joseph Bruchac. An old man—*Birdfoot's Grampa*—keeps insisting that the car be stopped so he can climb out and "gather into his hands the small toads blinded by our lights and leaping, live drops of rain." Finally, the others object, complaining that they have places to go.

> But, leathery hands full
> of wet brown life,
> knee deep in the summer
> roadside grass,
> he just smiled and said
> they have places to go to
> too. (see Hobson, 1979, p. 34)

Themes of loving and losing encompass an enormous range from fear of losing a romantic partner to a universal sense of love for life that also includes the responsibility for the enhancement and protection of all life. It is a long way from the tears-in-my-beer songs of jilted affection to a Gandhi or Schweitzer's reverence for life, and this perhaps can be considered a distance measured in moral development. Nevertheless, whether our desires and fears are completely self-centered or on a high plane of philosophical/spiritual awareness, the story of our lives often centers on the dynamics of loving and losing.

This brief and selective exploration of loving and losing as part of lifespan development begins with a frame of reference that has exercised considerable influence in the formation of attitudes and expectations in the United States and, to a lesser extent, in some other nations. This reminiscence of the classical Hollywood version is followed by attention to theories of love and loss, and then to research and other observations concerning the present scene.

The Classical Hollywood Version

"Boy meets girl. Boy loses girl. Boy gets girl." This was once the standard formula for a Hollywood movie. The "storybook ending" satisfied most viewers because "love had found a way" and one could leave the theater secure in the fantasy that Billy Handsome and Mary Sweetkins would indeed "live happily ever after." The promise of love everlasting was protected by quickly rolling the credits while the couple were hopping into the car or onto the horse to begin their life together. This highly predictable type of scenario drew much of its appeal from the fact that dreams and desires were at considerable risk away from the silver screen. In real life, the right boy did not always get the right girl, or might not be able to keep her—or the couple might spend half a century finding new ways to make life miserable for each other. (The possibility that the "right boy" might be looking for another "right boy" was beyond the pale.)

The most popular and common movies "wrapped everything up" neatly at the end. This held true for deathbed scenes as well. The typical Hollywood deathbed scene until recent times revealed as little about dying as the romantic scenes did about actual sexual interactions. Dying seldom interfered with anyone's hairdo, and only an occasional stifled groan would remind us that the person was (supposedly) in physical distress. The dialogue and interactions tended to be highly stereotyped and rich in bromides bearing little resemblance to the complexities, ambiguities, and diversities of actual deathbed scenes (Kastenbaum, 1992). The main point of the love story usually was to get the right couple married (and, by implication, off to offscreen ecstasy) after a few suspenseful and entertaining delays. The main point of the death story usually was to send the character off to offscreen bliss in a manner that relieved the viewers' anxieties and affirmed their beliefs. For some time, the Hollywood version of loving and losing spared us realistic confrontations with either sex or death. It substituted a set of scenarios that many people attempted to use as models for their own lives. Lacking a producer, director, script writer, sound track, and other devices, however, few could impose the media-promulgated images of loving and losing with any consistency on their own lives.

The classic Hollywood version of loving and losing has since been challenged and supplemented by a wider variety of approaches, including some that are probingly realistic or poetically imaginative. However, at least one general effect of the classic version continues to influence new generations: the disturbing suspicion that real love/lust and real response to loss are what are displayed for us on the silver screen or on television. Especially vulnerable are those who are just starting on their journey through the lifespan and are not yet secure in their own identities and values. Response tendencies honed by television images may prove of little value when these people are called on to face the vicissitudes of loving and losing in their own lives.

Loving as a Facet of Human Development and Experience

The social and behavioral sciences are showing signs of emerging from an era in which love was something of an embarrassment. The concept seemed too broad, too vague, too inspirational, too closely associated with popular images and sentiments. Perhaps not coincidentally, during this period of change attention to sexuality has also become more explicit and systematic. Today, some aspects of love are the topics of study under other headings (see, for example, **Attachment Across the Lifespan, Homosexuality, Marital Development, Sex in the Later Adult Years** and **Sexuality**). Significant gains in knowledge have resulted from dividing love-related issues into smaller, more manageable topics. Nevertheless, after many aspects have been removed for separate study, there still remains the basic concept of love and its implications for lifespan development.

A number of contemporary researchers, theoreticians, and service providers have so successfully violated the implicit taboo against discussing love that we now have a lively and interesting new literature on the subject. To supplement the brief presentation here, one may turn to resources such as

Irving Singer's (1984) brilliant three-volume history, *The Nature of Love* and Erich Fromm's (1956) pioneering *The Art of Loving*, as well as to useful contributions by Douglas and Atwell (1987), Fine (1985), Gaylin (1986), Gould and Iorio (1972), Greeley (1991), Mellen (1981); Miller and Siegel (1972), Pearson (1992), Sternberg (1988), and Sternberg and Barnes (1988).

Some Guiding Thoughts from the Past

One of the first tasks facing the new wave of contributors is to discover what remains most valuable from earlier observations and conceptions of love. Some of these ideas have been with us since the earliest surviving religious, philosophical, and historical writings. Other contributions—such as those engendered by the psychoanalytic approach—were made in much more recent times but have taken on an historical patina with the rapid and significant changes that have since taken place. The following selection represents a few of these past concepts that deserve consideration today. Emphasis is on observations, ideas, and values that are of particular relevance to lifespan development.

Sexual Love: Indispensable But Deadly Dangerous. Life without love would lack something essential. Of course, we seek passionate fulfillment; what could be more natural? There is great risk involved, however, at all phases of the lover's experience. The questing lover may not find love or may be rejected. Having found love and having won acceptance, one yet may lose it all. Even the lovers' embrace is perilous, and the moments after ecstasy are rehearsals for dying and death. These are among the observations about sexual love that were vividly expressed by poets of the ancient Greco-Roman world. Sappho of Lesbos (sixth century B.C.), considered by many to be the first woman poet, and Ovid, a lawyer of Rome (43 B.C.-17 A.D.), demonstrated markedly different ways of experiencing and coping with what both felt to be the truth: that love—if it really is

love—is deadly dangerous. Sappho is one of the first voices to come to us through the centuries with the feeling of dying for love. In one of her poems (*Seizure*) she watches the woman she loves succumbing to the charms and power of a man. As the poem concludes:

> My eyes are dead
> to light, my ears
> pound, and sweat pours over me.
> I convulse, greener than grass,
> and feel my mind slip as I
> go close to death.... (see Barnstone, 1988, p. 280)

Both love rejected and the postlude to sexual intercourse bring images of death to mind. As Barnstone comments, "She can no longer see, speak or hear. As her bodily functions weaken, she moves close to death, her analogue of the *via negativa*. The mystics would describe this state as dying away from space and time. In Taoist terminology, she is moving to the open country of emptiness" (p. 281).

Ovid's approach is usually lighter and more playful. Singer (1984) characterizes Ovid as idealizing "innocent merriment" (volume 1, p. 141). Love and sex are games to enjoy while we can. And yet, beneath this debonair attitude we find darker thoughts coming to the surface. For example, *The Dream* opens with the stark statement:

> That night I fell asleep as if forever
> and then the terrors came
> to haunt my soul.

When a soothsayer interprets his dream as prophesying that he is doomed to a cold and lonely bed,

> The air was chilled,
> blood left my face and Night stared in my eyes. (see Gregory, 1964, p. 92)

Ovid was an early and vivid advocate of the attempt to reduce the risks of sexual love by seeing it as a pleasantry, a diversion. Yet he recognized that it is a diversion from thoughts of the cold and lonely bed/grave, and that the game can turn perilous at any moment. Sappho's strong personality comes across most fully when she confronts desire as the life-giving and life-threatening enterprise it is. Both Sappho and Ovid take sexual love to be an essential condition of the fulfilled adult life and would therefore look askance at those who limit themselves to a spectator role, a preoccupation with material goods, or other trivial pursuits. And both would take us aside to confide that love is as deadly as it is beautiful.

Jen: Love as a Developmental Principle. During the same period when Sappho was writing her poetry, an agnostic political commentator was expressing his views to his students. Some of the students kept notes and shared them with others. Today these are known as the sayings or analects of Confucius. Although not organized as systematic treatises, these collected sayings (published in four books) offer one of the first major conceptions of human development (Kiefer, 1992; Ya, 1988; Ya & Thomas, 1988). Love was no less important to Confucius than to Sappho and Ovid, but it took a markedly different form.

For Confucius and his first great follower, Mencius, the development of the individual is intimately related to his or her social integration and place in the universe at large. Neither individual self-actualization nor engrossment in the delights and frights of sexual passion is emphasized by Confucius. Instead, each child has the potential to become a virtuous person and thereby to become truly human (jen). It is not a unique individuality that is to be sought for its own value, then, but rather the cultivation of the potential for virtue. Where does love come in?

> At the foundation of *jen* is love, meaning love for one's parents, for one's neighbors, and ultimately for all people. As a process, *jen* represents the way to build social relationships...*jen* is the core of virtue from which specific desirable traits arise. As such, *jen* reflects the perfect personality that is the goal of human development. (Ya, 1988, pp. 122-23)

The Confucian *jen* does not involve passionate devotion to one's own pleasures, sexual or otherwise, nor does it seek to win the approval of the gods or secure the re-

wards of eternal bliss. Love takes the form of a harmonious relationship between oneself and others and between the virtuous society and nature. People are born with the potential for "hearts of compassion," and this potential should be realized first by cultivating the traits of modesty, courtesy, and diligence and respecting one's parents, and then developing the ability to treat all people well.

Fear of loss, abandonment, loneliness, and despair are less evident in the Confucian literature (although separation, bereavement, and other stressful events can arouse such feelings in real-life situations). From the philosophical standpoint at least, individual human development should strengthen one's relationships with society and social institutions—so long as one maintains his or her personal virtue, one can lose a particular loved one but never one's loving relationship to all humankind.

Socrates/Plato: "Love is desire for the perpetual possession of the good." Singer (1984, volume 1, p. 53) selects this statement of Socrates from Plato's dialogue *Symposium* as representing the key idea that distinguishes this new theory of love from all that came before it. Socrates/Plato were not speaking against passionate sexual attractions nor against virtuous behavior in a well-ordered society. The platonic conception of love, however, rises to a higher level of abstraction.

Love is an idea or form that cannot be limited to the relationship between lovers or between wise parent and obedient child. All throughout our lives we seek that which is "good," "true," and "beautiful"—terms that represent different facets of the same value. In daily life we are more or less pleased and satisfied by available concrete manifestations that embody or hint at something of the good. And so we love sunsets, chocolate, ninth inning rallies, and, imperfectly, our own imperfect lovers. Nevertheless, there is within us a persistent search for that which is *most* good, true, and beautiful, and, therefore, most deserving of our highest love. Yes, there might be that most beautiful sunset, most delicious chocolate, and most glorious lover. Even the most sublime concrete manifestations of a particular goodness-truth-beauty, however, can only approximate to the very idea of perfect or absolute goodness. And if we think we love sunsets, chocolate, or our mate, just think what depths and heights of love we would experience if we could but stand in the presence of absolute goodness.

Furthermore, if goodness turned into mediocrity, truth into deception, and beauty into shambles, then we would hardly honor it as absolute and absolutely desirable. This is precisely one of the great defects of everyday life. All that we value in the temporal flow of life is subject to change, decay, and destruction. Time seems to mock us all, depriving both individuals and entire cultures of the most cherished manifestations of the good, the true, and the beautiful. Loss, although long delayed, is finally experienced even by those lovers who have shared their lives with each other for half a century or more, accepting the loss of youthful charms in exchange for deepening affection (Pearson, 1992). And so we are back to the opening statement: "Love is desire for the *perpetual* possession of the good." In other words, all we want is the best, now and forever.

Human development is largely the quest for absolute goodness in order to actualize our potential for love. People remain in an underdeveloped condition, perhaps hobbled by self-deceit, if they mistake the affections and passions of life in the temporal flow for the apprehension of absolute goodness, truth, and beauty. Much of Socrates/Plato's work throughout the dialogues is concerned with the process of discovering or evoking these absolute values. Theories of knowledge, education, and the relationship between the individual and society are proposed, theories that have been influential down to the present day.

What is most germane here is the idea that we must continue to develop our abilities to discern and appreciate that which is most deserving of our wholehearted, wholeminded love. The progression from childhood to maturity is a kind of schooling in love. For the youth, what pleases immediately and delights the senses will be taken as the representation of love. This should be

only a temporary state of affairs, but some people never move beyond the superficial identification of goodness-truth-beauty with whatever glitters and pleases the senses. Nevertheless, the wisest philosopher has reached this level only by passing through several intermediary approximations. At the highest level, one will still value the lesser forms of affection and passion, but will value most deeply the perfect, harmonious, and everlasting form of absolute love.

One cannot develop fully as a human being, then, without becoming more discerning and sophisticated regarding the nature of love. And this understanding, once achieved, provides a kind of safety net against catastrophic loss. People can and will lose anything and everything, including their lives. But absolute goodness is forever, and one enters into its vibrating harmony through a perfected capacity for love:

> Beholding beauty with the eye of the mind, he will be enabled to bring forth, not images of beauty, but realities (for he has hold not of an image but of a reality), and bringing forth and nourishing true virtue to become the friend of God and be immortal, if mortal man may. (Plato: Symposium, in *Great Books*, 1971, p. 167)

Christian Love: Spiritual Quest and Carnal Sin. As Christianity emerged from Judaism, the new religion offered alternative conceptions of both loving and losing. The life and sayings of Jesus became the basis for doctrines in which love was the dominant theme. No previous religion had given so central a position to love. At the same time, Christianity announced a joyous triumph over the loss so memorably characterized in the Old Testament: "for all flesh is as grass." Essentially, it was love that had triumphed over death. The basic implications for human development were quickly grasped by some who were drawn to the new creed. One should attempt to follow the precepts of Jesus, to live as he lived and believe as he believed. A life devoted to Christian love would not only be virtuous for its own sake but would also prepare one to enter the kingdom of heaven.

At this point, it might appear that the Christian message regarding love is simple, direct, and unified: Follow the example of Jesus as best as one can. Whether or not the message was ever that simple is a matter of controversy, but it is clear that over time the Christian concept of love has become more complex, diverse, and—seemingly—self-contradicting. Many believers do try to keep their focus on the life and sayings of Jesus, ignoring as much as they can the various doctrines and interpretations that have risen in competition. Taken as a whole, however, Christian beliefs, attitudes, and practices are far from simple or settled. An attempt to signal this complexity was already made by characterizing Christian love as both spiritual quest and carnal sin because there is no responsible way to encapsulate the complex set of Christian messages on love into a single and consistent statement.

The spiritual quest tradition is an edifice that Church fathers build upon the materials furnished both by the Gospels and by philosophers such as Plato and Plotinus (an Egyptian who developed an important neoplatonic theory in the third century of the Christian era). The transformation of the Gospel-told life of Jesus into an entire system of Church dogma has been hailed by some as a mighty achievement and has been decried by others as a distortion and obfuscation of the original message. Centuries after the life and death of Jesus, the official version of the Christian love message had taken a relatively settled form (those who had differing interpretations of Christian love would be in jeopardy for torture and death as heretics).

- There is a highest good, just as Socrates/Plato insisted. It is enduring and far beyond the pleasures and values of everyday life.
- Furthermore, those who would be virtuous and wise will devote themselves to the quest for incorporating this highest good into their own lives.
- However, this highest good is no longer a potential that is within individuals themselves: It is an attribute of God, who is now conceived as a Supreme Being. It is God's love that one seeks. In fact, all of creation exists to praise and serve God. Instead of themselves, or other creatures, ideas, or things, people should love God above all, and on God's terms. In return, and unlike Plato's absolute ideas, God will love them, too.

- Jesus provides a model and focus for love that people can understand more easily than the abstract Supreme Being. He represents a link between humanity and divine love, a being who is both of and beyond our world.
- Through God's infinite love and the sacrifice and compassion of Jesus, imperfect and mortal humans can achieve their salvation: Death will no longer have its sting. In their more limited way, as creatures of God and imitators of Christ, humans can also bestow love on their neighbors and forgive their errors and transgressions.

This portrait of Christian love is challenging enough in itself. Believers are asked to transcend the mean and the superficial by developing a life consecrated to God, taking Jesus as the model. No human relationship or achievement compares with the infinite love of God. But the actual challenge is far greater. Up to this point, the portrait has neglected the earthier side of love evidenced in sexual and other power relationships among people.

The three major complications have little if any foundation in the life and sayings of Jesus. In fact, they appear inconsistent with his character and message:

- Sexual activity is sinful.
- Women are inferior to men.
- Death is punishment for sin.

Leaving aside the historical derivation of these ideas, it can be seen that sexual love not only has been isolated from the conception of divine love but also has been construed as adversarial, negative, and dangerous. Lovers are at risk for damnation simply by being lovers. This is a relatively new conception. In the Greco-Roman world one could be guilty of sexual wrongdoing, as in marital infidelity, but sexual behavior itself was not offensive to the gods (who were rather active in that department themselves), and devotion to one's mate was a virtue. In the great Hindu tradition, sexual love and even sexual playfulness were admired as attributes of the life-giving gods. Significantly, the female principle was salient in Hindu worship but was markedly neglected or repressed in Christianity until the emergence of the Cult of Mary and courtly love about 1,200 years after the life and death of Jesus.

For centuries, Christian dogma and practice have assumed male superiority and hegemony. Love between equal partners has been made much more difficult because of the belief that women are inherently inferior, passive, and somehow especially responsible for sexual temptations and transgressions, just as they are especially associated with the dark anxieties of fertility. The institutionalized inequality between the sexes has tended not only to make the female the guilty party (e.g., even today, prostitution is treated largely as a crime on the part of the woman), but to affirm male advantages over women in a variety of power relationships, including the home, the legal system, and the workplace.

A life devoted to Christian love might be coherent and natural if it meant the attempt to model oneself after the teachings attributed to Jesus, whose way of life has impressed Jews, Muslims, and others who do not count themselves as Christians. However, as Christianity has passed from one generation to another through the centuries, it has taken on characteristics that place exceptional strain on those who would both pursue the highest good and enjoy fulfilling lives as men and women here on earth. Over both sexes hovers the traditional view that death is not just the end of life but that this loss is in consequence of original sin and constitutes a punishment for same. Over females hovers the tradition that developmental pathways through life are more restricted and narrow because they are here basically to serve men who are here basically to serve God. Over lovers hovers the tradition that there is something fundamentally wrong and

offensive to God in a relationship and an activity that brings such intimacy and pleasure.

In practice, Christian views of love vary considerably, depending on the cultural context and the experiences and personalities of the individuals concerned. Around the turn of the present century, however, there was an increasing perception that many of the miseries people visit on themselves and each other could be related to unresolved sexual conflicts, and that Christianity had contributed to this misfortune because "frequently...and perhaps in most cases, Christianity ceased to be a religion of love and became a religion of fear" (Pfister, 1923, p. 24). Oskar Pfister, Protestant minister who became one of the first lay psychoanalysts, was alarmed by the neurosis, ill will, and violence that had come to be so characteristic of the Christian enterprise that he cherished. For Pfister, "The removal of neurotic traits from religion is effected in principle in the same way as the cure of non-religious neurotics, i.e., mainly by the restoration of love and its elevation to be the dominant factor in life" (p. 23). It was Pfister's friend, a physician by the name of Sigmund Freud, who brought this challenging new view to prominence.

Psychoanalysis (Freudian version). Love is a union of tender and sexual feelings toward another person, but this type of relationship is very difficult to develop in the oppressive and hostile conditions of modern society. The concept of love is as central to Freud's psychoanalytic theory as it is to Greco-Roman or Christian thought, although one is perhaps more likely to be startled by the differences than to recognize the similarities. Essentially, Freud reconstructed what he called the *psychosexual stages* of development through which the earliest infantile desire for instant fulfillment of needs is transformed into an adult's ability to love and cherish another person. (It was left to others actually to observe and study child development directly instead of drawing inferences from the retrospective self-reports of adults.)

Several of Freud's ideas about love proved alarming and controversial. First, he traced the origins of sexuality to early childhood. This unsettling proposition was accompanied by accounts of family influences on the early development of sexuality and personality in general. Long before puberty, the child already has organized his or her personality around either normal or disturbing experiences within his or her network of relationships. One fortunate child, for example, has fallen temporarily in love with the opposite sex parent, whom the child fully intends to marry some day. Reaching physical maturity, this person now is ready to bring his or her confidence, self-esteem, and readiness for love to the quest for a mate. There are all too many unfortunate children, however, who are tantalized, encouraged, shamed, threatened, and punished by ambivalent parents and others. At one end of the continuum is the all-too-rare child who has moved through the psychosexual stages as normally as one moves through the stages of sensorimotor coordination. At the other end is the confused, traumatized, abused child for whom protosexuality already means hurt and who has had little experience with nurturant love. Still very much in the news today and still controversial is the question of the incidence of sexual molestation of children, although few knowledgeable people now doubt that early traumatic experiences do long-term harm.

Perhaps the best known (or best misunderstood) facet of Freud's theory is the proposition that sexuality should be expressed, not inhibited. Some individuals have used this misconception as a license for unbridled promiscuity; others have attacked it as an ungodly and immoral incitation. Freud's actual position—and his own life-style—were not nearly so extreme. Yes, Freud had learned from his patients that inhibited and conflicted sexuality does add to one's miseries, and in many ways. People live more balanced and enjoyable lives when they have a mutually satisfying sexual relationship. A therapeutic aim, for example, might be to help a woman feel that she is not a harlot or a sinner if she enjoys sexual feelings, or to help a man regain his potency by overcoming his childhood fear of a menacing father-figure who would punish him for daring to act like a husband/father himself. Wild sexual indulgences—such as rampant promiscuity or preference for deviant practices—were seen by Freud as immature or distorted forms of sexual expression.

Along with Pfister, Freud (1931/1978) believed that we would have a kinder, more harmonious, less hostile society if people could learn to love themselves and others—and to love themselves in others and others in themselves. Sexual love was seen as a natural, beneficial, and significant component of human love in general, although this source of intimacy and support could all too easily be distorted by traumatic childhood experiences and/or harsh and hypocritical social attitudes.

The relationship between loving and losing is explored in many ways by Freud. Perhaps his two most important contributions have been to the development of grief theory, particularly in one of his most famous essays, "On Mourning and Melancholia" (Freud, 1917). Through his own observations and through the many subsequent studies they have stimulated, Freud has enriched our awareness of the psychological response to loss of the loved person.

On a more philosophical—even mystical—level, the aging Freud (1920) offered a radically revised instinct theory in which impulses toward love, growth, and experience *(Eros)* are incessantly in competition with impulses toward withdrawal, cessation, and death *(Thanatos)*. This is seen as a grand cosmic contest in which, inevitably, death takes the palm. However, it is in the individual's best interest to avoid becoming thoroughly dominated by either Thanatos or Eros. In other words, people should stay in touch with both their loving and creative impulses on the one hand and their destructive and retreating impulses on the other.

The Postmodern Challenge

According to some observers, modern times are already behind us. In the postmodern world, communication of symbols and persuasion is gaining dominance over the production and distribution of material goods. The old rules are changing, and changing rapidly, in every domain of life. One's most intimate relationships are not immune from this exciting but disorienting process, nor are one's sense of personal identity and one's value priorities.

Some of the changes that can already be clearly observed seem to be mostly disruptive and stressful. The high rates of divorce, teen pregnancy, and single-parent households are among these disruptive changes. To these must be added the resurgence of previously known sexually transmitted diseases and the AIDS epidemic. Less visible casualties include people who have come to experience anxiety, depression, and a sense of alienation after discovering that the "sexual revolution" did not meet their deeper needs for intimacy and companionship, leading instead to a trail of broken relationships. What developmental implications all of this will have for several generations of children remains to be seen. Many observers deplore what is seen as the excessive influence of television and other media images on the formation of personality and values, including but by no means limited to love and sexuality.

Social institutions are also under pressure from postmodern changes. Federal and local governments, for example, are confronted by a constituency that is intensely divided on such issues as abortion and sex education. Churches face internal divisions as well. Is cohabitation still sinful? Should priests once again have permission to marry? (And what about nuns?) Must all clergy be heterosexual or asexual?

Some changes, however, may hold promise for an improved state of affairs. Increased empowerment of women in all facets of life may encourage the development of more mature and equitable sexual relationships. A more sophisticated public may be turning away from consumerism to values that are more directly related to significant relationships and creative activities. Negative stereotypes toward love relationships among older adults may be giving way to admiration and encouragement. Traditional biases against interethnic and interracial marriage may be losing ground to the opportunities and fascinations of a "global community."

Interestingly, in all of these postmodern changes there is little or no indication that love is becoming less valued. On the contrary, there seems to be a renewed exploration of the possibilities inherent in the love relationship, whether between mates or between generations. Recent studies indicate that "romantic love" is still with us, that it takes a variety of forms among youth (Marston, Hecht, & Roberts, 1987), and that the quality of relationships is still a major consideration (Hecht, Marston, & Larkey, 1988). Furthermore, what Douglas and Atwell (1987) characterize as "caring love" may emerge as a dominant principle in a world that is growing ever older and, one may hope, just a little wiser as well.

▼ ROBERT KASTENBAUM

See also: Adult Children and Their Parents; Age and Mate Choice; Attachment Across the Lifespan; Cohort and Generational Effects; Criminal Behavior; Divorce; Gender as a Shaping Force in Adult Development; Gender Differences in the Workplace; Homosexuality; Interethnic Relationships; Loneliness; Marital Development; Maturity; Religion and Coping with Crisis; Sex in the Later Adult Years; Sexuality; Widowhood: The Coping Response.

References

Barnstone, W. (1988). *Sappho and the Greek Lyric Poets.* New York: Schocken.

Douglas, J. D., & Atwell, F. C. (1987). *Love, Intimacy, and Sex.* Newbury Park, CA: Sage.

Fine, R. (1985). *The Meaning of Love in Human Experience.* New York: Wiley.

Freud, S. (1917). On mourning and melancholia. In *Collected Papers.* Volume 4, pp. 152-72.

———. (1920). *Beyond the Pleasure Principle.* Standard Edition. Volume 18.

———. (1931/1978). *Why War? The Correspondence Between Albert Einstein and Sigmund Freud.* Chicago: Chicago Institute for Psychoanalysis.

Fromm, E. (1956). *The Art of Loving*. New York: Harper & Row.

Gaylin, W. (1986). *Rediscovering Love*. New York: Viking.

Gould, J., & Iorio, J. (1972). *Love, Sex, and Identity*. San Francisco: Boyd & Fraser.

Greeley, A.. M. (1991). *Faithful Attraction: Discovering Intimacy, Love, and Fidelity in American Marriage*. New York: Tom Doherty Associates.

Gregory, H. (1964). *Love Poems of Ovid*. New York: Mentor.

Hecht, M. L., Marston, P. J., & Larkey, L. K. (1988). Relational quality and the maintenance of romantic loveships. Presented at annual convention of the Speech Communication Association, New Orleans, November 1988.

Hobson, G. (Ed.). (1979). *The Remembered Earth: An Anthology of Contemporary Native American Literature*. Albuquerque, NM: University of New Mexico Press.

Kastenbaum, R. (1992). *The Psychology of Death*. Revised Edition. New York: Springer.

Kiefer, C. W. (1992). Aging in Eastern cultures: An historical overview. In T. R. Cole, D. D. Van Tassel, & R. Kastenbaum (Eds.), *Handbook of the Humanities and Aging*. New York: Springer, pp. 96-124.

Marston, P. J., Hecht, M. L., & Roberts, T. (1987). "True love ways": The subjective experience and communication of romantic love. *Journal of Personal and Social Relationships, 4:* 387-407.

Mellen, S. L. W. (1981).*The Evolution of Love*. Oxford: W. H. Freeman.

Miller, B. S. (Ed.). (1977). *Love Song of the Dark Lord*. New York: Columbia University Press.

Miller, H. L., & Siegel, P. S. (1972). *Loving. A Psychological Approach*. New York: Wiley.

Pearson, J. C. (1992). *Lasting Love. What Keeps Couples Together*. Dubuque, IA: William C. Brown.

Pfister, O. (1923). *Some Applications of Psychoanalysis*. London: Allen & Unwin.

Plato. (1971). Symposium. In R. M. Hutchins (Ed.), *Great Books of the Western World*. Volume 7: *Plato*. Chicago: Encyclopedia Britannica.

Silkin, J. (1981). (Ed.). *First World War Poetry*. Second Edition. Harmondsworth, Middlesex, England: Penguin.

Singer, I. (1984). *The Nature of Love*. 3 vols. Chicago: University of Chicago Press.

Sternberg, R. J. (1988). *The Triangle of Love*. New York: Basic Books.

Sternberg, R. J., & Barnes, M. L. (Eds.). (1988). *The Psychology of Love*. New Haven, CT: Yale University Press.

Watson, B. (Ed.). (1984). *The Columbia Book of Chinese Poetry. From Early Times to the Thirteenth Century*. New York: Columbia University Press.

Ya, L. H. (1988). A Confucian theory of human development. In R. M. Thomas (Ed.), *Oriental Theories of Human Development*. New York: Peter Lang, pp. 117-33.

Ya, L. H., & Thomas, R. M. (1988). Confucianists' replies to questions about development. In R. M. Thomas (Ed.), *Oriental Theories of Human Development*. New York: Peter Lang, pp. 243-68.

M

MARITAL DEVELOPMENT

Marital development refers to the ways in which families begin, change, and develop as they progress through a lifetime. People may sometimes think that marriages remain the same. They may even count on a certain stability. Marriages are dynamic, however, and successful marital relationships change when there is a need to do so. This article addresses some of the major demands that arise in various stages of life as these influence and are influenced by the marital relationship.

If we compare the 1950s with the 1990s, we find an increase in the number of possible ways in which a marriage can be defined. In the U.S. culture of the 1950s, wives and husband knew what they were expected to do to be successful marital partners. The roles were clear but limited, especially for the wife. Research at that time indicated that many married women were dissatisfied, partly because they did not have the option of working outside the home and partly because they were expected to take primary responsibility for child care. This dissatisfaction influenced the way these wives felt about their husbands.

Today people have many more options and tend to be more satisfied with their marital relationships, but these expanded options increase the problems making choices. Both women and men are finding it difficult to cope with all the changes. The many possibilities that arise when one wishes to start a relationship with someone generate the need for a series of decisions about how to pick out a person with whom to become romantically involved, how to judge the appropriate way to communicate one's feelings, and how to know when one is in love.

Another series of decisions and changes begins when one moves from the status of a single to a married person. It seems to the newly married couple that everyone has expectations for them: their parents, friends, and employers, as well as each other. Both partners must work out a definition of their own unique marriage that is comfortable for them. Most couples find marriage to be hard work that requires agreeing on the level of commitment to the relationship and coming to terms with the growing feelings of attachment. Both husband and wife are more satisfied with the relationship when they have established a way of thinking about themselves as a marital couple. The inability to arrive at a mutually acceptable concept of their marriage can lead to termination. Divorce is more acceptable than it was in the 1950s, e.g., divorced families are no longer referred to as "broken homes," and no stigma is attached to being from a divorced family. Having had one marital relationship end in divorce, an individual is more likely to proceed with caution before remarriage. People often live together before remarriage to test the strength of the relationship.

Another change in the 1990s is that adult children often live at home longer. This can have a negative impact on the marital relationship of the parents. Many of these parents are looking forward to retirement.

One or both marital partners may be retiring younger because they are financially able to do so, and this life event has a definite impact on their marriage as well.

This brief survey of patterns of marital development begins with a focus on finding a romantic partner and then considers progression into marriage, the life of a marriage itself, the traditional concerns of marital development, and current issues related to divorce adjustment, single-parent dating, and remarriage.

Finding a Romantic Partner

One of life's greatest challenges is finding a romantic partner. In years past and in other cultures, arranged marriages were the norm. At the turn of the nineteenth century, the balance shifted to marriages based on affection rather than economic needs (Degler, 1983). Choice of a marital partner became a matter of attraction and interest. Since that time, U.S. culture has focused much attention on the definition and value of attractiveness (Berscheid & Walster, 1974).

Three types of attraction have been identified: physical, task/status, and social (McCroskey & McCain, 1974). Most people think only about physical attraction when they discuss romantic partners. The other types of attraction, however, may also lead to thinking about a person in a romantic way. For example, with task attraction, one might be attracted to a coworker who is very competent in performing a difficult job. This person is noticed more carefully and other positive attributes also become evident. Social attraction can also begin the process that leads to romantic involvement. A person with an engaging personality may attract attention because he or she is so pleasant to be with. As one learns more about this person, other aspects, not so readily noticed as the social attractiveness, may also come to the fore.

Physical attraction has been most often studied by researchers. This form of attraction is most important when one first meets another person. However, as people come to know each other better, the initial perception of physical attractiveness may be either enhanced or diminished. For example, a man of exceptional physical attractiveness may at first impress a woman as "wonderful," but if he turns out to be arrogant or unkind the woman may see him as less handsome physically as time goes by. Basically, though, people more often like physically attractive people, give them a more positive evaluation early in an interaction, and are more willing to do things for them (Berscheid & Walster, 1974).

There is a big leap from that initial phase of being attracted to a person to falling in love. In U.S. culture, being "in love" is regarded as an important prerequisite for marriage. Lee (1976) points out that there is more than one style or form of love. One experiences love of beauty (Eros) when there is an intense physical attraction. Playful love (Ludus) derives from enjoying the game of relationship interaction. This type of love relationship may be more diverting than enduring, an episode that one or both partners do not intend to convert into a lifetime commitment. A person who adopts the Ludus style does not seem to take love relationships very seriously.

People may also adopt a companionate love style (Storge). The relationship is based on friendship, affection, and mutual interests, not solely on physical attraction. Obsessive love (Mania) is characterized by the partners' fierce need to possess each other. This type of love relationship is difficult to sustain over a long period of time and often is accompanied by tension and distress. In realistic love (Pragma) the partners are not overly passionate or out of control. Instead they are careful planners who minimize the importance of feelings and emphasize the role of logic and rationality. Still another love style represents a classical ideal. Altruistic love (Agape) exists when the partners see love as unselfish giving and never demand that the partner reciprocate (Knapp, 1984).

Problems arise when the partners do not adopt the same way of feeling love. Thinking about possible combinations of love styles is useful in understanding the relational problems that many people experience. If, for instance, one person in a relationship feels realistic love and the other person feels obsessive love, the differences in orientation may lead to arguments and hurt feelings. Suppose instead that one person in a relationship feels altruistic love. There is the feeling that the partner is expected to allow that person to give all the time. Many people feel uncomfortable with this unspoken rule because they do not like to take from a loved one constantly and never be allowed to give anything in return.

Still another way to think about the concept of love is suggested by Shaver and Hazan (1988). They believe that love is an emotion that originates in feelings that were originally experienced in early childhood when attachment to the mothering person is so intense. In this view, it is from their earliest experience with love that people learn to give their love to others as adults. Shaver and Hazan identify three ways in which people learn to love: (a) secure love, (b) avoidant love, and (c) anxious/ambivalent love. The secure love style comes from parents who are responsive to a child's needs. As an adult, this person is likely to be warm and giving. Avoidant love results when parents are unwilling to be responsive to the child and to provide affectionate caregiving. The child in such a family develops into an adult who has difficulty showing affection and is unable to bond with others easily. Anxious/ambivalent love results from having parents who are inconsistent in their responsiveness. The parents were giving when it was convenient or served some purpose for them. As an adult, the child from such a family often seems in need of love from others and may give in a compulsive, driven manner to make sure the needed affection is received in return (Shaver & Hazan, 1988).

Progression into Marriage

Deciding to marry is considered a major step by most couples. Marrying for the first time has its own set of issues, and marrying for the second or third time is often a very different kind of experience.

The first-marriage couple goes through at least three stages (Rapoport, Rapoport, & Strelitz, 1980). The first period is marked by commitment to getting married. The honeymoon period follows, giving way inevitably to an early adjustment period. The commitment to marriage is signaled by a public statement that symbolizes the couple's willingness to enter into the marriage contract. Typically, engagements are communicated by rings, parties, and celebrations that publicly mark the agreement. During this engagement period, the couple must also prepare themselves to enter into a long-term relationship that requires the modification of other relational ties. For example, previous boyfriends or girlfriends should no longer have the same priority they once did for the engaged couple. Additionally, the engaged couple must begin to define the division of labor that each will adopt when they marry. In times past, women were the primary caretakers of the home and children, while men provided the financial support. Today, however, the division of labor for marital couples is more complex. Both men and women often work outside the home and more frequently negotiate the tasks necessary to maintain the household. The couple will have to decide who will cook and clean, how they will manage their finances, whose parents they will visit at holidays, whether they will have children and, if so, who will be the primary caregiver, and so forth.

Given the greater ambiguity in our society today, the period of negotiation between the partners during the engagement period may be more critical than ever. Although engagement periods sometimes are brief, they still serve an important function. The way that couples negotiate during this time may set patterns of decision making that will be used during the course of the marriage. Negotiations continue throughout a couple's marital life, and a successful marriage is one in which the partners are willing to communicate with each other and reach agreement on the issues they find important.

The honeymoon period is a significant transition that helps the couple become acquainted with the status of marriage (Aldous, 1978). In previous decades this was also a time when couples developed sexual competence. More frequently today, however, couples spend this time learning more about each other and their new responsibilities. The honeymoon period helps to ease the couple into its early marriage period.

If the couple has not lived together prior to marriage, the early marital stage provides the opportunity to work out a host of issues related to everyday life. What may seem like trivial concerns often become points of conflict because each person comes to the marriage with his or her own way of doing things. As Rapoport, Rapoport, & Strelitz (1980) point out, expectations for daily living are often held implicitly and not discussed until a disagreement is discovered. For example, a new husband may assume that they will go to his parents' home for the holidays. He makes these arrangements and does not think to consult with his new wife because he has always spent the holidays with his own family. When this plan is discovered, the husband is as taken aback as the wife. She had assumed that they would be spending the holidays with her family—or at least that she would have been consulted before a decision was made.

Newly married couples find it difficult to anticipate these types of everyday expectations because they have been so much a part of their lives. These events mark the beginning phase of marital life. As the marriage develops, the couple will experience many other stages in their lives together.

The Life of a Marriage

A marriage goes through a number of stages that are often influenced by the career of the family in general. Not every couple goes through all of the stages listed, but this framework indicates the complexity of marital life. For example, changes may occur:

1. When the couple is newly established without children

2. During the childbearing years when the couple is adjusting to infant and preschool children
3. When the couple has school-age children
4. When one or more of the children are adolescents
5. When the couple has at least one young adult child for whom they are still responsible
6. When the children have been launched and the couple is in its middle years of marriage
7. When the couple is in its later years (Mattessich & Hill, 1987)

During each of these periods, family issues influence the way that marital couples define their relationship. If a couple has children, they play a significant role in the way a marital relationship is perceived by the husband and wife. Many researchers and therapists believe that the family is a system and that everything that happens to any of its members has an effect on all of them. "They interlock so that a change in any part of the family affects the other parts" (Mattessich & Hill, 1987, p. 441).

Although the family functions as an interrelated group of people, it also maintains boundaries that protect the privacy of individuals and couples (Petronio, 1991). For example, when the husband and wife are newly married, they have private information that belongs only to them. They draw a boundary around this information to keep it confidential. As children appear, the couple's privacy boundary remains intact, signaling the right to have private information and private territory apart from the children. This process helps the couple protect its relationship and recognize that they are partners to each other as well as sharing parental responsibility.

Marital Types and Their Predicaments

Fitzpatrick (1988) offers a promising typology for the ways that marital couples might define their relationship. She introduces pure types and mixed types. The pure types are "those in which the husband and wife independently agree on a definition of their relationship...but...share the same ideological views of relationships,...experience the same level of autonomy and interdependence in their marriage, and share the same view of conflict expression" (p. 78).

Three couple types are also distinguished: the Traditionals, Independents, and Separates. Couples who define themselves as Separates tend to be emotionally and psychologically less involved with each other than other couples. They usually talk less to each other and tend to avoid conflict. Autonomy is emphasized over togetherness, and they appear to be relatively distant from each other. Independents tend to be sensitive to their family environment. They balance both cohesion and autonomy with their partner. These couples manage to maintain an intimate relationship, yet at the same time they also reserve their independence. The Traditionals emphasize harmony and consensus building in the family and with their partners. These couples define their relationships according to typical male/female role expectations. For example, wives are expected to stay at home with the children while husbands earn money to support the family.

Couples may also have mixed definitions, however. The mixed couple is one in which husband and wife disagree on their definitions of the relationship. Thus, one type of mixed couple would be the one "in which the husband defines the marriage as separate whereas the wife defines the same relationship as traditional" (Fitzpatrick, 1988, p. 78). A mixed couple may also comprise a husband who thinks of the relationship as separate and a wife who defines it as independent.

The identity of the couple as a couple will continue to develop over the course of the relationship, influenced by the partners' ways of seeing their own and each other's roles.

Marital Conflict

One way that people cope with conflict is to avoid acknowledging the problems. When avoiding conflict in marriage, partners may withdraw psychologically, as when a husband watches television while the wife is talking about a problem or when both partners physically withdraw from the situation altogether (Wilmot & Wilmot, 1978). Another way of coping is through accommodation. Yielding to the concerns or demands of the partner helps smooth problems over for the moment. There is danger in always giving in to the other spouse, however. Doing so may relinquish a person's rights or needs that are a legitimate part of the relationship (Wilmot & Wilmot, 1978). Additionally, a marital partner might use accommodation as a way to attain submissive power. By using guilt, the spouse may actually shift the power base in his or her favor at the expense of the partner. For example, a husband is asked what movie he would like to see. He replies, in his accommodating way, "Anything you would like, dear. I just want you to have a good time." The wife says "Fine!" and selects a movie. At the end, when they are walking out, she says she really enjoyed the movie and asks if he did as well. The husband replies that he did in a tone that suggests he did not. The wife pursues this dissatisfied tone, asking him what was wrong. "Nothing," insists the husband. "Everything is fine." Whatever she wanted was all right, even though he did not really want to see this movie. The husband accommodated but did so at a cost for the wife. This approach does not solve the conflict; it actually makes things worse.

Couples may also use a collaborative style of conflict management (Wilmot & Wilmot, 1978). With this style, a partner tries to solve the problems to the satisfaction of all involved. Cooperation is the main expectation for people who use this strategy, hoping that their needs, as well as the needs of the other spouse, can and will be met.

The last conflict management style is competition (Wilmot & Wilmot, 1978).

Couples who use this style see conflict as a win-lose game. One of the spouses must win and the other must lose. The person who views conflict resolution in this way tends to blame or demean the spouse's needs in order to achieve his or her own goals.

For couples to stay married, they must find a balance between conflict resolution and marital satisfaction. One potential problem arises when partners do not use the same conflict management style. If, for instance, one partner uses an avoidance style and the other a competitive style, resolution is not an easy task. The competitive person defines resolving a problem as a win-lose game. However, if the partner refuses to play the game and gives up immediately, conflict will remain as part of the incompatibility. It is useful, therefore, for couples to recognize differences in conflict management styles and to identify the ways each partner deals with conflicts. When inherent differences emerge, the couple can then try to work toward a better way of resolving their conflicts. If couples are unable or unwilling to work on their conflict management styles, their overall marital satisfaction can be negatively affected because conflicts are almost certain to arise in the normal course of life events.

Marital satisfaction is influenced by the conflicts that result from family responsibilities. For example, satisfaction for marital couples is "at its lowest point when the oldest child in the family is an adolescent (between 13 and 17 years of age) or is school-aged (between 7 and 12 years old)," according to observations by Steinberg and Silverberg (1987, p. 751).

During the preadolescent and adolescent years, parents and children experience a great many changes. The push-pull of the parent-child relationship during this time usually results in conflicts, minor or major, because the main task of an adolescent is to separate from the parents and become an independent adult. The residual of these conflicts often seeps into the marital relationship in one form or another. In addition, the marital partners may be so busy dealing with the adolescent's problems that they do not spend enough time on the maintenance of their own relationship.

When the adolescent becomes a young adult and leaves the home, the couple may go through a period of adjustment and then focus again on their own relationship. However, research has shown that there tends to be increased conflict between the parents and children when adult children remain in the household and continue to depend on their parents financially, or when adult children move back into the no longer empty nest (Suitor & Pillemer, 1987).

Conflict also arises when the marital couple become responsible for their elderly parents. Financial considerations and difficult decisions that have strong emotional connections can make this area an emotional minefield. Partners may fail to communicate their expectations about the way they will take care of an aged parent because they have just assumed that the other partner feels the same way. It may turn out, however, that the other partner is unwilling to commit large sums of money for elder care because he or she is worried about his or her own parents. There may also be significant unexplored differences between the partners in how much personal time and effort, as well as money, they feel ready to invest in caring for elderly parents.

As each phase evolves in the course of a marriage, there are many possibilities for misunderstandings, disagreements, and emotional reactions that influence the level of contentment and satisfaction with the marital relationship. Nevertheless, many couples find successful ways of overcoming the inevitable problems that occur when people live together and try to construct a shared life. The differences between the partners can also provide a source of insight and a stimulus to personal and marital growth. Being able to recognize the importance of differences and being willing to adjust are central to attaining satisfaction in marriage. And satisfaction is clearly a decisive factor in maintaining a relationship over time.

Divorce and Remarriage

Marital satisfaction may decline so significantly that the relationship deteriorates and terminates. With the onset of divorce comes the challenge of adjusting to a new lifestyle and possibly the experience of remarriage. Adjustment to divorce is difficult. Most people take approximately three years to divorce themselves psychologically from their ex-spouse (Petronio & Endres, 1986). The length and intensity of this reaction may vary depending on whether or not the couple was psychologically separated while still legally married. For example, in some situations one partner had already decided to end the relationship and did not share this intention with the spouse until the last moment. The person who is caught unaware may have the most trouble adjusting and take several years to separate himself or herself from the spouse. The deserted spouse may continue to play the same roles, such as giving in all the time or expecting the ex-spouse to help with his or her problems. It takes time to accept the new status. The spouse who did not initiate the divorce may experience periods of frustration and anger because the relationship is no longer the same. This is not to say that the initiator of the divorce is always the person who wants the divorce. Many times the partner who files for divorce feels compelled to do so because his or her spouse has a new relationship or creates an unpleasant home environment.

Part of adjusting to divorce is the realization that, in order to remarry, one must reenter the dating scene. This prospect often is both difficult and frightening to the divorced person. After many years of married life, reentry into the dating scene is felt to be intimidating (Petronio & Endres, 1986). If the divorced person has children, the anticipation of dating becomes even more complicated. Divorced persons must consider a number of issues, such as when to introduce their children to dating partners, how their children will react to dating partners, and how to cope with the issues of their own sexuality.

Interviews with single parents suggest that many of the people they date do not like the fact that they have children (Petronio & Endres, 1986). Yet, many feel that it is important for the child to be introduced to the dating partner early in the relationship. Mothers, in particular, want it made clear when they date someone that their children are part of the package.

For divorced parents, establishing a long term relationship is complicated because the new partner is also expected to develop a relationship with the children and even, at times, with the ex-spouse (Petronio & Endres, 1986). A new partner cannot enter into a relationship with the single parent without also coming to terms with the children. Simultaneously, then, the adults are developing their romantic relationship while they are attempting to facilitate a relationship for the new partner with the children.

Sometimes single parents want so much for the new partners to get along with the children that they inadvertently sabotage their success. For example, a father may want the children to like his new dating partner so much that he makes them feel guilty if they express their reservations. The children may not inherently dislike the new partner but may feel threatened and scared because they see change down the road. Sometimes the ex-spouse plays a role in undermining the success of a new relationship. For example, a mother may still feel resentful about the divorce (not being psychologically divorced) and tell the children that their father's new partner was the cause of their breakup. The new relationship is in jeopardy before it has a chance to succeed.

Single parents have a difficult task in finding and establishing new relationships. The process can be eased, however, by allowing the children and the new partner to find their own ways into a compatible relationship. Encouraging, prodding, and using guilt are techniques that are likely to be detrimental both to the children and to the feelings of the new partner.

Maintaining a nonhostile relationship with an ex-spouse is valuable in paving the way for a new partner. The children tend to be recipients of hostile feelings that pass between the ex-spouses. In turn, the children may ventilate these feelings on a new partner because they have relatively little to lose with that person. The children also need to feel confident that both the custodial and noncustodial parents are concerned about their welfare. This sense of security can be especially difficult to maintain with the noncustodial parent because he or she is not physically present on a continuous basis for the child.

One way to help the child establish and maintain a sense of relationship with the noncustodial parent is to encourage the child to write letters, even if the absentee parent lives nearby (Petronio & Carlson, 1990). Children see letters as tangible evidence that their noncustodial, absentee parent cares about them. They can read and re-read the contents whenever they miss the parent. Letters also give the child time to understand the contents without being hurried, as may be the case with telephone calls. The child can keep the letters private and not have to share the contents with anyone. In this way, the child feels that the letters are very special communications between himself or herself and the absentee parent. Letter writing can provide valuable communication between the absentee parent and the child, thereby strengthening the relationship. When the child feels secure with the absentee parent's feelings, and the noncustodial parent is sure that no one can replace him or her, then the noncustodial parent may have less need to meddle. The child may also feel more willing to accept a parent's new partner.

When divorced people succeed in establishing a new relationship, remarriage may be their next choice. Ihinger-Tallman and Pasley (1987) have written an excellent book on this topic. One of the many concerns they identify is the problem of merging households. First and foremost, remarrieds noted the difficulty of coping with financial arrangements. There are many ways to configure financial mergers for couples. These range from keeping finances completely separate to pooling all available sources of income. Most couples find that they need to negotiate in order to distribute resources to the children and themselves. This process can generate many conflicts.

Another area that causes difficulties is agreeing on rules for disciplining the children. It is likely that each parent has a different way of thinking about discipline, including both what constitutes an offense and what constitutes appropriate punishment. The new parents must first spend time learning how they differ and then negotiate a settlement. This is not an easy task, given that the children will intervene on their own behalf. Learning to cope with new parents is also difficult for the children. Becoming a step family puts strains on new marital relationships that are more complicated than those found in first-time marriages.

Long-Term Relationships

There are still some people who stay in their marriages for a lifetime. Weishaus and Field (1988) investigated a half century of marriage and found that there are several types of long-term marriages. For example, long-term marriages may be of the stable/positive type in which the couple maintain a close and vital relationship and work on becoming closer through the years. There may also be stable/neutral relationships. These are characterized as passive but congenial. The couples do not make a major emotional investment, but they experience little conflict. In addition, there are stable/negative types of marriages that are reliable and enduring but in which the couple have experienced disappointment and distress. A fourth type of long-term relationship was also identified. The curvilinear marriage starts at a high level of affect and satisfaction. Marital satisfaction decreases during the middle years but then increases in the later years. As is evident, these types of relationships are also found in younger marriages, although the curvilinear potential of some does not become evident until the later years. The key to success may be the ability of the partners to communicate effectively with each other in order to face problems head on and make the necessary changes and adjustments.

As this brief exploration has illustrated, marriage over the lifespan brings with it many issues and concerns. The nature of a marital relationship is dynamic and ever changing. It is influenced by children, relatives, financial security, and a whole host of life events. Marital relationships do not sustain themselves. It is the people in the relationships who must be ready to take chances and to show their courage by talking about difficult issues and lending their positive support to the values they hold most dear.

▼ SANDRA PETRONIO

See also: Adult Children and Their Parents; Attachment Across the Lifespan; Cohort and Generational Effects; Conflict as a Challenge in Adult Development; Divorce; Fairy Tales as Commentary on Adult Development and Aging; Housing as a Factor in Adult Life; Life Events; Loneliness; Menopause; Mental Health in the Adult Years; Military Service: Long-Term Effects on Adult Development; Privacy Issues; Sexuality; Social Relationships, Convoys of; Social Support for the Chronically Ill; Trust as a Challenge in Adult Development; Widowhood: The Coping Response.

References

Aldous, J. (1978). *Family Careers: Developmental Change in Families*. New York: Wiley.

Berscheid, E., & Walster, E. (1974). *Interpersonal Attraction*. Reading, MA: Addison-Wesley.

Degler, C. (1983). The emergence of the modern American family. In M. Gordon (Ed.), *The American Family in Socio-Historical Perspective*. New York: St. Martin's Press, pp. 18-42.

Fitzpatrick, M. (1988). *Between Husbands and Wives: Communication in Marriage*. Newbury Park, CA: Sage.

Ihinger-Tallman, M., & Pasley, K. (1987). *Remarriage*. Newbury Park, CA: Sage.

Knapp, M. (1984). *Interpersonal Communication and Human Relationships*. Newton, MA: Allyn & Bacon.

Lee, J. (1976). *The Colors of Love*. Englewood Cliffs, NJ: Prentice Hall.

Mattessich, P., & Hill, R. (1987). Life cycle and family development. In M. Sussman & S. Steinmetz (Eds.), *Handbook of Marriage and the Family*. New York: Plenum Press.

McCroskey, J., & McCain, T. (1974). The measurement of interpersonal attraction. *Speech Monographs, 41*: 261-66.

Petronio, S. (1991). Communication boundary management: A theoretical model of managing disclosure of private information between marital couples. *Communication Theory, 4*: 311-30.

Petronio, S., & Carlson, A. C. (1990). Navy children and their absentee fathers: The function of written communication. Paper presented at the International Communication Association Conference, Trinity College, Dublin, Ireland.

Petronio, S., & Endres, T. (1986). Dating and the single parent: Communication in the social network. *Journal of Divorce, 9*: 83-105.

Rapoport, R., Rapoport, R., & Strelitz, Z. (1980). *Fathers, Mothers, & Society: Perspectives on Parenting*. New York: Vintage Books.

Shaver, P., & Hazan, C. (1988). A biased overview of the study of love. *Journal of Social and Personal Relationships, 5*: 473-502.

Steinberg, L., & Silverberg, S. (1987). Influences on marital satisfaction during the middle stages of the family life cycle. *Journal of Marriage and the Family, 49*: 751-60.

Suitor, J., & Pillemer, K. (1987). The presence of adult children: A source of stress for elderly couple's marriage? *Journal of Marriage and the Family, 49*: 717-26.

Weishaus, S., & Field, D. (1988). A half century of marriage: Continuity or change? *Journal of Marriage and the Family, 50*: 763-74.

Wilmot, J., & Wilmot, W. (1978). *Interpersonal Conflict*. Dubuque, IA: William C. Brown.

MASTERY TYPES, DEVELOPMENT, AND AGING

The Mastery Types

Generally speaking, humans have available three primary modes of responding to circumstances so as to bring about conditions that are secure and comfortable in physical, social, and psychological terms. The present author has called these three modes of managing the internal (psychological) and external (social) domains Active Mastery, Passive Mastery, and Magical Mastery. Alternative and somewhat more technical terms that have also been offered for these modes are Alloplastic Mastery, Autoplastic Mastery, and Omniplastic Mastery.

Active Mastery. In the Active Mastery mode, the actor has a purpose and acts directly on the social or physical environment to achieve this purpose. The actor is sensitive to the realistic limits imposed by the nature of materials or by the needs and purposes of other individuals but acts effectively within these constraints to create the desired state of affairs. In this mode, the person is the center of initiative, a force for change, while the environment is perceived as open and malleable—an arena awaiting effective action. It is this facet of the situation that gives rise to the alternative title: *Alloplastic Mastery*. Alloplastic Mastery refers to disciplined force that is directed outward toward an environment whose materials can be modified or transformed in accord with some personal vision.

Passive Mastery. In the Passive Mastery mode, the position is decisively reversed: Now the physical and social domains are seen to be charged with power. The individual feels relatively weak, ineffectual, and subject to arbitrary forces over which he or she has little control.

The main recourse is to develop one's sensitivity—the better to apprehend and accommodate to the requirements of the powerful agents—whether these be the spouse, the boss, or the gods—that are seen as controlling one's fate and sense of security.

Passive Mastery can have at least two distinct sources. It can be the native style of people who have always depended on the power of others, those who trade passive compliance for security. Conversely, passivity may be born out of dynamic conflict. It can represent a last-ditch defense against powerful but dangerous consequences of action. *Autoplastic Mastery*, the alternative term for this style, captures the essence of this idea:

Rather than changing circumstances to meet the priorities of the self, it is the self that is altered to fit the perceived demands of the world.

Magical Mastery. Despite their clear differences, Active Mastery and Passive Mastery share an important characteristic: Both are instrumental modes of acting and being. In other words, they lead to changes in the outer world (Active Mastery) or in the self (Passive Mastery) that are in accord with the real possibilities and limitations of the physical, social, or personal domain. The Magical Mastery mode is not instrumental. Instead of actually changing the outer world or the inner self, the "magic-prone" individual revises his or her perception of these domains and does so by fiat, without intervening action.

Only the eye of the beholder is altered. The object of vision remains, in actuality, untouched. For example, the Magical Mastery individual does not act in the world so as to change a threatening situation into a favorable one. Instead, like Voltaire's Dr. Pangloss, this person blithely insists that the enemy is really a friend or that disaster is really a blessing: "Everything is for the best in the best of all possible worlds."

This version of Magical Mastery, in which badness in the outer world is transformed into goodness, corresponds to the primitive ego defense of *denial*. The individual's awareness of the inner self also can be revised in an arbitrary, magical manner: Personal flaws and sources of guilt and shame can be denied in the self and then transposed, via the equally primitive defense of *projection*, to become a "bad" feature of the outer world. Through this "magical cleansing," people render themselves pure in their own sight but discover corruption or threat in others. The term *Omniplastic Mastery* captures the same idea: Any troubling experience can be revised by a change in perception, instead of by effective action.

Using the Mastery Styles

Each of us has all of these major modes available, though we use them selectively, in response to situational pressures and opportunities. Thus, for example, the subordinate of an autocratic boss may adopt the Passive Mastery style when at the office out of fear and expediency. But that same person may switch to the Active Mastery style at home, becoming an effective decision maker for the family. At night, in sleep, Magical Mastery takes over: In his dreams, the subordinate can indulge, without risk, the pleasant fantasy of murdering the boss...slowly and with feeling.

In addition, many individuals are *blended* or ambivalent as to mastery type. They will uneasily vacillate, even within the same situation, between versions of Active and Passive Mastery in which each posture is reactive against the other. Thus, the subordinate employee referred to earlier may knuckle under to the autocratic employer on one occasion, then feel ashamed of this cowardly passivity, and, in reaction, stand up to that same boss on a subsequent occasion.

Other individuals may blend the Active and the Magical Mastery tendencies. Like certain paranoid characters, they may go out of their way to see others as hostile, menacing, or immoral, thereby gaining the right to act against them--to "take arms against a sea of troubles." In these blendings of styles, Magical Mastery "runs interference" for a kind of Active Mastery, for aggressive (even preemptory) action. Still other individuals blend Passive and Magical Mastery. They picture the world as so hostile, so charged with "bad power," that action is impossible and passive resignation their only recourse. In such cases, the use of Magical Mastery allows these individuals to indulge their passive tendencies without shame: "You can't fight city hall."

Studying the Mastery Orientations

Despite the fact that individuals shift and blend their mastery orientations, most people do favor one particular mode of mastery over the alternative possibilities. People are most apt to reveal their dominant style in unrehearsed and ambiguous situations. When external guides to proper action are absent, they fall back on inner direction, on their own native, preferred action propensities.

Thus, faced with their first battle, some soldiers will deploy strongly against the enemy, although with due regard for their own safety (Active Mastery). Other troopers—from the same unit, with the same training—will discover, under fire, that they have always been pacifists and will surrender at the first opportunity (Passive Mastery). A third group may handle their fear by denying the threat. Curling into a fetal position, they treat their foxhole as though it were a crib (Magical Mastery).

By the same token, the mastery orientations are best studied through the use of instruments that confront respondents with novel stimuli, the kind that do not clearly signal the "right" or customary interpretations. For this reason, projective tests are particularly useful in studying mastery style. Instruments such as the Rorschach, the Thematic Apperception Test (TAT), and the Sentence Completion Test confront the respondent with unfamiliar stimuli. There is an ink blot to interpret (Rorschach) or a picture of a boy and a violin in ambiguous relation to each other (TAT) or a set of sentence stems, each of which could be completed in a number of different ways (the Sentence Completion Test).

In each case, the respondent is provided with the "raw" stimulus materials and asked, in effect, to fashion out of these a representation, a metaphor of the psychosocial milieu that best conforms to his or her preferred mastery style. Thus, as we interpret a respondent's TAT story, her preferred organization of an ambiguous situations helps us to ascertain her mastery orientation. For example, from the various features of the TAT card, does she create an arena for effective action by a central figure (Active Mastery)? Or does she instead generate a story in which the central figure is seen as being blocked from effective action, either by personal inadequacy or by external forces (Passive Mastery)? Finally, are significant card features misconstrued so as to sponsor an avoidance, a *denial* of the implicit problem that is set by the stimulus card (Magical Mastery)?

In general, TAT findings regarding individual mastery type correlate with independent measures generated from the same respondents by other "depth" psychological instruments. By the same token, such findings do not correlate well with findings generated by the same people in response to self-report, precoded interview instruments. Given these discrepancies between psychological tests, many authorities in the field of personality and psychometrics have discredited findings from projective instruments on the grounds that their results have not been "seconded" or validated by independent measures. However, while such authorities may understand statistics, they do not seem to understand the nature and functions of fantasy. There is actually no *psychologically* sound reason why TAT-derived data should correlate with the data generated by the more "objective" tests. The projective tests are intentionally *unstructured*. They withhold clues as to the correct or socially desirable interpretation. In contrast, "objective" tests do signal the "right" or proper answer, thereby permitting respondents to exercise conscious control over their public relations. The objective tests reveal the respondent's knowledge of the social norms that bear on his or her life; the projective tests reveal that same person's subjective stance, including private opposition to norms and to those who set the norms.

Fantasy Activity

It can be seen, then, that the fantasy activity that is tapped by projective tests is often the antagonist rather than the counterpart of "proper," norm-governed behavior. Fantasy is a form of alternative action, a way of keeping dangerous promptings out of direct behavior, if not out of consciousness. The potentially risky or novel action tendencies are tried out in fantasy, rehearsed long before they are "released" into the real world. Thus, Shanan (1985) and Jacobowitz (1984) have shown that the findings from projective tests do indeed correlate with the findings from "objective" tests, but only when a significant time interval is introduced. For example, a tendency toward Passive Mastery that shows up in the TAT of a middle-aged individual at Time One will probably not correlate with his or her self-report, elicited by paper and pencil tests given during the same period. After a lapse of five years, however, the passive tendencies that could only have been enjoyed in fantasy at Time One have now become detoxified, and by Time Two these tendencies have become part of the self-concept and of the "normal" behavioral repertoire.

In short, fantasy, as elicited by projective tests, does predict overt behavior and conscious attitude in the future but does not necessarily represent one's dominant tendencies at the present moment. Consequently, we *should* get negative rather than positive statistical correlations between objective and projective tests given to the same respondent during the same time period. By the same token, however, the Time One TAT profile is very likely to show a high correlation with the conscious self-report of the same individual taken at Time Two several years later.

Mastery Type, Development, and Aging

Although most men and women are characterized by a dominant mastery style, this is not a lifetime commitment. Mastery orientations change not only in response to current situations but also developmentally, in predictable sequence, over time. Along these lines, this author's studies have been focused particularly on the effects of the aging process on the mastery orientations of adults across a variety of cultures, both modern and premodern (Gutmann, 1987).

In general, younger men, whether American Indian, Mexican Indian, Middle Eastern Druse, or urban American have been found to be characterized by Active Mastery. Older men are characterized by Passive Mastery or by some blending of Passive and Magical Mastery (in which Magical Mastery serves to protect a dominant passive orientation).

Women tend to reverse this drift, moving in later life toward Active Mastery or toward some combination of Active and Magical Mastery in which the magical overlay serves to protect and justify a vigorous and sometimes intrusive engagement with the world.

Figures 1-4 show this universal trend as it shapes TAT data from male Navajo respondents, ranging in age from 40 to 70. Each respondent was tested with the same TAT cards at two times: 1966 and 1971. Thus, the mastery profile generated by respondents who were in the age range 35-49 at Time One (Figure 1) shows that, as a group, they peaked

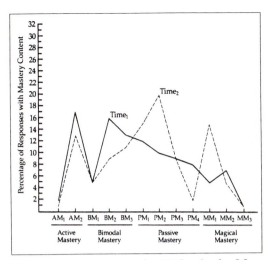

Figure 2. Distribution of TAT Stories by Mastery Orientations at Time$_1$ and Time$_2$, 50- to 59-Year-Old Navaho (Time$_1$ Ages). Reprinted from D. Gutmann, *Reclaimed Powers: Toward a New Psychology of Men and Women in Later Life*, copyright © 1987 by Basic Books, Inc. Reprinted by permission of Basic Books, a division of HarperCollins Publishers.

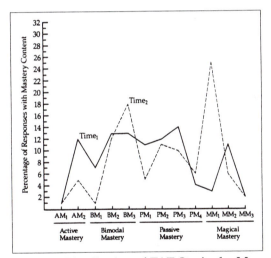

Figure 3. Distribution of TAT Stories by Mastery Orientations at Time$_1$ and Time$_2$, 60- to 69-Year-Old Navaho (Time$_1$ Ages). Reprinted from D. Gutmann, *Reclaimed Powers: Toward a New Psychology of Men and Women in Later Life*, copyright © 1987 by Basic Books, Inc. Reprinted by permission of Basic Books, a division of HarperCollins Publishers.

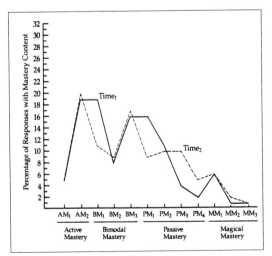

Figure 1. Distribution of TAT Stories by Mastery Orientations at Time$_1$ and Time$_2$, 35- to 49-Year-Old Navaho (Time$_1$ Ages). Reprinted from D. Gutmann, *Reclaimed Powers: Toward a New Psychology of Men and Women in Later Life*, copyright © 1987 by Basic Books, Inc. Reprinted by permission of Basic Books, a division of HarperCollins Publishers.

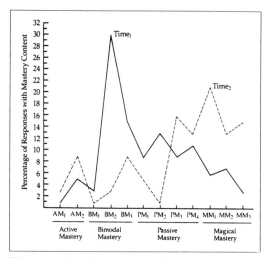

Figure 4. Distribution of TAT Stories by Mastery Orientations at Time₁ and Time₂, Navaho 70 Years Old and Older (Time₁ Ages). Reprinted from D. Gutmann, *Reclaimed Powers: Toward a New Psychology of Men and Women in Later Life,* copyright © 1987 by Basic Books, Inc. Reprinted by permission of Basic Books, a division of HarperCollins Publishers.

on Active Mastery. There is little change from Time One to Time Two. The Time One profile predicts with exactitude the Time Two profile. But for those respondents who were in the age range 50-59 at Time One (Figure 2), there is a moderate but distinct swing toward the Passive and Magical Mastery stations. This movement is intensified in the most senior groups (Figures 3 and 4), so that for the 70-year-old cohort, the separation between the Time One and Time Two profiles is almost complete.

Aging, then, not only brings about a movement from active to passive, but it also accelerates this movement. The older the male, the more rapidly he traverses the mastery track toward the passive and magical positions. The closer the lip of the waterfall, the faster the current; the closer one is to death, the more rapid is the sweep through the mastery positions.

More recent analyses of the author's Druse and urban U.S. data indicate that it is not only chronological age that brings about this "tectonic" shift in mastery orientations: The ending of the parental emergency seems to be an equally important factor in bringing out the transition from Active toward Passive Mastery in the case of men and from Passive toward Active Mastery in the case of postparental women. In other words, when controlled for age, the data show that postparental, postlaunch men are decisively more passive in their TAT responses than are their prelaunch age peers. Similarly, postlaunch women are decisively tilted toward Active Mastery TAT responses when compared with their prelaunch age peers.

In sum, both men and women are freed up in later life to live out the mastery styles that they had to "keep on hold" during their earlier years, particularly during the season of adult life that is dominated by the parental emergency.   ▼ DAVID GUTMANN

See also: Disengagement Theory; Fairy Tales as Commentary on Adult Development and Aging; Gender as a Shaping Force in Adult Development and Aging; Mexican Americans: Life Course Transitions and Adjustment; Mid-Life Crisis; Native American Perspectives on the Lifespan; Parental Imperative.

References

Gutmann, D. (1987). *Reclaimed Powers: Toward a New Psychology of Men and Women in Later Life.* New York: Basic Books.

Jacobowitz, J. (1984). *Stability and Change of Coping Patterns During the Middle Years as a Function of Personality Type.* Doctoral Dissertation. Department of Psychology, Hebrew University at Jerusalem, Israel.

Shanan, J. (1985). Personality types and culture in late adulthood. In J. Meacham (Ed.), *Contributions to Human Development.* Basel: S. Karger, pp. 1-144.

MATURITY

Maturity is one of those words that Mark Twain must have had in mind when he said we know the meaning—until someone asks us to define it. We use this word frequently enough in everyday speech; for example, one of the strongest adjectives we can insert into a letter of recommendation is "mature." By and large, however, social scientists have avoided using this term because its meaning can be so difficult to pin down. Recently, there has been increased interest in refining and using the maturity concept. Boelen (1978), a philosopher who has spent several decades wrestling with this concept, observes that "People are no longer indifferent to the question of maturity. On the contrary, the meaning of maturity has become a problem which haunts each of us" (p. vii).

The absence of an agreed upon definition of maturity is a significant problem in considering any and all theories of development. At this point in the study of adult development and aging, then, it becomes necessary to focus on the concept of maturity to help prepare the way for effective and constructive applications of this term.

Historical Perspective

Up until the present century, the term "character" was widely used to described the desired end of personality development. In their pioneering studies of deceit, Hartshorne and May (1928-1930) failed to find unified character traits in a large sample of schoolchildren. This negative finding cut the ground from under the assumption that people could be described simply as having "good" or "bad" character. Whether or not a child behaved in a deceitful manner seemed to "depend" on a number of circumstances and conditions.

The abandonment of "character" as a goal of development left a void. Trait psychologist Gordon Allport (1937) was among the first and most influential to propose maturity as an appropriate and viable replacement. In his classic personality text, Allport devoted a chapter to "the mature personality." He suggested that the mature person could be characterized by three traits (pp. 213-14):

- A variety of autonomous interests
- Self-objectification
- A unifying philosophy of life

In a subsequent edition of his text, Allport (1963) expanded this list to six. Other theorists have offered different combinations of traits that are said to characterize maturity. Perhaps the most exhaustive list is that provided by Maslow (1973). Choosing the term "self-actualization" in preference to maturity, Maslow identified 14 traits that characterize persons who exhibit an optimum level of personality development. There is overlap with Allport's list. Both, for example, speak of realistic perception and acceptance of self and others. Maslow added other characteristics, however, that had not previously been associated with maturity-type concepts, e.g., quality of detachment and a philosophical sense of humor. Overall, self-actualizing people were seen as those who "have developed or are developing to the full stature of which they are capable" (Maslow, 1973, p. 178).

Like Allport, Maslow listed various characteristics of optimal personality development without specifying a sequence in which they occur or the age at which their development might be complete. He did note, however, that he was unable to find any college students who could qualify as fully self-actualizing. In fact, he was forced to turn to literature and public figures to find sufficient examples of such persons.

Developmental Approaches

Freud's (1933) theory of psychosexual development is the "great granddaddy" of personality stage theories. Since the Freudian model ends with late adolescence (genital sexuality), it has not proven very helpful in defining lifespan maturity. Erik Erikson, a student of Anna Freud, extended the original formulation into a lifespan theory of psychosocial development that is probably the most widely accepted model of adult development today. Erikson's eighth and final developmental task calls for the individual to face issues of integrity vs. despair. By "integrity," Erikson (1968) means "the acceptance of one's one and only life cycle and the people who have become significant to it as something that had to be and that, by necessity, permitted no substitutions" (p. 139).

As with each of Erikson's developmental stages, the strengths and antipathies of all the previous developmental tasks are at play in the final stage. These dynamics involve a reworking of issues related to "care-rejectivity," "love-exclusivity," "fidelity-repudiation," and so forth. Especially salient is the basic issue of "hope-withdrawal" (Erikson, 1982, p. 64).

C. G. Jung represents the other seminal developmental theorist for understanding the maturity concept. Unlike Erikson, his work is not widely known to American professionals or the lay public, but it has influenced other well-known theorists such as Levinson (1978) and Gould (1978), for whom Jung's individuation concept plays a central role.

The complexity of Jung's theory makes it difficult to summarize. Its broad outlines were clearly stated by Jung, however, in his influential essay on the "Stages of Life" in which he posits the concept of a mid-life reversal:

> We cannot live in the afternoon of life according to the programme of life's morning—for what was great in life's morning (money-making, social existence, family and posterity) will be little at evening....Whoever carries over into the afternoon the law of the morning...must pay for so doing with damage to his soul. (Jung, 1933, pp. 108-09)

The second half of life, Jung argues, must have "a significance of its own," distinct from that of the morning of individual (ego) development. The name he gives to the final goal of development is *individuation*. This is the process through which individuals confront the unconscious elements that were repressed in the earlier years as they developed the "dominant function" of their personality. "The aim of individuation is nothing less than to divest the self of the false wrappings of the persona on the one hand, and of the suggestive power of the primordial images on the other" (Jung, 1972, p. 174).

To understand this task, it is necessary to note that Jung did not limit his view of the unconscious to the personal conflicts and repressions of the particular individual. Instead, he believed there was also a *collective unconscious*. This collective unconscious contains the primordial images and archetypes that have come down to us through the millennia and which we hold in common with all humanity at all times of history. Individuation involves establishing contact with these collective symbols—without becoming overwhelmed by them. Although the tasks of the first half of life can be accomplished by the functioning of the individual ego and conscious thought, those of the second half require a different mode. When successful, the polarities of the psyche are transcended, particularly those of the feminine and masculine components. This is a daunting challenge that few are able to master.

The individuation process leads to the discovery of the "Self," which Jung sees as the mediator between the conscious and the unconscious, between the ego and the non-ego. And the goals of the Self are seen to differ from those of the ego. The meaning and purpose of the Self has to do with "culture," by which Jung means not just the larger aims of current society, but the meanings, purposes, and larger realities that direct and inform society at its deepest level. Put simply, individuation—or maturity—is for Jung the process of discovering and living out the Self, with all its difficulties and perils, and its promise for the fulfilling of our human potential for growth and development.

Critique of Stage Theories

Two criticisms have been leveled against developmental stage theories and apply to any concepts of maturity derived from them. A long-standing reservation has to do with the question of *cultural relativism*. Cultures are known to vary considerably in their values, particularly with respect to what constitutes "the good life." Because concepts of maturity or self-actualization are based on such values, one must ask to what extent any formulation can be generalized beyond the culture in which it was formulated. The sec-

ond reservation might be termed *gender relativism*. The best known theories of personality development and maturity have been constructed by men: How well do they apply to women?

In his historical and cross-cultural survey of concepts of optimal personality, Coan (1977) provides a comprehensive statement of the cultural relativist position. He points out that different cultures have different ideals of the "good life," ranging from saint, to hero, to artist. Because our concepts of maturity are intimately related to basic cultural values, Coan offers little encouragement for finding any definitions that are not culture-bound. This, of course, is the position that is held to a greater or lesser degree by most social scientists and that has led to the neglect of such concepts as maturity and optimal personality.

Coan's formulation has a problem of its own, however, one that is shared also by the approach taken by many other social scientists. The traditional cultural relativist position fails to take into account the possibility that one criterion of maturity may not apply to all ages. When Coan (1977) seeks to determine what constitutes the "ideal person, personality, or life-style...the highest goal of living" (p. 3), he seems to assume that this ideal would apply to every age. This is the kind of assumption that Norton (1976) has termed "the anachronistic fallacy," by which one seeks to impose the same criteria on all stages of life. This problem can also be seen in the nondevelopmental theorists cited earlier. Allport (1937), despite his own nondevelopmental trait approach, noted in passing that if the behaviors of a healthy two-year-old were observed in a grown man, he would be seen as a sociopath or worse.

In addition, a closer look at the values underlying the maturity concept indicate that there may not be as much variation as Coan suggests. Norton (1976) offers a detailed analysis of the concept of maturity in the Western philosophic tradition, noting that the Greek concept of *eudaimonism* underlies most developmental theories, including those of both Erikson and Jung. As Norton (1976) explains,

eudaimonism "is the term for the ethical doctrine...that each person is obliged to know and live in the truth of his *daimon* (or genius), thereby progressively actualizing an excellence that is his innately and potentially" (p. ix). This concept provides the foundation for the concept of the essential nature of the person within the Western tradition, according to Norton.

The second criticism of the maturity concept has been raised by Gilligan (1982) and other feminist scholars who point out the male bias in our theoretical formulations. Theorists from Freud onward—not excluding Erikson and Jung—have seen maturation as involving progressive separation and independence. Feminist scholars hold that this is not normative for women, for whom relationships are of great importance at every developmental stage. Rather than seeing the salience of relationships as deviant and evidence of lower levels of development, they suggest that adequate theories of development—and of the end state of maturity—must take the feminine voice into account. And, one might add, the voices of other cultures and traditions as well.

Conclusion

Without denying the validity of these claims—and the feminist critique is a needed corrective to the one-sidedness of our developmental theories—it should be noted that the ideal of *eudaimonism* may well apply to both genders, particularly at the level of Norton's analysis. Whether or not this ideal, which has informed Western culture since the time of classical Greek philosophy, applies equally to other cultural traditions is a question that stands in need of examination. Based on preliminary data, Thomas (1991) finds certain similarities between Western and Indian views of maturity. What is at issue is not questions of empirical facts (at least, as narrowly defined by most social scientists) but a careful examination of cultural values and assumptions that inform our concepts of maturity. When we deal with the questions of meaning and purpose that underlie our con-

ceptions of maturity, we have moved into the domain of the humanities (Cole, Van Tassel, & Kastenbaum, 1992). Moody (1986, p. 39) suggested that consideration of issues of this nature must draw upon the "three C's": critical questioning (philosophy), continuity of time (history), and communication of shared meanings (literature). Only as social scientists join forces with others in the human sciences can we hope to come to grips with the complexities that inhere in the maturity concept. ▼ L. EUGENE THOMAS

See also: Adult Children and Their Parents; Age 40; Contextualism; Development and Aging in Historical Perspective; Fairy Tales as Commentary on Adult Development and Aging; Gender as a Shaping Force in Adult Development and Aging; Individuality; Japanese Perspectives on Adult Development; Mastery Types, Development, and Aging; Metaphors of the Life Course; Native American Perspectives on the Lifespan; Place and Personality in Adult Development; Spiritual Development and Wisdom: A Vedantic Perspective.

References

Allport, G. W. (1937). *Personality: A Psychological Interpretation.* New York: Holt, Rinehart & Winston.

———. (1963). *Pattern and Growth in Personality.* New York: Holt, Rinehart & Winston.

Boelen, B. (1978). *Personal Maturity: The Existential Dimension.* New York: Seabury.

Coan, R. W. (1977). *Hero, Artist, Sage or Saint?* New York: Columbia University Press.

Cole, T. R., Van Tassel, D. D., & Kastenbaum, R. (Eds.). (1992). *Handbook of the Humanities and Aging.* New York: Springer.

Erikson, E. H. (1968). *Identity, Youth and Crisis.* New York: Norton.

———. (1982). *The Life Cycle Completed: A Review.* New York: Norton.

Freud, S. (1964). *New Introductory Lectures on Psychoanalysis.* New York: Norton. (Original work, 1933.)

Gilligan, C. (1982). *In a Different Voice: Psychological Theory of Women's Development.* Cambridge, MA: Harvard University Press.

Gould, R. L. (1978). *Transformations: Growth and Change in Adult Life.* New York: Simon & Schuster.

Hartshorne, H., & May, M. A. (1928-1930). Volume 1. *Studies in Deceit.* Volume 2. *Studies in Service and Self-Control.* Volume 3. *Studies in Organization of Character.* New York: Macmillan.

Jung, C. G. (1933). *Modern Man in Search of a Soul.* New York: Harcourt, Brace.

———. (1972). *Two Essays on Analytical Psychology.* Princeton, NJ: Princeton University Press.

Levinson, D. J. (1978). *The Seasons of a Man's Life.* New York: Knopf.

Maslow, A. H. (1973). *Dominance, Self-Esteem, Self-Actualization.* Monterey, CA: Brooks/Cole.

Moody, H. R. (1986). The meaning of life and the meaning of old age. In T. R. Cole & S. A. Gadow (Eds.), *What Does It Mean to Grow Old? Reflections from the Humanities.* Durham, NC: Duke University Press.

Norton, D. L. (1976). *Personal Destiny: A Philosophy of Ethical Individualism.* Princeton, NJ: Princeton University Press.

Thomas, L. E. (1991). Dialogues with three religious renunciates and reflections on wisdom and maturity. *International Journal of Aging and Human Development,* 32: 211-27.

MEMORY

Instances of forgetfulness in middle-aged and older adults have been the subject of many jokes. One of the more frequently told jokes goes like this: "There are three things that decline with aging. First, you begin to lose your memory, and...I can't remember the other two!"

Jokes about memory problems reflect adults' deep-seated anxiety about losing the very essence of their being, that is, the ability to relate to their surroundings, make cogent decisions, and reminisce. Colloquial information about the devastating effects of Alzheimer's disease contributes greatly to this anxiety. In fact, studies have found that middle-aged and older adults identify the fear of losing their memory as one of their two major worries (the other relates to the loss of energy).

Table 1. Cross-sectional Experimental Evidence for Age-related Slowing of Memory Processes

	Memory Store				
Component affected	*Sensory*	*Primary*	*Secondary*	*Working*	*Tertiary*
Perceptual motor	positive	positive	positive	___	positive
Decision making	___	positive	positive	___	negative

Reprinted from L.W. Poon, *Aging in the 1980's: Psychological Issues*, Washington, DC: American Psychological Association, copyright © 1980 by the American Psychological Association. Reprinted by permission.

What Age-Related Changes Occur in Memory Functioning?

All cognitive processes are closely interrelated. However, age-related changes in memory have received by far the largest share of research effort (Poon & Siegler, 1991). Fozard (1980) provides a concise summary of research findings (see Table 1).

Registration of information is also known as *sensory memory*, a pre-attention stage that occurs before conscious recognition of the information. Primary and secondary memory are responsible for the acquisition and retention of new information. *Primary memory* is conceptualized as a limited capacity store in which information is still "in mind" as it is being used. This information will be lost if it is not rehearsed or processed instantaneously so that it can be stored in secondary memory. The term *secondary memory* refers to the repository of newly acquired information. *Working memory* is what we use to manipulate information for the

next stage of processing. Finally, *tertiary memory* is the repository for information that has been well learned and safely entered into our permanent memory bank.

Table 1 summarizes the existing cross-sectional experimental evidence for age-related slowing of memory processes, and Table 2 presents findings from both cross-sectional and longitudinal studies that have examined age decline in memory capacities across the adult lifespan. These two tables show that the rate of processing that is involved in practically all aspects of memory is slowed as we advance in age. Older adults are particularly disadvantaged in the retention of newly acquired information (secondary memory). These two tables also show that in normal aging the acquisition of new information (primary memory) and decision-making speed with familiar and well-practiced tasks (tertiary memory) tend to remain intact.

West (1985) echoes Fozard's research summary in a somewhat different way. She notes that in normal aging (a) thinking is

Table 2. Evidence for Age-related Declines in Memory Capacity

Type of study and type of evidence	Memory Store				
	Sensory	*Primary*	*Secondary*	*Working*	*Tertiary*
Cross-sectional studies					
Anecdotal	___	positive	positive	positive	positive
Psychometric	___	negative	positive	___	negative
Experimental	positive	negative	positive	positive	negative
Longitudinal Studies					
Anecdotal	___	___	___	___	___
Psychometric	___	negative	positive	___	negative
Experimental	___	___	positive	___	___

Reprinted from L.W. Poon, *Aging in the 1980's: Psychological Issues*, Washington, DC: American Psychological Association, copyright © 1980 by the American Psychological Association. Reprinted by permission.

slower, (b) best memory strategies are used less, (c) paying attention and ignoring distractions become more difficult, (d) learning something new takes more time, and (e) more cues are needed to recall something previously learned.

She also found that the following processes tend to remain stable in adulthood: (a) immediate memory, (b) recall of world knowledge, (c) susceptibility to interference, (d) forgetting rates, and (e) search process.

Relationships Between Memory and Other Cognitive Processes

As noted earlier, memory functioning is intimately connected to other cognitive processes in our daily lives. The effects of aging on four such processes are reviewed here.

Intellectual Functioning. Research on intellectual functioning has one of the longest and most productive records in the psychology of aging (Schaie, 1990). Three general patterns of findings can be summarized

1. The data show a high degree of regularity in intellectual functioning across the adult years.
2. Crystallized abilities, or knowledge acquired in the course of the socialization process, tend to remain stable over the adult lifespan. Fluid abilities (involved in the solution of novel problems) tend to decline gradually from young to old adulthood.
3. Disease and pathology exert profound effects on intellectual functioning. There is congruence between the findings on the basic ability to remember and retain simple information on the one hand and findings on the utilization of information necessary for intellectual pursuits on the other hand.

Understanding and Remembering Written Information. Reading and writing are everyday functions practiced throughout one's life. The first generation of research on whether the memory components of these well-practiced activities change with aging

presented conflicting and even contradictory findings (Poon, 1985). Some studies found clear-cut age deficits, while others did not. To address these discordant results, the second generation of research examined in detail the possible contributions of individual differences, the properties of the text to be processed, and the task demand on the observed performance. This set of results seems to support the finding of cognitive slowing with increasing age so that the difficulty of a task would have more effect on the recall performance of older as compared with younger adults.

An individual's level of education and verbal intelligence was found to account for a significant proportion of the age deficit on text recall performance. Age deficits in prose recall were found to be significant for adults with average and low verbal ability. Older adults with high verbal ability tended to utilize text structure as well as young adults and to take advantage of organized structure to enhance their performance. In contrast, older adults with low verbal ability showed less sensitivity to text structures that could assist them in the processing task. Clearly, then, the individual's basic level of verbal ability is a significant determinant of memory for text materials in the later years of life. Current research programs are attempting to understand the impact of everyday processing demands on older adults.

Speech Comprehension. One of the major contributions to age-related peripheral hearing decline is presbycusis (which includes the loss of sensitivity to higher auditory frequencies), and an increased probability of phonemic regression or decreased speech intelligibility (Olsho, Harkins, & Lenhardt, 1985). An important question for current research is how peripheral hearing deficits interact with available cognitive resources and experiences of older persons. This is an important question both for the understanding of speech comprehension by older individuals and for the design of methods to compensate for the observed deficits.

Some studies have already examined adults' ability to understand word-sentence context in a noisy background as well as their ability to process words presented at varying levels of speed and linguistic redundancy. Results indicate that older adults rely on the redundancy and familiar structure of language and linguistic constraints to maintain an acceptable level of performance. It appears that older listeners can compensate for peripheral hearing decline and that therapeutic procedures should take into account the individual's distinctive strengths and experiences.

Problem Solving. Given the existence of some age-related deficits in memory, what effect do they have on everyday problem-solving abilities? Although answers to this question are not yet definitive, the available studies allow three sets of general observations (Denney, 1989).

1. Tests of everyday problem-solving tasks show that middle-aged adults can perform better than young adults in some situations, but performance decline is evident for aged adults.
2. Traditional problem-solving tasks conducted under laboratory conditions provide useful predictions of older adults' ability to deal with problem-solving situations in the everyday world.
3. There appear to be changes in problem-solving styles and strategies in the later adult years that may be related to declining physical and cognitive abilities, but much further research is needed to identify and understand these changes.

Chronological age seems to provide little explanatory power regarding all differences that have been observed in memory and other cognitive processes throughout the adult years. Instead, individual variations in education, intelligence, experiential history, knowledge, cognitive strategies, and health may provide more meaningful clues to memory changes. Additionally, attention must also be given to the particular demands of the situation in which the individual is called upon to use his or her memory.

Memory Assessment

The assessment of possible memory dysfunction is not an easy task, especially in its early stages. The assessment problem is complicated by the likelihood that different types of memory could be affected by different factors, as well as by the fact that there is a very large range of memory performances that could be considered "normal." George Talland (1968), a pioneer investigator of normal and abnormal memory functioning, noted:

> Occasional failures in recall or a temporary difficulty in learning need not be taken as symptomatic of a disorder in a function. All our functions are exercised within limits and, with such heterogeneous and often complex functions as remembering and learning, the limits are wide. Every so often one's performance can exceed as well as fall short of those mean values that correspond to the bulk of one's efforts and achievements. We infer a disorder from a permanent or extensive disability in comparison with previous performance or in comparison with a suitably defined control group. (p. 24)

The fluid nature of memory makes it a challenge to estimate the probability of dysfunction and to isolate the locus of its disorder. Memory is involved in practically all aspects of their daily lives, and yet people tend not to think consciously or intentionally about how they acquire and remember information until they perceive that there is a problem. Consequently, studies have shown that patients often do not articulate their memory complaints accurately. On the other hand, clinician-scientists can misclassify the degree of cognitive and memory dysfunction in diagnosing cases of possible Alzheimer's disease. The percentage of misdiagnosis has been estimated to run between 10 to 50 percent, admittedly a large range, thereby indicating a lack of definitive information on the extent of misdiagnosis. Although memory and cognitive dysfunction are only two of the presenting factors in dementia, this range of estimated misdiagnosis indicates a need to improve our current understanding of memory and cognitive assessment, diagnostic criteria, and selection of diagnostic instruments.

If memory functioning is difficult to assess and there are many memory assessment instruments in the market, can some approaches be especially recommended? Are some tests better than others? How many tests are sufficient to evaluate all the factors involved in memory functioning?

The answers to these questions depend on the orientation of the clinician or researcher (see Poon et al., 1986 for a comprehensive review). There is no one correct answer. Because memory tests are used to confirm clinical hypotheses, a number of tests may be appropriate if they are suitable for the milieu of a particular individual and provide a qualitative profile of the underlying mechanisms that are the basis of the clinical hypothesis. The selection of a test or of a set of tests should therefore be guided by the prototypical behavioral symptoms of the disease, the hypotheses of the clinician, and the previously demonstrated sensitivity and specificity of a test.

This process necessitates informed decision making on the part of the clinician regarding (a) factors influencing memory functioning, (b) intake of signs and symptoms, (c) classification of severity of symptoms, and (d) understanding experimental findings and clinical assessment demands. A standardized memory test may be completely appropriate for one individual but provide incomplete data about another individual. This philosophy argues against holding that one standardized memory battery is necessarily more appropriate or useful than another and, instead, places the responsibility for effective assessment squarely on the individual.

Memory Training

Can an adult who wants to improve his or her memory do so? The answer by all researchers in memory over the adult age span would be a resounding "Yes!" (see Poon, Rubin, & Wilson, 1989, for a review). Memory improvement techniques have been known since the day of Socrates, and research has repeatedly demonstrated that significant improvement can be made *if an individual is motivated to practice and maintain the learned memory skills.*

In spite of the demonstrated efficacies of memory training techniques, the learning and maintenance of memory skills have been found to be difficult tasks for most adults. After improving their memory skills, most adults eventually retreat to their former, less efficient methods of remembering. This tendency led West (1989) to make the following suggestions for the planning of training programs for adult learners. The training programs should (a) be designed for the memory demands of the particular individual, (b) focus on strategies that this particular individual is likely to use, and (c) incorporate approaches that are likely to enhance maintenance and generalization of the newly learned memory skills.

Conclusion

Research on memory functioning during the adult years has led to some important and well-documented findings.

1. Some memory functions decline with age.
2. One's level of memory functioning is influenced not only by individual characteristics such as health, intelligence, and task familiarity, but also by task difficulty and situational demands.
3. Accurate diagnosis of memory dysfunction requires a thorough understanding of underlying mechanisms and contributing factors, and requires the use of appropriate hypothesis-testing techniques.
4. Memory functions can be improved in adults who have the motivation to practice and maintain the learned skills.

▼ LEONARD W. POON

See also: Cardiac Health; Humor; Information Processing; Intelligence—Crystallized and Fluid; Language Development; Learning and Memory in Everyday Life; Listening; Mental Health in the Adult Years.

References

Denney, N. W. (1989). Everyday problem solving: Methodological issues, research findings, and a model. In L. W. Poon, D. Rubin, & B. Wilson (Eds.), *Everyday Cognition in Adulthood and Late Life*. New York: Cambridge University Press.

Fozard, J. L. (1980). The time for remembering. In L. W. Poon (Ed.), *Aging in the 1980s: Psychological Issues*. Washington, DC: American Psychological Association.

Olsho, L. W., Harkins, S. W., & Lenhardt, M. L. (1985). Aging and the auditory system. In J. E. Birren & K. W. Schaie (Eds.), *Handbook of the Psychology of Aging*. New York: Van Nostrand Reinhold.

Poon, L. W. (1985). Differences in human memory with aging: Nature, causes, and clinical implications. In J. E. Birren & K. W. Schaie (Eds.), *Handbook of the Psychology of Aging*. New York: Van Nostrand Reinhold.

Poon, L. W., & Siegler, I. C. (1991). Psychological aspects of normal aging. In J. Sadavoy, L. W. Lazarus, & L. F. Jarvik (Eds.), *Comprehensive Review of Geriatric Psychiatry*. Washington, DC: American Psychiatric Press.

Poon, L. W., et al. (1986). *Handbook for Clinical Memory Assessment of Older Adults*. Washington, DC: American Psychological Association.

Poon, L. W., Rubin, D., & Wilson, B. (1989). *Everyday Cognition in Adulthood and Late Life*. New York: Cambridge University Press.

Schaie, K. W. (1990). Intellectual development in adulthood. In J. E. Birren & K. W. Schaie (Eds.), *Handbook of the Psychology of Aging*. New York: Academic Press.

Talland, G. (1968). *Disorders of Memory and Learning*. Harmondsworth, Middlesex, England: Penguin.

West, R. (1989). *Mental Fitness Over 40*. Gainesville, FL: Triad.

MENOPAUSE

Menopause (from the Greek *menos*, meaning monthly and *pausis*, a cessation) is the point in a woman's life that menstruation ends. In actuality, her body has been responding to signals that the ending is imminent for several years. Menopause is not an illness and it is not an accident. Menopause is part of normal development in women. It is a significant process that requires attention to the entire context of gender-specific influences, a phase of life. The terms "climacteric" or "change of life" indicate passage of time more effectively than the term "menopause." Just as puberty was a time of preparation for attaining the ability to reproduce life, so menopause represents the decline and then cessation of reproductive capacity.

There is no true counterpart to menopause in males. Although sperm production decreases as males age, the male does not experience the profound changes in hormone production that occur in the female.

Little is known about this significant process in the development of women. We are only beginning to understand the physiological changes. The emotional and social aspect remain to be explored by the generation that now approaches menopause.

"It is expected that by 2025 almost 24% of the 1.4 billion people living in developed regions will be aged 60 and over..." (Diczfalusy, 1991, p. 4). Women have an increasing lifespan. Females born in 1950 in a developed region of the world have a life expectancy of almost 69 years. Females born in the year 2000 can expect to live almost 80 years (Diczfalusy, 1991). Women outnumber men in older age groups.

In the 1990s nineteen million women will be between the ages of 45 and 54 (Sheehy, 1992). Baby boom generation women are moving into their late forties and fifties. More women than ever in history are surviving childbirth and living into their eighties and nineties. It is safe to say more women will have menopause this decade than any other decade in history. In addition there will be more postmenopausal women than ever before.

Answers are not readily available to questions about what happens to a woman's body, and what, if anything, should be done about it. Research, both of normal and abnormal aspects, is only now beginning. The coming generations will have many more answers than we do now. So in this article we will review what we think we know and what the questions are about menopause.

What Happens Physiologically?

A woman is born with all of the eggs she will ever have. Around the age of 12, she begins a monthly cycle of readying an egg for conception. At first cycles are irregular and eggs are not produced each time. Soon her body settles into a cycle of 26-28 days. The pituitary gland, the ovaries, and the uterus are joined together through production of hormones to release an egg and prepare the uterus for implantation and nourishment of the embryo if fertilization occurs. If the egg is not fertilized, she has menstruation and the cycle starts again (Cutler & Garcia, 1992).

A woman's feelings about her ability to bring a new human being to life are affected by her understanding of her body and family and societal attitudes related to reproduction. Problems of encouraging or preventing pregnancy affect a woman's feelings about her body. Feelings of fear, shame, reverence or just acceptance mix with feelings about her femaleness and sexuality.

If the ovaries are not surgically removed earlier, most women in their forties begin to experience the effects of ovarian aging. Cycles occur but no egg is produced. Gradually production of estrogen decreases and stops. The monthly bleeding periods become unpredictable, irregular, and then stop. Technically, menopause is said to occur when there have been no periods for a year (Cutler & Garcia, 1992).

Other changes occur. The ovaries and uterus become smaller. The vaginal entry contracts and the vagina becomes more shallow. The cells that line the vagina produce less lubrication and become less responsive to sexual arousal. The breasts become less firm. The pubic and axillary hair thins. About half of American women reach menopause by age 50 (Diczfalusy, 1991).

As during puberty, changes in hormone levels introduce challenging physiologic and emotional shifts for the woman. The hot flash (flush) is the most commonly recognized sign of menopause. Fat cells in the body are capable of producing estrogen. If the woman's fat cells produce enough estrogen to prevent wide swings in body estrogen levels, a woman may not experience hot flashes or other symptoms. However, most women (85%) do have hot flashes of the face, neck, and upper body (Edman, 1983). These may be accompanied by sudden, excessive perspiration. Hot flashes tend to occur more frequently late in the day, during hot weather, after consumption of hot foods or drinks, and with increased tension. Night sweats may wake the woman, causing insomnia and fatigue. The cause has received recent attention from researchers but still is not understood (Ginsburg & Hardiman, 1991). Whatever the cause, hot flashes are uncomfortable and embarrassing as they advertise that a woman's body is "aging."

Changes in the vagina include itching and dryness with increased susceptibility to urinary infection and incontinence. The most distressing change is lack of lubrication, causing pain during intercourse. Decreases in sexual desire may accompany decreases in testosterone (produced in the ovary), which mediates desire in both men and women (McCoy, 1991).

Loss of estrogen is associated with loss of bone mass—osteoporosis. The most loss occurs between ages 45 and 70. Half of all women have clinical osteoporosis by age 60 (Cutler & Garcia, 1992). With loss of bone mass comes back pain, loss of height, and the risk of bone fractures, particularly of the hip and vertebral bodies in the back. Smoking, immoderate drinking, obesity, and sedentary life-style increase the risk of osteoporosis and cardiovascular disease.

Other changes reported during the perimenopausal period include: increased risk of cardiovascular disease, skin changes (loss of thickness and increased susceptibility to ultraviolet rays), visual deficits, formication (sensation of insects crawling on the skin), memory loss, and emotional distress (depression, anxiety, insomnia) (Cutler & Garcia, 1992). Psychosocial distress may be based in loss of youth, loss of femininity, decreased sexual attractiveness, and inability to conceive. There is not enough research to know causes and relationships.

The Need for Knowledge

Until this century most women died during their childbearing years. Those who reached menopause did not talk about the experience except to say that it was a relief "to be done with all that." Even among women, sharing one's experience of menopause has not been considered polite. There is little research to tell us about socioeconomic and cultural differences in the experience of menopause (Standing & Glazer, 1992). There are no old wives' tales. Myths and fears include only a few whispers about ill health or worse — craziness. Even our literature has limited words to offer about the postmenopausal woman (Low, 1983).

In this age of TV, advertising is directed to feminine needs including estrogen patches, and vaginal moisturizing solutions. Can research and true knowledge of the experience of menopause be far behind? The research agenda might include the following questions: What happens to a woman's self-concept? How can these changes be integrated into the fabric of a lifetime? Will menopause be different in a high-tech society?

Women are beginning to share what menopause was like for them. The baby boomers will leave a very different legacy about menopause!

Coping with the Changes of Menopause

The "change of life" challenges women to find measures to adjust physically and emotionally. It is probable that coping with menopause requires consideration of lifestyle issues and of the recommendations offered by the medical community.

Prepare with a Lifelong Healthy Lifestyle. The following healthy habits can help prepare for menopause:

- Protect bones with a diet that has adequate Vitamin D and calcium.

- Promote healthy bones and reduce stress with exercise and good posture.
- Protect the cardiovascular system with a diet high in fiber and low in fat. Vitamin C plays an important role in healing wounds, reducing atherosclerosis, and strengthening bones.
- Avoid smoking, immoderate drinking, and obesity.

Cope with Changes. The following actions can help one to cope with the changes of menopause:

- Seek information. Understand what is normal.
- Take the opportunities to understand feelings of loss and change.
- Share knowledge and feelings with your partner and friends.
- Seek professional help when physical or emotional distress threatens to overwhelm you.

Understand Hormone Replacement Therapy. While menopause is not a disease, the disagreeable aspects of it can be modified or avoided through hormone replacement therapy (HRT). Hormone replacement therapy consists of supplementing a woman's depleted estrogen with natural or synthetic estrogen. It may include progesterone, and in some situations androgens (testosterone) may also be added (Sitruk-Ware, 1991).

Estrogen is normally formed in the ovary and adrenal cortex. Some weak forms (estrone) are produced by fat cells. Estrogen is responsible for female secondary sex characteristics and for the growth of the uterine lining in preparation for implantation of an embryo. Progesterone is produced by the corpus luteum of the ovary after release of an egg. It promotes changes in the tubes and uterus to nurture a fertilized egg. It is also responsible for sore breasts and bloating felt by many women at the beginning of pregnancy or before a menstrual period. If there is no fertilized egg, the corpus luteum disappears, progesterone levels fall, and menstruation occurs. The ovaries also produce androgens, such as testosterone. These hormones seem to play a role in a woman's sexual desire. They are found at their highest blood levels around the time of ovulation (Cutler & Garcia, 1992).

Supplementation of estrogen stops the hot flashes. It reduces loss of bone. It protects the cardiovascular system. Sexual desire returns and sexual activities become pleasurable again.

The advantages of HRT are clear. What about disadvantages? The lining of the uterus proliferates but does not shed without the opposition of progesterone. Chances of endometrial and breast cancer are small but real potential problems. Present-day hormone replacement therapy (HRT) includes a balance of low doses of estrogen and progesterone to protect against development of these cancers (Sitruk-Ware, 1991). With the addition of progesterone, periods and the feelings that accompany them continue.

The long-term effects of HRT are not known. HRT is not recommended for women who have preexisting cancer. Also estrogen, when taken orally, can affect the liver and gall bladder, so those with problems in these organs may avoid HRT (Sitruk-Ware,1991).

Is HRT just another way to avoid the fact that we age? Or is it natural to supplement something our body is no longer producing if we can? Are there other, more natural approaches to dealing with the consequences of menopause? Each woman must balance the advantages and disadvantages of using HRT within the context and meaning of her life.

What Does the Future Hold?

With the aging of baby boomers, drug manufacturers are anticipating billion dollar sales in the menopause business. Surprisingly, an estimated one-third of women given prescriptions for hormones never fill them. And the average length of time women continue on replacement is only nine months (Sheehy, 1992). Why is this? Clearly women know something the drug manufacturers do not.

In her book, *The Silent Passage*, Gail Sheehy (1992) suggests a different state of equilibrium, which she calls "coalescence." Perimenopausal women in our society are looking forward to a new liberation. The children are grown. Financial stability may have been attained. Fear of pregnancy is gone from sexual relationships. A celebration of self-esteem and well-being may launch women into new careers, politics, volunteer activities, and pursuit of long-delayed wishes. Perhaps women find that life without the pull of the moon and tides is more comfortable than they thought possible.

▼ Beatrice K. Kastenbaum

See also: Gender Differences as a Shaping Force in Adult Development and Aging; Marital Development; Mid-Life Crisis; Sex in the Later Adult Years; Sexuality.

References

Cutler, W., & Garcia, C. (1992). *Menopause: A Guide for Women and the Men Who Love Them.* New York: W. W. Norton and Company.

Diczfalusy, E. (1991) Demographic aspects: The menopause in the next century. In R. Sitruk-Ware, & W. Utian (Eds.), *The Menopause and Hormonal Replacement Therapy.* New York: Marcel Dekker, Inc., pp.1-14.

Edman, C. (1983). The climacteric. In H. J. Buchsbaum (Ed.), *The Menopause.* New York: Springer-Verlag, pp. 23-33.

Ginsburg, J. & Hardiman, P. (1991). What do we know about the pathogenesis of the menopausal hot flush? In R. Sitruk-Ware & W. Utian (Eds.), *The Menopause and Hormonal Replacement Therapy.* New York: Marcel Dekker, Inc., pp. 15-46.

Low, M. (1983). The perimenopausal woman in literature. In H. J. Buchsbaum (Ed.), *The Menopause.* New York: Springer-Verlag, pp. 205-13.

McCoy, N. (1991). The menopause and sexuality. In R. Sitruk-Ware & W. Utian (Eds.), *The Menopause and Hormonal Replacement Therapy.* New York: Marcel Dekker, Inc., pp. 73-100.

Sheehy, G. (1992). *The Silent Passage.* New York: Random House.

Sitruk-Ware, R. (1991). Hormonal replacement therapy: What to prescribe, how, and for how long. In R. Sitruk-Ware & W. Utian (Eds.), *The Menopause and Hormonal Replacement Therapy.* New York: Marcel Dekker, Inc., pp. 259-82.

Standing T., & Glazer, G. (1992). Attitudes of low-income clinic patients toward menopause. *Health Care for Women International, 12*: 271 280.

MENTAL HEALTH IN THE ADULT YEARS

The complex relationship between developmental change and mental health has been the subject of many studies and theories. Most of this concern, however, has been limited to the years of childhood and adolescence. There are few general theories of mental health and development through adulthood. Psychosocial research on adulthood has focused upon various "developmental tasks" whose "successful" resolution is considered essential for maintaining equilibrium, reducing stress, and preventing mental health problems.

The adult years have often been subdivided by researchers and theorists into several phases. Levinson (1978), for example, proposed three age-based categorizations: early adulthood, encompassing the period from the end of adolescence to approximately age 40; middle adulthood, continuing until about age 65; and later adulthood and old age, following age 65. Some other experts make additional distinctions, e.g., between the "young-old" (up to age 75) and the "old-old."

The Erikson-Levinson Model

Eric Erikson (1968) considered the early adult years a time when individuals must develop intimate relationships that include intense and long-term friendships and associations. Failure to establish intimate relationships with others was thought to result in isolation and self-absorption. From the perspective of Erikson, as more recently developed by Daniel Levinson (1978), mental health may be related to the resolution of developmental tasks in early adulthood. These tasks center around occupation, marriage and relationships, and parenthood.

Early adulthood begins with the development of an "entry life structure" in the early twenties, in which occupational choices are made and most people marry (at least, for the first time). Various sociocultural and psychosocial factors may influence mental health at this time. For example, unemployment has many psychological effects and is related to such problems as alcoholism, suicide, and mental illness. Successful completion of the early adult developmental task of creating an identity can be endangered by unemployment and its deprivation of job or career as a source of self-esteem.

Although marriages are still popular, with most Americans wedding in their mid-twenties, about half end in divorce. Most divorced people marry again, usually more successfully than the first time. Even if the marriage survives and improves, difficulties in the marital relationship are a frequent source of stress for young adults.

Parenthood is another important psychosocial challenge in early adulthood. Most persons have established families by age 30 and are faced with both the rewards and complications associated with raising a child. Having children introduces important changes in life-style, and learning to cope with the new responsibilities of parenthood can at times overtax young adults. Furthermore, divorced and other single parents often experience even greater pressure and stress. One in every five households in the United States that includes a child has only one parent on duty. The percentage of single-parent families is even higher among certain minority and socioeconomic groups; e.g., nearly 50 percent of black families are headed by unmarried women.

Middle adulthood was characterized by Erikson as a period of reviewing how one's life has been going and making decisions about the future. The central conflict at this stage involves generativity vs. stagnation. Generativity refers to raising children but also to a variety of other activities that can enhance one's sense of producing and creating. The failure to continue personal and social development during middle adulthood results in a sense of stagnation. Major sources of stress during the middle years include divorce, concerns about sexual adequacy and satisfaction, and the "empty-nest syndrome" (when children grow up and leave home). Physical health problems have also been shown to have significant consequences for mental health at this time of life (Vaillant, 1977).

In later adulthood and old age the major developmental task, according to Erikson, is obtaining a sense of integrity rather than despair and isolation. Neugarten (1968) elaborates on this concept by suggesting that one is faced specifically with the challenge of giving up previous positions of authority and yet still maintaining a sense of worth. This is usually accomplished, she believes, by basing one's sense of integrity on past rather than current achievements. This view has been challenged by a number of subsequent researchers (e.g., Mishara & Riedel, 1985) who believe men and women can find both continuing and new sources of self-esteem in the later adult years; they do not have to rely entirely on "credits" built up in the past. Almost all theorists and researchers also emphasize the great range of individual differences in patterns of development through the later years. No one statement about mental health in old age will do justice to the many varied ways in which people strive and cope.

Psychiatric Disorders

Erikson's influential concepts of adult development emphasize the importance of resolving a series of sociopsychological challenges that everybody faces in one form or another. Mental health problems can interfere with the ability to master these challenges and can also result from the failure to do so. For some individuals, mental health problems become so distressing and lead to such dysfunction that they are labeled as "psychiatric disorders."

It is generally recognized today that psychiatric disorders have multiple deter-

mining factors that are related not only to developmental issues but also to many other biological, sociocultural, and psychological influences. Biological influences include neurochemical imbalances and maturational differences. Sociocultural variables include vulnerabilities that can be associated with family stability, poverty, child-rearing problems, and victimization by socioeconomic discrimination. Psychological factors include stressful mother-infant interactions, the effects of divorce and bereavement, problems in identity development, and ineffective problem-solving skills. These are but a few of the influences that have been shown to bear a relationship to psychiatric disorder throughout the life span.

The most common method for evaluating adult mental health problems in North America is to follow the *Diagnostic and Statistical Manual of Mental Disorders* (DSM-III) of the American Psychiatric Association (1980). DSM-III conceptualizes mental health problems along five interacting "axes" or dimensions that, together, provide a picture of an individual's overall status. Most emphasis is often placed on axes I and II, "Clinical psychiatric syndromes" and "Personality disorders and specific developmental disorders." It is essential, however, to consider all five dimensions to obtain a complete picture of a person's mental health status:

Axis I: Clinical psychiatric syndromes
Axis II: Personality disorders and specific developmental disorders
Axis III: Physical disorders
Axis IV: Psychosocial stressors in the vocational and social spheres
Axis V: Highest level of adaptive function in the past year

Psychosocial stressors (Axis IV) can vary from none to catastrophic. The highest level of recent adaptive functioning (Axis V) can range from superior to grossly impaired.

According to this model, all individuals are challenged by their physical and psychosocial environments, and all must adapt psychologically to threats, challenges, and stressors. The outcome of this adaptation effort is determined by one's abilities to cope (Lazarus & Folkman, 1984). These abilities themselves are determined by the availability of current support systems as well as the personal resources that people have developed over the years. When adaptation to life events and circumstances is not successful, problems may be expressed in psychiatric disorders of thought, feeling, and behavior. Psychiatric symptoms range from common emotions such as "feeling depressed" to more pervasive and persistent problems such as schizophrenia, in which there is severe disturbance of one's ability to function in everyday life, sometimes accompanied by delusions and hallucinations.

Determining the prevalence of various mental health problems in adult life is difficult because many individuals with psychiatric disorders never come to the attention of mental health professionals. A number of studies of the general, noninstitutionalized adult population have attempted to discover the lifetime and short-term prevalence of the disorders that are classifiable by DSM-III. Usually these studies assess the presence of mental health problems on the basis of interviews with a random sample of the population. One of the more extensive studies, conducted by the National Institute of Mental Health (Regier & Burke, 1989), found that 15.4 percent of the population of the United States could be classified as having suffered from some form of mental disorder during the sampled year of 1978. Only 3 percent of the population received care from mental health specialists. Another 9 percent received treatment for mental disorders by a primary care physician (not a psychiatrist).

Regier and Burke (1989) reported the lifetime prevalence of having any DSM-III disorder as 32.2 percent. This means that one of every three people living in the United States is likely to experience a period of mental or emotional disorder at some point in life. Substance and alcohol abuse problems were found to be the most prevalent. Of the 16.4 percent of the general population with disorders of this type, most (13.3 percent) had problems associated with alcohol abuse-dependence. Drug abuse-dependence counted for another 5.9 percent.

Phobias of various type constituted the next most prevalent problem (12.5 percent), followed by affective mood disorders, particularly having experienced a major depressive episode (5.8 percent). Antisocial personality (2.5 percent) and schizophrenia (1.5 percent) added to the total of people afflicted by psychiatric disorders.

The scope of mental health and disorder can be enlarged by including the relatively minor but still disturbing problems that are encountered in everyday life. These range from anxiety over studying for an exam or speaking in public to difficulty in falling asleep at night or marital conflicts that result in an atmosphere of tension and insecurity. However, most people whom one would categorize as having mental health problems do not seek help from specialists and, except in the case of low-prevalence disorders such as schizophrenia, the difficulties either cease after a period of time or the individuals find more effective ways to cope with them.

Positive Mental Health

Instead of focusing on problems and disorders, one might consider what constitutes a mentally healthy psychosocial life and what factors contribute to positive well-being. From a developmental perspective, positive mental health is related to success in meeting the tasks and challenges that present themselves at different stages of life. Many interpersonal and ecological factors also relate to positive mental health, for example, having a comfortable income, a stable marriage or intimate relationship, a satisfying job, interesting activities, and so forth.

The issue of individual differences in the determination of mental health is still subject to wide debate. One position (e.g., Lazarus & Folkman, 1984) is that individual differences in coping ability and style have the most effect on positive mental health. Why is it that two people with almost identical life stressors may react very differently? One develops serious mental disorders and the other copes effectively with the stressors and lives a happy and fulfilled life. Observations and questions of this type guide the inquiries into coping ability as a major influence on mental health in adult life. Another position is rooted in the many observations that social support can have a positive influence on mental health. However, a significant question remains: Is having a large and supportive network of friends and families something that just comes as good fortune to some individuals, or are some people especially gifted in creating and developing the interpersonal networks that enhance positive mental health? This question is also the focus of much current research on the social and psychological determinants of mental health and mental disorders.

▼ BRIAN L. MISHARA

See also: Alcohol Use and Abuse; Depression; Divorce; Loneliness; Mental Health Resources for Adults; Mid-Life Crisis; Narcissism; Stress.

References

American Psychiatric Association. (1980). *Diagnostic and Statistical Manual of Mental Disorders.* Third Edition. Washington, DC: American Psychiatric Association.

Erikson, E. H. (1968). The human life cycle. In *International Encyclopedia of the Social Sciences.* New York: Macmillan.

Lazarus, R. S., & Folkman, S. (1984). *Stress, Appraisal and Coping.* New York: Springer.

Levinson, D. J. (1978). *The Season of a Man's Life.* New York: Knopf.

Mishara, B. G., & Riedel, R. (1985). *Le Vieillissement* (Aging). Paris: Presses Universitaires de France.

Neugarten, B. L. (Ed.). (1968). *Middle Age and Aging.* Chicago: University of Chicago Press.

Regier, D. A., & Burke, J. D. (1989). Epidemiology. In H. I. Kaplan & B. J. Sadock (Eds.), *Comprehensive Textbook of Psychiatry.* Fifth Edition. Baltimore: Williams & Wilkins, pp. 308-32.

Vaillant, G. E. (1977). *Adaptation to Life.* Boston: Little, Brown.

MENTAL HEALTH RESOURCES FOR ADULTS

The word *resource* suggests potential. Something is a resource, however, only if we know that it exists. Mental health resources for adults do indeed exist, but considerable exploration may be needed to find them. For mental health professionals, computers make the task of locating books and articles much easier than it was even a few years ago. However, the task of locating other resources such as professional organizations, self-help groups, pamphlets, booklets, and audiovisual materials may be much more difficult. For the general public, the process of locating information on organizations, written materials, audiovisual aids, and mental health services may seem daunting.

Fortunately, mental health self-help and advocacy groups have devoted systematic efforts in recent years to directing the general public to mental health resources. The select group of organizations, books, and audiovisual materials offered here is intended to be a general map for locating mental health resources throughout the United States. Persons interested in finding mental health services should remember that the family physician, minister, priest or rabbi, and local hospital all are likely to be knowledgeable about resources in the local community.

Organizations

The following is an annotated list of organizations that may be useful for obtaining specific details about mental health services and/or general information on this subject. The list includes professional organizations as well as self-help groups for persons with mental health problems and their families and friends.

Alcoholics Anonymous (AA)
General Service Board of Alcoholics Anonymous, Inc.
475 Riverside Drive

New York, NY 10115
(212) 870-3400
AA is an organization with the goal of helping people attain and maintain sobriety. Members of AA groups take an active role in running local activities; the groups are not directed by professionals. Local AA groups often are listed in the phone book. AA distributes printed and audiovisual materials that may be obtained at minimal cost.

The Alzheimer's Association

919 North Michigan Avenue, Suite 1000
Chicago, IL 60611-1676
(312) 335-8700   Toll free: (800) 272-3900
The Alzheimer's Association was founded by families of people with dementia and by scientists and physicians. It sponsors more than 200 local chapters that provide support groups and other services for people with dementia and their families. The location of a local chapter and information on Alzheimer's disease are available from the Association.

American Association for Geriatric Psychiatry

PO Box 376A
Greenbelt, MD 20768
(301) 220-0952
The American Association for Geriatric Psychiatry is an organization of psychiatrists with an interest in mental health care for older adults. It publishes a membership directory that indicates whether or not particular members accept patient referrals.

American Psychiatric Association (APA)

1400 K Street, NW, Department ENC
Washington, DC 20005
(202) 682-6220
The APA is the primary professional organization for psychiatrists in the United States. Individuals desiring information about psychiatric services in their area may contact the APA for the location of the nearest APA "psychiatric society," which may be able to provide assistance. The APA publishes a wide variety of brochures and pamphlets on mental health problems and has also produced videotapes on this topic.

American Psychological Association (APA)

750 First Street, NE
Washington, DC 20002-4242
(202) 336-5500

The APA is a scientific and professional organization of more than 60,000 psychologists. Although it does not offer assistance in locating psychological services, many of its state affiliates may provide help. Some affiliates have established referral systems to psychologists. The APA publishes books for professionals and has available a number of pamphlets for consumers of psychological services.

The Department of Veterans Affairs (VA)

810 Vermont Avenue, NW
Washington, DC 20420
The VA provides a number of benefits to U.S. veterans and their families. The VA operates hospitals and medical services throughout the nation, which often include mental health services. The VA also sponsors regional Geriatric Research, Education, and Clinical Centers (GRECCs), some of which provide specialized services for persons with dementia and depression. Local VA offices should be contacted for information on eligibility as well as the location of nearest services.

Family Service America

11700 West Lake Park Drive
Park Place
Milwaukee, WI 53224
(414) 359-1040 Toll free: (800) 221-2681
Family Service America is the parent organization of almost 300 private, nonprofit agencies in the United States and Canada that help individuals and their families with a variety of problems that include difficulties related to mental health. Those interested in locating a Family Service America affiliate may call the above-listed toll-free number. The organization also distributes books and audiovisual materials.

National Alliance for the Mentally Ill (NAMI)

2101 Wilson Boulevard, Suite 302
Arlington, VA 22201
(703) 524-7600
NAMI is an organization founded by families and friends of people with serious mental illnesses. It sponsors self-help groups for people with mental illness and for their families and friends. NAMI also advocates for mental health services and engages in public education activities. There are local NAMI affiliates throughout the country. NAMI also publishes educational materials and sells carefully selected books on mental illness at below retail cost. Interested individuals may write NAMI at the above-listed address and request the Resource Catalog that lists available materials.

National Association of Social Workers (NASW)

750 First Street, NE, Suite 700
Washington, DC 20002
(202) 408-8799 Toll free: (800) 638-8799
NASW is a professional organization of social workers. Although it does not provide direct services to the general public, NASW publishes a register of names and telephone numbers of clinical social workers throughout the United States. NASW may be contacted for the name of a nearby clinical social worker.

National Depressive and Manic-Depressive Association

730 North Franklin, Suite 501
Chicago, IL 60610
(312) 642-0049
The National Depressive and Manic-Depressive Association is an organization founded and directed by people with mood disorders and their families. The group educates the public about mood disorders, lobbies for persons with these problems, and sponsors support groups throughout the United States. The Association also sells books at discount and audiovisual materials on mental health.

National Institute of Mental Health (NIMH)

5600 Fisher Lane
Rockville, MD 10857
(301) 443-4513
The NIMH is the federal agency dedicated to research, training, and education on mental health problems. The Mental Disorders of the Aging Research Branch is the focus of the organization's activities on mental health and aging. The NIMH is an excellent source of brochures and pamphlets on mental health that may be obtained by writing to: Public Inquiries Branch, Room 15C-05, Office of Scientific Information, at the above-mentioned address. Many publications are available free of charge.

National Institute on Aging Information Center (NIA)

PO Box 8057
Gaithersburg, MD 20898-8057
(301) 495-3455
The National Institute on Aging (NIA) is charged with the responsibility for conducting and supporting research and training on various aspects of aging. Through its Information Center, NIA produces and distributes a variety of publications on aging both for the professional and for the general public. These include information packets about the NIA, Alzheimer's disease, research and grant opportunities, health education, and disease prevention, as well as technical reports and research summaries. *Age Pages* is an NIA publication series that offers brief health summaries for the general public on various topics. Some NIA publications are also available in Spanish and Chinese.

For information specific to the Alzheimer's Disease Research Centers (ADRC) sponsored by the government, as well as where to find help for persons with dementia throughout the country, the following NIA Center may be contacted: **Alzheimer's Disease Education and Referral Center**, PO Box 8250, Silver Spring, MD 20907-8250, (301) 495-3311.

National Mental Health Association

1021 Prince Street
Alexandria, VA 22314-2971
(703) 684-7722   Toll free: (800) 969-6642
The National Mental Health Association is an educational and social advocacy organization for mental health. Its local mental health affiliates provide information to the community at large and support and assist persons with mental illness and their families. The National Mental Health Association may be contacted at the above-mentioned address or through its toll-free number to obtain the name of the nearest Association affiliate or for a listing of brochures on mental health that are available from the organization.

Books on Mental Health

The books listed below are divided between those for mental health professionals and those for the general public. In view of the abundance of books for professionals on mental health problems, only those in the area of mental health and aging are listed. Books that are listed for the general public are divided between those on general topics in mental health and those on mental health and aging. The professional/nonprofessional distinction is somewhat arbitrary, since publications from each list often contain information that would be of interest both to professionals and the public.

The list of books offered below is not exhaustive but does include what are regarded as the better resources currently available on mental health. Some of these books can be obtained at below retail cost from the National Alliance for the Mentally Ill and also from the National Depressive and Manic-Depressive Association, whose addresses were given earlier in the section titled "Organizations." It is important to note that among the best sources of printed information on mental health problems for the general public are pamphlets, booklets, and brochures that are available from many of the organizations described earlier.

Books for Professionals

Birren, James E., Sloane, R. B., & Cohen, G. D. (Eds.). (1992). *Handbook of Mental Health and Aging.* Second Edition. San Diego: Academic Press. 976 pp. $85. ISBN-0-12-1012770-8.

Busse, Ewald W., & Glazer, Dan G. (Eds.). (1989). *Geriatric Psychiatry.* Washington, DC: American Psychiatric Press. 725 pp. $60. ISBN 0-88048-279-6.

Edinberg, Mark. (1985). *Mental Health Practice with the Elderly.* Englewood Cliffs, NJ: Prentice-Hall. 320 pp. $43.20. ISBN 0-13-575994-3.

Gwyther, Lisa P. (1985). *Care of the Alzheimer's Patient: A Manual for Nursing Home Staff.* Co-published by the American Health Care Association and the Alzheimer's Association. 122 pp. $6.95 (paperback). Available from the Alzheimer's Association.

Kermis, Marguerite D. (1986). *Mental Health in Late Life: The Adaptive Process.* Boston: Jones and Bartlett. 392 pp. $30. ISBN 0-86720-353-6.

Knight, Bob G. (1986) *Psychotherapy with Older Adults.* Beverly Hills, CA: Sage. 192 pp. $29.95. ISBN 0-8039-2633-2.

———. (1989). *Outreach with the Elderly: Community Education, Assessment, and Therapy.* New York: New York University Press. 168 pp. $35. ISBN 0-8147-4597-0. Paperback: $15. ISBN 0-8147-4607-1.

Light, Enid, & Lebowitz, Barry D. (Eds.). (1991). *The Elderly with Chronic Mental Illness.* New York: Springer. 370 pp. $49.95. ISBN 0-8261-7280-6.

Lurie, Elinor E., & Swan, James H. (Eds.). (1987). *Serving the Mentally Ill Elderly: Problems and Perspectives.* Lexington, MA: Lexington Books. 352 pp. $35. ISBN 0-669-14113-5.

Miller, Nancy E., & Cohen, Gene D. (Eds.). (1987). *Schizophrenia and Aging: Schizophrenia, Paranoia, and Schizophreniform Disorders in Later Life.* New York: Guilford Press. 367 pp. $40. ISBN 0-89862-228-X.

National Council of Community Mental Health Centers. (1989). *Serving the Elderly: A Mental Health Resource Guide.* 127 pp. $45 (paperback). Available from The National Council of Community Mental Health Centers, 12300 Twinbrook Parkway, Suite 320, Rockville, MD 20852.

Saltzman, Carl, & Lebowitz, Barry D. (Eds.). (1990). *Anxiety in the Elderly: Treatment and Research.* New York: Springer. 336 pp. $38.95. ISBN 0-8261-7090-0.

Smyer, Michael A., Cohen, Margaret, D., & Brannon, Diane (Eds.). (1989). *Mental Health Consultation in Nursing Homes.* New York: New York University Press. 304 pp. $28. ISBN 0-8147-7879-8.

Sunderland, Trey, Lewis, Myrna I., & Butler, Robert N. (1991). *Aging and Mental Health.* Fourth Edition. Riverside, NJ: Macmillan. 608 pp. $27 (paperback). ISBN 0-675-20920-X.

Toseland, Ronald W. (1990). *Group Work with Older Adults.* New York: New York University Press. 231 pp. $35. ISBN 0-8147-9189-6.

Zarit, Steven H., Orr, Nancy K., & Zarit, Judy M. (1985). *The Hidden Victims of Alzheimer's Disease: Families Under Stress.* New York: New York University Press. 224 pp. $32.50. ISBN 0-8147-96621-1. Paperback: $15. ISBN 0-8147-9663-X.

Books for the General Public—Mental Health Across the Lifespan

Committee on Psychiatry and the Community Group for the Advancement of Psychiatry. (1986). *A Family Affair: Helping Families Cope with Mental Illness.* New York: Bruner/Mazel. 110 pp. $20. ISBN 0-87630-444-7. Paperback: $9.95. ISBN 0-87630-443-9.

Greist, John H., & Jefferson, James. W. (1984). *Depression and Its Treatment: Help for the Nation's No. 1 Mental Problem.* Washington, DC: American Psychiatric Press. 128 pp. $7.95 (paperback). ISBN 0-88048-025-4.

Greist, John H., Jefferson, James W., & Marks, Isaac M. (1986). *Anxiety and Its Treatment: Help is Available.* Washington, DC: American Psychiatric Press. 216 pp. $14.95. ISBN 0-88048-212-5.

Korpell, Herbert S. (1984). *How You Can Help: A Guide for Families of Psychiatric Hospital Pa-*

tients. Washington, DC: American Psychiatric Press. 156 pp. $17.50. ISBN 0-88048-016-5. Paperback: $11. ISBN 0-88048-026-2.

Lewinsohn, Peter M., Munoz, Ricardo, F., Youngren, Mary Ann, & Zeiss, Antonette M. (1985). *Control Your Depression.* New York: Prentice-Hall. 272 pp. $16.95. ISBN 0-13-171927-0. Paperback: $10.95. ISBN 0-13-171893-2.

Papolos, Demitri, F., & Papolos, Janice. (1988). *Overcoming Depression.* New York: Harper & Row. 336 pp. $9.95 (paperback). ISBN 0-06-091488-2.

Torrey, E. F. (1988). *Surviving Schizophrenia: A Family Manual.* Revised Edition. New York: Harper & Row. 460 pp. $10.95 (paperback). ISBN 0-06-096249-6.

Zane, Manuel D., & Milt, Harry (1984). *Your Phobia: Understand Your Fears Through Contextual Therapy.* Washington, DC: American Psychiatric Press. 304 pp. $17.50. ISBN 0-88048-008-4.

Books for the General Public—Mental Health and the Older Adult

Billig, Nathan (1987). *To Be Old and Sad: Understanding Depression in the Elderly.* Lexington, MA: Lexington Books. 128 pp. $10.95 (paperback). ISBN 0-669-12279-3.

Cohen, Donna, & Eisdorfer, Carl (1986). *The Loss of Self: A Family Resource for the Care of Alzheimer's Disease and Related Disorders.* New York: W. W. Norton. 381 pp. $19.95. ISBN 0-393-02263-3. Paperback: $9.95. ISBN 0-452-25946-0.

Hinrichsen, Gregory A. (1990). *Mental Health Problems and Older Adults.* Santa Barbara, CA: ABC-CLIO. 300 pp. $39.50. ISBN 0-87436-240-7.

Mace, Nancy L., & Rabins, Peter V. (1991). *The 36-Hour Day: A Family Guide to Caring for Persons with Alzheimer's Disease, Related Illnesses, and Memory Loss in Later Life.* Revised Edition. Baltimore, MD: The Johns Hopkins University Press. 352 pp. $35. ISBN 0-8018-4033-3. Paperback: $9.95. ISBN 0-8018-4034-1.

Audiovisual Materials

The number of audiovisual programs on mental health continues to grow. Many of these materials are directed to persons with mental health problems and their families.

One valuable source is the National Alliance for the Mentally Ill, which also publishes a listing of selected videotapes about mental illness. The American Psychiatric Association has produced several videotapes on mental health issues, and a large selection of audiotapes is offered by the National Depressive and Manic-Depressive Association. There are fewer resources in the field of mental health and aging. *The Gerontologist,* published by the Gerontological Society of America, is the best source for critical reviews of audiovisual material on many topics in aging.

The following is a select list of films and videotapes.

Alcohol, Drugs, and Seniors: Tarnished Dreams

Problems of alcohol and drug abuse in the aged. Video and 16mm film. 23 minutes.
Purchase: video $370; film $495. Rental: $75 (film).
Source: AIMS Media, 6901 Woodley Avenue, Van Nuys, CA 91406-4878.

The Caregiver Kit

A set of five videotapes on different facets of caring for a family member with dementia: Meeting Daily Challenges; Communicating; Safety First; Managing Difficult Behavior; Caring for the Caregiver. Other instructional materials are included with the kit. Videos range in length from 18 to 21 minutes.
Purchase: kit $399; individual videos $100 each. Loan or rental might be arranged through local Alzheimer's Association chapter.
Source: Alzheimer's Association, 919 North Michigan Avenue, Suite 1000, Chicago, IL 60611-1676.

The Case of John R: Depression among Older Persons

Clinical case conference on a 73-year-old man who is depressed. Video. 15 minutes.
Purchase: $230. Rental: $30.
Source: Growing Edge Productions, PO Box 6296, Evanston, IL 60202.

Depression: The Storm Within

Orientation to basic issues in depressive illness. Video and 16mm film. 28 minutes.
Purchase: 1/2" VHS $100; 1/2" beta, 3/4", or PAL $125; 16mm film $250. Prices are less for members of the American Psychiatric Association. Contact the address below for information on free preview or loan.

Source: American Psychiatric Association Division of Public Affairs, 1400 K Street, NW, Dept. ENC, Washington, DC 20005.

Faces of Anxiety
Orientation to basic issues concerning anxiety disorders.
Video and 16mm film. 28 minutes.
Purchase: 1/2" VHS $100; 1/2" beta, 3/4", or PAL $125; 16mm film $250. Prices are less for members of the American Psychiatric Association. Contact the address below for free preview or loan.
Source: American Psychiatric Association Division of Public Affairs, 1400 K Street, NW, Dept. ENC, Washington DC 20005.

Four Lives: A Portrait of Manic Depression
Nature, causes, consequences, and treatments for manic-depression. Video and 16mm film. 60 minutes.
Purchase: video $430; film $700. Rental: $75 per day or $150 per week (video only).
Source: Fanlight Productions, 47 Halifax Street, Boston MA 02130.

Moods and Music
Music, depressive disorders, and creativity. Video. 58 minutes.
Purchase: $25.
Source: National Depressive and Manic-Depressive Association, 730 North Franklin, Suite 501, Chicago IL 60610.

Orientation to Alzheimer's Disease
Basic information on Alzheimer's disease and its effect on the patient and family. Video. 17 minutes.
Purchase: video only $125; video with written materials $160. Loan or rental might be arranged through local Alzheimer's Association chapter.
Source: Alzheimer's Association, 919 North Michigan Avenue, Suite 1000, Chicago, IL 60611-1676.

The Panic Prison
Orientation to basic issues concerning panic disorder. Video and 16mm film. 28 minutes.
Purchase: 1/2" VHS $100, 1/2" beta, 3/4", or PAL $125; 16mm film $250. Prices are less for members of the American Psychiatric Association. Contact the address below for free preview or loan.
Source: American Psychiatric Association Division of Public Affairs, 1400 K Street, NW, Dept. ENC, Washington, DC 20005.

To Paint the Stars
The relationship of manic-depressive disorder to creativity. Video. 58 minutes.
Purchase: $25.

Source: National Depressive and Manic-Depressive Association, 730 North Franklin, Suite 501, Chicago, IL 60610.

Reminiscence: Finding Meaning in Memories
Training program to help those who work with the elderly to facilitate reminiscence to reduce social isolation. 80 color slides. 13-minute audiocassette. Trainer's guide. Ten resource material booklets.
Purchase: $30.
Source: American Association of Retired Persons, Program Resources Dept. (B4), PO Box 51040, Station R, Washington, DC 20091.

▼ GREGORY A. HINRICHSEN
See also: Alcohol Use and Abuse; Depression; Drug Use and Abuse; Mental Health in the Adult Years; Widowhood: The Coping Response.

METAPHORS OF THE LIFE COURSE

Types of Metaphor

Metaphors represent a link between one semantic field and another when a term from one context is substituted for a term from another context (Ricoeur, 1975). For example, in using the expression "the spring of life," one links human aging to the change of seasons. This bestows a feeling of fertility and budding on the concept of youth, but it also adds a feeling of youth to a particular time of the year. The relation is symmetrical in this case. If one of the terms is difficult to comprehend or express, however, it will tend to be assimilated into the other term (Corradi, in press). A "hazy" idea often can be visualized more clearly when its essence is captured by a metaphor.

This function of metaphors is especially useful in the language of the human life course. It is difficult to "visualize" and "grasp" (both terms themselves being metaphorical) the life course, as time is elusive. One does not have an immediate perception of time, let alone of the continuing flow of time from the past through the present to the future. Furthermore, the most important life course is one's own—which is still in process and therefore incomplete so that it cannot be seen as a whole. Links with fields that lend themselves more to visual imagery will therefore help in discussing the life course. This is especially true when the evanescent course of life is connected to some external and more stable pattern.

Four kinds of links will be discussed here:

1. The division of the continuity of immediate experience of the life course into separate stages
2. The link of the progress of human lives to the steady sequences that can be discerned from the outside, such as the times of day, the seasons of the year, or the larger sweep of history
3. The transformation of temporal into spatial patterns
4. The use of terms of change and movement for the course of time

More than one relation may be used in each application. They will be discussed here as elements in the construction of metaphors.

Time and Space

The use of familiar temporal processes as metaphors for the life course is a conventional technique. For instance, using spring as a metaphor for childhood, summer for youth, fall for maturity, and winter for old age presents itself quite naturally. Similarly, use of the diurnal changes, like "the morning of life," provides an easy connection. On the other hand, the periods of history offer potential metaphors that require more creative effort. Here a linkage of the two—individual human life and history—will influence the perception of both and generate ideas about the human life course as well as a philosophy of history. The process of making metaphors exposes the mutual influence of individual lives and social patterns. The expression of both sequences tends to be associated with a general perspective on time.

Individual human lives as well as their cumulative impact in history are expressions of the workings of time, but time cannot be experienced directly. Measurement of time is achieved through verbal symbols, such as numbers, or in translation to space, such as the position of clock hands. It is understandable, therefore, that language about time is metaphorical and is especially rich in spatial metaphors. In fact, it would be difficult to discuss the present topic at all without using such expressions. "Life course, "life cycle," and the "path of life" all evoke visual representations of relations in space. Discussion about the several parts of life and their relationship will have to follow the same pattern. A discussion of metaphors of the life course cannot avoid calling upon spatial metaphors. "Life course" itself is one such metaphor.

The spatial metaphor of "time's arrow" defines one spatial dimension. The additional vertical dimension serves as a metaphor for qualitative aspects of the flow of time. In general, "up" is seen as better, showing achievement and reward, but it is also the direction of effort and difficulty. Thus the common picture of the life course—at least in modern Western society—is an arc that reaches its peak and then declines, with the zero-point reached at death. This image graphically reflects the achievement of upright posture, a decisive human trait. The antiquity of this metaphor is apparent in the Sphinx's riddle: "What goes on four legs in the morning, on two legs at noon, and on three in the evening?" The answer, of course, is the human being who first scrambles on all fours in infancy, stands proudly in his or her prime, but then needs the assistance of a walking stick in old age.

Individual use of this vertical metaphor is reflected in such terms as "the ups and downs of life" or "the peak of life." It represents a common way of thinking, and most people can represent their own actual and projected life in this graphic fashion. For example, in a sample of the general U.S. population, two-thirds of the respondents were able to use these metaphors appropriately (Back & Bourque, 1970).

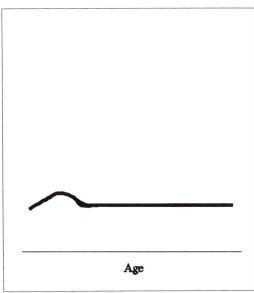

Figure 1. Consistently Low

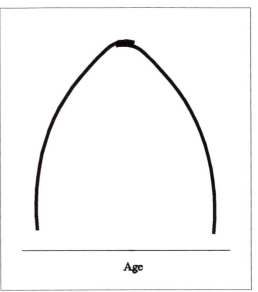

Figure 2. Bell-Shaped Curve

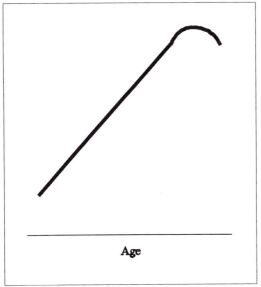

Figure 3. Peaking Ogive

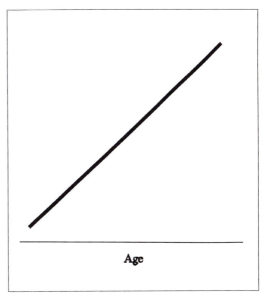

Figure 4. Upward Ogive

The four graphs shown above could be assigned to four patterns: consistently low (Figure 1), bell-shaped (Figure 2), peaking ogive (Figure 3), and upward ogive (Figure 4). These four shapes represented increased degrees of optimism on the part of the respondents and also a later "peak of life," respectively 40 and below, 45 to 55, 60 to 70, and 75 to 80. The different types as well as the peaks can be taken as metaphors, and the spatial representation shows a general perspective on the life course (Back & Averett, 1985).

Contrasted with this persistent picture we find an image of *progress*, which is associated with the religions of salvation and their medieval heritage of images and metaphors. Here the spatial connection looks to a contin-

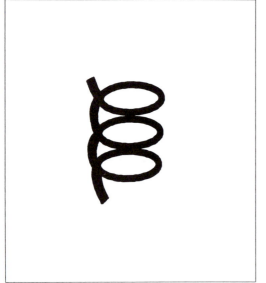

Figure 5. Upward Spiral

ued upward spiral (Figure 5): Even if physical aspects decline with age, the spiritual side can keep developing and death may be the prelude to salvation. This approach led to an image of striving toward individual as well as social perfection (Sears, 1986). There is a similarity to the upward ogive in the individual graphic metaphors. The spatial metaphor for this kind of move is the single or double spiral, combining the cyclical metaphor with the translation to the higher level (Tyng, 1978). It is interesting to note that in modern molecular biology the double helix has become the image of the progression of life.

History and Human Lives

St. Augustine was the most influential of the early Christian thinkers in his comparison of historical time with the periods of an individual's life (Augustine, 1958). For Augustine, the time from Adam to Noah is equivalent to infancy—an interval that is forgotten in adulthood, just as The Flood extinguished human memory. The second period, from Noah to Abraham, is likened to childhood, when language is acquired. The third, from Abraham to David, represented the adolescence of the world. During this period, the people of God were engendered—corresponding to the procreative maturity.

The fourth historical period recognized by Augustine lasted from David to the Babylonian exile. This was an epoch of splendor and, therefore, was regarded as the parallel to the prime of life. The birth of Jesus also constituted the birth of the fifth historical period: The individual equivalent is the decline from maturity toward old age. The Christian era, the sixth historical stage, was likened by Augustine to old age. This period includes the weakening of the flesh—the destruction of the temple—but also the birth of a new spirit.

Augustine's extended metaphor has been given in detail partly because it has been so influential that its traces are still part of the language and partly because it can be taken as a model of this comparison process and its many possibilities for expansion. For example, the sequence corresponds to the six days of the working week, with Sunday, the day of rest, taken as the opening to eternity. It also demonstrates the mutual influence of the metaphor, generating a new way of looking both at the human life course and cosmology.

Theories of Development

Current relationships of the same kind can be seen in theories of development in which the languages of economic and human development are used almost interchangeably and the millennium is promised at the next stage. But the purely two-dimensional metaphor of advance and decline has also found an historical application. Theories of the decline of civilization are often linked to this aspect of human development. The most obvious example is Oswald Spengler's (1927/1934) *Decline of the West*. Spengler equates such periods as youth, maturity, and aging with different world cultures, moving back and forth between these two realms of discourse. Again, the widespread use of this metaphor influences the perspective in both fields. This is particularly evident in such situations as the lives of young people in an aging culture: They may feel influenced both by their own youth and by their culture's age. The result might be an unfortunate lapsing into a kind of decadence instead of vigorously pursuing one's individual developmental career.

Comprehension of a process is also made easier by dividing it into separate parts that can be named and otherwise distinguished. The division of the life course into *stages* is made popular by its convenience. The particular number of stages identified and named seems to derive from our preference for those numbers, rather than from any necessity in the subject matter. Sears (1986) has observed that most theories settle on either four or seven stages.

Language and its metaphoric use provide names for these stages—and the names then foster the assumption that there are real entities that correspond to them Thus, the metaphors become part of the verbal environment within a society. In this case, the division of the life course into a number of stages has led to the still prevalent belief that this particular number of stages actually exists. The example from St. Augustine has shown that the model of the combination of numerology (or arithmology), life stages, historical periods, and mythology leads to the mutual connection of these fields—even today we are influenced by Shakespeare's seven stages of life.

The combination of number of stages and the arc metaphor has led to the image of ascent and descent, emphasizing childhood and youth on one side and senescence on the other. The middle period is then represented by a plateau or an undistinguished and undistinguishable period. This image is still reflected in the relative neglect of the middle period of life in social and psychological science. In the Augustinian example, this period was divided by the break from mature splendor to incipient decline and was marked by a violent crisis.

In individual lives this break in the curve has become known as the mid-life crisis (Jaques, 1970). It is marked by a turn-around in direction—from the metaphor of unlimited expansion to the realization of finitude and approaching death. Here the negative view of the passage of time and of death leads to the use of more dynamic metaphors of time and death. "A quiet, motionless ocean," for example, gives way to "a galloping horseman" or a "trumpet sounding alarm," linking these networks of images to time, death, and the life course (Back, 1974; Knapp & Garbutt, 1958).   ▼ KURT W. BACK

See also: Age 40; Contextualism; Development and Aging in Historical Perspective; Individuality.

References

Augustine (1958). *On Christian Doctrine.* New York: Liberal Arts Press.

Back, K. W. (1974). Metaphors as test of the personal philosophy of aging. In E. Palmore (Ed.), *Normal Aging II.* Durham, NC: Duke University Press, pp. 201-07.

Back, K. W., & Averett, C. P. (1985). Stability and change in life graph types. In E. Palmore (Ed.), *Normal Aging III.* Durham, NC: Duke University Press, pp. 290-305.

Back, K. W., & Bourque, L. B. (1970). Life graphs: Aging and cohort effects. *Journal of Gerontology,* 25: 249-55.

Corradi, C. (In press). The autobiographical metaphor: Narrative structure and explanatory function in autobiography. *Current Sociology.*

Jaques, E. (1970). *Work, Creativity, and Social Justice.* New York: International Universities Press.

Knapp, R. H., & Garbutt, J. T. (1958). Time imagery and the achievement motive. *Journal of Personality,* 26: 426-34.

Ricoeur, P. (1975). *The Rule of Metaphor.* Toronto: Toronto University Press.

Sears. E. (1986). *The Ages of Man: Medieval Interpretations of the Life Cycle.* Princeton, NJ: Princeton University Press.

Spengler, O. (1927/1934). *The Decline of the West.* New York: Knopf.

Tyng, A. G. (1978). Seeing order: Systems and symbols. In D. B. Brisson (Ed.), *Hypergraphics, Visualizing Complex Relationships in Art, Science, and Technology.* Boulder, CO: Westview Press, pp. 71-108.

MEXICAN AMERICANS: LIFE COURSE TRANSITIONS AND ADJUSTMENT

Data from the 1990 Census show that the Hispanic population of the United States is now in excess of 20 million, with approximately two-thirds being of Mexican origin. The recent rapid growth of the Mexican-American population is expected to continue throughout this decade. This growth has been accompanied by a realization that more needs to be known about this population. Although there has been interest in Mexican Americans for some time, it is only over the past few years that systematic studies have been conducted of their physical health, mental health, family structure, and related issues.

Early writings on Mexican Americans tended to project both negative and positive stereotypes, especially with regard to use of health care (e.g., Weaver, 1973) and family structure and relations. This stereotyping was based on studies of small samples in atypical areas—or on no studies at all. In reviewing the published literature on Mexican-American families during the 1980s, Vega (1990) concluded that despite the recent growth of empirical research "there remains much conjecture and recitation of old work, with few hard facts on which to base a viable resynthesis of heuristic models" (p. 1021).

This article purposefully avoids both conjecture and reliance on old studies. Rather, the focus is on recent studies of life course transitions and how these transitions influence the adaptation of Mexican Americans. The term *adaptation* is used broadly and is operationalized in terms of physical and mental health outcomes. Particular attention is given to marriage and divorce, the period of the empty nest, relationships with elderly parents, widowhood, and retirement.

Marriage and Adjustment

The literature on the Mexican-American family has long emphasized marriage as an important component of the population's strong familistic orientation (e.g., Becerra, 1988). In reviewing data from the 1980 Census, Bean and Tienda (1987) documented slightly higher marriage rates among Mexican Americans as compared with the general population. They also noted, however, that we can no longer assume that rates of marital stability are significantly higher among Mexican Americans because of rising divorce rates as well as high rates of marital separation.

How do marriage and its dissolution influence individual adaptation? The broader literature has shown a lively interest in the relationship between marital status and both physical and mental health. Ross, Mikrowski, and Goldsteen (1990) found that "overall, the married are in better health than the non-married, but parents are not better off than non-parents" (p. 1059). Studying Mexican Americans in San Antonio, Farrell and Markides (1985) and Markides and Farrell (1985) found that being married was associated with better physical and mental health in young adulthood and middle age, but not in old age. They concluded that the absence of a marital status effect in old age, particularly among women, reflects the fact that widowhood is more of an expected or "scheduled" transition to which older women seem to adapt successfully, even in a familistic group such as Mexican Americans. It is also possible that widowed older women benefit from strong extended family support. However, it is not clear why such supports should not be as effective in the middle and younger years. A more reasonable interpretation is that widowhood can have serious consequences when it occurs early in life—as an "unscheduled" transition—and that divorce takes its toll on people of any age.

The impact of divorce on well-being is not a simple process. For example, when Krause and Markides (1985) investigated the impact of Mexican-American women's employment on their psychological well-being, no overall effect was found. Employment did appear to be beneficial among divorced/separated women, but the opposite effect was found for divorced/separated women who had small children at home. The negative relationship between employment and psychological well-being for women who functioned as single parents has also been found in the general population (Ross, Mikrowski, & Goldsteen, 1990). Similar findings were obtained in a separate analysis with regard to physical illness and illness behavior (Krause & Markides, 1987). The employment role appears to counteract the negative consequences of divorce/separation. However, the added obligation of caring for small children has a synergistic or intensifying negative effect on women's well-being. Despite the traditional familistic emphasis, these supports do not always relieve the negative effects of multiple burdens on young Mexican-American women.

Alcohol Consumption

Another health-related factor that has been studied extensively in recent years is alcohol consumption (Caetano, 1987; Gilbert & Cervantes, 1986; Markides & Krause, 1990). This focus on alcohol consumption reflects the possibility that it may represent an index of adaptation or mental health, particularly among males. It has been suggested, for example, that while women become depressed in the face of stress, men turn to alcohol. This would make alcohol consumption a marker and substitute symptom for depression or psychological distress in males (Dohrenwend & Dohrenwend, 1976). This pattern also seems to hold true among Mexican Americans. A strong association has been found between levels of alcohol consumption and marital problems in younger Mexican-American men but not in younger women, whose marital problems were accompanied by high levels of depressive symptomatology. The association between alcohol consumption and marital problems was rather weak among middle-aged men, leading the authors to conclude that drinking is more tolerated by middle-

aged wives, who are more traditional (Markides & Krause, 1990). Thus, while heavy alcohol consumption among males may be tolerated in the Mexican-American family and community, changes may be underway in younger generations.

One of the most popular concepts in the literature on Mexican Americans has been that of acculturation, or the adoption of the values of the larger society. Acculturation has been much emphasized in the mental health literature (Roberts, 1987) and more recently in the literature on alcohol use (Gilbert & Cervantes, 1986). However, little attention has been given to the differential impact of acculturation at different stages in the life course. It is now becoming evident that acculturation does indeed have different meanings and takes different forms at various points in the life cycle, although much remains to be learned on this subject. For example, acculturation seems to be associated with higher levels of alcohol consumption in younger Mexican-American women in whom traditional norms regulating the drinking of women are more likely to be relaxed (Gilbert and Cervantes, 1986). Among males, however, acculturation seems to have the most influence on drinking patterns in middle age, a time when alcohol consumption is greater among less acculturated men and when perhaps it is more likely to reflect the influence of acculturative stress (Markides, Krause & Mendes de Leon, 1988).

Women in Middle Age

Middle age is a period of significant change in all groups, including Mexican Americans. One of the life course transitions of middle age to which considerable research has been devoted in the general population is the transition to the "empty nest." Given the importance of parenthood in the Mexican-American family (Alvirez & Bean, 1976), one would predict that the departure of children from the household would have a particularly negative effect on middle-aged Mexican-American women. However, Rogers and Markides (1989) found no differences in the physical and psychological well-being of middle-aged Mexican-American women in the postparental stage and women with children still in the home.

Although there is considerable knowledge regarding middle-aged women in the general population, little is known specifically about Mexican-American women. Data from a three-generation study of Mexican Americans in San Antonio have suggested that women in the middle years are engaged in strong networks with their extended families, particularly elderly parents and adult children. At the same time that they are relied on a great deal for advice and support, middle-aged women were also found to seek much support from their mothers and daughters (Markides & Martin, 1990). There seems to be an optimum level of reliance between generations. Patterns of minimum and heavy reliance are associated with negative psychological outcomes in middle-aged Mexican-American women, a result that has also been found in research with other familistic groups such as Italian Americans and Polish Americans (Cohler, 1983). These findings underscore the need for caution when conceptualizing and measuring social networks and social supports in these populations.

Old Age Transitions

Old age may well be the period in the Mexican-American life course about which the least is known. The early literature emphasized the warmth and supportive qualities of the extended family that were thought to ensure a secure place for older family members. This positive stereotype became open to question in the 1970s as concern grew that Mexican-American elders might be deprived of needed services because it was assumed that all their needs were being met by the extended family (Maldonado, 1975). Elderly Mexican Americans have higher expectations for their children regarding such matters as financial assistance and care during illness than is the case with the general population. Because these expectations are so high, they are less likely to be fulfilled. The

elders tend to see the younger generations as moving away from them and being neglectful—not visiting often enough, not being sensitive enough to their physical and emotional needs. Although a recent study has revealed strong relationships between Mexican-American elders and their children (Markides & Martin, 1990), the subjective feeling that one's children are not living up to expectations may be more important. The mental health consequences of this conflict between expectations and reality have not yet been adequately explored.

In the traditional Mexican-American family structure elderly people are held in high esteem and are viewed as "wise, knowledgeable, and deserving of respect" (Becerra, 1988, p. 149). It is apparent that even though younger generations subscribe to these traditional values, the Mexican-American family is undergoing changes that are threatening the actualization of these values, at least in the eyes of the older generation.

A final word is in order regarding the two major life course transitions in old age: widowhood and retirement. As noted earlier, widowhood in Mexican-American women does not appear to have lasting negative consequences when it occurs in old age, perhaps because it is an expected or "scheduled" transition; however, it does have negative consequences when it occurs early in life as an unexpected or "unscheduled" event. We know virtually nothing about the effect of widowhood on Mexican-American men. Information about retirement among Mexican-American men is just begininning to be developed. It has been suggested that the traditional concept of retirement is not very applicable, not for cultural reasons per se, but because the Mexican-American population is concentrated on the lower end of the occupational structure (Zsembik & Singer, 1990). There is some evidence that retirement occurs gradually and usually in response to health problems. Because this suggests a form of involuntary retirement, the finding that older Mexican Americans show poor adjustment to a life without work is not surprising (Markides, Martin, & Gomez, 1983). Much more needs to be learned about the retirement experience of Mexican Americans, including women, whose labor force participation rates have risen steadily in recent decades.

Conclusions

If anything can be concluded about the nature and consequences of adult life course transitions in Mexican Americans, it is that this group is much less unique and mysterious than earlier thought. Although Mexican Americans have more children, they experience marriage and marital dissolution rates that are similar to those in the broader society. Moreover, marriage and marital dissolution appear to have the same consequences, and so does the transition to the empty nest and to widowhood. There are some distinctive features in this population, however, with regard to the place of elderly people in the family and community. All generations continue to value old people and intergenerational relationships are strong. Nevertheless, because of their high expectations, elderly Mexican Americans are more likely to feel neglected by their children than is the case in the general population.

It is becoming increasingly clear that Mexican Americans are an overwhelmingly urban population living in a rapidly changing and complex society. And, while this population owes much to its Mexican roots, it is also greatly influenced by the larger American society.   ▼ KYRIAKOS S. MARKIDES

See also: Alcohol Use and Abuse; Divorce; Gender as a Shaping Force in Adult Development and Aging; Housing as a Factor in Adult Life; Interethnic Relationships; Marital Development; Mastery Types, Development, and Aging; Mental Health in the Adult Years; Retirement: An Emerging Challenge for Women; Retirement Preparation; Social Support for the Chronically Ill; Widowhood: The Coping Response.

References

Alvirez, D., & Bean, F. D. (1976). The Mexican American family. In C. H. Mindel & R. W. Habenstein (Eds.), *Ethnic Families in America.* New York: Elsevier, pp. 272-92.

Bean, F. D., & Tienda, M. (1987). *The Hispanic Population of the United States.* New York: Russel Sage Foundation.

Becerra, R. M. (1988). The Mexican American family. In C. H. Mindel, R. W. Habenstein, & R. Wright, Jr. (Eds.). *Ethnic Families in America.* Third Edition. New York: Elsevier, pp. 141-59.

Caetano, R. (1987). Acculturation and drinking practices among U.S. Hispanics. *British Journal of Addictions, 82*: 789-99.

Cohler, B. (1983). Autonomy and interdependence in the family of adulthood: A psychological perspective. *The Gerontologist, 23*: 33-39.

Dohrenwend, B., & Dohrenwend, B. (1976). Sex differences in psychiatric disorders. *American Journal of Sociology, 81*: 1447-59.

Farrell, J., & Markides, K. S. (1985). Marriage and health: A three generations study of Mexican Americans. *Journal of Marriage and the Family, 47*: 1029-36.

Gilbert, M. J., & Cervantes, R. C. (1986). Patterns and practices of alcohol use among Mexican Americans: A comprehensive review. *Hispanic Journal of Behavioural Sciences, 8*: 1-60.

Krause, N., & Markides, K. S. (1985). Employment and psychological well-being in Mexican American women. *Journal of Health & Social Behavior, 26*: 15-26.

------. (1987). Gender roles, illness, and illness behavior in a Mexican American population. *Social Sciences Quarterly, 68*: 102-21.

Maldonado, D. (1975). The Chicano aged. *Social Work, 20*: 213-16.

Markides, K. S., & Farrell, J. (1985). Marital status and depression among Mexican Americans. *Social Psychiatry, 20*: 86-91.

Markides, K. S., & Krause, N. (1990). Alcohol consumption in three generations of Mexican Americans: The influence of marital satisfaction, sex-role orientation, and acculturation. In B. Forster & J. C. Salloway (Eds.), *The Socio-Cultural Matrix of Alcohol and Drug Use.* Lewiston, NY: The Edwin Mellen Press.

Markides, K. S., Krause, N., & Mendes de Leon, C. F. (1988). Acculturation and alcohol consumption among Mexican Americans: A three-generation study. *American Journal of Public Health, 78*: 1178-81.

Markides, K. S., & Martin, H. W. (1990). *Older Mexican Americans: Selected Findings from Two Studies.* San Antonio, TX: The Tomas Rivera Center.

Markides, K. S., & Martin, H. W., with Gomez, E. (1983). *Older Mexican Americans: A Study in an Urban Barrio*. Monograph of the Center for Mexican American Studies. Austin, TX: University of Texas Press.

Roberts, R. E. (1987). An epidemiological perspective on the mental health of people of Mexican origin. In R. Rodriquez & M. T. Coleman (Eds.), *Mental Health Issues of the Mexican Origin Population of Texas*. Austin, TX: The Hogg Foundation for Mental Health.

Rogers, L. P., & Markides, K. S. (1989). The postparental stage and psychological well-being in Mexican American women. *Research on Aging, 11*: 508-16.

Ross, C. E., Mikrowski, J., & Goldsteen, K. (1990). The impact of family on health: The decade in review. *Journal of Marriage and the Family, 52*: 1059-78.

Vega, W. A. (1990). Hispanic families in the 1980's: A decade of research. *Journal of Marriage and the Family, 52*: 1015-24.

Weaver, J. L. (1973). Mexican American health care behavior: A critical review of the literature. *Social Science Quarterly, 54*: 85-102.

Zsembik, B. A., & Singer, A. (1990). The problem of defining retirement among minorities: The Mexican Americans. *The Gerontologist, 30*: 749-57.

MID-LIFE CRISIS

Does a mid-life crisis await every individual in the journey from youth to age? The expectation that a period of turbulence will be experienced in the middle years of life has gained rapid acceptance in popular culture. Although there is a tendency to accept mid-life crisis as proven, universal, and inevitable, the facts do not entirely support this view. A brief review of the origin of this concept will be followed by a consideration of the available evidence, and, finally, a comparison of crisis theory with other ways of looking at the middle years of adult development.

"Mid-Life Crisis": Birth of a Concept

The middle adult years have often been passed over in studies of human development. Researchers have tended to give almost all of their attention to infancy, childhood, and adolescence. It was understandable that early development would be the focus of developmental research and theory because the first years of life are marked by rapid growth and have a powerful shaping influence on adult personality. The relative lack of attention to adult development, however, made it difficult to comprehend the overall course of human growth and experience throughout the lifespan.

This situation began to change shortly after the end of World War II. As nations returned to the challenge of coping with their own social and economic issues, many observers were struck by a new and pervasive population trend. It was becoming apparent that most nations were "graying," i.e., undergoing an unprecedented increase in the proportion of long-lived citizens. Aging-and-the-aged emerged as a major research and policy agenda. Gerontology—the study of aging—attracted researchers, scholars, and clinicians from many disciplines. This new emphasis significantly expanded the range of developmental attention, but it left a hole in the middle. Society had become concerned about meeting the health, financial, and social needs of the aged, and therefore sought more knowledge about the aging process. By contrast, the middle generation remained semi-invisible. This "sandwich generation" shouldered much of the responsibility for social and financial support of both the young and the old, yet was seldom taken as the subject of developmental research itself.

By the middle of the 1960s there were occasional expressions of scholarly interest in the middle adult years. Neugarten (1964) and her colleagues and students at the University of Chicago were among the first to identify some of the issues that come to the fore during the middle adult years. The disengagement theory of aging (Cumming &

Henry, 1961) had also given some prominence to the transition from middle to old age. Furthermore, a psychoanalytic essay had even introduced the term "mid-life crisis" with respect to the individual's growing awareness of personal mortality (Jacques, 1965). Although these and a few other stimulating contributions had started to appear, the middle adult years were still relatively neglected in the scholarly literature, and had yet to attract much attention from the media and general public. It seemed as though scholarly interest in mid-life development would continue to grow at a reasonable pace until, eventually, there would be a sufficient body of knowledge to offer to society at large.

Instead, there was a sudden burst of attention that resulted in the almost instant popularization of the mid-life crisis concept. The main instrument of change was the book *Passages: Predictable Crises of Adult Life* (Sheehy, 1976). Gail Sheehy, a skillful author, had interviewed two researchers who were themselves conducting interviews and observations with mid-life adults. Psychiatrist R. L. Gould (1978) and psychologist Daniel Levinson (1978) would soon publish their findings and interpretations in their own books. Although these two subsequent books became influential in their own right, it was Sheehy's presentation of their in-progress observations that made the first and decisive impact on the public. *Passages* had become a best-seller, and "mid-life crisis" had become a buzzword for talk shows on radio and television.

From this point forward, the concept of mid-life crisis has had its own public career, bearing increasingly little resemblance to the continued studies of behavior and experience in the middle adult years. This episode was neither the first nor the last to establish a concept in the media/public mind well before the scientific community has had the opportunity to compile and evaluate the relevant findings.

Defining the Mid-Life Crisis

Precisely what is the mid-life crisis, when does it occur, and what, if anything is to be done about it?

Common to most versions of the mid-life crisis is the idea that people settle into a fairly predictable routine after their youth. (Statisticians often specify "youth" as the decade between ages 15 and 24.) The crisis does not arise until one has experienced a period of relative stability. Gould (1978) believes the crisis is encountered around age 35 and takes about a decade to resolve. Most other theoreticians refrain from specifying a particular age, but tend to see the crisis as coming in the forties or fifties. One of the difficulties in trying to be precise about the timing of a mid-life crisis, of course, is the lack of consensus as to when "middle age" begins and ends. Two of the most influential writers propose a twenty-year span for middle age, although not quite the same twenty years: ages 40-60 for Levinson and 35-55 for Neugarten.

All versions of the mid-life crisis assert that there is a surge of self-doubt, anxiety, and stress. The "smooth sailing" of successful adult experience encounters storm clouds and agitated seas. This zone of jeopardy awaits all voyagers, although each individual will have his or her own distinctive experience. Just as children must cope with pubescent changes as they enter adolescence, so mid-life adults must deal with a set of new challenges that are no less formidable for being less visible. Unlike young adolescents with their physical growth spurts and sexual maturation, men and women at mid-life have to contend with feelings of dissatisfaction and uneasiness. The source of this distress usually is not immediately apparent to the individual and his or her family and friends. A process of self-discovery or rediscovery is needed if the person is to recognize and cope with the vague but relentless sense that one's life seems to be taking a disturbing turn into uncharted territory.

Several theorists see the mid-life crisis as existential, i.e., an encounter with the questions of who one really is and what one's life really means. This encounter is thought by some to be precipitated by the dawning awareness that life will not go on forever in a comfortable adult groove—as a matter of fact, it will not go on forever. Prior to the public emergence of crisis theory, Cumming & Henry (1961) and Jacques (1965) had already hypothesized that it is the recognition of limited life expectancy that prompts mid-life adults to pause and take stock of their situation. From childhood onward, most people regard time as an almost unlimited resource—one's energies and desires will explode into the future. There is plenty of time to do and to enjoy, even time to waste. Death was a certainty, of course, but also an abstraction from which one was protected by a comfortable "space of time."

This simple view is first shaken, then shattered, by mid-life experiences. One's parents may grow frail and die. Some friends and colleagues of one's own age may become stricken. Younger people may seem to be moving up in status and influence, threatening one's career advancement or social standing. Evidences of one's own physical aging may cause twinges of anxiety ("Another gray hair!"). A mid-life adult may even feel uncomfortable because others are starting to treat him or her as though a respectable senior. "The check-out clerk called me 'Ma'am,'" one fortyish woman complained, "Am I a Ma'am already! I haven't stopped being a chick!" All in all, it becomes increasingly difficult to maintain the fiction that one has the key to permanent youthfulness and that one can just go on and on with the pleasant routines that have been established in middle adult life. People must now face, in some manner, the normative encounter with decline, loss, and mortality.

Furthermore, the mid-life adult is up against another formidable challenge: his or her own established self. It is not only that illusions of perpetual youth, invulnerability, and endless time have been rudely assaulted—one must now also recognize limitations and distortions in one's own development. Gould (1978) emphasizes the tendency

to admit that there is irrationality and evil within one's own self as well as in the external world. The belief that one has always been a fair-minded and ethical person gives way to the realization that one has been motivated at times by greed, lust, and vengeance, and has engaged in hypocrisy, deception, and other practices that one considers to be unworthy. The mid-life crisis is intensified by the feeling that one has not turned out to be a perfectly admirable person and is, in fact, one of the contributors to as well as one of the victims of the evils and miseries of the world. Forced to deal both with mortality and with the blemishes of one's own character and accomplishments, the mid-life adult must take an extra and more difficult step along the road to maturity. He or she must learn to "own" his or her own self: to accept an imperfect self that is essentially alone in an imperfect world.

Symbolically, one has become transformed from a child in an adult's body who is still counting on parental guidance and protection to becoming one's own parent. This process does not take place overnight. It will be several years before one can achieve this more realistic and seasoned sense of selfhood. Not everybody succeeds in making this mid-life developmental transformation; some men and women remain trapped in anxiety and self-doubt, trying various ways of escaping their dilemma, but unable to do so because the true source of the crisis has not been confronted and mastered.

For Gould, this resolution of the mid-life crisis—at about age 50—is the final challenge in the course of adult development. (Other theorists, such as Erikson, 1979, see developmental challenges continuing well into old age).

Levinson (1978) also calls attention to the role of the self in the mid-life crisis. Before reaching mid-life, a person has already passed through several stages of life, each of which involved the anxiety of transition or passage. These stages are universal, occurring in all societies when one comes of age for the next move ahead. The person who has made it through the earlier stages with some success arrives at mid-life with the sense of having reached a long-sought destination. At last, one is confident, established, and able to enjoy the fruits of one's accomplishments, including supportive and loving relationships.

This sense of well-being does not persist, however, for reasons such as have already been described. It is at this point that Levinson's approach differs somewhat from the other views that have been mentioned. Forced to reexamine their own lives, people must consider the choices that they have made along the way. Was it wise to have put so much effort into making money while the children were young that one did not have nearly enough time to spend with them? Should one have chosen the career that promised the higher status, or the line of work that one would actually have enjoyed doing? About their successes, people must ask: "Were these accomplishments worth the effort? Is this where my life really should be now?" About their failures: "Can I accept the disappointments and shortcomings for what they were, and get on with the life I have now?"

Although not usually regarded as a mid-life crisis theorist, David Gutmann (1987 and **Mastery Types, Development, and Aging**) has offered still another variation on the theme. Drawing upon observations made in several world cultures, Gutmann reports a strong tendency for mid-life men and women to give increasing expression to their other-gender personality inclinations. This tendency continues to grow with advancing age so that elderly women revel in their heightened assertiveness and elderly men in their newfound ability to nurture and enjoy without feeling the need to take command. For both men and women, the second half of life offers the potential for becoming a whole or completed person (a view that has its roots in the developmental theories of C. G. Jung, 1933). To achieve this late-life developmental goal, one must first pass through a mid-life crisis or its equivalent to transcend the partial self that carried the responsibility for achievements in the first half of life.

Taken together, the crisis theories do serve to call needed attention to the middle

adult years and do identify some of the challenges that are likely to occur during that period. Nevertheless, an important question remains to be answered: How do these theories stand up to empirical research?

Evaluation of Mid-Life Crisis Theory

The pioneering studies of Gould and Levinson were useful in raising possibilities and stimulating ideas. The interview/biography method was well suited to bringing forth detailed life experiences from a relatively small number of individuals. It was less well suited to testing alternative hypotheses in large and diverse populations. Studies of this type are more likely to provide a promising start to a line of inquiry than to provide definitive proof for a set of propositions. The Gould and Levinson studies offer glimpses into the lives of mid-life men in the United States during the 1970s; they tell us less about women and people of various cultural and subcultural backgrounds in other time frames.

In recent years a number of studies, both large and small, and employing a variety of methodologies, have provided further information on the middle adult years. The thesis that the middle adult years is dominated by a normative crisis has not fared well. For example, Clausen (1986) finds that most adults tend to evaluate themselves on an ongoing basis, and therefore are not faced by the sudden and unprecedented need to do so at mid-life. In her study of *Men in Their Forties* (1982), Tamir found a strong tendency for work values to become less important, while family and personal development values became more important. Although this shift supports the idea that personal values may be readjusted at mid-life, it did not usually carry the connotations of a crisis. Similarly, in their middle adult years, many women begin careers or renew their education, endeavors that break up existing patterns but that do not necessarily involve a crisis orientation (Schaie & Willis, 1986). Studies such as these suggest that the middle adult years may indeed be a time of reconsidering values and reorienting one's energies; however, these changes often occur without the sense of urgency, panic, and pressure that would usually be associated with a crisis situation.

Perhaps the most discouraging studies so far as mid-life crisis theory is concerned are those conducted and/or stimulated by Robert McCrae and Paul T. Costa, Jr (e. g., 1990). These researchers devised a Mid-life Crisis Scale that indexes the behaviors and feelings that are supposed to occur at this time of life. Studies using this instrument (e.g., Farrell & Rosenberg, 1981) have failed to discover a peak of distress at mid-life. Some people show most signs of distress earlier, some later: There is no clear overall pattern that confirms the crisis part of mid-life crisis theory. An examination of crisis-related behaviors (e. g., suicide attempts, admissions to mental health facilities, alcoholism, etc.) also failed to reveal a peak in the middle adult years (McCrae & Costa, 1983). Moreover, there is not much support for the proposition that mid-life adults in general experience an intensification of death anxiety (Kastenbaum, 1992).

All in all, the rather dramatic idea that every adult must expect a major period of crisis at mid-life has not been well supported by the available data. If the idea lingers on, then, it is for reasons other than its scientific validity.

Some Other Ways of Looking at Mid-Life Development

Loss, stress, and challenge can emerge powerfully at mid-life. The evidence, however, suggests that when this kind of situation does develop it is useful to look beyond the idea of a universal and unavoidable mid-life crisis. For example, historical events and situations can produce a mid-life crisis for one particular cohort of people and not for others (Riegel, 1975). Periods of high unemployment or rampant inflation similarly can touch off personal crises in mid-life but, again, these episodes do not demonstrate that mid-life itself is intrinsically a crisis-dominated period.

A major alternative is continuity theory. This approach holds that personality remains fairly stable throughout the adult years. Knowing what a person is like in youth is the most useful kind of information to have regarding that person's life-style in old age. Change does occur, but it is change within the particular type of personality that has already been established. McCrae and Costa are among the leading advocates of continuity theory and have conducted a number of studies that support this position (e. g., Costa & McCrae, 1977, 1980, 1989; McCrae & Costa, 1984). Within this perspective, mid-life can be a time of reflection and reorientation for those who have a knack for self-examination, but will be a time of crisis only if urgent problems arise (e. g., bereavement, health, finances).

Other theories emphasize dialectical processes through which continued development may be fostered throughout the adult years. The general dialectical position has been offered by Riegel (1975, 1976), and a number of specific theories are concerned with dialectical factors in development (e. g., Erikson, 1979; Kastenbaum, 1984, and **Habituation: A Key to Lifespan Development and Aging?**). Common to most dialectical theories is the implication that the impetus toward continued self-development may become stagnant at any point in the life course, but may also be renewed either spontaneously or through interaction with others. The middle adult years may be distinctive in this regard because the individual is likely to have a combination of health, vigor, and life experience that can provide the basis for significant advances in personal and interpersonal development.

▼ Robert Kastenbaum

See also: Adult Development and Aging, Models of; Age 40; Development and Aging; Development and Aging in Historical Perspective; Disengagement Theory; Habituation: A Key to Lifespan Development and Aging?; Life Events; Mastery Types, Development, and Aging; Menopause; Reminiscence and Life Review; Stress.

References

Clausen, J. A. (1986). *The Life Course: A Sociological Perspective*. Englewood Cliffs, NJ: Prentice-Hall.

Costa, P. T., Jr., & McCrae, R. R. (1977). Age differences in personality structure revisited: Studies in validity, stability, and change. *International Journal of Aging and Human Development*, 8: 261-75.

———. (1980). Still stable after all these years: Personality as a key to some issues in adulthood and old age. In P. B. Baltes & O. G. Brim, Jr. (Eds.), *Life-Span Development and Behavior*. Volume 3. New York: Academic Press, pp. 65-102.

———. (1989). Personality continuity and the changes of adult life. In M. Storandt & G. R. VandenBos (Eds.), *The Adult Years: Continuity and Change*. Washington, DC: American Psychological Association, pp. 45-77.

Cumming, E. M., & Henry, W. E. (1961). *Growing Old*. New York: Basic Books.

Erikson, E. H. (1979). Reflections on Dr. Borg's life cycle. In D. Van Tassel (Ed.), *Aging, Death, and the Completion of Being*. Pittsburgh: University of Pennsylvania Press, pp. 28-66.

Farrell, M. P., & Rosenberg, S. D. (1981). *Men at Mid-life*. Boston: Auburn House.

Gould, R. L. (1978). *Transformations: Growth and Change in Adult Life*. New York: Simon & Schuster.

Gutmann, D. (1987). *Reclaimed Powers*. New York: Basic Books.

Jacques, E. (1965). Death and the mid-life crisis. *International Journal of Psychoanalysis*, 46: 502-14.

Jung, C. G. (1933). *Modern Man in Search of a Soul*. New York: Harvest.

Kastenbaum, R. (1984). When aging begins: A lifespan developmental approach. *Research on Aging*, 6: 105-18.

———. (1992). *The Psychology of Death*. Revised Edition. New York: Springer Publishing Co.

Levinson, D. J. (1978). *The Seasons of a Man's Life*. New York: Alfred E. Knopf.

McCrae, R. R., & Costa, P. T., Jr. (1983). Psychological maturity and subjective well-being: Toward a new synthesis. *Developmental Psychology*, 19: 243-48.

———. (1984). *Emerging Lives, Enduring Dispositions: Personality in Adulthood*. Boston: Little, Brown.

———. (1990). *Personality in Adulthood*. New York: Guilford Press.

Neugarten, B. L. (Ed.). (1964). *Personality in Middle and Late Life*. New York: Atherton.

Riegel, K. F. (1975). Adult life crises: A dialectic interpretation of development. In N. Datan & L. H. Ginsberg (Eds.), *Life-Span Developmental Psychology: Normative Life Crises*, pp. 99-128.

———. (1976). The dialectics of human development. *The American Psychologist*, 31: 689-700.

Schaie, K. W., & Willis, S. L. (1986). *Adult Development and Aging*. Second Edition. Boston: Little, Brown.

Sheehy, G. (1976). *Passages: Predictable Crisis of Adult Life*. New York: Dalton.

Tamir, L. (1982). *Men in Their Forties*. New York: Springer Publishing Co.

MILITARY SERVICE: LONG-TERM EFFECTS ON ADULT DEVELOPMENT

Military service is a significant developmental experience in the lives of many men and women. Delineating its effects on the life course is not an easy task because one must consider a variety of moderating factors (see Figure 1). These include *ecological* variables such as branch of service, location of service, and amount of combat exposure; *personal* variables such as age, gender, ethnicity, social class, personality, and military rank; and *temporal* variables, i.e., cohort and period effects. One must also consider multiple levels of outcome—physical, psychological, and social well-being—all of which may be either positive or negative. Furthermore, the effects of military service, like other developmental experiences, unfold over time. A pattern of outcomes observed 5 years after discharge may differ markedly from the outcomes ob-

Preparation of this article was supported in part by a FIRST award to Dr. Aldwin (NIA AG07465).

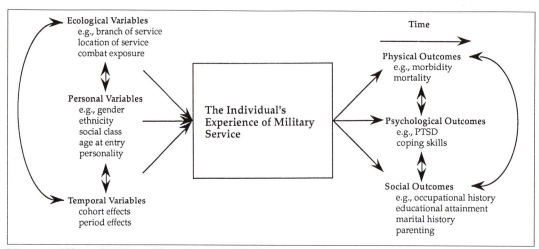

Figure 1. Effect of Military Variable on Adult Outcomes

served 20 years later (Aldwin & Stokols, 1988). Given these complexities, the best one can do is to delineate general patterns, knowing that they may not hold for all cohorts, social classes, sexes, ethnic groups, or individuals.

Physical Health Outcomes

Because of their initial selection for good physical health, veterans generally have lower rates of mortality than civilians, at least through mid-life. However, mortality rates are increased in lower ranks relative to higher ranks (Keehn, 1980), and externally caused mortality (suicides and accidents) is elevated in the first five years after discharge (Centers for Disease Control, 1987; Seltzer & Jablon, 1974). Prisoners of war who were subjected to extreme deprivation during their internment show increased mortality for approximately 10 years after release. Rates of hospitalization are also higher throughout their adult lives for prisoner of war survivors as compared with other veterans (Keehn, 1980).

Veterans with service in the Vietnam theater of operations, and apparently those with heavy combat exposure, report more physical health problems at mid-life than other Vietnam-era veterans or civilians (Card, 1983; Centers for Disease Control, 1988a; Kulka et al., 1990). Concerns still linger about

the long-term effects of Agent Orange exposure. Studies on cancer incidence have yielded equivocal results (Boyle, Decouflé, & O'Brien, 1989). Vietnam theater veterans report more birth defects in their offspring, but this has been substantiated by hospital records only for African-American veterans (Centers for Disease Control, 1988b).

In contrast to self-reports, physical examinations of a large group of male Vietnam veterans showed few differences between theater and era veterans. Hearing loss was more prevalent in theater veterans, most likely from damage caused by combat noise (Centers for Disease Control, 1988a). Men exposed to heavy combat also are more likely than other veterans or civilians to be physically disabled (Kulka et al., 1990).

Psychological Outcomes

Most veterans believe that military service affected their personal development (Card, 1983; Elder, 1987; Elder & Clipp, 1989). Negative outcomes include disruption of the life course, separation from others, and painful memories. Positive benefits include increases in maturity, coping skills, self-discipline, independence, cooperation, and sensitivity to others. Men and women in the military often confront adult responsibilities at an earlier age than civilians and may develop lifelong adaptive coping strategies from their experiences in facing extreme stress. Indeed, World War II and Korean conflict veterans are less likely than civilians to have a psychiatric disorder, although this is not true of veterans who served during or after the Vietnam War (Norquist et al., 1990). Also, troubled youth who join the military have better outcomes at age 30 than their civilian peers (Werner, in press).

Exposure to combat appears to be the most important of the many moderator variables for the effect of military service on psychological well-being. The demands of combat could provide valuable learning experience that would enhance coping skills and self-confidence (Elder & Clip, 1989). On the other hand, heavy combat exposure is associated with primarily negative outcomes.

One of these negative outcomes is the greater likelihood of posttraumatic stress disorder (PTSD). This is a psychiatric condition that is characterized by intrusive recollections of a traumatic event, such as combat. The syndrome often includes avoidance of reminders of the trauma, psychological numbing, and hyperarousal. Roughly one-third of male and female Vietnam theater veterans experienced PTSD at some point after discharge. When interviewed at mid-life, 15 percent of males and 8 percent of females still had the disorder. Current prevalence estimates are twice as high in veterans exposed to heavy combat. Additional risk is conferred by witnessing or participating in atrocities (Breslau & Davis, 1987).

The prevalence of PTSD in veterans of wars prior to Vietnam is unknown. Symptoms may emerge or intensify following events associated with aging, such as retirement or declining health (Elder & Clipp, 1989). World War II and Korean conflict veterans are less likely than Vietnam veterans to have PTSD (Blake et al., 1990; Rosenheck & Fontana, in press). Nevertheless, the symptom patterns are highly similar in all three groups (Rosenheck & Fontana, in press).

A host of ecological and personal variables are associated with the occurrence of PTSD. In male Vietnam veterans, PTSD prevalence was higher in African-Americans and Hispanics, relative to whites. The Army and Marine Corps had a higher prevalence than other branches of the service, and in all services men in the lower ranks were more likely to experience PTSD than those in higher ranks (Kulka et al., 1990). These differences may be due in part to combat exposure. For example, controlling for combat exposure eliminates the relatively higher prevalence of PTSD among African-Americans. However, the relatively high rate among Hispanics could not be explained on the basis of differential exposure to combat.

Combat-related PTSD is an outcome of military service that predicts numerous other problems (Kulka et al., 1990). At mid-life, male and female Vietnam veterans with PTSD are more likely than those without PTSD to have another psychiatric diagnosis as well as an alcohol problem. Males are also more likely to be substance abusers. Socially, veterans with PTSD have more marital and family problems, and are more isolated. They also have lower educational attainment, both overall and relative to premilitary education, and higher levels of occupational instability and unemployment. The list of misfortunes continues with more problems with vagrancy, homelessness, and criminal activity. Vietnam veterans with PTSD have more perceived physical health problems (but not physical disability) and are more likely to use the medical services that are available to veterans.

Less is known about the outcomes associated with PTSD in later life, except for the increased likelihood of current stress symptoms (Elder & Clipp, 1989). Relative to Vietnam veterans with PTSD, however, older veterans with PTSD show better social and occupational adjustment (Rosenheck & Fontana, in press).

Social Outcomes

Military service offers a means for upward social mobility through active duty occupational training and educational programs known as the "G.I. Bill." Since World

War II, approximately 20 million veterans have furthered their education through such programs (Department of Veterans Affairs, 1989). Men and women are equally likely to use veterans' educational benefits. African-Americans and Hispanics are more likely than whites to do so. Vietnam veterans have been making more use of their educational benefits than veterans of either World War II or the Korean conflict.

Veterans are slower than civilians to complete their education, especially if they enter the service at an early age. They catch up eventually to civilians, however, in the mean number of years of education attained (Card, 1983; Elder, 1986, 1987; Kulka et al., 1990). Significant subgroup differences also exist. Females and minority male veterans are more educated than their civilian counterparts, a difference that in females and Hispanic males reflects upward mobility (Kulka et al., 1990).

Military service neither facilitates nor impedes the attainment of an occupation appropriate to one's background (Elder, 1986) or education (Kulka et al., 1990). It may delay the transition to one's primary career, but by mid-life civilians and veterans generally hold jobs of similar status. Despite this similarity, male and female veterans have higher incomes than civilians. This difference has been observed in cohorts from World War II to the Vietnam era and is most notable in African-Americans and Hispanics (Martindale & Poston, 1979). Among veterans, income varies with combat exposure. In 1989, combat veterans from World War II and the Korean conflict earned less than noncombatants, but the reverse was true for Vietnam veterans (Rosenheck & Fontana, in press).

Male veterans are more likely than other adult males to be married (Department of Veterans Affairs, 1989), but they are slower to enter into marriage and parenthood (Card, 1983; Elder, 1986). Less is known about marital outcomes for female veterans, but they are somewhat less likely than other female adults to be married. Among males and females, those exposed to heavy combat are more likely than civilians or other veterans to have

marital and family problems (Kulka et al., 1990).

Much has been written about the camaraderie that develops among individuals who serve in the military, yet service friendships are retained by relatively few. Among World War II and Korean conflict veterans, these ties are most likely to be retained by men who lost a friend or comrade in combat, or who were exposed to heavy combat (Elder & Clipp, 1988). Among Vietnam veterans, heavy combat exposure is associated with a sense of social isolation in both males and females; even those with PTSD are more likely than those without PTSD to participate in a veterans organization (Kulka et al., 1990).

Special Developmental Considerations

There are similarities and differences between older and younger veterans. For example, combat-related PTSD has been diagnosed in both, but in older veterans the prevalence is lower and PTSD is not as strongly associated with impaired occupational and social functioning. Unfortunately, most studies on the effects of military service are either cross-sectional or, at best, follow only one cohort longitudinally. This makes it difficult to distinguish developmental effects from period and cohort effects.

Some intriguing developmental issues are raised by contradictory findings between cohorts of veterans on the effects of the timing of service entry. Vietnam veterans who entered the service as adolescents have had poorer outcomes later in life than older entrants, especially in psychological adjustment (Kulka et al., 1990). In contrast, World War II veterans who entered at an older age have had poorer outcomes in social and occupational functioning, likely because of the disruption they experienced in family life and career (Elder, 1987).

Obviously, methodological and other artifactual problems may account for this discrepancy. However, it is reasonable to speculate that the difference arises from an interaction between social context and the process of identity formation in early adulthood. From an Eriksonian perspective, individuals in late adolescence are at the stage of "identity vs. role confusion," caught between the "morality learned by the child and the ethics to be developed by the adult" (Erikson, 1963, pp. 262-63). At this stage, the adolescent is particularly sensitive to social influences. Eager for affirmation by their peers, adolescents may be vulnerable to ideologies because they rely on social mores for identity formation.

During World War II, it may have been easier for an adolescent soldier to construct a positive identity because he was likely to experienced a high degree of social cohesiveness. There was a great deal of popular support for the troops. Moreover, the men trained and went to war in the same groups, thereby having the opportunity to form and maintain social bonds. During the Vietnam War, however, it may have been difficult for an adolescent soldier to construct a positive identity. There was much opposition to the war in the United States, and soldiers did not stay with the same groups but rather rotated in and out of platoons on an individual basis. Thus, young soldiers in the Vietnam era may not have been provided with the type of social support needed to positively integrate the meaning of their soldiering activities into the personal identity. Older soldiers presumably had resolved issues related to identity and role confusion. Furthermore, with their more extensive life experience, they may have been in a better position to withstand the negative feedback about their actions from the broader social context despite the absence of consistent support from the same peer group. Obviously, this is a highly speculative line of reasoning, but it illustrates the types of issues that should be considered when trying to understand how military service influences adult development.

Conclusions

Military service has long-term positive and negative effects on adult development, and these effects depend on preexisting individual characteristics and on the dimensions of the military service. Serving in the military appears to accelerate psychological maturation but delays higher education and the transition to work, marriage, and parenthood. By mid-life, veterans typically have caught up to or surpassed their civilian counterparts, although women tend to remain unmarried. Upward mobility is most evident in minority groups. Far-reaching psychological and social consequences are limited primarily to those who had extensive combat experience or who encountered war-related atrocities. Less is known about the effects of military service in late life. More longitudinal research is needed, both to determine the similarities and differences between younger and older cohorts and to examine how these effects unfold over the lifespan.

▼ Paula P. Schnurr and Carolyn M. Aldwin

See also: Career Age; Cohort and Generational Effects; Friendships through the Adult Years; Gender Differences in the Workplace; Happiness, Cohort Measures of; Listening; Loneliness; Longevity; Marital Development; Mental Health in the Adult Years; Stress; Work Organization Membership and Behavior.

References

Aldwin, C. A., & Stokols, D. (1988). The effects of environmental change on individuals and groups: Some neglected issues in stress research. *Journal of Environmental Psychology, 8:* 67-75.

Blake, D. D., et al. (1990). Prevalence of PTSD symptoms in combat veterans seeking medical treatment. *Journal of Traumatic Stress, 3:* 15-27.

Boyle, C. A., Decouflé, P., & O'Brien, T. R. (1989). Long-term health consequences of military service in Vietnam. *Epidemiologic Reviews, 11:* 1-27.

Breslau, N., & Davis, G. C. (1987). Posttraumatic stress disorder: The etiology of specific wartime stressors. *American Journal of Psychiatry, 144:* 578-83.

Card, J. J. (1983). *Lives After Vietnam: The Personal Impact of Military Service.* Lexington, MA: Lexington Books.

Centers for Disease Control. (1987). Postservice mortality among Vietnam veterans. *Journal of the American Medical Association, 259:* 790-95.

————. (1988a). Health status of Vietnam veterans: II. Physical health. *Journal of the American Medical Association, 259:* 2708-14.

————. (1988b). Health status of Vietnam veterans: III. Reproductive outcomes and child health. *Journal of the American Medical Association, 259:* 2715-19.

Department of Veterans Affairs. (1989). *1987 Survey of Veterans.* Washington, DC: Department of Veterans Affairs.

Elder, G. H., Jr. (1986). Military times and turning points in men's lives. *Developmental Psychology, 22:* 233-45.

————. (1987). War mobilization and the life course: A cohort of World War II veterans. *Sociological Forum, 2:* 449-71.

Elder, G. H., Jr., & Clipp, E. C. (1988). Wartime losses and social bonding: Influences across 40 years in men's lives. *Psychiatry, 51:* 177-198.

————. (1989). Combat experience and emotional health: Impairment and resilience in later life. *Journal of Personality, 57:* 311-41.

Erikson, E. H. (1963). *Self and Society.* Second Edition. New York: Norton.

Keehn, R. J. (1980). Follow-up studies of World War II and Korean conflict prisoners. *American Journal of Epidemiology, 111:* 194-211.

Kulka, R. A., et al. (1990). *Trauma and the Vietnam War Generation.* New York: Bruner/Mazel.

Martindale, M., & Poston, D. L. (1979). Variations in veteran/nonveteran earnings patterns among World War II, Korea, and Vietnam War cohorts. *Armed Forces and Society, 5:* 219-43.

Norquist, G. S., et al. (1990). Psychiatric disorder in male veterans and nonveterans. *Journal of Nervous and Mental Disease, 178:* 328-55.

Rosenheck, R., & Fontana, A. (In press). Long-term sequelae of combat in World War II, Korea, and Vietnam: A comparative study. In R. Ursano, B. McCaughy, & C. Fullerton (Eds.), *Individual and Community Responses to Trauma and Disaster.* New York: Oxford University Press.

Seltzer, C., & Jablon, S. (1974). Effects of selection on mortality. *American Journal of Epidemiology, 100:* 367-72.

Werner, E. (In press). *Against the Odds.* Ithaca, NY: Cornell University Press.

N

NARCISSISM

Narcissism is an exaggerated self-love and sense of self-importance. The concept of narcissism derives from the Greek myth of Narcissus, who rejected the maiden Echo. As a punishment, the god Nemesis made him fall in love with his reflection in the water, and eventually he languished of self-admiration. Havelock Ellis first gave psychological significance to the term in 1898. Another early contribution was Sigmund Freud's work from 1914. More recent contributions include Heinz Kohut (1971) and Otto Kernberg (1975). These writers represent the psychoanalytic tradition. In the literature of psychoanalysis, "narcissistic" may refer to a sexual perversion, a developmental phase (Freud distinguished between the stages primary narcissism, in which the infant's pleasure drive is turned toward its own body, and secondary narcissism, which develops out of the desire of the child to identify with the parents), a mode of object choice (narcissistic object-choice is based on identification with an object similar to the subject), self-esteem, or a personality type (which can be either normal or pathological, and, if pathological, either neurotic, psychotic, or borderline). Narcissistic disorder has also been discussed from a number of other theoretical frameworks, such as social-learning theory. Because the concept of narcissism is used in so many different ways, its popularity carries the risk of confusion. This article focuses on the influences and circumstances that lead to narcissism as a salient characteristic of adult personality.

Early Development of Narcissism

All stages of human development have narcissistic components. Normal development is characterized by a growth from childhood love of self to adult love for others. In contrast, the narcissistic person retains an extreme self-absorption. A narcissistic person possesses a grandiose sense of self-importance. Narcissistic individuals have a great need for approval and admiration, but show little empathy for the feelings of others. Charming and engaging manners are merely a surface. Narcissistic people are ruthless and cold to people from whom they expect nothing, but may idealize people they believe they can use to their own advantage. Their relationships with other people are exploitative and possessive.

Most discussion of the development of narcissism has focused on the individual. However, structural and group level factors, such as social institutions, role expectations, and social networks, must also be examined. Structural factors may explain the possible increase in narcissistic difficulties in our time. If the observation that narcissism has become more prevalent holds true, then the explanation for this must be found on a societal level unless we engage in far-fetched speculation about a sudden increase in birth rate among narcissists.

Many scholars agree that narcissistic difficulties appear in the family setting during the early years. A basic question is whether one or both parents need to have narcissistic difficulties in order to transmit this characteristic to their child. The early transmission of narcissistic tendencies is most commonly illustrated by a narcissistic mother interacting with her child; in a wider perspective, this explanation of narcissism seems too simplified and static. The narrowness of the view that influence is strictly person-to-person is shown by using a longer time perspective. Explaining the continuation of narcissism over the generations with the person-to-person view would constitute a variation on the theology of original sin.

Love Withdrawal and Other Parental Control Mechanisms

In his seminal article, "The Middle-Class Child and Neurosis," Green (1946) does not explicitly mention the term narcissism, but the implications of what he calls "the most characteristic neurosis of modern society," do fall under the manifestations of narcissism. Green identifies three elements in childrearing that are responsible for this deficiency: (1) love withdrawal; (2) personality absorption; and (3) a conflict between initial adjustment through submission and later assumptions of goal achievement.

The threat of *love withdrawal* is one of the mechanisms used for the "soft" control of the child. Nonconforming behavior is punished by real or threatened abandonment, which causes feelings of guilt in the child. When the child conforms, the process of building a *pseudo ego* (or false self) is begun. The child is unable to express anger or disappointment because of the threat of love withdrawal. The child represses his or her anger, and so will be unaware of his or her real needs, and will also lack self-consciousness.

Narcissistic children are often described by their parents as "nice" or "good-natured" and unaggressive. Anger threatens the emotional equilibrium of the family and is therefore suppressed to maintain an illusion of normalcy and warmth. The price paid by offspring, however, is difficulty in initiating

or maintaining satisfying relationships outside the family system. A "family myth," meaning a series of beliefs shared by all family members, is fostered. The myth usually emphasizes "the theme of happiness" that aims at maintaining the status quo. The child's impression of a family of warmth and without aggressions generally remains unaffected by later experiences.

The influence from the primary caregiver is described as an *absorption of the personality* of the child, when the child is used to justify the parent's existence and serves as a substitute for the parent's own ego-ideal, (which is the self's notion of how he or she wishes to be). Such children have difficulties in developing a clear sense of self because they remain mere extensions of their parents.

The child whose personality has been absorbed is expected to accomplish, to "do things." But the earliest social condition in which children find themselves is dependence or submission, which is not an effective preparation for achievement. Thus, *conflict arises between initial submission and later expectations for achievement.* The accomplishments therefore are likely to take place in fantasy. Any striving or pressure to compete is painful and exaggerates anxiety, guilt, and feelings of inadequacy because it violates the initial submissive adjustment. On the other hand, not attempting an effort to achieve leads to an equal amount of guilt: a double-bind situation.

These three processes—love withdrawal, absorption of personality, and the conflict between submission and achievement—illustrate behavior that can be intensified by life within a secluded family, and in particular if the family is projected as "warm" in combination with secluded. In this context, "warmth" can be interpreted as inhibited aggressions. Parental intrusion may cause the child difficulties in becoming differentiated from one or both parents and in developing a self-identity as an independent autonomous person. The child also develops an exaggerated sense of importance that may lead to difficulties in forming healthy bonds with others in adult life. The overall long-range consequence can be a narcissistic personality trait that may include prominent feelings of loneliness.

Societal Influences

A fundamental question is how seclusion is conceptually connected to narcissistic difficulties. In line with the idea that structural factors and family setting are of importance for the development of narcissistic difficulties, there is reason to separate different forms of withdrawal. Slater (1963) identifies three principal forms of withdrawal.

1. Withdrawal of interest and energy from larger aggregates to within the confines of the nuclear family (*family withdrawal*)
2. Withdrawal of interest and energy from larger aggregates to a single intimate dyad (*dyadic withdrawal*)
3. Withdrawal of interest and energy from all objects to the self (*narcissistic withdrawal*)

Kernberg (1975) holds that a child may not attain object love (love of an object that is recognized as a person other than oneself) because of cold and rejecting parents, and Kohut (1971) suggests that a child may not be able to idealize the parents because of indifference or rejection. In either case, the result is said to be pathological narcissism.

An opposite model is based on the above distinction of different forms of withdrawal. Andersson (1990) claims that it is the *intrusive* parent who injects narcissism into the child. According to this two-step model, situations of *family withdrawal* foster narcissistic difficulties in the child, while *narcissistic withdrawal* fosters anxiety.

In the first step, certain societal conditions are suggested as influences on the family structure and sex roles. The family structure affects the interaction within the family, which in turn exerts an influence on the socialization of the child. In the case of familial withdrawal, the family is seen as an island of security in a turbulent, frightening, or unfamiliar environment. Such a secluded lifestyle may predispose the parent to a narcis-

sistic intrusion, lavishing "choking watchfulness" on the child. The parent's vigilance initiates a striving to secure a self of one's own—separation. In the case of familial withdrawal, however, the chances for a successful separation are minimal.

In the second step, the child of the first step has now become an adult and taken on the role of parent. He or she has become the parent described by Kernberg as cold, hostile, and rejecting, with moments of superficial devotion and interest. During the attachment period (a process that occurs between the infant and the parents, in particular the mother, and is significant in the formation of affectionate ties), the child in step two has difficulties in developing a clear sense of self for reasons that are opposite those present in the first-step situation. The child *fears* a separation. This developmental picture shows itself as anxiety, insecurity, and low self-worth.

Narcissism in the Middle and Late Adult Years

In mid-life, the narcissistic sense of self-importance can be maintained by the perceived adoration of others or by fantasies about future accomplishments. The most severe challenge for the person with narcissistic difficulties often comes in old age. The elderly person suffers a number of personal losses, such as loss of paid employment and occupational status, sexual attractiveness and interests, economic restrictions, former roles, health, and, finally, the approaching prospect of losing life. Losses also occur at younger ages, of course. However, the capacity for restitution is greater in mid-life than in advanced old age, and it is also possible to envision various new plans.

To the elderly person, the losses produce a *narcissistic hurt* that can result in a number of reactions. Of central concern is how the losses affect the individual's self-esteem and self-image. As an effect of the losses, the gratification received from perceived mastery and power declines as when, for example, social relationships connected with the individual's positions are lost. Earlier, these social contacts compensated for inner emptiness or emotional isolation.

The reactions to loss may include feelings of heightened anxiety, anger, and rage. The narcissistic trauma may also manifest itself in depression, hypochondriasis, paranoid tendencies, abuse of drugs and alcohol, and retreat into fantasy. In mid-life, the fantasies generally are directed toward the future. By contrast, the fantasies of the elderly person with narcissistic difficulties are directed toward the past and its real or imagined accomplishments.

In summary, it is important to look for factors extraneous to the individual or person-to-person perspective, to explain the transmission as well as the possible variation of narcissistic disorder. In that vein, in addition to more traditional explanations, a model is emphasized that is based on the division into three forms of withdrawal. According to this model, family withdrawal with its attribute, a secluded and "warm" family, is a major risk factor for the transmission of narcissistic disorder.

Old age is also a risky period for a person with narcissistic disorder in that losses and the futility of fantasizing about future accomplishments lead to a narcissistic hurt.

▼ LARS ANDERSSON

See also: Attachment Across the Lifespan; Depression; Loneliness; Mastery Types, Development, and Aging; Mental Health in the Adult Years; Parental Imperative.

References

Andersson, L. (1990). Narcissism and loneliness. *International Journal of Aging and Human Development*, 30: 81-94.

Ellis, H. (1898/1927). The conception of narcissism. *Psychoanalytical Review*, 14: 129-53.

Freud, S. (1914/1957). *On Narcissism, an Introduction.* Standard Edition, Volume 14. London: Hogarth, pp. 73-102.

Green, A. (1946). The middle-class child and neurosis. *American Sociological Review*, 11: 31-41.

Kernberg, O. (1975). *Borderline Conditions and Pathological Narcissism.* New York: Jason Aronson.

Kohut, H. (1971). *The Analysis of the Self.* New York: International University Press.

Slater, P. (1963). On social regression. *American Sociological Review*, 28: 339-58.

NATIVE AMERICAN PERSPECTIVES ON THE LIFESPAN

Native American perspectives on the lifespan can be approached in two ways. The sociocultural approach views the Native American Indian adult population as being distinct racially, ethnically, and historically from the dominant population. These differences are studied in an attempt to understand their origins and to adapt public policies and social services to the particular needs of this group.

The ethnophilosophical approach looks at the truly native views held by this population group itself. This different approach to the Native American life cycle shows that it is part of an entire world view that considers everything—"material" or "immaterial"—to be interrelated. The ethnophilosophical approach can be helpful in overcoming the existing compartmentalized and segmented system of policies, regulations, and services that are alien to the more integrated worldview held by Native Americans themselves.

This article begins with the ethnophilosophical approach and then considers the sociocultural perspective.

Spiritual Realities and the Lifespan

Spirituality is at the heart of traditional Native American life. One of the least known facts about the many native peoples who populated the American continent is that their entire lives were based on reverence to a system of spiritual realities (Deloria, 1973). Not all tribes, bands, or clans had the same beliefs, yet most adhered to a view that placed humans as equals among all creation—the air and minerals as well as the plants and animals. Within this worldview, humans were not considered central to existence. Native American conceptions of the lifespan did not emphasize human experience. The right to a "good life" did not place all of creation under human dominance—rather, it placed human beings in a position of responsibility and interdependence. This belief in interdependence influenced the relationships among the various passages of an individual's life.

For the traditional Native American, everything comes full circle, as do the sun and moon each day and night. Death is not seen as the end of life but as an event that makes possible the completion of the circle of life. Four phases of life comprise the complete circle: infancy, adolescence, adulthood, and old age. Each phase is complete in itself and each merits respect and reverence, just as each season of the year is complete and merits respect. The seasons have no clear beginning or end, and it is difficult to say which comes first, winter or spring. Likewise, there is no clear beginning of life phases, and each has its own gifts to benefit the others.

Some trace this perspective to Mayan philosophies, which greatly influenced native cultures throughout the Americas well over 1,000 years ago (Peterson, 1990). The Mayan concept of time is circular, implying that one always returns to a familiar place in the movement around a circle. This is in contrast to a linear view of time in which one always moves to a new place. Nothing in life is truly new. All experience is a repetition. This cyclical repetition brings comfort, and all the phases of life reflect a circular nature. Each phase is anticipated as part of a never-ending cycle, rather than as an indicator that youth is a limited resource that is followed by a wasting away.

To the Native American, one is always young in spirit, but one can always demonstrate wisdom also. The hierarchical systems of respect for elders do not mean that children are less respected. On the contrary, children are acknowledged as having much wisdom to teach through their actions. They are considered much closer to the spirit than are most sophisticated and socialized adults. During the first year of life there was always an awareness of the chance that the infant might "return home" (Powers, 1986, p. 53).

Rituals and Transitions

As with seasons, entrances and exits from one phase of life to another are traditionally marked with ceremony and ritual. These rituals serve as definitional rites that indicate to everyone what behaviors are subsequently appropriate and expected in traditional life. For instance, a solstice celebration would mark the beginning of seasonally appropriate preparation behaviors. Other rituals such as a naming ceremony, a puberty rite, or a young man's first vision quest would mark for everyone the phase of life within which one was walking (Walker, 1980). Each person was expected to participate in many significant rituals and ceremonies with other members of the community as all moved through the phases of life.

Most tribes no longer practice all of the traditional rituals. Many rituals, however, are still incorporated into the spiritual lives of modern-day Native Americans. An example is the Apache puberty rite through which girls become women. These rites are elaborate and grueling, but through them, the girl is united to the earth and to her people as a woman. The entire community shares spiritually in her new phase of life (Beck, Walters, & Francisco, 1990). The young woman is given the opportunity to let herself be known and accepted as a woman within her entire community. Among the Lakota, adolescence signaled the new communication rules that were to be followed. Because women and men did not speak to one another directly, adolescents spoke to their peers only through younger siblings, who were not bound by the same restrictions (Powers, 1986).

Each tribe, band, or clan had its own traditions and methods for indicating phases of life. Some were radically different, others shared many common elements. Although the basic overarching system of beliefs was similar, it should not be mistakenly concluded that members of the various Indian nations all practiced some common "religion" (Deloria, 1973). Everyday beliefs varied, with gods and spirits represented in many ways. One of the common elements was the belief in "the people," or "human beings," who walked with two legs unlike their four-legged, crawling, swimming, and flying brothers and sisters. The phases in a human being's life were part of a grand spiritual scheme. It was not uncommon for this conception to be accompanied by a belief in reincarnation, through which the spirit can approach perfection (Ross, 1989). Such a view makes it possible for infancy and old age to be seen equivalently, as distinguished from the assumption that life terminates with the death of the aged human body.

One tradition that highlights the acknowledgment of the new spirit in body is the Plains ceremony in which a newborn infant's umbilical cord is placed in a turtle-shaped leather pouch that is decorated with bead or quill work. The buried pouch is then a protection for the newborn child, whose spirit is still newly on earth. The turtle is often the symbol for the earth, with the Americas referred to as Turtle Island. The symbolism of this practice unites the earth with the flesh of a newborn. Again, interconnectedness is highlighted, as it also is when a deceased person is placed high on a butte or in an elevated canoe for the winds to come and take the spirit to the grandfathers. From the beginning of the earthly walk to the end, the spirit is connected to the elements. All phases are equally sacred.

When the phases of life are viewed equivalently, the concerns of each also become equivalent (Four Worlds Development Project, 1989). The extended, transgenerational family is taken for granted in native cultures, although adaptations have been made to modern nuclear family life-styles. It is important to understand, however, that a family is not defined as extended solely on the basis of cohabitation. The extended family, or *tiyospaye* in Lakota, is a perspective for human relations, not a demographic label. The idea of *tiyospaye* makes it always possible

and acceptable for transgenerational cohabitation to be seen as normal but not required. This is an extremely important consideration when dealing with issues of placement during various life phases. The extended family is a collection of people who are in equivalent, yet different, phases of life. In a society that views the different phases of life as distinct, it becomes easy to see how prevailing policies and services can contribute to the fragmenting of the traditional Native American community.

From the Sociocultural Perspective

The sociocultural approach to the Native American lifespan requires us to look first at history. It is well documented that hundreds of bands, clans, and tribes were forcibly displaced. This upheaval required the Indian peoples to abandon and radically alter much of their routine life-styles (Gonzalez-Santin & Lewis, 1989). These changes in life-style were so abrupt that some now believe that genetically evolved aspects of Native American physiology were unable to adapt to the sudden changes in diet and mobility. Many of the health problems that plague adult Native Americans—such as high blood pressure, obesity, diabetes, and lactose intolerance—can be tied to genetic predispositions. It thus becomes important for health professionals working with Native American adult populations to be familiar with relevant new research. For instance, the return to a traditional native diet seems to be successful in overcoming diabetes. This insight into problems that are common during later life phases in Native Americans might also be helpful in working with other adult populations.

Other common problems among Native American adults are alcoholism and drug abuse. Theories of adult development lead to the conclusion that the special concerns and issues that arise at certain points in the lifespan might predispose one to attempt to cope through substance abuse. The substance abuse patterns in the dominant society seem to support this explanation. The motivating factors for drinking binges among Native Americans might also be seen as paralleling similar phenomena in the general U.S. population. However, there are confounding factors. Alcohol and drug abuse were not traditional characteristics of Native American adults; rather, they were historically induced (Gonzalez-Santin & Lewis, 1989).

The disruption caused by removing Native American children from their families and forcing them to attend boarding schools— often intensified by forced religious conversion—resulted in whole generations of Indian people who were lacking in skills for developing healthy, trusting interpersonal relationships. Parenting skills were not learned, and the severe physical abuse suffered at the boarding schools provided dangerous models for discipline. Depression and poor self-images resulting from this situation created fertile ground for substance abuse in a people who were genetically incapable of tolerating alcohol.

Although not all Native Americans suffered the boarding school experience directly, the return of those who did to their communities allowed for the spread of the psychological damages incurred. One salient aspect of this historical reality has been the loss of significant roles for the Native American adult male, who, with the forced confinement on reservations, still struggles to find roles that allow him a viable place in his community. The resulting problems in identity and self-esteem contribute to a distortion of the traditional respect for all phases of life experience. Many problems in family life and marital relationships are linked to this damaging historical process.

Developing and Healing

Unfortunately, these psychoemotional problems are now often viewed as though characteristic of adult Native Americans, whereas they are actually the outcome of a massive disturbance of the traditional lifestyle. It is necessary to plan and deliver intervention and therapeutic services that ad-

dress the healing of the appropriate wounds. Fortunately, within the modern Native American community itself there is an awareness that generational healing needs to be incorporated into their spiritual and wellness agenda from infancy through old age.

Those working with Native American populations face the challenge of developing health and healing programs that recognize the actual origins and causes of malaise. Currently, there are the beginnings of new healing traditions for modern Native Americans, who must learn to accept their history as part of what has contributed to the present condition. The American Indian Institute of Norman, Oklahoma, hosts annual nationwide conferences to unite Native Americans with workers in the areas of mental health and child abuse prevention and intervention. Organizations such as the National Association for Native American Children of Alcoholics have been created to deal with the culturally specific nature of the many healing issues among Native American peoples.

A Native American view of the life span that addresses these sociocultural concerns recommends treating today's adults as part of an historical reality that has been passed down through generations. One aspect of this historical reality has been the loss of significant roles for the Native American adult male caused by the forced confinement on reservations. The Native American population struggles to maintain a dynamic culture in the present. This effort requires awareness both of the traumatic past and of modern influences. The circular views of life phases and the accompanying rituals and traditions are the cultural ideals for many members of this population. No developmental stage ever leaves behind the influences or needs of a prior stage. Likewise, the experiences of modern Native American adults are traditionally linked to historical experience. Perhaps in acquiring the wisdom to accept and value the past while moving resourcefully into the challenges of the future, Native Americans may offer a model of transgenerational understanding that is of value to all people everywhere.

▼ M. Christina Gonzalez

See also: Alcohol Use and Abuse; Attachment Across the Lifespan; Depression; Development and Aging in Historical Perspective; Drug Use and Abuse; Interethnic Relationships; Mastery Types, Development, and Aging; Parental Imperative; Religion and Coping with Crisis; Religion in Adult Life; Risk to Life through the Adult Years; Spiritual Development and Wisdom: A Vedantic Perspective.

References

Beck, P. V., Walters, A. L., & Francisco, N. (1990). *The Sacred.* Tsaile, AZ: Navajo Community College Press.

Deloria, V., Jr. (1973). *God Is Red.* New York: Anchor.

Four Worlds Development Project. (1989). *The Sacred Tree.* Lethbridge, Alberta, Canada: University of Lethbridge.

Gonzalez-Santin, E., & Lewis, A. (1989). *Collaboration: The Key. Defining Entry Level Competencies for Public Child Welfare Workers Serving Indian Communities.* Tempe, AZ: Arizona State University.

Hall, E. T. (1983). *The Dance of Life.* New York: Anchor.

Mails, T. E. (1988) *Secret Native American Pathways.* Tulsa, OK: Council Oaks Books.

McGaa, E. Eagle Man. (Ed.). (1990). *Mother Earth Spirituality.* New York: Harper & Row.

Peterson, S. (1990). *Native American Prophecies.* New York: Paragon.

Powers, M. N. (1986). *Oglala Women: Myth, Ritual, and Reality.* Chicago: University of Chicago Press.

Ross, A. C. (1989). *Mitakuye Oyasin.* Kyle, SD: Bear.

Walker, J. R. (1980). *Lakota Belief and Ritual.* Lincoln, NE: University of Nebraska Press.

P

PARENTAL IMPERATIVE

The psychoanalyst Erik Erikson once remarked to the author that human development across the lifespan is driven by a central and unique characteristic of our species: the protracted helplessness and vulnerability of the human child. For the most part, however, psychologists do not apply this insight to the study of human development across the lifespan. Instead they limit this consideration to the domain of childhood. Thus, while psychologists have given great attention to the sequences of human development under the condition of *being* parented, they have paid relatively slight attention to the impressive maturation that takes place in adult life as a consequence of being *parental*. By concentrating so much of their attention on children, researchers have largely ignored the major role that parenthood plays in fostering psychological development in adulthood and even in later life.

The Special Burden of the Human Parent

Given the child-centered bias of developmental theorists, the author was made aware of the adult parental imperative not by psychologists but by personal experience and by contact with older male respondents in the course of fieldwork among the Mexican Maya, the Middle-Eastern Druze, and the Navajo. The core message from these middle-aged and older respondents was that marriage and particularly parenthood had ended for them the fun and games of young manhood. Furthermore, these former pleasures were largely unregretted. Now these more mature men drew pleasure from their children's happiness: "I am content when there is peace in the home, my family is healthy, and there is peace in the village" was a typical statement from a Druze informant, and similar thoughts were voiced by middle-aged and elderly males in the other groups as well.

The parental imperative thesis that grew out of this fieldwork holds that this blunt, inescapable feature of our species sets the requirements of human development not only in the early years but in the adult and later years as well. This centrality of parenting in human affairs (and in primate affairs, generally) is based on a paradox. It is an inescapable consequence of cognitive liberation, of the relative human freedom from the tyranny of "old learning" and inflexible, wired-in instincts. By contrast with all nonprimate species, humans are born with very few instinctually guaranteed and reliable skills. Although smooth operation of the inner or physiological apparatus is ensured by wired-in features, the individual's relations with the outer physical and social worlds must all be laboriously, even painfully organized through new learning.

Thus, the human neonate is blind, the nervous system is not morphologically mature, and save for the inborn capacity to orient toward and suck the mother's breast, the infant lacks a repertoire of formed, reliable behaviors. Instead, the infant has a large reserve of unformed cognitive, behavioral, and social potentials, each of which requires special tending and shaping if it is to develop from the original, diffuse state to its matured outcome as an executive capacity of the individual mind or body. In the human case, innate biological clocks account chiefly for the surgent phase of development—for the arousal on schedule of the still unformed potentials. Devoted social nurturing is required at every critical point by parents, teachers, and other caregivers, however, if the maturing process is to move ahead for any given executive capacity.

In effect, the human species has traded the advantages of an old, "pre-wired" brain for the *tabula rasa* of the neocortex. The result is a learning explosion that advances each generation over the preceding one and that has, in a few millennia, made humans the masters of this planet and its near-space environs. If the species is to reap the evolutionary advantage of this marvelous human cortex, though, the parent's already matured functions must keep the vulnerable offspring alive and well until its own formed skills develop. The capable parent is thus a crucial link in the embellishment of new learning for the species.

Gender Roles and the Parental Imperative

The human species' freedom from the restrictions of old learning commits the young to a long childhood and the human adult to a long period of parental servitude. Mothers and fathers must meet children's needs for physical and emotional security until their offspring are ready to supply these requirements for themselves—and, ultimately, for their own children in turn. However, the child's basic and irreducible need for physical and emotional security cannot be met by the same provider. Physical safety from predators and human enemies can only be fought for and won on the perimeter of the community. But the child's emotional security, the sense of *basic trust*, can only be nurtured by a provider who stays close to home, within hail and reach of the child's cry. The evolutionary

process has had the effect of sorting these great parental responsibilities by gender. Men have been assigned the task of ensuring the child's physical security through their protective efforts at the periphery. Women have accepted the task of providing emotional security, the assurance of a reliable and soothing domestic presence.

This parenting arrangement is universal. It is based in biology and the irreducible needs of the child, rather than on the politics of patriarchy. Men are assigned the task of providing physical security not because they are superior to women, but because they represent a kind of "inflated currency." From the species perspective there is, generally speaking, an oversupply of males. One man can inseminate many females, but women, on the average, can gestate only one child every two years during their relatively brief period of fertility. Surplus males—usually those who are unmarried and pre-parental—can be assigned to the dangerous, high-casualty perimeter tasks that underwrite the community's physical security and even its survival. Thus, the more expendable male sex, armed with large muscles and the greater store of intrinsic aggression, is generally assigned to hunt large game; to open, maintain, and defend distant tillage; to guard against human and nonhuman predators; or to raid other communities for their wealth. By the same token, the female sex, on whom the population level ultimately depends, is less expendable. The sex whose body is designed to create life and whose emotional nature is designed to nurture life is generally assigned to more secure areas, there to supervise the formative experiences that sponsor emotional security in children.

Cultural rules must carry some of the burden of maintaining these distinct roles. The basic division of labor by gender, however, is an aspect not only of human but of general primate nature. The lower primates share with the human species the protracted period of childhood vulnerability. This distinguishing fact of primate life seems to have fostered an equivalent sexual division, among apes, of parenting roles. Thus, the ground-dwelling primate troop is protected by a defense force that is composed mainly of adult males. These guardians move out to the perimeter when predators approach and form a scouting line. When the troop is on the move, the adult males serve as a protective screen. The females look mainly to adult males to provide physical security for themselves and for the offspring who cling to their fur. The best fighters, the dominant males, have privileged sexual access to females. In effect, by the promise of sexual access, the females bribe the males into using their superior strength for defensive and parental purposes. In both humans and apes, adult life is circumscribed by the stringent requirements of primate motherhood and fatherhood.

Again, in human affairs, the natural propensities that distinguish the genders must be trained and refined through social influence in order to meet the prevailing cultural standards. In a pioneering study, Barry, Bacon, and Child (1957) abstracted ethnographic data concerning early socialization from 110 marginal sustenance groups. It was found that these communities routinely prepare young males, through play and initiation rites, for life in the lands beyond the perimeter, in a world they never made. Whether as trader, hunter, soldier, rebel, itinerant merchant, or laborer, the candidate moves from the inward, central location of his mother's world to the outward perimeter of his father's world. This transitional process often requires a stressful and painful set of ritualistic experiences.

Similarly, the girls are pressed to cultivate the qualities that will fit them for their roles as providers of physical and emotional nurture within the heart of the family and the community. Across cultures, the central themes in female socialization are nurturance, responsibility, and, to a lesser degree, obedience. Women can be aggressive. Men can be nurturing. However, each sex is called upon by its culture to develop those qualities that are most needed to meet the rigorous demands of the parental imperative.

Although the sex-role training begins early in life, its consequences are not fully evident until the actual onset of parenthood. The coming of the first child often brings a sense of shock, which the author has called the "chronic sense of parental emergency" (Gutmann, 1987). In response, each sex mobilizes the gender-specific parental qualities that have already been biologically ordained, developmentally scheduled, and culturally patterned.

Prior to parenthood, and despite their earlier sex-role training, in most societies young men and women are allowed to play out a wide range of psychological potentials with some degree of freedom. Conserving their narcissism for themselves, they can be *omnipotential*. They can indulge the masculine and feminine sides of their nature without having to make a final choice between them. However, this developmental holiday usually comes to an end as the individual confronts the chronic emergency of parenthood. In the service of their parental role, men put the tender side of their nature on hold. This aspect, desirable in itself, could interfere with their basic parental assignment. From this point on, the men will experience the tender side of their nature vicariously, through their wives.

Women at this time will turn away from their own aggression—the anger that could frighten their vulnerable children and possibly even drive away the provident husband. Denying herself the full measure of her potential aggression, as the man has his tenderness, the wife lives this side of her being vicariously, through her spouse. Each parent concedes to the other those characteristics that would interfere with their particular parental duty. In effect, both parents accomplish one of the great psychological transformations of the entire life cycle: They relinquish much of their own narcissism and concede it to the child. Now it is the child rather than the parent who—in the parent's own eyes—becomes a creature of infinite promise, a unique being who will never die.

Incidentally, this parent-centered view of human development places the trait of narcissism in a more positive light. Narcissism is not only designed to provide emergency rations of self-love; it is also designed by human evolution to protect the vulnerable but endlessly demanding child from his or her own parents. If parents did not concede their narcissism to the child, if they did not idealize their continuously needy child, then parental sacrifice would have no meaning—and the child would be at risk from its own progenitors.

Gender Roles in the Post-Parental Period

As time passes, the once-helpless children begin to demonstrate that they can provide for their own physical and emotional security, and that they can survive on their own. They develop a marketable labor capacity. They find lovers. Through adolescent rebellion they demonstrate that they are not the bearers of their parents' unsurrendered dreams. Emerging from their long period of dependency and helplessness, they take over from the parents the executive functions that had been held in escrow for them.

With the concomitant phasing out of the parental emergency, fathers and mothers can relax: The child is safely launched and no longer needs to be protected by heavy endowments of parental narcissism. In the post-parental years, adults are liberated from the psychological tax that is levied on the human species in compensation for its freedom from the programmed rigidities of instinct. Having raised the next generation of viable and potentially procreant children, the parents have earned the right to again be all-including, omnipotent. This regained freedom is usually expressed in token or symbolic ways.

Post-parental men and women can reclaim the sexual bimodality that was hitherto repressed and parceled out between husband and wife. Because their bimodality will no longer interfere with proper parenting, senior men and women can reclaim for themselves those aspects of self that were once disowned inwardly, though lived out externally, vicariously through the spouse. As a consequence, a significant sex role turnover takes place for both men and women. For

example, older men begin to live out directly, to own as part of themselves the more passive, sentient, and tender potentials that they had earlier conceded to the wife.

The universality of this shift is confirmed by the author's cross-cultural data (Gutmann, 1987) and by a number of other clinicians and researchers in various societies (Atchley, 1976; Benedek, 1952; Brenneis, 1975; Brown, 1985; Feldman, Biringen, & Nash, 1981; Galler, 1977; Gold, 1969; Hurlbert, 1962; Jaslow, 1976; Jung, 1933; Leonard, 1967; Lewis, 1965; Lowenthal et al., 1975; Ripley, 1984; Shanan, 1985; Streib, 1968; Tachibana, 1962; Van Arsdale, 1981).

The opposite effect is seen in older women across a great many societies. As post-parental men become milder, women become more assertive. Instead of continuing to devote themselves to serving the emotional needs of others, post-parental women generally become more domineering, independent, unsentimental, and even self-centered. They begin to assert their own desires, particularly those toward social dominance. Just as men in late middle life reclaim title to their denied "femininity," so middle-aged women repossess the aggressive "masculinity" that they once experienced only vicariously through their husbands.

The consequence of this internal revolution, this shift in the politics of self, is that the sharp gender distinctions of the peak parental period break down, and each sex becomes to some degree what the other used to be. When men and women stand down from the condition of parental emergency, they reclaim the condition of relative androgeny that characterized the pre-parental years. Finally, as the parental emergency subsides, mothers and fathers can reclaim also the quotient of narcissism that had been transformed to the service of children and that had constituted the social binding force in the child-centered, child-tending family. As that social structure is partially dismantled, narcissism again becomes available to the post-parental self. Depending on the social circumstances under which it emerges, that fund of narcissism can become the basis of late-onset vulnerabilities, or it can be recruited to the formation of new, more extensive social bonds.

The prosocial derivatives of senior narcissism can tie the generations to each other, and—as managed by powerful elders—they can link and bond the community to its great traditions and to its gods.

▼ David Gutmann

See also: Adult Children and Their Parents; Age 40; Attachment Across the Lifespan; Cohort and Generational Effects; Gender as a Shaping Force in Adult Development and Aging; Habituation: A Key to Lifespan Development and Aging?; Loneliness; Marital Development; Mastery Types, Development, and Aging; Narcissism; Native American Perspectives on the Lifespan; Trust as a Challenge in Adult Development.

References

Atchley, R. (1976). Selected social and psychological differences between men and women in later life. *Journal of Gerontology, 31:* 204-11.

Barry, H., Bacon, M., & Child, I. (1957). A cross cultural survey of some sex differences in socialization. *Journal of Social and Abnormal Psychology, 55:* 327-432.

Benedek, T. (1952). *Psychosexual Functions in Women.* New York: Ronald Press.

Brenneis, C. B. (1975). Developmental aspects of aging in women. *Archives of General Psychiatry, 32:* 429-35.

Brown, J. (1985). *In Her Prime: A New View of Middle-Aged Women.* South Hadley, MA: Bergin & Garvey.

Feldman, S., Biringen, C., & Nash, S. (1981). Fluctuations of sexual-related self-attributions as a function of stage of family life cycle. *Developmental Psychology, 17:* 24-35.

Galler, S. (1977). *Women Graduate Student Returnees and Their Husbands: A Study of the Effects of the Professional and Academic Graduate School Experience on Sex Role Perceptions, Marital Relationships, and Family Concepts.* Doctoral dissertation, The School of Education, Northwestern University, Evanston, IL.

Gold, S. (1969). Cross-cultural comparisons of role change with aging. *Student Journal of Human Development* (University of Chicago), *1:* 11-15.

Gutmann, D. (1964). An exploration of ego configurations in middle and later life. In B. Neugarten (Ed.), *Personality and Later Life.* New York: Atherton.

———. (1987). *Reclaimed Powers: Towards a New Psychology of Men and Women in Later Life.* New York: Basic Books.

Hurlbert, J. (1962). *Age as a Factor in the Social Organization of the Hare Indians of Port Good Hope, Northwest Territories.* Ottawa, Ontario, Canada: Northern Coordination and Research Centre, Department of Northern Affairs and National Resources.

Jaslow, P. (1976). Employment, retirement and morale among older women. *Journal of Gerontology, 31:* 212-18.

Jung, C. G. (1933). *Modern Man in Search of a Soul.* New York: Harcourt, Brace, & World.

Leonard, O. (1967). The older Spanish-speaking people of the Southwest. In E. Youmans (Ed.), *The Older Rural Americans.* Lexington: University of Kentucky Press, pp. 239-61.

Lewis, O. (1965). *Life in a Mexican Village: Tepoztlan Restudied.* Urbana: University of Illinois Press.

Lowenthal, M. F. et al. (1975). *Four Stages of Life.* San Francisco: Jossey-Bass.

Ripley, D. (1984). *Parental Status, Sex Roles, and Gender Mastery Style in Working Class Fathers.* Chicago: Department of Psychology, Illinois Institute of Technology. Unpublished doctoral dissertation.

Shanan, J. (1985). Personality types and culture in late adulthood. In J. Meacham (Ed.), *Contributions to Human Development.* Basel: S. Karger, pp. 1-144.

Streib, G. (1968). Family patterns in retirement. In M. S. Sussman (Ed.), *Sourcebook in Marriage and the Family.* Boston: Houghton Mifflin, pp. 215-40.

Tachibana, K. (1962). A study of introversion-extraversion in the aged. In C. Tibbitts & W. Donahue (Eds.), *Social and Psychological Aspects of Aging: Aging Around the World.* New York: Columbia University Press, pp. 426-41.

Van Arsdale, P. W. (1981). The elderly Asmat of New Guinea. In P. T. Amoss & S. Harrell (Eds.), *Other Ways of Growing Old: Anthropological Perspectives.* Stanford: Stanford University Press, pp. 111-23.

PLACE AND PERSONALITY IN ADULT DEVELOPMENT

It is ironic that developmentalists know so little about person-place relations across adulthood. After all, individuals are place-located at each moment of their existence. By necessity, behavior always occurs in a specific physical context. Among the constants of life, like death and taxes, one might add "environmental surround."

Until recently, however, adult developmentalists have usually sought within-person causes of behavior change, giving less attention to environmental factors that influence the life course (Baltes, 1987). Environmental psychology has produced useful information about the influences of real-world contexts on behavior. To date, though, we have no systematic empirical account of person-place dialectics across the adult lifespan. However, a small group of behavioral ecologists is now building on earlier research (Barker, 1963; Proshansky, Ittelson, & Rivson, 1970) to create a body of thought and research on what might be called *a psychology of place*. These researchers are diverse in their backgrounds and worldviews. There are *subjectivists*, who view environments as solely (though not merely) perceptual representations; *objectivists*, who avoid reference to perceptual processes altogether; and *transactionalists*, who allow for interactions with the actual, real-world everyday environment as well as its derived meanings for individuals (Stokols & Shumaker, 1981).

Given this diversity, it is not surprising to find researchers employing differing methodologies and analytical strategies. In addition, much research in this area has been descriptive rather than explanatory, hypothesis-generating rather than hypothesis-confirming. This is typical of a new field of inquiry. Here a few contributions that have powerful implications for understanding the adult life course are briefly reviewed.

The Quality of Place

Place is not easily defined. The term possesses ineffable features that are not easily captured. "It is," as someone once remarked, "a quality without a name." Phenomenologists (subjectivists) frequently define place existentially as "a centre of action and intention" (Relph, 1976, p. 42) or "a focus where we experience the meaningful events of our existence" (Norberg-Schulz, 1971, p. 19).

Some employ Chinese puzzle box approaches: "Places occur at all levels of identity, my place, your place, street, community, towns, country, region, and continent, but places never conform to the tidy hierarchies of classification. They overlap and interpenetrate one another...and are wide open to a variety of interpretations" (Donat, 1967, p. 9).

Even dictionaries offer diverse and sometimes contradictory signifiers for place: space, physical surroundings, atmosphere, an indefinite region or expanse, a particular region or location (*Webster's Ninth New Collegiate Dictionary*, 1983, p. 897). Following the lead of Camus (1955), Relph (1976) defines three elements of place: the physical setting, the activities occurring in this setting, and their meanings (symbols). Many of the definitional approaches used by place theorists include these three elements. It is the inclusion of behavior (e.g., activities) and imbued psychological meanings that make place of particular interest to psychologists.

Theorists disagree, however, about how the physical and behavioral aspects of place are related. Is "self" (an aspect of one's personality or behavior) a subcomponent or co-component of an actual physical setting? Or is it more appropriate to view place as a psychological representation, a subcomponent of self?

For example, the pioneering theory of Roger Barker (1963) locates ongoing behavior and its programs within a physical milieu, producing a unit of analysis he calls the *behavior setting*. Individuals enact the unique behavioral programs of each particular setting as they enter. Settings exert a strong conforming influence on the people who function within them. On the other hand, some researchers view place as an entity that resides primarily in the head, consisting of "memories, ideas, feelings, attitudes, values, preferences, meanings" related to physical settings in the everyday world (Proshansky, Fabian, & Kaminoff, 1983, p. 59). In these contrasting views, place is partially defined through behavior and the self is partially defined through place.

Place Identity and Self-Identity

In the view of Proshansky, Fabian, and Kaminoff (1983), place identity is influenced by "a wide range of person/physical setting experiences" accrued from the moment of birth until death" (p. 62). Place identity is thereby conceived as an integral part of the developmental process. A similar view is espoused by Howell (1980, 1983):

> Built environments are integral to virtually all stimulus configurations that enter into social learning, personality, and cognitive development in modern humans. As such environmental experiences "resonate" in memory storage and relate themselves to this or that purpose or context...bits of psychoenvironmental history are utilized as hypothetical constructs in transactional measures with the current environment and serve to test "who am I" contextually. (Howell, 1980, p. 426)

In this view, places not only constitute the hiding places of the ego, but also play a crucial role in defining the self. Places afford one a sense of stability and continuity, providing an immediate template of experience against which new environments can be judged (Proshansky, Fabian, and Kaminoff, 1983). Places guide behavior across the adult life course through their normative social meanings and allow individuals to express personal tastes and preferences and, in varying degrees, to exercise a sense of environmental control.

It is useful to distinguish among degrees of psychological involvement in personal and place identity. Rubinstein (1989)

has contributed a useful continuum of psychological involvement in a study of the ways in which the lifespan is expressed in the home environment. Using ethnographic interviews, Rubinstein identified four types of involvement:

- *Accounting:* Individual awareness of environmental features
- *Personalization:* Limited attribution of personal meaning to these features
- *Extension:* Intense psychological involvement with the environment
- *Embodiment:* Subjective merging of self with the environmental feature

Through embodiment, "environmental features may be assigned the task of carrying the load of personal meaning and thereby aid in the maintenance of self when it is threatened. Enlisted as an ally, the environmental features can come to function as part prosthetic self" (Rubinstein, 1989, p. 50).

An example drawn from a study of older individuals who reside in a tiny "ghost town" located in the midwestern United States aptly illustrates extreme extension, and perhaps also embodiment (Scheidt & Norris-Baker, 1990). Reminiscing about the past "glory days" of the community, a 92-year-old man paused by the river that borders the community:

> I was born right down there by the river bridge. I was in the hardware business several years ago with my father-in-law. And we furnished the cement to build that (current) bridge, the dam, and the powerhouse and all of that. And I hired a man to help me haul. And we hauled cement day and night all the whole time while they worked. There's the old bridge across the river right there. I was born right there. And at that time, a man brought a bunch of cattle in from the East. He was going to divide the bunch. They stampeded and they all went down with the bridge into the river. They had a lot of loss. Anyway, I was a baby. They built the bridge back. And that's been tore out now, too. I've seen three bridges across that river in my time.

He also recalled riding across the bridge in a horse-drawn buggy as a boy, following immediately behind a wagon carrying his mother's coffin to the cemetery. For this man, the bridges denoted his birth site, his first memory, the death of his mother, and his contribution to the construction of the community. After 90 years, in both literal and remembered forms, the bridges continued to validate an important aspect of his environmental identity. For this man and other older people in this community, even the stark ruins and remnants of former places served psychological functions, such as stimulating and nurturing a review of the meaning of one's past life (Butler, 1963).

Many phenomenologically oriented place theorists believe it is futile to attempt to separate elements of place from persons. "An authentic 'sense of place,'" writes Relph (1976, p. 65) "is rather like the type of relationship characterized by Martin Buber as 'I-Thou,' in which the subject and object, person and place, divisions are wholly replaced by the relationship itself." Questions of "Who am I?" are answered in terms of "Where I am." Place and self are fused.

Place Attachment

Regardless of their theoretical dispositions, scholars acknowledge that through socialization and direct experience, we understand places in terms of both our individual and our shared meanings. These meanings may be evaluated and expressed in terms of degrees of *place attachment*. This concept has been described as "a system of interlocked attitudes and behaviors that...reflect the intimacy of the strength of one's times to a locale" (Shumaker & Taylor, 1983, p. 237). On balance, positive feelings produce attachment while negative feelings produce alienation, detachment, or placelessness. Place attachments may be healthful or pathological for different individuals. Transactionalists have developed a number of models to explain the formation of place attachment under varying conditions (see Stokols & Schumaker, 1981).

Older adults frequently display a history of lifelong attachments to significant places in their lives. It is not surprising, therefore, that theorists have given much attention to the significance of place attachment for this age group. No theorist has articulated this sense of attachment with greater clarity than Graham Rowles (1983). He holds that small towns, for example, exhibit a social, physical, and autobiographical *insidedness* that encourages place attachment.

One particularly interesting facet is *autobiographical insidedness*. This refers to the meanings that are attached to current and remembered places, meanings that can span space and time. "The same location may be remembered as a wooded lot where a person stole her first kiss, a grocery store built some time later where she worked for several years, and as an abandoned fire-gutted building in the present" (Rowles, 1983, p. 305). Rowles believes these attachments to be "self-created" fictions to some extent magnified and reconstructed in memory. Howell (1983) also describes the ways in which places are emotionally redefined through reminiscence, life reviews, and attempts at adaptive problem solving. These views reinforce those voiced by Sarbin (1983), who advocates that greater attention be paid to the process of *emplotment*—the ways in which individuals construct personal narratives containing "plots, dramatis personae, settings, goals, beginnings and endings, climaxes, and anticlimax," and "how a particular 'where am I' question is answered and then rendered into an ongoing story" (Sarbin, 1983, p. 340).

Place Loss

Attachment to place often remains out of awareness unless environmental change threatens to disrupt person-place relations. Place bonds are threatened by conditions such as disasters and accidents (e.g., earthquakes, fires) and international and civil disorders (e.g., wars, terrorism) that may alter or destroy the places themselves or the character of their surrounding environments. Other conditions may dislodge persons while leaving places intact. Examples of the latter include the redefining of place boundaries, health problems necessitating relocation, and frequent migration associated with occupation (e.g., corporate employees, military families, farm migrants) or circumstance (e.g., homelessness, famine).

Information regarding the possible effects of these conditions has been derived largely from broader studies of relocation stress. Often such studies do not distinguish between behavioral consequences that are specifically related to the loss of former places and those associated with the numerous readjustments necessitated by a new and possibly strange environment. These studies also tend to focus on immediate, short-term effects.

Some types of environmental stress may produce long-salutary effects for individuals under some circumstances (Aldwin & Stokols, 1988). There have even been suggestions that threats to physical setting actually may serve useful defense functions for one's sense of self (Proshansky, Fabian, & Kaminoff, 1983; Shalit, 1987). Often, however, environmental changes that threaten or sever emotional bonds with place will have harmful impacts on physical and mental health. This seems particularly true for individuals who are locked into place-specific activity patterns which produce high place dependency (Stokols & Shumaker, 1981). Loss of place through destruction or forced relocation may produce a grief syndrome characterized by depression and illness.

Two examples of forced relocations are illustrative. In a classic study, Fried (1972) conducted before-and-after interviews with 500 residents of Boston's West End who were forced to move because of urban renewal. In addition to suffering severe short-term grief reactions, almost half of the respondents reported feeling depressed up to one year after the move, and one-fourth were still depressed up to two years later. These reactions were attributed to the loss of friends and support networks that had become intrinsic aspects of their sense of social place. Such forced relocations may also affect one's ability to establish place bonds to the new environment. "Groups who are dislocated from their residential 'turf' because of urban programs or other governmental or social interventions often feel 'lost' in their new setting and long for the old home and neighborhood. Depending on the stage of the lifecycle that the person is at, and the discrepancy between the old and new locations, a sense of belongingness to the new neighborhood may never be achieved" (Proshansky, Fabian, & Kaminoff, 1983, p. 66).

Several meanings of place loss are illustrated by the forced removal of Israeli settlers from the northern Sinai in 1982 (Dasberg & Sheffler, 1987; Kliot, 1987). The Israelis established settlements in this region in the early 1970s after its capture in the Six-Day War with Egypt. Following the signing of the peace treaty between Israel and Egypt, Israel ceded all of the Sinai to Egypt, forcing the relocation of Israeli settlers in the region.

Many evacuees reported feelings of humiliation and rootlessness, and exhibited mental and physical distress (Kliot, 1987). A team of mental health professionals in one settlement reported several types of disorder that were believed to have resulted from both the anticipated and the actual stress of the move. These effects included obsessive neurosis, depressive moods, posttraumatic stress disorder, and psychosomatic complaints (Dasberg & Sheffler, 1987). It was also reported (Kliot, 1987) that the relocation stress was greater for settlers who had made psychological investments in several features of the environment. For these persons, the embodiment of self in the settlements included (a) ideological and cultural investments consistent with the principles of pioneering Zionism (e.g., views of settlements as security outposts, images of desert conquest); (b) alteration of the habitat (e.g., creation of greenery around the settlements); (c) attachment to the physical landscape, including the sand dunes, sea, and palms; and (d) the symbolic value of the settlements as monuments to those who died during the Holocaust.

The psychological consequences of place loss are most frequently and dramatically evidenced by the disruptions suffered by such displaced populations (Fischman, 1986). We know less, however, of the outcomes experienced by individuals whose life-styles or occupations require or involve frequent place disruption. Furthermore, at present it is impossible to draw meaningful comparisons among these subpopulations. Again, it is difficult to separate the specific consequences of place loss and place disruption from the numerous stressors that are associated with relocation in general.

Studies indicate that frequent moves may result in harmful outcomes for some individuals and families. The research findings on corporate families parallel those for military families (Gullota & Donohue, 1983). For example, Gaylord and Symons (1986) found that loss of friends and community contributed to lowered feelings of self-worth among a variety of corporate employees who relocated frequently. Specifically, some employees reported feelings of anger, loneliness, anxiety, depression, alcohol or drug abuse, and a variety of somatic disorders that seemed attributable to relocation stress. There is also evidence indicating that high mobility may lead to a sense of rootlessness among homeless children (Gwirtzman & Fodor, 1987), among children of migrants (Cole, 1970), and among adolescents (Allen, 1987).

Of course, the impacts of place loss or place disruption will vary across contexts, among individuals within the same context, and among individuals at different phases of the adult life course. Several factors in the individual as well as the environment may influence how these impacts are experienced:

- The scope and magnitude of change or disruption
- The rate of disruption (sudden vs. gradual)
- The degree to which the disruption or loss may be anticipated (predictable vs. unpredictable)
- The degree of psychological control that the individual exerts over the disruption and its consequences
- The strength of one's attachment to place

- The availability of alternative places to meet one's needs
- The contrast between the disrupted or lost place and the new or alternative place
- The efficacy of one's repertoire of personality resources and coping responses

Clearly, developmental considerations associated with life phase may also moderate the impacts of place loss upon adults. For example, the move of a 20-year-old college student from home to a university environment carries entirely different implications than the move of an older individual from his or her own home to a nursing home. Although there is disruption of place bonds in both cases, the symbolic meaning of each is quite different. The former implies increases in independence, while the latter implies just the opposite.

Generally, the harmful impacts of both place loss and relocation are eased when such moves are voluntary—when the mover is allowed to participate in the decision to relocate, is able to anticipate the move, is allowed to become familiarized with the new residence, and brings familiar and meaningful furnishings from the previous residence into the new place (Schulz & Ewen, 1988).

A different condition—*placelessness*—also threatens the existence of place bonds. Relph (1976) warns of the subtle, everyday dehumanizing effects of creeping placelessness. Some environments appear to be devoid of significant places or are constructed with an attitude that fails to acknowledge significance of place. He decries other-directedness, e.g., landscapes made for tourists, commercial strips, "Disneyfied" and "museumised" places. Alienating placelessness is also generated by uniformity and standardization in the design of an environment. The formlessness and lack of human scale found in some environments (e.g., the gigantism of skyscrapers) are other factors that make it difficult for people to achieve a sense of being in a personally meaningful place. Finally, placelessness is intensified by the impermanence and instability of many places as a result of continuous redevelopment or abandonment. "To live in an environment which has to be endured or ignored rather than enjoyed is to be diminished as a human being" (Gauldie, 1969, p. 182).

Hummon (1986) challenges speculation that increasing modernization has erased regional characteristics that contribute to sense of place.

> The modern individual—highly mobile, socially rootless, living in a gray landscape of sterile houses, mass-produced neighborhoods, Manhattanized cities, and disappearing regions—has supposedly become homeless, with little sense of the place in which he or she resides, little attachment to home, neighborhood, settlement, or region.... Recent research on various forms of place identity has done much to undermine this indictment." (p. 3)

In a rare study of this issue, Hummon (1986) discovered regional differences in community identity existing among a sample of Californians who lived variously in cities, suburban areas, small towns, and country locales. Eighty percent of these individuals expressed clear regional identities that were distinguished by varying sentiments, interests, values, and expressed knowledge. For example, urban dwellers cited sentimental ties to the city and a sense of shared values and interests as definers of their community identity. Small-town residents reflected an emphasis on community, domesticity, and tradition, while open-country residents presented an identity embodying nature and outdoor activities, openness, and friendliness of residents, along with a sense of rugged individualism.

Hummon found that community identity had relatively little significance to the suburbanists compared with the significance it held for urbanists, townspeople, or country people, though some suburbanists mentioned home and yard, family and children, and community activity as central to their sense of community. About 20 percent of the residents in all these locales exhibited no sense of community identity, instead indicating a sense of "symbolic placelessness." Among these, some viewed their own environments as being indistinguishable from others. The "adaptables," in contrast, distinguished them-

selves as "fitting anywhere," thereby minimizing the significance of where they live. The remainder were classified as "the divided," expressing a split sense of community. They had grown up in one type of community and then moved to another community type under some pressure or constraint.

As this study illustrates, community identity blends features of self, the physical environment, and, more prominently, the symbolic or idealized environment. Hummon holds that it is mobility, not community decline, that is largely responsible for engendering a sense of placelessness. Mobility creates an identity conflict (as opposed to identity erosion) within the "divided" and may be creating a new form of community identity among the "adaptables," one that is based on varied community experiences and skills (Hummon, 1986, p. 21).

With the exception of a few studies like this, we still know little of the diversity of regional place identities, and even less about the myriad ways in which environmental instability may affect the development of self-identity in adults. As Proshansky, Fabian, & Kaminoff (1983) pointed out, there is "an almost complete neglect of the role of places and spaces in this aspect of human psychological development" (p. 57).

Conclusion

Perhaps the most useful contribution of the growing psychology of place is the insertion of the physical context (and its mental representations) into the study of adulthood. To date, however, an important contextual element remains missing from most research—the context of age-related change. As indicated earlier, present theory and research lend more to our understanding of place in adult psychology than to the role of place in adult development. We need, but do not yet have, a lifespan environmental psychology. Though we have information about place meaning among some populations of older adults, we have almost no *comparative* knowledge of person-place interactions *across* phases of the adult lifespan, including young adulthood and middle age. Studies tracking these interactions within individuals over time might yield a greater understanding of the developmental, historical, and personal factors that underlie the orchestration of the "place ballet" (Seamon, 1989) of the adult life course. ▼ RICK J. SCHEIDT

See also: Contextualism; Friendships through the Adult Years; Happiness, Cohort Measures of; Housing as a Factor in Adult Life; Life Events; Loneliness; Memory; Mental Health in the Adult Years; Political Beliefs and Activities; Reminiscence and Life Review; Rural Living: What Influence on Adult Development?.

References

Aldwin, C., & Stokols, D. (1988). The effects of environmental change on individuals and groups: Some neglected issues in stress research. *Journal of Environmental Psychology, 8:* 57-75.

Allen, B. (1987). Youth suicide. *Adolescence, 22:* 271-90.

Baltes, P. (1987). Theoretical propositions of lifespan developmental psychology: On the dynamics between growth and decline. *Developmental Psychology, 23:* 611-26.

Barker, R. (1963). *Ecological Psychology.* Stanford, CA: Stanford University Press.

Butler, R. (1963). The life review: An interpretation of reminiscence in the aged. *Psychiatry, 26:* 65-76.

Camus, A. (1955). *The Myth of Sisyphus.* New York: Vintage Books.

Cole, R. (1970). *Uprooted Children.* Pittsburgh: University of Pittsburgh Press.

Dasberg, H., & Sheffler, G. (1987). The disbandment of a community: A psychiatric action research project. *The Journal of Applied Behavioral Science, 23:* 89-101.

Donat, J. (Ed.). (1967). *World Architecture 4.* London: Studio Vista.

Fischman, J. (1986). A journey of hearts and minds. *Psychology Today, 20:* 42-47.

Fried, M. (1972). Grieving for a lost home. In R. Gutman (Ed.), *People and Buildings.* New York: Basic Books, pp. 188-210.

Gauldie, S. (1969). *Architecture: The Appreciation of the Arts.* London: Oxford University Press.

Gaylord, M., & Symons, E. (1986). Relocation stress: A definition and a need for services. *Employee Assistance Quarterly, 2:* 31-36.

Gewirtzman, R., & Fodor, I. (1987). The homeless child at school: From welfare hotel to classroom. *Child Welfare, 66:* 237-45.

Gullotta, T., & Donohue, K. (1983). Families, relocating, and the corporation. *United Social and Mental Health Services.* Na 20 (Dec); 15-24.

Howell, S. (1980). Environments as hypotheses in human aging research. In L. Poon (Ed.), *Aging in the 1990's: Psychological Issues.* Washington, DC: American Psychological Association.

——. (1983). The meaning of place in old age. In G. Rowles & R. Ohta (Eds.), *Aging and Milieu.* New York: Academic Press, pp. 97-107.

Hummon, D. (1986). City mouse, country mouse: The persistence of community identity. *Qualitative Sociology, 9:* 3-25.

Kliot, N. (1987). Here and there: The phenomenology of settlement removal from Northern Sinai. *The Journal of Applied Behavioral Science, 23:* 35-51.

Norberg-Schulz, C. (1971). *Existence, Space and Architecture.* New York: Praeger.

Proshansky, H., Fabian, A., & Kaminoff, R. (1983). Place identity: Physical world socialization of the self. *Journal of Environmental Psychology, 3:* 57-83.

Proshansky, H., Ittelson, W., & Rivson, L. (1970). *Environmental Psychology.* New York: Holt, Rinehart, and Winston.

Relph, E. (1976). *Place and Placelessness.* London: Pion Limited.

Rowles, G. (1983). Place and personal identity in old age: Observations from Appalachia. *Journal of Psychology, 3:* 299-313.

Rubinstein, R. (1989). The home environments of older people: A description of the psychosocial processes linking person to place. *Journal of Gerontology, 44:* 45-53.

Sarbin, T. (1983). Place identity as a component of self: An addendum. *Journal of Environmental Psychology, 3:* 337-42.

Scheidt, R., & Norris-Baker, C. (1990). A transactional approach to environmental stress among older residents of rural communities. *Journal of Rural Community Psychology, 11:* 5-30.

Schulz, R., & Ewen, R. C. (1988). *Adult Development and Aging: Myths and Emerging Realities.* New York: Macmillan.

Seamon, D. (1989). *Geography of the Life World.* New York: St. Martin's Press.

Shalit, E. (1987). Within borders and without: The interaction between geopolitical and personal boundaries in Israel. *Political Psychology, 8*: 365-78.

Shumaker, S., & Taylor, R. (1983). Toward a clarification of people-place relationships: A model of attachment to places. In N. Feimer & E. Geller (Eds.), *Environmental Psychology: Directions and Perspectives*. New York: Praeger, pp. 219-51.

Stokols, D., & Shumaker, S. (1981). People in places: A transactional view of settings. In J. Harvey (Ed.), *Cognition, Social Behavior, and the Environment*. Hillsdale, NJ: Lawrence Erlbaum, pp. 441-48.

POLITICAL BELIEFS AND ACTIVITIES

The United States was founded on the principles of a democratic state. The belief that the citizens of a community should all have a voice in shaping its direction, policies, and future was unique. Most European governments at that time were monarchies with highly structured class systems that denied the average citizen a voice in its decisions. The fact that the average U.S. citizen could vote and thereby exercise an influence on the government led the visiting observer Alexis de Tocqueville (1957) to comment: "The political activity that pervades the United States must be seen in order to be understood. No sooner do you set foot on American ground than you are stunned by a kind of Tumult" (1957, p. 259). Clearly, de Tocqueville believed that politics was the American passion and that the average citizen was caught up in political activity.

Undoubtedly the average citizen did have a larger voice in the government of the United States than in that of most other nations, but was this citizen really as politically involved as de Tocqueville believed? The evidence of current involvement of U.S. citizens in political activities is not convincing.

Thomas Dye's (1991) concept of the range of political activities in which citizens may be involved, along with the approximate percentage of the public that engages in each of these activities, is given in Table 1.

Table 1. Political Participation in the United States

Type of Activity	Percentage Involved
Run for public office	Less than 1%
Active in parties & campaigns	4 to 5%
Make campaign contribution	10%
Wear button or use bumper sticker	15%
Write or call a public official	17-20%
Belong to an organization	30-33%
Talk politics to others	30-35%
Vote	30-55%
Nonparticipants	30-45%

Source: Figure 1, p. 89: T. R. Dye, *Politics in States and Communities*, 7th edition. New York: Prentice-Hall, 1991. Used by permission of Prentice-Hall, Inc., Englewood Cliffs, NJ.

The lowest level of involvement is the nonparticipant, who does not even show up to vote on Election Day. Depending on the election, this group can actually be as high as 70 percent of those eligible to vote. It is difficult to believe today that the average citizen is enthralled with political activity when 45 percent or more do not vote in a given election. About one person in three discusses politics with others, although some of these people still may not vote. Approximately one-third of the population belongs to an organization that could be considered an interest group. About one person in five writes or calls a public official, somewhat fewer sport buttons or bumper stickers, and only 1 in 10 makes a campaign contribution. As for actual participation in parties and campaigns, only about 1 person in 20 engages in this high degree of political activity. Finally, it is the rare person who ever runs for public office, the figure being consistently under 1 percent.

"Gladiators" and "Spectators"

In terms of political activity, James McDowell (1990) has divided the American public into what he calls the "Gladiators" and the "Spectators." The Gladiators include the 6 percent of the public who either run for office themselves or actively campaign on behalf of a candidate. These are the activists who are in the public eye and periodically in the news. They knock on doors and try to persuade the public to vote for their favored candidate. The other 94 percent are the Spectators. This overwhelming majority of the public may watch reports of the campaign on television and occasionally read newspaper accounts of the campaigns, but they do not get involved personally. In McDowell's view, making a financial contribution to the candidate or party of one's choice, wearing a campaign button, or placing a bumper sticker on one's vehicle actually involves a minimum of effort on the citizen's part and should be considered at best a low level of involvement in political activity.

The actual political Gladiators compose such a distinct minority of the American population that one cannot help but wonder what de Tocqueville would say if he could observe the current level of political activity of the average U.S. citizen.

Voter Turnout in Historical Perspective

In colonial America, the rules of voter eligibility were considerably more restrictive than they are today. Generally, the only people allowed to vote were adult males of "good character" who were property owners and had paid their taxes (McGooney, 1949). In 1832, for example, only 22 percent of the adult population cast a ballot. Women and nonwhite citizens were denied this right (Johnson, 1980).

Voter turnout continued to increase, however, and by 1876 37.6 percent of the adult population cast ballots in the presidential election. Women were finally given the right to vote in 1920, a development that increased the turnout that year to 42.5 percent of the adult population.

As Table 2 indicates, voter turnout climbed to an all-time high in the 1968 election, when 67.8 percent of the adult population voted, but has since declined.

The record of sustained participation in the electoral process is considerably lower than one might expect. One study of voter

Table 2. Voter Registration and Turnout, 1966-1988

Year	Percent Registered	Percent Voting
1966	70.3	55.4
1968	74.3	67.8
1970	69.1	54.6
1972	72.3	63.0
1974	62.2	44.7
1976	66.7	59.2
1978	62.6	45.9
1980	66.9	59.2
1982	64.1	48.5
1984	68.3	59.9
1986	64.3	56.0
1988	66.6	57.4

Sources: U. S. Department of Commerce, Bureau of the Census, "Voter Participation in November, 1972," Population Characteristics, Series P-20, No. 244; "Voting and Registration in the Election of November, 1988," Series P-20, No. 440. Washington, DC: Government Printing Office.

participation over 10 elections (ranging from local to presidential elections) indicated that only 4 percent of the eligible voters cast a ballot in 9 or all 10 of the elections. Only 26 percent voted in half of the 10 elections, and 38 percent did not vote in any of the elections. Thus, not only are there more Spectators than Gladiators in American politics, but nearly two of every five Spectators never bother to vote in any election (Sigelman, 1985).

The high percentage of people who never vote in any election is probably a result of the fact that the individual receives no immediate or tangible benefit from voting and realizes that his or her vote is not likely to determine the outcome. Most people vote out of a sense of duty, patriotism, and commitment to democracy rather than because they expect their vote to make a concrete difference.

Social Determinants of Political Participation

Political participation is largely determined by a number of individual demographic and social circumstances that include age, race, education, occupation, and income. Table 3 indicates the effects of many of these variables in the 1984 election. (Note that some people tell pollsters that they voted when they really did not. While 59.9 percent of the voting age population reported that they voted, the actual number of votes cast showed that only 53.5 percent did so.)

As a general rule, older people are much more likely to vote in any election than young people. Although younger people may talk about politics at great length and with considerable emotion, their seniors are more likely actually to turn out and vote. For example, in the 1984 election, only about two of every five voters under age 25 reported going to the polls (grouping together the 18-20 and 21-24 categories). The number voting increased gradually to nearly 7 of every 10 in the age groups 45-64 and 65 and over. Similar age-related voting patterns were also found in the 1988 election. Engeller (1988) reports that voters in the age range 60-69 boasted the nation's highest turnout rate for the presidential election, 72.8 percent.

Age is probably the best single predictor of sustained political activity. As a general rule, older people are more interested and better informed about political developments and are more likely to participate actively in the process themselves. Probably the most significant single explanation of the influence of age would draw on differential social and community integration. Young

Table 3. Characteristics of Voters: 1984 Election

Percent Reporting They Voted	
Age	
18-20	36.7
21-24	43.5
25-34	54.5
35-44	63.5
45-64	69.8
65 & over	67.7
Employment status	
Employed	61.8
Unemployed	44.0
Education	
8 years or less	42.8
High school	58.7
College	79.1

Source: Statistical Abstract of the United States, 1989, p. 257.

people often have just moved from their hometown and do not identify with or consider themselves to be permanent residents of their new community. They may be in the military service, for example, or attending a trade school or college. It has been well established that geographic mobility is higher in the young adult years. Once established in an occupation, people are likely to remain in the same place for a number of years and thus have the opportunity to develop social and organizational ties and become integrated into a web of activities that make them feel that they are really a part of the community. As they come to feel that this is their community, too, they are more likely both to vote and to participate in other facets of the political process on a much more regular basis.

As a general rule, African Americans vote less frequently than whites. In 1984, 40.6 percent of the voting age African-American population reported themselves as having voted; this level had fallen to 35 percent for the 1988 election. Hispanics and Asian Americans are less likely to participate in the political process than are African Americans or whites. However, the longer immigrants live in the nation and in a particular community, the more socially integrated they tend to become, and the more likely they are to vote and participate in political activities. This process of becoming rooted in a community and then becoming more politically active seems to parallel what has already been noted about young adults.

The higher the level of education, the more likely a person is to vote, work in campaigns, and participate as a member of a political party. Even among individuals with the same income level, those with higher education participate more frequently (Welfinger & Rosenstone, 1980). In the 1988 election, 41.7 percent of those with a grade school education reported themselves as voters, whereas 58.2 percent of those with a high school education and 82.4 percent of those with a college education did so. The more educated person is more likely to understand how the political system works and how it can impinge on his or her life. The idea that one can have an impact on the government through voting and other political activities is also stronger among the more educated spectrum of the population.

Occupation and political activity also are connected. Employed people are considerably more likely to vote than the unemployed. Apparently, the unemployed become so preoccupied with their personal problems and concerns that they have little time or energy left to follow the political process. Those who are financially worse off than they were previously, for any reason, are also less likely to vote (Rosenstone, 1982).

People whose occupations are immediately affected by government policies and programs are somewhat more likely to vote than those who do not see a direct connection. A higher percentage of farm owners and government employees vote than do workers in many other occupations. Most farmers raise products that receive some form of government subsidy or are grown on some form of quota system. Any change in quotas or government subsidies can have a substantial effect on the farmer's income.

Similarly, a high percentage of government employees vote, recognizing that their careers also can be significantly affected by political decisions and policies. They are more likely than most people to follow politics closely in the mass media and to participate in the political process to the extent that their jobs will allow.

People with higher incomes participate more in the political process than those with lower incomes. When the level of education is equal, the person with a higher income is likely to be more active in the political process. Three explanations have been offered for this pattern. Some argue that the poor must put so much into acquiring the necessities of life that they have little time left over for political activity. Another explanation is that those with a higher income are more likely to live and work in environments that stimulate and encourage political participation. Access to political information in the workplace tends to increase the individual's interest in voting and other forms of participation. A third explanation is that higher income persons have more to gain or lose by government decisions and therefore are more highly motivated by their own self-interest to participate in the political process.

Conclusion

Age, race, education, occupational status, and income all influence voter turnout and other forms of political participation. Elderly, employed, well-educated, and high-income members of the dominant ethnic group are more likely to vote than the young, the unemployed, the less educated, lower income earners, and members of minority groups. In attempting to understand these voting patterns, two underlying factors come to mind. First, the more socially integrated and identified people are with their particular community, the more likely they are to vote. Second, the more directly people perceive a connection between government actions and their own lives, the more likely they are to vote.

A minority of approximately 6 percent of the public actually run for office themselves or campaign on behalf of a candidate they favor. The American public at large (about 94 percent) are but spectators of the political process, and a substantial number (about 35 percent) never bother to vote in any election and should, therefore, be considered to be alienated from the political process.

▼ HAROLD COX

See also: Gender as a Shaping Force in Adult Development and Aging; Generational Equity; Mexican Americans: Life Course Transitions and Adjustment; Place and Personality in Adult Development; Social Class and Adult Development; Work Capacity Across the Adult Years.

References

Conway, M. M. (1991). *Political Participation in the United States.* Washington, DC: Congressional Quarterly, Inc.

Dye, T. R. (1991). *Politics in States and Communities.* Seventh Edition. New York: Prentice-Hall.

Engeller, G. H. (1988). The impact of older voters in the 1988 elections. *Aging Network News*, 4: 1-6.

Johnson, C. E., Jr. (1980). Nonvoting Americans. *Current Population Reports, Series.* Washington, DC: Government Printing Office, p. 23.

McDowell, J. (1990). "Problems and Opportunities in Later Life." Lecture, Indiana State University Workshop, May 17.

McGooney, D. A. (1949). *The American Suffrage Medley.* Chicago: University of Chicago Press.

Rosenstone, S. J. (1982). Economic adversity and voting turnout. *American Journal of Political Science, 26:* 300-13.

Sigelman, L. (1985). Voting and nonvoting: A multi-election perspective. *American Journal of Political Science, 29:* 749-65.

de Tocqueville, A. (1957). *Democracy in America.* New York: Vintage Books.

Welfinger, R. E., & Rosenstone, S. J. (1980). *Who Votes.* New Haven, CT: Yale University Press, pp. 287-324.

POSSESSIONS

Possessions extend the self beyond the body. The self extends to objects that have become part of the person through habit, usefulness, or symbolic association. Just as mastery of objects is a distinguishing trait of humanity, resulting in part from the ability to use tools, so possession of objects has become an integral part of the human experience. Possessions extend the experience of the self through space and time—through space because of the extension of effective action and through time because objects endure through personal changes and seem to give assurance of the continuity of the self even beyond death.

Personal possessions occupy an intermediate position between the self and the outside world. During individual development the child learns to distinguish the outside world from the self and at the same time begins to acquire mastery of these separated objects. Thus, the individual starts to see objects as tools for the satisfaction of needs, as extensions of the body. Gradually, these objects themselves acquire value and emotional attractiveness. For the adult, possessions and material objects can form parts of the self, more or less distinguished from the center or "essence" of the self.

Thus, the ability to use tools leads to ownership and possessions. Objects become valuable for their uses and the advantages gained by their control, but objects also acquire value apart from their utility and become important as part of the personal self. The significance of possessions depends not only on the nature of the object itself but also on the social role of the owners. This role of possessions is controlled to a large degree by social and cultural situations. In turn, these situations vary with the individual's position within society, as marked, for example, by social status and age. Exploring some pertinent characteristics of material possessions can help clarify their role during the life course. Beginning with the helpless infant's need for external support, objects become useful as well as targets for strong feelings. This combination of instrumental and affective relations tells the story of one's personal relations to possessions throughout the life course.

Possessions and the World View

Different disciplines and theoretical perspectives tend to stress certain qualities of possessions. For example, a sociologist might be drawn to possessions primarily because of the ways in which they confer status upon the individual, while a cultural historian might be most interested in the ability some possessions have to endure over the whole lifespan and beyond. In discussing the place of objects and possessions in the different stages of the life course, consideration must be given to a variety of viewpoints.

The role of objects for the person involves a degree of inherent uncertainty; the objects are different from the individual, yet they become part of the individual's self and his or her personal world. These traits include some contradiction, and the exact position of possessions will depend on the general organization of the individual and the social world.

The place of possessions in human life is therefore always shifting. It depends on the intrinsic features of human development but simultaneously also on the historical, social, and cultural situation. Internal psychological development of the importance of possessions to the individual can be seen to be a standard because it is derived from general human experience. It is the approach of psychologists to study possessions and show the sequences from using possession for the sake of mastery of the environment to valuing possessions for their own sake for the validation of the continuity of the self (Furby, 1978).

The relation of individuals to possessions is clearly only part of the total worldview of the person. The ambivalence toward the objects is also an expression of the attitude of a culture toward material and spiritual values. Objects can be seen as means of distinction, as a means of asserting power over others, or as expressions of superior status. Possessions can separate individuals from each other. But sharing possessions can also bring people closer to each other and make them more fully members of a community. These variations have been studied by sociologists and anthropologists (Czikszentmihaly & Rochberg-Halton, 1981; Douglas & Isherwood, 1979).

Objects can be made to symbolize a number of social circumstances. Transitions between stages of life are frequently symbolized by relinquishing objects appropriate to the old stage before receiving those of a new one (Van Gennep, 1960). Even where this is not done in formal passage rite, people will give up possessions appropriate to one stage when they arrive at the next. For example, children will give up toys they now consider to be too babyish; retirees will abandon the tools of the trade. However, when the transition is accomplished, the question of identity still remains, and the adult will treasure the toys of childhood.

Psychogenic Theories

Throughout life, one's point of view regarding possessions will change according to one's perceived relationship to the outer world, in space and time. If one can dominate the environment, one can keep expanding the acquisition and use of goods; under other conditions some adaptations have to be made. From this perspective one can divide life course development into roughly three periods:

1. Infancy is a period of dependency when one tries to acquire any attractive object that may be available. The infant and young child look for immediate gratification of all needs. Possessions are put to immediate use but are also endowed with strong affect because of the dependency relation.

2. In young adulthood, mastery over the environment has been established and objects are valued for detached enjoyment over longer time frames as well as for their current use.

3. In late adulthood and senescence, direct mastery diminishes, but the longer past provides an increasing awareness of permanence and associated values. Few psychologists have linked this development directly to possessions, but it is often implied in their theories of the individual's changing relationship to the social and physical environment (e.g., Erikson, 1977).

It would follow that during maturity the value of particular objects would increase, simply because more time has accumulated to accord intrinsic value to different objects. These objects can then represent not only the original aims to be achieved (such as eating utensils representing food gratification) but continuity and a feeling of identity over time.

This model of human experience reflects an internal, purely psychogenic perspective. It is developed most distinctively in psychoanalytic theory. According to Freud, the earliest experience is the relation to the mother as the source of all comfort and nourishment, and the first stage of development is individuation—the separation of the self from other people and other objects. Childhood and adolescence are devoted to this task of recognizing the difference between oneself and other objects in the world. Some psychoanalysts, such as Melanie Klein, have built the main part of their work on the concept of object relations (Segal, 1964).

Psychoanalytic theory also distinguishes two kinds of relationship of the person to things in a partly metaphoric explanation that emphasizes the oral and the anal. Orality is the first mode encountered by the infant, deriving from the nursing experience, the protective, life-giving activity which is gradually seen as coming from a friendly source. This provides the model for the acquisition of mastery over the world's resources. A different pattern develops on the basis of experience with the anal modality. The anal relationship derives from the increasing ability to retain and control bodily waste. This leads to the ability to possess what one does not really want, whose control by itself gives pleasure. This model represents another kind of relation to possessions, one in which the goal is enduring relation and identity, not instrumental mastery and consumption. These two developmental stages in psychoanalytic theory can also be seen as representations of two views toward possessions in later life, as well as in a variety of social and ethical evaluations.

The dissociation between the person and other objects is never complete, and many objects are seen through a strong emotional lens. This relation is called object-cathexis. The bias toward the early life stages in psychoanalytic work puts the emphasis on the early development of the object-cathexis relationship but leaves much unsaid about its course in later life. It does provide a common framework of standard individual development from which social variations can be evaluated.

Social Theories

The distinction between the immediate utility of possessions and their enduring value has been recognized in a number of social and economic theories, especially by Marx in his concepts of use-value and exchange-value. This analysis is often marred by normative concerns, such as Marx's attacks on the capital-amassing bourgeoisie. However, the func-tion of possessions is deeper than the excesses of any particular economic system; both kinds of value are present in human relationships to objects, but they are affected differently by cultural positions and standing in society.

Social norms can determine what kinds of objects will have intrinsic worth. The clearest examples are precious stones and metals and money, the medium of exchange. The characteristic process goes in one direction—from instrumental to intrinsic value. An object must be seen as a tool for reaching a desired goal before it can itself acquire the characteristics of the goal. However, a similar process occurs also in the general cultural setting: Some useful objects can become collectors' items or museum pieces and win admiration for their own sake (e.g., eating utensils or articles of clothing). However, it would be extremely rare that these museum pieces would be used again for their original purposes. In his *Rubbish Theory*, Michael Thompson (1979) has demonstrated how these transformations go through regular stages and can be represented through mathematical models.

These models reveal the impact of the life-style of social classes (Bergmann, 1983). For example, working-class people tend to have a shorter active time perspective than the middle class. This difference in turn manifests itself in the middle class's preference for delayed gratification, which leads to an emphasis on the exchange and symbolic value of possessions, as compared with the working class's priority on the immediate use value. This class difference becomes especially important in the evaluation of possessions during the later years of life. Working-class people tend to continue to regard their possessions according to their immediate use value, while middle-class people tend to see in them symbols of the continuity of the self, as objects of memory, as well as assurance of extension into the future through bequests and inheritance (Redfoot & Back, 1988).

The Value of Possessions

The double position of objects as instrumental tools and as "objects of affection" has also led to an ambivalent attitude toward the value of possessions. Socially and individually, the relation to objects can be positive as well as negative. The need for objects to achieve important goals makes things morally positive and their possession a socially valuable achievement. On the other hand, the acquisition of objects for themselves and the lavishing of affect on them is seen as morally objectionable. Attraction to possessions may be seen as a deviation from the natural human life, and pejorative terms such as fetishism, materialism, splintering of the self, or alienation will be used.

The multifaceted role of possessions leads also to their ambivalent place in ethical discussions. While the value of possessions is accepted as contributing to human welfare, acknowledgment of this fact and its enjoyment is looked at with suspicion. By a strange transposition, material possessions themselves are seen as evil, and anti-materialism is extolled. This confusion is shown in the way that the a biblical injunction has been revised by the public mind. "The love of money is the root of all evil" has become "Money is the root of all evil."

▼ Kurt W. Back

See also: Development and Aging in Historical Perspective; Generational Equity; Mastery Types, Development, and Aging; Privacy Issues; Social Class and Adult Development; Subcultural Influences on Lifelong Development.

References

Bergmann, W. (1983). Das problem der zeit in der soziologie. *Kolner Zjeitschrift fur Sociologie und Sozialpsychogogie*, 35: 462-502.

Czikszentmihaly, M., & Rochberg-Halton, E. (1981). *The Meaning of Things: Domestic Symbols and the Self*. New York: Cambridge University Press.

Douglas, M., & Isherwood, B. (1979). *The World of Goods*. New York: Basic Books.

Erikson, E. H. (1977). *Toys and Reasons: Stages in the Ritualization of Experience*. New York: Norton.

Furby, L. (1978). Possessions: Toward a theory of their meaning and function throughout the life cycle. In P. Baltes (Ed.), *Life-Span Development and Behavior*. Volume 1. New York: Academic Press, pp. 198-336.

Redfoot, D. L., & Back, K. W. (1988). The perceptual presence of the life course. *International Journal of Aging & Human Development*, 28: 155-70.

Segal, H. (1964). *Introduction to the Work of Melanie Klein*. New York: Basic Books.

Thompson, M. (1979). *Rubbish Theory: The Creation and Destruction of Value*. Oxford: Oxford University Press.

Van Gennep, A. (1960). *Rites of Passage*. Chicago: University of Chicago Press.

PREMATURE AGING

Common experience suggests that people of the same chronological age may wear their years differently. A person who is a "young fifty," for example, may consider a friend rediscovered at a high school reunion to be an "old fifty." The apparent differences can be deceiving, of course. The friend may have been exhausted, depressed, or trying to fight off an illness. Temporary states that tax one's energies and overwhelm one's psychobiological resources can make one look—and feel—like a person many years older. This kind of "transient oldness" may vanish after the pressure has lifted, life events have taken a favorable turn, and the sleep deficit has been repaid.

Most adults studied report that they look and feel younger than their chronological age (e.g., Kastenbaum et al., 1972). Their claims may not simply reflect wishful thinking or self-flattery. More adults seem to enjoy good health and retain their vigor today as compared with men and women of earlier generations, who received less adequate medical care throughout their lives and encountered more burdens and hazards whether working within or outside the home.

The differences in real or apparent aging among adults in the general population are trivial, however, when compared with the changes seen in the very small number of individuals who are afflicted with *progeria*— a medical term often applied to premature aging. This condition is important not for its frequency—which, fortunately, is low—but for reasons of compassion and scientific investigation. The individual afflicted with a progeroid syndrome does not have the opportunity for a long and healthful life, and the family must cope with the caregiving responsibilities as well as the sorrows involved. Some gerontologists and other scientists believe progeria provides an unusual opportunity to learn more about normal development and aging. In many fields of research valuable knowledge has been gained by studying phenomena that deviate from the expected.

The growth of knowledge about premature aging in its extreme (progeroid) forms has been rather slow, chiefly because the low incidence of this condition has limited opportunities to study it. Nevertheless, some useful facts have emerged, and more can be expected in the future as longitudinal studies proceed.

1. *Premature aging usually makes itself known in early childhood.* The infant may appear normal at first. Within a year or two, however, an unusual pattern emerges that leads to the overall impression that this is an aged rather than a young individual. Brown (1987) offers a textbook-type description of progeria:

> They appear old, lose hair, and become bald in the first few years of life. There is widespread loss of subcutaneous fat. As a result, the veins over their scalps often become particularly noticeable. The skin appears aged and there are pigmentary age spots....They have thin, high-pitched voices and...a characteristic facial appearance, with prominent eyes, and a beak nose. A large balding head and small face give progeria subjects an extremely aged appearance. (p. 543)

However, there are also later-appearing syndromes that have progeroid characteristics.

2. *Life expectancy is markedly less than normal for individuals afflicted with a progeroid syndrome.* The extent of this reduced life expectancy varies with the particular form of premature aging. The type described above is an example of the Hutchinson-Guilford syndrome, often considered to be the primary or purest form of progeria. McKusick (1986) reports that the age of survival with this condition ranges from 10 to 20.

3. *Intellectual level and functioning do not seem to be affected.* Despite this pervasive impression of accelerated aging and its unfortunate implications for longevity, the individual is likely to function at a normal or above average level of intelligence. The implications of this divergence between physical and mental aspects of progeria have yet to be clarified.

4. *Accelerated aging is also a characteristic of Down's syndrome (DS).* The pattern here differs significantly from the Hutchinson-Guilford syndrome. The individual with DS is at high risk for senile dementia: a configuration of deficits in attention, orientation, learning, memory, and planning that is usually associated with such conditions as Alzheimer's disease. Other changes that are most often encountered in the neuropathology of aging are also found in DS, including neuronal deterioration as revealed by postmortem examination (Tice & Setlow, 1985). One of the most promising of the clues that have so far emerged from research on progeroid syndromes is the finding that both DS and Alzheimer patients have aberrations of the twenty-first chromosome.

5. *Still another form of premature aging— Werner syndrome (WS)—makes its first appearance in adolescence.* Typically, the individual has developed without any unusual difficulties until age 15 or so. At this point, two unexpected events occur: (a) growth comes to a halt, just when the individual is starting to reach full physical maturity; and (b) aging-like changes start to manifest themselves. Often the first obvious sign is the graying or whit-

ening of the hair. Skin changes are likely to follow. By the time the individual is in his or her mid-twenties there are usually a variety of other characteristics of aging, unfortunately all moving in the direction of reduced functional capacity and heightened risk. For example, wound healing becomes inefficient, and there is a much greater than average chance of developing diabetes mellitus, cataracts, and tumors.

6. *At present there is no cure or effective treatment for these and other progeroid syndromes.* One can imagine how especially stressful this situation must be for those who are unimpaired intellectually and who come to realize what the future does and does not hold for them.

7. *Progress has been made in identifying the causes of several progeroid syndromes.* These advances offer hope for prevention of these disorders in the future and, perhaps, for effective genetic engineering interventions. Problems in genetic structure have been discovered in all the major types of progeroid syndrome described here (Tice & Setlow, 1985). As already noted, DS has been traced to difficulties with a particular chromosome, the twenty-first. WS is an inherited recessive trait. The Hutchinson-Guilford syndrome also is thought to be a (different) inherited recessive trait, although further research is needed to provide details and confirmation.

Apparently there is no concern about any form of progeria having a contagious mode of dissemination, nor have there been reports of increased incidence.

Implications for Understanding Adult Development and Aging

Several implications and questions are worth considering briefly. First, the diversity of patterns among the progeroid syndromes (which have only been sampled here) suggests that premature aging should not be regarded simply as an early and accelerated version of normal aging. Taken separately, none of the syndromes reviewed is identical to the type of aging that occurs over extended periods of time in the later adult years, and, taken together, they represent three distinctive patterns of change. It is probable that much useful information will continue to be acquired from studies of individuals with progeroid syndromes. It would appear, though, that one cannot generalize with much confidence from any or all of these syndromes to the normal course of development and aging.

Another implication concerns the connection between development and aging. In all three syndromes the pattern of normal development goes awry in conjunction with the appearance of aging-like features. A reckless overinterpretation of this set of patterns could lead one to characterize *aging as a disorder of development.* This is not really such an overinterpretation when restricted to the progeroid syndromes. The more speculative and untested implication would be that *all* aging is the result of development disorder—therefore, prevent or correct these disorders, and aging will join the list of distressing conditions that have been vanquished by science. There are many difficulties with this idea, e. g., the problems that would arise if the growth process did *not* turn itself off in early adulthood. Nevertheless, it can be stimulating to have at least one radical notion to contend with.

For a more responsible line of inquiry, one might conceive of the progeroid syndromes as occupying extreme positions along a continuum of life-prolonging and life-shortening forces. These dramatic and uncommon disorders may be less significant for the well-being of the general population than many other genetic conditions that are less well known at present but perhaps more pervasive. In a magnificent contribution to the gerontological sciences, Caleb Finch (1990) has provided a comprehensive yet in-depth exploration of *Longevity, Senescence, and the Genome.* The *genome* is defined by Finch as "The total inventory of heritable nucleic acids, usually DNA..." (p. 675). Much of his book is devoted to examining development, aging, and longevity in a variety of species including humans. Within this broad framework, "premature aging" is but one subsector of genetic influence. Caleb concludes that "Without question, specific genes and combinations of genes ultimately determine the characteristics of senescence and the potential lifespan" (p. 656).

Perhaps one of the most effective uses to be made of the progeroid syndromes is to recognize them as examples of a larger class of genetic phenomena that bear on development, aging, and longevity. And—who knows—perhaps tomorrow somebody will discover the elusive chromosome that will fulfill the fantasy of centuries by granting both youth and long life.

▼ ROBERT KASTENBAUM

See also: Chronic Pain as a Lifespan Problem; Longevity; Risk to Life through the Adult Years; The Voice.

References

Brown, W. T. (1987). Progeroid syndromes. In G. L. Maddox (Ed.), *The Encyclopedia of Aging.* New York: Springer, pp. 542-43.

Finch, C. E. (1990). *Longevity, Senescence, and the Genome.* Chicago: University of Chicago Press.

Kastenbaum, R., et al. (1972). "The ages of me": Toward personal and interpersonal definitions of functional aging. *International Journal of Aging and Human Development, 3:* 197-211.

McKusick, V. A. (1986). *Mendelian Inheritance in Man: Catalogs of Autosomonal Dominant, Autosomonal Recessive, and X-linked Phenotypes.* Seventh Edition. Baltimore: Johns Hopkins University Press.

Tice, R. R., & Setlow, R. B. (1985). DNA repair and replication in aging organisms and cells. In C. E. Finch & E. L. Schneider (Eds.), *Handbook of the Biology of Aging.* New York: Van Nostrand Reinhold, pp. 173-224.

PRIVACY ISSUES

For many years people have been told that disclosing their every thought and feeling is critical to their happiness and mental health. Recently, however, a body of research literature has emerged that challenges these assumptions and suggests that disclosing one's problems may not be so beneficial as earlier proclaimed. People who practice self-disclosure give away some of their privacy. Often they do not think about this trade-off because they have such a strong need to talk about their problems with others. Nevertheless, disclosing private information does have an effect on the listener. Research suggests that one should be more aware of the listener and how this person may be influenced by the information one shares.

Westin (1967) provides a definition that focuses on private information: "Privacy is the claim of individuals, groups, or institutions to determine for themselves when, how, and to what extent information about themselves is communicated to others" (p. 7). Burgoon (1982) suggests that privacy issues span a number of different dimensions. She identifies four types of privacy: physical, social, psychological, and informational.

Physical privacy is defined as "the degree to which one is physically inaccessible to others" (Burgoon, 1982, p. 211). This represents the space people need around their bodies, without which they feel anxious or encroached upon by others. Privacy needs of this type differ cross-culturally. For example, people in the Mediterranean countries tend to feel the need for less personal space around them than do most people in the United States.

Social privacy refers to one's control over unwanted interactions with others. A person may achieve social privacy on an individual level simply by withdrawing from the company of others. Two or more people may also seek social privacy. For example, when a dating couple goes off to be alone, they are jointly constructing a privacy boundary that communicates to others that they do not want to be social at that time.

Burgoon also observes that people need a degree of *psychological privacy* in their lives as well. They need the opportunity to think private thoughts and experience their emotions apart from others. By doing so, they are able to maintain a sense of autonomy and to recognize their differences. Through psychological privacy people also engage in self-evaluation and may observe their own actions to assess whether or not they meet the standards set for themselves.

The last type of privacy suggested by Burgoon is *informational privacy*. This type accords mostly closely with self-disclosure and with Westin's (1967) definition presented earlier. There are many things about themselves that people might consider to constitute private information. Particular experiences they have had, relationships with others, and problems they have encountered in their lives are among the personal phenomena that people might prefer to enclose in informational privacy. Some of these experiences might be defined as positive and others as negative. For example, people might consider information about their salaries to be private in the workplace. They might not want people to read their personnel files without permission. They might object to having others listening in on their telephone conversations. The United States guarantees the right of privacy, but individuals must also be alert and active to ensure this right. New technologies such as satellite communication and new problems such as AIDS have led to increased opportunities or demands for invasion of privacy.

Although not always recognized as such, privacy is a fundamental issue across the lifespan. It is useful, therefore, to examine the way in which privacy is conceptualized in general as well as its specific manifestations at various periods of life.

Conceptualizing Privacy

Wolfe and Laufer (1974) point out that privacy involves the expression of the self and the protection of space or possessions, but it also presupposes that others are often recipients or violators of privacy. People manage past information about themselves and gauge the future consequences of sharing private information. Wolfe and Laufer believe that all people try to keep some type of control over their possessions, space, and information. They select the persons to whom they do or do not disclose private information. Similarly, they also exercise control over who is or is not admitted to their personal space. Furthermore, people are selective in the degree of access they allow. For example, one might tell Person A only part of an incident that one shares in full detail with Person B; one might offer Person C a ride in his or her car, but loan the car itself only to Person D. People also attempt to control the amount and type of stimulation that affects them, e.g., by turning off television shows they do not wish to see.

In addition to issues of personal control, Wolfe and Laufer (1974) observe that their culture influences the way people define privacy. For example, the Israeli culture includes fewer norms for privacy than that of the United States. On the other hand, privacy norms are more extensive in the German culture than in the U.S. culture (Spiro, 1971). People also have a variety of rituals both for maintaining and for giving up privacy. Parents in the United States, for example, discipline their children differently in public than they do in private (Petronio, Bourhis & Berquiste, 1987).

People frequently think about privacy as something that they themselves maintain and control. However, those who receive disclosures of private information often feel a sense of responsibility for the problems or issues involved. This kind of situation may develop, for example, when a stranger sitting beside you on a plane, train, or bus starts to disclose his or her personal problems. The stranger might say that he or she is thinking seriously of getting divorced and ask if you think that is a good idea. You have not asked for this information, yet you have become involved in somebody else's problems and might feel even a small sense of responsibility to provide an answer. This sense of responsibility on the part of the recipient of private information is felt more acutely when the self-disclosure is being made by a spouse or child (Petronio, 1991). Accompanying this feeling of responsibility can be the sense that the recipient has also experienced privacy invasion. This is the other side of privacy. People attempt to control their privacy both in terms of protecting themselves from others and by regulating a desire to become close to others by revealing themselves, opening up their space, or lending their possessions.

Altman (1975) proposes a concept that helps in understanding the regulation of privacy. He suggests a tendency to use a metaphoric boundary that protects one's privacy from others and regulates openness. To regulate their privacy boundary, people use a set of rules or criteria to know when to reveal private information, allow someone into their space, or give possessions, and when to protect their privacy. Petronio (1991) notes that people regulate their privacy boundary with varying degrees of control, ranging from loose to very tight. If one is very open with someone, then the boundary is relaxed and one is willing to risk vulnerability. People are most likely to behave this way because they like and trust another person. They tighten up their privacy boundaries when they are not willing to risk vulnerability.

A useful way to think about privacy, then, is as the need to achieve a balance between being open to others so one can know them better and protecting oneself from intrusions and vulnerability. This "balancing act" enables people to develop and maintain friendships and intimacies while keeping an independent self-concept as they move through the lifespan. A person's concept of privacy changes as he or she reaches different stages in life, from childhood through old age.

Privacy in Childhood and Adolescence

When children are young, they do not have many opportunities to control their privacy. Parents and older siblings control space or possessions and may act intrusively toward younger children. By testing situations, children begin to learn when they must comply and when they can take control (Wolfe & Laufer, 1974). For example, an older child may take a possession away from a younger sibling while playing. The younger child may decide to reclaim the toy. If the effort is successful, this behavior in defense of his or her own possessions and boundaries is more likely to be used again in the future.

It is through such little experiments that children learn about privacy.

> A true understanding that one can have thought and engage in behaviors that will not be known to others does not seem to be achieved for a number of years.... Freud once explained that the child's first lie (the first secret—one way of maintaining privacy of information by control) is one of the first signs of the beginning of separation and individuation.... When the child has been successful in its first lie or in its first hidden behavior there is awareness finally that many things are not known unless volitionally revealed. (Wolfe & Laufer, 1974, p. 35)

By the time children enter school, they begin to have a clearer sense of separation from their parents. Being independent from their parents gives children a greater sense of control over environment and provides the ground for learning about control over space, possessions, and personal information. Children also learn by observing their parents and other siblings, following the examples set by the family.

Adolescence is the time when privacy issues are most apparent for the child. Because of the increased motivation to separate from the family, particularly the parents, the adolescent claims more privacy than earlier in life. Granting privacy becomes one way in which parents can communicate their acceptance of their maturing child's new status. The parents send a positive message by not entering the adolescent's room without permission, not eavesdropping, and not expecting the adolescent to reveal personal kinds of information. Violations of privacy by parents can lead to problems within the parent-child relationship, while consenting to privacy rights communicates respect for the adolescent.

Parents and adolescent children often have different goals during this period. The child wishes to become more independent, while adults may wish to retain a significant measure of control. Many conflicts can erupt between parents and adolescent children because their needs are at odds. The adolescent wants increased control over his or her environment and rights to privacy, while the parents believe that by denying privacy rights they will be able to maintain their control, including continuing to make a variety of decisions that adolescents would prefer to make for themselves. Not all parents follow this route, but the sphere of privacy often is a prime "battlefield" between the adolescent's striving for independence and the parents' determination to keep power in their own hands.

Privacy in Adulthood

Adults face many issues regarding privacy. These concerns arise in friendships, intimate relationships, in the workplace, and in the family. Although all people learn to regulate or control their privacy as they grow up, they may have different rules by which they balance privacy with openness.

One study found that men and women use different rules or criteria when judging whether or not to share private information with others (Petronio, Martin, & Littlefield, 1984). Women prefer the criteria of trusting and liking a person, as well as not having the sense of being forced to reveal private information. Thus, the target person—the one who may or may not be given the opportunity to receive the private information—is critical to the disclosure decisions made by women.

The same study found that men tended to use a completely different criterion when judging whether or not to disclose private information. Men need to perceive the situation to be appropriate before they will talk about personal matters. Taking both findings together, we begin to see a pattern emerge.

For example, consider a woman who is disclosing her innermost personal feelings about their marriage to her husband. This scene happens to be taking place in a shopping mall. She is talking about these issues here and now because her criteria are whether she likes and trusts the person to whom she is talking. The husband, however, decides about disclosure based on the appropriateness of the situation, not the person to whom he is talking. In this situation, the husband is likely to become annoyed at his wife for violating his rule for disclosure, and the wife becomes annoyed at her husband because he refuses to talk about these issues. The problem is not that the husband is necessarily unwilling to talk about his wife's concerns, but that she wants him to talk about these things in what he feels is an inappropriate place.

Another perspective on the decision to talk about private matters has been offered by Derlega and Grzelak (1979), who propose five criteria as the basis for whether or not disclosure is appropriate in general. They note that people may wish to disclose for the purposes of expression, self-clarification, social validation, relational development, or social control. The need for *expression* may be generated by a painful experience, leading a person to say, "I feel terrible about what happened." The communication is felt to be appropriate because it conveys one's state of mind to others. People may also disclose private information because they have a need for *self-clarification*. Perhaps, for example, a person is not quite sure why she or he has behaved in a certain way. By disclosing the belief or opinion that led to this action, she or he may seek to rectify a misunderstanding. *Social validation* is another purpose that one might attempt to achieve through disclosure. This happens when a person offers a message that it is hoped will lead to feedback that confirms his or her sense of self-worth.

Relational development is also seen as a legitimate reason for disclosure. Many times a person enters into a self-disclosure as a way of encouraging the other person to reciprocate. Jourard (1971) observes that disclosure begets disclosure, and numerous studies support the phenomenon of reciprocity. Telling a person something that is rather private about oneself is likely to lead the recipient to feel obligated to reveal something of like nature in return. Mutual self-disclosure often plays an important role in the development of a relationship.

The last purpose for disclosure of private information is concerned with *social control*. Sometimes people disclose their feelings in a bid to control or manipulate others. Petronio (1982) found that wives often reported that their husbands used disclosure as a means of control. For example, one wife stated that her husband would make comments every time she bought something for the house. The wife interpreted this behavior as an implicit attempt at control because he would never come right out and say that she should stop buying things for the home, but he complained about his financial situation only when she did so.

Decisions about whether or not disclosure of private information is appropriate may be closely related to the way that a particular family defines the nature of privacy. Karpel (1980) observes that families have three levels of secrecy or privacy functioning at the same time. On one level, each person within a family has individual secrets or private information. As individuals they hold information about events, beliefs, or experiences that they do not wish to share with the other family members. A wife, for example, may live with the secret that she had an extramarital affair, or a son with the hidden knowledge that his girlfriend is pregnant. On another level, there are internal family secrets that involve two or more family members who keep certain information from others in the family. For example, the son may tell his mother that his girlfriend is pregnant, but not tell anyone else and not give permission for the mother to tell any other family member. Finally, there are shared family secrets: Everybody in the family knows that dad is an alcoholic, for example, but the family members are pledged to keep this information within the family.

Of these three levels, the most difficult type to manage is the internal family secret.

The individual who shares the private information often sets up the rules for how restrictive the recipient must be in disseminating or withholding this knowledge to other family members. In a recent study, Petronio and Bantz (1991) found that people often use prior restraint phrases as a way of indicating the importance of a particular piece of information. "Don't tell *anybody* this, OK?" would be a typical way of emphasizing the importance of the information involved. The individual who is disclosing this information thereby marks its personal significance to him or her and stipulates the rule for further disclosure (in this case: no further disclosure).

To Tell or Not to Tell?

There are times when keeping private information to oneself is important to the individual's own mental health. On the other hand, there are also times when it is vitally important to share information or feelings with another person. Pennebaker and O'Heeron (1984) examined the disclosure of private feelings after the death of a spouse. In general, people tended to have increased health problems after the death of their spouse. But the study found that the more time the survivors spent talking about the death, the less likely they were to become ill. Drawing upon the findings of his overall research program, Pennebaker suggests that talking about the event that causes a stress reduces negative outcomes for the individual. Private information and feelings that might be kept private under ordinary circumstances might be important to articulate and share with others when one is faced with stressful and demanding situations. Friends and family members have an improved opportunity to help each other cope with loss and stress when a greater degree of openness prevails in their communication patterns.

The coexisting needs to talk about life crisis and yet to maintain privacy is a paradox most often noted among elderly people. Health and financial concerns may generate highly stressful situations. An elderly person's need to talk about the problems must often be managed in conjunction with the need to remain in control of his or her life. Many years of mixed experiences with interpersonal relationships may have led the older person to fear that sharing a confidence might lead to being pressured to give up some measure of autonomy as well as to further invasions of private domains. Elderly people often require private time in order to survey and evaluate their own lives (Tamir, 1982). Additionally, the sense of self-esteem and self-worth is reinforced when one maintains control over privacy and makes one's own decisions about when it is appropriate to be open and with whom. Because elderly men and women are too often treated as though they had no privacy rights, they are likely to experience problems in regulating their boundaries.

As we journey through our lifespan, we encounter many instances in which we must control or regulate privacy. From youth we learn that people feel a sense of ownership about their space, possessions, and information. This sense of ownership is one of the guiding systems that enables us to differentiate ourselves from others. Furthermore, privacy may have differing definitions and functions within our own lives as we move from youth through age. The very definition of who we are is inextricably woven into our sense of privacy. Without privacy it is difficult either to achieve or to maintain autonomy. And yet we must always balance the need for privacy with the need for positive human interaction.   ▼ SANDRA PETRONIO

See also: Conflict as a Challenge in Adult Development; Gender as a Shaping Force in Adult Development and Aging; Housing as a Factor in Adult Life; Listening; Marital Development; Mental Health in the Adult Years; Possessions; Reminiscence and Life Review; Stress; Subcultural Influences on Lifelong Development.

References

Altman, I. (1975). *Environment and Social Behavior: Privacy, Personal Space, Territory, and Crowding.* Belmont, CA.: Wadsworth.

Bloom, M. (1980). *Adolescent-Parental Separation.* New York: Gardner.

Burgoon, J. (1982). Privacy and communication. In M. Burgoon (Ed.), *Communication Yearbook 6.* Beverly Hills, CA: Sage.

Derlega, V., & Grzelak, J. (1979). Appropriateness of self-disclosure. In G. Chelune (Ed.), *Self-Disclosure.* San Francisco, CA: Jossey-Bass.

Jourard, S. (1971). *The Transparent Self.* New York: Van Nostrand Reinhold.

Karpel, M. (1980). Family secrets. I. Conceptual and ethical issues in the relational context; II. Ethical and practical considerations in therapeutic management. *Family Process, 19:* 295-306.

Pennebaker, J., & O'Heeron, R. (1984). Confiding in others and illness rate among spouses of suicide and accidental death victims. *Journal of Abnormal Psychology, 93:* 473-76.

Petronio, S. (1982). The effect of interpersonal communication on women's family role satisfaction. *Western Journal of Speech Communication, 46:* 208-22.

———. (1991). Communication boundary management: A theoretical model of managing disclosure of private information between marital couples. *Communication Theory, 1:* 311-35.

Petronio, S., & Bantz, C. (1991). Controlling the ramifications of disclosure: "Don't tell anybody but..." *Journal of Language and Social Psychology, 10:* 1-7.

Petronio, S., Bourhis, J., & Berquiste, C. (1987). Families in public places: But Mom, you promised! In J. DeVito and M. Hecht (Eds.), *The Nonverbal Communication Reader.* Prospect Heights, IL: Waveland Press.

Petronio, S., Martin, J., & Littlefield, R. (1984). Prerequisite conditions for self-disclosure: A gender issue. *Communication Monographs, 51:* 268-73.

Rawlins, W. (1983). Openness as problematic in ongoing relationships: Two conversational dilemmas. *Communication Monographs, 50:* 1-13.

Spiro, H. (1971). Privacy in comparative perspectives. In J. R. Pennock & J. W. Chapman (Eds.), *Privacy.* New York: Atherton.

Tamir, L. (1982). *Communication and the Aging Process: Interaction Throughout the Life Cycle.* New York: Pergamon.

Westin, A. (1967). *Privacy and Freedom.* New York: Atheneum.

Wolfe, M., & Laufer, R. (1974). *The Concept of Privacy in Childhood and Adolescence.* New York: Environmental Design Research Association.

R

RELIGION AND COPING WITH CRISIS

"When misery is the greatest, God is the closest" (Gross, 1982, p. 242). Religion and God often become especially significant personally when one's life and happiness are threatened. Whether it be the twenty-third or ninety-first psalm, the promise is that the deity will provide protection and comfort. For most people, these needs are likely to increase with age. Growing threats of infirmity, disease, social isolation, helplessness and death are concomitants of aging. At these times, "the most important problem in regard to religious beliefs is not their logical truth, but their functional significance" (Wise, 1942, p. 131).

Many observers have suggested that religious faith benefits both mental and physical health (e.g., Levin & Schiller, 1988; Pollner, 1989). Concurrently, however, the role of faith is paradoxical: It may either encourage or inhibit well-being (Spilka, Hood, & Gorsuch, 1985). The mechanisms that produce these contradictory effects have not been clearly identified and will be looked into here.

Calling on Religion

Religious explanations are commonly sought when threat and ambiguity are especially troubling (Spilka & Schmidt, 1983). In addition, under such conditions, religion's potential to influence one's life increases for several reasons. First, religion offers the troubled individual meanings that connote wish fulfillment and hope. Second, religious faith endows the person with a sense of control when little else counters the powerlessness that accompanies severe personal distress. Third, in dire circumstances, feelings of despair and depression may dominate, and religion can maintain or enhance self-esteem. Finally, religious institutions usually offer a wide variety of supports through services, church and synagogue groups, and the ministrations of clergy and pastoral counselors.

The Role of Religious Meaning

From Aristotle to modern attribution theories, it has been assumed that people have a fundamental need to understand what underlies their experiences. Argyle (1959) claims that "a major mechanism behind religious beliefs is a purely cognitive desire to understand" (p. 167). Clark (1958) observes that "religion more than any other human function satisfies the need for meaning in life" (p. 419). Relative to crisis, Fichter (1981) sees "religious reality as the only way to make sense out of pain and suffering" (p. 20).

Bulman and Wortman's (1977) noted study of young adult paraplegics revealed that religious meanings endowed their plight with constructive purpose and direction. Research with cancer patients also shows that those who view their lives in a context of transcendent meaning cope better with their condition than do patients who lack such outlooks (Acklin, Brown, & Mauger, 1983). Religion provides breast cancer patients with valued meanings. One woman stated that "I had no idea God could answer so many of my questions." Another "felt that God had spared me somehow for a purpose that he would make apparent later" (Johnson & Spilka, 1988). Such self-affirming meanings have been seen as constituting "the essential nature of every being and as such its highest good" (Tillich, 1952, p. 23). These meanings are essential if one is to cope successfully with crisis.

In a similar vein, McIntosh, Silver, & Wortman (1989) suggest that religion may offer people a meaning system to cope with severe stress. Studying the mothers of sudden infant death syndrome (SIDS) babies, they found that religion not only helped these mothers deal with their loss but the importance of religion increased for those who were already religiously committed.

Religion and Control

Among the meanings that religion often conveys is the idea that crisis and tragedy can be overcome. The issue is not whether one can really control objective circumstances but whether people believe they can surmount even impossible obstacles. Claiming that the illusion of control can be a powerful force in supporting constructive coping with adversity, Lefcourt (1973) also suggests that it may be "the bedrock on which life flourishes" (p. 425).

Control is a complex phenomenon. A distinction must be made between primary and secondary control, i.e., between changing the world and changing the self. Kazantzakis (1961) put it well when he quoted a mystic's advice: "Since we cannot change reality, let us change the ideas which see reality" (p. 45). Religion offers opportunities for those in crisis to modify their perceptions of control. Rothbaum, Weisz, and Snyder (1982) suggest various means of accomplishing these ends. The remarks of breast cancer patients well illustrate these forms of secondary control (Johnson & Spilka, 1988). For example, *interpretive control* construes a distressing situation in less troubling or even

positive terms. One patient claimed that "God did not tell us that we would not have illness and other problems, but that we would be given his strength to carry us through."

A variant is *predictive control*. This approach assures the individual of a satisfactory outcome; the future is secured. Another patient stated that "Because of my relationship with God, I had faith that this cancer was not going to take my life." Lastly, *vicarious control* enables one to invoke the aid of others in order to resolve the problem. In this instance, God becomes a support or substitute for one's own actions. One woman declared, "I could talk to my God and ask for his help in healing."

Seeking help from the deity involves at least two relational patterns (Pargament et al., 1988). In one, the person may pray for aid and perceive this action as placing the problem "in the hands of God." In this *deferring* mode, the person is passive, but God is active. A *collaborative* style pictures a relationship in which both the person and the deity are active. One might pray for aid but also hold the view that "God helps those who help themselves."

Research supports the significant role of mastery and control in relation to religion and coping with crisis. Among long-term hemodialysis patients, O'Brien (1982) found that powerlessness diminishes as religious commitment increases. Patients with advanced cancer who believe that prayer is helpful (secondary vicarious control) demonstrate less pain and higher levels of well-being than their less religious counterparts (Yates et al., 1981).

Studying stress among older African-Americans, Krause and Van Tranh (1989) found that religiosity correlated with greater feelings of personal control. In like manner, indications suggestive of deferring and possibly collaborative control favorably affect well-being (Peterson & Roy, 1985). Collaborative control not only is strongly and positively affiliated with a sense that God is involved in health matters but also appears to counter a number of signs of real physical illness (McIntosh & Spilka, 1990). Faith may also find expression through the helping activities that religion supports both subjectively and institutionally. If those who help others see their efforts as beneficial, they apparently gain a sense of increased control (Krause, 1986).

Lack of a sense of control is also involved in how one looks at death. Negative images of death in terms of pain, loneliness, punishment, and failure run in parallel to perceptions of helplessness and the acceptance of a superficial, utilitarian faith orientation. In contrast, a religion of deep commitment opposes such negative feelings and is associated with a view of death in terms of an afterlife of courage and reward (Minton & Spilka, 1976; Spilka & Schmidt, 1983).

Religion offers people in crisis the hope of mastery and control over their situation. It may motivate them to try to change the existing state of affairs. If that is impossible, faith always has the potential of modifying the way reality is perceived.

Self-Esteem

A need for positive self-regard has often been seen as the most fundamental of human motives (Wylie, 1974). Whether it be through the provision of information or a sense of control, religion can make people feel good about themselves. Supporting fragile feelings of self-worth in stressful circumstances, religious explanations often take precedence over naturalistic ones, particularly if the latter suggest no hope. Brown and Siegel (1987) even suggest that "the relation between life events and illness is...mediated by changes in self-concept" (p. 1).

As with meaning and control, the research clearly demonstrates that religion is favorably related to self-esteem in difficult situations. Generally, well-being in late life is a correlate of religiosity, and this relationship holds in the areas of financial security and health problems (Koenig, Kvale, & Ferrel, 1988). Idler's (1987) work on some 2,811 elderly people also reveals that religiosity is negatively associated with functional disability and a depressive outlook. Studying

elderly African-Americans, Krause and Van Tranh (1989) found that religious involvement countered the negative effects of stress on self-esteem. A similar pattern appears to hold for cancer patients (Acklin, Brown, & Mauger, 1983). The social support that religious institutions offer also appears to maintain self-esteem (Brown & Siegel, 1987).

Conclusions

A considerable body of research supports the view that religion buffers the negative effects of crisis by providing people with religious explanations that convey positive meanings. In addition, a strong faith supports one's sense of mastery and self-esteem in severely distressing circumstances. Further research to define the cognitive and emotional aspects of these dimensions is merited. ▼ BERNARD SPILKA

See also: Chronic Pain as a Lifespan Problem; Happiness, Cohort Measures of; Mastery Types, Development, and Aging; Mental Health in the Adult Years; Native American Perspectives on the Lifespan; Religion in Adult Life; Stress; Suffering; Widowhood: The Coping Response.

References

Acklin, M. W., Brown, E. C., & Mauger, P. A. (1983). The role of religious values in coping with cancer. *Journal of Religion and Health*, 22: 322-33.

Argyle, M. (1959). *Religious Behavior*. Glencoe, IL: Free Press.

Brown, J. D., & Siegel, J. M. (1987). Stress and illness: The mediating role of changes in self-concept. Paper presented at the convention of the American Psychological Association, New York, August 1987.

Bulman, R. J., & Wortman, C. B. (1977). Attributions of blame and coping in the real world: Severe accident victims react to their lot. *Journal of Personality and Social Psychology*, 35: 351-63.

Clark, W. H. (1958). *The Psychology of Religion*. New York: Macmillan.

Fichter, J. H. (1981). *Religion and Pain*. New York: Crossroads.

Gross, L. (1982). *The Last Jews in Berlin*. New York: Simon & Schuster.

Idler, E. L. (1987). Religious involvement and the health of the elderly: Some hypotheses and an initial test. *Social Forces, 66*: 226-38.

Johnson, S., & Spilka, B. (1988). Coping with breast cancer: The role of religion. Paper presented at the convention of The Society for the Scientific Study of Religion, Chicago, October 1988.

Kazantzakis, N. (1961). *Report to Greco.* New York: Simon & Schuster.

Koenig, H. G., Kvale, J. N., & Ferrel, C. (1988). Religion and well-being in later life. *The Gerontologist, 28*: 18-28.

Krause, N. (1986). Social support, stress, and well-being among older adults. *Journal of Gerontology, 41*: 512-19.

Krause, N., & Van Tranh, T. (1989). Stress and religious involvement among older Blacks. *Journal of Gerontology, 44*: 4-13.

Lefcourt, H. M. (1973). The function of the illusions of control and freedom. *American Psychologist, 28*: 417-25.

Levin, J. S., & Schiller, P. L. (1988). Is there a religious factor in health? *Journal of Religion and Health, 26*: 9-36.

McIntosh, D. N., Silver, R. C., & Wortman, C. B. (1989). Parental religious change in response to the child's death. Paper presented at the convention of the Society for the Scientific Study of Religion, Salt Lake City, UT, October 1989.

McIntosh, D. N., & Spilka, B. (1990). Religion and physical health: The role of personal faith and control beliefs. *Research in the Social Scientific Study of Religion.* Volume 2. New York: JAI Press, pp. 167-94.

Minton, B., & Spilka, B. (1976). Perspectives on death in relation to powerlessness and form of personal religion. *Omega, Journal of Death and Dying, 7*: 261-67.

O'Brien, M. E. (1982). Religious faith and adjustment to long-term hemodialysis. *Journal of Religion and Health, 21*: 68-80.

Pargament, K. I., et al. (1988). Religion and the problem-solving process: Three styles of developing. *Journal for the Scientific Study of Religion, 27*: 90-104.

Peterson, L. R., & Roy, A. (1985). Religiosity, and meaning and purpose: Religion's consequences for psychological well-being. *Review of Religious Research, 27*: 49-63.

Pollner, M. (1989). Divine relations, social relations, and well-being. *Journal of Health and Social Behavior, 30*: 92-104.

Rothbaum, F., Weisz, J. R., & Snyder, S. S. (1982). Changing the world and changing the self:

A two process model of perceived control. *Journal of Personality and Social Psychology, 42*: 5-37.

Spilka, B., Hood, R. W., & Gorsuch, R. L. (1985). *The Psychology of Religion: An Empirical Approach.* Englewood Cliffs, NJ: Prentice-Hall.

Spilka, B. & Schmidt, G. (1983). General attribution theory for the psychology of religion: The influence of event-character on attributions to God. *Journal for the Scientific Study of Religion, 16*: 169-78.

Tillich, P. (1952). *The Courage to Be.* New Haven, CT: Yale University Press.

Wise, C. A. (1942). *Religion in Illness and Health.* New York: Harper & Bros.

Wylie, R. C. (1974). *The Self Concept.* Second Edition. Lincoln, NE: University of Nebraska Press.

Yates, J. W., et al. (1981). Religion in patients with advanced cancer. *Medical and Pediatric Oncology, 9*: 121-28.

RELIGION IN ADULT LIFE

For most of their history, the social and behavioral sciences have concerned themselves with infancy, childhood, and adolescence. Only within the past three decades has the remainder of the lifespan been "discovered." The "middle" years of adulthood, however, are still relatively ignored, as a rapidly growing population of elderly persons has directed our attention toward this group.

The psychological study of religion also has an atypical history. Prior to 1915, this was a burgeoning field, with such notables as G. Stanley Hall and William James making religion an acceptable area for psychological investigation. The introduction of behaviorism and psychoanalysis forced the psychology of religion out of the universities and into the seminaries, where for half a century it received little attention. Now, however, this trend has been reversed. Although still on the periphery of "respectable" psychology, religion is receiving consideration through new scientific journals, a spate of texts, research, and theory books, and a division of its own within the American Psychological Association

The Complexity of Religion

To examine personal faith at any age, one must appreciate its complexity. Behaviorally, people engage in a wide variety of religious activities: church attendance and participation in formal and informal ceremonies, plus the observations of various institutional rules and requirements. Cognitively, individual faith involves belief systems that include well-established theological principles which often are reinterpreted and reintegrated on the personal level. Experientially, intense religious experiences, often identified as mystical, may trigger new commitments and major changes in both religious and nonreligious behavior and beliefs. Each of these aspects of religion merits attention.

Another central consideration is that laypeople and most psychologists treat individual religious expression as a unitary phenomenon with a range from antireligious to orthodox. The majority of the data collected is therefore presented simplistically. Current models of religious orientation are multidimensional, yet most of the published research has not employed these refinements.

The relationship between religion and lifespan development appears to be a function of the needs that one's faith satisfies at different ages or different points in the life course. One theory suggests that religion helps people make sense out of complex, ambiguous, and threatening situations (Spilka, Shaver, & Kirkpatrick, 1985). To attribute an event to "God's will" can be reassuring and aid acceptance of tragedy. Religion also maintains or enhances one's sense of control in distressing circumstances via such actions as prayer or participation in ritual. Hope is one manifestation of this need for control. Religion also fulfills the desire for esteem. Positive meanings and a sense of control support a favorable self-image, and beliefs about forgiveness, God's mercy, identification with God, and so forth favor such perceptions.

Lastly, formal religious activity brings individuals of like mind together, thus meeting social needs. Churches frequently offer counseling, educational, and recreational programs as well to help their members cope with a variety of problems.

Religious Behavior

The most obvious behavioral indices of religious significance are religious affiliation, church attendance, and other activities such as home ritual observance, Bible reading, and engaging in private prayer. Recent Gallup poll data reveal that nationally 68 percent of the population are formally affiliated with religious institutions, and 43 percent attend services weekly (De Stefano, 1990).

Both of these indicators increase with age. While 61 percent of those aged 20 to 29 belong to a religious body and 34 percent regularly participate in services, these numbers respectively rise to 76 and 52 percent for persons aged 50 and older. As might be expected, these trends are accentuated among those who are formally affiliated with religious bodies. Studying more than 11,000 church members, Benson and Eklin (1990) found that 65 percent of those aged 20 to 29 attend church once a week or more. This tendency strengthens with age until 80 percent of those over 60 act similarly (Benson & Eklin, 1990). A similar pattern is evidenced when one looks at members who volunteer 11 or more hours a week to their church. The data show a steady rise from 4 percent of those in their twenties to 19 percent for church members 60 and older. (It is possible, of course, that the higher percentage of elderly people engaging in this kind of religious behavior reflects cohort differences to some extent and not necessarily changes with age in the same individual.)

These observations prompt one to ask whether churches offer programs and opportunities for senior adults. With 20 to 30 percent of church members being over the age of 65 and another 10 to 15 percent in the group aged 50 to 65, it is evident that institutionalized religion ministers extensively to the older segments of the population. Despite the fact that this represents a programmatic challenge, religious bodies have not been developing agendas to provide special services for those over 50. One survey of more than 3,000 churches found that none had budgeted funds to tailor programs for the aged (Culver, 1991). In other words, those who make up the majority of attendees at weekly services, and who may be the primary supporters of churches and synagogues, seem to get little or no attention from religious groups.

Similar age trends are apparent in religious behavior other than church participation. More Protestant church members of age 60 read the Bible at least several times a week, as compared with younger members. Although the differences are not greater (24 percent and 16 percent), fewer of the younger members deal with scripture. A like pattern is evident for prayer and meditation other than at church or meals. Forty-nine percent of those over 60 engage in these behaviors. With a slight reversal among 40-year-olds, there is a declining trend down to 35 percent for members in their twenties (Benson & Eklin, 1990).

Among Catholics in the general population, the trend is smaller but in the same direction. Asked if they had read the Bible within the preceding month, affirmative responses were given by 28 percent of those above 50 as compared with 18 percent of those aged 18 to 29. For meditation, the respective numbers are 35 and 23 percent (Gallup & Poling, 1980).

These figures clearly reveal that religious involvement is more common and intense among older adults. The reasons for such activity are not always evident, however. One argument suggests intergenerational differences in that the older segment of the population was brought up in a world where religion was more significant in the general culture. If so, we would expect senior adults to have attended church for a longer time when young than their junior counterparts. For church members, this is apparently true (Benson & Eklin, 1990). That people who are now at older adult ages attended church for a longer period of time in childhood can be seen in Table 1.

The overall trend is for a higher percentage of church members who are now in their middle and later adult years to have attended church for 10 or more years as a child. The trend reverses for those in their twenties at the time the survey was made. This could be a function of the increasing conservatism of the 1980s and the popularity of the born-again movement (Gallup & Poling, 1980; Roberts, 1984).

In addition to early training, the issue of what religious behavior does for people—particularly older people—needs to be confronted. Prayer and participation in ceremonies are *active cognitive coping strategies* that moderate stress (Holahan & Moos, 1987). In early and middle adulthood, religion helps to integrate people into the community and serves as a support for family life. It might also reduce job and achievement stress. Stress is often greater in the later years, however, because of growing awareness of the increasing probability of retirement, poor health, bereavement, the loss of a number of sources of satisfaction, and death. The relative lack of opportunities to regain or replace age-associated losses can impair morale and self-esteem. Despite the prevalence of mitigating terminology, the "golden years" are not favorably regarded in our society, leaving religion and the church as one of the few remaining need-fulfilling avenues open to many elderly persons.

Religious behavior and church involvement can provide alternative positive meanings and buttress self-esteem. The promise of

Table 1. Church Attendance in Childhood as Reported by Adults

Age of Adults	Percent Attending Church 10 Years or More During Childhood
20-29	6%
30-39	3%
40-49	5%
50-59	8%
60-69	9%

Based on data reported by P.L. Benson and C.H. Eklin, *Effective Christian Education: A National Study of Protestant Congregations*, Minneapolis, MN: Search Institute, 1990.

life after death and engaging in behaviors that ally one with the deity are viewed as reducing anxiety and empowering people (Fromm, 1950; Pruyser, 1968). Beit-Hallahmi (1989) further discusses "the production and control of emotion...in religious ritual" (p. 82). Through religious ritual one is doing something, and hope is a likely result.

Religious Beliefs

Religious beliefs both follow and condition religious behavior, therefore, as church involvement increases with age, so does the significance of religious belief. The personal significance of faith is rated as very important by 43 percent of respondents aged 18 to 29, 55 percent of those aged 30 to 49, and 70 percent of those 50 and older (Gallup & Newport, 1990).

The statement that religious beliefs constitute the center of their lives is claimed as "mostly" to "absolutely" true by church members. This view increases from 39 percent for those aged 20 to 29 to 50 to 59 percent for those above 60. Still, some unexpected contradiction is present—strong belief in life after death increases from the twenties through the fifties, but declines from 83 percent in the fifties to 73 percent for those over 60. One may speculate about a potential rejection of these ideas, leading to a sense of resignation as life nears its end. Despite this decline in the percentage of those expressing a belief in life after death, most church members do hold onto this belief late in life. The role of the church is considered to be of major importance to more church members in their sixties (48 percent) as compared with those in their twenties (30 percent). A similar pattern holds for the view that older church members "have a real sense that God is guiding" them. Whereas 27 percent of members in their twenties claims this is "almost always" to "always" true, 49 percent of those above 60 signal their assent (Benson & Eklin, 1990).

Looking to broad religious patterns rather than responses to single items, Benson and Eklin (1990) show steady increases in age for what they term *vertical and horizontal forms of faith.* Vertical implies "having a deep personal relationship with a loving God," while horizontal faith translates "this personal affirmation into acts of love, mercy, and justice" (p. 13).

These findings with religious beliefs parallel observations of religious activity, and undoubtedly each realm feeds the other. Beliefs are fundamentally meanings, and religious meanings possess the potential for empowerment and the enhancement of self-esteem. To the extent that nature and society may limit the options available to people as they age, religious faith offers promise and potential.

Religious Experience

The perception that one has had an intense religious or mystical experience can have powerful life-changing repercussions. Depending on how the question is phrased, 25 to 50 percent of the American population claim such an encounter with the divine. This is a controversial area. The older research pictures these events as primarily adolescent phenomena. The "born again" movement of the past three decades challenges this view. National data claim that 29 percent of 18- to 29-year-olds report born again experiences (Gallup, 1987). Similar occurrences are reported by 36 percent of those above 50. These data are consonant with our knowledge of religious beliefs and actions.

There is little doubt that the American people are strongly committed to traditional religion in its behavioral, cognitive, and experiential forms. These manifestations evidently increase with age. If, as contended here, one's faith offers meaning, control, and esteem to its adherents, we would expect to find evidence of its benefits in the lives of adults, especially older people. This hypothesis is rather well supported.

Correlates of Religion in Adult Life

With surprisingly little contradiction, research tells us that religion serves positive functions throughout adulthood, particularly among elderly persons in the areas of life satisfaction, mental health, and physical health.

Study after study, many using national adult samples, show that church attendance, religious beliefs, and the social dimension of religion counter distress, loneliness, depression, and personal adversity (Clemente & Sauer, 1976; McCann, 1962; Pollner, 1989; Ross, 1990). Faith accomplishes these ends by providing religionists with a sense of meaning and purpose that lessens anxiety (Peterson & Roy, 1985). Stress is reduced by the use of prayer and religious involvement, both of which apparently support self-esteem (Krause & Van Tranh, 1989; McCann, 1962).

Religion has also been found to promote health and actually decrease illness, possibly by bolstering the body's immune system (King, 1990). Levin and Schiller (1987) surveyed more than 200 empirical studies in this area, observing negative associations between religiosity and cardiovascular disease, hypertension, the rates of some cancers, and a variety of digestive disorders. In like manner, general health status and longevity correlated positively with religious commitment and involvement.

Many religious groups counsel and teach good health habits, and oppose unhealthy behaviors. The Mormons (members of the Church of Jesus Christ of Latter-day Saints) are noted for their emphasis on good nutrition and wellness, and their health statistics clearly show the benefits of these recommendations (King, 1990). The social support that some churches offer ill members may also aid in their recovery as well as enhancing their resistance to illness. Lastly, the well-known relationship between the sense of internal control and good health may be further buttressed by the conviction that the deity offers believers the strength to face life and adversity.

Conclusions

Religion is an integral part of the lives of most Americans and seems to be of the great-est significance among elderly persons. It apparently serves many people well, aiding them to cope with the trials and hardships of life by providing a positive sense of meaning, while also supporting desires for mastery and esteem. In our society, these needs usually become more critical as we age. Religious institutions could enhance their contribution to the mental and physical well-being of the population by attending more explicitly to these necessities. ▼ BERNARD SPILKA

See also: Cardiac Health; Individuality; Japanese Perspectives on Adult Development; Loneliness; Mental Health in the Adult Years; Native American Perspectives on the Lifespan; Religion and Coping with Crisis; Social Support for the Chronically Ill; Stress; Work Organization Membership and Behavior.

References

Beit-Hallahmi, B. (1989). *Prolegomena to the Psychological Study of Religion*. Lewisburg, PA: Bucknell University Press.

Benson, P. L., & Eklin, C. H. (1990). *Effective Christian Education: A National Study of Protestant Congregations*. Minneapolis, MN: Search Institute.

Clemente, F., & Sauer, W. J. (1976). Life satisfaction in the United States. *Social Forces, 54*: 621-31.

Culver, V. (1991). Congregations "Graying": Churches ignore older people, expert on aging says. *The Denver Post*, May 4, p. 6b.

De Stefano, L. (1990). Church/synagogue membership and attendance levels remain stable. *The Gallup Poll Monthly, 292* (August): 32-34.

Fromm, E. (1950). *Psychoanalysis and Religion*. New Haven, CT: Yale University Press.

Gallup, G., Jr. (1987). Religion in America. *The Gallup Report*, April, p. 259.

Gallup, G., Jr., & Newport, F. (1990). More Americans now believe in a power outside of themselves. *The Gallup Poll Monthly, 297* (June): 33-39.

Gallup, G., Jr. & Poling, D. (1980). *The Search for America's Faith*. Nashville, TN: Abingdon.

Holahan, C. J., & Moos, R. H. (1987). Personal and contextual determinants of coping strategies. *Journal of Personality and Social Psychology, 52*: 946-55.

King, D. G. (1990). Religion and health relationships: A review. *Journal of Religion and Health, 29*: 101-12.

Krause, N., & Van Tranh, T. (1989). Stress and religious involvement among older Blacks. *Journal of Gerontology, 44*: S4-S13.

Levin, J. S., & Schiller, P. L. (1987). Is there a religious factor in health? *Journal of Religion and Health, 26*: 9-36.

McCann, R. V. (1962). *The Churches and Mental Health*. New York: Basic Books.

Peterson, L. R., & Roy, A. (1985). Religiosity, anxiety, and meaning and purpose: Religion's consequences for psychological well-being. *Review of Religious Research, 27*: 49-62.

Pollner, M. (1989). Divine relations, social relations, and well-being. *Journal of Health Behavior, 30*: 92-104.

Pruyser, P. (1968). *A Dynamic Psychology of Religion*. New York: Harper & Row.

Roberts, K. A. (1984). *Religion in Sociological Perspective*. Homewood, IL: Dorsey.

Ross, C. E. (1990). Religion and psychological distress. *Journal for the Scientific Study of Religion, 29*: 236-45.

Spilka, B., Shaver, P., & Kirkpatrick, L. A. (1985). A general attribution theory for the psychology of religion. *Journal for the Scientific Study of Religion, 24*: 1-20.

REMINISCENCE AND LIFE REVIEW

Life review is a developmental process of adulthood that encourages one to recall and examine one's history. In this examination, one assigns greater value to certain life events than to others. For example, successfully graduating from high school is likely to be recalled as a pleasurable life event. An event of this kind contributes to a sense of satisfaction and accomplishment when it is brought back to mind. Not graduating from high school is likely to be viewed as an unsuccessful event that arouses bad feelings when recalled. In coping with the memory of negative personal events from the past, one must examine and work through them. In this instance, a middle-aged or elderly adult might judge that not graduating was the only course of action that was possible at the time and, therefore, is not a reason to feel regret or self-

anger now. However, if the individual's life review leads to the recall of negative events that cannot be resolved, set right, or dismissed in retrospect, these events remain as "unfinished business," ever ready to cause additional moments of sadness and decreased self-esteem.

Reminiscing is primarily a pleasurable event, often occurring as an interaction between people who share similar histories. This process can also occur within one's own memory as a sort of private dialogue, conducted in the manner of a gently drifting daydream. Sometimes reminiscing occurs spontaneously; at other times it is a more purposeful activity.

External events often trigger the reminiscence process. For example, a class reunion encourages people to relive the past and is usually a pleasurable time for sharing memories that produce warm feelings. The positive nature of these sharing episodes has raised the idea in many observers that reminiscence may not only be pleasurable but possibly therapeutic as well.

Early Observations of Reminiscing and Life Review

Literary works presented effective examples of both reminiscing and life review before these concepts became well established in the social and behavioral sciences. Among the outstanding examples is Tolstoy's 1882 novel, *The Death of Ivan Ilych*. During his fatal illness, Ilych feels a terrible loneliness. Eventually, pictures of his past life rise before him, one after another. The memories begin with what was nearest in time and then go back to early childhood. As he continues to explore his past, the same question repeatedly occurs to Ilych: "What if my whole life has really been wrong?" Once he could accept that painful possibility, Ilych started to pass his life in review in quite a new way and was finally able to transcend his pain and loneliness and achieve a peaceful death.

One of the first professionals to notice the therapeutic effectiveness of reminiscing was Robert Butler (1963). A psychiatrist, Butler worked with older people and wrote of the universal occurrence of life review in his patients. He noticed that some people completed successful life reviews and then moved on to other things in their lives. Others were stuck in the past, remembering events that disturbed them. These people became depressed and unable to cope with new challenges or take advantage of new opportunities. As a consequence, Butler believed that reminiscence should be encouraged, especially in older adults. Furthermore, his observations suggested that those who reminisced with a listener had more successful and therapeutic experiences.

Butler and Lewis (1974) later conducted reminiscing groups for older people and reported that these experiences helped the participants to understand the meaning of life. Butler (1974) further visualized life review as being prompted by crises that require one to reconsider one's identity and examine one's life-style. He suggested the need for a participant observer to act as a sounding board and to assist the reviewers in coming to terms with their lives.

The first empirical studies in this area were stimulated by Butler's early observations. McMahon and Rhudick (1964) found that veterans who reminisced had higher self-esteem than those who did not. In a more recent study, Haight (1988) conducted a six-week structured life review process with 60 homebound elderly adults and found that the life review experience significantly improved life satisfaction and psychological well-being.

Not all studies have had confirming results. Hedgepeth and Hale (1983) reported that their one-hour reminiscence intervention did not lead to a significant improvement in affect. Lieberman and Falk (1971) examined data from past interviews and concluded that there was no empirical support for a correlation between reminiscence and adaptation. Thus, a controversy began about the therapeutic efficacy of reminiscing and life review. The concepts themselves became blurred, and this blurring led to increased ambivalence about their usefulness.

Several reviewers have examined the work on reminiscing and life review (Hughston & Merriam, 1982; LoGerfor, 1980-1981; Molinari & Reichlin, 1984-1985; Taft & Nehrke, 1990). These reviews provide an excellent foundation for future studies and for a clearer understanding of the concepts. In essence, the reviews reiterate the need to define and differentiate the concepts of life review and reminiscing and to show that the processes differ. Only when the dimensions of each process are carefully studied and related to specific adaptation outcomes will practitioners be able to use these processes effectively.

The Eriksonian Connection

Theoretically, the work in reminiscence fits well into the epigenetic developmental concepts of Erik Erikson (1950). Erikson was among the first to explore developmental roles throughout the entire lifespan. He holds that a person must accomplish specific developmental tasks at a particular time in life in order to move on effectively to the next developmental position. For example, the first task faced by the infant is trust versus mistrust. The infant must learn to trust and gain hope before moving on to the next task of autonomy versus shame. If the infant does not achieve trust, it becomes stunted developmentally, limited by its mistrusting orientation (which, like trust, is strongly influenced by experiences with other people). The process is similar to stair climbing. If one cannot climb up the first step, one will never get to the second, or reach the top.

How does an infant learn mistrust rather than trust? Consider the loved child. When the loved child becomes hungry and cries, an adult brings a bottle. When the loved child becomes wet and cries, an adult changes the diaper. The caregiver holds and cuddles the loved child. Soon the loved child trusts that this adult will answer the child's needs, and there is a foundation for interpersonal trust.

Now consider the abused child. When the abused child becomes hungry and cries, an adult spanks the child until it stops crying.

When the abused child becomes wet and cries, again it is exposed to an adult's rage. The caregiver does not cuddle and love the abused child; instead the child's needs are often ignored. Soon the abused child does not cry for food and diaper changes; it has learned to mistrust the adult caregiver. In a word, the infant does not have hope. In this way the child learns mistrust in a primary relationship, and this feeling is transferred to encounters with others. As the child grows up, it may never place trust in another person and, therefore, never move on to Erikson's second stage (achieving a sense of autonomy).

Erikson's last stage is ego integrity versus despair. Integrity is said to be the acceptance of one's one-and-only life cycle as something that had to be and that by necessity permitted no substitutions. Ego integrity is a comradeship with the ways of distant times and a comfortableness with the inevitability of the life cycle. It is an emotional integration. Similarly, the process of life review incorporates a return to consciousness of past experiences that are resolved and reintegrated (Butler, 1963). Thus, the life review process facilitates the acceptance of life and the attainment of ego integrity and wisdom.

Erikson (1950) proposes that the opposite of integrity is despair. If an older person does not master the developmental task of integrity, this person may end up in despair, which signifies hopelessness and the feeling that the time remaining to one is too short to repair one's life and achieve a sense of positive wholeness. This view is similar to Butler's (1974) description of people who are "stuck" in their life reviews as depressed and despairing. Such a result occurs when there are particular events from the past that a person cannot reintegrate into his or her present life view. Thus, an unsuccessful life review results in an unsuccessful reintegration of remembered life events, accompanied by despair and hopelessness.

Unblurring the Life Review/ Reminiscing Confusion

Because these concepts became popular so quickly, their relationship soon became intermingled and confused. Writers on both topics failed to define the methodology for a successful life review, nor did they clearly differentiate life review from reminiscing. Instead, they examined different types of reminiscing and reported on them all as if they were the same.

This blurring of definitions led to a blurring of results and a lack of understanding about both processes. For example, as already noted, researchers would refer to a single interview session as a life review and then conclude that the results were not therapeutic. Some said the reminiscence process was ineffective and itself occasionally caused depression. In fact, however, an hour's worth of remembering is quite different from an integrative life review, and the differences in types of intervention produce different outcomes. To help "unblur" the definitions, Table 1 delineates the differences between reminiscing and life review.

Table 1. Differences Between Life Review and Reminiscence

Life Review	Reminiscence
Effort & Work	Pleasure
Self	Other
Evaluative	Nonevaluative
Integrative	Nonintegrative
Lifespan	Occasional times
Individual	Group
Prompted by Need or Crisis	Any Cue
Reframing Events	Accepting Events
Repetition & Catharsis	Repetition is Optional
Structured	Random

Source: B. K. Haight, College of Nursing, University of South Carolina, 1990.

Although some writers continue to use the terms "life review" and "reminiscing" interchangeably, they are two separate modalities and should be discussed individually. Certainly, reminiscing is a part of the life review process, but a true life review is more complicated than simple reminiscing. First, a life review is hard work, whereas reminiscing is often just a pleasurable moment. Life review is evaluative and integrative; reminiscing need not be.

In a life review, one recalls, assesses, evaluates, reframes, and then integrates. Participants cry over sad times and rework issues. They often rework issues so much that repetition becomes a part of the life review. Repetition may serve as a catharsis and ease the reintegration of the self. Life review examines the actions of the self at the time, place, or event. Reminiscence occurs about the events, times, and places as they were, and does not necessarily involve reflections on the self. Furthermore, life review encompasses the total lifespan; reminiscence does not need to do that. For example, if one is with old high school friends, the reminiscence is usually limited to shared experiences in those particular "good old days." Lastly, life review has structure; reminiscence does not.

Therapeutic Reminiscing

The question remains: What makes reminiscing therapeutically successful? In an effort to answer this question, Haight (1991) examined selected variables by conducting the reminiscing process in eight different ways. She examined the variables of individuality, structure, and evaluation. One set of interventions included all three variables; another set included two of the variables. All combinations of variables were used in the reminiscing processes to determine the most effective variables or combination of variables. Each of the sets of reminiscing processes was conducted over an eight-week period, so length of time was not a variable.

The results showed that *evaluation* was the most important part of a therapeutic reminiscing process. Without evaluation—an examination and valuing of life—there were no significant therapeutic effects on life satisfaction, psychological well-being, depression, and self-esteem.

Structure was also important. Structure means covering the entire lifespan rather than covering the lifespan in sequence. It did not matter if the reviewer discussed marriage before centering on preschool experience—but it did matter that the reviewer discussed all developmental levels and included both marriage and preschool.

The last component, *individuality*, refers to a private life review, performed on a one-to-one basis with the assistance of another person. Privacy helped people to resolve problems that were too personal to discuss in group settings and also proved to be a factor in a successful life review.

When the eight types of reminiscing processes were compared with one another and with two current events processes, the most therapeutic modality was found to be the individual structured evaluative life review process. This reminiscence process included all three concepts: individuality, structure, and evaluation.

Conclusion

Reminiscing and life review are pleasurable activities that enhance the developmental process in adults. Of the two, reminiscence is the more generic: Life review is one type of reminiscence. Scholars and researchers have used these terms interchangeably for many years. This lack of definition clouded the usefulness of both processes, leading to calls for clarification by those who reviewed the literature.

It is useful to couch life review within the framework of Erikson's lifespan developmental approach. The goal of a successful life review is the achievement of integrity. *Life review is an effective therapeutic modality for the entire adult lifespan.* Although most of the reported work in life review and reminiscing is with older people, the modality also seems to be effective for younger adults. For example, the high school student contemplating the future may find it useful to review his or her past life and list those events that are positively valued as well as those that were troublesome or disappointing. A consideration of events and experiences elicited through a life review can contribute to thoughtful decision making about future options.

In the middle adult years, there are many occasions for adjustment and the possibility of facing crises in many spheres. Typical problems include adjusting to the children leaving (or *not* leaving) home and dealing with frustrations and stresses experienced in the workplace. With a life review, the past can be valued and these values can then serve as a basis to plan for the future. The individual assessing his or her life can feel satisfaction over accomplishments and also work through and reframe failures—and then can begin again. Often, a life review performed therapeutically provides a new beginning at any age.   ▼ BARBARA K. HAIGHT

See also: Grandparent Education to Enhance Family Strength; Intelligence; Memory; Mental Health in the Adult Years; Mid-Life Crisis; Place and Personality in Adult Development; Privacy Issues; Trust as a Challenge in Adult Development; Widowhood: The Coping Response.

References

Butler, R. N. (1963). The life review: An interpretation of reminiscence in the aged. *Psychiatry, 26*: 65-76.

———. (1974). Successful aging and the role of the life review. *Journal of the American Geriatric Society, 22*: 529-34.

Butler, R. N. & Lewis, M. (1974). *Aging and Mental Health.* Second Edition. St. Louis, MO: Mosby.

Erikson, E. (1950). *Childhood and Society.* New York: W. W. Norton.

Haight, B. K. (1988). The therapeutic role of a structured life review process in homebound elderly subjects. *Journal of Gerontology, 43*: 40-44.

———. (1991). *The Examination of a Nursing Intervention: The Life Review.* Richmond, VA: Proceedings of the Southern Nursing Research Society.

Hedgepeth, B. E., & Hale, D. (1983). Effect of a positive reminiscing intervention on affect, expectancy, and performance. *Psychological Reports, 53*: 867-70.

Hughston, G. A., & Merriam, S. B. (1982). Reminiscence: A non-formal technique for improving cognitive functioning in the aged. *International Journal of Aging and Human Development, 15*: 139-49.

Lewis, M. I., & Butler, R. N. (1974). Life review therapy: Putting memories to work in individual and group psychotherapy. *Geriatrics, 29*: 165-73.

Lieberman, M., & Falk, J. (1971). The remembered past as a source of data for research on the life cycle. *Human Development, 14*: 132-71.

LoGerfo, M. (1980-1981). Three ways of reminiscence in theory and practice. *International Journal of Aging and Human Development, 12*: 39-48.

McMahon, A. W., & Rhudick, P. J. R (1964). Reminiscing in the aged: An adaptational response. In S. Levin & R. J. Kahana (Eds.), *Psychodynamic Studies on Aging: Creativity, Reminiscing, and Dying.* New York: International Universities Press.

Molinari, V., & Reichlin, R. E. (1984-1985). Life review reminiscence in the elderly: A review of the literature. *International Journal of Aging and Human Development, 20*: 81-92.

Taft, L. B., & Nehrke, M. F. (1990). Reminiscence, life review, and integrity in nursing home residents. *International Journal of Aging and Human Development, 30*: 189-96.

RETIREMENT: AN EMERGING CHALLENGE FOR WOMEN

In the numerous studies of retirement and its implications for society and the individual, particular attention has been given to the relationship between retirement and life satisfaction, morale, and personal identity (Erdner & Guy, 1990). Not surprisingly, the bulk of these studies have been concerned with men's adjustment to retirement since, traditionally, retirement has been primarily a male phenomenon. The notion of retirement as a male phenomenon rests largely on two basic arguments: (a) more men than women retire, and (b) this transition is more significant for men than for women. However, the veracity of these two arguments is being challenged seriously by a growing body of evidence.

In 1960, 23 million women were gainfully employed outside the home. By 1988 this figure had exceeded 55 million. At present, 57 percent of women work outside the home, as do 76.5 percent of men. In short, women presently represent approximately 40 percent of the U.S. labor force (U.S. Department of Labor, 1991). Additionally, by 1988, 73.6 percent of women with children between ages 6 and 17 were working, and

56.1 percent of women with children under age 6 were working.

It is estimated that by the year 2000, 80 percent of women between the ages of 25 and 49 will be in the labor force. This means that women would represent 47 percent of the labor force by the end of the present decade and century. This high rate of labor force participation by women—even those with preschool children—is a strong indicator that many women will be spending most of their lives in paid employment. It is this set of impressive and undeniable facts that pronounces retirement to be an emerging challenge for women.

Factors Influencing Women's Labor Force Participation

No single factor provides a complete explanation of the dramatic changes in women's work patterns. Rather, there is evidence that three important trends are largely responsible for this historic shift.

A substantial body of research identifies *financial need* as one of the primary extrinsic motivations for working women. Like men, most women are employed out of economic necessity. In fact, 44 percent of the women in the paid labor force are single, divorced, or widowed (U.S. Department of Labor, 1991). Likewise, most married women's earnings are a critical component of total family income.

A second trend viewed as an explanation for the rise of women in the work force is *increasing education*. In 1988, women represented 53.5 percent of the college population. In that same year, women earned 51.5 percent of all bachelor's degrees and 51 percent of all master's degrees (U.S. Department of Education, 1991). Between 1967 and 1987, the representation of women in such male-dominated occupations as architecture, medicine, and law more than doubled—and in some cases tripled or quadrupled. Since postsecondary education greatly increases the likelihood of women being in the labor force, it is logical to infer that college-educated males

can expect increasing career competition from college-educated females.

A third trend explaining the increase of women in the work force is changing gender roles. Today, women have considerable freedom to choose how they will fulfill their gender roles. It is becoming increasingly acceptable for women to have fewer children or to remain childless or even single. The number of single women between ages 25 and 29 rose from 11 percent in 1970 to 29 percent in 1987 (U.S. Bureau of the Census, 1988). Patterns observed during the period 1979-1980 have led to estimates that the average American woman can expect to spend 29.4 years of her life in the work force, compared with 38.8 years for men.

These statistics clearly demonstrate the potentially high rate of female employment and retirement over the next few decades. As the proportion of women in the work force continues to expand, and as women remain in the work force for longer periods of time, it seems probable that their retirement experience will become, at last, a "societally significant phenomenon" (Szinovacz, 1986-1987, p. 302).

Gender Bias in Early Retirement Research

The most common rite of passage symbolizing movement from middle age to old age is retirement. As early as 1949, Talcott Parsons called attention to the problem faced by men as they approached this transition period:

> By comparison with other societies the United States assumes the extreme position in the isolation of old age from participation in the most important social structures and interests....In view of the very great significance of occupational status...retirement leaves the older man in a peculiarly functionless situation. (Parsons, 1949, pp. 230-31)

The retirement literature of the 1950s and 1960s totally embraced this Parsonian position. For men, retirement was thought to represent a serious identity and status crisis, which was only exacerbated by society's inability to offer a compensatory role. Research specifically concerned with female retirement was virtually nonexistent before 1975. Early studies that did give lip service to the adaptation of women to retirement simply assumed that the adjustment was easy because women's primary role was not founded in work but, rather, in family. These studies did not consider work necessary to a woman's self-esteem since she lacked commitment to work (Cumming & Henry, 1961).

The rationale for this widely accepted approach to women's retirement issues was grounded in role theory's emphasis on the social and psychological losses incurred by males in the transition from work to retirement. These assumptions led to the conclusion that only the American male constructed his identity in work. Hence, males were said to have difficulty in adjusting to retirement, while females did not. "Retirement...deprives a man of the respect accorded the breadwinner in the American family and constrains him to assume a role similar to that of women. In this respect retirement is a more demoralizing experience for men than for women" (Blau, 1973, p. 29).

In the 1970s, social scientists influenced by feminism criticized the unverified notion that females adapt easily to retirement. "These critics argued that women had a strong commitment to work, that retirement deprived them of social contacts and isolated them in a domestic sphere they sought to escape, and that the loss of a meaningful work life, when combined with widowhood, led to substantial declines in their subjective well being" (Gratton & Haug, 1983, p. 62). It was this bold challenge to long held but empirically untested assumptions that opened the door for new studies of women and retirement.

Emerging Research Findings on Women's Retirement

Szinovacz (1986-1987, p. 302) writes that the emphasis on men in past retirement research would be of little consequence if men and women experienced retirement in similar ways and if major predictors of retirement satisfaction did not vary by sex. Unfortunately, the evidence on sex differences and the retirement experience is contradictory and confusing. Some studies suggest that females experience less anxiety about retirement than males; others suggest just the opposite. For example, several studies have reported that working women express more negative attitudes toward retirement than men and are more anxious about their nonworking years (Szinovacz, 1986-1987). In marked contrast, others have reported that retired women adjust very well to this life transition and view retirement as an opportunity to set their own schedules and commitments (Gigy, 1985-1986). This picture is further complicated by recent studies that demonstrate few, if any, sex differences. There is some evidence that the forces shaping men's retirement patterns are becoming increasingly important to women (Hayward, Grady, & McLaughlin, 1988).

The contradictory nature of research findings on sex differences in retirement clearly demonstrates the need to look beyond this factor if the retirement experience is to be thoroughly understood. It becomes of extreme importance to include personal, social, and work-related variables in both theoretical and research models on retirement. Cumming and Henry (1961), for example, have explained sex differences in adjustment to retirement by underscoring male-female differences in instrumental versus socioemotional approaches to coping. They argue that the less obligated, more discretionary time framework of the post-employed person may be more comprehensible and useful to women because of their higher priority and superior skills in the realm of interpersonal relations. An alternative explanation has been offered by Block (1982), who argues that sex differences in adjustment to retirement may be attributable to the lengthy and continuous work history experienced by most men and uncommon to most women. Understanding the extent to which these and other personal, social, and work-related variables contribute to sex differences in the retirement experience is just one of the many challenges awaiting future research.

Job attachment, work identity, activity level, income, and health are among the variables that are now being explored (Erdner & Guy, 1990). For the most part, this research has demonstrated that job attachment and work identity are negatively related to retirement attitudes, while activity level, income, and health are positively related. Additionally, there is some evidence to suggest that gradual as opposed to abrupt retirement results in a more successful transition for women (Usher, 1981). Similarly, a number of investigators have reported that retirement planning is positively related to satisfaction with and adjustment to the retirement years (Dorfman, 1989). There is also some evidence to suggest that working women's perceptions of retirement vary by age, marital status, and occupational status (Block, 1982). More specifically, older women and those in professional work roles have reported fewer positive perceptions concerning retirement. Additionally, a greater percentage of unmarried women in professional work roles have reported adverse concerns related to retirement.

Despite the increased research on female retirement, the literature remains critically deficient in several areas. First, research on women facing retirement has been extremely narrow in focus—concentrating on a relatively small set of variables and relationships, and spanning a relatively short period of time. Second, samples have been less than adequate, primarily because there are not yet large numbers of retired professional women from which samples can be selected. Third, little is known about possible ethnic and racial differences in retirement; the retirement of African-American women in particular remains virtually unaddressed.

Policy Implications

Individuals aged 65 and over represent the fastest growing age category in the United States. At present, elderly people comprise 12 percent of the total population. By the year 2025, this percentage is expected to increase to 21 percent, which translates to about 59 million people.

Stated in another way, in 1987, there were approximately 19.8 million Americans 65 and over for every 100 working-age adults. This figure, known as the *elderly dependency ratio*, is expected to double by the year 2030 (U.S. Department of Commerce, 1989). The majority of these older Americans today are women, and this will also be the case in the future. It is estimated that the current female life expectancy of 79 will rise to 81 within the first decade of the twenty-first century (U.S. Department of Commerce, 1989). This overall pattern means an increase in the number of years that people—especially women—spend outside of the labor force and in retirement.

The perception that retirement is not of equal significance for men and women is undergoing rapid change. With increasing numbers of women entering and remaining in the work force—including traditionally male-dominated occupations—it is possible that work is becoming the primary source of identification and self-worth for most adults, regardless of gender. Women in high-prestige, professional occupations might be expected to have particularly strong commitments to their careers and, therefore, misgivings about retirement.

A substantial body of evidence suggests that the importance of work in people's lives does indeed influence their attitudes toward retirement (Erdner & Guy, 1990). In fact, it has been argued that strong attachment to occupation *prevents* a positive attitude toward retirement, whereas low attachment to one's work *precipitates* a positive attitude. Additionally, there is evidence demonstrating that individuals who view their occupation as the central organizing factor in their lives tend to regard retirement as disrupting and threatening to their primary role identification. In contrast, those who view their occupation primarily as a source of income are more prone to perceive retirement as an opportunity to pursue other activities.

As the work roles of men and women become increasingly similar, we should start to see fewer and fewer differences in retirement attitudes and adjustment. Considerably more women will face problems similar to those faced by men.

Future research will demand larger and more representative samples from all races, social classes, and occupational groups as well as the inclusion of longitudinal designs. Careful attention must also be given to the measurement of crucial attitudinal variables such as perceived health, and expectations and beliefs regarding retirement, life satisfaction, and work satisfaction. Once the relationships among these and other variables are better understood, we will be able to use our knowledge not just to *predict* successful retirement but rather to help women as well as men *experience* successful retirement.

▼ REBECCA F. GUY AND RUTH ANN ERDNER

See also: Disengagement Theory; Gender as a Shaping Force in Adult Development and Aging; Life Events; Longevity; Mexican Americans: Life Course Transitions and Adjustment; Retirement Preparation.

References

Blau, Z. S. (1973). *Old Age in a Changing Society*. New York: New Viewpoints.

Block, M. R. (1982). *Women's Retirement: Policy Implications of Recent Research*. Beverly Hills, CA: Sage.

Cumming, E., & Henry, W. E. (1961). *Growing Old*. New York: Basic Books.

Dorfman, L. T. (1989). Retirement preparation and retirement satisfaction in the rural elderly. *The Journal of Applied Gerontology*, 8: 432-50.

Erdner, R. A., & Guy, R. F. (1990). Career identification and women's attitudes toward retirement. *International Journal of Aging and Human Development*, 30: 129-39.

Gigy, L. L. (1985-1986). Preretired and retired women's attitudes toward retirement. *International Journal of Aging and Human Development*, 22: 31-44.

Gratton, B., & Haug, M. R. (1983). Decision and adaptation. *Research on Aging*, 5: 59-76.

Hayward, M. D., Grady, W. R., & McLaughlin, S. D. (1988). The retirement process among older women in the United States. *Research on Aging*, 10: 358-82.

Parsons, T. (1949). *Essays in Sociological Theory, Pure and Applied*. Glencoe, IL: Free Press.

Szinovacz, M. (1986-1987). Preferred retirement timing and retirement satisfaction in women. *International Journal of Aging and Human Development*, 24: 301-17.

U.S. Bureau of the Census. (1988). *Marital Status and Living Arrangements: March, 1987*. Current Population Reports, Series P-20, No. 423. Washington, DC: U.S. Government Printing Office.

U.S. Department of Commerce. (1989). *Population of the United States, by Age, Sex, and Race: 1988-2000*. Series P-25, No. 1018. Washington, DC: U.S. Government Printing Office.

U.S. Department of Education. (1991). *Digest of Education Statistics 1990*. Washington, DC: U.S. Government Printing Office.

U.S. Department of Labor. (January, 1991). *Employment and Earnings*. Washington, DC: U.S. Government Printing Office.

Usher, C. E. (1981). Alternative work options for older workers: Part I—employees' interest. *Aging and Work*, 4: 74-80.

RETIREMENT PREPARATION

As individuals approach the end of their working lives, they often begin to think about retirement. Like most major events in life, retirement require a series of adjustments. The individual and his or her family face many challenges in making the transition from the work role to a new life situation. Learning to live on a reduced income, reallotting work time into other meaningful activities, and dealing with the expectations of others are among the adjustments that many retirees must manage. Additionally, the retiree must cope with health concerns, develop leisure activities, and adjust to the loss of the work role (Atchley, 1988; Hayslip & Panek, 1989). Individuals vary markedly in the ease with which they make this series of adjustments.

One way to enhance the retirement adjustment of middle-aged and older persons is through retirement preparation. Retirement can be conceptualized as an ongoing process that begins with the anticipation of eventually leaving one's employment. People may begin to formulate plans and make decisions early in life (e.g., choosing a retirement fund) with the implicit goal of protecting the quality of their lives when they are no longer working. This constitutes what can be termed the informal preparation for retirement. Actions of this type may be initiated by the individual, but may also simply represent the individual's compliance with expectations. A more active and systematic approach to retirement preparation can prove valuable in the long run.

Goals for Retirement Preparation

In an early review of the literature, Kasschau (1974) found that there was a great deal of confusion regarding the goals of most retirement preparation programs. Such ambiguity hinders efforts at evaluation and lessens the confidence that both individuals and employers might have in such efforts. More recent examinations of the literature continue to find that retirement preparation programs differ greatly in their content, modes of delivery, evaluation efforts, and goal specificity (Ekerdt, 1989).

Over and above the diversity of retirement preparation programs themselves, a distinction can be made between programs with a planning emphasis and those with a counseling emphasis. The former focus on the dissemination of information for the purpose of stimulating the individual's own efforts at planning in such areas as income maintenance, housing, or health care. Thoughtful planning based on accurate and timely information about finances is essential, given the possibility of unforeseen changes in a person's health status and the increased longevity of the population in general (Ekerdt, 1989; Quinn & Burkhauser, 1990).

The counseling function that retirement preparation can fulfill is to develop attitudes that are both positive and realistic. Additionally, effective programs can ease the emotional acceptance or management of the transition to a retired role. Retirement is not always a difficult role adjustment (Friedmann

& Orbach, 1974). It does pose serious problems for some people, however, particularly if their adaptational styles have been ineffective in the past (Neugarten, 1977) or if the changes from the work role to that of retiree are drastic or unforeseen (Lieberman, 1975).

The process of postretirement adjustment is a gradual one, even in the best of circumstances. Ekerdt and Bosse (1985) suggest that individuals progress through several phases of retirement adjustment: the *honeymoon phase*, the *disenchantment phase*, and a *stability (reorientation) phase*. Immediately after retirement, people often enter into a euphoric "honeymoon stage." They are very enthusiastic and look forward to doing things they did not have time to enjoy previously. New projects might be started, and involvements begin or increase in a variety of physical activities such as golf, bowling, tennis, or jogging. After about a year, however, there is a tendency to become disenchanted. There is less involvement in physical activities and an emotional letdown is experienced. Retirees find that their expectations may have been unrealistic or that they have underestimated the changes that retirement brings. In this second phase, they come to terms with the loss of structure in their daily lives that had been provided by their work schedule and obligations. They see less of their working friends, often feel lost and bored, and tend to focus on the past. A final phase is thought to begin about a year and a half after retirement. This phase is characterized by stability. It involves a reorientation to the everyday realities of being a retired person. The retiree now finds a predictable and satisfying daily routine and life-style. A new circle of friends has been established, and choices and decisions about the future can be made with confidence (Ekerdt & Bosse, 1985).

Preretirement training that is effective should lessen unrealistic expectations of the retirement experience. These unrealistic expectations are largely responsible for the honeymoon and disenchantment phases of adjustment.

The most effective programs would encompass both the planning and counseling objectives (Ekerdt, 1989; Kasschau, 1974). Because retirement is most usefully regarded as a complex process, programs with multiple goals are likely to be especially helpful. Persons anticipating retirement should give particular attention to comparing their present financial and social situation with what is likely to be the case after leaving work. One's decision to retire early or continue working as long as possible can be influenced by consideration of the job situation, the availability of flexible work options, financial inducements to continue to work or to retire, the general economic climate, and the attitudes and wishes of one's spouse (Atchley, 1979; Quinn & Burkhauser, 1990; Robinson, Coberly, & Paul, 1985).

Retirement preparation has both advantages and disadvantages (Ekerdt, 1989). In addition to benefiting individuals, preparation can also help companies test new methods for educating and training employees, as well as lessen turnover by increasing morale. A controversial objective of retirement planning is the employer's interest in cutting pension costs, which can lead to pressures for early retirement whether or not this would be in the best overall interest of the individual.

Although early retirement may be beneficial for those with viable work options, good health, and sufficient interpersonal and emotional resources, many people choose to work longer. This is especially true for those who enjoy their work and those who anticipate a significant drop in their income. For such persons, adopting a retirement-oriented mind-set as a function of a retirement preparation program may be counterproductive.

Retirement preparation often reduces the company's financial obligation to the employee (Ekerdt, 1989). However, the argument has been made that, through retirement planning, employees can improve early decision making on private investments. The result can be a situation that not only proves to be more financially advantageous to the employee but also causes a shift in the prevailing attitude that the government and the employer should bear the principal burden in the employee's retirement security.

Who Prepares for Retirement?

The expectation that preparation programs should fully prepare one for retirement depends upon whether one regards retirement as a discrete event or as an ongoing process. Many people see retirement as a specific event that occurs at a particular time and becomes increasingly significant as one moves closer to a fixed retirement age. The more useful alternative is to see retirement as an ongoing process that one begins through plans and decisions that are envisioned as early as one's twenties or thirties and then revised as personal experience increases and socioeconomic conditions change.

Anticipatory socialization and early planning for retirement have the advantage of avoiding the shock and stress of being caught unprepared when the time comes. For example, as mentioned above, morale may be increased among employees, thereby lessening turnover. In addition, pension costs to the company may be reduced by encouraging private saving, and employees who have taken part in a retirement preparation seminar may take better care of themselves after retirement, thus reducing health care costs to company-sponsored insurance programs. The later the planning begins, the greater is the risk of making costly and potentially irreversible decisions (Ekerdt, 1989). Greater attention to the more extended future in terms of health maintenance and income security should be encouraged, as distinguished from exclusive focus on immediate career advancement. Retirement planning should also prove beneficial in that one's identity and circle of friends will not revolve primarily around work. Flexibility and breadth would replace the single-mindedness that can be useful in achieving short-term career goals but is less effective for long-term planning and flexible coping.

Those with more extensive educational backgrounds usually enjoy a higher level of income as well. With both of these advantages, people have more alternatives for income, access to health care, and sources of life satisfaction (Verdi & Hayslip, 1991). Those who are less highly skilled and educated are also less likely to engage in preparatory retirement activities (Campione, 1988; Ekerdt, 1989; Verdi & Hayslip, 1991). This pattern suggests that special efforts may be needed to induce such persons to anticipate and plan for their retirement. Those who literally cannot afford to retire—the people who have held the lowest paying jobs and consequently contributed less to company-sponsored pension plans or Social Security—find themselves in double jeopardy: fewer resources and less preparation.

The available data suggest that the majority of Americans do not engage in systematic self-initiated retirement preparation activities. There is also a good deal of misunderstanding of retirement provisions among those with company-sponsored pensions (Ekerdt, 1989). Additionally, more recent cohorts seems to be preparing for their retirement even less actively (Ferraro, 1990).

Data on the prevalence of retirement preparation programs are difficult to access. Ekerdt's (1989) review suggests that the figures depend on the type of program. Nearly 90 percent of the firms contacted reported offering some type of planning assistance, but the more ambitious types of programs were offered by only about 15 percent. As Morrison and Jedrziewski (1988) observe, employers could do a better job in developing retirement planning programs that build on what is known about the retirement process, as well as in improving the overall design and administration of such programs.

One of the difficulties in evaluating both the prevalence and efficacy of retirement planning lies in the fact that not all persons who could enroll in formal programs do so. As already noted, the socioeconomically advantaged are those most likely to enroll (Campione, 1988), though the distinction between formal and informal planning is relevant here. A study of nearly 2,800 university employees has found that only a few had engaged in any form of planning other than financial (Turner, Scott, & Bailey, 1990). This omission was especially salient for those who were less advantaged. Higher education, greater family income, maleness, and increased age were related to more extensive planning activities.

Those who are experiencing job burnout and for whom leisure activities are important may choose to retire earlier (Rowe, 1990); therefore, these people engage in both formal and informal planning to a greater extent. Perhaps such persons are most likely to be found in formal, company-sponsored programs. For those who choose not to be involved, fear or ignorance of retirement is a likely explanation for their behavior (Research and Forecasts, Inc., 1980). However, poor program quality may also explain nonparticipation (Palmore, 1982). Given the diversity in how programs are defined and in what constitutes participation, one should be somewhat cautious in concluding that the available data are comprehensive and thoroughly accurate.

Content and Delivery of Retirement Planning Programs

There is considerable diversity in retirement planning programs with respect to content, design, and implementation. Nevertheless, most programs focus on the following issues: income and finances, health maintenance, living arrangements, relationships, leisure-time use, and relevant features of development and aging (e.g., widowhood, postretirement life). Although most programs are dominated by attention to income, health, and leisure, there probably needs to be more flexibility in content depending upon local resources and the needs of the persons to be served (Ekerdt, 1989).

More controversy exists regarding how such programs can be delivered effectively. The "how" of retirement planning varies with program goals and with one's assumptions about people in general (e.g., whether adults are primarily active or passive) and about retirement and aging in particular (e.g., retirement itself as a desirable or undesirable step in life).

The distinction between information and counseling also will influence the extent to which lecture or discussion format is used, whether an audience or participant mode of presentation is employed, and whether planning is carried out individually or in groups. Given the diversity of goals, target audiences, and resources, it would be premature to argue that one method or approach is invariably more effective than another. It does seem clear that there should be some effort to match those who deliver such programs with their audience so that individuals of lower authority, rank, or power are not being taught or led by persons who hold greater authority, rank, or power, e.g., supervisory vs. nonsupervisory personnel, white collar vs. blue collar workers (Ekerdt, 1989).

Is Retirement Planning Effective?

Judging the effectiveness of retirement planning depends upon the criteria for program efficacy. Those programs whose intent is simply to convey information should be evaluated differently from those whose focus is on individual counseling, attitude change, and well-being. Moreover, employers and employees may use different criteria in evaluating the worth of a program. In spite of the importance of this issue, there is surprisingly little research into program efficacy. Often, the samples studied are small, and self-selection of participants' biases results, as does the selective attrition from the sample. Random assignment of participants to treatment and control groups frequently is overlooked or simply impossible. Furthermore, goals may be ill defined and the measures may be poorly designed.

Available data suggest that retirement preparation programs are more effective in facilitating short-term attitude change than in generating long-term changes in attitudes and actual retirement planning behaviors (Abel & Hayslip, 1987; Glamser, 1981). Those who enroll in such programs and who benefit to the greatest extent may be more likely to engage in retirement planning anyway—their participation in the program is itself a form of planning (Glamser, 1981). However, definitive conclusions about the long-term effectiveness of retirement preparation programs remain elusive at this time.

Indeed, the realities of retirement may force people to redefine what is desirable or even attainable, undermining styles of adaptation and/or goals that they may have established in the program years earlier (Abel & Hayslip, 1987). There is a pressing need for well-designed, long-term longitudinal studies that attend to differential goals, methods of delivery, and degrees of participation. Much remains to be learned about the degree to which retirement planning is effective, what type is best, and for whom it is most helpful.   ▼ BERT HAYSLIP, JR.

See also: Gender as a Shaping Force in Adult Development and Aging; Life Events; Mexican Americans: Life Course Transitions and Adjustment; Retirement: An Emerging Challenge for Women; Subcultural Influences on Lifelong Development; Suffering; Trust as a Challenge in Adult Development; Work Capacity Across the Adult Years.

References

Abel, B., & Hayslip, B. (1987). Locus of control and retirement preparation. *Journal of Gerontology, 42:* 165-67.

Atchley, R. C. (1979). Issues in retirement research. *The Gerontologist, 19:* 44-54.

———. (1988). *Social Forces and Aging.* Fifth Edition. Belmont, CA: Wadsworth.

Campione, W. A. (1988). Predicting participation in retirement preparation programs. *Journal of Gerontology, 43:* 591-95.

Ekerdt, D. J. (1989). Retirement preparation. In M. P. Lawton (Ed.), *Annual Review of Gerontology and Geriatrics.* Volume 9. New York: Springer, pp. 321-56.

Ekerdt, D. J., & Bosse, R. (1985). An empirical test for phases of retirement: Findings from the Normative Aging Study. *Journal of Gerontology, 40:* 95-101.

Ferraro, K. F. (1990). Cohort analysis of retirement preparation. *Journal of Gerontology, 45:* 521-31.

Friedmann, E. A., & Orbach, H. L. (1974). Adjustment to retirement. In S. Arieti (Ed.), *American Handbook of Psychiatry.* Volume 1: *Foundations of Psychiatry.* Second Edition. New York: Basic Books, pp. 609-45.

Glamser, F. D. (1981). The impact of preretirement programs on the retirement experience. *Journal of Gerontology, 36*: 244-50.

Hayslip, B., & Panek, P. (1989). *Adult Development and Aging*. New York: Harper & Row.

Kasschau, P. L. (1974). Reevaluating the need for retirement preparation programs. *Industrial Gerontology, 1*: 42-59.

Lieberman, M. A. (1975). Adaptive processes in later life. In N. Datan & L. Ginsberg (Eds.), *Life-span Developmental Psychology: Normative Life Events*. New York: Academic Press, pp. 135-59.

Morrison, M. H., & Jedrziewski, M. K. (1988). Retirement planning: Everybody benefits. *Personnel Administrator, 33*: 74-80.

Neugarten, B. (1977). Personality and aging. In J. E. Birren & K. W. Schaie (Eds.), *Handbook of the Psychology of Aging*. New York: Van Nostrand Reinhold, pp. 626-49.

Palmore, E. B. (1982). Preparation for retirement: The impact of preretirement programs on retirement and leisure. In N. J. Osgood (Ed.), *Life After Work: Retirement, Leisure, Recreation, and the Elderly*. New York: Praeger, pp. 330-41.

Quinn, J. F., & Burkhauser, R. B. (1990). Work and retirement. In R. Binstock & L. George (Eds.), *Handbook of Aging and the Social Sciences*. Third Edition. New York: Academic Press, pp. 304-27.

Research and Forecasts, Inc. (1980). Retirement preparation: Growing corporate involvement. *Aging and Work, 3*: 1-13.

Robinson, P. K., Coberly, S., & Paul, C. E. (1985). Work and retirement. In R. Binstock & E. Shanas (Eds.), *Handbook of Aging and the Social Sciences*. Third Edition. New York: Van Nostrand Reinhold, pp. 503-27.

Rowe, G. P. (1990). Retirement transition of state employees: A ten year follow-up. Paper presented at the annual scientific meeting of the Gerontological Society of America, Boston, November.

Turner, M. J., Scott, J. P., & Bailey, W. C. (1990). Factors impacting attitude toward retirement and retirement planning behavior among midlife university employees. Paper presented at the annual scientific meeting of the Gerontological Society of America, Boston, November.

Underwood, D. (1984). Toward self-reliance in retirement planning. *Harvard Business Review, 62*: 18-20.

Verdi, J. W., & Hayslip, B. (1991). Occupational level and retirement satisfaction: A path analytic solution. Paper presented at the annual convention of the American Psychological Association, San Francisco, August.

RISK TO LIFE THROUGH THE ADULT YEARS

The major threats to life vary in their specific level of risk at particular ages and among particular demographic groups. Awareness of the changing and differential pattern of mortality can help guide intervention efforts to lessen the risk to life for each age and demographic grouping.

Mortality Data

Taylor (1991) observes that "in the past 90 years, patterns of disease in the United States of such acute infectious disorders as tuberculosis, influenza, measles, and poliomyelitis have declined because of treatment innovations and changes in public health standards" (1991, p. 53). Simultaneously, however, Taylor noted an increase over time in "preventable disorders" such as cardiovascular disease, lung cancer, automobile accidents, and alcohol and drug abuse. Jenkins (1988) attributed increases in cardiovascular disease from the early part of the century to "the changed composition of the U.S. population, with greater numbers of people living until the older ages when heart disease is most common" (p. 324). Cardiovascular diseases have been the number one cause of death throughout the twentieth century, although the rate has been declining since the 1960s (Holinger, 1987). Malignant neoplasms (cancer) and violence (accident, homicide, suicide) occupy the second and third positions.

Risk to life for specific causes is associated with sex, race, and age.

Gender/Sex and Mortality

As can be seen in Table 1, males have higher mortality rates than females (all rates are per 100,000 population in the specified group). In addition, male death rates exceed those for females for the highest-ranking specific causes, particularly heart disease and cancer. External causes of death are generally higher for males than females, and they rank higher among the leading causes of male deaths.

Many explanations have been advanced for the heightened male susceptibility to death in general and from specific causes, as well as for the associated differences in life expectancy. *Biogenetic differences* between the sexes take several forms that could influence survival. For example, chromosomal differences could make females less susceptible to many diseases, relatively high metabolic rates in males might contribute to some disorders, and the diet favored by males could be related to the higher metabolic rates and also lead to more vulnerability to cancer. *Environmental differences* include risks associated with the type of work engaged in by males and females as well as differential experiences with stress, cigarette smoking, and exercise. *Psychosocial factors* could influence risk to life through the differential expectations and demands made on males and females. As Stillion (1985) suggests, all three categories of explanation should be incorporated into any attempt to gain a complete understanding of the differential mortality rates of males and females. These factors undoubtedly operate both independently and in combination with one another in producing mortality differences. In addition, changes in many of these factors occur through historical time. For example, if female and male roles have become less distinct as occupational and environmental differences lessen, there may also be a gradual reduction of the sex differential in mortality.

Race and Mortality

White mortality rates exceed those for nonwhites (Table 1). The rankings of the leading causes of death are essentially the same, with the white rates more often higher. Jackson (1980) has shown that these higher rates for whites are most accurate for older adult groups.

One difference between the races is the higher ranking of homicide and lower ranking of suicide for nonwhites compared with whites. The much higher ranking and rates of causes of death originating in the perinatal period among nonwhites are another racial group difference. Other age and sex differences also exist by race (Jackson, 1980, Chapter 4), and the differential population age distributions of whites and nonwhites also have an influence on the rankings of the causes of death.

As an example of these age-sex-race differences, Table 1 implies that nonwhites have slightly higher rates of accidents than do whites (in 1987, the respective rates were 40.9 and 38.6). What these aggregated data mask, however, is the fact that this race differential exists primarily among males. Nonwhite male rates of 62.1 and black male rates of 67.1 compare with 53.7 for white males (data for 1988; National Center for Health Statistics, 1990).

An aggregate table such as Table 1 also hides the fact that these racial differences in accidents for males are clear at all but the extreme age groupings of 15-24 and 85+. The accident rate is most divergent between nonwhite and white males in the "young old." In the age range 65-74, nonwhite males show an accidental death rate of 108.4 compared with 64 for white males. For males in the age range 75-84, the nonwhite rate is 178.6 for nonwhites compared with 139.9 for whites. Jackson (1980) speculates that the higher black male accidental death rates are associated with "less efficient motor vehicles, and less access to good medical care" (p. 68). The generalization that nonwhites are at greater risk than whites for accidental death turns out to be much less useful than close attention to the relative vulnerability of males at particular points in their lives.

Table 1. Causes of Death by Gender and Race

Males Causes of Death	Number	Mean Rate	%	Females Causes of Death	Number	Mean Rate	%
Total Deaths	1115896.0	931.9	100.0	Total Deaths	1031366.7	818.1	100.0
Heart Disease	379607.0	317.0	34.0	Heart Disease	343185.0	272.2	33.3
Malignant				Malignant			
Neoplasms	258683.3	216.0	23.2	Neoplasms	227359.0	180.3	22.0
Accidents	64849.7	54.2	5.8	Cerebrovascular			
Cerebrovascular				Diseases	89920.7	71.3	8.7
Diseases	58714.0	49.0	5.3	Pneumonia &			
Pulmonary Diseases	48052.0	40.1	4.3	Influenza	39113.3	31.0	3.8
Pneumonia &				Pulmonary Diseases	33807.0	26.8	3.3
Influenza	35365.7	29.5	3.2	Accidents	30866.3	24.5	3.0
Suicide	24338.7	20.3	2.2	Diabetes Mellitus	24263.7	19.2	2.4
Diabetes Mellitus	17647.3	14.7	1.6	Atherosclerosis	13302.7	10.6	1.3
Chronic Liver				Septicemia	11194.7	8.9	1.1
Disease	17185.7	14.4	1.5	Nephritis	11163.3	8.9	1.1
Homicide	16751.0	14.0	1.5	**Other Causes**			
Other Causes				Chronic Liver			
HIV	15552.3	13.0	1.4	Disease	9249.0	7.3	0.9
Nephritis	10690.7	8.9	1.0	Perinatal Conditions	7949.3	6.3	0.8
Perinatal Conditions	10448.7	8.7	0.9	Suicide	6887.7	5.5	0.7
Septicemia	8863.3	7.4	0.8	Homicide	5263.7	4.2	0.5
Atherosclerosis	8003.0	6.7	0.7	HIV	1831.7	1.5	0.2

Whites Causes of Death	Number	Mean Rate	%	Nonwhites Causes of Death	Number	Mean Rate	%
Total Deaths	1857938.0	895.9	100.0	Total Deaths	289324.7	752.9	100.0
Heart Disease	637374.7	307.4	34.3	Heart Disease	85417.3	222.3	29.5
Malignant				Malignant			
Neoplasms	425923.0	205.4	22.9	Neoplasms	60119.3	156.4	20.8
Cerebrovascular				Cerebrovascular			
Diseases	128546.3	62.0	6.9	Diseases	20088.3	52.3	6.9
Accidents	80013.3	38.6	4.3	Accidents	15702.7	40.9	5.4
Pulmonary Diseases	75740.7	36.5	4.1	Homicide	10847.3	28.2	3.7
Pneumonia &				Pneumonia &			
Influenza	66411.3	32.0	3.6	Influenza	8067.7	21.0	2.8
Diabetes Mellitus	34046.7	16.4	1.8	Diabetes Mellitus	7864.3	20.3	2.7
Suicide	27810.3	13.4	1.5	Perinatal Conditions	7064.7	18.5	2.5
Chronic Liver				Pulmonary Diseases	6118.3	15.9	2.1
Disease	21967.0	10.6	1.2	HIV	5487.3	14.3	1.9
Atherosclerosis	19592.7	9.4	1.1	**Other Causes**			
Other Causes				Chronic Liver			
Nephritis	17428.7	8.4	0.9	Disease	4467.7	11.6	1.5
Septicemia	16145.3	7.8	0.9	Nephritis	4425.3	11.5	1.5
HIV	11896.7	5.7	0.6	Septicemia	3912.7	10.2	1.4
Perinatal Conditions	11303.3	5.5	0.6	Suicide	3416.0	8.9	1.2
Homicide	11167.3	5.4	0.6	Atherosclerosis	1713.0	4.5	0.6

Based on 1980 U.S. Census data.

Age and Mortality

As already noted, infectious and communicable diseases such as measles, polio, and influenza have decreased over time because of public health advances and improved treatment measures, e.g., immunization, better nutrition and sanitation procedures, and more effective medications. These modes of death are traditionally associated with early-life risk (Cook & Oltjenbruns, 1989; Garrison & McQuiston, 1989; Taylor, 1991).

Decreases in mortality rates among the young have been one factor in the increase in the older adult population. Higher proportions of individuals now survive the threat of early-life diseases and become long-lived adults. Few treatments or public health measures have (thus far) proven highly successful in reducing the primary causes of death for the adult and older adult populations. Chronic degenerative disorders such as heart disease and cancer are pervasive. In other words, "demographically, death has become more and more the property of the old" (Kamerman, 1988, p. 8).

Kamerman (1988) points out that in 1900 those under age 15 represented 34 percent of the U.S. population—but also represented 53 percent of the deaths. Those 65 and above in 1900 were only 4 percent of the population but accounted for 17 percent of the deaths. By dramatic contrast, in 1989, children under 15 accounted for 21.7 percent of the population (U.S. Bureau of the Census, 1990b) but only 2.6 percent of the deaths (National Center for Health Statistics, 1992), compared with figures of 12.5 percent and 71.5 percent for the elderly population.

The overwhelming number of deaths among the old notwithstanding, one general finding in mortality trends by age shows that among children, youth, and young adults, the external causes of death—accidents, homicide, suicide—rank relatively high. On the other hand, leading causes of death are predominantly disease-related in middle-aged and older adults (see Table 2). In other words, the young most often die by their own or someone else's hand or through carelessness (Holinger, 1987; Rivara, 1983-1985), whereas middle-aged and elderly people typically succumb to diseases and other body conditions.

Accidents are clearly the leading cause of mortality among the children and youth of our society (Table 2). For those aged 5 to 14, the three external modes of death combine to represent more than half of all deaths (55 percent). By adolescence and young adulthood (15 to 24), this proportion increases to the point where 3 of every 4 deaths (76.4 percent) are the result of accident, homicide, or suicide. This is the peak age period for external causes of mortality. After young adulthood, the proportion of deaths that are attributable to external (nondisease or physical disorder) causes declines markedly:

Ages 25-44	4 of 10
Ages 45-64	.7 of 10
Ages 65+	.3 of 10

Firearm mortality—whether by accident, homicide, or suicide—is one subcategory of violent death that has increased substantially in recent years among young people. Deaths from this cause accounted for 20 percent of all deaths for those aged 15 to 24 in 1988 (Fingerhut et al., 1991).

Patterns associated with specific causes of mortality by age can be attributed in part to the prevention of major risks in infancy, childhood, and youth along with the relative lack of prevention for major late life causes. Some attention should also be given, however, to other possible influences on mortality risk. Holinger, (1987, Chapter 12) provides documentation of the *strong correlations between population changes and violent deaths (aggregation of and separate considerations of accident, homicide, suicide).* In particular, he demonstrates strong predictive potential for the changes from 1933 to 1982 in the size of the young adult population and the levels of violent death in that group. Violent deaths (especially suicides and homicides) among the young increased from the 1950s through the 1970s. This alarming pattern is associated with the large size of the "baby boomer" cohort as it moved through the ages 15 to 24.

Table 2. Causes of Death by Age

5-14 Yrs. Causes of Death	Number	Mean Rate	%	15-24 Yrs. Causes of Death	Number	Mean Rate	%
Total Deaths	8860.7	25.6	100.0	Total Deaths	37559.3	100.4	100.0
Accidents	4167.7	12.0	47.0	Accidents	17980.0	48.1	47.9
Malignant				Homicide	5770.0	15.4	15.4
Neoplasms	1129.7	3.3	12.7	Suicide	4907.7	13.1	13.1
Congenital Anomalies	475.7	1.4	5.4	Malignant			
Homicide	458.7	1.3	5.2	Neoplasms	1894.7	5.1	5.0
Heart Disease	314.3	0.9	3.5	Heart Disease	1030.0	2.8	2.7
Suicide	244.7	0.7	2.8	HIV	546.7	1.5	1.5
Pneumonia &				Congenital Anomalies	482.3	1.3	1.3
Influenza	114.3	0.3	1.3	Pneumonia &			
Pulmonary Diseases	111.7	0.3	1.3	Influenza	268.3	0.7	0.7
Benign Neoplasms	89.7	0.3	1.0	Cerebrovascular			
Cerebrovascular				Diseases	247.3	0.7	0.7
Diseases	76.0	0.2	0.9	Pulmonary Diseases	187.7	0.5	0.5
Other Causes				**Other Causes**			
HIV	55.0	0.2	0.6	Diabetes Mellitus	124.7	0.3	0.3
Septicemia	44.7	0.1	0.5	Benign Neoplasms	97.7	0.3	0.3
Diabetes Mellitus	31.3	0.1	0.4	Septicemia	96.7	0.3	0.3
Nephritis	21.7	0.1	0.2	Nephritis	75.7	0.2	0.2
Chronic Liver Disease	6.3	0.0	0.1	Chronic Liver Disease	60.3	0.2	0.2
Atherosclerosis	0.3	0.0	0.0	Atherosclerosis	2.0	0.0	0.0

25-44 Yrs Causes of Death	Number	Mean Rate	%	45-64 Yrs. Causes of Death	Number	Mean Rate	%
Total Deaths	136399.3	172.8	100.1	Total Deaths	384929.7	836.9	100.0
Accidents	28064.0	35.6	20.6	Malignant			
Malignant				Neoplasms	136111.7	295.9	35.4
Neoplasms	20717.7	26.2	15.2	Heart Disease	118090.0	256.8	30.7
Heart Disease	15587.7	19.7	11.4	Cerebrovascular			
HIV	12787.3	16.2	9.4	Diseases	15703.3	34.1	4.1
Suicide	11866.0	15.0	8.7	Accidents	15010.0	32.6	3.9
Homicide	10749.3	13.6	7.9	Pulmonary Diseases	12847.3	27.9	3.3
Chronic Liver				Chronic Liver			
Disease	4588.7	5.8	3.4	Disease	11644.3	25.3	3.0
Cerebrovascular				Diabetes Mellitus	8836.3	19.2	2.3
Diseases	3345.3	4.2	2.5	Suicide	7093.0	15.4	1.8
Pneumonia &				Pneumonia &			
Influenza	2141.7	2.7	1.6	Influenza	5662.3	12.3	1.5
Diabetes Mellitus	1997.0	2.5	1.5	HIV	3415.7	7.4	0.9
Other Causes				**Other Causes**			
Pulmonary Diseases	925.7	1.2	0.7	Homicide	2944.7	6.4	0.8
Congenital Anomalies	865.3	1.1	0.6	Nephritis	2739.3	6.0	0.7
Septicemia	847.0	1.1	0.6	Septicemia	2655.7	5.8	0.7
Nephritis	714.3	0.9	0.5	Benign Neoplasms	1229.0	2.7	0.3
Benign Neoplasms	448.7	0.6	0.3	Atherosclerosis	965.3	2.1	0.3
Atherosclerosis	54.3	0.1	0.0	Congenital Anomalies	783.7	1.7	0.2

Based on 1980 U.S. Census data.

Table 2. Causes of Death by Age (continued)

65+ Yrs. Causes of Death	Number	Mean Rate	%
Total Deaths	1532547.7	5046.8	100.0
Heart Disease	616817.0	2031.2	40.2
Malignant Neoplasms	325530.7	1072.0	21.2
Cerebrovascular Diseases	129063.0	425.0	8.4
Pulmonary Diseases	67676.7	222.9	4.4
Pneumonia & Influenza	65426.7	215.5	4.3
Diabetes Mellitus	30907.3	101.8	2.0
Accidents	26555.3	87.4	1.7
Atherosclerosis	20280.0	66.8	1.3
Nephritis	18070.0	59.5	1.2
Septicemia	16057.3	52.9	1.0
Other Causes			
Chronic Liver Disease	10103.0	33.3	0.7
Suicide	6351.7	20.9	0.4
Benign Neoplasms	4681.3	15.4	0.3
Homicide	1323.3	4.4	0.1
Congenital Anomalies	1080.0	3.6	0.1
HIV	367.0	1.2	0.0

Based on 1980 U.S. Census data.

Why would such a correlation exist? The most likely explanation is that large cohorts generate increased competition and stress, which, in turn, contribute to higher mortality by violent means as well as other outcomes (Easterlin, 1987). This hypothesis has led to predictions of stability and even decline in these causes in the near future because succeeding cohorts of young people are expected to be smaller. On the other hand, some authors (e.g., Manton, Blazer, & Woodbury, 1987; Pollinger-Haas & Hendin, 1983) have used essentially these same data to argue that the suicide rate will be markedly *higher* than it is at present when the baby boomers reach older adulthood in the next century. Holinger (1987, Chapter 12, pp. 191-93), utilizes population-based model data to predict future elderly rates that are lower than those of present-day elderly. Similarly, McIntosh (1992) has argued that even though elderly suicide will remain at high levels

compared to other age groups in the population, there are arguments that might predict lower rates for the aged baby boomers than among today's old.

Implications for the Prevention of Premature Death

Because death is inevitable, the central focus of a discussion of risk to life is not death per se but rather premature death. The emphasis is on which causes of death are amenable to intervention and which produce death before it would occur by natural processes alone. Chief among the causes of premature death are those related directly or indirectly to personal patterns of behavior and life-styles. The Centers for Disease Control estimate that "overall...50% of all deaths from the ten leading causes of death in this country are due to modifiable lifestyle factors" (Taylor, 1991, p. 53).

Modifiable Behaviors

One important modifiable aspect of lifestyles can be referred to as *health compromising behaviors.* Particularly important among these behaviors are smoking, alcoholism, and problem drinking. Taylor (1991) estimates that smoking accounts for approximately 125,000 cancer deaths in the United States each year—about 30 percent of all cancer deaths. Green and Shellenberger (1991) maintain that 350,000 annual deaths are connected to smoking and call tobacco "the leading cause of death in the United States" (p. 604). Obviously, this suggested top ranking includes deaths by other causes that were related to smoking. It is not only lung cancer, but also heart disease, respiratory disorders, and the effects of secondhand smoke on others that have been linked to premature death. Taylor (1991) and many others conclude that many deaths from cancer and heart disease could be avoided by eliminating smoking from one's behavior and life-style.

Alcohol abuse and alcoholism contribute to death by liver cirrhosis, some forms of cancer, and drunk driving (which kills other people as well as the abuser). Green and Shellenberger (1991) assert that, after tobacco, "alcohol is the second-leading cause of death in the United States" (p. 606). Once again, alcohol's contributions to deaths listed under other causes are pooled to produce this ranking. For example, it is estimated that 50 percent of all automobile accident fatalities (there were 417,575 in 1989; National Center for Health Statistics, 1992) are the result of drinking and driving. Green and Shellenberger would also include 30,000 of the deaths attributed each year to homicide, falls, and fires.

In a more traditional compilation of mortality statistics, and as shown in Tables 1 and 2, cardiovascular disease is the leading killer in the United States, accounting for one-third of all deaths (see also Jenkins, 1988). Although this cause of death is physiological, it is often brought about by life-styles and behavior. Taylor (1991) labels many of these deaths as premature because they occur before age 75. Increased risk of heart disease has been linked to diet and particularly to cholesterol and obesity, as well as to sedentary lifestyles, smoking and alcohol abuse, and emotional and environmental stress (Green & Shellenberg, 1991; Heaton, 1988; Taylor, 1991). Personality characteristics such as Type A behavior have also been associated with increased risk in some studies, although this picture has become more complex lately. The majority of these contributing factors are amenable to modification or elimination.

Prescriptions for Prevention

To reduce premature death, it is necessary both to modify or eliminate health-compromising behaviors and to increase health-enhancing behaviors. Smoking, alcohol abuse, and obesity can be reduced by the promotion of good health habits, particularly if these are introduced early in life and continued into and through adulthood and old age. Reductions in mortality from the other leading causes of death—heart disease, cancer, etc.—are also feasible through a number of measures that would often affect more than one

of these causes. Among the good health habits are exercise, weight control, healthy dietary choices, breast and testicular self-examination, smoking cessation, alcohol intake in moderation with abstinence in some circumstances, and training in stress reduction and coping skills (Green & Shellenberger, 1991; Heaton, 1988; Taylor, 1991).

Other specific behavioral modifications would reduce mortality from such leading causes as accidents and suicides. The risk of fatalities in automobile and other vehicular accidents would be lowered by the installation of air bags, the use of seat belts and child restraint seats, the use of helmets by motorcyclists, and driving at slower speeds. Other accident prevention measures are available that would lower deaths by poisoning, at work, in the home, and in many other contexts of daily life. Environmental modifications as well as education and behavioral alteration have been suggested for a great many accidental death situations (e.g., Rivara, 1983-1985; Williams, 1983-1985). A reduction of accidents, suicides, and homicides would result from less availability and access to handguns (Moscicki & Boyd, 1983-1985).

To these prevention prescriptions, Michael (1982) would add the lessening of environmental hazards that increase risk of death, as well as "eliminating inadequacies in the existing health care system" (p. 937). Taylor (1991) further suggests that there has been excessive emphasis on mortality rather than morbidity. In calling for a reversal in priority, Taylor asserts that "reorienting the focus of health promotion toward reducing the period of morbidity, rather than delaying mortality, may ultimately do more for quality of life" (p. 514).

The changes required to reduce risk to life across the adult years are known. What is needed is the readiness to apply this knowledge in our lives and culture.

▼ John L. McIntosh

See also: Alcohol Use and Abuse; Happiness, Cohort Measures of; Mental Health in the Adult Years; Native American Perspectives on the Lifespan; Religion in Adult Life; Stress; Suffering; Widowhood: The Coping Response.

References

Cook, A. S., & Oltjenbruns, K. A. (1989). *Dying and Grieving: Lifespan and Family Perspectives.* New York: Holt, Rinehart & Winston.

Easterlin, R. A. (1987). *Birth and Fortune.* Second Edition. Chicago: University of Chicago Press.

Fingerhut, L. A., et al. (1991). Firearm mortality among children, youth, and young adults 1-34 years of age, trends and current status: United States, 1979-1988. *NCHS Monthly Vital Statistics Report, 39* (11, Supplement).

Garrison, W. T., & McQuiston, S. (1989). *Chronic Illness During Childhood and Adolescence: Psychological Aspects.* Newbury Park, CA: Sage.

Green, J., & Shellenberger, R. (1991). *The Dynamics of Health and Wellness: A Biopsychosocial Approach.* Fort Worth, TX: Holt, Rinehart and Winston.

Heaton, R. K. (Ed.). (1988). Cardiovascular Disease. (Special series). *Journal of Consulting and Clinical Psychology, 56:* 323-92.

Holinger, P. C. (1987). *Violent Deaths in the United States: An Epidemiologic Study of Suicide, Homicide, and Accidents.* New York: Guilford.

Jackson, J. J. (1980). *Minorities and Aging.* Belmont, CA: Wadsworth.

Jenkins, C. D. (1988). Epidemiology of cardiovascular diseases. *Journal of Consulting and Clinical Psychology, 56:* 324-32.

Kamerman, J. B. (1988). *Death in the Midst of Life: Social and Cultural Influences on Death, Grief and Mourning.* Englewood Cliffs, NJ: Prentice-Hall.

Manton, K. G., Blazer, D. G., & Woodbury, M. A. (1987). Suicide in middle age and later life: Sex and race specific life table and cohort analyses. *Journal of Gerontology, 42:* 219-27.

McIntosh, J. L. (1992). Older adults: The next suicide epidemic? *Suicide and Life-Threatening Behavior, 22,* 322-32.

Michael, J. M. (1982). The second revolution in health: Health promotion and its environmental base. *American Psychologist, 37:* 936-41.

Moscicki, E. K., & Boyd, J. H. (1983-1985). Epidemiologic trends in firearm suicides among adolescents. *Pediatrician, 12:* 52-62.

National Center for Health Statistics. (1989). Advance report of final mortality statistics, 1987. *NCHS Monthly Vital Statistic Report, 38* (5, Supplement).

------. (1990). *Vital Statistics of the United States, 1988.* Volume 2. *Mortality. Part A.* Washington, DC: U.S. Government Printing Office.

------. (1991). Advance report of final mortality statistics, 1988. *NCHS Monthly Vital Statistics Report, 39* (7, Supplement).

------. (1992). Advance report of final mortality statistics, 1989. *NCHS Monthly Vital Statistics Report, 40* (8, Supplement 2).

Pollinger-Haas, A., & Hendin, H. (1983). Suicide among older people: Projections for the future. *Suicide and Life-Threatening Behavior, 13:* 147-54.

Rivara, F. P. (1983-1985). Epidemiology of violent deaths in children and adolescents in the United States. *Pediatrician, 12:* 3-10.

Stillion, J. M. (1985). *Death and the Sexes: An Examination of Differential Longevity, Attitudes, Behaviors, and Coping Skills.* Washington, DC: Hemisphere.

Taylor, S. E. (1991). *Health Psychology.* Second Edition. New York: McGraw-Hill.

U.S. Bureau of the Census (1990a). United States population estimates, by age, sex, race, and Hispanic origin: 1980 to 1988. *Current Population Reports,* Series P-25, No. 1045.

------. (1990b). U.S. population estimates by age, sex, race, and Hispanic origin: 1989. *Current Population Reports,* Series P-25, No. 1057.

Williams, A. F. (1983-1985). Fatal motor vehicle crashes involving teenagers. *Pediatrician, 12:* 37-40.

RURAL LIVING: WHAT INFLUENCE ON ADULT DEVELOPMENT?

Many rural contexts in the United States stand in gloomy contrast to the idyllic images of rural life portrayed by Norman Rockwell, Thornton Wilder, and Courier and Ives. And, contrary to the nostalgic picture of pastoral life offered by Garrison Keillor, the news from the real Lake Woebegone is not good (Olson-Sierra, 1987).

Dramatic changes are occurring in rural environments that have the potential to alter the life course of millions of adults. Given the limited number of adult developmental studies devoted to understanding the rural developmental context, this brief examination of the meanings of these changes for rural residents and their implications for the contextual study of adult development will draw upon selected multidisciplinary research from adult psychology, sociology, anthropology, and behavioral geography.

Because "adult development" and "rural" are concepts that resist easy definition, a scientific model is introduced which places these terms in a mutual defining context. The multiple meanings of "rural" as used by students of rural life are examined, and the diversity of both rural contexts and the populations within them are considered. Finally, the rural developmental context is discussed in light of the striking physical, social, and cultural changes that are taking place in many rural areas in the United States.

A Contextual Model of Adult Development

The contextual perspective on adult development represents a relatively new and refreshing turn of scientific thinking. For most of this century, developmentalists have focused primarily on the study of children and on one question in particular: Is the course of human development "directed primarily by structures in the environment that are external to the person, or is development guided principally by the genetic program within?" (Scarr, 1982, p. 852).

Although this question still influences the narrower research agenda of strict environmentalists (Baer, 1989) and behavior geneticists (Plomin, DeFries, & McClearn, 1989), contextualists have a broad view of adult development. In this view, personal, cultural, and historical factors interact with ontogenetic (within-person, biologically regulated) factors to produce behavior change (Baltes, 1987; Lerner & Kauffman, 1985). Adult development can be simultaneously influenced by idiosyncratic experiences and pervasive cultural norms, values, and expectations, as well as both trivial and momentous historical occurrences—and the biological aging process. Contextualists play no favor-

ites regarding which of these factors may be responsible for changes in adult development. Each factor must be taken into account if one is to understand the myriad programs of adulthood.

Developmental change may also reflect both positive and negative outcomes, both growth and decline, across varying domains of behavior and experience. In short, development cannot be adequately described or explained without a full accounting of the developmental context. Most importantly, this view differs from other developmental approaches in its emphasis on the diversity of developmental outcomes that may occur both within and between lives across the adult life course. It provides an extremely useful model for understanding the way in which specific contexts—such as the rural environment—shape the adult life course.

What Does "Rural" Mean?

Though rural contexts have been depicted in the imagery of art and literature for thousands of years (Lutwack, 1984), it is still necessary to translate "rural" into terms more useful for a scientific study. From a contextual perspective, there is real value in examining the diverse definitional approaches here since they contribute to an understanding of rural living. These contrasts allow us to see that rural context has diverse meanings that are negotiated by researchers as well as by rural residents. The approaches fall into four general categories: *geodemographic characteristics, definers of the physical milieu, sociocultural values,* and *phenomenological dimensions.* Each will be briefly considered.

Geodemographic Characteristics. Many rural psychologists and sociologists in the United States continue to define rural by using objective criteria that are based on population attributes such as distribution, density, and composition (Windley & Scheidt, 1988). This approach has yielded several different and sometimes confusing numerical definers of rurality. The most commonly used criterion is the urban-rural distinction of the U.S. Bureau of the Census. A place is defined as rural if it comprises a farm or a place of 2,500 or fewer residents (rural nonfarm).

Another major designation breaks down populations into metropolitan and nonmetropolitan statistical areas. A metropolitan statistical area is defined as a geographic area with a large population nucleus, along with adjacent communities that are socially and economically integrated with this nucleus (U.S. Department of Commerce, 1988). Under this definition, about 65 million people (or about 25 percent of the U.S. population) live in nonmetropolitan or rural areas, with only 2 percent living on farms. In comparison with the urban population, the total rural population has proportionately more whites, fewer African-Americans, and fewer Hispanics. Almost 10 million persons (18 percent) live in poverty in rural areas of the United States (Wagenfeld, 1988). Rural residents constitute about 30 percent of all the impoverished people in this nation, a figure that is somewhat higher than their representation in the population at large. Some rural areas have increased and some have decreased in population since 1980.

As Krout (1988) has noted, these statistical configurations of rurality add little to our direct understanding of the life course. To some extent, however, indicators of population composition, density, and geographic dispersion may be useful as predictors of behavioral outcomes. For example, we know that the low population density and greater population dispersion in rural areas make access to services more difficult for many rural residents. This situation may require different coping strategies for accessing resources among rural residents than might be customary in urban settings (Krout, 1988). It would be valuable to examine changes in these indicators over time and correlate them with behavioral or life-style changes across adulthood. At the moment, however, there are few studies charting these person-environment changes within a developmental perspective.

Definers of the Physical Milieu. The context of adult life is enriched to a degree by approaches that define rurality through the physical milieu. As Rowles (1984) notes, physical contrasts with the city are most apparent, with rural settings being most closely associated with natural environments—plant life, trees, and spaciousness. There is also less verticality among building forms in rural areas. Blues, greens, and browns characterize rural environments, while whites, reds, and grays are found more often in urban settings. In contrast to urban environments, rural settings "present lower levels of cognitive complexity and stimulus input" and remain "fairly stable through time" (Rowles, 1984, p. 132). Little attention has been given to the impact of rural physical settings upon adult development (see **Place and Personality in Adult Development**).

Sociocultural Values. Some scholars judge that both demographic and physical environmental definitions are inadequate for capturing the essence of rurality. One group has suggested that the essence of rural life can be better discerned by identifying the distinguishing sociocultural and psychological values and attitudes that are held by rural residents (Flax et al., 1979). These include such values and attitudes as practicality, efficiency, work, friendliness, honesty, patriotism, deep religious commitment, social conservatism, and mistrust of government (Ford, 1962). Another observer of rural life has added the further pervasive characteristics of a slower pace of life, an emphasis on self-reliance, a greater chance of being known, and an extensive social support network (Rowles, 1984).

Some hold that rural and urban lifestyles are closer than they have ever been before (Rasmussen & Bowers, 1988) because of changes in rural economies and modern communication technologies. Others hold that "just because rural society in America has changed socially and economically does not mean that its distinctive value structure has disappeared" (Krout, 1988, p. 107). The jury is still out on this point, however, and there is little research which examines the lifespan implications of being socialized into rural versus urban value systems.

Phenomenological Dimensions. Rowles (1984) has made a significant contribution to the contextual understanding of rural living, using a phenomenological approach. He conducted an extensive ethnographic study of a small rural community in Appalachia, focusing primarily upon elderly persons. Rowles asserts that "there will be no one conceptualization of rural suitable for all occasions: its use is situated" (Rowles, 1984, p. 121). Broader ecological definitions will yield little of value for understanding adult development and aging unless they are tied to the personal contexts in which individuals reside. Rowles holds that we must gain greater understanding of the way in which the "people themselves hold images of and impute meaning and value to the concept of rural" (Rowles, 1984, p. 122). For example, one rural resident might feel isolated from the mainstream of society and develop a sense of frustration and bitterness regarding the perceived lack of amenities and access to opportunities. In contrast, another rural resident might feel at home and protected in a familiar and neighborly environment against the perceived frenzy and impersonality of urban centers.

Diversity in Rural Living

Regardless of how researchers choose to define "rural," it is generally recognized that there is considerable diversity among rural contexts: One place is not just the same as another. Some definitional approaches do a better job than others in revealing this variation. Demographic summaries conceal the tremendous complexity that exists among rural subpopulations. One scholar notes that the 1,380 nonmetropolitan counties in the United States "differ in their geographic dispersion as well as in their proportion of minorities, average income, age structure, and remoteness from urban centers. In sum, demographic data suggest a considerable diversity in rural America" (Wagenfeld, 1988, p. 8). It is probable that demographic summaries perpetuate a stereotype of rural typicality that is based upon a fictional norm and masks the actual diversity of rural settings in the United States.

It is also easy to blur distinctions among rural contexts when using the physical environmental definitions. Differences among the physical elements of rural places can be as great as those found in rural-urban contrasts. There are considerable physical contrasts among rural locations found in the hollows of Appalachia, the deserts of the Southwest, the Great Plains, the Colorado Rockies, and the mountains of Vermont. One would surely expect differences in the ways in which these physical contexts influence the definition of rural life that is held by their residents as well as the pattern of development through the lifespan.

The sociocultural approach that attributes common values to rural populations may also be oversimplified (Krout, 1988). There is evidence of considerable variation in the value structure of rural Americans (Larson, 1978). For instance, small towns display tremendous diversity in their "covenants"—the general tacit agreement among residents about what is important (Schroeder, 1980, p. 112). Town covenants are often expressed in physical and architectural features that signal their cultural meanings. One may learn to "read" a town by understanding its covenants, as illustrated in this example of Schroeder's (1980) drive-through observation of the small town of Dixon, Illinois:

> The main thing one notices in Dixon on a summer day is what Dixon wanted noticed. Touted in signs at the end of town as the Petunia City, Dixon delivers the goods. The highway is named Petunia Boulevard, and it is not the only civic property planted with petunias: the street borders of private residences are also planted for a dozen or more city blocks. The petunias are not showy. They are widely spaced, not bunched profusely as one sees in professionally planned horticultural gardens.... They are plain, honest, grandma's petunias.... Dixon's message was clear; it had chosen to be a floral oasis, and it brought city and citizen together to do this. Adding all the factors together, my dozen minutes reading of Dixon recommended this starting point for closer read-

ing: the covenant is with *community.*" (pp. 127-29)

Other important concepts expressed as covenants include people, nature, progress, comfort, work, history, youth, morals, class, production, god, privacy, and uniqueness (Schroeder, 1980). The diversity produced by these covenants stands in stark contrast to the stereotype that all small towns are alike. Indeed, there are several types of small communities, each expressing its own covenant. These include agricultural towns, government centers, industrial towns, polynuclear suburbs, recreational communities, art colonies, religious communities, college towns, Native-American reservation towns, crossroad hamlets, senior adult ("retirement") communities, and terminuses of highways and railroads, to name but a few (Schroeder, 1980). These differing sociocultural contexts may have diverse impacts upon the nature and quality of their inhabitants' lives.

The Changing Rural Landscape: Impacts on Adult Lives

Contextual researchers have determined that adult life trajectories can be strongly influenced by historical events. These events may generate "life crises" that result from the friction that occurs when outerworld demands threaten one's self-identity (Riegel, 1975). For example, Harel (1981) has examined the long-term impacts of the Holocaust on the lives of survivors, and Elder (1974) has conducted extensive research on the way in which the Great Depression altered the lives of men raised during that era. Residents of rural areas are familiar with their own versions of traumatic events, particularly with natural disasters such as tornadoes and floods. There is, however, a more pervasive normative event occurring in many rural areas that is redefining and, in some cases, erasing rural contexts. This event is the restructuring of the rural economy that was initiated by the "farm crisis" of the 1980s. Research on this life-altering event is only now beginning, and it warrants more atten-

tion by adult developmentalists (Scheidt & Norris-Baker, 1990).

Rural life today differs dramatically from rural life in the early part of the twentieth century. At that time, about 60 percent of the population lived in rural areas, with about 42 percent on farms. As already noted, today about 25 percent of the U.S. population resides in rural areas, with about 2 percent living on farms. The rural economy is much less dependent upon farming now than at the turn of the century. Today only one-third of rural counties depend heavily upon agriculture. The reasons most often cited for this change include international forces, the shift to service industries, deregulation, and the modernization of agriculture (Drabenstott, 1988).

The most difficult times in recent years occurred during the 1980s.

> Agricultural exports began declining after reaching an all-time high in 1981. Farm income became increasingly unstable, and the cost of government price support programs escalated because of lower prices and heavy surpluses. The credit picture became even worse. Farmers that had borrowed heavily...began suffering as incomes dropped and farmland values plummeted. Farm bankruptcies increased and the entire rural credit system was affected. Farmers found themselves increasingly at the mercy of macroeconomic forces beyond the control of traditional agricultural policies. (Rasmussen & Bowers, 1988, p. 10)

Short- and long-term changes in the rural economy are changing the physical, social, and cultural environments of many small towns. This is particularly evident in the Cornbelt and the Great Plains. Business losses have translated into population losses in the more remote communities, resulting in decreased purchasing power among residents, leakage of retail trade to regional centers, an inadequate tax base to maintain the community infrastructure, and declining property values (Daniels & Lapping, 1987).

Data on rural poverty indicate that the decline of small towns is widespread. Many are turning into "rural ghettos" (Jacobsen & Albertson, 1987). For example, towns with

2,500 or fewer residents comprise 87 percent of all the communities in Kansas. By conservative estimate, at least half of these communities are dying, with many turning into rural neighborhoods or ghost towns (Scheidt & Norris-Baker, 1990).

As a contextual perspective would predict, there is evidence that these changes have carried different meanings for various subpopulations of rural residents, affecting their lives in different ways. Epidemiological research indicates that the numerous stressors connected with these changes have taken many forms and have already had harmful effects at both individual and environmental levels.

> Thousands of rural Americans suffer severe emotional stress because they have lost their land, homes, jobs, sense of well-being, life-style, and in some extreme instances, the lives of their loved ones. The emotional problems most frequently cited as consequences of the rural crisis include depression, anxiety, marital conflicts, anger, abusive and self-abusive behavior, alcohol and drug abuse, and contemplation of suicide. (Adams & Benjamin, 1988, pp. 49-50)

More specifically, the North Dakota Department of Human Services reported a 300 percent increase in cases of domestic violence between 1980 and 1986 (Bergland, 1988). Reported cases of child abuse almost doubled during the same period, and suicide rates increased by 27 percent. Bergland cites evidence that mental health problems are increasing faster in rural communities than in urban areas. Higher rates of alcohol abuse, alcohol dependence, and cognitive deficit problems have been found among rural than among urban residents (Blazer et al., 1985).

The people at greatest risk for mental disorder in rural areas are the elderly, the chronically ill, the poor, and the dependent— all of whom are overrepresented in rural settings. These residents are also at higher risk than urban residents for health problems in general. These problems include more chronic and persistent diseases, more days of disability, higher rates of fetal and infant mortality, and higher rates of accidental inju-

ries (Human & Wasem, 1991). Not all of these maladies are caused by the recent rural economic crisis; there is evidence that long-term, macro-level social, cultural, and economic changes have threatened rural life-styles for several years.

Although the numbers emerging from epidemiological studies are informative at one level, they tell us little about how people actually cope with these changes in their everyday lives over time. The statistics tell us about the consequences of adaptive failure, but they reveal nothing about adaptive resilience. The lifespan effects of historical changes such as the rural crisis may vary not only according to the previous state of the person and available resources but also according to the person's stage of life. For example, one would expect that younger residents would differ from older residents in their encounters with hard times. These differences presumably would reflect age-related social roles and options. From the contextualist view, it is wise to examine similarities and differences in the responses to these stressors, remembering that people are producers, not merely products, of historical change "through their construction of historical interpretations and their actions in the present" (Elder, Liker, & Jaworski, 1984, p. 68). Research is only beginning to be pursued along these lines.

One of the few studies to examine positive as well as negative outcomes associated with the rural crisis involved in-depth interviews with older residents of four small Kansas communities (Norris-Baker & Scheidt, in press; Scheidt & Norris-Baker, 1990). Many small, dying towns contain a large proportion of older residents who were left behind to "age in place" as younger generations sought employment opportunities elsewhere.

Some notable positive aspects were emerging from these elders' efforts to deal with the physical, social, and cultural declines in their hometowns. For example, while many older adults admitted having little control over the larger, external causes of community decline, they demonstrated considerable influence and autonomy by filling formal and informal roles essential to maintaining the towns. Some older adults assumed new roles as "culture bearers" and local historians, preserving the sense of community identity for others as well as themselves. The high level of volunteerism in these towns bolstered the self-esteem of some individuals whose skills and talents may not have been so highly valued in more prosperous and functional communities.

The lack of easy access to health care facilities served as an additional incentive for some to maintain life-styles that supported health and fitness. With few long-term care facilities available locally, the small towns developed extensive informal social support systems that allowed frail elders to remain in their own homes. The adaptive hardiness of such residents, however, may not be representative of those who live in economically healthier rural communities. There is reason to be concerned that

> most of the actions and benefits we have observed are largely reactive, as opposed to proactive. Almost invariably, they occur in response to negative events brought about by forces that are unlikely to disappear. Adopting the metaphor of the death trajectory, we wonder whether these reactive, seemingly beneficial behaviors displayed by older residents of endangered towns are part of a normal pattern of behaviors found in terminally ill communities. (Norris-Baker & Scheidt, in press)

To extend the metaphor, are these small communities analogous to cells within a dying organ? And are these high-control, apparently beneficial behaviors of older residents analogous to the valiant but doomed efforts of antibodies fighting disease in a terminally ill patient? Should rural practitioners be looking beyond community revitalization models, developing instead a "hospice" model that could guide service delivery policy in these dying communities?

Conclusion

Commenting on the existing state of knowledge in a different area, a researcher once conceded that "we know just enough to know what we don't know." This aptly describes our knowledge of the mutual dynamics existing between rural contexts and the adult life course. We know little, for instance, about the specific ways in which the changes in small towns may impact upon adult lives over time. We do know that those who are immediately affected by these changes face difficult times and painful choices. From the contextual perspective, historical moments such as the restructuring of the rural economy in the United States will almost assuredly have developmental "ripple effects" that will change lives indelibly. These changes, similar to the death event, may "fall like an iron gate, trapping some of the survivors in the past and liberating others to go forth to a new life style" (Kastenbaum, 1975, p. 25).

What is learned from these survivors can inform interventions designed to enhance the development of adults residing within rural contexts and other environments that are characterized by complexity, diversity, and perennial change.   ▼ RICK J. SCHEIDT

See also: Alcohol Use and Abuse; Cohort and Generational Effects; Contextualism; Depression; Life Events; Place and Personality in Adult Development; Religion in Adult Life; Stress.

References

Adams, R., & Benjamin, M. (1988). Innovative approaches to mental health service delivery in rural areas. *Journal of Rural Community Psychology, 9:* 41-50.

Baer, D. (1989). Behavior analysis of human development. Abstract. *Society for Research in Child Development, 6:* 117.

Baltes, P. (1987). Theoretical propositions of life-span developmental psychology: On the dynamics between growth and decline. *Developmental Psychology, 23:* 611-26.

Bergland, B. (1988). Rural mental health: Report of the National Action Commission on the mental health of rural Americans. *Journal of Rural Community Psychology, 9:* 29-39.

Blazer, D., et al. (1985). Psychiatric disorders: A rural/urban comparison. *Archives of General Psychiatry, 42:* 653-56.

Daniels, T., & Lapping, M. (1987). Small town triage: A rural resettlement policy for the American Midwest. *Journal of Rural Studies, 3:* 273-80.

Drabenstott, M. (1988). Executive summary. *Rural America in Transition*. Kansas City: Federal Reserve Bank of Kansas City.

Elder, G. (1974). *Children of the Great Depression*. Chicago: University of Chicago Press.

Elder, G., Liker, G., & Jaworski, B. (1984). Hardship in lives: Depression influences from the 1930's to old age in postwar America. In K. McCluskey & H. Reese (Eds.), *Life-span Developmental Psychology: Historical and Generational Effects.* New York: Academic Press, pp. 161-201.

Flax, J., et al. (1979). *Mental Health and Rural America: An Overview and Annotated Bibliography.* Washington, DC: U.S. Department of Health, Education, and Welfare.

Ford, T. (1962). *The Southern Appalachian Region*. Lexington, KY: University of Kentucky Press.

Harel, Z. (1981). The long range impact of the holocaust on survivors. Abstract. *The Gerontologist, 21:* 63

Human, J., & Wasem, C. (1991). Rural mental health in America. *American Psychologist, 46:* 232-39.

Jacobsen, G., & Albertson, B. (1987). Social and economic change in rural Iowa: The development of rural ghettos. *Human Services in the Rural Environment, 10-11:* 58-65.

Kastenbaum, R. (1975). Is death a life crisis? On the confrontation with death in theory and practice. In N. Datan & L. Ginsberg (Eds.), *Life-span Developmental Psychology: Normative Life Crises.* New York: Academic Press, pp. 19-50.

Krout, J. (1988). The elderly in rural environments. *Journal of Rural Studies, 4:* 103-14.

Larson, O. (1978). Values and beliefs of rural people. In T. Ford (Ed.), *Rural U.S.A.: Persistence and Change.* Ames, IA: Iowa State University, pp. 38-61.

Lerner, R., & Kauffman, M. (1985). The concept of development in contextualism. *Developmental Review, 5:* 309-33.

Lutwack, L. (1984). *The Role of Place in Literature*. Syracuse, NY: Syracuse University Press.

Norris-Baker, C., & Scheidt, R. (in press). A contextual approach to serving older persons of economically-threatened small towns. *Journal of Aging Studies.*

Olson-Sierra, M. (1987). News from the real Lake Woebegone, or what Garrison Keillor won't tell you. *The Rural Sociologist, 7:* 107-11.

Plomin, R., DeFries, J., & McClearn, G. (1989). *Behavior Genetics: A Primer.* Second Edition. San Francisco: Freeman.

Rasmussen, W., & Bowers, D. (1988). *Rural America in Transition*. Kansas City: Federal Reserve Bank of Kansas City.

Riegel, D. (1975). Adult life crises: A dialectic interpretation of development. In N. Datan & L. Ginsberg (Eds.), *Life-span Developmental Psychology: Normative Life Crises.* New York: Academic Press, pp. 99-128.

Rowles, G. (1984). Aging in rural environments. In I. Altman, M. P. Lawton, & J. Wohwill (Eds.), *Elderly People and the Environment.* New York: Plenum, pp. 129-57.

Scarr, S. (1982). Development is internally guided, not determined. *Contemporary Psychology, 27:* 852-53.

Scheidt, R., & Norris-Baker, L. (1990). A transactional approach to environmental stress among older residents of rural communities. *Journal of Rural Community Psychology, 11:* 5-30.

Schroeder, F. (1980). Types of American small towns and how to read them. *Southern Quarterly, 19:* 104-35.

U.S. Department of Commerce. (1988). Rural and rural farm population. *Current Population Reports.* Series P-20, No. 439.

Wagenfeld, M. (1988). Rural mental health and community psychology in the post community mental health era. *Journal of Rural Community Psychology, 9:* 5-12.

Windley, P., & Scheidt, R. (1988). Rural small towns: An environmental context for aging. *Journal of Rural Studies, 4:* 151-58.

S

SEX IN THE LATER ADULT YEARS

My Parents Never Had Sex is the title of a book (Hammond, 1987) that aptly describes the prevailing attitudes toward sex in the later years. If it is difficult for young people to think of their 30- or 40-year-old parents having sex, it can seem inconceivable that Grandma and Grandpa could also be interested—and beyond credulity that they could actually be "doing it." Yet recent studies reveal a different picture of sex after 60. In fact, since this area was opened to research, the findings have consistently contradicted the stereotypes.

The revised portrait of sexual interest and behavior among older adults can be sketched through attention to the following 10 points.

1. *People over 60 are interested in, think about, and desire sex.* Surveys of older people reveal that more than 95 percent express interest in sex (Brecher, 1984; Starr & Weiner, 1981). Individual comments are even more revealing (Starr & Weiner, 1981):

   - "Yes, still need sex and enjoy it" (female, age 68).
   - "Yes, like everything about it" (male, age 68).
   - "It makes me feel good and improves my disposition" (female, age 78).
   - "Yes, it is one of the supreme pleasures of living" (male, age 74).
   - "I like sex tremendously with my sweetheart" (female, age 74).
   - "Yes, I believe it relieves pressures of life. I feel much better physically and mentally when enjoying a good sex life" (male, age 72).

   What these and many other comments remind us is that people remain the same more than they change over the years. Although we readily accept this truism in regard to younger people, we quickly forget it when looking at older people. Sexuality is a vital part of a person's self-image; therefore, like any other vital function it is likely to continue in some form throughout the lifespan

   In fact, when sexuality apparently is *not* present, there should be concern about where it is hiding and what effect denial, repression, or frustration has on the overall quality of life. When younger people show signs of depression, it is commonplace to query them about their social and sexual lives, recognizing that these are essential to personal fulfillment. Yet these areas are rarely explored with older people because of the false assumption that sexuality somehow mysteriously disappears after a certain age. To counteract this trend, one geriatric physician recommends that "with the same casual comfort that we have always asked intimate questions of women about vaginal discharge, urinary flow, and constipation, so now let us also ask older women: 'How do you handle your normal sexual feelings?'" (Renshaw, 1982).

2. *Older adults consider sex important to their physical and psychological well-being.* Many men and women in their sixties and beyond are aware of the negative effects on their overall functioning when sexuality vanishes from their lives. There is also medical evidence that ailments such as arthritis and insomnia are helped by continued sexual activity through raising cortisone levels in the blood (Butler & Lewis, 1990). Other complaints, aches, pains, and depression have also been associated with cessation of sexual activity. One investigator has even suggested that sexuality can be a deterrent to suicide in elderly adults (Leviton, 1973). These findings testify to the importance of sexuality for overall feelings of well-being.

3. *Sexual activity patterns in the later adult years are consistent with the patterns established by the individuals in their earlier years.* Those who were active continue to be active. Those who were inactive continue their pattern of inactivity. This finding also confirms what we know about personality and behavior in general: People tend to be consistent over time unless something happens that interferes with the established pattern (e.g., loss of a partner).

4. *Older men and women engage in a variety of sexual practices, including oral sex, consistent with their earlier repertoire.* We usually associate "fancy sex" with young people who are supposed to have a lock on imagination and variety. Our age stereotypes lead us to believe that older people, if they engage in sex at all, do it in the most routine and detached manner. Why should this be so? If a couple enjoyed certain activities when younger, why shouldn't they continue to do so? The quotes speak for themselves (Starr & Weiner, 1981):

   • "Clitoral stimulation, manual and oral, hugging, kissing, sexy talk, massage" (female, age 61).
   • "Freedom to explore my partner's body and her initiative and aggression in doing the same for me" (male, age 75).
   • "When I know that I'm going to have an orgasm and my husband kisses me" (female, age 74).
   • "Kissing—rousing nipples with kissing and sucking" (male, age 70).
   • "Kissing the man I care about and making love to him—also orally" (female, age 63).

5. *A majority of older people find sexual experiences to be as satisfying or more satisfying than they were earlier in their lives.* This finding is rather surprising since it is a physiological fact that the sexual response in men (not women) declines with age. But when we look closely at the responses to this question, it is clear that pleasure is a highly subjective experience. Many older couples feel that sex is better now because it is more relaxed, without the fear of pregnancy. Furthermore, retired couples can engage in sex at whatever time of the day most suits them. For those couples who remain active in the later years, these factors can contribute to the perception of equal or better sex compared with the years of the "quickie" after the 11 o'clock news, a tiring day, and preoccupation with the pressures of work, economics, and child rearing.

6. *Maintaining sexually gratifying relationships requires readjustments since the male sexual response (arousal and orgasm) declines sharply in later life while the female response remains at a high plateau.* The male capacity for arousal and orgasm reaches a peak in late adolescence and early adulthood. Thereafter, it declines slowly throughout adulthood with an accelerated decline in response after age 60. About 50 percent of men past age 60 report occasional difficulty in getting an erection (Brecher, 1984; Starr & Weiner, 1981). Many older men report difficulty in sustaining an erection, and there is a longer recovery period after orgasm. Even so, most men over 60—and even into their eighties—are capable of erec-

tion and orgasm. There are also individual differences so that some men barely decline while others have more accelerated declines.

Women experience a different pattern of sexual response over the adult years. A peak of arousal and orgasmic response is reached in the mid-thirties and remains at about that level throughout their lives. In others words, the woman of 70 is as capable of orgasm as a 35-year-old woman.

The disparity of sexual response between men and women requires readjustment for older couples if they are to remain active. The man must learn to accept his declining sexual response and not have the expectations of his younger years. The inability of many men to adjust to declining response accounts for much of the reduction in sexual activity among some older couples. Some men withdraw entirely from sex because of the fear of sexual failure or disappointment that their response is not what it was when younger. Couples who remain more active make better adjustments to changing patterns of sexual response, giving more time for male arousal and focusing on "pleasuring" rather than a scorecard of performance.

7. *The single most important factor in reduced sexual activity or no sexual activity is the unavailability of a partner.* This is especially true for single, widowed, and divorced older women. Since women tend to marry men a few years older than themselves and then to outlive them by an average of seven years, there are far more older women than older men—and with each advancing decade the gap widens. After age 65 there are five times as many widows as widowers. Although most older women express interest, need, and desire for sexuality, they lack the opportunity for heterosexual activity.

8. *Masturbation is a common practice among older adults.* This may come as a shock to many people, since masturbation at one time was a great taboo thought to have all kinds of dire consequences, including insanity and blindness. That view dramatically changed during the sexual revolution of the 1960s and 1970s. As a matter of fact, masturbation even became a prescribed technique for developing sexual responses and dealing with the lack of a partner. This transformation in attitude prompted comments such as, "The practice once thought to cause warts is now recommended to all but cure them" (Tavris & Sadd, 1977).

This trend did not escape the notice of older people. According to the *Starr-Weiner Report*, 82 percent of the respondents accepted masturbation in principle, 46 percent acknowledged masturbating, and there was strong evidence that many others were reluctant to tell the truth. Masturbation was highest for single (81 percent), divorced (66 percent), and widowed (47 percent) women.

9. *For women who are sexually active, menopause does not reduce sexual interest or activity* (Hite, 1976; Starr & Weiner, 1981; Tavris & Sadd, 1977). The dictum "use it or lose it" has real meaning here. This comes as good news for those who fear that menopause marks the decline or end of sexuality. In many cases the elimination of a fear of pregnancy introduces a renewed sense of freedom in sexual activity. Also, since the female response does not decline with age, there is no reason for menopause to impact negatively on sexual behavior. The vaginal walls tend to thin with age and secretions diminish, but these changes can easily be compensated for with lubrication, as many couples have discovered.

Gynecologists do report that patients after menopause frequently experience painful intercourse, dryness, and lowered interest in sex. These symptoms have been reported to respond to estrogen replacement therapy (Beard & Curtis, 1991). It may be that physicians get a skewed view of the effects of menopause since they are more likely to see patients who have complaints. It must also be borne in mind that it has been well established that the most important organ for sexual activity is the mind.

10. *Emerging generations of elderly men and women are likely to forge new solutions to the sexual and social problems of the later years.* A person born in 1950 will turn 60 in the year 2010. Her generation undoubtedly will be different from her parents' or grandparents' generation when they were elderly. The generation that grew up during the sexual revolution and beyond will have broader conceptions of their sexual and social lives. Certainly, practices such as masturbation will be more readily accepted.

The emerging generations of elderly persons are also likely to develop new solutions to the sexual and social problems of the later years because of their more open attitudes and their history of tuning in to sexual and social needs. It is difficult to predict what course their solutions will take, but the revolution of the old may finally change some of our stereotyped views of sexuality throughout the life span.

▼ BERNARD D. STARR

See also: Adult Children and Their Parents; Chronic Pain as a Lifespan Problem; Cohort and Generational Effects; Depression; Divorce; Happiness, Cohort Measures of; Individuality; Marital Development; Menopause; Mental Health in the Adult Years; Sexuality.

References

Beard, M., & Curtis, L. (1991). *Menopause and the Years Ahead*. Tucson, AZ: Fisher Books.

Brecher, E. (1984). *Love, Sex, and Aging*. Boston: Little, Brown.

Butler, R. N., & Lewis, M. I. (1990). *Love and Sex After 60*. New York: Harper & Row.

Hammond, D. B. (1987). *My Parents Never Had Sex*. New York: Prometheus.

Hite, S. (1976). *The Hite Report*. New York: Dell.

Leviton, D. (1973). The significance of sexual activity as a deterrent to suicide among the aged. *Omega, 4*: 163-74.

Renshaw, D. C. (1982). Sex and older women. *Medical Aspects of Human Sexuality, 16*: 132-39.

Starr, B. D. (1985). Sexuality and aging. In C. Eisdorfer (Ed.), *Annual Review of Gerontology and Geriatrics*. Volume 5. New York: Springer, pp. 97-126.

Starr, B. D., & Weiner, M. B. (1981). *The Starr-Weiner Report on Sex and Sexuality in the Mature Years*. New York: McGraw-Hill.

Tavris, C., & Sadd, S. (1977). *The Redbook Report on Female Sexuality*. New York: Delacorte.

SEXUALITY

An obvious fact of human development is that, with a few exceptions, each of us goes through our lives as either a female or a male. Sexual differentiation contributes to every facet of our experience. For example, being female has placed babies at a higher risk for infanticide throughout history, but today confers an advantage in life expectancy. Being male is correlated with relatively greater height and muscularity, but also with relatively slower socio-emotional development in early childhood. Furthermore, cultural expectations and pressures operate throughout the life course along sex-specific lines, whether one is male, female, or hermaphroditic (intersexual). To ignore sexuality would be to ignore one of the essential dimensions of human experience from youth to age.

Sexuality involves more than participation in sexual activities. "Having sex" is an expression of sexuality, but sexuality is an enduring characteristic regardless of one's pattern of sexual behavior. Both a nun and a priest may honor their vows of chastity, but the former remains a woman and the latter a man. Physiological functioning, social roles, and personal identity cannot be separated from sexuality except by esoteric research methods. In other words, we may behave *sexually* from time to time, but *sexuality* is one of the defining characteristics of our being.

Gender, reproduction/fertility, and *sensuality* are terms often associated with sexuality. It is probably most useful to think of *gender* as a sociocultural marker. Socialization processes, career opportunities, and many other influences tend to be differentiated according to male/female status (see **Gender as a Shaping Force in Adult Development and Aging** and **Gender Differences in the Workplace**). These patterns are rooted in biological differentiations between the sexes, but are expressed primarily on the interpersonal and symbolic levels. Today it is less unusual for women to pursue professional careers and for men to share in household responsibilities. This shift represents a partial reconstruction of attitudes and expectations rather than a transformation of sex-linked biological characteristics. Gender roles in society, then, constitute a cultural overlay on the basics of sexual differentiation. This overlay is subject to modification as conditions and attitudes change, e.g., the greater acceptance of women into "men only" work situations during World War II, and subsequent attempts to restore the traditional bias that a woman's "place" is in the home.

Reproduction and *fertility* are the core functions of sexuality. (*Reproduction* denotes the process by which the species is perpetuated; *fertility* refers to the capacity to engage in the reproductive process.) Biologists, animal breeders, epidemiologists, and economists often treat reproduction as though it is the only purpose of sexuality. From these standpoints, sexuality is but a means through which populations are replenished. This position is conveyed through the old joke that "A hen is just nature's way of making another egg." Economists seldom inquire as to whether or not the hen (and rooster) feel content to have actualized their social role obligations, nor do farmers routinely meditate about the hen's sense of sexual fulfillment or maternal gratification.

Students of human development, however, are entitled to operate from a different perspective. Making babies is not invariably the uppermost thought when people engage in sexual activities. Although the reproductive function is crucial for the species, the sexual behavior of individuals may be at the service of a great many blended motivations. These motivations can include tension release, pleasure-bonding, a need to control the other, or an expression of love. Furthermore, the motivations are not necessarily identical for both partners. And, obviously, the attempt to equate sexuality with reproduction is not a promising approach to understanding homosexual activity.

Sensuality is at times a salient characteristic of courtship and love-making. Consider, for example, the romantic image of candlelight, roses, and wine. The subdued, flickering light of the candle, the beguiling scent of the flowers, the taste of the wine and its warming afterglow—each of these components arouses the senses; together the effect is heightened. The sights, the scents, the tastes, the glow do not in themselves produce a state of complete gratification or tension-release. It is all preparation, expectation. A light touch of one companion's hand upon the other's hand may at this point be thrilling. It has been known for centuries that subtle and patient enhancement of sensory experience can contribute to deeply satisfying and memorable love-making. Perfume-making was regarded as the highest art form among the Japanese elite a millennium ago, and almost every culture has poems, songs, dances, feasts, love gifts, and other customs intended to create a state of heightened sensuous awareness in preparation for sexual activity.

Nevertheless, the relationship between sensuality and sexuality is not as simple and invariant as the romantic image might suggest. Sexual episodes can also be sudden, brief, and violent, usually because of an aggressive male. When one or both partners are bored or otherwise unenthusiastic, intercourse can be routine and nearly anesthetic. Although shared sensuality can transform a sexual episode into an exceptional experience, not all sexual episodes are rich in sensuality. People often feel disappointed in their early sexual encounters because "bells did not ring" and "rockets did not go off"; only a physical act occurred. Although such disappointments have many possible causes (including overheated, media-fueled expectations), the lack of refined sensory preparation and participation is often involved.

Sensuality also appears in nonsexual contexts. The child who is happiest playing in mud puddles and in adult life enjoys work that "dirties" the hands finds pleasure in direct contact with nature. The ardent gardener, for example, delights in handling soil, seeds, plants, and tools while taking in the ever-changing array of outdoor sights, sounds, and scents. "Nature sensuality" may have a deep connection to reproduction and survival, but to interpret the gardener's experiences as "sexual" would be a loose interpretation indeed. People may find sensuous pleasure in a flight of geese overhead, the sound of the breeze through the forest, or the scent of a campfire as well as in works of art or commercial design. Societies that have been especially fearful of sexual expression have sometimes attempted to prohibit virtually all sensuous experiences, but that is akin to ordering water not to be wet and children not to enjoy splashing.

The development of an individual's sexuality throughout the life course, then, proceeds along several major dimensions. Sexual development can lead one to conform to or deviate from society's gender expectations. Sexual development can lead to participation or nonparticipation in the reproduction of the species. And sexual development can produce a vibrant or a restrained sensuality that either enhances or is absent from sexual activity. No existing body of thought and research integrates all these dimensions into a comprehensive framework, but some information and insights on the development of adult sexuality are available. And the emerging picture has its share of surprises.

Sexuality and the Brain

One of these surprises merits our immediate attention. The current "politically correct" view holds gender stereotypes responsible for most of the observed differences in the lives of females and males. Females still must combat entrenched patterns of discrimination, but removing the culturally imposed barriers will leave little difference between the sexes in personality, interests, life style, and achievement. This view assumes that biological differences are largely limited to primary and secondary sexual characteristics. Females and males are thought to differ in those anatomical and physiological respects related to reproductive function, but to have identical brains. This assumption is being challenged, however, by recent advances in neural research. Consider the following statement:

> With the development of the field of neuroendocrinology it has become clear that the brain is an integral component of the reproductive system. Not surprisingly, therefore, the brain also undergoes the process of sexual differentiation. In fact, it appears that the mammalian brain is either inherently feminine or at least bipotential and that its functional and morphological characteristics, which are recognized as typical of the male, are induced by the action of testicular testosterone (and its derivatives) during specific "critical periods" of development. (Gorski, 1989, p. 33)

Although the above statement was offered within a scientific context, it cannot help but have implications for social and political action. The assertion that the mammalian (and, thus, human) brain is sexually differentiated might at first seem to support gender-linked role patterns imposed by society. This argument for the status quo is quickly upset by the revelation that the brain is more likely to be inherently feminine than masculine. The male brain appears to be a revised version of the female brain that is given its variant structure through hormonal sculpturing shortly before and shortly after birth. "Maleness" also seems to be more vulnerable to subsequent events. Rat studies have shown that removal of the ovaries in the newborn female has no major effect on sexual behavior in adult life, but castration leads to the development of feminized rather than masculine behavior in males.

Sex differences in the structure of the central nervous system (CNS) have been discovered in many species, including the canary, zebra finch, guinea pig, and human. The influence of gonadal hormones is most obvious in a functional system of the brain that is sometimes known as "the surge center," which includes the anterior sector of the hypothalamus and the preoptic area of the brain. Soon after birth, this area grows much more rapidly in the male and is much larger when the peak of development is reached. This means that more neurons (nerve cells) are generated in males than females within this area of the brain, and, consequently, more become available to migrate to other positions in the CNS.

Nevertheless, the term "surge center" has been given to this area because of a phenomenon that occurs only with females: a hormone produced by the surge center stimulates the pituitary to release a substance required for ovulation (Jones, 1991). Perhaps it is not so surprising after all that there would be differential structures and processes in the CNS to regulate the differential sexuality of females and males.

Studies are also finding that female and male brains differ in characteristics of the opiate-like binding sites (Hammer, 1985). It may be that significant sex differences exist with respect to the entire array of neuropeptide receptors that mediate our emotional states. Sensitivity to pain, ability to call upon self-sedating neural mechanisms, and many other facets of our emotional response to the world may be differentiated by sexuality as mediated through the CNS.

One of the most significant differences may be that the "female brain is somewhat less hemispherically specialized than the male brain . . . and the corpus callosum that joins the two hemispheres is somewhat thicker in females. This corresponds with the fact that women are superior to men in integrating verbal and nonverbal information and that language loss after traumatic damage of the left hemisphere in women is easier to cure by therapy than comparable traumatic injuries in men. Whereas, in women, language is more a means of social communication, in men it is perhaps more a means of analytical thought" (Eibl-Eibesfeldt, 1989, p. 272). If confirmed by subsequent research, these findings and their accompanying interpretations would contribute much to our understanding of sex-linked behavior patterns and feeling-states. At present it might be wise to

regard such findings with interest and an open mind, but to reserve total acceptance until all the major results have been supported by independent research and all alternative explanations have been carefully considered.

Even at the present stage of knowledge, it is difficult to deny differences in the brain structure and function of males and females. The number of neurons in the preoptic area, the pre-ovulatory "surge," the differential patterns of opiate receptor sites, and the tendency toward more unified functioning of the hemispheres in females are not the only differences that have been observed, and more such findings may be expected in the future. The sexual differentiation of the brain, whether we like it or not, is rapidly becoming a fact that cannot be ignored in understanding human development. It should be kept clearly in mind that differences do not denote superiority of inferiority. There is no compelling biological or psychosocial basis for assuming that one sex-linked brain configuration is more valuable or effective than the other. First, the differences are relatively small in comparison with the CNS structures and functions that are held in common by both sexes. Secondly, the differences probably contribute to the versatility and adaptability of the species. Instead of being misappropriated as an excuse for further sex-linked social discrimination, the neurobiology of sexual differentiation provides another opportunity to appreciate that both females and males have something valuable to offer.

Sexual Maturation: The Basics

The new wave of research into sexual differentiation of the brain and CNS may eventually require us to rethink our entire conception of human development. In the meantime, a large and useful body of knowledge regarding the basics of sexual maturation has been accumulating over many years.

Primary Sexual Differentiation. Each parent contributes a set of 22 autosomal chromosomes to the child. Most of the child's genetic inheritance is represented by these 22 pairs, including eye and hair color, height, etc. The 23rd chromosome determines the child's sex. The mother will always contribute an X chromosome. The father will contribute either an X or a Y. If fertilization is achieved by an X sperm (also known as *gynosperm*), the child will be a female. If the ovum is fertilized by a Y sperm (*androsperm*), the child will be a male. In past centuries a patriarch might blame his wife for bearing a daughter rather than the desired male heir, but research shows the patriarch should blame his own androsperm for not winning the race to the ovum. (The androsperm is actually smaller and swifter, but this does not guarantee victory.)

Anatomical differences do not appear in the embryo until about the sixth week. At this time, testes start to develop in embryos that have the XY configuration of sex chromosomes. The testes contribute to further sexual differentiation by secreting testosterone and other male hormones (collectively known as *androgens*). The testicles will migrate to their permanent location in the scrotum, bringing along its associated blood vessels and nerves.

Sexual differentiation in the female (XX) embryo begins a little later. Ovaries start to develop around the third month following conception, and an earlier ductile structure withers away, to be replaced by the genital tract that will eventually support the reproductive process. A structure that becomes the penis for males becomes the clitoris for females, whose labia majora and vestibule are counterparts of the scrotum.

Guided either by the X or Y control mechanism, then, the fertilized ovum becomes well differentiated sexually while still in its prenatal state. Nature starts with the same basic structures, sculpturing them toward female or male orientation through differential hormonal action.

Childhood. The facts of childhood sexuality can be difficult to separate from the fears, prohibitions, and myths that have long surrounded this subject. From a broad historical and cultural perspective it appears that Western society has attempted to per-petuate the beliefs that children (a) do not and (b) should not have sexual dimensions to their lives. In his challenging reconstruction of *The History of Sexuality*, Michel Foucault (1980) argues that this intensive effort to repress and deny sexuality in childhood has had quite the opposite effect

> Take the secondary schools of the eighteenth century, for example. On whole, one can have the impression that sex was hardly spoken of at all in these institutions. But one only has to glance over the architectural layout, the rules of discipline, and their whole internal organization: the question of sex was a constant preoccupation . . . . The space for classes, the shape of the tables, the planning of the recreation lessons, the distribution of the dormitories (with or without partitions, with or without curtains), the rules for monitoring bedtime and sleep periods—all this referred, in the most prolix manner, to the sexuality of children. (Volume 1, pp. 27-28)

Many studies, however, have made clear that sexuality is part of childhood experience throughout the world (e.g., Goldman & Goldman, 1982; Spiro, 1982.) A particular culture—or family—might be "uptight" about the slightest expression of interest in one's own or another's genital organs, or might regard young children's curiosity and play with relaxed indulgence. These differential responses on the part of society are likely to affect the child's attitudes toward sexuality and his or her openness in expressing curiosity, but are not likely to quell the natural fascination.

Changing attitudes toward sexuality in general have lead to generational differences in views of sexual behavior in childhood. Many of today's "oldest old" can recall having heard stern warnings about what happens to little boys or girls who "touch themselves." Masturbation was once thought to be a major cause of physical, mental, emotional, and moral disorder. Babies were sometimes swaddled to overcome the temptation to explore their own bodies, and anti-masturbation harnesses were available for parents who were determined to exercise control over their children night and day. As Fisher

(1989) and others have commented, the body was often regarded as a danger zone in childhood as well as in the adult years. Those who came to age from such an upbringing had one more difficulty to overcome in accepting their own and their partner's body as a part of the natural world that can be the source of pleasurable and guiltless sharing.

In the ordinary course of infant and child development, exploring and playing with one's sex organs is but one dimension of testing self and world for their possibilities. Preoccupation with sexuality at an early age would suggest the existence of tensions, pressure, and unresolved problems that may be either organic or situational in origin. Passing episodes of mutual sexual exploration by young children, for example, are not likely to be problematic, but molestation by teenagers or adults can generate anxieties that disturb the individual's development and well-being for many years.

As already described, sexuality plays a significant role in prenatal development. Sexual differentiation continues to be influential in shaping the character and experience of the young child. Studies in many cultures reveal that boys and girls tend to show different patterns of interests and activities. Expert opinion has been swinging back and forth with respect to the role of cultural and biological factors in determining these patterns. Margaret Mead (1935, 1949) was for a time extremely influential with her thesis that society is almost entirely responsible for the differential personality development of females and males. One problem with this thesis, however, is that it is not what Mead actually said, but, rather, reflects the sociopolitical uses that were made of her observations. The distinguished ethologist Irenaus Eibl-Eibesfeldt (1989, p. 265) points out that Mead was quite appreciative of the biological side of development and did not believe that any society could easily induce females and males to behave in ways that ran counter to their natural temperaments. Furthermore, in reviewing more recent studies of sex role behavior, Eibl-Eibesfeldt finds that "boys are boys" and "girls are girls"

wherever they have been studied carefully. Boys, for example, tend to be more physically active and adventuresome, and girls more collaborative in their play. Both girls and boys generally prefer to seek those of their own gender for companionship and play.

Puberty (Adolescence). There is both truth and exaggeration in the familiar statement that the child becomes a sexual being with the advent of puberty. The biological changes that occur at this time are certainly eventful and consequential. However, as already noted, the child has been thinking, feeling, and acting in accordance with biological and cultural sex-linked paths of development almost since the moment of conception.

It is most accurate to think of pubescence as a process through which the child reaches his or her sexual maturity. Pubescence represents a second "growth spurt." Children develop at a phenomenal rate during the first few months of life. This rate eventually slows and provides a welcome period of stability that enables the child to adjust socially, emotionally, and cognitively. This second and final growth spurt involves a quickening of change both in overall characteristics (e.g., height, voice), and in sexual characteristics (the adult "figure" starts to emerge). For females and males alike, the increased secretion of a pituitary hormone that is known, logically enough, as the growth hormone (GH) plays a crucial role in the sexual maturation and overall development. Other hormones are also at work, however. The thyroid gland contributes hormones that increase the metabolic rate and stimulates general development. Androgens (male hormones) also contribute to sexual maturation in both females and males, while estrogens (secreted by the ovaries) play an additional role in female development. Incidentally, the temporary blemish of acne is a side-effect of androgen secretion in about 3 of 10 youths of both sexes. It can be helpful to realize that acne is "not caused by improper hygiene, spread by touch, associated with long hair, caused by masturbation, or cured by frequent sex" (Jones, 1991, p. 130). This condition usually disappears when the pubescent rush of hormones subsides.

In general, girls experience pubescence at an earlier age than boys, and also reach sexual maturity at an earlier age. Researchers on this topic caution that there are marked individual differences and, therefore, one should not expect a particular boy or girl to follow a particular schedule. With this caution in mind, it may be useful to summarize typical pubescent changes for both sexes.

Females tend to experience their new growth spurt at around age 10. They become hungrier and "tall up" in a hurry. Some months later, breast development begins, the pelvis widens, and pubic hair appears. At about age 12 it is not unusual for girls to become impatient with the seeming delay in the development of a womanly shape. However, at this time much development of the internal organs necessary for reproduction takes place. In about the 13th year, the breast development that often serves as the public "badge" of womanhood in the U.S. appears. This development continues for another year or so as does the general reshaping of the body from "girl" to "woman," but adult stature will not be reached until about age 16.

Two very important developments have been left out of this picture because they deserve special attention. *Menarche* (the first menstruation) most often occurs during the first half of the twelfth year, but varies between age 11 and 15. The girl's response to her menarche may be complex, including pride and fear. It is a fortunate young woman who can count upon accurate, caring, and open communication with her parents, particularly her mother, at this time. Less fortunate are those young women who have to "figure it out" by themselves, with the dubious assistance of peers whose own knowledge may be limited and, all too often, flawed with demeaning cultural stereotypes and superstitions about menstruation. It is helpful to be aware that some menstrual cycles may be absent or abbreviated after the menarche; this is not necessarily a cause for alarm.

The first ovulation is the other major development. Most often, the first menstrual cycle is infertile: no ovum is released. The beginning of regular ovulation may not occur for months—or even a year or two—after menarche. Again, it is helpful to be aware of these normal variations. And, considering the tendency toward very early sexual activity over the past few decades, there should be awareness of the possibility that ovulation has accompanied the menarche. Although the odds are against this timing, some young females have become pregnant soon after their menarche.

Males tend to show obvious signs of pubescent change around age 12 (always allowing for individual differences). The visible indices are preceded by physiological preparations for sexual maturity, particularly the emergence of the capacity to secrete androgens and manufacture sperm. After a year or so of this preparation, the testes start to enlarge. Bone and muscle develop at a quickened pace (starting to narrow the gap between males and the females, who experienced the growth spurt about two years before). Sexual development expresses itself through enlargement of the penis and scrotum and appearance of pubic hair.

For the 12-year-old, another of the new developments may prove to be a mingled source of delight, concern, and confusion. Most males will have already experienced erections from time to time. Now the frequency of spontaneous erections increases markedly. These occurrences are subject to misinterpretation by adults and may puzzle the young males themselves. Generally, these spontaneous erections do not represent an "oversexed" disposition or even a response to sexual stimuli. Because the capacity for adult sexual functioning is intensely "under construction" at this time, spontaneous erections may arise as a response to any intensification of experience, such as entering a new situation, encountering stress, etc. It will be a while before erections become integrated into the youth's overall approach to life and love.

There is no male pubescent development comparable to menarche in the female. The occurrence of *nocturnal emissions* around age 13, however, can become a source of anxiety and misapprehension. Just as a young female may not know quite what to make of her first menstruation cycle, so the young male may fear that something is going amiss. The passing of seminal fluid during sleep has sometimes been interpreted by the youth as an indication that he is not normal, and by parents as proof that he has masturbated and is, therefore, on the road to moral and physical decay.

About age 14, the characteristic male voice starts to resound from the enlarged larynx. This development often boosts the young man's self-esteem, helping him to achieve more status with his peers and to advance his cause among adults. It is also about this time that a visible as well as an audible change occurs--the peach fuzz of childhood begins to resemble the virile facial hair of adult males. "His first shave" can become a family celebration, signifying one more step toward adulthood. Again, individuals can differ markedly in the timing of these developments, and these differences should not be taken seriously as a basis for assessing masculinity.

From the biological standpoint, the most important development is the ability to procreate. Fertile ejaculations usually begin about age 15. This general guideline should not be taken to mean that there is no risk of pregnancy from sexual intercourse prior to that age. Over the next two or three years, the young male will become taller, more broad shouldered, and more muscular. Genetic endowment willing, the youth will also start to sprout chest hairs. Even by age 18, though, full adult stature and strength is seldom attained. There is still some "filling out" to do. It is helpful for young males (and everybody in their lives) to be aware that some awkwardness in coordination and some periods of low energy may accompany this long progression toward physical maturity. Those who criticize young males as "clumsy" or "lazy" may not know their developmental biology.

For both females and males, physical attractiveness is likely to become a salient issue. It is not just that a person wants to be appealing to potential romantic partners—there is also the need for peer approval and self-respect. Researchers emphasize that support and approval from parents is particularly important at this time so that youth have a basis for security that is not entirely dependent on how they think they look to other youths (Tobin-Richards et al., 1983).

Sexuality in the Adult Years

The physical side of sexual maturity is achieved through pubescence and is usually well established by the eighteenth year. Emotional and social maturity is another matter. The capacity to engage in sexual intercourse and to beget offspring is not necessarily accompanied by a sense of perspective, awareness of options and consequences, and overall good judgment. The limited experience of young females and males often contributes to their difficulties; years later, "older and wiser" as the cliche goes, they might have made different decisions and suffered fewer adverse consequences. However, there is nothing magic about accumulating more experiences if few lessons are learned. Perhaps most critical is the commitment to understanding the other person. It is less difficult to understand how a young couple might have difficulty in sharing their needs, desires, hopes, and fears than to understand how people in midlife can still complain that "I have no idea what s/he wants!"

Physical maturity, then, only provides a foundation upon which people may develop insights and skills that contribute to a rewarding sexual life. Physical development will take care of itself in most instances. The development of a mature "sexual self," however, requires rising to the challenge.

Although this challenge is continuous, it is useful to divide adult sexuality into the reproductive and the postreproductive years. To assert that there is a sharp and universal cross-over point would be to court ridicule. Many a "postreproductive" person has become a parent, and traditional beliefs about sexuality in the later adult years are losing credibility (See **Sex in the Later Adult Years**).

Nevertheless, there are major differences between sexuality during the prime reproductive years and in the middle and later adult years, if only because general life situations are likely to be so different.

The Reproductive Years. Many generations have been asked to conform to a model of adult sexual relationships that its proponents characterize as virtuous and moral and its critics assail as hypocritical and unrealistic. This model remains influential today, although it can no longer be said to reign uncontested. In the most idealized version, a heterosexual couple enters marriage without either partner having engaged in sexual activity beyond the hand-holding and good-night kiss stage. The wedding contract then confers upon the husband the "right" and the wife the "obligation" for intercourse. Sex is to be confined to the bedroom. Even there, all embraces will remain within the confines of socially approved maneuvers. The respectable husband will never think of making an indelicate suggestion or initiating an exotic move, and the shy and sheltered wife would not know what was happening even if he did. The couple is to remain strictly monogamous, of course. Open discussion of sex-related matters is out of the question, especially when women or children are involved. The socially responsible person will discuss neither sex nor death (Gorer, 1965), and the most admired widows will be those who "honored the memory" of their departed husbands by eschewing subsequent relationships.

Sexual intercourse is not to be overvalued for its inherent satisfactions. Indeed, sexual pleasures can be dangerous, disrupting the "moral fabric" of society (a subtle material that seems to exist only to be disrupted every now and then). The acceptance of sexual relationships between husband and wife is a concession made to certain brute realities: (a) for most men, it is better to engage in sex with a lawful mate than to "burn" in restless passion or seek relief with the "wrong kind" of woman; (b) no sex—no babies, and (c) marriage provides the most secure financial and interpersonal context within which to raise the next generation.

In practice, the sex life of humans has strayed from this ideal more often than not. Because of the notorious double standard of morality, men were given considerable latitude to "have their flings" both before and during wedlock, an option not available to respectable women. Furthermore, the ideal was hardly ideal from the woman's standpoint. Instead of enjoying equal opportunities to develop her own interests and potential, the married woman was expected to serve as *The Mother Machine*, to use Gena Corea's (1986) telling phrase. As historian Peter Gay (1984) has documented, pregnancy struck fear into the hearts of many women over the centuries, and for ample reason.

Women died in childbirth or soon after. Others survived a harrowing experience (or many harrowing experiences, given the multiple pregnancies), but never recovered their health and vitality. Gay makes a strong case for the proposition that so-called "frigidity" and avoidance of sex on the part of wives was a reaction to anxieties associated with the complications of pregnancy prior to modern public health and medical techniques. And to this must be added the ravages of sexually transmitted diseases. Syphilis in particular was a menace to "respectable wives" who contracted the disease from their dallying husbands and often had a stillborn fetus as a result.

This brief history is important as prelude to the sexual choices and challenges that adults confront today. These choices arise within a socio-technological context that differs from the past in many significant ways. Among the important differences are:

- Availability of effective (though not 100% effective) contraception devices
- Availability of effective (though not 100% effective) treatment for some sexually transmitted diseases
- Increased social acceptance of divorce
- Changing public health and economic factors that reduce the perceived value of having many children

- Emergence of a mass media culture in which "sex appeal" is used relentlessly to sell products, services, and entertainments
- Emergence of a strong equal rights movement, still in progress, that has already "rocked the boat" with respect to a wide variety of human relationships, including, although not limited to, the sexual

Any one of these developments would have had some effect on adult sexual choices and behaviors. But the situation is far more complex, because all these developments interact with each other, and because these changes keep changing. For example, opportunistic sexual behavior increased when penicillin was found to be an effective treatment for venereal disease. This apparent reduction in health risk reinforced the sense of freedom from concern that accompanied the increased availability of improved contraceptives. Both developments fostered the belief that one could have any number of sexual partners without taking a significant risk. This belief was then "writ in large" by the mass media and the entertainment industry. Sex became more explicit in magazines, motion pictures, and television, as did the "playboy philosophy" of sex as fun and games.

One hears less about the playboy philosophy today because, as already noted, the changes themselves have changed. The "traditional" venereal diseases mutated to defend themselves against the available treatments, a relatively rare condition (*Chalamydia trachomatis*) became more common, and AIDS appeared to loom like a death-head over the prospect of carefree fun and games. Moreover, society has been forced to recognize that the availability of contraceptives does not necessarily guarantee sex without consequences. The high and still rising incidence of teenage pregnancies is generating severe problems for the individuals involved and for society at large. The anxiety of a pregnant 14-year-old and the decisions and responsibilities that confront her belong to a sobering real world that has little in common with media-enhanced fantasies of risk-free sexual frolics.

In recent years, much has been said about the ticking of the "biological clock." As more women pursue advanced studies and managerial and professional careers, more of their time and energies must be given to these activities. The prime years for having babies and the prime years for establishing oneself in a career tend to be the same years. Additionally, when both females and males are functioning under the pressure of trying to establish themselves in their careers, it may be more difficult to devise an arrangement that is satisfying from the personal, occupational, and family-building standpoints. The farmer's granddaughter, now in her late 20s and completing a graduate degree, is not as likely to want a dozen children of her own (to help out around her nonexistent farm and serve as social security for her old age). But she may well have a strong desire for a child or two, along with the growing concern that either career or motherhood "will have something to give."

Complicating the situation is the heritage of sexual, economic, and political inequality. These issues are both broader and deeper than the double standard that has long countenanced male sexual adventuring but which demanded perpetual "purity" from the woman. Kate Millett (1970) called attention to many of these issues in her influential book, *Sexual Politics*. This thoughtful exploration places sexual relationships firmly within an historical economic and political context. According to Millett, the sexual relationship is also a power relationship. In fact, it is often *more* a power than a specifically sexual relationship. In *Sex and Destiny* (1984), Germaine Greer focused on "the politics of human fertility." Once again, the case is made that sexual experience and its consequences are part and parcel of dominant socio-political values. Within the seeming privacy and uniqueness of a particular couple's sexual activities there are likely to be strong socio-political forces at work. The female's role is obedience and compliance: she is primarily the man's wife and mother of his children.

Although much remains controversial about sexual politics, it is clear that adults today cannot as easily slip into traditional female and male roles. For example, what some men might have regarded as their natural right to tease and embarrass a woman is today looked upon as harassment and is subject to legal action. Similarly, a woman is more likely today than in the past to be forthcoming about her own sexual needs instead of passively accepting whatever her partner happens to offer. Furthermore, people with a homosexual orientation are also more likely to affirm their sexual life-styles while at the same time demanding equal treatment in their nonsexual roles (e.g., worker, citizen).

People who are now entering into their reproductive years have distinctive opportunities as well as challenges. The availability of contraceptive devices can help monogamous couples plan their families in accordance with their mutual long-term goals. The more open communication pattern can help people learn how to meet each other's emotional and sexual needs and prevent misunderstandings. When sexual questions or problems do arise, there are more resources available for consultation (Friedman & Chernen, 1987). And even that source of anxiety—the shifting and ambiguous rules governing human relationships in general and sexual relationships in particular—can lead to fresh and creative outcomes. Liberated from the compulsion to take on any pre-existing role, lovers may discover rewarding new ways to make a life together.

The Postreproductive Years. The "greying" of the population in most technologically advanced nations is adding not just years, but quality years to the lives of many men and women. It is no longer unusual to find elderly people who are energetic and fully engrossed in life. Often, the difference between having and not having an active sex life depends on having or not having a healthy and willing partner. Women tend to be more disadvantaged in this respect because of the higher mortality rate among aging men (see **Risk to Life through the Adult Years**). There is also a sex difference in fertility. During menopause, women lose their reproductive capacity. The capacity to produce fertile sperm continues into the ninth decade in some men.

Overall, the decline in potency and virility is slow and gradual, as contrasted with the fairly sudden and dramatic physiological changes that women experience at menopause. There is also some evidence that men who remain sexually active continue at a higher level of fertile potency and virility into their advanced years (Nieschlag & Michel, 1986).

Once a taboo subject, sex in the later adult years is being studied by both biomedical and sociobehavioral researchers. It is also apparent that more people are speaking openly about the sexual facets of their own lives. This seems to be part of a more general process through which adults are preserving vitality and sensual enjoyment in the postreproductive years. The implicit "age politics" that has expected people to step aside, expect less, and "act their age" is giving way to the awareness of continuing rights and abilities. Indeed, both knowledge and the ability to give pleasure to others can be enhanced by a long life's experience.

▼ Robert Kastenbaum

See also: Divorce; Gender as a Shaping Force in Adult Development and Aging; Gender Differences in the Workplace; Homosexuality; Loving and Losing; Menopause; Sex in the Later Adult Years.

References

Corea, G. (1986). *The Mother Machine*. New York: Harper & Row.

Eibl-Eibesfeldt, I. (1989). *Human Ethology*. New York: Aldine de Gruyter.

Fisher, S. (1989). *Sexual Images of the Self*. Hillsdale, NJ: Lawrence Earlbaum Associates.

Foucault, M. (1980). *The History of Sexuality*. 3 volumes. New York: Vintage.

Friedman, J.M., & Chernen, L. (1987). Sexual dysfunction. In L. Michelson & L.M. Ascher (Eds.), *Anxiety and Stress Disorders*. New York: Guilford, pp. 442-64.

Gay, P. (1984). *Education of the Senses*. New York: Oxford.

Goldman, R.J., & Goldman, J.D.G. (1982). *Children's Sexual Thinking*. London: Routledge & Kegan Paul.

Gorer, G. (1965). The pornography of death. In G. Gorer, *Death, Grief, and Mourning*. Garden City, NY: Doubleday, pp. 192-99.

Gorski, R.A. (1989). Structural sex differences in the brain: Their origin and significance. In J.M. Lakoski, et al. (Eds.), *Neural Control of Reproductive Function*. New York: Alan R. Liss, pp. 33-44.

Greer, G. (1984). *Sex and Destiny*. New York: Harper & Row.

Hammer, R.P., Jr. (1985). The sex hormone dependent development of opiate receptors in the rat medial preoptic area. *Brain Research*, 360: 65-74.

Jones, R.E. (1991). *Human Reproductive Biology*. San Diego: Academic Press.

Mead, M. (1935). *Sex and Temperament in Three Primitive Societies*. New York: William Morrow.

-----. (1949). *Male and Female*. New York: William Morrow.

Millett, K. (1970). *Sexual Politics*. Garden City, NY: Doubleday.

Nieschlag, E., & Michel, E. (1986). Reproductive functions in grandfathers. In L. Mastroianni, Jr., & C.A. Paulsen (Eds.), *Aging, Reproduction, and the Climacteric*. New York: Plenum, pp. 59-72.

Spiro, M.E. (1982). *Oepidus in the Trobriands*. Chicago: University of Chicago Press.

Tobin-Richards, M.H., Boxer, A.M., & Petersen, A.C. (1983). The psychological significance of pubertal change. Sex differences in perception of self during early adolescence. In J. Brooks-Gunn & A.C. Petersen (Eds.), *Girls at Puberty*. New York: Plenum, pp. 127-54.

SIBLING RELATIONSHIPS

The sibling relationship may begin as early as infancy and extend throughout the lifespan. In fact, most people over age 65 (between 75 percent and 93 percent, depending on the study) have at least one living sibling (Cicirelli, 1980; Shanas et al., 1968). For many people the sibling relationship is a significant part of their later years of life (Cicirelli, 1980; Gold, 1987; Troll, 1971). The sibling relationship, then, is one of the earliest to form and it persists through the adult life course for many people.

Early Developmental Course of the Sibling Relationship

Sibling relationships have been defined as the total of the interactions—actions, verbal and nonverbal communication—of two or more individuals who share common biological parents. This definition also encompasses their knowledge, perceptions, attitudes, beliefs, and feelings regarding each other, from the time when one sibling first becomes aware of the other. This comprehensive definition draws attention to some distinctive aspects of the sibling relationship such as a shared biological background and a long history. Many researchers, however, limit themselves to specific markers such as the age span between siblings, the number of living siblings, and / or the presence of a spouse or children. These limitations in the scope of research also impose limitations on the generalizations that can be drawn.

The relationship between two siblings is usually described as having a developmental course of its own, complementing the individual development of each sister or brother. This course or trajectory can be divided into phases of *initiation, maintenance,* and *decline and dissolution* (Cicirelli & Nussbaum, 1989). The initiation phase includes the development of attachments between siblings. It typically occurs in early childhood. The relationship then enters an extended maintenance phase. This phase usually spans the lives of the individuals involved. A wide range of factors are likely to influence each sibling's involvement in the relationship as major changes affect one sibling or another. In the dissolution phase, the relationship may end abruptly with the death of one of the siblings or gradually with a decline in functions late in life. Occasionally, a disagreement will occur of such magnitude that the relationship will be dissolved prematurely.

Given the length of the maintenance phase, it is likely that events could happen at a variety of points along the lifespan to influence the quality or intensity of the relationship at a later point. Additionally, the dynamic nature of relationships and the variety of personalities involved make it likely that similar events might have widely different consequences. Some commonality may be identified, however, by looking at the factors that influence and characterize different types of sibling relationships, with an emphasis on the later adult years.

Types of Sibling Relationships

Deborah Gold (1989) has developed a useful typology of sibling relationships based on exploratory interviews with men and women over age 65. All were white, middle class, and healthy. Additionally, all the respondents had living siblings, had been married, and had children. None were twins. This sampling procedure helped to avoid individuals with either an atypically intense relationship or no relationship with a sibling. Obviously, siblings representing a wider variety of racial, ethnic, and socioeconomic subpopulations will need to be included in future research (the first examples will be touched on later).

Gold (1989) described five relationship types: intimate, congenial, loyal, apathetic, and hostile.

The *intimate* relationship, characterized by ardent devotion and psychological closeness, was found in 14 percent of the sample. These brothers and sisters enter each others' inner lives, confiding their most personal thoughts and feelings. Communication is consistent and frequent—often daily—and includes visits, telephone calls, and letters.

The *congenial* relationship was found in 30 percent of the siblings. These people also share strong feelings of friendship and caring, but they do not develop the capacity for intimacy that is shared by intimate siblings. Consistent contact occurs; however, it is on a weekly or monthly basis.

The *loyal* sibling relationship (34 percent) was a little more common than any of the other types in this first sample. The bond between loyal siblings is based primarily on shared family background rather than shared personal involvement. These siblings see their role as comprising a unique set of responsibilities and rewards, governed by a strong sense of family obligation. They tend to have little contact regardless of proximity. However, loyal siblings do attend major family events such as weddings and funerals.

The three types just described all represent positive relationships between siblings; together they comprise 78 percent of the total sample population.

The two remaining groups include siblings whose relationships were characterized as *apathetic* (11 percent) or *hostile* (11 percent). *Apathetic* siblings do not operate on an exchange basis. No actual or potential emotional or instrumental support is involved in these relationships. These siblings show no signs of psychological involvement. They rarely think about one another, and if they do, it is usually because someone else has brought up the topic. *Hostile* sibling relationships are characterized by resentment, anger, and enmity. No closeness exists between these siblings, and contact is nonexistent except when it occurs inadvertently.

These latter two groups involve relationships in which siblings are not positive components in each others' lives. They differ, however, in that while one involves no psychological involvement, the other involves a level of negative psychological involvement that is comparable to the positive psychological involvement of intimate siblings.

Clearly, significant differences exist in the overall character—positive or negative—and the level of involvement—very high to nonexistent in sibling relationships. Attention now turns to the way that sibling relationships reach their final shape in the later adult years.

Factors Influencing the Sibling Relationship

Situational, relational, and *demographic* variables all influence the type of relationship that is experienced by elderly adult siblings. Overall, Spitzberg and Hecht (1984) conclude that communication skill and motivation are the key factors that predict satisfaction in sibling and other enduring relationships.

Situational Variables. Situational variables characterize the context within which the sibling relationship operates. These variables include the siblings' physical proximity to each other, the existence of a spouse and/or parents, the stage of child rearing, sibling health, and economic situation.

It might be expected that the siblings' physical proximity would influence both frequency of contact and quality of the relationship.

However, siblings do not necessarily have to interact frequently in order to be satisfied with their relationship (Lee & Ihinger-Tallman, 1980; McGhee, 1985). The mere availability of a sister has been found to be associated with greater life satisfaction for some elderly people (McGhee, 1985). It is difficult to generalize about the actual frequency of face-to-face contact among siblings. For example, weekly contacts occur between as few as 17 percent or as many as 69 percent of elderly siblings, depending upon the particular study consulted (Allan, 1977; Cicirelli, 1980, 1982; Scott, 1983; Shanas, 1973). It is rare, however, for siblings to go without contact for an extended period of time (Cicirelli, 1979). Telephone contacts are much more frequent than writing as supplementary ways of staying in contact; for example, only one person in five writes as often as monthly to his or her sibling (Scott, 1983).

Mere physical proximity does not guarantee a satisfying sibling relationship, just as distance does not necessarily mean that the relationship is meaningless or in trouble. Gold (1987) notes instances in which siblings who lived close to one another rarely spoke or had a hostile relationship, and others who enjoyed intimate, congenial, or loyal relationships although separated by thousands of miles.

The existence of an immediate family for either sibling could also influence the nature of their relationship. The death of a spouse seems to increase both frequency of contact and the sense of closeness between siblings (Anderson, 1984; Gold, 1986). Having children at home decreases the frequency of interaction but seems to have little impact on how close the siblings feel to each other (Bedford, 1989). It appears that having a spouse may make siblings less dependent on each other, but that children do not replace the role of siblings in each others' lives.

When faced with health or financial problems, most older people consider siblings to be on call in a crisis, but only a few (7 percent) regarded a sibling as a primary source of help (Cicerelli, 1979). This crisis support seems to be a benefit that flows from the relationship rather than a factor that actually shapes the relationship. Individuals with apathetic or hostile sibling relationships would not ask a sibling for assistance and did not expect to be asked for assistance (Gold, 1987). Most would turn to federal or state programs before they would turn to their siblings, even though they knew the sibling was in a position to help them. Although many siblings in the other three types would be willing to ask for or give assistance if needed, this again was an outcome of the relationship rather than an influence on the nature of the relationship.

Relational Variables. A core aspect of the sibling relationship is the set of attitudes, beliefs, and feelings that each individual holds toward the other and toward the relationship as such. These factors include shared reminiscence, caring, responsibility, rivalry, and feelings that remain from the initiation phase of the relationship.

Shared reminiscence plays a unique role in the sibling relationship. Because only brothers and sisters have these common lifelong memories, they become a distinctive factor in shaping sibling relationships in later life. The ability to share these memories often is more satisfying for elderly adults than personal reminiscence. Gold (1987) contends that this shared reminiscence plays a significant life-validation role for elderly adults and that siblings are uniquely suited to meeting this need. The desire to engage in shared reminiscence becomes a strong motivation for sibling interaction and can result in high levels of satisfaction with the relationship. Those who maintain positive sibling relationships in old age often value the opportunity to engage in shared reminiscence.

The sense of responsibility and caring also influences the sibling relationship in later adulthood. Gold (1987) found that only men used the word "responsibility" to describe their psychological attachment to a sibling—women tended to express this feeling as "caring." The intensity of the relationship was equal for men and women, although framed differentially as either "responsibility" or "caring." The emotional power of the sibling relationship was evident among men as well as women; several men wept throughout the discussion. This sense of emotional attachment seems to be a significant influence for all who have a positive relationship with their siblings. The expression of caring seems to be identified with the siblings' closeness, expressiveness, and attention to the needs of the other, which Spitzberg and Hecht (1984) associate with high relational satisfaction. Emotional attachment also seems to be a factor in those relationships typed as hostile—but in the opposite direction. The apathetic group is the only one in which this close emotional attachment seems to have dissipated, if it ever did exist.

Sibling rivalries also seem to have an important influence in shaping the relationship. These rivalries may begin at an early point in the relationship or emerge because of some actual or perceived transgression later in life. Although there is no question that sibling rivalries do exist, their forms and impact differ so much that generalization is difficult. Some siblings have little contact with each other for years because of some ancient conflict or grievance but suddenly decide in old age that it is time to forget or forgive. For others, however, these conflicts are carried through to the end of the lifespan. No clear pattern has yet been discovered to explain what allows some pairs to overcome chronic antagonisms or compels others to remain at odds with each other every day of their lives. It would be useful to study communication skills and patterns in those sibling pairs who remain antagonists to each other and perhaps, by communicational interventions, help them to reconcile their differences and forge a more constructive relationship.

Events from early in the relationship and family influences may also provide a foundation for the nature of the sibling relationship later in life. Dunn (1983) suggests that early sibling interactions may have an influence on the relationship later in life. She notes that first interactions that were marked by interest, affection, and imitative behavior on the part of the older sibling resulted in a friendlier relationship 14 months later. Although these results were not followed into adulthood, the implications are there. There is at least the possibility that these early attachments set the tone for a relationship that can be maintained despite subsequent strains.

Demographic Variables. The final group of variables includes gender, ethnicity, and age. Gender influences seem to be twofold: (a) women generally view sibling relationships in a more positive way, and (b) sisters seem to be more important to both brothers and sisters. Gold (1989) discovered that relationships including at least one sister tended to cluster more in the positive categories of the typology, while brother-brother relationships tended to cluster in the types that represent less sibling involvement. Furthermore, both Gold (1989) and Cicirelli (1991) reported higher levels of relational satisfaction for siblings with sisters.

Ethnicity also seems to influence the nature of sibling relationships in later life. As already reported, most elderly whites (78 percent) had positive sibling relationships, distributed among the intimate, congenial, and loyal types. In a second study, Gold (1988) found that positive sibling relationships were even more common (95 percent) in an African-American sample. Italian-American sibling relationships were characterized by more emotional involvement than those of American adults of European Protestant backgrounds (Johnson, 1982). Cultural background appears to have a significant effect on the type of relationship siblings are likely to experience and deserves further study.

Finally, age may play a role in how siblings relate to one another. The sibling relationship seems to be more important to elderly than to middle-aged adults (Cicirelli, 1985). Several of the stories reported by Gold (1987) involved people who felt that the sibling relationship had become more important to them as they realized where they were in their lifespan. Elderly people were more willing to overlook previous conflicts, and more willing and able to devote time to the relationship than in earlier years.

Conclusions

Relational and demographic factors seem to be more important than situational variables in shaping adult sibling relationships. The ability to share reminiscences seems to be an especially important factor in the development of satisfying relationships later in life. For these siblings, issues of rivalry and conflict become subordinate to the intrinsic value of the relationship. For a small number of siblings, though, long-term mutual grievances become so important that they prevent the achievement of a positive relationship.

At this point no research has charted particular sibling relationships across long periods of time; therefore, it is difficult to discern clear relationships between the early and the later stages. Studies that use cross-sectional analysis or ask elders to recall childhood experiences and events suggest that there is little residual influence from early childhood, but this conclusion may not stand up when more adequate methods are applied. It seems plausible that childhood influences such as family values and early sibling interactions do lay a foundation for the sibling relationship in the adult years. We must continue to enrich our understanding of the sibling relationship if we are to appreciate the interpersonal side of the journey across the lifespan. ▼ Marty Birkholt

See also: Attachment Across the Lifespan; Conflict as a Challenge in Adult Development; Fictive Kin; Gender as a Shaping Force in Adult Development and Aging; Reminiscence and Life Review; Social Relationships, Convoys of; Social Support for the Chronically Ill; Subcultural Influences on Lifelong Development; Twins through the Lifespan.

References

Allan, G. (1977). Sibling solidarity. *Journal of Marriage and the Family, 39*: 177-84.

Anderson, T. B. (1984). Widowhood as a life transition: Its impact on kinship ties. *Journal of Marriage and the Family, 46:* 105-14.

Bedford, V. H. (1989). A comparison of thematic apperceptions of sibling affiliation, conflict, and separation at two points of adulthood. *International Journal of Aging and Human Development, 28:* 53-66.

Cicirelli, V. G. (1979). *Social Services for Elderly in Relation to the Kin Network.* Washington, DC: NRTA-AARP Andrus Foundation.

———. (1980). Sibling relationships in adulthood. *Aging in the 1980's: Psychological Issues.* Washington, DC: American Psychological Association, pp. 455-62.

———. (1982). Sibling influence throughout the lifespan. In M. E. Lamb & B. Sutton-Smith (Eds.), *Sibling Relationships: Their Nature and Significance Across the Lifespan.* Hillsdale, NJ: Lawrence Erlbaum, pp. 267-84.

———. (1985). The role of siblings as family caregivers. In W. J. Sauer & R. T. Coward (Eds.), *Social Support Networks and the Care of the Elderly: Theory, Research, Practice, and Policy.* New York: Springer, pp. 93-107.

———. (1991). Sibling relationships in adulthood. *Marriage and Family Review, 16:* 291-310.

Cicirelli, V. G., & Nussbaum, J. F. (1989). Relationships with siblings in later life. In J. F. Nussbaum (Ed.), *Life-Span Communication: Normative Processes.* Hillsdale, NJ: Lawrence Erlbaum, pp. 283-99.

Dunn, J. (1983). Sibling relationships in early childhood. *Child Development, 54:* 787-811.

Gold, D.T. (1986). Sibling relationships in retrospect. Unpublished doctoral dissertation, Northwestern University, p. 16.

———. (1987a). *Siblings in Old Age: Their Roles and Relationships.* Chicago: Center for Applied Gerontology.

———. (1987b). Later-life sibling relationships: Does race affect typological distribution? Paper presented at annual meetings of The Gerontological Society of America, San Francisco, November.

———. (1989). Sibling relationships in old age: A typology. *International Journal of Aging and Human Development, 28:* 37-51.

Johnson, C. L. (1982). Sibling solidarity: Its function in Italian-American families. *Journal of Marriage and the Family, 44:* 155-67.

Lee, G. R., & Ihinger-Tallman, M. (1980). Sibling interactions and morale. *Research on Aging, 2*: 367-91.

McGhee, J. L. (1985). The effects of siblings on the life satisfaction of the rural elderly. *Journal of Marriage and the Family, 47*: 85-91.

Scott, J. P. (1983). Siblings and other kin. In T. H. Brubaker (Ed.), *Family Relationships in Later Life.* Beverly Hills, CA: Sage, pp. 47-62.

Shanas, E. (1973). Family-kin networks and aging in cross-cultural perspective. *Journal of Marriage and the Family, 35*: 505-11.

Shanas, E., et al. (1968). *Older People in Three Industrial Societies.* New York: Atherton.

Spitzberg, B. H., & Hecht, M. L. (1984). A component model of relational competence. *Human Communication Research, 10*: 575-99.

Troll, L. E. (1971). The family in later life: A decade review. *Journal of Marriage and the Family, 33*: 263-90.

SLEEP AND DREAMS

One's waking life might be likened to a workplace that is brightly illuminated. A clock steadfastly records each passing moment while people go about their tasks in a logical and predictable manner. The scene is familiar and its events make sense. By comparison, one's slumber might be likened to a room that has been abandoned by the authorities: The lights have been turned out, all rules of logic and purpose appear to be suspended, and even the clock has given itself a vacation. Perhaps it is not surprising that (a) humankind has long been fascinated by what takes place in this mysterious zone, and (b) objective scientists have often felt uncomfortable and unequipped to deal with these phenomena.

In recent years some of the mystery of sleep and dreams has yielded to breakthroughs in research methodology. Progress has been considerably more impressive with respect to sleep, but some illuminating information has also been acquired about dreams and dreaming. Much remains to be understood, however.

In examining sleep and dreams from a developmental perspective, the results of scientific investigations will be emphasized. However, it is useful to remember at the outset that individual and sociocultural temperament also influence one's conceptions. When we call a person a dreamer, for example, we may be intending to bestow praise, in other words, this person is a "visionary," a person who sees possibilities where others see only what is in front of their nose. But we may also intend to chastise people by calling them dreamers—idle folk who prefer to lie around and indulge in fantasies while the rest of us are hard at work. In a time-conscious, goal-oriented, materialistic society, there seems to be a built-in suspicion and enmity toward the sleeper and the dreamer—along with a bit of envy.

There are also two distinctly different attitudes toward the significance of sleep and dream life. In one tradition, sleep is regarded as part of the background or periphery of life, deserving of attention only when a problem such as insomnia arises. In the competing tradition, sleep is regarded as a special state of being in which the mind is opened to spiritual, mystic, and philosophical experiences that are seldom available in waking life. A variant is the scientific hypothesis that sleep and/or dreams perform vital functions for the organism. It is possible to think of sleep as a significant process that deserves systematic research while at the same time dismissing dreams as side effects or "emissions" that have little to do with development and well-being. In this article the position is taken that the study of both sleeping and dreaming can reveal much about people at the neurophysiological, personal, and interpersonal levels.

After reviewing current knowledge and theory about sleep and dreams in general, their roles in adult development will be considered, along with a few suggestions for everyday—or perhaps that should be everynight—life.

The Nature and Functions of Sleep

Much of what has been learned about the nature and functions of sleep is based on studies that record the electrical activity of the brain. In sleep laboratories throughout the world, volunteers consent to having electrodes placed on their forehead, scalp, and face that detect electrical potentials so small they are expressed in microvolts: one-millionth of a volt. The electroencephalogram (EEG) is a continuous graphic record of this activity as it occurs in the cerebral cortex, the top stratum of neural tissue in the brain. Additionally, a pair of electrodes is usually attached to the face to detect eye movements. Depending on the particular purposes of the study, other measures of psychophysiological activity (such as respiration and heart rate) may also be recorded by attaching additional electrodes to various muscle groups.

Over the course of a night's sleep, pens attached to the monitoring apparatus will produce an EEG record that exceeds the length of two football fields. Fortunately for research purposes, most participants adjust quickly to these unusual conditions and are even able to go back to sleep if awakened for questioning, as is sometimes required. The abundant quantitative information yielded by studies in the sleep laboratory over the past four decades has enabled scientists to replace guesswork with detailed and well-verified conclusions regarding several major aspects of the sleep process.

First, it has become clear that the sleeping person is not entirely "off duty." Although less responsive to the environment and less active physically than during the waking state, the sleeping person goes through a sequence of stages that involve changes in both neural functioning and general bodily state. Second, one of these stages of sleep—known as REM for "rapid eye movements"—has proven to be of particular significance. Third, these stages are recycled several times during a full night's sleep.

Five stages have been identified in the normal sleep process, consisting of REM and four sequential non-REM phases (Borbely, 1986; Foulkes, 1966; Kleitman, 1963). Generally, this is what happens as one moves from wakefulness through the first sleep cycle of the night.

- *Wakefulness.* There are eye movements, muscular tension, and other signs of general activity. The EEG pattern takes the form of the *alpha wave*, an electric potential that operates in the range of 8 to 12 cycles per second (CPS). There is also a background mixture of other low-voltage activity.

- *Stage One.* This is the transitional stage from waking to sleep. One is most "lightly" asleep at this point. The "brain wave" has now slowed to about half of its waking tempo and has become somewhat *desynchronized* (less regular and unified). Very little time is spent in Stage One—only about 3 percent of the total sleep time (Webb, 1982).

- *Stage Two.* This is the longest phase of sleep, lasting about half of the night. The basic waves become larger and are overlapped by *sleep spindles*—faster bursts of electrical activity. To make this pattern even more complex, there are also occasional waves that are a good deal slower. These are known as the *K-complexes.* Meanwhile, the muscles relax and the eyes show minimal movement. Although much is happening on the EEG record, the body is at ease. Unlike Stage One, there is no question but that a person in Stage Two is really asleep.

- *Stage Three.* The sleeper is entering the realm of what is sometimes called *delta sleep.* At this point, the EEG reveals the arrival of very slow waves (one to four CPS) of high amplitude. During this relatively brief phase (about 7 percent of total sleep time) the sleeper remains still and relaxed.

- *Stage Four.* The large, slow waves now become even more dominant as the sleeper continues in the second phase of delta sleep.

This is often considered to be the deepest phase of sleep. The distinction between stages three and four is somewhat a matter of convenience for researchers; for most purposes one can regard these adjacent stages as an overall period of time in which one is most removed from the neurophysiological patterns associated with wakefulness. Stage four per se occupies about 15 percent of total sleep time. People who have been deprived of delta sleep compensate by spending more time in this phase at their next opportunity.

- *REM sleep.* As the name suggests, the REM episode is characterized by rapid eye movements. But this is not all that happens. There is a sudden re-arousal of bodily activity—an excitement. Pulse and respiration rates increase, as does blood flow. The EEG pattern is complex and can differ from one person to another, with mixed indices of waking and sleeping waves. One may easily form the impression that this person is somehow both asleep and awake at the same time. Perhaps there is something to be said for this impression because it is during REM episodes that we experience our most vivid dreams. It was the discovery of REM episodes and their connection to dreams that introduced the modern era of sleep research. For a while it was thought that all dreams are experienced during REM episodes. It was later discovered that dreams also occur in other stages, although content analysis indicates that non-REM dreams are more concerned with events of everyday life and have less of the vivid, bizarre, and surrealistic character of one's most fantastical dreams (Hall, 1984; Spiegel, 1981).

In an adult's normal night's sleep, there will be several recyclings of the stages, although each time the proportion of time spent in a particular phase will change. On the average, it takes about 100 minutes to move all the way through the stages. During eight hours of sleep, one experiences somewhere between four and six cycles, each of which includes segments of REM and non-REM sleep. The proportion of REM to total sleep increases throughout the night, while delta sleep is sharply reduced. By the time one has entered the third cycle, one is likely to experience no Stage Four sleep at all, but the REM episode may now be three times longer than in its first appearance of about 10 minutes. As is the case with delta sleep, people who are interrupted during REM episodes will experience a REM rebound effect at their earliest opportunity.

There is general agreement that REM and non-REM sleep differ markedly in their nature and function, although beyond this point there remain controversy and questions yet to be resolved. Some of these issues will be considered after a survey of what has been learned about changes in sleep patterns throughout the lifespan.

Sleep from Infancy through Old Age

Patterns of wakefulness and sleep change in a systematic manner as one moves through the lifespan. More is known about the changes that occur during infancy and childhood, but knowledge is gradually being acquired about the adult years as well.

The earliest period of human development is accompanied by significant changes in the relationship between wakefulness and sleep, as well as in the nature of sleep. Newborns typically sleep about 16 hours a day. This pattern is approximately reversed in adulthood, although not everybody experiences or feels the need for eight hours of sleep a day. It is also characteristic of infants to distribute their sleeping episodes throughout the day. Weary parents can hardly wait until baby "decides" to do most of his or her sleeping at night, along with a nap or two during the day. Said more technically, infants begin with a polyphasic sleep pattern and gradually acquire the monophasic pattern associated with adult life. (Polyphasia is not such a bad idea for adults, though; many grown-ups feel the need for restorative naps at particular times of the day, often in the middle of the afternoon, as Coleman, 1992, has recently documented.) Most children still take daily naps until they go off to school, at which point individual differences express themselves.

The sleep cycle of infants and young children is shorter than that of adults. A one-year-old, for example, is likely to move through his or her entire cycle in about half the time required by mom and dad. The proportion of time spent in the various stages also differs. Infants spend approximately half of their sleep time in REM phases, which, except for their duration, appear similar to those experienced by adults. Unlike adults, however, young children seem to move directly into a REM episode right after falling asleep and then eventually go on to the other stages.

The stronger biological need for sleep in infancy and early childhood probably arises from the incomplete state of the central nervous system in early childhood, and the demands made on the body by the fast pace of general development. Being a baby can be hard work! An interesting theory offered by Hobson (1988) should be tested out:

> Early in development, REM sleep could provide the brain with a highly organized program of internal action. This program is stereotyped, redundant, and reliable—all features useful to a developing system. For example, REM sleep could help prepare the organism's reflex repertoire.... It would make sense at first for such a system to be overprogrammed. (p. 292)

Hobson's theory suggests that REM sleep activates a set of genetic instructions that enable the infant to start organizing its potentials. The startle reflex, habituation, and a variety of other early-appearing behaviors might be guided and stimulated by the processes at work in REM sleep. Older children and adults would have much less need for this kind of basic internal guidance, and therefore less need for REM sleep, or so Hobson's theory implies.

What changes occur in sleep patterns during the adult years? In a useful review of the research literature, Prinz, Dustman, and Emmerson (1990) conclude that "The most prominent age difference in the sleep EEG is reduced amplitude and amount of the high voltage delta waves that characterize slow wave (Stage 3 and Stage 4) sleep" (p. 136). In other words, as one moves into the later adult years, deep sleep is no longer quite so deep. This neurophysiological evidence is consistent with what many elderly persons report of their own experiences: "I don't sleep as well as I used to—I may be getting my hours in, but I don't feel completely rested when I wake up."

As most adults age, delta sleep not only becomes less deep but also is reduced in duration. At age 20, a person is likely to experience about 100 minutes of delta sleep per night—but at age 70 not much more than 10 minutes (Dement et al., 1985). The older person is also more likely to spend time awake during the night, thereby losing the benfits of a long, uninterrupted rest. "Taken together, these age differences in sleep and wakefulness are in the direction of impaired sleep maintenance and depth, a conclusion that is further supported by observations that older subjects are more easily aroused from nighttime sleep by auditory stimuli" (Prinz, Dustman, & Emmerson, 1985, pp. 137-38.)

Unfortunately, these changes have been found to occur in healthy as well as ailing and disabled individuals. Because elderly men and women selected for good health show a consistent pattern of sleep impairment (as compared with younger adults), such changes are now assumed to be part of the "built-in" life-span program for human development and aging, rather than the outcome of specific impairments. Nevertheless, a variety of acquired difficulties (e.g., cardiovascular ailments, depression, and drug effects) can intensify sleep loss.

It is not surprising, then, that many older adults "nod off" one or more times during the day. On the positive side, people tend to compensate for sleep deprivation by moving more rapidly into delta sleep, spending less time in the preliminary stages. This is true of both young and elderly adults (Carskadon, Harvey, & Dement, 1981; Webb, 1982). By implication, several short naps might be more beneficial than one long period of lying abed because relatively more delta sleep is experienced right after dozing off.

Another major change is the progressive reduction in REM sleep through the adult years. As already noted, REM sleep occurs most extensively in infancy and early childhood. The reduction in REM sleep appears to be a strong marker of the developmental/aging process across the lifespan, continuing to operate in the later adult years.

Dreams and Dreaming

Despite the close connections between sleep and dreams, progress in understanding dreams and dreaming has not matched the dramatic progress achieved with sleep in recent years. Two explanations for this lag can be offered. In all probability, the more influential factor is the lack of a breakthrough in research methodology. Before the invention of the EEG technique and its application to sleep research, researchers could observe the sleeping person, alter the conditions under which sleep took place, ask questions before, during, or after sleep, and so forth, but not actually track the neurophysiological processes associated with sleep. Dream researchers can still use these traditional techniques and acquire some knowledge in these ways, but no revolutionary new research tool or technique gives them a direct, objective, and easily repeated method for studying dreams as such. In fact, the most famous technique remains psychoanalysis, a procedure that requires a highly trained researcher, a trusting relationship with the participant, many repeated sessions, and the always open-to-doubt analysis of complex verbal material.

The second explanation must be sought in the attitude of many scientists toward the topic of dreams. Over the centuries dreams have been the subject of spectacular claims such as the following: "Dreams predict the future." "Dead souls return to advise us in our dreams!" "She often dreams of bridges that are too short to reach the other side—obviously this means that she has not over-

come her desire to be a man and possess the male organ." Few biological, social, and behavioral scientists care to be identified with topics that invite fascinating but unsupported and perhaps unsupportable assertions. Not quite sure how to deal with dreams from a methodological and conceptual standpoint and uncomfortable with the possibility of being stigmatized by even showing an interest in this topic, many a scientist simply turns away. The cumulative effect can be discerned in the meager attention given to dreams and dreaming in major reference works and textbooks devoted to adult development. The nature and significance of dreams and dreaming in adult life is seldom even mentioned.

This deficit in scholarly attention cannot be overcome here. However, a few observations are offered that might be useful as a guide for future inquiry. To begin with, one can make the challenge a little more manageable by distinguishing firmly between dreams and dreaming. Asking what a particular dream signifies requires a different approach than asking about the fundamental nature and function of the act of dreaming. Much of the popular controversy has concerned the interpretation of dreams rather than the explication of dreaming.

Consider first the nature and function of dreaming. As earlier noted, researchers have found that vivid dreaming is an activity that occurs during highly distinctive episodes within the overall sleep process. Some researchers (e.g., Dement, 1968) consider REM sleep to represent such a special state of the organism that it should be regarded as a third condition to be added to the usual dichotomy of wakefulness and sleeping. Because REM episodes are so eventful, it becomes plausible to suggest that, whatever else dreaming might be, it is not an isolated and insignificant activity. It is difficult to believe that REM would exist and follow systematic patterns from infancy through old age if it did not have some important function in development and well-being. The systematic decrease in REM sleep from infancy through the older adult years suggests that dreaming is indeed related to some core aspects of human development and aging. The direction of this change provides still a further clue: If less and less REM sleep is available to adults as they grow older, perhaps they have fewer dreams with the "animated and pictorial" qualities (Spiegel, 1981) that are associated with the REM episode. If true, this would reduce the total frequency of dreams experienced by aging adults. If older adults continue to dream in non-REM stages, more of their dreams will resemble the thoughts that move through their minds in the waking state. Interestingly, this change would be in the opposite direction from the position taken by **Disengagement Theory,** which holds that people experience a heightened interiority with advancing age as they withdraw from many of their previous social and occupational obligations. One would seem to undergo an impoverishment rather than an enrichment of inner life with the marked decrease in REM-type dreams.

At this point it becomes reasonable to offer a set of alternative hypotheses:

- *People do not need to dream as much* as they mature and grow old. Dreaming performs or is involved in functions that are more important to the developing than to the relatively stable or aging person.

- *One's ability to dream diminishes with age,* along with a variety of other abilities that depend upon the status of the central and peripheral nervous system, e.g., visual acuity, auditory discrimination, ability to process several types of information at the same time.

- *Individual developmental histories influence REM sleep and dream life in old age.* The suggestion here is that many people make little use of their fantasy and imaging capacities, maintaining a well-defended borderline between the realities of waking life and "all that nonsense" that happens in dreams. As a common tendency, this would give rise to the generalization that people dream less in the later adult years and therefore place no demands on their central nervous systems to produce REM episodes. However, *some* people may have

established a pattern of cultivating dreams and other fantasy-level ideation, thereby not only continuing to encourage the "dream factory" but introducing innovations and refinements along the way.

Support for the first hypothesis would suggest that reduction in dreaming activity is a relatively trivial aspect of the aging process. Support for the second hypothesis would raise concern that with reduced dreaming one is losing whatever benefits are contributed by that process—whether dreaming itself actually performs functions that are vital for well-being or is simply an experiential representation for neurophysiological processes that are doing the actual work. (Another alternative, of course, would be to argue that dreaming—the representation of certain integrative processes—may diminish or even vanish while the underlying processes themselves continue to function smoothly.) Support for the third hypothesis would emphasize the importance of Individuality in human development and aging. What one makes of oneself not only influences health, longevity, personality, and interpersonal relationships, but even the extent and nature of the adventures one has while asleep.

To state these hypotheses is not to prove them, nor to eliminate still other possibilities. These are simply examples of possibilities that are inherent in the current knowledge provided by sleep research.

One consistent pattern of findings does indicate that sleep quality diminishes with advancing age, and that this trend is not favorable for our health and vigor. In some studies of sleep and related phenomena, the author attempted to obtain dream reports from elderly adults. So few dreams were reported—even from healthy elders living independently in the community—that no conclusions could be drawn. At present no definitive evidence exists regarding the frequency of dreams over the course of years in the same individuals. Until the needed studies are conducted, one is left with the observation that older men and women *seem* to have fewer dreams and that few of these dreams are vivid and eventful. One cannot dismiss the possibility, however, that failure to remember or reluctance to report dreams might be contributing factors to the apparent reduction. A somewhat more radical possibility is also worth suggesting. Perhaps dreaming and the processes that it represents become intensified and more efficient with advancing adult age: It takes less dreaming activity to accomplish whatever functions dreams are intended to accomplish. If, however, one takes the available information at its face value, the extent and quality of both sleep and dreams appear to decline as one grows older. It is difficult to place these parallel changes in a favorable light.

A thorough understanding of dreams would require in-depth attention to the *content, structure, processes,* and *purposes* that characterize these attractions that play in the theater of the mind. A useful behavioral science approach to dream *content* has been established by C. S. Hall and his colleagues (Hall, 1984; Hall & Nordby, 1972; Hall & Van de Castle, 1966). They have found that men and women tend to dream about different things, and that an individual's dreams have about the same type of content over a period of several years. There are no critical methodological barriers to more extensive studies of dream content through the adult years, except for concerns about the relationship between dreams recalled and dreams forgotten.

The founder of psychoanalysis found dreams indispensable as a source of information regarding the general functioning of a person's mental and emotional lives. Freud (1967) distinguished between the *manifest* and the *latent* content of dreams. It is not enough to observe the people, objects, and events that occur in dreams: Beneath this manifest presentation is a set of deeper or latent meanings that provide "the royal pathway to the Unconscious." Freud is at his most creative in attempting to attempting to explain how one's conflicts and tensions are transformed into the stuff of dreams. In today's computer-aware world, we might speak of this as a process of coding that is guided by system rules. *Dream-work* was the term Freud introduced. Unresolved anxieties can be expressed in the language of dreams only when they have been subjected to a set of transformations. Among the major processes that contribute to the construction of dreams from the mingled substances of conscious and unconscious concerns are *condensation, displacement,* and *symbolization.* One or two dream images are able to represent people, events, and conflicts that would usually require lengthy presentation if one were depending on the language and logic of waking life. Complexities are therefore condensed into images. Displacement is a process of substitution in which the dream-work disguises its true concerns. One might, for example, divide one's own personality up among several different dream characters. Symbolization is still another way of presenting concerns in a dream while at the same time disguising or coding them enough to avoid alarming one's "censor." According to Freud, sexual impulses that are unacceptable to the waking self are often represented in a symbolic manner in dreams.

In Freud's view, dreaming is a process that safeguards sleep by enabling people to express their conflicts and thereby discharge tension that would otherwise interfere with rest. This process does not always work, however, as Freud (1967) acknowledges, and one may awaken with the vivid memory of a nightmare. Carl C. Jung (1965, 1974), a disciple of Freud before going his own way, offered a different pathway to dream interpretation. Jung believed that dreams can represent deep layers not only of a person's own personality, but of humanity in general. Giving less prominence to the role of sexual conflict in dreams, Jung saw an even more creative process involved in dreams. Of particular interest for students of aging, Jung suggested that in the second half of life one has the challenge of actualizing aspects of oneself that were relatively neglected in one's youth. Dreams are thought to play an important role in this process, as well as in coping with a variety of other crises and opportunities.

The views of Freud and Jung remain influential today—even when unrecognized as such—but it cannot be said that a solid consensus has been reached on the functions of dreams and their relationship to sleep. Researchers such as Hobson (1988) believe that one can bypass much of the decoding work required by Freudian and Jungian theories and "read" dreams more directly as information-processing sequences that attempt to integrate the various bits of data that have lodged in one's mind "even if it must resort to creative storytelling" (Hobson, 1988, p. 219). Conflict remains a factor in the construction and interpretation of dreams, but it is not necessarily the most powerful force. Finally, on a welcome note, Hobson suggests that dreams are sometimes just a way to entertain oneself and need not be analyzed to within an inch of their lives.

Sleeping Well

Nobody appreciates the value of a good night's sleep better than the person who has been deprived. Although most people can adjust to temporary sleep deprivation, they eventually feel the subjective and objective consequences of prolonged deprivation. (How much sleep a person requires to feel his or her best and how much sleep deprivation is "too much" varies from individual to individual.)

Sleep difficulties can take a number of forms, including:

- Problems in falling asleep
- Problems in remaining asleep
- Sleep apnea (brief episodes during which breathing ceases)
- Falling asleep at inappropriate and unintended times
- Oversleeping
- Abnormal sleep that does not perform the functions of normal sleep (often related to drug use)

Any of these difficulties can be primarily physical or primarily psychological in origin, or may result from a combination of circumstances. At times the individual may be well aware that his or her sleeping problems are related to a particular life situation and will be relieved when the situation passes (e.g., adjustment to a new neighborhood, worry about a family member's health). Prolonged or intensifying sleep disturbances may signify underlying problems that should be given professional attention. Sleep problems should be taken seriously not only for the direct discomfort they generate but also because they may be clues to underlying physical problems. A breakdown in the individual's normal and satisfying sleep patterns may also signify unresolved grief or some other type of depressive action. Health care professionals have good reason for their routine inquiries into a patient's sleeping patterns.

As already reported, overall sleep quality tends to diminish in the later adult years, although there are marked individual differences here as in other spheres of functioning. Many remedies have been advocated. Spiegel (1981) refers to a book in which a German physician lists more than 70 techniques that somebody has thought useful in helping older people get a good night's rest (Rubinstein, 1976). Many of these techniques involve rituals of some kind. Arrange your little world in the way that is best suited to you, and make sure everything is in place every night is what some people suggest. Charles Dickens was one of the many celebrities who resorted to personal rituals at bedtime:

> Whenever he moved into a new room the first thing he did was march to the bed, draw out his pocket compass, and shove the bed around until its head was pointing due north. According to a theory of the time, magnetic currents streamed north and south between the poles and the sleeping person was thought to reap innumerable benefits if he allowed these currents to flow in a straight line through his body. (Luce & Segal, 1966, p. 19)

No doubt there are people who feel just as strongly that one ought to sleep from east to west!

"Sleeping pills" are among the most popular types of medicine consumed by the

U.S. public. Barbiturates were once the most frequently used substance to produce sleep, but they had a number of undesirable side effects. One of the most popular replacements for barbiturates—thalidomide—proved to be responsible for major deformities in newborns. Physicians today usually prefer to prescribe drugs of the benzodiazepine family. This hypnotic has proven to be appreciably safer than barbiturates but still can lead to problems if used in combination with alcohol and some other drugs or used to excess. Furthermore, drug-induced sleep is not identical with spontaneous sleep and may not have as much benefit for the individual.

In work with elderly patients the author has found that sleeping problems can sometimes be minimized when people are encouraged to be more active during the day. Sitting around all day, perhaps half dozing in front of a television set, adds to sleep problems. Physically active people of any age are more likely to sleep well at night. Persons afflicted with Alzheimer's disease and other dementing conditions can be helped to maintain sleeping patterns closer to those of normal adults if they are provided with a safe environment that includes opportunities for walking and other forms of physical activity. Unfortunately, in all institutions staff members tend to seek control over the residents' sleeping habits for sake of convenient management. A more flexible approach that considered the resident's own needs and limitations would be beneficial to those elderly men and women who require supervisory care.

In a series of studies, a glass of wine in the middle of the afternoon or after dinner was found to help many elderly people to sleep better and also was associated with higher morale, increased interpersonal communication, and other favorable indices (Mishara & Kastenbaum, 1980, Chapters 7 and 8). Although wine has some intrinsic sleep-inducing qualities, the favorable effects of its consumption in the fairly minimal amounts tested seemed to result in part from its being seen as a symbol of good living.

(Drinking alcohol in quantity, as well as taking in caffeine, tends to make it more difficult to sleep well.)

The man or woman who is determined to sleep well tonight will probably improve his or her chances by engaging in some form of pleasurable exercise during the day, enjoying leisure and companionship during the evening, eating a light snack ("Milk" say the dairy people; "Bananas" say the fruit vendors, etc.), and settling down on a not-too-squishy bed in a darkened room. Should one not immediately enter the realm of slumber, experts suggest that before reaching for a pill, one reach instead for a good book, a half-knit sweater, or one's mate (not necessarily in that sequence).   ▼ Robert Kastenbaum

See also: Alcohol Use and Abuse; Conflict as a Challenge in Adult Development; Depression; Disengagement Theory; Drug Use and Abuse; Exercise; Habituation: A Key to Lifespan Development and Aging?; Individuality; Information Processing; Longevity; Mental Health in the Adult Years; Spiritual Development and Wisdom: A Vedantic Perspective.

References

Borbely, A. (1986). *Secrets of Sleep*. New York: Basic Books.

Carskadon, M. A., Harvey, K., & Dement, W. C. (1981). Sleep loss in young adolescents. *Sleep, 4:* 299-312.

Coleman, R. (1992) *Wide Awake at 3:00 A.M.* Palo Alto, CA: Stanford University Press.

Dement, W. C. (1968). A new look at the third state of existence. *Stanford, M.D., 8:* 2-8.

Dement, W. C., et al. (1985). Changes of sleep and wakefulness with age. In C. E. Finch & E. L. Schneider (Eds.), *Handbook of the Biology of Aging*. New York: Van Nostrand Reinhold, pp. 692-717.

Foulkes, D. (1966). *The Psychology of Sleep*. New York: Scribners.

Freud, S. (1965). *New Introductory Lectures on Psychoanalysis*. New York: W. W. Norton (Original publication 1933).

———. (1967). *The Interpretation of Dreams*. New York: Avon. (Original publication 1900).

Hall, C. S. (1984). Dreams. In R. J. Corsini (Ed.), *Encyclopedia of Psychology*, Volume 1. New York: Wiley Interscience, pp. 388-90.

Hall, C. S., & Nordby, V. J. (1972). *The Individual and His Dreams*. New York: New American Library.

Hall, C. S., & Van de Castle, R. L. (1966). *The Content Analysis of Dreams*. New York: Appleton-Century-Crofts.

Hobson, J. A. (1988). *The Dreaming Brain*. New York: Basic Books.

Jung, G. C. (1965). *Memories, Dreams, Reflections*. New York: Vintage.

————. (1974). *Dreams*. In *The Collected Works of C. G. Jung*, Volumes 4, 8, 12, 16. Princeton, NJ: Princeton University Press.

Kleitman, N. (1963). *Sleep and Wakefulness*. Revised Edition. Chicago: University of Chicago Press.

Luce, G. G., & Segal, J. (1966). *Sleep*. New York: Lancer.

Mishara, B. L., & Kastenbaum, R. (1980). *Alcohol and Old Age*. New York: Grune & Stratton.

Prinz, P. N., Dustman, R. E., & Emmerson, R. (1985). Electrophysiology and aging. In J. E. Birren & K. W. Schaie (Eds.), *Handbook of the Psychology of Aging*. Third Edition. New York: Academic Press, pp. 135-49.

Rubinstein, H. (1976). *Das Kopfkissenbuch fur Sclaflose*. Hamburg: Roholt.

Spiegel, R. (1981). *Sleep and Sleeplessness in Advanced Age*. Jamaica, NY: Spectrum.

Webb, W. B. (1982). Sleep in older persons: Sleep structures of 50- to 60-year-old men and women. *Journal of Gerontology, 37:* 581-86.

SLOWING OF BEHAVIOR WITH AGE

One of the most consistent findings in the study of adult development is the slowing of behavior with increasing age. Briefly discussed here are the magnitude and significance of this effect of aging, contemporary explanations for it, and some attempts that are being made to mitigate and cope with its consequences. For ease of reading, conclusions are italicized and sources of additional information appear at the end of each section.

Magnitude and Significance of Slowing

The general slowing of behavior that comes with aging is defined as the increase in time taken to perform tasks or activities involving such cognitive functions as perception, attention, memory, reasoning, motor preparation, and movement execution. For instance, nearly all of the studies that have compared 20-year-olds and 60-year-olds, have reported slowing (13 to 20 percent) in reaction time (RT) with age. Longitudinal studies (repeated testing on the same people) of RT and movement time (reciprocal tapping) have further corroborated this slowing effect. *So reliable is behavioral slowing with age that some suggest it be considered formally identified as a "marker" or "index" of the aging process and the integrity of the central nervous system.*

Slowness increases with task difficulty and complexity and with the extent to which higher mediating neural structures are involved. Between ages 20 and 96, humans can be expected to slow on simple auditory RT tasks by about 0.006 second (0.06 ms) per year. On disjunctive RT tasks in which one must decide whether or not to react, the general trend is to slow by about 0.015 second (1.5 ms) per year (Figure 1). With increases in task difficulty comes increasingly greater slowing (e.g., four-choice RT might slow by 3 ms/year and complex RT by as much as 10 ms/year).

Remember, this is slowing on a single RT trial. In real life, responses usually involve a series of discrete trials (e.g., a 70-year-old, compared with a 20-year-old, performing a task involving three four-choice RT components might be nearly half of a second slower— 70 - 20 years = 50 years X 3 parts = 450 ms slower).

Because psychomotor speed is embedded in a matrix of relationships with physiological and behavioral parameters, *the consequence of slowing affects nearly every aspect of human performance and daily life,* from the obvious impaired initiation and timing of motor functions to the less obvious disrup-

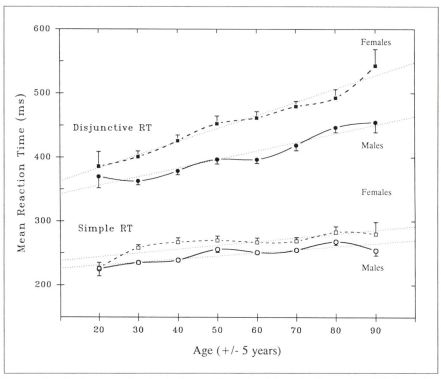

Figure 1. Slowing on Simple Auditory Reaction Time Tasks and on Disjunctive Reaction Time Tasks. Adapted from Fozard et al., (in press).

tion of perceptual and cognitive processing. This slowing may cause difficulties in completing such everyday tasks as walking, eating, bathing, dressing, opening containers, dialing a telephone, picking up small objects, performing intricate assemblies, and toileting, not to mention more complex tasks like operating vehicles and machinery, manipulating controls, or monitoring displays.

Researchers have shown that *older adults may be living in a qualitatively and functionally different environment from that of younger people,* and that equipment (products) and environment must be designed with specific factoring for operator characteristics, especially age. Because of changes that occur in attention, vision, and perceptual-motor reaction time, elderly persons are more prone to accidents, injuries, and fatalities. Older adults have more injuries than the young from motor vehicles, falls, fires, burns, and other accidents, and have higher death, dysfunction, and disability rates than any other age group.

(See Barrett et al., 1977; Birren & Schaie, 1990; Birren, Vercruyssen, & Fisher, 1990; Birren, Woods, & Williams, 1980; Cerella, 1985, 1990; Cerrella, Poon, & Williams, 1980; Charness & Bosman, 1990; Fozard et al., in press; Greene, 1983; Hertzog, 1992; McDowd, Vercruyssen, & Birren, 1991; Salthouse, 1985; Schneider & Rowe, 1990; Smith, 1990; Spirduso & MacRae, 1990; Sterns, Barrett, & Alexander, 1985; Vercruyssen, 1991; Welford, 1968, 1977a, 1984, 1985a, 1988; Welford & Birren, 1965)

Three Prediction Models of Age-Related Slowing

Plotting RT as a function of task difficulty (Figure 2), three models attempt to predict RT differences between young and old subjects.

The Additive Model of Slowing. Welford (1977a) proposed an additive relationship between young and old on RT tasks

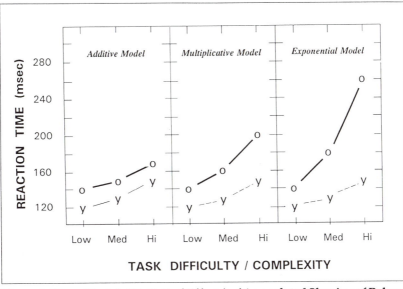

Figure 2. Three Models (Statistical Effects) of Age-related Slowing of Behavior. Adapted from J. Botwinick, (1984).

of varying difficulty that describes elderly adults as being slowed by a constant amount (Figure 2), regardless of task difficulty, with the expression:

$$RT_o = RT_y + c$$

(o = old subjects; y = young subjects, c = a constant or main effect of age that is added to RT_y). This function produces a linear relationship between age and task difficulty.

The Multiplicative Model of Slowing. In the multiplicative model, the age constant described in the additive model takes on a multiplicative role with the expression

$$RT_o = RT_y(c)$$

(o = old subjects; y = young subjects; c = a constant that is multiplied times the RT_y) and attributes slowing to the actions of a single mechanism, assumed to affect the central nervous system (CNS) as a whole in a general way (Figure 2). This function describes a linear relationship between age and task difficulty with a slope greater than 1.0.

The Exponential Model of Slowing. Greene (1983) proposed a dynamic model of slowing (also called the exponential model) characterized by an exponential increase in

RT with increasing task difficulty, expressed as

$$RT_o = RT_y^{c}$$

(o = old subjects; y = young subjects; c = a constant that is a power function or exponent of RT_y, e.g., c = 1.3 in Figure 2), related to the exponentially increasing loss of neurons and neuronal connectivity with advancing age.

All three models have received some empirical support, but the majority of evidence substantiates the multiplicative model of slowing with age.

(See Botwinick, 1984; Cerella, 1985, 1990; Cerella, Poon, & Williams, 1980; Fozard et al., in press; Greene, 1983; Welford, 1977a).

A Working Model of Information Processing

One example of the many models of cognition is presented in Figure 3. Information flow is illustrated through a schematic diagram that divides cognitive processes into at least three sequential steps (also called stages). These begin with stimulus encoding and end with production of an overt response. While the degree to which informa-

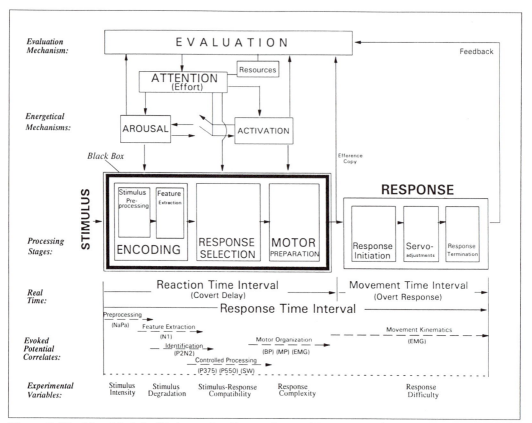

Figure 3. Working Model of Information Processing and Human Performance. Illustrated is the subdivision of response time into reaction and movement time intervals, each containing serial processing stages that are influenced by energetical mechanisms and regulated by an omnibus evaluation controller. Also shown are electrophysiological-evoked potential correlates and experimental variables used to differentially load processing stages. Adapted from Mulder, 1986; Pribram & McGuinness, 1975; Sanders, 1983; and Vercruyssen, 1984.

tion is processed in parallel varies from task to task, a serial model like this one permits theoretical comparisons of the time required at each processing stage, and therefore may be suitable for describing RT tasks. *Some studies have found that slowing is generalized and evident in nearly all stages of information processing, while others suggest that slowing may be stage specific.*

(See Mulder, 1986; Pribram & McGuinness, 1975; Sanders, 1983; Vercruyssen, 1984.)

Neurobiological Perspective on Slowing with Age

Two major types of explanation for this pattern of slowing with age have been of-

fered: the *neurobiological* ("hardware") and the *psychological* ("software") perspective.

Neurobiological 1: Central or Peripheral? *The peripheral hypothesis* states that the sensory and motor changes that accompany aging are the cause of delays in getting information to the brain and/or from the brain to the muscles. In other words, slowing with age is attributable to declines in peripheral processes such as sensory discrimination and change in the speed of motor responses. What does research find? *Although peripheral factors such as reduced conduction velocity through afferent and efferent pathways may contribute somewhat to slowing with age, there is sufficient evidence to presume that the primary focus of slowing is central rather than peripheral. In other words, slowing is mainly attributable to deterio-*

ration of primary cognitive functions rather than of impaired sensory and motor functions.

(See Birren & Schaie, 1990; Birren, Woods, & Williams, 1980; Botwinick, 1984; Cerrella, 1985, 1990; Cerrella, Poon, & Williams, 1980; Salthouse, 1985; Schneider & Rowe, 1990; Spirduso & MacRae, 1990; Welford, 1977a, 1984.)

Neurobiological 2: Generalized vs. Specific Slowing. Several studies have found a slight increase in neural conduction time with age in humans. This finding led many to believe that a small increase in time per event could produce a relatively large slowing of behavior because of the large number of neural events that occur nearly simultaneously in the brain. But is this slowing generalized throughout the CNS or specific to certain cognitive processes, mechanisms, or functions? Following are three of the major explanations related to this query.

The neural-noise theory states that response times and most neural events are slower in older adults because the CNS needs more time to integrate information and to compensate for increased levels of distracting "neural noise," such as background sounds, brain cell irregularity, or subvocal task-unrelated thought. However, slowing with age cannot be attributed entirely to neural conduction velocity and the neural noise theory.

The alpha wave and cycle-time hypothesis suggests that processing rate is a function of internal clock (cycle-time) speed. The alpha rhythm pattern of electrical activity in the brain is thought to serve as a central timing mechanism for most or all neural operations. Many processing operations can be performed only at specific periods in a timing cycle, making nearly all resulting behaviors slower in cases where the alpha wave is slow.

Some studies have found high correlations between age and alpha period and between alpha period and reaction time, but other studies have failed to support these relationships. Feedback techniques have been used to speed up and slow down cycle-time, thereby producing corresponding changes in simple RT. One prediction from this hypoth-

eses is that slowing should be generalized and evident in nearly all stages, not specific to one. Some studies have supported this prediction while others have indicated that slowing may be stage specific. Another prediction that has been well substantiated is that the magnitude of correlations across both speeded and unspeeded dependent measures should increase with advancing age.

The *generalized slowing hypothesis* (Birren, Woods, & Williams, 1980) states that information travels through the same processes in the old as in the young. The process is slower in elderly adults because of the generalized slowing of central mediated functions of the CNS. In lectures, Birren has likened information processing to the transport of people up and down an escalator. The older CNS is simulated by simply turning the speed down on the transport machine. Nothing changes the internal workings of the escalator, it just takes longer to move the same number of people as before. Popular opinion, based on considerable evidence, is that there are few age differences in *how* the young and old process information: The old are simply slower than the young.

Until there is better evidence to the contrary, presume that slowing is a generalized phenomenon, affecting nearly all cognitive processes.

(See Birren & Schaie, 1990; Birren, Vercruyssen, & Fisher, 1990; Birren, Woods, & Williams, 1980; Salthouse, 1985; Schneider & Rowe, 1990; Surwillo, 1968; Welford, 1977a, 1984; Welford & Birren, 1965.)

Neurobiological 3: Structural and System Decomposition. *The cell loss hypothesis* suggests that slowness of behavior with age may be attributable to cell loss, particularly in the extrapyramidal or "fast" motor system. These cell losses would cause declines in the efficiency and capacity of neuronal transmissions, probably through the reduction of synaptic density. Cell loss would also be associated with reduced levels of neurotransmitters and other defects in neural networks, as well as changes in the norepinephrine system, locus coeruleus, basal ganglia, brain hormones (dopamine, serotonin, and norepinephrine), cerebral metabolic rate, cerebral blood flow, cerebellum, and extrapyramidal motor system.

The disease explanation states that disease may account for much of the slowing seen in relatively healthy older adults. Even mild disease could impair cognition, particularly memory retrieval and storage, as well as speed of responding. Patients with cardiovascular disorders perform psychomotor tasks more slowly than healthy people of the same age. Patients with cerebrovascular disorders are even slower. Reduced cardiac output may lead to oxygen deprivation in the brain (a condition called *anoxia*) and disrupt functional efficiency of neural systems, thereby slowing behavior.

Examples of structural and system decomposition correlate with, but do not necessarily cause, behavioral slowing. Needed are models that show causal relationships between organic changes in old age (pathologies and morbidity) and speed of performance.

(See Birren & Schaie, 1990; Birren, Woods, & Williams, 1980; Bondareff, 1985; Cerella, 1990; Greene, 1983; Salthouse, 1985; Schneider & Rowe, 1990; Welford, 1977b, 1984; Welford & Birren, 1965.)

Neurobiological 4: Genetic and Other Factors. Intelligence is closely related to a person's physiological functioning. Likewise, speed of behavior may have a biological basis which is most affected by the physiological changes that accompany aging. The correlation of age, intelligence, and speed of performance cannot be overlooked (Birren & Schaie, 1990; Birren, Woods, & Williams, 1980; Botwinick, 1984; Hertzog, 1992; Schneider & Rowe, 1990). *Speed is fundamental to fluid intelligence: As speed declines, so do fluid intelligence scores.*

Psychological Perspective of Changes with Age

The psychological (software) perspective of age changes in speed of behavior is based on the notion that information-processing (computing) speed may vary as a function of the effectiveness and efficiency of mental operations (control language software).

Psychological 1: Information Overload and Task Complexity. The degree of slowing with age depends on the task. With relatively easy tasks age differences are small, but as task difficulty / complexity increases the performance of elderly adults is degraded exponentially. This decline is presumed to be caused by an overload of the information-processing system. Complexity may be defined in terms of such factors as increased cognitive demands (mental load), increased numbers of stimuli or responses to be processed, increased number of movement components, or increased attentional requirements. This scenario is less likely to occur, however, if the individuals are highly skilled. *So salient and reliable is the task complexity hypothesis that it deserves to be added to the definition of the slowing phenomenon: With increasing age comes a general slowing of behavior, the magnitude of which is determined by task difficulty/complexity.*

(See Birren, Woods, & Williams, 1980; Cerella, 1985, 1990; McDowd, Vercruyssen, & Birren, 1991; Salthouse, 1985.)

Psychological 2: Memory Changes. Speed of behavior has been shown to be related to memory ability. *Compared with young adults, elderly persons are less effective at data storage and retrieval, and sometimes in the recall of distant events. For elderly adults, slower performance in many tasks may be related to their slower rate of memory scanning. Whether or not the actual capacity of working memory is affected by age has not yet been determined.*

(See Birren, Woods, & Williams, 1980; Salthouse, 1985; Welford, 1984.)

Psychological 3: Changes in Mental Set, States, or Biases. Cautiousness is a tendency to respond with great care because of the importance attached to making a mistake. Elderly adults tend to monitor their actions more carefully than do young adults. *The learned consequences of responding quickly and wrongly, as well as a limited ability to respond to other stimuli while engaged in processing one stimulus, may influence older adults to adopt a habit of being slow and cautious.*

The accuracy-emphasis hypothesis predicts that age differences in speed should disappear in tasks that minimize or eliminate variations in strategy or control processes. However, age differences in speed remain even when individuals of different ages are compared at precisely the same level of accuracy. *Conclusion: A shift from speed to accuracy is to be expected as people grow older, but is insufficient to account for much of the observed slowing.*

Response variability reflects the difficulty elderly adults have in controlling their RT task responses. They perform slower overall than young adults, have greater slowing following an error (thus increasing overall variability), and are less able to maintain an optimal range of performance.

The rigidity explanation claims that elderly people are less flexible than young adults. Elderly people are generally assumed to be unable to switch easily from one action or task to another and to regulate moment-to-moment sets, instead sticking firmly to their original routines. However, this explanation may be overly simplistic and inappropriate. Research exploring age changes in rigidity, attention switching, strategy shifts, and response biases is much needed.

The CNS arousal/activation hypothesis proposes that levels of CNS arousal or activation may be related to slowness of behavior with age. However, conflicting results have emerged. Some studies suggest that an *over*aroused CNS is responsible for age-related slowing while others point to an *under*aroused CNS. Psychophysiological studies show that neural excitability decreases with age. Enhanced arousal (through noise, posture, and exercise) has led to greater improvements in performance of elderly persons as compared with young adults. However, there is also evidence supporting the exact opposite hypothesis.

Societal and individual expectations that older adults should slow in most behaviors may function like a self-fulfilling prophecy, inducing older adults to conform to these expectations by being slow.

Cautiousness and the shift from speed to accuracy cannot account for a great deal of slow-ing with age. Elderly people perform slower, more variably, and with greater individual differences than young adults, especially when doing complicated tasks and in situations where the sequencing of stimuli are externally paced. Age changes in rigidity, response preparedness, and mental sets are uncertain, but they may account for some slowing. The debate continues as to whether elderly adults are under- or overaroused compared with the young. Also unknown is the extent to which elderly people are unalterably (biologically) slow or choose to be slow as a means of coping response.

(See Birren, Woods, & Williams, 1980; Fozard et al., in press; Pribram & McGuinness, 1975; Salthouse, 1985; Sanders, 1983; Welford, 1984.)

Psychological 4: Attentional Changes. *Older adults are less able than young adults to sustain attention (vigilance), focus attention on relevant and ignore irrelevant information, recover from distraction, and concurrently process multiple pieces of information. Elderly persons also are more easily distracted and more susceptible to distraction, possibly because they have more task-unrelated thoughts, reduced attentional capacities, and misallocation of processing resources.*

(See Birren, Vercruyssen, & Fisher, 1990; Birren, Woods, & Williams, 1980; McDowd, Vercruyssen, & Birren, 1991; Welford, 1977a.)

Attempts to Mitigate Slowing

Task practice helps individuals to have faster and less variable RTs. While most studies show remaining effects of age after extensive practice, some unreplicated studies have been able to completely remove age differences through extended practice. *Practice is especially beneficial to elderly adults when successful task performance involves remembering complex rules.*

A physically and mentally active life-style may maintain an individual's level of physical work capacity, delay the age at which environmental demands exceed physical capabilities, and reduce the rate of cognitive slowing. Physically fit older adults have faster RTs than do sedentary and unfit people of the same age. However, although aerobic training programs offer many positive benefits to participants, there is no consistent evidence supporting reaction time decreases with improvements in aerobic fitness.

Extended practice on a task may diminish age differences in speed, particularly in cases where experience, knowledge, and wisdom are factors determining response rate. Life-styles involving daily exercise, physical activity, and high-level mental stimulation may be successful in thwarting declines in cognitive functions, but it is too early to state this proposition definitively. Also, speed of behavior has been improved via stimulating drugs, electric shock to punish slow responses, practice and money as incentives, and feedback and instructions for rapid responding, but in all these cases age differences remained.

(See Birren, Vercruyssen, & Fisher, 1990; Kozma & Stones, 1990; Salthouse, 1985; Spirduso & MacRae, 1990; Vercruyssen, 1984.)

Ergonomic Interventions to Cope with Slowing

Speed of behavior will become increasingly more important for successfully coping with advances in our complex, automated, and fast-paced high-tech society. Designs for many products and environments need to be altered for elderly users. Geroergonomists are making significant advances in task design, personnel selection, performance prediction, accident analysis, human tests and measurements, demographic norms, differential diagnosis indicators, and more.

Task Selection. How well elderly adults perform often depends on the task. Older adults are at a distinct disadvantage compared with young adults when performing complex or complicated tasks, even if initial performance levels are equated. Age differences are greater for the written than the oral version of the symbol-digit substitution test of the Wechsler Adult Intelligence Scale, but age differences in simple RT may disappear by substituting vocal responses for manual ones. Older adults may be faster in recalling the names of dated objects, while the young may be faster at retrieving contemporary

unique items. Older individuals may be able to compensate for biological slowing and perform as well as young adults, especially in tasks utilizing their wealth of experiences. For instance, older typists may type as fast as or faster than young typists (despite performing slower on tapping and other speed tasks) by looking further ahead in the test, thus increasing their preparation time (Figure 4).

Changes in the Environment. Home and work environment design have to be improved for elderly adults to live safely and comfortably. Accessibility and acceptability are even mandated now as part of the Americans With Disabilities Act. The high number of potentially serious falls at home experienced by older people may be related to losses in hearing, vision, and balance, but 38 percent are caused by environmental hazards. In order to reduce the risk of falls, hazards such as exposed electrical cords, loose rugs, and uneven surfaces should be eliminated. Other suggestions for home design improvements include easy access for emergency medical assistance, gas-detecting sensors over gas ranges, cutoff switches or timers on cooking/heating appliances, telephone ringer and earpiece adjustments for the hearing impaired, well-labeled hot water controls, and water temperature regulators to prevent scalding. Workplace design examples include avoiding high frequency (4,000 Hz) communications and using high levels of lighting while avoiding glare. Older workers are underrepresented in externally paced industrial tasks, and, in light of the probability of mishap due to slowed responses, this is probably to their benefit. Fitting the person to the task and the task to the person are important goals in workplace design.

Transportation Systems. Behavioral slowing with age may lead to severe problems in properly operating vehicles, controlling equipment, and monitoring displays. Individuals aged 75 and older have the highest per capita fatality rate of any age group in automobile accidents. Driving difficulties encountered by those over age 60 affect driv-

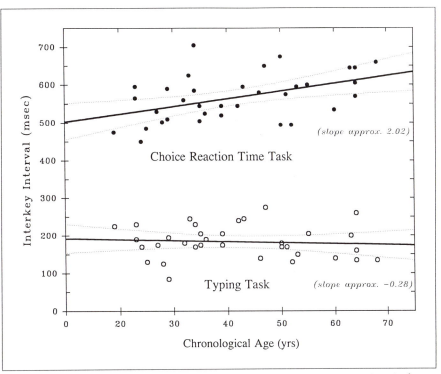

Figure 4. Typing Reaction Times. Median typing interkey interval and choice reaction time as a function of age (age range = 19-72 years) with each point representing a single typist. Adapted from Salthouse, 1984, p. 354; see also Salthouse, 1985, 1987.

ing at night, reading of traffic signs and instruments, backing and merging, and ease of entry and egress. Necessary highway design features include roadway delineation and signage, street and walkway lighting, intersection layout, traffic and pedestrian control devices, and emergency communication systems. Much work remains to make transportation safer and more convenient for everyone.

Increasing attention is being given to the design of products and environments with usability by elderly and/or disabled individuals in mind. Geroergonomists are making changes in everyday living that improve functional utility, career duration, and performance on the job, while decreasing the risk of accidents and health problems.

(See Birren, Vercruyssen, & Fisher, 1990; Charness & Bosman, 1990; Lawton, 1990; Salthouse, 1985; Smith, 1990; Welford, 1977a, 1977b, 1988.)

Conclusions

With increasing age come certain physiological and psychological changes which are responsible for a generalized slowing of most physical and mental performance. The magnitude of this effect increases as a power function of task demand (e.g., task difficulty, task complexity, mental load, degree of higher cortical operations required). However, there are wide inter- and intraindividual differences. This diversity makes it vital to distinguish whether observed changes are attributable to aging itself or other causes such as declining physical activity, societal expectation, and common illnesses.

Furthermore, declines in neurobiological processes that accompany aging are not necessarily predictive of performance degradation since years of experience may lead to expertise and high-level performance for older adults. In other words, for some, psychological changes may compensate for biological "dust" and "rust" such that functional capacity remains high throughout life. The research literature is filled with cases that show huge age differences, many of which are exaggerations. It is important to understand the etiology and factors regulating speed of behavior, both when speed is viewed as a dependent measure and as an independent variable. Although wisdom, experience, vocabulary, and greater crystallized intelligence benefit older people in employing more successful strategies and tactics, senior adults still take longer to perform most physical activities and mental operations than do young adults. Optimistically, whatever slowing cannot be prevented by good health, fitness, and wisdom may be compensated for in the near future by innovative product and environmental designs.

(See Birren & Schaie, 1990; Birren, Vercruyssen, & Fisher, 1990; Cerella, Poon, & Williams, 1980; Hertzog, 1992; McDowd, Vercruyssen, & Birren, 1991; Salthouse, 1985; Spirduso & MacRae,1990; Vercruyssen, 1984.)

▼ MAX VERCRUYSSEN

See also: Age 65; Cardiac Health; Driving: A Lifespan Challenge; Exercise; Information Processing; Intelligence; Memory; Work Capacity Across the Adult Years.

References

Barrett, G. V., et al. (1977). Information processing skills predictive of accident involvement for younger and older commercial drivers. *Industrial Gerontology, 4:* 173-82.

Birren, J. E.., & Schaie, K. W. (Eds.). (1990). *Handbook of the Psychology of Aging.* Third Edition. New York: Academic Press.

Birren, J. E., Vercruyssen, M., & Fisher, Laurel M. (1990). Aging and speed of behaviour: Its scientific and practical significance. In M. Bergener, M. Ermini, & H. B. Stahelin (Eds.), *Challenges in Aging: The 1990 Sandoz Lectures in Gerontology*. New York: Academic Press, pp. 3-23.

Birren, J. E., Woods, A. M., & Williams, M. V. (1980). Behavioral slowing with age: Causes, organization, and consequences. In L. W. Poon (Ed.), *Aging in the 1980s: Psychological Issues.* Washington, DC: American Psychological Association, pp. 293-308.

Bondareff, W. (1985). The neural bases of aging. In J. E. Birren and K. W. Schaie (Eds.), *Handbook of the Psychology of Aging.* Second Edition. New York: Van Nostrand Reinhold, pp. 95-112.

Botwinick, J. (1984). *Aging and Behavior: A Comprehensive Integration of Research Findings.* Third Edition. New York: Springer.

Cerella, J. (1985). Information processing rates in the elderly. *Psychological Bulletin, 98,* 67-83.

———. (1990). Aging and information-processing rate. In J. E. Birren & K. W. Schaie (Eds.), *Handbook of the Psychology of Aging.* Third Edition. New York: Academic Press, pp. 201-21.

Cerella, J., Poon, L. W., & Williams, D. M. (1980). A quantitative theory of mental processing time and age. In L. W. Poon (Ed.), *Aging in the 1980s: Selective Contemporary Issues in the Psychology of Aging.* Washington, DC: American Psychological Association, pp. 532-40.

Charness, N., & Bosman, E. A. (1990). Human factors and design for older adults. In J. E. Birren & K. W. Schaie (Eds.), *Handbook of the Psychology of Aging.* Third Edition. New York: Academic Press, pp. 446-62.

Fozard, J. L., et al. (in press). Age changes and sex differences in reaction time: The Baltimore Longitudinal Study of Aging. *Journal of Gerontology.*

Greene, V. L. (1983). Age dynamic models of information-processing task latency: A theoretical note. *Journal of Gerontology, 38,* 46-50.

Hertzog, C. (1992). Aging, information processing speed, and intelligence. In K. W. Schaie (Ed.), *Annual Review of Gerontology and Geriatrics.* Volume 11. New York: Springer, pp. 55-79.

Kozma, A., & Stones, J. J. (1990). Decrements in habitual and maximal physical performance with age. In M. Perlmutter (Ed.), *Later Life Potential.* Washington DC: The Gerontological Society of America, pp. 1-22.

Lawton, M. P. (1990). Aging and performance of home tasks. *Human Factors, 32:* 527-36.

McDowd, J. M., Vercruyssen, M., & Birren, J. E. (1991). Aging, divided attention, and dual-task performance. In D. L. Damos (Ed.), *Multiple-task Performance.* London: Taylor & Francis, pp. 387-414.

Mulder, G. (1986). The concept and measurement of mental effort. In G.R.J. Hockey, A.W.K. Gaillard, & M.G.H. Coles (Eds.), *Energetics and Human Information Processing.* Martinus Nijhoff, pp. 86-112.

Pribram, K. H., & McGuinness, D. (1975). Arousal, activation, and effort in the control of attention. *Psychological Review, 82:* 116-49.

Salthouse, T. A. (1984). *Adult Cognition: An Experimental Psychology of Human Aging.* New York: Springer-Verlag.

———. (1985). Speed of behavior and its implications for cognition. In J. E. Birren & K. W. Schaie (Eds.), *Handbook of the Psychology of Aging.* Second Edition. New York: Van Nostrand Reinhold, pp. 400-26.

———. (1987). Speed-accuracy trade-off. In G. L. Maddox (Ed.) *The Encyclopedia of Aging.* New York: Springer, pp. 643-44.

Sanders, A. F. (1983). Towards a model of stress and human performance. *Acta Psychologica, 53:* 61-97.

Schneider, E. L., & Rowe, J. W. (1990). *Handbook of the Biology of Aging.* Second Edition. New York: Academic Press.

Smith, D. B. D. (1990). Human factors and aging: An overview of research needs and application opportunities. *Human Factors, 32:* 509-26.

Spirduso, W. W., & MacRae, P. G. (1990). Motor performance and aging. In J. E. Birren & K. W. Schaie (Eds.), *Handbook of the Psychology of Aging.* Third Edition. New York: Academic Press, pp. 183-200.

Sterns, H. L., Barrett, G. V., & Alexander, R. A. (1985). Accidents and the aging individual. In J. E. Birren & K. W. Schaie (Eds.), *Handbook of the Psychology of Aging.* Second Edition. New York: Van Nostrand Reinhold, pp. 703-21.

Surwillo, W. W. (1968). Timing of behavior in senescence and the role of the central nervous system. In G. A. Talland (Ed.), *Human Aging and Behavior: Recent Advances in Research and Theory.* New York: Academic Press, pp. 1-35.

Vercruyssen, M. (1984). *Carbon Dioxide Inhalation and Information Processing: Effects of an Environmental Stressor on Cognition.* Unpublished doctoral dissertation, The Pennsylvania State University, University Park, PA.

———. (1991). Age-related slowing of behavior. *Proceedings of the Human Factors Society—35th Annual Meeting.* Santa Monica, CA: Human Factors Society, pp. 188-92.

Welford, A. T. (1968). *Aging and Human Skills.* London: Oxford University Press.

———. (1977a). Motor performance. In J. E. Birren & K. W. Schaie (Eds.), *Handbook of the Psychology of Aging.* Second Edition. New York: Van Nostrand Reinhold, pp. 450-96.

———. (1977b). Causes of slowing of performance with age. *Interdisciplinary Topics in Gerontology, 11:* 43-51.

———. (1984). Between bodily changes and performance: Some possible reasons for slowing with age. *Experimental Aging Research, 10:* 73-88.

———. (1985). Changes of performance with age: An overview. In N. Charness (Ed.), *Aging and Human Performance.* Chichester, UK: Wiley, pp. 333-69.

———. (1988). Preventing Adverse Changes of Work with Age. *International Journal of Aging and Human Development, 27:* 283-91.

Welford, A. T., & Birren, J. E. (Eds.). (1965). *Behavior, Aging, and the Nervous System.* Springfield, IL: Charles C. Thomas.

Acknowledgments: Ideas presented in this paper benefited from discussions with J. E. Birren, A. T. Welford, M. E. Christina, A. F. Sanders, V. D. Buckles, J. L. Fozard, P. A. Hancock, J. M. McDowd, and B. D. B. Smith. N. Hasebe and A. Matsumura helped organize material for an earlier version of this article.

SOCIAL CLASS AND ADULT DEVELOPMENT

Social class and the life course are closely linked. Social class imposes patterns on the temporal sequences, duration, and structure on the way life unfolds. Adult development may be woven from many threads, but none is isolated from the effects of membership in important social categories. Participation in these categories determines when social roles become available, how they are activated, and how they are played out. In fact, much of the way a person experiences life comes about as a consequence of socioeconomic status (Clausen, 1986), including the substance and meaning of occupational careers, marital-family roles, and adjustments to the life-course changes.

The transition to early adulthood is thought by many to provide the principal anchor for what follows (Spilerman, 1977). Undoubtedly, the timing of that transition is mediated through membership in social class categories. The first phase of adulthood is marked by participation in the labor force and earning a livelihood. Therefore, the necessity, indeed, the opportunity, to be self-supporting is a consequence of an individual's membership in certain social categories. Those who are able to enter on a voluntary instead of a compulsory basis are able to defer one phase of life while prolonging the preceding phase. The same could be said of those who extend their education, defer marriage or parenthood, or postpone any of the rites of passage that are commonly thought to signify different phases of the life course.

The notion that development is strictly a maturational process that unfolds from within according to some built-in imperative has been increasingly challenged in recent years. The new view is represented by Clausen's assertion: "The trajectory of human life is the product of many forces— genetic, physiological, ecological, social and cultural" (1972, p. 462). In other words, human beings are shaped both by biological and contextual factors, and it is perilous to ignore the latter if adult development is to be explained.

Riegel was among the first to propose that development is an interactive process. Ontogenetic approaches, stressing patterns that emerge from within, must be alloyed with a holistic view that recognizes the importance of contextual and social variables (Gergen, 1977; Hagestad, 1990; Riegel, 1973). The malleability of both child and adult development has been explored and found to be influenced by a wide range of extrinsic socio-economic and cultural factors (Bronfenbrenner, 1979; Sorensen, Weinert, & Sherrod, 1986).

It is one thing to claim that no one lives and develops in isolation, and another to integrate that contention into research designs that can illuminate the processes involved. Much further attention is needed to the processes by which extrinsic factors provide the contexts that give shape to development (Kohli & Meyer, 1986). Furthermore, we cannot expect to understand stability as well as development during the adult years

unless we give systematic attention to all the factors that contribute to the social organization of the life course.

Many social scientists contend that development is a characteristic not only of individuals but of entire subgroups of the population (Featherman, 1986). How groups of people experience life will influence the way that individual life courses are experienced. Individuals from similar cultures, locales, and racial, social, or gender categories are likely to demonstrate characteristic patternings in the way life unfolds because they have comparable experiences and resources. The nature of a person's social opportunities or obligations is as telling a marker of a certain period of life as is any physiological or psychological attribute. A corollary is that roles and their effects emerge from memberships in identifiable social categories that mediate individual development (Dowd, 1990; Featherman & Lerner, 1985).

The Relevance of Social Class

In technical terms, sociologists who study adult development see it as an outgrowth of positions attained and status transitions that are shaped by institutionalized pathways and opportunity structures (Featherman, 1986; O'Rand, 1990). Social class background, like other structural factors, gives substance to recognized age-graded commonalities that define the trajectories of human development. Hogan and Astone assert, "This means that the pace of biological, psychological, and social development may vary between individuals, and there need be no uniformity in the ordering in which developmental stages on the different dimensions occur" (1986, p. 111). Rowe and Kahn (1987) go further still, pointing out that the fundamental biological or physiological states that influence the way we look at adult development are themselves not insulated from social factors.

Individuals from disparate socioeconomic statuses may not encounter the same things in the course of life because they vary so much in personal resources and access to opportunity. Depending on socioeconomic characteristics, developmental trajectories may be quite dissimilar. It may be that some adjective other than development would be a more apt characterization of the adult years among those groups for whom constancy is more common than change. Some researchers maintain that the growing routinization of the life course is driven by changes in the work-a-day world (Kohli & Meyer, 1986). Historically, the shift of productive sphere from home to factory presaged changes in the way the life course was viewed. When factory work became commonplace, many changes followed: Child labor and retirement laws were instituted, for example, and educational requirements became more formalized. As the world of work grew in importance job-related factors came to be embodied in our basic concepts of adulthood. The rights and responsibilities of the job, the nature of reward, the kind of benefits received, and financial autonomy are among the foundations upon which the concept of social class rests. Eventually, our ideas of what adulthood is all about became very much related to the work role and situation. Dowd is unequivocal: "First and most tangibly, social class influences development through the allocation of economic and cultural resources that are the enabling requisites of development" (1990, p. 150).

The Meaning of Social Class

Social class or socioeconomic status (the terms are often used interchangeably) refers to the social hierarchy. Customarily, lower, middle, and upper classes are distinguished. Internal gradations of each may also be identified. Social class categories are a composite measure of income, occupation, and educational backgrounds. These, in turn, lead to comparable life-styles, worldviews, and life chances for members of a given class. Traditionally, social class was seen as a consequence of two types of characteristics: *ascribed characteristics*, those into which a person is born; and *achieved characteristics*, those people earn or attain in their own lives. The relative importance accorded these characteristics mirrors the logic of the marketplace and the social distribution of valued attributes.

Although social class underlies both the apportionment of opportunities and the distribution of rewards, there is much debate about the basis of assignment for any particular social class. Originally, social class was thought to be a consequence of human capital—those skills and qualifications a person brought to the world of work. In recent years an element of political economy has been added as commentators have asserted that social class membership is not merely a result of status attainment, but also reflects the allocation of opportunities to various subgroups of the population. Regardless of the basis for assignment, position in the hierarchical ranking is a major influence on access to opportunity and life chances.

The centrality of social class in predicting all manner of outcomes raises many questions. How do the accoutrements of life-style affect developmental processes? How are transitions and opportunities based on socioeconomic status incorporated into the way that adult development is defined? To resolve these questions it is important to point out that social class is a relational construct. In other words, it provides a foundation for the way that people interact with and label one another. It would not be going too far to suggest that socioeconomic status also has a significant role in shaping a person's self-definition and the way that others define this person.

Social Class and Adult Development

There is a high risk of confusing socioeconomic status with what are oftentimes viewed as developmental patterns. Think of how difficult it is to describe any aspect of adulthood without reference to social roles, certain aspects of marital status, changes in opportunities and obligations, and occupational mobility and advancement. Think, too, about how many factors affect one's ability to participate in various types of roles. If all these potential influences color the way life is experienced, what, then, is left as the kernel of adult development? The contribution of sociology to the solution of this puzzle is that social stratification established the parameters within which the experience of adult development plays out (Kohli & Meyer, 1986).

Researchers have often observed that adult development takes a wide variety of individual styles and patterns. Part of this heterogeneity actually may stem from differences in socioeconomic variables. Patterns of social stratification leverage the timing of major life events, and thereby influence the nature of adult development. Indeed, socioeconomic status is a principal factor in establishing normative pathways of adult development (Hogan & Astone, 1986; Lacy & Hendricks, 1980). The interactions among socioeconomic statuses, events undergone, their timing, duration, and subsequent transitions in the life course constitute the sociology of adult development. One sociological approach in particular, what has been called "event history analysis," has become a major analytic strategy for identifying how life-course development is linked to social experience (Marini, 1984).

All developmental models assume that the various facets of development are synchronous, that they all occur on a coordinating schedule. This assumption may itself be linked to social class. Disorder in the timing of life transitions indicates, at the very least, an absence of synchronization that derives from personal and social instabilities (Rindfuss, Swicegood & Rosenfeld, 1987). For example, membership in lower socioeconomic statuses may be accompanied either by disrupted occupational involvements or flat career tracks. A person who occupies a succession of entry-level positions, rather than moving through a career-like progression, may later experience a number of disordered or disrupted transitions. Societal disruptions—such as recessions, depressions, civil unrest, or wars—may also be inimical to the scheduling process (Elder, 1974; Elder, Pavalko & Hastings, 1991). Which gender, social class, or other category of people is the

most affected by societal disruptions can be determined only through empirical research. If the evidence suggests that the consequences are not uniform, then the problems of delineating the stages or sequences of adult development become even more complex.

One thing is clear: Socioeconomic status, the division of labor, and the distribution of rights and resources play major roles in shaping the content of adult development. Involvement in the world of work or other class-linked activities may underpin transitions and achievements to such an extent that later outcomes are inextricably linked to those occurring earlier (Elder, Pavalko & Hastings, 1991; Featherman, 1983; O'Rand, 1990).

The way people think about the future is also closely tied to socioeconomic status. Whether or not people look to the future and anticipate new horizons and opportunities may be a reflection of their jobs. Employment that provides retirement annuities will foster a different sort of middle age than employment that provides neither security nor opportunity for personal growth. As already mentioned, a succession of entry-level jobs is unlikely to be supportive of either. Jobs providing pension coverage, and thereby an element of economic security, will affect the timing of retirement and the sense of futurity very differently than jobs without pensions (O'Rand, 1990). Similarly, those in the middle classes have relatively less latitude in the timing of retirement than do either their lower- or upper-status counterparts.

It should come as no surprise that socioeconomic status imposes a degree of standardization on available roles. After all, it is through our institutions and our membership in diverse status categories that normative boundaries or benchmarks are given meaning. They are the heart of what is sometimes termed the "normative timetables" of life (Hagestad & Neugarten, 1985). Some observers have gone so far as to assert that social classes and what they portend are the building blocks of the social construction of the life course—and that development is nothing but an accommodation to patterns imposed by one's social context (Guillemard, 1982).

Summary

Many social scientists see adult development as a process contingent on any number of possible influences. This interactive perspective is redefining the way we see development so that the interaction of psychological, social, and historical forces wherein transitions and timing circumscribe what were once thought to be ontogenetic stages unfolding from within (Dannefer, 1984; Hendricks, 1984; Kastenbaum, 1987). Over the past few decades widespread agreement has been reached on the importance of personal resources as a prime factor in explaining why some people age one way and others another. Should the evidence indicate that social class and associated variables structure the way that life is lived, then the utility of the concept of adult development and the use of chronological age in its demarcation must be approached with caution. Although this caveat will not deconstruct the concept of adult development as an intrinsic psychological process, it may first blur and then in the long run facilitate more meaningful conceptualizations. Even so basic a feature of development as stages or sequences may be shown to be highly malleable and perhaps best laid to rest (Featherstone & Hepworth, 1989; Lacy and Hendricks, 1980).

Aside from the structural implications of membership in any particular socioeconomic status, there is also a social psychological dimension. The way that people think of themselves flows from the available roles and the meanings they derive from these roles. Every life course transition implies that self-definitions are reformulated in terms of the previous roles that have been relinquished and the new roles that are being assumed. However they occur, transitions can not be considered apart from the concomitants of socioeconomic status that give them meaning. By attending to social class differences we may be better able to identify the constituent elements of adult development.

▼ JON HENDRICKS

See also: Conflict as a Challenge in Adult Development; Disengagement Theory; Fictive Kin; Habituation: A Key to Lifespan Development and Aging?; Intelligence—Crystallized and Fluid; Japanese Perspectives on Adult Development; Life Events; Political Beliefs and Activities; Work Capacity Across the Adult Years; Work Organization Membership and Behavior.

References

Bronfenbrenner, U. (1979). *The Ecology of Human Development*. Cambridge, MA: Harvard University Press.

Clausen, J. (1972). The life course of individuals. In M. W. Riley, M. Johnson, & A. Foner (Eds.), *Aging and Society. Volume 3: A Sociology of Age Stratification*. New York: Russell Sage Foundation, pp. 457-514.

———. (1986). *The Life Course: A Sociological Perspective*. Englewood Cliffs, NJ: Prentice-Hall.

Dannefer, D. (1984). Adult development and social theory: A paradigmatic reappraisal. *American Sociological Review, 49:* 100-16.

Dowd, J.J. (1990). Ever since Durkheim: The socialization of human development. *Human Development, 33:* 138-59.

Elder, G. H., Jr. (1974). *Children of the Great Depression: Social Change in Life Experience*. Chicago: University of Chicago Press.

Elder, G. H., Jr., Pavalko, E. K., & Hastings, T. J. (1991). Talent, history, and the fulfillment of promise. *Psychiatry, 54:* 251-67.

Featherman, D. L. (1983). The life-span perspective in social science research. In P. B. Baltes & O. Brimm, Jr. (Eds.), *Life-Span Development and Behavior*. Volume 5. New York: Academic Press, pp. 1-49.

———. (1986). Biography, society and history: Individual development as a populations process. In A. Sorensen, F. Weinert, & L. Sherrod (Eds.), *Human Development and the Life Course: Multidisciplinary Perspectives*. Hillsdale, NJ: Erlbaum, pp. 99-152.

Featherman, D. L., & Lerner, R. M. (1985). Ontogenesis and sociogenesis: Problematics for theory and research about development and socialization across the lifespan. *American Sociological Review, 50:* 659-76.

Featherstone, M., & Hepworth, M. (1989). Ageing and old age: Reflections on the postmodern life course. In B. Bytheway, T. Keil, P. Allat, & A. Bryman (Eds.), *Becoming and Being Old: Sociological Approaches to Later Life*. London: Sage, pp. 143-57.

Gergen, K. J. (1977). Stability, change, and chance in human development. In N. Datan & H. W. Reese (Eds.), *Life-Span Developmental Psychology*. New York: Academic Press, pp. 135-58.

Guillemard, A. M. (1982). Old age, retirement, and the social class structure: Toward an analysis of the structural dynamics of the latter stage of life. In T. K. Haraven & K. J. Adams (Eds.), *Aging and Life Course Transitions: An Interdisciplinary Perspective*. London: Tavistock, pp. 221-44.

Hagestad, G. O. (1990). Social perspectives on the life course. In R. H. Binstock & L. K. George (Eds.), *Handbook of Aging and the Social Sciences*. Third Edition. San Diego: Academic Press, pp. 221-44.

Hagestad, G. O., & Neugarten, B. L. (1985). Age and the life course. In R. L. Binstock & E. Shanas (Eds.), *Handbook of Aging and the Social Sciences*. Second Edition. New York: Van Nostrand Reinhold, pp. 35-61.

Hendricks, J. (1984). Lifecourse and structure: The fate of the art. *Ageing and Society, 4:* 93-98.

Hogan, D., & Astone, N. M. (1986). The transition to adulthood. In R. H. Turner (Ed.), *Annual Review of Sociology*. Volume 12. Palo Alto, CA: Annual Reviews, Inc.

Kastenbaum, R. (1987). Life-Course. In G. L. Maddox (Ed.), *The Encyclopedia of Aging*. New York: Springer, pp. 388-90.

Kohli, M., & Meyer, J. W. (1986). Social structure and the social construction of the life stages. *Human Development, 29:* 145-56.

Lacy, W. B., & Hendricks, J. (1980). Developmental models of adult life: Myth or reality? *International Journal of Aging & Human Development, 11:* 89-110.

Marini, M. M. (1984). The order of events in the transition to adulthood. *Sociology of Education, 57:* 63-84.

O'Rand, A. M. (1990). Stratification and the life course. In R. H. Binstock & L. K. George (Eds.), *Handbook of Aging and the Social Sciences*. Third Edition. San Diego: Academic Press, pp. 130-48.

Riegel, K. F. (1973). An epitaph for a paradigm. *Human Development, 16:* 1-7.

Rindfuss, R. R., Swicegood, C. G., & Rosenfeld, R. A. (1987). Disorder in the life course: How common and does it matter? *American Sociological Review, 52:* 785-801.

Rowe, J. W., & Kahn, R. L. (1987). Human aging: Usual and successful. *Science, 237:* 143-49.

Sorensen, A. B., Weinert, F. E., & Sherrod, L. R. (Eds.). (1986). *Human Development and the Life Course: Multidisciplinary Perspectives*. Hillsdale, NJ: Erlbaum.

Spilerman, S. (1977). Careers, labor market structure, and socioeconomic achievement. *American Journal of Sociology, 83:* 551-93.

Thompson, E. P. (1971). The moral economy of the English crowd in the eighteenth century. *Past and Present, 50:* 76-136.

SOCIAL RELATIONSHIPS, CONVOYS OF

The concept of convoys of social relationships was first introduced by the anthropologist David Plath and further developed by Kahn and Antonucci (1980; Antonucci, 1985; Kahn, 1979). This term incorporates the theoretical perspectives of attachment, social roles, and social support research within a lifespan perspective. The fundamental importance of social relationships to adult development is now widely accepted. The impact of social relationships is best understood within a lifespan context that is sensitive both to the continuity and stability in social relationships and to the potential for discontinuity and change.

Social relationships influence the individual at every level of development and interaction, and this influence should not be underestimated. Individuals are surrounded by people who are central to their socialization and development. The convoy describes a group of people, usually close family and friends, who help and protect the individual. Through this group individuals come to understand the world around them, to develop a sense of their own strengths and weaknesses. It is to these people, their convoy members, that individuals turn when they need help, information, or affection. Although the convoy is a source of help and support, in some circumstances the individual can be limited or made vulnerable by these relationships. For example, convoy members may make too many demands on the individual, establish a pattern of overprotection, or convey a sense of inadequacy or inferiority.

Continuity of Relationships over the Lifespan

Almost two decades ago it was suggested that adult social relationships could best be understood as a continuation of attachment across the lifespan (Antonucci, 1976; Lerner & Ryff, 1978; Parkes & Stevenson-Hinde, 1982). More recently, it has been suggested that the concepts of lifespan attachment and social support be integrated to provide a broader perspective on the nature, mechanisms, and effects of social relationships in adulthood (Antonucci, 1985, 1990; Antonucci & Jackson, 1987; Kahn & Antonucci, 1980; Levitt, 1990). The following paragraphs summarize this proposed integration and identify critical questions concerning social relationships.

Attachment research has traditionally focused on children and their primary attachment figures. Whether as specific as mother-infant dyads or as general as adult-child relationships, the term "attachment" clearly refers to those social contacts that are especially significant or close. The convoy that surrounds the adult is thought to include relationships that are based on parent-child connections as well as other close and significant relationships that are formed over the years. Prime examples include relationships with spouse and children. Some friends, colleagues, and coworkers may also become important members of the convoy.

People whose attachment relationships during infancy and childhood have been optimal are thought to enter adulthood with clear advantages over those whose early attachment relationships have been flawed or limited (Rutter, 1987). It has become increasingly clear that troubled adults are more likely to have had a troubled childhood. These early difficulties are often marked by poor attachment and either by poor patterns of interactions (nonresponsive or uncaring caregivers) or by major losses, such as the death of a parent (Brown & Harris, 1976).

At the core of the convoy notion is the assertion that social relationships are continuous over the life course. Thus, the individual who has positive social relationships or attachments as a child not only enters adulthood with these advantages but also is much more likely to be competent in seeking and maintaining optimal social relationships in moving through adulthood. An appropriate analogy would be that a firm foundation allows one to build a better house. Attachment in childhood is not a unitary phenomenon, however. The child may have a poor relationship with one close attachment figure but compensate for this problem somewhat by having a better relationship with other emotionally significant people. Indeed, both positive and negative relationships are dynamic and subject to change. Relationships evolve over time, thereby providing the individual with the opportunity to recover from earlier problematic interactions.

The convoy of social relationships not only helps people feel that they are loved and "belong" but also provides companions on whom they can depend in times of stress and crisis. The larger and more varied the membership of the convoy, the more options are available to the individual when problems arise in any one particular relationship. It should be noted that convoy relationships are not unidirectional. Just as an individual is able to call on members of his or her convoy for help, members of the convoy similarly have access to that individual when they need assistance. Under normal circumstances this continuing exchange of support is likely to contribute to the mental health of all involved. Although little research has examined reciprocity in social relationships, findings do suggest both that people prefer to exchange support and that healthy people are likely to report that they give more support to convoy members than they receive from them (Antonucci, 1990).

Antonucci and Jackson (1987) suggested that this expectancy of exchange might represent a highly adaptive set of behaviors. People may prefer to provide more support than they receive because they are comforted by the idea that close convoy members are available for one another when they are needed. With such a history of providing to others in need, individuals can feel assured that they themselves will be provided for at some future time when confronted by loss or stress. Antonucci (1985) coined the term "Support Bank" to describe this phenomenon. People make deposits into their Support Bank by providing instrumental assistance and affectional support to their convoy members. Since people are much more likely to face functional impairments as they grow older, having a resource such as this to draw on can be seen as especially adaptive.

In sum, it is proposed that individuals move through life surrounded by a convoy of social relationships. This convoy, as in the usual sense of the term, is meant to help and protect people. For the most part, when convoys are operating optimally they represent a built-in, long-term, and diverse support system. Although we still know very little about the mechanisms through which the convoy provides this protection, the available evidence indicates that people who are surrounded by supportive others are better able to cope with the normal stresses and strains of daily living and also enjoy better health and greater well-being.

▼ Toni C. Antonucci and Hiroko Akiyama

See also: Adult Children and Their Parents; Attachment Across the Lifespan; Fictive Kin; Friendships through the Adult Years; Gender as a Shaping Force in Adult Development and Aging; Grandparent Communication Skills; Loneliness; Marital Development; Sibling Relationships; Twins through the Lifespan; Widowhood: The Coping Response.

References

Antonucci, T. C. (1976). Attachment: A life-span concept. *Human Development, 19:* 135-42.

———. (1985). Personal characteristics, social support, and social behavior. In R. H. Binstock & E. Shanas (Eds.), *Handbook of Aging and the Social Sciences.* Second Edition. New York: Van Nostrand Reinhold, pp. 94-128.

———. (1990). Social supports and social relationships. In R. H. Binstock & L. K. George (Eds.), *Handbook of Aging & the Social Sciences.* Third Edition. Orlando, FL: Academic Press, pp. 205-26.

Antonucci, T. C., & Jackson, J. S. (1987). Social support, interpersonal efficacy, and health. In L. L. Carstensen & B. A. Edelstein (Eds.), *Handbook of Clinical Gerontology.* New York: Pergamon Press, pp. 291-311.

———. (1989). Successful aging and life course reciprocity. In A. Warnes (Ed.), *Human Ageing and Later Life: Multidisciplinary Perspectives.* London: Hodder & Stoughton, pp. 83-95.

Bretherton, I., & Waters, E. (1985). *Growing Points of Attachment Theory and Research. Monographs of the Society for Research in Child Development, 50:* 1-2.

Brown, G. W., & Harris, T. (1978). *Social Origins of Depression.* New York: Free Press.

Kahn, R. L. (1979). Aging and social support. In M. W. Riley (Ed.), *Aging from Birth to Death.* Boulder, CO: Westview, pp. 77-91.

Kahn, R. L., & Antonucci, T. C. (1980). Convoys over the life course: Attachment, roles, and social support. In P. B. Baltes & O. Brim (Eds.), *Life-Span Development and Behavior.* Volume 3. New York: Academic Press, pp. 234-86.

Lerner, R., & Ryff, C. (1978). Implementation of the life-span view of human development: The sample case of attachment. In P. B. Baltes (Ed.), *Life-Span Development and Behavior.* Volume 1. New York: Plenum Press, pp. 2-45.

Levitt, M. J. (1990). Attachment and close relationships: A life span perspective. In J. L. Gewirtz & W. F. Kurtines (Eds.), *Intersections with Attachment.* Hillsdale, NJ: Erlbaum, pp. 38-55.

Main, M., Kaplan, N., & Cassidy, J. (1985). Security in infancy, childhood and adulthood: A move to the level of representation. In I. Bretherton & E. Waters (Eds.), *Growing Points of Attachment Theory and Research, Monographs of the Society for Research in Child Development, 50:* 66-104.

Parkes, C. M., & Stevenson-Hinde, J. (Eds.). (1982). *The Place of Attachment in Human Behavior.* New York: Basic Books.

Plath, D. (1980). *Long Engagements.* Stanford, CA: Stanford University Press.

Rutter, M. (1987). Continuities and discontinuities. In J. Osofski (Ed.), *Handbook of Infant Development.* New York: Wiley, pp. 214-38.

SOCIAL SUPPORT FOR THE CHRONICALLY ILL

The idea that social relationships can improve the lives of adults with chronic illness, both physically and emotionally, has generated a great deal of public policy interest. Social scientists, hoping to contribute to more enlightened public policy, have started to provide answers to the question: Does social support make a difference to the well-being of chronically ill adults? In search of these answers, they have also asked the more specific questions: What kind of social support is most valuable? What social provisions are truly supportive to the chronically ill?

Social scientists use the term "social support" to encompass a variety of actions and tasks: offering tangible assistance, such as housing and money; offering advice; reassuring the person that he or she is loved; and affirming the individual's membership in a group or network of caring others. What these actions have in common is the goal of either offsetting the physical problems created by chronic illness or countering the negative emotional reactions (e.g., depression and anxiety) that often develop with illness.

Social support theory proposes that the "active ingredient" of social support is its ability to buffer people from the expectable negative consequences of stress. By and large, studies of people experiencing bereavement, pregnancy, unemployment, and work stress have been consistent with the theory. Social support does seem to act as a buffer against the emotional toll of stress, particularly when the support creates in recipients the perception that caring people are available to them when life becomes stressful (Cohen & Wills, 1985; House & Kahn, 1985; Kessler & McLeod, 1985).

Links Between Social Support and Health

The role of social support in chronic illness is of particular interest because of (a) the ongoing stresses experienced by those who have a long-term health problem and (b) the known link between social relationships and physical health. Large-scale epidemiological studies have shown that people who are socially integrated are much more likely to be among the living after a substantial period of time has elapsed, e.g., 13 years in the research reported by House, Landis, & Umberson (1988).

Social relationships have not been found to have a definitive causal role in the onset of illness, however. Epidemiological studies have not shown lack of social integration to be related to the development of specific illnesses. Furthermore, those studies that have linked social relationships with specific conditions such as myocardial infarction (e.g., Bruhn, 1965) have been retrospective. This leaves open the possibility that lessened social involvement was the result, rather than the cause of illness.

One important role that social support does appear to play in chronic illness is in shaping the course of the illness. Recovery from acute episodes or health crises seems to have a particularly close relationship with social support. For example, quicker recovery from myocardial infarction has been found for men whose wives reported receiving help from more sources during the recovery period (Finlayson, 1976) and whose families expressed less worry about the patient's health (Garrity, 1973). Strong social support among breast cancer patients has been found to predict slower disease progression, though it is unrelated to five-year survival (Levy et al., 1991).

More rapid physical rehabilitation and greater improvement in rehabilitation have also been linked to the receipt of social support (see review by Wallston et al., 1983). The fact that the beneficial effects of social support on recovery emerge both in studies of naturally occurring support and in intervention studies underscores the strength of this finding. Clearly, a stress-buffering model is important for understanding the role of social relationships in health throughout the lifespan.

Probably social support's most important role in chronic illness is its ability to influence emotional well-being. Emotional adjustment among elderly people who are disabled has been linked to the receipt of assistance from others (Arling, 1987). This link may also hold true throughout the entire life course, but this remains to be studied. It has been found, however, that a generalized perception of being supported can successfully offset depression in disabled adults (Turner & Noh, 1988). Additionally, emotional state and cognitive ability following a stroke have been successfully predicted on the basis of the individuals' available social support (Stephens et al., 1987).

Types of Social Support Effective in Chronic Illness

Despite the accumulating evidence for social support's role in chronic illness, we have only a minimal understanding of the process through which support exerts its beneficial influence. Analysis of the types of social support that have proved effective is helpful in illustrating the means through which social support helps the chronically ill. Research findings indicate that a variety of types of social support can be beneficial but point quite consistently to the importance of *instrumental* and *emotional* support. The two types operate in distinct ways and may offer different kinds of benefit.

Instrumental Support. The provision of assistance with day-to-day problems is of both practical and emotional significance to the chronically ill. Possibly the most important role played by instrumental assistance is in preventing, or at least forestalling, institutionalization (Tobin & Kulys, 1981). Kin, the most typical and most preferred providers of instrumental assistance to elderly persons, act as informal brokers of medical care use (Coe et al., 1985). For many elders, kin provide alternative living arrangements that offer a choice other than living alone or living in an institution (Magaziner et al., 1988). A vast amount of daily care is regularly provided to

elderly persons by their kin (e.g., Branch & Jette, 1983; Chatters, Taylor, & Jackson, 1985).

The psychological benefits of receiving such instrumental assistance seem to be mixed. Some social scientists have suggested that practical forms of social support often are less beneficial than more generalized emotional support—perhaps because practical assistance can be given in grudging and demeaning ways (Heller, Swindle, & Dusenbury, 1986). But a number of studies have found that the receipt of practical assistance is linked to well-being (e.g., Arling, 1987; Felton & Berry, in press), suggesting that, at least under some conditions, instrumental aid has emotional as well as practical benefits.

Emotional Support. Emotional support seems to be the component of social support that is most consistently related to adjustment. This result has been found in studies of all types of stressors (House & Kahn, 1985). However, giving emotional support to the chronically ill can be difficult. The studies offering the strongest evidence for positive effects of social support in chronic illness have measured social support as a perception or a sense that one is supported. These studies evaluate the overall quality of social support (e.g., Turner & Noh, 1988). Studies that simply assess whether or not a person is being given sympathy or has someone to talk to about personal matters generally find this support less strongly related to emotional well-being among the chronically ill. Lowenthal and Haven's (1968) classic study showed that having a *confidant* offset the negative emotional effects of retirement and widowhood—but did not do so for illness.

A few studies have even found that being the recipient of emotional support was linked to poorer emotional outcomes among cancer patients, at least under conditions of severe disability (Dunkel-Schetter & Wortman, 1982; Revenson, Wollman, & Felton, 1983). Some studies have shown both the benefits of social support and the effects of negative social interaction. Lewis's (1966) findings regarding family overprotectiveness among men recovering from congestive heart failure are an example. Such studies imply that effective social support—especially emotional support—does not flow uniformly from all social ties, not even from all intimate ties.

The Right Kind of Support? The difficulties involved in obtaining the right kind of social support for illness have been illustrated in studies of adults with cancer. People with cancer have been found to feel that the quality of their interactions with others declines and to experience increased feelings of alienation as the illness advances (Wortman & Conway, 1985). In one study, cancer patients perceived that others treated them differently—72 percent reported being misunderstood, and more than half thought that they were being avoided and/or feared (Peters-Golden, 1982).

Misunderstandings about the specific needs of the physically ill for different kinds of support at different stages of the illness are important sources of support-providers' errors. However, the ill individual's own repulsion at physical changes and negative reactions to helplessness, fear, and sadness play significant roles as well.

It is probable that one of the ways in which social support achieves its beneficial results is through enhancing identity and self-esteem. The chronically ill person is encouraged to adopt a problem-solving stance (Ross & Mirowsky, 1989). Other ways in which social support might work are currently being explored. Umberson (1987) has provided data indicating that at least one way in which being married reduces mortality is through its lessening of the propensity to engage in risk-taking behaviors such as excessive drug and alcohol use.

Social support seems to have two ways of providing a beneficial influence on depression. There is a straightforward effect associated with emotional support; i.e., feeling supported makes one feel less depressed. An indirect effect also seems to exist: People who feel supported experience fewer of the day-to-day hassles that reinforce depression (Cutrona & Russell, 1991). Different kinds of mechanisms are undoubtedly at work at different stages of the health-to-illness con-tinuum: The broadly based social integration that seems effective in preventing illness differs from the help-giving types of social support that protect ill people from unpleasant emotional states (e.g., Cutrona, Russell, & Rose, 1986).

Source of Social Support

Recent studies suggesting that the *source* of the social support is more significant than previously thought make it more complicated to determine what kind of social support is most valuable. Lieberman's (1986) review of studies of social support to the bereaved led him to suggest that people develop normative schema about who is the appropriate helper for them in a given set of circumstances. This helper is the person whose support is most counted upon and is perceived as most effective. Support from sources other than the normatively expected provider may become meaningless in light of such schema.

Gerontologists (Cantor, 1979; Rook, 1987) have described older adults' "substitution hierarchy," or their ranking of preferred caregivers:

- Spouses are preferred over children.
- Children are preferred over more distant relatives.
- Distant relatives are preferred over friends and neighbors.

One recent study found that the emotional benefits of practical or instrumental assistance were insignificant if that assistance was provided by nonkin but substantial if provided by kin. On the other hand, reassurance of worth had emotional benefits if provided by nonkin but not if provided by kin (Felton & Berry, in press). Most social relationships are multifaceted; therefore, we must have finely grained assessments of the source as well as the nature, extent, and timing of support.

The possibility that different types of social support are particularly valuable to the individual in meeting different kinds of stressors, needs, or "adaptive tasks" (Wortman & Conway, 1985) implies that long-term assessments of social support are needed. Cohen (1988) describes evidence favoring the proposition that social integration enhances the probabilities of survival most among those who are already ill and proposes that social support may be more beneficial for health at some stages than at others.

Very few longitudinal studies of social support have been undertaken among the chronically ill, however. Johnson & Catalano (1983) showed that the frequency of family contact declined over an eight-month period following elderly patients' discharge from a hospital. Contact with friends remained the same but at a lower level than family contact. We know very little about possible changes in the value of social support as illness continues or worsens, and even less about possible changes in the quality of social relationships over time. Certain functions served by social relationships simply may be abandoned by the chronically ill, especially if these functions require the involvement of nonkin and/or the exercise of energy-intensive abilities (Felton, 1990). Given the centrality of social relationships in people's images of successful adjustment (e.g., Ryff, 1989), changes in social support may be as important as reflections of the chronically ill adult's physical state in predicting her or his continued physical and emotional health.

▼ Barbara J. Felton

See also: Cardiac Health; Chronic Pain as a Lifespan Problem; Depression; Divorce; Gender as a Shaping Force in Adult Development and Aging; Life Events; Longevity; Marital Development; Mexican Americans: Life Course Transitions and Adjustment; Religion in Adult Life; Risk to Life through the Adult Years; Stress.

References

Arling, G. (1987). Strain, social support, and distress in old age. *Journal of Gerontology, 42:* 107-13.

Branch, L. G., & Jette, A. M. (1983). Elder's use of informal assistance. *The Gerontologist, 23:* 51-56.

Bruhn, J. G. (1965). An epidemiological study of myocardial infarctions in an Italian-Ameri-can community. *Journal of Chronic Diseases, 18:* 353-65.

Cantor, M. (1979). Neighbors and friends: An overlooked resource in the informal support system. *Research on Aging, 1:* 434-63.

Chatters, L. M., Taylor, R. J., & Jackson, J. S. (1985). Size and composition of the informal helper networks of elderly blacks. *Journal of Gerontology, 40:* 605-14.

Coe, R. M., et al. (1985). Elderly persons without family support networks and use of health services: A follow-up report on social network relationships. *Research on Aging, 7:* 617-22.

Cohen, S. (1988). Psychosocial models of the role of social support in the etiology of physical disease. *Health Psychology, 7:* 269-97.

Cohen, S., & Wills, T. A. (1985). Stress, social support, and the buffering hypothesis. *Psychological Bulletin, 98:* 310-57.

Cutrona, C. E., & Russell, D. W. (1991). Social support, stress, and depressive symptoms among the elderly: Test of a process model. *Psychology and Aging, 6:* 190-201.

Cutrona, C. E., Russell, D. W., & Rose, J. (1986). Social support and adaptation to stress by the elderly. *Psychology and Aging, 1:* 47-54.

Dunkel-Schetter, C., & Wortman, C. (1982). The interpersonal dynamics of cancer: Problems in social relationships and their impact on the patient. In H. Friedman & M. R. DiMatteo (Eds.), *International Issues in Health Care.* New York: Academic Press, pp. 69-100.

Felton, B. J. (1990). Coping and social support in older people's experiences of chronic illness. In M. A. P. Stephens et al. (Eds.), *Stress and Coping in Later-Life Families.* New York: Hemisphere, pp. 153-71.

Felton, B. J., & Berry, C. A. (in press). Do the sources of the urban elderly's social support determine its psychological consequences? *Psychology and Aging.*

Finlayson, A. (1976). Social networks as coping resources: Lay help and consultation patterns used by women in husband's post-infarction career. *Social Science and Medicine, 10:* 97-103.

Garrity, T. F. (1973). Vocational adjustment after first myocardial infarction: Comparative assessment of several variables suggested in the literature. *Social Science and Medicine, 7:* 705-17.

Heller, K., Swindle, R. W., Jr., & Dusenbury, L. (1986). Component social support processes: Comments and integration. *Journal of Consulting and Clinical Psychology, 54:* 466-70.

House, J. S., & Kahn, R. L. (1985). Measures and concepts of social support. In S. Cohen & S. L. Syme (Eds.), *Social Support and Health.* New York: Academic Press, pp. 83-108.

House, J. S., Landis, K. R., & Umberson, D. (1988). Social relationships and health. *Science, 241:* 540-45.

Johnson, C. L., & Catalano, D. J. (1983). A longitudinal study of family supports to impaired elderly. *The Gerontologist, 23:* 612-18.

Kessler, R. C., & McLeod, J. D. (1985). Social support and mental health in community samples. In S. Cohen & S. L. Syme (Eds.), *Social Support and Health.* New York: Academic Press, pp. 219-40.

Krause, N. (1987). Chronic financial strain, social support, and depressive symptoms in older adults. *Psychology and Aging, 2:* 185-92.

Levy, S. M., et al. (1991). Immunological and psychosocial predictors of disease recurrence in patients with early-stage breast cancer. *Behavioral Medicine, 17:* 67-75.

Lewis, C. E. (1966). Factors influencing the return to work of men with congestive heart failure. *Journal of Chronic Diseases, 19:* 1193-1209.

Lieberman, M. A. (1986). Social supports—The consequences of psychologizing: A commentary. *Journal of Consulting and Clinical Psychology, 54:* 461-65.

Lowenthal, M. F., & Haven, C. (1968). Interaction and adaptation: Intimacy as a critical variable. *American Sociological Review, 33:* 20-30.

Magaziner, J., et al. (1988). Health and living arrangements among older women: Does living alone increase the risk of illness? *Journal of Gerontology, 42:* M127-33.

Peters-Golden, H. (1982). Breast cancer: Varied perceptions of social support in the illness experience. *Social Science and Medicine, 16:* 483-91.

Revenson, T. A., Wollman, C. A., & Felton, B. J. (1983). Social supports as stress buffers for adult cancer patients. *Psychosomatic Medicine, 45:* 321-31.

Rook, K. S. (1987). Reciprocity of social exchange and social satisfaction among older women. *Journal of Personality and Social Psychology, 52:* 145-54.

Ross, C. E., & Mirowsky, J. (1989). Explaining the social patterns of depression: Control and problem-solving—or support and talking? *Journal of Health and Social Behavior, 30:* 206-19.

Ryff, C. D. (1989). In the eye of the beholder: Views of psychological well-being among middle-aged and older adults. *Psychology and Aging, 4:* 195-210.

Stephens, M. A., et al. (1987). Social networks as assets and liabilities in recovery from stroke by geriatric patients. *Psychology and Aging, 2:* 125-29.

Tobin, S. S., & Kulys, R. (1981). The family in the institutionalization of the elderly. *Journal of Social Issues, 37:* 145-57.

Turner, R. J., & Noh, S. (1988). Physical disability and depression: A longitudinal analysis. *Journal of Health and Social Behavior, 29:* 23-37.

Umberson, D. (1987). Family status and health behaviors: Social control as a dimension of social integration. *Journal of Health and Social Behavior, 28:* 306-19.

Wallston, B. S., et al. (1983). Social support and physical health. *Health Psychology, 2:* 367-91.

Wortman, C. B., & Conway, T. L. (1985). The role of social support in adaptation and recovery from physical illness. In S. Cohen & S. L. Syme (Eds.), *Social Support and Health.* New York: Academic Press, pp. 281-302.

Wortman, C. B., & Dunkel-Schetter, C. (1979). Interpersonal relationships and cancer: A theoretical analysis. *Journal of Social Issues, 35:* 120-55.

SPIRITUAL DEVELOPMENT AND WISDOM: A VEDANTIC PERSPECTIVE

Adult development can be seen as an evolutionary feedback process through which people construct and maintain patterns of inner meaning and social relationship (Atchley, 1989). This concept of development can also be applied to the evolution of spiritual awareness and wisdom. The Vedantic perspective from India offers insight into the nature of spiritual development that can be used to link spiritual development, aging, and wisdom.

Vedanta refers to a philosophy reflected at the end of the Hindu Vedas, which date back to at least 1500 B.C. According to this perspective, the body-mind is a vehicle through which consciousness appears. Because the body-mind is embedded in a social environment, early life socialization emphasizes a narrow definition of consciousness as merely an outgrowth of the body-mind and its personality and social roles. First psychological and then social development are given priority in the socialization process. Even religious socialization tends to emphasize the integration of religious practices and concerns into the personality and social roles of the individual. However, psychological and social development, including high achievement and competence in religious behavior, may not satisfy the inner need for meaning. It is this hunger for something more than can be provided by the everyday world, a sense of the true significance of human life, that impels consciousness to seek spiritual development.

"I Am": Turning Inward

Many other religious philosophies presume that spiritual connections and development occur in relation to some entity or principle outside the individual. Vedanta, however, presumes that the ultimate can be found only by turning inward. Conscious presence, the sense "I am," is the vantage point from which the calculating mind can be seen as a limited vehicle for understanding.

Spiritual development is a process of decoupling or detaching consciousness from identification with the body-mind and its personality and external relationships and developing a sense of identification with the inner spirit. One cannot define spirit in concrete terms because it is a quality of existence, not part of the subject-object, dualistic, conceptual world. Thus, one becomes aware of spirit by turning attention inward and slowing down the flow of thought.

Detachment is gained by rising above one's attachments, not by denying them, because denial is a strong form of attachment. To rise above attachments, it is necessary to study the mind and its desires and fears and to learn to experience desires and fears without acting on the impulse to do something

about them. One must learn to be passionately dispassionate.

That which witnesses the mind and its various states is the "I am." As practice is gained at witnessing the mind, experience dwelling in the "I am" increases. Eventually the mind slows down, and then existence without thought is experienced. For those who do not fear it, a no-thought state of consciousness is experienced as a vast warm emptiness full of spiritual joy. Into this serenely happy void often comes another kind of voice than that usually heard within the mind: the voice of nonpersonal consciousness, sometimes called the voice of God. From the vantage point of nonpersonal consciousness, the body-mind with its mélange of fabricated desires and fears is seen as a self-centered entity no better or worse than the other self-centered entities that populate everyday consciousness. The reaction to this perception is often compassion for all beings and an attitude of detachment.

Witnessing thought teaches that "peace of mind" is only a fleeting possibility because the essence of mind is creating differences, analyzing them, and solving problems. There is real peace only *beyond* mind; in the no-thought state, it can be found even in the midst of mental chaos. It exists in the space between thoughts. It is the limitless tableau that forms the background of thought. It is pure "I am."

Flowing with Life

Coming at the world from the sense "I am" means going with the flow of life. "Between the banks of pain and pleasure flows the river of life. It is only when the mind refuses to flow with life and gets stuck at the banks that life becomes a problem. By flowing with life I mean acceptance—letting come what comes and go what goes" (Nisargadatta Maharaj, as quoted in Frydman, 1973, pp. 6-7). "When effort is needed, effort will appear. When effortless becomes essential, it will assert itself. You need not push life about. Just flow with it and give yourself completely to the task of the present moment, which is the now" (Nisargadatta Maharaj, as quoted in Powell, 1984, p. 57). Living a simple life on automatic pilot creates opportunities to just be, which is a spiritual experience that illuminates values.

The work of early life is to create the fully functional social being that is able to fulfill its responsibilities and survive in the world. Lifelong habits of responsibility and action are the automatic pilot that frees the aging individual to turn attention inward and uncover the spirit.

A key to spiritual development is the opportunity and desire to pay intense attention to the fundamental self. "The desire to find the Self will be surely fulfilled, provided you want nothing else. But you must be honest with yourself and really want nothing else. If in the meantime you want many other things and are engaged in their pursuit, your main purpose may be delayed until you grow wider and cease being torn between contradictory urges. Go within, without swerving" (Nisargadatta Maharaj, as quoted by Frydman, 1973, p. 167). One advantage that aging brings to this picture is that long-lived people have by and large achieved their external objectives and are freer to turn their attentions inward.

Vedantic Self-Realization

In the Vedantic tradition, self-realization is the development of nonpersonal consciousness. It is not absorption with one's personal agenda, nor is it a realization of some hidden personality. It is the flowering of a world within that has hitherto been obscured by the drama of everyday life, which persistently claims attentions from one's awareness. "The gospel of self-realization, once heard, will never be forgotten. Like a seed left in the ground, it will wait for the right season and sprout and grow into a mighty tree" (Nisargadatta Maharaj, as quoted by Frydman, 1973, p. 209). Enlightenment can be thought of as a state in which nonpersonal consciousness is ever-present, even in the midst of personal turmoil.

Realizing nonpersonal consciousness is a powerful experience, and it can occur quite suddenly. But to remain steadily in this consciousness, as a context for life, requires persistent and earnest attention. Ripening and flowering are two metaphors often used to describe the process. Known as *sadhana*, this process prepares the way for clarity and charity.

Sustaining the process of self-realization requires faith, trust, patience, insight, and witnessing. Perhaps central is the practice of meditation. The primary purpose of meditation is to become conscious of and familiar with and at one with the inner life. "You begin by letting thoughts flow and watching them. The very observation slows down the mind until it stops altogether. Once the mind is quiet, keep it quiet. Don't get bored with peace, be in it, go deeper into·it" (Nisargadatta Maharaj, as quoted in Frydman, 1973, p. 257).

It is not necessary or even desirable to reject everyday life. "Do your work. When you have a moment free, look within. What is important is not to miss the opportunity when it presents itself.... That is enough.... These moments of inner quiet will burn out all obstacles" (Nisargadatta Maharaj, as quoted by Frydman, 1973, pp. 247-48).

It is worth noting that the model of spiritual development articulated by Nisargadatta Maharaj is not unique to Hinduism. Similar perspectives can be found in the mystical religious texts of Christianity, Islam, Buddhism, Judaism, Taoism, Sufism, and many other religions (Hixon, 1978).

Meditative Prayer in Later Adulthood

What evidence do we have that might support the notion that aging people increase their level of interest in spiritual development? Peacock and Paloma (1991) analyzed data from a 1988 Gallup survey and found a sharp increase with age in meditative prayer. In fact, the age difference in meditative prayer was much greater than that for other types of prayer such as talking to God, ritual prayer, or petitionary prayer. At ages 26 to 45, about 45 percent of the respondents achieved high scores on meditative prayer. Meditative prayer scores were appreciably higher for adults at more advanced age levels: 58 percent for those between 46 and 65, 71 percent of those 66 to 75, and 77 percent among respondents aged 75 or over.

These data were cross-sectional, so the age differences could be the result of cohort differences in perspectives on prayer. To evaluate this possibility, the author analyzed longitudinal data from two studies (Atchley, 1989). As part of the surveys, respondents were asked to rank "being a religious person" on a four-point scale ranging from very important to very unimportant. This measure does not address the issue of meditative prayer but does provide an opportunity to look at changes over time in values related to spiritual issues.

The proportion who rated being religious as very important increased with age in the cross-sectional results for 1977; more importantly, from 1977 to 1982 the percent who scored being religious as very important increased *within* each group. The increase was greater for the older age groups. For example, the proportion of those between age 60 and 69 who rated being religious as very important increased from 21 percent in 1977 to 28 percent in 1981, and the proportion of those 70 to 79 increased from 31 percent to 38 percent. Those aged 80 and older increased from 38 percent to 47 percent. It should be noted that this was a panel study, so the responses were from the same individuals followed over time. Thus, the importance of being religious did actually increase over time, in fact quite markedly so over the relatively short time span of only four years. In sum, data from these two studies support the notion that interest in spirituality increases with age even in the older population.

An Increased Capacity for Wisdom?

Does increased spiritual development in later life increase the capacity for wisdom?

Obviously, a key to answering this question is a definition of wisdom. Achenbaum and Orwoll (1991) provide a comprehensive definition of wisdom based on their excellent review of the literature. In their model, wisdom is a multidimensional construct. Three dimensions deal with emotional (affective), cognitive, and conative (mental processes directed toward action and striving) components of consciousness. Three other dimensions relate to three varieties of target for thought: intrapersonal, interpersonal, and transpersonal.

These two sets of concepts, when cross-classified, yield nine components of wisdom. At the *intrapersonal* level, wisdom consists of self-development, self-knowledge, and integrity. Self-development involves self-examination for purposes of honest evaluation. Self-knowledge is an acceptance of what one is actually like. Integrity involves attaching meaning to the self's existence.

All three qualities of intrapersonal wisdom require the ability to view oneself from a vantage point outside oneself. At the *interpersonal* level, wisdom consists of empathy, understanding, and maturity in relationships. All three components of interpersonal wisdom require the ability to stand outside one's own self-centered perspective to view others with acceptance. Thus, the *transpersonal* level—the capacity to transcend the personal self—is the key to wisdom. It allows one to transcend narrow personal emotions, comprehend the limits of personal knowledge and understanding, and strive for spiritual rather than personal worldly aims. And this transpersonal perspective allows wisdom to be brought into the intrapersonal and interpersonal arenas of life. The transpersonal perspective cited by Achenbaum and Orwoll (1991) is quite similar to the nonpersonal consciousness discussed earlier.

Aging may be related to spiritual development and wisdom through both internal and external shifts that occur over the life course. The increase in interiority that has been found to occur in personality in later adulthood was referred to earlier. This turning inward can serve as a stimulus for spiritual development, presuming that spiritual development lies within. Contemplation of one's inner life produces the perspective needed for intrapersonal wisdom. Contemplation can also reveal much about the nature of human relationships that can result in their transformation in the direction of interpersonal wisdom. Finally, contemplation requires an attitude of dispassionate witnessing that promotes the development of nonpersonal consciousness, which is a crucial final step toward transpersonal wisdom.

External changes over the lifespan also promote contemplation, spiritual development, and wisdom. The age-related reduction in external responsibilities, which can accompany the completion of child rearing and retirement from employment, simplifies life and reduces external conflicts to an extent that can create added opportunities for meditation and contemplation. For example, Larson, Zuzanek, and Mannell (1985) studied 92 retired adults who carried electronic pagers for one week. The respondents were paged at random times throughout the week and asked to fill out self-reports about their relationships and internal states. The researchers found that the respondents voluntarily spent almost half of their waking hours alone, but being alone was not a negative experience for a large majority of them. When they were alone, the respondents tended to be doing things that required concentration and challenge, which suggested to the researchers that they were highly engaged, but *not* interpersonally. Solitude was not a negative, vegetative state, but rather an opportunity for focused thought and absorption.

When this single-minded concentration is turned upon spiritual issues, the prospects for spiritual development are probably high. Thus, there is evidence that the social conditions for many people in later life are conducive to spiritual development. Opportunity is not enough, however. There must also be a desire to go beyond personal existence in the search for meaning. That such motivation exists is reflected in the data on the increased importance of religiosity and meditative prayer.

Combining ideas from religious philosophy, human development, and social science provides a broad view of spiritual development and wisdom that perhaps gets us closer to understanding these enigmatic phenomena. In particular, it makes the case that spiritual development, which is often ignored in adult developmental research, is crucial to the relationship of aging to wisdom. It is spiritual development that brings wisdom, not aging per se.

▼ ROBERT C. ATCHLEY

See also: Adult Development and Aging, Models of; Attachment Across the Lifespan; Cohort and Generational Effects; Development and Aging in Historical Perspective; Religion in Adult Life; Trust as a Challenge in Adult Development.

References

Achenbaum, W. A., & Orwoll, L. (1991). Becoming wise: A psychogerontological interpretation of the Book of Job. *International Journal of Aging & Human Development, 32*: 21-39.

Atchley, R. C. (1989). A continuity theory of normal aging. *The Gerontologist, 29:* 183-90.

Balsekar, R. S. (1982). *Pointers from Nisargadatta Maharaj.* Durham, NC: Acorn Press.

Frydman, M. (1973). *I Am That.* Bombay: Chetana.

Hixon, L. (1978). *Coming Home: The Experience of Enlightenment in Sacred Traditions.* New York: Anchor Books.

Larson, R., Zuzanek, J., & Mannell, R. (1985). Being alone versus being with people: Disengagement in the daily experience of older adults. *Journal of Gerontology, 40:* 375-81.

Peacock, J. R., & Paloma, M. M. (1991). Religiosity and life satisfaction across the life course. Paper presented at the annual conference of the Society for the Scientific Study of Religion. Pittsburgh, PA, November.

Powell, R. (1984). *The Blissful Life.* Durham, NC: Acorn Press.

STRESS

The field of stress research emerged in the early 1940s and has subsequently undergone many changes. To provide an understanding of where the field is today, this review first presents basic information on matters of definition and social significance. Next, attention is given to three complementary approaches that have been used effectively to study stress: *catastrophe research, life event research,* and research on the *stressors of everyday life.* Although each approach has its flaws, each also has something to contribute to the present-day study of how "the slings and arrows of outrageous fortune" affect people's lives.

Definitions and Social Significance of Stress

When encountering the world of stress research for the first time, people often are dismayed to find how differently the word *stress* itself has been used. Many clinical and laboratory-based experiments, for example, define stress in terms of behaviors that follow exposure to stress conditions (e.g., Selye, 1956). Among humans, heart rate and depression are common indicators of stress. Defecation or urination after exposure to an electric grid is a typical measure of stress in studies involving rats and mice.

On the other hand, researchers who study stress in the community often use the term "stress" to refer not to the responses but to the provoking condition or stressor. Still others use the term much more broadly and refer to a model or paradigm that includes both the stressor and the response, as well as various mediating factors. Perhaps one needs a certain amount of stress tolerance to study the studies of stress.

Simple and Complex Stress Paradigms. The simplest stress paradigm includes only two elements: the stressor and the stress response. For example, many early studies of so-called life events were trying to learn whether or not stress events predicted physical illness. While most of these studies found significant but weak relationships, the guiding paradigm has been criticized as being overly mechanical since it implies a direct relationship between stressor and response. The assumption that a stressor has a direct and powerful response-producing effect is also the assumption that the organism/person itself does not have much to do with the matter.

Central to more recent stress paradigms is the notion that the relationship between stress exposure and response is orchestrated by a variety of mediators. These include social supports, self-esteem, and coping strategies (Ensel & Lin, 1991; Lazarus & Folkman, 1984). The basic paradigm includes three elements: stressors, mediators, and responses. The *stressors* are impinging or provoking agents, including life events as well as more chronic strains and daily hassles. *Mediators* include characteristics of both the person and the environment. *Responses* can be divided into those that occur shortly after stress exposure and those that reflect long-term adaptation. Most investigators consider physical health responses ranging from hypertension to the common cold and psychological responses such as anxiety or depression.

Positive and Negative Stressors. Since they represent conditions that create disruption or a need for readjustment, stressors can run the gamut from death and divorce to vacations and promotions. A number of stress inventories, especially those dealing with specific events, either include both positive and negative items (e.g., Holmes & Rahe, 1967) or allow respondents to make such distinctions themselves (e.g., Chiriboga, 1977; Dohrenwend, 1986; Landerman et al., 1989). Negative stressors usually correlate more strongly with mental or physical problems, while positive stressors are associated with well-being.

Why Study Stress? The rapid growth of stress research owes much to the fact that stressors predict a variety of significant problems related to social, physical, and mental health. Stressors have been associated with everything from coronary heart disease to general psychiatric symptomatology (e.g., Dohrenwend, 1986; Fiske & Chiriboga, 1990) to major depression (Brown & Harris, 1989). The diagnostic categories of Post Traumatic Stress Disorder and Adjustment Disorders are now viewed as consequences of stress exposure (Noshpitz & Coddington, 1990).

Stress and Depression

The most well-documented outcome of stress exposure is depression. Whether the predictor is a comprehensive summary of stressors or a specific condition such as chronic stress at work or sudden unemployment, higher levels of depression are reported for adults of all ages.

Stress in the family has received the bulk of the attention, perhaps because family relationships and situations endure for prolonged periods of time, and any real or threatened change may therefore have greater impact (Pearlin & Turner, 1987). The death of family members can result in depression and even death among the survivors (Brown & Harris, 1989), and similar findings have been reported for divorce.

The caregiving role is also of concern. For example, low-income adolescent mothers of infants report greater depression (McKenry et al., 1990). Chronic parenting stress can lead to depression in young adults (Quittner, Glueckauf, & Jackson, 1990), as can providing care for an older, dependent spouse or parent (Chiriboga, Yee, & Weiler, 1992; Zarit, Orr, & Zarit, 1985).

New Directions. Perhaps the most exciting new avenue of stress research deals with the specific linkage between stress and physical health. For example, in a carefully controlled study of viral infections in blood and nasal secretions, Cohen, Tyrell, and Smith (1991) found that stress responses predict rates of infection. One explanation is that a response such as depression leads to compromised immunological functioning which, in turn, lowers host resistance to disease (e.g., Kiecolt-Glaser & Glaser, 1988; Vogt, 1992).

But whether the focus of attention be on physiological processes or mental health outcomes, most researchers today would agree that the critical predisposing factor is *not* some objectively determined level of stress exposure. Instead, the critical factor is the individual's appraisal of how threatening or challenging the situation is (Fiske & Chiriboga, 1990; Lazarus & Folkman, 1984).

Developmental Perspectives on Stress

Stressors deserve study not only because of their effects on health but also because they constitute an important set of determinants of continuity and change in adult personality. For example, a study in which a panel of men and women were repeatedly interviewed over a period of 12 years found that those who had been subjected to fewer stress events showed greater stability in measures of self-concept and psychological symptoms (Fiske & Chiriboga, 1990). The life-course implications of stressors can be far-reaching, as evidenced by Elder's (1974) finding that the Great Depression, when experienced during particular stages of childhood, continued to influence the individuals' lives some 30 or 40 years later.

Age differences in the experiencing of stressful situations are another source of interest to students of adult development. Over the past two decades, one finding has been repeated over and over again: Younger people are more likely to report life events—both positive and negative—than are older adults. There is also evidence that, when asked about similar events, older people appraise them as less threatening or undesirable than do younger adults.

The frequency of stressful events may begin to decline at some point in later middle age, and older adults may generally perceive events in less negative terms. However, significant exceptions must be recognized. For example, stressors related to deaths of family members and friends, and to personal health problems, are reported more frequently by those aged 70 and over (Fiske & Chiriboga, 1990; Hurwicz et al., 1992).

Older people are also more likely to report as personally stressful the situations their children and friends are facing (e.g., Kastenbaum, 1988). And, as will be seen in the following section, older people may also be more threatened by natural disasters or disruptive situations such as involuntary relocation.

Research Based on Catastrophe Models

Current stress research represents an amalgamation of methodologies that have been tried since the 1940s. Early studies focused on how people responded to extremely disruptive life circumstances. Lindemann's (1944) observations on survivors of the Coconut Grove fire and Grinker and Spiegel's (1945) classic study of American soldiers in World War II serve as pioneering examples of this genre of stress research.

Stress as a Given. A hallmark of the catastrophe model is the assumption that all the individuals involved were subjected to extremely distressing life circumstances. This line of research often draws on the survivors of life-threatening conditions such as combat, internment in concentration camps, and exposure to severe floods, hurricanes, and tornadoes. The underlying question is how individuals fare, given their exposure to high levels of stress.

An example taken from aging research deals with the nature of significance of relocation. As early as the 1920s, concerns were being raised about the impact of involuntary relocation upon older persons. In the 1950s and 1960s, studies demonstrated significant mortality and morbidity both shortly after relocation and over periods of a year or more. More recent work (e.g., Tobin, 1989) has focused on mediating factors and outcome. Results indicate that being provided with information concerning the new environment and feeling some level of control over the relocation itself may alleviate distress.

The Evolving Stress Response. One of the more impressive contributions of catastrophe research is a well-replicated clinical description of how behaviors and symptoms emerge following exposure to major threat. The stages of stress response can be characterized as (1) emotional numbing, (2) outcry, (3) denial, (4) intrusive thoughts, (5) working through, and (6) resolution and acceptance (Horowitz, 1986). Although equally appropriate to younger and older persons, the stages may not always unfold in the same order.

Heightened Risk of Elderly Persons. From the early work of Friedsam (1960) to the present (Phifer, 1990), researchers have emphasized the special vulnerabilities of elderly people to many catastrophic conditions. On the other hand, there is evidence that *for all age groups the unexpected crisis is more devastating*: Looking just at bereavements, widowers may be more vulnerable than widows, young adults may react more strongly than old, and the death of a child may be the most disruptive loss of all.

The Potential of Catastrophe Research. By focusing on people who have experienced major stressors, this genre of research has the advantage of a clearly defined population and it also addresses problems of compelling social and personal significance. However, a number of problems are associated with this approach, including:

1. *Heterogeneity of response.* Studies based on this model often assume that the stress situation is essentially equivalent across individuals. Nevertheless, there are often marked variations in how people perceive what to an external observer might appear to be similar situations.
2. *Sampling problems.* When attempting to study people who have just experienced a devastating event, more problems than usual may be encountered in identifying prospective respondents and in securing their cooperation while they are still in a highly distraught state (Baum, 1987).
3. *Generalizability.* Given the presumed severity, and the rarity, of extreme stressful conditions, questions can be raised concerning how generalizable the results might be to problems faced by most people in their everyday stress experiences.

During the late 1980s and the early 1990s, a new cohort of clinicians and researchers has emerged who are following catastrophe models of research, but with a broadening of the definition of catastrophe. Topics now include the psychological and social trauma associated with problems such as rape and cancer (e.g., Taylor & Dakoff,

1988; Wortman & Silver, 1987). Studies of occupational stress or caregiving can also be subsumed under this model (Zarit, Orr, & Zarit, 1985).

Research Based on Life Events

The catastrophe approach may be appropriate when studying particular groups of distressed individuals. Other approaches, however, may be more suitable to studies of the general population. This may explain the appearance of a new genre of research, the so-called life events approach, in the 1960s. The first instruments were brief checklists of relatively common situations. Life events research began in earnest, however, only when an instrument became available that combined a more comprehensive list of events with a standard weighting scale for event severity: the Schedule of Recent Events (SRE).

Measures of Life Events. The 42-item SRE (Holmes & Rahe, 1967) was first seen as relevant to all age groups. For many years the "gold standard" in assessing stress exposure, the SRE included a sophisticated weighting system based on the assumption that each life event imposed an equivalent demand for readjustment on people representing diverse economic and cultural groups. The SRE was brief and readily comprehensible by both researchers and respondents.

After problems surfaced with item content and standardization procedures, the instrument was revised and expanded to included 77 items (Rahe, 1978). Other instruments also emerged, including the Psychiatric Epidemiology Research Interview (PERI) Events Scale (Dohrenwend, 1986) and the Life Events Questionnaire (Chiriboga, 1977).

Perhaps the most widely accepted alternative to the SRE is the PERI Events Scale. With 102 items, the PERI is one of the more comprehensive event inventories and has lifespan applicability. It was designed to overcome the problems identified in the SRE, including ambiguous phrasing and a scarcity of positive or desirable events. Several alternative standardized weightings are available, in addition to a simple count of events.

Selection of the appropriate scoring system depends on the situation and sample.

One advantage of event inventories is that they are readily adapted for use with specialized populations such as children, surgical patients, graduate students, or older persons. For example, Coddington (1972) has developed inventories specific to different stages of childhood, and a number of investigators have revised the original SRE for use with older populations (e.g., Kahana, Kahana, & Young, 1987). Several other inventories have been either revised or developed specifically for older populations.

The PERI has also been adapted for use with older populations. For example, Cohen, Teresi, and Holmes (1985) reduced the PERI scale to 15 items. Modifications are not always so drastic. In creating a more age-relevant instrument, Krause (1986) reduced the PERI scale but added items from other scales to obtain a 77-item inventory.

Still another useful procedure is The Louisville Older Persons Events Scale (LOPES). Murrell, Norris, and Grote (1988) developed LOPES as a broad-spectrum inventory of older persons. The instrument is unusual in that the 54 items were selected on the basis of extensive pretesting with older populations. LOPES also elicits information on life events that are experienced over a shorter time period (six months) than is usually the case with event inventories.

Lewinsohn and his colleagues have developed several stress inventories that have lifespan relevance. The Pleasant Events Schedule (PES) and Unpleasant Events Schedule were developed on the basis of reports by respondents primarily of college age but including older individuals as well. The instrument has been revised by considering impact and frequency of occurrence of events among persons aged 50 and over (Teri & Lewinsohn, 1982).

Evaluating the Life Events Approach. A problem inherent to life event inventories is that there are limits to the number of events that respondents can be expected to review, and no one instrument can possibly cover all stressors. Most event inventories therefore include items appropriate only to limited segments of the population. The geriatric event inventories, for example, contain items relevant primarily to older adults, while at least half the items contained in the Schedule of Recent Events are relevant only to young and middle-aged adults.

The use of standardized weighting systems is also suspect because group variations have been found in the assessment of event impact (Chiriboga, 1977). For example, in later analyses of data used to develop the original SRE weighting system of Holmes and Rahe (1967), significant age differences on assigned rates were found for approximately two-thirds of life events. Some instruments circumvent this problem by asking the respondents themselves to rate events on characteristics such as their expectedness, degree of control over the situation, or desirability (e.g., Landerman et al., 1989).

Despite their drawbacks, life event inventories with standardized weights do continue to be the method of choice for many researchers. When inventories appropriate to the particular populations are used, much valuable information can be obtained. However, all these inventories exhibit one inherent flaw: By definition, they assess only life events.

Stressors of Everyday Life

From the mid-1970s onward, a number of instruments have been developed either to supplement or replace life event inventories. These alternatives focus on conditions that range from daily hassles to the more enduring or chronic stressors. Anticipated events and "nonevents" (things that did not happen) have also been suggested as relevant to all ages. There is evidence that, for persons in the middle and later years, stressful experiences of their children and friends play an increasingly important role (Fiske & Chiriboga, 1990).

The alternative approaches may be grouped into three categories, the micro, mezzo, and macro.

Stressors at the *micro* level focus on the seemingly minor problems of everyday life. Examples include getting caught in a traffic jam or running out of hot water while taking a shower. Although probably the most commonly experienced type of stressors, they are also the least investigated. Several studies conclude that day-to-day events or "hassles" are more strongly correlated than life events with physical and psychosocial outcomes (Lazarus & Folkman, 1984; Zautra et al., 1988).

The most studied of the three levels, *mezzo* stressors are found in situations that are generally more memorable and important than micro stressors. Life events fall into this category, as do stressors of a more chronic or enduring nature (Pearlin, 1985). Other mezzo stressors include anticipated stressors, nonevents, and transitions (Fiske & Chiriboga, 1990; Kemeny et al., 1989).

Stressors at the *macro* level are those that occur to such elements of society as a community, a state, or even the nation as a whole. War in the Middle East, major economic downturns, a flurry of near-misses in the air lanes, or oil spills not only create headlines but also arouse anxiety and a generally heightened sense of distress. For example, Brenner (1985) reported a very strong linkage between downturns in the U.S. economy and upturns in admission rates to mental institutions. Among gerontologists, perhaps the best known macro-level research is Glen Elder's (1974) previously mentioned analysis of the long-term impact of the Great Depression. Elder and others suggest that the entire course of adult life is profoundly affected by the social and physical environment.

Toward an Integrated Model of Social Stressors

Letting go of the Schedule of Recent Events as the gold standard has freed researchers to explore more innovative and diverse approaches to stress measurement. The active pursuit of alternatives to life event methodologies has generated a wealth of concepts and instruments designed to assess stressors. The result is that researchers today, whether they be gerontologists or child counselors, have available a number of options when selecting instruments.

One drawback to the rapid proliferation of stress indices over the past decade has been that there may be too many choices. Many of the newer instruments are still in the developmental stage, their psychometric properties are not well described, and their interrelationships are poorly understood. Overall, stress research today is entering an age of complexity in which the empirical models not only are very sophisticated but also incorporate multiple approaches to measuring the stressor component of the stress paradigm.

A Final Comment. Research on social stress has not only theoretical but also immensely practical implications. While scientists may be fascinated by the linkages between stress exposure and psychological functioning and physical health, the lay reader may be equally encouraged by the many daily life applications of this area of vigorous research. Already, for example, many health facilities offer special therapeutic programs focused on helping people cope with stressors such as work stress and job loss, sexual assault, and bereavement. Many employers provide special programs to help alleviate work-related stress, and most insurance companies now recognize the authenticity of stress disorders. Public school systems commonly utilize stress management interventions with students when classmates are injured or killed in accidents or by the unfortunate shootings that occur with increasing frequency today, both on and off campus. Even the pharmaceutical companies are entering the scene, with specialized vitamin formulas for periods of unusual stress.

The attention currently paid to stress research by the media, as well as by professionals, may have some undesirable side effects, such as unreasonable expectations for quick solutions and cures. However, it may also contribute to a heightened public awareness of personal stress experiences and their consequences for both children and adults.

Surprisingly, it is not uncommon for people to be completely unaware that they are stressed to the point of breakdown. In the future, people may be as likely to take their "stress temperature" via simple inventories as to monitor their body temperature with thermometers.　　　▼ David A. Chiriboga

See also: Age 40; Alcohol Use and Abuse; Cardiac Health; Chronic Pain as a Lifespan Problem; Conflict as a Challenge in Adult Development; Depression; Divorce; Expressive Arts; Life Events; Mid-Life Crisis; Military Service: Long-Term Effects on Adult Development; Privacy Issues; Religion and Coping with Crisis; Risk to Life through the Adult Years; Rural Living: What Influence on Adult Development?; Social Support for the Chronically Ill; Travel: Stimulus to Adult Development; Widowhood: The Coping Response; Work Capacity Across the Adult Years.

References

Baum, A. (1987). Toxins, technology, and natural disasters. In G. R. VandenBos & B. K. Bryant (Eds.), *Cataclysms, Crises, and Catastrophes: Psychology in Action.* Washington, DC: American Psychological Association.

Brenner, M. H. (1985). Economic change and the suicide rate: A population model including loss, separation, illness, and alcohol consumption. In M. R. Zales (Ed.), *Stress in Health and Disease.* New York: Brunner/Mazel.

Brown, G. W., & Harris, T. O. (1989). Depression. In G. W. Brown & T. O. Harris (Eds.), *Life Events and Illness.* New York: Guilford Press.

Chiriboga, D. A. (1977). Life event weighting systems: A comparative analysis. *Journal of Psychosomatic Research, 21:* 415-21.

Chiriboga, D. A., Yee, B. W. K., & Weiler, P. G. (1992). Stress in the context of caring. In L. Montada, S. Filipp, & M. J. Lerner (Eds.), *Life Crises and Experience of Loss in Adulthood.* Hillsdale, NJ: Lawrence Erlbaum, pp. 95-118.

Coddington, R. D. (1972). The significance of life events as etiologic factors in the diseases of children. II. A study of a normal population. *Journal of Psychosomatic Research, 16:* 205-13.

Cohen, C. I., Teresi, J. & Holmes, D. (1985). Social networks, stress, and physical health. *Journal of Gerontology, 40:* 478-86.

Cohen, S., Tyrell, D. A. J., & Smith, A. P. (1991). Psychological stress and susceptibility to the common cold. *New England Journal of Medicine, 325*: 506-12.

Dohrenwend, P. B. (1986). Note on a program of research on alternative social psychological models of relationships between life stress and psychopathology. In M. H. Appley & R. Turnbull (Eds.), *Dynamics of Stress: Physiological, Psychological, and Social Perspectives.* New York: Plenum.

Elder, G. H., Jr. (1974). *Children of the Great Depression.* Chicago: University of Chicago Press.

Ensel, W. M., & Lin, N. (1991). The life stress paradigm and psychological distress. *Journal of Health and Social Behavior, 32:* 321-41.

Fiske, M., & Chiriboga, D. A. (1990). *Change and Continuity in Adult Life.* San Francisco: Jossey-Bass.

Friedsam, H. J. (1960). Older persons as disaster casualties. *Journal of Health and Human Behavior, 1:* 269-73.

Grinker, R. R., & Spiegel, J. P. (1945). *Men Under Stress.* New York: McGraw-Hill.

Holmes, T., & Rahe, R. (1967). The social readjustment rating scale. *Journal of Psychosomatic Research, 11:* 213-18.

Horowitz, M. J. (1986). *Stress Response Syndromes.* Second Edition. New Jersey: Jason Aronson.

Hurwicz, M. L., et al. (1992). Salient life events in three generation families. *Journal of Gerontology, 47:* P11-13.

Kahana, E. F., Kahana, B., & Young, R. (1987). Infuences of diverse stress on health and well-being of community aged. In A. M. Fowler (Ed.), *Post Traumatic Stress.* Washington, DC: Veterans Administration.

Kastenbaum, R. (1988). Vicarious grief: An intergenerational phenomenon? *Death Studies, 12:* 447-53.

Kemeny, M. E., et al. (1989). Psychological and immunological predictors of genital herpes recurrence. *Psychosomatic Medicine, 51:* 195-208.

Kiecolt-Glaser, J. K., & Glaser, R. (1988). Behavioral influences on immune function: Evidence for the interplay between stress and health. In T. M. Field, P. M. McCabe, & N. Schneiderman (Eds.), *Stress and Coping Across Development.* Hillsdale, NJ: Lawrence Erlbaum.

Krause, N. (1986). Life stress as a correlate of depression among older adults. *Psychiatry-Res, 18:* 227-37.

Landerman, R., et al. (1989). Alternative models of the stress buffering hypothesis. *American Journal of Community Psychology, 17:* 625-42.

Lazarus, R. S., & Folkman, S. (1984). *Stress Appraisal, and Coping.* New York: Springer.

Lindemann, E. (1944). Symptomatology and management of acute grief. *American Journal of Psychiatry, 101:* 141-48.

McKenry, P. C., et al. (1990). Mediators of depression among low-income, adolescent mothers of infants: A longitudinal perspective. *Journal of Youth & Adolescence, 19:* 327-47.

Murrell, S. A., Norris, F. H., & Grote, C. (1988). Life events in older adults. In L. H. Cohen (Ed.), *Life Events and Psychological Functioning.* Newbury Park, CA: Sage.

Noshpitz, J. D., & Coddington, R. D. (Eds.). (1990). *Stressors and the Adjustment Disorders.* Somerset, NJ: John Wiley & Sons.

Pearlin, L. I. (1985). Life strains and psychological distress among adults. In A. Monat & R. S. Lazarus (Eds.), *Stress and Coping: An Anthology.* Second Edition. New York: Columbia University Press.

Pearlin, L. I., & Turner, H. A. (1987). The family as a context of the stress process. In S. V. Kasl & C. L. Cooper (Eds.), *Stress and Health: Issues in Research Methodology.* Chichester, England: John Wiley & Sons.

Phifer, J. F. (1990). Psychological distress and somatic symptoms after natural disasters: Differential vulnerability among older adults. *Psychology and Aging, 5:* 412-20.

Quittner, A. L., Glueckauf, R. L., & Jackson, D. N. (1990). Chronic parenting stress: Moderating versus mediating effects of social supports. *Journal of Personality & Social Psychology, 59:* 1266-78.

Rahe, R. H. (1978). Life change measurement clarification. *Psychosomatic Medicine, 40:* 95-98.

Selye, H. (1956). *The Stress of Life.* New York: McGraw-Hill.

Taylor, S. E., & Dakoff, G. A. (1988). Social support and the cancer patient. In S. Spacapan & S. Oskamp (Eds.), *The Social Psychology of Health.* Newbury Park, CA: Sage.

Teri, L., & Lewinsohn, P. (1982). Modification of the pleasant and unpleasant events schedules for use with the elderly. *Journal of Consulting and Clinical Psychology, 50:* 444-45.

Tobin, S. S. (1989). The effects of institutionalization. In K. S. Markides & C. L. Cooper (Eds.), *Aging, Stress, and Health.* New York: John Wiley & Sons.

Vogt, T. M. (1992). Aging, stress and illness: Psychobiological linkages. In M. G. Ory, R. P. Abeles, & P. D. Lipman (Eds.), *Aging, Health and Behavior*. Newbury Park, CA: Sage.

Wortman, C., & Silver, R. (1987). Coping with irrevocable loss. In G. R. VandenBos & B. K. Bryant (Eds.), *Cataclysms, Crises, and Catastrophes: Psychology in Action*. Washington, DC: American Psychological Association.

Zarit, S. H., Orr, N. K., & Zarit, J. M. (1985). *The Hidden Victims of Alzheimer's Disease: Families Under Stress*. New York: New York University Press.

Zautra, A. J., et al. (1988). The contribution of small events to stress and distress. In L. H. Cohen (Ed.), *Life Events and Psychological Functioning*. Newbury Park, CA: Sage.

SUBCULTURAL INFLUENCES ON LIFELONG DEVELOPMENT

Many social structures and systems help to shape the individual's development as an adult. These influences include social and economic class, ethnic and cultural background, family relations, and interpersonal relationships. When examining contemporary Western societies, however, one must add *subculture* to this list. Subcultures are very common in most industrialized nations. Punks, mods, skinheads, hippies, beatniks, gays, and even Rastafarians are all examples of the wide variety of groups that are associated with identifiable subcultures.

Subcultures have a profound effect upon their members, providing social contacts, values, and a sense of belonging. Indeed, for many people, the subculture may constitute their primary social system. To understand more fully the influence of subcultures on lifelong development, one must consider first the nature of subcultures themselves.

Nature and Functions of Subcultures

What is a subculture? Providing a strict, exact definition of subculture is difficult because subcultures take so many different forms in contemporary society. Most subcultures, however, do share three features.

First, subcultures typically are associated with recognizable life-styles. Motorcycle clubs, punk rockers, and retirement communities are all identified with particular life-styles. By this term is meant a generally uniform set of values and behaviors that is shared by the members of the subculture. Paul Willis (1978) describes the life-style of a subculture as a *homology*: The values and behaviors of a subculture are systematically related in a way that "makes sense" to its members but that may seem alien or lawless to outsiders. A good example of such a homology was the hippie life-style, which combined the values of "dropping out" and "turning on" with drug use, "love-ins," and psychedelic fashions and music in a way that was, at once, coherent and meaningful for its members but confusing and foreign to the dominant culture.

Second, individuals within a subculture are separated from the larger culture only in terms of this life-style. There are rarely strict geographic or language barriers isolating subcultures; therefore, interactions with the larger culture remain relatively frequent. This, in fact, is what makes a subculture a *sub*culture: It is *part* of a larger cultural system. An urban gang member, for example, is likely to encounter people from the larger culture in a variety of settings: in the supermarket or liquor store, on public transit, in school, or even, in the worst case, in the judicial system.

Third, subcultures tend to develop social institutions that are parallel to, but distinct from, those in the larger culture. These may include alternative media (magazines, newspapers, radio stations), segregated leisure activities (nightclubs, games), and even economic structures (retail outlets, mail-order houses). Many youth subcultures, for example, are organized around various forms of pop music: heavy metal, speed metal, punk, and industrial/noise, to name just a few. Members of these cultures typically read magazines and listen to radio stations that are devoted to their particular genre of music. They attend clubs where their music is played or performed. They buy their music and often their clothing at "alternative" stores that cater to their subculture. Such social institutions provide social contacts for members of a subculture and, further, help to stabilize and clarify the life-styles that identify various subcultures.

Why are subcultures important in lifelong development? Subcultures provide their members with what Erving Goffman (1963) calls *ego identity*: a sense of one's own personal character and of one's situation in relation to society as a whole. The life-style of a subculture, as noted above, helps its members make sense of their experience in the world and, as such, provides a focus for self-definition.

A subculture also contributes to the social identity of its members. Undoubtedly, one of the most important social functions of a subculture is the provision of social contacts and a sense of belonging to its members. However, subcultural affiliation also indicates separation from the larger culture. A member of a subculture is saying, in effect: "I *belong* to this particular group, and I am *different* from the rest of society." Thus, it is through both a sense of belonging and a sense of separation that subcultures provide their members with a social identity.

Of course, the extent to which subcultures contribute to ego identity can vary. For some members, subcultural affiliation is the central component of both their self-concept and their social identity. Such members are said to be highly ego-involved in relation to the subculture. Other members, however, may view their participation in a subculture as only one part of their overall self-concept and social identity.

In addition to this central function of providing ego identity, subcultures may also fulfill political functions, seeking to empower their members. Sometimes this political function is implicit, as in the case of the mods, a subculture that responded to high youth unemployment by adopting the affluent fashions of upwardly mobile white-collar workers (Hall & Jefferson, 1976). In other cases,

however, a political function is quite explicit. The punk subculture, for example, was explicitly—and often militantly—political, as evidenced in the lyrics of punk groups such as the Sex Pistols and Clash. Similar political functions are apparent in groups associated with elderly adults, such as the Gray Panthers.

When, in the course of their lives, are people most likely to join a subculture? Many people never join a subculture. However, when such affiliation does occur, it is typically during periods of transition in life, periods in which individuals may experience an "identity crisis." Thus, the most common type of subculture is the youth subculture. Young adults breaking away from the family often require a new social group to provide a sense of self and social identity and, accordingly, join subcultures. In such situations, subcultures offer not only a system of social support but also a means for youths to distinguish themselves from their parents and to resist the perceived oppression of family life (Hall & Jefferson, 1976).

However, the transition to adult independence is not the only transition in life. Another common transition that may lead to subcultural affiliation occurs at retirement. Retiring workers often suffer a loss of identity and therefore seek new social support and identity in retirement communities and leisure clubs that may be organized around such activities as playing golf, bridge, or bingo, or, increasingly, travel and renewed education. Although not all such social organizations are truly subcultural, many demonstrate the essential features of subcultures outlined above, especially senior adult communities such as Sun City and Leisure World.

There is a second common scenario in which individuals are likely to join a subculture—one that also relates to the identity functions of subcultures. Sometimes an individual forms a close friendship or romantic relationship with an individual who is already a member of a subculture. To increase identification with this friend or lover, the individual may join the subculture himself or herself. If and when such a personal relationship comes to an end, the initiated member may or may not leave the subculture, depending on the extent to which this new member has restructured his or her identity in relation to the subculture.

Since individuals typically go through a series of identity transitions and close relationships in the course of their lives, subcultural affiliation, when it occurs, tends to be a *stage* in adult development. A given individual may go through one or more periods during which he or she joins and then leaves a subculture. It is less common for individuals to remain with a single subculture throughout the entire adult life course, although this does happen on occasion.

Given that people tend to join different types of subcultures at different points in life, the following discussion of the types of subcultural affiliation that are associated with different stages in life is useful.

Youth Subculture

As already noted, youth subcultures are the most common and most easily recognized subcultures. There are several explanations for this. First, the transition from adolescence to adult independence may be the most disruptive identity transition in most people's lives, leading to a greater need for subcultural affiliation. Second, young people have relatively high levels of leisure time, which makes them susceptible to the lifestyle attractions of subcultures. Third, the social circles of youths typically consist of others of very similar age—people who are going through the same transition process. This facilitates the formation of (and recruitment into) social collectives such as subcultures.

Youth subcultures typically provide a "way station" in adult development. Between the security of the family and the construction of a new independent identity, youths find comfort and resistance in subcultures. In examining the mod and teddy-boy subcultures in post-World War II Britain, Hall and Jefferson (1976) concluded that these two divergent groups fulfilled essentially the same functions: They let their members know that they were not alone in their alienation from family and society, and they provided a means for their members to facilitate their alienation and separation from the family. Allegiance to a youth subculture is seldom met with parental approval and, as such, the members of such subcultures are provided with a focus and framework for interpreting and expressing their feelings of isolation and of being misunderstood by their families.

However, because of this emphasis on resistance and alienation, the value systems of youth subcultures are rarely functional in the long run and membership in youth subcultures is usually temporary. The long-term costs of adhering to the values of resistance and alienation are considerable. Such values make it difficult for members of youth subcultures to secure satisfactory employment in mainstream society. These values also constrain interpersonal relationships with individuals outside of the subculture, including restored relationships with parents and siblings.

Thus, once members of youth subcultures complete the transition to adult independence, membership in the subculture becomes less appealing both economically and socially. New social systems start to provide support and identity as youths secure career employment, get married, or have children. It then becomes increasingly unsatisfactory to adhere to a value system that is based on alienation and resistance. As a result, most members of youth subcultures eventually leave the subculture.

Subcultures in Middle Age

There has been virtually no research into the role of subcultures in middle age, perhaps because mid-life traditionally has been regarded as a relatively stable period in terms of the individual's ego identity. However, almost everyone has heard of adults in "mid-life crisis" who have radically reformed their lives, sometimes in relation to subcultural groups. For example, there is the stereotypical story of the adult American male who finds himself in an identity crisis, severs his primary ties to his family, and joins a motorcycle club such as Hell's Angels. The rarity of such examples suggests that subcultural affiliation in mid-life is idiosyncratic, grounded in a variety of individual factors that resist generalization. Nevertheless, the fact that such changes do occur demonstrates the potential significance of subcultural affiliation at any stage in life.

Subcultures and the Elderly Adult

As noted earlier, a second common transition in life that may lead to subcultural affiliation occurs during retirement. As people leave the workplace, they lose an important source of identity and social support. Such displaced retirees may find new identity and support in senior adult communities, leisure clubs, or other social collectives. Such affiliations are often an effective strategy in dealing with the disorientation that can accompany retirement (Rosow, 1967).

The most recognized senior adult subculture is the self-contained "retirement" community. (Many residents raise plausible objections to this term, pointing to the active quality of their lives.) Such communities have appeared throughout the United States but are most prevalent in the warmer climates of Arizona, Florida, and Southern California. The life-styles associated with these retirement communities are typically organized around leisure activities such as golf, bingo, bridge, and dancing.

Senior adult or retirement communities, however, are relatively expensive places in which to live and are available to only a small percentage of retirees. The "leisure lifestyle" has also emerged in other social structures, many of which are also subcultural in nature. Most cities have a number of leisure clubs that are typically heavily populated with elderly members. Again, bridge clubs, bingo halls, senior golf associations, and dance clubs are among the most common. Such social groups also arise informally in a variety of contexts, e.g., groups of men who meet to play chess and checkers in parks, and groups of women who meet to make quilts and socialize.

To be sure, not all social structures that are organized around leisure activities for elderly people are truly subcultures. Many such structures, however, do fulfill important subcultural functions. They provide a sense of belonging and purpose in the lives of those who participate and, further, promote a value system that can, in part, replace the lost values of the workplace. This can ease the feelings of displacement that often occur, especially during the early retirement period. Perhaps the most succinct statement of this value system is the slogan that was coined for the Sun City retirement community by founder Del Webb: "Happiness equals activity plus friendliness" (Aiken, 1989).

Members of retirement subcultures usually remain active in the subculture for the remainder of their lives, as long as health permits. Although this permanence may suggest that retirement subcultures are more socially viable than youth subcultures, it is more likely the result of the dearth of other available social systems for elderly people in our society.

Of course, not all retirees find the leisure life-style of retirement subcultures to their liking. These individuals may join a retirement subculture for a brief period of time and then leave. In such cases, the subculture fulfills a transition function between retirement and the development of new social roles. These new roles may include a revitalized marriage, new activities and responsibilities as a grandparent, or new interpersonal relationships.

Conclusion

The study of subcultures is still a relatively new field. To date, only the most preliminary findings and theories are available. Nonetheless, two general conclusions have been clearly established. First, many people affiliate with subcultural groups at one or another point in their lives. Second, for those who establish such affiliations, subcultures fulfill important personal and social functions. Further, as the preceding discussion of youth and retirement subcultures has shown, subcultural affiliation may play an important role in adult development at any stage in life.

Many people, however, discount the role of subcultures, noting that some people never affiliate with subcultures or observing that subcultures often consist of the disaffected or disenfranchised. Yet, there is a saying—usually invoked by followers of various mystical doctrines—that goes: "For those who understand, no explanation is necessary; for those who do not understand, no explanation is possible." This saying applies equally well to subcultures. For those who do not understand what it means to be disaffected, to be disenfranchised, subcultures may always appear alien and marginal. However, for those who have participated in such groups, subcultures are an important part of life— and, as the discussion here has sought to demonstrate, an important part of understanding life. ▼ PETER J. MARSTON

See also: Disengagement Theory; Fictive Kin; Housing as a Factor in Adult Life; Intelligence—Crystallized and Fluid; Interethnic Relationships; Learning and Memory in Everyday Life; Possessions; Retirement Preparation; Sibling Relationships; Work Organization Membership and Behavior.

References

Aiken, L. R. (1989). *Later Life*. Third Edition. Hillsdale, NJ: Lawrence Erlbaum.

Goffman, E. (1963). *Stigma*. Englewood Cliffs, NJ: Prentice-Hall.

Hall, S., & Jefferson, T. (1976). *Resistance Through Rituals*. London: Hutchinson.

Hebdige, D. (1979). *Subculture: The Meaning of Style*. New York: Methuen.

Rosow, I. (1967). *Social Integration of the Aged*. New York: Free Press.

Willis, P. (1978). *Profane Culture*. London: Routledge & Kegan Paul.

SUFFERING

Suffering, like love or death or friendship, can be given no single exhaustive definition. Suffering is heterogeneous; it shadows life at all points and takes many individual and cultural forms. Consciousness can no more stand beyond suffering than it can transcend the course and meaning of life itself. Even today, in a society that often seems dedicated to "happiness," suffering can make itself well known to the middle-aged person and become a close companion to the old.

Suffering can be defined in several ways (Amato, 1990). It can be equated to and identified with severe pain. In spiritual and religious literature, however, suffering is often contrasted to pain. The latter is understood primarily to pertain to the body, where it is localized, discrete, and of limited duration. Suffering, in contrast, afflicts the spirit and can be understood to shape a person's whole life. Suffering's companions are not just types of pain but great dark chunks of life that are marked by misery, misfortune, grief, tragedy, disaster, and catastrophe. These ordeals go to the issue of human destiny and shape the great tests of the human spirit. Of such stuff great art and the most profound religious speculations are made.

As the author argues in *Victims and Values: A History and a Theory of Suffering* (Amato, 1990), humans must fashion the meaning of individual and collective selves both out of and in opposition to suffering. As all humans learn, no other form of suffering is so terrible as purposeless and senseless suffering.

All humans must interpret, judge, and value the pains of their suffering and that of others and must even, on occasion, consider the suffering of animals and of God. To a degree, people know and value pain and suffering on an individual basis. But they also consider and judge suffering within the context of their given cultures, and the truths, myths, stereotypes, prejudices, and contradictions that shape their consciousness. Religious, ethnic, national, popular, and mass cultures teach one what suffering is, who should suffer, and who, at what age, stage, and condition, should suffer what (Miller, 1978; Rowe, 1982; Zborowski, 1969). The issue is made more complex and daunting by the fact that these diverse sources of instruction sometimes contradict one another.

Cultures assign and value sufferings. For example, cultures commonly teach that men and women, the young and the old, the rich and the poor, and the educated and the uneducated should suffer different experiences in different ways. Much of what the middle-aged and old suffer—and how they express their suffering—turns not just on the strengths and weaknesses of the character they have spent a lifetime fashioning but also on the cultures they have inherited.

Suffering is a profound and complex matter of self-interpretation. As humans age, they increasingly conceive of themselves in relation to what they suffer, what they can and should suffer, and how and why they suffer. In a significant sense, individuals know and define themselves by their social transactions of suffering. By the nature of living in groups, people benefit from one another's suffering. On the ever arguable territory of suffering and sacrifices given and received, forced and volunteered, humans define their obligations to one another: child to parent, husband to wife, young to old, living to dead, mortals to the gods. Through sacrifice—understood as suffering concentrated and symbolized—people trade in human lives with one another and with the gods. These exchanges of suffering and sacrifice define one's fundamental sense of obligation and gratitude, just as they shape public discourses about victims and heroes (Amato, 1982). Unless people recognize how much they identify with and argue over the worth of sacrifices, they cannot comprehend the powerful claims of Judaism and Christianity or the ethical content of contemporary political discourse.

In its most intense forms, suffering has since time immemorial threatened to overwhelm humanity with a sense of futility. The modern world—less than three centuries old—has broken with the past by declaring suffering in all its forms to be an enemy. The modern attitude holds that suffering has no intrinsic value: It neither saves nor makes wiser or more beautiful. The contention is that suffering can claim no permanent and commanding place in humanity's transactions, whether earthly or eternal. Suffering, the modern world asserts, is not an inescapable matter of human destiny but is one of many disagreeable conditions that are subject to analysis, reform, therapy, and dissolution.

From the standpoint of adult development, this modern orientation has the effect of rejecting the traditional place and role of suffering in middle and old age. This historical contrast is at the center of the exploration undertaken here. The discussion will not only consider the place of suffering in various stages of human life but also attempt to decipher some of the most divided, perplexing, and irreconcilable voices within people and the array of institutions around them.

The Suffering of the Old

Many middle-aged and old people in the modern world live with both traditional and contemporary cultural attitudes about the worth and necessity of suffering. Inescapably, they confront two cultures. One culture argues that life in its natural course of aging proves to be a matter of pain and suffering; the other conceives of life as a continuous and broadening opportunity for pleasure and happiness. This latter, more modern view, is buttressed by the presumption that pain and suffering can be relieved by therapeutic measures when these negative experiences do arise.

The older the person, the more likely he or she is to experience pain and suffering as inseparably joined and as irreversibly present in life. To be old means that one's pains and sufferings are many. In this view, the failures of one's body lead to interminable trips to medical experts who cannot really help. One becomes increasingly cut off from the world as sight, hearing, work, friends, and even family are lost. Worse, there is even loss of the autonomy of body and the integrity of spirit. But worst of all, one's suffering does not seem to count for anything or to anyone.

This is the way my mother sees being old since my father died, ending more than half a century of marriage. "The old suffer all bad things," she aggressively contends. At first my mother tried to live alone. She failed and had to leave her home, give up the places and the people she knew for a lifetime, and relocate in another state. She tried to start over, but an early burst of enthusiasm fell short of producing a new world. Since taking up residence in a well-provided and benign congregate housing situation, she has found the everyday conditions of life to be more manageable. However, she persists in acting as though she were but a guest there, waiting for damnably tarrying death to do its work and take her where she believes she belongs.

Her friends' letters from Detroit do not often console her. "Dear Ethel," wrote one of her friends in a wavering hand, "I hope this letter finds you feeling better. I am not so good either. I fell down thirteen times, and now I have to pay...." Another wrote, "1990 does not go down as a banner year for us. A stroke (for me) requiring carotid artery surgery.... (My wife) too took a bad fall on the pavement at the local shopping center, resulting in severe facial bruises and a right shoulder hairline fracture which only time will heal. But our outlook is positive and we thank the Dear Lord for many blessings." Still another friend, apologizing for not writing for a long while, wrote in her Christmas card: "I've been busy taking Melvin to the doctors and dentist. He can't drive the car. He had the frozen shoulder ailment, and had to go to therapy treatments for fourteen days, three times a week.... He had to get new dentures. Today I took him for a bone scan at St. John's Hospital. Next week I've got to take him to Bon Secours Hospital. He has an infected big toe and they have to shoot dye in his leg to see what they can do. He doesn't go to play cards anymore."

My mother does not write back.

The Harvest of Age

In the past the majority of those who reached the blessed age of 60 plus 10 believed that they had lived too long. Age, they discovered, harvested more pains and suffering than could be subordinated to some worthwhile end. Although old age might bring wisdom and respect, more commonly it brought bitterness, disillusion, rejection, and despair.

Unlike the men and women of times past, people have become "medicalized." They look to medicine to control if not cure their pain and suffering. The very stages of the middle and late years are defined in relation to medical conditions. Increasing numbers repudiate all those past cultures that regarded suffering and death as the price of salvation. No longer conceding a natural course to life, the old are approaching the point where they may be left without a corresponding folk wisdom and popular wisdom to meet inescapable pain and suffering. Furthermore, both the middle-aged and the old tend to look at themselves through the mirror of the idealized young, rather than the portrait of the venerated old (Goodich, 1990; Kastenbaum, 1990).

In the traditional world, a small literary elite depicted old age as the culminating stage of character, power, and wisdom. The great majority, however, remained oblivious to such idealizations. For the greatest majority—the peasants of the traditional order—old age was not a matter of being blessed. It was the condition of being worn out, the sense of being useless, and the threat of being discarded. The peasants knew that their life in many respects was like that of the animals. Life proceeded by pain and ended in pain. At every stage, from birth to death, life was shadowed by suffering and death.

Peasants and workers of the old order were as different as possible from members of the contemporary developed world in their assumptions about life. What was life about? Incurable pain (Weber, 1976). Magic trees, saints, and priests might help out from time to time, and God might grant a miracle. For everyday life from youth through age, however, one had best inure oneself to pain.

New Ages and New Stages

The men and women of the old order voiced the necessity of suffering throughout life (Amato, 1982, 1986). Pain, work, and suffering formed the essential currency of exchange in the traditional rural order. In exchange for their gifts, the gods demanded lives and sacrifices. Heroes paid for their glory in agony, ordeal, and death. Women anguished in pain to bear children. Peasants paid in labor for their bread, and mystics in self-abnegation for their visions. Accomplishments had a cost in suffering, and the perversity and obdurateness of one's fellow humans guaranteed the inevitability of suffering (Amato, 1990).

For the vast majority in the old order, the kingdom of suffering was all encompassing. Accident, illness, violence, madness, and death ambushed all. Each stage of life was vulnerable to risk, pain, suffering, and death. Tenderness, sympathy, and compassion, while known and appreciated, were not to be expected. Men often were old at 40. Women aged even more rapidly, being spared no labors. Even children were not long cuddled or understood to have special developmental needs. Centuries had to pass before it was generally recognized that childhood can be differentiated into its own stages that have their particular needs and demands.

Unlike today, a relatively safe middle age did not exist. There was no middle period of life during which, still enjoying good health, one had the opportunity to consolidate possessions and survey the fruits of one's early labors and sacrifices. Instead, one still struggled just to survive.

The old did not anticipate "golden years." Those who had land would attempt to negotiate contracts to assure themselves perpetual use of a room, a garden, and tools so that they would not have to spend their last days suffering at the hands of their fickle children.

The absence of goods, the random course of events, the limit of human powers, and the minimum of sympathy and empathy did not foster the articulation of the stages of life. The differentiation of life into full, expected, and natural stages remained far more an artifact of literature—belonging to the Bible and the classics—than a description of the normal course of everyday life. One had only to notice that queens often died birthing and princes perished in droves before ascending to their rightful thrones. What assurance, what protection, what prospects, then, for the peasant? Furthermore, one's own will and efforts did not necessarily count for very much. Even Aristotle believed that the gods' blessings were far more important for happiness than a sound character.

Modernity's Assault against Suffering

The modern world launched a direct assault against the kingdoms of pain and suffering. The Enlightenment initiated this assault with its commitment to put human reason and institutions in the service of earthly happiness and pleasure. It rejected the inevitability of suffering and the efficacy of sacrifice. It opened the entire human kingdom, including the territories of suffering and pain, to understanding and cure.

Romanticism added a second great element to the assault. As the Enlightenment made earthly happiness the end of human powers, so Romanticism made youth the measure of the good life and regarded youthfulness and energy as an important part of every stage of life. (This radical movement had more impact on the middle classes than on the still beleaguered peasantry and the increasing hordes of urban poor.) Even though it dramatized the anguish of artists and found creativity in people's collective suffering, Romanticism valued youth and youthfulness on an unprecedented scale (Fischer, 1978).

Nevertheless, ideas and shifts in sensibility alone did not completely define modernity's assault against suffering and its revolutionary redefinition of life and its stages. Institutions also defined ideals of life and its stages. The central state rationalized social reality. Democracy implied the equality of all. In the West, national social security and workers' insurance in the late nineteenth and twentieth centuries not only declared a commitment to the well-being of workers and their families but also divided society into the two great groups: those who work, and those who have retired (Haber, 1983). With this division there eventually came the benefit of being guaranteed a basic right to earn one's living and to collect a pension. This was accompanied, however, by the opprobrium of being nonproductive and, therefore, useless. Work—economic work—became the measure of being fully and legitimately alive.

Other trends also profoundly define modern life and its stages. The mounting tendency of moderns to have a limited number of children and to migrate has made both children and the nuclear family ever more precious. For the upper classes, the death of a child—or even a domestic pet—frequently accounts for the deepest suffering of the modern person. For all stages, modern suffering is increasingly understood as a matter of emotions and individual psychology.

Increased well-being and longevity, to choose another trend, have made middle age a far more distinct period of life. There is a much greater likelihood that one will enjoy good health, even the prolonged vigor of youth, while having the further pleasures of amassing property and witnessing one's children successfully exploit the advantages of a society of multiple opportunities. One's sacrifice of time and energy will be seen as vindicated. Of course, unexpected illness, loss of work or health, failure in marriage, and disappointment in one's children all produce suffering, especially in light of the enhanced expectations. The suffering can become intense and all-consuming if at mid-life one comes to the terrible recognition that one has failed one's promise, opportunities, family, and friends—and that it is (or seems) too late to redeem these failures.

The trend of living longer in an ever more mobile society also contributes to shaping old age. In fortunate times, old age can prolong what was best in middle age. Dislocation and loss, however, can convert old age into a matter of loneliness, uselessness, and irrelevance.

Differentiating and Defining New Old Ages

In the developed world, individuals live longer, and they mature and age more slowly (Stearns, 1976). More ages and stages are differentiated. Textbooks now offer the standard classifications of "adult development" (Cook, 1983; Hughes & Noppe, 1985; Mishara & Riedel, 1984; Rybash, Roodin, & Santrock, 1985). Just as childhood and adolescence were differentiated in the first half of this century so in the second half researchers are busily at work differentiating several old ages (Hareven, 1978). Many epidemiologists now differentiate the later years of life into three old ages, starting with a "young old age" at 65, moving through a "middle old age," and concluding with an "old old age" starting at 85 (Siegel, 1980). One might even argue that potentially there are as many "middle ages" or "old ages" as there are keen analysts.

Beyond historical trends, there are many notions about life's stages. People rapidly accept and as rapidly reject these ideas, depending on their needs and inclinations. One of the more recent inventions, for example, is the mid-life crisis. Said by some of its enthusiasts to be an inevitable event, the mid-life crisis is modeled on Erikson's fashionable "adolescent crisis" (Erikson, 1958, 1978).

Life's stages, and the pains and the suffering associated with them, increasingly are being defined in reference to individuals who make more choices, have more opportunities, and expect fuller lives than their parents experienced. In turn, these individuals are correctly depicted as having less bodily pain but as far more prone to cultivate their emotional suffering. They are commonly understood to have crises involving choice. It is optimistically assumed that if these choices are properly resolved the individual will then (somehow) continue to preserve his or her youthfulness.

The disadvantages of class, the play of events, and the limits of human nature can defy this optimism. Nothing, however, so ironically contradicts the optimist's faith in the prolongation of life as does the multiplication of nursing homes. A conservative estimate would be that 11,500 new nursing homes will be needed in the United States by the year 2020. Even without replacing old nursing homes, this project would require building 364 new facilities every four days for the next 30 years. Building nursing homes does not seem to qualify as an emblem to optimism; rather, it is a reaction to more and more people living longer and longer.

The old person's long and frequently painful journey to death does not fit into modernity's quest for pleasure and fulfillment. The old seem to embody the worst form of suffering, i.e., purposeless suffering, suffering that redeems nothing. Living wills and reinvigorated moves toward euthanasia are among the likely responses to the threatening image of hordes of Methuselah-like 80-year-olds and growing legions of vacant-eyed 90- and 100-year-olds guarding the entrances to an infinite horizon of nursing homes.

Repulsed by the pains and sufferings of the old, contemporary men and women do battle against the enemies of a long and full life. Moderns welcome models of aging that promise happiness and offer therapy. They set aside old standbys such as character, prayer, good luck, and fate. They praise those who work and play right up to the end—the 86-year-old woman sky diver and the 84-year-old man who still runs the marathon.

In their increasingly differentiated middle age, the men and women of the middle class start IRAs, evaluate investments, cultivate hobbies, establish athletic regimens, attempt to follow healthful diets, and calculate the advantages of early retirement—while simultaneously doing all they can to avoid suffering and to claim all the available pleasures. They compete as hard as they can to live as long and to be as happy as they can. They judge a long and happy life to be the measure of their intelligence and competitive edge.

A Paradox for the Modern Age

The differentiation of life and its stages increasingly has made pain and suffering seem a matter of choice, sensibility, therapy, reform, argument, and politics. (Again, this is especially true for the middle classes.) The old have become another class of victims in modern society. They compete on the basis of their suffering for preferential treatment by an increasingly therapeutic state (Quadagno, 1982). In mobilized, centralized, and democratized society, people contend for attention and benefits on the basis of innocent suffering. From this perspective the old argue that they should have their suffering alleviated by the society for which they have suffered. In contemporary society, then, the stages of life are a matter of politics.

Yet there remains a sharp paradox: Prolonging life also increases the possibility of suffering. In particular the possibility of senseless and purposeless being, the type of exit so insidiously prepared by Alzheimer's disease or small strokes, increases. Furthermore, as pain and suffering become the domain of physicians and therapists, people sacrifice their own will and consciousness. They lose the capacity to inure themselves to suffering—their own and others'—as an inevitable condition of life and nature and, possibly, the wages of sins (Pernick, 1985; Williams, 1987).

In fact, the modern assumption that ties life to the promise of therapy and happiness does not prepare aging humans well for the pain and suffering that come their way. Indeed, this assumption, so important to humanity's collective progress and well-being, has the effect of undercutting character, prayer, and religion, which have been humanity's longest and most reliable responses to incurable pain and suffering. The promise of happiness and therapy runs counter to the reality that humans were not born to be happy and were not meant to live forever.   ▼ Joseph Amato

See also: Age 65; Chronic Pain as a Lifespan Problem; Depression; Development and Aging in Historical Perspective; Fairy Tales as Commentary on Adult Development and Aging; Generational Equity; Longevity; Religion and Coping with Crisis; Retirement Preparation; Rural Living: What Influence on Adult Development?; Widowhood: The Coping Response.

References

Amato, J. (1982). *Guilt and Gratitude: A Study of the Origins of Contemporary Conscience.* Westport, CT: Greenwood Press.

———. (1985). *Death Book: Terrors, Consolations, Contradictions, and Paradoxes.* Marshall, MN: Venti Amati / Peoria, IL: Ellis Press.

———. (1986). A world without intimacy: A portrait of a time before we were individuals and lovers. *International Social Science Review, 61:* 155-68.

———. (1990). *Victims and Values. A History and a Theory of Suffering.* Westport, CT: Greenwood Press / New York: Praeger Press.

Cook, A. (1983). *Contemporary Perspectives on Adult Development and Aging.* New York: Macmillan.

Erikson, E. H. (1958). *Young Man Luther: A Study in Psychoanalytic History.* New York: Norton.

———. (1978). Reflections on Dr. Borg's life cycle. In E. H. Erikson (Ed.), *Adulthood.* New York: Norton, pp. 1-32.

Fischer, D. (1978). *Growing Old in America.* New York: Oxford University Press.

Goodich, M. (1990). The virtues and vices of old people in the late middle ages. *International Journal of Aging and Human Development, 30:* 119-27.

Haber, C. (1983). *Beyond Sixty-Five. The Dilemma of Old Age in America's Past.* Cambridge, MA: Cambridge University Press.

Hareven, T. (1978). The last stage: Historical adulthood and old age. In E. H. Erickson (Ed.), *Adulthood.* New York: Norton, pp. 201-16.

Hughes, F., & Noppe, L. (1985). *Human Development Across the Life Span.* St. Paul, MN: West Publishing.

Kastenbaum, R. (1989). Old men created by young artists: Time-transcendence in Tennyson and Picasso. *International Journal of Aging and Human Development, 28:* 81-104.

———. (1990). The age of saints and the saintliness of age. *International Journal of Aging and Human Development, 30:* 95-118.

Marshall, V. (1978-1979). No exit: A symbolic interactionist perspective on aging. *International Journal of Aging and Human Development, 9:* 345-58.

Miller, J. (1978). *The Body in Question.* New York: Random House.

Mishara, B., & Riedel, R. (1984). *Le Vieillissement.* Paris: Presses Universitaire de France.

Pernick, M. (1985). *A Calculus of Suffering: Pain, Professionalism, and Anesthesia in Nineteenth Century America.* New York: Columbia University Press.

Quadagno, J. (1982). *Aging in Early Industrial Society: Work, Family, and Social Policy in Nineteenth-Century England.* New York: Academic Press.

Rowe, D. (1982). *The Construction of Life and Death.* New York: Wiley.

Rybash, J., Roodin, P., & Santrock, P. (1985). *Adult Development and Aging.* New York: William C. Brown.

Siegel, J. S. (1980). Recent and prospective demographic trends for the elderly population and some implications for health care. In S. G. Haynes & L. Stallones (Eds.), *Epidemiology of Aging.* Bethesda, MD: National Institutes of Health, pp. 289-316.

Stearns, P. (1976). *Old Age in European Society.* New York: Holmes and Meier.

Weber, E. (1976). *Peasants into Frenchmen: The Modernization of Rural France, 1870-1914.* Stanford, CA: Stanford University Press.

Williams, G. (1987). *Age of Miracles: Medicine and Surgery in the Nineteenth Century.* Chicago: Academy Publishers.

Zborowski, M. (1969). *People in Pain.* San Francisco: Jossey-Bass.

Zeldin, T. (1977). *France, 1848-1945: Intellect, Taste, and Anxiety.* Volume 2. Oxford: Oxford University Press.

SUICIDE

It is sometimes assumed that the "will to live" is the most powerful motivating force for all organisms. The frail-seeming plant pushing its way up to the light through a paved surface, the elephant herd laboriously transporting their bulky bodies over long distances in search of water, the person with a life-threatening illness who refuses to give up the struggle—all may be taken as examples of a universal striving for survival. Both the wilderness and human society offer many examples that are consistent with the belief that life seeks to preserve life.

What is one to make, then, of suicide? Each year, more than 30,000 people take their own lives in the United States according to the official cause of death certification, and many experts consider this number an underestimate. Suicidal behavior occurs in all contemporary societies and is reported in the literature and historical records that have come down through the centuries from many parts of the world. That suicidal behavior has been so widely observed in so many times, places, and cultures raises many questions for those with a philosophical or psychological turn of mind. Why would a person choose death over life? The moral/spiritual questions rapidly follow. *Should* a person have the right to choose death? Does one have an obligation to go on living no matter what— and, if so, to whom is this obligation owed? Are there circumstances when suicide is actually the moral alternative? Does it matter from a moral standpoint whether one ends one's life through a single decisive action, slowly but systematically erodes one's ability to survive, or hastens death by failing to take actions that could preserve health or reduce risk? In other words: How important is the modality—suicide—as compared with the outcome—premature death?

The following consideration of some of the basic facts and concepts that have emerged in studies of suicidal behavior and therapeutic contacts with suicidal individuals and their families will not automatically answer the philosophical and moral questions that arise, but it will offer a framework within which each reader can form his or her own judgments.

Basic Terms and Concepts

Suicide is the intentional act of killing oneself. It is a straightforward coinage from the Latin *sui* (= oneself) and *cidium*, from *caedere* (= to kill). According to Shneidman (1976), this term was not introduced until the middle of the seventeenth century, although self-killing has been known since ancient times. *Parasuicide* is a term that has come into circulation only in recent years. This is now the term commonly used when referring to suicide attempts. Unless otherwise noted, then, suicide refers to a completed act of self-destruction and parasuicide to attempts that did not result in death.

Although the primary meanings of these terms are clear enough, each presents significant difficulties from a practical standpoint. How does one know whether or not an act of suicide or parasuicide was intentional? The underlying problem here is the difficulty in establishing intentionality for *any* human action. Often one's actions are influenced by multiple considerations and circumstances. Even a seemingly trivial action, such as opening the door of a refrigerator, may be the result of a number of both converging and competing impulses. Many suicidologists (to use the awkward term that has established itself in this field) find that it is not useful to regard suicide/parasuicide in terms of simple cause-and-effect sequences. Instead, an effort is made to understand the total context from which a self-destructive action emerges.

In some instances there is not enough detailed and comprehensive information available to make a secure judgment about intentionality: Did that driver become inebriated and then "accidentally" suffer a fatal collision with a tree, or did that person drink with the definite intention of finding death on the highway? Sometimes the individual who survives a nearly fatal incident does not know the answer himself or herself.

Overall, one can neither easily dispense with the concept of intentionality nor easily draw conclusions about intentionality in many instances of suicide/parasuicide. Suicidologists have learned to proceed with caution. Procedures such as the *psychological autopsy*, a multidisciplinary review of ambiguous deaths, are sometimes employed to bring a variety of information and perspectives to bear on the question of intentionality and other factors (e.g., Farberow, Kang, & Bullman, 1990; Shneidman & Farberow, 1961).

Parasuicide presents difficulties to caregivers and researchers because such incidents do not necessarily come to their attention. A person may have already made several suicide attempts without their being recognized as such. Unless the individual is known to have in fact engaged in parasuicidal behavior, a potential caregiver may not be attentive to indices of additional self-destructive attempts, nor can researchers be entirely confident in their studies of parasuicidal trends since many such incidents do not come to official notice. In reading the suicide literature, one often notices that statistical tables are provided rather abundantly for suicide rates, but that attempted suicides are estimated on the basis of the limited information available.

The *suicide rate* is a basic statistical tool that is particularly useful in comparing two or more populations and in examining changes over time within the same population. To calculate this rate, one must know both the number of suicides and the size of the total population. The standard formula is

$$\text{Suicide Rate} = \frac{\text{Number of Suicides}}{\text{Population}} \times 100,000$$

Among other concepts that are often discussed in attempting to understand, predict, or prevent suicidal behavior, it is useful to be familiar with the following.

Rational suicide. This term refers to an act of self-destruction carried out (or contemplated) by an individual whose mental functioning is clear, logical, and unaffected by strong emotions, by significant distortions of reality, or by use of alcohol or other drugs. This concept is frequently introduced to counter the once-common but erroneous assumption that people who commit suicide must be out of their minds at the time.

Anomic, egoistic, altruistic, and fatalistic suicide. Emil Durkheim, a founder of modern sociology as well as the study of suicide, suggested that individual acts of self-destruction are strongly influenced by the strength and nature of the person's connection to society (Durkheim, 1951). *Anomie* can contribute to suicidality because the individual feels abandoned by society, as in unemployment, forced retirement, and other forms of exclusion. *Egoistic* suicide occurs among people who live by their own rules and have little involvement with the larger society;

high-ranking executives, creative artists, and celebrities are thought to be at particular risk. *Altruistic* suicide occurs when the individual is motivated to give his or her life for the preservation of the larger community and its traditions. The now illegal Indian ritual of *Suttee (Sati)* required a widow to die at her husband's funeral. Aged, ill, or disabled people who commit suicide with the idea of not being a burden on others are among present-day examples of altruistic suicide. *Fatalistic* suicide may be the outcome when a person feels blocked and frustrated in all efforts to reach his or her goals. Although this pathway toward suicide has been less systematically studied than the others, it is thought that people who are lifelong victims of discrimination and oppression may be particularly vulnerable.

Assisted suicide. This term refers to situations in which another person or persons contribute to self-intentioned death. Assisted suicide is a highly controversial issue. The same action is likely to be described as "mercy death" or "deliverance" by advocates and as "murder" by opponents. Physician Jack Kevorkian, inventor of the so-called suicide machine, has now expressed his views at book length (Kevorkian, 1991). An examination of more diverse positions is offered by Battin and Maris (1983).

Basic Facts on Adult Suicidal Behavior

Suicide rates have increased markedly for youths (ages 15 to 24) in the United States and many other nations since 1950. This trend, strongest among males, has remained at about the same high level in recent years. Valuable explorations of youth suicide are offered by Farberow (1989); Motto (1984); Peck, Farberow, and Litman (1985); and Shaffer et al. (1988).

Focusing on the adult years, one finds the following major facts about suicidal behavior.

- Males have a higher suicide rate than females at every adult age. This is true for both whites and nonwhites. (A note about the term *nonwhites* follows this list.)

- Male suicide rates rise sharply with increasing age from mid-life (ages 45 to 50) onward.

- Female suicide rates increase moderately until mid-life and then decline slightly.

- Elderly people have the highest suicide rates, with those classified as the old-old (75+) having the highest age-associated rates of all.

- White suicide rates are higher than African-American rates at all adult ages.

- Unlike the overall pattern for suicide rates among whites, combined nonwhite populations show an increased rate until about age 35. There are relatively small changes in the rate from that point forward, with a slight increase in the later adult years that remains below the peak rate observed in the third decade of life.

It is unsatisfactory from every standpoint to combine all ethnic and racial subpopulations into a category designated as "nonwhite." This has been an unfortunate necessity in many instances because of the lack of data that offer reliable breakdowns by specific groups. McIntosh (1992) has provided the best available information by culling from census reports and other official documents. He finds that there is "tremendous variability" within the "nonwhite" spectrum of the U.S. population. McIntosh's calculations yield the pattern shown in Table 1. Comparable data were not available for Hispanics, but McIntosh notes that suicide rates for this population are fairly similar to those of the African-American population.

Table 1
Suicide Rates of U.S. Ethnic & Racial Subpopulations

Native Americans	13.6
Whites	12.9
Japanese Americans	9.1
Chinese Americans	8.3
African Americans	5.7
Filipino Americans	3.6

Two different age-related patterns occur. Suicide rates increase from the middle to the later adult years among Chinese-Americans, Japanese-Americans, and Filipino-Americans. African-Americans, Hispanic-Americans, and Native Americans show instead a pattern in which suicide rates reach a peak in the early adult years.

The data presented up to this point (which deal only with completed suicides) show that age, sex, and ethnicity or race all have a bearing on suicide rates in adulthood. Examining all age, sex, and ethnic or racial combinations, it also becomes clear that the person most at risk for suicide is the old, white man. Nevertheless, even in this relatively high-risk group, most do *not* commit suicide: Among old-old white men the suicide rate is approximately 60 per 100,000.

It is important, then, to identify other predictors of suicidal behavior. Such predictors not only would be useful in their primary functions of detection and prevention but also would help in understanding the contexts from which suicidal actions emerge. Much research has been devoted to this quest. In his recent review of the literature, Maris (1992) has confirmed that all of the following factors contribute to the prediction of suicidal behavior in adulthood: depressive illness, alcoholism and drug abuse, suicidal ideation and communication, prior suicide attempts, use of lethal methods, social isolation, hopelessness, cognitive rigidity, having had another person in the family commit suicide, work and financial problems, marital problems, stress, anger, physical illness, and a combination of any of these.

A brief look at some of these influences on suicidality as they occur in combinations at various points in adult life follows. For an in-depth examination of all the predictors taken individually, see Maris et al. (1992).

Several types of life events can lead to a depressive response as one moves through the adult years. Among younger adults these events often include marital problems, divorce, and other disturbances in intimate relationships; difficulties in establishing oneself financially; and lack of experience in coping with stressful situations. Furthermore, some individuals turn to drinking or drugs in an attempt to escape their anxieties. Should a depressive response develop, such a person is likely to have even more difficulties in communicating and problem solving. Feeling that one has failed or that one can see no other way out of the situation—and perhaps under the momentary influence of alcohol or drugs—suicidal action may be taken.

In the later adult years, the loss of significant personal relationships can also be a factor. In addition to marital problems, however, older people are also more likely to experience the incapacitation or death of the spouse, as well as the deaths of other members of their developmental convoys. Furthermore, they are also more likely to face pain, disabilities, and illnesses that are becoming chronic and not easily overcome. Financial problems may arise as fixed income and limited assets appear inadequate to meet rising expenses. All of these changes in life circumstances contribute to increased social isolation: One has lost companions, easy mobility, and disposable income and often does not feel "up" for new adventures.

There are many other scenarios that lead to suicidal attempts in both the earlier and the later adult years. Individual differences are important at all points in the lifespan and should not be neglected when examining suicidal ideation and behavior. Nevertheless, there are at least two ways in which suicidal behavior tends to differ among younger and older adults: (a) older adults are more likely to contemplate or attempt suicide in a planned and rational rather than an impulsive manner, and (b) older adults are more likely to use methods with a higher probability of lethality. The use of firearms, for example, is considered to be a more lethal modality than the ingestion of a drug overdose—and elderly people (especially the old, white man, again) more often do use firearms in their suicidal attempts. It has long been recognized that alcohol is frequently a contributing factor to sudden death through suicide, homicide, and accidents. Although alcohol and drugs are sometimes involved in the suicides of older adults, these mind-altering substances are more often found to be contributing factors in the suicides of younger adults.

It might be useful to turn the suicide predictors to their reverse signs and consider some of the factors that contribute to a relatively *low* risk for self-destruction through the adult years. Adults protect themselves from suicidal ideation and behavior when they have a number of mutually rewarding relationships (including a companionable marriage), when they think in a clear and flexible manner, when they have learned from previous life experiences and are therefore able to cope with the stress of new situations, when they are in good physical health and/or have developed ways of compensating for limitations and disabilities, and when they have some peace of mind regarding their ability to meet financial needs and obligations.

Pragmatic and Moral Issues

There is a close relationship between the pragmatic and moral issues that are associated with adult suicide. For example, as just noted, concern about financial status has a bearing on suicidality. Among numerous observations that have confirmed this connection is a set of studies revealing that the suicide rate among farmers increases during lean economic times (Ragland & Berman, 1990-1991). Other analyses show that the suicide rate among elderly Americans declines during periods of economic prosperity and increases during recessions (Lester & Yang, 1992). It is worth keeping this connection in mind when one encounters assertions that suicide is somehow more natural or acceptable among elderly people. This type of assertion is sometimes used as justification for limiting the access of senior adults to health, social, and other entitlements. Overall, the facts indicate that older people as a group become more or less suicidal depending on the stresses and threats they face and the resources that are available to them. The number of elderly people who see suicide as their only remaining option is, in part, a function of social attitudes and policy priorities.

In judging whether or not it is "right" to take one's own life, people are often influenced by their personal experiences, fears, stresses, and special interests. What people express as though it were an objective or philosophical proposition may be only a way of rationalizing their own biases. This phenomenon has been particularly evident in the willingness to assume that a person who is experiencing hardships associated with age, disability, or chronic illness no longer holds life to be precious and would not be much of a loss to society. It has become increasingly, clear, however, that the individual's own perspective is often quite different from what has been attributed to him or her. Life can still be precious to an aged person, and that person's life still precious to others.

Through all the adult years, many people have shown the ability to accept the inevitability of death without rushing forward to embrace it, and to discover constructive alternatives to suicide even in their darkest hours (Kastenbaum, 1992, in press).

Moral questions certainly remain about the "right" to live, to die, and to take the life of others. Philosophical questions also remain about the significance of suicide as an individual choice and as a violation or as a fulfillment of cultural expectations. From a practical standpoint, however, the suicidal adult is still a living person whose ultimate choice may depend much on the sensitivity, integrity, and affirmation that others are able to bring to their relationship with him or her.

▼ Robert Kastenbaum

See also: Alcohol Use and Abuse; Chronic Pain as a Lifespan Problem; Depression; Disengagement Theory; Divorce; Drug Use and Abuse; Friendships through the Adult Years; Gender as a Shaping Force in Adult Development and Aging; Life Events; Loneliness; Marital Development; Mental Health in the Adult Years; Mexican Americans: Life Course Transitions and Adjustment; Native American Perspectives on the Lifespan; Religion and Coping with Crisis; Retirement Preparation; Risk to Life through the Adult Years; Social Relationships, Convoys of; Social Support

for the Chronically Ill; Stress; Suffering; Widowhood: The Coping Response.

References

Battin, M. P., & Maris, R. W. (Eds.). (1983). *Suicide and Ethics*. New York: Human Sciences Press.

Durkheim, E. (1951). *Suicide*. New York: The Free Press. (Original work published 1897).

Farberow, N. L. (1989). Suicide: Youth. In R. Kastenbaum & B. Kastenbaum (Eds.), *Encyclopedia of Death*. Phoenix, AZ: The Oryx Press, pp. 239-42.

Farberow, N. L., Kang, H. K., & Bullman, T. A. (1990). Combat experience and postservice psychosocial status as predictors of suicide in Vietnam veterans. *Journal of Nervous and Mental Disease, 178*: 32-37.

Kastenbaum, R. (1992). Death, suicide, and the older adult. *Suicide & Life-Threatening Behavior, 22*: 1-14.

———. (in press). Alternatives to suicide. In L. Tallmer & D. Lester (Eds.), *Suicide in the Elderly: Counseling Needs and Management*. Boston: Charles Press.

Kevorkian, J. (1991). *Prescription: Medicide*. New York: Prometheus.

Lester, D., & Yang, B. (1992). Correlates for the elderly suicide rate. *Suicide & Life-Threatening Behavior, 22*: 36-47.

Maris, R. W. (1992). Overview of the study of suicide assessment and prediction. In R. W. Maris et al. (Eds.), *Assessment and Prediction of Suicide*. New York: The Guilford Press, pp. 3-24.

Maris, R. W., et al. (Eds.). (1992). *Assessment and Prediction of Suicide*. New York: The Guilford Press.

McIntosh, J. (1992). Epidemiology of suicide in the elderly. *Suicide & Life-Threatening Behavior, 22*: 36-58.

Motto, J. A. (1984). Suicide in male adolescents. In H. S. Sudak, A. B. Ford, & N. B. Rushworth (Eds.), *Suicide in the Young*. Boston: John Wright, pp. 227-44.

Peck, M. L., Farberow, N. L., & Litman, R. E. (Eds.). (1985). *Youth Suicide*. New York: Springer.

Ragland, J. D., & Berman, A. L. (1990-1991). Farm crisis and suicide: Dying on the vine? *Omega, 22*: 173-86.

Shaffer, D., et al. (1988). Preventing teenage suicide: A critical review. *Journal of the Ameri-*

can *Academy of Child and Adolescent Psychiatry, 27*: 675-87.

Shneidman, E. S. (1976) Introduction: Current overview of suicide. In E. S. Shneidman (Ed.), *Suicide: Contemporary Developments.* New York: Grune & Stratton, pp. 1-24.

Shneidman, E. S., & Farberow, N. L. (1961). Sample investigations of equivocal suicidal deaths. In N. L. Farberow & E. S. Shneidman (Eds.), *The Cry for Help.* New York: McGraw-Hill, pp. 118-28.

T

TASTE AND SMELL

Unlike a number of other species, humans generally give highest priority to vision and hearing. Predatory animals often track their prey through olfactory clues and many a beast marks its turf by bodily excretions. On the amorous side of the ledger, some types of female moths can attract males at a great distance by scenting the air with the slightest hint of a fragrant message. Despite their relatively low position on the human sensory hierarchy, however, taste and smell remain significant modalities for orienting oneself to the possibilities and dangers of one's environment. "Is something burning?" and "This milk doesn't taste right" are examples of self-protective responses to smell and taste signals. Much pleasure is experienced through savoring certain tastes and fragrances, while certain objects and places may be quite aversive to us because they "smell bad."

It has been argued that all of the various senses possess an underlying unity (Marks, 1978). Although each sense gives its own distinctive set of messages, both the workings of the nervous system and one's imagination tend to create equivalences (e.g., "warm colors" or "sharp taste") and integrate these varied sensory inputs into overall impressions. Taste and smell are among those senses that seem most closely interrelated. The acts of preparing and eating food involve a combination of taste and smell. A delicious aroma can arouse one's taste buds and at times may

even disguise the fact that the food itself has little flavor.

A presentation of the biological foundations for taste and smell will be followed by a summary of what has been learned about changes in these senses that occur during the adult years. It should be noted at the outset that the lifespan developmental course of taste and smell has not received nearly as much study as vision or hearing.

Olfaction (Smelling)

Olfaction is generally considered to be a relatively primitive sensory modality. The structures and connections that serve this modality are simple compared with the incredible complexity of other types and levels of the human information-processing system and are thought to have evolved earlier. Speculation aside, the olfactory system is primarily *chemical* in its action. The reception of olfactory information requires physical contact between a volatile molecule and one's sensing apparatus. This process differs markedly from vision. Visual information can be obtained about a mountaintop in the distance without having a little piece of that mountain physically enter one's eye. (A good thing, too, or the great peak might soon be diminished by having so many eyes taking it in.)

The basic act of olfaction involves the following elements and sequence:

1. A gaseous molecule
2. Becomes airborne and
3. Enters the nasal cavity when the person breathes in or sniffs at it.

4. If the molecule is at least partially soluble in water, it will then interact chemically with the mucus cells in the top portion of the nasal cavity.

5. Sniffing increases the "smellability" of an olfactory stimulus because it draws the flow of air into the upper chambers.

6. From this point, the olfactory message passes upward through very small apertures in the ethmoid bone and reaches the olfactory bulb. It is then routed to the olfactory tract of the brain after this input has been analyzed and coded by this subcortical center.

There will be no olfactory sensation unless these conditions are met (with the exception of sensations of smell that can be experienced in certain pathological conditions of the nervous system). The ability to detect lower levels of olfactory stimulation and to distinguish one type from another can be impaired by trauma or disease. Unfortunately, the olfactory sense also declines with advancing adult age. It has been found that the ability to detect, differentiate, and identify odors is relatively less efficient among elderly adults (e.g., Corso, 1981; Schiffman, 1979; Van Toller, 1985).

Much remains to be learned, however, about the pattern, extent, and inevitability of olfactory loss in the later adult years. Few of the available studies are longitudinal (following the same individuals), and the mechanisms involved have not been firmly identified. Hayslip and Panek (1989) observe that "damage to the olfactory bulb and tract and therefore changes in sensitivity to smell are more likely attributable to environmental factors, such as occupational odors, airborne toxic agents, and smoking, rather than age per se" (p. 136). They also cite a study by Engen (1977) that suggests that people who make extensive use of their olfactory skills are more likely to keep them functioning well over the years.

Another observation is also worth keeping in mind. Cotman and Holets (1985) point out that "The olfactory bulb is interesting because it shows continual neurogenesis and synaptic growth throughout life" (p. 626).

Although this finding comes from research with rats, it does raise the possibility that this "primitive" sensory modality may have an advantage not so obviously enjoyed by more evolved sensory systems. The adroit sniffer may indeed stimulate his or her olfactory system to ever greater achievements throughout the years, but only further research will tell.

Gustation (Tasting)

The sensation of taste begins with the arrival of a physical (molecular) stimulus that is either already in an aqueous form or can be dissolved in saliva. Such a stimulus can activate the taste buds, located on the tongue. The "bumps" or projections on the tongue are known as *papillae*. Contrary to common assumptions, many of these papillae contain no taste buds at all. Other papillae, however, are the sites for the four basic types of taste receptors that have been clearly identified: sweet, sour, salt, and bitter. The more complex taste sensations are built up from combinations of these buds that specialize in these various basic "tastes."

In general, each of these subjective experiences (e.g, "bitter") is related to stimulation by particular types of chemicals. Many bitter tastes, for example, are produced by contact with alkaloids, while the experience of "sweetness" follows stimulation by sugars and many other carbohydrates. Nevertheless, research has not demonstrated a clear and fixed relationship among the precise structure of the chemical stimuli, the receptors, and the experience of a particular taste (Corso, 1981). In part, this lack of definitive conclusions is related to methodological problems in separating out the components of stimulation and in finding ways to obtain well-differentiated and standard responses from the participants. The possibility remains that the subjective experience of taste actually does depend on more than the chemical structure of the stimuli, at least in some instances, and so cannot be reduced to the kind of simple regularities that most researchers would prefer to find.

The taste buds are also interesting structures because, like the olfactory bulb, they have the ability to regenerate; in fact, it is their normal operating procedure to go through degenerative/regenerative cycles. It would appear, then, that the "lower" senses of olfaction and gustation have growth and self-repair functions that operate on a different principle and are perhaps more resilient than what are found in the more advanced visual and auditory systems.

Like all receptor systems, the taste buds on the tongue must connect to the brain, and they do so through the ninth cranial nerve (the *glossopharyngeal*, a tough customer to encounter in a spelling bee). There are also some taste buds in the larynx and pharynx; these make their connections through the tenth *(vagus)* nerve. Arriving in the upper levels of the central nervous system, the gustatory inputs pass through several subcortical structures (the *medulla, pons,* and *thalamus*) before being routed to their cortical destination, the *parietal* area of the brain. Neuroscientists probably were not that surprised when they discovered that the taste pathway ends up right behind the area that is active when one chews food.

The acuity and sensitivity of the gustatory system shows age-associated declines, although, as was the case with olfaction, much remains to be learned about the nature, extent, and inevitability of this process. Recent studies confirm earlier indications that all four basic taste sensations are less readily detected as one enters the sixth decade of life (Markson, 1991; Weiffenbach, Count, & Baun, 1988). A stronger sensory input is necessary for the older adult to experience and identify the taste. This diminished ability to experience tastes could well be related to the decreased number of taste buds and decreased saliva flow that have been found in elderly adults (Engen, 1977). Note again, however, that these are cross-sectional studies and so disclose only age differences, not necessarily changes with age. Furthermore, relatively small numbers of elderly adults have been studied in this regard, and one cannot be sure that all conditions that could have affected taste perception were controlled or ruled out. For example, both taste and smell acuity could be affected by medications and perhaps by untreated ailments or depressive mood. Corso (1981) points out that tongue disease in particular could affect taste sensitivity, yet little attention has been given to this area. There is little doubt that smoking reduces taste sensitivity at all age levels, and many years of smoking could do more damage than aging per se.

Implications

The available data indicate that both taste and smell are less effective in later adulthood than in youth. The changes appear to be relatively small and gradual over the years, but they either accumulate or accelerate around the sixth decade of life. It is likely that the nature of one's habits and experiences can either intensify or lessen the rate and extent of sensory loss. Nonsmokers who use their sniffers and taste buds with as much finesse and delight as their eyes and ears are probably increasing their chances of maintaining these abilities throughout the years. A professional wine taster or chef, for example, may continue to function well in later adulthood because his or her sensitivities have been exceptionally well developed and kept in good form.

One of the most common laments of older adults is that "Food just doesn't taste good any more." This judgment is sometimes turned into complaints against a particular cook or recipe. It is more likely that one's ability to detect nuances of fragrance and flavor have diminished to the point where the total experience of eating has become bland and disappointing.

Nutritionists and chefs who serve senior adult populations are taking this phenomenon increasingly into consideration. It is possible to plan meals that restore some of the savor and therefore entice the appetite. Both health and pleasure can be at stake here. Adequate nutritional status is an important safeguard for the health of an elderly person, so loss of interest in eating can have serious consequences. Vitamin deficiency is a particular risk. And, of course, it is unfortunate when a long-term source of pleasure is lost.

People generally prefer to make dining a social experience. The lonely elderly person is less likely to eat well and consistently. Good company, appetizingly served meals, and some knowledge and imagination in the choice and preparation of food often can compensate for the loss of some olfactory and gustatory acuity.

A great-grandmother of the author's acquaintance loads up on candies and cookies during her marketing expeditions. Holding a bag of M & Ms in one hand and a sack of miniature candy bars in the other, she closes her eyes and impersonates the scales of justice. "Why, you see, chocolate makes a perfectly well-balanced meal!"

▼ ROBERT KASTENBAUM

See also: Body Senses; Depression; Humor; Listening; Vision.

References

Corso, J. F. (1981). *Aging Sensory Systems and Perception*. New York: Praeger.

Cotman, C. W., & Holets, V. R. (1985). Structural changes at synapses with age: Plasticity and regeneration. In C. E. Finch & E. L. Schneider (Eds.), *The Biology of Aging*. Second Edition. New York: Van Nostrand Reinhold, pp. 617-44.

Engen, T. (1977). Taste and smell. In J. Birren & W. Schaie (Eds.), *Handbook of the Psychology of Aging*. New York: Van Nostrand Reinhold, pp. 554-61.

Hayslip, B., & Panek, P. E. (1989). *Adult Development and Aging*. New York: Harper & Row.

Marks, L. E. (1978). *The Unity of the Senses*. New York: Academic Press.

Markson, E. W. (1991). Physiological changes, illness, and health care use in later life. In B. B. Hess & E. W. Markson (Eds.), *Growing Old in America*. New Brunswick, NJ: Transaction Publishing, pp. 173-86.

Schiffman, S. (1979). Changes in taste and smell with age: Psychophysical aspects. In J. Ordy & K. Brizzee (Eds.), *Sensory Systems and Communication in the Elderly*. New York: Raven Press, pp. 227-46.

Van Toller, C. (1985). *Aging and the Sense of Smell*. Springfield, IL: Charles C. Thomas.

Weiffenbach, J. (1982). Taste thresholds: Quality specific variation with human aging. *Journal of Gerontology, 37:* 372-77.

Weiffenbach, J. M., Count, B. J., & Baun, B. J. (1986). Taste intensity perception in aging. *Journal of Gerontology, 41:* 460-68.

TRAVEL: STIMULUS TO ADULT DEVELOPMENT

People have always traveled, from the early nomads who wandered to find food for survival to the modern-day tourist who visits seven European nations in as many days. Whether sojourning for fun and adventure, a search for a better life, or involuntarily to escape war and oppression, the experience of travel has always presented a challenge to the individual psyche.

Much of travel in the early part of the twentieth century was intended to broaden and refine the character of young well-to-dos, as in Mark Twain's *Innocents Abroad*. Today, young people still travel to broaden their perspectives. For adults who work in other lands, the challenge is not just to broaden their horizons but to adjust to a new cultural environment while accomplishing the task at hand. The older sojourner may have additional concerns for health and security. Recent studies suggest that extended sojourns have differential impacts and present different challenges, depending on the traveler's age and stage of psychological and social development.

Traveling as a Child

"Third-culture kids" (TCKs) are children who spend their formative years abroad as dependents of parents who are employed overseas. Lacking broader comparisons, they tend to adapt to each new situation as it arises, regardless of the particular cultural expectations and demands. Neither guided by nor blinkered by extensive comparison experiences, children often are more adaptable than adults in new cultural contexts.

Ironically, the adaptability comes partly from the high mobility. Moving frequently as a family seems to have the effect of bringing the individual members closer together. Sharing the common experience of confronting an unfamiliar territory and providing mutual support offers the child the security to explore and learn from each new environment (Useem & Downie, 1976). As one TCK with Asian experience reported: "I guess I could live anywhere and be comfortable. I have always liked to think I get along with all different people. I don't feel bothered by a lack of roots, and I don't think I have a lot of problems because of that."

Children who spend a lot of time abroad seem to become both "a part of" and "apart from" whatever situation they are in. One who grew up in Africa and Asia explains, "I find myself sitting back and objectively observing Americans and Africans, occasionally smiling and occasionally shaking my head. I get along comfortably with both, but then again, there is a bit of me that remains apart." TCKs are particularly adept at learning second languages and are remarkably cosmopolitan, often having more contact with locals than do their parents (Torbiorn, 1982). In one study, 75 percent of the children surveyed reported that they feel most comfortable with people who are internationally oriented and who have lived abroad.

On the other hand, although they adapt well abroad, TCKs often suffer some stress in accommodating to life back home. While abroad they had become accustomed to being a bit marginal; individuals in the host countries assume the TCK will be different. Upon coming "home" to the United States they actually encounter what is a relatively new culture to them, but one in which friends and family are often unaware of or unsympathetic to their problems of reentry transition. After all, they look American, have American parents, and speak English (though sometimes it is not their first language)—so what's the problem? As one returning TCK comments: "I think part of the problem when I came to the States was I looked American but I did things that were not quite American.

I had fun trying to be an American. It was an act in a way."

However, most children eventually do adapt well upon their return and benefit from having sojourned in foreign settings.

Traveling as an Adolescent

As children grow into adolescence, they have increasing opportunities to travel abroad on their own. Approximately 750,000 young Americans go abroad each year to travel, study, or work. Such sojourns probably have more impact at this stage of life than at any other. Many go abroad during high school as exchange students, usually living with a host family. Others spend their junior year in college studying abroad. These sojourns are experienced differently, depending on the level of maturity and psychological development of the adolescent. Younger or less mature adolescents seem to benefit most personally, while those who are older or more mature for their age seem to benefit most in the intellectual and cognitive spheres (Kauffmann, Martin, & Weaver, in press).

Younger, less experienced adolescents who go abroad seem to grow up faster. High school or young college students often say that their experiences abroad gave them increased self-confidence, independence, autonomy from parents, and interpersonal flexibility. They seem to benefit simply from being away from home and learning to be independent and do things on their own. As one student from Iowa reported after his year in Malaysia, "I've become a new person and it's terrific. No one can take what I got away from me, and I try to share it. I've given 20-plus speeches so far. You took a frightened, self-conscious kid and turned him, ME, into a self assured, can-do person."

A teenager from Maryland who sojourned in Peru recalls: "The most significant effects of the summer were the changes I saw taking place in myself. I returned to the U.S. liking myself more than I ever had, ready to meet and set goals, to contribute and to explore. It seemed like the beginning of a new life for me, at least the beginning of an adult life."

The impact of sojourning for those who go abroad a second time or who are already more psychologically and socially mature seems to have a greater effect on their cognitive and intellectual aspects. They show increased global awareness and cultural knowledge:

"Before I went, I never really paid attention to what was happening in the world. I'd read the paper, but I didn't know any history or anything. Over there, I took political science courses and I started to realize that things aren't black and white. There's histories and ties all over that connect it all. I started paying more attention." "Now I see the interdependency in the world and have a lot more respect for other cultures and see that humanity really does have something universal that links us together...."

Traveled adolescents often experience a change in their perceptions of their own home culture, as well as changes in personal values and life-style priorities. These changes often are more profound than for children or adults because young people are in the process of more explicitly formulating their own values and beliefs (Perry, 1970). This process is not without its social friction. They may come back acting "German" or "French" and criticizing aspects of life in the United States. Furthermore, there are often some difficulties in readjusting to their home culture (Martin, 1985). As one young person reports: "There is almost no communication between my friend and me. It's as if there's a difference between us that can't be reversed. I know the changes are because I have lived abroad. She just doesn't understand what happened to me. We still talk, but I've stopped telling her about Germany."

Parents, other family members, and friends usually are a bit wary at first of the changes that have taken place in the thoughts and attitudes of the adolescent sojourner. They usually discover, however, that the positive effects outweigh the negative. The sojourners usually return more independent, more globally aware, and more sensitive to the connectedness between peoples (Carlson et al., 1990).

Traveling in Maturity

Most adults sojourn abroad for vacation or work. Those who travel for short periods of time and are relatively open-minded find this experience exciting and broadening. It is an especially illuminating experience if the travelers have the opportunity for meaningful interactions within the cultures and nations they visit. One could argue that a bus tour of seven countries in seven days is not really an intercultural experience, but more an experience of the "accidental tourist" type—where one tries to replicate home as much as possible while traveling abroad.

Adults who spend an extended time abroad (from six months to two years) may benefit in the same way as the more mature adolescent. They are likely to acquire increased global awareness and understanding of foreign cultures and peoples, as well as a heightened understanding of their own cultural background. However, the impact of an international sojourn may be less dramatic in mature adults for two major reasons. First, the adult's values and priorities are already solidified and therefore more resistant to revision than those of adolescents (Gullahorn & Gullahorn, 1963). Second, the adult sojourner who works abroad is more interested in coping effectively with *culture shock* and being successful on the job than in learning deeply from the experience. The learning that does take place from the overseas experience is sometimes an unexpected benefit.

Culture shock—the psychological and sometimes physical discomfort that comes from dealing with new and different ways of living and thinking—seems to affect everyone who actually comes in contact with another cultural group. (The accidental tourist is excepted because of his or her isolation from the people of the host nation or culture.) For example, when Americans visit the Middle East, they encounter women who are veiled from head to foot, as well as locals who refuse to give an honest answer. When the sojourners are given wrong directions or promised goods and services that never materialize, they feel confused, sometimes angry, and definitely out of sync with the local environment. In other words, they experience culture shock.

After much more contact and some reflection, the visitors may realize that their reactions are based on cultural differences in male and female roles or in the definitions of truth and honesty, rather than some inherent defect of the other culture. Culture shock also occurs for Middle Easterners visiting the United States. They may be very offended by the lack of modesty displayed by the women and shocked by Americans' insistence on telling the truth even when it makes the other person unhappy. Middle Easterners would rather tell a white lie and pass a pleasant time in conversation than tell the naked (unpleasant) truth.

In early research, culture shock was viewed as something to avoid. It was seen as a disease to which the unsuspecting visitor fell prey. This supposed disease came complete with symptoms, such as frequent washing of the hands, and a recovery period which could be hastened—not surprisingly—by learning more about the language and the people one was visiting (Oberg, 1960).

In current research, culture shock is viewed as a normal response of individuals to a new situation, a transition period that can be useful if managed productively, much the way that one learns from other difficult transitions in life (e.g., divorce, relocation, or the death of a loved one). To benefit the most from culture shock and ultimately to learn the most from the sojourn experience requires an open mind, tolerance for ambiguity, some self-examination, and the setting of realistic expectations by obtaining information about the new cultural environment prior to departure (Martin & Rohrlich, 1991).

Recent studies also suggest that the most effective personnel overseas are often those who experience the greatest degree of culture shock. In other words, the most effective person is not necessarily the one who sails through untouched by the new cultural experience but, rather, the individual who becomes involved in local culture, allows his or her own beliefs and assumptions to be challenged, and takes risks. This individual is likely to experience more culture shock at first but in the long run acquires a deeper understanding of the local culture and is able to build relationships that enable him or her to be more successful on the job.

There are some gender differences in adult sojourning. Young American women report having felt more concern prior to travel (Martin & Rohrlich, 1991) and more difficulty in the sojourning experience itself, as compared with men (Kim, 1988). This difficulty is related in part to different expectations for male and female travelers. In most countries, women still are not expected to travel alone. Those who violate this expectation may encounter bewilderment at best, and at worst harassment, from the locals. Women who accompany their husbands on work assignments overseas often are confronted with the difficult task of coping with an unfamiliar culture and language in their daily dealings with marketing, household responsibilities, children's education, and so forth while their husbands function in more structured and therefore more manageable work environments.

Adult sojourners returning home after working abroad experience the same reentry transition mentioned earlier in readjusting to the personal and social milieu (Miller, 1988). In addition, they often find difficulties in reentering their home organizations. This is especially true of those who are most effective abroad. Colleagues do not really want to hear about the time they spent in Kuala Lumpur or Cairo, but are mainly interested in their reintegrating, i.e., being the same person they were before they left (Adler, 1981). Most adults find that they make the transition and that life readjusts to "normal" after about six months. Having a sympathetic support network and friends who have also traveled makes this readjustment process easier.

The older adult sojourner may have concerns beyond coping with culture shock, being successful in an overseas job, or learning about new people and cultures. There continues to be an increase in mobility and travel among older Americans, for both pleasure and learning. Many adults travel extensively for the first time after retirement when they have fewer family responsibilities and (if they are fortunate) greater financial security.

At this stage of life, travel concerns relate primarily to safety, security, health precautions, and logistics. Therefore, many older men and women prefer structured group tours over individual travel. Tours have the advantages of reducing the individual's burden for logistical details and providing increased security and comfort. Varying degrees of individual independence and choice are available to the sojourner, depending on the structure of the particular tour. The tour experience can also provide a ready-made group of companions for those who travel alone, particularly after the death of a spouse.

Despite the advantages of tour arrangements, however, the older sojourner, like all travelers, will derive the most benefit from seeking opportunities to interact directly with the local cultures and people.

▼ Judith Martin

See also: Cohort and Generational Effects; Gender as a Shaping Force in Adult Development and Aging; Interethnic Relationships; Stress; Work Organization Membership and Behavior.

References

Adler, N. (1981). Managing cross cultural transitions. *Group and Organization Studies, 6:* 341-55.

Carlson, J. S., et al. (1990). *Study Abroad: The Experience of American Undergraduates.* Westport, CT: Greenwood Press.

Gullahorn, J. T., & Gullahorn, J. E. (1963). Extension of the U-curve hypothesis. *Journal of Social Issues, 19:* 33-47.

Kauffmann, N., Martin, J. N., & Weaver, H. (in press). *Students Abroad, Strangers at Home.* Yarmouth, ME: Intercultural Press.

Kim, Y. Y. (1988). *Communication and Cross-Cultural Adaptation.* Philadelphia: Multilingual Matters.

Martin, J. (1985). The impact of a homestay abroad on relationships at home. *AFS Occasional Papers in Intercultural Learning, No. 8.*

Martin, J. N., & Rohrlich, B. (1991). The relationship between college student study abroad, sojourners' expectations, and selected characteristics. *Journal of College Student Development, 32:* 39-46.

Miller, M. D. (1988). Reflections on reentry after teaching in China. *AFS Occasional Papers in Intercultural Learning, No. 14.*

Oberg, K. (1960). Cultural shock: adjustment to new cultural environments. *Practical Anthropology, 7:* 177-82.

Perry, W. G. (1970). *Forms of Intellectual and Ethical Development in the College Years.* New York: Holt, Rinehart & Winston.

Torbiorn, I. (1982). *Living Abroad.* New York: John Wiley.

Useem, R. H., & Downie, R. D. (1976). Third-Culture Kids. *Today's Education,* pp. 103-05.

TRUST AS A CHALLENGE IN ADULT DEVELOPMENT

Interpersonal trust has been regarded as crucial for the survival of society (Deutsch, 1973; Rotter, 1971). Many daily acts require depending on others to fulfill their promises or to act benevolently (e. g., accepting a person's check, walking to work in a large city). People would not engage in such acts unless they had a fundamental trust in others. Certainly, acts requiring goodwilled behavior on the part of others occur with great frequency throughout adulthood and, therefore, interpersonal trust is also a significant factor in our social functioning.

What Is Trust?

Interpersonal trust has been conceptualized in two ways. The first is in terms of an individual's beliefs about whether other people's verbal communications are reliable and correspond to their actual attitudes and behaviors. This is the approach taken by Rotter (1967), who defined interpersonal trust as the belief that others' words, statements, or promises can be relied upon. Guided by that principle, Schlenker, Helm, and Tedeschi (1973) conceptualized interpersonal trust as an individual's willingness to depend on another's promise in a risky interaction. By "risky interaction" is meant a situation that requires the exchange of behaviors between two or more persons and in which the outcomes are interdependent and therefore somewhat uncertain.

The second conceptualization of trust is similar but rests on benevolence. Rosenberg (1956) defined interpersonal trust as individuals' beliefs that others are benevolent, that is, inclined toward helping rather than harming others. Guided by that principle, various researchers have regarded interpersonal trust as the willingness to engage in benevolent behavior in a risky interaction (Deutsch, 1960; Wrightsman, 1966).

One other dimension of interpersonal trust has also attracted interest. Researchers have distinguished between individuals' interpersonal trust beliefs in "generalized others" and their trust in specific persons (Johnson-George & Swap, 1982). For example, an individual may believe that others in general fail to keep their promises and therefore are untrustworthy—but nevertheless believe that a given person does keep his or her promises and is therefore very trustworthy.

Research Findings

The bulk of the research has examined interpersonal trust during the late adolescent period (e.g., early college years). Attention has been given to establishing tests that measure interpersonal trust as a personality characteristic and the attributes with which it is associated (Rotter, 1971, 1980).

Individuals who hold high trust beliefs tend to differ from those with lower levels of interpersonal trust in several ways (Rotter, 1980). The high-trusting individual is

1. Less likely to lie and cheat
2. Happier and less conflicted and maladjusted
3. More popular with others and more sought out as a friend

Despite the high-trusting person's inclination toward a greater trust in other people, he or she is not excessively gullible. When there is some basis for distrust, the high-trusting person will be cautious. Overall, the available research supports the conclusion that high interpersonal trust is a positive characteristic.

Interpersonal trust has been studied to a more limited extent during adulthood. For example, it has been found that interpersonal trust is a characteristic of marriages in which the partners reported that they had strong feelings of love toward each other (Larzelere & Huston, 1980). These findings were consistent with the researchers' hypothesis that interpersonal trust contributes to the love experienced by marriage partners and is important for the survival of a marriage. Interpersonal trust beliefs of husbands and wives have also been found to be positively associated with their sensitivity to nonverbal cues (Sabatelli, Buck, & Dreyer, 1983). This supports the hypothesis that when adults form high interpersonal trusting beliefs, they achieve a high sensitivity to others' nonverbal cues and thereby have access to others' actual emotions, attitudes, beliefs, and dispositions. In that sense, adults who hold high interpersonal trust beliefs may prove to be superior spouses because they are more sensitive to their partners' nonverbal cues and thereby their emotional states and attitudes than are adults who hold low interpersonal trust beliefs.

What about interpersonal trust in later adulthood? The author modified Rotter's (1967) interpersonal trust belief scale for use with elderly adults (Rotenberg, 1990). Rotter's scale was modified because many of the questions were more appropriate to the experiences and interests of college students and were linguistically complex. A subsample of Rotter's questions was simplified linguistically and then administered to 140 individuals ranging from ages 60 to 89. One subgroup of individuals was asked to identify others within the group who were trusting and distrusting. Evidence was obtained for the reliability and validity of this "elder person" scale. The trust scores for individuals on this scale were found to be closely related to the trusting versus distrusting ratings they had received from their peers.

Additional analyses of the elderly person scale yielded evidence for four underlying qualities of interpersonal trust beliefs in later adulthood: (a) trust in the dependability of social-legal organizations, (b) fear of being cheated by others, (c) trust in the dependability of specific social groups, and (d) adherence to trustworthy ideals. The first of these—trust in social-legal organizations—appeared to change in a curvilinear fashion with age; it decreased from a young-old age group (ages 60 to 69) to a middle-old old age group (ages 70 to 79), and from then it increased to the old-old age group (ages 80 to 89). The first decrease in trust from the young-old to the middle-old age group was attributed to the effects of retirement. Because retirement is frequently accompanied by unexpected and dramatic reductions in income and social status, individuals may experience a decrease in their trust in social-legal organizations such as courts and politicians. The increase from the middle-old to old-old groups was attributed to a form of generativity during old age. When entering very old age, individuals may acquire a renewed hope for the future and show an increased trust in social-legal institutions (e.g., the United Nations) as a means of preserving peoples' welfare and the quality of life for future generations.

Stability and Change

With the exception of the author's work, researchers have not yet addressed the issue of whether individuals' interpersonal trust beliefs and behaviors remain stable, change, or develop across the adult period. A theoretical framework is proposed that may help to address this issue. This theory suggests that interpersonal trust across adulthood is the result of an interaction between (a) the personality characteristic of interpersonal trust beliefs/behavior and (b) trust-relevant life events. The first aspect has been examined (Rotenberg, 1990) as a derivative of Rotter's (1967, 1971, 1980) research.

The second aspect reflects individuals' encounters with new and significant others or with organizations that vary in trustworthiness (e.g., promise fulfillment versus violation, lying versus telling the truth). For example, suppose that an adult takes a new job and finds out that his or her boss is completely untrustworthy, given to lying, cheating, and deception. Such encounters can force adults to experience a crisis and reexamine their fundamental trust beliefs in others. Although such events might force dramatic changes, personality characteristics act to maintain some stability. Individuals' interpersonal trust beliefs have been developed over previous extensive life experience. Becoming part of the individual's overall personality, these beliefs influence the way a particular behavior or situation is interpreted. The course of interpersonal trust across the adult period is a product of the moderate change that results from new encounters and the stability that is inherent in personality characteristics.

A Theory of Trust Development

Based on the preceding theory, a developmental-like pattern should emerge of the extent to which individuals encounter trust-relevant events at common periods during adulthood. The following six trust-relevant age periods may be evident.

1. *Entry to the workplace.* During this period the crisis concerns individuals' interpersonal trust in subordinates, coworkers, and supervisors (Kruglanski, 1970).
2. *Marriage.* During this period the crisis concerns the trust that is placed in one's spouse, particularly the type of trust that is required for the achievement of significant mutual goals and intimacy (Larzelere & Huston, 1980).
3. *Parenthood.* During this period, the crisis concerns the adult's trust in persons who have limited but developing social competence—their children.
4. *Children's marriages.* During this period the crisis concerns individuals' interper-

sonal trust in in-laws who were not chosen by them as intimate others.

5. *Retirement.* During this period, the crisis concerns individuals' interpersonal trust in social organizations and the services or care they provide (Rotenberg, 1990).

6. *Mortality.* During this period, the crisis concerns individuals' interpersonal trust in social-legal organizations as a means of preserving people's welfare and the fundamental quality of life for future generations.

Sex differences in the preceding interpersonal trust periods should be evident to the extent to which the trust-relevant events are of differential importance or prevalence for men and women across adulthood. For example, given the intensive traditional role of the mother in child care, parenthood may become a predominant interpersonal trust period for women. In particular, women's interpersonal trust from early through middle adulthood may center largely around their trust in their children, who have limited but continually developing physical and social abilities. ▼ KEN J. ROTENBERG

See also: Fairy Tales as Commentary on Adult Development and Aging; Marital Development; Parental Imperative; Reminiscence and Life Review; Retirement Preparation; Spiritual Development and Wisdom: A Vedantic Perspective.

References

Deutsch, M. (1960). Trust, trustworthiness and the F scale. *Journal of Abnormal and Social Psychology, 61:* 138-40.

———. (1973). *The Resolution of Conflict: Constructive and Destructive Processes.* New Haven, CT: Yale University Press.

Johnson-George, C., & Swap, W. C. (1982). Measurement of specific interpersonal trust: Construction and validation of a scale to assess trust in a specific other. *Journal of Personality and Social Psychology, 43:* 1306-17.

Kruglanski, A. W. (1970). Attributing trustworthiness in supervisor-worker relations. *Journal of Experimental Social Psychology, 6:* 214-32.

Larzelere, R. E., & Huston, T. L. (1980). The dyadic trust scale: Toward understanding interpersonal trust in close relationships. *Journal of Marriage and the Family, 42:* 595-604.

Rosenberg, M. (1956). Misanthropy and political ideology. *American Sociological Review, 21:* 690-95.

Rotenberg, K. J. (1990). A measure of the trust beliefs of elderly individuals. *International Journal of Aging and Human Development, 30:* 141-52.

Rotter, J. B. (1967). A new scale for the measurement of interpersonal trust. *Journal of Personality, 35:* 651-65.

———. (1971). Generalized expectancies for interpersonal trust. *American Psychologist, 26:* 443-52.

———. (1980). Interpersonal trust, trustworthiness and gullibility. *American Psychologist, 35:* 1-7.

Sabatelli, R. M., Buck, R., & Dreyer, A. (1983). Locus of control, interpersonal trust and nonverbal communication accuracy. *Journal of Personality and Social Psychology, 44:* 399-409.

Schlenker, B. R., Helm, B., & Tedeschi, J. T. (1973). The effects of personality and situational variables on behavioral trust. *Journal of Personality and Social Psychology, 25:* 419-27.

Wrightsman, L. S. (1966). Personality and attitudinal correlates of trusting and trustworthy behaviors in a two-person game. *Journal of Personality and Social Psychology, 4:* 328-32.

TWINS THROUGH THE LIFESPAN

Twins have long been a subject of popular fascination. "Two of a kind" has novelty value because single births are far more common. In some cultures the birth of twins was once considered to be a favorable sign from the deity, but in other cultures, just the opposite. Dramatists have often seized upon twins as a plot device; e.g., the "long-lost twin" shows up in the final scene of an old-fashioned melodrama, or, as in Shakespeare's *The Comedy of Errors, two* sets of identical twins manage to confuse themselves and everyone else for the sake of comedy. That twin mischief and merriment was already an ancient idea can be seen in the fact that this sixteenth-century entertainment was based on two plays by Plautus, a satirist of the Greek classical period.

On a more symbolic level, the existence of actual twins may resonate with another idea that has been around for a very long time. This idea has been expressed in many different ways, e.g., as a "spirit double," a *doppelganger* (German), and an "altercast" (an imagined version of one's own self, in contemporary communication studies parlance). Terms such as these denote the belief that one's everyday self has a hidden or invisible companion. Depending on the context and the individual, this may take the form of an imaginary companion with whom one shares secrets and makes plans, a mystical inward essence, or a disturbing *Other* who has all the unacceptable impulses that have been vanquished (or have they?) from one's socially acceptable self.

To see twins for who they really are, then, requires the ability to distance ourselves from stereotypes and personal or sociohistorical resonances. Reviewing the biology of twinship is the first step to take in this direction.

Biological Basis of Twinship

It is usually held that there are two types of twins: monozygotics and dizygotics. When the same egg is fertilized by a single sperm, divides, and forms two separate embryos, the resultant offspring are known as *monozygotics* (MZ), or identical twins. *Dizygotics* (DZ), or fraternal twins, are thought to come into being when two eggs are released at about the same time from either one or both ovaries and are then fertilized by two different sperm.

From the genetic standpoint, identical and fraternal twins differ markedly. Coming as they do from separate ova and separate sperm, DZs develop as separate individuals, although they share the same parents. Theoretically, one would expect no greater genetic similarity between a pair of fraternal twins than between any two children of the same parents. In contrast, identical twins would be expected to share precisely the same genetic heritage.

One assumes, therefore, that all identical twins are of the same sex, while fraternal twins may be either of the same sex or of opposite sexes.

This picture is complicated a little by two considerations. First, it is not out of the realm of possibility that other types of twinning occur in nature. Twins with a shared MZ heritage might differ either at conception or at some later point because of mutation or chromosomal damage. This possibility has been raised in connection with the existence of Down's syndrome in one identical twin while the other is free of the disorder (Novitski, 1977). Another theoretical possibility is that two separate sperm would fertilize the same ovum. The offspring then would be expected to carry identical genetic instructions from the mother but would differ in their paternal contributions. From the practical standpoint, however, it has proven very difficult to identify such twins (MacGillivray, Nylander, & Corney, 1975).

There is also a phenomenon known as *superfecundation*, in which two or more ova produced in the same period of time by the same female are fertilized by sperm from more than one male. Farber (1981) reports that superfecundation occurs to some limited extent among animals (dogs and cows are mentioned) and that two instances have been verified in humans. Again, this variant in twinning is of more interest theoretically than as a substantive consideration in human development.

One variation, however, is worth keeping in mind, although its lifespan developmental implications have not yet been studied. Farber (1981) provides a concise description of the basic pattern:

> Mirror imaging, also known as *asymmetry*, refers to those sets of monozygotics who show some degree of mirror reversal in various physical traits. For example, many sets have one right-handed and one left-handed partner. The degree of mirror imaging can be extensive, including handedness, footedness, hair whorl, facial features, and

even aspects of the shape of internal organs. At other times, the asymmetry is only partial as, for example, in twins who have reversed hair whorls and facial characteristics but the same hand/foot dominance. Cases of situs inversus viscerum have been described, where the location of internal organs within the body is reversed. This occurs most frequently in conjoined, or Siamese, twins and is not frequent in monozygotics who are fully separated. (p. 10)

Two variations on this variation are especially interesting. First, the twins may be mirror images of each other in one or more domains in which an abnormal or pathological conditions exists. For example, pathological asymmetry may be manifested as congenital malformations that occur on the right side of one twin and the left side of the other. Second, some observers believe that there can be *psychological* asymmetry between identical twins. In other words, one of the pair has certain dominant psychological characteristics that are not evident in the other, and vice versa. One twin may be physically adventuresome and active, for example, and the other more inward and reflective. Presumably, these mirror image psychological traits represent inherited dispositions rather than child-rearing or other experiential influences. This provocative hypothesis has not been firmly demonstrated, although one can find twin pairs in which the psychological asymmetry concept seems applicable.

Twins: The Developmentalist's Delight

Twins are not just "interesting" to those who study biological or psychosocial development. Many researchers regard twin studies as the most effective and definitive way of distinguishing between the effects of heredity and individual experience. The "nature vs. nurture" controversy has been with the life sciences from the beginning and is still lively today. The controversy was once more extremist, vehement, and perhaps also more colorful. The greatest thinkers of their time often took positions on this issue. For ex-

ample, Immanuel Kant (1781) argued powerfully for the nature side of the controversy, convincing many that individuals bring a mental as well as physical structure with them in their journey through life—an active, questing, organized, and organizing faculty that was not itself created out of mere experience. John Locke (1690) had previously electrified the philosophical and political establishment with his radical doctrine of the *tabula rasa:* the mind as a "blank slate" upon which experience would write and personal character develop.

The nature/nurture controversy was significant then and is significant now for its social, political, and economic implications as well as for its relationship to individual development. One need look no further than the U.S. Constitution to realize that Locke's view, with its emphasis on environmental influences, provided the philosophical muscle behind the creation of a democratic republic in which the concept of equal rights and opportunity was fundamental. Kant's ideas also continue to be influential, however, and remain beneath the surface in many areas of contemporary inquiry, including studies of cognitive development.

Scientists from both the biological and the sociobehavioral disciplines were quick to recognize the potential value of twin studies in assessing the relative influence of genetic and experiential factors in human development. The early growth and later life characteristics of twins could be compared with those of nontwin siblings. Even more usefully, twins raised apart from each other could be compared with those who grew up in the same household.

Ethical and practical considerations, of course, limit the options available to scientists in designing such studies. One does not ask parents to separate their identical twins so that they can be reared in different environments to serve research purposes. Instead, researchers properly must rely on circumstances that arise spontaneously in the course of human events that happen to result in the separation of twins at some point in their lives. Various kinds of statistical and

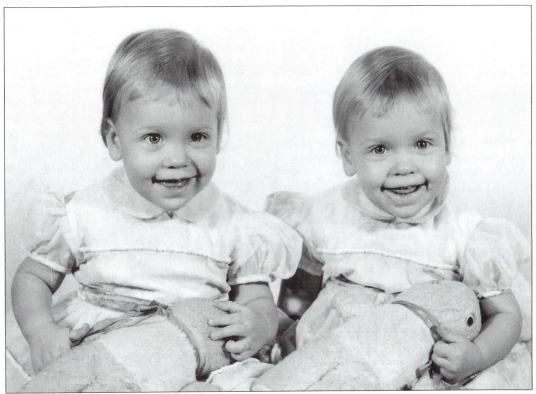

Figure 1. Identical Twins Karen (left) and Chris (right) at Age 1

Figure 2. Twins Karen (right) and Chris (left) in Their 30s

quasi-experimental designs can also be used to help distinguish between genetic and environmental influences. The methodology of twin research involves many complexities and contingencies—just keeping track of people over the years is itself a challenge—and there is room for criticism and alternative interpretations. Nevertheless, over the years, much has been learned from twin research that is useful to all who seek to understand the "nature/nurture" interaction in human development and aging.

Major Findings

Longevity. The correlation between the longevity of twins is stronger than that found for non-twin siblings, and the correlation is at its strongest for MZ (identical) twins (e.g, Harvald & Hauge, 1965; Pearl & Pearl, 1934). When specific pairs of MZ twins are considered, it is often found that they reached very similar ages. In Juel-Nielsen's (1980) study, for example, Twin A in one set died at age 83 and Twin B at 80, while in another set Twin A died at 92 and Twin B at 96. The pattern emerging from available data indicates that there is indeed something to the idea that identical twins do share very basic characteristics, including those that are influential in determining longevity.

There is probably more to this relationship than is presently known. For example, the Russian biologists Gavrilov and Gavrilova (1991) make a plausible case for the proposition that the influence of genetic endowment on longevity may differ at various points in the lifespan. Commenting on Jacquard's (1982) data, they suggest that the genetic contribution is strongest early in the lifespan, decreasing significantly through the adult years. "Thus in the analysis of lifespan, in addition to the two traditional sources of variation (environment and genotype), it is also necessary to take into account an additional third source of variation: the stochastic (kinetic) nature of the process" (Gavrilov & Gavrilova, 1991, p. 37). If additional studies bear out this contention, what we have learned from twins will include an enhanced appreciation for the complex ways in which genetic and environmental influences interact across the lifespan.

Physical Characteristics. Common observations about the physical "identicality" of identical twins are well confirmed by research. Studies of MZ twins reared apart have been reviewed by Farber (1981) and provide the following consistent pattern of findings.

- Identical twins are very similar in height as adults, often to within an inch.
- Skeletal structure ("build") is nearly identical.
- Characteristics of hair and skin match very closely (e.g., pigmentation and freckles).
- When visual abnormalities or difficulties exist for one member of the pair, the same problem is also present in the other member (but this does not mean that MZ twins have any greater likelihood of ophthalmic difficulties than do people in general).

- Measures of central nervous and cardiovascular performance are also highly concordant, as demonstrated through electroencephalograms, electrocardiograms, and blood pressure monitoring.

It is important to distinguish between basic physical characteristics such as those noted above and vulnerability to specific illnesses and syndromes. The available data from in-depth studies clearly support the common observation that MZ twins bear a strong likeness to each other that must be attributed to their shared genetic endowment. However, the data on incidence of illness and physical disorder are not comparable in either quantity or quality, thereby limiting the generalizations that can be made. Furthermore, within the limits of the available data, it appears that the concordance between basic physical characteristics of MZ twins does not extend to the broad range of illnesses and syndromes. For example, susceptibility to respiratory disease seems to be more closely associated with environmental than with genetic factors, but musculoskeletal disorders were highly concordant. It is probable that the contribution of genetic factors eventually will be found to vary according to the particular type of illness or syndrome.

Mental Development. Reliable conclusions are difficult to reach in this area because of ongoing methodological controversies as well as gaps in the available data base. Farber's (1981) painstaking reanalysis of the available studies yields several points worth considering, however.

- Mutual contact between identical twins seems to account for a substantial amount of the variance in IQ test scores, thereby emphasizing the role of interpersonal communication as a process that influences mental development.
- Environments are likely to exert much of their influence on mental development by either fostering or inhibiting the emergence of new intellectual abilities, e.g., the child may be ready to try out his or her next mode of intellectual exploration and infor-

mation processing, but the environment may be indifferent or even punitive.

- The genetic similarity between MZ twins may show itself primarily in terms of the sequence and timing with which various phases of mental development come to the fore, a possibility that has yet to be given systematic study.

The hypothesis that mental development and intellectual level are determined primarily by genetic endowment is favored by many lay people and a number of scientists. Twin research, especially involving DZ pairs whose members have been reared apart, would seem to provide an ideal test of this hypothesis. Nevertheless, it would be wise to refrain from drawing conclusions at this time. The data, when examined with great care (Farber, 1981), cannot be fully relied on in the area of mental development—a much more difficult topic than dealing with basic physical dimensions such as height, skeletal structure, and so forth.

Personality and Behavior. Common observation again suggests marked concordance between identical twins in the realm of personality and behavior. A and B often seem to laugh, feel sad, or become nervous at the same time. Researchers have also found many examples of simultaneous or matching behavior in twins and, again, especially among identical twins. The more dependable findings include the following.

- There are remarkable similarities in gestures and mannerisms among MZ twins (e.g., both would make the same half-humorous face before answering a question, or both would nod their heads in the same way as they spoke).

- Nervous, anxiety-expressing habits also tended to characterize both twins in the set—e.g., if A was a nail-biter, one could expect B to have this habit as well, and if B suffered from insomnia, this was probably also a problem for A.

- The psychophysiological responses of MZ twins to alcoholic beverages seem to be highly concordant, but their actual drink-

ing (or nondrinking) behavior seems to be influenced more by the social environment in which they are raised.

- Basic personality style and mood were usually very similar; e.g., both tended to be either cheerful or somber; A and B might differ in the extent or intensity of a characteristic, such as risk-taking or shyness, but both generally behaved in much the same way.

- Surprisingly, MZ twins who are reared apart are rated as showing greater similarity in personality; this tendency exists even when the twins were raised in very different types of home environments.

One dual-factor explanation for the last finding is that parents may treat an identical twin differently than other children, and that early contact between the twins continues to exercise a potent influence on personality development even when they are separated because of attempts to compensate for their loss of regular companionship with each other.

Twinship in Old Age. Several studies have tried to follow twins from infancy and childhood through to old age. From the information currently available, the following points are worth particular attention (Jarvik, Bennett, & Blumner, 1973).

- The pattern of greater similarity between MZ than DZ twins persists in the later years of life, thereby strengthening the case for genetic influence on overall development and aging.

- Mental abilities and coping skills tend to remain stable throughout the adult years, barring illness or trauma.

- A high degree of stability in mental functioning throughout the adult years is associated with a more active and enjoyable life-style in old age, despite changes in physical health. The last point is illustrated by twinship case histories such as this excerpt:

> Mrs. S....is a vital, self-confident, and poised 93 year-old woman who has maintained a quick wit, sharp reasoning

abilities, and good motor coordination. Findings from repeated series of psychological tests administered over a 20-year time span show her to be alert, free from psychiatry disorder, and capable at levels considered more than adequate for a person 30 years younger.... Mrs. S. looks much younger than her chronological age. Despite the fact that she has great difficulty walking, due to senile osteoarthritis, she continues to be an active woman—seeing friends, supplementing the household income by crocheting, making rugs and mats, and collecting buttons which she arranges and sews into pictures and onto baskets. Her twin sister, although dizygotic, aged with comparable success and remained self-sufficient until her fatal heart attack at age 86. (Jarvik, Bennett, & Blumner, 1973, p. 133)

Summary and Implications

The study of development and aging in twins has already provided information that is valuable in examining the relationship between "nature" and "nurture" factors for all people. By and large, the data support and extend the common observation that twins resemble each other in a broad range of physical, behavioral, and personality characteristics. This concordance, as one might expect, is especially strong for identical (MZ) twins. Genetic endowment plays a significant role in human development and aging, and twin data underscore this point in many ways.

Nevertheless, the matter cannot be considered fully resolved. Much needs to be learned about the modalities and processes through which particular facets of the genetic endowment exercise their influence. Moreover, it is also clear that environmental and experiential factors cannot be dismissed. No bioscientist today would assert that the environment is merely the arena in which "wired-in" developments make their predestined appearance. The significance of environmental/experiential factors has been touched on here with respect to differential vulnerability to disease, but it also extends throughout all the realms of physical, psychological, and

social functioning. We can appreciate the force of genetic endowment, especially as manifested so clearly among DZ twins, without losing sight of the unique experiences and socioenvironmental circumstances encountered by every individual.

One of the more neglected aspects of study has been the role of the active self in shaping experiences, forming relationships, and establishing skills. There has been a tendency to lose the active individual within a welter of nature vs. nurture dynamics. It is useful to bear in mind that a person is not simply the passive resultant of inner and outer forces. Each person is a unique identity with his or her own worldview and approach to life.

More attention to the distinctive intrapersonal and interpersonal world of twins (and triplets, for that matter) would also be welcome. Instead of studying identical twins for the information that can be gleaned for other purposes, it would be fascinating to know more about what is special about the twinship relationship itself. What does it mean to be an "individual," for example, when one is part of a set of DZ twins—and do loneliness, empathy, creativity, grief, and other experiences also take on distinctive characteristics? Perhaps it is time to study the special intimacies and communicational processes involved in twinship throughout the lifespan. Such a study could hardly fail to yield crucial information about the human experience. ▼ Robert Kastenbaum

See also: Alcohol Use and Abuse; Development and Aging in Historical Perspective; Longevity; Sibling Relationships; Social Relationships, Convoys of.

References

Farber, S. L. (1981). *Identical Twins Reared Apart*. New York: Basic Books.

Gavrilov, L. A., & Gavrilova, N. S. (1991). *The Biology of Life Span: A Quantitative Approach*. London: Harwood.

Harvald, B., & Hauge, M. (1965). Hereditary factors elucidated by twin studies. In J. V. Neel, M. W. Shaw, & W. J. Schull (Eds.), *Genetics and the Epidemiology of Chronic Diseases*. PHS

Publication 1163. Washington, DC: Department of Health, Education and Welfare, pp. 61-76.

Jacquard, A. (1982). Heritability of human longevity. In H. S. Preston (Ed.), *Biological and Social Aspects of Mortality and the Length of Life*. Liege, Belgium: Kaplow, pp. 39-92.

Jarvik, L. J., Bennett, R., & Blumner, B. (1973). Design of a comprehensive life history interview schedule. In L. F. Jarvik, C. Eisdorfer, & J. E. Blum (Ed.), *Intellectual Functioning in Adults*. New York: Springer, pp. 127-36.

Juel-Nielsen, N . (1980). *Individual and Environment: A Psychiatric-Psychological Investigation of MZ Twins Reared Apart*. New York: International Universities Press.

Kant, I. (orig. 1781). *The Critique of Pure Reason*.

Locke, J. (orig. 1690). *An Essay Concerning Human Understanding*.

MacGillivray, I., Nylander, P.P. S., & Corney, G. (1975). *Human Multiple Reproduction*. Philadelphia: W. B. Saunders.

Novitski, E. (1977). *Human Genetics*. New York: Macmillan.

Pearl, R., & Pearl, R. W. (1934). *The Ancestry of the Long-Lived*. London: Milford.

V

VISION

Vision is the dominant sense modality for most people. Not only do people depend extensively upon visual information in everyday life, but they also have a strong tendency to regard "seeing as believing," i.e., to consider vision the most trustworthy of the senses ("I have to see it with my own eyes!"). Common verbal imagery also expresses the influence of the visual modality, e.g., "Keep your eyes peeled" as a metaphor for alertness, "She's the apple of my eye" as an indicator of personal preferences, and "I'm in the dark about that" as a confession of ignorance or confusion. Both the practical and the symbolic importance of vision are good reasons to "look" carefully at the functional, developmental, and integrative facets of this modality, with particular attention to the changes that occur in the adult years.

The Basics of Vision

One's ability to detect and utilize information in the visual modality depends on (a) what the environment has to offer, (b) the status of one's visual receptors, and (c) the integrity of the central processing system through which sensory impressions are transformed into usable perceptions.

What one needs from the environment is electromagnetic radiation and the absence of physical barriers between oneself and the objects of one's visual attention. More specifically, one needs that spectrum of electromag- netic radiation called "light." Composed of particles known as *photons*, light behaves in some circumstances as though it were a stream of discrete units and in other circumstances as though a wave. (Physicists have occasionally tried to reconcile these two phenomena by describing light as moving in "wavicles.") The type of electromagnetic radiation that serves as light is within a narrow mid-range of wavelength, roughly from 380 to 760 *nanometers* (a billionth of a meter). When the wavelength is quite small, one is likely to be in the presence of gamma or ultraviolet rays. Longer wavelengths take such forms as "electricity" (still an imperfectly understood concept) and broadcasting signals. People respond in various ways to electromagnetic radiation of various lengths and intensities, but they depend on a narrow range of "wavicle" activity to light up their eyes.

The availability of light does not guarantee that one will have a successful look around. An unobstructed visual pathway between perceiver and target is necessary unless one has Clark Kent's X-ray vision. Although structurally and functionally vision is the most complex of the sensory modalities, it can be made inoperative by environmental barriers as well as under- or overillumination (e.g., a battery of flashbulbs exploding as we step from our limousines). In contrast, the morphologically humbler olfactory sense readily informs us that the neighbors are preparing a barbeque in their backyard even though our eyes don't have a clue.

The human visual system is constructed according to a basic plan that is shared with other vertebrates. The eyes feature a versatile *lens* that concentrates and focuses incoming light signals. Spherical when off duty, the lens has the ability to alter its shape to correct for the distance of the object one is attempting to view. This is the process known as *accommodation,* through which a flattening response puts distant objects into focus and a rounding response does the same for nearby objects. The lens is not perfectly transparent even in youth: A pale yellow pigment filters out some blue and ultraviolet light. Color perception is affected by the selective absorption of various wavelengths, and this makes each person his or her own color expert, ready to argue with the friend who sees that gray as blue or vice versa.

Before light reaches the real-honest-to-goodness lens, it passes through a bulging window that serves as a preliminary and nonadjusting lens device. This is the *cornea,* a simple structure that represents perhaps the most forward signal-detection station of the central nervous system. Behind the cornea is a chamber filled with a watery fluid, appropriately known as the *aqueous humor.* Light that passes through the cornea must also make its way past the *iris.* The opening itself is known as the *pupil.* From a decorator's standpoint, the iris is interesting because it provides the overall color impression made by a person's eyes. From a functional standpoint, however, the iris helps to protect delicate visual organs from overexposure by adjusting the amount of light admitted (dark eyes are more effective in this regard).

Another very important structure within the visual apparatus is the *retina.* Located at the back of the eye, the retina captures the image resulting from the influx of visual information. Here are found more than 100 million receptor cells that react to the light passed through by the lens and begin the process of organizing or coding the incoming sensations before forwarding this information to higher neural centers. The periphery of the retina is densely packed with *rods,* the receptor type that allows one to see under conditions of low illumination. The middle of the retina is occupied by *cones,*

receptor neurons that do their best work under conditions of bright illumination and that provide information on color.

The retina is supplied by an extensive network of blood vessels and is protected to some extent by a jellylike substance known as the *vitreous humor.* This miniature jelly sea is also home to various bits of floating debris, which on some occasions become visible in the form of moving shadows.

In assessing a person's visual system, one would give attention to its effectiveness in accommodation, already noted. Other measures of function include *absolute threshold, visual acuity, adaptation, glare sensitivity, depth perception,* and performance throughout the entire *visual field.*

Absolute threshold refers to the lowest level of illumination that is required for the person to detect visual information. The more effective one's visual system, the lower will be the absolute threshold: If a person bumps into a chair in the middle of the night while the cats pass through without incident, this may be just one of the many ways in which the gods are asserting their superiority. *Visual acuity* refers to the level of detail and accuracy a person is able to derive from visual inspection of the environment. This is what eye charts are intended to measure.

Adaptation refers to the ability to adjust to changes in illumination. There are two directions here: dark adaptation and light adaptation. As people move from a brightly to a dimly illuminated environment, their eyes compensate by expanding to allow more light to enter; the reverse process takes place when they move back from dim to bright lighting. *Glare sensitivity* refers to the tendency for vision to deteriorate when a person is exposed to bright lights. A person who is highly sensitive to glare is more likely to have his or her visual performance disrupted by the intrusion of relatively bright illumination, for example, the high-beaming headlights of an approaching vehicle on a dark night.

Depth perception refers to the visual system's effectiveness in determining the spatial relationships among objects and between these objects and oneself. Much but not all depth perception is lost when a person closes one eye. Even in this biomechanical sphere of functioning, the individual's experience and judgment play a role. One can make useful informed guesses about the spatial relationships among objects on the basis of past experiences with them. This is one of the ways in which central processes contribute to the transformation of electromagnetic radiation into visual perception.

The *visual field* is often assessed in terms of peripheral and central attention. What a person sees "out of the corner" of his or her eyes is peripheral vision. The person with unimpaired peripheral vision is more likely to notice people, signs, vehicles, and other objects that are not within direct view and thereby be in position to approach or avoid them. Excellent peripheral vision is often an attribute of athletes such as the basketball player who makes a seemingly "blind" pass to a teammate. Vision field is determined by testing the range of vision available to a person while his or her head remains in a fixed position.

What people see when they think they are seeing something depends on all the structures and functions that have been mentioned, and also on the activity of higher levels within the central nervous system. The "finished product" requires the following steps after the receptor system has generated a visual image on the retina:

- Long axons branching out from retinal neurons deliver the visual message through the optic nerve (the place where this nerve connects with the retina is the "blind spot").
- This semiprocessed or coded message is a representational summary of signals that were detected from millions upon millions of receptor cells.
- After an intermediary visit to the optic chiasma, the message reaches the *thalamus*, a subcortical organ, and then moves further upward to the *occipital lobe* at the back of the cerebral cortex.
- At this point, the refined message has arrived at its destination, the sector of the brain that is largely responsible for the integration and experience of visual information.
- Specialized sets of neurons within the visual cortex then perform analyses upon the incoming visual signal; the accurate and differentiated visual perceptions that one takes for granted are created or "fine tuned" through these complex and only partially understood operations.

This is a simplified sketch of the higher pathway processing of visual signals that are on their way up to the brain. A more complete picture would include the events that occur on the way back—as the central nervous system provides guidance for the actions one might initiate on the basis of the visual information that has just been processed. Eye-hand coordination, for example, relies heavily on rapid and accurate utilization of visual information and therefore on the complex processes that make this two-way translation possible (Bard, Fleury, & Hay, 1990).

Changes in Visual Functioning with Adult Age

There are four potential sources of change in visual functioning as people move from the early to the later adult years: (a) intrinsic physiological decline ("aging"), (b) illness, (c) trauma, and (d) life-style and experience. The simplest "wrap-up" would be to characterize all age-associated changes as decline and then to explain this decline in terms of "aging." In fact, there is a pattern of age-associated decline, and there is something to be said for the position that these changes are the expression of a psychobiological process that is first known as "development" and then as "aging." The total picture is more complex, however, and in practice it can be difficult to weigh the contributions of the various sources of change. For example, a child growing up in poverty may have some visual weaknesses and also suffer from dietary insufficiencies. With prompt and skilled care, this child could enter adulthood with normal visual functioning. Economic disadvantage and prevailing social policy, however, may deprive the child of opportunity for unimpaired development both visually and overall. Meeting this developmentally disadvantaged person when he or she is an elderly adult could lead to the erroneous impression that the observed disabilities are the function of "aging." A little patience and perseverance is needed to place visual functioning over the adult years in a useful perspective.

Changes in Specific Visual Functions

The status of the various visual functions changes as people move from early to later adulthood. In this review of what is known about these changes, a few practical suggestions are offered for dealing with the changes that have obvious implications for everyday life.

Absolute Threshold. Throughout the adult years there is an increase in the absolute threshold for detection of visual stimuli. This means that the older one is, the more light one needs (Verillo & Verillo, 1985). Older people are likely to be at a disadvantage when trying to find their way around in marginally lit public spaces such as parking lots and streets. Providing safe access to community resources for people of all ages might begin by ensuring that lighting is adequate for older adults.

Accommodation. It has been fairly well established that people have more difficulty in shifting their focus to targets of varying distances as they grow older (Panek et al., 1977). Older people usually have special difficulty in trying to refocus on nearby objects. This condition, known as *presbyopia*, is a consequence of the lens's reduced elasticity. Furthermore, the refocusing process also takes longer. Hayslip and Panek (1989) point out that this slower adjustment time makes driving difficult. "Drivers must constantly and alternately focus on the instrument panel and monitor the vehicles immediately in front of them (near), then refocus on exit signs and autos in the distance (far), and then refocus on objects that are near again. Since a longer time is often required to refocus with advanc-

ing age, many older drivers may accidentally miss important signs, since they cannot quickly focus.... They may consequently compensate for this increased time to accommodate by driving more slowly" (Hayslip & Panek, 1989, p. 124).

Visual Acuity. The ability to see accurately and in detail continues to improve from childhood until late adolescence or the mid-twenties. Many people experience little change until they reach their fifties. This means that if one makes only routine demands on visual acuity there will be a long period during which this ability holds more or less constant. Those who call upon their vision to make unusually precise judgments (e.g., jewelers) may find that even a small decrement is problematic and therefore schedule frequent eye examinations and change their glasses prescriptions promptly when so indicated. Decline in visual acuity accelerates markedly from the sixties onward. This adds up to a substantial decline when a person is compared at ages 40 and 80: The loss of acuity is in the 80 percent range (Weale, 1975).

There is an interaction between absolute threshold level and acuity: As one ages, one loses more acuity at lower levels of illumination (Richards, 1977). Moving objects also become more difficult to see clearly with advancing age (Panek, et al., 1977).

One consequence of the continuing decrement in visual acuity is the additional effort that aging adults must expend to fulfill those needs and desires that depend on vision. People start to prefer large-type versions of books (when available), move up to television sets with larger screens if they have the money and space for them, and perhaps acquire an assortment of glasses for various purposes. Publications, agencies, and businesses that would like to be "user friendly" to older adults would be well advised to avoid imposing extra burdens on their visual abilities by using "fancy printing" in which there is poor contrast between color of type and color of paper or by using small print in an effort to be economical. If the client or potential customer tosses the document aside because it is too difficult to read, this approach has proven not to be so economical after all.

Adaptation. Most people continue to make successful adaptations, to both light and dark, through most of the adult years. However, the process takes longer (Kline & Schieber, 1985). It would be wise to allow a little extra time when a person aged 60 or more will have to move from a brightly to a dimly lit environment or vice versa.

Glare Sensitivity. People become increasingly sensitive to glare through the later adult years. Scomatic glare is perhaps the most familiar and also the most dangerous in its possible consequences. This condition arises when confronted by a bright light (the high-beamed headlights on a dark road situation): The aging retina is overstimulated, and the lens, having thickened, is less effective in focusing the stimulation. As a result, the eye cannot filter out extraneous light. Veiling glare is a phenomenon generated by the retina itself that allows light to scatter instead of gather into a tight focus, thereby reducing the contrast between the viewed object and its background (Whitbourne, 1985).

Depth Perception. There appears to be little change in depth perception through the mid-forties. What happens to depth perception in the later adult years has not yet been firmly established, although it is thought that some decline does occur. The reduction in accommodation and visual field (below) are among the co-processes that could be involved in the decline of depth perception abilities.

Visual Field. Adults with some years on them are sometimes accused of being "narrow-minded." Whether or not that criticism is justified, there is abundant evidence that people do become relatively narrow-sighted. The visual field starts to shrink appreciably after the mid-forties (Kline & Schieber, 1985). A more direct contribution to this loss may come from reduced strength and flexibility in the muscles that enable the eyeball to move with speed and accuracy.

All of the above changes are considered to be primarily the result of intrinsic or age-related processes. The most solid and extensive evidence has been derived from studies of the visual receptor system and its components, e.g., cornea, lens, and retina.

Kuwabara (1979) has described many of these changes in detail. There is no doubt that both the structure and the functional capacities of the visual receptor system undergo systematic change of a negative type over the latter half of the life course, just as they undergo positive developmental changes earlier.

It is probable that a pattern of change also occurs at higher levels, especially in the complex and specialized work carried out by neurons in the visual cortex. These processes are inherently more difficult to study. Furthermore, the functioning of the visual cortex itself is but one facet of the central nervous system, and like every other aspect of psychobiological selves, it is also subject to change through time.

The whole story of vision through the adult years will not have been told until a good deal more is known about what is happening in the upper reaches of the brain and its overall integrative action. There is reason to believe, however, that age-associated changes are not limited to the receptor organs in visual and other sensory modalities. For example, the ability to monitor inner and outer signals—flowing through any sense modality—requires the availability of an intact, well-functioning *attentional* system. It is known that the attentional system is organized in a multilevel or hierarchical manner (Luria, 1973) and that age differences in attention are linked to changes occurring in the functioning of the "command structures" (Plude & Doussard-Roosevelt, 1989). Visual performance in the later adult years, then, is likely to be affected by changes in the multilevel structure of the visual system, as well as by changes that occur in related systems such as the attentional system. To conclude that "It's just my eyes going bad" would underestimate the role of age-related changes at various levels of operation throughout the nervous system.

Pathology and Trauma

Clearly, some visual dysfunctions through the adult years are the result of disease processes, physical disorders, or traumatic injury rather than aging. Prevent or treat these problems, and the deficits will not exist. A significant example is visual difficulty that is secondary to diabetes. Successful management of the diabetes can avoid visual impairment at any age. Not all examples are as clearly attributable to either aging or disease, however. Cataracts occur most frequently in the later adult years, as cloudy spots start to appear on the surface of the lens. Younger adults may also develop cataracts, however, and some elderly men and women seem to be spared this disability. This situation leaves room for competing points of view. One can choose to regard cataract formation as a "natural" correlate of the aging process, or one can hold that cataracts are unfortunate "add-ons" rather than an intrinsic and inevitable development. In the latter case, one might draw a parallel with conditions such as the Dutch elm disease, which, no matter how frequently appearing and devastating in its effects, can be sharply distinguished from the elm tree itself.

Gerontologists increasingly discover that conditions once thought to be intrinsic to the "aging process" actually have their own distinctive etiologies and are subject to some degree of prevention, modification, or reversal. Moreover, there is also a dynamic rather than a one-sided relationship between trauma and functional decline. Certain types of injury may accelerate the aging process, but some individuals seem exceptionally well equipped to recover function after external (e.g., accidental) or internal (e.g., stroke) trauma. It is highly possible that there will be a continuing shift toward prevention and intervention in visual dysfunctions that had previously been considered to be the inevitable outcomes of "aging" (whatever, precisely, "aging" is).

Optimizing Visual Functioning through the Adult Years

People are not entirely the passive victims of a relentless decline in acuity, accommodation, and other visual functions. Their knowledge, values, health care practices, and general life-style all have a bearing on how they make use of their visual processing apparatus and how they compensate for difficulties that arise.

A major example is provided by the *visual search* process. As the term suggests, this process comes into play when one seeks information through the visual modality to answer questions, obtain objects, increase security, or otherwise satisfy one's needs. Unlike a biomechanical process such as dark adaptation, visual search calls upon life experience, knowledge base, and personality style, and also may be strongly influenced by the particulars of the situation. How effective one is in visual search endeavors will depend on more than the status of visual apparatus. A person who is at the peak of his or her visual functioning may be less efficient in his or her search efforts than somebody with less acute vision but a more highly developed sense of search strategy and information processing.

Laboratory investigation of the visual search process is revealing that adults of all ages can improve their performances by more effective strategies. For example, the form of task preparation known as semantic priming has been found especially useful in helping people to carry out successful visual search operations (Fozard, 1990). Instead of relying on long-entrenched habits that were not very effective to begin with, one can develop approaches to visual search tasks that make better use of one's time, energies, and preexistent knowledge base.

Perhaps the time will come when child development practices and early education will include attention to the lifelong optimization of the visual system, and when people will consider it as natural to seek assistance to improve their cognitive mastery of visual function as to purchase a pair of glasses that will make the most of their aging but still faithful eyes.　▼ Robert Kastenbaum

See also: Body Senses; Driving: A Lifespan Challenge; Housing as a Factor in Adult Life; Humor; Information Processing; Listening; Taste and Smell; Work Capacity Across the Adult Years.

References

Bard, C., Fleury, M., & Hay, L. (Eds.). (1990). *Development of Eye-Hand Coordination.* Columbia, SC: University of South Carolina Press.

Fozard, J. L. (1990). Vision and hearing in aging. In J. E. Birren & K. W. Schaie (Eds), *Handbook of the Psychology of Aging.* Third Edition. New York: Academic Press, pp. 150-71.

Hayslip, B., Jr., & Panek, P. E. (1989). *Adult Development and Aging.* New York: Harper & Row.

Kline, D. W., & Schieber, F. (1985). Vision and aging. In J. E. Birren & K. W. Schaie (Eds.), *Handbook of the Psychology of Aging.* Second Edition. New York: Van Nostrand Reinhold, pp. 296-331.

Kuwabara, T. (1979). Age-related changes of the eye. In S. S. Han & D. H. Coons (Eds.), *Special Senses in Aging.* Ann Arbor, MI: University of Michigan Institute of Gerontology, pp. 46-78.

Luria, A. R. (1973) *The Working Brain.* London: Penguin.

Panek, P. E., et al. (1977). A review of age changes in perceptual information processing ability with regard to driving. *Experimental Aging Research, 3:* 387-449.

Plude, D. J., & Doussard-Roosevelt, J. A. (1989). Aging, selective attention, and feature integration. *Psychology and Aging, 4:* 98-105.

Richards, O. W. (1977). Effects of luminance and contrast on visual acuity ages 16 to 90 years. *American Journal of Optometry and Physiological Optics, 54:* 178-84.

Verillo, R. T., & Verillo, V. (1985). Sensory and perceptual performance. In N. Charness (Ed.). *Aging and Human Performance.* New York: Wiley, pp. 1-46.

Weale, R. A. (1975). Senile changes in visual acuity. *Transactions of the Ophthalamological Societies of the United Kingdom, 95:* 36-38.

Whitbourne, S. K. (1985). *The Aging Body.* New York: Springer-Verlag.

THE VOICE

What a marvelous instrument the human voice is. At birth it is used to signal one's presence in the human family. The birth cry announces one's arrival as if to say: "I am here. Please be aware of me." From the moment of birth, the organ of voice—the larynx—is capable of generating sound which is universally recognized as the birth cry. This cry occurs spontaneously, without practice, without instruction from a mother, and even without trial-and-error attempts to make it work. The cry of the infant from Canton, China, will be the same as that of the infant from College Park, Maryland, in terms of pitch, loudness, inflections, and quality. Regardless of the parental language spoken, this universal birth cry brings joy to parents the world over.

Anatomical and Physiological Foundations

Understanding this mechanism of sound, the larynx, and how it works from birth through the aging process requires a knowledge of the anatomical and physiological bases of the human voice. Although the anatomy of the larynx may change significantly over the lifespan, the physiological bases of sound will vary little.

Anatomy. The *larynx* is a valving mechanism which anatomically sits on top of the trachea, or windpipe, as a sentinel that protects the trachea and other structures of the respiratory tract from the invasion of foreign matter such as foods and liquids. This valve must be capable of closing to prevent aspiration of such substances, but it also must open efficiently to allow air into the system. The opening of the laryngeal valve for respiration and its closure during swallowing to prevent aspiration constitute the biological functions of the larynx. These biological functions are complex, but the usage of this same organ as a sound generator for the human voice—a process known as *phonation*—is a much higher level of function. Phonation involves the interaction of anatomy (structure), physiology (function), and acoustic principles of sound generation.

The larynx is the general organ involved in biological as well as sound, or phonatory, functions. It is a structure composed of three main cartilages which form its general shape, i.e., the cricoid, thyroid, and paired arytenoid cartilages. These cartilages are bound together into a functional unit by ligaments, muscles, and other forms of connective tissue. The muscle structure of the larynx is what opens and closes the valve to allow biological and phonatory processes to occur.

The most easily identified cartilage is the thyroid cartilage, which presents itself, particularly in mature males, as the *Adam's apple*. This structure, more technically called the laryngeal prominence, can be identified by touching the middle of the neck in front and feeling the hardest and most prominent structure. The thyroid cartilage is shaped like a shield to protect the inner structures of the larynx. Of special importance among these inner structures are the *vocal folds*, located immediately behind the walls of the thyroid cartilage. The vocal folds are the structures upon which the human voice is most dependent; in fact, they provide the basis for the voice. The muscles of the vocal folds are attached in front to the thyroid cartilage and in back to the arytenoid cartilages. The arytenoid cartilages are capable of complex movements which influence the vocal folds that are attached to them. These movements of the arytenoid cartilages cause the vocal folds to move in various states of opening and closing. If the arytenoid cartilages are moved apart, the vocal folds are likewise moved apart because of arytenoid attachment. The opposite is true when the arytenoids are moved together, causing vocal fold closure.

Both vocal folds are composed of a band of muscle tissue (thyroarytenoid, also called the vocalis muscle) that lies horizontally from the front to the back of the larynx. One vocal fold is exactly the same shape as the other. When viewed from above, the vocal folds appear as two bands of muscles that can move together or apart. When apart, there is a space between them through which air passes on the way to and from the lungs. This space is called the *glottis*. When the folds are brought together, the glottis is closed. This action prevents food or liquid from entering the respiratory tract.

Physiology and Acoustics. Two essential ingredients are needed for the vocal folds to produce the sound of a voice. First, there must be air flow from the lungs, as in exhalation. Second, the valving potential of vocal fold closure must impede, or somewhat obstruct, that flow of air. When air exhaled from the lungs is obstructed by the lightly closed vocal cords, pressure occurs below the vocal folds which sets them into vibration. This vibration of the vocal folds is the sound source of the voice.

The sound produced by the vibrating vocal folds is a neutral sound, like a buzz or a sound produced by a massage vibrator. It does not sound like any human vowel sound. For that to happen, vocal resonance must occur. The sound will have a specific frequency or *pitch, measured in hertz* (Hz), and a specific intensity or *loudness, measured in decibels*. For example, a newborn infant's cry typically has a frequency around 500 Hz. This value of 500 Hz means that the vocal folds are vibrating 500 times per second to generate that pitch.

The pitch produced in voice is dependent upon the length, mass, and tension of the vocal folds during vibration. Just as a string on a guitar will vibrate different pitches depending on the length, thickness (mass), and tension of the string, so the vocal folds will vibrate different pitches as a result of variance in those same properties.

The sound generated by the vibrating vocal folds must be resonated in order to be perceived as the human voice. Fortunately, humans have a natural "concert hall" for resonation in the form of the oral cavity, the nasal cavity, and the anatomical hallway that connects them, the throat or pharynx. Thus, sound generated by the vibrating folds is resonated into the various vowels and consonants of human speech in these cavities above the larynx (Baken, 1987; Zemlin, 1988).

The Pre-Puberty Voice

There is no difference in the voices of boys and girls in terms of pitch, loudness, and quality characteristic during the first years of life. It is not until puberty that gender differences begin to emerge.

Prior to puberty, the vocal folds grow and develop in a similar manner for both sexes. In infants, for example, the muscles of the vocal folds are very tiny, approximately 3 to 4 mm in tissue length. Think of it, all that crying sound comes from tissues only 3 mm long. The length and cross-sectional mass are the same regardless of the sex of the baby.

As the infant grows into childhood and early youth, the length and cross-sectional mass of the vocal folds increase, and the natural pitch of the voice lowers slightly year by year. Just prior to puberty, the vibrating vocal folds are approximately 10 mm long, regardless of gender. When the hormonal changes of puberty begin to generate significant differences in male and female bodies, the larynx grows in a manner corresponding to this general physical growth, and the voice begins to change.

Puberty and Voice

Puberty produces significant laryngeal dimorphism between males and females. As the male body grows, adding inches to height and bulkier muscles to a slender frame, the larynx also grows and becomes thicker. By the end of puberty, the typical male vocal folds will have increased at least 60 percent in length and a corresponding amount in cross-sectional mass. As a result of this increased size, the natural pitch of the typical male voice will lower nearly one octave. Thus a boy has become a man in terms of body structure and voice. If males do not make this vocal adjustment to the lower voice, a disorder called *puberphonia* occurs (Case, 1991, Chapter 6).

Female vocal folds will increase only about 30 percent in length, but they also

increase in cross-sectional mass. The corresponding pitch will also lower, but not nearly so drastically as with males.

In addition to the above laryngeal and vocal mechanism changes resulting from puberty, the following occur.

- Prepubertal female laryngeal dimensions are closer to adult size and weight than male counterparts, suggesting that the female larynx requires less growth over time to reach maturity.

- Laryngeal cartilage growth occurs through external expansion (called oppositional growth) as well as internal expansion (called interstitial growth), so the basic shape of the larynx is not changed during puberty growth spurts.

- Extensive regional growth characterizes the enhancement of the anterior aspect of the male thyroid cartilage. This growth produces the typical male Adam's apple, a thicker thyroid cartilage surface that develops on the male and can often be seen very easily, particularly in thin individuals.

- Vocal fold length and thickness grow independently. It is thought that thickness continues to increase after length has reached adult dimensions and that this increasing thickness is responsible for the truly mature male or female voice heard from age 20 through the fifties. A typical 50-year-old male's vocal pitch or frequency would be around 120 Hz. The typical female's vocal pitch or frequency at this same age would be about 22 Hz. Keep in mind that these figures are general averages and that there is much variability from person to person within each gender (Baken, 1987; Kahane, 1987).

The Adult Years

Once the larynx and vocal folds stabilize in terms of the growth and developmental changes associated with puberty, both males and females enter a relatively stable vocal period so far as pitch is concerned. This stage lasts from the thirties through the fifties and even into the seventies. Figure 1 displays the general pitch patterns of males and females from childhood through the adult years. The plotting of vocal frequency (pitch) over time demonstrates this relative stability after puberty. The pitch data for males and females are sufficiently stable that one bar graph can represent those decades.

The Aging Voice

We have described how a clear divergence of fundamental frequency or pitch occurs at puberty between males and females; the opposite trend appears to exist in the later years of life. A slight vocal convergence occurs, bringing the voices of men and women closer in pitch. This convergence takes place as the older male voice rises in pitch and the older female voice remains more stable, or lowers slightly in extreme old age. The voices do not become identical, however, and it is still possible to detect gender in most older persons merely by hearing the voice. The typical pitch or frequency of the male in his eighth decade will be about 150 Hz, while the typical woman of the same age will have a pitch or frequency of about 197 Hz.

The effect of aging on vocal intensity is not so well understood. The stereotype of the older voice is that loudness is increased to compensate for hearing loss. Some individuals may experience such vocal change from hearing loss, but it is more likely that the older speaker will have a reduced ability to produce loud tones because of decreased respiratory support for voice as a function of reduced energy levels.

Another commonly perceived aspect of the older voice is vocal tremor, a rhythmical fluctuation of pitch that is much like vocal vibrato in the singing voice. An actor playing the role of an older person may express that character by causing the voice to fluctuate in the tremorlike pattern. This, however, is merely a stereotypical representation of aging in the voice. Tremor is not a part of the aging voice as such. More likely, it is a manifestation of a clinical change in the innervation of the larynx and, therefore, a sign of a neurological disorder. Vocal tremor—known as *essential tremor*—should be evaluated medically. In the healthy older person, the voice may be weaker, the speech generally slower in articulation, and the duration of utterance somewhat shorter, but the vocal pitch should remain fairly steady (Aronson, 1990; Case, 1991, Chapter 5).

Care of the Voice Throughout the Lifespan

It is easy to take for granted one's ability to produce voice since in most cases it is

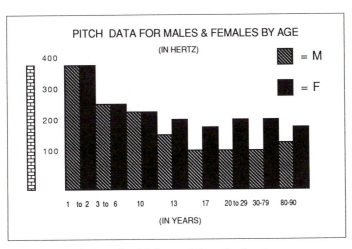

Figure 1. Pitch Data for Males and Females by Age

available from birth until one's dying breath. However, there are many disorders of the voice that can be prevented by applying principles of good vocal hygiene. These principles have been discovered and tested by professionals in the health fields that care for the voice as well as professionals in vocal performance, speech-language pathology, and voice science.

One significant principle involves avoiding the use of cigarettes, pipes, or cigars. Inhaling smoke through the larynx to the lungs is a damaging process. The heat and chemical irritants present in the smoke constitute harmful agents that lead to swelling of the vocal folds, the formation of polyps, and even cancer, which often requires surgical removal of the larynx (laryngectomy).

Another significant principle of good vocal hygiene involves the elimination of vocal abuse such as yelling, screaming, prolonged talking at pitch levels that are too high or low, and talking in noisy places such as factories, around machinery, and even in nightclubs that have loud music playing constantly. Many patients have been seen by professionals in voice management because of injury to the vocal folds as a result of these and similar activities.

The human voice certainly is a remarkable instrument. It serves to announce one's entry into the world. It provides the vocal basis for human speech (Baken, 1987). It signals joy through laughter (LaPointe, Mowrer & Case, 1987) and sadness or fear through crying (Moses, 1954). It is the basis for great inspiration when one hears arias sung by singers who control the pitch, loudness, and quality as precisely as the finest musical instrument. The voice is so basic to human communication that only when it is lost (as in the example of laryngeal cancer requiring surgical removal of the larynx) does one recognize how significantly life is altered (Case, 1991, Chapter 7). It is an organ that should be appreciated and cared for as the basis for human speech.   ▼ JAMES L. CASE

See also: Gender as a Shaping Force in Adult Development and Aging; Language Development; Listening.

References

Aronson, A. E. (1990). *Clinical Voice Disorders.* Third Edition. New York: Thieme Inc.

Baken, R. J. (1987). *Clinical Measurement of Voice and Speech.* Austin, TX: PRO-ED.

Case, J. L. (1991). *Clinical Management of Voice and Speech.* Second Edition. Austin, TX: PRO-ED.

Kahane, J. C. (1987). Connective tissue changes in the larynx and their effects on voice. *Journal of Voice, 1:* 27-30.

LaPointe, L. L., Mowrer, D. E., & Case, J. L. (1987). A comparative acoustic analysis of the laugh response of 20 and 70 year-old males. *International Journal of Aging and Human Development, 31:* 1-9.

Moses, P. J. (1954). *The Voice of Neurosis.* New York: Grune and Stratton.

Zemlin, W. R. (1988). *Speech and Hearing Science: Anatomy and Physiology.* Third Edition. Englewood Cliffs, NJ: Prentice-Hall.

W

WIDOWHOOD: THE COPING RESPONSE

The death of a spouse is an increasingly common experience among aging adults, particularly women. The 1990 Census revealed that only 1 percent of the population between ages 18 and 54 were widowed, but 34 percent of those 65 and over and 67 percent of those 85 and over were widowed (U.S. Bureau of the Census, 1991). A gender difference becomes increasingly apparent in the later years of life. After age 65, nearly 49 percent of the women but only 14 percent of men were widowed. In the 85+ category, 80 percent of women and 43 percent of men were widowed. These high percentages actually underestimate the number of persons who experience the death of a spouse because they do not include those who remarried.

Adjustment to Bereavement

Although the death of a spouse is a common experience, many people are not well prepared for the bereavement process that follows the death. Bereavement refers to both the situation and the long-term process of adjusting to the death of someone with whom a person feels close. The adjustment process is multidimensional in that the loss can affect nearly every aspect of a person's life, including emotions, spirituality, identity, social interactions and relationships, sexuality, work productivity, health, and even death. The term *bereavement* also has been used in reference to losses other than death, such as the loss of a home or personal belongings because of a fire or a natural disaster. It is more common, however, to use the term bereavement in situations following the death of a friend or relative, or even an animal companion.

Other terms associated with the bereavement process include *grief* and *mourning*. These terms are distinguishable from bereavement in that they refer to specific aspects of the broader process. Grief is characterized by the affective or emotional responses that people often experience during the early phases of the bereavement process. These feelings frequently include disbelief, confusion, shock, numbness, sadness, and sometimes anger and guilt. Feeling abandoned, lonely, or depressed and being preoccupied with thoughts of the deceased person and the events surrounding the death are often components of grief.

Not all persons experience these feelings and the degree of intensity varies in those who do, but it is common for bereaved persons to feel a wide range of emotions that come and go quickly and can reappear over many months or even years.

Culture plays a role in shaping how people experience and express bereavement (Chigier, 1988; Stroebe & Stroebe, 1987). Most professionals use the term *mourning* to refer to the commonly accepted or culturally patterned ways people express themselves during the adjustment process. Mourning does not refer to the individual's inner feelings and thoughts but to such behaviors as crying; missing work; altering daily routines; attending funerals, cremations, and burials; following standards for dress and appearance; and participating in other rituals that are influenced by the surrounding culture. The diversity in how people grieve and mourn helps to illustrate the importance of understanding the context in which bereavement takes place. Age, gender, social class position, ethnicity, and race of the bereaved will influence how they feel and behave during the process. Also, these two terms help us to recognize the complex, multidimensional nature of bereavement.

In the case of spousal bereavement, the adjustment process leads to a new role with additional social expectations. The bereaved spouse is expected to redefine his or her self-concept to fit with the new social position of widowhood. These widowhood adjustments are difficult to separate from the long-term bereavement process because they occur at the same time. With widowhood, however, the emphasis is placed on changing patterns of interaction with others, as well as altering the self-concept to reflect what has been called an "uncoupled identity" (Saunders, 1981). In U.S. society, married couples often form their identity around their partner so that John sees himself as Mary's husband and Mary perceives herself as John's wife. After years of marriage and doing things together, it is difficult to accept a new uncoupled identity based upon the absence of the partner and the loss of shared activities.

Changing Views about the Bereavement Process

Throughout history, all human societies have struggled to develop satisfying views about life and death. Much less attention has been given to understanding the experiences of survivors and helping them find effective ways to cope with bereavement. Most of our knowledge about coping with the death of others has come from clinical observations (Freud, 1957), autobiographical accounts (Caine, 1974), and early descriptive studies of small samples of bereaved persons (Lindemann, 1944).

For many years it was widely accepted that the bereavement process follows an orderly sequence of stages, phases, or steps; that normal and abnormal grief could easily be distinguished; and that people eventually recover from the loss in much the same way that a wound heals over time (Glick, Weiss, & Parkes, 1974). We are now beginning to question many of these assumptions on the basis of recent large-scale studies that have examined random samples of bereaved persons over several years (Wortman & Silver, 1989).

A great deal has been learned from studies that extended beyond those who sought help from professional clinicians or those who survived unusual life-threatening situations. Research in the 1980s and 1990s has included younger and older spouses, both men and women, and those who have coped very well along with those who have managed poorly. Whereas earlier studies often waited until 6 to 18 months after the death, more recent studies have interviewed spouses as early as two or three weeks after the death, and in some cases even before the death occurred.

Bereavement research is important because recent studies have revealed new information that has changed our understanding of the course of spousal bereavement and clarified the factors that contribute to more successful coping.

Research Highlights

There is growing recognition that although the death of a spouse might be the most stressful event that a person will experience, many bereaved spouses, including those who are older, do find ways to manage and rebuild their lives. The course of spousal bereavement is often characterized by *resiliency*, which allows depression, loneliness, and sadness to be followed by feelings of pride, confidence, and personal growth. Although it has been estimated that between 15 and 25 percent of bereaved spouses have long-term difficulty in coping, many more gradually discover effective ways (Lund, 1989).

Resiliency following the death of a spouse might best be explained by a life course or developmental perspective that emphasizes the importance of growth, maturation, adaptability, and previous life experiences in coping with stressful events. When we experience bereavement at earlier times in our life course, we are likely to be less prepared to make the needed adjustments. Spousal bereavement in later life is considered to be more "on time" because we expect deaths to occur with greater frequency as we age. Older adults also have had more opportunities than younger adults to successfully manage a variety of losses and thereby develop effective strategies and interpersonal skills.

This advantage, however, does not mean that older adults automatically cope better than others. Unsuccessful coping with earlier losses can lead to poor coping skills later. Another problem is "bereavement overload" (Kastenbaum, 1991), in which coping becomes exceedingly difficult because several losses or deaths occur in a very short time. The key to resiliency during bereavement is developing successful interpersonal coping strategies for coping with each new loss.

Recent studies have revealed that the bereavement process is more like a roller coaster ride than an orderly progression of stages with clear time frames associated with each stage. The bereavement rollercoaster is characterized by the rapidly changing emotions of grief; meeting the challenges of learning new skills; recognizing personal weaknesses and limitations; developing new patterns of behavior; experiencing fatigue, loneliness, and helplessness; and forming new friendships and relationships.

Research has been unable to identify clear time markers associated with these many ups and downs. In fact, the highs and lows can occur within minutes, days, months, or years. Fortunately, most bereaved spouses experience a roller-coaster ride that becomes more manageable over time, with fewer abrupt highs and lows. This gradual improvement may never lead to an end or

resolution, however, because many bereaved spouses report: "You never get over it—you learn to live with it."

Another theme emerging from recent studies is that of being more cautious in using the term "normal" to describe grief or bereavement. There is a great deal of diversity among people. Furthermore, the same individual may experience and express herself or himself in a variety of ways during bereavement. What would have been considered outside the realm of "normal" grief several years ago may now be considered a normal part of the process. For example, talking to a deceased spouse would once have been defined as abnormal or even pathological, but recent research findings show that this is actually a very common practice among bereaved spouses—and it is now often encouraged as a therapeutic technique.

Rather than applying rigid labels such as "normal" or "abnormal," it is more appropriate to use terms such as "common" or "uncommon" to describe bereavement feelings and behaviors. A bereaved person is far less stigmatized and assaulted by being told that she or he is experiencing some uncommon feelings than by being told, "You are abnormal."

What Helps?

One often hears people say that the passage of time will heal the wound. This statement is problematic and inaccurate because it implies that little or no effort is required to cope with the situation. Simply allowing time to pass is supposed to bring about successful adjustment. Although it is a fact that most bereaved spouses experience less difficulty and more positive adjustments over time, it is important to recognize that it is what people *do* with their time that determines the outcomes. Successful adjustments require active rather than passive coping strategies.

Previously bereaved spouses have told others that it is most helpful to take one day at a time and to remain active, busy, and socially connected with other people (Lund,

1989). Being physically and socially active during the process can help to reduce the feelings of despair, helplessness, loneliness, and being overwhelmed that often contribute to a long-term strategy of waiting—often in vain—for time to bring about healing.

In addition to these active coping strategies, recent studies have documented the importance of having social support from others and opportunities for self-expression available, especially in the early months of bereavement. Some of the most difficult and stressful bereavement experiences occur in the first few months when grief issues are especially intense.

Researchers have also learned that how a person copes with loss early in the process appears to be one of the best predictors of long-term coping. Those who report having effective coping experiences in the first couple of months usually cope better than others a few years later. Bereaved spouses therefore are likely to benefit most from social support that they receive early in the process and from opportunities to express how they feel at this time. Some of the most appreciated and helpful support comes from those who allow the bereaved to openly express anger, sadness, and other emotions without passing along advice and counsel. It is important for bereaved persons to know that their reactions are common and that others respect their feelings and care about their well-being. Self-help groups for bereaved persons provide good opportunities for self-expression, particularly for those who do not already have someone in whom they can confide.

The relevancy of a lifespan developmental perspective in understanding spousal bereavement is supported by research that has focused on the role of self-esteem and self-efficacy. Both concepts represent personal coping resources that individuals develop throughout their lives. Self-esteem refers to the positive or negative judgments or evaluations that one makes about self-worth. Self-efficacy refers to one's ability to meet the changing demands of everyday life.

The way people feel about themselves and how skilled they are in managing the many tasks of daily living—maintaining a household, paying bills, driving a car, knowing how to access resources, etc.—will influence how effectively they adjust to the death of a spouse or partner. People who develop positive self-esteem and competencies such as social, interpersonal, and instrumental skills are likely to have more favorable bereavement outcomes than those who develop negative self-images and lack self-efficacy.

Self-esteem and self-efficacy are highly interrelated because people who have confidence and pride in themselves are usually more motivated to learn new skills, and the process of becoming more competent in daily life itself creates more positive self-esteem. Bereaved spouses with these positive characteristics are likely to cope quite well because they will not be content with a passive approach to coping. Conversely, bereaved spouses who never developed these personal coping resources are likely to experience long-term difficulties because they are more inclined to believe that they deserve to remain depressed, lonely, and incapacitated. These people tend to feel overwhelmed and take few constructive actions on their own behalf.

The predictors of adjustment to spousal bereavement are similar for both men and women and for young and older adults. Age and gender are *not* the most influential factors in the course of bereavement. What is of greater importance is to develop positive feelings about oneself early in life, continue to enhance these views over the life course, and develop skills that help one to meet the changing circumstances and demands of daily living. People with these traits are more likely than others to adjust well to nearly any major life stress or transition.

Development is a lifelong process. In the case of spousal bereavement, which is most commonly experienced in later life, the developmental process is challenged. During this transition period, the bereaved spouse can remain physically, psychologically, and socially disrupted or can emerge with a sense of growth from learning new skills, becoming more independent, and developing a clearer self-identity. A wide range of possible

outcomes can result from the death of a spouse, and they are not limited by a person's age. ▼ Dale A. Lund

See also: Depression; Life Events; Loneliness; Marital Development; Mental Health Resources for Adults; Mexican Americans: Life Course Transitions and Adjustment; Religion and Coping with Crisis; Reminiscence and Life Review; Social Relationships, Convoys of; Stress; Suffering.

References

Caine, L. (1974). *Widow.* New York: Bantam.

Chigier, E. (Ed.). (1988). *Grief and Bereavement in Contemporary Society.* London: Freund Publishing House Ltd.

Freud, S. (1957). Mourning and melancholia. *The Standard Edition of the Complete Psychological Works of Sigmund Freud.* Volume 14. London: Hogarth Press.

Glick, J., Weiss, R., & Parkes, C. (1974). *The First Year of Bereavement.* New York: John Wiley & Sons.

Kastenbaum, R. (1991). *Death, Society, and Human Experience.* Fourth Edition. New York: Macmillan/Merrill.

Lindemann, E. (1944). The symptomatology and management of acute grief. *American Journal of Psychiatry, 101:* 141-48.

Lund, D. (1989). Conclusions about bereavement in later life and implications for interventions and future research. In D. Lund (Ed.), *Older Bereaved Spouses: Research with Practical Applications.* New York: Hemisphere, pp. 217-31.

Saunders, J. (1981). A process of bereavement resolution: Uncoupled identity. *Western Journal of Nursing Research, 3:* 319-32.

Stroebe, W., & Stroebe, M. (1987). *Bereavement and Health: The Psychological and Physical Consequences of Partner Loss.* London: Cambridge University Press.

U.S. Bureau of the Census (1991). Marital status and living arrangements: March, 1990. *Current Population Reports,* Series P-20, No. 450. Washington, DC: Government Printing Office.

Wortman, C., & Silver, R. (1989). The myths of coping with loss. *Journal of Consulting and Clinical Psychology, 57:* 349-57.

WORK CAPACITY ACROSS THE ADULT YEARS

Experience versus Biology

The ability to meet the requirements of work situations, or indeed any other challenge of everyday living, depends fundamentally on two sets of factors. The capacities of the chain of biological mechanisms of the body—sensory, muscular, and cerebral—make up the first set of factors, and the individual's knowledge and experience make up the second set. The first set of factors decline with age during adulthood; the second accumulate and improve over the years, often offsetting biological declines.

Biological capacities rise to an early peak around age 20 and then, on average, fall—slowly at first and more rapidly later. For example, visual acuity and adjustment of focus to distance decline so much that by age 40 few avoid the need for spectacles for either distance viewing or reading, or for both. Similarly, sensitivity of the ears to high frequencies declines so that by about the same age few can hear the squeak of a bat. By the sixties there may be difficulty in distinguishing consonants such as *s* from *f* or *p* from *t*.

Muscular strength has been found to decline, on average, by about 2.5 percent from the twenties to the thirties, 7 percent to the forties, 14 percent to the fifties, and 23 percent to the sixties. This decline is the result of the progressive loss of muscle fibers and their reduced activation by nerve impulses (Larsson, 1982). The amount of heavy muscular work achieved over given periods of time also falls because of decreasing function of the respiratory and circulatory systems, which result in reduced oxygen supply to the muscles. Other limitations such a stiffness of joints and arthritic pains also increase with age, although they seldom become important until the sixties or seventies.

It had been assumed for some time that all changes of performance with age could be attributed to declines in the various sensory

and muscular mechanisms. This assumption has been proven incorrect by the (unpopular) finding that there are similar changes in central or mental operations with age. For instance, average scores on intelligence tests have been found to decline by about 0.7 percent per year from the twenties to the fifties (Pacaud & Welford, 1989; Slater, 1948; Vincent, 1952). The decline proceeds more rapidly thereafter (Foulds & Raven, 1948).

Reaction times lengthen and many mental activities become slower from the twenties onward by amounts that increase both absolutely and proportionately as the tasks of relating stimuli to responses and integrating information become more complex (Welford, 1977). The control of movements that require relatively little muscular strength becomes a little slower or less accurate, or both, from about the thirties onward (Welford, Norris, & Shock, 1969; York & Biederman, 1990). Registering new material in memory becomes more difficult, but once it has been firmly registered it seems not to be forgotten with advancing age, even though older people may take longer to retrieve information from memory when it is needed.

An "Index of Aging"?

It has been suggested that overall capacity for work can be determined by combining measures of these various sensory, motor, and central capacities into an "index of aging." This, however, is clearly a wrong approach for three reasons:

1. Different jobs and types of work make different demands. For example, work that requires great muscular strength may make only slight demands on vision, hearing, or intelligence, and work requiring fine visual acuity may make little demand on muscular strength. In general, performance is *limited* by the capacity which its demands load fully, and its demands on other capacities are, over a wide range, unimportant.
2. The *rate* of change of capacities with age differs greatly between and within individuals. Thus, one person may become hard of hearing but preserve excellent sight and muscular physique, while another may have a significant reduction in muscular strength but experience little change of mental acumen. In other words, capacity for work depends upon a match between the particular demands of the job and the pattern of capacities of the particular individual.
3. An "index of aging" ignores the essential contribution of knowledge and experience to the effective use of capacities.

Experience and resulting knowledge obviously increase rapidly through childhood and adolescence and continue to accumulate and improve during adulthood. The abilities gained provide what might be termed the "tactics" and "strategies" of work performance. These consist not only in knowing what to do and having a basic understanding of tools and materials used but also in refining methods and attaining accuracy so that actions can be carried out quickly and without continually checking the correctness of results. Experience and knowledge lead to the efficient deployment of capacities so that job demands can be met more efficiently and with less capacity than would otherwise be required. The terms *skill* and *expertise* are used to describe this astute form of cognitive guidance over actions. Their effects are well expressed in an observation heard both in industry and sports: "The skilled expert always seems to have all the time in the world."

The decline of biological capacities, together with the increase of knowledge and experience during adulthood, means that for any work or task there is an average age at which performance will be optimal according to the balance of demands it makes on the biological and the experiential factors. This optimal age will be younger if the main demand is on biological factors, older if it is on the experiential and knowledge factors. The word "average" again needs to be emphasized: The variation among individuals already noted in both biological capacities and knowledge/experience means that some individuals will reach their peak performance at any particular task earlier or later than most.

Production Work in Industry

Studies of output by persons of different ages engaged in industrial production work have found that average speed and accuracy both tend to increase up to age 35 to 45. Thereafter, accuracy remains high while speed either remains constant or declines slowly (Welford, 1977), but at the same time the number of people employed falls. The trends are well illustrated in Figure 1.

The rise of performance from the teens to the thirties could be due in part to the dropout of less efficient workers. Mainly, though, it reflects increasing expertise that results from longer experience at the work being done. This view is reinforced by the much steeper rise for skilled work, in which, by definition, there is more to be learned before full expertise is attained.

It appears that up to the thirties or forties experience compensates for declines in biological capacities, but that after that age biological decline begins to assert itself in most jobs. The no-longer-young employee then tends to move on to other types of work. The variation between individuals already

noted means that some are able to carry on, but they are examples of "survival of the fittest." This conclusion is supported by studies that have found that those who remain in the same jobs had been superior performers during their earlier years (King, 1956) and those who move to other types of work tend to be less physically fit than those who remain (Powell, 1973).

Age distributions such as those shown in Figure 1 can be misleading if a job has expanded so that young recruits have not had time to grow old or has contracted so that recruiting of young workers has ceased. Nevertheless, comparisons between age distributions and average ages of those employed on different jobs are probably the best, even if somewhat crude, measures available of how suitable particular types of work are for people of different ages. Studies have shown that the age distributions and mean ages of workers on various jobs correspond well with the extent to which the jobs make physiological and psychological demands that would be expected to be taxing for those in later middle age (Smith, 1973; Welford, 1966).

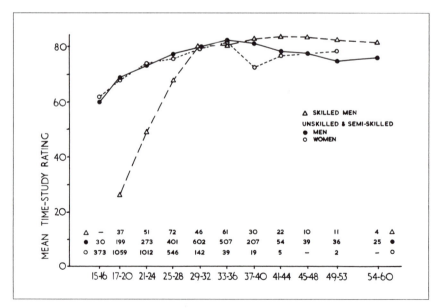

Figure 1. Time-Study Measures of Performance, and Numbers at Work in Different Age Ranges at a Factory Making Electrical Apparatus. Plotted from data tabulated by Wackwitz (1946).

Demands Made by Production Work.
The following demands on individual capacity have been identified for production work.

1. *Speed* demanded by piece-rate work and, especially, the combination of speed with rigid pacing, as on many conveyor lines, place rigorous and incessant demands on the worker that become especially difficult in the middle and later adult years (Belbin, 1953; Featherstone & Cunningham, 1963). A classical example of the differing age distributions for work with and without speed pressure is shown in Figure 2.

2. *Heavy muscular effort* is required in many mining and quarrying jobs. Differences in performance on more and less physically demanding coal-mining jobs are shown in Figure 3. Work involving both

speed and heavy muscular effort is especially unfavorable for the middle-aged worker (Belbin, 1953). However, people in later middle age have been found to meet substantial demands for physical effort well (Barkin, 1933) when speed is not also a prime consideration. Examples have been observed of people moving successfully from fast-paced jobs to work that is physically more demanding (Belbin, 1955). Older people have also been found to tolerate such adverse work conditions as dust, drafts, noise, and heat (Heron & Chown, 1961).

3. *Complex instructions and elaborate working drawings* present difficulties for the older worker (Murrell & Tucker, 1960). Table 1 shows the average ages of men employed in a large precision engineering factory in England. The youngest groups in the

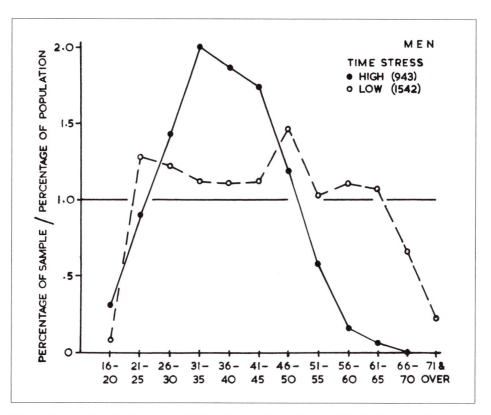

Figure 2. Age Distribution of 2,485 Men Engaged in Industrial Work. The data shown are the ratios of the percentages in each age range divided by the percentage of the corresponding age range in the general population. Data from Welford (1958) and the United Kingdom Census of 1951.

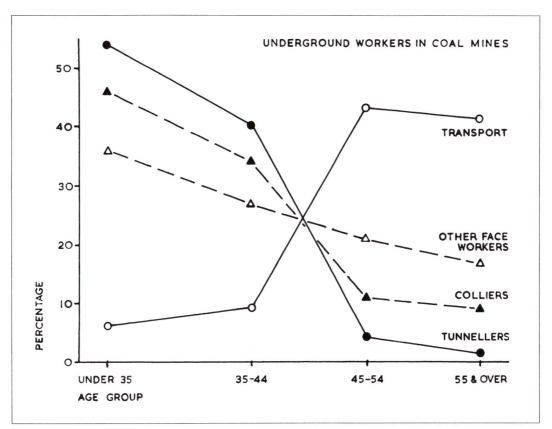

Figure 3. Percentages of Men in Four Age Ranges on Underground Work in Coal Mines. Tunnelling is regarded as the most severely demanding work, that of colliers as less, and that of transport as least. Plotted from data tabulated by Powell (1973).

factory are the pattern makers and electricians, whose work makes significant demands of this kind.

4. *Fine visual acuity and high degrees of accuracy* also become increasingly difficult with advancing age (Murrell & Tucker, 1960). The average ages of those shown in Table 1 as employed on work highly demanding of close visual inspection and concentration were lower than of those employed on work requiring less skill. Both groups of employees were on average younger than those in nonproduction jobs which, although benefiting from knowledge and experience, were less demanding of sensory and mental capacities.

Laboratory studies and observations in industrial settings suggest three further sources of difficulty for those in later middle age.

5. *Substantial changes of working method,* such as are often required with new machinery, present problems. As noted earlier, difficulties in learning increase during the adult years, but these often seem to be accompanied by problems of motivation. Although new methods might make work easier once they are well mastered, the immediate effect of their introduction may be difficulty and frustration (Welford, 1976, 1981).

6. *Keeping track of several developing situations simultaneously* (Maule & Sanford, 1980) is a taxing responsibility for older workers and, therefore, also an unpopular one. Safety concerns also increase if the job is one in which a temporary fail-

Table 1. Median Ages (in years) of Men in Various Types of Work in an Engineering Factory

(The total workforce included over 3,000 men.)

Type of Work	Median Age
Requires use of complex working diagrams	
Pattern makers	31.5
Electricians	35.2
Skilled work demanding high precision	
Millers	35.4
Grinders	37.5
Turners	37.9
Borers	38.0
Skilled work requiring less precision	
Drillers	42.8
Polishers	43.7
Welders	44.5
Fitters	44.9
Foundry workers	45.0
Plating and heat treatment	48.8
Nonproduction work	
Storekeepers	52.2
Factory services	56.8
Laborers	57.1
Packers	58.1

A similar pattern of age differences on these types of work was also found in six other, smaller engineering factories.

Data from Murrell, Griew, & Tucker (1957).

ure of attention or concentration could lead to injury.

7. *Envisaging processes that cannot be directly observed* has been found to be more difficult for older workers (Welford, 1960). This kind of work often involves the additional task of inferring processes from readings on meters or other symbolic displays, which also tends to be more of a problem with advancing age. Both of these difficulties are illustrated in large-scale industrial operations such as the generation of electricity or the manufacture of chemicals, which involve many remote control operations.

Where Do Workers Go When They Leave the Production Line? The substantial fall in numbers of women between the early twenties and early thirties shown in Figure 1 is probably attributable to many leaving to marry and start a family. Reduction in the numbers of both men and women from the thirties onward can be attributed to several causes.

Some workers, especially those with superior skills, are promoted to foremen or other managerial positions, which tend to be filled with persons who are older than the average production worker.

Additionally, a few suffer accidents that lead to disablement. As shown in Table 2, types of accident change with age. Accidents typical of younger workers have been found to be attributable to carelessness, impulsivity, or lack of skill. In contrast, workers in later middle age and beyond are more likely to have accidents that are attributable to slowness as, for example, in recovering balance when tripped or in getting out of the way of moving objects. Such accidents more often occur in job situations that appear to be unduly demanding of older people (Griew, 1958; King, 1955; Whitfield, 1954).

Additionally, researchers in France have emphasized the *cumulative incidence of disease and of working conditions injurious to health.* Industrial workers, for example, have poorer health than schoolteachers and other people holding professional positions (Clement, 1969; Tieger & Villatte, 1983). Loss of time from work because of sickness may increase with age, and some industrial conditions do injure health. For example, it has been estimated that safe loads for lifting should be reduced by about 25 percent from the twenties to the fifties if low back pain and related disorders are to be avoided (Stubbs, 1985).

It is probably an exaggeration, however, to attribute the main decline of numbers on production work to such causes. First, it is possible that people with professional careers, as a group, started off with a genetic advantage and, therefore, show less decline with age in at least some biological capacities (e.g., Foulds & Raven, 1948; Pacaud & Welford, 1989). Furthermore, ill health is sometimes a rationalization for moves to a less demanding type of work. It has been found that, as many production workers en-

Table 2. Age Differences (in years) in Causes of Agricultural Accidents

Cause of Accident	Number	Percentages of each type of accident		
		Age group: 15-30	31-50	51-80
Increases with age				
Falls	453	13.0	23.9	31.5
Hit by moving or falling objects	339	14.9	15.8	21.4
Decreases with age				
Caught in machine	202	12.6	10.3	7.2
Using tool	184	12.6	8.2	7.9
Bodily or muscular strain	127	6.9	7.1	3.6
Starting an engine	98	10.3	4.3	1.2
No significant change				
Moving heavy object	103	4.0	5.5	4.6
Knocked against or trod on object	90	5.0	5.1	3.6
Action of animal	79	2.6	4.2	4.4
Miscellaneous	175	9.9	8.5	8.7
Unspecified	141	8.2	7.1	6.3

Data from King (1955).

ter their forties, they carry on their jobs under increasing strain, working more continuously, taking fewer informal breaks, and generally making more effort. Eventually, they have some minor illness and go to their doctors, who take the opportunity to prescribe "lighter" work. The change is entered in the factory records as "for medical reasons" but is really due to the changes of capacity normal to aging reaching a critical point (Richardson, 1953).

Further studies have found little association between work done and fitness in a medical sense (Richardson, 1956; Richardson & Weir, 1961). These studies noted in passing that some of those who moved took the opportunity to express their pent-up feelings against the job, the foreman, and the employers in a splendid final row and were therefore recorded as "left dissatisfied." Such reasons perhaps help to explain the surprising lack of awareness of problems of aging among industrial management.

Most of the moves from production work are to jobs that lack the crucial demand that was found insupportable in the old jobs. Thus, the coal miners whose ages are shown in Figure 3 were found to move in their forties from the extremely demanding work of tunnelers and colliers at the coal-face to support jobs such as transporting coal from the face and above ground. Men doing the paced work of car production lines tended to move to the unpaced work of rectifying faults at the side of the lines. A few people choose to become self-employed and thus are able to regulate their work themselves. Otherwise, the moves are usually to nonproduction work, such as that of storemen, janitors, and repairers, the average ages of whom in the example shown in Table 1 were substantially higher than those of production workers (Murrell, Griew, & Tucker, 1957). The conscious reason for moving is probably not that the former job can no longer be done at all but that it has become too much of an effort—awareness therefore serves as an "early warning."

The "shakedown" with age that occurs with these moves seems to be generally welcome. Satisfaction with work is commonly found to rise with age. Older employees also tend to be rated as more reliable and to engage in fewer incidences of voluntary absenteeism (Davies & Sparrow, 1985). However, the jobs to which the moves are made tend to be less skilled, and this implies a waste of potential. It must be emphasized that, of the many capacities required to meet the demands of any particular job, only one mismatch between capacity and demand is enough to limit performance. *If this one limitation could be removed, the change of job would be unnecessary.*

Reducing the Need to Move. In some cases the limitation can be removed by a change in the method of working. This sometimes happens spontaneously as when, for instance, a person discovers how a change of posture makes it possible to lift with less effort or how to save time by arranging tools and materials so that they are ready to hand in the required sequence. When not innovated and adopted spontaneously, beneficial changes sometimes can be introduced by a short course of retraining on the job. Such retraining can also overcome the boredom induced by a job that has become excessively routinized.

In other cases, a limitation could be removed by modification of the job or of the conditions under which it is done. Perhaps the best recognized example is that lighting of relatively high intensity but arranged so as not to cause glare can substantially offset the loss of visual acuity with age. Arranging a conveyor line so that each item is not passed immediately to the next operative but has to wait a little until he or she has completed work on a previous item does not reduce the speed of the line, but makes the timing more flexible.

Several other points of design can reduce limitations:

- Clearer working drawings and circuit and flow diagrams
- Arranging machine tools and workbenches so as to avoid stooping and other awkward postures
- Judicious use of power assistance to lessen physical effort required
- Layout of consoles in automated plants so that indicators and controls that belong together are placed together, and are arranged so that they are inspected and operated in an easily understood order
- Designing machinery, seating, and workplaces to take proper account of the dimensions of human operators.

Attention to such points—many of which may at first sight appear trivial—could prevent or at least postpone the need for many people to move from production positions in mid-life. It would open up a wider range of jobs to those who have to move because of redundancy or technical change.

Training for New Work. When a change of work must be made, an individual's potential is likely to be most fully realized if two steps are taken. First, tests of physical and mental capacity should be given to ensure that the new work will be suitable. Tests of physical capacity are well recognized. For mental capacity, standard tests have been found to be less reliable predictors of success in training than what are termed "work sample" tests, in which performance is measured on a simplified version of the task that incorporates its essential features.

Second, it is necessary to impart the required knowledge and develop the necessary skill for the new work. To do this, lectures and demonstrations may be unsatisfactory because the pace of instruction is not under the trainee's control. Since older people tend to be slower at comprehending new material and registering it in memory, they are likely to miss some points made in lectures and demonstrations. These omissions will leave gaps in their understanding and make it difficult for them to grasp the task as a whole. The difficulty can be reduced in the case of imparting knowledge by using clearly expressed written instructions which trainees can study at their own pace.

When teaching a skill, the difficulty encountered by older people in mastering complex movements and procedures has in a number of cases been greatly reduced by use of the "discovery method of training." In this method, trainees are given only a minimum of instruction and then asked to find out for themselves how the task should be done. The circumstances in which this exploratory behavior is carried out require them to make active decisions, but ensure that, if wrong, these will be immediately corrected so that ineffective methods do not become ingrained. The classical example of the use of this method was for teaching the invisible mending of woolen cloth. Middle-aged trainees successfully learned a job previously considered impossible to master after adolescence. Subsequent applications have been made with several other types of work (Belbin, Belbin, & Hill, 1957; Belbin, 1969). An important feature of this method is that trainees work at their own pace in the early stages. This same feature has also been effective in other situations such as giving trainees on commercial sewing machines control of the normally very fast pace during their early practice sessions (Nettelbeck & Kirby, 1976).

Testing and training must be carried out in a sensitive and sympathetic manner (Belbin & Belbin, 1972). Trainees may be resentful that their former jobs have ceased and anxious in the face of an unknown future which causes fears of failure and consequent loss of self-respect and social status. There is a need for all concerned to have respect for age. Trainers should be compatible in temperament with trainees. Patience is also a valuable quality because many middle-aged trainees who are slow to learn turn out to be successful performers later. When training is complete, care is needed to facilitate a smooth introduction to the new job. All of these considerations may sound expensive and unduly solicitous, but the reward is that successful adult trainees usually become competent, reliable, and long-staying workers.

Office, Professional, and Managerial Work

Office Work. Much less is known about office work, but the same pattern of well-maintained performance together with declining number of workers with advancing adult age is shown in Table 3 (Greenberg, 1961). The pace of work is more under the individual's control than in most factory operations, yet speed-related stress has also been found among officer workers in their forties and fifties (Welford, 1984). Whether such stress is relieved by office automation is not known; this procedure might cause diffi-

Table 3. Measured Output of Office Workers in Different Age Groups

(Output of 35-44 group provides standard of 100.)

Age Group	Number of Workers	Average Output
Under 25	1084	92.4
25-34	1506	99.4
35-44	1466	100.0
45-54	1023	100.1
55-64	429	98.6
65 and over	86	101.2

Data from Greenberg (1961).

culties at first in coping with new methods of work but then prove effective in the long run.

Professional and Managerial Work. The patterns previously noted for production and office work do not hold true here in all respects. There appears to be little decline with age in the number of persons occupied in professional work. There is a substantial rise with age of those engaged in management (Smith, 1973).

It is difficult to assess performance in professional and managerial work, but the ages at which significant original research and scholarly contributions have been made by academics are in line with the idea that they result from a balance between mental capacities and accumulated knowledge and comprehension. Some important contributions are made throughout the adult years, but the age at which they are most frequent varies with the subject of study. For example, the physical sciences depend heavily on particular types of mental capacity, and peak achievement in this field usually comes in the twenties and thirties (Lehman, 1953). The peak comes considerably later in fields such as history, law, and literature, presumably because it takes longer to gain the necessary knowledge, experience, and perspective. Some falloff in performance from the forties onward has been reported for design engineers, whose work embodies an imaginative use of mathematics of physics. Managers, for whom experience is important, have been found to maintain their effectiveness well into their later adult years but to change their methods somewhat: They tend to take account of more information when making decisions and to show less confidence. Perhaps this is an understandable correlation because extra information increases the likelihood of ambiguity and conflict (Birren, 1969; see also **Creativity**).

Changes of work common among professionals can be construed as, in a sense, moves from production to nonproduction work—from creative activities to service, development, and maintenance. Thus, many academics move from research to teaching and administration, and among other professionals senior partners tend to assume more administrative roles, guiding and organizing the work of their productive junior partners.

The danger for professional and manager in the later adult years is probably failure to keep abreast of new specialized knowledge. Time should be set aside for study, even if this conflicts with the pressing responsibilities that come with seniority. There is an increasing need for authoritative digests of new knowledge written concisely and in plain language with the busy practitioner or manager in mind. The requirement that some professionals attend conferences and seminars where new knowledge is presented can also be valuable by providing occasions when normal responsibilities can be shed with a good conscience.

Retirement

Changes in biological capacities with age tend to accelerate during the sixties. To their effects often are added stiffening joints, arthritic twinges, and other minor or major aches and pains. At the same time, problems of a different kind frequently arise. Working situations seldom remain static. Managements change, legal restrictions are tightened, and new knowledge suggests revised techniques. Difficulties typical of late middle age and beyond in learning and adjustment make such changes unwelcome—all the more so if adjustment seems to imply the rejection of expertise and beliefs built up over the years of which the individual is proud.

The situation can be even more distressing because for many people the accumulated wisdom of many years was never formulated in words. This lack of a ready means of expression hinders efforts to argue against change and defend the status quo. In consequence, older people often feel—with justification—that younger colleagues are rushing into innovations that eventually will prove disastrous, an outcome that is far from unusual in many fields of human endeavor, including the teaching profession.

As a result, demands of work begin again to exceed capacities so that the effort becomes more than seems worthwhile. People become impatient of hassles with fellow workers and others with whom they have to deal. Finally, with mixed feelings of defeat and relief, they decide to retire. The differences among individuals already noted mean that the age at which this happens will vary, but the tendency for this to occur around age 65 has been widely recognized.

Retirement from the job that one has been doing for a number of years does not necessarily mean ceasing to work if the retiree wants to continue and the opportunity is there. Many kinds of work can still be done without having to deal with the onerous physical, mental, or social demands that may have made retirement welcome in the first place. For factory and office workers there are jobs in which they could use their knowledge and expertise in less demanding circumstances. Many skilled workers have opportunities for occasional work, which can easily add up to nearly full time. Academics often continue scholarly activities after they are relieved of administrative chores. Retired professionals and managers may do valuable work as consultants. For all, there are opportunities for service in voluntary organizations, although in recent years professional restrictive practices and fear of opportunistic lawsuits following minor errors have caused some organizations to make less than full use of their volunteers' expertise.

An increasing number of retirees are taking university and adult education courses in subjects they had to leave aside in earlier years. For some, however, use of leisure time is a problem. Learning new ways of filling their time is likely to be accompanied by the same type of difficulties already noted for older people in the work force. The only certain way of avoiding these difficulties is to develop leisure-oriented interests and skills before retirement. Indeed, since skills once acquired are seldom lost with age, there is much to be said for equipping schoolchildren with a broad range of skills, including the use of tools and materials, that could be put to good use when discretionary time comes their way in the retirement years.

Postscript

Our knowledge and understanding of work capacity is far from complete, even after more than half a century of research. Clearly, however, if a person's capacities are to be used to full advantage, he she will need a change of work at least once during a career. What these changes should be, when they should be made, and how they should vary between jobs and individuals would become clearer if we could trace the courses of working careers of people in various walks of life. To attempt to do this by following a group of young adults through to retirement would obviously be unrealistic, but much could be learned by tracing back the careers of those who have retired. If this were done, it would almost certainly be found that many people had made several moves between their twenties and retirement.

The author's personal experience and observation suggest that many people in all walks of life would benefit from changing their work at about 10-year intervals. This could be accomplished by doing a different job in the same place or the same job in a different place. After a decade at the same job, what started as an exciting exploration has all too often become dull routine. Making changes in middle life can present practical difficulty if it involves uprooting home and family and making bureaucratic arrangements such as for the transfer of pension rights, and there may be regrets when leaving old friends. However, the challenge that can come from a carefully chosen move—or even from a forced move—can lead to a rejuvenation that will greatly enhance the quality of life and increase one's abilities to serve both others and oneself to the full extent of one's powers.   ▼ ALAN T. WELFORD

See also: Age 40; Age 65; Exercises; Gender Differences in the Workplace; Political Beliefs and Activities; Retirement Preparation; Slowing of Behavior with Age; Social Class and Adult Development; Stress; Vision; The Voice; Work Organization Membership and Behavior.

References

Barkin, S. (1933). *The Older Worker in Industry.* New York Legislative State Document No. 60. Albany, NY: Lyon.

Belbin, R. M. (1953). Difficulties of older people in industry. *Occupational Psychology, 27:* 177-90.

———. (1955). Older people and heavy work. *British Journal of Industrial Medicine, 12:* 309-19.

———. (1969). *The Discovery Method: An International Experiment in Retraining.* Paris: Organization for Economic Cooperation and Development.

Belbin, E., & Belbin, R. M. (1972). *Problems in Adult Retraining.* London: Heinemann.

Belbin, E., Belbin, R. M., & Hill, F. (1957). A comparison between the results of three different methods of operator training. *Ergonomics, 1:* 39-50.

Birren, J. E. (1969). Age and decision strategies. In A. T. Welford & J. E. Birren (Eds.), *Decision Making and Age.* Basel: Karger, pp. 23-36. (Reprinted in 1980 by Arno Press, New York.)

Clement, F. (1969). The relative development of several psychophysiological and psychometric variables with different occupations and intellectual levels. In A. T. Welford & J. E. Birren (Eds.), *Decision Making and Age.* Basel: Karger, pp. 56-65. (Reprinted in 1980 by Arno Press, New York.)

Davies, D. R., & Sparrow, P. R. (1985). Age and work behavior. In N. Charness (Ed.), *Aging and Human Performance.* Chichester, England: Wiley, pp. 293-332.

Featherstone, M. S., & Cunningham, C. M. (1963). Age of manual workers in relation to conditions and demands of work. *Occupational Psychology, 37:* 197-208.

Foulds, G. A., & Raven, J. C. (1948). Normal changes in the mental abilities of adults as age advances. *Journal of Mental Science, 94*: 133-42.

Greenberg, L. (1961). Productivity of older workers. *The Gerontologist, 1*: 38-41.

Griew, S. (1958). A study of accidents in relation to occupation and age. *Ergonomics, 2*: 17-23.

Heron, A., & Chown, S. M. (1961). *Ageing and the Semi-Skilled: A Survey in Manufacturing Industry on Merseyside.* Medical Research Council Memo. No. 40. London: Her Majesty's Stationery Office.

King, H. F. (1955). An age-analysis of some agricultural accidents. *Occupational Psychology, 29*: 245-53.

———. (1956). An attempt to use production data in the study of age and performance. *Journal of Gerontology, 11*: 410-16.

Larsson, L. (1982). Aging in mammalian skeletal tissue. In J. A. Mortimer, F. J. Pirozzolo, & G. J. Maletta (Eds.), *The Aging Motor System.* New York: Praeger, pp. 60-97.

Lehman, H. C. (1953). *Age and Achievement.* Princeton, NJ: Princeton University Press.

Maule, A. J., & Sanford, A. J. (1980). Adult age differences in multi-source selection behaviour with partially predictable signals. British *Journal of Psychology, 71*: 69-81.

Murrell, K. F. H., Griew, S., & Tucker, W. A. (1957). Age structure in the engineering industry: A preliminary study. *Occupational Psychology, 31*: 150-68.

Murrell, K. F. H., & Tucker, W. A. (1960). A pilot job-study of age-related causes of difficulty in light engineering. *Ergonomics, 3*: 74-79.

Nettelbeck, T., & Kirby, N. H. (1976). Training the mentally handicapped to sew. *Education and Training of the Mentally Retarded, 11*: 31-36.

Pacaud, S., & Welford, A. T. (1989). Performance in relation to age and educational level: A monumental research. *Experimental Aging Research, 15*: 123-36.

Powell, M. (1973). Age and occupational change among coal-miners. *Occupational Psychology, 47*: 37-49.

Richardson, I. M. (1953). Age and work: A study of 489 men in heavy industry. *British Journal of Industrial Medicine, 10*: 269-84.

———. (1956). A socio-medical study of 200 unemployed men. *Medical Officer, 96*: 165-70.

Richardson, I. M., & Weir, R. D. (1961). Age and disability. *The Gerontologist, 1*: 185-90.

Slater, P. (1948). The association between age and score on the Progressive Matrices Test. *British Journal of Psychology, 1*: 64-69.

Smith, J. M. (1973). Age and occupation: The determinants of male occupational age structures—hypothesis H and hypothesis A. *Journal of Gerontology, 28*: 484-90.

Stubbs, D. A. (1985). Human constraints on manual working capacity: Effects of age on intertruncal pressure. *Ergonomics, 28*: 107-14.

Tieger, C., & Villatte, R. (1983). Conditions de travail et vieillissement differential. *Travail et Emploi, 16*: 27-36.

Vincent, D. F. (1952). The linear relationship between age and score of adults in intelligence tests. *Occupational Psychology, 26*: 243-49.

Wackwitz, J. D. (1946). *Het Verband Tusschen Arbeidsprestatie en Leeftijd.* Delft, The Netherlands: Waltman.

Welford, A. T. (1958). *Ageing and Human Skill.* Oxford: Oxford University Press for the Nuffield Foundation. (Reprinted in 1973 by Greenwood Press, Westport, CT.)

———. (1960). *Ergonomics of Automation.* D. S. I. R. Problems of Progress in Industry, No. 8. London: Her Majesty's Stationery Office.

———. (1966). Industrial work suitable for older people: Some British studies. *The Gerontologist, 6*: 4-9.

———. (1976). Motivation, capacity, learning, and age. *International Journal of Aging and Human Development, 7*: 189-99.

———. (1977). Motor performance. In J. E. Birren & K. W. Schaie (Eds.), *Handbook of the Psychology of Aging.* New York: Van Nostrand Reinhold, pp. 450-96.

———. (1981). Signal, noises, performance and age. *Human Factors, 23*: 97-109.

———. (1984). Between bodily changes and performance: Some possible reasons for slowing with age. *Experimental Aging Research, 10*: 73-88.

———. (1988). Preventing adverse changes of work with age. *International Journal of Aging and Human Development, 27*: 283-91.

Welford, A. T., Norris, A. H., & Shock, N. W. (1969). Speed and accuracy of movement and their changes with age. *Acta Psychologica, 30*: 3-15.

Whitfield, J. W. (1954). Individual differences in accident susceptibility among coal miners. *British Journal of Industrial Medicine, 11*: 126-39.

York, J. L., & Biederman, I. (1990). Effects of age and sex on reciprocal tapping performance. *Perceptual and Motor Skills, 71*: 675-84.

WORK ORGANIZATION MEMBERSHIP AND BEHAVIOR

The importance of work as a means to identify who and what we are has long been an article of faith in the United States. (Mowsesian, 1986, p. xviii)

Most adults in the United States work in organizations for most of their lives. The development of more numerous and larger work organizations has been a distinctive characteristic of the twentieth century. Not long ago there were but a few large organizations (such as the armed forces), and most people worked in agriculture or mining. Now we are an urbanized society in which literally thousands of organizations each employ tens of thousands of people. Because work life is so central to the definition and maintenance of identity in the United States and many other Euro-American nations, it would be difficult to understand the total pattern of adult development without giving consideration to organizational membership.

An individual's relationship with work organizations occurs in a developmental manner (Jablin, 1985, 1987; Osipow, 1986). In fact, an individual's relationship with organizations is tri-developmental. First, the individual experiences an *individual lifespan process* of entering the work force, working, and exiting. This process encompasses personal physical development and change, and the accruing of experience and skills. These individual stages are often described as adolescence, early adulthood, middle adulthood, and late adulthood (Hayslip & Panek, 1989).

Second, the individual experiences *within-organizational development.* This process includes the achievements, relationships, and transitions that occur within a particular work organization as well as a person's move-ments from one organization to another. Most individuals will work for more than one organization during their careers.

Third, the character of work and of organizations continues to change over the course of an individual's life and during his or her service with a particular organization. This facet of development is *societal change.* Many types of work did not exist 50 years ago (e.g., computer programming, laser surgery). Work organizations have changed significantly along with changes in technology (e.g., cellular phones, electronic mail, fax machines), personnel (e.g., a more culturally diverse work force), and geography (e.g., the growth of the suburbs, along with suburban office parks and shopping malls).

With transitions simultaneously occurring across the lifespan, within organizations, and across society, the pattern of change in organizational membership and behavior is very complex. Furthermore, it is clear that the character of an individual's membership in work organizations is the result of an interaction among the individual, organizations, and work. Individuals both influence and are influenced by organizations and work.

Four developmental stages are especially important in understanding organizational membership and behavior: *anticipatory socialization, organizational assimilation, organizational membership,* and *organizational exit* (based on Jablin, 1987). These stages may occur through the various phases of lifespan development (e.g., early adulthood), so that each stage of organizational membership is complicated by lifespan factors.

Anticipatory Socialization

People learn about organizations before they join them through a process called anticipatory socialization. This process is part of the generalized lifespan development experience as individuals learn about a wide variety of work and organizations. They learn about vocations through their families, friends, education, the media, and their own part-time employment (Jablin, 1987). Television provides particularly vivid portrayals of work organizations (Vande Berg & Trujillo, 1989). Thus, individuals become acquainted with the images of numerous types of organizations before entering any of them. Anticipatory socialization continues to be important well into early adulthood as students learn specific details of their careers.

The hiring process provides additional anticipatory socialization that emphasizes the within-organizational experience. Interviewers inform potential employees regarding specifics of the organization through conversation and written materials—but also indirectly through the way in which they behave toward the potential employees. Before actually starting work, then, the individual will know something about the life and character of this particular organization. As individuals repeat the joining process throughout their life, they will again experience this process of anticipatory socialization and continue to build up a storehouse of knowledge about organizations.

The hiring socialization process differs across the lifespan. Adolescents tend to experience very brief hiring procedures; organizations seldom are willing to invest much effort. Moving through the lifespan, individuals and organizations both are likely to invest much more time in the hiring process, thus providing the older individual with the opportunity to learn more about the organization before joining it.

Organizational Assimilation

The process of actually learning the ropes in organizations has received a great deal of attention over the past two decades. In reviewing the extensive literature on organizational assimilation, Jablin (1985, 1987) observes that it is a two-way process. The organization attempts to shape the newcomer's behavior, socializing the individual to the organization's way of life. At the same time, however, the newcomer tries to individualize the organization to fit his or her needs and preferences. Few people accept everything about an organization when they join it.

The reciprocal process of organization influencing individual and individual influencing organization occurs during both the "encounter" and the "metamorphosis" phases of assimilation. In the encounter phase, the first experiences with a new organization produce change, contrast, surprise, and an attempt at sense-making by the newcomer (Louis, 1980). In the metamorphosis phase, the newcomer works out his or her relationship with the organization.

The organizational assimilation process is central to the within-organization experience of individuals throughout their lives (Osipow, 1986). The complexity of the assimilation process and the difficulty of explaining it led Baum (1990) to develop a new perspective on organizational assimilation and membership that seeks to understood an individual's relationships with organizations in psychoanalytic terms. How useful this perspective will be remains to be seen.

The assimilation process will vary across the individual's lifespan as a result of different types of position, changing levels of experience, and differences in peer involvement. For example, adolescents often have little or no work experience and are hired into less-skilled positions that have a strong peer culture. Thus, their assimilation is likely to be structured firmly by the organization (e.g., training programs at fast-food restaurants), yet also influenced heavily by their adolescent peers. In contrast, young adults who are hired into a first "permanent" position may experience widely differing types of assimilation, ranging from a formal three-month process through an immediate "sink or swim" approach: "OK, kid, get out there and sell!" The availability of peer or family support in such situations will also vary widely, partly because young adults often are mobile and may take a position far away from the supportive people in their lives.

Organizational Membership

There is a vast literature on the careers of organization members. Psychological, sociological, management, and communication studies range across nearly every aspect of the organizational behavior and experience of individuals. The focus here is on five issues that will continue to shape organizational membership and behavior well into the next century: *partial inclusion, job conditions, vitality, diversity,* and *health.*

Partial Inclusion. Not all people are equally a part of an organization. People approach their work life with varying degrees of commitment. A person may believe his or her work is a job, a career, or a calling. Individuals who view work only as a source of money and security hold jobs. Those who also view work as advancement in an occupation have careers. Individuals who view their work as having responsibilities, power, and impact beyond themselves have a calling. The type of relationship an individual has with work and the level of commitment will affect the character of that person's organizational membership and behavior.

The concept of partial inclusion deals with the varying levels of individual participation in work organizations (Weick, 1969, 1979). Partial inclusion indicates that all members of an organization are investing only parts of themselves and their behavior in the organization; everyone has some life outside of work. Understanding that all organizational participation is partial enables one to look more closely at the degree of a person's involvement. This degree of involvement is likely to change substantially as the individual moves simultaneously through transitions within the organization and through his or her personal lifespan.

Competing external demands are one important source of variance across the lifespan. For example, adolescents and young adults may have relatively low levels of involvement in their work organizations because of the high demands made on them by peer culture or by becoming parents. In contrast, in middle adulthood, people are more likely to become "empty nesters." With their children grown and living independently, they face fewer competing demands at home and may thus increase their organizational involvement.

Job Conditions. Self-direction and autonomy are two of the most influential job conditions that affect organizational membership. When individuals are given the opportunity to have an increased voice in how they go about their work, they are likely to show greater intellectual flexibility and experience greater satisfaction (Miller, Slomczynski, & Kohn, 1985). Further, increased autonomy is also related to more positive occupational values, self-competence estimates, work commitment, self-esteem, and job involvement (Mortimer, 1988). Providing workers with independence in responsibilities and judgment has significantly positive effects on organizational life. This finding holds true from early through later adulthood. For adolescents, the stereotypical pattern of low self-direction for young, entry-level workers could contribute to less positive work experiences.

Vitality. With the elimination of mandatory retirement and the increase in the average age in the United States, numerous questions have been raised about stimulating "older workers" (e.g., Humple & Lyons, 1983; Rosen & Jerdee, 1985). The question often is framed as one of a worker's vitality, that is, the potential for continuing productivity across time. In fact, however, concern about maintaining organizational members' vitality should not be limited to older employees. Age by itself is *not* directly related to decline in productivity.

Instead of worrying about aging, what is essential to continuing vitality is the organization's effort to stimulate its members' growth through opportuntiies to learn new tasks and develop new ideas. The vitality of university faculty members might be enhanced by the provision of sabbatical leaves for projects and study, travel support to attend conferences and learn new material, support for an intellectual community, and financial support for faculty improvement (e.g., course development). Similar provisions might have similarly positive effects in other types of work organizations.

Vitality is an important issue in organizational membership throughout the adult years, and the organizations themselves must play an active role in supporting individuals' efforts to grow and develop throughout all their work years. However, research does not support the stereotypical notion that vitality is related to age. Those who continue to make the assumption that the older worker necessarily suffers a loss of vitality are themselves victimized by "old" and, in this case, outworn notions.

Diversity. The workplace has become significantly diversified over the past three decades. More women, more African Americans, more Mexican Americans, more Asian Americans, more single parents, and more disasbled individuals are working in organizations. Increased cultural diversity of work organizations in the United States is already a fact, and it influences organizational membership in several ways.

The increased number of women and ethnic minorities in the workplace raises issues of racism and sexism (Osipow, 1986). In *Men and Women of the Corporation,* a classic analysis of organizational membership and diversity, Kanter (1977) suggested that different pressures are felt by the minorities as the relative number of men and women or blacks and whites changes in an organization. When very few women or African Americans are included in an organization, they tend to be perceived as tokens who represent all women or all African Americans. This spotlight can place an enormous burden on the individual. As the numbers of women or African Americans increase, however, each individual is seen more as an individual, and the pressure to represent an entire group of people diminishes. If Kanter is correct, the next few years will be a time of major adjustment in work organizations as female and ethnic minority group members are "reclassified" as individuals rather than as representatives of groups.

The increased diversity of the work organization will also bring a richness and strength of ideas. Individuals of varying backgrounds and experiences will offer new viewpoints on old problems, new understandings of a changing world, and alternative strategies for organizing. The stimulus and challenge of a more diverse organizational membership could improve the efficiency and versatility of organizations in the next century.

The change in the work force composition will also influence organizational membership and behavior by introducing altered family contexts. Although an individual's family situation has always influenced his or her organizational behavior, changes in the demographics of the work force in recent years have made family context even more salient. Two changes are notable. First, the number of single parents in the workplace has increased. Second, there has been an evolution of the middle-class family from single career (typically the husband) with a spouse as "support staff" (Kanter, 1977) to dual career, especially among the middle-class. Both of these changes have the effect of making work organization membership more of an individual than a family responsibility.

The stereotypical assumption that people become increasingly rigid with age has come under serious criticism by adult developmentalists (e.g., Hayslip & Panek, 1989). Yet there is still relatively little research into the question of how individuals respond to diversity all across their lifespan. Given the number and magnitude of changes that are related to diversity, exploring patterns of individual response might well become a major research topic for the next decade.

Health. Work and work organization membership are part of a paradox:

> Work creates a double-bind situation for many people in our society. It is something they can not live healthily with or without. Excessive work demands and dangerous conditions can damage both mind and body. Yet work can be an important source of psychic rewards, without which both body and mind can deteriorate. (Schwalbe & Gecas, 1988, pp. 127-238)

Work is important to the health and well-being of individuals, yet it is also dangerous. Throughout one's work life the likelihood of work-related disability increases

(Schwalbe & Gecas, 1988). Stress is also a major risk of work. The many negative effects of stress can include heart disease and a variety of other illnesses (Sorenson & Mortimer, 1988). Thus, membership in work organizations places one at risk—literally risk of life and limb—while simultaneously stimulating, energizing, and making life more positive.

The complexity of organizational life is an outcome of the interplay among these membership factors: partial inclusion, job conditions, vitality, diversity, and health. For example, the increased diversity of the workplace might encourage organizations to offer members more opportunity for self-direction, which in turn would stimulate involvement and reduce stress. In this and in many other ways, changing job conditions could improve the quality of organizational membership or, if handled poorly, could instead endanger both the individual and the organization.

Organizational Exit

Individuals leave organizations for a variety of reasons—some by choice, others by necessity. Whatever the reasons, it is clear that organizational exit is common and many would argue that it is also becoming more frequent. The "problem" of organizational exit is typically framed as "turnover," which is expensive and time consuming for organizations that must hire and retrain a replacement and wait while a new person becomes productive. Jablin's (1987) model of the relationship between communication and turnover identifies eight factors that can lead to members' becoming dissatisfied and eager to leave. Louis (1980) proposes that joining an organization involves changes that differ from the individual's previous experiences and require the newcomer to make sense of the new organization. In both of these approaches, turnover is seen as a problem in organizational membership.

Alternatively, organizational exit can be considered part of the member's growth in a career. For example, leaving one organization for another is sometimes necessary for promotion and continued growth. In such careers, organizational exit becomes a regular part of an individual's work experience, even though it may have disruptive effects on family as well as work relationships (Kanter, 1977).

The character of organizational exit clearly varies throughout the lifespan. Adolescents are expected to leave their current employment, which generally is of the "first job" type. Similarly, those in late adulthood are expected to retire from their jobs (although they may continue to work in other jobs). For other stages of lifespan development, organizational exit can result from such widely differing circumstances as a layoff during organizational downsizing, a personal mid-life crisis, or an opportunity for career advancement in another organization.

Conclusion

Individual membership and behavior in work organizations develop across the lifespan. This is a multiple pattern in which an individual continues to develop as he or she functions within an organization that is undergoing change and is itself embedded in a larger society that is inclined toward major techological, economic, and social change.

Throughout much of their adult lives, individuals anticipate organizational membership, assimilate into organizations, function as organization members, and exit from organizations. The many different factors influencing organizational membership include the partial inclusion character of membership, job conditions, vitality, member diversity, and health.

As the composition of society and organizations continues to change—with increasing age and education, for example—the character of organizational membership and behavior will also change. The challenge of studying organizational life is that its collective character ensures that an organization will change as its membership changes—yet at the same time organizations influence both who is a member and what means to be a member.

Organization life is created by people while, in turn, the people in organizations are recreated by organizations.

▼ Charles R. Bantz

See also: Age 40; Career Age; Disengagement Theory; Friendships through the Adult Years; Gender Differences in the Workplace; Individuality; Intelligence; Japanese Perspectives on Adult Development; Mental Health in the Adult Years; Mexican Americans: Life Course Transitions and Adjustment; Military Service: Long-Term Effects on Adult Development; Social Class and Adult Development; Stress; Subcultural Influences on Lifelong Development; Travel: Stimulus to Adult Development; Work Capacity Across the Adult Years.

References

Baum, H. S. (1990). *Organizational membership: Personal Development in the Workplace.* Albany, NY: State University of New York Press.

Bellah, R. H., & Corcoran, M. (1988). Vitality of midcareer and older professionals: Problems and prospects. In J. T. Mortimer & K. M. Borman (Eds.), *Work Experience and Psychological Development Through the Life Span.* Washington, DC: American Association for the Advancement of Science, pp. 201-32.

Hayslip, B., Jr., & Panek, P. E. (1989). *Adult Development and Aging.* New York: Harper & Row.

Humple, D. S., & Lyons, M. (1983). *Management and the Older Workforce: Policies and Programs.* New York: American Management Associations.

Jablin, F. M. (1985). Task/work relationships: A life-span perspective. In M. L. Knapp & G. R. Miller (Eds.), *Handbook of Interpersonal Communication.* Beverly Hills, CA: Sage, pp. 615-54.

———. (1987). Organizational entry, assimilation, and entry. In F. M. Jablin et al. (Eds.), *Handbook of Organizatational Communication: An Interdisciplinary Perspective.* Newbury Park, CA: Sage, pp. 679-740.

Kanter, R. M. (1977). *Men and Women of the Corporation.* New York: Basic Books.

Louis, M. R. (1980). Surprise and sensemaking: What newcomers experience in entering unfamiliar organizational settings. *Administrative Science Quarterly, 25:* 226-51.

Miller, J., Slomczynski, K. M., & Kohn, N. L. (1985). Continuity of learning-generalization: The effect of job on men's intellective process in the United States and Poland. *American Journal of Sociology, 91:* 593-615.

Mortimer, J. T. (1988). Introduction. In J. T. Mortimer & K. M. Borman (Eds.), *Work Experience and Psychological Development Through the Lifespan.* Washington, DC: American Association for the Advancement of Science.

Mowsesian, R. (1986). *Golden Goals, Rusted Realities: Work and Aging in America.* Far Hills, NJ: New Horizon Press.

Osipow, S. H. (1986). Career issues through the life span. In M. S. Pallak & R. Perloff (Eds.), *Psychology and Work: Productivity, Change, and Employment.* Washington, DC: American Psychological Association, pp. 141-68.

Rosen, B., & Jerdee, T. H. (1985). *Older Employees: New Roles for Valued Resources.* Homewood, IL: Dow Jones-Irwin.

Schwalbe, M. L., & Gecas, V. (1988). Social psychological dimensions of job-related disability. In J. T. Mortimer & K. M. Borman (Eds.), *Work Experience and Psychological Development Through the Lifespan.* Washington, DC: American Association for the Advancement of Science, pp. 233-71.

Sorenson, G., & Mortimer, J. T. (1988). Implications of the dual roles of adult women for their health. In J. T. Mortimer & K. M. Borman (Eds.), *Work Experience and Psychological Development Through the Lifespan.* Washington, DC: American Association for the Advancement of Science, pp. 157-97.

Vande Berg, L., & Trujillo, N. (1989). *Organizational Life on Television.* Norwood, NJ: Ablex Publishing.

Weick, K. E. (1969). *The Social Psychology of Organizing.* Reading, MA: Addison-Wesley.

———. (1979). *The Social Psychology of Organizing.* Second Edition. Reading, MA: Addison-Wesley.

Index

Abilities, differential, 233-234
Absolute threshold, visual, 527, 529
Accidental injuries
    due to slowing with age, 458
    of rural residents, 426
Accidents
    predictors of, 138
    of workers by age, 546-547
Accommodation, visual, 527, 529
Acculturation, Mexican-Americans, 343
Accuracy-emphasis hypothesis, slowing and, 463
Achievement vs. submission, child development and, 358
Active mastery, 312-316
Acuity, visual, 527, 529
Adam's apple (thyroid cartilage), 533
Adaptation to new situations, intelligence and, 249
Adolescence
    developmental tasks during, 4
    sexuality and, 437-439
    travel and, 512-513
Adolescent pregnancy, 441
Adoptive fathers, generativity and, 5
Adult Attachment Interview, 4
Adult children, parents and, 1-6
Adult development
    aging and, 7-18, 112-119
    contextual model of, 422
    influence of rural living, 421-428
    life events as markers of, 277-278

military service and, 351-356
    models of, 7-18, 112-119
    social class and, 467-472
Adult learner, characteristics of, 266-267
Adult register development, 263
Aerobic capacity, 145
Affect attunement, 72
Affirmative action, 253
African cultures, marriage patterns, 29
African-American families, grandparents and, 192-193
African Americans
    experiences of, 18-26
    housing and, 218
    labels for, 255
    religion and, 394-395
    suicide and age, 504
    as voters, 379
Agape (altruistic love), 304
Age
    anxiety related to, 348
    causes of death by (statistical table), 418-419
    civil rights and attitudes toward, 255
    compensation for declines related to, 240
    creativity and, 95-96
    crime and, 98-105
    depression and, 109
    divorce and 130-131
    ethnic relationships and, 255-256
    fairy tales and, 154-157
    forty (40), 31-35
    four humors and four qualities and, 120
    friendships and, 160-164
    humor appreciation and, 224-225
    mate choice and, 26-30

memory declines related to, 321-322
    mortality and, 417-418
    pride in, 258
    productivity and, 95-96
    religiosity and, 395, 397-399
    sibling relationships and, 446-447
    sixty-five (65), 35-37
    slowing of behavior and, 457-467
    slowing of information processing and, 239
    subcultures and, 494
    suffering and, 496-497
    suicide and, 504-506
    twenty-one (21), 30-31
    vision and, 528-530
    voice changes and, 534-536
    voting behavior and, 378-379
    wisdom and, 497
Age changes, twins and, 523-524
Age differences
    crystallized and fluid intelligence and, 249-250
    drivers and, 135-136
    housing and, 217
    inductive reasoning ability and, 238
    information processing and, 237-240
    intelligence and, 242-244
    life events and, 275-276
    memory and, 237-238
    series completion tests and, 237-238
    spatial abilities and, 238
Age discrimination, 32
Age homogeneity, friendship and, 161
Ageism, 258

creativity and 96
gay men and, 212
Age-segregated communica-
tion, 180-181
Age-standardized mortality
rate, 287
Aggression, women, life cycle
and, 367
Aging
development and, 112-119
as disorder of develop-
ment, 386-387
as evolutionary process,
290-291
death and, 113
fall of humanity and, 122-
123
Galen's theory of, 121
in historical perspective,
119-126
other species and, 291
rate of, 291
sleep patterns and, 451-454
Aging process, slowing as
index of, 457
AIDS, gay community and,
213
Alcohol
Mexican Americans and,
343
military personnel and, 353
Native Americans and, 363
premature death and, 419-
420
as recreational drug, 139
suicide and, 504
use and abuse of, 37-40
Alcoholism, treatment, 39
Alpha wave, 449
Alpha wave and cycle-time
hypothesis, slowing and,
461
Altercast, twins and, 519
Altruistic love (Agape), 304
Altruistic suicide, 503
Alzheimer's disease, 57-58, 61
control and, 87
diagnosis of, 323-324
resemblance to premature
aging, 385
sleep and, 456
Ambivalence toward elders,
260-261
American Association of
Retired Persons (AARP),
90, 142

American College of Emer-
gency Physicians, 57
Americans for Generational
Equity, 176-177
Anachronistic fallacy, 319
Androgens, sexual maturation
and, 437
Animals, olfactory clues and,
508
Anomie, suicide and, 503
Anticipatory socialization
retirement and, 411-412
for work organizations,
553-554
Anxiety
humor and, 223
related to age, 348
Apnea, 455
"Appropriate death," health
education and, 207
Aristotle
ages of life, 120-121
comedy theory, 223-224
middle age as prime of life,
113
potentiality to actuality,
113
theory of development,
112-114
Art therapies, 151
Arthritis, 65
sexual activity and, 430
Arts, expressive, 150-153
Asian Americans, as voters,
379
Assisted suicide, 503
Attachment, 40-44
Bowlby's theory of, 40-41
figures, 43
loneliness and, 284
relationships, 40-44
social convoys and, 473
Attention, divided, and
learning, 267
Attention changes, slowing
and, 463
Attentional system, brain and,
530
Attractiveness, sexual maturation and, 439
Auditory recognition, of
infants and children, 281
Augustine, St., theory of
development, 340
Australians, parent-child
bond and, 3

Autobiographical insidedness,
372
Autonomy vs. shame, 402
Autopsy, psychological, 502

Baby boom women, meno-
pause and, 325
Baby boomer cohort, 176, 417-
418
Beauty, love of (Eros), 304
Bedtime rituals, sleep and, 455
"Behaving oldly," 197
Behavior settings, (Roger
Barker), 370-371
Behavioral modifications,
mortality reduction and,
420
Behaviorism, 17
Benny, Jack, age anxiety and,
32
Bereavement
culture and, 537-538
depression and, 107
overload and older adults,
539
widow's adjustment to,
537-538
"Best friends," 163
Bible
age and reading of, 398
age 21 and, 30-31
Biblical patriarchs, longevity
and, 285
Biological clock
fertility and, 441
surgent development and,
366
Biological decline, work-
related capacities and age,
542
Biological limit, longevity
and, 291
Bipolar disorder ("manic
depression"), 107
Birdfoot's Grampa (Bruchac),
293
Birthrate, fictive kin and, 159-
160
Bits, uncertainty reduction
and, 236
Blood pressure, exercise and,
145
Body senses, 45-51
Body water, changes with age,
38
Books, mental health, 334-336

"Born again" movement, 399
Boundaries, privacy and, 389
Bowlby, John, 40
Brain
    attentional system and, 530
    integrative action of, 530
    opiate-like binding sites in, 435
    sexual differentiation and, 435
    sexuality and, 434-435
    surge center of, 435
Brain chemistry, depression and, 108
Brain damage, coping ability and, 249
Brainstorming, older adult groups, 183
Brothers and sisters, 444
Bunyan, John, 122-124
Burden
    of caregivers, 59
    fear of becoming, 3
Butler, Robert, life review theory, 401-402

Caffeine, lifespan patterns, 141
Cancer
    depression and, 108
    social interactions and, 477
"Canes vs. kids" argument, 177
Cardiac disease, gender and, 53
Cardiac health, 38-39, 52-54
Cardiovascular disease
    among females, 167
    mortality and, 414
Cardiovascular function, exercise and, 144-145
Cardiovascular system, 53
Career age, 55-57
Career criminals, 99
Caregivers, gender and, 168-169
Caregiving, 57-63
Caring love, 301
Carnal sin, love as, 297-298
Cataracts, 531
Catastrophe research, 484
Catastrophic loss, love and, 297
Cautiousness, slowing and, 462-463
Centenarians, 63-64

Central nervous system, arousal hypothesis, 463
Chalamydia trachomatis, increasing incidence of, 441
Channel capacity, 236
Channels of communication, 70
"Character," as goal of development, 317
Childbirth, death and 440
Childhood, sexuality and, 436-437
Childhood separation, adult loneliness and, 284-285
Children
    abuse and development of trust, 402-403
    as defective adults, 114
    pain and, 65
    sleep cycle of, 451
    stages of development, 14-15
Chinese-Americans, age, suicide and, 504
Choice, crisis of, 499
Cholesterol, exercise and, 146
"Chosen relatives," 157
Christian love, 297-298
Chromosomal damage, twins and, 519
Chromosome pairs, sex and, 166
Chromosomes, sexual differentiation and, 435-436
Chronic pain, 64-67
Chronically ill, social support for, 475-479
Chronological age
    convenience of, 36
    happiness and, 200
    memory and, 323
    self-attitudes toward, 384
Church programs for elders, 397-398
Cicero, journey of life and, 120
Circumlocatory speech, age and, 263
Civil rights, age and attitudes toward, 255
Civil Rights Movement, 20-21
Class distinctions, developmental processes and, 469
Clergy, sexuality of, 301
"Climacteric, grand," 124

"Climacteric." *See* Menopause
Clinical depression, defined, 106
Cognitive decline, cardiac disease and, 54
Cognitive development (Piaget), 14-15
Cognitive differentiation, gender and, 166
Cognitive functioning, humor and, 225
Cohort analysis, 68-69
Cohort differences
    drivers and, 153
    intelligence and, 245
Cohort effects, 67-70
    caregivers and, 62
    crime and, 98
    depression and, 109
    divorce and, 130
    generational effects and, 67-70
    happiness and, 200-202
Cohorts
    baby boomers and, 176, 417-418
    defined, 67
    generational equity and, 175
    military service and, 354-355
Collective unconscious (Jung), 318
College education, employment and, 406
Combat, exposure to and adult well-being, 353
The Comedy of Errors, (Shakespeare), 518
"Coming out," 209
Communication, 70-77
    channels of, 70
    creative-expressive activities and, 153
    dementia and, 76
    egocentric, 73
    models of, 279
    sibling relationships and, 444-445
    skills of grandparents, 180-186
    techniques of, 73-74
    written and age, 264
Communion, interpersonal, 72
Community identity, 375
Companionate love style, 304

Companions, social convoys and, 473

Compensation, age-related declines and, 240

Competence, environmental and age, 219

Competency, driving, 136-137

Complementary characteristics, friendship and, 162

Complex humor, 225-226

Complexity, slowness and, 457, 462

Compliance, with medications, 142-143

Concrete operations, 14

Confidantes, 3

Conflict, 77-81
creativity and, 97
eccentric behavior and, 80
management of, 78-81
marital, 307-308
stress and, 77

Confucian love (Jen), 296

Confucian precepts, age and, 259

Confucianism, longevity and, 285

Confucius, 9

Consciousness, nonpersonal, 481

Contact theory, prejudice and, 254

Contemplation, age and, 114-115, 483

Contextual model of adult development, 422

Contextualism, 81-86

Contingent feedback experiences, 42

Continuity of relationships, 473-474

Continuity theory, mid-life development and, 350

Contraceptive devices, 440

Control, 86-92
illusion of, 394

Conversations
intergenerational, 191
monopolizing of, 183

Convoy (supporting people), 163

Convoys, social relationships and, 472-474

Coping
gender differences in, 407-408

with loss by widows, 539-540
mechanisms, 19-20

Corea, Gena, 440

Cortisone levels, sexual activity and, 430

Counseling, retirement preparation and, 410

Creative development, discontinuities in, 150

Creative-expressive therapy, 151

Creativity, 92-98
definitions of, 92-93
developmental flow and, 150
in individuals, 93-95
peak periods, 95
renewal of, 96
stress and, 150
Tennyson and, 97

Criminal behavior, 98-105

Crisis
age and risk of, 486
religion and hope during, 195
support from siblings during, 445
as stimulus for life review, 402
theory of, 348

Cross-gender understanding, 169-170

Cross-sex friendships, 163

Crude death rates, Third World nations, 287

Crystallized intelligence, 241, 248-253, 322

Cultural influences, intelligence and, 249

Cultural relativism, 318

Cultural relativity, 26

Culture
bereavement and, 537-538
value of suffering to, 496

Culture shock, 513-514

Cyclical repetition, Native American world view and, 361

Cyclothymia, 107

"Dangerous age," 124

Darwin, Charles, 7

Death
accepting inevitability of, 506

age and belief in afterlife, 399
aging and, 113
causes of (statistical table), 416
causes of by age (statistical table), 418-419
childbirth and, 440
communication and, 74
gender and, 167-168
methods for determining rates of, 287
as punishment for sin, 298
recovery from spouse's, 539
sense of control and, 395
of spouse, 391
violent, 417-418

The Death of Ivan Ilych, (Tolstoy), 401

Deathbed scenes, Hollywood version, 294

Decline and dissolution, sibling relationship and, 443

Delta sleep, 449

Dementia, communication and, 76

Democracy, suffering and, 498

Dependence, on self or others, 88

Dependency ratio, of elderly, 408

Depression, 106-111
age and, 330-331
age and exercise, 146-147
age 40 and, 31
bereavement and, 107
brain chemistry and, 108
ECT and, 110
major episodes of, 106-107
risk factors for, 109
social support and, 477
stress and, 108, 485
suicide and, 107
taste sensitivity and, 510
theories of, 108
treatment of, 110-111
twins and, 108

Depth perception, 527-528

Detachment, transcendence of, 480

Development
aging and, 112-119
communication and, 70-77

conflict management and, 77

context of, 8-9

contextualism and, 83-85

differential, 231-232

early, 7-8

as evolutionary process, 83

history of, 119-126

individuality in, 229-236

Japanese perspective on, 258-261

language and, 262-265

marital, 304-311

parent-centered view of, 367-368

place and personality, 370-377

privacy needs and concepts of, 389-390

as quest for absolute goodness, 297

sense of humor and, 225-226

spiritual, 91

theories of disengagement and, 126-130

Developmental changes, mastery styles and, 314-316

Developmental flow, creativity and, 150

Developmental loneliness, 283-284

Developmental models, 112-119

Developmental pattern, work career, 553

Developmental stage theories, critique of, 318-319

Developmental tasks, mental health and (Erikson), 329-330

Developmental trajectories, social class and, 469

Deviance, crime and age, 100

Diabetes, vision and, 531

Dialectical theory, mid-life development and, 350

Dialectical thinking, 83-84

Diet, 53

diabetes and, 362

menopause and, 327

Disability

communication and, 72

control of life and, 85

"Disappointment generation," 20-21

Disasters, older people and, 485-487

Disclosing private feelings, stress reduction and, 391

Discrimination

ethnicity and, 253-254

in racially divided society, 22

Disease

as cause of death (statistical tables), 416, 418-419

listening ability and, 281

slowing as explanation of, 462

Disempowered groups, 254

Disengagement, conflict and, 80

Disengagement theory, 7, 10, 126-130, 346-347

Disidentifier, drivers' license as, 136

Diversity in workplace, gender and ethnicity, 556

Divided attention, learning and, 267

Division of labor

adult development and, 470

gender and, 366-367

Divorce, 130-134, 309-310, 329

caregiving and, 59-60

children of, 132

depression and, 109

life events and, 131

Mexican Americans and, 343-344

rates of, 130

social support and, 131-132

stepchildren and, 132-133

stress and, 131-132

Domestic violence, rural communities and, 426

Doppelganger, twins and, 519

Double standard of sexuality, 440-441

Down's syndrome, 385, 519

"Dream factory," individual differences in, 453

Dreams, 448-457

content of, 454-455

"dreamer" as negative stereotype in, 448

functions of, 452-453

latent and manifest content of, 454

sleep and, 448-457

theory of, 454

Drinking patterns, age and, 37-38

Driving, 134-139

competency, 136-137

difficulties due to age, 464-465

information processing and, 236

safety, 136-137

Drugs

adverse effects of interactions, 142

illegal, 141

"maturing out," 141

military personnel and, 353

Native Americans and, 363

"recreational," 139-140

risk factors and, 143

stress and use of, 141-142

suicide and, 504

use and abuse of, 139-143

Druse, Middle Eastern

mastery style and, 315-316

parental imperative and, 365

Dualistic conceptions, 480

Duration dependence, life course and, 277

Durkheim, Emil, suicide typology, 503

Dyadic withdrawal, narcissism and, 359

Dying for love, 295

Dyslexia, 72

Dysthmia, 107

Early development, 7-8

Eccentric behavior, conflict and, 80

Ecological validity, 265-266

Ecology model, individual development, 230-231

Economic opportunity, gender and, 168-169

Economy, rural, farm crisis and, 425

ECT, depression and, 110

Education

adult learner and, 266-267

creativity and, 96

grandparents and, 186-194

health and age, 202-208

Education *(continued)*
language, age, and level of, 264-265
military service and, 353-354
patient, 206
voting behavior and level of, 379-380
EEG (electroencephalogram), sleep and, 449
Ego identity, subculture and, 492
Ego identity vs. despair, life review and, 403
Ego integrity vs. despair (Erikson), 13
Ego psychology, 12
Egocentric communication, 73
Egocentric thinking, 156
Egoistic suicide, 503
Eibl-Eibesfeldt, Irenaus, 437
Eight Ages of Man (Erikson), 124-125
Elder tales, 154-156
Elderly, risk of falling, 50-51
Elderly dependency ratio, 408
Elderly parents, marital conflict and, 308
Electroencephalogram (EEG), sleep and, 449
Electromagnetic radiation, vision and, 526
Embeddedness, contextualism and 82-83
Embodiment, personal meanings and, 371
Embryo, sexual differentiation of, 436
Emotional support, chronically ill and, 476-477
Emplotment, 372
Employment
discrimination against homosexuals and, 213
women and, 342-343, 405-406
Empty Nest, 2
age 40 and, 32
Mexican Americans and, 343
Encoding, information processing and, 237-238
Engagement, marital, stages of, 305-306
Entering and exiting workforce, 553

"Entry life structure," 329
Environmental competence, age and 219
Environmental docility, age and, 219
Epigenetic theory (Erikson) 1, 9, 12-14, 114
Equity
generational, 175-180
intergenerational conflict and, 177
theory of, 1, 3-4
Ergonomics, 464-465
Erikson, Erik, 1, 9, 11-14, 82
developmental tasks and, 329-330
eight stages of man, 124-125
mental health and, 329-330
"psychosocial crisis," 12
reminiscence in life review and, 402-403
Eros, 300, 304
Essential tremor, aging and, 535
Estrogen replacement therapy, 431
Estrogens, sexual maturation and, 437
Ethnic relations, lifespan development of, 255-256
Ethnicity
homosexuality and, 212
sibling relationships and, 446
suicide and, 504
Event history analysis, 470
Everyday intelligence, 246
Everyday life
learning and, 265-274
memory and 265-274
slowing and tasks of, 458
stressors of, 484, 488
Evolutionary process, aging and, 290-291
Exchange of support, expectations of, 473-474
Exercise, 144-150
blood pressure and, 145
cardiovascular function and, 144-145
cholesterol and, 146
depression and, 146-147
health benefits of, 144-146
health education and, 206
physical fitness and, 147

psychological benefits of, 147-148
pulmonary function and, 145
stamina and, 146
types of, 147-148
Existential crisis, middle age and, 347-348
Expressive arts, 150-153
Ex-spouse, relationship with, 309-310
Extended family
bean-pole shape of, 1
elders and, 344
of Native Americans, 362

Fairy tales, age and, 154-157
Fall of humanity, aging and, 122-123
Fallacy, anachronistic, 319
Family
caregivers, 58
changes in life of, 1-2
changes in structure of, 159
contact with of chronically ill, 477
divorce and structure of, 132-133
effects of military life on, 374
grandparents and, 186-194
housing and values of, 216
Mexican-American, 342-343
narcissism and, 359
reconstituted, 132-133
respect for aged members of, 259
secrets of, 391
stress and, 485
Farm crisis, rural economy and, 425
Fatalism, 21
Fatalistic suicide, 503
Faults, facing one's own, 156
Female parenting, basic trust, 366
Feminist critique, developmental theories and, 319
Fertility, 433
Fictive kin, 157-160
Fiji, marriage patterns in, 29,
Filial piety, 258-259
Filipino-Americans, age, suicide and, 504

Financial need, working women and, 406

Firearms, age, suicide and, 505

The Fixed Period (Trollope), 175

Flirtation gestures, cross-cultural universals in, 28

Fluid intelligence, 241, 248-253, 322

Forced relocations, 373-374

Forgetfulness, jokes about, 320

Formal operations, 14

Formal vs. postformal reasoning (Piaget), 241

"Forty year jitters," 31

Foucault, Michel, 436

Four humors and four qualities, age and, 120

Fourteenth Amendment, age 21 and, 30

Fraternal twins *(dizygotics)*, 519

Freud, Sigmund, 7, 10-11
  dream theory of, 454-455
  love and sexuality theory of, 299-300

Friendships, 161-164

Future-oriented communication, conflict and, 81

Galen, 121

"Gay," defined, 209

Gay bashing, 213

Gay communities, 211

Gay couples, 159

Gender, 165-170
  bias and age, 120
  cardiac disease and, 53
  caregivers and, 168-169
  chances of marriage by, 29
  cognitive differentiation and, 166
  death and, 167-168
  depression and, 109
  division of labor and, 366-367
  divorce and, 131
  economic opportunity and, 168-169
  employment and status, 171-172
  friendships and, 162-163
  health and, 167-168
  identity, 165-166

influence on development and aging, 165-170
  mid-life crisis and, 349
  military service and, 354
  mortality rates and, 418
  parental imperative and, 366-368
  pitch and, 535
  power and, 169
  pubescent changes and, 438-439
  risk factors and, 167-168
  roles and careers, 406
  salaries and, 171
  sex and, 165
  voice and, 534-536
  workplace segregation and, 171-172

Gender differences
  adjusting to retirement, 407
  caregivers and, 58
  communication and, 73
  coping and, 407-408
  criminal behavior and, 101-103
  disengagement and, 127-128
  mastery style and, 315
  models of, 166-167
  privacy and, 390
  relationship intensity and, 446
  suicide and, 503-504
  travel and, 514
  trust and, 518
  in the workplace, 171-174

Generalized slowing hypothesis, 462

Generation gap, 2, 180

Generational equity, 175-180

Generations, compared with cohorts, 69

Generativity vs. stagnation, (Erikson), 5, 13, 75, 329-330

Genetic engineering, premature aging and, 386

Genetic epistemology, 13-14

Genetic inheritance, 435-436

Genitals, children's curiosity about, 436

Genome, premature aging and, 386-387

Geodemographic characteristics, 422

Geriatric medicine, origins of, 124

Germans, Jewish American attitudes toward, age and, 256

Glare sensitivity, 527, 529

Glass ceiling, 173-174

Glossopharyngeal nerve, 510

Gompertz curve (Gompertz-Makeham Law), 289-290

"Grand climacteric," 124

Grandparents
  communication skills of, 180-186
  comparison of grandmothers with grandfathers, 192
  divorcing child and, 132
  education and, 186-194
  responsibilities of, 187-188
  satisfactions of, 189

"Granny-dumping," 57

Great Britain, age as a marker, 30

Greer, Germaine, 441

Grief, health education and, 207

Growth and deficiency motives (Maslow), 16

Growth hormone, 437

Gustation (taste), decline in sense of, 510

Gustatory system, 509

Habituation, 195-200

Happiness, cohort effects and, 200-202

Harassment, legal action and, 442

Healing, Native American, 363

Health
  belief model, 204
  benefits of exercise, 144-146
  compromising behaviors, 419
  defined, 203
  and disease of Native Americans, 362-363
  education and age, 202-208
  gender and, 167-168
  illness and religiosity, 400
  military service and, 352
  problems of rural residents, 426
  rural access to care, 427

Health *(continued)*
 social support for crises, 475
 stress and, 484
 work organization membership and, 556-557
Healthy People Year 2000, 203
Hearing and listening, 278-279, 281
Hearing difficulties, 181
Heart rate, as indicator of stress, 484
Heat, age and (Aristotle), 113-113, 120-121
Heightened interiority, 127, 453
Helplessness, learned, 88-90
Hick-Lyman Law , stimulus-response relationship and, 236
Higher education, career age and, 55-56
High-trusting individual, 516
Hispanic Americans
 depression and, 109
 housing and, 218
 population in the U.S., 342
 suicide and, 504
 as voters, 379
Historical perspective, development and aging, 119-126
The History of Sexuality, (Foucault), 436
Holland, marriage patterns in, 29
Hollywood deathbed scenes, 294
Homicide patterns, 28
"homosexual," defined, 209
Homosexual culture, changes in, 209
Homosexuality, 208-215
 affirmation of lifestyle, 442
 parenthood and, 210-211
 race and, 212
 religion and, 211
Honeymoon period, 305-306
Hormone replacement therapy, 327
"Hot flash," menopause and, 326, 328
Housing, 215-222
 for disabled, 219-220
 issues of center city residence, 218-219

neighbors and, 216
privacy and, 216
subsidized rental, 220
Humor, 222-228
 age and, 222-228
 appreciation and age, 224-225
 cognitive functioning and, 225
 complex, 225-226
Hutchinson-Guilford syndrome, 385
Hyperhabituation, 197-199

Identical twins *(monozygotics)* 519
"Identicality," twins and, 522
Identity, 4
 community and, 375
 driving and, 134
 ego and, 492
 military service and, 355
 transitions and subcultural affiliations, 493
Illegal drugs, 141
Illusion of control, 394
Images of development and aging, 114-116
Imaginary playmates, 157
Imaginative play, self-expression and, 152
Immortals, 286
Immune system, age and, 289
Income level, voting behavior and, 380
Independence, driving, and 135
Index of aging, the search for, 542
Index of aging process, slowing as, 457
Individual differences
 centenarians, 64
 creativity and, 95
 emergence of, 232-233
 intelligence and, 246
Individuality, 229-236
Individuation, development and (Jung), 318
Inductive reasoning ability, age differences in, 238
Industrial society, age and crime and, 98-99
Industrial work, age and, 543-544

Infant morbidity and mortality, 18
Infant-mother attachments, 41
Information filtering, habituation, age and, 296
Information overload, slowing and, 462
Information processing, 16-17, 90-91, 236-241
Information processing model, slowing and, 459-460
Informational privacy, 388
Injustice, sense of, 169
Innocents Abroad (Twain), 511
Insomnia, sexual activity and, 430
Institutional residence, communication and 75-76
Instrumental support, chronically ill and, 476
Integrative processes, dreaming and, 453
Integrity, as final developmental stage (Erikson), 317-318
Intellectual decline, studies of, 245-246, 250-251
Intellectual development, later adulthood and, 246
Intelligence, 241-248
 creativity and, 94
 crystallized, 241, 248-253, 322
 cultural influences and, 249
 everyday, 246
 fluid, 241, 248-253, 322
 IQ, 241-242
 mandatory retirement and, 241
 multiple, 242
 psychometric, 241
 sensory-motor, 14
Intentionality, suicide and, 502
Interactional theory, development and, 229
Interethnic relationships, 253-257
Intergenerational communication, 1-3
Intergenerational conflict, equity and, 177
Intergenerational conversations, 191

Intergenerational discussion groups, guidelines, 181-185
Intergenerational relationships, 187
Intergenerational transfer of assets, 177-178
Interpersonal communion, 72
Interpersonal trust, 515-516
Interpretive control, 394
Intimacy, 4
IQ (intelligence quotient), 241-242
Isolation, social and emotional, 283

Japanese, 258-261
  age and attitudes toward, 256
  ambivalence toward elders, 260-261
  bowing to elders, 259
  developmental perspective of, 258-261
  hierarchical relationships and age, 258-259
  Obasute (abandoning the aged), 260
  Onyakoka (obligation to parents), 259
  power of elderly, 261
  suicide and, 504
Japanese Americans, age, suicide and, 504
Jen, Confucian love, 296
Jewish Americans, attitudes toward Germans, age and, 256
Job conditions, organizational membership and, 555
Job discrimination, age and, 32
Job requirements, age and, 542
Jobs, minimum wage, 23
Journey of life, concept of, 120-121, 125
Journey through life, vi, 7
Jung, Carl, 11-12, 31, 318
  dream theory of, 454-455
  tasks for later life, 156
  theory of creativity, 94

Kaiser Wilhelm II, 35
Kansas City Study, 127

Kant, Immanuel, theory of development, 520
Kevorkian, Jack, assisted suicide, 503
Kin, fictive, 157-160
Kinesthesia (sense of position and balance), 47-48
Krupp workers, retirement benefits and, 35

Labor, division of, gender and, 366-367
Language, respect for age and, 260
Language development, 262-265
Larynx, sound production and, 532-533
Latency, 13
Latent and manifest content, dreams, 454
Learned helplessness, 88-90
Learned optimism, 89
Learning
  memory and, 265-274
  self-directed, 272-274
  style and age, 271
  versus memory, 267-268
Length of life, factors influencing, 288-289,
"Lesbian," defined, 209
Lesbian couples, 159
Levinson, Daniel, adult age categorizations, 329
Life after death beliefs, age and, 399
Life care communities, 220-221
Life course
  duration dependence and, 277
  sexual differentiation and, 432
Life events, 274-278
  divorce and, 131
  negative, 276-277
  research into, 484, 487-488
  suicide and, 504-505
Life expectancy, 63
Life expectation, basic concept, 286-287
Life experience, 5
Life review
  death and, 114
  reminiscence and, 401-405
  theory of (Butler), 401-402

Life satisfaction
  retirement and, 411-412
  siblings and, 445
Life stories, 9
Life transitions
  caregivers and, 60
  divorce and, 133
Life-style
  sexual, 442
  slowing and, 463-464
  subcultures and, 491
Lifelong learning, 188
Lifespan, mortality rate changes and, 289-290
Light, vision and, 526
Listening, 278-282
Locke, John, theory of development, 115-116
Loneliness, 282-285
  in The Death of Ivan Ilych, 401
Long-lived people, inwardness and, 481
Long-term marriages, 310-311
Longevity, 285-292
  Biblical patriarchs and, 285
  biological limit and, 291
  centenarians and, 63
  Confucianism and, 285
  gender and, 167-168
  premature aging and, 386-387
  twins and, 521-522
"Lookism" (male beauty), 212
Lost Horizon (Hilton), 286
Love
  altruistic (Agape), 304
  of beauty (Eros), 304
  caring, 301
  as carnal sin, 297-298
  catastrophic loss and, 297
  Christian message of, 297-299
  companionate style of, 304
  Confucian (Jen), 296
  of the good (Socrates/Plato), 296-297
  for life, 293
  obsessive (Mania), 304
  playful (Ludus), 304
  in postmodern world, 301
  psychosexual stages of development and, 299
  realistic (Pragma), 304
  romantic, 301
  and sex as a game, 295

Love (*continued*)
  sexual as deadly danger-
    ous, 295-296
  withdrawal of and narcis-
    sism, 358
Love Song of the Dark Lord
  (Sanskrit), 293
Loving and losing, 292-302
Low back pain, 65
Ludus (playful love), 304

Magic, erupting in ordinary
  lives, 155
Magical mastery, aging,
  development and, 312-
  316
Male sexual response, aging
  and, 430-431
Male superiority, Christian
  dogma and, 298-299
Males
  as protectors, 367
  surplus, 366
Managerial work, age and
  549-550
Mandatory retirement,
  intelligence and, 241
Mania (obsessive love), 304
Marital development, 303-311
Marital types, 306-307
Markers of adult develop-
  ment, life events as, 277-
  278
Marriage
  chances of by age and
    gender, 29
  long-term, 310-311
  patterns of, 29
  relationship changes and,
    306
  remarriage, 309-310
  trust and, 517
Maslow, Abraham, 15-16
Mastery types, 311-316
  active, 312-316
  magical, 312-316
  mid-life crisis and, 349
  passive, 312-316
  satisfaction, 308
Masturbation
  mistaken beliefs about,
    436-437
  older adults and, 431
Mate choice, age and, 26-30
Mathematical models,
  slowing and, 458-459

Maturation
  rate of, 499
  sexual, 436-439
  social approval and crime,
    100
Mature personality traits
  (Allport), 317
"Maturing out" (drug use),
  141
Maturity, 316-320
Mauritius, marriage patterns
  in, 29
Mayan philosophies, cyclical
  repetition and, 361, 365
Mead, Margaret, culture,
  sexuality and, 437
Meanings, creativity and, 94
Mediators of stress, 484
Medication
  depression and, 108
  taste sensitivity and, 510
Meditative prayer, age and,
  481
Memory, 320-325
  age differences in, 237-238
  changes and slowing, 462
  control, 90
  crystallized and fluid
    intelligence and, 322
  declines related to age, 321-
    322
  everyday life and, 265-274
  learning and, 265-274
  primary, 321
  secondary, 321
  sensory, 321
  speech comprehension,
    322-323
  storage of and information
    processing, 237-238
  tertiary, 321
  thinking and, 322-323
  training and age, 324
  versus learning, 267-268
  of written information, 322
Menarche, 438
Menopause, 325-329, 431
Menstruation, 325
Mental abilities, primary
  (Thurstone), 241
Mental development, twins,
  522-523
Mental health, 329-332
  positive, 331-332
  problems of rural resi-
    dents, 426

  resources, 332-337
  services, 332-334
Mental imagery, self-discovery and, 152
Metamemory, age and, 269-
  270
Metaphors of the life course,
  337-341
Mexican Americans, 342-346
  acculturation of, 343
  divorce and, 343-344
  empty nest and, 343
  respect for elders of, 344
  retirement and, 344
  social support and, 344
Mexican Indians, mastery
  style and, 315
Middle adult years, neglect of,
  346
Mid-life crisis, 7-8, 346-351
  subcultures and, 493-494
  theories of, 348-350
Military service, 351-356
  effect of frequent moves on
    families, 374
  effect on adult develop-
    ment, 351-356
  women in, 172-173
Millett, Kate, 441
Minimum wage jobs, 23
Mirror imaging, twins and,
  519
Mobility, 375, 512
Models of adult development
  and aging, 7-17
Mortality
  age and, 417-418
  trends in data, 414-415
  trust in socio-legal organi-
    zations and, 518
Mortality rate
  basic concept of, 287
  changes over lifespan, 289-
    290
  race and, 415-416
Moses, 33
The Mother Machine, (Corea),
  440
Mother-child communication,
  71-72
Motor vehicles, functions in
  adult life, 134-135
Moves, frequent, effects of,
  374
Multigenerational households,
  3

Multiple intelligence, theory of (Gardner), 242
Muscular strength, age and, 541-542
Mutual aid, 159
Mutual withdrawal, elder and society, 126-127

Naps, age and, 451-452
Narcissism, 357-360, 367
Narcissistic withdrawal, 359
National Alzheimer's Association, 61
Native Americans, 360-364
 boarding school experiences of, 363
 cyclical world view of, 361
 healing, 363
 life phase rituals of, 361-362
 perspectives on lifespan, 360-364
 reincarnation and, 362
 respect for elders and, 361
 suicide and, 504
Nature vs. nurture controversy, twins and, 520
Navajos
 mastery style of men, 315
 parental imperative of, 365
Necropolis, as depository for elderly adults, 175
Negative life events, 276-277
Neglectful upbringing, adult loneliness and, 284-285
Negotiating for control, 86-87
Neighbors, housing and, 216
Neural-noise theory, slowing and, 461
Neurobiological models, slowing and, 460-461
Neurotransmitters, 108
Newborns, communication ability, 71
Nocturnal emissions, 438-439
Noise, 70, 270
Noncognitive factors, learning and, 267
Nondevelopmental models, 16-17
Nonhuman species, aging and 291
Nonpersonal consciousness, 481
Number symbolism, age 40 and, 33-34

Nursing home residents, control and, 90

Obasute (abandoning the aged), 260
Objects, value of, developmental process and, 382-383
Obligation to parents *(Onyakoka)*, 259
Obsessive love (Mania), 304
Occupation, attachment to, 408-409
Occupational crisis, age 40 and, 31-32
Office work, age and, 549
"Old Man Mad about Painting" (Manji/Hokusai), 92
"Oldness," result of hyperhabituation, 198
Olfactory bulb, regeneration of, 510
Olfactory system, 508-509
Onyakoko (obligation to parents), 259
Opiate-like binding sites, brain, 435
Optimism, learned, 89
Oral language, age and, 263
Oral sex, older people and, 430
Organizational assimilation, 554
Organizational exit, age and, 557
Organizations, trust and, 517
Orienting reflex, 195
Osteoporosis, 326
Ovaries, changes with age, 326
"Overbenefit," parent-child relationship and, 4
Ovid, sexual love and, 295-296
Ovulation, 438

Pain
 chronic, 64-67
 public policy and, 66
 sensitivity in old age, 65-66
 suffering and, 495
Parasuicide, 502
Parental emergency, narcissism and, 368-369
Parental imperative, 365-369

Parental intrusion, narcissism and, 358
Parent-child bond, among Australians, 3
Parenthood
 gay and lesbian, 210-211
 Mexican-American, 343-344
 stress and, 485
 trust and, 517
Parents
 adult children and, 1-6
 marital conflict of elderly, 308
Partial inclusion, organizations, 555
Partner availability, sexual activity and, 431
Passages (Sheehy), 347
Passive master, aging development and, 312-316
Patient education, 206
"Peak of life," as metaphor of life course, 336-338
Peak periods, creativity, 95
Peership, social-age and, 1-2
Pension costs, retirement planning and, 411
Pepper Commission Report, 178-179
PERI (Psychiatric Epidemiology Research Interview), 487
Personal space, need for, 387
Personality, 370-377
Personality characteristics, differential, 233-234
Phobias, 331
Physical attraction, marital choice and, 304
Physical decline, centenarians, 64
Physical fitness, exercise and, 147
Piaget, Jean, 13-14, 82
Picasso, Pablo, 97
Pilgrim's Progress (Bunyan), 122-124
Pitch, 535
Place, 370-377
Place identity, 371-372
Placebos, 47
Placelessness, 374-375
Play, creative expression as, 151

"Playboy philosophy,"
venereal disease and, 441
Playmates, imaginary, 157
Pleasure, sexual, older people
and, 430
Political beliefs and activities,
377-381
Political functions, subcul-
tures and, 492
Political involvement, of
average citizen, 377
Polyphasic sleep pattern, 450-
451
Population losses, rural areas,
425
Poro, marriage patterns in, 29
Positive mental health, 331-
332
Possessions, 381-384
"POSSSLQ" relationships, 159
Post-parental period, 368-369
"Postreproductive person,"
439
Postreproductive years, 442
Postretirement adjustment,
410
Posttraumatic stress disorder
(PTSD), 353
Potentiality to actuality
(Aristotle), 113
Poverty
fear of, 155-156
rural, 423, 425-426
Power, age, gender and, 169
Practice, slowing and, 463-464
Pragma (realistic love), 304
Prayer, 398, 481-482
Predictive control, 394
Predictive models of age-
related slowing, 458-463
Pregnancy
adolescent, 441
anxiety and, 440
feelings about, 326
Preindustrial societies, role of
elders, 156
Prejudice, contact theory of,
254
Premature aging, 384-387
Premature death, prevention
of, 419-420
Preoperational thought, 14
Preparation for retirement,
409-414
Preretirement training, 410-
411

Prescription drugs, lifespan
patterns, 141
Primary caregivers, 61
Primary memory, 321
Primary mental abilities
(Thurstone), 241
Prime of life, middle age as
(Aristotle), 113
Privacy, 387-392
boundaries and, 389
caregiving and, 62
housing and, 216
psychological, 388
social, 387-388
therapeutic reminiscing
and, 404
violations of, 389-390
Problem solving, 80-81
age differences and, 251
memory and, 323
training for, 250
Production work, age and, 546
Professional work, age and,
549-550
Progeria. *See* Premature aging
Progress, as metaphor of life
course, 338-340
Proximity, relationship
satisfaction and, 445
Psychiatric disorders, 330-331
Psychiatric Epidemiology
Research Interview
(PERI), 487
Psychoanalysis, dream theory,
454
Psychoanalytic model,
development, aging and,
10-14
Psychoanalytic theory, of
possessions, 382-383
Psychogenic pain, 65
Psychological autopsy, 502
Psychological privacy, 388
Psychometric intelligence, 241
Psychomotor speed, 457
Psychosexual stages of
development, love and,
299
"Psychosocial crisis"
(Erikson), 12
Ptolemy, ages ruled by
planets, 121
Pubescent changes, gender
and, 438-439
Public policy
caregiving, 62

pain and, 66
Public policy crisis, crime and,
103
Public policy debate, genera-
tional equity and, 175-178
"Pull" theories, 8
Pulmonary function, exercise
and, 145
Punishment for crime, age
and, 100-102
"Push" theories, 8

Quality of Life Educational
Program, 152-153

Race
homosexuality and, 212
mortality rates and, 415-
416
suicide and, 504
Racial discrimination , 22, 24
Racism in workplace, 556
Rapid eye movements (REM),
sleep and, 449
Rational suicide, 503
Reaction time, 457-458, 541-
542
Realistic love (Pragma), 304
Reciprocal relationship, fictive
kin, 158
Reciprocity, adult friendships
and, 163
Reconstituted family, 132-133
"Recreational drugs," frequency of use, 139-140
Reengagement with society,
127
Rehabilitation, social support
and, 475-476
Reincarnation, Native
Americans and, 362
Relational development,
disclosure and, 390-391
Relationship changes, mar-
riage and 306
Relationship deterioration,
communication, 74-75
Relationship intensity, gender
differences and, 446
Relationship types, siblings,
444
Relationships
conflict and, 77-81
continuity over lifespan,
473-474
control and, 87-88

interethnic, 253-257
marital, 304
with parents, 5
POSSSLQ, 159
reciprocal with fictive kin, 158
sexual, 440
sibling, 443-448
wisdom and, 482
Religion, 393-401
in adult life, 396-401
church programs for elders and, 397-398
coping with crisis and, 393-396
homosexuality and, 211
Religiosity
age and, 201, 395, 397-399, 482
health and illness, 400
Religious explanations, 393
Religious heritage, Mediterranean, 34
Religious socialization, 480
Relocations, forced, 373-374
REM (rapid eye movements), sleep and, 440, 450
Remarriage, 309-310
Reminiscence, 401-405
life review and, 401-405
shared by elderly adults, 445
Reproduction, sexual activities and, 433
Reproductive ability, age and, 27
Residential proximity, friendship and, 161
Respite services, 61
Retirement
age and benefits, 35-36
gender differences in adjustment to, 407
mandatory, 241
Mexican Americans and, 344
pension costs, 411
preparation for, 409-414
preretirement training, 410-411
"sixty-five and out," 36
studies of gender bias in, 406-407
subculture, 494
trust and, 517
as women's challenge, 405-409

workplace alternatives to, 550
Retrieval (of memory), information processing and, 237-238
Riddle of the Sphinx, 338
"Right to die," 506
Rigidity, slowing and, 463
Risk factors
drugs and, 143
gender and, 167-168
heart disease and hypertension, 52-53
modifiable, 419-420
Risk to life, 414-421
Rites of passage, possessions and, 382
Rituals, life phases, Native Americans and, 361-362
Rivalries, sibling, 446
Rogers, Carl, 15-16
Roman law, age and, 31
Romantic love, 301
Romanticism, suffering and, 498
Root metaphors, contextualism 81-83
Rousseau, Jean Jacques, theory of development, 116
Routinization, age, habituation and, 199
Rural economy, farm crisis and, 425
Rural living, influence on adult development, 421-428
Rural population losses, 425
Rural poverty, 423, 425-426

Safety
driving, 136-137
housing and, 216
Saliva flow, age and, 510
Same-sex attraction, 208-209
Same-sex marriages, 210
"Sandwich generation," responsibilities of, 346
Sappho, 295
Sati (Suttee), widows and, 503
Satisfaction, marital, 308
Secondary memory, 321
Secrets, family, 391
Sedentary behavior, attitude toward, 147

Seizure (Sappho), 295
Seligman, Martin , learned helplessness, 88-90
Self-absorption, early development of, 357-358
Self-actualization (Maslow), 15-16, 150, 317
Self-confrontation and reformation, 156
Self-discovery, mental imagery and, 152
Self-doubt, middle age and, 347
Self-esteem
bereavement recovery and, 540
male voice and, 439
Self-image, sexuality and, 429
Self-realization, Vedantic tradition and, 481
Self-regulation, 87
Senior adult communities, as subcultures, 492, 494
Senior narcissism, 36
Senses, 45-51, 508
Sensory loss, communication and, 75
Sensory memory, 321
Sensory-motor intelligence, 14
Sensuality, compared with sexuality, 433-434
Series completions tests, age differences in, 237-238
Setting Limits (Callahan), 175
Seven ages of life, 121
Sex
chromosome pairs and, 166
gender and, 165
in later adult years, 429-432
Sex and Destiny (Greer), 441
"Sex appeal," mass media and, 441
Sexism, 174
in the workplace, 556
Sex-role behavior, culture and, 437
Sex-role shifting, age, parenting status and, 368-369
Sex-role training, parenthood and, 367
Sexual activity
continued virility and, 442
insomnia and, 430
as sinful, 298-299

Sexual differentiation, life course and, 432
Sexual energy, reduction, 31
Sexual equality, adult generations and, 2
Sexual feelings, older people, 429
Sexual intercourse, expectations of, 440
Sexual interest, age and, 26
Sexual love, as
   deadly dangerous, 295-296
Sexual mores, crime, age and, 102
Sexual Politics (Millett), 441
Sexuality, 432-443
   brain and, 434-435
   clergy and, 301
   early development of, 300
   homosexuality, 208-215
   in postmodern world, 301
Sexually transmitted diseases, 440
Shakespeare, William, 518
Shared reminiscence, elderly adults, 445
The Shining Fish, elder tale, 154-155
Sibling relationships, 443-448
Sibling rivalries, 446
Signal response types, habituation (197
Similarity, friendship and, 161-162
Single parent families, 329
Skin, receptors in, 48
Sleep, 448-457
   age and quality of, 453-454
   Alzheimer's disease and, 456
   apnea, 455
   bedtime rituals, 455
   delta, 449
   deprivation, 451-452
   dreams and, 448-457
   EEG and, 449
   laboratories, 449
   patterns of wakefulness and, 450-452
   polyphasic pattern, 450-451
   problems, 455-456
   rapid eye movements (REM), 449
   spindles, 449
   stages of, 449-450

wine and, 456
"Sleeping pills," 455-456
Slowing
   of behavior with age, 457-467
   in centenarians, 64
   in information processing with age, 239
   mathematical models of, 458-459
   memory changes and, 462
   memory processes and, 321-322
   neurological models of, 460-461
Small towns, decline of, 425-426
"Smart" houses, 221
Smell, sense of, 508-511
Smoking
   cardiac health and, 52
   effects on voice, 536
   lifespan patterns of, 140-141
   premature death and, 419-420
   sense of smell and, 510
   sense of taste and, 510
Social-age peership, 1-2
Social class
   adult development and, 467-472
   possessions and, 383
Social integration, health and, 475
Social learning theory, 17
Social life, caregiving and, 60
Social privacy, 387-388
Social relationships, convoys of, 472-474
Social Security, benefits and taxes, 176, 178
Social support
   chronically ill and, 475-479
   divorce and, 131-132
   Mexican Americans and, 344
   Polish Americans and, 344
   stress and, 475
Socialization, anticipatory, retirement and, 411-412
Socioeconomic status, 467-472
Socrates/Plato, love of the good 296-297
Somesthetic senses, 46-47

Spatial abilities, age differences in, 238
Speech comprehension, memory and 322-323
Speed demands, age, work and , 544
Sperm
   age and production of, 325
   X and Y, 436
Sphinx, riddle of, 338
Spiritual ages, 121
Spiritual development, 91,
   Vedantic philosophy and, 479-483
Spiritual quest, love as, 297-298
Spiritual realities, Native Americans and, 360-361
Spouse, death of, 391
Stage theories, 116-118
Stages of sleep, 449-450
Stamina, exercise and, 146
Stepchildren, divorce and, 132-133
Stereotypes, female and male, 169-170
Stimulus-response relationship, Hick-Lyman Law and, 236
Stochastic theory, longevity and, 522
Storybook endings, 294-295
Strange Meeting (Owen), 293
Strange Situation (Ainsworth), 41
Strength training, age and, 146
Stress, 483-491
   caregivers and, 59-60
   conflict and, 77
   creativity and, 150
   depression and, 108
   divorce and, 131-132
   drug use and, 141-142
   personality and, 485
   play and, 152
   reduction, 391
   religious meaning and, 393-394
   relocation and, 373-374
   returning home and, 512
   social support and, 475
   stages of response to, 486
Stressors of everyday life, 484
Subcultural influences, development and, 491-495

Submission vs. achievement, child development and, 358
Subsidized rental housing, 220
Substitution hierarchy, older adults and, 477
Suburban residence, age and, 217-218
Suffering, 495-501
Suicide, 501-507
    age and, 417
    altruistic, 503
    anomie and, 503
    assisted, 503
    depression and, 107
    Durkheim's typology, 503
    egoistic, 503
    ethnicity and, 504
    farmers and, 505
    fatalistic, 503
    Filipino Americans and, 504
    firearms and, 505
    gender differences and, 503-504
    intentionality and, 502
    Japanese Americans and, 504
    life events and, 504-505
    as moral question, 502
    Native Americans and, 504
    parasuicide, 502
    race and, 504
    rates of, 503
    rational, 503
Superfecundation, 519
Surge center, brain, sexual differentiation and, 435
Surplus males, 366
Suttee (Sati), widows and, 503
Symbolic interaction theory, health education and, 205

Task difficulty, slowness and, 457
Taste, sense of, 508-511
Taste buds, 509-510
TAT findings, mastery styles and, 312-313
Technological change, grandparents and, 186
Teleos, life journey and 113
Telephone contacts, siblings, 445
Ten steps of life, 123

Tenderness, men, life cycle and, 367
Tennyson, Alfred, Lord, creativity, 97
Tertiary memory, 321
Thanatos, 300
Therapeutic reminiscing, 404
Therapeutic technique, humor as, 226
Therapy, depression, 110-111
Thermal (temperature) sense, 47, 49
Thinking, relationship to memory, 322-323
"Third-culture kids", 511-512
Time, running out, 127
Time's arrow, as metaphor of life course, 338
Tolerance, attitude toward other ethnic groups, 253
Tolstoy, Count Lev, 401
Touch (cutaneous sense), 46, 49
Town covenants, rural living and, 424
Towns, small, decline of, 425-426
Training for new work, age and, 548-549
Transfer of assets, intergenerational, 177-178
Transition to early adulthood, 467-468
Transpersonal wisdom, 482
Transportation systems, age and, 464
Travel, adult development and, 511-515
Trust
    adult development and, 515-518
    age and, 516-517
Turtle Island, symbolism of, 362
Twain, Mark, 511
Twins, 518-525
    age changes and, 523-524
    altercast and, 519
    chromosomal damage and, 519
    depression and, 108
    Doppelganger and, 519
    fraternal, 519
    identical, 519
    identicality, 522
    longevity, 521-522

mental development of, 522-523
    mirror imaging and, 519
    nature vs. nurture controversy, 520
    personality of, 523
Type A behavior, health risk and, 420

Uncertainty reduction, bits and, 236
"Unconditional positive regard" (Rogers), 16
"Unfinished business," life review and, 401
Unity of the senses, 508
U-shaped hypothesis, conflict management, 77-78, 80

Vagina, changes with menopause, 326
Vagus nerve, 510
Value structure, rural Americans, 424
Values, age, happiness and, 201
Vedantic philosophy, spiritual development and, 479-483
Verbal listening responses, 279-280
Vertical society and respect for aged, 258
Vestibular sense, 47-48
Vicarious control, 394
Vietnamese immigrants, age and attitudes toward, 256
Violations of privacy, 389-390
Violent deaths, trends in, 417-418
Vision, 137, 526-532
Visual acuity, 527, 545
Visual field, 527, 529
Visual search process, age and, 531
Visual system, 526-528
"Vital force," bodily processes and, 123-124
"Vitality," as workplace issue, age and, 555-556
Vocal folds, 533
Vocal intensity, age and, 535
Voice, 532-536
Voter turnout, age and, 378-379
Voting age, 30

Vulnerability, 50, 86-92

Wakefulness and sleep, patterns of, 450-452
Waking life, attitudes toward, 448
Wechsler Adult Intelligence Scale, 241
Wellness, 204
Werner syndrome, 385
Widowhood, 537-541
    sexuality during, 440
    Suttee (Sati) and, 503
"Will to live," as motivation, 501
Wine, sleep and, 456
Wisdom, spiritual development and, 479-483
Wise old man, 156
Withdrawal, narcissistic, 359

Women
    age and sexual response, 431
    aggression and, 367
    challenge of retirement for, 405-409
    employment trends for, 405-406
    entry into "male occupations," 172-173
    menopause and baby boomers, 325
    military service and, 172-173
    wellbeing of during employment, 342-343
Women's rights movement, 172
Work capacity, 541-553

Work organization membership, 553-558
Work role, loss of, 409
Workers, difficulties of in middle age, 545-546
Workforce, entering and exiting, 553
Working memory, 321
Workplace
    gender and, 171-174
    trust and, 517
World views (Pepper), 81
Written information, memory of, 322
Written language, age and, 264

Young adult, tasks of, 4
Youth subcultures, 491-493